GEORGIA STUDENT EDITION

PRENTICE HALL
LITERATURE

Timeless Voices, Timeless Themes

GOLD LEVEL

PEARSON

Prentice
Hall

Upper Saddle River, New Jersey

Needham, Massachusetts

ISBN 0-13-062454-3

2 3 4 5 6 7 8 9 10   08 07 06 05 04

Your Georgia Quality Core Curriculum

Think about it. Although you may not realize it, you use your language arts skills every day. Whether you're writing an e-mail, reading your favorite magazine, or describing a new movie, your language arts skills are active. The key to your success in language arts is your ability to use language arts skills in the real world. To guide you toward this goal, the Georgia State Board of Education has established the comprehensive Quality Core Curriculum. The QCC describe what you should know and be able to do in each grade, from kindergarten to grade 12. As you work through this book, you will work toward the mastery of each and every Georgia QCC for Language Arts. The more you build on each standard, the stronger and more confident you will grow.

Ninth Grade Principles of Literature and Composition Georgia Quality Core Curriculum

Here is a complete list of this year's QCC so that you can know what you're expected to learn this year. The ninth grade QCC begins with Standard 26 and ends with 50.

Critical Thinking

Standard 26: Solves word analogy problems.

Analogy problems ask you to identify the relationship between a pair of words and to identify a second pair of words that has the same relationship. In the example shown here, the relationship is cause and effect. An earthquake causes disaster, just as nourishment causes growth.

> **EXAMPLE** Complete the analogy.
>
> EARTHQUAKE : DISASTER
> A. knowledge : wisdom
> B. nourishment : growth
> C. decoration : beauty
> D. logic : reason

Reading/Literature

Standard 27: Uses the features of print materials appropriately (e.g., table of contents, preface, introduction, titles and subtitles, index, glossary, appendix, and bibliography).

You use the different parts of a book, encyclopedia, newspaper, and other print sources to locate information.

> **EXAMPLE:** In which part of a science textbook would you most easily find the definition of a science term?
>
> A. preface   C. glossary
> B. index   D. bibliography

Standard 28: Varies reading speed and methods according to the type of material and purpose of reading.

Depending on the type of material you are reading and your purpose for reading, you will adjust your reading speed.

> **EXAMPLE:** If you were going to read and take notes from a book for a research report, how would you read the material?
>
> A. scan quickly to find details
> B. skim quickly to find main points
> C. read carefully to understand and remember
> D. read comfortably to enjoy

Standard 29: Identifies the structural elements of literature (e.g., plot, characterization, setting, mood, tone, and point of view).

Most fiction includes plot, characters, setting, mood, tone, and point of view. You will learn to identify these elements in novels and short stories.

> **EXAMPLE:** The character described here is
>
> A. a scientist. C. an engineer.
> B. an astronaut. D. a teacher.

Standard 30: Reads and responds to mythology.

Many Greek myths were written as epic poems and include epic heroes who must overcome almost insurmountable odds to reach their goal. You will study the historical context of Greek mythology and you will learn to identify different elements of mythology.

> **EXAMPLE:** In this passage, what qualities mark Odysseus as a hero?
>
> A. He "learned the minds of many distant men."
> B. He "weathered many bitter nights and days."
> C. He is a wanderer.
> D. He could not save his men.

Standard 31: Reads, discusses, and analyzes technical literature and general exposition.

You will read, discuss, and analyze technical literature and nonfiction essays. Be aware of the generalizations writers make and the specific details they use to support them. You should also recognize that some writers do not provide specifics to support their opinions.

EXAMPLE: Which statement from the passage is a generalization?

A. His music is similar to Beethoven's.
B. The rhythm in the first refrain is too choppy.
C. All classical music is wonderful.
D. The piano is crucial to the success of this composition.

Standard 32: Experiences a variety of nonprint resources (film, recordings, theatre, computers, and databases) as a part of the study of literature and vocational/technical writings.

You will study written works through a variety of sources, such as film adaptations of written works, film reviews, song lyrics, dramatic plays, and computer and database information.

EXAMPLE: If you were going to write a movie script for Edgar Allan Poe's poem "The Raven," what do you think is the most important element of the poem that the movie should convey?

A. mood   C. speaker
B. stanzas   D. rhythm

Standard 33: Expands reading vocabulary.

As you read, you will come across words that are unfamiliar to you. You will learn what these words mean and understand how they are used in context.

EXAMPLE: Within the context of the passage, the word <u>provoke</u> means

A. to follow through.
B. to create excitement.
C. to avoid getting involved.
D. to stir or arouse to action.

Standard 34: Applies word recognition strategies through the use of graphophonic, semantic, syntactic, and orthographic cueing systems.

Sometimes you can define unfamiliar words by analyzing prefixes, suffixes, root words, and context clues.

EXAMPLE: In this passage, the word <u>dynamic</u> means

A. tall.   C. powerful.
B. distant.   D. intelligent.

Standard 35: Interprets literal and nonliteral meanings of words and phrases.

Many words and phrases that you will come across in your reading have both literal meanings (denotations) and nonliteral meanings (connotations). You can often determine the meaning of a word or phrase based on how it is used in context.

EXAMPLE: What does the word <u>firm</u> most likely mean, as used in this passage?

A. fast   C. fallen
B. lost   D. strict

Standard 36: Adjusts reading speed according to purpose and rereads for comprehension.

When you read to understand and remember information, you read slower. When you read to enjoy or to skim for details, you read faster. Sometimes, you will need to reread material to make sure you understand it.

EXAMPLE: To help you understand and remember the complex process of how the human body turns food into fuel, (1) read about the process carefully and slowly, and (2) reread for comprehension.

Standard 37: Analyzes explicit and implicit main ideas, details, sequence of events, and cause/effect relationships.

You will read a wide variety of texts. Being able to identify a text's main idea will help you to understand better the work as a whole. Sometimes, a writer states the main idea explicitly—directly in the text. At other times, the main idea is implied, and you must identify it based on other information in the text.

> **EXAMPLE:** To analyze a text, (1) identify the main idea, (2) look for supporting details, (3) determine the sequence of events, (4) identify cause/effect relationships, and (5) think about whether the information in the text supports the main idea.

Standard 38: Makes comparisons, predictions, generalizations, and draws conclusions.

As you read, you will often use a variety of reading strategies, such as making comparisons, predictions, or generalizations, and drawing conclusions.

> **EXAMPLE:** To understand, get involved with, and analyze a text, ask yourself questions as you read. Here are some examples:
> - How are these things similar?
> - What will happen next?
> - What is the general meaning of this passage?
> - What generalizations has the author made? Are they supported by specific details?
> - Why did that happen?

Standard 39: Analyzes fact and opinion, persuasion, bias, and stereotyping.

Many authors use persuasion to get readers to agree with their opinions. Be aware of different persuasive techniques.

> **EXAMPLE:** To analyze persuasive writing, (1) distinguish between fact and opinion, and (2) recognize bias and stereotyping.

Standard 40: Recognizes different contextual structures and adapts vocabulary and comprehension strategies appropriately.

You will identify the type, purpose, tone, and audience of different forms of writing. For example, a thank-you letter is a form of social writing. Its purpose is to offer thanks, its tone is usually friendly, and its audience is usually someone the writer knows.

EXAMPLE: For what audience did Martin Luther King, Jr. write his speech "I Have a Dream"?

A. the citizens of Alabama
B. the children of former slaves
C. all the people in the United States
D. all the people in the world

Speaking/Listening

Standard 41: Engages critically and constructively in discussions by speaking and listening.

Whether you are speaking or listening, you must know your purpose, role, and audience. As a speaker, your purpose might be to persuade or to inform. Your role might be to lead a group discussion, and your audience could be a group of 8th graders or school officials. As a listener, your purpose could be to appreciate and/or comprehend. Your role might be to evaluate what you hear and give feedback.

EXAMPLE: To play a critical and constructive role in a discussion, ask yourself these questions prior to participating:

- What information am I providing?
- Why am I providing it?
- Who is my audience?
- What do I want to learn from this discussion?
- What can I contribute?
- How will I evaluate what I hear?

Standard 42: Follows multipart instructions and asks questions for clarification.

When following instructions, make sure you don't miss a step or get the steps out of order. Ask questions if you need help or clarification.

EXAMPLE: To follow multipart instructions: listen to each step; make sure to get the steps in order; take notes if you need to; visualize each step; and ask questions.

Standard 43: Adapts words and strategies to various situations and audiences.

When you speak or write, you will choose specific words and strategies for presenting information. You will make these choices based on the situation and who is listening to you or reading what you wrote.

EXAMPLE: Because of language and tone in this letter, you can assume the writer's audience is his

A. friend.   C. classmate.

B. parent.   D. principal.

Standard 44: Conceives and develops ideas about a topic for the purpose of speaking to a group; chooses and organizes related ideas; presents them clearly in standard American English; and evaluates similar presentations by others.

In presenting information orally, you need to make sure you have chosen an interesting topic and considered your audience. Your topic and main idea should be clear and supported with relevant details. Your speech should also be well organized to avoid confusion, and you should use standard American English appropriate to your audience. In addition to giving speeches, you will also listen to and evaluate speeches by your peers and other public speakers.

EXAMPLE: When you arrive to give your speech to the Future Farmers of America, you discover that your audience is actually the Young Scientists of America. In order to adapt your speech to your new audience, which of the following approaches would you take in presenting your speech?

A. use scientific jargon

B. treat the audience as you would any other

C. wear a lab coat and latex gloves

D. be very serious and avoid humor

Standard 45: Evaluates the messages and effects of mass media.

You see and listen to messages from mass media every day—on television and radio commercials, on billboards, the Internet, in magazines, and so on. To evaluate mass media messages, ask yourself the following questions: What is the purpose? Is the information correct and up-to-date? What information is left out? What type of language is used?

EXAMPLE: The writer of this advertisement is appealing to the listener's

A. need to be socially different.
B. need to buy quality products.
C. desire to save money.
D. desire to be different.

Standard 46: Identifies verbal and nonverbal components of interpersonal communications.

Any time you speak with or listen to someone, you can find verbal and nonverbal signals. These signals tell a lot about the speaker's knowledge, confidence, preparation, and feelings about his or her topic.

EXAMPLE: Nonverbal signals include eye contact, facial expressions, gestures, and posture. Verbal signals include diction, mood, pitch, pace of speech, and volume.

Writing/Usage/Grammar

Standard 47: Writes well-developed paragraphs with clear, controlling ideas.

You will read and write many paragraphs and essays. A paragraph contains a topic sentence that states or implies the main idea. Other sentences in the paragraph should support the main idea and be clearly organized.

EXAMPLE: The implied main idea of this paragraph is

A. science is a difficult subject to study.
B. science can be fun and exciting.
C. anyone can be a scientist.
D. it takes special skills to be a scientist.

Standard 48: Writes in narrative, descriptive, persuasive, and expository modes with emphasis on persuasive writing.

In ninth grade, you will be given writing assignments with different purposes. These purposes will include writing to entertain, describe, persuade, or inform.

EXAMPLE: In which situation would the writer's purpose be primarily to persuade?

A. a children's play performed in a circus
B. a report on a new scientific discovery for a health class
C. a report on the effects of earthquakes
D. a campaign poster for a candidate for student council president

Standard 49: Uses precise punctuation, capitalization, spelling, and other elements of manuscript form.

When you write, you want your readers to pay attention to what you have to say, not the errors you might have made. Writing that does not include correct grammar, usage, and mechanics makes it difficult for your readers to understand the heart of the message that you are attempting to convey in your writing.

EXAMPLE: Find the capitalization error in the following sentence.

Tuesday, November 28, 1952, was the coldest day of Winter, if not the year.

A. Tuesday should not be capitalized.
B. November should not be capitalized.
C. Winter should not be capitalized.
D. Year should be capitalized.

Standard 50: Writes for a variety of purposes including, but not limited to, technical (process, explanation), business (letters of order, request, application, complaint), personal (journals, diaries, stories), social (friendly letters, thank-you notes, invitations), and academic (themes, reports, essays, analyses, critiques).

What you are writing (such as an essay explaining a process, or a thank-you note) often determines your purpose for writing. When you write about a specific topic for a specific purpose, you must also consider who your audience is and what your tone will be. For example, if you are writing a letter to a business requesting information, your audience would most likely be a professional person, and your tone would be formal and polite.

EXAMPLE: The situation that would be most appropriate for a persuasive argument in a playful tone is

A. a flyer to garner support for a new recycling program.
B. an advertisement for a healthy snack for kids.
C. a letter to the President supporting tax cuts for small businesses.
D. a phone call to your state representative about tourism.

What Is a Rubric?

A rubric is a tool, often in the form of a chart or grid, that helps you assess your work. Rubrics are particularly helpful for writing and speaking assignments.

To help you or others assess, or evaluate, your work, a rubric offers several specific criteria to be applied to your work. Then the rubric helps you or an evaluator indicate your range of success or failure according to those specific criteria. Rubrics are often used to evaluate writing for standardized tests like the Georgia High School Writing Test (GHSWT).

When you know what the rubric will be before you begin writing a persuasive essay, for example, you will be aware as you write of specific criteria that are important in that kind of essay. As you evaluate the essay before giving it to your teacher, you will focus on the specific areas that your teacher wants you to master—or on areas that you know present challenges for you.

How are rubrics constructed?

Rubrics can be constructed in several different ways.

- Your teacher may assign a rubric for a specific assignment.
- Your teacher may direct you to a rubric in your textbook.
- Your teacher and your class may construct a rubric together.
- You and your classmates may construct a rubric together.
- You may create your own rubric with criteria you want to evaluate in your work.

How will a rubric help me?

A rubric will help you assess your work on a scale. Scales vary from rubric to rubric but usually range from 6 to 1, 5 to 1, or 4 to 1, with 6, 5, or 4 being the highest score and 1 being the lowest. If the rubric is being used by someone else to assess your work, the rubric will give your evaluator a clear range within which to place your work. If you are using the rubric yourself, it will help you make improvements to your work.

What are the types of rubrics?

- A **holistic rubric** has general criteria that can apply to a variety of assignments.
- An **analytic rubric** is specific to a particular assignment. The criteria for evaluation address the specific issues important to that assignment. See pp. GA 15–16 for examples of the analytic rubric used to assess the GHSWT.

PRENTICE HALL
LITERATURE

Timeless Voices, Timeless Themes

Copper

Bronze

Silver

Gold

Platinum

The American Experience

The British Tradition

CONTRIBUTING AUTHORS

The contributing authors guided the direction and philosophy of *Prentice Hall Literature: Timeless Voices, Timeless Themes*. Working with the development team, they helped to build the pedagogical integrity of the program and to ensure its relevance for today's teachers and students.

Kate Kinsella

Kate Kinsella, Ed.D., is a faculty member in the Department of Secondary Education at San Francisco State University. A specialist in second-language acquisition and adolescent reading and writing, she teaches coursework addressing language and literacy development across the secondary curricula. She has taught high-school ESL and directed SFSU's *Intensive English Program* for first-generation bilingual college students. She maintains secondary classroom involvement by teaching an academic literacy class for second-language learners through the University's *Step to College* partnership program. A former Fulbright lecturer and perennial institute leader for TESOL, the California Reading Association, and the California League of Middle Schools, Dr. Kinsella provides professional development nationally on topics ranging from learning-style enhancement to second-language reading. Her scholarship has been published in journals such as the *TESOL Journal,* the *CATESOL Journal,* and the *Social Studies Review.* Dr. Kinsella earned her M.A. in TESOL from San Francisco State University and her Ed.D. in Second Language Acquisition from the University of San Francisco.

Kevin Feldman

Kevin Feldman, Ed.D., is the Director of Reading and Early Intervention with the Sonoma County Office of Education (SCOE). His career in education spans thirty-one years. As the Director of Reading and Early Intervention for SCOE, he develops, organizes, and monitors programs related to K–12 literacy and prevention of reading difficulties. He also serves as a Leadership Team Consultant to the California Reading and Literature Project and assists in the development and implementation of K–12 programs throughout California. Dr. Feldman earned his undergraduate degree in Psychology from Washington State University and has a Master's degree in Special Education, Learning Disabilities, and Instructional Design from U.C. Riverside. He earned his Ed.D. in Curriculum and Instruction from the University of San Francisco.

Colleen Shea Stump

Colleen Shea Stump, Ph.D., is a Special Education supervisor in the area of Resource and Inclusion for Seattle Public Schools. She served as a professor and chairperson for the Department of Special Education at San Francisco State University. She continues as a lead consultant in the area of collaboration for the California State Improvement Grant and travels the state of California providing professional development training in the areas of collaboration, content literacy instruction, and inclusive instruction. Dr. Stump earned her doctorate at the University of Washington, her M.A. in Special Education from the University of New Mexico, and her B.S. in Elementary Education from the University of Wisconsin–Eau Claire.

Joyce Armstrong Carroll

In her forty-year career, Joyce Armstrong Carroll, Ed. D., has taught on every grade level from primary to graduate school. In the past twenty years, she has trained teachers in the teaching of writing. A nationally known consultant, she has served as president of TCTE and on NCTE's Commission on Composition. More than fifty of her articles have appeared in journals such as *Curriculum Review, English Journal, Media & Methods, Southwest Philosophical Studies, English in Texas,* and the *Florida English Journal.* With Edward E. Wilson, Dr. Carroll co-authored *Acts of Teaching: How to Teach Writing* and co-edited *Poetry After Lunch: Poetry to Read Aloud.* She co-directs the New Jersey Writing Project in Texas.

Edward E. Wilson

A former editor of *English in Texas,* Edward E. Wilson has served as a high-school English teacher and a writing consultant in school districts nationwide. Wilson has served on both the Texas Teacher Professional Practices Commission and NCTE's Commission on Composition. Wilson's poetry appears in Paul Janeczko's anthology *The Music of What Happens.* With Dr. Carroll, he co-wrote *Acts of Teaching: How to Teach Writing* and co-edited *Poetry After Lunch: Poetry to Read Aloud.* Wilson co-directs the New Jersey Writing Project in Texas.

PROGRAM ADVISORS

The program advisors provided ongoing input throughout the development of *Prentice Hall Literature: Timeless Voices, Timeless Themes*. Their valuable insights ensure that the perspectives of the teachers throughout the country are represented within this literature series.

Diane Cappillo
English Department Chair
Barbara Goleman Senior High School
Miami, Florida

Anita Clay
Language Arts Instructor
Gateway Institute of Technology
St. Louis, Missouri

Ellen Eberly
Language Arts Instructor
Catholic Memorial High School
West Roxbury, Massachusetts

Nancy Fahner
L.A.M.P. Lansing Area Manufacturing
  Partnership
Ingham Intermediate School District
Mason, Michigan

Terri Fields
Instructor of Language Arts,
  Communication Arts, and Author
Sunnyslope High School
Phoenix, Arizona

Susan Goldberg
Language Arts Instructor
Westlake Middle School
Thornwood, New York

Margo L. Graf
English Department Chair, Speech,
  Yearbook, Journalism
Lane Middle School
Fort Wayne, Indiana

Christopher E. Guarraia
Language Arts Instructor
Lakewood High School
Saint Petersburg, Florida

V. Pauline Hodges
Teacher, Educational Consultant
Forgan High School
Forgan, Oklahoma

Karen Hurley
Language Arts Instructor
Perry Meridian Middle School
Indianapolis, Indiana

Lenore D. Hynes
Language Arts Coordinator
Sunman-Dearborn Community
  Schools
Sunman, Indiana

Linda Kramer
Language Arts Instructor
Norman High School North
Norman, Oklahoma

Thomas S. Lindsay
Assistant Superintendent of Schools
Manheim District 83
Franklin Park, Illinois

Agathaniki (Niki) Locklear
English Department Chair
Simon Kenton High School
Independence, Kentucky

Ashley MacDonald
Language Arts Instructor
South Forsyth High School
Cumming, Georgia

Mary Ellen Mastej
Language Arts Instructor
Scott Middle School
Hammond, Indiana

Nancy L. Monroe
English, Speed Reading Teacher
Bolton High School
Alexandria, Louisiana

Jim Moody
Language Arts Instructor
Northside High School
Fort Smith, Arkansas

David Morris
Teacher of English, Writing,
  Publications, Yearbook
Washington High School
South Bend, Indiana

Rosemary A. Naab
English Department Chair
Ryan High School
Archdiocese of Philadelphia
Philadelphia, Pennsylvania

Ann Okamura
English Teacher
Laguna Creek High School
Elk Grove, California

Tucky Roger
Coordinator of Languages
Tulsa Public Schools
Tulsa, Oklahoma

Jonathan L. Schatz
English Teacher/Team Leader
Tappan Zee High School
Orangeburg, New York

John Scott
Assistant Principal
Middlesex High School
Saluda, Virginia

Ken Spurlock
Assistant Principal, Retired
Boone County High School
Florence, Kentucky

Dr. Jennifer Watson
Secondary Language Arts
  Coordinator
Putnam City Schools
Oklahoma City, Oklahoma

Joan West
Assistant Principal
Oliver Middle School
Broken Arrow, Oklahoma

CONTENTS IN BRIEF

Learn About Literature

Themes in Literature

Literary Genres

Resources

Handbooks

Indexes

UNIT 1

THEME: *Spine Tinglers*

SKILLS WORKSHOPS

THEME: *Challenges and Choices*

SKILLS WORKSHOPS

UNIT 3

THEME: *Moments of Discovery*

SKILLS WORKSHOPS

UNIT 4

THEME: *The Lighter Side*

UNIT 5

THEME: *Visions of the Future*

	Why Read Literature?		442
	How to Read Literature: **Use Critical Reading Strategies**		443
Bill Gates	*from* The Road Ahead	Nonfiction	446
Isaac Asimov	The Machine That Won the War	Short Story	456

Connections: *Literature and Technology*

Julia Alvarez	Aha Moment	Article	466

Comparing Literary Works

Robert Frost	Fire and Ice	Poetry	472
Sara Teasdale	"There Will Come Soft Rains" (War Time)	Poetry	473
Edwin Muir	The Horses	Poetry	474
Richard Brautigan	All Watched Over by Machines of Loving Grace	Poetry	476

Reading Informational Materials: *Product Information*

Technical Directions and Warranty	Product Information	480

Comparing Literary Works

Arthur C. Clarke	"If I Forget Thee, Oh Earth . . ."	Short Story	486
Rachel Carson	*from* Silent Spring	Nonfiction	491
Bryan Woolley	To the Residents of A.D. 2029	Nonfiction	495

Comparing Literary Works

Shu Ting Translated by Donald Finkel	Gifts	Poetry	504
Nelson Mandela	Glory and Hope	Speech	506

SKILLS WORKSHOPS

Writing Workshop: Exposition: How-to Essays 512

Listening and Speaking Workshop: Effective Listening and Note Taking 516

Assessment Workshop: Generalizations 517

Contents ◆ *xi*

UNIT 6

GENRE: *Short Stories*

SKILLS WORKSHOPS

GENRE: *Nonfiction*

SKILLS WORKSHOPS

UNIT 8

GENRE: *Drama*

SKILLS WORKSHOPS

UNIT 9

GENRE: *Poetry*

(Continued on page xvi.)

Genre: *Poetry* (continued)

Skills Workshops

UNIT 10 · GENRE: *The Epic*

SKILLS WORKSHOPS

Complete Contents by Genre

COMPARING LITERARY WORKS

READING INFORMATIONAL MATERIALS

CONNECTIONS

How to Read Literature

Writing Workshops

Listening and Speaking Workshops

Assessment Workshops

Learn About Literature

Forms of Literature

Short Story • Nonfiction • Drama • Poetry • Folk Literature

Just as there are different styles of music, such as classical or rock, so too are there different forms of literature. Each is called a genre and has its own distinct characteristics. These pages present a brief explanation and an example of each genre. They will help you understand and appreciate the literature when you read these various works in their entirety.

Short Story

A **short story** is a brief work of fiction. In most short stories, one main character faces a conflict that is resolved in the plot. In addition, a short story usually conveys a theme, or message about life. Good craftsmanship goes into the writing of a good story, which must accomplish its purpose in relatively few words.

● **What do you learn about a character's conflict in this story's opening?**

She was one of those pretty, charming young women who are born, as if by an error of Fate, into a petty official's family. She had no dowry, no hopes, not the slightest chance of being appreciated, understood, loved, and married by a rich and distinguished man; so she slipped into marriage with a minor civil servant at the Ministry of Education.

FROM "THE NECKLACE," GUY DE MAUPASSANT, P. 608

Nonfiction

Nonfiction is writing that tells about real people, places, objects, events, and ideas. Many of the nonfiction articles in this book are either essays or biographical or autobiographical sketches. All discuss the real world as opposed to an imaginary one. The author of a nonfiction article may wish to convey and explain information, convince readers to accept a particular idea or opinion, or simply entertain and amuse readers.

● **Based on its opening, what do you sense is the author's purpose in this nonfiction article?**

The essence of childhood, of course, is play, which my friends and I did endlessly on streets that we reluctantly shared with traffic. As a daring receiver in touch football, I spent many happy years running up and down those asphalt fields, hoping that a football would hit me before a Chevrolet did.

FROM "GO DEEP TO THE SEWER," BILL COSBY, P. 368

> "In the midst of any adventure, a born writer has a desire to hurry home and put it into words."
>
> —Maxine Hong Kingston

Drama

Drama is written to be performed by actors. The script is made up of dialogue and monologue—the words the actors say—and stage directions, which comment on how and where the action occurs.

○ **How does the appearance of this dramatic text differ from the appearance of a short story?**

> **HORACE.** That's a pretty piece.
> **MARY CATHERINE.** Yes, it is.
> [*A pause. They dance again.* HORACE *stops.*]
> **HORACE.** I'm ready to go if you are, Mary Catherine.
> **MARY CATHERINE.** I'm ready. [*They start out.*] Scared?
>
> FROM "THE DANCERS," HORTON FOOTE, P. 734

Poetry

Poetry is literature that appears in verse form. It often has a regular rhythm and, sometimes, a rhyme scheme. Some poems tell a story, while other poems present a single image or express a single emotion or thought. Most poems use concise, musical, and emotionally charged language to convey an idea.

○ **How do the lines of poetry below differ in form from the prose paragraphs on the facing page?**

> Some say the world will end in fire,
> Some say in ice.
> From what I've tasted of desire
> I hold with those who favor fire.
>
> FROM "FIRE AND ICE," ROBERT FROST, P. 472

Folk Literature

Folk literature is the unwritten lore of a specific people or culture, passed down through the generations by word of mouth until, at some point, it is put into writing. Folk literature includes myths, folk tales, fairy tales, legends, and fables. Such stories express the hopes, fears, loves, dreams, and values of the people who tell them and pass them on.

○ **What does the beginning of this myth indicate about the values of people in ancient Greece?**

> King Acrisius of Argos had only one child, a daughter, Danaë. She was beautiful above all the other women of the land, but this was small comfort to the King for not having a son.
>
> FROM "PERSEUS," EDITH HAMILTON, P. 214

Short Stories

Plot • Characters • Setting • Point of View • Theme

Short stories invite you to travel to fictional places, meet interesting and unusual people, and get involved with the problems they face. This book presents a variety of short stories. No two are exactly the same, although all the stories share certain characteristics and follow a prescribed structure.

Plot

The **plot** of a short story is its sequence of events. It involves both characters and a problem, or conflict. The plot begins with an exposition that introduces the characters, setting, and basic story. The action rises as characters try to resolve the problem. Tension increases as events lead to a climax, or high point of interest or suspense. The climax is followed by falling action, leading to the resolution of the conflict.

Climax

Rising Action Falling Action

Conflict Introduced

Exposition **Resolution**

⬤ **Which plot details do you learn from the opening sentence of this short story?**

I had called upon my friend, Mr. Sherlock Holmes, one day in the autumn of last year and found him in deep conversation with a very stout, florid-faced, elderly gentleman with fiery red hair.

FROM "THE RED-HEADED LEAGUE," SIR ARTHUR CONAN DOYLE, P. 96

Characters

The **characters** in a short story are the people or animals who participate in the action. Writers can develop characters in a variety of ways. Details about characters are revealed through their physical description and their words and actions. In addition, writers reveal characters through their interaction with other characters in the story.

⬤ **What do the details in the following passage tell you about Nat's character?**

Nat Hocken, because of a wartime disability, had a pension and did not work full-time at the farm. He worked three days a week, and they gave him the lighter jobs: hedging, thatching, repairs to the farm buildings.

Although he was married, with children, his was a solitary disposition; he liked best to work alone. It pleased him when he was given a bank to build up, or a gate to mend at the far end of the peninsula, where the sea surrounded the farmland on either side. Then, at midday, he would pause and eat the pasty that his wife had baked for him, and, sitting on the cliff's edge, watch the birds.

FROM "THE BIRDS," DAPHNE DU MAURIER, P. 50

"They ghosted you up a swell story . . ."   —Langston Hughes

Point of View

The **point of view** in a story is the vantage point from which the story is told. In *first-person narration*, the storyteller is a character in the action. In *third-person narration*, the story-teller reports events, taking no direct part in the action.

⦿ **Which clues in this sentence indicate the point of view of this short story?**

I was six when my mother taught me the art of invisible strength.

FROM "RULES OF THE GAME," AMY TAN, P. 262

Setting

The **setting** of a story is the time and place of the action. Time can include not only the historical period—past, present, or future—but also a specific year, season, or time of day. Place may involve not only the geographical place—a region, country, state, or town—but also the social, economic, or cultural environment.

In some stories, setting serves as a decorative but nonessential background. In contrast, the setting of other stories may drive the action by providing a problem that the characters must face and overcome.

⦿ **Which details in this passage help you to identify the setting of the story?**

I belong in Cleveland, Ohio. One winter's night, two years ago, I reached home just after dark, in a driving snowstorm, and the first thing I heard when I entered the house was that my dearest boyhood friend and schoolmate, John B. Hackett, had died the day before, and that his last utterance had been a desire that I would take his remains home to his poor old father and mother in Wisconsin. I was greatly shocked and grieved, but there was no time to waste in emotions; I must start at once.

FROM "THE INVALID'S STORY," MARK TWAIN, P. 596

Theme

The **theme** of a short story is the central message or insight into life revealed through the work. In some stories, the theme may be stated directly. In most stories, however, the theme is only implied. You must use the story's events to help you draw conclusions about its theme.

⦿ **Based on the following passage, what might be the theme of this story?**

He also felt the warmth of the earth. He sensed he was inside someone. Then he understood what Don Trine was doing. He was not crazy, he simply liked to feel the earth when it was sleeping.

FROM "THE HARVEST," TOMÁS RIVERA, P. 616

Nonfiction

Autobiography • Biography • Essay • Informational Text

Nonfiction is prose writing that presents and explains ideas or that tells about real people. Among nonfiction forms are essays, newspaper and magazine articles, journals, travelogues, biographies, and autobiographies. In this book, you will read several kinds of nonfiction and have the opportunity to explore the similarities and differences among them.

Autobiography

An **autobiography** is a form of non-fiction in which a person relates his or her own life story. It may tell about the person's whole life or only part of it. The author's purpose may be to explain his or her values, to teach lessons about life, to entertain or amuse readers, or any combination of these.

● **What does this passage from Rosa Parks's autobiography suggest about her purpose for writing?**

As I sat there, I tried not to think about what might happen. I knew that anything was possible. I could be manhandled or beaten. I could be arrested. People have asked me if it occurred to me then that I could be the test case the NAACP had been looking for. I did not think about that at all. In fact if I had let myself think too deeply about what might happen to me, I might have gotten off the bus. But I chose to remain.

FROM ROSA PARKS: MY STORY, ROSA PARKS, P. 168

Biography

A **biography** is a form of nonfiction in which a writer tells the life story of another person. Biographies have been written about many famous people, historical and contemporary, but they can also be written about "ordinary" people. As with an autobiography, a biography is factual and may be written to express a person's values, to teach lessons about life, or to entertain or inspire readers. A biography usually emphasizes the causes and effects of a person's actions.

● **Why might a writer have included the information presented here in a biography of Arthur Ashe?**

He once described his life as "a succession of fortunate circumstances." He was in his twenties then. More than half of his life was behind him. His memory of his mother was confined to a single image: in a blue corduroy bathrobe she stood in a doorway looking out on the courts and playing fields surrounding their house, which stood in the center of a Richmond playground. Weakened by illness, she was taken to a hospital that day, and died at the age of twenty-seven. He was six.

FROM "ARTHUR ASHE REMEMBERED," JOHN MCPHEE, P. 682

> "It has always seemed to me that truth is not just 'stranger than fiction,' but also more interesting."
> —Jim Haskins

Essay

An **essay** is a short nonfiction work about a particular subject. It presents a main idea and supports it with examples, facts, statistics, or anecdotes.

- A *narrative essay* tells a true story.
- An *expository essay* gives information, discusses ideas, or explains a process.
- A *persuasive essay* tries to convince readers to do something or to accept the writer's point of view.
- A *reflective essay* presents the writer's reflections or thoughts on a topic of personal importance.

● **What does this opening from an essay suggest about its main idea?**

It has taken me a good number of years to come to any measure of respect for summer. I was, being May-born, literally an "infant of the spring" and, during the later childhood years, tended, for some reason or other, to rather worship the cold aloofness of winter. . . . For the longest kind of time I simply thought that *summer* was a mistake.

FROM "ON SUMMER," LORRAINE HANSBERRY, P. 656

Informational Text

Informational text is writing that provides the knowledge to guide and educate you. Informational texts include magazine and newspaper articles on current topics, as well as instructional manuals and textbooks.

● **Based on this lead paragraph from a newspaper article, how might you expect the text to educate or enlighten you?**

San Francisco—In dim light they appear to be sleeping, but they've been dead up to 4,000 years: more than 100 astoundingly well-preserved mummies unearthed in a Chinese desert, whose inexplicably blond hair and white skin could topple dogmas about early human history.

FROM "CAUCASIAN MUMMIES MYSTIFY CHINESE," KEAY DAVIDSON, P. 132

Drama

*Types of Plays • Dialogue and Monologue •
Stage Directions • Plot and Conflict*

Drama consists of writing that is intended to be performed by actors for an audience. The script combines dialogue—the words the actors say—with stage directions—the author's comments on how and where the actors should move and speak. As you read drama, you "set the stage" in your own mind, using your imagination to visualize the scenery, lighting, costumes, and actors.

Types of Plays

Not all plays are the same in their tone, style, or message. A **comedy** is a humorous play with a happy ending. A **tragedy** is a play in which a hero suffers a major downfall. A **drama** is a serious play, although the consequences are not necessarily as dire as those in a tragedy.

● **From what type of play do you think the following passage comes? Why?**

> BENVOLIO.
> O noble Prince, I can discover all
> The unlucky manage of this fatal
>   brawl.
> There lies the man, slain by young
>   Romeo,
> That slew thy kinsman, brave
>   Mercutio.
>
> FROM THE TRAGEDY OF ROMEO AND JULIET,
> WILLIAM SHAKESPEARE, P. 770

Dialogue and Monologue

The action of a play is conveyed mainly through **dialogue**—the conversations between two or more characters. A **monologue** is a lengthy speech that one character addresses to others on stage. Both dialogue and monologue reveal character traits and advance the story action in drama.

● **What do you learn about the speakers in this brief piece of dialogue?**

> MARY CATHERINE. I love to dance.
> HORACE. Well . . . I don't dance too well.
> MARY CATHERINE. There's nothing to it but confidence.
> HORACE. That's what my sister says. . . .
> MARY CATHERINE. I didn't learn for the longest kind of time for lack of confidence and then Emily gave me a long lecture about it and I got confidence and went ahead and learned. Would you like to come in for a while?
> HORACE. Well . . . if it's all right with you. . . .
> MARY CATHERINE. I'd be glad to have you.
> HORACE. Thank you.
>
> FROM THE DANCERS, HORTON FOOTE, P. 734

Upstage Right	Upstage Center	Upstage Left
Right	Center	Left
Downstage Right	Downstage Center	Downstage Left

Stage Directions

Stage directions are the instructions for performing the play and the descriptions of settings, characters, and actions. When you read dramatic literature, the stage directions can help you visualize the play. Using a staging chart like the one shown above, you can imagine where the scenery is and how the actors move by following the indications of downstage, upstage, left, and right.

● **What information in these stage directions helps you visualize the setting of the play?**

[Scene: The stage is divided into four acting areas: downstage left is the living room of INEZ and HERMAN STANLEY. Downstage right is part of a small-town drugstore. Upstage right is the living room of ELIZABETH CREWS. Upstage left, the yard and living room of MARY CATHERINE DAVIS.]

FROM THE DANCERS, HORTON FOOTE, P. 734

Plot and Conflict

A play, much like a short story, contains a **plot,** or series of events, involving a **conflict,** or problem, that one or more characters face. The conflict is introduced early in the play, perhaps in its opening scene. Tension builds to the climax, and by the final scene of the play, the conflict has been resolved, either happily or unhappily, for the main characters.

● **What kind of conflict is indicated in this dialogue?**

EMILY. I don't feel good . . . . [She begins to cry.] Oh, Mother, I don't want to go to the dance tonight. Please, ma'm, don't make me. I'll do anything in this world for you if you promise me . . .

ELIZABETH. Emily. This is all settled. You are going to that dance. Do you understand me? You are going to that dance. That sweet, nice brother of Inez Stanley's will be here any minute. . . .

FROM THE DANCERS, HORTON FOOTE, P. 734

Poetry

Types of Poetry • Poetic Form • Figurative Language • Rhyme and Rhythm

Poetry is writing that combines language, images, and sounds to create a special emotional effect. A poem's sound and structure are different from those of prose, the writing you find in short stories and nonfiction. Poetry is arranged in lines and stanzas, and its language is more visual and musical than prose. A story speaks to readers, but a poem sings to them.

Types of Poetry

There are many different types of poems. A **narrative poem,** like a short story, tells a story that includes a plot, characters, and a setting. A **lyric poem** expresses the observations and feelings of a speaker in a musical way. A **dramatic poem** uses the techniques of drama in the form of a monologue for one speaker or dramatic dialogue for two or more speakers.

● **Which details in this passage help you to recognize it comes from a lyric poem?**

I like hot days, hot days
Sweat is what you got days
Bugs buzzin from cousin to cousin
Juices dripping
Running and ripping
Catch the one you love days
FROM "SUMMER," WALTER DEAN MYERS,
P. 927

Poetic Form

Poetic form refers to the way the lines of a poem are shaped and arranged. Often, a poet groups lines into formal units called *stanzas.* A stanza may have any number of lines. Poetic form affects the way the poem is read aloud and, to a degree, the message that the poem conveys.

● **Why do you think the last lines of this poem have been set apart?**

Harlem

What happens to a dream deferred?

    Does it dry up
    like a raisin in the sun?
    Or fester like a sore——
    And then run?
    Does it stink like rotten meat?
    Or crust and sugar over——
    like a syrupy sweet?

    Maybe it just sags
    like a heavy load.

    Or does it explode?
"DREAM DEFERRED," LANGSTON HUGHES, P. 904

Figurative Language

Figurative language is writing or speech that is not meant to be taken literally. It is often used to create vivid impressions by setting up fresh comparisons between dissimilar things.

In a **simile,** *like* or *as* is used to compare two basically different things. For example, the simile "I wandered lonely as a cloud" compares the speaker to a cloud and emphasizes the speaker's aimlessness.

In contrast to a simile, a **metaphor** states a comparison of two things directly. In the metaphor "if dreams die / Life is a broken-winged bird," the poet compares life to an injured bird and shows the effect of losing hope.

In **personification,** a nonhuman subject is given human characteristics. In the lines "Let the rain kiss you. / Let the rain sing you a lullaby," the poet personifies the rain, making it seem vital and alive.

● **What comparisons do you find in these lines of poetry?**

Continuous as the stars that shine
And twinkle on the milky way,
They stretched in never-ending line
Along the margin of a bay:
Ten thousand saw I at a glance,
Tossing their heads in sprightly dance.
FROM "I WANDERED LONELY AS A CLOUD,"
WILLIAM WORDSWORTH, P. **896**

Rhythm and Rhyme

In addition to poetic conventions like figurative language and stanza structure, the elements of rhythm and rhyme give poetry its musical qualities.

Rhythm in a poem is the pattern of stressed (´) and unstressed (˘) syllables in each line. Notice the regular rhythm in this line:

Once upon a midnight dreary . . .

Rhyme in a poem is the repetition of sounds at the ends of words. For example:

Once upon a midnight <u>dreary</u>,
While I pondered, weak and <u>weary</u> . . .

● **What rhythm and rhyme do you find in these lines of poetry?**

Two roads diverged in a yellow wood,
And sorry I could not travel both
And be one traveler, long I stood
And looked down one as far as I could
To where it bent in the undergrowth;
FROM "THE ROAD NOT TAKEN," ROBERT FROST,
P. **188**

Folk Literature

Myth • Folk Tale • Tall Tale • Epic

Not all stories were written down when they were first told. Folk literature comes from generations of peoples or cultures that passed down their favorite tales orally before ever recording them. Folk literature includes myths, folk tales, tall tales, and epics. Like a favorite family recipe, folk literature holds special enjoyment for all those who know it and pass it on.

Myth

A **myth** is a fictional tale that explains the actions of gods or the causes of natural phenomena. It involves supernatural elements and has little historical truth to it. Among the most familiar myths today are those of the ancient Greeks and Romans.

Myths have several purposes. They serve as a cultural history, explaining natural phenomena such as oceans and mountains. They also reinforce a culture's values. Finally, they are a source of entertainment.

● **Which details in this passage indicate that it is from a myth?**

King Acrisius of Argos had only one child, a daughter, Danaë. She was beautiful above all the other women of the land, but this was small comfort to the King for not having a son. He journeyed to Delphi to ask the god if there was any hope that some day he would be the father of a boy. The priestess told him no, and added what was far worse: that his daughter would have a son who would kill him.

FROM "PERSEUS," EDITH HAMILTON, P. 214

Folk Tale

A **folk tale** is a story composed orally and then passed from person to person by word of mouth. As part of an oral tradition, folk tales originated among people who could neither read nor write. They entertained one another by telling stories aloud, often about heroes, adventure, magic, or romance. Like mythology, folk tales also help reinforce a culture's values and explain the natural world.

● **This passage comes from an African folk tale. Which elements make it an appealing story to hear?**

Once, not far from the city of Accra on the Gulf of Guinea, a country man went out to his garden to dig up some yams to take to market. While he was digging, one of the yams said to him, "Well, at last you're here. You never weeded me, but now you come around with your digging stick. Go away and leave me alone!"

FROM "TALK," HAROLD COURLANDER AND GEORGE HERZOG, P. 412

Tall Tale

A **tall tale** is a kind of humorous story in which characters possess superhuman abilities and impossible happenings occur. Tall tales were common on the American frontier, when characters like Paul Bunyan and Febold Feboldson were favorites. Tall tales are told in common, everyday speech and employ some realistic detail in addition to exaggeration.

● **Which details from this passage indicate that it is from a tall tale?**

. . . The sun shone on his cornfield until the corn began to pop, while the rain washed the syrup out of his sugar cane.

Now the cane field was on a hill and the cornfield was in a valley. The syrup flowed downhill into the popped corn and rolled it into great balls. Bergstrom says some of them were hundreds of feet high and looked like big tennis balls from a distance. You never see any of them now, because the grasshoppers ate them all up in one day, July 21, 1874.

FROM "FEBOLD FEBOLDSON," PAUL R. BEATH, IN WRITERS OF THE AMERICAN MIDWEST, PRENTICE HALL LITERATURE LIBRARY, P. 23

Epic

An **epic** is a long narrative poem about the deeds of gods or heroes in war or travel. An epic is written in ornate, poetic language. It incorporates myth, legend, and history and often includes the intervention of the gods in human affairs.

In an epic, the poet begins by announcing the subject and asking a Muse, one of the nine goddesses of the arts, literature, and sciences, to help.

Homer's epic *Odyssey* (p. 980) tells the story of the Greek hero Odysseus, the king of Ithaca.

● **Which characteristics of an epic do you find in this opening verse of Homer's *Odyssey*?**

Sing in me, Muse, and through me
    tell the story
of that man skilled in the ways of
    contending,
the wanderer, harried for years on end,
after he plundered the stronghold
of the proud height of Troy.

FROM THE ODYSSEY, HOMER, P. 980

UNIT 1 *Spine Tinglers*

Exploring the Theme

Turn the page to enter a world of suspense and mystery. Here, extraordinary events are commonplace, and desperate acts or unexplained phenomena can change the course of a life forever. Experience these stories, poems, and essays—if you dare! Your heart will race, your fists will clench, and your spine will tingle.

In "The Cask of Amontillado," a man is driven to cold-blooded, methodical murder for reasons known only to himself. Follow the condemned man as he is unknowingly led to a terrifying end. Scream out a warning to him if you choose, but he is not likely to hear you. His fate has already been decided by others more powerful.

▲ **Critical Viewing** Which details in this painting create a sense of mystery or suspense? **[Analyze]**

Why Read Literature?

Whenever you read a work of suspense, you have a purpose, or reason. You might just want to experience the feeling of a good scare, but you may have other reasons for reading as well. Preview these three purposes you might set before reading works in this unit.

1 Read for the Love of Literature

Edgar Allan Poe was obsessed with the fear of being buried alive. Poe conveyed this horror so imaginatively in his stories that he inspired one Russian reader to patent his own device. The mechanism enabled the "deceased" to signal those above ground that they had acted a little too hastily. You may understand why someone would go to such lengths when you read **"The Cask of Amontillado,"** page 6.

What happens when the hunter becomes the hunted? That is the ominous question Richard Connell seeks to answer in a frightening story about a different kind of hunt. You may not be able to resist rushing to the end to learn what happens in **"The Most Dangerous Game,"** page 18.

2 Read to Be Entertained

Sometimes the most unexpected events happen at the end of a close contest when the entire game is on the line. Find out what happens when it all comes down to the final man in Ernest Thayer's **"Casey at the Bat,"** page 42.

If you have ever heard footsteps echoing loudly on an empty street at night or imagined a lurking shadow behind every tree, you will sympathize with the spooked horseman in Walter de la Mare's **"The Listeners,"** page 122.

3 Read for Information

The discovery of 100 Caucasian mummies in a remote region of China challenges established beliefs about ancient Chinese history. Learn more about these mysterious mummies by reading Keay Davidson's article **"Caucasian Mummies Mystify Chinese,"** page 132.

Take It to the Net

Visit the Web site for online instruction and activities related to each selection in this unit.
www.phschool.com

How to Read Literature

Use Literal Comprehension Strategies

Your first goal in reading is to understand what the writer is saying. This task becomes more difficult when writers use unfamiliar words or construct sentences that do not make sense when you first read them. You can use the following literal comprehension strategies to help clear up confusion.

1. Break down long sentences.

- Read sentences in meaningful groups of words, not word by word.
- Figure out the subject of the sentence. Then, determine what the sentence is saying about that subject.
- Rearrange the sentence if you are confused by word order, as the example at right demonstrates.

2. Use context clues.

Context refers to the words, phrases, sentences, and ideas that surround a word. Use clues contained in the context to help determine the meaning of unfamiliar words or phrases. Look at this sample passage:

> "I wanted the ideal animal to hunt," explained the general. "So I said: 'What are the attributes of an ideal *quarry*?' "
>
> — *from* "The Most Dangerous Game"

If the word *quarry* is unfamiliar, you could determine its meaning by looking at the previous sentence and noticing how the word *ideal* is repeated. The general is looking for the *ideal* animal to hunt, so you can conclude that *quarry* probably means a hunted animal.

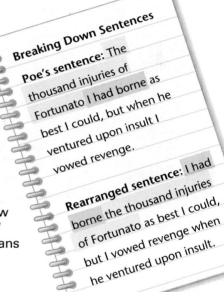

Breaking Down Sentences

Poe's sentence: The thousand injuries of Fortunato I had borne as best I could, but when he ventured upon insult I vowed revenge.

Rearranged sentence: I had borne the thousand injuries of Fortunato as best I could, but I vowed revenge when he ventured upon insult.

3. Summarize.

Summarizing involves picking out key events, describing them briefly in your own words, and then placing them in order of occurrence to concisely report the action or main idea of a selection. Prepare a summary to serve these purposes:

- Make sure you understand what happens in a story as you read.
- Remind yourself of basic plot events later on.

4. Predict.

Predicting, or making guesses about what will happen later in a selection, keeps you actively involved in a story. Use prediction to avoid missing important details and to check your understanding of what you have read.

As you read this unit's selections, apply these strategies to increase your understanding of the text.

Prepare to Read

The Cask of Amontillado

 Take It to the Net

Visit www.phschool.com for interactive activities and instruction related to "The Cask of Amontillado," including
- background
- graphic organizers
- literary elements
- reading strategies

Preview

Connecting to the Literature

Often, it does not take much to spark a desire for revenge. It can start with a simple insult or an unresolved dispute. You encounter these situations in books, movies, television shows, and in real life. Sometimes, as in this story, a quest for revenge can get out of hand.

Background

Much of the action in this story takes place in catacombs. These long passageways and side tunnels stretch out like cities of the dead. In past centuries, many wealthy European families held funerals in catacombs beneath the family manor. The dead were then laid to rest, surrounded by the bones of their ancestors. The most extensive known catacombs are found outside Rome.

Literary Analysis

Mood

The **mood** of a work of literature is the primary feeling that the reader experiences while reading it. In "The Cask of Amontillado," Edgar Allan Poe carefully chooses words and details to create a mood of eerie suspense. In this example, notice how the italicized words affect the mood.

> We passed through a *range of low arches*, *descended*, passed on, and *descending* again, arrived at a *deep crypt*, in which the *foulness* of the air caused our flambeaux rather to *glow* than flame.

As the story unfolds, see how quickly the mood changes.

Connecting Literary Elements

A **description** is a portrait painted in words of a person, place, or object. In "The Cask of Amontillado," description creates the eerie mood. For example, details such as *drops of moisture* that *trickle among the bones* help readers picture the scene and sense the mood. Take note of dark descriptions that contribute to the mood.

Reading Strategy

Breaking Down Confusing Sentences

When you approach Poe's writing, you may need to **break down confusing sentences**. To do this:

- Read sentences in meaningful sections, not word by word.
- Figure out the subject—who or what the sentence is about. Then, determine what the sentence is saying about that subject.
- Rearrange, change, or take out words to make the sentence clearer.

If you come to a difficult sentence while you are reading, use a chart like this one to break the sentence into sections and clarify information about the subjects. The example on the right breaks down the first sentence in the story.

Subject	Information About the Subject
I (narrator)	had borne the thousand injuries of Fortunato
he (Fortunato)	ventured upon insult
I (narrator)	vowed revenge

Vocabulary Development

precluded (prē klōōd′ id) *v.* prevented; made impossible in advance (p. 7)

retribution (re′ trə byōō′ shən) *n.* payback; punishment for a misdeed (p. 7)

accosted (ə kôst′ id) *v.* greeted, especially in an aggressive way (p. 7)

afflicted (ə flikt′ id) *v.* suffering or sickened (p. 8)

explicit (eks plis′ it) *adj.* clearly stated (p. 8)

recoiling (ri koil′ iŋ) *v.* staggering back (p. 10)

termination (tʉr′ mə nā′ shən) *n.* end (p. 10)

subsided (səb sīd′ id) *v.* settled down; became less active or intense (p. 11)

The Cask of Amontillado[1]

Edgar Allan Poe

The Court Jester, 1875 (detail), William Merritt Chase, Pennsylvania Academy of the Fine Arts, Philadelphia

▲ **Critical Viewing** How does this costume compare with your image of the costume worn by Fortunato? **[Compare and Contrast]**

The thousand injuries of Fortunato I had borne as I best could, but when he ventured upon insult I vowed revenge. You, who so well know the nature of my soul, will not suppose, however, that I gave utterance to a threat. At *length* I would be avenged; this was a point definitely settled—but the very definitiveness with which it was resolved <u>precluded</u> the idea of risk. I must not only punish but punish with impunity.[2] A wrong is unredressed when <u>retribution</u> overtakes its redresser. It is equally unredressed when the avenger fails to make himself felt as such to him who has done the wrong.

It must be understood that neither by word nor deed had I given Fortunato cause to doubt my good will. I continued, as was my wont, to smile in his face, and he did not perceive that my smile *now* was at the thought of his immolation.[3]

He had a weak point—this Fortunato—although in other regards he was a man to be respected and even feared. He prided himself on his connoisseurship[4] in wine. Few Italians have the true virtuoso[5] spirit. For the most part their enthusiasm is adopted to suit the time and opportunity, to practice imposture upon the British and Austrian millionaires. In painting and gemmary, Fortunato, like his countrymen, was a quack, but in the matter of old wines he was sincere. In this respect I did not differ from him materially; I was skillful in the Italian vintages myself, and bought largely whenever I could.

It was about dusk, one evening during the supreme madness of the carnival season, that I encountered my friend. He <u>accosted</u> me with excessive warmth, for he had been drinking much. The man wore motley.[6] He had on a tight-fitting parti-striped dress, and his head was surmounted by the conical cap and bells. I was so pleased to see him that I thought I should never have done wringing his hand.

I said to him, "My dear Fortunato, you are luckily met. How remarkably well you are looking today. But I have received a pipe[7] of what passes for Amontillado, and I have my doubts."

"How?" said he. "Amontillado? A pipe? Impossible! And in the middle of the carnival!"

"I have my doubts," I replied: "and I was silly enough to pay the full Amontillado price without consulting you in the matter. You were not to be found, and I was fearful of losing a bargain."

"Amontillado!"

"I have my doubts."

"Amontillado!"

"And I must satisfy them."

"Amontillado!"

---

1. **Amontillado** (ə män´ tə ya´ dō) *n.* a pale, dry sherry.
2. **impunity** (im pyoō´ ni tē´) *n.* freedom from consequences.
3. **immolation** (im´ ə lā´ shən) *n.* destruction.
4. **connoisseurship** (kän´ ə sur´ ship) *n.* expert judgment.
5. **virtuoso** (vur´ choō ō´ sō) *adj.* masterly skill in a particular field.
6. **motley** (mät´ lē) *n.* a clown's multicolored costume.
7. **pipe** (pīp) *n.* large barrel, holding approximately 126 gallons.

---

precluded (prē kloōd´ id) *v.* prevented; made impossible in advance

retribution (re trə byoō´ shən) *n.* payback; punishment for a misdeed

accosted (ə kôst´ id) *v.* greeted, especially in a forward or aggressive way

Reading Check

Why does the speaker vow revenge on Fortunato?

"As you are engaged, I am on my way to Luchesi. If any one has a critical turn it is he. He will tell me—"

"Luchesi cannot tell Amontillado from sherry."

"And yet some fools will have it that his taste is a match for your own."

"Come, let us go."

"Whither?"

"To your vaults."

"My friend, no; I will not impose upon your good nature. I perceive you have an engagement. Luchesi—"

"I have no engagement—come."

"My friend, no. It is not the engagement, but the severe cold with which I perceive you are <u>afflicted</u>. The vaults are insufferably damp. They are encrusted with niter."

afflicted (ə flikt´ id) v. suffering or sickened

"Let us go, nevertheless. The cold is merely nothing. Amontillado! You have been imposed upon. And as for Luchesi, he cannot distinguish sherry from Amontillado."

Thus speaking, Fortunato possessed himself of my arm; and putting on a mask of black silk and drawing a *roquelaure*[8] closely about my person, I suffered him to hurry me to my palazzo.

There were no attendants at home; they had absconded to make merry in honor of the time. I had told them that I should not return until the morning, and had given them <u>explicit</u> orders not to stir from the house. These orders were sufficient, I well knew, to insure their immediate disappearance, one and all, as soon as my back was turned.

explicit (eks plis´ it) adj. clearly stated

I took from their sconces two flambeaux, and giving one to Fortunato, bowed him through several suites of rooms to the archway that led into the vaults. I passed down a long and winding staircase, requesting him to be cautious as he followed. We came at length to the foot of the descent, and stood together upon the damp ground of the catacombs of the Montresors.

The gait of my friend was unsteady, and the bells upon his cap jingled as he strode.

"The pipe," he said.

"It is farther on," said I; "but observe the white webwork which gleams from these cavern walls."

He turned towards me, and looked into my eyes with two filmy orbs that distilled the rheum of intoxication.

"Niter?" he asked, at length.

"Niter," I replied. "How long have you had that cough?"

"Ugh! ugh! ugh!—ugh! ugh! ugh!—ugh! ugh! ugh!—ugh! ugh! ugh!—ugh! ugh! ugh!"

My poor friend found it impossible to reply for many minutes.

"It is nothing," he said, at last.

"Come," I said, with decision, "we will go back; your health is precious. You are rich, respected, admired, beloved; you are happy, as once I was.

Literary Analysis
Mood How does Fortunato's cough add to the eerie mood?

---

8. roquelaure (räk´ ə lôr) *n.* knee-length cloak.

You are a man to be missed. For me it is no matter. We will go back; you will be ill, and I cannot be responsible. Besides, there is Luchesi—"

"Enough," he said; "the cough is a mere nothing; it will not kill me. I shall not die of a cough."

"True—true," I replied; "and, indeed, I had no intention of alarming you unnecessarily—but you should use all proper caution. A draft of this Medoc will defend us from the damps."

Here I knocked off the neck of a bottle which I drew from a long row of its fellows that lay upon the mold.

"Drink," I said, presenting him the wine.

He raised it to his lips with a leer. He paused and nodded to me familiarly, while his bells jingled.

"I drink," he said "to the buried that repose around us."

"And I to your long life."

He again took my arm, and we proceeded.

"These vaults," he said, "are extensive."

"The Montresors," I replied, "were a great and numerous family."

"I forget your arms."

"A huge human foot d'or, in a field azure; the foot crushes a serpent rampant whose fangs are imbedded in the heel."

"And the motto?"

"Nemo me impune lacessit."[9]

"Good!" he said.

The wine sparkled in his eyes and the bells jingled. My own fancy grew warm with the Medoc. We had passed through long walls of piled skeletons, with casks and puncheons[10] intermingling, into the inmost recesses of the catacombs. I paused again, and this time I made bold to seize Fortunato by an arm above the elbow.

"The niter!" I said; "see, it increases. It hangs like moss upon the vaults. We are below the river's bed. The drops of moisture trickle among the bones. Come, we will go back ere it is too late. Your cough—"

"It is nothing," he said; "let us go on. But first, another draft of the Medoc."

I broke and reached him a flagon of De Grâve. He emptied it at a breath. His eyes flashed with a fierce light. He laughed and threw the bottle upwards with a gesticulation I did not understand.

I looked at him in surprise. He repeated the movement—a grotesque one.

▲ Critical Viewing
Which details of this photograph reflect the mood of the story? **[Connect]**

✔**Reading Check**
Where is Montresor bringing Fortunato?

---

9. *Nemo me impune lacessit* Latin for "No one attacks me with impunity."
10. **puncheons** (pun´ chənz) *n.* large barrels.

"You do not comprehend?" he said.

"Not I," I replied.

"Then you are not of the brotherhood."

"How?"

"You are not of the masons."[11]

"Yes, yes," I said; "yes, yes."

"You? Impossible! A mason?"

"A mason," I replied.

"A sign," he said, "a sign."

"It is this," I answered, producing from beneath the folds of my *roquelaure* a trowel.

"You jest," he exclaimed, <u>recoiling</u> a few paces. "But let us proceed to the Amontillado."

"Be it so," I said, replacing the tool beneath the cloak and again offering him my arm. He leaned upon it heavily. We continued our route in search of the Amontillado. We passed through a range of low arches, descended, passed on, and descending again, arrived at a deep crypt, in which the foulness of the air caused our flambeaux rather to glow than flame.

At the most remote end of the crypt there appeared another less spacious. Its walls had been lined with human remains, piled to the vault overhead, in the fashion of the great catacombs of Paris. Three sides of this interior crypt were still ornamented in this manner. From the fourth side the bones had been thrown down, and lay promiscuously upon the earth, forming at one point a mound of some size. Within the wall thus exposed by the displacing of the bones, we perceived a still interior crypt or recess, in depth about four feet, in width three, in height six or seven. It seemed to have been constructed for no especial use within itself, but formed merely the *interval* between two of the colossal supports of the roof of the catacombs, and was backed by one of their circumscribing walls of solid granite.

It was in vain that Fortunato, uplifting his dull torch, endeavored to pry into the depth of the recess. Its <u>termination</u> the feeble light did not enable us to see.

"Proceed," I said: "herein is the Amontillado. As for Luchesi—"

"He is an ignoramus," interrupted my friend, as he stepped unsteadily forward, while I followed immediately at his heels. In an instant he had reached the extremity of the niche, and finding his progress arrested by the rock, stood stupidly bewildered. A moment more and I had fettered him to the granite. In its surface were two iron staples, distant from each other about two feet, horizontally. From one of these depended a short chain, from the other a padlock. Throwing the links about his waist, it was but the work of a few seconds to secure it. He was too much astounded to resist. Withdrawing the key I stepped back from the recess.

"Pass your hand," I said, "over the wall; you cannot help feeling the

recoiling (ri koil′ iŋ) v. staggering back

Reading Strategy
Breaking Down Confusing Sentences
Restate the sentence starting "Within the wall . . ." What is the narrator describing?

termination (tʉr mə nā′ shən) n. end

---

11. masons the Freemasons, an international secret society.

niter. Indeed, it is *very* damp. Once more let me *implore* you to return. No? Then I must positively leave you. But I must first render you all the little attentions in my power."

"The Amontillado!" ejaculated my friend, not yet recovered from his astonishment.

"True," I replied; "the Amontillado."

As I said these words I busied myself among the pile of bones of which I have before spoken. Throwing them aside, I soon uncovered a quantity of building stone and mortar. With these materials and with the aid of my trowel, I began vigorously to wall up the entrance of the niche.

I had scarcely laid the first tier of the masonry when I discovered that the intoxication of Fortunato had in a great measure worn off. The earliest indication I had of this was a low moaning cry from the depth of the recess. It was *not* the cry of a drunken man. There was then a long and obstinate silence. I laid the second tier, and the third, and the fourth; and then I heard the furious vibrations of the chain. The noise lasted for several minutes, during which, that I might hearken to it with the more satisfaction, I ceased my labors and sat down upon the bones. When at last the clanking <u>subsided</u>, I resumed the trowel, and finished without interruption the fifth, the sixth, and the seventh tier. The wall was now nearly upon a level with my breast. I again paused, and holding the flambeaux over the masonwork, threw a few feeble rays upon the figure within.

A succession of loud and shrill screams, bursting suddenly from the throat of the chained form, seemed to thrust me violently back. For a brief moment I hesitated, I trembled. Unsheathing my rapier, I began to grope with it about the recess; but the thought of an instant reassured me. I placed my hand upon the solid fabric of the catacombs, and felt satisfied. I reapproached the wall; I replied to the yells of him who clamored. I reechoed, I aided, I surpassed them in volume and in strength. I did this, and the clamorer grew still.

It was now midnight, and my task was drawing to a close. I had completed the eighth, the ninth, and the tenth tier. I had finished a portion of the last and the eleventh; there remained but a single stone to be fitted and plastered in. I struggled with its weight; I placed it partially in its destined position. But now there came from out the niche a low laugh that erected the hairs upon my head. It was succeeded by a sad voice, which I had difficulty in recognizing as that of the noble Fortunato. The voice said—

▲ **Critical Viewing**
Explain how the context of a story might make a festive mask such as this one appear sinister. **[Interpret]**

subsided (səb sīd´ id) v. settled down; became less active or intense

✔ **Reading Check**

What has Montresor done to Fortunato?

"Ha! ha! ha!—he! he! he!—a very good joke, indeed—an excellent jest. We will have many a rich laugh about it at the palazzo—he! he! he!—over our wine—he! he! he!"

"The Amontillado!" I said.

"He! he! he!—he! he! he!—yes, the Amontillado. But is it not getting late? Will not they be awaiting us at the palazzo, the Lady Fortunato and the rest? Let us be gone."

"Yes," I said, "let us be gone."

"*For the love of God, Montresor!*"

"Yes," I said, "for the love of God!"

But to these words I hearkened in vain for a reply. I grew impatient. I called aloud—

"Fortunato!"

No answer. I called again—

"Fortunato!"

No answer still. I thrust a torch through the remaining aperture and let it fall within. There came forth in return only a jingling of the bells. My heart grew sick; it was the dampness of the catacombs that made it so. I hastened to make an end of my labor. I forced the last stone into its position; I plastered it up. Against the new masonry I reerected the old rampart of bones. For the half of a century no mortal has disturbed them. *In pace requiescat!*[12]

---

12. *In pace requiescat!* Latin for "May he rest in peace!"

Review and Assess

Thinking About the Selection

1. **Respond:** At what point in the story do you find Montresor most disturbing? Explain.

2. **(a) Recall:** How does Montresor describe Fortunato's actions and attitudes early in the story? **(b) Analyze Causes and Effects:** Which character traits make Fortunato such an easy prey for Montresor?

3. **(a) Recall:** What specific steps does Montresor take to ensure that his plan works? **(b) Interpret:** Why does Montresor keep urging Fortunato to turn back?

4. **(a) Recall:** Why does Montresor hate Fortunato? **(b) Support:** Why does Montresor feel he has the right to take justice into his own hands?

5. **Evaluate:** Montresor acts as judge and executioner in this story. Explain whether you think individuals are ever justified in taking justice into their own hands.

Edgar Allan Poe

(1809–1849)

One of the first great American storytellers, Edgar Allan Poe blazed the trail for writers like Stephen King.

Poe's amazing but dark imagination may have had its roots in his troubled childhood, for he was orphaned by the age of three. Trouble plagued Poe in his adult life, too. He had to leave the University of Virginia when John Allan, his foster father, refused to pay the gambling debts that Poe had amassed. Later, Poe's dismissal from West Point caused Allan to disown him.

Poe found some happiness when he married Virginia Clemm. After she died of tuberculosis in 1847, however, Poe became increasingly antisocial. In 1849, he was discovered in a delirious condition in a Baltimore street. Three days later, he was dead at the age of forty.

Review and Assess

Literary Analysis

Mood

1. Name at least three images that contribute to the story's eerie **mood**.
2. (a) Describe the mood of the scene in which Montresor first tells Fortunato about the Amontillado. (b) How does the mood change as the story unfolds?
3. How does Montresor's response to Fortunato's screams add to the mood as the story reaches its high point?

Connecting Literary Elements

4. Which **descriptions** of Fortunato shape your impression of him the most? Explain.
5. Using a chart like the one below, show how the descriptions of the catacombs contribute to the mood.

Description of Catacomb	Mood Created

Reading Strategy

Breaking Down Confusing Sentences

6. To **break down** the following sentence, make a flowchart like the one below to show the three things that Montresor does after Fortunato grabs his arm.

   "Thus speaking, Fortunato possessed himself of my arm; and putting on a mask of black silk and drawing a *roquelaure* closely about my person, I suffered him to hurry me to my palazzo."

7. Break down this sentence to explain what has happened: "A moment more and I had fettered him to the granite."

Extend Understanding

8. **Career Connection:** If you were a lawyer, what evidence would you use to prove Montresor's guilt?

Quick Review

Mood is the feeling that a piece of literature creates in the reader.

A **description** is a portrait in words of a person, place, or object.

To **break down** a confusing sentence, rearrange, change, or take out words in order to identify its subject and what is being said about that subject.

 Take It to the Net
www.phschool.com
Take the interactive self-test online to check your understanding of the selection.

Integrate Language Skills

Vocabulary Development Lesson

Word Analysis: Latin Prefix *pre-*

The Latin prefix *pre-*, as found in *precluded*, means "before" or "in advance." Identify the word from the list below that best fits each definition.

preview   precaution   prejudice

1. To see in advance
2. Judgment without sufficient facts
3. Care taken in advance

Spelling Strategy

When you add an ending that begins with a vowel to a word that ends in a silent *e*, the *e* is usually dropped. For example, when adding *-ing* to the word *subside*, drop the silent *e* to form *subsiding*. Write the word formed by adding the ending to each word below.

1. smile + *-ing*
2. jingle + *-ed*
3. believe + *-able*
4. face + *-ing*

Grammar Lesson

Common Nouns and Proper Nouns

A **common noun** names any one of a class of people, places, or things—for example, *man*, *city*, or *month*. A **proper noun** names a specific person, place, or thing and always begins with a capital letter—for example, *William*, *Los Angeles*, or *September*.

In the following excerpt from "The Cask of Amontillado," the common nouns are underlined, and the proper noun is in boldface.

Example: I paused again, and this <u>time</u> I made bold to seize **Fortunato** by an <u>arm</u> above the <u>elbow</u>.

Concept Development: Antonyms

Identify the antonym, or opposite, of the first word.

1. precluded: (a) prevented, (b) aided, (c) started
2. retribution: (a) reward, (b) disaster, (c) assignment
3. accosted: (a) sought, (b) retreated, (c) discovered
4. subsided: (a) increased, (b) created, (c) challenged
5. afflicted: (a) weary, (b) skeptical, (c) blessed
6. explicit: (a) unnecessary, (b) vague, (c) impatient
7. recoiling: (a) unfastening, (b) releasing, (c) advancing
8. termination: (a) height, (b) beginning, (c) extension

Practice Copy each sentence below. Draw one line under each common noun and two lines under each proper noun.

1. Edgar Allan Poe wrote the story.
2. A modern writer might set the story in New Orleans.
3. Mardi Gras, held in February or March, is a wild celebration.
4. Montresor led him through the catacombs.
5. It would be difficult to find Montresor in the French Quarter.

Writing Application Write a paragraph about a scene from the story. Use at least three common nouns and three proper nouns.

W͞G Prentice Hall Writing and Grammar Connection: Chapter 16, Section 1

Writing Lesson

Description of a Set

Imagine that "The Cask of Amontillado" is being made into a movie. Choose a scene from the story. Use your imagination to expand upon Poe's description as you prepare a vivid, precise description of a set design for that scene.

Prewriting Review the scene you have chosen and picture it in your mind. Jot down precise details of sight, sound, smell, taste, and texture.

Model: Gathering Precise Details

Scene: Montresor meets Fortunato.

Poe: "It was about dusk, one evening during the
                 supreme madness of the carnival season, . . ."

Set Details: rough cobblestone street, lit by flickering torches
                 distant sound of singing; people in costumes

> Precise details, such as *rough cobblestones* and *flickering torches*, will help the audience "see" the scene.

Drafting Organize your set description by describing it spatially, moving from left to right or from the foreground to the background. Refer to your notes, and include the specific elements of the set.

Revising Read your draft aloud to a classmate. Add or change any details that you feel will help readers see your set more clearly.

Prentice Hall Writing and Grammar Connection: Chapter 6, Section 2

Extension Activities

Listening and Speaking Retell part of "The Cask of Amontillado" from Fortunato's perspective. Include the following in your **retelling:**

- Fortunato's thoughts about Montresor in the beginning and at the end of the story
- Fortunato's feelings about the situation

Present your retelling to your class, using tones and gestures you think Fortunato would use. After your retelling, ask your classmates for feedback.

Research and Technology In a group, create a **storyboard** outlining the main events of the plot for a movie version of "The Cask of Amontillado." Draw each important scene in comic-book style. For each frame, write a brief description of the action. Include Poe's main events and any important events that you add. Use graphics software to help create the storyboard scenes. **[Group Activity]**

 **Take It to the Net**   www.phschool.com

Go online for an additional research activity using the Internet.

Prepare to Read

The Most Dangerous Game

 Take It to the Net

Visit www.phschool.com for interactive activities and instruction related to "The Most Dangerous Game," including
- background
- graphic organizers
- literary elements
- reading strategies

Preview

Connecting to the Literature

Some competitions can be friendly, while others can be fierce. If one side takes the competition more seriously than the other, the situation can become unpleasant, or even dangerous. In "The Most Dangerous Game," a competition becomes a life-or-death situation.

Background

The main characters in this story enjoy hunting big game—large animals, such as lions or bears—for sport. For hunting enthusiasts, big-game hunting is the ultimate test of skill. In recent times, however, this sport has become controversial as populations of big-game animals have dwindled or have even become endangered.

Literary Analysis

Suspense

Suspense is the reader's feeling of curiosity, uncertainty, or even anxiety about the outcome of events in a story. Writers can create suspense by putting characters into tense or risky situations. In this example from the story, the uncertainty of the situation helps to create suspense.

> For a seemingly endless time he fought the sea. He began to count his strokes; he could do possibly a hundred more and then—

As you read, pay attention to events and details that create suspense.

Connecting Literary Elements

Conflict plays a key role in establishing suspense. A **conflict** is a struggle between opposing forces, setting one character against another character, a character against nature, or a character against himself or herself. In "The Most Dangerous Game," suspense grows as the conflict between the story's two main characters intensifies.

Reading Strategy

Using Context Clues

As you read, use **context clues** to figure out the approximate meaning of an unfamiliar word.

- Look at the words, phrases, and sentences that surround the unfamiliar word. These "surroundings" are the context. In particular, look for words or details that might describe or rename the word.
- Once you find clue words, create a definition that makes sense to you. Reread your sentence using your new definition in place of the difficult word to see whether the sentence now makes more sense.

Use a chart like this to gather context clues and figure out meanings.

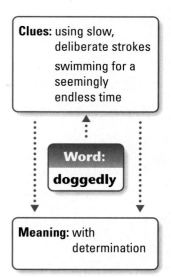

Clues: using slow, deliberate strokes

swimming for a seemingly endless time

Word: doggedly

Meaning: with determination

Vocabulary Development

palpable (pal´ pə bəl) *adj.* able to be touched or felt (p. 19)

indolently (in´ də lənt lē) *adv.* lazily; idly (p. 20)

bizarre (bi zär´) *adj.* odd in appearance (p. 23)

naive (nä ēv´) *adj.* unsophisticated (p. 27)

scruples (scrōō´ pəlz) *n.* misgivings about something one feels is wrong (p. 27)

blandly (bland´ lē) *adv.* in a mild and soothing manner (p. 28)

grotesque (grō tesk´) *adj.* having a strange, bizarre design (p. 29)

futile (fyōōt´ 'l) *adj.* hopeless (p. 31)

▲ **Critical Viewing** How does this painting create
a feeling of suspense? **[Analyze]**

The Most Dangerous Game

Richard Connell

"Off there to the right—somewhere—is a large island," said Whitney. "It's rather a mystery—"

"What island is it?" Rainsford asked.

"The old charts call it 'Ship-Trap Island,' " Whitney replied. "A suggestive name, isn't it? Sailors have a curious dread of the place. I don't know why. Some superstition—"

"Can't see it," remarked Rainsford, trying to peer through the dank tropical night that was <u>palpable</u> as it pressed its thick warm blackness in upon the yacht.

"You've good eyes," said Whitney, with a laugh, "and I've seen you pick off a moose moving in the brown fall bush at four hundred yards, but even you can't see four miles or so through a moonless Caribbean[1] night."

"Not four yards," admitted Rainsford. "Ugh! It's like moist black velvet."

"It will be light in Rio," promised Whitney. "We should make it in a few days. I hope the jaguar guns have come from Purdey's. We should have some good hunting up the Amazon.[2] Great sport, hunting."

"The best sport in the world," agreed Rainsford.

"For the hunter," amended Whitney. "Not for the jaguar."

"Don't talk rot, Whitney," said Rainsford. "You're a big-game hunter, not a philosopher. Who cares how a jaguar feels?"

palpable (pal′ pə bəl) *adj.* able to be touched or felt

✔ **Reading Check**

How do sailors feel about the mysterious "ship-trap island"?

---

1. **Caribbean** (kar′ ə bē′ ən) the Caribbean Sea, a part of the Atlantic Ocean, bounded by South America, Central America, and the West Indies.
2. **Amazon** (am′ ə zän′) large river in South America.

"Perhaps the jaguar does," observed Whitney.

"Bah! They've no understanding."

"Even so, I rather think they understand one thing—fear. The fear of pain and the fear of death."

"Nonsense," laughed Rainsford. "This hot weather is making you soft, Whitney. Be a realist. The world is made up of two classes—the hunters and the huntees. Luckily, you and I are the hunters. Do you think we've passed that island yet?"

"I can't tell in the dark. I hope so."

"Why?" asked Rainsford.

"The place has a reputation—a bad one."

"Cannibals?" suggested Rainsford.

"Hardly. Even cannibals wouldn't live in such a God-forsaken place. But it's gotten into sailor lore, somehow. Didn't you notice that the crew's nerves seemed a bit jumpy today?"

"They were a bit strange, now you mention it. Even Captain Nielsen—"

"Yes, even that tough-minded old Swede, who'd go up to the devil himself and ask him for a light. Those fishy blue eyes held a look I never saw there before. All I could get out of him was: 'This place has an evil name among sea-faring men, sir.' Then he said to me, very gravely: 'Don't you feel anything?'—as if the air about us was actually poisonous. Now, you mustn't laugh when I tell you this —I did feel something like a sudden chill.

"There was no breeze. The sea was as flat as a plate-glass window. We were drawing near the island then. What I felt was a—a mental chill; a sort of sudden dread."

"Pure imagination," said Rainsford. "One superstitious sailor can taint the whole ship's company with his fear."

"Maybe. But sometimes I think sailors have an extra sense that tells them when they are in danger. Sometimes I think evil is a tangible thing—with wave lengths, just as sound and light have. An evil place can, so to speak, broadcast vibrations of evil. Anyhow, I'm glad we're getting out of this zone. Well, I think I'll turn in now, Rainsford."

"I'm not sleepy," said Rainsford. "I'm going to smoke another pipe on the afterdeck."

"Good night, then, Rainsford. See you at breakfast."

"Right. Good night, Whitney."

There was no sound in the night as Rainsford sat there, but the muffled throb of the engine that drove the yacht swiftly through the darkness, and the swish and ripple of the wash of the propeller.

Rainsford, reclining in a steamer chair, indolently puffed on his favorite brier. The sensuous drowsiness of the night was on him. "It's so dark," he thought, "that I could sleep without closing my eyes; the night would be my eyelids—"

An abrupt sound startled him. Off to the right he heard it, and his ears, expert in such matters, could not be mistaken. Again he heard the sound, and again. Somewhere, off in the blackness, someone had fired a gun three times.

Literary Analysis
Suspense What effect does Rainsford's response have on the reader?

indolently (in′ də lənt lē)
adv. lazily; idly

Rainsford sprang up and moved quickly to the rail, mystified. He strained his eyes in the direction from which the reports had come, but it was like trying to see through a blanket. He leaped upon the rail and balanced himself there, to get greater elevation; his pipe, striking a rope, was knocked from his mouth. He lunged for it; a short, hoarse cry came from his lips as he realized he had reached too far and had lost his balance. The cry was pinched off short as the blood-warm waters of the Caribbean Sea closed over his head.

He struggled up to the surface and tried to cry out, but the wash from the speeding yacht slapped him in the face and the salt water in his open mouth made him gag and strangle. Desperately he struck out with strong strokes after the receding lights of the yacht, but he stopped before he had swum fifty feet. A certain cool-headedness had come to him; it was not the first time he had been in a tight place. There was a chance that his cries could be heard by someone aboard the yacht, but that chance was slender, and grew more slender as the yacht raced on. He wrestled himself out of his clothes, and shouted with all his power. The lights of the yacht became faint and ever-vanishing fireflies; then they were blotted out entirely by the night.

Hat, Knife, and Gun in Woods, David Mann, Sal Barracca & Associates

Rainsford remembered the shots. They had come from the right, and doggedly he swam in that direction, swimming with slow, deliberate strokes, conserving his strength. For a seemingly endless time he fought the sea. He began to count his strokes; he could do possibly a hundred more and then—

Rainsford heard a sound. It came out of the darkness, a high screaming sound, the sound of an animal in an extremity of anguish and terror.

He did not recognize the animal that made the sound; he did not try to; with fresh vitality he swam toward the sound. He heard it again; then it was cut short by another noise, crisp, staccato.

"Pistol shot," muttered Rainsford, swimming on.

Ten minutes of determined effort brought another sound to his ears—the most welcome he had ever heard—the muttering and growling of the sea breaking on a rocky shore. He was almost on the rocks before he saw them; on a night less calm he would have been shattered against them. With his remaining strength he dragged himself from the swirling waters. Jagged crags appeared to jut into the opaqueness, he forced

▲ **Critical Viewing**
Based on this painting, predict what might happen in the story. **[Predict]**

 **Reading Check**

What happens to Rainsford after he hears a gunshot while on the ship?

himself upward, hand over hand. Gasping, his hands raw, he reached a flat place at the top. Dense jungle came down to the very edge of the cliffs. What perils that tangle of trees and underbrush might hold for him did not concern Rainsford just then. All he knew was that he was safe from his enemy, the sea, and that utter weariness was on him. He flung himself down at the jungle edge and tumbled headlong into the deepest sleep of his life.

When he opened his eyes he knew from the position of the sun that it was late in the afternoon. Sleep had given him new vigor; a sharp hunger was picking at him. He looked about him, almost cheerfully.

"Where there are pistol shots, there are men. Where there are men, there is food," he thought. But what kind of men, he wondered, in so forbidding a place? An unbroken front of snarled and ragged jungle fringed the shore.

He saw no sign of a trail through the closely knit web of weeds and trees; it was easier to go along the shore, and Rainsford floundered along by the water. Not far from where he had landed, he stopped.

Some wounded thing, by the evidence a large animal, had thrashed about in the underbrush; the jungle weeds were crushed down and the moss was lacerated; one patch of weeds was stained crimson. A small, glittering object not far away caught Rainsford's eye and he picked it up. It was an empty cartridge.

"A twenty-two," he remarked. "That's odd. It must have been a fairly large animal too. The hunter had his nerve with him to tackle it with a light gun. It's clear that the brute put up a fight. I suppose the first three shots I heard was when the hunter flushed his quarry[3] and wounded it. The last shot was when he trailed it here and finished it."

He examined the ground closely and found what he had hoped to find—the print of hunting boots. They pointed along the cliff in the direction he had been going. Eagerly he hurried along, now slipping on a rotten log or a loose stone, but making headway; night was beginning to settle down on the island.

Bleak darkness was blacking out the sea and jungle when Rainsford sighted the lights. He came upon them as he turned a crook in the coast line, and his first thought was that he had come upon a village, for there were many lights. But as he forged along he saw to his great astonishment that all the lights were in one enormous building—a lofty structure with pointed towers plunging upward into the gloom. His eyes made out the shadowy outlines of a palatial château;[4] it was set on a high bluff, and on three sides of it cliffs dived down to where the sea licked greedy lips in the shadows.

"Mirage," thought Rainsford. But it was no mirage, he found, when he

▲ **Critical Viewing**
What does this picture suggest about Rainsford's struggle to climb out of the water and on to land? **[Analyze]**

Literary Analysis
Conflict and Suspense
Which details of Rainsford's struggle build suspense?

---

3. **flushed his quarry** (kwôr´ ē) drove his prey into the open.
4. **palatial château** (pə lā´ shəl sha tō´) a mansion as luxurious as a palace.

opened the tall spiked iron gate. The stone steps were real enough; the massive door with a leering gargoyle[5] for a knocker was real enough; yet about it all hung an air of unreality.

He lifted the knocker, and it creaked up stiffly, as if it had never before been used. He let it fall, and it startled him with its booming loudness. He thought he heard steps within; the door remained closed. Again Rainsford lifted the heavy knocker, and let it fall. The door opened then, opened as suddenly as if it were on a spring, and Rainsford stood blinking in the river of glaring gold light that poured out. The first thing Rainsford's eyes discerned was the largest man Rainsford had ever seen—a gigantic creature, solidly made and black-bearded to the waist. In his hand the man held a long-barreled revolver, and he was pointing it straight at Rainsford's heart.

Out of the snarl of beard two small eyes regarded Rainsford.

"Don't be alarmed," said Rainsford, with a smile which he hoped was disarming. "I'm no robber. I fell off a yacht. My name is Sanger Rainsford of New York City."

The menacing look in the eyes did not change. The revolver pointed as rigidly as if the giant were a statue. He gave no sign that he understood Rainsford's words, or that he had even heard them. He was dressed in uniform, a black uniform trimmed with gray astrakhan.[6]

"I'm Sanger Rainsford of New York," Rainsford began again. "I fell off a yacht. I am hungry."

The man's only answer was to raise with his thumb the hammer of his revolver. Then Rainsford saw the man's free hand go to his forehead in a military salute, and he saw him click his heels together and stand at attention. Another man was coming down the broad marble steps, an erect, slender man in evening clothes. He advanced to Rainsford and held out his hand.

In a cultivated voice marked by a slight accent that gave it added precision and deliberateness, he said: "It is a very great pleasure and honor to welcome Mr. Sanger Rainsford, the celebrated hunter, to my home."

Automatically Rainsford shook the man's hand.

"I've read your book about hunting snow leopards in Tibet, you see," explained the man. "I am General Zaroff."

Rainsford's first impression was that the man was singularly handsome; his second was that there was an original, almost <u>bizarre</u> quality about the general's face. He was a tall man past middle age, for his hair was a vivid white; but his thick eyebrows and pointed military mustache were as black as the night from which Rainsford had come. His eyes, too, were black and very bright. He had high cheek bones, a sharp-cut nose, a spare, dark face, the face of a man used to giving orders, the face of an aristocrat. Turning to the giant in uniform, the general made a sign. The giant put away his pistol, saluted, withdrew.

"Ivan is an incredibly strong fellow," remarked the general, "but he

---

5. **gargoyle** (gär´ goil) *n.* strange and distorted animal form projecting from a building.
6. **astrakhan** (as´ trə kan´) *n.* loosely curled fur made from the skins of young lambs.

Reading Strategy
Using Context Clues
Which context clues can you use to determine the meaning of *discerned*?

bizarre (bi zär´) *adj.* odd in appearance

Reading Check
What does Rainsford find when he finally makes it to the island?

The Most Dangerous Game ◆ 23

has the misfortune to be deaf and dumb. A simple fellow, but, I'm afraid, like all his race, a bit of a savage."

"Is he Russian?"

"He is a Cossack,"[7] said the general, and his smile showed red lips and pointed teeth. "So am I."

"Come," he said, "we shouldn't be chatting here. We can talk later. Now you want clothes, food, rest. You shall have them. This is a most restful spot."

Ivan had reappeared, and the general spoke to him with lips that moved but gave forth no sound.

"Follow Ivan, if you please, Mr. Rainsford," said the general. "I was about to have my dinner when you came. I'll wait for you. You'll find that my clothes will fit you, I think."

It was to a huge, beam-ceilinged bedroom with a canopied bed big enough for six men that Rainsford followed the silent giant. Ivan laid out an evening suit, and Rainsford, as he put it on, noticed that it came from a London tailor who ordinarily cut and sewed for none below the rank of duke.

The dining room to which Ivan conducted him was in many ways remarkable. There was a medieval magnificence about it; it suggested a baronial hall of feudal times with its oaken panels, its high ceiling, its vast refectory table where twoscore men could sit down to eat. About the hall were the mounted heads of many animals—lions, tigers, elephants, moose, bears; larger or more perfect specimens Rainsford had never seen. At the great table the general was sitting, alone.

"You'll have a cocktail, Mr. Rainsford," he suggested. The cocktail was surpassingly good; and, Rainsford noted, the table appointments were of the finest—the linen, the crystal, the silver, the china.

They were eating *borsch*, the rich, red soup with whipped cream so dear to Russian palates. Half apologetically General Zaroff said: "We do our best to preserve the amenities of civilization here. Please forgive any lapses. We are well off the beaten track, you know. Do you think the champagne has suffered from its long ocean trip?"

"Not in the least," declared Rainsford. He was finding the general a most thoughtful and affable host, a true cosmopolite.[8] But there was one small trait of the general's that made Rainsford uncomfortable. Whenever he looked up from his plate he found the general studying him, appraising him narrowly.

"Perhaps," said General Zaroff, "you were surprised that I recognized your name. You see, I read all books on hunting published in English, French, and Russian. I have but one passion in my life, Mr. Rainsford, and it is the hunt."

"You have some wonderful heads here," said Rainsford as he ate a particularly well cooked filet mignon. "That Cape buffalo is the largest I ever saw."

"Oh, that fellow. Yes, he was a monster."

Literary Analysis
Suspense What is your impression of the general? Can he be trusted?

Reading Strategy
Using Context Clues Which context clues suggest the approximate meaning of *amenities*?

---

7. **Cossack** (käs′ ak) member of a people from southern Russia, famous for their fierceness.
8. **cosmopolite** (käz mäp′ ə līt′) *n.* person at home in all parts of the world.

"Did he charge you?"

"Hurled me against a tree," said the general. "Fractured my skull. But I got the brute."

"I've always thought," said Rainsford, "that the Cape buffalo is the most dangerous of all big game."

For a moment the general did not reply; he was smiling his curious red-lipped smile. Then he said slowly: "No. You are wrong, sir. The Cape buffalo is not the most dangerous big game." He sipped his wine. "Here in my preserve on this island," he said in the same slow tone, "I hunt more dangerous game."

Rainsford expressed his surprise. "Is there big game on this island?"

The general nodded. "The biggest."

"Really?"

"Oh, it isn't here naturally, of course. I have to stock the island."

"What have you imported, general?" Rainsford asked. "Tigers?"

The general smiled. "No," he said. "Hunting tigers ceased to interest me some years ago. I exhausted their possibilities, you see. No thrill left in tigers, no real danger. I live for danger, Mr. Rainsford."

The general took from his pocket a gold cigarette case and offered his guest a long black cigarette with a silver tip; it was perfumed and gave off a smell like incense.

"We will have some capital hunting, you and I," said the general. "I shall be most glad to have your society."

"But what game—" began Rainsford.

"I'll tell you," said the general. "You will be amused, I know. I think I may say, in all modesty, that I have done a rare thing. I have invented a new sensation. May I pour you another glass of port, Mr. Rainsford?"

"Thank you, general."

The general filled both glasses, and said: "God makes some men poets. Some He makes kings, some beggars. Me He made a hunter. My hand was made for the trigger, my father said. He was a very rich man with a quarter of a million acres in the Crimea,[9] and he was an ardent sportsman. When I was only five years old he gave me a little gun, specially made in Moscow for me, to shoot sparrows with. When I shot some of his prize turkeys with it, he did not punish me; he complimented me on my marksmanship. I killed my first bear in the Caucasus[10] when I was ten. My whole life has been one prolonged hunt. I went into the army—it was expected of noblemen's sons—and for a time commanded a division of Cossack cavalry, but my real interest was always the hunt. I have hunted every kind of game in every land. It would be impossible for me to tell you how many animals I have killed."

The general puffed at his cigarette.

"After the debacle[11] in Russia I left the country, for it was imprudent for an officer of the Czar to stay there. Many noble Russians lost

Literary Analysis
Suspense How does this discussion about the biggest game create suspense?

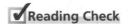
Reading Check
Why has Zaroff lost interest in hunting tigers?

---

9. **Crimea** (krī mē′ ə) region in southwestern Russia on the Black Sea.
10. **Caucasus** (kô′ kə səs) mountain range in southern Russia.
11. **debacle** (di bäk′ əl) *n.* bad defeat—Zaroff is referring to the Russian Revolution of 1917, a defeat for upper-class Russians like himself.

The Most Dangerous Game ◆ 25

everything. I, luckily, had invested heavily in American securities, so I shall never have to open a tea room in Monte Carlo or drive a taxi in Paris. Naturally, I continued to hunt—grizzlies in your Rockies, crocodiles in the Ganges, rhinoceroses in East Africa. It was in Africa that the Cape buffalo hit me and laid me up for six months. As soon as I recovered I started for the Amazon to hunt jaguars, for I had heard they were unusually cunning. They weren't." The Cossack♦ sighed. "They were no match at all for a hunter with his wits about him, and a high-powered rifle. I was bitterly disappointed. I was lying in my tent with a splitting headache one night when a terrible thought pushed its way into my mind. Hunting was beginning to bore me! And hunting, remember, had been my life. I have heard that in America business men often go to pieces when they give up the business that has been their life."

"Yes, that's so," said Rainsford.

The general smiled. "I had no wish to go to pieces," he said. "I must do something. Now, mine is an analytical mind, Mr. Rainsford. Doubtless that is why I enjoy the problems of the chase."

"No doubt, General Zaroff."

"So," continued the general, "I asked myself why the hunt no longer fascinated me. You are much younger than I am, Mr. Rainsford, and have not hunted as much, but you perhaps can guess the answer."

"What was it?"

"Simply this: hunting had ceased to be what you call 'a sporting proposition.' It had become too easy. I always got my quarry. Always. There is no greater bore than perfection."

The general lit a fresh cigarette.

"No animal had a chance with me any more. That is no boast; it is a mathematical certainty. The animal had nothing but his legs and his instinct. Instinct is no match for reason. When I thought of this it was a tragic moment for me, I can tell you."

Rainsford leaned across the table, absorbed in what his host was saying.

"It came to me as an inspiration what I must do," the general went on.

"And that was?"

The general smiled the quiet smile of one who has faced an obstacle and surmounted it with success. "I had to invent a new animal to hunt," he said.

"A new animal? You're joking."

"Not at all," said the general. "I never joke about hunting. I needed a new animal. I found one. So I bought this island, built this house, and here I do my hunting. The island is perfect for my purpose—there are jungles with a maze of trails in them, hills, swamps—"

Literature
in context History Connection

Czar Nicholas II, overthrown in the Russian Revolution of 1917

Literary Analysis
Suspense What do you think Zaroff is going to identify as the "most dangerous game"? Explain.

"But the animal, General Zaroff?"

"Oh," said the general, "it supplies me with the most exciting hunting in the world. No other hunting compares with it for an instant. Every day I hunt, and I never grow bored now, for I have a quarry with which I can match my wits."

Rainsford's bewilderment showed in his face.

"I wanted the ideal animal to hunt," explained the general. "So I said: 'What are the attributes of an ideal quarry?' And the answer was, of course: 'It must have courage, cunning, and, above all, it must be able to reason.' "

"But no animal can reason," objected Rainsford.

"My dear fellow," said the general, "there is one that can."

"But you can't mean—" gasped Rainsford.

"And why not?"

"I can't believe you are serious, General Zaroff. This is a grisly joke."

"Why should I not be serious? I am speaking of hunting."

"Hunting? General Zaroff, what you speak of is murder."

The general laughed with entire good nature. He regarded Rainsford quizzically. "I refuse to believe that so modern and civilized a young man as you seem to be harbors romantic ideas about the value of human life. Surely your experiences in the war—"

"Did not make me condone cold-blooded murder," finished Rainsford stiffly.

Laughter shook the general. "How extraordinarily droll you are!" he said. "One does not expect nowadays to find a young man of the educated class, even in America, with such a <u>naive</u>, and, if I may say so, mid-Victorian point of view.[12] It's like finding a snuff-box in a limousine. Ah, well, doubtless you had Puritan ancestors. So many Americans appear to have had. I'll wager you'll forget your notions when you go hunting with me. You've a genuine new thrill in store for you, Mr. Rainsford."

"Thank you, I'm a hunter, not a murderer."

"Dear me," said the general, quite unruffled, "again that unpleasant word. But I think I can show you that your <u>scruples</u> are quite ill founded."

"Yes?"

"Life is for the strong, to be lived by the strong, and, if need be, taken by the strong. The weak of the world were put here to give the strong pleasure. I am strong. Why should I not use my gift? If I wish to hunt, why should I not? I hunt the scum of the earth—sailors from tramp ships—lascars,[13] blacks, Chinese, whites, mongrels—a thoroughbred horse or hound is worth more than a score of them."

"But they are men," said Rainsford hotly.

"Precisely," said the general. "That is why I use them. It gives me pleasure. They can reason, after a fashion. So they are dangerous."

"But where do you get them?"

---

12. **mid-Victorian point of view** a point of view emphasizing proper behavior and associated with the time of Queen Victoria of England (1819–1901).
13. **lascars** (las´ kərz) *n.* Oriental sailors, especially natives of India.

naive (nä ēv´) *adj.* unsophisticated

scruples (scroo´ pəlz) *n.* misgivings about something one feels is wrong

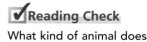

Reading Check

What kind of animal does Zaroff hunt?

The general's left eyelid fluttered down in a wink. "This island is called Ship-Trap," he answered. "Sometimes an angry god of the high seas sends them to me. Sometimes, when Providence is not so kind, I help Providence a bit. Come to the window with me."

Rainsford went to the window and looked out toward the sea.

"Watch! Out there!" exclaimed the general, pointing into the night. Rainsford's eyes saw only blackness, and then, as the general pressed a button, far out to sea Rainsford saw the flash of lights.

The general chuckled. "They indicate a channel," he said, "where there's none: giant rocks with razor edges crouch like a sea monster with wide-open jaws. They can crush a ship as easily as I crush this nut." He dropped a walnut on the hardwood floor and brought his heel grinding down on it. "Oh, yes," he said, casually, as if in answer to a question, "I have electricity. We try to be civilized here."

"Civilized? And you shoot down men?"

A trace of anger was in the general's black eyes, but it was there for but a second, and he said, in his most pleasant manner: "Dear me, what a righteous young man you are! I assure you I do not do the thing you suggest. That would be barbarous. I treat these visitors with every consideration. They get plenty of good food and exercise. They get into splendid physical condition. You shall see for yourself tomorrow."

"What do you mean?"

"We'll visit my training school," smiled the general. "It's in the cellar. I have about a dozen pupils down there now. They're from the Spanish bark San Lucar that had the bad luck to go on the rocks out there. A very inferior lot, I regret to say. Poor specimens and more accustomed to the deck than to the jungle."

He raised his hand, and Ivan, who served as waiter, brought thick Turkish coffee. Rainsford, with an effort, held his tongue in check.

"It's a game, you see," pursued the general <u>blandly</u>. "I suggest to one of them that we go hunting. I give him a supply of food and an excellent hunting knife. I give him three hours' start. I am to follow, armed only with a pistol of the smallest caliber and range. If my quarry eludes me for three whole days, he wins the game. If I find him"—the general smiled—"he loses."

"Suppose he refuses to be hunted?"

"Oh," said the general, "I give him his option, of course. He need not play the game if he doesn't wish to. If he does not wish to hunt, I turn

▲ Critical Viewing
What might it be like to hunt in an environment such as the one pictured here? **[Speculate]**

blandly (bland´ lē) *adv.* in a mild and soothing manner

him over to Ivan. Ivan once had the honor of serving as official knouter[14] to the Great White Czar, and he has his own ideas of sport. Invariably, Mr. Rainsford, invariably they choose the hunt."

"And if they win?"

The smile on the general's face widened. "To date I have not lost," he said.

Then he added, hastily: "I don't wish you to think me a braggart, Mr. Rainsford. Many of them afford only the most elementary sort of problem. Occasionally I strike a tartar.[15] One almost did win. I eventually had to use the dogs."

"The dogs?"

"This way, please. I'll show you."

The general steered Rainsford to a window. The lights from the windows sent a flickering illumination that made <u>grotesque</u> patterns on the courtyard below, and Rainsford could see moving about there a dozen or so huge black shapes; as they turned toward him, their eyes glittered greenly.

"A rather good lot, I think," observed the general. "They are let out at seven every night. If anyone should try to get into my house—or out of it—something extremely regrettable would occur to him." He hummed a snatch of song from the Folies Bergère.[16]

"And now," said the general, "I want to show you my new collection of heads. Will you come with me to the library?"

"I hope," said Rainsford, "that you will excuse me tonight, General Zaroff. I'm really not feeling at all well."

"Ah, indeed?" the general inquired solicitously. "Well, I suppose that's only natural, after your long swim. You need a good, restful night's sleep. Tomorrow you'll feel like a new man, I'll wager. Then we'll hunt, eh? I've one rather promising prospect—"

Rainsford was hurrying from the room.

"Sorry you can't go with me tonight," called the general. "I expect rather fair sport—a big, strong black. He looks resourceful—Well good night, Mr. Rainsford; I hope you have a good night's rest."

The bed was good, and the pajamas of the softest silk, and he was tired in every fiber of his being, but nevertheless Rainsford could not quiet his brain with the opiate of sleep. He lay, eyes wide open. Once he thought he heard stealthy steps in the corridor outside his room. He sought to throw open the door; it would not open. He went to the window and looked out. His room was high up in one of the towers. The lights of the château were out now, and it was dark and silent, but there was a fragment of sallow moon, and by its wan light he could see, dimly, the courtyard; there, weaving in and out in the pattern of shadow, were black, noiseless forms; the hounds heard him at the window and looked up, expectantly, with their green eyes. Rainsford went back to the bed

grotesque (grō tesk´) *adj.* having a strange, bizarre design

---

14. **knouter** (nout´ ər) *n.* someone who beats criminals with a leather whip, or knout.
15. **tartar** (tär´ tər) *n.* stubborn, violent person.
16. **Folies Bergère** (fô´ lē ber zher´) musical theater in Paris.

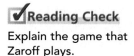

Reading Check

Explain the game that Zaroff plays.

and lay down. By many methods he tried to put himself to sleep. He had achieved a doze when, just as morning began to come, he heard, far off in the jungle, the faint report of a pistol.

General Zaroff did not appear until luncheon. He was dressed faultlessly in the tweeds of a country squire. He was solicitous about the state of Rainsford's health.

"As for me," sighed the general, "I do not feel so well. I am worried, Mr. Rainsford. Last night I detected traces of my old complaint."

To Rainsford's questioning glance the general said: "Ennui. Boredom."

Then, taking a second helping of crêpes suzette, the general explained: "The hunting was not good last night. The fellow lost his head. He made a straight trail that offered no problems at all. That's the trouble with these sailors; they have dull brains to begin with, and they do not know how to get about in the woods. They do excessively stupid and obvious things. It's most annoying. Will you have another glass of Chablis, Mr. Rainsford?"

"General," said Rainsford firmly, "I wish to leave this island at once."

The general raised his thickets of eyebrows; he seemed hurt. "But, my dear fellow," the general protested, "you've only just come. You've had no hunting—"

"I wish to go today," said Rainsford. He saw the dead black eyes of the general on him, studying him. General Zaroff's face suddenly brightened.

He filled Rainsford's glass with venerable Chablis from a dusty bottle.

"Tonight," said the general, "we will hunt—you and I."

Rainsford shook his head. "No, general," he said. "I will not hunt."

The general shrugged his shoulders and delicately ate a hothouse grape. "As you wish, my friend," he said. "The choice rests entirely with you. But may I not venture to suggest that you will find my idea of sport more diverting than Ivan's?"

He nodded toward the corner to where the giant stood, scowling, his thick arms crossed on his hogshead of chest.

"You don't mean—" cried Rainsford.

"My dear fellow," said the general, "have I not told you I always mean what I say about hunting? This is really an inspiration. I drink to a foeman worthy of my steel—at last."

The general raised his glass, but Rainsford sat staring at him.

"You'll find this game worth playing," the general said enthusiastically. "Your brain against mine. Your woodcraft against mine. Your strength and stamina against mine. Outdoor chess! And the stake is not without value, eh?"

"And if I win—" began Rainsford huskily.

"I'll cheerfully acknowledge myself defeated if I do not find you by midnight of the third day," said General Zaroff. "My sloop will place you on the mainland near a town."

The general read what Rainsford was thinking.

"Oh, you can trust me," said the Cossack. "I will give you my word as

▲ **Critical Viewing**
How does Rainsford's room, high in a tower, add to the suspense of the story? **[Connect]**

Literary Analysis
Suspense and Conflict
Why does this conflict between Rainsford and Zaroff escalate the suspense?

a gentleman and a sportsman. Of course you, in turn, must agree to say nothing of your visit here."

"I'll agree to nothing of the kind," said Rainsford.

"Oh," said the general, "in that case— But why discuss that now? Three days hence we can discuss it over a bottle of Veuve Cliquot, unless—"

The general sipped his wine.

Then a businesslike air animated him. "Ivan," he said to Rainsford, "will supply you with hunting clothes, food, a knife. I suggest you wear moccasins; they leave a poorer trail. I suggest too that you avoid the big swamp in the southeast corner of the island. We call it Death Swamp. There's quicksand there. One foolish fellow tried it. The deplorable part of it was that Lazarus followed him. You can imagine my feelings, Mr. Rainsford. I loved Lazarus; he was the finest hound in my pack. Well, I must beg you to excuse me now. I always take a siesta after lunch. You'll hardly have time for a nap, I fear. You'll want to start, no doubt. I shall not follow till dusk. Hunting at night is so much more exciting than by day, don't you think? Au revoir,[17] Mr. Rainsford, au revoir."

General Zaroff, with a deep, courtly bow, strolled from the room.

From another door came Ivan. Under one arm he carried khaki hunting clothes, a haversack of food, a leather sheath containing a long-bladed hunting knife; his right hand rested on a cocked revolver thrust in the crimson sash about his waist. . . .

Reading Strategy
Using Context Clues
Which clues help you determine the meaning of *hence*?

▲ **Critical Viewing**
Based on this photograph, what adjective might best describe Zaroff's dogs? **[Analyze]**

Rainsford had fought his way through the bush for two hours. "I must keep my nerve. I must keep my nerve," he said through tight teeth.

He had not been entirely clear-headed when the château gates snapped shut behind him.

His whole idea at first was to put distance between himself and General Zaroff, and, to this end, he had plunged along, spurred on by the sharp rowels of something very like panic. Now he had got a grip on himself, had stopped, and was taking stock of himself and the situation.

He saw that straight flight was <u>futile</u>; inevitably it would bring him face to face with the sea. He was in a picture with a frame of water, and his operations, clearly, must take place within that frame.

"I'll give him a trail to follow," muttered Rainsford, and he struck off from the rude paths he had been following into the trackless wilderness. He executed a series of intricate loops; he doubled on his trail again and again, recalling all the lore of the fox hunt, and all the dodges of the fox. Night found him leg-weary, with his hands and face lashed by the branches, on a thickly wooded ridge. He knew it would be insane to blunder on through the dark, even if he had the strength. His need for rest was imperative and he thought: "I have played the fox, now I must

futile (fyōōt′ əl) *adj.* useless; hopeless

✔ **Reading Check**
What is Rainsford's initial strategy?

---

17. au revoir (ō′ rə vwär′) French for "until we meet again."

play the cat of the fable." A big tree with a thick trunk and outspread branches was nearby, and, taking care to leave not the slightest mark, he climbed up into the crotch, and stretching out on one of the broad limbs, after a fashion, rested. Rest brought him new confidence and almost a feeling of security. Even so zealous a hunter as General Zaroff could not trace him there, he told himself; only the devil himself could follow that complicated trail through the jungle after dark. But, perhaps, the general was a devil—

An apprehensive night crawled slowly by like a wounded snake, and sleep did not visit Rainsford, although the silence of a dead world was on the jungle. Toward morning when a dingy gray was varnishing the sky, the cry of some startled bird focused Rainsford's attention in that direction. Something was coming through the bush, coming slowly, carefully, coming by the same winding way Rainsford had come. He flattened himself down on the limb, and through a screen of leaves almost as thick as tapestry, he watched. The thing that was approaching was a man.

It was General Zaroff. He made his way along with his eyes fixed in utmost concentration on the ground before him. He paused, almost beneath the tree, dropped to his knees and studied the ground. Rainsford's impulse was to hurl himself down like a panther, but he saw the general's right hand held something metallic—a small automatic pistol.

The hunter shook his head several times, as if he were puzzled. Then he straightened up and took from his case one of his black cigarettes; its pungent incense-like smoke floated up to Rainsford's nostrils.

Rainsford held his breath. The general's eyes had left the ground and were traveling inch by inch up the tree. Rainsford froze there, every muscle tensed for a spring. But the sharp eyes of the hunter stopped before they reached the limb where Rainsford lay; a smile spread over his brown face. Very deliberately he blew a smoke ring into the air; then he turned his back on the tree and walked carelessly away, back along the trail he had come. The swish of the underbrush against his hunting boots grew fainter and fainter.

The pent-up air burst hotly from Rainsford's lungs. His first thought made him feel sick and numb. The general could follow a trail through the woods at night; he could follow an extremely difficult trail; he must have uncanny powers; only by the merest chance had the Cossack failed to see his quarry.

Rainsford's second thought was even more terrible. It sent a shudder of cold horror through his whole being. Why had the general smiled? Why had he turned back?

Rainsford did not want to believe what his reason told him was true, but the truth was as evident as the sun that had by now pushed through the morning mists. The general was playing with him! The general was saving him for another day's sport! The Cossack was the cat; he was the mouse. Then it was that Rainsford knew the full meaning of terror.

"I will not lose my nerve. I will not."

Literary Analysis
Suspense Which words in this paragraph help create suspense?

Literary Analysis
Suspense and Conflict How are the conflict and suspense intensified at this point?

He slid down from the tree, and struck off again into the woods. His face was set and he forced the machinery of his mind to function. Three hundred yards from his hiding place he stopped where a huge dead tree leaned precariously on a smaller, living one. Throwing off his sack of food, Rainsford took his knife from its sheath and began to work with all his energy.

The job was finished at last, and he threw himself down behind a fallen log a hundred feet away. He did not have to wait long. The cat was coming again to play with the mouse.

Following the trail with the sureness of a bloodhound, came General Zaroff. Nothing escaped those searching black eyes, no crushed blade of grass, no bent twig, no mark, no matter how faint, in the moss. So intent was the Cossack on his stalking that he was upon the thing Rainsford had made before he saw it. His foot touched the protruding bough that was the trigger. Even as he touched it, the general sensed his danger and leaped back with the agility of an ape. But he was not quite quick enough; the dead tree, delicately adjusted to rest on the cut living one, crashed down and struck the general a glancing blow on the shoulder as it fell; but for his alertness, he must have been smashed beneath it. He staggered, but he did not fall; nor did he drop his revolver. He stood there, rubbing his injured shoulder, and Rainsford, with fear again gripping his heart, heard the general's mocking laugh ring through the jungle.

"Rainsford," called the general, "if you are within the sound of my voice, as I suppose you are, let me congratulate you. Not many men know how to make a Malay mancatcher. Luckily, for me, I too have hunted in Malacca. You are proving interesting, Mr. Rainsford. I am going now to have my wound dressed; it's only a slight one. But I shall be back. I shall be back."

When the general, nursing his bruised shoulder, had gone, Rainsford took up his flight again. It was flight now, a desperate, hopeless flight, that carried him on for some hours. Dusk came, then darkness, and still he pressed on. The ground grew softer under his moccasins; the vegetation grew ranker, denser; insects bit him savagely. Then, as he stepped forward, his foot sank into the ooze. He tried to wrench it back, but the muck sucked viciously at his foot as if it were a giant leech. With a violent effort, he tore his foot loose. He knew where he was now. Death Swamp and its quicksand.

His hands were tight closed as if his nerve were something tangible that someone in the darkness was trying to tear from his grip. The softness of the earth had given him an idea. He stepped back from the quicksand a dozen feet or so, and, like some huge prehistoric beaver, he began to dig.

Rainsford had dug himself in in France* when a second's delay meant death. That had been a placid pastime compared to his digging now.

Literature in context Social Studies Connection

♦ **WWI Trenches**

When Rainsford "digs himself in," he is drawing on his experience as a soldier. In World War I, soldiers protected themselves from their enemies by digging deep trenches. The soldiers then lived in the trenches and took turns charging the enemy's trenches in the face of machine-gun fire. Imagine the fear Rainsford must feel if his experience as a soldier is considered "a placid pastime compared to his digging now."

Canadian Troops Leave the Trenches, World War I

✓**Reading Check**

What does Rainsford build in an effort to save himself?

The pit grew deeper; when it was above his shoulders, he climbed out and from some hard saplings cut stakes and sharpened them to a fine point. These stakes he planted in the bottom of the pit with the points sticking up. With flying fingers he wove a rough carpet of weeds and branches and with it he covered the mouth of the pit. Then, wet with sweat and aching with tiredness, he crouched behind the stump of a lightning-charred tree.

He knew his pursuer was coming; he heard the padding sound of feet on the soft earth, and the night breeze brought him the perfume of the general's cigarette. It seemed to Rainsford that the general was coming with unusual swiftness; he was not feeling his way along, foot by foot. Rainsford, crouching there, could not see the general, nor could he see the pit. He lived a year in a minute. Then he felt an impulse to cry aloud with joy, for he heard the sharp crackle of the breaking branches as the cover of the pit gave way; he heard the sharp scream of pain as the pointed stakes found their mark. He leaped up from his place of concealment. Then he cowered back. Three feet from the pit a man was standing, with an electric torch in his hand.

"You've done well, Rainsford," the voice of the general called. "Your Burmese tiger pit has claimed one of my best dogs. Again you score. I think, Mr. Rainsford, I'll see what you can do against my whole pack. I'm going home for a rest now. Thank you for a most amusing evening."

At daybreak Rainsford, lying near the swamp, was awakened by a sound that made him know that he had new things to learn about fear.

Literary Analysis
Suspense How does Rainsford feel after his efforts? How does this passage make you, the reader, feel?

◀ **Critical Viewing**
Imagine Rainsford at the edge of the cliff. What would result from his leaping into the crashing waves? **[Speculate]**

It was a distant sound, faint and wavering, but he knew it. It was the baying of a pack of hounds.

Rainsford knew he could do one of two things. He could stay where he was and wait. That was suicide. He could flee. That was postponing the inevitable. For a moment he stood there, thinking. An idea that held a wild chance came to him, and, tightening his belt, he headed away from the swamp.

The baying of the hounds drew nearer, then still nearer, nearer, ever nearer. On a ridge Rainsford climbed a tree. Down a watercourse, not a quarter of a mile away, he could see the bush moving. Straining his eyes, he saw the lean figure of General Zaroff; just ahead of him Rainsford made out another figure whose wide shoulders surged through the tall jungle weeds; it was the giant Ivan, and he seemed pulled forward by some unseen force; Rainsford knew that Ivan must be holding the pack in leash.

They would be on him any minute now. His mind worked frantically. He thought of a native trick he had learned in Uganda. He slid down the tree. He caught hold of a springy young sapling and to it he fastened his hunting knife, with the blade pointing down the trail; with a bit of wild grapevine he tied back the sapling. Then he ran for his life. The hounds raised their voices as they hit the fresh scent. Rainsford knew now how an animal at bay feels.

He had to stop to get his breath. The baying of the hounds stopped abruptly, and Rainsford's heart stopped too. They must have reached the knife.

He shinnied excitedly up a tree and looked back. His pursuers had stopped. But the hope that was in Rainsford's brain when he climbed died, for he saw in the shallow valley that General Zaroff was still on his feet. But Ivan was not. The knife, driven by the recoil of the springing tree, had not wholly failed.

"Nerve, nerve, nerve!" he panted, as he dashed along. A blue gap showed between the trees dead ahead. Ever nearer drew the hounds. Rainsford forced himself on toward that gap. He reached it. It was the shore of the sea. Across a cove he could see the gloomy gray stone of the château. Twenty feet below him the sea rumbled and hissed. Rainsford hesitated. He heard the hounds. Then he leaped far out into the sea. . . .

When the general and his pack reached the place by the sea, the Cossack stopped. For some minutes he stood regarding the blue-green expanse of water. He shrugged his shoulders. Then he sat down, took a drink of brandy from a silver flask, lit a perfumed cigarette, and hummed a bit from *Madame Butterfly*.[18]

General Zaroff had an exceedingly good dinner in his great paneled dining hall that evening. With it he had a bottle of Pol Roger and half a bottle of Chambertin. Two slight annoyances kept him from perfect enjoyment. One was the thought that it would be difficult to replace Ivan; the other was that his quarry had escaped him; of course the

---

18. *Madame Butterfly* an opera by Giacomo Puccini.

Literary Analysis
Suspense How does this peaceful scene add to the suspense?

**Reading Check**
What happens to Ivan during the hunt?

American hadn't played the game—so thought the general as he tasted his after-dinner liqueur. In his library he read, to soothe himself, from the works of Marcus Aurelius.[19] At ten he went up to his bedroom. He was deliciously tired, he said to himself, as he locked himself in. There was a little moonlight, so, before turning on his light, he went to the window and looked down at the courtyard. He could see the great hounds, and he called: "Better luck another time," to them. Then he switched on the light.

A man, who had been hiding in the curtain of the bed, was standing there.

"Rainsford!" screamed the general. "How in God's name did you get here?"

"Swam," said Rainsford. "I found it quicker than walking through the jungle."

The general sucked in his breath and smiled. "I congratulate you," he said. "You have won the game."

Rainsford did not smile. "I am still a beast at bay," he said, in a low, hoarse voice. "Get ready, General Zaroff."

The general made one of his deepest bows. "I see," he said. "Splendid! One of us is to furnish a repast for the hounds. The other will sleep in this very excellent bed. On guard, Rainsford. . . ."

He had never slept in a better bed, Rainsford decided.

---

19. **Marcus Aurelius** (ô rē´ lē əs) Roman emperor and philosopher (A.D. 121–180).

Review and Assess

Thinking About the Selection

1. **Respond:** What do you admire or dislike about Rainsford?

2. **(a) Recall:** What, according to Zaroff, is the most dangerous game? **(b) Analyze:** Based on his attitude, would you call Zaroff "civilized"? Why or why not?

3. **(a) Recall:** Early in the story, what do you learn about Rainsford's views on hunting? **(b) Compare and Contrast:** How does Rainsford's attitude toward hunting compare with Zaroff's?

4. **(a) Recall:** What happens at the end of the story? **(b) Infer:** In the last scene of the story, why does Rainsford say "I am still a beast at bay"?

5. **Draw Conclusions:** How do you think the hunting experience with Zaroff changed Rainsford?

6. **(a) Analyze:** What words would you use to describe Zaroff's character? **(b) Apply:** Do you think people like Zaroff exist in real life? Explain.

Richard Connell

(1893–1949)

Richard Connell seemed destined to become a writer: He was a sports reporter at the age of ten! By the time he was sixteen, Connell was editing his father's newspaper in Poughkeepsie, New York. He stayed involved in journalism at Harvard University, where he was an editor for the *Daily Crimson*. During World War I, Connell edited his division's newspaper and reported on wartime events.

In 1924, Connell published the story you have just read. A year later, he settled in Beverly Hills, California. The film version of "The Most Dangerous Game" was released in 1932 and has inspired many other adventure movies. Connell's success as a movie screenwriter continued for the rest of his life, and he received two Academy Award nominations for his work.

Review and Assess

Literary Analysis

Suspense

1. (a) Find three details that provide early clues about Zaroff's hobby. (b) How do these clues create **suspense**?

2. Using a chart like the one below, show how the details of Rainford's first night build a sense of dread.

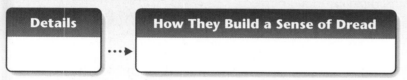

Details	How They Build a Sense of Dread

3. In your opinion, what are the three most suspenseful events in the story? Why?

Connecting Literary Elements

4. Early in the story, Rainsford says, "The world is made up of two classes—the hunters and the huntees." How does his **conflict** with Zaroff help Rainsford understand this expression in a new way?

5. In addition to conflicts between characters, stories may include conflicts between a character and nature and internal conflicts within a character. Use a chart like this one to explain each conflict.

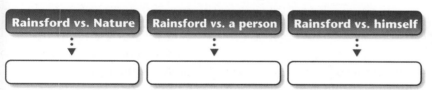

Rainsford vs. Nature	Rainsford vs. a person	Rainsford vs. himself

Reading Strategy

Using Context Clues

6. For each passage from the story, give an approximate meaning for the italicized word and explain which **context clues** helped you.

   (a) He heard [the sound] again; then it was cut short by another noise, crisp, *staccato*. "Pistol shot," muttered Rainsford, swimming on. (b) To Rainsford's questioning glance the general said: "*Ennui*. Boredom."

Extend Understanding

7. **Career Connection:** What careers, other than hunter, would be suited to someone with Rainsford's skills and attitudes? Why?

Quick Review

Suspense is the reader's feeling of curiosity, uncertainty, even anxiety about the outcome of events in a story.

A **conflict** is a struggle between opposing forces.

Context clues—hints in surrounding words, phrases, and sentences—can help you to figure out the approximate meaning of an unfamiliar word.

 Take It to the Net

www.phschool.com

Take the interactive self-test online to check your understanding of the selection.

Integrate Language Skills

Vocabulary Development Lesson

Word Analysis: Forms of *scruples*

The noun *scruples* refers to the uncomfortable feeling one has about doing something one thinks is wrong. By adding the suffix *-ous*, you form *scrupulous*, which means "having scruples."

Use *scruples*, *scrupulous*, and *unscrupulous* in a paragraph.

Spelling Strategy

The suffixes *-able* and *-ible* have the same meaning but slightly different spellings. The suffix *-able*, as in *palpable*, is more common, but *-ible*, as in *tangible*, sometimes applies.

Review each item below. Write *Correct* if the spelling is correct. If the spelling is incorrect, write the correct spelling.

1. terrable   3. regrettible
2. unquenchable   4. impossable

Fluency: Clarify Word Meaning

Complete each item with a vocabulary word from the list on page 17.

1. The farmer was ___?___ about city life.
2. "Surrender now," commanded the conqueror. "Resistance is ___?___."
3. The silence was so ___?___ that you could cut it with a knife.
4. He lounged on the couch ___?___.
5. They met under rather ___?___ circumstances: a camel auction.
6. With its fans and twisted features, the mask was amazingly ___?___.
7. The officer phrased his sentences ___?___ to avoid making people angry.
8. She had her ___?___ and would not give in to peer pressure.

Grammar Lesson

Pronouns and Antecedents

Pronouns are words that stand for nouns or for words that take the place of nouns. **Antecedents** are the words for which pronouns stand. Some of the most common pronouns are *I/me/my/mine*, *you/your/yours*, *he/him/his*, *she/her/hers*, *we/us/our/ours*, and *they/them/their/theirs*.

In these examples, the pronouns are set in italics; the antecedents are underlined.

> **Examples:** <u>Rainsford</u> feared for *his* life.
>
> Zaroff's <u>dogs</u> used *their* sense of smell.
>
> The <u>jungle</u> is a unique place with *its* wild animals and dense trees.

Practice Copy these sentences. Underline each pronoun and circle its antecedent.

1. One superstitious sailor can taint the whole company with his fear.
2. Rainsford remembered the shots. They had come from the right.
3. Follow Ivan, if you please, Mr. Rainsford. . . .
4. The general said, "I was about to have my dinner."
5. He had never slept better, Rainsford decided.

Writing Application Write sentences that include pronouns by using *Rainsford* and *jungle* as the antecedents.

*W*ᴳ *Prentice Hall Writing and Grammar Connection: Chapter 16, Section 2*

Writing Lesson

Survival Manual

Rainsford triumphs because he has the knowledge he needs to survive. Think about Rainsford's situation, and create a set of detailed instructions on how to survive a ruthless pursuer that you think Rainsford would write.

Prewriting   Review the story and note the techniques Rainsford uses. Make a list of questions readers might have about techniques. Then, arrange your notes into a logical order.

> ### Model: Anticipating Readers' Questions
>
> What materials would I need if I were building a trap?
>
> Could I build a trap if I didn't have tools? How?
>
> How large or deep should the trap be?

> A list of potential trouble spots can help a writer plan an effective guide.

Drafting   Using your questions and answers, write a first draft of Rainsford's survival manual. Give precise measurements or other specifications, define terms, and provide examples when necessary.

Revising   To improve your draft, try to follow the instructions. For example, if you have described how to create a trap, try drawing the trap based on your instructions. Add any details necessary to ensure that your readers can follow the directions.

W͛G Prentice Hall Writing and Grammar Connection: Chapter 11, Section 2

Extension Activities

Listening and Speaking With a group of classmates, put Rainsford on trial for killing Zaroff. These tips will help you plan a **video trial:**

- Plan arguments for both the prosecution and the defense.
- Have the two sides use props or diagrams to make their arguments accurate and persuasive.

Videotape your trial and show it to the rest of your class. After classmates see the video, discuss the effect of this form of media on viewers' perceptions of the trial. **[Group Activity]**

Research and Technology Hunting has threatened the population of many big-game species. Create a **database** of information about two or three big-game species, such as moose, jaguar, lion, tiger, elephant, crocodile, grizzly bear, or Cape buffalo. Use the database to help prepare a presentation about these species and their status today.

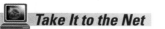 **Take It to the Net**   www.phschool.com

Go online for an additional research activity using the Internet.

Prepare to Read

Casey at the Bat

Baseball Players Practicing, 1875, Thomas Eakins Museum of Art, Rhode Island School of Design

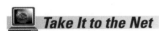

Take It to the Net

Visit www.phschool.com for interactive activities and instruction related to "Casey at the Bat," including

- background
- graphic organizers
- literary elements
- reading strategies

Preview

Connecting to the Literature

Sporting events can really keep you on the edge of your seat! An athlete can break a world record, or a losing team can charge to victory at the last minute. This poem may remind you of nail-biting moments you have experienced while either watching or playing a sport.

Background

In most cases, a baseball game does not end until all innings have been played and one team has scored the most runs. As a result, a team that is behind always has the chance for a comeback as long as players keep getting base hits and avoid making the final out. "Casey at the Bat" captures the hopes of a team that is behind by two runs as they go to bat for a final time.

Literary Analysis

Climax and Anticlimax

The **climax** of a story, or any type of narrative, is its biggest moment. During the climax, you can expect the following:

- The action of the story is at its peak.
- The feelings of the readers are at their most intense.

At the climax, you know that you are about to discover how the story's main problem or struggle will turn out.

If the action starts in a grand manner but the outcome is trivial or disappointing, the story has an anticlimax, too. An **anticlimax** is the point at which you learn that the story has not turned out the way you had expected. As you read "Casey at the Bat," notice how the story builds to its climax, and decide whether or not the story has an anticlimax.

Connecting Literary Elements

The climax is a key element in a story—whether that story is told in a movie, a novel, a short story, or a narrative poem. "Casey at the Bat" is an example of a **narrative poem,** a poem that tells a story. Like other stories, a narrative poem has a sequence of events and characters whose lives are set in a specific time and place.

Reading Strategy

Summarizing

Summarizing sections of a poem or story can help you better understand what you are reading. Follow these steps as you summarize:

- State the main points and details of a passage briefly and in your own words.
- Notice important story details and fit them into your picture of what is happening.
- Use your own language and style to express that information.

Use a chart like the one shown here to help you summarize.

Main Points
- a baseball game - one team is losing - fans are watching

Details
Mudville: the home-team fans are worried

Summary
"In the last inning of its game, Mudville is losing. There are two outs against them, and the fans are worried."

Vocabulary Development

pallor (pal´ ər) *n.* paleness (p. 43)

wreathed (rēth̶d) *v.* curled around (p. 43)

writhing (rīth´ iŋ) *v.* twisting; turning (p. 43)

tumult (too̅´ mult) *n.* noisy commotion (p. 44)

Casey at the Bat

Ernest Lawrence Thayer

Baseball Players Practicing, 1875, Thomas Eakins Museum of Art, Rhode Island School of Design

▲ **Critical Viewing** Compare and contrast the stance and attitude of the batter in this painting with Casey's stance and attitude. **[Compare and Contrast]**

It looked extremely rocky for the Mudville nine that day;
The score stood two to four, with but an inning left to play.
So, when Cooney died at second, and Burrows did the same,
A <u>pallor</u> <u>wreathed</u> the features of the patrons of the game.

pallor (pal´ ər) *n.* paleness

wreathed (rēt*h*d) *v.* curled around

5   A straggling few got up to go, leaving there the rest,
With that hope which springs eternal within the human breast.
For they thought: "If only Casey would get a whack at that,"
They'd put even money now, with Casey at the bat.

But Flynn preceded Casey, and likewise so did Blake,
10   And the former was a pudd'n, and the latter was a fake.
So on that stricken multitude a deathlike silence sat;
For there seemed but little chance of Casey's getting to the bat.

But Flynn let drive a "single," to the wonderment of all.
And the much-despised Blakey "tore the cover off the ball."
15   And when the dust had lifted, and they saw what had occurred,
There was Blakey safe at second, and Flynn a-huggin' third.

Literary Analysis
Climax and Anticlimax
What expectation for Casey do the successes of Flynn and Blake create?

Then from the gladdened multitude went up a joyous yell—
It rumbled in the mountaintops, it rattled in the dell;[1]
It struck upon the hillside and rebounded on the flat;
20   For Casey, mighty Casey, was advancing to the bat.

There was ease in Casey's manner as he stepped into his place,
There was pride in Casey's bearing and a smile on Casey's face;
And when responding to the cheers he lightly doffed[2] his hat,
No stranger in the crowd could doubt 'twas Casey at the bat.

25   Ten thousand eyes were on him as he rubbed his hands with dirt,
Five thousand tongues applauded when he wiped them on his shirt;
Then when the <u>writhing</u> pitcher ground the ball into his hip,
Defiance glanced in Casey's eye, a sneer curled Casey's lip.

writhing (rīt*h*´ iŋ) *v.* twisting; turning

And now the leather-covered sphere came hurtling through the air,
30   And Casey stood a-watching it in haughty grandeur there.
Close by the sturdy batsman the ball unheeded sped;
"That ain't my style," said Casey. "Strike one," the umpire said.

From the benches, black with people, there went up a muffled roar,
Like the beating of the storm waves on the stern and distant shore.
35   "Kill him! kill the umpire!" shouted someone on the stand;
And it's likely they'd have killed him had not Casey raised his hand.

✔Reading Check
What happens when the first ball is thrown to Casey?

---

1. dell (del) *n.* small, secluded valley.
2. doffed (däft) *v.* lifted.

With a smile of Christian charity great Casey's visage[3] shone;
He stilled the rising <u>tumult</u>, he made the game go on;
He signaled to the pitcher, and once more the spheroid flew;
40   But Casey still ignored it, and the umpire said, "Strike two."

"Fraud!" cried the maddened thousands, and the echo answered
    "Fraud!"
But one scornful look from Casey and the audience was awed;
They saw his face grow stern and cold, they saw his muscles strain,
And they knew that Casey wouldn't let the ball go by again.

45   The sneer is gone from Casey's lips, his teeth are clenched in hate.
He pounds with cruel vengeance his bat upon the plate:
And now the pitcher holds the ball, and now he lets it go,
And now the air is shattered by the force of Casey's blow.

Oh, somewhere in this favored land the sun is shining bright,
50   The band is playing somewhere, and somewhere hearts are light:
And somewhere men are laughing, and somewhere children shout,
But there is no joy in Mudville: Mighty Casey has struck out.

---

3. visage (viz´ ij) *n.* face.

tumult (too´ mult) *n.* noisy commotion

Reading Strategy
Summarizing State the main points and details of these two stanzas briefly and in your own words.

Review and Assess

Thinking About the Selection

1. **Respond:** Did you expect the poem to end the way it did? Why or why not?

2. **(a) Recall:** What happens in the first two stanzas? **(b) Analyze Causes and Effects:** How does the first part of the poem make you want to keep reading?

3. **(a) Recall:** Describe Casey, citing details of his appearance and actions. **(b) Infer:** What type of player would you say Casey is? Why?

4. **(a) Recall:** How is Casey described before the last pitch? **(b) Draw Conclusions:** How might Casey's attitude have affected his game?

5. **(a) Recall:** What is the outcome of Casey's turn at bat? **(b) Speculate:** Based on what you know about Casey, what do you think was his reaction? Why?

6. **(a) Analyze:** Why do you think this poem—written more than a century ago—has remained one of the most popular sports poems to this day? **(b) Evaluate:** Do you think the poem deserves this status? Why or why not?

Ernest Lawrence Thayer

(1863–1940)

It is not surprising that "Casey at the Bat" reads like a sports story in verse. The poet, Ernest Lawrence Thayer, spent many years working as a newspaper reporter. Thayer began his reporting career working on *The Lampoon*, Harvard University's humor magazine. He later worked at newspapers in New York and California.

"Casey at the Bat" first appeared in the *San Francisco Examiner* on June 3, 1888, under Thayer's pen name, Phin. The poem became such a favorite that in 1953 it inspired an operetta called *The Mighty Casey.*

Review and Assess

Literary Analysis

Climax and Anticlimax

1. What problem or struggle sets the stage for the **climax**?
2. Which lines of the poem present the climax itself? Explain.
3. Is the outcome of the poem an **anticlimax**? Why or why not?

Connecting Literary Elements

4. Complete a chart like this one to show that "Casey at the Bat" has the three major elements of a **narrative poem**.

Characters	Time and Place	Sequence of Events

5. To which elements in the chart did Thayer give the most attention? Explain.
6. (a) How would "Casey at the Bat" be different if it were written as a short story or play? (b) Would the story be as effective if it were not told in the form of a poem?

Reading Strategy

Summarizing

7. What information is left out of the following summary of lines 5–8? "Some fans left, but most stayed because they were hopeful."
8. Use a chart like this one to explain what happened at the beginning, middle, and end of the poem. Then, in three sentences, summarize the entire poem.

Beginning	Middle	End
Summary:		

Extend Understanding

9. **Sports Connection:** How might defeat add to a player's popularity?

Quick Review

The **climax** of a narrative is its moment of peak action and greatest intensity.
An **anticlimax** occurs when the outcome is trivial or disappointing when compared to the reader's expectations.

A **narrative poem** is a poem that tells a story.

When you **summarize** a passage, you briefly state its main points and details in your own words.

 Take It to the Net
www.phschool.com
Take the interactive self-test online to check your understanding of the selection.

Integrate Language Skills

Vocabulary Development Lesson

Word Analysis: Forms of *tumult*

Learning other forms of a word can expand your vocabulary. *Tumult*, a noun, is changed into an adjective, *tumultuous*, by adding the suffix -*ous*. You may already know that the adjective *tumultuous* means "wild and noisy." If so, when you come across the noun *tumult* in "Casey at the Bat," you will be able to figure out that it means "a noisy commotion."

On your paper, complete each sentence with one of the following words.

tumult   tumultuous   tumultuously

1. Her supporters gave the senator a ____?____ greeting following her speech.
2. An explosion caused a ____?____ downtown.
3. The crowd responded ____?____ when he struck out.

Fluency: Words in Sentences

For each item below, write a sentence that uses a word from the vocabulary list on page 41.

1. Write the first sentence of a news article describing a noisy demonstration in the city.
2. Describe the way a snake moves.
3. Explain why you think that your friend may not be feeling well today.
4. Tell about an old house that has ivy growing around its pillars.

Spelling Strategy

When you add the suffix -*ous* to a word, you may need to make additional spelling changes. For example, when you add -*ous* to *tumult*, you add a *u* before the suffix to form *tumultuous*.

Write the adjective form of each noun below.

1. glory   2. tempest   3. religion

Grammar Lesson

Possessive Nouns

A **possessive noun** is used to show ownership. It serves as an adjective by modifying another noun.

In these lines, the possessive nouns are set in italics. Notice that, in the first example, the underlined word that is "owned" is not a physical object but an aspect of Casey's personality.

> **Examples:** There was ease in *Casey's* <u>manner</u> as he stepped into his place, . . .
>
> The *team's* <u>defeat</u> was discouraging.
>
> The *player's* <u>fans</u> roared loudly.

Practice List the five possessive nouns in the following paragraph, as well as the word that is "owned" by each one.

> Casey's face broke into a grin when he connected with the ball. Every fan's eyes followed the ball as it flew over the pitcher's head. The ball reached the top of its arc and then fell—right toward an outfielder's glove. It took only a moment's work to catch the ball and declare Casey "out."

Writing Application For each noun below, write a sentence using it as a possessive noun.

1. catcher   2. coach   3. fan

 Prentice Hall Writing and Grammar Connection: Chapter 29, Section 6

46 ◆ *Spine Tinglers*

Writing Lesson

Sportscast

Like "Casey at the Bat," a good sportscast uses vivid and lively language. Vivid language captures the thrills and disappointments of a sports event. Write a sportscast about Casey's experience that hooks your audience and tells a good story.

Prewriting   Create a list of the vivid verbs—action words with a punch—that describe Casey's experience. For example, list ways that Casey might swing the bat or ways the pitcher might throw the ball to Casey.

Drafting   As you draft, picture the game in your mind. Make sure the verbs you choose are appropriate for describing a baseball game.

Revising   Reread your draft. Using this model as an example, circle the verbs in your draft and decide whether more lively action words would make your writing sparkle.

Model: Revising to Include Vivid Verbs

raced
Ana Moreno ~~ran~~ down the court, the Panthers in hot pursuit.

spotted   *slipped*
She ~~saw~~ a teammate's signal and ~~gave~~ Keisha Washington the

bagged
ball. Washington's play ~~got~~ the victory.

> Vivid verbs make the action in these sentences more exciting and easier to visualize.

Prentice Hall Writing and Grammar Connection: Chapter 4, Section 4

Extension Activities

Listening and Speaking   With a partner, role-play a **sports interview** with Casey. Follow these suggestions as you plan:

- Identify your audience and list the questions that would interest them.
- Practice verbal strategies, such as changing the pitch and tone of your voice. For example, if Casey is upset about the recent loss, he should sound disappointed or angry.

Role-play your interview in front of your class, and ask classmates to evaluate your work. **[Group Activity]**

Research and Technology   In "Casey at the Bat," the fans have very high expectations of Casey, Mudville's famous player. Write a **research report** comparing a famous baseball player in history to a famous present-day baseball player. Use library resources such as the Internet, newspapers, and books to research the experiences of each player. In your report, compare their lifestyles and successes.

Take It to the Net   www.phschool.com
Go online for an additional research activity using the Internet.

Prepare to Read

The Birds

 Take It to the Net

Visit www.phschool.com for interactive activities and instruction related to "The Birds," including
- background
- graphic organizers
- literary elements
- reading strategies

Preview

Connecting to the Literature

You step outside and the sky is dark and threatening. Low rumbles of thunder are becoming louder. You look at the threatening scene and fear makes your blood run cold. Daphne du Maurier's "The Birds" will probably evoke these same eerie feelings as you read about nature itself brooding and eventually striking out.

Background

Imagine sitting in a dark movie theater, watching images of flocks of birds descending upon average people in an unsuspecting town. This is what it was like to see *The Birds*, which filmmaker Alfred Hitchcock adapted from this story. After reading "The Birds," you will probably see why Hitchcock decided to adapt the story into his frightening film.

Literary Analysis

Foreshadowing

As its name suggests, **foreshadowing** is the author's use of clues to hint at future events. In this passage from "The Birds," for instance, du Maurier hints at danger to come.

The birds had been more restless than ever this fall of the year.

Keep an eye out for other examples of foreshadowing as you read; in particular, watch for details that seem unusual or disturbing.

Connecting Literary Elements

Imagery is language that a writer uses to create word pictures for the reader. These pictures, or images, are created by details of sight, sound, taste, touch, smell, or movement. In "The Birds," vivid images help bring the scenes to life. They also call attention to details—and help you discover the foreshadowing clues that du Maurier provides.

Reading Strategy

Predicting

Predicting, or making guesses about what will happen before a story ends, can often help you check your understanding of a story.

- To make a prediction, start by looking for small but unusual details. These details might be minor events that catch your attention but that the characters in the story seem to ignore.
- Ask yourself what would happen if the detail were to become more important. In "The Birds," for example, think about what would happen if a disturbing detail were multiplied many times.
- Note your predictions, but be prepared to revise your guesses as the story develops.

Use a chart to help you record your predictions. The chart shown here presents a small but unusual detail from "The Birds."

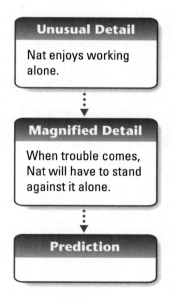

Unusual Detail

Nat enjoys working alone.

Magnified Detail

When trouble comes, Nat will have to stand against it alone.

Prediction

Vocabulary Development

placid (plas´ id) *adj.* calm (p. 51)

garish (gar´ ish) *adj.* too bright (p. 54)

recounted (ri kount´ ed) *v.* told in detail; narrated (p. 61)

sullen (sul´ ən) *adj.* gloomy (p. 62)

furtively (fur´ tiv lē) *adv.* stealthily, so as to avoid being heard (p. 67)

imperative (im per´ ə tiv) *adj.* urgent; absolutely necessary (p. 69)

reconnaissance (ri kän´ ə səns) *adj.* exploratory in nature, as when observing to seek information (p. 70)

fretful (fret´ fəl) *adj.* irritable and discontented (p. 77)

The Birds

Daphne du Maurier

Attack of the Birds, 1994, Lev Tabenkin, Maya Polsky Gallery

▲ **Critical Viewing** Based on this painting, what do you think might happen in this story? **[Predict]**

n December the third the wind changed overnight and it was winter. Until then the autumn had been mellow, soft. The leaves had lingered on the trees, golden-red, and the hedgerows were still green. The earth was rich where the plow had turned it.

Nat Hocken, because of a wartime disability, had a pension and did not work full-time at the farm. He worked three days a week, and they gave him the lighter jobs: hedging, thatching, repairs to the farm buildings.

Although he was married, with children, his was a solitary disposition; he liked best to work alone. It pleased him when he was given a bank to build up, or a gate to mend at the far end of the peninsula, where the sea surrounded the farmland on either side. Then, at midday, he would pause and eat the pasty[1] that his wife had baked for him, and, sitting on the cliff's edge, watch the birds. Autumn was best for this, better than spring. In spring the birds flew inland, purposeful, intent; they knew where they were bound; the rhythm and ritual of their life brooked no delay. In autumn those that had not migrated overseas but remained to pass the winter were caught up in the same driving urge, but because migration was denied them followed a pattern of their own. Great flocks of them came to the peninsula, restless, uneasy, spending themselves in motion; now wheeling, circling in the sky, now settling to feed on the rich new-turned soil, but even when they fed it was as though they did so without hunger, without desire. Restlessness drove them to the skies again.

Black and white, jackdaw and gull, mingled in strange partnership, seeking some sort of liberation, never satisfied, never still. Flocks of starlings, rustling like silk, flew to fresh pasture, driven by the same necessity of movement, and the smaller birds, the finches and the larks, scattered from tree to hedge as if compelled.

Nat watched them, and he watched the sea birds too. Down in the bay they waited for the tide. They had more patience. Oyster catchers, redshank, sanderling, and curlew watched by the water's edge; as the slow sea sucked at the shore and then withdrew, leaving the strip of seaweed bare and the shingle churned, the sea birds raced and ran upon the beaches. Then that same impulse to flight seized upon them too. Crying, whistling, calling, they skimmed the <u>placid</u> sea and left the shore. Make haste, make speed, hurry and begone; yet where, and to what purpose? The restless urge of autumn, unsatisfying, sad, had put a spell upon them and they must flock, and wheel, and cry; they must spill themselves of motion before winter came.

"Perhaps," thought Nat, munching his pasty by the cliff's edge, "a message comes to the birds in autumn, like a warning. Winter is coming. Many of them perish. And like the people who, apprehensive of death before their time, drive themselves to work or folly, the birds do likewise."

---

1. pasty (pas′ tē) *n.* a meat pie.

Reading Strategy
Predicting How could this scene of "strange partnership" hint at a danger later on?

placid (plas′ id) *adj.* calm

**Reading Check**
What happens to the birds that do not migrate?

The birds had been more restless than ever this fall of the year, the agitation more marked because the days were still. As the tractor traced its path up and down the western hills, the figure of the farmer silhouetted on the driving seat, the whole machine and the man upon it would be lost momentarily in the great cloud of wheeling, crying birds. There were many more than usual; Nat was sure of this.

Always, in autumn, they followed the plow, but not in great flocks like these, nor with such clamor.

Nat remarked upon it when hedging was finished for the day. "Yes," said the farmer, "there are more birds about than usual; I've noticed it too. And daring, some of them, taking no notice of the tractor. One or two gulls came so close to my head this afternoon I thought they'd knock my cap off! As it was, I could scarcely see what I was doing, when they were overhead and I had the sun in my eyes. I have a notion the weather will change. It will be a hard winter. That's why the birds are restless."

Nat, tramping home across the fields and down the lane to his cottage, saw the birds still flocking over the western hills, in the last glow of the sun. No wind, and the gray sea calm and full. Campion in bloom yet in the hedges, and the air mild. The farmer was right, though, and it was that night the weather turned. Nat's bedroom faced east. He woke just after two and heard the wind in the chimney. Not the storm and bluster of a sou' westerly gale, bringing the rain, but east wind, cold and dry. It sounded hollow in the chimney, and a loose slate rattled on the roof. Nat listened, and he could hear the sea roaring in the bay. Even the air in the small bedroom had turned chill: a draft came under the skirting of the door, blowing upon the bed. Nat drew the blanket round him, leaned closer to the back of his sleeping wife, and stayed wakeful, watchful, aware of misgiving without cause.

Then he heard the tapping on the window. There was no creeper on the cottage walls to break loose and scratch upon the pane. He listened, and the tapping continued until, irritated by the sound, Nat got out of bed and went to the window. He opened it, and as he did so something brushed his hand, jabbing at his knuckles, grazing the skin. Then he saw the flutter of the wings and it was gone, over the roof, behind the cottage.

It was a bird; what kind of bird he could not tell. The wind must have driven it to shelter on the sill.

He shut the window and went back to bed, but, feeling his knuckles wet, put his mouth to the scratch. The bird had drawn blood. Frightened, he supposed, and bewildered, the bird, seeking shelter, had stabbed at him in the darkness. Once more he settled himself to sleep.

Literary Analysis
Foreshadowing What might the birds' restlessness and large numbers foreshadow?

Literary Analysis
Foreshadowing and Imagery What image of the wind does this description generate, and what might it foreshadow about the next day?

Presently the tapping came again, this time more forceful, more insistent, and now his wife woke at the sound and, turning in the bed, said to him, "See to the window, Nat, it's rattling."

"I've already seen to it," he told her; "there's some bird there trying to get in. Can't you hear the wind? It's blowing from the east, driving the birds to shelter."

"Send them away," she said, "I can't sleep with that noise."

He went to the window for the second time, and now when he opened it there was not one bird upon the sill but half a dozen; they flew straight into his face, attacking him.

He shouted, striking out at them with his arms, scattering them; like the first one, they flew over the roof and disappeared. Quickly he let the window fall and latched it.

"Did you hear that?" he said. "They went for me. Tried to peck my eyes." He stood by the window, peering into the darkness, and could see nothing. His wife, heavy with sleep, murmured from the bed.

"I'm not making it up," he said, angry at her suggestion. "I tell you the birds were on the sill, trying to get into the room."

Suddenly a frightened cry came from the room across the passage where the children slept.

"It's Jill," said his wife, roused at the sound, sitting up in bed. "Go to her, see what's the matter."

Nat lit the candle, but when he opened the bedroom door to cross the passage the draft blew out the flame.

There came a second cry of terror, this time from both children, and stumbling into their room, he felt the beating of wings about him in the darkness. The window was wide open. Through it came the birds, hitting first the ceiling and the walls, then swerving in midflight, turning to the children in their beds.

"It's all right, I'm here," shouted Nat, and the children flung themselves, screaming, upon him, while in the darkness the birds rose and dived and came for him again.

"What is it, Nat, what's happened?" his wife called from the further bedroom, and swiftly he pushed the children through the door to the passage and shut it upon them, so that he was alone now in their bedroom with the birds.

He seized a blanket from the nearest bed and, using it as a weapon, flung it to right and left about him in the air. He felt the thud of bodies, heard the fluttering of wings, but they were not yet defeated, for again and again they returned to the assault, jabbing his hands, his head, the little stabbing beaks sharp as pointed forks. The blanket became a weapon of defense; he wound it about his

Reading Strategy
Predicting Based on this detail and others, predict what will happen in the children's room.

**Reading Check**

What happens in the children's room?

The Birds ◆ 53

head, and then in greater darkness beat at the birds with his bare hands. He dared not stumble to the door and open it, lest in doing so the birds should follow him.

How long he fought with them in the darkness he could not tell, but at last the beating of the wings about him lessened and then withdrew, and through the density of the blanket he was aware of light. He waited, listened; there was no sound except the fretful crying of one of the children from the bedroom beyond. The fluttering, the whirring of the wings had ceased.

He took the blanket from his head and stared about him. The cold gray morning light exposed the room. Dawn and the open window had called the living birds; the dead lay on the floor. Nat gazed at the little corpses, shocked and horrified. They were all small birds, none of any size; there must have been fifty of them lying there upon the floor. There were robins, finches, sparrows, blue tits, larks, and bramblings, birds that by nature's law kept to their own flock and their own territory, and now, joining one with another in their urge for battle, had destroyed themselves against the bedroom walls or in the strife had been destroyed by him. Some had lost feathers in the fight; others had blood, his blood, upon their beaks.

Literary Analysis
Foreshadowing and Imagery What might the imagery of this description foreshadow?

Sickened, Nat went to the window and stared out across his patch of garden to the fields.

It was bitter cold, and the ground had all the hard black look of frost. Not white frost, to shine in the morning sun, but the black frost that the east wind brings. The sea, fiercer now with the turning tide, white-capped and steep, broke harshly in the bay. Of the birds there was no sign. Not a sparrow chattered in the hedge beyond the garden gate, no early missel-thrush or blackbird pecked on the grass for worms. There was no sound at all but the east wind and the sea.

Nat shut the window and the door of the small bedroom, and went back across the passage to his own. His wife sat up in bed, one child asleep beside her, the smaller in her arms, his face bandaged. The curtains were tightly drawn across the window, the candles lit. Her face looked garish in the yellow light. She shook her head for silence.

garish (gar´ ish) *adj.* too bright

"He's sleeping now," she whispered, "but only just. Something must have cut him, there was blood at the corner of his eyes. Jill said it was the birds. She said she woke up, and the birds were in the room."

His wife looked up at Nat, searching his face for confirmation. She looked terrified, bewildered, and he did not want her to know that he was also shaken, dazed almost, by the events of the past few hours.

"There are birds in there," he said, "dead birds, nearly fifty of them. Robins, wrens, all the little birds from hereabouts. It's as though a madness seized them, with the east wind." He sat down on the bed beside his wife and held her hand. "It's the weather," he said, "it must be that, it's the hard weather. They aren't the birds, maybe, from here around. They've been driven down from upcountry."

"But, Nat," whispered his wife, "it's only this night that the weather turned. There's been no snow to drive them. And they can't be hungry yet. There's food for them out there in the fields."

"It's the weather," repeated Nat. "I tell you, it's the weather."

His face, too, was drawn and tired, like hers. They stared at one another for a while without speaking.

"I'll go downstairs and make a cup of tea," he said.

The sight of the kitchen reassured him. The cups and saucers, neatly stacked upon the dresser, the table and chairs, his wife's roll of knitting on her basket chair, the children's toys in a corner cupboard.

He knelt down, raked out the old embers, and relit the fire. The glowing sticks brought normality, the steaming kettle and the brown teapot comfort and security. He drank his tea, carried a cup up to his wife. Then he washed in the scullery,[2] and, putting on his boots, opened the back door.

The sky was hard and leaden, and the brown hills that had gleamed in the sun the day before looked dark and bare. The east wind, like a razor, stripped the trees, and the leaves, crackling and dry, shivered and scattered with the wind's blast. Nat stubbed the earth with his boot. It was frozen hard. He had never known a change so swift and sudden. Black winter had descended in a single night.

The children were awake now. Jill was chattering upstairs and young Johnny crying once again. Nat heard his wife's voice, soothing, comforting. Presently they came down. He had breakfast ready for them, and the routine of the day began.

"Did you drive away the birds?" asked Jill, restored to calm because of the kitchen fire, because of day, because of breakfast.

"Yes, they've all gone now," said Nat. "It was the east wind brought them in. They were frightened and lost, they wanted shelter."

"They tried to peck us," said Jill. "They went for Johnny's eyes."

"Fright made them do that," said Nat. "They didn't know where they were in the dark bedroom."

"I hope they won't come again," said Jill. "Perhaps if we put bread for them outside the window they will eat that and fly away."

She finished her breakfast and then went for her coat and hood, her schoolbooks and her satchel. Nat said nothing, but his wife looked at him across the table. A silent message passed between them.

"I'll walk with her to the bus," he said. "I don't go to the farm today."

And while the child was washing in the scullery he said to his wife, "Keep all the windows closed, and the doors too. Just to be on the safe side. I'll go to the farm. Find out if they heard anything in the night." Then he walked with his small daughter up the lane. She seemed to have forgotten her experience of the night before. She danced ahead of him, chasing the leaves, her face whipped with the cold and rosy under the pixie hood.

"Is it going to snow, Dad?" she said. "It's cold enough."

He glanced up at the bleak sky, felt the wind tear at his shoulders.

---

2. **scullery** (skul′ ər ē) *n.* a room next to the kitchen where pots and pans are washed and stored.

Literary Analysis
Foreshadowing
Overnight, "black winter" has taken hold of the countryside. What might the suddenness of this change foreshadow?

Reading Check

What does Nat ask his wife to do before he leaves the house?

"No," he said, "it's not going to snow. This is a black winter, not a white one."

All the while he searched the hedgerows for the birds, glanced over the top of them to the fields beyond, looked to the small wood above the farm where the rooks and jackdaws gathered. He saw none.

The other children waited by the bus stop, muffled, hooded like Jill, the faces white and pinched with cold.

Jill ran to them, waving. "My dad says it won't snow," she called, "it's going to be a black winter."

She said nothing of the birds. She began to push and struggle with another little girl. The bus came ambling up the hill. Nat saw her on to it, then turned and walked back towards the farm. It was not his day for work, but he wanted to satisfy himself that all was well. Jim, the cowman, was clattering in the yard.

"Boss around?" asked Nat.

"Gone to market," said Jim. "It's Tuesday, isn't it?"

He clumped off round the corner of a shed. He had no time for Nat. Nat was said to be superior. Read books, and the like. Nat had forgotten it was Tuesday. This showed how the events of the preceding night had shaken him. He went to the back door of the farmhouse and heard Mrs. Trigg singing in the kitchen, the wireless[3] making a background to her song.

"Are you there, missus?" called out Nat.

She came to the door, beaming, broad, a good-tempered woman.

"Hullo, Mr. Hocken," she said. "Can you tell me where this cold is coming from? Is it Russia? I've never seen such a change. And it's going on, the wireless says. Something to do with the Arctic Circle."

"We didn't turn on the wireless this morning," said Nat. "Fact is, we had trouble in the night."

"Kiddies poorly?"

"No . . ." He hardly knew how to explain it. Now, in daylight, the battle of the birds would sound absurd.

He tried to tell Mrs. Trigg what had happened, but he could see from her eyes that she thought his story was the result of a nightmare.

"Sure they were real birds," she said, smiling, "with proper feathers and all? Not the funny-shaped kind that the men see after closing hours on a Saturday night?"

"Mrs. Trigg," he said, "there are fifty dead birds, robins, wrens, and such, lying low on the floor of the children's bedroom. They went for me; they tried to go for young Johnny's eyes."

▲ **Critical Viewing**
Compare and contrast the mood of the painting with the mood of the story so far. **[Compare and Contrast]**

---

3. wireless (wīr′ lis) *n.* radio.

Landscape From a Dream, 1936-38, Paul Nash, Tate Gallery, London

Mrs. Trigg stared at him doubtfully.

"Well there, now," she answered, "I suppose the weather brought them. Once in the bedroom, they wouldn't know where they were to. Foreign birds maybe, from that Arctic Circle."

"No," said Nat, "they were the birds you see about here every day."

"Funny thing," said Mrs. Trigg, "no explaining it, really. You ought to write up and ask the *Guardian*. They'd have some answer for it. Well, I must be getting on."

She nodded, smiled, and went back into the kitchen.

Reading Check

What is Mrs. Trigg's response to Nat's story?

Nat, dissatisfied, turned to the farm gate. Had it not been for those corpses on the bedroom floor, which he must now collect and bury somewhere, he would have considered the tale exaggeration too.

Jim was standing by the gate.

"Had any trouble with the birds?" asked Nat.

"Birds? What birds?"

"We got them up our place last night. Scores of them, came in the children's bedroom. Quite savage they were."

"Oh?" It took time for anything to penetrate Jim's head. "Never heard of birds acting savage," he said at length. "They get tame, like, sometimes. I've seen them come to the windows for crumbs."

"These birds last night weren't tame."

"No? Cold, maybe. Hungry. You put out some crumbs."

Jim was no more interested than Mrs. Trigg had been. It was, Nat thought, like air raids in the war.♦ No one down this end of the country knew what the Plymouth folk had seen and suffered. You had to endure something yourself before it touched you. He walked back along the lane and crossed the stile to his cottage. He found his wife in the kitchen with young Johnny.

"See anyone?" she asked.

"Mrs. Trigg and Jim," he answered. "I don't think they believed me. Anyway, nothing wrong up there."

"You might take the birds away," she said. "I daren't go into the room to make the beds until you do. I'm scared."

"Nothing to scare you now," said Nat. "They're dead, aren't they?"

He went up with a sack and dropped the stiff bodies into it, one by one. Yes, there were fifty of them, all told. Just the ordinary, common birds of the hedgerow, nothing as large even as a thrush. It must have been fright that made them act the way they did. Blue tits, wrens—it was incredible to think of the power of their small beaks jabbing at his face and hands the night before. He took the sack out into the garden and was faced now with a fresh problem. The ground was too hard to dig. It was frozen solid, yet no snow had fallen, nothing had happened in the past hours but the coming of the east wind. It was unnatural, queer. The weather prophets must be right. The change was something connected with the Arctic Circle.

The wind seemed to cut him to the bone as he stood there uncertainly, holding the sack. He could see the white-capped seas breaking down under in the bay. He decided to take the birds to the shore and bury them.

*L*iterature

in context World History Connection

♦ *Preparing for the Blitz*

As he prepares for the birds' attack, Nat again draws a parallel between this situation and World War II. After striking British Royal Air Force (RAF) bases in August and September of 1940, German forces believed that they had destroyed the RAF. They then began to bomb civilian targets in what was called the *Blitz* (the German word for "lightning"). The Blitz continued until May of 1941, with raids almost every night. Blackout boards and shelters became a familiar part of British life during that difficult time.

A World War II Bomb Shelter

Literary Analysis
Foreshadowing What might the "unnatural" weather foreshadow?

When he reached the beach below the headland he could scarcely stand, the force of the east wind was so strong. It hurt to draw breath, and his bare hands were blue. Never had he known such cold, not in all the bad winters he could remember. It was low tide. He crunched his way over the shingle[4] to the softer sand and then, his back to the wind, ground a pit in the sand with his heel. He meant to drop the birds into it, but as he opened up the sack the force of the wind carried them, lifted them, as though in flight again, and they were blown away from him along the beach, tossed like feathers, spread and scattered, the bodies of the fifty frozen birds. There was something ugly in the sight. He did not like it. The dead birds were swept away from him by the wind.

"The tide will take them when it turns," he said to himself.

He looked out to sea and watched the crested breakers, combing green. They rose stiffly, curled, and broke again, and because it was ebb tide the roar was distant, more remote, lacking the sound and thunder of the flood.

Then he saw them. The gulls. Out there, riding the seas.

What he had thought at first to be the whitecaps of the waves were gulls. Hundreds, thousands, tens of thousands . . . They rose and fell in the trough of the seas, heads to the wind, like a mighty fleet at anchor, waiting on the tide. To eastward, and to the west, the gulls were there. They stretched as far as his eye could reach, in close formation, line upon line. Had the sea been still they would have covered the bay like a white cloud, head to head, body packed to body. Only the east wind, whipping the sea to breakers, hid them from the shore.

Nat turned and, leaving the beach, climbed the steep path home. Someone should know of this. Someone should be told. Something was happening, because of the east wind and the weather, that he did not understand. He wondered if he should go to the call box by the bus stop and ring up the police. Yet what could they do? What could anyone do? Tens of thousands of gulls riding the sea there in the bay because of storm, because of hunger. The police would think him mad, or drunk, or take the statement from him with great calm. "Thank you. Yes, the matter has already been reported. The hard weather is driving the birds inland in great numbers." Nat looked about him. Still no sign of any other bird. Perhaps the cold had sent them all from upcountry? As he drew near to the cottage his wife came to meet him at the door. She called to him, excited. "Nat," she said, "it's on the wireless. They've just read out a special news bulletin. I've written it down."

"What's on the wireless?" he said.

"About the birds," she said. "It's not only here, it's everywhere. In London, all over the country. Something has happened to the birds."

Together they went into the kitchen. He read the piece of paper lying on the table.

"Statement from the Home Office at 11 A.M. today. Reports from all over the country are coming in hourly about the vast quantity of birds

---

4. shingle *n.* area of beach covered with waterworn gravel.

Reading Strategy
Predicting Do you think Nat will call the police? Why?

**Reading Check**

What does Nat see riding the seas?

flocking above towns, villages, and outlying districts, causing obstruction and damage and even attacking individuals. It is thought that the Arctic airstream, at present covering the British Isles, is causing birds to migrate south in immense numbers, and that intense hunger may drive these birds to attack human beings. Householders are warned to see to their windows, doors, and chimneys, and to take reasonable precautions for the safety of their children. A further statement will be issued later."

A kind of excitement seized Nat; he looked at his wife in triumph.

"There you are," he said. "Let's hope they'll hear that at the farm. Mrs. Trigg will know it wasn't any story. It's true. All over the country. I've been telling myself all morning there's something wrong. And just now, down on the beach, I looked out to sea and there are gulls, thousands of them, tens of thousands—you couldn't put a pin between their heads—and they're all out there, riding on the sea, waiting."

"What are they waiting for, Nat?" she asked.

He stared at her, then looked down again at the piece of paper.

"I don't know," he said slowly. "It says here the birds are hungry."

He went over to the drawer where he kept his hammer and tools.

"What are you going to do, Nat?"

"See to the windows and the chimneys too, like they tell you."

"You think they would break in, with the windows shut? Those sparrows and robins and such? Why, how could they?"

He did not answer. He was not thinking of the robins and the sparrows. He was thinking of the gulls . . .

He went upstairs and worked there the rest of the morning, boarding the windows of the bedrooms, filling up the chimney bases. Good job it was his free day and he was not working at the farm. It reminded him of the old days, at the beginning of the war. He was not married then, and he had made all the black-out boards for his mother's house in Plymouth. Made the shelter too. Not that it had been of any use when the moment came. He wondered if they would take these precautions up at the farm. He doubted it. Too easygoing, Harry Trigg and his missus. Maybe they'd laugh at the whole thing. Go off to a dance or a whist drive.[5]

"Dinner's ready." She called him, from the kitchen.

"All right. Coming down."

He was pleased with his handiwork. The frames fitted nicely over the little panes and at the bases of the chimneys.

When dinner was over and his wife was washing up, Nat switched on the one o'clock news. The same announcement was repeated, the one which she had taken down during the morning, but the news bulletin enlarged upon it. "The flocks of birds have caused dislocation in all areas," read the announcer, "and in London the sky was so dense at ten

Literary Analysis
Imagery and Foreshadowing Which details found in Nat's description foreshadow unusual events to come?

---

5. whist drive *n.* a card game organized for a group.

o'clock this morning that it seemed as if the city was covered by a vast black cloud.

"The birds settled on rooftops, on window ledges, and on chimneys. The species included blackbird, thrush, the common house sparrow, and, as might be expected in the metropolis, a vast quantity of pigeons and starlings, and that frequenter of the London river, the black-headed gull. The sight has been so unusual that traffic came to a standstill in many thoroughfares, work was abandoned in shops and offices, and the streets and pavements were crowded with people standing about to watch the birds."

Various incidents were <u>recounted</u>, the suspected reason of cold and hunger stated again, and warnings to householders repeated. The announcer's voice was smooth and suave. Nat had the impression that this man, in particular, treated the whole business as he would an elaborate joke. There would be others like him, hundreds of them, who did not know what it was to struggle in darkness with a flock of birds. There would be parties tonight in London, like the ones they gave on election nights. People standing about, shouting and laughing . . . "Come and watch the birds!"

Nat switched off the wireless. He got up and started work on the kitchen windows. His wife watched him, young Johnny at her heels.

"What, boards for down here too?" she said. "Why, I'll have to light up before three o'clock. I see no call for boards down here."

"Better be sure than sorry," answered Nat. "I'm not going to take any chances."

"What they ought to do," she said, "is to call the Army out and shoot the birds. That would soon scare them off."

"Let them try," said Nat. "How'd they set about it?"

"They have the Army to the docks," she answered, "when the dockers strike. The soldiers go down and unload the ships."

"Yes," said Nat, "and the population of London is eight million or more. Think of all the buildings, all the flats and houses. Do you think they've enough soldiers to go around shooting birds from every roof?"

"I don't know. But something should be done. They ought to do something."

Nat thought to himself that "they" were no doubt considering the problem at that very moment, but whatever "they" decided to do in London and the big cities would not help the people here, three hundred miles away. Each householder must look after his own.

"How are we off for food?" he said.

"Now, Nat, whatever next?"

"Never mind. What have you got in the larder?"[6]

"It's shopping day tomorrow, you know that. I don't keep uncooked

---

6. **larder** (lärd´ ər) *n.* place where food is kept; pantry.

Reading Strategy
Predicting Based on the reaction to the birds, predict what you think might happen.

recounted (ri kount´ ed) *v.* told in detail; narrated

✓Reading Check

What steps does Nat take to protect his family and his home?

food hanging about, it goes off. Butcher doesn't call till the day after. But I can bring back something when I go in tomorrow."

Nat did not want to scare her. He thought it possible that she might not go to town tomorrow. He looked in the larder for himself, and in the cupboard where she kept her tins. They would do for a couple of days. Bread was low.

"What about the baker?"

"He comes tomorrow too."

He saw she had flour. If the baker did not call she had enough to bake one loaf.

"We'd be better off in the old days," he said, "when the women baked twice a week, and had pilchards[7] salted, and there was food for a family to last a siege, if need be."

"I've tried the children with tinned fish, they don't like it," she said.

Nat went on hammering the boards across the kitchen windows. Candles. They were low in candles too. That must be another thing she meant to buy tomorrow. Well, it could not be helped. They must go early to bed tonight. That was, if . . .

He got up and went out of the back door and stood in the garden, looking down toward the sea. There had been no sun all day, and now, at barely three o'clock, a kind of darkness had already come, the sky <u>sullen</u>, heavy, colorless like salt. He could hear the vicious sea drumming on the rocks. He walked down the path, halfway to the beach. And then he stopped. He could see the tide had turned. The rock that had shown in midmorning was now covered, but it was not the sea that held his eyes. The gulls had risen. They were circling, hundreds of them, thousands of them, lifting their wings against the wind. It was the gulls that made the darkening of the sky. And they were silent. They made not a sound. They just went on soaring and circling, rising, falling, trying their strength against the wind.

Nat turned. He ran up the path, back to the cottage.

"I'm going for Jill," he said. "I'll wait for her at the bus stop."

"What's the matter?" asked his wife. "You've gone quite white."

"Keep Johnny inside," he said. "Keep the door shut. Light up now, and draw the curtains."

"It's only just gone three," she said.

"Never mind. Do what I tell you."

He looked inside the tool shed outside the back door. Nothing there of much use. A spade was too heavy, and a fork no good. He took the hoe. It was the only possible tool, and light enough to carry.

He started walking up the lane to the bus stop, and now and again glanced back over his shoulder.

The gulls had risen higher now, their circles were broader, wider, they were spreading out in huge formation across the sky.

He hurried on; although he knew the bus would not come to the top of the hill before four o'clock he had to hurry. He passed no one on the

sullen (sul′ ən) *adj.* gloomy

**Literary Analysis
Foreshadowing** What might the circling gulls foreshadow?

---

7. pilchards (pil′ chərdz) *n.* small fish similar to sardines.

way. He was glad of this. No time to stop and chatter.

At the top of the hill he waited. He was much too soon. There was half an hour still to go. The east wind came whipping across the fields from the higher ground. He stamped his feet and blew upon his hands. In the distance he could see the clay hills, white and clean, against the heavy pallor of the sky. Something black rose from behind them, like a smudge at first, then widening, becoming deeper, and the smudge became a cloud, and the cloud divided again into five other clouds, spreading north, east, south, and west, and they were not clouds at all; they were birds. He watched them travel across the sky, and as one section passed overhead, within two or three hundred feet of him, he knew, from their speed, they were bound inland, upcountry; they had no business with the people here on the peninsula. They were rooks, crows, jackdaws, magpies, jays, all birds that usually preyed upon the smaller species; but this afternoon they were bound on some other mission.

"They've been given the towns," thought Nat; "they know what they have to do. We don't matter so much here. The gulls will serve for us. The others go to the towns."

He went to the call box, stepped inside, and lifted the receiver. The exchange would do. They would pass the message on.

"I'm speaking from Highway," he said, "by the bus stop. I want to report large formations of birds traveling upcountry. The gulls are also forming in the bay."

"All right," answered the voice, laconic, weary.

"You'll be sure and pass this message on to the proper quarter?"

"Yes . . . yes . . ." Impatient now, fed-up. The buzzing note resumed.

"She's another," thought Nat, "she doesn't care. Maybe she's had to answer calls all day. She hopes to go to the pictures tonight. She'll squeeze some fellow's hand and point up at the sky and say 'Look at all them birds!' She doesn't care."

The bus came lumbering up the hill. Jill climbed out, and three or four other children. The bus went on towards the town.

"What's the hoe for, Dad?"

They crowded around him, laughing, pointing.

"I just brought it along," he said. "Come on now, let's get home. It's cold, no hanging about. Here, you. I'll watch you across the fields, see how fast you can run."

He was speaking to Jill's companions, who came from different families, living in the council houses.[8] A short cut would take them to the cottages.

"We want to play a bit in the lane," said one of them.

"No, you don't. You go off home or I'll tell your Mammy."

They whispered to one another, round-eyed, then scuttled off across the fields. Jill stared at her father, her mouth sullen.

"We always play in the lane," she said.

"Not tonight, you don't," he said. "Come on now, no dawdling."

---

8. **council houses** n. housing units built by the government.

Reading Strategy
Predicting What might happen if these details about the birds were multiplied many times?

Reading Check

What important message is Nat trying to report when he goes to the call box?

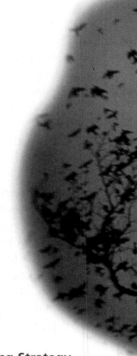

He could see the gulls now, circling the fields, coming in toward the land. Still silent. Still no sound.

"Look, Dad, look over there, look at all the gulls."

"Yes. Hurry, now."

"Where are they flying to? Where are they going?"

"Upcountry, I dare say. Where it's warmer."

He seized her hand and dragged her after him along the lane.

"Don't go so fast. I can't keep up."

The gulls were copying the rooks and crows. They were spreading out in formation across the sky. They headed, in bands of thousands, to the four compass points.

"Dad, what is it? What are the gulls doing?"

They were not intent upon their flight, as the crows, as the jackdaws had been. They still circled overhead. Nor did they fly so high. It was as though they waited upon some signal. As though some decision had yet to be given. The order was not clear.

"Do you want me to carry you, Jill? Here, come pick-a-back."

This way he might put on speed; but he was wrong. Jill was heavy. She kept slipping. And was crying too. His sense of urgency, of fear, had communicated itself to the child.

"I wish the gulls would go away. I don't like them. They're coming closer to the lane."

He put her down again. He started running, swinging Jill after him. As they went past the farm turning he saw the farmer backing his car out of the garage. Nat called to him.

"Can you give us a lift?" he said.

"What's that?"

Mr. Trigg turned in the driving seat and stared at them. Then a smile came to his cheerful, rubicund face.

"It looks as though we're in for some fun," he said. "Have you seen the gulls? Jim and I are going to take a crack at them. Everyone's gone bird-crazy, talking of nothing else. I hear you were troubled in the night. Want a gun?"

Nat shook his head.

The small car was packed. There was just room for Jill, if she crouched on top of petrol tins on the back seat.

"I don't want a gun," said Nat, "but I'd be obliged if you'd run Jill home. She's scared of the birds."

He spoke briefly. He did not want to talk in front of Jill.

"O.K.," said the farmer, "I'll take her home. Why don't you stop behind and join the shooting match? We'll make the feathers fly."

Jill climbed in, and turning the car, the driver sped up the lane. Nat followed after. Trigg must be crazy. What use was a gun against a sky of birds?

Now Nat was not responsible for Jill, he had time to look about him. The birds were circling still above the fields. Mostly herring gull, but the black-backed gull amongst them. Usually they kept apart. Now they were united. Some bond had brought them together. It was the black-

Reading Strategy
Predicting What do you predict will happen if Nat and Jill do not move along more quickly?

▲ **Critical Viewing**
What do the scraggly tree and the scores of birds in the photograph convey about the setting of this story? **[Infer]**

backed gull that attacked the smaller birds, and even newborn lambs, so he'd heard. He'd never seen it done. He remembered this now, though, looking above him in the sky. They were coming in towards the farm. They were circling lower in the sky, and the black-backed gulls were to the front, the black-backed gulls were leading. The farm, then, was their target. They were making for the farm.

Nat increased his pace toward his own cottage. He saw the farmer's car turn and come back along the lane. It drew up beside him with a jerk.

"The kid has run inside," said the farmer. "Your wife was watching for her. Well, what do you make of it? They're saying in town the Russians have done it. The Russians have poisoned the birds."

"How could they do that?" asked Nat.

"Don't ask me. You know how stories get around. Will you join my shooting match?"

"No, I'll get along home. The wife will be worried else."

☑**Reading Check**

Why does Nat ask Mr. Trigg to take Jill home?

"My missus says if you could eat gull there'd be some sense in it," said Trigg. "We'd have roast gull, baked gull, and pickle 'em into the bargain. You wait until I let off a few barrels into the brutes. That'll scare 'em."

"Have you boarded your windows?" asked Nat.

"No. Lot of nonsense. They like to scare you on the wireless. I've had more to do today than to go round boarding up my windows."

"I'd board them now, if I were you."

"Garn. You're windy. Like to come to our place to sleep?"

"No, thanks all the same."

"All right. See you in the morning. Give you a gull breakfast."

The farmer grinned and turned his car to the farm entrance.

Nat hurried on. Past the little wood, past the old barn, and then across the stile to the remaining field.

As he jumped the stile he heard the whir of wings. A black-backed gull dived down at him from the sky, missed, swerved in flight, and rose to dive again. In a moment it was joined by others, six, seven, a dozen, black-backed and herring mixed. Nat dropped his hoe. The hoe was useless. Covering his head with his arms, he ran toward the cottage. They kept coming at him from the air, silent save for the beating wings. The terrible, fluttering wings. He could feel the blood on his hands, his wrists, his neck. Each stab of a swooping beak tore his flesh. If only he could keep them from his eyes. Nothing else mattered. He must keep them from his eyes. They had not learned yet how to cling to a shoulder, how to rip clothing, how to dive in mass upon the head, upon the body. But with each dive, with each attack, they became bolder. And they had no thought for themselves. When they dived low and missed, they crashed, bruised and broken, on the ground. As Nat ran he stumbled, kicking their spent bodies in front of him.

He found the door; he hammered upon it with his bleeding hands. Because of the boarded windows no light shone. Everything was dark.

"Let me in," he shouted, "it's Nat. Let me in."

He shouted loud to make himself heard above the whir of the gulls' wings.

Then he saw the gannet, poised for the dive, above him in the sky. The gulls circled, retired, soared, one after another, against the wind. Only the gannet remained. One single gannet above him in the sky. The wings folded suddenly to its body. It dropped like a stone. Nat screamed, and the door opened. He stumbled across the threshold, and his wife threw her weight against the door.

They heard the thud of the gannet as it fell.

His wife dressed his wounds. They were not deep. The backs of his hands had suffered most, and his wrists. Had he not worn a cap they would have reached his head. As to the gannet . . . the gannet could have split his skull.

The children were crying, of course. They had seen the blood on their father's hands.

"It's all right now," he told them. "I'm not hurt. Just a few scratches.

Reading Strategy
Predicting Based on this conversation, what do you think will happen to the farmer? Explain your prediction.

Literary Analysis
Foreshadowing What future events might the words with each attack, they became bolder foreshadow?

You play with Johnny, Jill. Mammy will wash these cuts."

He half shut the door to the scullery so that they could not see. His wife was ashen. She began running water from the sink.

"I saw them overhead," she whispered. "They began collecting just as Jill ran in with Mr. Trigg. I shut the door fast, and it jammed. That's why I couldn't open it at once when you came."

"Thank God they waited for me," he said. "Jill would have fallen at once. One bird alone would have done it."

<u>Furtively</u>, so as not to alarm the children, they whispered together as she bandaged his hands and the back of his neck.

"They're flying inland," he said, "thousands of them. Rooks, crows, all the bigger birds. I saw them from the bus stop. They're making for the towns."

"But what can they do, Nat?"

"They'll attack. Go for everyone out in the streets. Then they'll try the windows, the chimneys."

"Why don't the authorities do something? Why don't they get the Army, get machine guns, anything?"

"There's been no time. Nobody's prepared. We'll hear what they have to say on the six o'clock news."

Nat went back into the kitchen, followed by his wife. Johnny was playing quietly on the floor. Only Jill looked anxious.

"I can hear the birds," she said. "Listen, Dad."

Nat listened. Muffled sounds came from the windows, from the door. Wings brushing the surface, sliding, scraping, seeking a way of entry. The sound of many bodies, pressed together, shuffling on the sills. Now and again came a thud, a crash, as some bird dived and fell. "Some of them will kill themselves that way," he thought, "but not enough. Never enough."

"All right," he said aloud. "I've got boards over the windows, Jill. The birds can't get in."

He went and examined all the windows. His work had been thorough. Every gap was closed. He would make extra certain, however. He found wedges, pieces of old tin, strips of wood and metal, and fastened them at the sides to reinforce the boards. His hammering helped to deafen the sound of the birds, the shuffling, the tapping, and more ominous—he did not want his wife or the children to hear it—the splinter of cracked glass.

"Turn on the wireless," he said, "let's have the wireless."

This would drown the sound also. He went upstairs to the bedrooms and reinforced the windows there. Now he could hear the birds on the roof, the scraping of claws, a sliding, jostling sound.

He decided they must sleep in the kitchen, keep up the fire, bring down the mattresses, and lay them out on the floor. He was afraid of the bedroom chimneys. The boards he had placed at the chimney bases might give way. In the kitchen they would be safe because of the fire. He would have to make a joke of it. Pretend to the children they were playing at camp. If the worst happened, and the birds forced an entry down

furtively (fụr´ tiv lē) *adv.* stealthily, so as to avoid being heard

Literary Analysis
Foreshadowing Think about what Nat has done to get his house ready for this attack. What might the cracked glass foreshadow, and why?

**Reading Check**

What steps does Nat take to prepare his house against the birds?

the bedroom chimneys, it would be hours, days perhaps, before they could break down the doors. The birds would be imprisoned in the bedrooms. They could do no harm there. Crowded together, they would stifle and die.

He began to bring the mattresses downstairs. At sight of them his wife's eyes widened in apprehension. She thought the birds had already broken in upstairs.

"All right," he said cheerfully, "we'll all sleep together in the kitchen tonight. More cozy here by the fire. Then we shan't be worried by those silly old birds tapping at the windows."

He made the children help him rearrange the furniture, and he took the precaution of moving the dresser, with his wife's help, across the window. It fitted well. It was an added safeguard. The mattresses could now be laid, one beside the other, against the wall where the dresser had stood.

"We're safe enough now," he thought. "We're snug and tight, like an air-raid shelter. We can hold out. It's just the food that worries me. Food, and coal for the fire. We've enough for two or three days, not more. By that time . . ."

No use thinking ahead as far as that. And they'd be giving directions on the wireless. People would be told what to do. And now, in the midst of many problems, he realized that it was dance music only coming over the air. Not Children's Hour, as it should have been. He glanced at the dial. Yes, they were on the Home Service all right. Dance records. He switched to the Light program. He knew the reason. The usual programs had been abandoned. This only happened at exceptional times. Elections and such. He tried to remember if it had happened in the war, during the heavy raids on London. But of course. The B.B.C.[9] was not stationed in London during the war. The programs were broadcast from other, temporary quarters. "We're better off here," he thought; "we're better off here in the kitchen, with the windows and the doors boarded, than they are up in the towns. Thank God we're not in the towns."

At six o'clock the records ceased. The time signal was given. No matter if it scared the children, he must hear the news. There was a pause after the pips.[10] Then the announcer spoke. His voice was solemn, grave. Quite different from midday.

"This is London," he said. "A National Emergency was proclaimed at four o'clock this afternoon. Measures are being taken to safeguard the lives and property of the population, but it must be understood that these are not easy to effect immediately, owing to the unforeseen and unparalleled nature of the present crisis. Every householder must take

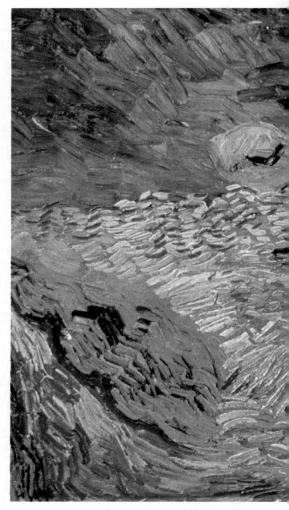

▲ **Critical Viewing**
What feelings conveyed through this painting might be similar to those conveyed through the story? **[Describe]**

---

9. B.B.C. British Broadcasting Corporation.
10. pips *n.* beeping sounds that indicate the time.

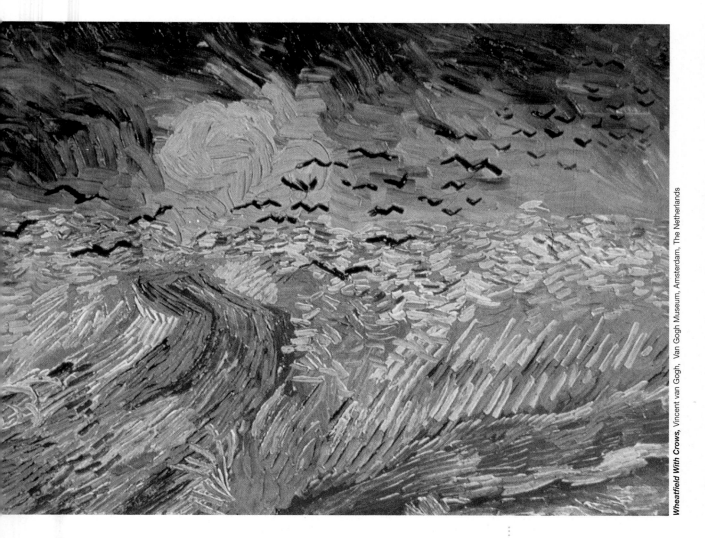

Wheatfield With Crows, Vincent van Gogh, Van Gogh Museum, Amsterdam, The Netherlands

precautions to his own building, and where several people live together, as in flats and apartments, they must unite to do the utmost they can to prevent entry. It is absolutely <u>imperative</u> that every individual stay indoors tonight and that no one at all remain on the streets, or roads, or anywhere withoutdoors.[11] The birds, in vast numbers, are attacking anyone on sight, and have already begun an assault upon buildings; but these, with due care, should be impenetrable. The population is asked to remain calm and not to panic. Owing to the exceptional nature of the emergency, there will be no further transmission from any broadcasting station until 7 A.M. tomorrow."

They played the National Anthem. Nothing more happened. Nat switched off the set. He looked at his wife. She stared back at him.

"What's it mean?" said Jill. "What did the news say?"

"There won't be any more programs tonight," said Nat. "There's been a breakdown at the B.B.C."

---

11. withoutdoors *adv.* old-fashioned variation of "outdoors."

imperative (im per´ ə tiv) *adj.* urgent; absolutely necessary

Reading Check

What important news is revealed through the broadcast?

"Is it the birds?" asked Jill. "Have the birds done it?"

"No," said Nat, "it's just that everyone's very busy, and then of course they have to get rid of the birds, messing everything up, in the towns. Well, we can manage without the wireless for one evening."

"I wish we had a gramophone,"[12] said Jill, "that would be better than nothing."

She had her face turned to the dresser backed against the windows. Try as they did to ignore it, they were all aware of the shuffling, the stabbing, the persistent beating and sweeping of wings.

"We'll have supper early," suggested Nat, "something for a treat. Ask Mammy. Toasted cheese, eh? Something we all like?"

He winked and nodded at his wife. He wanted the look of dread, of apprehension, to go from Jill's face.

He helped with the supper, whistling, singing, making as much clatter as he could, and it seemed to him that the shuffling and the tapping were not so intense as they had been at first. Presently he went up to the bedrooms and listened, and he no longer heard the jostling for place upon the roof.

"They've got reasoning powers," he thought; "they know it's hard to break in here. They'll try elsewhere. They won't waste their time with us."

Literary Analysis
Foreshadowing What might this quiet moment foreshadow?

Supper passed without incident, and then, when they were clearing away, they heard a new sound, droning, familiar, a sound they all knew and understood.

His wife looked up at him, her face alight. "It's planes," she said; "they're sending out planes after the birds. That's what I said they ought to do all along. That will get them. Isn't that gunfire? Can't you hear guns?"

It might be gunfire out at sea. Nat could not tell. Big naval guns might have an effect upon the gulls out at sea, but the gulls were inland now. The guns couldn't shell the shore because of the population.

Reading Strategy
Predicting What do you predict will happen to the planes?

"It's good, isn't it," said his wife, "to hear the planes?" And Jill, catching her enthusiasm, jumped up and down with Johnny. "The planes will get the birds. The planes will shoot them."

Just then they heard a crash about two miles distant, followed by a second, then a third. The droning became more distant, passed away out to sea.

"What was that?" asked his wife. "Were they dropping bombs on the birds?"

"I don't know," answered Nat. "I don't think so."

He did not want to tell her that the sound they had heard was the crashing of aircraft. It was, he had no doubt, a venture on the part of the authorities to send out <u>reconnaissance</u> forces, but they might have known the venture was suicidal. What could aircraft do against birds that flung themselves to death against propeller and fuselage, but hurtle to the ground themselves? This was being tried now, he supposed, over

reconnaissance (ri kän´ ə səns) *adj.* exploratory in nature, as when observing to seek information

---

12. gramophone (gram´ ə fōn´) *n.* phonograph; record player.

the whole country. And at a cost. Someone high up had lost his head.

"Where have the planes gone, Dad?" asked Jill.

"Back to base," he said. "Come on, now, time to tuck down for bed."

It kept his wife occupied, undressing the children before the fire, seeing to the bedding, one thing and another, while he went round the cottage again, making sure that nothing had worked loose. There was no further drone of aircraft, and the naval guns had ceased. "Waste of life and effort," Nat said to himself. "We can't destroy enough of them that way. Cost too heavy. There's always gas. Maybe they'll try spraying with gas, mustard gas. We'll be warned first, of course, if they do. There's one thing, the best brains of the country will be on to it tonight."

Somehow the thought reassured him. He had a picture of scientists, naturalists, technicians, and all those chaps they called the back-room boys, summoned to a council; they'd be working on the problem now. This was not a job for the government, for the chiefs of staff—they would merely carry out the orders of the scientists.

"They'll have to be ruthless," he thought. "Where the trouble's worst they'll have to risk more lives, if they use gas. All the livestock, too, and the soil—all contaminated. As long as everyone doesn't panic. That's the trouble. People panicking, losing their heads. The B.B.C. was right to warn us of that."

Upstairs in the bedrooms all was quiet. No further scraping and stabbing at the windows. A lull in battle. Forces regrouping. Wasn't that what they called it in the old wartime bulletins? The wind hadn't dropped, though. He could still hear it roaring in the chimneys. And the sea breaking down on the shore. Then he remembered the tide. The tide would be on the turn. Maybe the lull in battle was because of the tide. There was some law the birds obeyed, and it was all to do with the east wind and the tide.

He glanced at his watch. Nearly eight o'clock. It must have gone high water an hour ago. That explained the lull: the birds attacked with the flood tide. It might not work that way inland, upcountry, but it seemed as if it was so this way on the coast. He reckoned the time limit in his head. They had six hours to go without attack. When the tide turned again, around one-twenty in the morning, the birds would come back . . .

There were two things he could do. The first to rest, with his wife and the children, and all of them snatch what sleep they could, until the small hours. The second to go out, see how they were faring at the farm, see if the telephone was still working there, so that they might get news from the exchange.

He called softly to his wife, who had just settled the children. She came halfway up the stairs and he whispered to her.

"You're not to go," she said at once, "you're not to go and leave me alone with the children. I can't stand it."

Her voice rose hysterically. He hushed her, calmed her.

"All right," he said, "all right. I'll wait till morning. And we'll get the wireless bulletin then too, at seven. But in the morning, when the tide

Literary Analysis

Foreshadowing and Imagery In what ways does this image of experts gathering add to the tension of the story?

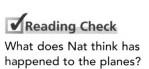

Reading Check

What does Nat think has happened to the planes?

ebbs again, I'll try for the farm, and they may let us have bread and potatoes, and milk too."

His mind was busy again, planning against emergency. They would not have milked, of course, this evening. The cows would be standing by the gate, waiting in the yard, with the household inside, battened behind boards, as they were here at the cottage. That is, if they had time to take precautions. He thought of the farmer, Trigg, smiling at him from the car. There would have been no shooting party, not tonight.

The children were asleep. His wife, still clothed, was sitting on her mattress. She watched him, her eyes nervous.

"What are you going to do?" she whispered.

He shook his head for silence. Softly, stealthily, he opened the back door and looked outside.

It was pitch dark. The wind was blowing harder than ever, coming in steady gusts, icy, from the sea. He kicked at the step outside the door. It was heaped with birds. There were dead birds everywhere. Under the windows, against the walls. These were the suicides, the divers, the ones with broken necks. Wherever he looked he saw dead birds. No trace of the living. The living had flown seaward with the turn of the tide. The gulls would be riding the seas now, as they had done in the forenoon.

In the far distance, on the hill where the tractor had been two days before, something was burning. One of the aircraft that had crashed; the fire, fanned by the wind, had set light to a stack.

He looked at the bodies of the birds, and he had a notion that if he heaped them, one upon the other, on the windowsills they would make added protection for the next attack. Not much, perhaps, but

something. The bodies would have to be clawed at, pecked, and dragged aside before the living birds could gain purchase on the sills and attack the panes. He set to work in the darkness. It was queer; he hated touching them. The bodies were still warm and bloody. The blood matted their feathers. He felt his stomach turn, but he went on with his work. He noticed grimly that every windowpane was shattered. Only the boards had kept the birds from breaking in. He stuffed the cracked panes with the bleeding bodies of the birds.

When he had finished he went back into the cottage. He barricaded the kitchen door, made it doubly secure. He took off his bandages, sticky with the birds' blood, not with his own cuts, and put on a fresh bandage.

His wife had made him cocoa and he drank it thirstily. He was very tired.

"All right," he said, smiling, "don't worry. We'll get through."

He lay down on his mattress and closed his eyes. He slept at once. He dreamt uneasily, because through his dreams there ran a thread of something forgotten. Some piece of work, neglected, that he should have done. Some precaution that he had known well but had not taken, and he could not put a name to it in his dreams. It was connected in some way with the burning aircraft and the stack upon the hill. He went on sleeping, though; he did not awake. It was his wife shaking his shoulder that awoke him finally.

"They've begun," she sobbed, "they've started this last hour. I can't listen to it any longer alone. There's something smelling bad too, something burning."

▲ Critical Viewing
Which images found in this picture foreshadow danger? **[Describe]**

✔ Reading Check
Briefly describe what Nat finds when he steps outside the cottage.

The Birds ◆ 73

Then he remembered. He had forgotten to make up the fire. It was smoldering, nearly out. He got up swiftly and lit the lamp. The hammering had started at the windows and the doors, but it was not that he minded now. It was the smell of singed feathers. The smell filled the kitchen. He knew at once what it was. The birds were coming down the chimney, squeezing their way down to the kitchen range.

He got sticks and paper and put them on the embers, then reached for the can of paraffin.[13]

"Stand back," he shouted to his wife. "We've got to risk this."

He threw the paraffin onto the fire. The flame roared up the pipe, and down upon the fire fell the scorched, blackened bodies of the birds.

The children woke, crying. "What is it?" said Jill. "What's happened?"

Nat had no time to answer. He was raking the bodies from the chimney, clawing them out onto the floor. The flames still roared, and the danger of the chimney catching fire was one he had to take. The flames would send away the living birds from the chimney top. The lower joint was the difficulty, though. This was choked with the smoldering, helpless bodies of the birds caught by fire. He scarcely heeded the attack on the windows and the door: let them beat their wings, break their beaks, lose their lives, in the attempt to force an entry into his home. They would not break in. He thanked God he had one of the old cottages, with small windows, stout walls. Not like the new council houses. Heaven help them up the lane in the new council houses.

"Stop crying," he called to the children. "There's nothing to be afraid of, stop crying."

He went on raking at the burning, smoldering bodies as they fell into the fire.

"This'll fetch them," he said to himself, "the draft and the flames together. We're all right, as long as the chimney doesn't catch. I ought to be shot for this. It's all my fault. Last thing, I should have made up the fire. I knew there was something."

Amid the scratching and tearing at the window boards came the sudden homely striking of the kitchen clock. Three A.M. A little more than four hours yet to go. He could not be sure of the exact time of high water. He reckoned it would not turn much before half-past seven, twenty to eight.

"Light up the Primus,"[14] he said to his wife. "Make us some tea, and the kids some cocoa. No use sitting around doing nothing."

That was the line. Keep her busy, and the children too. Move about, eat, drink; always best to be on the go.

He waited by the range. The flames were dying. But no more blackened bodies fell from the chimney. He thrust his poker up as far as it could go and found nothing. It was clear. The chimney was clear. He wiped the sweat from his forehead.

"Come on now, Jill," he said, "bring me some more sticks. We'll have

---

13. paraffin (par´ ə fin) *n.* kerosene.
14. Primus (prī´ məs) *n.* small, portable stove.

Spine Tinglers

Reading Strategy
Predicting What do you predict will happen next inside the house? Which details led you to this prediction?

Literary Analysis
Foreshadowing What effect does the sound of the clock have on the story? Explain.

a good fire going directly." She wouldn't come near him, though. She was staring at the heaped singed bodies of the birds.

"Never mind them," he said. "We'll put those in the passage when I've got the fire steady."

The danger of the chimney was over. It could not happen again, not if the fire was kept burning day and night.

"I'll have to get more fuel from the farm tomorrow," he thought. "This will never last. I'll manage, though. I can do all that with the ebb tide. It can be worked, fetching what we need, when the tide's turned. We've just got to adapt ourselves, that's all."

They drank tea and cocoa and ate slices of bread and Bovril.[15] Only half a loaf left, Nat noticed. Never mind though, they'd get by.

"Stop it," said young Johnny, pointing to the windows with his spoon, "stop it, you old birds."

"That's right," said Nat, smiling, "we don't want the old beggars, do we? Had enough of 'em."

They began to cheer when they heard the thud of the suicide birds.

"There's another, Dad," cried Jill, "he's done for."

"He's had it," said Nat. "There he goes, the blighter."

This was the way to face up to it. This was the spirit. If they could keep this up, hang on like this until seven, when the first news bulletin came through, they would not have done too badly.

"Give us a cigarette," he said to his wife. "A bit of a smoke will clear away the smell of the scorched feathers."

"There's only two left in the packet," she said. "I was going to buy you some from the Co-op."

"I'll have one," he said, "t'other will keep for a rainy day."

No sense trying to make the children rest. There was no rest to be got while the tapping and the scratching went on at the windows. He sat with one arm round his wife and the other round Jill, with Johnny on his mother's lap and the blankets heaped about them on the mattress.

"You can't help admiring the beggars," he said; "they've got persistence. You'd think they'd tire of the game, but not a bit of it."

Admiration was hard to sustain. The tapping went on and on and a new rasping note struck Nat's ear, as though a sharper beak than any hitherto had come to take over from its fellows. He tried to remember the names of birds; he tried to think which species would go for this particular job. It was not the tap of the woodpecker. That would be light and frequent. This was more serious, because if it continued long the wood would splinter as the glass had done. Then he remembered the hawks. Could the hawks have taken over from the gulls? Were there buzzards now upon the sills, using talons as well as beaks? Hawks, buzzards, kestrels, falcons—he had forgotten the birds of prey. He had forgotten the gripping power of the birds of prey. Three hours to go, and while they waited, the sound of the splintering wood, the talons tearing at the wood.

---

15. Bovril (bō′ vril) *n.* thick beef-flavored liquid used to make broth.

Reading Strategy
Predicting Based on the spirit Nat and his family are showing, what do you predict will happen?

Reading Check
How do the birds get into the house?

Over and Above #13, 1964, Clarence H. Carter

Nat looked about him, seeing what furniture he could destroy to fortify the door. The windows were safe because of the dresser. He was not certain of the door. He went upstairs, but when he reached the landing he paused and listened. There was a soft patter on the floor of the children's bedroom. The birds had broken through . . . He put his ear to the door. No mistake. He could hear the rustle of wings and the light patter as they searched the floor. The other bedroom was still clear. He went into it and began bringing out the furniture, to pile at the head of the stairs should the door of the children's bedroom go. It was a preparation. It might never be needed. He could not stack the furniture against the door, because it opened inward. The only possible thing was to have it at the top of the stairs.

"Come down. Nat, what are you doing?" called his wife.

"I won't be long," he shouted. "Just making everything shipshape up here."

He did not want her to come; he did not want her to hear the

▲ **Critical Viewing**
Would you expect a bird in this story to look like the bird in this picture? Explain. **[Describe]**

pattering of the feet in the children's bedroom, the brushing of those wings against the door.

At five-thirty he suggested breakfast, bacon and fried bread, if only to stop the growing look of panic in his wife's eyes and to calm the <u>fretful</u> children. She did not know about the birds upstairs. The bedroom, luckily, was not over the kitchen. Had it been so, she could not have failed to hear the sound of them up there, tapping the boards. And the silly, senseless thud of the suicide birds, the death and glory boys, who flew into the bedroom, smashing their heads against the walls. He knew them of old, the herring gulls. They had no brains. The black-backs were different; they knew what they were doing. So did the buzzards, the hawks . . .

He found himself watching the clock, gazing at the hands that went so slowly round the dial. If his theory was not correct, if the attack did not cease with the turn of the tide, he knew they were beaten. They could not continue through the long day without air, without rest, without more fuel, without . . . His mind raced. He knew there were so many things they needed to withstand siege. They were not fully prepared. They were not ready. It might be that it would be safer in the towns after all. If he could get a message through on the farm telephone to his cousin, only a short journey by train upcountry, they might be able to hire a car. That would be quicker—hire a car between tides . . .

His wife's voice, calling his name, drove away the sudden, desperate desire for sleep.

"What is it? What now?" he said sharply.

"The wireless," said his wife. "I've been watching the clock. It's nearly seven."

"Don't twist the knob," he said, impatient for the first time. "It's on the Home where it is. They'll speak from the Home."

They waited. The kitchen clock struck seven. There was no sound. No chimes, no music. They waited until a quarter past, switching to the Light. The result was the same. No news bulletin came through.

"We've heard wrong," he said. "They won't be broadcasting until eight o'clock."

They left it switched on, and Nat thought of the battery, wondered how much power was left in it. It was generally recharged when his wife went shopping in the town. If the battery failed they would not hear the instructions.

"It's getting light," whispered his wife. "I can't see it, but I can feel it. And the birds aren't hammering so loud."

She was right. The rasping, tearing sound grew fainter every moment. So did the shuffling, the jostling for place upon the step, upon the sills. The tide was on the turn. By eight there was no sound at all. Only the wind. The children, lulled at last by the stillness, fell asleep. At half-past eight Nat switched the wireless off.

"What are you doing? We'll miss the news," said his wife.

"There isn't going to be any news," said Nat. "We've got to depend upon ourselves."

fretful (fret´ fəl) *adj.* irritable and discontented

**Reading Check**

Why does Nat put the furniture at the top of the stairs?

He went to the door and slowly pulled away the barricades. He drew the bolts and, kicking the bodies from the step outside the door, breathed the cold air. He had six working hours before him, and he knew he must reserve his strength for the right things, not waste it in any way. Food, and light, and fuel; these were the necessary things. If he could get them in sufficiency, they could endure another night.

He stepped into the garden, and as he did so he saw the living birds. The gulls had gone to ride the sea, as they had done before; they sought sea food, and the buoyancy of the tide, before they returned to the attack. Not so the land birds. They waited and watched. Nat saw them, on the hedgerows, on the soil, crowded in the trees, outside in the field, line upon line of birds, all still, doing nothing.

He went to the end of his small garden. The birds did not move. They went on watching him.

"I've got to get food," said Nat to himself. "I've got to go to the farm to find food."

He went back to the cottage. He saw to the windows and the doors. He went upstairs and opened the children's bedroom. It was empty, except for the dead birds on the floor. The living were out there, in the garden, in the fields. He went downstairs.

"I'm going to the farm," he said.

His wife clung to him. She had seen the living birds from the open door.

"Take us with you," she begged. "We can't stay here alone. I'd rather die than stay here alone."

He considered the matter. He nodded.

"Come on, then," he said. "Bring baskets, and Johnny's pram.[16] We can load up the pram."

They dressed against the biting wind, wore gloves and scarves. His wife put Johnny in the pram. Nat took Jill's hand.

"The birds," she whimpered, "they're all out there in the fields."

"They won't hurt us," he said, "not in the light."

They started walking across the field towards the stile, and the birds did not move. They waited, their heads turned to the wind.

When they reached the turning to the farm, Nat stopped and told his wife to wait in the shelter of the hedge with the two children.

"But I want to see Mrs. Trigg," she protested. "There are lots of things we can borrow if they went to market yesterday; not only bread, and . . ."

"Wait here," Nat interrupted. "I'll be back in a moment."

The cows were lowing, moving restlessly in the yard, and he could see a gap in the fence where the sheep had knocked their way through, to roam unchecked in the front garden before the farmhouse. No smoke came from the chimneys. He was filled with misgiving. He did not want his wife or the children to go down to the farm.

"Don't gib[17] now," said Nat, harshly, "do what I say."

Literary Analysis
Foreshadowing and Imagery Do you think the image of the birds waiting and watching foreshadows an end to danger?

---

16. pram *n.* baby carriage.
17. gib (jib) *v.* hesitate.

She withdrew with the pram into the hedge, screening herself and the children from the wind.

He went down alone to the farm. He pushed his way through the herd of bellowing cows, which turned this way and that, distressed, their udders full. He saw the car standing by the gate, not put away in the garage. The windows of the farmhouse were smashed. There were many dead gulls lying in the yard and around the house. The living birds perched on the group of trees behind the farm and on the roof of the house. They were quite still. They watched him.

Jim's body lay in the yard . . . what was left of it. When the birds had finished, the cows had trampled him. His gun was beside him. The door of the house was shut and bolted, but as the windows were smashed it was easy to lift them and climb through. Trigg's body was close to the telephone. He must have been trying to get through to the exchange when the birds came for him. The receiver was hanging loose, the instrument torn from the wall. No sign of Mrs. Trigg. She would be upstairs. Was it any use going up? Sickened, Nat knew what he would find.

"Thank God," he said to himself, "there were no children."

He forced himself to climb the stairs, but halfway he turned and descended again. He could see her legs protruding from the open bedroom door. Beside her were the bodies of the black-backed gulls, and an umbrella, broken.

"It's no use," thought Nat, "doing anything. I've only got five hours, less than that. The Triggs would understand. I must load up with what I can find."

He tramped back to his wife and children.

"I'm going to fill up the car with stuff," he said. "I'll put coal in it, and paraffin for the Primus. We'll take it home and return for a fresh load."

"What about the Triggs?" asked his wife.

"They must have gone to friends," he said.

"Shall I come and help you, then?"

"No; there's a mess down there. Cows and sheep all over the place. Wait, I'll get the car. You can sit in it."

Clumsily he backed the car out of the yard and into the lane. His wife and the children could not see Jim's body from there.

"Stay here," he said, "never mind the pram. The pram can be fetched later. I'm going to load the car."

Her eyes watched his all the time. He believed she understood, otherwise she would have suggested helping him to find the bread and groceries.

They made three journeys altogether, backwards and forwards between their cottage and the farm, before he was satisfied they had everything they needed. It was surprising, once he started thinking, how many things were necessary. Almost the most important of all was planking for the windows. He had to go round searching for timber. He wanted to renew the boards on all the windows at the cottage.

Literary Analysis

Foreshadowing Do you think that the deaths of everyone at the farm foreshadow a similar fate for Nat and his family? Why or why not?

**Reading Check**

What does Nat find at the Triggs' farm?

Candles, paraffin, nails, tinned stuff; the list was endless. Besides all that, he milked three of the cows. The rest, poor brutes, would have to go on bellowing.

On the final journey he drove the car to the bus stop, got out, and went to the telephone box. He waited a few minutes, jangling the receiver. No good, though. The line was dead. He climbed on to a bank and looked over the countryside, but there was no sign of life at all, nothing in the fields but the waiting, watching birds. Some of them slept—he could see the beaks tucked into the feathers.

"You'd think they'd be feeding," he said to himself, "not just standing in that way."

Then he remembered. They were gorged with food. They had eaten their fill during the night. That was why they did not move this morning . . .

No smoke came from the chimneys of the council houses. He thought of the children who had run across the fields the night before.

"I should have known," he thought; "I ought to have taken them home with me."

He lifted his face to the sky. It was colorless and gray. The bare trees on the landscape looked bent and blackened by the east wind. The cold did not affect the living birds waiting out there in the fields.

"This is the time they ought to get them," said Nat; "they're a sitting target now. They must be doing this all over the country. Why don't our aircraft take off now and spray them with mustard gas? What are all our chaps doing? They must know, they must see for themselves."

He went back to the car and got into the driver's seat.

"Go quickly past that second gate," whispered his wife. "The postman's lying there. I don't want Jill to see."

He accelerated. The little Morris bumped and rattled along the lane. The children shrieked with laughter.

"Up-a-down, up-a-down," shouted young Johnny.

It was a quarter to one by the time they reached the cottage. Only an hour to go.

"Better have cold dinner," said Nat. "Hot up something for yourself and the children, some of that soup. I've no time to eat now. I've got to unload all this stuff."

He got everything inside the cottage. It could be sorted later. Give them all something to do during the long hours ahead. First he must see to the windows and the doors.

He went round the cottage methodically, testing every window, every door. He climbed on to the roof also, and fixed boards across every chimney, except the kitchen. The cold was so intense he could hardly bear it, but the job had to be done. Now and again he would look up, searching the sky for aircraft. None came. As he worked he cursed the inefficiency of the authorities.

Literary Analysis
Foreshadowing What might the dead phone line foreshadow?

"It's always the same," he muttered. "They always let us down. Muddle, muddle, from the start. No plan, no real organization. And we don't matter down here. That's what it is. The people upcountry have priority. They're using gas up there, no doubt, and all the aircraft. We've got to wait and take what comes."

He paused, his work on the bedroom chimney finished, and looked out to sea. Something was moving out there. Something gray and white amongst the breakers.

"Good old Navy," he said, "they never let us down. They're coming down-channel, they're turning in the bay."

He waited, straining his eyes, watering in the wind, towards the sea. He was wrong, though. It was not ships. The Navy was not there. The gulls were rising from the sea. The massed flocks in the fields, with ruffled feathers, rose in formation from the ground and, wing to wing, soared upwards to the sky.

The tide had turned again.

Nat climbed down the ladder and went inside the kitchen. The family were at dinner. It was a little after two. He bolted the door, put up the barricade, and lit the lamp.

"It's nighttime," said young Johnny.

His wife had switched on the wireless once again, but no sound came from it.

"I've been all round the dial," she said, "foreign stations, and that lot. I can't get anything."

"Maybe they have the same trouble," he said, "maybe it's the same right through Europe."

She poured out a plateful of the Triggs' soup, cut him a large slice of the Triggs' bread, and spread their dripping upon it.

They ate in silence. A piece of the dripping ran down young Johnny's chin and fell on to the table.

"Manners, Johnny," said Jill, "you should learn to wipe your mouth."

The tapping began at the windows, at the door. The rustling, the jostling, the pushing for position on the sills. The first thud of the suicide gulls upon the step.

"Won't America do something?" said his wife. "They've always been our allies, haven't they? Surely America will do something?"

Nat did not answer. The boards were strong against the windows, and on the chimneys too. The cottage was filled with stores, with fuel, with all they needed for the next few days. When he had finished dinner he would put the stuff away, stack it neatly, get everything shipshape, handy-like. His wife could help him, and the children too. They'd tire themselves out, between now and a quarter to nine, when the tide would ebb; then he'd tuck them down on their mattresses, see that they slept good and sound until three in the morning.

He had a new scheme for the windows, which was to fix barbed

Reading Strategy
Predicting What do you think will happen next?

**Reading Check**

What theory does Nat develop to explain why the birds do not move in the morning?

wire in front of the boards. He had brought a great roll of it from the farm. The nuisance was, he'd have to work at this in the dark, when the lull came between nine and three. Pity he had not thought of it before. Still, as long as the wife slept, and the kids, that was the main thing.

The smaller birds were at the window now. He recognized the light tap-tapping of their beaks and the soft brush of their wings. The hawks ignored the windows. They concentrated their attack upon the door. Nat listened to the tearing sound of splintering wood, and wondered how many million years of memory were stored in those little brains, behind the stabbing beaks, the piercing eyes, now giving them this instinct to destroy mankind with all the deft precision of machines.

"I'll smoke that last cigarette," he said to his wife. "Stupid of me, it was the one thing I forgot to bring back from the farm."

He reached for it, switched on the silent wireless. He threw the empty packet on the fire, and watched it burn.

Daphne du Maurier

(1907–1989)

Du Maurier was born in London into a family of actors, artists, and writers. Her father was an actor and theater manager who specialized in playing criminals on the stage, and her grandfather was a novelist who illustrated his own writing.

The Loving Spirit (1931), du Maurier's first novel, became a bestseller, propelling her into a lifelong career as a writer. She followed with a series of romantic novels that were tinged with mystery and suspense.

Du Maurier's stories caught the attention of director Alfred Hitchcock, who specialized in suspenseful films. In addition to *The Birds*, Hitchcock made two other films based on du Maurier's tales, including *Rebecca*, which won the Academy Award for Best Picture in 1940.

Review and Assess

Thinking About the Selection

1. **Respond:** Did you find "The Birds" suspenseful? Explain.

2. **(a) Recall:** In the beginning of the story, what does the narrator say about Nat and how he spends his days?
   (b) Analyze: Do his actions suggest that Nat is sensitive to the natural world? Why or why not?

3. **(a) Recall:** According to Nat, what is different about the birds this fall? **(b) Analyze:** How might this new difference in the birds contribute to their destructive nature?

4. **(a) Recall:** When Nat cleans up after the first attack, how does he explain the birds' behavior? **(b) Evaluate:** How strongly do you think he believes his own explanation?

5. **(a) Draw Conclusions:** Why do you think the birds have begun attacking and trying to kill people? **(b) Connect:** Do you think that an animal population could suddenly turn against people? Why? **(c) Generalize:** What message do you think the story conveys about the relationship between humans and the natural world?

6. **(a) Connect:** What ending do you think most readers expect?
   (b) Evaluate: Why might this story have an inconclusive ending?

Review and Assess

Literary Analysis

Foreshadowing

1. How does Nat's sighting of masses of gulls riding the sea **foreshadow** possible disaster?
2. What does the BBC announcement of a national emergency foreshadow?
3. Using a chart like this one, explain what you think the scene at Triggs' farm at the end of the story foreshadows for Nat's family.

Scene at Triggs' Farm	Possible Outcomes

Connecting Literary Elements

4. (a) Reread the description of the children's bedroom after Nat has fought off the birds in the dark of the night (p. 53). Use a chart like the one shown here to record the **imagery** in that description. (b) Explain the effect that you think each image is meant to have.

Image		Explanation of Effect
	···▶	

5. (a) Review the last three paragraphs of the story, and find at least two vivid details. (b) How do these details add to the suspense?

Reading Strategy

Predicting

6. What were the first hints that led you to **predict** the outcome?
7. Review the predictions you made as you read. (a) Identify one prediction that was accurate and one that you later revised. (b) For each, explain how details later in the story supported or contradicted your prediction.

Extend Understanding

8. **Science Connection:** What questions about the bird invasion might a scientist raise to help understand the events of the story?

Quick Review

Foreshadowing is the author's use of clues that hint at events to come.

Imagery is the use of language to create word pictures in a reader's mind.

When you **predict,** use details to make educated guesses about what will happen later in the story.

 Take It to the Net
www.phschool.com
Take the interactive self-test online to check your understanding of the selection.

Integrate Language Skills

Vocabulary Development Lesson

Word Analysis: Anglo-Saxon Suffix *-ful*

In "The Birds," the children are described as *fretful* about the frightening situation they face. The word *fretful* contains the Anglo-Saxon suffix *-ful*. The suffix means "having the quality of," as in *forgetful*; "having the quality that would fill," as in *handful*; or "full of," as in *fretful*. Therefore, *fretful* literally means "full of fret or worry," and it is no surprise that a fretful person is irritable or discontented.

Add the suffix *-ful* to these words. Then, using your knowledge of the suffix *-ful*, provide a definition for each of the words you generate.

1. sorrow
2. teaspoon
3. help
4. regret
5. spite
6. rest

Fluency: Clarify Word Meaning

Match each vocabulary word with its synonym.

1. placid
2. garish
3. reconnaissance
4. sullen
5. furtively
6. imperative
7. recounted
8. fretful

a. gloomy
b. urgent
c. calm
d. exploratory
e. gaudy
f. stealthily
g. irritable
h. narrated

Spelling Strategy

Most words ending in silent *e* keep the *e* before a suffix beginning with a consonant. For example, *grace* + *-ful* = *graceful*. Write the correct spelling of each word below.

1. securly
2. housful
3. discouragment

Grammar Lesson

Reflexive and Intensive Pronouns

A **reflexive pronoun** ends in *-self* or *-selves* and indicates that someone or something performs an action to, for, or upon itself. Reflexive pronouns point back to a noun or pronoun that appears earlier in the sentence. They are essential to the meaning of a sentence. In contrast, an **intensive pronoun** also ends in *-self* or *-selves* but simply adds emphasis to a noun or pronoun in the same sentence.

> **Reflexive:** "Once more he settled *himself* to sleep."
>
> **Intensive:** "You had to endure something *yourself* before it touched you."

Practice Identify whether each underlined pronoun below is reflexive or intensive.

1. Jill read <u>herself</u> a story after supper.
2. Her parents <u>themselves</u> had encouraged her.
3. They said, "If you children want to play, you will have to see to it <u>yourselves</u>."
4. Nat whispered, "I will go outside and take a look around <u>myself</u>."
5. He convinced <u>himself</u> they were safe.

Writing Application Write two sentences that include these pronouns, used as indicated.

1. himself (reflexive)
2. ourselves (intensive)

WG Prentice Hall Writing and Grammar Connection: Chapter 16, Section 2

Writing Lesson

Bird's-Eye View of a Place

Imagine how different "The Birds" would be if it were told from the point of view of one of the birds. The action would be described from above rather than below. Write a description of a scene in the story as it would look to a bird flying overhead.

Prewriting   To see the scene from above, make a blueprint of the scene by drawing what you have chosen to describe. Label the key places.

Drafting   Refer to your sketch as you draft your bird's point of view. Include details that indicate a downward-looking perspective. For example, a bird in the sky would be able to see Nat's entire house, but it would not, for example, see the color of Nat's eyes.

Revising   Reread your description, checking for inconsistencies in viewpoint. Correct any passages that describe something from the ground up.

Model: Revising to Maintain a Consistent Viewpoint

The shingled roof of the library peeked through the ~~oak~~ trees. A~~look through the windows showed that it was a busy place today~~.

> To keep this viewpoint consistent, details that could be seen only from ground level are eliminated.

WG   *Prentice Hall Writing and Grammar Connection: Chapter 6, Section 4*

Extension Activities

Listening and Speaking   In "The Birds," people try to protect themselves from birds. In real life, birds often need protection from people. In a small group, hold a **panel discussion** in which you answer the following questions:

- What dangers do humans pose to bird populations?
- What can be done to protect birds and their habitats?

Each participant should research the topic and prepare a set of concise notes for easy reference during the discussion. **[Group Activity]**

Research and Technology   Prepare a research report and give a **presentation** on any four of the birds mentioned in this story. For each bird, research size, distinguishing features, natural habitats, and behaviors. Use the Internet or the CD-ROM edition of an encyclopedia to locate photographs and factual information.

 Take It to the Net   www.phschool.com

Go online for an additional research activity using the Internet.

from
The Perfect Storm
Sebastian Junger

"The Birds" draws its power from the transformation of a common, harmless animal into something dark and sinister.

Other authors tap the same power to transform the ordinary in nature into the extraordinary. In his 1997 book "The Perfect Storm," Sebastian Junger uses the true story of boats caught in a major storm to demonstrate the power extreme weather has on our imagination. He shows how extreme weather can transform familiar landscapes, like a gently rolling sea, into territory that is suddenly alien and hostile. In the following excerpt, people are exposed to the furious side of nature, providing insight into the different ways that people cope with danger and risk.

2:30 AM—s/v [sailing vessel] is running out of fuel, recommend we try to keep Falcon o/s [on-scene] until Tamaroa arrives.
5:29 AM—Falcon has lost comms [communication] with vessel, vessel is low on battery power and taking on water. Pumps are keeping up but are run by ele [electric].
7:07 AM—Falcon o/s, vessel has been located. Six hours fuel left. People on board are scared.

The H-3 arrives on scene around 6:30 and spends half an hour just trying to locate the *Satori*. The conditions are so bad that she's vanished from the Falcon's radar, and the H-3 pilot is almost on top of her before spotting her in the foam-streaked seas. The Falcon circles off to the southwest to prepare a life-raft drop while the H-3 takes up a hover directly over the boat. In these conditions the Falcon pilot could never line up on something as small as a sailboat, so the H-3 acts as a stand-in. The Falcon comes back at 140 knots, radar locked onto the helicopter, and at the last moment the H-3 falls away and the jet makes the drop. The pilot comes screaming over the *Satori's* mast and the copilot pushes two life-raft packages out a hatch in the floorboards. The rafts are linked by a long nylon tether, and as they fall they cartwheel apart, splashing down well to either side of the *Satori*. The tether, released at two hundred feet into a hurricane-force wind, drops right into Bylander's hand.

The H-3 hovers overhead while the *Satori* crew haul in the packages, but both rafts have exploded on impact. There's nothing at either end of the line. The *Tamaroa* is still five hours away and the storm has retrograded[1] to within a couple of hundred miles of the coast; over the next twenty-four hours it will pass directly over the *Satori*. A daylight rescue in these conditions is difficult, and a nighttime rescue is out of the question. If the *Satori* crew is not taken off in the next few hours, there's a good chance they won't be taken off at all. Late that morning the second H-3 arrives and the pilot, Lieutenant Klosson, explains the situation to Ray Leonard. Leonard radios back that he's not leaving the boat.

It's unclear whether Leonard is serious or just trying to save face. Either way, the Coast Guard is having none of it. Two helicopters, two Falcon jets, a medium-range cutter, and a hundred air- and seamen have already been committed to the rescue; the *Satori* crew are coming off now. *"Owner refuses to leave and says he's sailed through hurricanes before,"* the Comcen[2] incident log records at 12:24 that afternoon. *"Tamaroa wants manifestly unsafe voyage so that o/o [owner-operator] can be forced off."*

A "manifestly unsafe voyage" means that the vessel has been deemed an unacceptable risk to her crew or others, and the Coast Guard has the legal authority to order everyone off. Commander Brudnicki gets on the radio with District One and requests a manifestly unsafe designation for the *Satori,* and at 12:47 it is granted. The *Tamaroa* is just a couple of miles away now, within VHF[3] range of the *Satori,* and Brudnicki raises Leonard on the radio and tells him he has no choice in the matter. Everyone is leaving the boat. At 12:57 in the afternoon, thirteen hours after weighing anchor, the *Tamaroa* plunges into view.

There's a lot of hardware circling the *Satori*. There's the Falcon, the H-3, the *Tamaroa*, and the freighter *Gold Bond Conveyor*, which has been cutting circles around the *Satori* since the first mayday call. Hardware is not the problem, though; it's time. Dark is only three hours away, and the departing H-3 pilot doesn't think the *Satori* will survive another night. She'll run out of fuel, start getting knocked down, and eventually break apart. The crew will be cast into the sea, and the helicopter pilot will refuse to drop his rescue swimmer because he can't be sure of getting him back. It would be up to the *Tamaroa* to maneuver alongside the swimmers and pull them on board, and in these seas it would be almost impossible. It's now or never.

The only way to take them off, Brudnicki decides, is to shuttle them back to the *Tamaroa* in one of the little Avons. The Avons are twenty-one-foot inflatable rafts with rigid hulls and outboard engines;

---

1. **retrograded** (re′trə grād′ ed) *v.* moved backward.
2. **Comcen** (käm′ sen) *abbrev.* Coast Guard abbreviation for the Command Center, which keeps track of rescue operations.
3. **VHF** *abbrev.* Very High Frequency; radio frequency used by ships for communication.

tether (te*th*′ ər) *n.* rope or chain attached to an object.

mayday (mā′ dā′) radio distress signal used for ships in trouble.

Thematic Connection
What steps do the rescue crew take to battle nature?

 **Reading Check**

Why is it critical to save the *Satori* crew before nightfall?

one of them could make a run to the *Satori*, drop off survival suits, and then come back again to pick up the three crew. If anyone wound up in the water, at least they'd be insulated and afloat. It's not a particularly complicated maneuver, but no one has done it in conditions like this before. No one has even *seen* conditions like this before. At 1:23 PM the *Tamaroa* crew gathers at the port davits,[4] three men climb aboard the Avon, and they lower away.

It goes badly from the start. What passes for a lull between waves is in fact a crest-to-trough change of thirty to forty feet. Chief bosun[5] Thomas Amidon lowers the Avon halfway down, gets lifted up by the next wave, can't keep up with the trough and freefalls to the bottom of the cable. The lifting eye gets ripped out of its mount and Amidon almost pitches overboard. He struggles back into position, finishes lowering the boat, and makes way from the *Tamaroa*.

The seas are twice the size of the Avon raft. With <u>excruciating</u> slowness it fights its way to the *Satori*, comes up bow-to-stern,[6] and a crew member flings the three survival suits on deck. Stimpson grabs them and hands them out, but Amidon doesn't back out in time. The sailboat rides up a sea, comes down on the Avon, and punctures one of her air bladders. Things start to happen very fast now: the Avon's bow collapses, a wave swamps her to the gunwales,[7] the engine dies, and she falls away astern. Amidon tries desperately to get the engine going again and finally manages to, but they're up to their waists in water and the raft is crippled. There's no way they can even get themselves back onto the *Tamaroa*, much less save the crew of the *Satori*. Six people, not just three, now need to be rescued.

The H-3 crew watches all this <u>incredulously</u>. They're in a two o'clock hover with their jump door open, just over the tops of the waves. They can see the raft dragging heavily through the seas, and the *Tamaroa* heaving through ninety-degree rolls. Pilot Claude Hessel finally gets on the radio and tells Brudnicki and Amidon that he may have another way of doing this. He can't hoist[8] the *Satori* crew directly off their deck, he says, because the mast is <u>flailing</u> too wildly and might entangle the hoist. That would drag the H-3 right down on top of the boat. But he could drop his rescue swimmer, who would take the people off the boat one at a time and bring them up on the hoist. It's the best chance they've got, and Brudnicki knows it. He consults with District One and then gives the okay.

▲ **Critical Viewing**
What dangers does a rescue like the one shown here present? **[Analyze]**

excruciating (eks krōō′ shē āt′ iŋ) *adj.* agonizing

incredulously (in krej′ oo ləs lē) *adv.* unwilling or unable to believe

flailing (flāl′ iŋ) *v.* swinging freely

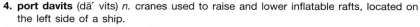

4. **port davits** (dā′ vits) *n.* cranes used to raise and lower inflatable rafts, located on the left side of a ship.
5. **Chief bosun** (bō′ sən) *n.* officer in charge of the ship's crew and equipment; also spelled boatswain.
6. **bow-to-stern** (bou tōō stʉrn) *nautical term.* from the front of a ship (*bow*) to its rear (*stern*).
7. **gunwales** (gun′ əls) *n.* upper edge of the side of a boat or ship.
8. **hoist** *v.* lift by means of a special apparatus.

The rescue swimmer on Hessel's helicopter is Dave Moore, a three-year veteran who has never been on a major rescue. ("The good cases don't come along too often—usually someone beats you to them," he says. "If a sailboat gets in trouble far out we usually get a rescue, but otherwise it's just a lot of little stuff.") Moore is handsome in a baby-faced sort of way—square-jawed, blue-eyed, and a big open smile. He has a dense, compact body that is more seallike than athletic. His profession of rescue swimmer came about when a tanker went down off New York in the mid-1980s. A Coast Guard helicopter was hovering overhead, but it was winter and the tanker crew were too <u>hypothermic</u> to get into the lift basket. They all drowned. Congress decided they wanted something done, and the Coast Guard adopted the Navy rescue program. Moore is twenty-five years old, born the year Karen Stimpson graduated from high school.

Moore is already wearing a neoprene wetsuit. He puts on socks and hood, straps on swim fins, pulls a mask and snorkel down over his head, and then struggles into his neoprene gloves. He buckles on a life vest and then signals to flight engineer Vriesman that he's ready. Vriesman, who has one arm extended, gatelike, across the jump door, steps aside and allows Moore to crouch by the edge. That means that they're at "ten and ten"—a ten-foot hover at ten knots. Moore, who's no longer plugged into the intercom, signals final corrections to Vriesman with his hands, who relays them to the pilot. This is it; Moore has trained three years for this moment. An hour ago he was in the lunch line back on base. Now he's about to drop into the <u>maelstrom</u>.

Hessel holds a low hover with the boat at his two o'clock. Moore can see the crew clustered together on deck and the *Satori* making slow, plunging headway into the seas. Vriesman is seated next to Moore at the hoist controls, and avionicsman[9] Ayres is behind the copilot with the radio and search gear. Both wear flightsuits and crash helmets and are plugged into the internal communication system in the wall. The time is 2:07 PM. Moore picks a spot between waves, takes a deep breath, and jumps.

---

9. **avionicsman** (ā´ vē än´ iks man) *n.* crew member in charge of electronic equipment.

hypothermic (hī´ pō *thur*´ mik) *adj.* having a dangerously low body temperature

maelstrom (māl´ strəm) *n.* violent or turbulent whirl of air and water

Sebastian Junger

(b. 1962)

The widespread popularity of *The Perfect Storm* surprised even its author, Sebastian Junger. Though *The Perfect Storm* was his first book, Junger has written many articles for *Outside*, *Men's Journal*, and *The New York Times Magazine*.

Junger is drawn to the subject of ordinary people performing dangerous work. He might feel a connection to them because he has participated in dangerous work himself. His past jobs have included a freelance writing assignment in war-torn Bosnia and work as a climber for a tree removal service.

Connecting Literature Past and Present

1. How do characters in both this excerpt from *The Perfect Storm* and "The Birds" employ science and technology to deal with a natural threat?
2. (a) How are the two stories similar in their portrayal of human beings facing natural disasters? (b) Does the fact that "The Birds" is fiction affect the way you feel about the characters? Why or why not?
3. Explain the similarities and differences in the ways that characters in each selection face danger.

READING INFORMATIONAL MATERIALS

Movie Reviews

About Movie Reviews

Reviews of new films are published in most newspapers on the day they open. In addition, reviews can be found in many magazines, as well as on the Internet, radio, and TV. Writers of movie reviews usually summarize the film's plot and comment on whether they feel the film is worth seeing. Movie critics support their opinions by analyzing the plot, acting, visual appeal, and other elements of the film. Before you allow a review to influence your opinion, follow these steps:

- Distinguish between fact and opinion in the review.
- Analyze the critic's arguments.
- Evaluate the persuasive language the critic uses.

Reading Strategy

Identifying Support for Response

Reviewers know that in order to sway readers, they need to defend their views with convincing reasons. To persuade readers that their opinions are valid, film critics respond to particular elements of a film, providing examples that support their response.

For example, the author of this review of Alfred Hitchcock's *The Birds* finds the movie frightening. As you read the review, look for details he provides to support his response. Use a chart like the one below to jot down the reviewer's responses to particular elements of the film. Identify his support of those responses through his examples and explanations.

Element	Reviewer's Opinion	Support
Special Effects: Bird swooping down on townspeople in scene with gas station explosion	". . . special effects in *The Birds* provide believable and extraordinary horror . . ."	Special effects experts handled bird scenes so well that moviegoers exiting the theater would probably glance up at the sky fearfully.

The Birds

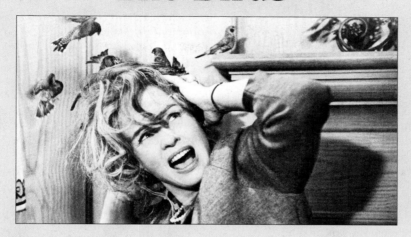

DeWitt Bodeen

[In his film, Hitchcock] has the cinematic advantage [over du Maurier's short story] of being able to show the birds graphically, as they gather and wait like [an evil] army and then swoop in to destroy and kill. In one scene, for example, a bird authority named Mrs. Bundy (Ethel Griffies) sits in a restaurant assuring her listeners that there are many varieties of birds, all of which stick to their own kind, making it impossible for them to unite for any form of attack. As she speaks, however, the birds outside gather and then inexplicably dive down upon the people, seemingly at random. Hitchcock has a special photographic adviser named Ub Iwerks, who, with the aid of special effects expert Laurence A. Hampton, handled the bird scenes in such an effective way that anyone coming out of a theater where *The Birds* had been screened as a matinee attraction was likely to glance up to the sky warily. *The Birds* was nominated for a special effects Academy Award in 1963, but lost to *Cleopatra* for no apparent reason, a fact that upset many critics, since the special effects in *The Birds* provide believable and extraordinary horror and are uncannily executed.

Hitchcock begins his story in San Francisco, where a bachelor attorney, Mitch Brenner (Rod Taylor), meets a wealthy, cool blonde named Melanie Daniels (Tippi Hedren). The two flirt and tease each other, and Melanie is especially taken with Mitch. She impulsively decides to visit Brenner at his home in Bodega Bay, a little north of the city, where he spends weekends with his sister Cathy (Veronica Cartwright) and mother (Jessica Tandy). Brenner's former girlfriend, Annie Hayworth (Suzanne Pleshette), also lives there, teaching at an elementary school a little apart from the main village center.

When Melanie arrives, bringing a cage with two lovebirds which she has bought for Mitch as a joke, the townspeople eye her ominously, for the birds in the area are already gathering around the town, behaving queerly and

> The reviewer provides a summary of the film's plot in paragraphs 2, 3, and 4.

> The writer identifies actors and actresses by name.

> The first part of this sentence presents a fact, while the second part offers an opinion.

The Birds

setting the people on edge. Melanie decides to rent a boat, take the birds across the bay to Mitch's house, give them to Cathy, then quietly return and wait for Mitch's reaction. When they do meet again he begins to like her more, and they fall in love, against his mother's wishes.

After these events, the birds begin more attacks. In one instance they swoop down on a service station, where an attendant is frightened and drops the gasoline line, allowing a spill to spread over the area. A driver watching the birds moving in to attack absentmindedly lights his cigarette and drops the lighted match in the path of the gasoline. There is a huge explosion, and that whole area of the town square is set afire. The camera pulls back for a full overhead shot of the disaster, while the birds sweep through the sky overhead and screech in triumph.

. . .

Hitchcock puts this dark, bizarre, frightening fairy tale before the camera with rare skill. The birds in all their terror and power were manipulated by a trainer named Ray Berwick; without him and the special effects crew, the film would not have been so believable. The picture is handsomely photographed in Technicolor by Robert Burks, and Hitchcock intensifies the spellbound, eerie atmosphere of his story by having no musical background score. Instead, he uses an electronic sound device called a Trautonium, designed by

Oskar Sala, and upon this device a toneless, monotonous, but frightening and otherworldly composition by Remi Gassman is played. The advance publicity campaign for the film was expertly handled; on billboards all over numerous cities as well as in the newspapers there appeared the warning message "The Birds Is Coming," piqueing interest in the story.

. . .

There is . . . much more to the film than merely birds. There are some seeming inconsistencies in the plot, and allusions which were criticized by contemporary reviewers are now analyzed at great length. As with all Hitchcock films there is more than a mere story; the complexities of this film are perhaps more difficult to decipher than most. It is never really clear in the film why the birds are attacking, or what, if anything, Melanie's love birds have to do with their behavior. The birds may be avenging something, but there is no evidence of what that something is. The children who are attacked are certainly innocent of any wrongdoing, and in some cases the people killed inadvertently cause their own deaths by panicking.

. . .

The true meaning of the film . . . cannot be pinpointed. This perhaps illustrates one of the greatest aspects of Hitchcock's films: so many questions are left unanswered that they can reveal new insights and nuances of meaning even after repeated viewings.

After a summary, the reviewer offers his opinion. Here, he offers praise.

The reviewer uses specific descriptive words to illustrate his opinion of film elements such as cinematography and music.

Check Your Comprehension

1. According to the reviewer, what advantage does the filmmaker have over the short story writer?
2. What did Ub Iwerks, Laurence A. Hampton, Ray Berwick, Robert Burks, Oskar Sala, and Remi Gassman contribute to the film?
3. (a) According to the reviewer, what are some of the unanswered questions raised by the film? (b) What is the reviewer's opinion of these questions?
4. How did those in charge of publicity do a good job?

Applying the Reading Strategy

Identifying Support for Response

5. Cite three examples DeWitt Bodeen gives to support his opinion that the movie is made "with rare skill."
6. Bodeen finds parts of the film "difficult to decipher," yet he does not think that this is a flaw. How does he defend this response?
7. Complete your own evaluation of the ideas in Bodeen's review. View Alfred Hitchcock's *The Birds*, and then write a brief summary comparing your response to the reviewer's.

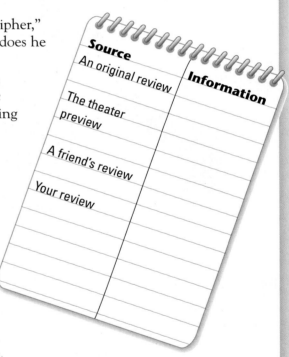

Activity

Evaluating Movie Reviews

Choose a film currently showing in theaters. Using a chart like the one shown, record review information from a variety of sources. Then, see the film and write your own review, providing reasons for your opinion.

Compare your findings to decide which sources gave accurate, convincing, or reliable reviews and whether you agreed with the opinions stated. Then, summarize what you have learned from this exercise.

Contrasting Informational Materials

Movie Reviews and Advertisements

1. Find several movie advertisements and review them to determine the key characteristics of this form of informational material.
2. (a) What do reviews and advertisements have in common? (b) How are they different?
3. Which form do you find more reliable? Explain.

Prepare to Read

The Red-headed League

Take It to the Net

Visit www.phschool.com
for interactive activities and
instruction related to "The
Red-headed League,"
including

- background
- graphic organizers
- literary elements
- reading strategies

Preview

Connecting to the Literature

Just a quick glance at a person can give you clues to his personality. This sizing up of people is part of the unpaid detective work of everyday life. As you read "The Red-headed League," notice how the brilliant detective Sherlock Holmes uses the technique of keen observation to solve a mystery.

Background

This story is one of many tales about the exploits of the world's most famous fictional detective, Sherlock Holmes. Often shown wearing a cape and deerstalker cap, Holmes is recognized even by people who have never read a Sherlock Holmes mystery.

Literary Analysis

The Mystery

A **mystery** is a story of suspense that usually contains a crime, a crime-solver, a criminal, suspects, and key details such as clues, alibis, and characters' possible reasons for committing a crime. When you read a line like the following from "The Red-headed League," you know that you are embarking on detective work and there is a mystery to solve.

> ". . . I want to find out about them, and who they are, and what their object was in playing this prank—if it was a prank—upon me. It was a pretty expensive joke for them, for it cost them two and thirty pounds."

Read "The Red-headed League" carefully to find details the writer has provided to help you solve the mystery.

Connecting Literary Elements

In "The Red-headed League," **characterization**, the way in which characters are developed, provides vital clues to solving the mystery. Writers reveal characters through a variety of techniques, including direct statements, descriptions, and characters' words, thoughts, and actions. Notice how each character in the story is developed and which details are clues to solving the mystery.

Reading Strategy

Finding Key Details

Readers of mysteries try to solve the crime along with—or even before—the detective. This is done by noting **key details**, pieces of information that have a bearing on the crime. These key details are often clues to the mystery. For example, subtleties in a character's actions may reveal something significant. Use a chart like the one shown to record the key details that you find as you read. For each detail, note its possible importance to the case.

> **Key Detail**
>
> Wilson's assistant is willing to work for half wages.
>
> ↓
>
> **Importance**
>
> It's odd that someone volunteers for less pay.

Vocabulary Development

singular (siŋ´ gyə lər) *adj.* rare; extraordinary (p. 97)

avail (ə vāl´) *v.* be of help (p. 103)

hoax (hōks) *n.* deceitful trick (p. 104)

introspective (in´ trə spek´ tiv) *adj.* causing one to look into one's own thoughts and feelings (p. 107)

vex (veks) *v.* annoy (p. 108)

conundrums (kə nun´ drəmz) *n.* puzzling questions or problems (p. 108)

astuteness (ə st‾oot´ nis) *n.* shrewdness (p. 108)

formidable (fôr´ mə də bəl) *adj.* awe-inspiring (p. 108)

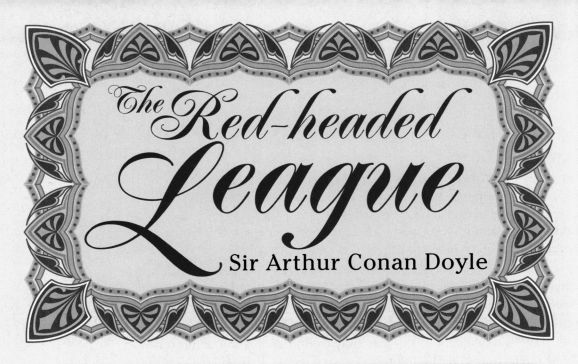

The Red-headed League

Sir Arthur Conan Doyle

I had called upon my friend, Mr. Sherlock Holmes, one day in the autumn of last year and found him in deep conversation with a very stout, florid-faced, elderly gentleman with fiery red hair. With an apology for my intrusion, I was about to withdraw when Holmes pulled me abruptly into the room and closed the door behind me.

"You could not possibly have come at a better time, my dear Watson," he said cordially.

"I was afraid that you were engaged."

"So I am. Very much so."

"Then I can wait in the next room."

"Not at all. This gentleman, Mr. Wilson, has been my partner and helper in many of my most successful cases, and I have no doubt that he will be of the utmost use to me in yours also."

The stout gentleman half rose from his chair and gave a bob of greeting, with a quick little questioning glance from his small, fat-encircled eyes.

"Try the settee,"[1] said Holmes, relapsing into his armchair and putting his finger tips together, as was his custom when in judicial moods. "I know, my dear Watson, that you share my love of all that is bizarre and outside the conventions and humdrum routine of everyday life. You have shown your relish for it by the enthusiasm which has prompted you to chronicle, and, if you will excuse my saying so, somewhat to embellish so many of my own little adventures."

"Your cases have indeed been of the greatest interest to me," I observed.

"You will remember that I remarked the other day, just before we went into the very simple problem presented by Miss Mary Sutherland, that for strange effects and extraordinary combinations we must go to life itself, which is always far more daring than any effort of the imagination."

"A proposition which I took the liberty of doubting."

"You did, Doctor, but none the less you must come round to my view, for otherwise I shall keep on piling fact upon fact on you until your reason breaks down under them and acknowledges me to be right. Now, Mr. Jabez Wilson here has been good enough to call upon me this morning, and to begin a narrative which promises to be one of the most singular which I have listened to for some time. You have heard me remark that the strangest and most unique things are very often connected not with the larger but with the smaller crimes, and occasionally, indeed, where there is room for doubt whether any positive crime has

---

1. **settee** (se tē′) *n.* small sofa.

Literary Analysis
The Mystery What does Holmes's comment about Watson indicate about the crime-solver in this mystery?

singular (sin′ gyə lər) *adj.* rare; extraordinary

Reading Check

Who has helped Holmes in many of his cases?

been committed. As far as I have heard it is impossible for me to say whether the present case is an instance of crime or not, but the course of events is certainly among the most singular that I have ever listened to. Perhaps, Mr. Wilson, you would have the great kindness to recommence your narrative. I ask you not merely because my friend Dr. Watson has not heard the opening part but also because the peculiar nature of the story makes me anxious to have every possible detail from your lips. As a rule, when I have heard some slight indication of the course of events, I am able to guide myself by the thousands of other similar cases which occur to my memory. In the present instance I am forced to admit that the facts are, to the best of my belief, unique."

The portly client puffed out his chest with an appearance of some little pride and pulled a dirty and wrinkled newspaper from the inside pocket of his great coat. As he glanced down the advertisement column, with his head thrust forward and the paper flattened out upon his knee, I took a good look at the man and endeavored, after the fashion of my companion, to read the indications which might be presented by his dress or appearance.

I did not gain very much, however, by my inspection. Our visitor bore every mark of being an average commonplace British tradesman, obese, pompous, and slow. He wore rather baggy gray shepherd's check trousers, a not over-clean black frock coat, unbuttoned in the front, and a drab waistcoat with a heavy brassy Albert chain, and a square pierced bit of metal dangling down as an ornament. A frayed top hat and a faded brown overcoat with a wrinkled velvet collar lay upon a chair beside him. Altogether, look as I would, there was nothing remarkable about the man save his blazing red head, and the expression of extreme chagrin and discontent upon his features.

Reading Strategy
Finding Key Details
Which details of Wilson's appearance does Watson seem to regard as most important?

Sherlock Holmes's quick eye took in my occupation, and he shook his head with a smile as he noticed my questioning glances. "Beyond the obvious facts that he has at some time done manual labor, that he takes snuff,[2] that he is a Freemason,[3] that he has been in China, and that he has done a considerable amount of writing lately, I can deduce nothing else."

Mr. Jabez Wilson started up in his chair, with his forefinger upon the paper, but his eyes upon my companion.

"How, in the name of good fortune, did you know all that, Mr. Holmes?" he asked. "How did you know, for example, that I did manual labor? It's as true as gospel, for I began as a ship's carpenter."

"Your hands, my dear sir. Your right hand is quite a size larger than your left. You have worked with it, and the muscles are more developed."

"Well, the snuff, then, and the Freemasonry?"

"I won't insult your intelligence by telling you how I read that, especially as, rather against the strict rules of your order, you use an arc-and-compass breastpin."

Literary Analysis
The Mystery Why are Holmes's observations of Wilson more meaningful than Watson's?

---

2. **snuff** powdered tobacco.
3. **Freemason** member of a secret society.

"Ah, of course, I forgot that. But the writing?"

"What else can be indicated by that right cuff so very shiny for five inches, and the left one with the smooth patch near the elbow where you rest it upon the desk?"

"Well, but China?"

"The fish that you have tattooed immediately above your right wrist could only have been done in China. I have made a small study of tattoo marks and have even contributed to the literature of the subject. That trick of staining the fishes' scales of a delicate pink is quite peculiar to China. When, in addition, I see a Chinese coin hanging from your watch-chain, the matter becomes even more simple."

Mr. Jabez Wilson laughed heavily. "Well, I never!" said he. "I thought at first that you had done something clever, but I see that there was nothing in it, after all."

"I begin to think, Watson," said Holmes, "that I make a mistake in explaining. *'Omne ignotum pro magnifico,'*[4] you know, and my poor little reputation, such as it is, will suffer shipwreck if I am so candid. Can you not find the advertisement, Mr. Wilson?"

"Yes, I have got it now," he answered with his thick red finger planted halfway down the column. "Here it is. This is what began it all. You just read it for yourself, sir."

I took the paper from him and read as follows:

To THE RED-HEADED LEAGUE:

On account of the bequest of the late Ezekiah Hopkins, of Lebanon, Pennsylvania, U. S. A., there is now another vacancy open which entitles a member of the League to a salary of £4◆ a week for purely nominal services. All red-headed men who are sound in body and mind, and above the age of twenty-one years, are eligible. Apply in person on Monday, at eleven o'clock, to Duncan Ross, at the offices of the League, 7 Pope's Court, Fleet Street.

"What on earth does this mean?" I ejaculated after I had twice read over the extraordinary announcement.

Holmes chuckled and wriggled in his chair, as was his habit when in high spirits. "It is a little off the beaten track, isn't it?" said he. "And now, Mr. Wilson, off you go at scratch and tell us all about yourself, your household, and the effect which this advertisement had upon your fortunes. You will first make a note, Doctor, of the paper and the date."

"It is *The Morning Chronicle* of April 27, 1890. Just two months ago."

"Very good. Now, Mr. Wilson?"

"Well, it is just as I have been telling you, Mr. Sherlock Holmes," said Jabez Wilson, mopping his forehead; "I have a small pawnbroker's business at Coburg Square, near the City. It's not a very large

---

4. *Omne ignotum pro magnifico* (äm´ nā ig nō´ təm prō mag nē´ fē kō) Latin for "Whatever is unknown is magnified."

Literature
in context Math Connection

◆ *Pound Conversions*

The advertisement announces a League salary of four pounds a week. The pound is the monetary unit of Great Britain. Its equivalency in American dollars fluctuates, depending on current economic conditions. At the time Doyle wrote the story, one British pound equaled about $4.85, so four pounds would have equaled about $19.40. This was considered a large amount at the time in which the story is set, particularly for such simple work.

✔Reading Check

Who is eligible for the position posted in the advertisement?

affair, and of late years it has not done more than just give me a living. I used to be able to keep two assistants, but now I only keep one; and I would have a job to pay him but that he is willing to come for half wages so as to learn the business."

"What is the name of this obliging youth?" asked Sherlock Holmes.

"His name is Vincent Spaulding, and he's not such a youth, either. It's hard to say his age. I should not wish a smarter assistant, Mr. Holmes; and I know very well that he could better himself and earn twice what I am able to give him. But, after all, if he is satisfied, why should I put ideas in his head?"

"Why, indeed? You seem most fortunate in having an employee who comes under the full market price. It is not a common experience among employers in this age. I don't know that your assistant is not as remarkable as your advertisement."

"Oh, he has his faults, too," said Mr. Wilson. "Never was such a fellow for photography. Snapping away with a camera when he ought to be improving his mind, and then diving down into the cellar like a rabbit into its hole to develop his pictures. That is his main fault, but on the whole he's a good worker. There's no vice in him."

"He is still with you, I presume?"

"Yes, sir. He and a girl of fourteen, who does a bit of simple cooking and keeps the place clean—that's all I have in the house, for I am a widower and never had any family. We live very quietly, sir, the three of us; and we keep a roof over our heads and pay our debts, if we do nothing more.

"The first thing that put us out was that advertisement. Spaulding, he came down into the office just this day eight weeks, with this very paper in his hand, and he says:

" 'I wish to the Lord, Mr. Wilson, that I was a red-headed man.'

" 'Why that?' I asks.

" 'Why,' says he, 'here's another vacancy on the League of the Red-headed Men. It's worth quite a little fortune to any man who gets it, and I understand that there are more vacancies than there are men, so that the trustees are at their wits' end what to do with the money. If my hair would only change color, here's a nice little crib all ready for me to step into.'

" 'Why, what is it, then?' I asked. You see, Mr. Holmes, I am a very stay-at-home man,

Reading Strategy
Finding Key Details
Which details about Vincent Spaulding are unusual enough to interest Sherlock Holmes?

and as my business came to me instead of my having to go to it, I was often weeks on end without putting my foot over the doormat. In that way I didn't know much of what was going on outside, and I was always glad of a bit of news.

" 'Have you never heard of the League of the Red-headed Men?' he asked with his eyes open.

" 'Never.'

" 'Why, I wonder at that, for you are eligible yourself for one of the vacancies.'

" 'And what are they worth?' I asked.

" 'Oh, merely a couple of hundred a year, but the work is slight, and it need not interfere very much with one's other occupations.'

"Well, you can easily think that that made me prick up my ears, for the business has not been over-good for some years, and an extra couple of hundred would have been very handy.

" 'Tell me all about it,' said I.

" 'Well,' said he, showing me the advertisement, 'you can see for yourself that the League has a vacancy, and there is the address where you should apply for particulars. As far as I can make out, the League was founded by an American millionaire, Ezekiah Hopkins, who was very peculiar in his ways. He was himself red-headed, and he had a great sympathy for all red-headed men; so when he died it was found that he had left his enormous fortune in the hands of trustees, with instructions to apply the interest to the providing of easy berths to men whose hair is of that color. From all I hear it is splendid pay and very little to do.

" 'But,' said I, 'there would be millions of red-headed men who would apply.'

" 'Not so many as you might think,' he answered. 'You see it is really confined to Londoners, and to grown men. This American had started from London when he was young, and he wanted to do the old town a good turn. Then, again, I have heard it is no use your applying if your hair is light red, or dark red, or anything but real bright, blazing, fiery red. Now, if you cared to apply, Mr. Wilson, you would just walk in; but perhaps it would hardly be worth your while to put yourself out of the way for the sake of a few hundred pounds.'

"Now, it is a fact, gentlemen, as you may see for yourselves, that my hair is of a very full and rich tint, so that it seemed to me that if there was to be any competition in the matter I stood as good a chance as any man that I had ever met. Vincent Spaulding seemed to know so much about it that I thought he might prove useful so I just ordered him to put up the shutters for the day and to come right away with me. He was very willing to have a holiday,[5] so we shut the business up and started off for the address that was given us in the advertisement.

"I never hope to see such a sight as that again, Mr. Holmes. From north, south, east, and west every man who had a shade of red in his hair had tramped into the city to answer the advertisement. Fleet

---

5. **holiday** a day off from work; a vacation.

Literary Analysis
The Mystery The Red-headed League seems too good to be true. What appears most suspicious about this club?

**Reading Check**
Why did Wilson believe he had a good chance of being chosen for the position?

Street was choked with red-headed folk, and Pope's Court looked like a coster's orange barrow.[6] I should not have thought there were so many in the whole country as were brought together by that single advertisement. Every shade of color they were—straw, lemon, orange, brick, Irish-setter, liver, clay: but, as Spaulding said, there were not many who had the real vivid flame-colored tint. When I saw how many were waiting, I would have given it up in despair: but Spaulding would not hear of it. How he did it I could not imagine, but he pushed and pulled and butted until he got me through the crowd, and right up to the steps which led to the office. There was a double stream upon the stair, some going up in hope, and some coming back dejected: but we wedged in as well as we could and soon found ourselves in the office."

"Your experience has been a most entertaining one," remarked Holmes as his client paused and refreshed his memory with a huge pinch of snuff. "Pray continue your very interesting statement."

"There was nothing in the office but a couple of wooden chairs and a deal table, behind which sat a small man with a head that was even redder than mine. He said a few words to each candidate as he came up, and then he always managed to find some fault in them which would disqualify them. Getting a vacancy did not seem to be such a very easy matter, after all. However, when our turn came the little man was much more favorable to me than to any of the others, and he closed the door as we entered, so that he might have a private word with us.

" 'This is Mr. Jabez Wilson,' said my assistant, 'and he is willing to fill a vacancy in the League.'

" 'And he is admirably suited for it,' the other answered. 'He has every requirement. I cannot recall when I have seen anything so fine.' He took a step backward, cocked his head on one side, and gazed at my hair until I felt quite bashful. Then suddenly he plunged forward, wrung my hand, and congratulated me warmly on my success.

" 'It would be injustice to hesitate, said he. 'You will, however, I am sure, excuse me for taking an obvious precaution.' With that he seized my hair in both his hands, and tugged until I yelled with the pain. 'There is water in your eyes,' said he as he released me. 'I perceive that all is as it should be. But we have to be careful, for we have twice been deceived by wigs and once by paint. I could tell you tales of cobbler's wax which would disgust you with human nature.' He stepped over to the window and shouted through it at the top of his voice that the vacancy was filled. A groan of disappointment came up from below, and the folk all trooped away in different directions until there was not a red head to be seen except my own and that of the manager.

" 'My name,' said he, 'is Mr. Duncan Ross, and I am myself one of the pensioners upon the fund left by our noble benefactor. Are you a married man, Mr. Wilson? Have you a family?'

Reading Strategy
Finding Key Details What do you notice about how the League interviewer receives Wilson?

Literary Analysis
The Mystery What is suspicious about the way in which the vacancy was filled?

---

6. **coster's orange barrow** pushcart of a seller of oranges.

"I answered that I had not.

"His face fell immediately.

" 'Dear me!' he said gravely, 'that is very serious indeed! I am sorry to hear you say that. The fund was, of course, for the propagation and spread of the red-heads as well as for their maintenance. It is exceedingly unfortunate that you should be a bachelor.'

"My face lengthened at this, Mr. Holmes, for I thought that I was not to have the vacancy after all: but after thinking it over for a few minutes he said that it would be all right.

" 'In the case of another,' said he, 'the objection might be fatal, but we must stretch a point in favor of a man with such a head of hair as yours. When shall you be able to enter upon your new duties?

" 'Well, it is a little awkward, for I have a business already,' said I.

" 'Oh, never mind about that, Mr. Wilson!' said Vincent Spaulding. 'I should be able to look after that for you.'

" 'What would be the hours?' I asked.

" 'Ten to two.'

"Now a pawnbroker's business is mostly done of an evening, Mr. Holmes, especially Thursday and Friday evening, which is just before pay-day: so it would suit me very well to earn a little in the mornings. Besides, I knew that my assistant was a good man, and that he would see to anything that turned up.

" 'That would suit me very well,' said I. 'And the pay?'

" 'Is £4 a week.'

" 'And the work?'

" 'Is purely nominal.'

" 'What do you call purely nominal?'

" 'Well, you have to be in the office, or at least in the building, the whole time. If you leave, you forfeit your whole position forever. The will is very clear upon that point. You don't comply with the conditions if you budge from the office during that time.'

" 'It's only four hours a day, and I should not think of leaving,' said I.

" 'No excuse will <u>avail</u>,' said Mr. Duncan Ross: 'neither sickness nor business nor anything else. There you must stay, or you lose your billet.'[7]

" 'And the work?'

" 'Is to copy out the Encyclopedia Britannica. There is the first volume of it in that press. You must find your own ink, pens, and blotting-paper, but we provide this table and chair. Will you be ready tomorrow?'

" 'Certainly,' I answered.

" 'Then, good-bye, Mr. Jabez Wilson, and let me congratulate you once more on the important position which you have been fortunate enough to gain.' He bowed me out of the room, and I went home with my assistant, hardly knowing what to say or do, I was so pleased at my own good fortune.

---

7. billet (bil´ it) *n.* position; job.

avail (ə vāl´) *v.* be of help

Literary Analysis
The Mystery What is it about the nature of Wilson's job that sounds suspicious?

**Reading Check**
Who offered to look after Wilson's pawnbroker business while he was at his other job?

"Well, I thought over the matter all day, and by evening I was in low spirits again: for I had quite persuaded myself that the whole affair must be some great <u>hoax</u> or fraud, though what its object might be I could not imagine. It seemed altogether past belief that anyone could make such a will, or that they would pay such a sum for doing anything so simple as copying out the Encyclopedia Britannica. Vincent Spaulding did what he could to cheer me up, but by bedtime I had reasoned myself out of the whole thing. However, in the morning I determined to have a look at it anyhow, so I bought a penny bottle of ink, and with a quill-pen, and seven sheets of foolscap paper,[8] I started off for Pope's Court.

"Well, to my surprise and delight, everything was as right as possible. The table was set out ready for me, and Mr. Duncan Ross was there to see that I got fairly to work. He started me off upon the letter A, and then he left me; but he would drop in from time to time to see that all was right with me. At two o'clock he bade me good-day, complimented me upon the amount that I had written, and locked the door of the office after me.

"This went on day after day, Mr. Holmes, and on Saturday the manager came in and planked down four golden sovereigns for my week's work. It was the same next week, and the same the week after. Every morning I was there at ten, and every afternoon I left at two. By degrees Mr. Duncan Ross took to coming in only once of a morning, and then, after a time, he did not come in at all. Still, of course, I never dared to leave the room for an instant, for I was not sure when he might come, and the billet was such a good one, and suited me so well, that I would not risk the loss of it.

"Eight weeks passed away like this, and I had written about Abbots and Archery and Armor and Architecture and Attica, and hoped with diligence that I might get on to the B's before very long. It cost me something in foolscap,and I had pretty nearly filled a shelf with my writings. And then suddenly the whole business came to an end."

"To an end?"

"Yes, sir. And no later than this morning. I went to my work as usual at ten o'clock, but the door was shut and locked, with a little square of cardboard hammered on to the middle of the panel with a tack. Here it is, and you can read for yourself."

hoax (hōks) *n.* deceitful trick

---

8. foolscap paper writing paper.

He held up a piece of white cardboard about the size of a sheet of notepaper. It read in this fashion:

THE RED-HEADED LEAGUE

IS

DISSOLVED.

October 9, 1890.

Sherlock Holmes and I surveyed this curt announcement and the rueful face behind it, until the comical side of the affair so completely overtopped every other consideration that we both burst out into a roar of laughter.

"I cannot see that there is anything very funny," cried our client, flushing up to the roots of his flaming head. "If you can do nothing better than laugh at me, I can go elsewhere."

"No, no," cried Holmes, shoving him back into the chair from which he had half risen. "I really wouldn't miss your case for the world. It is most refreshingly unusual. But there is, if you will excuse my saying so, something just a little funny about it. Pray what steps did you take when you found the card upon the door?"

"I was staggered, sir. I did not know what to do. Then I called at the offices round, but none of them seemed to know anything about it. Finally, I went to the landlord, who is an accountant living on the ground floor, and I asked him if he could tell me what had become of the Red-headed League. He said that he had never heard of any such body. Then I asked him who Mr. Duncan Ross was. He answered that the name was new to him.

" 'Well,' said I, 'the gentleman at No. 4.'

" 'What, the red-headed man?'

" 'Yes.'

" 'Oh,' said he, 'his name was William Morris. He was a solicitor[9] and was using my room as a temporary convenience until his new premises were ready. He moved out yesterday.'

" 'Where could I find him?'

" 'Oh, at his new offices. He did tell me the address. Yes, 17 King Edward Street, near St. Paul's.'

"I started off, Mr. Holmes, but when I got to that address it was a manufactory of artificial kneecaps, and no one in it had ever heard of either Mr. William Morris or Mr. Duncan Ross."

"And what did you do then?" asked Holmes.

"I went home to Saxe-Coburg Square, and I took the advice of my assistant. But he could not help me in any way. He could only say that if I waited I should hear by post. But that was not quite good enough, Mr. Holmes. I did not wish to lose such a place without a struggle, so, as I had heard that you were good enough to give advice to poor folk who were in need of it, I came right away to you."

"And you did very wisely," said Holmes. "Your case is an exceedingly remarkable one, and I shall be happy to look into it. From what

---

9. **solicitor** member of the legal profession.

Literary Analysis
The Mystery At this point, another suspect enters the picture. Which clues point toward this character as a suspect?

**Reading Check**
After eight weeks at his new job, what does Wilson find posted on the door?

you have told me I think that it is possible that graver issues hang from it than might at first sight appear."

"Grave enough!" said Mr. Jabez Wilson. "Why, I have lost four pound a week."

"As far as you are personally concerned," remarked Holmes, "I do not see that you have any grievance against this extraordinary league. On the contrary, you are, as I understand, richer by some £30, to say nothing of the minute knowledge which you have gained on every subject which comes under the letter A. You have lost nothing by them."

"No, sir. But I want to find out about them, and who they are, and what their object was in playing this prank—if it was a prank—upon me. It was a pretty expensive joke for them, for it cost them two and thirty pounds."

"We shall endeavor to clear up these points for you. And, first, one or two questions, Mr. Wilson. This assistant of yours who first called your attention to the advertisement—how long had he been with you?"

"About a month then."

"How did he come?"

"In answer to an advertisement."

"Was he the only applicant?"

"No, I had a dozen."

"Why did you pick him?"

"Because he was handy and would come cheap."

"At half-wages, in fact."

"Yes."

"What is he like, this Vincent Spaulding?"

"Small, stout-built, very quick in his ways. No hair on his face, though he's not short of thirty. Has a white splash of acid upon his forehead."

Holmes sat up in his chair in considerable excitement. "I thought as much," said he. "Have you ever observed that his ears are pierced for earrings?"

"Yes, sir. He told me that a gypsy had done it for him when he was a lad."

"Hum!" said Holmes, sinking back in deep thought. "He is still with you?"

"Oh, yes, sir; I have only just left him."

"And has your business been attended to in your absence?"

"Nothing to complain of, sir. There's never very much to do of a morning."

"That will do, Mr. Wilson. I shall be happy to give you an opinion upon the subject in the course of a day or two. Today is Saturday, and I hope that by Monday we may come to a conclusion."

"Well, Watson," said Holmes when our visitor had left us, "what do

Literary Analysis
The Mystery and Characterization Explain what is revealed in this passage about Holmes as a crime-solver.

you make of it all?"

"I make nothing of it," I answered frankly. "It is a most mysterious business."

"As a rule," said Holmes, "the more bizarre a thing is the less mysterious it proves to be. It is your commonplace, featureless crimes which are really puzzling, just as a commonplace face is the most difficult to identify. But I must be prompt over this matter."

"What are you going to do, then?" I asked.

"To smoke," he answered. "It is quite a three pipe problem, and I beg that you won't speak to me for fifty minutes." He curled himself up in his chair, with his thin knees drawn up to his hawk-like nose, and there he sat with his eyes closed and his black clay pipe thrusting out like the bill of some strange bird. I had come to the conclusion that he had dropped asleep, and indeed was nodding myself, when he suddenly sprang out of his chair with the gesture of a man who has made up his mind and put his pipe down upon the mantelpiece.

"Sarasate[10] plays at the St. James's Hall this afternoon," he remarked. "What do you think, Watson? Could your patients spare you for a few hours?"

"I have nothing to do today. My practice is never very absorbing."

"Then put on your hat and come. I am going through the City first, and we can have some lunch on the way. I observe that there is a good deal of German music on the program, which is rather more to my taste than Italian or French. It is <u>introspective</u>, and I want to introspect. Come along!"

We traveled by the Underground as far as Aldersgate; and a short walk took us to Saxe-Coburg Square, the scene of the singular story which we had listened to in the morning. It was a poky, little, shabby-genteel place, where four lines of dingy two-storied brick houses looked out into a small railed–in enclosure, where a lawn of weedy grass and a few clumps of faded laurel bushes made a hard fight against a smoke-laden and uncongenial atmosphere. Three gilt balls and a brown board with "JABEZ WILSON" in white letters, upon a corner house, announced the place where our red-headed client carried on his business. Sherlock Holmes stopped in front of it with his head on one side and looked it all over, with his eyes shining brightly between puckered lids. Then he walked slowly up the street, and then down again to the corner, still looking keenly at the houses. Finally he returned to the pawnbroker's, and, having thumped vigorously upon the pavement with his stick two or three times, he went up to the door and knocked. It was instantly opened by a bright-looking, clean-shaven young fellow, who asked him to step in.

"Thank you," said Holmes, "I only wished to ask you how you would go from here to the Strand."

"Third right, fourth left," answered the assistant promptly, closing the door.

---

10. **Sarasate** (sä rä sä´ tä) Spanish violinist and composer.

introspective (in´ trə spek´ tiv) *adj.* causing one to look into one's own thoughts and feelings

Reading Strategy
Finding Key Details
Which key details in this passage seem to be clues that help Holmes solve the crime?

☑ **Reading Check**

What reasons does Mr. Wilson give for hiring Vincent Spaulding?

"Smart fellow, that," observed Holmes as we walked away. "He is, in my judgment, the fourth smartest man in London, and for daring I am not sure that he has not a claim to be third. I have known something of him before."

"Evidently," said I, "Mr. Wilson's assistant counts for a good deal in this mystery of the Red-headed League. I am sure that you inquired your way merely in order that you might see him."

"Not him."

"What then?"

"The knees of his trousers."

"And what did you see?"

"What I expected to see."

"Why did you beat the pavement?"

"My dear doctor, this is a time for observation, not for talk. We are spies in an enemy's country. We know something of Saxe-Coburg Square. Let us now explore the parts which lie behind it."

The road in which we found ourselves as we turned round the corner from the retired Saxe-Coburg Square presented as great a contrast to it as the front of a picture does to the back. It was one of the main arteries which conveyed the traffic of the City to the north and west. The roadway was blocked with the immense stream of commerce flowing in a double tide inward and outward, while the footpaths were black with the hurrying swarm of pedestrians. It was difficult to realize as we looked at the line of fine shops and stately business premises that they really abutted on the other side upon the faded and stagnant square which we had just quitted.

"Let me see," said Holmes, standing at the corner and glancing along the line, "I should like just to remember the order of the houses here. It is a hobby of mine to have an exact knowledge of London. There is Mortimer's, the tobacconist, the little newspaper shop, the Coburg branch of the City and Suburban Bank, the Vegetarian Restaurant, and McFarlane's carriage-building depot. That carries us right on to the other block. And now, Doctor, we've done our work, so it's time we had some play. A sandwich and a cup of coffee, and then off to violin land, where all is sweetness and delicacy and harmony, and there are no red-headed clients to <u>vex</u> us with their <u>conundrums</u>."

My friend was an enthusiastic musician, being himself not only a very capable performer but a composer of no ordinary merit. All the afternoon he sat in the stalls wrapped in the most perfect happiness, gently waving his long, thin fingers in time to the music, while his gently smiling face and his languid, dreamy eyes were as unlike those of Holmes, the sleuthhound, Holmes the relentless, keen-witted, ready-handed criminal agent, as it was possible to conceive. In his singular character the dual nature alternately asserted itself, and his extreme exactness and <u>astuteness</u> represented, as I have often thought, the reaction against the poetic and contemplative mood which occasionally predominated in him. The swing of his nature took him from extreme languor to devouring energy; and, as I knew

Literary Analysis
The Mystery What might be Holmes's motive for familiarizing himself with the order of the buildings behind Saxe-Coburg Square?

vex (veks) *v.* annoy

conundrums (kə nun′ drəmz) *n.* puzzling questions or problems

astuteness (ə stōōt′ nis) *n.* shrewdness

formidable (fôr′ mə də bəl) *adj.* awe-inspiring

well, he was never so truly <u>formidable</u> as when, for days on end, he had been lounging in his armchair amid his improvisations and his black-letter editions. Then it was that the lust of the chase would suddenly come upon him, and that his brilliant reasoning power would rise to the level of intuition, until those who were unacquainted with his methods would look askance at him as on a man whose knowledge was not that of other mortals. When I saw him that afternoon so enwrapped in the music at St. James's Hall I felt that an evil time might be coming upon those whom he had set himself to hunt down.

"You want to go home, no doubt, Doctor," he remarked as we emerged.

"Yes, it would be as well."

"And I have some business to do which will take some hours. This business at Coburg Square is serious."

"Why serious?"

"A considerable crime is in contemplation. I have every reason to believe that we shall be in time to stop it. But today being Saturday rather complicates matters. I shall want your help tonight."

"At what time?"

"Ten will be early enough."

"I shall be at Baker Street at ten."

"Very well. And, I say, Doctor, there may be some little danger, so kindly put your army revolver in your pocket." He waved his hand, turned on his heel, and disappeared in an instant among the crowd.

I trust that I am not more dense than my neighbors, but I was always oppressed with a sense of my own stupidity in my dealings with Sherlock Holmes. Here I had heard what he had heard, I had seen what he had seen, and yet from his words it was evident that he saw clearly not only what had happened but what was about to happen, while to me the whole business was still confused and grotesque. As I drove home to my house in Kensington I thought over it all, from the extraordinary story of the red-headed copier of the Encyclopedia down to the visit to Saxe-Coburg Square, and the ominous words with which he had parted from me. What was this nocturnal expedition, and why should I go armed? Where were we going, and what were we to do? I had the hint from Holmes that this smooth-faced pawnbroker's assistant was a formidable man—a man who might play a deep game. I tried to puzzle it out, but gave it up in despair and set the matter aside until night should bring an explanation.

It was a quarter past nine when I started from home and made my way across the Park, and so through Oxford Street to Baker Street. Two hansoms* were standing at the door, and as I entered the passage I heard the sound of voices from above. On entering his room I

Literature in context Cultural Connection

♦ **Hansoms**

The hansom, also known as the hansom cab, is a two-wheeled covered carriage for two passengers, pulled by one horse. The cab was named for its inventor, Joseph Hansom (1803–1882), a London architect. By the late 1850s, the hansom was popular in New York and Boston as well as in London. Customers could enjoy a scenic and romantic ride in private with an unobstructed view, since the driver sat above and behind the passengers' cab. Today, hansom cabs are still a popular feature in New York's Central Park. However, in this story, they are a common form of transportation.

☑ **Reading Check**

Where do Holmes and Watson go after investigating at Saxe-Coburg Square?

found Holmes in animated conversation with two men, one of whom I recognized as Peter Jones, the official police agent, while the other was a long, thin, sad-faced man, with a very shiny hat and oppressively respectable frock coat.

"Ha! our party is complete," said Holmes, buttoning up his pea-jacket and taking his heavy hunting crop from the rack. "Watson, I think you know Mr. Jones, of Scotland Yard? Let me introduce you to Mr. Merryweather, who is to be our companion in tonight's adventure."

"We're hunting in couples again, Doctor, you see," said Jones in his consequential way. "Our friend here is a wonderful man for starting a chase. All he wants is an old dog to help him to do the running down."

"I hope a wild goose may not prove to be the end of our chase," observed Mr. Merryweather gloomily.

"You may place considerable confidence in Mr. Holmes, sir," said the police agent loftily. "He has his own little methods, which are, if he won't mind my saying so, just a little too theoretical and fantastic, but he has the makings of a detective in him. It is not too much to say that once or twice, as in that business of the Sholto murder and the Agra treasure, he has been more nearly correct than the official force."

"Oh, if you say so, Mr. Jones, it is all right," said the stranger with deference. "Still, I confess that I miss my rubber.[11] It is the first Saturday night for seven-and-twenty years that I have not had my rubber."

"I think you will find," said Sherlock Holmes, "that you will play for a higher stake tonight than you have ever done yet, and that the play will be more exciting. For you, Mr. Merryweather, the stake will be some £30,000: and for you, Jones, it will be the man upon whom you wish to lay your hands."

"John Clay, the murderer, thief, smasher, and forger. He's a young man, Mr. Merryweather, but he is at the head of his profession, and I would rather have my bracelets on him than on any criminal in

---

11. rubber card games.

London. He's a remarkable man, is young John Clay. His grandfather was a royal duke, and he himself has been to Eton[12] and Oxford.[13] His brain is as cunning as his fingers, and though we meet signs of him at every turn, we never know where to find the man himself. He'll crack a crib[14] in Scotland one week, and be raising money to build an orphanage in Cornwall the next. I've been on his track for years and have never set eyes on him yet."

"I hope that I may have the pleasure of introducing you tonight. I've had one or two little turns also with Mr. John Clay, and I agree with you that he is at the head of his profession. It is past ten, however, and quite time that we started. If you two will take the first hansom, Watson and I will follow in the second."

Sherlock Holmes was not very communicative during the long drive and lay back in the cab humming the tunes which he had heard in the afternoon. We rattled through an endless labyrinth of gas-lit streets until we emerged into Farrington Street.

"We are close there now," my friend remarked. "This fellow Merryweather is a bank director, and personally interested in the matter. I thought it as well to have Jones with us also. He is not a bad fellow, though an absolute imbecile in his profession. He has one positive virtue. He is as brave as a bulldog and as tenacious as a lobster if he gets his claws upon anyone. Here we are, and they are waiting for us."

We had reached the same crowded thoroughfare in which we had found ourselves in the morning. Our cabs were dismissed, and, following the guidance of Mr. Merryweather, we passed down a narrow passage and through a side door, which he opened for us. Within there was a small corridor, which ended in a very massive iron gate. This also was opened, and led down a flight of winding stone steps, which terminated at another formidable gate. Mr. Merryweather stopped to light a lantern, and then conducted us down a dark, earth-smelling passage, and so, after opening a third door, into a huge vault or cellar, which was piled all round with crates and massive boxes.

"You are not very vulnerable from above," Holmes remarked as he held up the lantern and gazed about him.

"Nor from below," said Mr. Merryweather, striking his stick upon the flags which lined the floor. "Why, dear me, it sounds quite hollow!" he remarked, looking up in surprise.

"I must really ask you to be a little more quiet!" said Holmes severely. "You have already imperiled the whole success of our expedition. Might I beg that you would have the goodness to sit down upon one of those boxes, and not to interfere?"

The solemn Mr. Merryweather perched himself upon a crate, with a very injured expression upon his face, while Holmes fell upon his knees upon the floor and, with the lantern and a magnifying lens, began to

Literary Analysis
The Mystery A new suspect's name is mentioned here. What evidence suggests that John Clay might really be Vincent Spaulding?

---

12. **Eton** famous British secondary school for boys.
13. **Oxford** oldest university in Great Britain.
14. **crack a crib** break into and rob a house.

✔**Reading Check**
Who is Mr. Merryweather?

examine minutely the cracks between the stones. A few seconds sufficed to satisfy him, for he sprang to his feet again and put his glass in his pocket.

"We have at least an hour before us," he remarked, "for they can hardly take any steps until the good pawnbroker is safely in bed. Then they will not lose a minute, for the sooner they do their work the longer time they will have for their escape. We are at present, Doctor—as no doubt you have divined—in the cellar of the City branch of one of the principal London banks. Mr. Merryweather is the chairman of directors, and he will explain to you that there are reasons why the more daring criminals of London should take a considerable interest in this cellar at present."

"It is our French gold," whispered the director. "We have had several warnings that an attempt might be made upon it."

"Your French gold?"

"Yes. We had occasion some months ago to strengthen our resources and borrowed for that purpose 30,000 napoleons from the Bank of France. It has become known that we have never had occasion to unpack the money, and that it is still lying in our cellar. The crate upon which I sit contains 2,000 napoleons packed between layers of lead foil. Our reserve of bullion is much larger at present than is usually kept in a single branch office, and the directors have had misgivings upon the subject."

"Which were very well justified," observed Holmes.

"And now it is time that we arranged our little plans. I expect that within an hour matters will come to a head. In the meantime, Mr. Merryweather, we must put the screen over that dark lantern."

"And sit in the dark?"

"I am afraid so. I had brought a pack of cards in my pocket, and I thought that, as we were a *partie carrée*,[15] you might have your rubber after all. But I see that the enemy's preparations have gone so far that we cannot risk the presence of a light. And, first of all, we must choose our positions. These are daring men, and though we shall take them at a disadvantage, they may do us some harm unless we are careful. I shall stand behind this crate, and do you conceal yourselves behind those. Then, when I flash a light upon them, close in swiftly. If they fire, Watson, have no compunction about shooting them down."

I placed my revolver, cocked, upon the top of the wooden case behind which I crouched. Holmes shot the slide across the front of his lantern and left us in pitch darkness—such an absolute darkness as I have never before experienced. The smell of hot metal remained to assure us that the light was still there, ready to flash out at a moment's notice. To me, with my nerves worked up to a pitch of expectancy, there was something depressing and subduing in the sudden gloom, and in the cold dank air of the vault.

"They have but one retreat," whispered Holmes. "That is back

---

15. *partie carrée* (pär tē′ cä rā′) French for "group of four."

Literary Analysis
The Mystery A mystery usually includes a suspect's motive for committing a crime. What possible motive is indicated by Merryweather's revelation?

Literary Analysis
The Mystery and Characterization What do the words *they may do us some harm* reveal about the criminals?

through the house into Saxe-Coburg Square. I hope that you have done what I asked you, Jones?"

"I have an inspector and two officers waiting at the front door."

"Then we have stopped all the holes. And now we must be silent and wait."

What a time it seemed! From comparing notes afterwards it was but an hour and a quarter, yet it appeared to me that the night must have almost gone, and the dawn be breaking above us. My limbs were weary and stiff, for I feared to change my position; yet my nerves were worked up to the highest pitch of tension, and my hearing was so acute that I could not only hear the gentle breathing of my companions, but I could distinguish the deeper, heavier in-breath of the bulky Jones from the thin, sighing note of the bank director. From my position I could look over the case in the direction of the floor. Suddenly my eyes caught the glint of a light.

At first it was but a lurid spark upon the stone pavement. Then it lengthened out until it became a yellow line, and then, without any warning or sound, a gash seemed to open and a hand appeared; a white, almost womanly hand, which felt about in the center of the little area of light. For a minute or more the hand, with its writhing fingers, protruded out of the floor. Then it was withdrawn as suddenly as it appeared, and all was dark again save the single lurid spark which marked a chink between the stones.

Its disappearance, however, was but momentary. With a rending, tearing sound, one of the broad, white stones turned over upon its side and left a square, gaping hole, through which streamed the light of a lantern. Over the edge there peeped a clean-cut, boyish face, which looked keenly about it, and then, with a hand on either side of the aperture, drew itself shoulder-high and waist-high, until one knee rested upon the edge. In another instant he stood at the side of the hole and was hauling after him a companion, lithe and small like himself, with a pale face and a shock of very red hair.

"It's all clear," he whispered. "Have you the chisel and the bags? Great Scott! Jump, Archie, jump, and I'll swing for it."

Sherlock Holmes had sprung out and seized the intruder by the collar. The other dived down the hole, and I heard the sound of rending cloth as Jones clutched at his skirts. The light flashed upon the barrel of a revolver, but Holmes's hunting crop came down on the man's wrist, and the pistol clinked upon the stone floor.

"It's no use, John Clay," said Holmes blandly. "You have no chance at all."

"So I see," the other answered with the utmost coolness. "I fancy that my pal is all right, though I see you have got his coattails."

"There are three men waiting for him at the door," said Holmes.

"Oh, indeed! You seem to have done the thing very completely. I must compliment you."

"And I you," Holmes answered. "Your red-headed idea was very new and effective."

Literary Analysis
The Mystery Which details contribute to the suspense of the mystery at this point?

**Reading Check**

How long do Holmes and his party wait for the criminals to arrive?

"You'll see your pal again presently," said Jones. "He's quicker at climbing down holes than I am. Just hold out while I fix the derbies."[16]

"I beg that you will not touch me with your filthy hands," remarked our prisoner as the handcuffs clattered upon his wrists. "You may not be aware that I have royal blood in my veins. Have the goodness, also, when you address me always to say 'sir' and 'please.'"

"All right," said Jones with a stare and a snigger. "Well, would you please, sir, march upstairs, where we can get a cab to carry your Highness to the police station?"

"That is better," said John Clay serenely. He made a sweeping bow to the three of us and walked quietly off in the custody of the detective.

"Really, Mr. Holmes," said Mr. Merryweather as we followed them from the cellar, "I do not know how the bank can thank you or repay you. There is no doubt that you have detected and defeated in the most complete manner one of the most deter-mined attempts at bank robbery that have ever come within my experience."

"I have had one or two little scores of my own to settle with Mr. John Clay," said Holmes. "I have been at some small expense over this matter, which I shall expect the bank to refund, but beyond that I am amply repaid by having had an experience which is in many ways unique, and by hearing the very remarkable narrative of the Red-headed League."

"You see, Watson," he explained in the early hours of the morning as we sat over a glass of whisky and soda in Baker Street, "it was per-fectly obvious from the first that the only possible object of this rather

---

16. derbies handcuffs.

fantastic business of the advertisement of the League, and the copying of the Encyclopedia, must be to get this not over-bright pawnbroker out of the way for a number of hours every day. It was a curious way of managing it, but, really, it would be difficult to suggest a better. The method was no doubt suggested to Clay's ingenious mind by the color of his accomplice's hair. The £4 a week was a lure which must draw him, and what was it to them, who were playing for thousands? They put in the advertisement, one rogue has the temporary office, the other rogue incites the man to apply for it, and together they manage to secure his absence every morning in the week. From the time that I heard of the assistant having come for half wages, it was obvious to me that he had some strong motive for securing the situation."

"But how could you guess what the motive was?"

"Had there been women in the house, I should have suspected a mere vulgar intrigue. That, however, was out of the question. The man's business was a small one, and there was nothing in his house which could account for such elaborate preparations, and such an expenditure as they were at. It must, then, be something out of the house. What could it be? I thought of the assistant's fondness for photography, and his trick of vanishing into the cellar. The cellar! There was the end of this tangled clue. Then I made inquiries as to this mysterious assistant and found that I had to deal with one of the coolest and most daring criminals in London. He was doing something in the cellar—something which took many hours a day for months on end. What could it be, once more? I could think of nothing save that he was running a tunnel to some other building.

"So far I had got when we went to visit the scene of action. I surprised you by beating upon the pavement with my stick. I was ascertaining whether the cellar stretched out in front or behind. It was not in front. Then I rang the bell, and, as I hoped, the assistant answered it. We have had some skirmishes, but we had never set eyes upon each other before. I hardly looked at his face. His knees were what I wished to see. You must yourself have remarked how worn, wrinkled, and stained they were. They spoke of those hours of burrowing. The only remaining point was what they were burrowing for. I walked round the corner, saw that the City and Suburban Bank abutted on our friend's premises, and felt that I had solved my problem. When you drove home after the concert I called upon Scotland Yard and upon the chairman of the bank directors, with the result that you have seen."

"And how could you tell that they would make their attempt tonight?" I asked.

"Well, when they closed their League offices that was a sign that they cared no longer about Mr. Jabez Wilson's presence—in other words, that they had completed their tunnel. But it was essential that they should use it soon, as it might be discovered, or the bullion might be removed. Saturday would suit them better than any other day, as it would give them two days for their escape. For all these reasons I expected them to come tonight."

Reading Strategy
Finding Key Details Even after the case is solved, Watson wonders how Holmes did it. Name the key details that explain the detective's solution.

✔**Reading Check**

As Holmes reveals his clues, what reason does he give for striking his stick against the pavement?

The Red-headed League ◆ 115

"You reasoned it out beautifully," I exclaimed in unfeigned admiration. "It is so long a chain, and yet every link rings true."

"It saved me from ennui,"[17] he answered, yawning. "Alas! I already feel it closing in upon me. My life is spent in one long effort to escape from the commonplaces of existence. These little problems help me to do so."

"And you are a benefactor of the race," said I.

He shrugged his shoulders. "Well, perhaps, after all, it is of some little use," he remarked. " *'L'homme c'est rien—l'oeuvre c'est tout,'*[18] as Gustave Flaubert wrote to George Sand."[19]

---

17. **ennui** (än′ wē) boredom.
18. ***L'homme c'est rien—l'oeuvre c'est tout*** (lum sā rē en′ lɵvr sā too) French for "Man is nothing—the work is everything."
19. **Gustave Flaubert** (goos täv′ flō ber′) . . . **George Sand** notable French novelists of the nineteenth century.

Review and Assess

Thinking About the Selection

1. **Respond: (a)** What did you think of the solution to the mystery? **(b)** Did you find it a satisfying ending to the story? Explain.

2. **(a) Recall:** Why does Jabez Wilson come to see Sherlock Holmes? **(b) Infer:** Why does Holmes find Jabez Wilson's story interesting?

3. **(a) Recall:** As a member of the exclusive Red-headed League, what job is Wilson given? **(b) Analyze:** How does Wilson's menial job with the Red-headed League help the criminals with their attempted burglary?

4. **(a) Recall:** What happens the night of the attempted burglary? **(b) Analyze:** Which clues found at Saxe-Coburg Square help Holmes solve the crime?

5. **(a) Summarize:** What strategies would you say Holmes uses to solve crimes? **(b) Apply:** Would a real detective in today's world be able to solve a crime using Holmes's methods? Why or why not?

6. **(a) Speculate:** How would this story be different if it were told by Holmes rather than by Watson? **(b) Evaluate:** Would it be more or less effective? Why?

7. **Generalize:** The main purpose of detective stories like this one is to entertain audiences. Is it also possible to learn lessons from detective stories that can be applied to your own life? Support your answer, using this story as an example.

Sir Arthur Conan Doyle

(1859–1930)

Sir Arthur Conan Doyle began his career as an eye doctor. Finding little success, he began to write mystery stories. He probably modeled his detective, Sherlock Holmes, after a medical school professor who could diagnose illnesses from clues other doctors missed.

After several rejections from publishers, Doyle sold his first detective novel, *A Study in Scarlet*, in 1887. Perhaps remembering his own medical background, Doyle made the narrator Dr. John Watson, Holmes's devoted companion.

Readers grew to love the odd detective who solved puzzling crimes. When Doyle killed off Holmes in a story in 1893, readers protested so strongly that he was forced to bring back the beloved detective.

Review and Assess

Literary Analysis

The Mystery

1. Identify the elements of a **mystery** within Jabez Wilson's story.
2. Which clues point to Vincent Spaulding as the probable criminal? Use a chart like the one shown here to list at least three clues. Then, show how the clues point to Spaulding as a probable criminal.

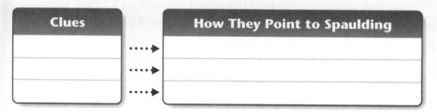

Clues		How They Point to Spaulding
	····▶	
	····▶	
	····▶	

Connecting Literary Elements

3. (a) How would you **characterize** Vincent Spaulding? (b) What techniques does Doyle use to reveal Spaulding's character?
4. (a) How would you characterize Sherlock Holmes? (b) Which of his personality traits help him solve mysteries? Record your answer in a chart like this one.

Holmes's Characteristics	How They Help Solve the Mystery

Reading Strategy

Finding Key Details

5. At the mystery's outset, Wilson relates his story to Holmes and Watson. Review his story and identify four **key details** that are clues to the mystery.
6. Explain how each of the four key details in Wilson's story suggests a solution to the mystery.

Extend Understanding

7. **Career Connection:** What are three other professions in which Holmes's reasoning skills could be useful? Give reasons for your choices.

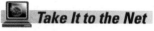

Integrate Language Skills

Vocabulary Development Lesson

Word Analysis: Latin Root -spec-

The Latin root -spec- means "see" or "look." The root appears in the word *introspective*, which means "looking inward." It also appears in the words *spectator*, *inspector*, and *spectacle*. Match each word with its definition.

1. spectator
2. inspector
3. spectacle

a. a remarkable sight
b. one who observes
c. one who looks into a matter

Spelling Strategy

When you add a prefix to a word or root, do not change the spelling of the word or root. For example, *intro- + spective = introspective*. Add a prefix such as *un-, re-, pre-,* or *mis-* to the following words to make three English words.

1. clear   2. consider   3. judge

Fluency: Context

On your paper, write the following paragraph. Using the clues you find there, fill in the blanks with words from the vocabulary list on page 95.

I'm rather shy and ___?___, but my uncle has an extremely unusual and ___?___ personality. He is both impatient and brilliant. When confronted with perplexing ___?___, he has been known to shout wildly, "Do not ___?___ me!" at no one in particular. Despite this brashness, he solves the problem. My uncle's ___?___ is regarded as ___?___ by those who respect him and as an elaborate ___?___ by those who don't. Whenever I ask for help, however, he will ___?___ himself immediately. I must say, my uncle is a very fascinating and entertaining person to know.

Grammar Lesson

Coordinate Adjectives

Adjectives are words that modify a noun or pronoun. **Coordinate adjectives** are adjectives of equal rank that separately modify the noun they precede. Use commas to separate coordinate adjectives.

To test whether adjectives are coordinate, switch their order. If the sentence still makes sense, the adjectives are coordinate.

Coordinate: . . . a very *stout, florid-faced, elderly* gentleman . . .
. . . an *elderly, florid-faced, stout* gentleman . . .

Not coordinate: In a *few short* hours, we'll know the outcome.

Practice On your paper, write the following sentences. Supply adjectives to complete them. Separate coordinate adjectives with a comma.

1. The ___?___ ___?___ goblet was stolen.
2. The ___?___ ___?___ book contained a clue.
3. The detective outwitted the ___?___ ___?___ villain.
4. People were shocked that such a ___?___ ___?___ citizen had committed the crime.
5. The detective wore a ___?___ ___?___ coat.

Writing Application Create sentences by adding nouns to each of the following pairs of coordinate adjectives.

1. sly, perceptive   2. sneaky, greedy

WG Prentice Hall Writing and Grammar Connection: Chapter 29, Section 2

Writing Lesson

Detective Story

In his story, Doyle created a detective so real that readers still write to him! Write your own detective story that will appeal to today's readers.

Prewriting Brainstorm to come up with possible crimes. Choose one of your ideas as the focus of your story. Create a diagram like the one shown, putting the crime in the center box. Elaborate with key details about the detective, the suspects, their motives, alibis, and other clues.

Detective: Sergeant Smith—intelligent, thin, quiet

Key detail: Company just changed its leadership.

Computer laptop stolen from corporate office

Suspect: Boris, janitor, works overnight

Suspect: James, office assistant, in debt

Drafting Using your diagram as a guide, write your story. Provide readers with hints to the solution of the mystery.

Revising Ask a classmate to read your story and use a highlighter to mark each clue he or she encounters. See if your classmate has noticed the hints you have provided. You may want to add hints or strengthen ones you have included.

*W*G *Prentice Hall Writing and Grammar Connection: Chapter 5, Section 2*

Extension Activities

Listening and Speaking With a partner, **role-play an interrogation** of Spaulding by Officer Jones. When you act out the scene, focus on these kinds of body language:

- posture—the way a character stands or sits and holds his head
- gestures—how a person points or waves his hand when he talks
- eye contact—the way a person does or does not look directly at another person

After a few rehearsals, present your role play to your class. **[Group Activity]**

Research and Technology Research the science of detective work. Study fingerprinting, lie detectors, or other techniques used by detectives to arrest criminals. Refer to multiple sources, such as the Internet, journals, and criminology books, to gain more information on the subject you choose. Then, prepare a **written report.**

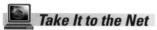 **Take It to the Net** www.phschool.com

Go online for an additional research activity using the Internet.

Prepare to Read

The Listeners ◆ Beware: Do Not Read This Poem ◆ Echo

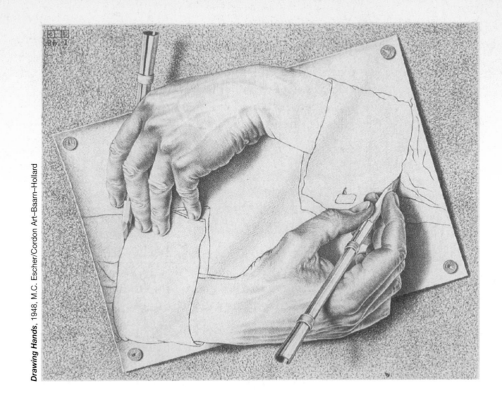

Drawing Hands, 1948, M.C. Escher/Cordon Art–Baarn–Hollard

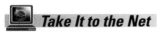
Preview

Connecting to the Literature

A man knocks on a moonlit door. A parrot screams in a jungle. A woman disappears into a mirror. Images like these are strange, and you are not sure how they connect, yet they seem to hint at an unknown story. These poems use such images to hint at mysteries and possibilities.

Background

Just as poets create mystery in lines of poetry, artists create mysterious images with the lines they draw. Dutch artist M. C. Escher (1898–1972), for example, specialized in drawings that challenge the mind and delight the imagination. Look carefully at the Escher image above and consider why it is mysterious.

Literary Analysis

Imagery

Poets do not draw pictures with pens and brushes. However, they can use picture-painting words, called **imagery**, to help you experience their ideas with all your senses—touch, taste, smell, hearing, and sight. The poems in this section use imagery in a special way to create pictures of worlds that are haunted by mystery. Notice the vivid imagery in this passage from "Echo":

> Thousands of parrots
> screamed together
> and rock echoed.

As you read the selections, look for images that appeal strongly to your senses and paint pictures of worlds haunted by mystery.

Comparing Literary Works

Just as individual artists have their own techniques for painting a picture, individual poets have their own ways of creating imagery. Much depends on each poet's **diction**, or word choice. The poet's choice of vocabulary and vividness of language contribute to the imagery and affect its ultimate forcefulness. As you read the selections, compare the diction in the poems. Pay particular attention to the following:

- unique or interesting words that contribute to an image
- vivid or intense language that paints a clear picture

Reading Strategy

Using Your Senses

By **using your senses** when you read a poem, you let the poem's language create a picture in your mind. As you read, experience each poem through your senses by focusing on language that tells how something looks, sounds, feels, smells, or tastes. Use a diagram like the one shown to record the sensory language in each selection. Write the words and phrases you find in their appropriate boxes.

Vocabulary Development

perplexed (pər plekst´) *adj.* puzzled; full of doubt (p. 122)

thronging (thrôŋ´ iŋ) *adj.* crowding into (p. 122)

legendary (lej´ ən der´ ē) *adj.* based on legends, stories handed down from one generation to the next (p. 124)

strafing (strāf´ iŋ) *adj.* attacking with machine-gun fire (p. 126)

The Listeners

Walter de la Mare

'Is there anybody there?' said the Traveler,
    Knocking on the moonlit door;
And his horse in the silence champed¹ the grasses
    Of the forest's ferny floor:
5 And a bird flew up out of the turret,
    Above the Traveler's head:
And he smote² upon the door again a second time;
    'Is there anybody there?' he said.
But no one descended to the Traveler;
10   No head from the leaf-fringed sill
Leaned over and looked into his gray eyes,
    Where he stood <u>perplexed</u> and still.
But only a host of phantom listeners
    That dwelt in the lone house then
15 Stood listening in the quiet of the moonlight
    To that voice from the world of men:
Stood <u>thronging</u> the faint moonbeams on the dark stair,
    That goes down to the empty hall,
Hearkening in an air stirred and shaken
20   By the lonely Traveler's call.
And he felt in his heart their strangeness,

---

1. **champed** (champt) *v.* chewed.
2. **smote** (smōt) *v.* struck hard.

▲ Critical Viewing
Does this painting convey the same feeling as "The Listeners"? Why or why not? **[Explain]**

Literary Analysis
Imagery Which words convey clear images in the first ten lines?

perplexed (pər plekst´) *adj.* puzzled; full of doubt

thronging (thrôŋ´ iŋ) *adj.* crowding into

Their stillness answering his cry,
While his horse moved, cropping the dark turf,
'Neath the starred and leafy sky;
25 For he suddenly smote on the door, even
        Louder, and lifted his head:—
    'Tell them I came, and no one answered,
        That I kept my word,' he said.
    Never the least stir made the listeners,
30   Though every word he spake[3]
    Fell echoing through the shadowiness of the still house
        From the one man left awake:
    Ay, they heard his foot upon the stirrup,
        And the sound of iron on stone,
35 And how the silence surged softly backward,
        When the plunging hoofs were gone.

3. **spake** (spāk) v. spoke.

Literary Analysis
Imagery Which words paint a vivid image of a forest setting?

Review and Assess

Thinking About the Selection

1. **Respond:** Did you find this poem spooky and chilling? Why or why not?

2. **(a) Recall:** Briefly describe the time and place in which the action of the poem occurs. **(b) Analyze:** Why are the time and place important?

3. **(a) Recall:** Which words are used to describe the house? **(b) Interpret:** Which other details create the eerie, dreamlike atmosphere of the poem?

4. **(a) Recall:** What information does the poet leave out? **(b) Infer:** Why do you think there are so many unanswered questions in the poem? **(c) Speculate:** What are some possible answers to these questions?

5. **(a) Recall:** What do you learn about the traveler in the poem? **(b) Infer:** Why do you think de la Mare called the poem "The Listeners" rather than "The Traveler"?

6. **Synthesize:** Would knowing more about the Traveler's actions lessen the poem's mystery? Explain.

7. **Evaluate:** Why do you think people are compelled by mysteries like this one?

Walter de la Mare

(1873–1956)

Walter de la Mare's most famous poems, like "The Listeners," tell mysterious, incomplete stories. Perhaps de la Mare, an Englishman, used his poetry to live a more intriguing life because his daytime jobs were so unmysterious. At age seventeen, for example, he worked in the statistics department of the Anglo-American Oil Company. Poems may have been his escape from numbers!

In addition to composing poems, de la Mare wrote short stories, novels, and plays. He also edited poetry anthologies.

The Listeners ◆ 123

BEWARE:
Do Not Read This Poem

Ishmael Reed

tonite, *thriller* was
abt an ol woman, so vain she
surrounded her self w/
    many mirrors

It got so bad that finally she
locked herself indoors & her
whole life became the
    mirrors

one day the villagers broke
into her house, but she was too
swift for them. she disappeared
    into a mirror
each tenant who bought the house
after that lost a loved one to
    the ol woman in the mirror:
    first a little girl
    then a young woman
    then the young woman/s husband

the hunger of this poem is legendary
it has taken in many victims
back off from this poem
it has drawn in yr feet
back off from this poem
it has drawn in yr legs
back off from this poem
it is a greedy mirror
you are into this poem. from
    the waist down
nobody can hear you can they?

Literary Analysis
Imagery What is most impressive about the image of the woman's house?

legendary (lej´ ən der´ ē) *adj.* based on legends, stories handed down from one generation to the next

```
30    this poem has had you up to here
             belch
      this poem aint got no manners
      you cant call out frm this poem
      relax now & go w/ this poem
35    move & roll on to this poem

             do not resist this poem
             this poem has yr eyes
             this poem has his head
             this poem has his arms
40           this poem has his fingers
             this poem has his fingertips

      this poem is the reader & the
             reader this poem

      statistic: the us bureau of missing persons reports
45           that in 1968 over 100,000 people disappeared
             leaving no solid clues
             nor trace        only
      a space        in the lives of their friends
```

Review and Assess

Thinking About the Selection

1. **Respond:** What feelings did Reed's poem evoke in you? Explain.

2. **(a) Recall:** What is unique about the woman's house? **(b) Analyze:** How does the description of this house add to the mystery of the poem?

3. **(a) Recall:** What does the poem say happens to those who read it? **(b) Interpret:** What does the idea of the reader's interaction suggest about the mystery of reading?

4. **(a) Recall:** Which lines in the poem refer to the poem and the reader as one? **(b) Interpret:** What message is the speaker trying to convey when he says "this poem is the reader & the/reader is this poem"? **(c) Infer:** How would you describe the speaker's tone of voice? Support your answer.

5. **(a) Analyze:** How does the sound of the poem change in the last stanza, beginning with line 44? **(b) Evaluate:** How does such an ending extend the mystery?

6. **(a) Analyze:** What details could the poet add to clarify the poem's story? **(b) Take a Position:** Considering the ways these details might alter the poem's effectiveness, would you want to include them? Explain.

Ishmael Reed

(b. 1938)

Ishmael Reed is as mysterious, many-sided, and hilarious as his poem "Beware: Do Not Read This Poem." Born in Chattanooga, Tennessee, and raised in Buffalo, New York, Reed has worked as a hospital attendant, market researcher, newspaper manager, and unemployment-office clerk.

In addition to poetry collections like *Chattanooga* (1973), Reed has written satiric novels that make fun of American westerns, as well as slave narratives, essays, plays, songs, and even operas.

Echo

Henriqueta Lisboa
Translated by
Hélcio Veiga Costa

Green parrot
let out a shrill scream.
Rock in sudden
anger, replied.

5   A great uproar
invaded the forest.
Thousands of parrots
screamed together
and rock echoed.

10   From all sides
strafing space
steely screams rained
and rained down.

Very piercing screams!

But no one died.

Literary Analysis
Imagery and Diction
What do you "hear" when you read the first stanza?

strafing (strāf′ iŋ) *adj.*
attacking with machine-gun fire

Henriqueta Lisboa

(1903–1985)

A Brazilian poet, Lisboa uses a few well-chosen words to create powerful poems. By the age of twenty, she had already published her first book of poetry. Her early lyrics deal with traditional poetic themes, while her later poems tell about the history of her region. The themes she touched upon later in her life were not uncommon ones. Many of her contemporaries, such as Brazilian writer and poet Mário de Andrade, also spoke about the significance of Brazil in their works.

Review and Assess

Thinking About the Selection

1. **Respond:** What did you find pleasant or unpleasant about the sounds in the poem?

2. **(a) Recall:** What happens in the poem? **(b) Distinguish:** Which details in the poem could realistically occur, and which could not?

3. **(a) Recall:** What does the rock do when the green parrot first screams? **(b) Speculate:** What might the rock have been demanding of the parrot?

4. **(a) Analyze:** What effect does the poem's last line have on the meaning of the poem? **(b) Interpret:** What might be the message in this poem?

5. **(a) Evaluate:** Do you think the last line improves or weakens the poem? Explain.

Review and Assess

Literary Analysis

Imagery

1. Explain how the **imagery** in "The Listeners" helps you to hear "silence" and see invisible "listeners." Identify at least one sound-based image and one sight-based one.

2. In "Beware: Do Not Read This Poem," how does the image of "a greedy mirror" help you to experience the strangeness of reading?

3. Find two examples of imagery in "Echo" and show how they create a feeling of uncertainty.

Comparing Literary Works

4. For each example of **diction** below, explain the image created by the italicized words.

Title of Poem	Examples of Diction	Image Created
The Listeners	"*echoing* through the *shadowiness* of the *still* house"	
Beware: Do Not Read This Poem	"this poem has *yr* eyes"	
Echo	"parrot let out a *shrill* scream"	

5. How does the vividness of language in "The Listeners" compare to that in "Echo"?

6. In your opinion, which of the three poets creates the most powerful images? Justify your answer with details from the poem.

Reading Strategy

Using Your Senses

7. (a) Why is sound as important as sight in experiencing the world of "The Listeners"? (b) In which of the other two poems do you *hear* a mystery? Explain.

8. (a) Which of the poems asks you to picture yourself? (b) How are you invited to see yourself?

Extend Understanding

9. **Music Connection:** If you were setting these poems to music, what type of music would you choose for each? Explain.

Integrate Language Skills

Vocabulary Development Lesson

Word Analysis: Poetic License and Vocabulary in Poems

Poetic license is a poet's freedom to break rules of vocabulary, grammar, or spelling in order to create a literary effect. For example, in "The Listeners," de la Mare uses *spake* for *spoke*. The word suggests an old-fashioned feeling. Answer these questions:

1. What other unusual word does de la Mare use in lines 5–7? What does it connote, or suggest to you?
2. Find an example of poetic license in line 32 of Ishmael Reed's poem. What connotation or association does the word have?
3. (a) What poetic license does Henriqueta Lisboa take in line 14 of her poem? (b) What effect does this violation of grammar have?

Fluency: Context

Copy the following paragraph. Fill in each blank with a word from the vocabulary list on page 121.

The detective entered the deserted house and stood in front of the mirror, ___?___. Deep inside the mysterious glass, he could see the ___?___ parrots, a species that had never existed. Hundreds of them were ___?___ a forest clearing, ___?___ the trees with their steely cries.

Spelling Strategy

When you add a suffix starting with a vowel to a base word ending with a consonant, do not change the spelling of the base word: *legend* + *-ary* = *legendary*. Add each suffix indicated to form a new word.

1. travel (*-er*) 2. appear (*-ance*) 3. green (*-ish*)

Grammar Lesson

Types of Adjectives

An **adjective** is a word used to describe a noun or pronoun or to give a noun or pronoun a more specific meaning. Adjectives modify nouns and pronouns by telling *what kind, which one, how many,* or *how much.* Sometimes a noun, pronoun, or verb may serve as an adjective.

> **Adjective:** the *lone* house (modifies *house*)
> **Noun as Adjective:** *phantom* listeners (modifies *listeners*)
> **Pronoun as Adjective:** felt in *his* heart (modifies *heart*)
> **Verb as Adjective:** an air *stirred* and *shaken* (modify *air*)

Practice Identify each word that serves as an adjective. Then, determine whether the word is an *adjective, noun, pronoun,* or *verb.*

1. They saw the faint moonbeams on the dark stair.
2. The silence surged backwards when the plunging hoofs disappeared.
3. Her whole life became the mirrors.
4. The forest bird let out a shrill scream.
5. Green parrots screamed piercing screams.

Writing Application Use each of the following words as an adjective in a sentence.

1. echoing   3. paper
2. strange   4. your

*W*_G *Prentice Hall Writing and Grammar Connection: Chapter 18, Section 1*

Writing Lesson

Comparison-and-Contrast Essay

The poems in this section use imagery to create pictures. Write a comparison-and-contrast essay comparing the imagery found in two of the poems.

Prewriting   Decide which two poems generated the strongest or clearest word pictures for you. Then, complete a Venn diagram in which you jot down the similarities and differences between these two poems.

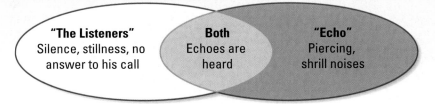

"The Listeners"
Silence, stillness, no answer to his call

Both
Echoes are heard

"Echo"
Piercing, shrill noises

Drafting   Write a sentence to identify the comparison or contrast you will address. In each body paragraph of your essay, focus on one poem, citing examples of vivid language that produces an image.

Revising   Reread your essay to make sure you have used appropriate transition words. To show similarities, use words such as *all*, *similarly*, *both*, *in the same way*, and *equally*. To show differences, use words such as *on the other hand*, *in contrast*, and *however*.

 Prentice Hall Writing and Grammar Connection: Chapter 9, Section 2

Extension Activities

Listening and Speaking   In a small group, write a **dramatic scene** that takes place in "the lone house" of "the listeners" after the Traveler has galloped away. Assign each group member one of the following roles: actor, director, or set designer.

- Use your scene to answer some of the questions left unanswered by the poem.
- Then, act out the scene you have created.
- You may choose to videotape your drama or produce it onstage.

After acting out your scene, ask your audience to help you analyze the production. **[Group Activity]**

Research and Technology   "Echo" is set in Brazil's tropical rain forest. Give a **multimedia presentation** on this environment, taking the class on a magical mystery tour through its wonders. Use an atlas to gather information about the locations of Brazil's rain forests. Then, use the Internet to research the kinds of plants, animals, and weather found in those locations. Present your findings to the class.

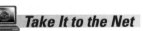 **Take It to the Net**   www.phschool.com

Go online for an additional research activity using the Internet.

Prepare to Read

Caucasian Mummies Mystify Chinese

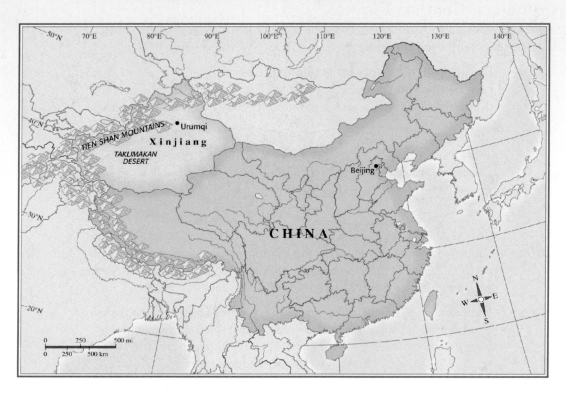

 Take It to the Net

Visit www.phschool.com
for interactive activities
and instruction related to
"Caucasian Mummies
Mystify Chinese," including
- background
- graphic organizers
- literary elements
- reading strategies

Preview

Connecting to the Literature

Unsolved mysteries, such as how the Egyptian pyramids were built or why huge slabs of rock were placed in circles at Stonehenge, are popular subjects for books, articles, and television programs. This article focuses on the discovery of mysterious Caucasian mummies in what is now China.

Background

While you may connect mummies with ancient Egypt, they actually have been found all over the world, including China, Europe, Peru, and Mexico. Because people often were buried with their clothes, tools, and even food, mummies can teach us much about how ancient peoples lived.

Literary Analysis

News Article

The purpose of a **news article** such as "Caucasian Mummies Mystify Chinese" is to inform you—the reader—by providing facts that answer six questions: *Who? What? When? Where? Why?* and *How?* To help you answer these questions, pay close attention to the following parts of the article:

- the lead, or opening sentences
- details in the form of facts, statistics, and summaries
- opinions and quotations from experts and eyewitnesses

As you read the article, answer as many questions as you can after reading the first paragraph. Then, continue to look for additional answers in the facts and expert opinions that follow.

Connecting Literary Elements

News reporters are taught to write with **objectivity,** presenting the facts only, without opinions or judgments on the subject. By using objective language, the writer lets readers form their own opinions without influence. Pay close attention to the presentation of information in this article. Ask yourself if the writer is being objective, and notice whether certain words or details suggest an opinion or position.

Reading Strategy

Finding the Main Idea

When reading a news article, **finding the main idea** is a critical skill. The main idea in a news article is its most important point. Often, the main idea is stated in the lead paragraph. You can also determine the main idea by answering the six questions addressed in the article, and then deciding on the main point based on your answers.

As you read the article, use a chart like the one shown to record answers to the six questions: *Who? What? When? Where? Why?* and *How?*

Who?	
What?	
When?	
Where?	
Why?	
How?	

Vocabulary Development

dogmas (dôg′ məz) *n.* firmly held beliefs or doctrines (p. 133)

parched (pärcht) *adj.* dried up by heat (p. 133)

archaeologist (är′ kē äl′ ə jist) *n.* person who studies the remains of ancient ways of life (p. 133)

imperialist (im pir′ ē əl ist) *adj.* here, describing a person from a country that seeks to dominate weaker countries (p. 134)

subjugation (sub′ jə gā′ shən) *n.* enslavement (p. 136)

reconcile (rek′ ən sīl′) *v.* bring into agreement (p. 136)

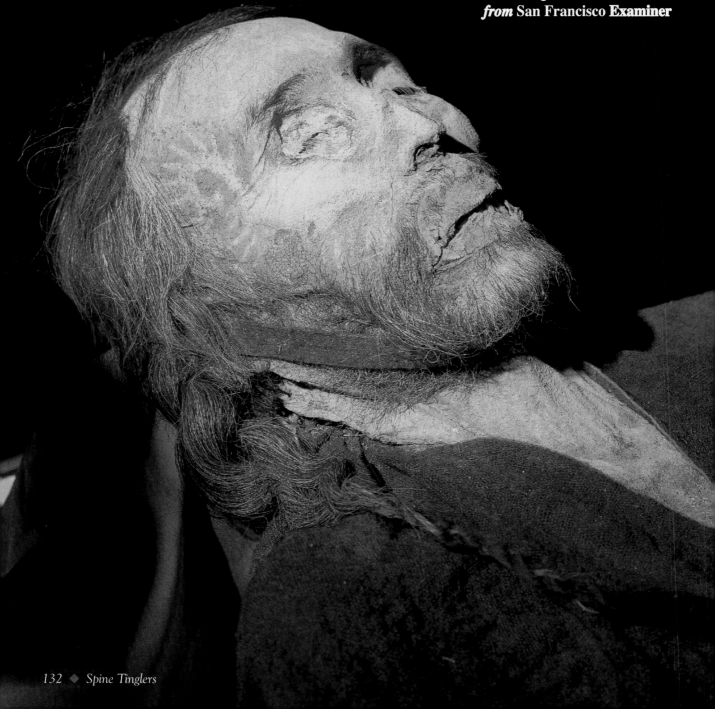

Caucasian Mummies Mystify Chinese

Keay Davidson
from San Francisco **Examiner**

San Francisco—In dim light they appear to be sleeping, but they've been dead up to 4,000 years: more than 100 astoundingly well-preserved mummies unearthed in a Chinese desert, whose inexplicably blond hair and white skin could topple <u>dogmas</u> about early human history.

A former Stanford scientist is analyzing the mummies' DNA in hopes of answering haunting questions: Who are they? Where did they come from? And what on earth were these European-looking men, women and children doing in China's <u>parched</u> out-back 2,000 years before Jesus, when Europe was largely a dark forest? Sixteen years after the first mummies were found, the Chinese government has granted Western researchers their first close look at these faces from prehistory: a baby in colorful swaddling clothes; a 20-year-old girl with braided hair, found buried in a curled-up position with her hands by her chest, as if dozing; a man with a pigtail, scarlet-colored clothes and red, blue, and amber leg wrappings. . . .

The discovery—which could have far greater impact on our understanding of societal evolution than the lone, ancient "ice man" uncovered in the Alps in 1991—is described in an article by science writer Evan Hadingham in the April 1994 issue of *Discover* magazine. Based on the *Discover* article and *San Francisco Examiner* interviews with experts on genetics and Chinese history and culture, here's how the discoveries unfolded. In 1978 and 1979, Chinese <u>archaeologist</u> Wang Binghua found the first of what would prove to be more than 100 mummies in Xinjiang (zin jē ang´) Province. They had white skin, blond hair, long noses and skulls, and deep-set eyes—Caucasians,[1] perhaps from Northern Europe.

Little Attention in the West

Only scanty press reports have reached the West, at least partly because of the region's isolation, Chinese bureaucratic inertia and the regime's suppression of foreign contacts, particularly after the Tiananmen Square massacre[2] of 1989.

Now the cloud of mystery is lifting thanks to an investigation organized by University of Pennsylvania China scholar Victor Mair, in collaboration with researchers in China, the United States and Italy. The collaboration required delicate negotiations with Chinese officials.

It would have been "absolutely unthinkable" for Chinese authorities

---

1. **Caucasian** (kô kā´ zhən) *adj.* belonging to one of the major geographical groups of human beings, including the native peoples of Europe, who are loosely called the white race, though their skin colors may vary.
2. **Tiananmen** (tyen´ ə mən) **Square massacre** the murder of approximately 3,000 pro-democracy demonstrators by Chinese soldiers in Beijing, the capital of China, on June 3 and 4, 1989.

◀ **Critical Viewing** What features of this mummy might help scientists to deduce facts about the man and his life? **[Deduce]**

dogmas (dôg´ məz) *n.* firmly held beliefs or doctrines

parched (pärcht) *adj.* dried up by heat

Literary Analysis
News Article What questions does the writer answer in this paragraph?

archaeologist (är´ kē äl´ ə jist) *n.* person who studies the remains of ancient ways of life

✓**Reading Check**
Where were more than 100 mummies found?

▲ **Critical Viewing** Find the Xinjiang province on the map. Based on its location, explain why Europeans might have settled in that particular part of China. **[Draw Conclusions]**

to grant Westerners such access—including tissue samples from the mummies—only five years ago, Mair told *The Examiner*. "In the 1910s and 1920s, it was a game of the <u>imperialist</u> (Western) archaeologists to go in and take away important stuff—ancient manuscripts, artworks, paintings, statues . . . (Chinese officials are) very sensitive to that and they don't want to make the same situation recur," Mair said.

He also speculates that some Chinese officials may have initially hesitated to ballyhoo the find because they didn't know what to make of all those Caucasian faces. They date from a time when, according to regional histories and national pride, China was advancing—developing writing and metal artifacts and wheeled vehicles—without help from foreign meddlers.

imperialist (im pir´ ē əl ist) *adj.* here, describing a person from a country that seeks to dominate weaker countries

Bodies' Condition Excellent

The mummies were unearthed at scattered burial sites in an approximately 500-mile-wide region of northwest China, between the so-called Celestial (Tian Shan) Mountains and the Taklimakan (täk´ li mä kän´) Desert. They range in age from 2000 B.C. to 300 B.C., based largely on radiocarbon dating.

Reading Strategy
Finding the Main Idea
How does this subhead and others help you to determine the article's main idea?

Where do they come from? At the University of Sassari in Italy, anthropological geneticist[3] Paolo Francalacci—who worked at Stanford until recently—hopes to determine the mummies' likely place of origin by comparing their DNA, or genetic material, with modern DNA from different societies.

"It will take time before we know anything (from the DNA analysis)," cautions Francalacci's Stanford colleague, Luigi Luca Cavalli-Sforza, a population geneticist. "It's a very tricky type of analysis. Old DNA is generally very damaged.

"What I find most surprising of all is that these mummies were in such perfect condition," Cavalli-Sforza said. Their European-looking features are "sufficient, I think, to say these people came from Northern Europe. . . . My guess is that these (people) were kind of 'scouts' (who) were, most probably, traveling east and maybe settled there (in Xinjiang)." He believes thousands of mummies may yet be found.

Why has it taken so long for the news to get Western scholars' attention? While Western news media trumpeted the 5,000-year-old "ice man" found in the Austrian and Italian Alps, they have ignored the Chinese find—almost. . . .

Poor Chinese public relations could be partly to blame. Mair suspects that in the late 1970s, Chinese scholars were so startled by the Caucasian mummies that they weren't sure what to do with them.

"I think it flummoxed them when they found these Caucasian people out there . . . it's not what they expected," he said. "They didn't know how to put it into any of their schemes for history; it just didn't make sense to them. . . ."

Nagging Questions

In 1987, Mair happened to be touring China when he entered a museum in Urumqi (ür üm´ chē) that displayed mummies of a man, woman and child—a family, as it appeared. They had died 3,000 years earlier, "yet the bodies looked as if they were buried yesterday," he said.

What left him "thunderstruck," though, was their faces: They were Caucasians, apparently of European origin. "The questions kept nagging at me: Who were these people? How did they get out here at such an early date?"

The April 1994 issue of *Discover* includes a gallery of color photos of the corpses. They include a man with a painted image of the sun— a religious symbol?—on the temple of his head; the baby in swaddling clothes, its eyes covered with stones—a burial ritual?; a woman in a tall, peaked hat, . . . and a woman wearing a fur-lined coat, leather mittens and a two-pointed hat that, according to Chinese archaeologists, indicates she might have had *two husbands*—a possible result of a shortage of females. They were buried in simple graves, roughly 6 feet deep, with mats at the bottom. Some graves contain artifacts

Reading Strategy
Finding the Main Idea
How does this question in the article help you to determine the main idea?

Literary Analysis
News Article and Objectivity Is objective writing evident in this paragraph? Why or why not?

**Reading Check**

Why does one scientist say it is difficult to analyze the DNA of the mummies?

---

3. **anthropological geneticist** one who studies the historical development of human beings through the examination of their genes.

hinting that the living mourned the dead: For example, a baby was buried with a sort of milk bottle fashioned from a sheep's udder.

"This is my favorite story in the seven years that I've edited *Discover* . . . because we were able to publish something monumental before anyone else," said the magazine's editor, Paul Hoffman.

Traditionally, Chinese historians insist that their society evolved on its own with little foreign input. That view has played well in modern China, which resents its past <u>subjugation</u> to foreign imperialists.

But Mair says the traditional view is hard to <u>reconcile</u> with the discovery of so many Caucasians who lived in what is now the westernmost edge of China, thousands of years before Marco Polo.[4] "The archaeological, linguistic, and textual evidence forces me to conclude that China has both significantly influenced and been influenced by other civilizations throughout history and, indeed, prehistory," Mair said. . . .

subjugation (sub′ jə gā′ shən) *n.* enslavement

reconcile (rek′ ən sīl′) *v.* bring into agreement

---

4. **Marco Polo** (1254–1324) Italian traveler and trader considered to be the first European to cross the length of Asia.

Review and Assess

Thinking About the Selection

1. **Respond:** What else would you like to know about the Caucasian mummies and the way these ancient people lived?

2. **(a) Recall:** What is remarkable about the mummies' appearance? **(b) Analyze:** Why did Chinese officials react as they did to the discovery of the mummies?

3. **(a) Recall:** Where do experts think the people found in the Chinese desert originally lived? **(b) Infer:** How has the discovery of the mummies changed historians' views of early Chinese culture?

4. **(a) Recall:** In what year were the first mummies unearthed? **(b) Interpret:** Why was there a delay between this event and the involvement of Western scholars and scientists?

5. **(a) Recall:** What tests are scientists conducting on the mummies? **(b) Speculate:** How will the tests help unlock the mystery surrounding this discovery?

6. **(a) Evaluate:** Do you think the reporter clearly communicated why the discovery of the mummies was so important? Why or why not? **(b) Assess:** What did you find most interesting about this article? Why?

7. **Extend:** Explain whether you think that real-life mysteries, like this one, are more or less interesting than those made up by storytellers.

Keay Davidson

(b. 1953)

Keay Davidson loves to write about science and technology. As a science reporter and author of books and magazine articles, he tracks the latest information on everything from NASA to tornadoes.

Davidson began as a newspaper reporter in Georgia while still in college. He moved to Florida in 1976 and later began to write about the space program. In 1981, he became a science reporter for the *Los Angeles Times* and, later, the *San Francisco Examiner*.

As a writer, Davidson coauthored *Wrinkles in Time*, a book about new scientific theories on the origins of the universe. In 1996, when the movie *Twister* swept through theaters, Davidson explained the science behind the special effects in his book *Twister: The Science of Tornadoes*.

Review and Assess

Literary Analysis

News Article

1. (a) Which details of the **news article's** lead are written to grab a reader's attention? (b) Does it make you want to read on? Why or why not?
2. (a) How do the quotations from an expert on China help you understand the news that is being reported? (b) Identify at least two quotations and explain how they extend your understanding.
3. How might this story have been different if it had been written as an encyclopedia article?

Connecting Literary Elements

4. To maintain a position of **objectivity,** the writer links positions he presents to specific authorities. Identify three opinions in the article. For each, indicate the source, or who gave the opinion.
5. How objective is Davidson's article? Support your answer.
6. How might your reaction to the article have been different if Davidson had been less objective—for example, more enthusiastic or more critical?

Reading Strategy

Finding the Main Idea

7. (a) Review the article and answer the questions in the chart shown. (b) Based on your answers to the questions, what do you think is the **main idea** of the article?

What is being tested?		**When** were the mummies found?	
Who is performing the testing?		**Why** is the discovery of these mummies important?	
Where were the mummies found?		**How** does the discovery change historians' views on early Chinese culture?	

Extend Understanding

8. **Science Connection:** In what way does the work of archaeologists have an impact on the way we live today?

Quick Review

A **news article** is written to inform you about a topic by answering six questions: *Who? What? When? Where? Why?* and *How?*

Objectivity in a news article requires the presentation of facts only, free of the writer's opinions or judgments.

The **main idea** in a news article is its most important point.

 Take It to the Net
www.phschool.com
Take the interactive self-test online to check your understanding of the selection.

Integrate Language Skills

Vocabulary Development Lesson

Word Analysis: Greek Suffix -ist

The Greek suffix -ist means "one who practices." For example, the suffix appears in the word archaeologist, which means "one who practices archaeology." Use your knowledge of -ist to define each of these words:

1. geneticist   2. linguist   3. nutritionist

Spelling Strategy

When you add an ending to a word that ends in y preceded by a consonant, change the y to i before adding the suffix. For example, when you add -ous to mystery, you form the word mysterious. For each item, write the new word formed.

1. history + -an   3. rely + -able
2. mummy + -fy   4. carry + -ed

Concept Development: Synonyms

For each item below, write the word that is the best synonym, or closest match, for the first word.

1. dogmas: (a) documents, (b) beliefs, (c) rumors
2. parched: (a) dried, (b) sophisticated, (c) curved
3. archaeologist: (a) leader, (b) caretaker, (c) scientist
4. imperialist: (a) dominating, (b) wise, (c) proud
5. subjugation: (a) enslavement, (b) freedom, (c) celebration
6. reconcile: (a) interpretation, (b) settle, (c) begin

Grammar Lesson

Proper and Compound Adjectives

A **proper adjective** is a proper noun used as an adjective or an adjective formed from a proper noun. A **compound adjective** is an adjective that is made up of more than one word. Compound adjectives are usually hyphenated. In a few cases, they are written as combined words.

> **Proper Adjective:** *February* weather (a proper noun used as an adjective)
>
> **Proper Adjective:** *Chinese* government (a form of a proper noun, *China*, used as an adjective)
>
> **Compound Adjective:** *fur-lined* coat; *underpaid* researchers

Practice Identify the proper and compound adjectives in each sentence below.

1. The mummy of a young woman in a curled-up position was found.
2. A Chinese archaeologist found the first of the mummies.
3. The mummies had deep-set eyes.
4. The Chinese government allowed Western researchers to see the findings.
5. Some of the photos of the corpses showed a woman in a fur-lined coat.

Writing Application Write four sentences, using at least two proper adjectives and at least two compound adjectives.

W̶G Prentice Hall Writing and Grammar Connection: Chapter 18, Section 1

Writing Lesson

News Feature

Though usually based at least indirectly on a news event, news features, like Davidson's article, provide information of general interest, explore the human-interest angle of a news story, or describe a personality. Write your own news feature about a subject of interest—perhaps a hobby, sports hero, or fashion trend.

Prewriting   Start by planning a lead that will grab the reader's attention. If none comes to mind, think of the questions you will answer in the feature. One of your answers may spark an idea.

Model: Grabbing the Reader's Attention

It stretches. It twists. It comes in all sizes and colors. And it never needs washing. What's the latest fad to hit high schools all across America? It's rubber-band jewelry.

> This lead gets the reader's attention by offering several details about the subject before identifying it.

Drafting   Once you have created an attention-grabbing lead, keep readers interested with details that answer *who, what, when, where, why,* and *how* about your subject. Remember to offer facts only, without your personal opinion.

Revising   Read your news feature as though you know nothing about the topic. Circle words or ideas that need more elaboration, and then add any details that will clarify the writing.

WG *Prentice Hall Writing and Grammar Connection: Chapter 12, Section 2*

Extension Activities

Listening and Speaking Imagine that you were the first archaeologist to uncover the Caucasian mummies of China. Now, you have been invited by colleagues to do a **visual presentation** of your findings at an archaeology conference. Using maps and photographs, explain to your colleagues

- how you came to discover the mummies.
- what happened as a result of your discovery.
- why your discovery is so important.

Answer as many *who, what, where, when, why,* and *how* questions as possible in your presentation.

Research and Technology In a group, create a **travel brochure** promoting a tour of archaeological sites in China where mummies have been uncovered. Make sure your brochure includes maps, illustrations, and detailed explanations of the important sites. Use library resources to find photographs and information about the sites included in your brochure. **[Group Activity]**

 Take It to the Net   www.phschool.com

Go online for an additional research activity using the Internet.

Writing WORKSHOP

Narration: Autobiographical Narrative

In an **autobiographical narrative,** a writer relates an experience from his or her life. In this workshop, you will write an autobiographical narrative that tells a story from your life.

Assignment Criteria. Your autobiographical narrative should have the following characteristics:

- Yourself as the main character
- A sequence of events that suggests an insight you gained
- Action that accommodates shifts in time and mood
- Concrete details that describe sights, sounds, smells, and physical sensations
- Your personal feelings, thoughts, or views

To preview the criteria on which your autobiographical narrative may be assessed, see the Rubric on page 143.

Prewriting

Choose a topic. Write your autobiographical narrative about a topic of importance to you. Try **blueprinting** to identify an idea. First, sketch a blue-print of a place you remember well. Label each room or area. Then, jot down words or phrases you associate with these areas. Choose one of these ideas as the topic of your narrative.

Gather details. Record as many details as possible about the idea you have chosen. One idea may remind you of others. Review your notes and narrow your list to the details you will include in your narrative.

Structure the sequence. Create a detailed record of the order of events in your narrative by making a **timeline.** Write down the first event related to the subject of your narra-tive. Record subsequent events in the order in which they occurred.

Timeline

1 Dreamed of riding bike with no training wheels.

2 Dad took off training wheels.

3 Rode two-wheeled bike and fell.

4 Improved riding. Tried other activities.

Add personal thoughts. Look at the list of events you will include in your narrative, and note what you were thinking when each event occurred. Consider adding these thoughts to your narrative to enrich the writing.

Example

Event:	My mom suggested I play outside.
First Thought:	I thought of riding my bike without training wheels.
Second Thought:	I worried about whether I could ride a two-wheeled bike without falling.

Student Model

Before you draft your autobiographical narrative, read this student model and review the characteristics of effective autobiographical narrative.

Albert Kim
Palos Verdes, CA

Leaving Fear Behind

It all happened one day when my mom suggested that I go outside and play, not just stay inside as I usually did. At five years old, I really enjoyed staying inside my cozy house. The only outdoor activity that I ever did up to that point was ride a rusty bicycle with training wheels on it, but I often thought of what it would be like to ride it without those wheels.

> Albert is the main character in this narrative.

One night I dreamed of riding a bike with no training wheels. The bike felt large and unsteady. I couldn't keep my balance, and I fell down. I woke up right when I hit the ground. Then I was more scared than ever.

Every day I thought about riding that bike. Then I said to myself that I needed to do whatever I could to get rid of the tension. I decided that I had to do it. I had to ride a bike without those old wheels so I could feel good again.

> Words that indicate time passing suggest a sequence of events.

Late one afternoon, my dad used all kinds of tools to take off those old, rusty training wheels. My bike was ready. I got on, trying to sit still, while my dad held the back of the seat. I was still shaking because I was scared. Pedaling as fast as I could, I didn't realize that my dad had already let go. I was riding! This was unbelievable! I felt the soft, cool breeze rushing across my face.

Suddenly, something went wrong. My joy quickly faded. I couldn't stop my bike! I was barreling toward the end of the street. There was a very sharp and narrow curve ahead. To my horror, I realized I hadn't yet learned how to make a sharp turn, not even with wheels on. When I was about two feet from the curve, I turned the front wheel as hard as I could and my feet got stuck in the pedals. WHAM! I crashed and scraped my leg. The next thing I knew, I was laughing. Even though I was hurt, I was very happy and glad that I had accomplished what I had wanted to do.

> The writer describes the action using physical sensations and shifts in mood.

Since then I have tried many new things: swimming, games, and other activities. I found out that I am really good at the things I have tried. Learning to ride without training wheels was the first time I ever took a chance on trying something new. Because I was successful, I was not afraid to try other things. I crossed a threshold in my life and left fear behind.

> The writer suggests an insight he gained as a result of the experience.

Drafting

Identify your main point. As you draft your narrative, think about why the story you have chosen to tell might be meaningful to others. When you have determined what you want your audience to understand, organize your details to highlight the importance of that main point.

Organize events. The description of events adds substance to your autobiographical essay. Too much description, however, can distract a reader from your main point. Instead, choose details to accomplish these goals:

- Highlighting the central conflict that sets the events in motion.
- Creating tension that builds to a climax, or turning point.
- Offering insights related to your main point.

Elaborate. As you draft your autobiographical narrative, remember that you can make your story even more vivid by providing detailed information. The chart shown here provides some tips to help you elaborate further on an idea.

Basic Story Element	Elaboration Tip
Experience to narrate	Explain its main effect on you.
Time and place	Describe impressions using sensory details, including sights, smells, sounds, and tastes.
Suspense	Add details that raise the tension and heighten the story's problem.
Main events of story	Include thoughts or feelings that occurred to you at the time of the events.
Story outcome	Consider other possible outcomes of events.

Revising

Explode a moment. To help your readers experience the event as you did, add details that bring your thoughts and feelings to life. Read your draft and highlight moments in your narrative where you can expand your idea by telling more about what you were thinking, what it looked or felt like, or how others reacted. Then, jot down these details on a separate piece of paper and incorporate them into your revised draft.

Model: Exploding a Moment

The bike felt large and unsteady.

One night I dreamed of riding a bike with no training wheels. I couldn't keep my balance, and I fell down. I woke up right when I hit the ground. Then I was more scared than ever.

Albert adds details to describe the nervous feeling before he lost his balance.

Revise to vary your sentences. Even though your autobiographical narrative is about an event that happened to you, you should avoid beginning every sentence with *I*. Look closely at the sentences in your draft, and vary sentence beginnings to make your draft more interesting. Compare the model and the nonmodel. Why is the model more effective than the nonmodel?

Nonmodel	Model
I didn't realize that my dad had already let go. I was riding! I couldn't believe it! I felt the soft, cool breeze rushing across my face.	My dad had already let go without my realizing it. I was riding! This was unbelievable! I felt the soft, cool breeze rushing across my face.

Publishing and Presenting

Share your writing with a wider audience by presenting your story to your classmates.

Deliver an oral presentation. Practice reading your story aloud. Mark up a copy of your autobiographical narrative, underlining any dialogue, thoughts, or conversations that you believe your audience would enjoy. As you present to your classmates, emphasize those passages.

Post your essay. Create a bulletin board display of the essays written by you and your classmates. Have each writer supply a short comment about the event or idea that inspired the writing. Add photographs if they are available.

 Speaking Connection
To learn more about presenting an autobiographical narrative, see the **Listening and Speaking Workshop,** p. 144.

 Prentice Hall Writing and Grammar Connection: Chapter 4

Rubric for Self-Assessment

Evaluate your autobiographical narrative using the following criteria and rating scale:

Criteria	Rating Scale				
	Not very				Very
How central are you to the action of the story?	1	2	3	4	5
How clearly organized is the sequence of events?	1	2	3	4	5
How well does the action accommodate shifts in time and mood?	1	2	3	4	5
How powerfully are concrete and sensory details used to describe events?	1	2	3	4	5
How well do you convey your insights, thoughts, and feelings?	1	2	3	4	5

Listening and Speaking WORKSHOP

Delivering a Narrative Presentation

Narrative presentations use storytelling to describe a sequence of events with meaning for an audience. You give a narrative presentation every time you tell friends what happened in a movie or sports event. Certain qualities make a narrative presentation effective—a clear story line, a description of place and time, a sense of mood, and an indication of importance to the audience or speaker.

Prepare the Presentation

Choose a compelling story. The best stories are so interesting they actually compel the audience to pay attention. For your presentation, choose a true or fictional story that lends itself easily to retelling and will have an impact on your audience.

Practice telling the story. Practice delivering your narrative to family members or friends first. After you learn which parts people like best, you can emphasize those. Your story will get better with every retelling.

Deliver the Presentation

The same aspects that you enjoy when watching an exciting performance are the ones that will make your presentation enjoyable for an audience. Incorporate these strategies into your presentation:

Use variation to hook your audience. Make your narrative more interesting by varying your voice and body language.

- Let your voice rise and fall according to the effect you want to create. Add dramatic pauses to create suspense.
- Quicken your pace to show excitement or slow it down to indicate the passage of time.
- Use gestures and facial expressions to enhance story events.

Indicate significance. When you tell a personal narrative, communicate how the event had an impact on your life. If you are giving a narrative about a larger event, such as the Civil War, explain its influence on other events of the time.

Control nervous energy. As you speak before a group, you may fidget or sway. Work to stand still, making only movements that enhance your words.

> ### Narrative Presentation Self-Evaluation
>
> - Do you think your audience understood the point of your presentation? If not, how could you have communicated this better?
> - Which aspects of your story did others like best? Do you agree? Why?
> - Which parts of your narrative were hard to describe?
> - What changes would you make to improve your presentation?

Activity: Analyzing a Speech — Rehearse and deliver a short narrative presentation in front of a group. Use the feedback you get from others and the self-evaluation form above to help you critique your presentation.

Assessment WORKSHOP

Context Clues

The reading sections of some tests require you to read a passage and answer multiple-choice questions about word meanings. Frequently, you can determine the meanings of unfamiliar words by using context clues. The following strategies can help you answer test questions on word meanings:

- Skim the *context* of an unfamiliar word—words or phrases surrounding the word that might provide clues to its meaning.
- Search for explanations or descriptions that include details or examples.
- Consider the ideas presented in the sentences before and after an unfamiliar word or phrase. Determine a meaning consistent with the entire passage.

Sample Test Item

Directions: Read the passage, and then answer the question that follows.

Fred was furious that Jonathan hadn't put any gas in his car after borrowing it for the day. Even though they had not discussed it, Fred was sure they had a tacit understanding that Jonathan would return the car with a full tank.

1. The word tacit in this passage means ___?___

   A written

   B spoken

   C legal

   D unspoken

Answer and Explanation

D is the correct answer. There is no context that supports *A, B,* or *C.* The phrase "Even though they had not discussed it" provides a clue that *tacit* means "unspoken."

Practice

Directions: Read the passage, and then answer the questions that follow.

After the entry-level position had gone unfilled for two months, Ms. Harding reviewed Carl Borden's application. He had seemed somewhat reticent at the start of his interview, but perhaps his silent manner was due to nervousness. After a few rounds of light banter, he was talking comfortably about his qualifications.

1. In this passage, the word reticent means ___?___

   A untruthful

   B relaxed

   C reserved

   D argumentative

2. The word banter means ___?___

   A analysis

   B debate

   C persuasion

   D small talk

Human Achievement, Tsing-Fang Chen, Lucia Gallery, NYC

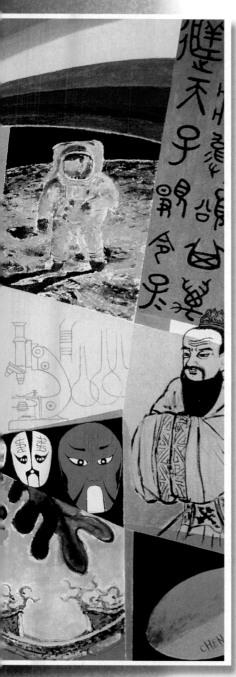

Exploring the Theme

An athlete challenges herself to be the best she can be. A powerful leader makes difficult decisions that can affect an entire nation. No matter who you are, life involves facing challenges and making choices. In these stories, poems, and essays, you will see how people in many different situations confront challenges and choices in their daily lives.

Rosa Parks did not know that her refusal to give up her seat on a Birmingham bus would spark a crucial struggle in the civil rights movement. In "My Story," Parks shows us that people approach challenges in different ways and make decisions for all kinds of reasons. Some decisions are made quietly, by ordinary people with little fanfare. But they can take as much courage, and have as much impact, as the decisions of a president.

▲ **Critical Viewing** What different types of human achievement are represented in this painting? **[Analyze]**

Why Read Literature?

Whenever you read, you have a purpose, or reason. Perhaps you choose a literary work because you know little about its subject. Or maybe you pick up a selection because the subject is familiar and you enjoy reading about it. Preview some purposes you might set before reading the works in this unit.

1 Read for the Love of Literature

Interestingly, certain stories seem enhanced by their predictability. The fun is in watching the details unfold and finding out whether you guessed right in the end. Predict the winner of a showdown in ancient China in Ray Bradbury's **"The Golden Kite, the Silver Wind,"** page 178.

Most of us would come up short if asked to describe the complex give and take, graceful arcs, and physical battering of a good pickup game of basketball. If it takes a poem to capture the twists and turns, fakes, and sudden soaring movements of a beautiful game, you could do no better than Yusef Komunyakaa's **"Slam, Dunk, and Hook,"** page 228.

2 Read for Information

Even if a story is completely mythical, it can still be a rich source of information. Greek myths tell us much about the values, views, and beliefs of the ancient Greeks. Find out why a little help from the gods was not considered dishonest for a hero with fate on his side in Edith Hamilton's **"Perseus,"** page 214.

3 Read to Be Inspired

In his autobiography, Martin Luther King, Jr., reveals that he stopped looking at his notes halfway through his speech at the March on Washington. Knowing that he spoke from spontaneous heartfelt emotion could explain the power of a speech considered one of the most eloquent in human history. Join the millions who drew inspiration from King's words as you read **"I Have a Dream,"** page 164.

 Take It to the Net

Visit the Web site for online instruction and activities related to each selection in this unit.
www.phschool.com

How to Read Literature

Use Interactive Reading Strategies

When you read, you are not just viewing words on a page. You are also thinking about the ideas, images, and information presented in the text. With difficult or unfamiliar topics, you might find it harder to interact with the text. Use these strategies to help you get involved.

1. Establish a purpose for reading.

- Determine the reason you wish to read a work of literature. For example, you might read for entertainment or to learn information.
- Read the selection and note the facts and details that help you achieve your original purpose.
- Use a K-W-L chart, like the one at right, to help define your purpose and evaluate the selection.

2. Respond.

Readers bring their own set of expectations, beliefs, and experiences to the literature they read. To tap your own responses:

- Compare events in the selection with your own experiences.
- Use the author's text as a way to examine your own feelings about the subject.
- Consider the lessons of the piece and how you might use them in your own life.

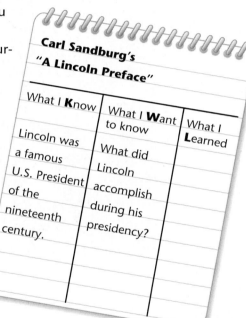

Carl Sandburg's "A Lincoln Preface"

What I **K**now	What I **W**ant to know	What I **L**earned
Lincoln was a famous U.S. President of the nineteenth century.	What did Lincoln accomplish during his presidency?	

3. Predict.

- Pause as you complete sections of a story to think about what might happen next.
- Base your predictions on what has already happened in the story, personal experience, or prior knowledge of the subject.

4. Generate questions.

To make sure you remain fully involved with a selection, generate questions to answer as you read.

- Use the common question words *who, what, where, when, why,* and *how* to review what you have read.
- Think about any unanswered questions you might still have as you read future passages.
- If you still have unanswered questions after finishing, discuss the work with others or do research to complete your understanding.

As you read the selections in this unit, apply these reading strategies to interact with the text.

Prepare to Read

from A Lincoln Preface

Lincoln Proclaiming Thanksgiving, Dean Cornwell, The Lincoln Museum, Fort Wayne, Indiana, a part of Lincoln National Corp.

 Take It to the Net

Visit www.phschool.com for interactive activities and instruction related to "A Lincoln Preface," including
- background
- graphic organizers
- literary elements
- reading strategies

Preview

Connecting to the Literature

Whether we admire them for their achievements, abilities, or fine qualities, we are often inspired to pay tribute to our heroes in some way. Imagine being inspired to write a six-volume biography, as Carl Sandburg did for his hero, Abraham Lincoln.

Background

Abraham Lincoln is remembered as one of our greatest presidents, yet at the time of his election in 1860, less than half the country supported him. One reason is that Lincoln was opposed to slavery—and many landowners in the south still kept slaves. After seven southern states left the Union, the Civil War broke out in April 1861. By June 1861, a total of eleven states had left the Union and joined the Confederacy.

Literary Analysis

Anecdote

An **anecdote** is a brief story about an interesting, amusing, or strange event told to illustrate a point. Carl Sandburg helps readers see Lincoln's attitude and sense of humor through anecdotes like this one:

> As [Lincoln] shook hands with the correspondent of the London *Times*, he drawled, "Well, I guess the London *Times* is about the greatest power on earth—unless perhaps it is the Mississippi River."

As you read the anecdotes in "A Lincoln Preface," jot down in a word or two what each one tells about Lincoln.

Connecting Literary Elements

Anecdotes are a type of **narration**—writing that tells a story. Sometimes, anecdotes are woven into a longer story. In this selection, for example, Sandburg weaves together anecdotes to tell the larger story of Lincoln's role in the Civil War.

Reading Strategy

Establishing a Purpose for Reading

Before you begin to read a selection, **establish a purpose**—decide *why* you are reading it. Sometimes, you read purely for enjoyment, but often you read to learn something new. For example, if you already know some information about Lincoln, you may be reading to learn more. Before reading the excerpt from "A Lincoln Preface," decide what else you would like to learn about Lincoln and start a K-W-L chart like the one shown here. Follow these steps:

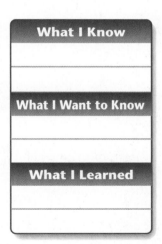

- Use the title and introductory paragraphs to determine the topic of a selection, and write down what you know about that topic.
- Jot down what you hope to learn from the selection, and focus on these points as you read.

Continue to complete your chart as you read.

Vocabulary Development

despotic (des pät′ ik) *adj.* like an absolute ruler or tyrant (p. 153)

chattel (chat′ əl) *n.* a movable item of personal property (p. 153)

cipher (sī′ fər) *adj.* code (p. 155)

slouching (slouch′ iŋ) *adj.* drooping (p. 155)

censure (sen′ shər) *n.* strong disapproval (p. 156)

gaunt (gônt) *adj.* thin and bony (p. 157)

droll (drōl) *adj.* comic and amusing in an odd way (p. 158)

from A Lincoln Preface
Carl Sandburg

▲ **Critical Viewing** What can you tell about Lincoln from this painting? **[Infer]**

In the time of the April lilacs in the year 1865, a man in the City of Washington, D.C., trusted a guard to watch at a door, and the guard was careless, left the door, and the man was shot, lingered a night, passed away, was laid in a box, and carried north and west a thousand miles; bells sobbed; cities wore crepe;[1] people stood with hats off as the railroad burial car came past at midnight, dawn or noon.

During the four years of time before he gave up the ghost, this man was clothed with despotic power, commanding the most powerful armies till then assembled in modern warfare, enforcing drafts of soldiers, abolishing the right of habeas corpus,[2] directing politically and spiritually the wild, massive forces loosed in civil war.

Four billion dollars' worth of property was taken from those who had been legal owners of it, confiscated, wiped out as by fire, at his instigation and executive direction; a class of chattel property recognized as lawful for two hundred years went to the scrap pile.

When the woman who wrote *Uncle Tom's Cabin*[3] came to see him in the White House, he greeted her, "So you're the little woman who wrote the book that made this great war," and as they seated themselves at a fireplace, "I do love an open fire: I always had one at home." As they were finishing their talk of the days of blood, he said, "I shan't last long after it's over."

An Illinois Congressman looked in on him as he had his face lathered for a shave in the White House and remarked, "If anybody had told me that in a great crisis like this the people were going out to a little one-horse town and pick out a one-horse lawyer for president, I wouldn't have believed it." The answer was, "Neither would I. But it was a time when a man with a policy would have been fatal to the country. I never had a policy. I have simply tried to do what seemed best each day, as each day came."

"I don't intend precisely to throw the Constitution overboard, but I will stick it in a

---

1. **crepe** (krāp) *n.* thin, black cloth worn to show mourning.
2. **habeas corpus** (hā bē əs kôr′ pəs) right of an imprisoned person to have a court hearing.
3. **woman . . . Cabin** Harriet Beecher Stowe (1811–1896), whose novel stirred up opinion against slavery.

despotic (des pät′ ik) *adj.* like an absolute ruler or tyrant

chattel (chat′ 'l) *n.* a movable item of personal property

Literary Analysis
Anecdote What point does this anecdote make about Lincoln's devotion to his country?

**Reading Check**

What did Lincoln do during the four years before he was killed?

hole if I can," he told a Cabinet officer. The enemy was violating the Constitution to destroy the Union, he argued, and therefore, "I will violate the Constitution, if necessary, to save the Union." He instructed a messenger to the Secretary of the Treasury, "Tell him not to bother himself about the Constitution. Say that I have that sacred instrument here at the White House, and I am guarding it with great care."

When he was renominated, it was by the device of seating delegates from Tennessee, which gave enough added votes to seat favorable delegates from Kentucky, Missouri, Louisiana, Arkansas, and from one county in Florida. Until late in that campaign of 1864, he expected to lose the November election; military victories brought the tide his way; the vote was 2,200,000 for him and 1,800,000 against him. Among those who bitterly fought him politically, and accused him of blunders or crimes, were Franklin Pierce, a former president of the United States; Horatio Seymour, the Governor of New York; Samuel F. B. Morse, inventor of the telegraph; Cyrus H. McCormick, inventor of the farm reaper; General George B. McClellan, a Democrat who had commanded the Army of the Potomac; and the *Chicago Times*, a daily newspaper. In all its essential propositions the Southern Confederacy had the moral support of powerful, respectable elements throughout the North, probably more than a million votes believing in the justice of the cause of the South as compared with the North.

Peculiarsome Abe, N. C. Wyeth, The Free Library of Philadelphia

▲ **Critical Viewing**
What message does this painting convey about Lincoln? **[Describe]**

While propagandas raged, and the war winds howled, he sat in the White House, the Stubborn Man of History, writing that the Mississippi was one river and could not belong to two countries, that the plans for railroad connection from coast to coast must be pushed through and the Union Pacific[4] realized.

His life, mind and heart ran in contrasts. When his white kid gloves broke into tatters while shaking hands at a White House reception, he remarked, "This looks like a general bustification." When he talked with an Ohio friend one day during the 1864 campaign, he

---

4. Union Pacific railroad chartered by Congress in 1862 to form part of a transcontinental system.

mentioned one public man, and murmured, "He's a thistle! I don't see why God lets him live." Of a devious Senator, he said, "He's too crooked to lie still!" And of a New York editor, "In early life in the West, we used to make our shoes last a great while with much mending, and sometimes, when far gone, we found the leather so rotten the stitches would not hold. Greeley is so rotten that nothing can be done with him. He is not truthful; the stitches all tear out." As he sat in the telegraph office of the War Department, reading <u>cipher</u> dispatches, and came to the words, Hosanna and Husband, he would chuckle, "Jeffy D.,"[5] and at the words, Hunter and Happy, "Bobby Lee."[6]

While the luck of war wavered and broke and came again, as generals failed and campaigns were lost, he held enough forces of the Union together to raise new armies and supply them, until generals were found who made war as victorious war has always been made, with terror, frightfulness, destruction, and valor and sacrifice past words of man to tell.

A <u>slouching</u>, gray-headed poet,[7] haunting the hospitals at Washington, characterized him as "the grandest figure on the crowded canvas of the drama of the nineteenth century—a Hoosier Michael Angelo."[8]

His own speeches, letters, telegrams and official messages during that war form the most significant and enduring document from any one man on why the war began, why it went on, and the dangers beyond its end. He mentioned "the politicians," over and again "the politicians," with scorn and blame. As the platoons filed before him at a review of an army corps, he asked, "What is to become of these boys when the war is over?"

He was a chosen spokesman: yet there were times he was silent; nothing but silence could at those times have fitted a chosen spokesman; in the mixed shame and blame of the immense wrongs of two crashing civilizations, with nothing to say, he said nothing, slept not at all, and wept at those times in a way that made weeping appropriate, decent, majestic.

His hat was shot off as he rode alone one night in Washington; a son he loved died as he watched at the bed; his wife was accused of betraying information to the enemy, until denials from him were necessary; his best companion was a fine-hearted and brilliant son with a deformed palate and an impediment of speech; when a Pennsylvania Congressman told him the enemy had declared they would break into the city and hang him to a lamppost, he said he had considered "the violent preliminaries" to such a scene; on his left thumb was a scar where an ax had nearly chopped the thumb off when he was a boy; over one eye was a scar where he had been hit with a club in the hands of a man trying to steal the cargo off a

cipher (sī′ fər) *adj.* code

slouching (slouch′ iŋ) *adj.* drooping

Reading Strategy
Establishing a Purpose for Reading What two sides of Lincoln's personality do these paragraphs reveal?

Reading Check
Name at least three people who fought against Lincoln politically.

---

5. **"Jeffy D."** Jefferson Davis (1808–1889), president of the Confederacy.
6. **"Bobby Lee"** Robert E. Lee (1807–1870), commander in chief of the Confederate army.
7. **slouching . . . poet** Walt Whitman (1819–1892).
8. **Michael Angelo** Michelangelo (mik′ əl an′ jə lō′), famous Italian artist (1475–1564).

Mississippi River flatboat; he threw a cashiered[9] officer out of his room in the White House, crying, "I can bear <u>censure</u>, but not insult. I never wish to see your face again."

As he shook hands with the correspondent of the London *Times*, he drawled, "Well, I guess the London *Times* is about the greatest power on earth—unless perhaps it is the Mississippi River." He rebuked with anger a woman who got on her knees to thank him for a pardon that saved her son from being shot at sunrise; and when an Iowa woman said she had journeyed out of her way to Washington just for a look at him, he grinned, "Well, in the matter of looking at one another, I have altogether the advantage."

He asked his Cabinet to vote on the high military command, and after the vote, told them the appointment had already been made; one Cabinet officer, who had been governor of Ohio, came away personally baffled and frustrated from an interview, to exclaim, to a private secretary, "That man is the most cunning person I ever saw in my life"; an Illinois lawyer who had been sent on errands carrying his political secrets, said, "He is a trimmer[10] and such a trimmer as the world has never seen."

He manipulated the admission of Nevada as a state in the Union, when her votes were needed for the Emancipation Proclamation,♦ saying, "It is easier to admit Nevada than to raise another million of soldiers." At the same time he went to the office of a former New York editor, who had become Assistant Secretary of War, and said the votes of three congressmen were wanted for the required three-quarters of votes in the House of Representatives, advising, "There are three that you can deal with better than anybody else. . . . Whatever promise you make to those men, I will perform it." And in the same week, he said to a Massachusetts politician that two votes were lacking, and, "Those two votes must be procured. I leave it to you to determine how it shall be done; but remember that I am President of the United States and clothed with immense power, and I expect you to procure those votes." And while he was thus employing every last resource and device of practical politics to constitutionally abolish slavery, the abolitionist[11] Henry Ward Beecher attacked him with javelins of scorn and detestation in a series of editorials that brought from him the single comment, "Is thy servant a dog?"

When the King of Siam sent him a costly sword of exquisite

Literature in context History Connection

♦ **The Emancipation Proclamation**

When Lincoln signed the Emancipation Proclamation, he recognized its enormous symbolic power while understanding its limitations. Some argued it was really only a partial emancipation—freeing slaves in unconquered Confederate territory—but it was an important first step. Not only did the document give Southern blacks cause to hope, rebel, and escape, it also served as a recruitment incentive for the new black regiments of the Union Army. As the army advanced, liberating slaves along the way, it was clear that the Emancipation Proclamation had done what it was designed to do: pave the way for the total abolition of slavery.

Lincoln at the Signing of the Emancipation Proclamation

---

9. **cashiered** (ka shird´) *v.* dishonorably discharged.
10. **trimmer** (trim´ ər) *n.* person who changes his opinion to suit the circumstances.
11. **abolitionist** (ab´ ə lish´ ən ist) *n.* person in favor of doing away with slavery in the United States.

embellishment, and two elephant tusks, along with letters and a photograph of the King, he acknowledged the gifts in a manner as lavish as the Orientals. Addressing the King of Siam as "Great and Good Friend," he wrote thanks for each of the gifts, including "also two elephant's tusks of length and magnitude, such as indicate they could have belonged only to an animal which was a native of Siam." After further thanks for the tokens received, he closed the letter to the King of Siam with strange grace and humor, saying, "I appreciate most highly your Majesty's tender of good offices in forwarding to this Government a stock from which a supply of elephants might be raised on our soil. . . . our political jurisdiction, however, does not reach a latitude so low as to favor the multiplication of the elephant, and steam on land as well as water has been our best agent of transportation . . . Meantime, wishing for your Majesty a long and happy life, and, for the generous and emulous people of Siam, the highest possible prosperity, I commend both to the blessing of Almighty God."

He sent hundreds of telegrams, "Suspend death sentence" or "Suspend execution" of So-and-So, who was to be shot at sunrise. The telegrams varied oddly at times, as in one, "If Thomas Samplogh, of the First Delaware Regiment, has been sentenced to death, and is not yet executed, suspend and report the case to me." And another, "Is it Lieut. Samuel B. Davis whose death sentence is commuted? If not done, let it be done."

While the war drums beat, he liked best of all the stories told of him, one of two Quakeresses[12] heard talking in a railway car. "I think that Jefferson will succeed." "Why does thee think so?" "Because Jefferson is a praying man." "And so is Abraham a praying man." "Yes, but the Lord will think Abraham is joking."

An Indiana man at the White House heard him say, "Voorhees, don't it seem strange to you that I, who could never so much as cut off the head of a chicken, should be elected, or selected, into the midst of all this blood?"

A party of American citizens, standing in the ruins of the Forum in Rome, Italy, heard there the news of the first assassination of the first American dictator, and took it as a sign of the growing up and the aging of the civilization on the North American continent. Far out in Coles County, Illinois, a beautiful, <u>gaunt</u> old woman in a log cabin said, "I knowed he'd never come back."

Of men taking too fat profits out of the war, he said, "Where the carcass is there will the eagles be gathered together."

An enemy general, Longstreet, after the war, declared him to have been "the one matchless man in forty millions of people," while one of his private secretaries, Hay, declared his life to have been the most perfect in its relationships and adjustments since that of Christ.

Between the days in which he crawled as a baby on the dirt floor of

---

12. **Quakeresses** (kwāk´ ər es əz) *n.* female members of the religious group known as the Society of Friends, or Quakers.

Literary Analysis
Anecdote What does this anecdote about gifts from Siam convey about Lincoln's personality?

gaunt (gônt) *adj.* thin and bony

**Reading Check**

What story regarding the Quakeresses did Lincoln appreciate?

a Kentucky cabin, and the time when he gave his final breath in Washington, he packed a rich life with work, thought, laughter, tears, hate, love.

With vast reservoirs of the comic and the <u>droll</u>, and notwithstanding a mastery of mirth and nonsense, he delivered a volume of addresses and letters of terrible and serious appeal, with import beyond his own day, shot through here and there with far, thin ironics, with paragraphs having raillery[13] of the quality of the Book of Job,[14] and echoes as subtle as the whispers of wind in prairie grass.

Perhaps no human clay pot has held more laughter and tears.

The facts and myths of his life are to be an American possession, shared widely over the world, for thousands of years, as the tradition of Knute or Alfred, Lao-tse or Diogenes, Pericles or Caesar,[15] are kept. This because he was not only a genius in the science of neighborly human relationships and an artist in the personal handling of life from day to day, but a strange friend and a friendly stranger to all forms of life that he met.

He lived fifty-six years of which fifty-two were lived in the West—the prairie years.

droll (drōl) *adj.* comic and amusing in an odd way

---

13. **raillery** (rāl′ ər ē) *n.* good-natured teasing.
14. **Book of Job** (jōb) book of the Old Testament in which a man named Job is tested by God.
15. **Knute** (knōōt) **or Alfred, Lao-tse** (lou′ dzu′) **or Diogenes** (dī äj′ ə nēz), **Pericles** (per′ ə klēz) **or Caesar** (sē′ zər) well-known thinkers and leaders from different eras and places.

Review and Assess

Thinking About the Selection

1. **Respond:** Which anecdote interested you the most?
2. **(a) Recall:** To whom did Lincoln refer as "the little woman who wrote the book that made this great war"? **(b) Infer:** Why do you think Lincoln wanted to meet with this woman?
3. **(a) Recall:** How did Lincoln justify admitting Nevada to the Union? **(b) Analyze:** What other examples can you find of Lincoln's use of "practical politics"?
4. **(a) Distinguish:** How does Sandburg show that Lincoln "packed a rich life with work, thought, laughter, tears, hate, love"? **(b) Evaluate:** What do you think Sandburg thought about his subject?
5. **Evaluate:** Do you think Lincoln was justified in violating the Constitution to save the Union? Why or why not?
6. **Extend:** How does Lincoln's life, based on Sandburg's portrait, compare to the lives of other great leaders?

Carl Sandburg

(1878–1967)

At the age of thirteen, Carl Sandburg dropped out of school; for the next seven years, he worked as a porter, scene changer, truck handler, dishwasher, potter, and farm worker. Sandburg served briefly in Puerto Rico during the Spanish-American War, and that experience brought on the strong antiwar feelings that Sandburg would hold throughout his life.

After the war, Sandburg discovered literature. He read a great deal and spent eighteen years researching and writing *Abraham Lincoln: The Prairie Years* and *Abraham Lincoln: The War Years*. Sandburg received two Pulitzer Prizes—one for his Lincoln biography and one for poetry. He also gained recognition for having written what many consider the greatest historical biography of the 1900s.

Review and Assess

Literary Analysis

Anecdote

1. Use an organizer like the one shown to analyze **anecdotes** from the selection. For each, summarize the story and then identify the personality trait it reveals.

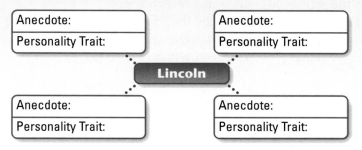

2. Why do you think Sandburg included in this work some anecdotes that portrayed Lincoln in a less-than-pleasing light?
3. Which of your previous notions about Lincoln does the narration change?

Connecting Literary Elements

4. What is the central problem that ties this **narrative** together?
5. How does Sandburg's narration paint a verbal picture of Lincoln?
6. (a) How does a biography built on anecdotes differ from other biographies you have read? (b) How do the anecdotes strengthen the narrative?

Reading Strategy

Establishing a Purpose for Reading

7. Identify two different **purposes** readers may bring to this selection.
8. Identify three pieces of information from the selection that helped you achieve the purpose of learning more about Abraham Lincoln.
9. If you were reading to learn more about the Civil War, which details in the selection would help you?

Extend Understanding

10. **Literature Connection:** Why do you think people are fascinated with political biographies that reveal the positive and negative inner workings of a politician's life?

Integrate Language Skills

Vocabulary Development Lesson

Word Analysis: Anglo-Saxon Suffix -ic

The Anglo-Saxon suffix -ic means "like" or "pertaining to." It creates the adjective form of many words, such as *despotic*, which means "like a despot, or tyrant." Define each of the following words, incorporating the definition of -ic into each answer.

1. artistic **2.** realistic **3.** problematic

Spelling Strategy

To add an ending like -ic to a word that ends in a consonant, simply add the suffix. For example, *carbon* becomes *carbonic*. Create the adjective form of the following words by adding the suffix -ic to each one. Then, write a sentence using the new word.

1. artist **3.** class

2. poet **4.** patriot

Concept Development: Analogies

When you analyze vocabulary analogies, first study the relationship between a given word pair, and then complete a second word pair to show the same relationship.

Copy the following analogies. Complete each one with the appropriate word from the vocabulary list on page 151.

1. tradition : custom :: possession : _____?_____
2. war : peace :: praise : _____?_____
3. garbled : speech :: _____?_____ : message
4. standing tall : alert :: _____?_____ : tired
5. tolerant : democratic :: repressive : _____?_____
6. well-fed : plump :: undernourished : _____?_____
7. strange : bizarre :: funny : _____?_____

Grammar Lesson

Transitive and Intransitive Verbs

An action verb is **transitive** if it directs action toward someone or something named in the same sentence. An action verb is **intransitive** if it does not direct action toward something or someone named in the same sentence. To determine whether a verb is transitive or intransitive, ask *Whom?* or *What?* after the verb. If you can find the answer in the sentence, the verb is transitive. If not, the verb is intransitive.

Transitive: The president <u>read</u> the documents.

Intransitive: The president <u>read</u> every day.

Practice: Identify each underlined verb as *transitive* or *intransitive*.

1. Several people bitterly <u>fought</u> him politically.
2. Propagandas <u>raged</u> and the war winds <u>howled</u>.
3. He <u>asked</u> his cabinet to vote on the issue.
4. He <u>spoke</u> forcefully during the war.
5. The telegrams <u>varied</u> at times.

Writing Application Write a brief paragraph about a modern-day leader. In your writing, use three transitive verbs and three intransitive verbs.

Writing Lesson

Character Profile

Write a short profile of Lincoln, describing the traits, talents, and special skills that helped him succeed as president. Use Sandburg's narrative and your own knowledge to create your profile.

Prewriting   Use a chart like the one shown to jot down descriptions of Lincoln. Then, provide evidence for each description you list.

Model: Gathering Details About a Person

Description	Evidence
determined	He manipulated the admission of Nevada as a state into the Union to win votes for the Emancipation Proclamation.

Drafting   As you draft, use a solid organization. You might begin by explaining some of Lincoln's minor personality traits and move to addressing his most impressive traits, or do the reverse.

Revising   Reread your draft. Check to make sure that each description of Lincoln is backed up with evidence. Add any details needed to present a clear profile of Lincoln.

Prentice Hall Writing and Grammar Connection: Chapter 5, Section 2

Extension Activities

Listening and Speaking   In a group, conduct a **panel discussion** on Lincoln's use of "practical politics" to end slavery with the passage of the Emancipation Proclamation.

- Panel members should prepare their remarks in advance.
- Each speaker can present a brief opening statement.
- The panel can then debate the issue to reach a conclusion.

After the discussion, ask audience members to evaluate the event. **[Group Activity]**

Research and Technology   Create a **timeline** of the most significant events in Lincoln's life and presidency as Sandburg reports them. In the appropriate places, include situations in which he made famous speeches or suffered personal tragedies. Use graphics software to create your timeline, and present it to your class.

 **Take It to the Net**   www.phschool.com

Go online for an additional research activity using the Internet.

Prepare to Read

I Have a Dream ◆ *from* Rosa Parks: My Story ◆
There Is a Longing ◆ I Hear America Singing

 Take It to the Net

Visit www.phschool.com
for interactive activities
and instruction related to
the selections, including
- background
- graphic organizers
- literary elements
- reading strategies

Preview

Connecting to the Literature

Think of a time when you were inspired by a speech, a work of writing, or even a conversation. Often, as you will see in these selections, we find inspiration in the words of people who challenge us to be the best we can be.

Background

The freedom of speech guaranteed by the United States Constitution is a civil right, a freedom that people are entitled to as members of a society. Some Americans have not always enjoyed these rights and have had to struggle for equality. Their fight—marked by demonstrations and legal challenges—is known as the civil rights movement. It began in the 1950s and was led by figures such as Martin Luther King, Jr., and Rosa Parks.

Literary Analysis

Author's Purpose

An **author's purpose** is his or her reason for writing. For example, an author may want to entertain, inform, or persuade the reader. This example from "I Have a Dream" reveals the author's purpose: to urge all Americans, regardless of background, to accept one another as equals.

> With this faith, we will be able to transform the jangling discords of our nation into a beautiful symphony of brotherhood.

As you read, determine each author's purpose, and evaluate the author's techniques to decide how successfully he or she has conveyed that purpose.

Comparing Literary Works

An author's purpose helps shape his or her **tone**—the attitude toward the subject that an author conveys in a piece of writing. Identify the tone of each piece by looking for words that indicate how the author feels. Try to select adjectives that capture each tone. Then, look at the similarities and differences in the tones of the four selections.

Reading Strategy

Responding

When you read something, you cannot help but **respond,** or react, to it.

- As you read, ask yourself how you are reacting.
- Note your feelings, such as anger or sympathy.
- Look for the words or ideas that have provoked your response.

Use a chart like this one to write down your responses as you read.

Vocabulary Development

creed (krēd) *n.* statement of belief (p. 165)

oppression (ə presh′ ən) *n.* keeping others down by the unjust use of power (p. 165)

oasis (ō ā′ sis) *n.* fertile place in the desert (p. 165)

exalted (eg zôlt′ əd) *v.* lifted up (p. 165)

prodigious (prə dij′ əs) *adj.* wonderful; of great size (p. 166)

hamlet (ham′ lit) *n.* small village (p. 166)

complied (kəm plīd′) *v.* carried out or fulfilled a request (p. 168)

manhandled (man′ han′ dəld) *v.* treated roughly (p. 169)

determination (dē tʉr′ mi nā′ shən) *n.* firm intention (p. 170)

endurance (en door′ əns) *n.* ability to withstand hardship and continue on (p. 170)

from Rosa Parks: My Story

Rosa Parks (with Jim Haskins)

The Beginning, Artis Lane

When I got off from work that evening of December 1, I went to Court Square as usual to catch the Cleveland Avenue bus home. I didn't look to see who was driving when I got on, and by the time I recognized him, I had already paid my fare. It was the same driver who had put me off the bus back in 1943, twelve years earlier. He was still tall and heavy, with red, rough-looking skin. And he was still mean-looking. I didn't know if he had been on that route before—they switched the drivers around sometimes. I do know that most of the time if I saw him on a bus, I wouldn't get on it.

I saw a vacant seat in the middle section of the bus and took it. I didn't even question why there was a vacant seat even though there were quite a few people standing in the back. If I had thought about it at all, I would probably have figured maybe someone saw me get on and did not take the seat but left it vacant for me. There was a man sitting next to the window and two women across the aisle.

The next stop was the Empire Theater, and some whites got on. They filled up the white seats, and one man was left standing. The driver looked back and noticed the man standing. Then he looked back at us. He said, "Let me have those front seats," because they were the front seats of the black section. Didn't anybody move. We just sat right where we were, the four of us. Then he spoke a second time: "Y'all better make it light on yourselves and let me have those seats."

The man in the window seat next to me stood up, and I moved to let him pass by me, and then I looked across the aisle and saw that the two women were also standing. I moved over to the window seat. I could not see how standing up was going to "make it light" for me. The more we gave in and <u>complied</u>, the worse they treated us.

I thought back to the time when I used to sit up all night and didn't

▲ Critical Viewing
How does this painting reflect the ideal of equal rights for all people? **[Analyze]**

Literary Analysis
Author's Purpose Why do you think Rosa Parks included this background information in her story of the encounter on the bus?

complied (kəm plīd´) v. carried out or fulfilled a request

sleep, and my grandfather would have his gun right by the fireplace, or if he had his one-horse wagon going anywhere, he always had his gun in the back of the wagon. People always say that I didn't give up my seat because I was tired, but that isn't true. I was not tired physically, or no more tired than I usually was at the end of a working day. I was not old, although some people have an image of me as being old then.

I was forty-two. No, the only tired I was, was tired of giving in.

The driver of the bus saw me still sitting there, and he asked was I going to stand up.

I said, "No." He said, "Well, I'm going to have you arrested." Then I said, "You may do that." These were the only words we said to each other. I didn't even know his name, which was James Blake, until we were in court together. He got out of the bus and stayed outside for a few minutes, waiting for the police.

As I sat there, I tried not to think about what might happen. I knew that anything was possible. I could be <u>manhandled</u> or beaten. I could be arrested. People have asked me if it occurred to me then that I could be the test case the NAACP[1] had been looking for. I did not think about that at all. In fact if I had let myself think too deeply about what might happen to me, I might have gotten off the bus. But I chose to remain.

---

1. **NAACP** *abbr.* National Association for the Advancement of Colored People.

Reading Strategy

Responding What is your reaction to this quotation by Rosa Parks: "No, the only tired I was, was tired of giving in"? Why?

manhandled (man´ han´ dəld) *v.* treated roughly

Review and Assess

Thinking About the Selection

1. **Respond:** What do you think about Rosa Parks's actions? Explain.

2. **(a) Recall:** In which section did Rosa Parks sit on the bus? **(b) Interpret:** Why did the bus driver ask the people in her row to give up their seats?

3. **(a) Recall:** Summarize her memory of her grandfather. **(b) Interpret:** How does her childhood memory affect her action that day, many years later?

4. **(a) Recall:** What reason does Rosa Parks give for staying in her seat? **(b) Interpret:** How did her refusal to stand up contribute to the civil rights movement?

5. **Compare and Contrast:** Both Rev. King and Rosa Parks helped win equality for minorities. How are their actions similar and different?

6. **Speculate:** Do you think that if Rosa Parks had given up her seat, integration would have taken place anyway? Explain.

Rosa Parks

(b. 1913)

In 1955, Rosa Parks was arrested for breaking an unjust law— she refused to give up her seat on a public bus to a white man. This incident sparked a boycott that led to the end of segregation on the Montgomery bus system. Her courageous action marked the start of the civil rights movement. In 1999, she was granted the Congressional Gold Medal. This is the highest honor given to a civilian in the United States.

from *Rosa Parks: My Story* ◆ 169

There Is a Longing

Chief Dan George

There is a longing in the heart of my people
to reach out and grasp that which is needed
for our survival. There is a longing among
the young of my nation to secure for themselves
5   and their people the skills that will
provide them with a sense of worth and
purpose. They will be our new warriors.
Their training will be much longer and
more demanding than it was in olden days.
10 The long years of study will demand more
<u>determination</u>; separation from home and
family will demand <u>endurance</u>. But they
will emerge with their hand held forward,
not to receive welfare, but to grasp the
15 place in society that is rightly ours.

I am a chief, but my power to make war
is gone, and the only weapon left to me
is speech. It is only with tongue and speech
that I can fight my people's war.

20 Oh, Great Spirit![1] Give me back the courage
of the olden Chiefs. Let me wrestle with
my surroundings. Let me once again,
live in harmony with my environment.
Let me humbly accept this new culture
25 and through it rise up and go on. Like
the thunderbird[2] of old, I shall rise again
out of the sea; I shall grab the instruments

determination (dē tu̇r´ mi nā´ shən) *n.* firm intention

endurance (en do͝or´ əns) *n.* ability to withstand hardship and continue on

Reading Strategy
Responding What do you think is the most persuasive part of the writer's message?

---

1. **Great Spirit** for many Native Americans, the greatest power or god.
2. **thunderbird** a powerful supernatural creature that was thought to produce thunder by flapping its wings and produce lightning by opening and closing its eyes. In the folklore of some Native American nations, the thunderbird is in constant warfare with the powers beneath the waters.

We the People, Kathy Morrow, Courtesy of the artist

of the white man's success—his
education, his skills. With these new tools
30 I shall build my race into the proudest
segment of your society. I shall see our
young braves and our chiefs sitting in
the houses of law and government, ruling
and being ruled by the knowledge and
35 freedoms of *our* great land.

▲ **Critical Viewing**
Which images in this
painting reflect ideas
found in the poem?
[Interpret]

Review and Assess

Thinking About the Selection

1. **Respond:** How did you feel as you read "There Is a Longing"? Explain.

2. **(a) Recall:** What does Chief Dan George say is his community's longing? **(b) Draw Conclusions:** What is his greatest fear?

3. **(a) Recall:** What is the training the new warriors will have to endure? **(b) Analyze:** Why does Chief Dan George think this training is necessary?

4. **(a) Infer:** In what way is Chief Dan George different from his predecessors? **(b) Interpret:** What does the chief mean by fighting a war "with tongue and speech"?

5. **(a) Analyze:** In what ways does Chief Dan George believe the Great Spirit will help his people? **(b) Deduce:** What do you think the Chief himself will have to do to help them?

6. **Assess:** Do you think the Chief's goal of achieving success through education and skills is the best means for improving his people's lives? Explain.

Chief Dan George

(1899–1981)

Chief Dan George had many careers, including actor and writer. Chief of a Salish Band of Native Americans in British Columbia, Canada, he was deeply concerned about developing mutual respect between Native Americans and other North Americans. As an actor, he accepted only roles that presented Native Americans with dignity. As a writer and public speaker, he emphasized respect and understanding among people.

There Is a Longing ◆ 171

I Hear America Singing

Walt Whitman

I hear America singing, the varied carols I hear,
Those of mechanics, each one singing his as it should be
    blithe and strong,
The carpenter singing his as he measures his plank or beam,
The mason singing his as he makes ready for work, or
    leaves off work,
5 The boatman singing what belongs to him in his boat, the
    deckhand singing on the steamboat deck,
The shoemaker singing as he sits on his bench, the hatter
    singing as he stands,
The wood-cutter's song, the ploughboy's on his way in the
    morning, or at noon intermission or at sundown,
The delicious singing of the mother, or of the young wife at
    work, or of the girl sewing or washing,
Each singing what belongs to him or her and to none else,
10 The day what belongs to the day—at night the party of
    young fellows, robust, friendly,
Singing with open mouths their strong melodious songs.

Literary Analysis
Author's Purpose Which word in the opening lines helps identify Whitman's purpose?

Walt Whitman

(1819–1892)

Walt Whitman, one of America's greatest poets, was a lover of democracy and a champion of the common individual. Part of Whitman's mission as a poet was to inspire and vitalize the United States through the ecstatic vision of democratic life. His expansive vision and spirit are reflected in "I Hear America Singing."

Review and Assess

Thinking About the Selection

1. **Respond:** Which of the "songs" speaks to you the most? Explain.

2. **(a) Recall:** Identify three singers Whitman names.
   (b) Interpret: What does Whitman mean when he says that he hears their songs?

3. **(a) Recall:** When does the mason sing? The ploughboy?
   (b) Distinguish: Why do you think Whitman pictures the American worker in various situations and times of day?

4. **Generalize:** What kind of nation does Whitman depict?

5. **Speculate:** Do you think modern-day America is similar to the world Whitman presents? Why or why not?

Review and Assess

Literary Analysis

Author's Purpose

1. Choose one of the selections you have just read. Using a chart like the one shown here, note details of content and style that help you determine the **author's purpose**.

2. How does King's use of repetition help to achieve his purpose?
3. Chief Dan George voices his appeal for his people's future. To whom is he speaking? Native Americans? Others? Explain.

Comparing Literary Works

4. (a) Analyze each writer's **tone** by completing a chart like the one shown here. For each selection, note words that reflect the writer's attitude toward the subject. Then, select a single adjective to identify the writer's tone. (b) In what ways does each writer use tone to emphasize the importance of his or her subject?

King	Word Choice	Parks
Chief Dan George		Whitman

5. Both King and Parks write about the civil rights movement in the United States. (a) How are the tones of the two pieces different? (b) What is the reason for this difference?

Reading Strategy

Responding

6. Choose one "carol" from "I Hear America Singing" and explain the **response** it generated in you.
7. Which selection provoked the strongest response in you? Explain.

Extend Understanding

8. **Social Studies Connection:** Do the ideas and issues in these selections still hold true today? Explain.

Quick Review

An **author's purpose** is his or her reason for writing.

The **tone** of a piece of writing is the author's attitude toward the subject.

When you **respond** to what you read, you acknowledge your personal reaction to the writing.

 Take It to the Net
www.phschool.com
Take the interactive self-test online to check your understanding of these selections.

Integrate Language Skills

Vocabulary Development Lesson

Word Analysis: Latin Root -cred-

Creed comes from the Latin verb *credere*, which means "to believe." Applying the meaning of *-cred-*, use each of the following words in a sentence.

a. credit

b. incredible

c. credentials

d. credibility

Spelling Strategy

Before adding a suffix beginning with a vowel to a word that ends in silent *e*, you usually drop the *e*. For example, when adding the suffix *-ance* to *endure*, the silent *e* is dropped and the word becomes *endurance*. Write the correct spelling of the following words. Then, write a sentence using each new word.

1. sense + *-ory*
2. imagine + *-ary*
3. like + *-able*
4. drive + *-ing*

Concept Development: Synonyms and Antonyms

Synonyms are words with similar meanings, such as *happy* and *cheerful*. Antonyms are words with opposite meanings, such as *light* and *dark*. Identify the relationships of the following word pairs. Use **S** for synonyms and **A** for antonyms.

1. creed, statement of doubt
2. oppression, liberty
3. oasis, desert
4. exalted, dignified
5. prodigious, remarkable
6. hamlet, city
7. complied, obeyed
8. manhandled, shoved
9. determination, weakness
10. endurance, stamina

Grammar Lesson

Action and Linking Verbs

Action verbs express physical or mental actions, like *jump* or *think*. In contrast, **linking verbs,** including forms of the verb *be*, express a state of being. They connect the subject to a word that renames or describes the subject.

Action verbs: I *saw* a seat and *took* it.

Linking verbs: I *was* tired of giving in.

Practice Copy the following sentences from the selections. Underline the action verbs and circle the linking verbs.

1. I am a chief, but my power is gone.

2. I hear America singing, the varied carols I hear.

3. I have a dream that one day every valley shall be exalted.

4. I shall build my race into the proudest segment of your society.

5. It was the same driver who had put me off the bus back in 1943, twelve years earlier.

Writing Application Write a paragraph about a person whose words or actions inspire you. Circle the verbs you have chosen, and then identify whether each is an action or a linking verb.

W̶G̶ Prentice Hall Writing and Grammar Connection: Chapter 17, Sections 1 and 2

Writing Lesson

Proposal for a School Speaker

Consider the benefit of having a great speaker, like Martin Luther King, Jr., speak at your school. Write a proposal to your principal, presenting a persuasive argument in favor of inviting a specific speaker to a school assembly.

Prewriting   Think about problems that your classmates face daily, and consider the ways a speaker might address them. Make a list of potential speakers, and describe the benefit that each speech would provide.

Model: Gathering Evidence

Speaker	Benefit speaker will provide
Toni Morrison	Her success could inspire students to express themselves through writing.

Drafting   As you draft, explain how the speaker you have chosen could help address important issues in your school. End with an appeal that will convince the principal to act on your proposal.

Revising   Review your proposal to see that your examples are persuasive and simply stated. Check your final paragraph to be sure that you end with an appeal noting the benefits of the speaker's visit.

*W*G *Prentice Hall Writing and Grammar Connection: Chapter 7, Section 2*

Extension Activities

Listening and Speaking Compose a **radio news report** in which you provide on-the-spot coverage of King's speech and explain his dream for America. Include the following in your report:

- background information about the civil rights movement
- excerpts from King's speech
- description of the effect it had on the crowd

Share your report with your class. Tape-record yourself while broadcasting so that you can evaluate your work later.

Research and Technology In a group, create a **multimedia presentation** on a single aspect of the American civil rights movement, such as laws, marches, or specific leaders. Assemble photographs for your presentation, as well as video or audio recordings of civil rights speeches and events. Present your findings to your class. **[Group Activity]**

 **Take It to the Net**   www.phschool.com

Go online for an additional research activity using the Internet.

Prepare to Read

The Golden Kite, the Silver Wind

Rectangular Box, Avery Brundage Collection, Asian Art Museum of San Francisco

 Take It to the Net

Visit www.phschool.com for interactive activities and instruction related to "The Golden Kite, The Silver Wind," including
- background
- graphic organizers
- literary elements
- reading strategies

Preview

Connecting to the Literature

Have you and a friend ever tried to outdo each other? The two of you may have become consumed by rivalry, but most likely, no one else was hurt as a result of it. In this story, a rivalry becomes so intense that it leads to widespread suffering.

Background

"The Golden Kite, the Silver Wind" was written during the Cold War, a period of intense rivalry between the United States and the former Soviet Union. During this time, each action by one country—the creation of a weapon, the launching of a satellite—was countered by a reaction from the other country. As you read, think about the parallels between the story events and the history of the Cold War.

Literary Analysis
Fable

"The Golden Kite, the Silver Wind" is a **fable**, a brief story that teaches a lesson. This lesson, or moral, may be directly stated, or it may be shown through the choices the characters make. In this fable, the actions of two rival towns teach a lesson about the value of cooperation over competition. The following example from the story highlights the unhealthy competition existing between the towns.

> "They build their wall," said the Mandarin, "in the shape of a pig! Do you see? Our own city wall is built in the shape of an orange. That pig will devour us, greedily!"

As you read, consider what lesson can be learned from this fable.

Connecting Literary Elements

A **dialogue** is a conversation between characters. As a complement to a writer's narration, dialogue is used to reveal more about a character and to advance action in a story. In this story, the dialogue quickens the action, introduces each Mandarin's tactics, and helps reveal the lesson of the fable.

Reading Strategy
Predicting Consequences of Actions

Try to **predict the consequences of each action** in a story by considering events that have already occurred. Then, read on to see whether your predictions were correct. To help you, follow these suggestions:

- Write down each event as it occurs.
- Before you read further, predict the consequences of that event.
- Look for a pattern that will lead you to the moral of the story.

Use a chart like the one shown to help you predict as you read.

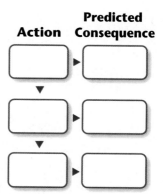

Vocabulary Development

portents (pôr´ tentz) *n.* things that are thought to be signs of events to come; omens (p. 179)

vile (vīl) *adj.* evil; wicked (p. 179)

ravenous (rav´ ə nəs) *adj.* greedily hungry (p. 179)

acclaimed (ə klāmd´) *v.* greeted with loud applause or approval (p. 180)

pandemonium (pan´ də mōn´ nē əm) *n.* wild disorder, noise, or confusion (p. 180)

spurn (spʉrn) *v.* reject in a scornful way (p. 180)

When his men had gone, smiling and bustling, the Mandarin turned with great love to the silken screen. "Daughter," he whispered, "I will embrace you." There was no reply. He stepped around the screen, and she was gone.

Such modesty, he thought. She has slipped away and left me with a triumph, as if it were mine.

The news spread through the city; the Mandarin was <u>acclaimed</u>. Everyone carried stone to the walls. Fireworks were set off and the demons of death and poverty did not linger, as all worked together. At the end of the month the wall had been changed. It was now a mighty bludgeon with which to drive pigs, boars, even lions, far away. The Mandarin slept like a happy fox every night.

"I would like to see the Mandarin of Kwan-Si when the news is learned. Such <u>pandemonium</u> and hysteria; he will likely throw himself from a mountain! A little more of that wine, oh Daughter-who-thinks-like-a-son."

But the pleasure was like a winter flower; it died swiftly. That very afternoon the messenger rushed into the courtroom. "Oh, Mandarin, disease, early sorrow, avalanches, grasshopper plagues, and poisoned well water!"

The Mandarin trembled.

"The town of Kwan-Si," said the messenger, "which was built like a pig and which animal we drove away by changing our walls to a mighty stick, has now turned triumph to winter ashes. They have built their city's walls like a great bonfire to burn our stick!"

The Mandarin's heart sickened within him, like an autumn fruit upon an ancient tree. "Oh, gods! Travelers will <u>spurn</u> us. Tradesmen, reading the symbols, will turn from the stick, so easily destroyed, to the fire, which conquers all!"

"No," said a whisper like a snowflake from behind the silken screen.

"No," said the startled Mandarin.

"Tell my stonemasons," said the whisper that was a falling drop of rain, "to build our walls in the shape of a shining lake."

The Mandarin said this aloud, his heart warmed.

"And with this lake of water," said the whisper and the old man, "we will quench the fire and put it out forever!"

The city turned out in joy to learn that once again they had been saved by the magnificent Emperor of ideas. They ran to the walls and built them nearer to this new vision, singing, not as loudly as before, of course, for they were tired, and not as quickly, for since it had taken a month to rebuild the wall the first time, they had had to neglect business and crops and therefore were somewhat weaker and poorer.

There then followed a succession of horrible and wonderful days, one in another like a nest of frightened boxes.

"Oh, Emperor," cried the messenger, "Kwan-Si has rebuilt their walls to resemble a mouth with which to drink all our lake!"

acclaimed (ə klāmd´) v. greeted with loud applause or approval; hailed

pandemonium (pan´ də mōn´ nē əm) n. wild disorder, noise, or confusion

spurn (spʉrn) v. reject in a scornful way

Reading Strategy
Predicting Consequences of Actions What do you think will be the consequence of this latest action?

"Then," said the Emperor, standing very close to his silken screen, "build our walls like a needle to sew up that mouth!"

"Emperor!" screamed the messenger. "They make their walls like a sword to break your needle!"

The Emperor held, trembling, to the silken screen. "Then shift the stones to form a scabbard to sheathe that sword!"[2]

"Mercy," wept the messenger the following morn, "they have worked all night and shaped their walls like lightning which will explode and destroy that sheath!"

Sickness spread in the city like a pack of evil dogs. Shops closed. The population, working now steadily for endless months upon the changing of the walls, resembled Death himself, clattering his white bones like musical instruments in the wind. Funerals began to appear in the streets, though it was the middle of summer, a time when all should be tending and harvesting. The Mandarin fell so ill that he had his bed drawn up by the silken screen and there he lay, miserably giving his architectural orders. The voice behind the screen was weak now, too, and faint, like the wind in the eaves.

"Kwan-Si is an eagle. Then our walls must be a net for that eagle. They are a sun to burn our net. Then we build a moon to eclipse their sun!"

Like a rusted machine, the city ground to a halt.

At last the whisper behind the screen cried out:

"In the name of the gods, send for Kwan-Si!"

Upon the last day of summer the Mandarin Kwan-Si, very ill and withered away, was carried into our Mandarin's courtroom by four starving footmen. The two mandarins were propped up, facing each other. Their breaths fluttered like winter winds in their mouths. A voice said:

"Let us put an end to this."

The old men nodded.

"This cannot go on," said the faint voice. "Our people do nothing but rebuild our cities to a different shape every day, every hour. They have no time to hunt, to fish, to love, to be good to their ancestors and their ancestors' children."

"This I admit," said the mandarins of the towns of the Cage, the Moon, the Spear, the Fire, the Sword and this, that, and other things.

"Carry us into the sunlight," said the voice.

The old men were borne out under the sun and up a little hill. In the late summer breeze a few very thin children were flying dragon kites in all the colors of the sun, and frogs and grass, the color of the sea and the color of coins and wheat.

The first Mandarin's daughter stood by his bed.

"See," she said.

"Those are nothing but kites," said the two old men.

Literary Analysis
Fable What lesson are the mandarins beginning to learn?

Reading Check
What kind of wall was built to defeat Kwan-si's sun?

---

2. **scabbard** (skab´ ərd) **to sheathe** (shēth) **that sword!** case to hold the blade of the sword.

"But what is a kite on the ground?" she said. "It is nothing. What does it need to sustain it and make it beautiful and truly spiritual?"

"The wind, of course!" said the others.

"And what do the sky and the wind need to make *them* beautiful?"

"A kite, of course—many kites, to break the monotony, the sameness of the sky. Colored kites, flying!"

"So," said the Mandarin's daughter. "You, Kwan-Si, will make a last rebuilding of your town to resemble nothing more nor less than the wind. And we shall build like a golden kite. The wind will beautify the kite and carry it to wondrous heights. And the kite will break the sameness of the wind's existence and give it purpose and meaning. One without the other is nothing. Together, all will be beauty and cooperation and a long and enduring life."

Whereupon the two mandarins were so overjoyed that they took their first nourishment in days, momentarily were given strength, embraced, and lavished praise upon each other, called the Mandarin's daughter a boy, a man, a stone pillar, a warrior, and a true and unforgettable son. Almost immediately they parted and hurried to their towns, calling out and singing, weakly but happily.

And so, in time, the towns became the Town of Golden Kite and the Town of the Silver Wind. And harvestings were harvested and business tended again, and the flesh returned, and disease ran off like a frightened jackal. And on every night of the year the inhabitants in the Town of the Kite could hear the good clear wind sustaining them. And those in the Town of the Wind could hear the kite singing, whispering, rising, and beautifying them.

"So be it," said the Mandarin in front of his silken screen.

Literary Analysis

Fable and Dialogue What do you learn from the dialogue between the daughter and the two mandarins?

Review and Assess

Thinking About the Selection

1. **Respond:** Do you think the Mandarin's daughter gave her father good advice? Explain.

2. **(a) Recall:** Which event at the beginning of the story upsets and angers the Mandarin? **(b) Infer:** What does his reaction tell you about his beliefs?

3. **(a) Recall:** How does the Mandarin's daughter advise her father? **(b) Infer:** Why do you think she needs to advise him in such a way?

4. **(a) Infer:** What can you infer about the townspeople based on their response to the Mandarin's plans? **(b) Evaluate:** Should they have continued to follow his advice?

5. **Apply:** How can the lesson from this story be applied to everyday life situations?

Ray Bradbury

(b. 1920)

Born in Waukegan, Illinois, Bradbury developed a love of fantasy and suspenseful writing at an early age. In 1932, Bradbury's family moved to Tucson, Arizona, where he wrote his first stories. In 1934, they moved to Los Angeles, where he has lived ever since.

A year after he graduated from high school, Bradbury founded and edited a publication called *Futuria Fantasia*. By this time, he was already writing at least one story a week.

One of America's most celebrated science-fiction writers, Bradbury has earned the World Fantasy Award for lifetime achievement and the Grand Master Award from the Science Fiction Writers of America.

Review and Assess

Literary Analysis

Fable

1. (a) What poor choices were made by both the Mandarin and his daughter in this **fable**? (b) What happened as a result?

2. Use a chart like this one to list key responsibilities of leaders. What lesson does this fable teach us about powerful leaders and their responsibilities to the people they represent?

Responsibilities		Mandarins' Leadership Abilities
	···▶	

3. In your own words, express the moral of the fable in one sentence.

Connecting Literary Elements

4. Most of the **dialogue** in the story is provided by the daughter speaking from behind a screen. What does this dialogue reveal to us about the daughter and the Mandarin?

5. (a) Note places in the story where dialogue moves the action along more quickly. (b) Why does dialogue work better than description in the story?

Reading Strategy

Predicting Consequences of Actions

6. What were the first hints that the rivalry between the two towns would be disastrous? Support your answer.

7. At what point were you able to **predict** the outcome? Explain.

8. (a) What do you predict will be the result of the actions taken at the end of the story? (b) Which details support your answer?

Extend Understanding

9. **World History Connection:** This story was written during the Cold War. (a) Why would the story have been especially appropriate for that time? (b) Which countries or cultures from today's world could the two villages represent? Explain.

Quick Review

A **fable** is a brief story that teaches a lesson, or moral. The moral may be directly stated, or indirectly shown through the choices the characters make.

Dialogue—a conversation between characters—is used to reveal more about the characters and to move the action of the story along.

To **predict consequences of actions,** guess the outcome of a story based on the events that have already occurred.

 Take It to the Net
www.phschool.com

Take the interactive self-test online to check your understanding of this selection.

Integrate Language Skills

Vocabulary Development Lesson

Word Analysis: Latin Root -clam-

In this story, the word *acclaimed*, meaning "greeted with loud applause or approval," contains *-claim-*, a variation of the Latin root *-clam-*, meaning "call out" or "shout." Applying the meaning of *-clam-*, write a sentence for each word below.

1. exclaim   **2.** proclamation   **3.** clamorous

Spelling Strategy

The final consonant of a prefix sometimes changes to match the first letter of the word to which it is attached. The result is a doubled consonant. For example, the prefix *in-* changes to *ir-* in *irregular*.

Rewrite each item below by adding the given prefix. Then, write a sentence using the new word.

1. *ex-* + centric   **2.** *ad-* + sign

Fluency: Context

Write each sentence below, filling in the blanks with words from the vocabulary list on page 177, or forms of those words.

The ____?____ for the kingdom were not good. The crops had failed, lightning had struck the bell tower, and a dragon was causing ____?____ across the countryside. Fierce and ____?____, the dragon terrified the peasants and devoured their livestock, leaving the people hungry and frightened. "That ____?____ dragon must be destroyed!" exclaimed the princess. ____?____ offers of assistance, she rode off to fight the dragon. On her triumphant return home, the dragon-slaying princess was ____?____ by her grateful people for her bravery and determination.

Grammar Lesson

Compound Verbs

A **compound verb** is two or more verbs that have the same subject and are joined by a conjunction such as *and* or *or*. In the following example from "The Golden Kite, the Silver Wind," the subject is underlined and the parts of the compound verb are italicized.

> S   V   V
> **Example:** "<u>They</u> *ran* to the walls and *built* them nearer to this new vision. . . ."

Both *ran* and *built* have the same subject, *They*, and the verbs are connected by the conjunction *and*.

Practice Identify the compound verbs in each sentence below.

1. She spoke and directed people through the silken screen.
2. The townspeople worked all night and shaped their walls like lightning.
3. The people moaned and wept.
4. They parted and hurried back to work.
5. The wind will carry and sustain the kite.

Writing Application Use each word below as the subject in a sentence, and create compound verbs to accompany each subject.

1. Mandarin   **2.** walls

W̶G̶ Prentice Hall Writing and Grammar Connection: Chapter 20, Section 1

Writing Lesson

Persuasive Letter

Imagine you were living in one of the cities featured in "The Golden Kite, the Silver Wind." Write a letter to the Mandarin, letting him know how concerned you are about the competition between the cities and urging him to resolve the conflict.

Prewriting Brainstorm a list of points you would like to make about the conflict. Keep your audience in mind and think about what you can say that would affect the Mandarin's thoughts about the issue.

Drafting As you draft, make sure your arguments are supported. Whenever possible, prove your point by providing examples, facts, or details.

Revising As you revise, underline all of your arguments and highlight the support. If a point needs more evidence, add details. If there is no stronger evidence, eliminate your point.

Model: Evaluating Support for Your Arguments

The people of the city will not survive the competition.

and people are dying

Everyone is working on the walls. Sickness has spread.

> Added information supports the argument that the people of the city will not survive.

---

*W*G *Prentice Hall Writing and Grammar Connection: Chapter 7, Section 4*

Extension Activities

Listening and Speaking In a small group, present a **dramatic interpretation** of Bradbury's story. Make these necessary decisions to organize your interpretation properly.

- Assign the roles of the two mandarins, the daughter, and a messenger.
- Assign the role of director to one person in the group who can listen objectively and give advice on pitch and tone of voice.

Present your interpretation to the class, and ask your audience to evaluate your presentation. **[Group Activity]**

Research and Technology Bradbury's fable addresses issues raised by the Cold War. Research some aspect of the Cold War. For example, you might study the alliances each side formed or the weapons buildup that took place. Use library resources like the Internet, an atlas, and history books. Then, compare the events in Bradbury's story to produce a **historical report.**

 **Take It to the Net**   www.phschool.com

Go online for an additional research activity using the Internet.

Prepare to Read

The Road Not Taken ◆ To be of use ◆ New Directions

 Take It to the Net

Visit www.phschool.com
for interactive activities
and instruction related to
the selections, including

- background
- graphic organizers
- literary elements
- reading strategies

Preview

Connecting to the Literature

You face choices big and small every day. The questions of how to challenge yourself in a new way or which career path to pursue present decisions with major implications. The selections that follow explore these kinds of life choices—critical forks in the road of life.

Background

In the early 1900s, job opportunities were limited for many Americans—particularly for African Americans like Annie Johnson in Maya Angelou's "New Directions." Then, the most common jobs for African American women were cleaning, childcare, and general household labor. For women who had families, caring for someone else's household was an extra burden. No wonder Annie Johnson struck off in a "new direction."

Literary Analysis

Figurative Language

Figurative language, language that means more than it says literally, is often used to create vivid impressions by introducing comparisons between dissimilar things. Look at the following example of figurative language found in Marge Piercy's "To be of use":

> The people I love the best
> jump into work head first,
> without dallying in the shallows.

Piercy is not stating that the people she loves best are deep-sea divers. Rather, she is expressing admiration for people who take on challenges courageously. As you read the selections, take note of vivid language that implies more than its literal meaning.

Comparing Literary Works

While making difficult decisions and working toward a goal, the people you will encounter in these selections have put themselves to the test. In the words of Robert Frost, "that has made all the difference." Compare and contrast the ways each writer uses figurative language to convey larger ideas about decisions and their impact.

Reading Strategy

Generating Questions

To better understand what you read, **generate questions** based on the text. Begin with the common questions words *who, what, where, when, why,* and *how.* Write questions that come to mind as you read a passage, and try to answer those questions as you progress. Use a chart like the one shown to jot down your questions and answers.

Who?	
What?	
When?	
Where?	
Why?	
How?	

Vocabulary Development

diverged (di vʉrjd′) *v.* branched out in different directions (p. 189)

dallying (dalˊ ē iŋ) *v.* wasting time; loitering (p. 190)

submerged (səb mʉrjd′) *adj.* covered with something; underwater (p. 190)

harness (härˊ nis) *v.* attach, as with straps for pulling or controlling (p. 190)

amicably (amˊ i kə blē) *adv.* agreeably (p. 191)

meticulously (mə tikˊ yo͞o ləs lē) *adv.* very carefully and precisely (p. 191)

specters (spekˊ tərz) *n.* ghostly images; phantoms (p. 191)

ominous (ämˊ ə nəs) *adj.* threatening; menacing (p. 192)

unpalatable (un palˊ it ə bəl) *adj.* distasteful; unpleasant (p. 192)

tempted by the hot meat pies which Annie ladled out of the fat. She wrapped them in newspapers, which soaked up the grease, and offered them for sale at a nickel each. Although business was slow, those first days Annie was determined. She balanced her appearances between the two hours of activity.

So, on Monday if she offered hot fresh pies at the cotton gin and sold the remaining cooled-down pies at the lumber mill for three cents, then on Tuesday she went first to the lumber mill presenting fresh, just-cooked pies as the lumbermen covered in sawdust emerged from the mill.

For the next few years, on balmy spring days, blistering summer noons, and cold, wet, and wintry middays, Annie never disappointed her customers, who could count on seeing the tall, brown-skin woman bent over her brazier, carefully turning the meat pies. When she felt certain that the workers had become dependent on her, she built a stall between the two hives of industry and let the men run to her for their lunchtime provisions.

She had indeed stepped from the road which seemed to have been chosen for her and cut herself a brand-new path. In years that stall became a store where customers could buy cheese, meal, syrup, cookies, candy, writing tablets, pickles, canned goods, fresh fruit, soft drinks, coal, oil, and leather soles for worn-out shoes.

Each of us has the right and the responsibility to assess the roads which lie ahead, and those over which we have traveled, and if the future road looms <u>ominous</u> or unpromising, and the roads back uninviting, then we need to gather our resolve and, carrying only the necessary baggage, step off that road into another direction. If the new choice is also <u>unpalatable</u>, without embarrassment, we must be ready to change that as well.

Reading Strategy
Generating Questions
What question does this paragraph spark in your mind?

ominous (ăm´ ə nəs) *adj.* threatening; menacing

unpalatable (un pal´ it ə bəl) *adj.* distasteful; unpleasant

Review and Assess

Thinking About the Selections

1. **Respond:** Would you rather meet Annie Johnson or the speaker of "To be of use"? Explain.

2. **(a) Recall:** In the first stanza of "To be of use," what kind of people does the speaker say she loves best? **(b) Analyze:** What kinds of qualities or traits do these people possess?

3. **(a) Recall:** Why does Annie Johnson have to find a source of income? **(b) Infer:** Why do you think Annie Johnson chose not to pursue a factory job or a job as a domestic?

4. **(a) Recall:** How does Annie Johnson earn a living? **(b) Draw Conclusions:** What does Johnson's achievement suggest about the human spirit in general?

5. **Apply:** What are the positive consequences of feeling useful?

Maya Angelou

(b. 1928)
Three decades after Frost's appearance at the Kennedy inauguration, President-elect Bill Clinton invited fellow Arkansan Maya Angelou to read one of her poems at his inaugural ceremonies. In both her poetry and her nonfiction, Angelou draws on her own experience, frequently exploring the problems of poverty, racism, and sexism.

Review and Assess

Literary Analysis

Figurative Language

1. Why is the description of life as a road or path an effective use of **figurative language**?
2. Use a chart like this one to record four examples of figurative language from "To be of use." Explain the meaning of each example.

Figurative Language:	1. _____ _____	2. _____ _____	3. _____ _____	4. _____ _____
Meaning:				

Comparing Literary Works

3. (a) Compare Frost's "less traveled" road with the "new path" that Johnson carves for herself. (b) What similar approaches to life do these images convey?
4. (a) Contrast the way Frost's speaker approaches the roads and the way the people in Piercy's opening stanza approach the water. (b) What different approaches to life does the figurative language convey?

Reading Strategy

Generating Questions

5. Using a chart like the one shown, identify at least three of the **questions** and answers you **generated** while reading the selections.

	Who?	What?	When?	Where?	Why?	How?
Question:						
Answer:						

6. Which questions helped you understand the selections best?

Extend Understanding

7. **History Connection:** Annie Johnson's situation shows the struggle that many African American women faced in the early 1900s. How have situations changed for African Americans in the United States over the last century?

Quick Review

Figurative language is language that means more than it says literally. It is often used to create vivid impressions by setting up comparisons between dissimilar things.

To better understand what you read, **generate questions** based on the text. Begin with the common question words *who, what, where, when, why,* and *how* about a selection.

 Take It to the Net
www.phschool.com

Take the interactive self-test online to check your understanding of the selections.

Integrate Language Skills

Vocabulary Development Lesson

Word Analysis: Anglo-Saxon Suffix -ly

Words that end in -ly are often adjectives turned into adverbs of manner—adverbs that tell *how* or *in what manner*. Use the suffix -ly to turn the following adjectives into adverbs.

1. amicable (friendly)
2. meticulous (very careful or thorough)
3. ominous (menacing; threatening)

Spelling Strategy

Do not double the letters *w*, *h*, *x*, or *y* at the end of a word before adding an ending such as -ing or -ed. For example, *box + -ed = boxed*. Write the new words formed by adding the given suffixes below, and then use each word in a sentence.

1. dismay + -ed
2. catch + -ing
3. flex + -ed
4. flow + -ing

Fluency: True or False

Indicate whether each of the following statements is true or false. Explain your answer.

1. If a stream *diverged*, two parts of it probably moved in different directions.
2. If you and your friend part *amicably*, you are most likely in a bad mood.
3. If you clean your room *meticulously*, it is messy.
4. Some children dress as *specters* on Halloween.
5. A smile is usually an *ominous* expression.
6. Most chefs try to cook *unpalatable* meals.
7. Window shoppers seem to enjoy *dallying*.
8. Flowers are *submerged* in the soil.
9. In Alaska, some people *harness* dogs to a sled.

Grammar Lesson

Regular Verbs

A **verb** has four principal parts: the present, the present participle, the past, and the past participle. Most of the verbs in the English language, such as the verb *talk*, are regular, and you can form these parts following a predictable pattern. Notice that the final *e* may be dropped in forming the present participle.

> **Present:** talk; race
> **Present Participle:** (is) talking; (is) racing
> **Past:** talked; raced
> **Past Participle:** (has) talked; (has) raced

Practice Write the four principal parts of each of the following verbs.

1. look
2. diverge
3. observe
4. harvest
5. work
6. walk
7. jump
8. cook
9. expect
10. cover

Writing Application Write four sentences using each of the principal parts of the regular verb *travel*. After each sentence, identify which part you used.

Writing Lesson

Evaluation of Figurative Language

By using figurative language—such as the image of a road in Frost's poem to suggest a life—writers hope to add clarity and color to their writing. Choose one of the selections and write an essay evaluating the writer's use of figurative language.

Prewriting List examples of figurative language that you find in your chosen selection. Identify the basic comparisons that are stated or implied. As you make your list, decide whether the language leaves you confused or if the choice of words is logical. Also, notice whether the comparison is an overused expression or a fresh, new idea.

Model: Evaluating Figurative Language

Figurative Language	Comments	
"[people] who pull like water buffalo, with massive patience"	This is original and makes a clear comparison to people who work diligently and patiently.	The comment evaluates the unique qualities of the poet's use of figurative language.

Drafting State your reaction to the figurative language, and then cite examples to support your reaction. Present the examples in order of importance or in the order in which they appear in the work.

Revising Make sure you have offered enough examples to support all general statements. Check to see that your sentences are logical.

WG *Prentice Hall Writing and Grammar Connection: Chapter 13, Section 2*

Extension Activities

Listening and Speaking Working with another student, role-play a **job interview** that might take place between Annie Johnson and a potential employer.

- Analyze the occasion and decide what each speaker needs to say.
- Decide what the potential employer wants to hear.

During the interview, use effective, formal language to convey the character and the situation. When appropriate, use gestures and eye contact to make a point.

Research and Technology Working in a small group, **videotape an interview** with a local businessperson, a teacher, or another professional to learn about the stages of that person's career. After watching the video, compare the aspects of your subject's career to those of Annie Johnson's. **[Group Activity]**

 **Take It to the Net** www.phschool.com

Go online for an additional research activity using the Internet.

Business Documents

About Business Documents

A business document is a formal piece of writing relating to the work-place. The purpose of a business document is to communicate specific information effectively by presenting facts and other pertinent details.

This chart shows the variety and function of business documents.

Types of Business Documents	
Print	Electronic
Letter: a formal, written message sent by regular mail	**Voice mail:** a spoken message recorded on an answering machine
Agenda: a schedule for a meeting	**E-mail:** a typed message sent by computer
Memo: a brief message with pertinent information for internal company use only	**Fax:** a printed copy of a handwritten or typed message transmitted via phone lines
Meeting minutes: the notes and a summary of a business meeting	
Form/application: a document filled out by an applicant	

A well-written business document meets these criteria:

- It imparts accurate information in a clear, direct, and concise way.
- It addresses specific issues and anticipates readers' questions.
- It is neatly formatted, well organized, and error-free.

Reading Strategy

Analyzing Document Structure and Format

The structure of a business document suits its purpose. Look at the structure and format of these common business documents:

A **business letter** addresses a work-related issue, such as a request for service or a clarification of company policy. The letter has six parts: the heading, inside address, salutation, body, closing, and signature. It is written in paragraph form that follows an acceptable format of indentation.

A **business agenda** outlines the schedule for a meeting. An agenda contains a title identifying the subject, a list of starting and ending times for scheduled events, and descriptions of each part of the agenda.

Letter of Welcome

In the following business letter, California senator Martha Escutia welcomes students to a college conference. Notice that the language of the letter, which uses block format, is welcoming but formal and polite.

The **heading** provides the business address of the senator.

The **salutation** identifies and greets the letter's recipients.

The **body** explains the letter writer's purpose for writing.

The **closing,** written in Spanish, means "It is possible." Typical English closings include "Sincerely" and "Yours truly."

Representing the communities of:

Bell

Bell Gardens

Commerce

Cudahy

East Los Angeles

Florence-Graham

Huntington Park

Maywood

Miramonte

Montebello

Norwalk

Pico Rivera

Santa Fe Springs

South El Monte

South Gate

Vernon

Walnut Park

Whittier

Senator
MARTHA ESCUTIA
California State Senate 30th District
400 N. Montebello Blvd. #101
Montebello, CA 90640

Dear Students:

I want to welcome you to the 8th Annual Southeast College Conference. It is my privilege to host this exciting event and to share the many educational opportunities at your disposal.

You have reached a critical time in your life, a time filled with questions. Where do you want to go in life? How will you get there? Education is definitely the vehicle to your success in any career you choose. Education will help develop you into leaders of the next generation. It will empower you intellectually and enable you to grow into valuable, contributing citizens of your community.

As a young girl I learned the importance of a college education. I armed myself with information that enabled me to pursue my dream. Believe me, my quest for higher education was not easy. I remember the financial and social obstacles my family and community had to overcome. Their sacrifices inspired me to educate myself and give back to my community.

When I was first elected to the Assembly, I was overjoyed. I finally had the opportunity to give back by passing legislation to improve the quality of life in my community. This year, as your Senator, I passed SB 1689, the Advanced Placement Challenge Grant Program. This measure allocated $16.5 million dollars to fund Advanced Placement (AP) classes in schools that lack teachers and support systems for AP students. I also passed SB 1683, which will ensure that every student at risk of not graduating will receive the extra academic help he or she needs. Its focus is to give the students the tools they need to establish a stronger educational foundation.

Please make today an opportunity of a lifetime. Ask questions, participate in the workshops, let your voice be heard and, most importantly, have fun. Today I am very proud to have the opportunity to meet the great minds of the future. I wish you the best of luck and continued success in your future educational endeavors.

SÍ, SE PUEDE

Senator Martha Escutia

Senator Martha Escutia

Conference Agenda

In addition to the business letter welcoming them to the 8th Annual Southeast College Conference, students attending also received this agenda. The agenda outlines activities from 8 A.M. to 2 P.M.

The agenda announces the exact times for each part of the program.

Descriptions in boldface letters identify what will happen during each scheduled time period.

Program Agenda

8:00 A.M.–9:00 A.M.
Registration/Continental Breakfast

9:00 A.M.–10:00 A.M.
Welcome
Mel Mares
Principal, Bell High School

Opening Remarks
Senator Martha Escutia

Keynote Speakers
Manny Medrano
Legal Issues Reporter, Channel 4 News

Claudio Trejos
Sports Anchor, KTLA News

10:15 A.M.–11:00 A.M.
Workshop Session I

11:15 A.M.–12:00 P.M.
Workshop Session II

12:00 P.M.–2:00 P.M.
Lunch/College Recruitment Fair

Check Your Comprehension

1. What is Senator Escutia's purpose for writing her business letter?
2. What personal information does the senator share to make her letter friendly to students?
3. According to the agenda, who is delivering the opening remarks?
4. When will Workshop Session I be held?

Applying the Reading Strategy

Analyzing Document Structure and Format

5. What is the relationship between the opening and closing paragraphs of this business letter?
6. What is the purpose of the paragraph in which the author discusses her accomplishments as senator?
7. Why do you think the senator chose to write her closing in Spanish?

Activity

Writing a Letter of Welcome to Parents

Write a business letter in which you welcome parents to a school event such as a parent-teacher conference or talent show. Assume that the letter will be distributed to parents as they enter the building. In your letter, include information that tells when and where the event takes place. Also, explain the purpose of the event. Use friendly but formal language. Keep track of the parts of your business letter by using the chart at right.

> **Outline for Letter of Welcome to Parents**
>
> **Heading:** Your Address
> **Salutation:** "Dear Parents:"
> **Body:**
> • Letter's Purpose (in opening paragraph)
> • Explanation of Event
> • Where and When
> **Polite Closing:**
> **Signature:**

Contrasting Informational Texts

Document Formats

1. For each situation below, indicate the best format to convey information. Choose voice mail, e-mail, fax, business letter, agenda, memo, meeting minutes, or application form. Explain your choice.

   (a) Formally introducing your business to a new client
   (b) Reminding a co-worker about an idea you had and asking for her input
   (c) Supplying the information needed to open a bank account
   (d) Sharing a sketch of your idea with someone in another office
   (e) Recording decisions made at a meeting
   (f) Instructing employees about a complex new policy

Prepare to Read

Old Man of the Temple

Preview

Connecting to the Literature

You see a shadow dart behind a tree, but when you reach the tree and
look, there is nothing there—what could it be? The narrator's experience
in this story is universal: He sees something and cannot believe his eyes.
It is this element of mystery that can make a story so much fun to read.

Background

"Old Man of the Temple" takes place near Malgudi, a fictional town in
southern India. Although it is imaginary, it could be any one of thousands
of rural southern Indian towns. Its roads are unpaved, and cattle roam the
dirt paths as farmers till the fields. It is a place where the ruins of temples
hundreds of years old decay amid the creeping tropical vines.

Literary Analysis

Fantasy

"Old Man of the Temple" is a **fantasy**—a work of fiction that includes characters, places, and events that could not really exist or happen. When you read fantasy, you leave the real world behind in order to enjoy the tale. Yet, fantasies always contain some realistic elements—just to give perspective to the fantastical elements. The following passage from the story presents the fantastic idea of a dead person coming back to life.

> "Don't feel hurt; I say you shouldn't be here any more because you are dead."

As you read, notice how reality combines with fantasy to create a ghostly tale.

Connecting Literary Elements

The **setting**—the time and place in which the action occurs—of this story contributes greatly to the fantasy. Because the story takes place in India, details of the action are interwoven with ideas and symbols from Indian history and legend. Notice how the setting contributes to the fantasy of the story.

Reading Strategy

Distinguishing Fantasy From Reality

As this story begins, a man and his driver are driving down a lonely rural road at night. That much can be established. Very soon, however, it becomes more and more difficult to **distinguish fantasy from reality**.

- If you feel confused by something that has happened in the story, reread the section.
- Determine which details could or could not happen in real life.

Use a chart like the one on the right to distinguish those elements that are real and those that are fantastic, or impossible.

Real
Taxi ride at night

Fantastic
The old man that only Doss sees

Vocabulary Development

sobriety (sə brī′ ə tē) *n.* moderation, especially in the use of alcoholic beverages (p. 203)

awry (ə rī′) *adj.* not straight (p. 204)

literally (lit′ ər əl ē) *adv.* actually; in fact (p. 206)

longevity (län jev′ə tē) *n.* the length or duration of a life (p. 206)

imperative (im per′ ə tiv) *adj.* absolutely necessary; urgent (p. 207)

venture (ven′ chər) *n.* chance (p. 208)

Old Man of the Temple

R. K. Narayan

The Talkative Man said:

It was some years ago that this happened. I don't know if you can make anything of it. If you do, I shall be glad to hear what you have to say; but personally I don't understand it at all. It has always mystified me. Perhaps the driver was drunk; perhaps he wasn't.

I had engaged a taxi for going to Kumbum, which, as you may already know, is fifty miles from Malgudi.[1] I went there one morning and it was past nine in the evening when I finished my business and started back for the town. Doss [däs], the driver, was a young fellow of about twenty-five. He had often brought his car for me and I liked him. He was a well-behaved, obedient fellow, with a capacity to sit and wait at the wheel, which is really a rare quality in a taxi driver. He drove the car smoothly, seldom swore at passers-by, and exhibited perfect judgment, good sense, and <u>sobriety</u>; and so I preferred him to any other driver whenever I had to go out on business.

It was about eleven when we passed the village

---

1. **Malgudi** (mäl gōō′ dē) fictional city about which Narayan often writes.

◄ **Critical Viewing** What mysterious events might occur in a temple like this? **[Speculate]**

Koopal [koo päl´], which is on the way down. It was the dark half of the month and the surrounding country was swallowed up in the night. The village street was deserted. Everyone had gone to sleep; hardly any light was to be seen. The stars overhead sparkled brightly. Sitting in the back seat and listening to the continuous noise of the running wheels, I was half lulled into a drowse.

All of a sudden Doss swerved the car and shouted: "You old fool! Do you want to kill yourself?"

I was shaken out of my drowse and asked: "What is the matter?"

Doss stopped the car and said, "You see that old fellow, sir. He is trying to kill himself. I can't understand what he is up to."

I looked in the direction he pointed and asked, "Which old man?"

"There, there. He is coming towards us again. As soon as I saw him open that temple door and come out I had a feeling, somehow, that I must keep an eye on him."

I took out my torch, got down, and walked about, but could see no one. There was an old temple on the roadside. It was utterly in ruins; most portions of it were mere mounds of old brick; the walls were <u>awry</u>; the doors were shut to the main doorway, and brambles and thickets grew over and covered them. It was difficult to guess with the aid of the torch alone what temple it was and to what period it belonged.

"The doors are shut and sealed and don't look as if they had been opened for centuries now," I cried.

"No, sir," Doss said coming nearer. "I saw the old man open the doors and come out. He is standing there; shall we ask him to open them again if you want to go in and see?"

I said to Doss, "Let us be going. We are wasting our time here."

We went back to the car. Doss sat in his seat, pressed the self-starter, and asked without turning his head, "Are you permitting this fellow to come with us, sir? He says he will get down at the next milestone."

"Which fellow?" I asked.

Doss indicated the space next to him.

"What is the matter with you, Doss? Have you had a drop of drink or something?"

"I have never tasted any drink in my life, sir," he said, and added, "Get down, old boy. Master says he can't take you."

"Are you talking to yourself?"

"After all, I think we needn't care for these unknown fellows on the road," he said.

"Doss," I pleaded. "Do you feel confident you can drive? If you feel dizzy don't drive."

"Thank you, sir," said Doss. "I would rather not start the car now. I am feeling a little out of sorts." I looked at him anxiously. He closed his eyes, his breathing became heavy and noisy, and gradually his head sank.

"Doss, Doss," I cried desperately. I got down, walked to the front seat, opened the door, and shook him vigorously. He opened his eyes, assumed a hunched-up position, and rubbed his eyes with his hands, which trembled like an old man's.

awry (ə rī´) *adj.* not straight

"Do you feel better?" I asked.

"Better! Better! Hi! Hi!" he said in a thin, piping voice.

"What has happened to your voice? You sound like someone else," I said.

"Nothing. My voice is as good as it was. When a man is eighty he is bound to feel a few changes coming on."

"You aren't eighty, surely," I said.

"Not a day less," he said. "Is nobody going to move this vehicle? If not, there is no sense in sitting here all day. I will get down and go back to my temple."

"I don't know how to drive," I said. "And unless you do it, I don't see how it can move."

"Me!" exclaimed Doss. "These new chariots! God knows what they are drawn by, I never understand, though I could handle a pair of bullocks[2] in my time. May I ask a question?"

"Go on," I said.

"Where is everybody?"

"Who?"

"Lots of people I knew are not to be seen at all. All sorts of new fellows everywhere, and nobody seems to care. Not a soul comes near the temple. All sorts of people go about but not one who cares to stop and talk. Why doesn't the king ever come this way? He used to go this way at least once a year before."

"Which king?" I asked.

"Let me go, you idiot," said Doss, edging towards the door on which I was leaning. "You don't seem to know anything." He pushed me aside, and got down from the car. He stooped as if he had a big hump on his back, and hobbled along towards the temple. I followed him, hardly knowing what to do. He turned and snarled at me: "Go away, leave me alone. I have had enough of you."

"What has come over you, Doss?" I asked.

"Who is Doss, anyway? Doss, Doss, Doss. What an absurd name! Call me by my name or leave me alone. Don't follow me calling 'Doss, Doss.' "

"What is your name?" I asked.

"Krishna Battar [krish′ nə bə tar′], and if you mention my name people will know for a hundred miles around. I built a temple where there was only a cactus field before. I dug the earth, burnt every brick, and put them one upon another, all single-handed. And on the day the temple held up its tower over the surrounding country, what a crowd gathered! The king sent his chief minister . . ."

"Who was the king?"

"Where do you come from?" he asked.

"I belong to these parts certainly, but as far as I know there has been only a collector at the head of the district. I have never heard of any king."

---

2. **bullocks** (bŏŏl′ əks) *n.* oxen; steer.

Hinduism and Reincarnation

Hinduism is the religion of the majority of people in India, the setting for "Old Man of the Temple." Drawing from a set of beliefs that is thousands of years old, Hinduism teaches that death is a temporary stage in an endless cycle of reincarnations, or rebirths. The actions that someone performs in one life, good and bad, will determine the conditions of future rebirths. Therefore, it is not surprising that Narayan includes aspects of reincarnation in his story.

Reading Strategy
Distinguishing Fantasy From Reality Which clues in this paragraph sound real and which sound fantastic?

✔**Reading Check**

How old does Doss say he is when he wakes up?

"Hi! Hi! Hi!" he cackled, and his voice rang through the gloomy silent village. "Fancy never knowing the king! He will behead you if he hears it."

"What is his name?" I asked.

This tickled him so much that he sat down on the ground, <u>literally</u> unable to stand the joke any more. He laughed and coughed uncontrollably.

"I am sorry to admit," I said, "that my parents have brought me up in such utter ignorance of worldly affairs that I don't know even my king. But won't you enlighten me? What is his name?"

"Vishnu Varma [vish′ nōō vär′ mə], the emperor of emperors . . ."

I cast my mind up and down the range of my historical knowledge but there was no one by that name. Perhaps a local chief of pre-British days, I thought.

"What a king! He often visited my temple or sent his minister for the Annual Festival of the temple. But now nobody cares."

"People are becoming less godly nowadays," I said. There was silence for a moment. An idea occurred to me, I can't say why. "Listen to me," I said. "You ought not to be here any more."

"What do you mean?" he asked, drawing himself up, proudly.

"Don't feel hurt; I say you shouldn't be here any more because you are dead."

"Dead! Dead!" he said. "Don't talk nonsense. How can I be dead when you see me before you now? If I am dead how can I be saying this and that?"

"I don't know all that," I said. I argued and pointed out that according to his own story he was more than five hundred years old, and didn't he know that man's <u>longevity</u> was only a hundred? He constantly interrupted me, but considered deeply what I said.

He said: "It is like this . . . I was coming through the jungle one night after visiting my sister in the next village. I had on me some money and gold ornaments. A gang of robbers set upon me. I gave them as good a fight as any man could, but they were too many for me. They beat me down and knifed me; they took away all that I had on me and left thinking they had killed me. But soon I got up and tried to follow them. They were gone. And I returned to the temple and have been here since . . ."

I told him, "Krishna Battar, you are dead, absolutely dead. You must try and go away from here."

"What is to happen to the temple?" he asked.

"Others will look after it."

"Where am I to go? Where am I to go?"

"Have you no one who cares for you?" I asked.

"None except my wife. I loved her very much."

"You can go to her."

"Oh, no. She died four years ago . . ."

Four years! It was very puzzling. "Do you say four years back from now?" I asked.

"Yes, four years ago from now." He was clearly without any sense of time.

literally (lit′ ər əl ē) *adv.* actually; in fact

longevity (län jev′ə tē) *n.* the length or duration of a life

Reading Strategy
Distinguishing Fantasy From Reality Does the old man's story sound fantastic or realistic to you? Explain.

◀ **Critical Viewing**
How do the details of this
painting compare to the
details of the story's
setting? **[Support]**

So I asked, "Was she alive when you were attacked by thieves?"

"Certainly not. If she had been alive she would never have allowed me
to go through the jungle after nightfall. She took very good care of me."

"See here," I said. "It is <u>imperative</u> you should go away from here. If
she comes and calls you, will you go?"

"How can she when I tell you that she is dead?"

I thought for a moment. Presently I found myself saying, "Think of her,
and only of her, for a while and see what happens. What was her name?"

"Seetha [sē´ thə], a wonderful girl . . ."

"Come on, think of her." He remained in deep thought for a while.
He suddenly screamed, "Seetha is coming! Am I dreaming or what? I
will go with her . . ." He stood up, very erect; he appeared to have lost
all the humps and twists he had on his body. He drew himself up,
made a dash forward, and fell down in a heap.

imperative (im per´ ə tiv)
adj. absolutely necessary;
urgent

✓**Reading Check**

According to the old man,
how many years ago did
his wife die?

Old Man of the Temple ◆ *207*

Doss lay on the rough ground. The only sign of life in him was his faint breathing. I shook him and called him. He would not open his eyes. I walked across and knocked on the door of the first cottage. I banged on the door violently.

Someone moaned inside, "Ah, it is come!"

Someone else whispered, "You just cover your ears and sleep. It will knock for a while and go away." I banged on the door and shouted who I was and where I came from.

I walked back to the car and sounded the horn. Then the door opened, and a whole family crowded out with lamps. "We thought it was the usual knocking and we wouldn't have opened if you hadn't spoken."

"When was this knocking first heard?" I asked.

"We can't say," said one. "The first time I heard it was when my grandfather was living; he used to say he had even seen it once or twice. It doesn't harm anyone, as far as I know. The only thing it does is bother the bullock carts passing the temple and knock on the doors at night . . ."

I said as a <u>venture</u>, "It is unlikely you will be troubled any more."

It proved correct. When I passed that way again months later I was told that the bullocks passing the temple after dusk never shied now and no knocking on the doors was heard at nights. So I felt that the old fellow had really gone away with his good wife.

venture (ven´ chər) *n.* chance

R. K. Narayan

(1906-2001)
Within a career that spanned more than sixty years, R. K. Narayan wrote more than fifteen novels, as well as numerous collections of short stories, travel books, and essays. Born in the city of Madras in southern India, he was one of nine children of a middle-class family. He attended Maharaja's College in Mysore, and after briefly working as a teacher, he became a writer.

In his novels, legends, and short stories, Narayan skillfully combines Western plots and themes with Indian subject matter. In 1958, he won the National Prize of the Indian Literary Academy, his nation's highest literary honor.

Review and Assess

Thinking About the Selection

1. **Respond:** The narrator tells you, "I don't know if you can make anything of it. If you do, I shall be glad to hear what you have to say. . . ." How would you answer him?

2. **(a) Recall:** Early in the story, what does Doss say he sees when he swerves the car? **(b) Analyze:** Why does the narrator find Doss's words unbelievable?

3. **(a) Recall:** Describe the transformation that happens to Doss. **(b) Analyze:** How does the narrator react to the change?

4. **(a) Recall:** What does the narrator say to cause the old man to think about his own situation? **(b) Infer:** Do you think the narrator is ruled more by his feelings or by reason? Why?

5. **Connect:** What purpose does the introduction of the family serve?

6. **Assess:** How might you respond if you found yourself in the narrator's situation?

Review and Assess

Literary Analysis

Fantasy

1. Why is "Old Man of the Temple" a **fantasy**?
2. How do the fantastic elements add to the story?
3. Using a chart like the one below, show how the realistic elements found in the story contribute to an atmosphere in which fantasy can develop.

Connecting Literary Elements

4. Use a chart like the one below to help you answer the following questions. (a) How does the **setting** contribute to the fantasy in the story? (b) How does the setting contribute to the reality in the story?

5. How might this story be different if it were set in a modern American city?

Reading Strategy

Distinguishing Fantasy From Reality

6. Name two elements of the story that are fantastic.
7. At what point in the story does the plot change from realistic to fantastic? Explain.
8. During which scenes in the story is it difficult to **distinguish fantasy from reality**? Explain.

Extend Understanding

9. **Media Connection:** Compare this story with fantasy movies. (a) Which elements are similar? (b) Which are different?

Quick Review

Fantasy is fiction that includes characters, places, and events that could not exist or happen in real life.

The **setting** of a story is the time and place in which the action occurs.

To **distinguish fantasy from reality**, determine which elements of a story could or could not happen in real life.

 Take It to the Net
www.phschool.com
Take the interactive self-test online to check your understanding of the selection.

Integrate Language Skills

Vocabulary Development Lesson

Word Analysis: Latin Suffix -ity

In the word *longevity*, you find the suffix *-ity*, meaning "state of" or "condition of." One way to define *longevity* is "the condition of having a long life." Using the meaning of *-ity*, write definitions for the following words:

1. agility
2. severity
3. generosity
4. individuality

Spelling Strategy

When spelling a word that contains the *j* sound before an *e*, you usually use a *g*, as in *longevity*. There are exceptions, however, such as *subject*. For each word below, write "Correct" if the word is spelled correctly. If the spelling is incorrect, write the proper spelling.

1. suggest   2. injection   3. magesty

Concept Development: Synonyms

In each numbered item, choose the word whose meaning is closest to that of the word from the vocabulary list on page 201.

1. sobriety: (a) sadness, (b) loneliness, (c) moderation
2. awry: (a) sophisticated, (b) crooked, (c) clever
3. literally: (a) actually, (b) scholarly, (c) differently
4. longevity: (a) height, (b) endurance, (c) duration
5. imperative: (a) essential, (b) unnecessary, (c) ruler
6. venture: (a) satisfaction, (b) risk, (c) university

Grammar Lesson

Adverbs

Adverbs are words that modify verbs, adjectives, and other adverbs. They answer the questions *Where? When? In what way?* and *To what extent?* about the words they modify. You can often make descriptions more meaningful by adding an adverb to a sentence. Look at the following examples:

Modifying a Verb: Doss <u>drove</u> the car *smoothly*. (*smoothly* modifies the verb *drove*)

Modifying an Adjective: He drove an *extremely* <u>large</u> car. (*extremely* modifies the adjective *large*)

Modifying an Adverb: He drove the car *very* <u>smoothly</u>. (*very* modifies the adverb *smoothly*)

Practice Copy each sentence. Underline the word or words modified by the adverb in italics. Then, identify whether the word modified is a verb, an adjective, or an adverb.

1. He *certainly* believed that he was right.
2. His wife took *very* good care of him.
3. Doss told him that he was *absolutely* dead.
4. He laughed *uncontrollably* at the news.
5. He needed to go *away* from there.

Writing Application Use each of the following adverbs in a sentence. At the end of the sentence, write which word each one modifies.

1. completely   2. entirely   3. quietly

Writing Lesson

Travel Brochure

India, where "Old Man of the Temple" takes place, is a land of ancient cultures, colorful ceremonies, and joyous celebrations—an excellent visitor destination. Using the setting of the story and additional information about India, write a travel brochure that will entice travelers to visit.

Prewriting   Decide on the features you will describe in your brochure. Review the selection and research India to gather appealing details.

Drafting   Many qualities can make the tone of your brochure persuasive. For instance, vivid descriptions will appeal to readers' imaginations and dreams, and a sense of humor will spark a receptive attitude.

Model: Using a Persuasive Tone

From mysterious and historical temple ruins to breathtaking views of snow-peaked mountains soaring to incredible heights, you can experience the splendor of a culture rich in beauty and tradition.

> Words like *breathtaking* and *soaring* convey the splendor of India and appeal to a tourist's desire for an unforgettable experience.

Revising   Reread your draft. Make sure that your readers will be persuaded to visit. Add information that can make your tone more persuasive and your travel brochure more appealing.

W͞G Prentice Hall Writing and Grammar Connection: Chapter 7, Section 3

Extension Activities

Listening and Speaking Prepare a **dramatic monologue** in which the old man relates the story from his point of view. Follow these suggestions as you write your monologue:

- Use appropriate word choice—select words that the old man would use.
- Describe experiences found in the story.
- Enhance your performance by adding new information about the old man that you did not learn in the story.

Perform your monologue for the class.

Research and Technology Southern India, where this story takes place, is overwhelmingly Hindu. In a group, do a **research report** on Hinduism and explain how Hinduism enriches your understanding of this story. Use library resources, including the Internet, to find information to strengthen your report. **[Group Activity]**

 **Take It to the Net**   www.phschool.com

Go online for an additional research activity using the Internet.

Prepare to Read

Perseus

Danaē with young Perseus arriving on the island of Seripo,
Museo Archeologico, Ferrara, Italy

 Take It to the Net

Visit www.phschool.com for interactive activities and instruction related to "Perseus," including
- background
- graphic organizers
- literary elements
- reading strategies

Preview

Connecting to the Literature

Some people love to rise to the challenge of difficult situations, while others prefer to keep their lives on an even keel. Perseus, the main character in this selection, is the first sort of person—the type who thrives on grappling with thorny problems. Before reading, consider which type of person you relate to more.

Background

"Perseus" takes place in a mythological world populated by Greek gods and goddesses. Among them are Zeus, the chief god, who fathered a number of human children; Athena, goddess of war and wisdom; and Hermes, the messenger god. Each god plays a pivotal role in Perseus' heroic adventure.

Literary Analysis

Hero in a Myth

A **hero in a myth** is a character who performs amazing feats in a tale involving supernatural beings and fantastic events. The hero in a myth is often aided by sympathetic gods and magical elements. Nevertheless, the hero must exhibit admirable qualities such as courage, loyalty, and fairness. The following excerpt shows the loyalty and courage of Perseus, the hero in this myth.

> [Perseus] did exactly what the King had hoped he would do, declared that he would . . . go off and kill Medusa and bring back her head as his gift. . . . No one in his senses would have made such a proposal.

As you read, think about how Perseus' positive traits make him worthy of the supernatural help he gets.

Connecting Literary Elements

An **antagonist** is a character or force in conflict with the main character or hero in a story. In this story, Perseus is faced with conflicts between two antagonists, his grandfather Acrisius and the king Polydectes. As you read, take note of the actions and choices of these antagonists, which create great struggles and challenges for the hero, Perseus.

Reading Strategy

Predicting

When you read, you can **predict** outcomes by thinking about the world presented in the literature and about the logical consequences of the characters' actions. Use these strategies to help you predict outcomes in "Perseus":

- Look for details and facts to suggest what may occur later.
- Decide what would be the likely outcome of an event.

Use a chart like the one shown here to note your predictions.

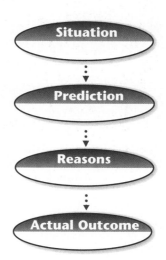

Vocabulary Development

kindred (kin´ drid) *n.* relatives (p. 215)

mortified (môrt´ ə fīd´) *adj.* embarrassed (p. 216)

despair (di sper´) *n.* hopelessness (p. 217)

wavering (wā´ vər iŋ) *adj.* flickering (p. 219)

revelry (rev´ əl rē) *n.* party (p. 219)

deity (dē´ ə tē) *n.* a god (p. 220)

reconciled (rek´ ən sīld´) *adj.* became friends again (p. 222)

Perseus

Edith Hamilton

Andromeda Liberated, Pierre Mignard. Louvre, Paris, France

▲ **Critical Viewing** The man with the sword is Perseus as an adult. Judging from this painting, how do you think others perceive him? Cite details in the art to support your answer. **[Draw Conclusions]**

K ing Acrisius [a kris´ ē əs] of Argos had only one child, a daughter, Danaë [dan´ ā ē]. She was beautiful above all the other women of the land, but this was small comfort to the King for not having a son. He journeyed to Delphi to ask the god if there was any hope that some day he would be the father of a boy. The priestess told him no, and added what was far worse: that his daughter would have a son who would kill him.

The only sure way to escape that fate was for the King to have Danaë instantly put to death—taking no chances, but seeing to it himself. This Acrisius would not do. His fatherly affection was not strong, as events proved, but his fear of the gods was. They visited with terrible punishment those who shed the blood of <u>kindred</u>. Acrisius did not dare slay his daughter. Instead, he had a house built all of bronze and sunk underground, but with part of the roof open to the sky so that light and air could come through. Here he shut her up and guarded her.

> So Danaë endured, the beautiful,
> To change the glad daylight for brass-bound walls,
> And in that chamber secret as the grave
> She lived a prisoner. Yet to her came
> Zeus in the golden rain.

As she sat there through the long days and hours with nothing to do, nothing to see except the clouds moving by overhead, a mysterious thing happened, a shower of gold fell from the sky and filled her chamber. How it was revealed to her that it was Zeus who had visited her in this shape we are not told, but she knew that the child she bore was his son.

For a time she kept his birth secret from her father, but it became increasingly difficult to do so in the narrow limits of that bronze house and finally one day the little boy—his name was Perseus—was discovered by his grandfather. "Your child!" Acrisius cried in great anger. "Who is his father?" But when Danaë answered proudly, "Zeus," he would not believe her. One thing only he was sure of, that the boy's life was a terrible danger to his own. He was afraid to kill him for the same reason that had kept him from killing her, fear of Zeus and the Furies who pursue such murderers. But if he could not kill them outright, he could put them in the way of tolerably certain death. He had a great chest made, and the two placed in it. Then it was taken out to sea and cast into the water.

In that strange boat Danaë sat with her little son. The daylight faded and she was alone on the sea.

Reading Strategy
Predicting What do you think will happen to Danaë and Perseus after they are sent off in the chest?

> When in the carven chest the winds and waves
> Struck fear into her heart she put her arms,
> Not without tears, round Perseus tenderly
> She said, "O son, what grief is mine.
> But you sleep softly, little child,
> Sunk deep in rest within your cheerless home,
> Only a box, brass-bound. The night, this darkness visible,
> The scudding waves so near to your soft curls,
> The shrill voice of the wind, you do not heed,
> Nestled in your red cloak, fair little face."

Through the night in the tossing chest she listened to the waters that seemed always about to wash over them. The dawn came, but with no comfort to her for she could not see it. Neither could she see

Reading Check

What was Acrisius told would happen to him when his daughter had a son?

that around them there were islands rising high above the sea, many islands. All she knew was that presently a wave seemed to lift them and carry them swiftly on and then, retreating, leave them on something solid and motionless. They had made land; they were safe from the sea, but they were still in the chest with no way to get out.

Fate willed it—or perhaps Zeus, who up to now had done little for his love and his child—that they should be discovered by a good man, a fisherman named Dictys. He came upon the great box and broke it open and took the pitiful cargo home to his wife who was as kind as he. They had no children and they cared for Danaë and Perseus as if they were their own. The two lived there many years, Danaë content to let her son follow the fisherman's humble trade, out of harm's way. But in the end more trouble came. Polydectes [pol i dek′ tēz], the ruler of the little island, was the brother of Dictys, but he was a cruel and ruthless man. He seems to have taken no notice of the mother and son for a long time, but at last Danaë attracted his attention. She was still radiantly beautiful even though Perseus by now was full grown, and Polydectes fell in love with her. He wanted her, but he did not want her son, and he set himself to think out a way of getting rid of him.

There were some fearsome monsters called Gorgons who lived on an island and were known far and wide because of their deadly power. Polydectes evidently talked to Perseus about them; he probably told him that he would rather have the head of one of them than anything else in the world. This seems practically certain from the plan he devised for killing Perseus. He announced that he was about to be married and he called his friends together for a celebration, including Perseus in the invitation. Each guest, as was customary, brought a gift for the bride-to-be, except Perseus alone. He had nothing he could give. He was young and proud and keenly <u>mortified</u>. He stood up before them all and did exactly what the King had hoped he would do, declared that he would give him a present better than any there. He would go off and kill Medusa and bring back her head as his gift. Nothing could have suited the King better. No one in his senses would have made such a proposal. Medusa was one of the Gorgons,

> And they are three, the Gorgons, each with wings
> And snaky hair, most horrible to mortals.
> Whom no man shall behold and draw again
> The breath of life,

for the reason that whoever looked at them were turned instantly into stone. It seemed that Perseus had been led by his angry pride into making an empty boast. No man unaided could kill Medusa.

But Perseus was saved from his folly. Two great gods were watching over him. He took ship as soon as he left the King's hall, not daring to see his mother first and tell her what he intended, and he sailed to Greece to learn where the three monsters were to be found. He went to Delphi, but all the priestess would say was to bid him

Reading Strategy
Predicting Do you think Danaë and Perseus will survive? Why?

mortified (môrt′ ə fīd′) *adj.* embarrassed

Literary Analysis
Hero in a Myth What is heroic about Perseus' offer to the King?

Danaë with young Perseus arriving on the island of Seripo,
Museo Archeologico, Ferrara, Italy

▲ Critical Viewing
Which scene in the story
does this art illustrate?
[Assess]

seek the land where men eat not Demeter's golden grain, but only
acorns. So he went to Dodona, in the land of oak trees, where the
talking oaks were which declared Zeus's will and where the Selli lived
who made their bread from acorns. They could tell him, however, no
more than this, that he was under the protection of the gods. They
did not know where the Gorgons lived.

When and how Hermes and Athena came to his help is not told in
any story, but he must have known <u>despair</u> before they did so. At last,
however, as he wandered on, he met a strange and beautiful person.
We know what he looked like from many a poem, a young man with
the first down upon his cheek when youth is loveliest, carrying, as no
other young man ever did, a wand of gold with wings at one end,
wearing a winged hat, too, and winged sandals. At sight of him hope
must have entered Perseus' heart, for he would know that this could
be none other than Hermes, the guide and the giver of good.

This radiant personage told him that before he attacked Medusa he
must first be properly equipped, and that what he needed was in the
possession of the nymphs of the North. To find the nymphs' abode,
they must go to the Gray Women who alone could tell them the way.
These women dwelt in a land where all was dim and shrouded in twilight. No ray of sun looked ever on that country, nor the moon by

despair (di sper′) *n.*
hopelessness

☑ **Reading Check**

Who is Hermes?

night. In that gray place the three women lived, all gray themselves and withered as in extreme old age. They were strange creatures, indeed, most of all because they had but one eye for the three, which it was their custom to take turns with, each removing it from her forehead when she had had it for a time and handing it to another.

All this Hermes told Perseus and then he unfolded his plan. He would himself guide Perseus to them. Once there Perseus must keep hidden until he saw one of them take the eye out of her forehead to pass it on. At that moment, when none of the three could see, he must rush forward and seize the eye and refuse to give it back until they told him how to reach the nymphs of the North.

He himself, Hermes said, would give him a sword to attack Medusa with—which could not be bent or broken by the Gorgon's scales, no matter how hard they were. This was a wonderful gift, no doubt, and yet of what use was a sword when the creature to be struck by it could turn the swordsman into stone before he was within striking distance? But another great deity was at hand to help. Pallas Athena stood beside Perseus. She took off the shield of polished bronze which covered her breast and held it out to him. "Look into this when you attack the Gorgon,"

▼ **Critical Viewing**
Who is portrayed in this art? How do you know? **[Connect]**

she said. "You will be able to see her in it as in a mirror, and so avoid her deadly power."

Now, indeed, Perseus had good reason to hope. The journey to the twilight land was long, over the stream of Ocean and on to the very border of the black country where the Cimmerians dwell, but Hermes was his guide and he could not go astray. They found the Gray Women at last, looking in the <u>wavering</u> light like gray birds, for they had the shape of swans. But their heads were human and beneath their wings they had arms and hands. Perseus did just as Hermes had said, he held back until he saw one of them take the eye out of her forehead. Then before she could give it to her sister, he snatched it out of her hand. It was a moment or two before the three realized they had lost it. Each thought one of the others had it. But Perseus spoke out and told them he had taken it and that it would be theirs again only when they showed him how to find the nymphs of the North. They gave him full directions at once; they would have done anything to get their eye back. He returned it to them and went on the way they had pointed out to him. He was bound, although he did not know it, to the blessed country of the Hyperboreans [hī per bō´ rē anz], at the back of the North Wind, of which it is said: "Neither by ship nor yet by land shall one find the wondrous road to the gathering place of the Hyperboreans." But Perseus had Hermes with him, so that the road lay open to him, and he reached that host of happy people who are always banqueting and holding joyful <u>revelry</u>. They showed him great kindness: they welcomed him to their feast, and the maidens dancing to the sound of flute and lyre paused to get for him the gifts he sought. These were three: winged sandals, a magic wallet which would always become the right size for whatever was to be carried in it, and, most important of all, a cap which made the wearer invisible. With these and Athena's shield and Hermes' sword Perseus was ready for the Gorgons. Hermes knew where they lived, and leaving the happy land the two flew back across Ocean and over the sea to the Terrible Sisters' island.

By great good fortune they were all asleep when Perseus found them. In the mirror of the bright shield he could see them clearly, creatures with great wings and bodies covered with golden scales and hair a mass of twisting snakes. Athena was beside him now as well as Hermes. They told him which one was Medusa and that was important, for she alone of the three could be killed; the other two were immortal. Perseus on his winged sandals hovered above them, looking, however, only at the shield. Then he aimed a stroke down at Medusa's throat and Athena guided his hand. With a single sweep of his sword he cut through her neck and, his eyes still fixed on the shield with never a glance at her, he swooped low enough to seize the head. He dropped it into the wallet which closed around it. He had nothing to fear from it now. But the two other Gorgons had awakened and, horrified at the sight of their sister slain, tried to pursue the slayer. Perseus was safe; he had on the cap of darkness and they could not find him.

wavering (wā´ vər iŋ) *adj.* flickering

Literary Analysis
Hero in a Myth Which heroic quality does Perseus reveal in his treatment of the Gray Women?

revelry (rev´ əl rē) *n.* party

Reading Strategy
Predicting How do you think Perseus will use the wallet and the cap that were gifts from the Hyperboreans?

Reading Check
What does Athena give to Perseus to help fight the Gorgon?

So over the sea rich-haired Danaë's son,
Perseus, on his winged sandals sped,
Flying swift as thought.
In a wallet of silver,
A wonder to behold,
He bore the head of the monster,
While Hermes, the son of Maia,
The messenger of Zeus,
Kept ever at his side.

On his way back he came to Ethiopia and alighted there. By this time Hermes had left him. Perseus found, as Hercules was later to find, that a lovely maiden had been given up to be devoured by a horrible sea serpent. Her name was Andromeda and she was the daughter of a silly vain woman,

That starred Ethiop queen who strove
To set her beauty's praise above
The sea-nymphs, and their power offended.

She had boasted that she was more beautiful than the daughters of Nereus, the Sea-god. An absolutely certain way in those days to draw down on one a wretched fate was to claim superiority in anything over any <u>deity</u>; nevertheless people were perpetually doing so. In this case the punishment for the arrogance the gods detested fell not on Queen Cassiopeia [kas´ ē ō pē´ ə], Andromeda's mother, but on her daughter. The Ethiopians were being devoured in numbers by the serpent; and, learning from the oracle that they could be freed from the pest only if Andromeda were offered up to it, they forced Cepheus [sē fəs], her father, to consent. When Perseus arrived the maiden was on a rocky ledge by the sea, chained there to wait for the coming of the monster. Perseus saw her and on the instant loved her. He waited beside her until the great snake came for its prey; then he cut its head off just as he had the Gorgon's. The headless body dropped back into the water; Perseus took Andromeda to her parents and asked for her hand, which they gladly gave him.

With her he sailed back to the island and his mother, but in the house where he had lived so long he found no one. The fisherman Dictys' wife was long since dead, and the two others, Danaë and the man who had been like a father to Perseus, had had to fly and hide themselves from Polydectes, who was furious at Danaë's refusal to marry him. They had taken refuge in a temple, Perseus was told. He learned also that the King was holding a banquet in the palace and all the men who favored him were gathered there. Perseus instantly saw his opportunity. He went straight to the palace and entered the hall. As he stood at the entrance, Athena's shining buckler on his breast, the silver wallet at his side, he drew the eyes of every man there. Then before any could look away he held up the Gorgon's head; and at the sight one and all, the cruel King and his servile courtiers, were turned into stone. There they sat, a row of statues,

Reading Strategy
Predicting What part do you think Andromeda will play in Perseus' journey? Why?

deity (dē´ ə tē) *n.* a god

Literary Analysis
Hero in a Myth What new challenge does Perseus face?

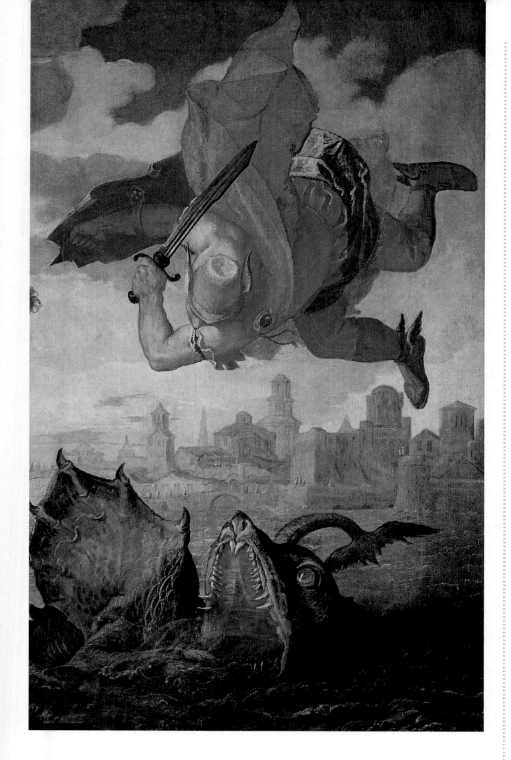

◀ **Critical Viewing**
Which heroic qualities
does this image illustrate?
[Support]

☑ **Reading Check**

What does Perseus learn
has happened to Dictys
and Danaë?

each, as it were, frozen stiff in the attitude he had struck when he
first saw Perseus.

When the islanders knew themselves freed from the tyrant it was easy
for Perseus to find Danaë and Dictys. He made Dictys king of the island,
but he and his mother decided that they would go back with Andromeda

to Greece and try to be <u>reconciled</u> to Acrisius, to see if the many years that had passed since he had put them in the chest had not softened him so that he would be glad to receive his daughter and grandson. When they reached Argos, however, they found that Acrisius had been driven away from the city, and where he was no one could say. It happened that soon after their arrival Perseus heard that the King of Larissa, in the North, was holding a great athletic contest, and he journeyed there to take part. In the discus-throwing when his turn came and he hurled the heavy missile, it swerved and fell among the spectators. Acrisius was there on a visit to the King, and the discus struck him. The blow was fatal and he died at once.

So Apollo's oracle was again proved true. If Perseus felt any grief, at least he knew that his grandfather had done his best to kill him and his mother. With his death their troubles came to an end. Perseus and Andromeda lived happily ever after. Their son, Electryon, was the grandfather of Hercules.

Medusa's head was given to Athena, who bore it always upon the aegis, Zeus's shield, which she carried for him.

reconciled (rek´ ən sīld´)
adj. became friends again

Review and Assess

Thinking About the Selection

1. **Respond:** Which of Perseus' adventures would make the best action-adventure movie? Why?

2. **(a) Recall:** What prediction does the priestess make to Acrisius? **(b) Connect:** What two actions does Acrisius take to prevent the prediction from coming true? **(c) Infer:** What is revealed about Acrisius' character through the actions he takes to escape fate?

3. **(a) Recall:** Why does Perseus set out to kill Medusa? **(b) Connect:** What help does he receive from Hermes and Athena? **(c) Infer:** What detail of Perseus' background might have led Athena and Hermes to help Perseus in his quest?

4. **(a) Recall:** How does Perseus manage to kill Medusa? **(b) Hypothesize:** What might have happened to Perseus if he had not received help from the gods?

5. **Make a Judgment:** Considering the actions he takes against Danaë and Perseus, does Acrisius deserve his fate? Why or why not?

6. **Draw Conclusions:** What does this myth suggest about one's ability to escape or control fate? Explain.

7. **Extend:** This myth from ancient Greece is thousands of years old. **(a)** What lessson do you think it taught its first audiences? **(b)** In what ways is it still relevant today?

Edith Hamilton

(1867–1963)

Edith Hamilton's long journey on Earth began soon after the Civil War and ended in the Space Age. Her heart took an even longer journey—back to the worlds of ancient Greece and Rome—to find messages that modern people could apply to their lives.

Hamilton started as a groundbreaking educator who helped found the Bryn Mawr School in Baltimore, the first college preparatory school for women. She taught a generation of young women the lesson she had learned: not to limit their goals simply because they were not men.

After leaving Bryn Mawr, Hamilton began writing articles about ancient Greece, which she later turned into a book entitled *The Greek Way,* published in 1930. Her other books include *The Roman Way* (1932), *The Prophets of Israel* (1936), and *Mythology* (1942).

Review and Assess

Literary Analysis

Hero in a Myth

1. Perseus accepts the help of Hermes and Athena in his pursuit of Medusa, but which **heroic qualities** of his own does he draw upon to accomplish his goals?
2. Which heroic quality does Perseus exhibit when he decides to return to Argos to see Acrisius?
3. Which of Danaë's qualities might Perseus have inherited from her? Use the following chart to analyze the connection between mother and son. In each case, provide an example of each quality you identify.

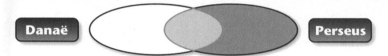

Connecting Literary Elements

4. In what ways are Acrisius and Polydectes **antagonists** of Perseus? In a chart like the following, trace their actions, the difficulties they create for Perseus, and the ways he overcomes these challenges.

Antagonist	Actions	Effect on Perseus	End Result

5. How do the actions of the two antagonists make Perseus an even stronger hero?

Reading Strategy

Predicting

6. What evidence in the story made it possible to **predict** that Perseus would be successful in killing Medusa?
7. (a) Why is Acrisius' death a logical outcome? (b) What aspects of his death could not have been predicted?

Extend Understanding

8. **Literature Connection:** (a) What situations from other works of literature, movies, or real life can you recall in which someone tried to escape or control fate? (b) What were the outcomes?

Quick Review

A **hero in a myth** is a character who performs amazing feats in a tale involving supernatural beings and fantastic events.

An **antagonist** is a character or force in conflict with the hero.

To **predict** story events, look for details and facts to suggest what may occur later.

 Take It to the Net

www.phschool.com

Take the interactive self-test online to check your understanding of the selections.

Integrate Language Skills

Vocabulary Development Lesson

Word Analysis: Latin Root -mort-

The word *mortified*, meaning "deeply humiliated," is based on the Latin root -mort-, meaning "death." Use the meaning of -mort- to help you define the following words.

1. immortality
2. mortician
3. mortally
4. immortalize

Spelling Strategy

When you add an ending that begins with a vowel to a word of more than one syllable that ends in a consonant preceded by a vowel, you normally do not double the final consonant. Thus, *cancel + -ed = canceled*. However, if the word's stress is on the final syllable, you usually double the consonant. Thus, *compel + -ing = compelling*. Add the ending shown to each of the words below.

1. wither + -ing 2. transmit + -ed 3. refer + -ed

Concept Development: Synonyms

On your paper, write the word or phrase whose meaning is closest to that of the first word. If necessary, review the vocabulary word list on page 213.

1. deity: (a) goodness, (b) god, (c) generosity
2. mortified: (a) cleansed, (b) stiff, (c) humiliated
3. revelry: (a) grand party, (b) rude awakening, (c) loud disagreement
4. despair: (a) hopelessness, (b) ruin, (c) sacrifice
5. reconciled: (a) guessed again, (b) became friends again, (c) forgot again
6. wavering: (a) greeting, (b) stumbling, (c) flickering
7. kindred: (a) relatives, (b) childhood, (c) hostility

Grammar Lesson

Active and Passive Voice

A verb in the **active voice** expresses an action done *by* its subject. A verb in the **passive voice** expresses an action done *to* its subject.

> **Active voice:** Edith Hamilton *wrote* "Perseus." [The subject, *Edith Hamilton*, performs the action of the verb *wrote*.]
>
> **Passive voice:** "Perseus" *was written* by Edith Hamilton. [The subject, *"Perseus,"* receives the action of the verb *was written*.]

Sentences written in the active voice are often less wordy and more direct than those written in the passive voice. Therefore, use the active voice to create more forceful and lively writing.

Practice Copy the following sentences and underline the verb or verbs in each one. Determine whether the underlined verbs are in the active or passive voice.

1. Danaë was imprisoned by Acrisius.
2. They were placed in a chest in the sea.
3. Dictys found them on the beach.
4. In his search for Medusa, Perseus was helped by Hermes and Athena.
5. Perseus rescued Andromeda.

Writing Application Write four sentences about Perseus' heroic actions, two in the active voice and two in the passive voice.

WG Prentice Hall Writing and Grammar Connection: Chapter 23, Section 2

Writing Lesson

Speech of Introduction

Imagine that you have to deliver a speech introducing Perseus at a large public gathering. Your speech should tell your audience something of Perseus' background and should go on to describe and praise his deeds before finally introducing him.

Prewriting   Start by listing the important facts of Perseus' life. Then, highlight the events that will appeal to the audience in various ways—by touching people's emotions or by amusing them, for example.

> ### Model: Listing Details That Appeal to Your Audience
>
> 1. Dictys found Perseus and his mother in a chest.
> 2. Perseus told Polydectes he would bring back Medusa's head.
> 3. He did not tell his mother, and he sailed off to Greece.
> 4. Perseus received help from Athena and Hermes.
>
> The highlighted information accents Perseus' heroic qualities—qualities audiences should find compelling.

Drafting   Organize your information in time order, or group the details into categories by focusing on each of Perseus' character traits. Then, cite details from his life that relate to each trait.

Revising   Reread your draft and make sure you have chosen the most appealing material from Perseus' story to help win over your audience.

*W*G *Prentice Hall Writing and Grammar Connection: Chapter 7, Section 2*

Extension Activities

Listening and Speaking Imagine that Acrisius escapes death and is brought to trial for his treatment of Danaë and Perseus. As a prosecuting attorney, present an **opening argument** to a jury of your classmates, accusing the king of intent to commit murder. Follow these tips to help you:

- Explain how Acrisius put Danaë and Perseus in a life-threatening situation.
- Point out Acrisius' motive—the reason he wanted to kill them.

Present your opening argument to the class.

Research and Technology In a group, prepare an **illustrated map** showing Perseus' travels from the time of his birth until the end of the story. Refer back to the story and list the places he goes to in his travels. Then, create your map. Illustrate the map with pictures of the various gods and monsters he meets. Use graphics software to design the map. [**Group Activity**]

 **Take It to the Net**   www.phschool.com

Go online for an additional research activity using the Internet.

Prepare to Read

Slam, Dunk, & Hook ◆ The Spearthrower ◆ Shoulders

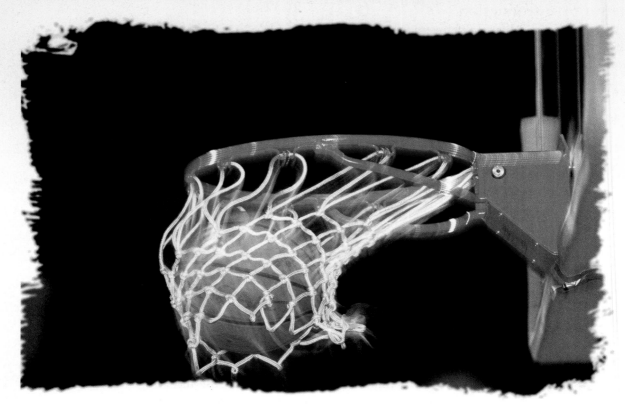

 Take It to the Net

Visit www.phschool.com
for interactive activities
and instruction related to
the selections, including
- background
- graphic organizers
- literary elements
- reading strategies

Preview

Connecting to the Literature

These poems are about the exhilaration of pure physical action that comes from a disciplined focus on an important goal. As you read, experience the sensation described and imagine what it means to spend every ounce of your strength for something you want with all your heart.

Background

The title "The Spearthrower" refers not only to a javelin thrower but also to a poet who sends her "signed song" of praise for women athletes into the "bullying dark" of athletic events once dominated by men. In associating the poet with the athlete, the poet Lillian Morrison follows a tradition from ancient Greece, where poets sang songs honoring Olympic athletics.

Literary Analysis
Theme in Poetry

On their surface, these poems vividly describe physical action, but underneath that surface is a **theme,** a central message or insight about life that sits at the center of each poem. The following lines from "The Spearthrower" address such a theme, suggesting that the athlete throws her javelin not only for herself but for other female athletes as well.

> her quick laps
> on the curving track,
> that the sprinter surge
> and the hurdler leap, . . .

As you read these poems, look for the insights or messages at their core.

Comparing Literary Works

In poetry, as in other literature, theme can be hinted at sideways or stated directly. In "The Spearthrower" and "Shoulders," the themes are stated directly. In contrast, in "Slam, Dunk, & Hook," the theme is implied; there seems to be much more than a game at stake. Compare and contrast the themes in each of the poems, paying close attention to the meaning that lies just beneath the words.

Reading Strategy
Forming Mental Images

A poet writes words that let you see pictures in your mind's eye. To **form mental images** of a poem, turn the poet's words into pictures by applying your own experiences. These strategies will help you form mental images as you read poetry:

- Picture the scene that the poet sketches for you in words.
- If a picture does not come to mind easily, relate the words to events in your own life or to another poem or story you have read.

Use the chart shown at the right to help you form mental images as you read.

Words: _____

_____

_____

↓

Image Created
in Your Mind: _____

_____

_____

Vocabulary Development

metaphysical (met´ə fiz´i kəl) *adj.* spiritual; beyond the physical (p. 229)

jibed (jībd) *v.* stopped short and turned from side to side (p. 229)

feint (fānt) *v.* deliver a pretended move to catch an opponent off guard (p. 229)

surge (sʉrj) *v.* increase suddenly; speed up (p. 231)

Slam, Dunk, & Hook

Yusef Komunyakaa

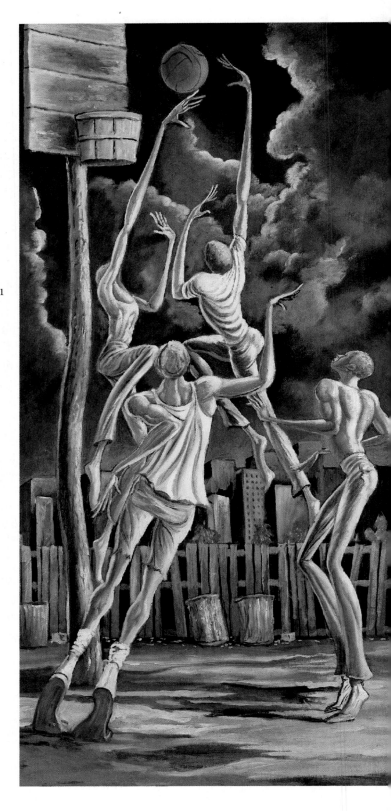

Fast breaks. Lay ups. With Mercury's[1]
Insignia[2] on our sneakers,
We outmaneuvered the footwork
Of bad angels. Nothing but a hot
5 Swish of strings like silk
Ten feet out. In the roundhouse[3]
Labyrinth[4] our bodies
Created, we could almost
Last forever, poised in midair
10 Like storybook sea monsters.
A high note hung there
A long second. Off
The rim. We'd corkscrew
Up & dunk balls that exploded

---

1. **Mercury's** Mercury was the Roman god of travel, usually depicted with wings on his feet.
2. **insignia** (in sig′ nē ə) *n.* emblems or badges; logos.
3. **roundhouse** *n.* area on the court beneath the basket.
4. **labyrinth** (lab′ ə rinth) *n.* maze.

▶ **Critical Viewing** Which details in this painting relate to lines in the poem "Slam, Dunk, & Hook"? **[Connect]**

15   The skullcap of hope & good
     Intention. Bug-eyed, lanky,
     All hands & feet . . . sprung rhythm.
     We were metaphysical when girls
     Cheered on the sidelines.
20   Tangled up in a falling,
     Muscles were a bright motor
     Double-flashing to the metal hoop
     Nailed to our oak.
     When Sonny Boy's mama died
25   He played nonstop all day, so hard
     Our backboard splintered.
     Glistening with sweat, we jibed
     & rolled the ball off our
     Fingertips. Trouble
30   Was there slapping a blackjack
     Against an open palm.
     Dribble, drive to the inside, feint,
     & glide like a sparrow hawk.
     Lay ups. Fast breaks.
35   We had moves we didn't know
     We had. Our bodies spun
     On swivels of bone & faith,
     Through a lyric slipknot
     Of joy, & we knew we were
40   Beautiful & dangerous.

metaphysical (met´ə fiz´i kəl) *adj.* spiritual; beyond the physical

jibed (jībd) *v.* stopped short and turned from side to side

feint (fānt) *v.* deliver a pretended move to catch an opponent off guard

Review and Assess

Thinking About the Selection

1. **Respond:** Which images in this poem were clearest to you? Explain your answer.

2. **(a) Recall:** How does the speaker describe the action in lines 3–4? **(b) Infer:** Who or what do you think are the "bad angels" to which Komunyakaa refers?

3. **(a) Recall:** How does Sonny Boy play on the day his mother dies? **(b) Infer:** Why do you think he plays this way?

4. **(a) Interpret:** How does the first line of the poem convey the fast action of a game? **(b) Infer:** What might have been the purpose of starting the poem in such a way?

5. **(a) Analyze:** Why might the basketball players be both "beautiful" and "dangerous"? **(b) Infer:** What does playing basketball help the neighborhood boys to do?

6. **Apply:** Do you think sports are just for fun or do you think they help in other ways?

Yusef Komunyakaa

(b. 1947)

Komunyakaa has said that he likes "connecting the abstract to the concrete," and that is precisely what he does in "Slam, Dunk, & Hook." Komunyakaa won the Pulitzer Prize for poetry for his book *Neon Vernacular: New and Selected Poems* (1993). He grew up in Bogalusa, Louisiana, and earned the Bronze Star in Vietnam, serving as reporter and editor of the military newspaper *The Southern Cross*. He now teaches at Princeton University.

The Spearthrower

Lillian Morrison

She walks alone
to the edge of the park
and throws into
the bullying dark
5 her javelin
of light,
her singing sign
her signed song
that the runner may run
10 far and long
her quick laps
on the curving track,
that the sprinter surge
and the hurdler leap,
15 that the vaulter soar,
clear the highest bar,
and the discus fly
as the great crowds cry
to their heroines
20 Come on!

Reading Strategy
Forming Mental Images
Describe the picture you
see in your mind as you
read lines 1–6.

surge (sʉrj) v. increase
suddenly; speed up

Review and Assess

Thinking About the Selection

1. **Respond:** How did this poem make you feel when you read it? Why?

2. **(a) Recall:** What surroundings does Morrison describe at the beginning of the poem? **(b) Analyze:** Which words add mood to this description? **(c) Interpret:** Why do you think Morrison refers to the dark as "bullying"?

3. **(a) Recall:** Who "walks alone" in the poem? **(b) Evaluate:** What is the effect of starting the poem this way?

4. **(a) Recall:** Which athletes does Morrison mention in lines 9–16? **(b) Interpret:** Which details in the poem support the interpretation that the spearthrower is not an athlete, but a poet?

5. **Analyze:** What benefit does the spearthrower "pass on" to other female athletes?

6. **Speculate:** What do you think motivates great athletes the most?

7. **Extend:** Do you believe that the successes and failures a person experiences can greatly affect others? Explain.

Lillian Morrison

(b. 1917)

Lillian Morrison has worked as a librarian and has written and compiled many books. She has published several books of her own poetry, including *Whistling the Morning In* (1992). She has also edited several anthologies of poems about sports (including one focused on basketball and entitled, coincidentally, *Slam, Dunk*), along with collections of riddles, playground chants, and autograph sayings.

Shoulders

Naomi Shihab Nye

A man crosses the street in rain,
stepping gently, looking two times north and south,
because his son is asleep on his shoulder.

No car must splash him.
5   No car drive too near to his shadow.

This man carries the world's most sensitive cargo
but he's not marked.
Nowhere does his jacket say FRAGILE,
HANDLE WITH CARE.

10   His ear fills up with breathing.
He hears the hum of the boy's dream
deep inside him.

We're not going to be able
to live in the world
15   if we're not willing to do what he's doing
with one another.

The road will only be wide.
The rain will never stop falling.

Literary Analysis
Theme in Poetry Why does the poet point out that the child is not marked "fragile"?

Naomi Shihab Nye

(b. 1952)

Naomi Shihab Nye spent her teenage years in Jerusalem and has since worked as a visiting writer at several colleges and universities, including the University of Texas. Her books of poems have received such awards as the Pushcart Prize. In addition, her work has received recognition from the American Library Association. Nye says, "For me poetry has always been a way of paying attention to the world. . . ."

Review and Assess

Thinking About the Selection

1. **Respond:** Which images in the poem "spoke" to you? Why?

2. **(a) Recall:** Where are the father and child as the poem begins?
   (b) Interpret: Why might the poet have chosen this setting?

3. **(a) Recall:** Why is the father in the poem "stepping gently"?
   (b) Speculate: What does the son represent in the poem?

4. **(a) Interpret:** What warning does the poet give to the world in lines 17–18? **(b) Draw Conclusions:** What dangers does this warning seem to suggest?

5. **(a) Infer:** What does the speaker of the poem say that people must do for one another? **(b) Apply:** Do you think most people treat each other the way this man treats his son? Explain.

Review and Assess

Literary Analysis

Theme in Poetry

1. (a) What does "Slam, Dunk, & Hook" say about the role of basketball in the street life of the neighborhood kids? (b) Which details of the poem suggest that **theme**?

2. How does the "spearthrower" (that is, the poet who sings of women athletes) enable the runner to run and the discus to fly?

3. Use the chart below to analyze the insights in "Shoulders." (a) What message does the speaker convey about the role of a parent in a child's life? (b) What message is implied about the responsibility of all human beings?

4. What idea about life is Nye expressing when she talks about the road always being wide and the rain always falling?

Comparing Literary Works

5. Using the chart below, compare the action, images, and themes of the three poems. (a) Which poem best conveys physical action? Explain. (b) Which poem best conveys emotional challenges? Explain.

Poem	Summary of Action	Images Created	Theme

Reading Strategy

Forming Mental Images

6. Which **image** in "Slam, Dunk, & Hook" creates the most vivid picture in your mind?

7. Describe what you see in the final image of "Shoulders."

Extend Understanding

8. **Sports Connection:** "The Spearthrower" shows women overcoming great obstacles in sports. Name a famous female athlete, and explain the impact she has had on sports and other athletes.

Integrate Language Skills

Vocabulary Development Lesson

Specialized Vocabulary: Jargon

Some poems use **jargon,** specialized vocabulary used in a particular occupation, sport, or other well-defined activity. For example, the term *feint* in "Slam, Dunk, & Hook" refers to a pretended move meant to take an opponent off guard. For each item, write the meaning of the jargon and the impression each word or phrase suggests.

1. dribble
2. drive to the inside
3. fast breaks
4. quick laps

Spelling Strategy

Remember the following rule: Place *i* before *e* except after *c* or when sounded like *a* as in *neighbor* and *weigh*. For each word, write "Correct" if the word is spelled correctly. If the spelling is incorrect, write the correct spelling.

1. yield
2. height
3. recieved
4. sieze

Fluency: Words in Context

Rewrite the following paragraph, filling in the blanks with words from the vocabulary list on page 227.

Emotions were high as the game entered the last quarter. The score was tied. The winning team would make it to the playoffs. We saw the center ____?____ left, then pass the ball to the right, confusing the player guarding her. The player who caught the ball then ____?____, looking for a teammate on either side of her who was closer to the basket. The moment was almost ____?____ as she found an opening among the group of girls that allowed her to ____?____ past the guard and make her shot. The home team was going to the playoffs, and the visiting team was left feeling stunned.

Grammar Lesson

Irregular Verbs

Unlike regular verbs, the past tense and past participle of **irregular verbs** are not formed by adding *-ed* to the present form. Instead, the past tense and past participle are formed in various ways. Some change vowels or consonants within the word. Others change both vowels and consonants. Some verbs use the same form for the present, past, and past participle. Look at the various forms of the verbs *run* and *catch*.

Present: run; catch

Past: ran; caught

Past Participle: (have) run; (have) caught

Practice

Test your knowledge of irregular verbs by identifying the past and past participle of each present-tense verb below. Use a dictionary if you are not sure about a particular form.

1. began
2. hang
3. spring
4. fall
5. drive
6. sing
7. stand
8. swing
9. lead
10. won

Writing Application Write three sentences using the present, past, and past participle of *spin*.

W̶G Prentice Hall Writing and Grammar Connection: Chapter 23, Section 1

Writing Lesson

Editorial

Write an **editorial**—a brief piece of writing that presents one side of an issue—related to one of the selections. For example, using information you gathered from "Slam, Dunk, & Hook," you could write an editorial about the need for more funding for neighborhood sports because of the effect sports have on self-esteem.

Prewriting   To persuade your readers, try to anticipate questions from those who might disagree with you. Imagine how opponents might question your opinions, and jot down questions and opposing viewpoints.

Model: Anticipating Readers' Questions

Topic: Our neighborhood needs more money for sports programs.

Questions: How much money will it cost our city?

Will funding come out of taxpayer money?

> Generating questions that readers might have helps you address all of the important aspects of an issue.

Drafting   Write your editorial by stating the issue clearly and expressing your opinion reasonably. Address the questions you anticipated.

Revising   Show your editorial to several people. Try to find at least one reader who disagrees with you. Ask that person whether your opinion sounds fair and if you have answered all objections effectively. If you hear a point you should have raised, consider adding it to your editorial.

W/G   *Prentice Hall Writing and Grammar Connection: Chapter 7, Section 2*

Extension Activities

Listening and Speaking   A good sportscast captures the thrills of the game. Choose one of the track-and-field events in "The Spearthrower." Create a **sportscast** describing the contest from start to finish. Use these tips to guide your preparation:

- Give a play-by-play of the game.
- Focus attention on exciting or disappointing moments.
- Use vivid and lively language.

When you have written your sportscast, rehearse it and then present it to your class.

Research and Technology   In a group, do a **research report** on some aspect of women's athletic competitions—for example, a biography of one outstanding athlete or an explanation of an exciting current topic. Use library resources, including the Internet and sports magazines, to help you with your research. Include photographs, recordings, and videotapes, if possible. **[Group Activity]**

 Take It to the Net   www.phschool.com

Go online for an additional research activity using the Internet.

Writing WORKSHOP

Workplace Writing: Business Letter

The form of writing commonly used by those in the workplace is a **business letter.** Business letters may take the form of job offer letters, requests for information, or letters of introduction. In this workshop, you will write a business letter to learn more about a profession.

Assignment Criteria. Your business letter should have the following characteristics:

- a heading, inside address, greeting, body, closing, and signature
- formal, polite language that outlines a clear purpose and provides relevant background information
- standard formatting with consistent spacing and indentation

To preview the criteria on which your business letter may be assessed, see the Rubric on page 239.

Prewriting

Choose a topic. To write a business letter, **list and itemize** to identify some of your strengths. In a chart like the one shown, match your strengths with "dream jobs" that require those abilities. Choose a profession from the list that you would like to learn more about. Use this career as the subject of your business letter.

Choose a Topic

Personal Strength	Dream Jobs Requiring This Strength
artistic	painter, sculptor
avid reader	teacher, writer, journalist
fast runner	professional running back
good joke teller	comedian

Make connections. Use the Internet, the classified section in the newspaper, or your local phone book to find the address, name, and title of the person to whom you will send your letter. Then, jot down any questions you might like to ask someone in that profession.

Research. Gather some background information about the dream job you have chosen. Use your school or local library or the Internet to research salary level, employment opportunities, and other pertinent information. Jot this down for use in the draft of your business letter.

Identify your purpose. Before you write your business letter, consider why you are writing. Review your notes and come up with a sentence that expresses this information clearly. You may want to incorporate this information later into the body of your draft.

> **Example:** I have taken guitar lessons for years, and I want to learn about the job of a studio musician.

Student Model

Before you begin drafting your business letter, read this model from Robin Weber, a student in St. Petersburg, Florida.

Intelligent Productions
220 Any Street, Suite 112
Any Town, NY 10000
December 13, 2001

> In his letter, Robin assumes the voice of a business that he created for this assignment.

G-2000 Computers
310 Infinite Loop
Any City, CA 94000

Dear Sirs:

My business is currently in the market for several high-end, reliable server computers. I would like to obtain more information about your line of server products.

> The author states his purpose clearly and concisely.

The computers we use are operating twenty-four hours a day, seven days a week, as servers hosting a high-traffic Internet Web site. Therefore, it would be unacceptable for my company to purchase computers that require periods of inactivity in order to remain in working condition. We are also concerned about technical support issues and cost.

> In this paragraph, the author provides important back-ground information.

I would appreciate if you could send me the exact specifications on cata-log items number 1444, as well as number 2314. There is no information on warranties in your product descriptions. Any information in this regard would be very helpful in making my purchasing decision. Also, would it be possible to obtain a high volume discount? How would such an order affect delivery time?

> The author uses modified block format.

> The letter includes specific questions that Robin would like answered.

Please send me any information you have on these issues. I look forward to hearing from you.

> The conclusion summarizes the request using polite language.

Sincerely,

Robin Weber

Robin Weber
Intelligent Productions

Drafting

Selecting a format. Select a standard format that uses traditional font and spacing. Acceptable formats for business letters include the following:

- **Block format**—each part of the letter begins at the left margin
- **Modified block format**—the heading, closing, and signature are indented to the center of the page

Adhere to standards. As you draft your business letter, be certain you have included all of the essential parts of the form. Use the checklist at right to verify that your business letter has all of the proper elements. Add any elements that are missing from your checklist.

Consider your audience. Remember that you are addressing a busy professional. Include only information that is essential; do not provide flowery elaboration that will detract from your main purpose. Make sure to provide information clearly and use formal vocabulary, style, and tone of address.

Call for action. As you draft, include information that tells your reader what you want him or her to do. For example, you may want to set up an interview, arrange a phone call, or you may want the recipient to provide you with some information. Make sure the outcome you want is clearly stated.

Business Letter Standards
☐ **Heading**—indicates the writer's address and affiliation (if any) and the date
☐ **Inside Address**—indicates where letter will be sent
☐ **Greeting**—always punctuated by a colon
☐ **Body**—states the writer's purpose
☐ **Closing**—an appropriate farewell
☐ **Signature**—a signed name

Revising

Revise to support your purpose. Your business letter must address the reasons for your writing. Verify that this reason is clearly stated early in the body of your business letter. To evaluate your letter, look over your draft to find places where you can offer detail to support your purpose.

1. Review your draft and underline your purpose for writing.

2. Highlight any other details in your business letter that reinforce your purpose for writing.

3. Cross out details that are not essential for the reader to know.

Model: Supporting Your Purpose

I would like to obtain more information about your line of server products. The computers we use are operating twenty-four hours a day, seven days a week, as servers hosting a high-traffic Internet Web site. ~~Intelligent Productions was the fastest-growing privately owned company in the year 2000.~~

> This information is not essential to the writer's purpose.

Revise to make language formal. Look for words in your business letter that can be replaced to create a more formal effect. In the following example, *excels* creates a more formal effect than *is good*.

> **Example:** He *is good* at playing chess.
> He *excels* at playing chess.

Compare the model and the nonmodel. Why is the model more effective than the nonmodel?

Nonmodel	Model
I want a good, reliable server. Can you get me some information on your products?	My business is currently in the market for several high-end, reliable server computers. I would like to obtain more information about your line of server products.

Publishing and Presenting

Consider sharing your writing with a wider audience in one of the following ways.

Send your letter. If your letter is written to an existing business, mail it. When you get a response, share it with classmates.

Apply your knowledge to another situation: write a letter of complaint. Pair up with a partner. Write a letter of complaint to your partner's fictional company, using formal language and following the standard format for a business letter. Ask your partner to draft a polite business letter addressing your complaint. Afterward, discuss whether you were each satisfied with the letter you received.

 Prentice Hall Writing and Grammar Connection: Chapter 15

**Read to Write**

To learn more about writing business documents, see **Reading Informational Materials,** p. 196.

Rubric for Self-Assessment

Evaluate your business letter using the following criteria and rating scale:

Criteria	Rating Scale				
	Not very				Very
How well does the letter incorporate all the elements of a business letter?	1	2	3	4	5
How clear and formal is the language of the letter?	1	2	3	4	5
How well does the letter follow appropriate formatting?	1	2	3	4	5
How well does the letter include appropriate background information?	1	2	3	4	5
How clearly is the purpose stated?	1	2	3	4	5

Listening and Speaking WORKSHOP

Conducting Interviews

You do not need to be a talk-show host to produce a good interview. All you need is curiosity about a subject, a willingness to put in some preparation time, and a chance to connect with someone who can provide the detailed information you need.

Prepare for the Interview

Whether you are using an interview to gather data for a research paper or to find a new job, you want to start off feeling prepared. To plan:

Identify your purpose. Determine what kind of information you need to obtain from an interview. Your purpose might be to find a few personal stories for a history paper or facts for a school newspaper article.

Do research. Perform enough preliminary research so that you can ask informed questions. For a job interview, find out more about the employer. Before interviewing an expert on the psychology of twins, look at studies on twin behavior.

Draw up questions. The best questions inspire answers in which people talk about themselves and their experiences. Everyone has a conversation "combination lock." Your challenge is to find the right combination of insightful, provocative questions that lets you open that lock.

Conduct the Interview

Once your preparation is complete, consider these tips for conducting a productive interview:

Build a question staircase. Think of the answers in your interview as the steps in a staircase you are building upward. Each *question* should build on the *answer* you just received, as well as the previous question. See the chart at right for guidance.

Stick to your subject. Maintain focus by keeping your original purpose in mind. If the other person seems confused, you may have gone off-topic or asked an overly complicated question. Simplify your question, make sure it is relevant, and give examples to get back on track.

Activity: Interview and Evaluation Practice your skills by interviewing a community member with a particular expertise. Use the graphic to help you evaluate the quality of information you receive. After the interview, determine what you did well and areas you could improve.

Building a Question Staircase

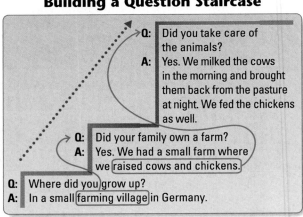

Q: Did you take care of the animals?
A: Yes. We milked the cows in the morning and brought them back from the pasture at night. We fed the chickens as well.

Q: Did your family own a farm?
A: Yes. We had a small farm where we raised cows and chickens.

Q: Where did you grow up?
A: In a small farming village in Germany.

Assessment WORKSHOP

Facts and Details

The reading sections of some tests require you to read a passage and answer multiple-choice questions about supporting ideas in a passage. The supporting ideas in a text are the facts and details that provide information about a main idea. Use the following strategies to help you answer test questions about supporting ideas:

- Think of a statement that summarizes the main idea of the passage.
- Look for facts or details that relate to the main idea.
- Check to see whether the test question is answered by the main idea or a supporting detail.
- Eliminate responses that supply details unrelated to the question.

Sample Test Item

Directions: Read the following passage, and then answer the question that follows.

As Yolanda read the application for summer camp counselor, she felt doubtful. She was interested in teaching art and sports, but the position required experience. Did she qualify? She made a list of what she had done: two terms of a child-development lab last year, babysitting for four years, one year as an art and soccer teacher for day camp.

1. Which of Yolanda's experiences is the closest match for the position?

   A her experience as a babysitter

   B the classes she took in child development

   C her experience as an art and soccer teacher

   D her certification in CPR

Answer and Explanation

The correct answer is *C,* which describes her art and sports experience. *A* and *B* are experiences that relate to the position, but neither is a close match. While Yolanda may be certified in CPR, this detail is not directly stated in the passage; *D* is therefore incorrect.

▶ Practice

Directions: Read the following passage, and then answer the question that follows.

Dr. Ellen Ochoa is a woman of many talents. She was born and raised in southern California, where her primary interests as a child included reading and playing flute. Graduating as the top-ranked math student in high school, she went on to earn an undergraduate degree in physics, as well as a master's and a doctorate in electrical engineering.

In 1993, she became the first Hispanic female astronaut to travel in space, where she and her team studied the sun's radiation levels. She even played the flute in space!

1. Dr. Ochoa's childhood interests included _____?_____.

   A reading

   B electrical engineering

   C band

   D physics

2. What success is not included in the passage?

   A earning a doctoral degree

   B becoming an astronaut

   C graduating from high school

   D leading a university marching band

Waiting Girl, 1978, Yan Hsia, Asian American Arts Center

Exploring the Theme

Any insight can be a moment of discovery—children identifying an entire animal from a fragment of jawbone or a woman suddenly recognizing a common thread that she shares with her mother and grandmother. Whether big or small, these moments of discovery teach people something about themselves, others, and the world around them.

In Amy Tan's "Rules of the Game," Waverly Jong gains sudden insights in successive waves during her childhood in San Francisco's Chinatown. Insight into the intricacies of chess allows her to succeed beyond everyone's expectations. This same success, though, alienates her from the rest of her family and a more carefree past. In just a few pages of the story, you will experience moments of discovery of every variety—exhilarating, bittersweet, and full of pain.

▲ **Critical Viewing** What emotions would you imagine this woman is experiencing? **[Analyze]**

Why Read Literature?

Perhaps we always read to gain insight or to learn more about the world around us. You might be interested in specific information or you might just enjoy the way an author puts words together. Preview these three purposes you might set before reading works in this unit.

1 Read for the Love of Literature

The early 1960s was an excruciating time for southern African American students attending formerly all-white schools. These students were pioneers, venturing into new territory where many angry voices were raised against them. Discover the meaning of personal courage in Charlayne Hunter–Gault's classic account "**In My Place,**" page 296.

Many readers enjoy stories that reveal inner truths about themselves. If you have ever regretted missing an opportunity to meet someone—for a reason too ridiculous to remember—then you may sympathize with the main character in Cynthia Rylant's "**Checkouts,**" page 282.

2 Read to Appreciate an Author's Style

When you read any of E. E. Cummings's poems, you will quickly realize that regular rules of grammar do not apply. Capital letters are reincarnated as lower case letters and parentheses appear magically out of nowhere. Although it may seem random, Cummings's style is closely tailored to the way the poem makes you feel. To gain an appreciation for Cummings's unusual choices, read "**maggie and milly and molly and may,**" page 328.

William Stafford's writing has a conversational style that can make you feel like you are listening to a friend tell a good story. See how Stafford creates this effect in "**Fifteen,**" page 286, a poem about a motorcycle and the intensity of youth.

3 Read for Information

The National Audubon Society was inspired by a group of Boston women who were horrified by the mistreatment of birds. In 1896, they banded together, boycotting products such as hats and clothing adorned with bird feathers. Their dedication, more than a century ago, has grown to include Audubon chapters nationwide. In addition to producing mailings and publications, the National Audubon Society has established a presence online to spread information and encourage action. To find out about navigating the Web to learn more about this group, see the **Audubon Society Web site,** page 257.

 Take It to the Net

Visit the Web site for online instruction and activities related to each selection in this unit.

www.phschool.com

How to Read Literature

Use Strategies for Constructing Meaning

You have to go a step beyond the literal meaning of each word on a page to fully understand what you are reading. Next steps include putting words and ideas together, forming judgments about plot and character, reading between the lines, and relating material to past experiences. This process is called constructing meaning. Use these strategies to help you construct meaning.

1. Relate generalizations and evidence.

- To find a generalization, look for a statement that is broad and strongly worded.

- Check to see whether an author backs up his or her generalization with convincing evidence. If the evidence is weak, you might decide that you disagree with the generalization.

2. Identify causes and effects.

- Find at least one reason *(cause)* for each result *(effect)* in a story.

- Use cause and effect to understand the chain of events in fiction and nonfiction. The chart at right shows the start of a cause-and-effect analysis of "The Interlopers."

3. Make inferences about character.

You can use inferences—reasonable conclusions based on details in the text—to predict how characters will react to certain situations.

- Consider the details that the author includes about characters.

- Pay close attention to physical descriptions and to actions that might shed light on character traits. Look at this example:

> I assumed he had learned from the hotel manager that I was to be in Herat for five days, and it was obvious that he felt confident that within that period he could wear me down and persuade me to buy a rug.
>
> —from **"The Rug Merchant"**

From this quotation, you can infer that the author is smart enough to know that he will be the target of a sales strategy. You might also infer that he is suspicious of others' motives.

4. Relate to personal experience.

Think about events in the selection and how they might resemble events in your life. Then, use your experiences to understand a story's characters and predict what might happen next.

As you read the selections in this unit, use these strategies for constructing meaning to enrich your understanding of the literature.

Cause and Effect

Question
Why does Ulrich hate Georg so deeply?

Cause
Georg repeatedly hunts without permission on land that legally belongs to Ulrich.

Effect
Ulrich is hunting down Georg so that he can settle this quarrel.

Prepare to Read

Children in the Woods

Preview

Connecting to the Literature

Some of your ideas about how the world works may have come from observations and discoveries you made as a child. Mixing red and yellow paint to get orange, for example, might have shown you how colors are formed. In "Children in the Woods," Barry Lopez shares his thoughts on how to help children discover and understand their world.

Background

At one time, the emphasis in science was to describe the natural world in as much detail as possible. In the early nineteenth century, in fact, collecting and cataloging such objects as birds' eggs and orchids was a popular hobby. Today, although scientists need to know the names of living things, they focus more upon theories and explanations.

Literary Analysis

Reflective Essay

A **reflective essay** is a short nonfiction work that focuses on the writer's thoughts about a personal experience. Most reflective essays have a friendly tone and convey a sense of discovery. Consider the reflective nature of this statement from the selection.

> Whenever I walk with a child, I think how much I have seen disappear in my own life.

As you read, consider Lopez's "discoveries."

Connecting Literary Elements

In a reflective essay, sensory language can help readers share in the experience that the writer explores. **Sensory language** is writing or speech that appeals to one or more of the senses. Sensory language often helps you "see" what the writer is describing, but some words or phrases can also suggest sounds, textures, smells, and tastes.

Reading Strategy

Relating Generalizations and Evidence

The key point of Lopez's reflective essay is a **generalization**—a broad principle that is supported by particulars, or **evidence**. Use these tips to relate generalizations and evidence:

- Look for broad personal opinions in the essay that might direct you toward generalizations. There may be small generalizations throughout, but somewhere there should be a large generalization that states the overall "point" of the essay.
- Find specific details to back up those generalizations.

Record your evidence and generalization on a chart like this one.

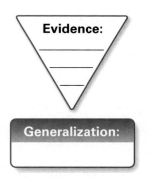

Vocabulary Development

charged (chärjd) *adj.* intense (p. 249)

acutely (ə kyōōt´ lē) *adv.* sharply (p. 249)

elucidate (ə lōō´ sə dāt´) *v.* explain (p. 249)

extrapolation (ek strap´ ə lā´ shən) *n.* conclusions drawn by speculation on the basis of facts (p. 250)

detritus (dē trīt´ əs) *n.* debris (p. 250)

effervesce (ef´ ər ves´) *v.* to be lively (p. 250)

myriad (mir´ ē əd) *adj.* countless; innumerable (p. 250)

insidious (in sid´ ē əs) *adj.* treacherous in a sly, tricky way (p. 250)

ineffable (in ef´ ə bəl) *adj.* too overwhelming to be expressed in words (p. 251)

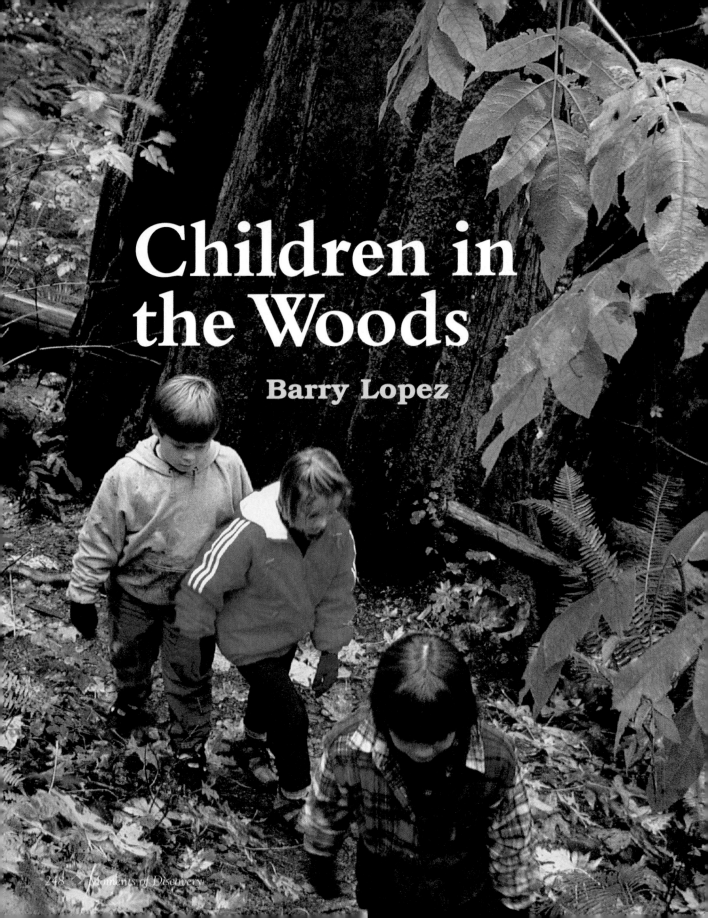

Children in
the Woods

Barry Lopez

When I was a child growing up in the San Fernando Valley in California, a trip into Los Angeles was special. The sensation of movement from a rural area into an urban one was sharp. On one of these <u>charged</u> occasions, walking down a sidewalk with my mother, I stopped suddenly, caught by a pattern of sunlight trapped in a spiraling imperfection in a windowpane. A stranger, an elderly woman in a cloth coat and a dark hat, spoke out spontaneously, saying how remarkable it is that children notice these things.

I have never forgotten the texture of this incident. Whenever I recall it I am moved not so much by any sense of my young self but by a sense of responsibility toward children, knowing how <u>acutely</u> I was affected in that moment by that woman's words. The effect, for all I know, has lasted a lifetime.

Now, years later, I live in a rain forest in western Oregon, on the banks of a mountain river in relatively undisturbed country, surrounded by 150-foot-tall Douglas firs,[1] delicate deerhead orchids, and clearings where wild berries grow. White-footed mice and mule deer, mink and coyote move through here. My wife and I do not have children, but children we know, or children whose parents we are close to, are often here. They always want to go into the woods. And I wonder what to tell them.

In the beginning, years ago, I think I said too much. I spoke with an encyclopedic knowledge of the names of plants or the names of birds passing through in season. Gradually I came to say less. After a while the only words I spoke, beyond answering a question or calling attention quickly to the slight difference between a sprig of red cedar and a sprig of incense cedar,[2] were to <u>elucidate</u> single objects.

I remember once finding a fragment of a raccoon's jaw in an alder thicket. I sat down alongside the two children with me and encouraged them to find out who this was—with only the three teeth still intact in a

---

1. **Douglas firs** tall evergreen trees of the pine family.
2. **sprig of red cedar . . . incense cedar** twigs from two types of trees of the pine family.

charged (chärjd) *adj.*
tensely expectant; intense

acutely (ə kyo͞ot′ lē) *adv.*
sharply

Reading Strategy
Relating Generalizations and Evidence What evidence supports the generalization that Lopez loves nature and is knowledgeable about plants and animals?

elucidate (ə lo͞o′ sə dāt′) *v.*
explain

✔**Reading Check**

When he first started his walks in the woods with children, how does Lopez say he spoke to them?

piece of the animal's maxilla[3] to guide them. The teeth told by their shape and placement what this animal ate. By a kind of visual extrapolation its size became clear. There were other clues, immediately present, which told, with what I could add of climate and terrain, how this animal lived, how its broken jaw came to be lying here. Raccoon, they surmised. And tiny tooth marks along the bone's broken edge told of a mouse's hunger for calcium.

We set the jaw back and went on.

If I had known more about raccoons, finer points of osteology,[4] we might have guessed more: say, whether it was male or female. But what we deduced was all we needed. Hours later, the maxilla, lost behind us in the detritus of the forest floor, continued to effervesce. It was tied faintly to all else we spoke of that afternoon.

In speaking with children who might one day take a permanent interest in natural history—as writers, as scientists, as filmmakers, as anthropologists[5]—I have sensed that an extrapolation from a single fragment of the whole is the most invigorating experience I can share with them. I think children know that nearly anyone can learn the names of things; the impression made on them at this level is fleeting. What takes a lifetime to learn, they comprehend, is the existence and substance of myriad relationships: it is these relationships, not the things themselves, that ultimately hold the human imagination.

The brightest children, it has often struck me, are fascinated by metaphor—with what is shown in the set of relationships bearing on the raccoon, for example, to lie quite beyond the raccoon. In the end, you are trying to make clear to them that everything found at the edge of one's senses—the high note of the winter wren, the thick perfume of propolis that drifts downwind from spring willows, the brightness of wood chips scattered by beaver—that all this fits together. The indestructibility of these associations conveys a sense of permanence that nurtures the heart, that cripples one of the most insidious of

> ## The brightest children, it has often struck me, are fascinated by metaphor . . .

extrapolation (ek strap′ ə lā′ shən) *n.* conclusions drawn by speculation on the basis of facts

detritus (dē trīt′ əs) *n.* debris

effervesce (ef ər ves′) *v.* to be lively

myriad (mir′ ē əd) *adj.* countless; innumerable

insidious (in sid′ ē əs) *adj.* treacherous in a sly, tricky way

---

3. **maxilla** (maks il′ ə) *n.* upper jaw.
4. **osteology** (äs′ tē äl′ ə jē) *n.* study of the structure and function of bones.
5. **anthropologists** (an′ *thr*ō päl′ ə jists) *n.* specialists in the study of mankind, especially the cultures of mankind.

▲ **Critical Viewing** Do you agree with the author that discoveries children make in nature can help them understand the world around them? **[Assess]**

human anxieties, the one that says, you do not belong here, you are unnecessary.

Whenever I walk with a child, I think how much I have seen disappear in my own life. What will there be for this person when he is my age? If he senses something <u>ineffable</u> in the landscape, will I know enough to encourage it?—to somehow show him that, yes, when people talk about violent death, spiritual exhilaration, compassion, futility, final causes, they are drawing on forty thousand years of human meditation on *this*—as we embrace Douglas firs, or stand by a river across whose undulating back we skip stones, or dig out a camas bulb,[6] biting down into a taste so much wilder than last night's potatoes.

The most moving look I ever saw from a child in the woods was on

ineffable (in ef´ ə bəl) *adj.* too overwhelming to be expressed in words

---

☑ Reading Check

What do the children learn from the raccoon jaw?

---

6. **camas** (kam´ əs) **bulbs** underground buds of a sweet and edible American plant.

a mud bar by the footprints of a heron.[7] We were on our knees, making handprints beside the footprints. You could feel the creek vibrating in the silt and sand. The sun beat down heavily on our hair. Our shoes were soaking wet. The look said: I did not know until now that I needed someone much older to confirm this, the feeling I have of life here. I can now grow older, knowing it need never be lost.

The quickest door to open in the woods for a child is the one that leads to the smallest room, by knowing the name each thing is called. The door that leads to the cathedral is marked by a hesitancy to speak at all, rather to encourage by example a sharpness of the senses. If one speaks it should only be to say, as well as one can, how wonderfully all this fits together, to indicate what a long, fierce peace can derive from this knowledge.

---

7. heron (her´ ən) wading bird with a long neck, long legs, and a long, tapered bill.

Review and Assess

Thinking About the Selection

1. **Respond:** Would you like to explore the woods or parks near your home with someone like Barry Lopez? Explain.

2. **(a) Recall:** What does the elderly woman in Los Angeles say to Lopez's mother? **(b) Infer:** Why do her words affect Lopez so greatly?

3. **(a) Recall:** List three activities that take place on Lopez's walks in the woods. **(b) Infer:** Why does Lopez use the method he does to teach children about nature?

4. **(a) Interpret:** Why is the author concerned about what he tells children? **(b) Draw Conclusions:** Why does the author change his approach to teaching children about nature? **(c) Analyze:** What do children gain from an understanding of relationships in nature?

5. **(a) Infer:** How do you think Lopez himself grows and develops from the moments of discovery he shares with children? **(b) Speculate:** Do you think that a greater understanding of nature can bring more peace to a person?

6. **(a) Interpret:** Which details in the essay indicate that Lopez is concerned with the passage of time? **(b) Speculate:** Why do you think this concern is intensified by his interaction with children?

7. **Assess:** What is the greatest benefit of learning about nature?

8. **Apply:** How could you apply Barry Lopez's ideas to teaching art to children?

Barry Lopez

(b. 1945)

If you have any interest in nature, you will be moved by the poetic nonfiction of Barry Lopez. In his writing, Lopez speaks for those that cannot speak for themselves— Santa Ana winds, wolves, cottonwood trees, and more. Lopez has said, "I like to use the word *isumatug*. It's of eastern Arctic Eskimo dialect and refers to the storyteller, meaning 'the person who creates the atmosphere in which wisdom reveals itself.'"

An avid explorer, Lopez has journeyed to Alaska, the Galapagos Islands, Australia, Africa, the Antarctic, and the Arctic. In fact, he defines himself as "a writer who travels. Some writers stay at home or inside a room. I am a writer who travels."

Review and Assess

Literary Analysis

Reflective Essay

1. Which elements of "Children in the Woods" make it a good exam-ple of a **reflective essay?** Use a chart like the one below to record your answer.

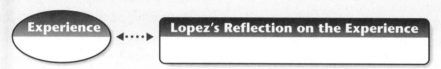

2. (a) If Lopez wrote "Children in the Woods" in the third person, telling about someone else's experiences, how would it differ from the essay he wrote? (b) Do you think it would be as effective?

Connecting Literary Elements

3. When Lopez recalls making handprints next to footprints of a heron, which **sensory language** brings that personal experience to life?
4. Using a chart like the one below, list examples of sensory language in the essay and explain why the language appeals to your senses.

Example		Sight	Sound	Taste	Touch	Smell

5. How do the images help you understand Lopez's personal thoughts?

Reading Strategy

Relating Generalizations and Evidence

6. (a) What **generalization** does the author make about speaking to children? (b) What **evidence** from his childhood in Los Angeles supports this?
7. (a) What do you think is the key point, or greatest generalization, of "Children in the Woods"? (b) Name three pieces of evidence that relate to the generalization.

Extend Understanding

8. **Career Connection:** Lopez believes that seeing relationships is better than just learning the names of things. Why might this approach help a person who is studying to be a doctor?

Integrate Language Skills

Vocabulary Development Lesson

Word Analysis: Latin Prefix *extra-*

Extrapolate contains the Latin prefix *extra-*, which means "outside." When you extrapolate, you put facts together to reach a conclusion that is "outside" the information you had when you started. Using the meaning of *extra-*, explain the following terms. Use a dictionary to check your answers.

1. extraordinary
2. extracurricular
3. extrasensory
4. extraterrestrial

Spelling Strategy

When adding an ending that begins with a vowel to a word that ends in a silent *e*, drop the *e* before you add the ending. For example, *make + -ing = making*. Write the word formed by adding each ending.

1. reside + *-ence*
2. invigorate + *-ing*

Fluency: Clarify Word Meaning

Identify the word from the vocabulary list on page 247 that answers each question.

1. What does soda do when you open the can?
2. What is another word for "explain"?
3. What do scientists get when they use facts to help them draw conclusions?
4. What word describes a tense game?
5. What would you find scattered around a junkyard?
6. How might someone experience a bad headache?
7. How might you describe a disease that is deadly but very hard to detect?
8. How many stars are in the sky?
9. How could you describe a feeling so strong that you could not put it into words?

Grammar Lesson

Prepositions

A **preposition** is a word that relates a noun or pronoun that appears with it to another word in the sentence. Although most prepositions, such as *at*, *by*, *in*, and *with*, are single words, some prepositions, such as *because of* and *in addition to*, are compound. In this example from "Children in the Woods," the prepositions are in italics:

> **Example:** The most moving look I ever saw *from* a child *in* the woods was *on* a mud bar *by* the footprints *of* a heron. We were *on* our knees, making handprints *beside* the footprints.

Practice Write each sentence, underlining all prepositions.

1. They saw rabbits across the stream.
2. The water flowed from the mountain and into the river.
3. The children walked along the path and looked at the roots of the tree.
4. Around the corner from the hiking trail we spotted a chipmunk.
5. The children can look at life a little differently because of the walk in the woods.

Writing Application Write a paragraph about nature using the following prepositions: *over*, *outside*, and *ahead of*.

WG Prentice Hall Writing and Grammar Connection: Chapter 19, Section 1

Writing Lesson

Field Guide

In "Children in the Woods," Barry Lopez vividly describes the woods around his home. A field guide provides detailed information about particular types of wildlife in a region. Write your own field guide about nature found right outside your home.

Prewriting   Brainstorm for a list of animals that live near your home. For each general group, itemize by naming specific examples. From your list, select the subjects for your field guide.

Model: Listing and Itemizing

Around My House

squirrels	cardinals
chipmunks	sparrows
birds	goldfinches
rabbits	

> Specific examples make a field guide clearer and more useful to its readers.

Drafting   As you draft, be specific, factual, and objective. Show what the animals look like and how they behave. For example, if you are describing the feeding habits of rabbits, tell exactly which plants they eat.

Revising   Have classmates read your field guide and list their unanswered questions. Use these questions to guide your revisions.

W̶G Prentice Hall Writing and Grammar Connection: Chapter 12, Section 2

Extension Activities

Listening and Speaking Keeping Barry Lopez's ideas in mind, devise a **lesson plan** to teach children about one aspect of nature. Use these suggestions as you plan:

- Select a topic that you know rather well.
- Use visuals to help inform your audience.
- Practice your lesson. If possible, videotape yourself to find room for improvement.

When you have finished preparing, teach your lesson to a child or a small group of children.

Research and Technology The woods described by Lopez are part of a temperate rain forest. In a group, prepare a **rain forest presentation.** Use resources at the library and on the Internet to find your facts. In your presentation, include a world map that shows where temperate rain forests are located. [**Group Activity**]

 **Take It to the Net**   www.phschool.com

Go online for an additional research activity using the Internet.

Web Sites

About Web Sites

A Web site is a collection of information located at a specific address on the World Wide Web, a part of the Internet accessible by computer. Software known as a browser enables an Internet user to access millions of Web sites around the world. To connect to a Web site, a user can either type a specific address or click on a word or picture that is electronically linked to the address. Often, a Web site begins with a home page, which is similar to the table of contents in a book. The user clicks on a specific home page listing, or link, to access the Web site's information on that topic.

Reading Strategy

Evaluating Credibility of Sources

When you access Web sites for information, it is important to evaluate the credibility of your sources. Use these questions to determine whether or not a source can be trusted:

- Who is the sponsor of the site?
- What are their credentials and background?
- Are both sides of issues represented?
- How current is the information?

You can trust the National Audubon Society, an established group, to give accurate Web site information on the Important Bird Area Program, a strictly factual topic. However, the Audubon Web page titled "Audubon View" sometimes presents an opinion, so you must treat that information more cautiously. Use a graphic organizer like the one shown here to rate the credibility of each link on the Audubon Web site home page.

Link	Credibility
Names of North American Birds	**Sponsor?** National Audubon Society. **Credentials?** 100-year-old organization that runs wildlife preservation programs. **Both sides shown?** Page presents factual information, not opinion. **Information current?** Yes. **Credible or not?** Credible. An organization dedicated to conservation would keep an accurate list of names of birds.

Audubon Web Site

If you are looking for information on wildlife conservation on the Internet, you are likely to come across the Web site for the National Audubon Society. The National Audubon Society is an organization that is dedicated to wildlife conservation and habitat restoration. The home page of the organization is shown below, providing a table of contents with links to the various pages of the site.

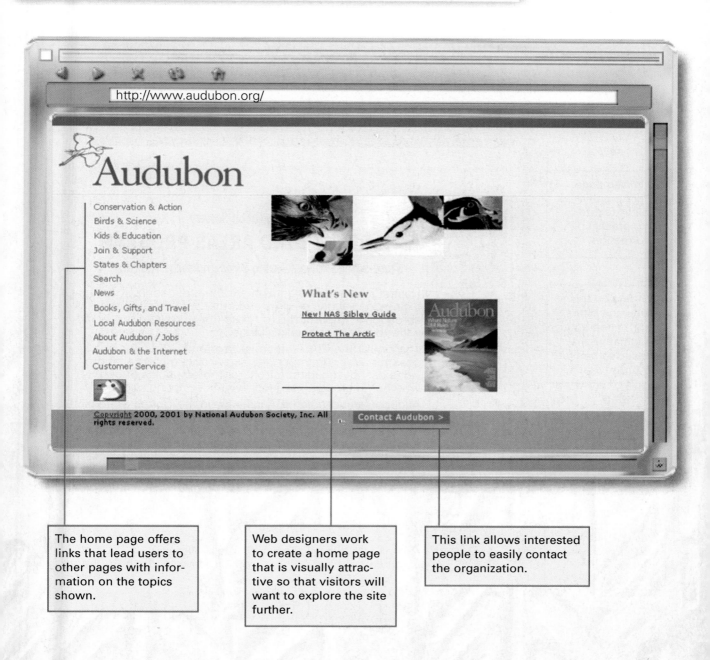

http://www.audubon.org/

Audubon

Conservation & Action
Birds & Science
Kids & Education
Join & Support
States & Chapters
Search
News
Books, Gifts, and Travel
Local Audubon Resources
About Audubon / Jobs
Audubon & the Internet
Customer Service

What's New

New! NAS Sibley Guide

Protect The Arctic

Contact Audubon >

The home page offers links that lead users to other pages with information on the topics shown.

Web designers work to create a home page that is visually attractive so that visitors will want to explore the site further.

This link allows interested people to easily contact the organization.

Internal Pages

Since there is too much information to fit on a single page, and because the Internet is suited to the presentation of unlimited information, the Audubon site is designed with multiple levels to organize its information. Users move down a level every time they click on a link on a page. The page shown below, from the third level of the site, provides detailed information about the Important Bird Areas Program.

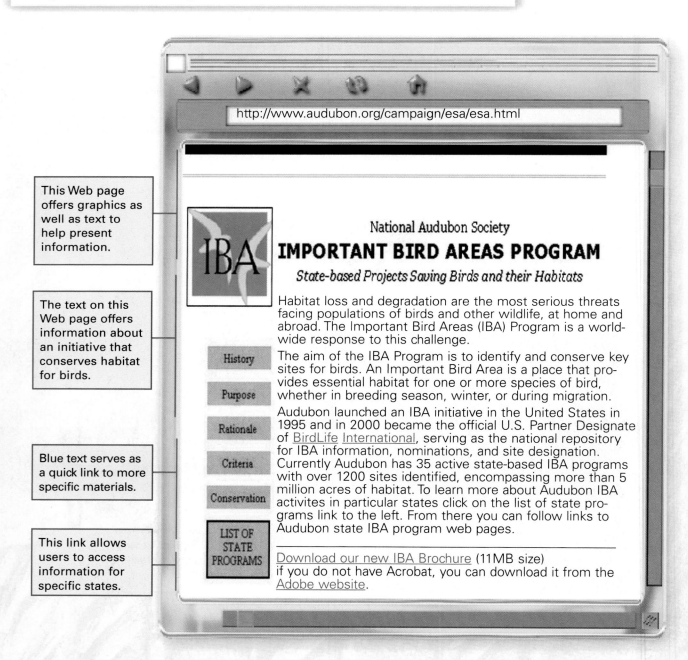

This Web page offers graphics as well as text to help present information.

The text on this Web page offers information about an initiative that conserves habitat for birds.

Blue text serves as a quick link to more specific materials.

This link allows users to access information for specific states.

http://www.audubon.org/campaign/esa/esa.html

National Audubon Society

IMPORTANT BIRD AREAS PROGRAM

State-based Projects Saving Birds and their Habitats

Habitat loss and degradation are the most serious threats facing populations of birds and other wildlife, at home and abroad. The Important Bird Areas (IBA) Program is a world-wide response to this challenge.

The aim of the IBA Program is to identify and conserve key sites for birds. An Important Bird Area is a place that provides essential habitat for one or more species of bird, whether in breeding season, winter, or during migration.

Audubon launched an IBA initiative in the United States in 1995 and in 2000 became the official U.S. Partner Designate of BirdLife International, serving as the national repository for IBA information, nominations, and site designation. Currently Audubon has 35 active state-based IBA programs with over 1200 sites identified, encompassing more than 5 million acres of habitat. To learn more about Audubon IBA activites in particular states click on the list of state programs link to the left. From there you can follow links to Audubon state IBA program web pages.

Download our new IBA Brochure (11MB size) if you do not have Acrobat, you can download it from the Adobe website.

History

Purpose

Rationale

Criteria

Conservation

LIST OF STATE PROGRAMS

Check Your Comprehension

1. Which link or links on the home page lead to information about education and resources?
2. Where would you find contact information?
3. What is the aim of the IBA program?

Applying the Reading Strategy

Evaluating Credibility of Sources

4. Cite two links on the Audubon home page that lead to information you can easily accept, along with two links you might evaluate more cautiously. Record your answers in the chart like the one below.

Credible	Explanation
Link:	

Evaluate More Cautiously	Explanation
Link:	

Activity

Researching a Web Site

You can find information on virtually any topic by using the World Wide Web. Choose a topic of interest to you. Then, use one or more Web sites to find information on your topic. For each site you visit, record information on an index card like the one shown here. Rank at least three sites in order of usefulness.

Conducting a Web Search

Topic:
Web address(es)
Web sponsor or author:
Credibility:
_____Excellent _____Good _____Fair
_____Poor
Date site was last updated:
Interesting facts:

Contrasting Informational Texts

Web Sites and Traditional Resources

1. Suppose that you wished to learn about the conservation of bird habitat without logging on to the Internet. (a) How could you find information on your topic in an encyclopedia? (b) Explain how this search process differs from using a Web site.
2. List resources other than the Internet and encyclopedias that you could use to find information on the conservation of bird habitat. Explain how to use each source and how using each one differs from using a Web site.

Prepare to Read

Rules of the Game

 Take It to the Net

Visit www.phschool.com
for interactive activities
and instruction related to
"Rules of the Game,"
including

- background
- graphic organizers
- literary elements
- reading strategies

Preview

Connecting to the Literature

In "Rules of the Game," a generational tug of war is complicated by a conflict between Chinese and American cultures. No matter what your cultural background might be, however, the battle of wills that takes place in this selection should be familiar to you.

Background

Chess, which plays a central role in this story by Amy Tan, is believed to have evolved from a game first played in India in the sixth century. The game spread to Persia (the present Iran), and the Arab invaders who conquered Persia in the seventh century later introduced chess to other lands around the Mediterranean Sea. Today, chess is played by people of all ages and cultural backgrounds around the world.

Literary Analysis

Generational Conflict

A **generational conflict** is a struggle that exists between characters when beliefs and values change from one generation to another. The following passage from "Rules of the Game" demonstrates the generational conflict that exists in the story.

> One day, after we left a shop I said under my breath, "I wish you wouldn't do that, telling everybody I'm your daughter." My mother stopped walking. . . . "Aiii-ya. So shame be with mother?"

As you read the story, pay attention to the conflicts, or struggles, between the characters and consider why the conflicts exist.

Connecting Literary Elements

Motivation is the reason behind a character's thoughts, feelings, and actions. The motives of characters often contribute to the conflict in a story. In "Rules of the Game," young Waverly's motivation to be a successful chess player, and her mother's motivation to become involved with Waverly's success, greatly contribute to the conflict.

Reading Strategy

Contrasting Characters

Throughout the story, you will see Waverly and her mother engaged in conflict. In order to follow the story, you need to understand how the two main characters are contrasted.

- As you read, **contrast,** or notice the differences in, the way each character expresses herself.
- Consider how each character feels about the other.

Use a chart like the one shown here to keep track of the actions, words, traits, and hopes of Waverly and her mother.

Waverly	Mrs. Jong
Born in the U.S.	Born in China
Significant Actions	
Significant Statements	
Personality Traits	
Hopes	

Vocabulary Development

pungent (pun´ jənt) *adj.* producing a sharp sensation of smell (p. 263)

benevolently (bə nev´ ə lent lē) *adv.* in a kind and well-meaning way (p. 267)

retort (ri tôrt´) *n.* sharp or clever reply (p. 267)

prodigy (präd´ ə jē) *n.* person who is amazingly talented or intelligent (p. 269)

malodorous (mal ō´ dər əs) *adj.* having a bad smell (p. 269)

concessions (kən sesh´ ənz) *n.* things given or granted as privileges (p. 270)

At the corner of the alley was Hong Sing's, a four-table cafe with a recessed stairwell in front that led to a door marked "Tradesmen." My brothers and I believed the bad people emerged from this door at night. Tourists never went to Hong Sing's, since the menu was printed only in Chinese. A Caucasian[4] man with a big camera once posed me and my playmates in front of the restaurant. He had us move to the side of the picture window so the photo would capture the roasted duck with its head dangling from a juice-covered rope. After he took the picture, I told him he should go into Hong Sing's and eat dinner. When he smiled and asked me what they served, I shouted, "Guts and duck's feet and octopus gizzards!" Then I ran off with my friends, shrieking with laughter as we scampered across the alley and hid in the entryway grotto[5] of the China Gem Company, my heart pounding with hope that he would chase us.

My mother named me after the street that we lived on: Waverly Place Jong, my official name for important American documents. But my family called me Meimei [mā´ mā´], "Little Sister," I was the youngest, the only daughter. Each morning before school, my mother would twist and yank on my thick black hair until she had formed two tightly wound pigtails. One day, as she struggled to weave a hard-toothed comb through my disobedient hair, I had a sly thought.

I asked her, "Ma, what is Chinese torture?" My mother shook her head. A bobby pin was wedged between her lips. She wetted her palm and smoothed the hair above my ear, then pushed the pin in so that it nicked sharply against my scalp.

"Who say this word?" she asked without a trace of knowing how wicked I was being. I shrugged my shoulders and said, "Some boy in my class said Chinese people do Chinese torture."

"Chinese people do many things," she said simply. "Chinese people do business, do medicine, do painting. Not lazy like American people. We do torture. Best torture."

M y older brother Vincent was the one who actually got the chess set. We had gone to the annual Christmas party held at the First Chinese Baptist Church at the end of the alley. The missionary ladies had put together a Santa bag of gifts donated by members of another church. None of the gifts had names on them. There were separate sacks for boys and girls of different ages.

One of the Chinese parishioners had donned a Santa Claus costume and a stiff paper beard with cotton balls glued to it. I think the only children who thought he was the real thing were too young to

Reading Strategy
Contrasting Characters
What does this conversation between Waverly and her mother reveal about each character's personality?

---

4. **Caucasian** (kô kā´ zhən) *adj.* person of European ancestry.
5. **entryway grotto** (grät´ ō) *n.* entryway resembling a cave.

know that Santa Claus was not Chinese. When my turn came up, the Santa man asked me how old I was. I thought it was a trick question; I was seven according to the American formula and eight by the Chinese calendar. I said I was born on March 17, 1951. That seemed to satisfy him. He then solemnly asked if I had been a very, very good girl this year and did I believe in Jesus Christ and obey my parents. I knew the only answer to that. I nodded back with equal solemnity.

Having watched the other children opening their gifts, I already knew that the big gifts were not necessarily the nicest ones. One girl my age got a large coloring book of biblical characters, while a less greedy girl who selected a small box received a glass vial of lavender toilet water. The sound of the box was also important. A ten-year-old boy had chosen a box that jangled when he shook it. It was a tin globe of the world with a slit for inserting money. He must have thought it was full of dimes and nickels, because when he saw that it had just ten pennies, his face fell with such undisguised disappointment that his mother slapped the side of his head and led him out of the church hall, apologizing to the crowd for her son who had such bad manners he couldn't appreciate such a fine gift.

As I peered into the sack, I quickly fingered the remaining presents, testing their weight, imagining what they contained. I chose a heavy, compact one that was wrapped in shiny silver foil and a red satin ribbon. It was a twelve-pack of Life Savers and I spent the rest of the party arranging and rearranging the candy tubes in the order of my favorites. My brother Winston chose wisely as well. His present turned out to be a box of intricate plastic parts; the instructions on the box proclaimed that when they were properly assembled he would have an authentic miniature replica of a World War II submarine.

Vincent got the chess set, which would have been a very decent present to get at a church Christmas party except it was obviously used and, as we discovered later, it was missing a black pawn and a white knight. My mother graciously thanked the unknown benefactor, saying, "Too good. Cost too much." At which point, an old lady with fine white, wispy hair nodded toward our family and said with a whistling whisper, "Merry, merry Christmas."

When we got home, my mother told Vincent to throw the chess set away. "She not want it. We not want it," she said, tossing her head stiffly to the side with a tight, proud smile. My brothers had deaf ears. They were already lining up the chess pieces and reading from the dog-eared instruction book.

I watched Vincent and Winston play during Christmas week. The chess board seemed to hold elaborate secrets waiting to be untangled. The chessmen were more powerful than Old Li's magic herbs that cured ancestral curses. And my brothers wore such serious faces that I was sure something was at stake that was greater than avoiding the tradesmen's door to Hong Sing's.

Literary Analysis
Generational Conflict and Motivation What motivates Waverly to produce the right answers for Santa Claus?

Reading Strategy
Contrasting Characters What do Mrs. Jong's statement and action regarding the chess set suggest about her sense of her own worth?

✔**Reading Check**
What gift does Vincent receive at the Christmas party?

"Let me! Let me!" I begged between games when one brother or the other would sit back with a deep sigh of relief and victory, the other annoyed, unable to let go of the outcome. Vincent at first refused to let me play, but when I offered my Life Savers as replacements for the buttons that filled in for the missing pieces, he relented. He chose the flavors: wild cherry for the black pawn and peppermint for the white knight. Winner could eat both. As our mother sprinkled flour and rolled out small doughy circles for the steamed dumplings that would be our dinner that night, Vincent explained the rules, pointing to each piece. "You have sixteen pieces and so do I. One king and queen, two bishops, two knights, two castles, and eight pawns. The pawns can only move forward one step, except on the first move. Then they can move two. But they can only take men by moving crossways like this, except in the beginning, when you can move ahead and take another pawn."

"Why?" I asked as I moved my pawn. "Why can't they move more steps?"

"Because they're pawns," he said.

"But why do they go crossways to take other men. Why aren't there any women and children?"

"Why is the sky blue? Why must you always ask stupid questions?" asked Vincent. "This is a game. These are the rules. I didn't make them up. See. Here. In the book." He jabbed a page with a pawn in his hand. "Pawn. P-A-W-N. Pawn. Read it yourself."

My mother patted the flour off her hands. "Let me see book," she said quietly. She scanned the pages quickly, not reading the foreign English symbols, seeming to search deliberately for nothing in particular.

"This American rules," she concluded at last. "Every time people come out from foreign country, must know rules. You not know, judge say, Too bad, go back. They not telling you why so you can use their way go forward. They say, Don't know why, you find out yourself. But they knowing all the time. Better you take it, find out why yourself." She tossed her head back with a satisfied smile.

I found out about all the whys later. I read the rules and looked up all the big words in a dictionary. I borrowed books from the Chinatown library. I studied each chess piece, trying to absorb the power each contained.

I learned about opening moves and why it's important to control the center early on; the shortest distance between two points is straight down the middle. I learned about the middle game and why tactics between two adversaries are like clashing ideas; the one who plays better has the clearest plans for both attacking and getting out of traps. I learned why it is essential in the endgame* to have foresight, a mathematical understanding of all possible moves, and patience; all weaknesses and advantages become evident to a strong adversary and are obscured to a tiring opponent. I discovered that for the whole game one must gather invisible strengths and see the endgame before the game begins.

I also found out why I should never reveal "why" to others. A little knowledge withheld is a great advantage one should store for future use. That is the power of chess. It is a game of secrets in which one must show and never tell.

I loved the secrets I found within the sixty-four black and white squares. I carefully drew a handmade chessboard and pinned it to the wall next to my bed, where at night I would stare for hours at imaginary battles. Soon I no longer lost any games or Life Savers, but I lost my adversaries. Winston and Vincent decided they were more interested in roaming the streets after school in their Hopalong Cassidy[6] cowboy hats.

On a cold spring afternoon, while walking home from school, I detoured through the playground at the end of our alley. I saw a group of old men, two seated across a folding table playing a game of chess, others smoking pipes, eating peanuts, and watching. I ran home and grabbed Vincent's chess set, which was bound in a cardboard box with rubber bands. I also carefully selected two prized rolls of Life Savers. I came back to the park and approached a man who was observing the game.

"Want to play?" I asked him. His face widened with surprise and he grinned as he looked at the box under my arm.

"Little sister, been a long time since I play with dolls," he said, smiling <u>benevolently</u>. I quickly put the box down next to him on the bench and displayed my <u>retort</u>.

Lau Po, as he allowed me to call him, turned out to be a much better player than my brothers. I lost many games and many Life Savers. But over the weeks, with each diminishing roll of candies, I added new secrets. Lau Po gave me the names. The Double Attack from the East and West Shores. Throwing Stones on the Drowning Man. The Sudden Meeting of the Clan. The Surprise from the Sleeping Guard. The Humble Servant Who Kills the King. Sand in the Eyes of Advancing Forces. A Double Killing Without Blood.

There were also the fine points of chess etiquette. Keep captured men in neat rows, as well-tended prisoners. Never announce "Check" with vanity, lest someone with an unseen sword slit your throat. Never hurl pieces into the sandbox after you have lost a game, because then you must find them again, by yourself, after apologizing to all around you. By the end of the summer, Lau Po had taught me all he knew, and I had become a better chess player.

---

6. **Hopalong Cassidy** character in cowboy movies during the 1950s.

Literature in context Cultural Connection

◆ **Endgame**

Endgame describes a tense period in a chess game when the end seems close at hand. With fewer pieces left, lines of attack and defense become clearer to both players. Mistakes are magnified in an endgame, when the margin between victory and defeat can be a single ill-considered move. In this story, Waverly develops a keen awareness of the strategies needed in the endgame to secure a victory.

benevolently (bə nev´ ə lent lē) adv. in a kind and well-meaning way

retort (ri tôrt´) n. sharp or clever reply

Reading Check

How does Waverly quench her desire to understand the rules of chess?

A small week-
end crowd of
Chinese people
and tourists would
gather as I played
and defeated my
opponents one by
one. My mother
would join the
crowds during
these outdoor
exhibition games.
She sat proudly on
the bench, telling
my admirers with
proper Chinese
humility, "Is luck."

A man who
watched me play
in the park sug-
gested that my
mother allow me
to play in local
chess tourna-
ments. My mother
smiled graciously,
an answer that
meant nothing. I
desperately want-
ed to go, but I bit
back my tongue. I
knew she would

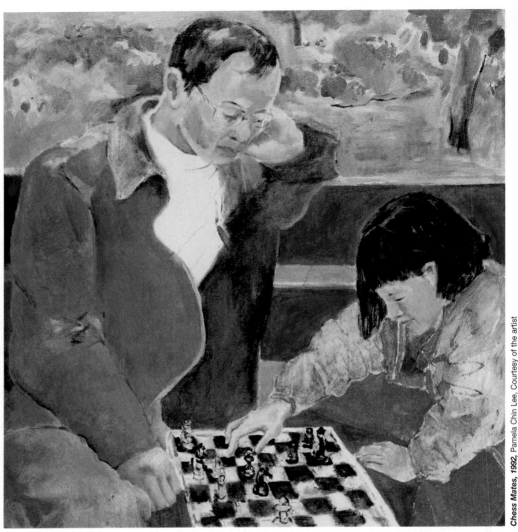

Chess Mates, 1992, Pamela Chin Lee, Courtesy of the artist

not let me play among strangers. So as we walked home I said in a
small voice that I didn't want to play in the local tournament. They
would have American rules. If I lost, I would bring shame on my family.

"Is shame you fall down nobody push you," said my mother.

During my first tournament, my mother sat with me in the front
row as I waited for my turn. I frequently bounced my legs to unstick
them from the cold metal seat of the folding chair. When my name
was called, I leapt up. My mother unwrapped something in her lap. It
was her chang, a small tablet of red jade which held the sun's fire. "Is
luck," she whispered, and tucked it into my dress pocket. I turned to
my opponent, a fifteen-year-old boy from Oakland. He looked at me,
wrinkling his nose.

As I began to play, the boy disappeared, the color ran out of the
room, and I saw only my white pieces and his black ones waiting on
the other side. A light wind began blowing past my ears. It whispered
secrets only I could hear.

▲ **Critical Viewing**
Based on details in the
painting, who do you
think is winning this chess
game? Why? **[Support]**

"Blow from the South," it murmured. "The wind leaves no trail." I saw a clear path, the traps to avoid. The crowd rustled. "Shhh! Shhh!" said the corners of the room. The wind blew stronger. "Throw sand from the East to distract him." The knight came forward ready for the sacrifice. The wind hissed, louder and louder. "Blow, blow, blow. He cannot see. He is blind now. Make him lean away from the wind so he is easier to knock down."

"Check," I said, as the wind roared with laughter. The wind died down to little puffs, my own breath.

My mother placed my first trophy next to a new plastic chess set that the neighborhood Tao society[7] had given to me. As she wiped each piece with a soft cloth, she said, "Next time win more, lose less."

"Ma, it's not how many pieces you lose," I said. "Sometimes you need to lose pieces to get ahead."

"Better to lose less, see if you really need."

At the next tournament, I won again, but it was my mother who wore the triumphant grin.

"Lost eight piece this time. Last time was eleven. What I tell you? Better off lose less!" I was annoyed, but I couldn't say anything.

I attended more tournaments, each one farther away from home. I won all games, in all divisions. The Chinese bakery downstairs from our flat displayed my growing collection of trophies in its window, amidst the dust-covered cakes that were never picked up. The day after I won an important regional tournament, the window encased a fresh sheet cake with whipped-cream frosting and red script saying, "Congratulations, Waverly Jong, Chinatown Chess Champion." Soon after that, a flower shop, headstone engraver, and funeral parlor offered to sponsor me in national tournaments. That's when my mother decided I no longer had to do the dishes. Winston and Vincent had to do my chores.

"Why does she get to play and we do all the work," complained Vincent.

"Is new American rules," said my mother. "Meimei play, squeeze all her brains out for win chess. You play, worth squeeze towel."

By my ninth birthday, I was a national chess champion. I was still some 429 points away from grand-master status, but I was touted as the Great American Hope, a child <u>prodigy</u> and a girl to boot. They ran a photo of me in *Life* magazine next to a quote in which Bobby Fischer[8] said, "There will never be a woman grand master." "Your move, Bobby," said the caption.

The day they took the magazine picture I wore neatly plaited braids clipped with plastic barrettes trimmed with rhinestones. I was playing in

---

Literary Analysis

Generational Conflict and Motivation What motivates the mother to advise Waverly, instead of complimenting her daughter on her win?

prodigy (präd´ ə jē) *n.* person who is amazingly talented or intelligent

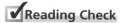

Reading Check

Why was Waverly featured in *Life* magazine?

---

7. **Tao** (dou) **society** group of people who believe in Taoism, a Chinese religion that stresses simplicity and unselfishness.
8. **Bobby Fischer** born in 1943, this American chess prodigy attained the high rank of grand master in 1958.

a large high school auditorium that echoed with phlegmy coughs and the squeaky rubber knobs of chair legs sliding across freshly waxed wooden floors. Seated across from me was an American man, about the same age as Lau Po, maybe fifty. I remember that his sweaty brow seemed to weep at my every move. He wore a dark, <u>malodorous</u> suit. One of his pockets was stuffed with a great white kerchief on which he wiped his palm before sweeping his hand over the chosen chess piece with great flourish.

In my crisp pink-and-white dress with scratchy lace at the neck, one of two my mother had sewn for these special occasions, I would clasp my hands under my chin, the delicate points of my elbows poised lightly on the table in the manner my mother had shown me for posing for the press. I would swing my patent leather shoes back and forth like an impatient child riding on a school bus. Then I would pause, suck in my lips, twirl my chosen piece in midair as if undecided, and then firmly plant it in its new threatening place, with a triumphant smile thrown back at my opponent for good measure.

I no longer played in the alley of Waverly Place. I never visited the playground where the pigeons and old men gathered. I went to school, then directly home to learn new chess secrets, cleverly concealed advantages, more escape routes.

But I found it difficult to concentrate at home. My mother had a habit of standing over me while I plotted out my games. I think she thought of herself as my protective ally. Her lips would be sealed tight, and after each move I made, a soft "Hmmmmph" would escape from her nose.

"Ma, I can't practice when you stand there like that," I said one day. She retreated to the kitchen and made loud noises with the pots and pans. When the crashing stopped, I could see out of the corner of my eye that she was standing in the doorway. "Hmmmmph!" Only this one came out of her tight throat.

My parents made many <u>concessions</u> to allow me to practice. One time I complained that the bedroom I shared was so noisy that I couldn't think. Thereafter, my brothers slept in a bed in the living room facing the street. I said I couldn't finish my rice; my head didn't work right when my stomach was too full. I left the table with half-finished bowls and nobody complained. But there was one duty I couldn't avoid. I had to accompany my mother on Saturday market days when I had no tournament to play. My mother would proudly walk with me, visiting many shops, buying very little. "This my daughter Wave-ly Jong," she said to whoever looked her way.

One day, after we left a shop I said under my breath, "I wish you wouldn't do that, telling everybody I'm your daughter." My mother stopped walking. Crowds of people with heavy bags pushed past us on the sidewalk, bumping into first one shoulder, then another.

"Aiii-ya. So shame be with mother?" She grasped my hand even tighter as she glared at me.

I looked down. "It's not that, it's just so obvious. It's just so embarrassing."

malodorous (mal ō′ dər əs) *adj.* having a bad smell

Reading Strategy
Contrasting Characters
What does this passage reveal about the way each character communicates?

concessions (kən sesh′ ənz) *n.* things given or granted as privileges

"Embarrass you be my daughter?" Her voice was cracking with anger.

"That's not what I meant. That's not what I said."

"What you say?"

I knew it was a mistake to say anything more, but I heard my voice speaking. "Why do you have to use me to show off? If you want to show off, then why don't you learn to play chess." My mother's eyes turned into dangerous black slits. She had no words for me, just sharp silence.

I felt the wind rushing around my hot ears. I jerked my hand out of my mother's tight grasp and spun around, knocking into an old woman. Her bag of groceries spilled to the ground.

"Aii-ya! Stupid girl!" my mother and the woman cried. Oranges and tin cans careened down the sidewalk. As my mother stooped to help the old woman pick up the escaping food, I took off.

I raced down the street, dashing between people, not looking back as my mother screamed shrilly, "Meimei! Meimei!" I fled down an alley, past dark curtained shops and merchants washing the grime off their windows. I sped into the sunlight, into a large street crowded with tourists examining trinkets and souvenirs. I ducked into another dark alley, down another street, up another alley. I ran until it hurt and I realized I had nowhere to go, that I was not running from anything. The alleys contained no escape routes.

My breath came out like angry smoke. It was cold. I sat down on an upturned plastic pail next to a stack of empty boxes, cupping my chin with my hands, thinking hard. I imagined my mother, first walking briskly down one street or another looking for me, then giving up and returning home to await my arrival. After two hours, I stood up on creaking legs and slowly walked home.

The alley was quiet and I could see the yellow lights shining from our flat like two tiger's eyes in the night. I climbed the sixteen steps to the door, advancing quietly up each so as not to make any warning sounds. I turned the knob; the door was locked. I heard a chair moving, quick steps, the locks turning—click! click! click!—and then the door opened.

"About time you got home," said Vincent. "Boy, are you in trouble."

He slid back to the dinner table. On a platter were the remains of a large fish, its fleshy head still connected to bones swimming upstream in vain escape. Standing there waiting for my punishment, I heard my mother speak in a dry voice.

"We not concerning this girl. This girl not have concerning for us."

Nobody looked at me. Bone chopsticks[9] clinked against the insides of bowls being emptied into hungry mouths.

---

9. **chopsticks** (chäp′ stiks′) two small sticks of wood, bone, or ivory, held together in one hand and used as utensils for eating, cooking, and serving food.

Literary Analysis
Generational Conflict
What makes Waverly upset with her mother's behavior?

✔**Reading Check**

What does Waverly say to her mother when they walk through the Saturday market?

I walked into my room, closed the door, and lay down on my bed. The room was dark, the ceiling filled with shadows from the dinner-time lights of neighboring flats.

In my head, I saw a chessboard with sixty-four black and white squares. Opposite me was my opponent, two angry black slits. She wore a triumphant smile. "Strongest wind cannot be seen," she said.

Her black men advanced across the plane, slowly marching to each successive level as a single unit. My white pieces screamed as they scurried and fell off the board one by one. As her men drew closer to my edge, I felt myself growing light. I rose up into the air and flew out the window. Higher and higher, above the alley, over the tops of tiled roofs, where I was gathered up by the wind and pushed up toward the night sky until everything below me disappeared and I was alone.

I closed my eyes and pondered my next move.

Review and Assess

Thinking About the Selection

1. **Respond:** Which character did you find most realistic? Explain.

2. **(a) Recall:** Explain the salted plums incident in the beginning of the story. **(b) Analyze:** Which strategy does Waverly use with her mother even before she starts playing chess?

3. **(a) Recall:** How does Mrs. Jong teach Waverly rules of behavior? **(b) Connect:** How does Waverly use these rules to win at chess? **(c) Extend:** How does she use them in her struggle with her mother?

4. **Speculate:** The story ends without a final showdown. Who do you think will eventually "win" the game? Why?

5. **Apply:** Referring to chess, Waverly says that "for the whole game one must gather invisible strengths and see the endgame before the game begins." In which more general situations does this idea apply? Explain.

6. **Interpret:** Why do you think Amy Tan called this story "Rules of the Game"?

7. **(a) Assess:** Which elements of the struggle between Waverly and her mother are universal, relating to people from all cultures? Explain. **(b) Extend:** Which elements are uniquely Chinese American? Explain.

8. **Take a Position:** Do you think that Waverly's anger toward her mother is justified? Why or why not?

Amy Tan

(b. 1952)

Like Waverly, the nine-year-old chess champion in this story, Amy Tan was something of a child prodigy, displaying literary promise at the ripe age of eight. As a young woman, Tan supported herself as a technical writer, playing piano and writing fiction for relaxation. Through writing, she discovered her own ethnic identity. She has said in interviews that she had tried to minimize her ethnicity when she was younger. All that changed when she began to write about the painful but rich experiences of Chinese American women.

In 1985, Tan wrote "Rules of the Game," which she later included in *The Joy Luck Club*, set in Oakland, California, where she was born. The novel weaves together the stories of four Chinese mothers and their American-born daughters.

Review and Assess

Literary Analysis

Generational Conflict

1. What does Waverly resent about her mother's behavior when they are shopping together?
2. What might Mrs. Jong feel that her child does not yet understand?
3. (a) Use a chart like the one shown below to list statements made by Waverly and her mother that suggest a conflict. (b) Based on their statements, how would you rate the **generational conflict** on a scale from 1 to 10? Explain.

Speaker	Statement

Connecting Literary Elements

4. What motivates Mrs. Jong's involvement in Waverly's chess success?
5. How does Waverly's **motivation** to be a successful chess player contribute to her conflict with her mother?

Reading Strategy

Contrasting Characters

6. In what ways are Waverly and Mrs. Jong more alike than they admit? Using a chart like the one below, analyze their similarities and differences.

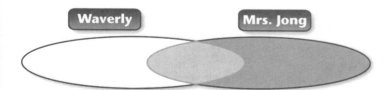

7. Why is Waverly in a better position than her mother to understand "American rules"?
8. What does Mrs. Jong want for her daughter that she does not have herself?

Extend Understanding

9. **Humanities Connection:** What other stories do you know in which a child uses success in some activity to outgrow a parent?

Quick Review

Generational conflict is the struggle between two characters that occurs when beliefs and values change from one generation to another.

Motivation is the reason that explains why a character thinks, feels, or behaves in a certain way.

To **contrast characters,** find the differences that exist between people in a story.

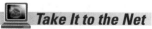 **Take It to the Net**
www.phschool.com

Take the interactive self-test online to check your understanding of the selection.

Integrate Language Skills

Vocabulary Development Lesson

Word Origins: Words From French

Several words found in "Rules of the Game" come from the French language, including *etiquette* (rules of behavior) and *souvenirs* (mementos).

In your notebook, write the English equivalent of these Old French words.

1. *rieules*　**2.** *circonstances*　**3.** *torneiement*

Spelling Strategy

Most English words ending in *-gy* are spelled with an *o* before the *-gy*. *Prodigy*, however, is one of only four words in common usage that do not follow this rule. Review the items below. If the spelling of a word is correct, write *Correct*. If the spelling is wrong, write the proper spelling.

1. strategy　**2.** apoligy　**3.** effegy

Concept Development: Synonyms

For each item below, identify the letter of the word or phrase whose meaning is closest to that of the first word.

1. concessions: (a) things granted, (b) large meetings, (c) secrets
2. retort: (a) foolish deed, (b) clever reply, (c) old wisdom
3. malodorous: (a) evil-minded, (b) bad-smelling, (c) beautiful-sounding
4. prodigy: (a) young child, (b) large amount, (c) talented person
5. pungent: (a) sweet-tasting, (b) sharp-smelling, (c) witty
6. benevolently: (a) wealthily, (b) attractively, (c) in a kind way

Grammar Lesson

Prepositional Phrases

A **prepositional phrase** is a group of words that includes a preposition and a noun or pronoun, called the *object of the preposition*. Generally, the object of the preposition is found after the preposition. In the following examples from the story, prepositional phrases are underlined, prepositions are italicized, and objects of prepositions are boldface.

> **Examples:** She won respect *from* **others**.
>
> No one knew it *at the* **time**.
>
> *During* the tense **game,** she showed great concentration.

Practice Find the prepositional phrases in the following sentences. For each, identify the object of the preposition.

1. Nobody looked at Waverly.
2. The gifts did not have names on them.
3. The tin globe had a slit for inserting money.
4. She loved the secrets she found in chess.
5. After the game, she put the pieces in the case.

Writing Application Write four sentences, using one of these prepositional phrases in each.

1. about me　　3. through a strategy
2. before the game　4. after Mrs. Jong

W̶G̶ Prentice Hall Writing and Grammar Connection: Chapter 19, Section 1

Writing Lesson

Advice Column

Imagine you are a newspaper advice columnist. Write a column that provides advice to Waverly and her mother about how they can resolve their conflict.

Prewriting   Jot down all of the issues between Waverly and Mrs. Jong. Next to each issue, make a suggestion about how the conflict can be resolved.

Drafting   Your column should include suggestions for both characters. Remember to keep an objective tone—do not favor one character over another, but instead show concern for both of them.

Revising   Read your draft, paying attention to the tone. Highlight and rewrite any language that sounds biased, or overly supportive of one character. Make sure you have addressed every issue and provided reasonable solutions to their problems.

Model: Revising to Keep an Objective Tone

Biased:	Objective:
It's not surprising that Waverly was completely embarrassed when you put her on display at the market.	It's obvious that you are very proud of your daughter, but it will help both of you if you express your pride differently.

> The objective statement shows concern for both people.

Prentice Hall Writing and Grammar Connection: Chapter 11, Section 4

Extension Activities

Listening and Speaking With a classmate, write a **dialogue** between Waverly and her mother that takes place years after the events in this story, when Waverly is an adult.

- Consider the character traits you think Waverly will have as an adult.
- Decide whether the dialogue will reflect conflict in their relationship or a better way of communicating.

Read your dialogue aloud to the class. **[Group Activity]**

Research and Technology Imagine that you are a radio announcer. Give a **radio commentary** describing a national chess tournament in which Waverly Jong is a finalist. Start your commentary by explaining the significance of the event. Remember to use a tone of voice that captures the mood of the scene. After practicing, present the commentary to your class.

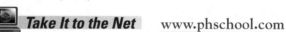 *Take It to the Net*   www.phschool.com

Go online for an additional research activity using the Internet.

CONNECTIONS
Literature and Media
From Printed Page to Silver Screen

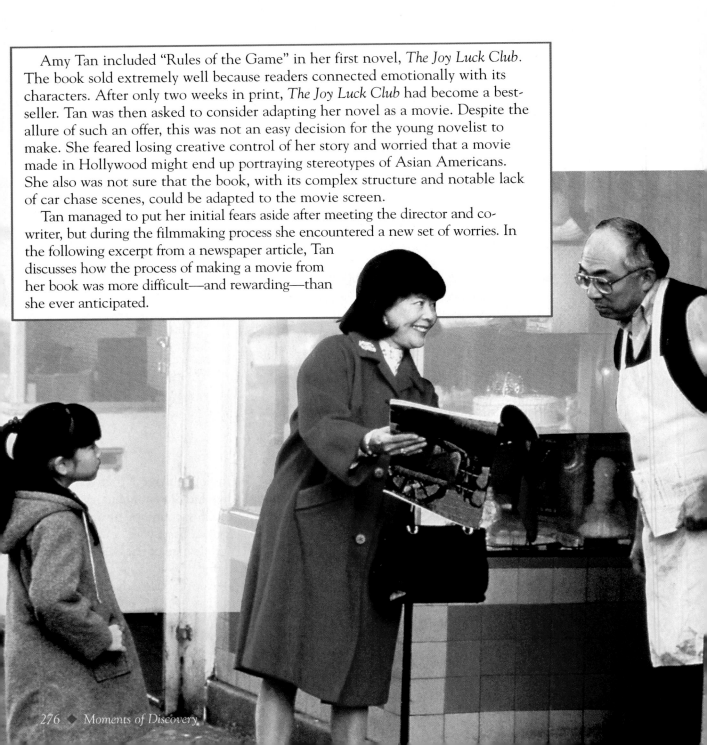

Amy Tan included "Rules of the Game" in her first novel, *The Joy Luck Club*. The book sold extremely well because readers connected emotionally with its characters. After only two weeks in print, *The Joy Luck Club* had become a best-seller. Tan was then asked to consider adapting her novel as a movie. Despite the allure of such an offer, this was not an easy decision for the young novelist to make. She feared losing creative control of her story and worried that a movie made in Hollywood might end up portraying stereotypes of Asian Americans. She also was not sure that the book, with its complex structure and notable lack of car chase scenes, could be adapted to the movie screen.

Tan managed to put her initial fears aside after meeting the director and co-writer, but during the filmmaking process she encountered a new set of worries. In the following excerpt from a newspaper article, Tan discusses how the process of making a movie from her book was more difficult—and rewarding—than she ever anticipated.

from Joy, Luck, and Hollywood

Amy Tan

Los Angeles Times, September 5, 1993

I CRIED MY EYES OUT

I saw all the dailies,[1] most of them on video format at home. I cried throughout the making of the movie. I was very moved by what I was seeing. I was exhausted watching what the actors went through. At major stages, Ron and I worked with Wayne and the editor, Maysie Hoy, as the movie was being cut. That process was fascinating but tedious. I ended up thinking Maysie was a saint.

Around April, I got to see a first rough cut.[2] I was supposed to watch it and take notes of problem areas and such. But I was too <u>mesmerized</u> to do anything but watch it pretty much like an ordinary moviegoer. I laughed, I cried. The second time I saw it, I said to Wayne: "I want you to remember this day. We're going to get a lot of different reactions to this film later down the road. But I want us to remember that on this day, you, Ron and I were proud with what we've accomplished. We made our vision."

> **mesmerized** (mez´mər ized´) *v.* hypnotized; fascinated

Ron insisted that I come to the test previews because there I'd get some of the biggest highs or lows of my life, seeing how a real audience reacted. Fortunately, it was the former. I was surprised, though, whenever people laughed during a scene I never considered funny. I suppose it was one of those <u>ironic</u> laughs, in which one recognizes the pain of some childhood humiliation.

> **ironic** (ī rän´ ik) *adj.* directly opposite to what is or what might be expected

I've now seen the movie about 25 times, and I am not ashamed to say I'm moved to tears each time.

By the time you read this, I will have seen the movie with my mother and my half sister, who just immigrated from China. So that'll be my version of life imitating art, or sitting in front of it. I'm nervous about what my mother will think. I'm afraid she'll be overwhelmed by

---

1. dailies (dā´ lēz) *n.* movie term to describe the photographic prints made from the previous day's filming. Directors and actors use dailies to assess the progress of the film and the quality of actors' performances.
2. rough cut *n.* early version of an entire film. The rough cut allows the director and writers to receive reactions and suggest additional revisions for the finished film.

✔**Reading Check**

What was Amy Tan's initial reaction to seeing the first rough cut?

Prepare to Read

Checkouts ◆ Fifteen

Food City, 1967, Richard Estes, Collection of the Akron Art Museum, Akron, Ohio

Take It to the Net

Visit www.phschool.com for interactive activities and instruction related to the selections, including

- background
- graphic organizers
- literary elements
- reading strategies

Preview

Connecting to the Literature

You get on the school bus and sit alone instead of taking a seat next to someone you do not know. You cannot go to a concert because you are battling the flu. Missed opportunities for new adventures occur just about every day. In these two selections, young people experience lost opportunities for different reasons.

Background

In "Checkouts," the main character is compared to "a Tibetan monk in solitary meditation." The Buddhist monks of Tibet live in seclusion, often meditating, or clearing the mind of all thoughts, to achieve a state of perfect calmness. In "Checkouts," the main character achieves this state by grocery shopping!

Literary Analysis

Irony

Irony is the contrast between an actual outcome and what the reader or the characters expect, or what might logically be expected. Irony can add humor to some situations; it can also invite readers to stop and think. In this example from "Checkouts," notice the discrepancy in ideas and how it creates irony.

> Then one day the bag boy dropped her jar of mayonnaise and that is how she fell in love.

You would probably expect a person to be frustrated if a bag boy dropped a jar of mayonnaise. In "Checkouts," however, the action generates an unexpected outcome.

Comparing Literary Works

The following selections share a theme of self-discovery. In "Checkouts," a girl falls in love, and in "Fifteen," a boy chances upon a riderless motorcycle. These opportunities for new experiences lead the teenagers to discoveries about themselves. As you read, compare and contrast the opportunities, losses, and discoveries each character faces.

Reading Strategy

Relating to Personal Experience

You can appreciate and understand a character's story by **relating it to your personal experience.** To do this, use the following strategies:

- Decide how the events in the story are like your own experiences.
- Consider how you or people you know would feel in the same situation.

Make a chart like the one shown here to keep track of your thoughts.

Story Detail

The bag boy's job

Personal Experience the Incident Recalls

My first job as a grocery store cashier

Feelings It Evokes

Nervousness, anxiety

Vocabulary Development

intuition (in´ to͞o ish´ ən) *n.* knowledge of something without reasoning (p. 283)

reverie (rev´ ər ē) *n.* dreamy thought of pleasant things (p. 283)

shards (shärdz) *n.* broken pieces (p. 283)

harried (har´ ēd) *adj.* worried (p. 283)

brazen (brā´ zən) *adj.* shamelessly bold (p. 283)

dishevelment (di shev´ əl ment) *n.* state of being untidy (p. 284)

perverse (pər vurs´) *adj.* contrary and willful (p. 284)

articulate (är tik´ yo͞o lāt´) *v.* express in words (p. 284)

lingered (liŋ´ gərd) *v.* stayed on, as if unwilling to leave (p. 285)

demure (di myoor´) *adj.* shy or modest (p. 286)

Checkouts

Cynthia Rylant

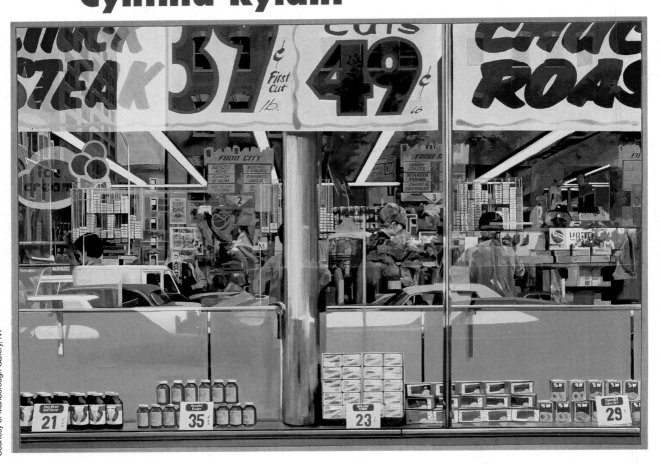

H er parents had moved her to Cincinnati, to a large house with beveled glass[1] windows and several porches and the *history* her mother liked to emphasize. You'll love the house, they said. You'll be lonely at first, they admitted, but you're so nice you'll make friends fast. And as an impulse tore at her to lie on the floor, to hold to their ankles and tell them she felt she was dying, to offer anything, anything at all, so they might allow her to finish growing up in the town of her childhood, they firmed their mouths and spoke from their chests and they said, It's decided.

> ▲ **Critical Viewing**
> What distractions found in a supermarket might help people take their minds off their troubles?
> **[Analyze]**

---

1. beveled (bev´ əld) **glass** glass having angled or slanted edges.

They moved her to Cincinnati, where for a month she spent the greater part of every day in a room full of beveled glass windows, sifting through photographs of the life she'd lived and left behind. But it is difficult work, suffering, and in its own way a kind of art, and finally she didn't have the energy for it anymore, so she emerged from the beautiful house and fell in love with a bag boy at the supermarket. Of course, this didn't happen all at once, just like that, but in the sequence of things that's exactly the way it happened.

She liked to grocery shop. She loved it in the way some people love to drive long country roads, because doing it she could think and relax and wander. Her parents wrote up the list and handed it to her and off she went without complaint to perform what they regarded as a great sacrifice of her time and a sign that she was indeed a very nice girl. She had never told them how much she loved grocery shopping, only that she was "willing" to do it. She had an <u>intuition</u> which told her that her parents were not safe for sharing such strong, important facts about herself. Let them think they knew her.

Once inside the supermarket, her hands firmly around the handle of the cart, she would lapse into a kind of <u>reverie</u> and wheel toward the produce. Like a Tibetan monk in solitary meditation, she calmed to a point of deep, deep happiness; this feeling came to her, reliably, if strangely, only in the supermarket.

Then one day the bag boy dropped her jar of mayonnaise and that is how she fell in love.

He was nervous—first day on the job—and along had come this fascinating girl, standing in the checkout line with the unfocused stare one often sees in young children, her face turned enough away that he might take several full looks at her as he packed sturdy bags full of food and the goods of modern life. She interested him because her hair was red and thick, and in it she had placed a huge orange bow, nearly the size of a small hat. That was enough to distract him, and when finally it was her groceries he was packing, she looked at him and smiled and he could respond only by busting her jar of mayonnaise on the floor, <u>shards</u> of glass and oozing cream decorating the area around his feet.

She loved him at exactly that moment, and if he'd known this perhaps he wouldn't have fallen into the brown depression he fell into, which lasted the rest of his shift. He believed he must have looked the fool in her eyes, and he envied the sureness of everyone around him: the cocky cashier at the register, the grim and <u>harried</u> store manager, the bland butcher, and the <u>brazen</u> bag boys who smoked in the warehouse on their breaks. He wanted a second chance. Another chance to be confident and say witty things to her as he threw tin cans into her bags, persuading her to allow him to help her to her car so he might learn just a little about her, check out the floor of the car for signs of hobbies or fetishes and the bumpers for clues as to beliefs and loyalties.

But he busted her jar of mayonnaise and nothing else worked out for the rest of the day.

Literary Analysis
Irony What is ironic about her love for grocery shopping?

intuition (in′ tōō ish′ ən) n. knowledge of something without reasoning

reverie (rev′ ər ē) n. dreamy thought of pleasant things

shards (shärdz) n. broken pieces

harried (har′ ēd) adj. worried

brazen (brā′ zən) adj. shamelessly bold

**Reading Check**

Why does the girl fascinate the bag boy?

Strange, how attractive clumsiness can be. She left the supermarket with stars in her eyes, for she had loved the way his long nervous fingers moved from the conveyor belt to the bags, how deftly (until the mayonnaise) they had picked up her items and placed them in her bags. She had loved the way the hair kept falling into his eyes as he leaned over to grab a box or a tin. And the tattered brown shoes he wore with no socks. And the left side of his collar turned in rather than out.

The bag boy seemed a wonderful contrast to the perfectly beautiful house she had been forced to accept as her home, to the *history* she hated, to the loneliness she had become used to, and she couldn't wait to come back for more of his awkwardness and <u>dishevelment</u>.

Incredibly, it was another four weeks before they saw each other again. As fate would have it, her visits to the supermarket never coincided with his schedule to bag. Each time she went to the store, her eyes scanned the checkouts at once, her heart in her mouth. And each hour he worked, the bag boy kept one eye on the door, watching for the red-haired girl with the big orange bow.

Yet in their disappointment these weeks there was a kind of ecstasy. It is reason enough to be alive, the hope you may see again some face which has meant something to you. The anticipation of meeting the bag boy eased the girl's painful transition into her new and jarring life in Cincinnati. It provided for her an anchor amid all that was impersonal and unfamiliar, and she spent less time on thoughts of what she had left behind as she concentrated on what might lie ahead. And for the boy, the long and often tedious hours at the supermarket which provided no challenge other than that of showing up the following workday . . . these hours became possibilities of mystery and romance for him as he watched the electric doors for the girl in the orange bow.

And when finally they did meet up again, neither offered a clue to the other that he, or she, had been the object of obsessive thought for weeks. She spotted him as soon as she came into the store, but she kept her eyes strictly in front of her as she pulled out a cart and wheeled it toward the produce. And he, too, knew the instant she came through the door—though the orange bow was gone, replaced by a small but bright yellow flower instead—and he never once turned his head in her direction but watched her from the corner of his vision as he tried to swallow back the fear in his throat.

It is odd how we sometimes deny ourselves the very pleasure we have longed for and which is finally within our reach. For some <u>perverse</u> reason she would not have been able to <u>articulate</u>, the girl did not bring her cart up to the bag boy's checkout when her shopping was done. And the bag boy let her leave the store, pretending no notice of her.

This is often the way of children, when they truly want a thing, to pretend that they don't. And then they grow angry when no one tried harder to give them this thing they so casually rejected, and they

Literary Analysis
Irony What is ironic about the teenagers' response to each other?

dishevelment (di shev′ əl ment) *n.* state of being untidy

Reading Strategy
Relating to Personal Experience Why might it be easy for a teenage reader to appreciate what the bag boy is feeling?

perverse (pər vurs′) *adj.* contrary and willful

articulate (är tik′ yə lāt) *v.* express in words

soon find themselves in a rage simply because they cannot say yes when they mean yes. Humans are very complicated. (And perhaps cats, who have been known to react in the same way, though the resulting rage can only be guessed at.)

The girl hated herself for not checking out at the boy's line, and the boy hated himself for not catching her eye and saying hello, and they most sincerely hated each other without having ever exchanged even two minutes of conversation.

Eventually—in fact, within the week—a kind and intelligent boy who lived very near her beautiful house asked the girl to a movie and she gave up her fancy for the bag boy at the supermarket. And the bag boy himself grew so bored with his job that he made a desperate search for something better and ended up in a bookstore where scores of fascinating girls <u>lingered</u> like honeybees about a hive. Some months later the bag boy and the girl with the orange bow again crossed paths, standing in line with their dates at a movie theater, and, glancing toward the other, each smiled slightly, then looked away, as strangers on public buses often do, when one is moving off the bus and the other is moving on.

lingered (lin´ gərd) *v.* stayed on, as if unwilling to leave

Review and Assess

Thinking About the Selection

1. **Respond:** Were you disappointed that the girl and boy did not get together? Explain.

2. **(a) Recall:** How does the girl feel about grocery shopping? **(b) Infer:** What do you learn about the girl from her attitude toward grocery shopping?

3. **(a) Recall:** What do the boy and girl think about while they are apart? **(b) Analyze:** How might their unacknowledged romance be useful to both the girl and the boy?

4. **(a) Recall:** What happens at the end of the story? **(b) Speculate:** How do you think the two characters feel when they see each other at the movie theater?

5. **(a) Compare:** How are the girl and the bag boy alike? **(b) Analyze:** What effect do their similarities have on the tension of the story?

6. **Evaluate:** One critic said that in some stories, Cynthia Rylant relies on telling rather than showing what her characters are like. Do you think this criticism applies to this story? Give examples to support your opinion.

7. **Draw Conclusions:** Does the experience described in the story seem like a missed opportunity or a necessary outcome? Explain.

Cynthia Rylant

(b. 1954)

Quiet, thoughtful characters who are isolated in some way are Cynthia Rylant's specialty. She has said, "I don't want to deal with the people who have what they want. I want to deal with people who don't have what they want, to show their lives, too."

Rylant discovered a love of good writing in college English classes. She never considered becoming a writer herself, however, until she took a job as a librarian and began reading children's books. Since publishing *When I Was Young in the Mountains* in 1982, Rylant has produced picture books, poetry, short stories, and novels. In 1993, her novel *Missing May* won the Newbery Award.

Fifteen

William Stafford

South of the bridge on Seventeenth
I found back of the willows one summer
day a motorcycle with engine running
as it lay on its side, ticking over
5   slowly in the high grass. I was fifteen.

I admired all that pulsing gleam, the
shiny flanks, the <u>demure</u> headlights
fringed where it lay; I led it gently
to the road and stood with that
10 companion, ready and friendly. I was fifteen.

We could find the end of a road, meet
the sky on out Seventeenth. I thought about
hills, and patting the handle got back a
confident opinion. On the bridge we indulged
15 a forward feeling, a tremble. I was fifteen.

Thinking, back farther in the grass I found
the owner, just coming to, where he had flipped
over the rail. He had blood on his hand, was pale—
I helped him walk to his machine. He ran his hand
20 over it, called me a good man, roared away.

I stood there, fifteen.

demure (di myoor´) *adj.*
shy or modest

William Stafford

(1914–1993)

Reading a poem by William Stafford is like conversing with the poet. According to commentator Robert Bly, Stafford's poems are "spoken like a friend over coffee."

Stafford grew up in Kansas but later taught and wrote in Oregon. He did not publish his first book, *West of Your City*, until he was forty-six. From then on, he was prolific. He wrote a poem every day and published numerous collections, including *Traveling Through the Dark*, winner of the National Book Award in 1963.

Review and Assess

Thinking About the Selection

1. **Respond:** What would you have done if you had been in the speaker's place? Why?

2. **(a) Recall:** Which words in the first half of the poem make the motorcycle seem human? **(b) Infer:** On what basis is the speaker first attracted to the motorcycle?

3. **(a) Recall:** What does the boy imagine doing with the motorcycle? **(b) Infer:** What does the motorcycle represent to him?

4. **(a) Recall:** How does the speaker help the owner of the motorcycle? **(b) Compare and Contrast:** How do the speaker's actions contrast with his fantasy? **(c) Draw Conclusions:** What does this contrast tell you about the speaker?

5. **Apply:** What message does this poem convey about the contrasts between fantasy and reality? Explain.

Review and Assess

Literary Analysis

Irony

1. Why is it **ironic** that the girl falls in love with the bag boy?
2. In "Fifteen," why is it ironic that the owner of the motorcycle calls the speaker "good man"?
3. (a) Using a chart like the one shown below, explain what is ironic about the endings of "Checkouts" and "Fifteen." (b) In each story, what point does the ironic ending make?

Action of Story	Expected Ending	

⋯▶ **Actual Ending**

Comparing Literary Works

4. (a) Using a chart like the one below, compare the two characters in "Checkouts" to the boy in "Fifteen." (b) Who do you think learns the most about himself or herself? Why?

Character	Experiences	Feelings	Missed Opportunity	Self-discovery

Reading Strategy

Relating to Personal Experience

5. (a) Which **personal experiences** do the events in "Fifteen" call to mind? (b) How do your memories of these experiences help you to appreciate the speaker's feelings and actions?
6. What advice would you have given the girl in "Checkouts"?
7. Do you think that the unacknowledged romance in "Checkouts" is true to life? Why or why not?

Extend Understanding

8. **Cultural Connection:** Teenagers sometimes are said to have a culture all their own. Do you think that reading either selection would help adults understand "teen culture" better? Why or why not?

Quick Review

Irony is the discrepancy between what readers or characters expect and what actually happens.

Relate a story **to personal experience** by connecting characters and events to people, situations, and feelings you know.

 Take It to the Net

www.phschool.com

Take the interactive self-test online to check your understanding of the selections.

Integrate Language Skills

Vocabulary Development Lesson

Word Analysis: Latin Suffix -ment

The Latin suffix -ment means "state or condition of." It can be added to some verbs to form nouns, changing *dishevel* to *dishevelment*. Change each verb below to a noun by adding -ment, and use each new word in a sentence.

1. amuse
2. enlighten
3. disappoint
4. disillusion

Spelling Strategy

When you add an ending to words ending in y preceded by a consonant, change the y to *i*, unless the ending begins with an *i*. For example, *carry + -ed = carried*, but *carry + -ing = carrying*.

If the spelling of each word is correct, write *Correct*. If it is wrong, write the correct spelling.

1. denyed   2. denying   3. varyable

Fluency: Clarify Word Meaning

For each numbered item, choose the letter of the word that is closest in meaning to the vocabulary list word.

1. intuition
2. reverie
3. shards
4. harried
5. brazen

6. dishevelment
7. perverse
8. articulate
9. lingered
10. demure

a. daydream
b. untidiness
c. willfully contrary
d. shy
e. a feeling beyond thought
f. broken pieces
g. stayed on
h. worried
i. express in words
j. bold

Grammar Lesson

Prepositional Phrases as Modifiers

A **prepositional phrase** is made up of a preposition and a noun or pronoun, called the object of the preposition.

A prepositional phrase can function as either an adjective or an adverb, depending on the word it modifies. An adjective phrase modifies nouns and pronouns. An adverb phrase modifies verbs, adjectives, and adverbs. Look at the following examples:

Adjective phrase: The <u>girl</u> *in the grocery store* fell in love. (modifies the noun *girl*)

Adverb phrase: She <u>smiled</u> *at the bag boy*. (modifies the verb *smiled*)

Practice Identify the prepositional phrases in these sentences. Then, for each phrase, identify the word it modifies and indicate whether it is an adjective or adverb phrase.

1. He took the motorcycle to the road.
2. At the store, she looked for the boy.
3. The jar of mayonnaise fell to the floor.
4. He didn't mention the color of the bike.
5. They were at a theater with their dates.

Writing Application Use the following prepositional phrases in sentences. Explain whether the phrase is an adjective or adverb phrase.

1. after the trip   2. on the motorcycle

WG Prentice Hall Writing and Grammar Connection: Chapter 21, Section 1

Writing Lesson

Character's Journal

In order to focus more on the feelings of the characters in "Checkouts," retell the events of the story by creating contrasting journals. For each date of an entry, prepare "he-said/she-said" entries.

Prewriting   Review the story to list three key events. For each event, note the likely response of each character.

Model: Finding Subjects for Each Journal

Girl	Event	Boy
thought the boy was very sweet	boy drops and breaks jar	mortified and wanted to hide

Drafting   Begin each paired journal entry with the date and a headline that summarizes the main idea of the entry. Then, in the voice of the character, write the ideas and emotions the event provoked.

Revising   Review your draft, looking for opportunities to tighten the connection between the entries. For example, if one character includes a specific detail, consider adding that detail—and a contrasting response—to the other character's journal.

WG *Prentice Hall Writing and Grammar Connection: Chapter 13, Section 2*

Extension Activities

Listening and Speaking Imagine you are the girl from "Checkouts," talking on the telephone to a friend in your old hometown. Tell the story of your infatuation with the bag boy.

- Start by telling your friend where you met the boy and why you like him.
- Use appropriate expressions to convey the emotions of the girl.

Write down the story you have created, practice reading it, and then present your **oral story** to your class.

Research and Technology In a group, develop a **script for a scene** from a teen soap opera based on the story from "Checkouts." In your script, make sure that you include stage directions to describe the action and the characters' emotions. Remember that you want your characters to speak and act in a way that will appeal to teenagers. **[Group Activity]**

 **Take It to the Net**   www.phschool.com

Go online for an additional research activity using the Internet.

Prepare to Read

Sympathy ◆ Caged Bird ◆ We never know how high we are ◆ *from* In My Place

 Take It to the Net

Visit www.phschool.com for interactive activities and instruction related to the selections, including

- background
- graphic organizers
- literary elements
- reading strategies

Preview

Connecting to the Literature

The writers in this group tell about the way a dream can focus our lives. If you have ever been driven by a dream, you will be able to relate to the authors' messages—even if you have had a very different experience.

Background

Until the 1950s, Southern public schools and universities were segregated; African American students did not attend the same schools as white students. In the landmark *Brown v. Board of Education* decision of 1954, however, the Supreme Court overturned the doctrine of "separate but equal" schools and ruled that separate schools for different races could not offer equivalent education. In the early 1960s, various African American students like writer Charlayne Hunter-Gault enrolled at formerly all-white institutions.

Literary Analysis

Symbol

A **symbol** is an object, person, or idea that represents something beyond itself. Authors may use symbols to make a point, create a mood, or reinforce a theme. For example, in literature, springtime often represents new life and hope. Notice how the bird in the following lines from "Caged Bird" symbolizes human circumstance:

> But a bird that stalks / down his narrow cage / can seldom see through / his bars of rage. . . .

In these selections, look for details that symbolize a larger meaning.

Comparing Literary Works

As these writers suggest, dreams are part of our identity. The dream may be to acquire freedom or love or success; it may come true, or it may not. As you read these selections, compare and contrast the message each author conveys about reaching for a dream.

Reading Strategy

Drawing Conclusions

Whether you are reading or just observing life, you often make sense of information by **drawing conclusions.**

- When you draw conclusions, you form an opinion about something based upon evidence that you can identify.
- Pay attention to ideas about the work that occur to you but that are not actually stated.

Each of the works in this group invites you to draw a particular conclusion about the value of aspiring to something beyond your current circumstances. Use a chart like the one shown to record your conclusions and the evidence for them.

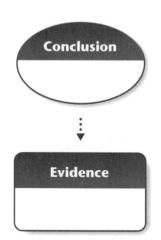

Vocabulary Development

keener (kēn´ ər) *adj.* sharper (p. 292)

warp (wôrp) *v.* twist; distort (p. 295)

epithets (ep´ ə thetz) *n.* abusive words or phrases (p. 297)

effigies (ef´ i jēz) *n.* crude figures representing hated people or groups (p. 297)

disperse (di spurs´) *v.* drive off or scatter in different directions (p. 297)

imbued (im byōōd´) *v.* inspired (p. 298)

perpetuated (pər pech´ ōō āt´ id) *v.* caused to continue indefinitely (p. 298)

Sympathy

Paul Laurence Dunbar

I know what the caged bird feels, alas!
When the sun is bright on the upland slopes;
When the wind stirs, soft through the springing grass,
And the river flows like a stream of glass;
5 When the first bird sings and the first bud opes,
And the faint perfume from its chalice[1] steals—
I know what the caged bird feels!

I know why the caged bird beats his wing
Till its blood is red on the cruel bars;
10 For he must fly back to his perch and cling
When he fain[2] would be on the bough a-swing;
And a pain still throbs in the old, old scars
And they pulse again with a <u>keener</u> sting—
I know why he beats his wing!

15 I know why the caged bird sings, ah me,
When his wing is bruised and his bosom sore,—
When he beats his bars and he would be free;
It is not a carol of joy or glee,
But a prayer that he sends from his heart's deep core,
20 But a plea, that upward to Heaven he flings—
I know why the caged bird sings!

---

1. **chalice** (chal´ is) *v.* cup or goblet; here, the cup-shaped part of a budding flower.
2. **fain** (fān) *adv.* gladly; eagerly.

Literary Analysis
Symbol What kind of situation do the details of the first stanza represent?

keener (kēn´ ər) *adj.* sharper

Paul Laurence Dunbar

(1872–1906)

He died before reaching his thirty-fifth birthday, but Paul Laurence Dunbar produced a tremendous outpouring of poetry and fiction during his brief lifetime. Born in Dayton, Ohio, the child of former slaves, Dunbar is widely recognized as the first African American poet of national stature.

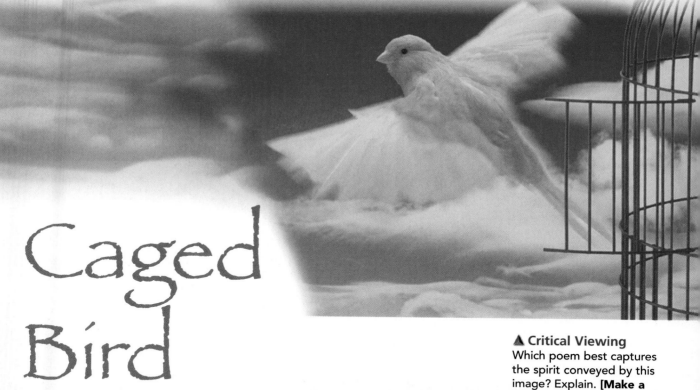

Caged Bird

Maya Angelou

A free bird leaps
on the back of the wind
and floats downstream
till the current ends
5 and dips his wing
in the orange sun rays
and dares to claim the sky.

But a bird that stalks
down his narrow cage
10 can seldom see through
his bars of rage
his wings are clipped and
his feet are tied
so he opens his throat to sing.

15 The caged bird sings
with a fearful trill
of things unknown
but longed for still
and his tune is heard
20 on the distant hill
for the caged bird
sings of freedom.

▲ Critical Viewing
Which poem best captures the spirit conveyed by this image? Explain. **[Make a Judgment]**

Reading Strategy
Drawing Conclusions
Can the bird in the second stanza expect to be free? Why or why not?

✔ Reading Check

According to "Caged Bird," how does a free bird interact with his environment?

The free bird thinks of another breeze
and the trade winds soft through the sighing trees
25   and the fat worms waiting on a dawn-bright lawn
and he names the sky his own.

But a caged bird stands on the grave of dreams
his shadow shouts on a nightmare scream
his wings are clipped and his feet are tied
30   so he opens his throat to sing.

The caged bird sings
with a fearful trill
of things unknown
but longed for still
35   and his tune is heard
on the distant hill
for the caged bird
sings of freedom.

Review and Assess

Thinking About the Selections

1. **Respond:** What, if anything, has made you feel like the caged bird that Dunbar describes?

2. **(a) Recall:** What outdoor scene does the first stanza of "Sympathy" describe? **(b) Infer:** What does the caged bird feel at this time?

3. **(a) Recall:** In the second stanza of "Sympathy," what is the bird's main activity? **(b) Infer:** Why does the caged bird beat its wing against the bars of its cage?

4. **(a) Recall:** What expression appears repeatedly in "Sympathy"? **(b) Interpret:** Why do you think the speaker can sympathize so well with the caged bird?

5. **(a) Recall:** In "Caged Bird," in which stanza do readers meet the caged bird? **(b) Analyze:** Why do you think that the life of the free bird is described first?

6. **(a) Recall:** How has the caged bird been crippled? **(b) Infer:** If he still sings "with a fearful trill" despite this experience, what can you conclude about his character?

7. **(a) Recall:** How do the caged birds sing in each of the poems? **(b) Infer:** Why do they sing as they do?

8. **Speculate:** What good, if any, results from each caged bird's singing?

Maya Angelou

(b. 1928)

Born Marguerite Johnson in St. Louis, Missouri, Maya Angelou grew up in Arkansas and California. Her difficult childhood became the source for her extremely popular autobiography, *I Know Why the Caged Bird Sings* (1969), which takes its title from Paul Laurence Dunbar's "Sympathy."

In her adult life, she achieved success as a singer, an actress, a civil rights worker, and a writer of non-fiction, fiction, poetry, and plays. In her book *Wouldn't Take Nothin' for My Journey Now* (1993), she shares her reflections on life.

We never know how high we are

Emily Dickinson

Bubbles, Watercolor, 39" x 29". Courtesy of Scott Burdick

We never know how high we are
Till we are asked to rise
And then if we are true to plan
Our statures touch the skies—
The Heroism we recite
Would be a normal thing
Did not ourselves the Cubits[1] <u>warp</u>
For fear to be a King—

---

1. **Cubits** (kyōo´ bitz) ancient measure using the length of the arm from the end of the middle finger to the elbow (about 18–22 inches).

warp (wôrp) *v.* twist; distort

Review and Assess

Thinking About the Selection

1. **Respond:** What personal experiences does this poem call to mind? Explain.

2. **(a) Recall:** According to the poem, what happens when we are asked to rise to an occasion? **(b) Hypothesize:** Why might this happen?

3. **(a) Recall:** What happens "if we are true to plan"?
   (b) Speculate: How might Dickinson define heroism?

4. **(a) Recall:** According to the poem, what prevents people from acting heroically all the time? **(b) Distinguish:** Does Dickinson think people do not live to their full potential or that they are too humble to accept praise? Explain.

5. **Extend:** What advice do you think Dickinson would give someone who was just offered a challenging job opportunity?

Emily Dickinson

(1830–1886)

Emily Dickinson was born and lived most of her life in Amherst, Massachusetts. Outwardly, her life was uneventful. The range and depth of her inner life, however, are suggested by the fact that she wrote at least 1,775 poems—each one compact with emotional power. She hid these poems in a bureau drawer, where they remained until after her death.

from

In My Place

Charlayne Hunter-Gault

On January 9, 1961, I walked onto the campus at the University of Georgia to begin registering for classes. Ordinarily, there would not have been anything unusual about such a routine exercise, except, in this instance, the officials at the university had been fighting for two and a half years to keep me out. I was not socially, intellectually, or morally undesirable. I was Black. And no Black student had ever been admitted to the University of Georgia in its 176-year history. Until the landmark *Brown* v. *Board of Education* decision that in 1954 declared separate but equal schools unconstitutional, the university was protected by law in its exclusion of people like me. In applying to the university, Hamilton Holmes and I were making one of the first major tests of the court's ruling in Georgia, and no one was sure just how hard it would be to challenge nearly two hundred years of exclusive white privilege. It would take us two and a half years of fighting our way through the system and the courts, but finally, with the help of the NAACP[1] Legal Defense and Educational Fund, Inc., and with the support of our family and friends, we won the right that should have been ours all along. With the ink barely dry on the court order of three days before, Hamilton Holmes and I walked onto the campus and into history.

We would be greeted by mobs of white students, who within forty-eight hours would hurl <u>epithets</u>, burn crosses and Black <u>effigies</u>, and finally stage a riot outside my dormitory while, nearby, state patrolmen ignored the call from university officials to come and intervene. Tear gas would <u>disperse</u> the crowd, but not before I got word in my dorm room, now strewn with glass from a rock through my window, that Hamilton and I were being suspended for our own safety. It might have been the end of the story but for the fact that the University of

---

1. **NAACP** *abbr.* National Association for the Advancement of Colored People.

◀ **Critical Viewing** Which character traits does Charlayne Hunter-Gault display in this photograph? **[Analyze]**

Reading Strategy
Drawing Conclusions
What evidence supports the conclusion that Hunter-Gault faced a major struggle?

epithets (ep´ ə thetz) *n.* abusive words or phrases

effigies (ef´ i jēz) *n.* crude figures representing hated people or groups

disperse (di spʉrs´) *v.* drive off or scatter in different directions

✔ **Reading Check**

What happened when Hunter-Gault walked onto the campus?

from *In My Place* ◆ 297

Georgia was now the lead case in a series of events that would become Georgia's entry into the Civil Rights Revolution. And we—like the legions of young Black students to follow in other arenas—were now imbued with an unshakable determination to take control of our destiny and force the South to abandon the wretched Jim Crow laws[2] it had perpetuated for generations to keep us in our place.

The newfound sense of mission that now motivated us evolved for me out of a natural desire to fulfill a dream I had nurtured from an early age. With a passion bordering on obsession, I wanted to be a journalist, a dream that would have been, if not unthinkable, at least undoable in the South of my early years. But no one ever told me not to dream, and when the time came to act on that dream, I would not let anything stand in the way of fulfilling it.

imbued (im byōōd´) v. inspired

perpetuated (per pech´ ōō āt´ id) v. caused to continue indefinitely

---

2. **Jim Crow laws** upholding or practicing discrimination against African Americans. Jim Crow was a derogatory name given to African Americans from the title of a nineteenth-century minstrel song.

Review and Assess

Thinking About the Selection

1. **Respond:** If you had faced the obstacles that Hunter-Gault did, how would you have handled the situation?

2. **(a) Recall:** What had been true of the University of Georgia for 176 years? **(b) Compare and Contrast:** How was Hunter-Gault's arrival on campus different from the experiences of most other students?

3. **(a) Recall:** What specific student actions met Hunter-Gault and Hamilton Holmes at the university during their first two days? **(b) Analyze:** Why was there such a violent reaction to Hunter-Gault's attempt to attend college?

4. **(a) Recall:** How did Hunter-Gault respond when she learned that she would be suspended? **(b) Deduce:** What qualities did she need in order to succeed in her mission?

5. **(a) Recall:** With which statement does Hunter-Gault conclude her essay? **(b) Draw Conclusions:** What conclusion can you draw from this idea?

6. **(a) Connect:** How does Hunter-Gault's chosen career connect with her experiences and dreams? **(b) Generalize:** How can a sense of pursuing a larger purpose, as well as one's personal goals, give someone strength?

7. **Evaluate:** Do you think Hunter-Gault is a hero? Why or why not?

Charlayne Hunter-Gault

(b. 1942)

Born into a minister's family in South Carolina, Charlayne Hunter-Gault showed writing talent early in life and was accepted into several universities. When she was encouraged by civil rights leaders to apply to the University of Georgia, however, she made history as one of the first African American students to enter an all-white institution.

As an adult, Hunter-Gault achieved her dream of becoming a journalist, working for the "MacNeil/Lehrer Report," the *New Yorker*, and the *New York Times*, among others. Her work in broadcast journalism has won her many awards, including two Emmys and a Peabody for excellence in broadcast journalism.

Review and Assess

Literary Analysis

Symbol

1. In Dunbar's poem, what might the cage **symbolize**?
2. In a chart like the one below, list the experiences of the birds, and then explain how their experiences symbolize those of humans.

3. In Dickinson's poem, what might *high* and *rise* symbolize?

Comparing Literary Works

4. Use a Venn diagram to compare and contrast the spirit and behavior of the caged birds in "Sympathy" and "Caged Bird."

5. Based on the message of her poem, do you think Dickinson would have seen people as caged or free? Explain.
6. Would you compare Hunter-Gault's experience to that of a caged or a free bird?

Reading Strategy

Drawing Conclusions

7. What **conclusion** can you draw from Dunbar's and Angelou's poems about freedom? Why?
8. What can you conclude from Dickinson's poem about who is responsible for a life falling short of its potential?
9. What conclusion can you draw from Hunter-Gault's circumstance about her commitment to her dream?

Extend Understanding

10. **World Events Connection:** Identify and explain a situation, past or present, in a different country from your own, in which you think one or more of these selections would apply.

Integrate Language Skills

Vocabulary Development Lesson

Levels of Diction

Diction is word choice. A writer's diction depends on his or her purpose, audience, and mood. For example, Dunbar uses elevated, or formal, diction when he refers to a song as a "carol," but Angelou uses the more down-to-earth "tune."

1. Find two more examples of old-fashioned or formal diction in "Sympathy."
2. What impression of the speaker is created?

Spelling Strategy

When adding an ending to a word that ends in more than one consonant, never double the final consonant. For example, *warp* + *-ed* = *warped*. If the spelling of each word below is correct, write *Correct*. If the spelling is incorrect, write the correct spelling.

1. protectted   2. wanting   3. deterring

Concept Development: Synonyms

For each item below, identify the letter of the word whose meaning is closest to that of the first word. If necessary, review the vocabulary words listed on page 291.

1. warp: (a) hit, (b) distort, (c) build
2. disperse: (a) scatter, (b) steal, (c) scold
3. perpetuated: (a) generated, (b) prolonged, (c) honored
4. effigies: (a) speeches, (b) insults, (c) dummies
5. keener: (a) sharper, (b) sweeter, (c) smarter
6. imbued: (a) painted, (b) placed, (c) inspired
7. epithets: (a) books, (b) slurs, (c) legends

Grammar Lesson

Preposition or Adverb?

Many words that act as prepositions can also act as adverbs, depending on their usage. A **preposition** must have an object and be part of a prepositional phrase. **Adverbs** modify verbs, adjectives, and adverbs but do not have objects.

> **Preposition:** She had to pass *through* an angry mob. (the object is *mob*)
>
> **Adverb:** She walked right *through*. (no object following *through*; modifies *walked*)

Practice Identify each underlined word as a preposition or an adverb.

1. Charlayne was not accepted <u>from</u> the moment she arrived.
2. The school had never admitted a black student <u>before</u>.
3. I'm sure she didn't even feel safe <u>inside</u>.
4. She received word that she was suspended <u>for</u> her own safety.
5. <u>After</u> the news, she decided she would continue to fight for equality.

Writing Application Use each of the following words in a sentence. Then, determine whether the word functions as a preposition or as an adverb.

1. throughout   4. around
2. outside   5. along
3. at   6. since

*W*_G *Prentice Hall Writing and Grammar Connection: Chapter 19, Section 1*

Writing Lesson

Editorial

Write an editorial, an essay that offers an opinion on an issue, for the student newspaper at the University of Georgia at the time of Charlayne Hunter-Gault's enrollment. Try to persuade the students at the university to change their behavior toward the new African American students.

Prewriting   Jot down your point of view on the topic. Make a list of reasons to explain why students should change their behavior. Highlight the most important reasons.

Drafting   As you draft, be sure to use a solid organization. You might choose to start with your least important reasons and build toward your most important reasons, or do the reverse.

Revising   Reread your draft to make sure you have made smooth transitions between sentences. Add transition words such as *also*, *since*, and *therefore* to smooth out your writing and clarify your ideas.

Model: Adding Transitions to Smooth Writing

Although

∧They came here to seek an education, they have only dealt with

                Therefore,

prejudice so far.∧It is time for us to make a change.

> Transitions like *although* and *therefore* help to connect ideas and make arguments more logical.

W/G   *Prentice Hall Writing and Grammar Connection: Chapter 11, Section 4*

Extension Activities

Listening and Speaking Plan and prepare an **oral presentation** that compares Hunter-Gault's experience with the experiences of the birds found in "Sympathy" and "Caged Bird."

- Jot down Hunter-Gault's experiences and the experiences of the free and caged birds.
- Note the similarities and differences.
- Organize your notes in a way that will clearly convey your comparison.

After you have given your presentation, ask your classmates if they agree with your views.

Research and Technology In a small group, prepare a **historical report** on the *Brown v. Board of Education* decision of 1954. In your report, explain how the Supreme Court ruling helped Charlayne Hunter-Gault attend a previously all-white school. Use library resources, including the Internet, to find information on the subject. **[Group Activity]**

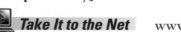 **Take It to the Net**   www.phschool.com

Go online for an additional research activity using the Internet

Prepare to Read

The Interlopers

 Take It to the Net

Visit www.phschool.com
for interactive activities
and instruction related
to "The Interlopers,"
including

- background
- graphic organizers
- literary elements
- reading strategies

Preview

Connecting to the Literature

All people get into arguments from time to time, but most disagreements do not last for a lifetime, as is the case with the characters in "The Interlopers." Think about how a long-standing dispute between two people can come to a disastrous end.

Background

A feud is a bitter, prolonged fight, typically between families or clans, that may continue for years or even generations. It may start with a single insult or injury, which provokes an act of revenge. This act in turn prompts a response, and the cycle of anger and violence is set in motion. The brutality of a feud can make for gripping drama, as it does in "The Interlopers."

Literary Analysis

Conflict

The **conflict** in a story is the struggle between opposing forces. A conflict may be internal or external. An **internal conflict** occurs within a character who experiences opposing ideas or feelings. In contrast, an **external conflict** occurs between characters or between a character and a force of nature. This passage shows a conflict between two men:

> The two enemies stood glaring at one another for a long silent moment. Each had a rifle in his hand, each had hate in his heart and murder uppermost in his mind.

As you read "The Interlopers," look for details that describe and explain the conflicts between and within the two main characters.

Connecting Literary Elements

To build the conflict of this story, the author uses **indirect characterization,** revealing only what a character does, says, and thinks. This leaves readers to draw their own conclusions about the nature of the characters and the conflict. In "The Interlopers," the writer allows the words and deeds of Ulrich and Georg to disclose what they are really like. Their actions and speech demonstrate and build the underlying conflict between them.

Reading Strategy

Identifying Causes and Effects

Understanding the causes and effects in a story can help clarify a conflict between characters.

- A **cause** is the reason for an action or event. In "The Interlopers," the cause of a long-standing feud is an old land dispute.
- An **effect** is the result of an action or event. In the story, the effect of the ancient land dispute is the personal feud between the two men.

Record the causes and effects of the story in a chart like this one.

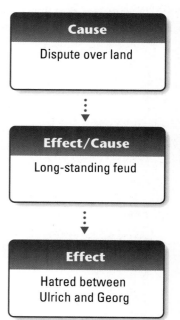

Vocabulary Development

precipitous (prē sip´ ə təs) *adj.* steep; sheer (p. 304)

marauders (mə rôd´ ərz) *n.* raiders; people who take goods by force (p. 305)

medley (med´ lē) *n.* mixture of things not usually found together (p. 306)

condolences (kən dō´ lən səz) *n.* expressions of sympathy with a grieving person's pain (p. 307)

languor (laŋ´ gər) *n.* lack of vigor; weakness; weariness (p. 307)

succor (suk´ ər) *n.* relief; aid; assistance (p. 309)

The Interlopers

Saki

In a forest of mixed growth somewhere on the eastern spurs of the Carpathians,[1] a man stood one winter night watching and listening, as though he waited for some beast of the woods to come within the range of his vision, and, later, of his rifle. But the game for whose presence he kept so keen an outlook was none that figured in the sportsman's calendar as lawful and proper for the chase: Ulrich von Gradwitz (oolʹ rik fôn grädʹ vitz) patrolled the dark forest in quest of a human enemy.

The forest lands of Gradwitz were of wide extent and well stocked with game; the narrow strip of <u>precipitous</u> woodland that lay on its outskirt was not remarkable for the game it harbored or the shooting it afforded, but it was the most jealously guarded of all its owner's territorial possessions. A famous lawsuit, in the days of his grandfather, had wrested it from the illegal possession of a neighboring family of petty landowners; the dispossessed party had never acquiesced in the judgment

precipitous
(prē sipʹ ə təs) *adj.*
steep; sheer

---

1. **Carpathians** (kär päʹ thē ənz) mountains in central Europe.

of the Courts, and a long series of poaching affrays[2] and similar scandals had embittered the relationships between the families for three generations. The neighbor feud had grown into a personal one since Ulrich had come to be head of his family; if there was a man in the world whom he detested and wished ill to it was Georg Znaeym (gā´ ôrg znä´ im), the inheritor of the quarrel and the tireless game-snatcher and raider of the disputed border-forest. The feud might, perhaps, have died down or been compromised if the personal ill will of the two men had not stood in the way; as boys they had thirsted for one another's blood, as men each prayed that misfortune might fall on the other, and this wind-scourged winter night Ulrich had banded together his foresters to watch the dark forest, not in quest of four-footed quarry, but to keep a lookout for the prowling thieves whom he suspected of being afoot from across the land boundary. The roebuck[3] which usually kept in the sheltered hollows during a storm wind, were running like driven things tonight, and there was movement and unrest among the creatures that were wont to sleep through the dark hours. Assuredly there was a disturbing element in the forest, and Ulrich could guess the quarter from whence it came.

Reading Strategy
Identifying Causes and Effects What event is the cause for the feud?

He strayed away by himself from the watchers whom he had placed in ambush on the crest of the hill, and wandered far down the steep slopes amid the wild tangle of undergrowth, peering through the tree trunks and listening through the whistling and skirling of the wind and the restless beating of the branches for sight or sound of the marauders. If only on this wild night, in this dark, lone spot, he might come across Georg Znaeym, man to man, with none to witness—that was the wish that was uppermost in his thoughts. And as he stepped round the trunk of a huge beech he came face to face with the man he sought.

marauders (mə rôd´ ərz) *n.* raiders; people who take goods by force

The two enemies stood glaring at one another for a long silent moment. Each had a rifle in his hand, each had hate in his heart and murder uppermost in his mind. The chance had come to give full play to the passions of a lifetime. But a man who has been brought up under the code of a restraining civilization cannot easily nerve himself to shoot down his neighbor in cold blood and without word spoken, except for an offense against his hearth and honor. And before the moment of hesitation had given way to action a deed of Nature's own violence overwhelmed them both. A fierce shriek of the storm had been answered by a splitting crash over their heads, and ere they could leap aside a mass of falling beech tree had thundered down on them. Ulrich von Gradwitz found himself stretched on the ground, one arm numb beneath him and the other held almost as helplessly in a tight tangle of forked branches, while both legs were pinned beneath the fallen mass. His heavy shooting-boots had saved his feet from being crushed to pieces, but if his fractures were not as serious

Literary Analysis
Conflict How is the bitterness between the two landowners evident in this passage?

☑**Reading Check**
What happens to the men when they come face to face?

---

2. **poaching affrays** (pōch´ iŋ ə frāz´) disputes about hunting on someone else's property.
3. **roebuck** (rō´ buk´) *n.* male deer.

as they might have been, at least it was evident that he could not move from his present position till someone came to release him. The descending twigs had slashed the skin of his face, and he had to wink away some drops of blood from his eyelashes before he could take in a general view of the disaster. At his side, so near that under ordinary circumstances he could almost have touched him, lay Georg Znaeym, alive and struggling, but obviously as helplessly pinioned down as himself. All round them lay a thick-strewn wreckage of splintered branches and broken twigs.

Relief at being alive and exasperation at his captive plight brought a strange <u>medley</u> of pious thank-offerings and sharp curses to Ulrich's lips. Georg, who was nearly blinded with the blood which trickled across his eyes, stopped his struggling for a moment to listen, and then gave a short, snarling laugh.

"So you're not killed, as you ought to be, but you're caught, anyway," he cried; "caught fast. Ho, what a jest, Ulrich von Gradwitz snared in his stolen forest. There's real justice for you!"

And he laughed again, mockingly and savagely.

"I'm caught in my own forest land," retorted Ulrich. "When my men come to release us you will wish, perhaps, that you were in a better plight than caught poaching on a neighbor's land, shame on you."

Georg was silent for a moment; then he answered quietly:

"Are you sure that your men will find much to release? I have men, too, in the forest tonight, close behind me, and *they* will be here first

medley (med´ lē) *n.* mixture of things not usually found together

▼ **Critical Viewing**
Why does the setting—a snowy forest like the one shown here—intensify the danger of the conflict? **[Connect]**

Untitled, Rob Wood, Illustration by Wood Ronsaville Harlin, Inc.

and do the releasing. When they drag me out from under these branches it won't need much clumsiness on their part to roll this mass of trunk right over on the top of you. Your men will find you dead under a fallen beech tree. For form's sake I shall send my <u>condolences</u> to your family."

"It is a useful hint," said Ulrich fiercely. "My men had orders to follow in ten minutes' time, seven of which must have gone by already, and when they get me out—I will remember the hint. Only as you will have met your death poaching on my lands I don't think I can decently send any message of condolence to your family."

"Good," snarled Georg, "good. We fight this quarrel out to the death, you and I and our foresters, with no cursed interlopers to come between us. Death and damnation to you, Ulrich von Gradwitz."

"The same to you, Georg Znaeym, forest-thief, game-snatcher."

Both men spoke with the bitterness of possible defeat before them, for each knew that it might be long before his men would seek him out or find him; it was a bare matter of chance which party would arrive first on the scene.

Both had now given up the useless struggle to free themselves from the mass of wood that held them down; Ulrich limited his endeavors to an effort to bring his one partially free arm near enough to his outer coat pocket to draw out his wine flask. Even when he had accomplished that operation it was long before he could manage the unscrewing of the stopper or get any of the liquid down his throat. But what a heaven-sent draft it seemed! It was an open winter, and little snow had fallen as yet, hence the captives suffered less from the cold than might have been the case at that season of the year; nevertheless, the wine was warming and reviving to the wounded man, and he looked across with something like a throb of pity to where his enemy lay, just keeping the groans of pain and weariness from crossing his lips.

"Could you reach this flask if I threw it over to you?" asked Ulrich suddenly; "there is good wine in it, and one may as well be as comfortable as one can. Let us drink, even if tonight one of us dies."

"No, I can scarcely see anything; there is so much blood caked round my eyes," said Georg, "and in any case I don't drink wine with an enemy."

Ulrich was silent for a few minutes, and lay listening to the weary screeching of the wind. An idea was slowly forming and growing in his brain, an idea that gained strength every time that he looked across at the man who was fighting so grimly against pain and exhaustion. In the pain and <u>languor</u> that Ulrich himself was feeling the old fierce hatred seemed to be dying down.

"Neighbor," he said presently, "do as you please if your men come first. It was a fair compact. But as for me, I've changed my mind. If my men are the first to come you shall be the first to be helped, as though you were my guest. We have quarreled like devils all our lives over this stupid strip of forest, where the trees can't even stand

condolences (kən dō′ lən sez) *n.* expressions of sympathy with a grieving person's pain

Literary Analysis
Conflict and Indirect Characterization What can you conclude about the men's characters from their exchange of comments here?

languor (laŋ′ gər) *n.* lack of vigor; weakness; weariness

 **Reading Check**

What happens to the two men after the tree falls?

upright in a breath of wind. Lying here tonight, thinking, I've come to think we've been rather fools; there are better things in life than getting the better of a boundary dispute. Neighbor, if you will help me to bury the old quarrel I—I will ask you to be my friend."

Georg Znaeym was silent for so long that Ulrich thought, perhaps, he had fainted with the pain of his injuries. Then he spoke slowly and in jerks.

"How the whole region would stare and gabble if we rode into the market square together. No one living can remember seeing a Znaeym and a von Gradwitz talking to one another in friendship. And what peace there would be among the forester folk if we ended our feud tonight. And if we choose to make peace among our people there is none other to interfere, no interlopers from outside . . . You would come and keep the Sylvester night beneath my roof, and I would come and feast on some high day at your castle . . . I would never fire a shot on your land, save when you invited me as a guest; and you should come and shoot with me down in the marshes where the wildfowl are. In all the countryside there are none that could hinder if we willed to make peace. I never thought to have wanted to do

▲ **Critical Viewing**
What kinds of encounters or incidents might occur in this setting? **[Analyze]**

Literary Analysis
Conflict How has the nature of the conflict between the two men now changed?

other than hate you all my life, but I think I have changed my mind about things too, this last half-hour. And you offered me your wine flask . . . Ulrich von Gradwitz, I will be your friend."

For a space both men were silent, turning over in their minds the wonderful changes that this dramatic reconciliation would bring about. In the cold, gloomy forest, with the wind tearing in fitful gusts through the naked branches and whistling round the tree trunks, they lay and waited for the help that would now bring release and <u>succor</u> to both parties. And each prayed a private prayer that his men might be the first to arrive, so that he might be the first to show honorable attention to the enemy that had become a friend.

Presently, as the wind dropped for a moment, Ulrich broke silence.

"Let's shout for help," he said; "in this lull our voices may carry a little way."

"They won't carry far through the trees and undergrowth," said Georg, "but we can try. Together, then."

The two raised their voices in a prolonged hunting call.

"Together again," said Ulrich a few minutes later, after listening in vain for an answering halloo.

succor (suk´ ər) *n.* relief; aid; assistance

 Reading Check

What response does Georg give when Ulrich asks him to be his friend?

"I heard something that time, I think," said Ulrich.

"I heard nothing but the pestilential wind," said Georg hoarsely.

There was silence again for some minutes, and then Ulrich gave a joyful cry.

"I can see figures coming through the wood. They are following in the way I came down the hillside."

Both men raised their voices in as loud a shout as they could muster.

"They hear us! They've stopped. Now they see us. They're running down the hill toward us," cried Ulrich.

"How many of them are there?" asked Georg.

"I can't see distinctly," said Ulrich; "nine or ten."

"Then they are yours," said Georg; "I had only seven out with me."

"They are making all the speed they can, brave lads," said Ulrich gladly.

"Are they your men?" asked Georg. "Are they your men?" he repeated impatiently as Ulrich did not answer.

"No," said Ulrich with a laugh, the idiotic chattering laugh of a man unstrung with hideous fear.

"Who are they?" asked Georg quickly, straining his eyes to see what the other would gladly not have seen.

"Wolves."

Review and Assess

Thinking About the Selection

1. **Respond:** With whom did you sympathize: Ulrich, Georg, neither, or both? Why?

2. **(a) Recall:** Whose family won possession of the disputed land in the lawsuit? **(b) Interpret:** Why does Georg not consider himself a poacher?

3. **(a) Recall:** How far back does the hatred between Ulrich and Georg go? **(b) Infer:** Which factors about the feud seem to contribute the most to Ulrich's anger at Georg?

4. **(a) Recall:** In what condition does the fallen tree leave each man? **(b) Draw Conclusions:** Why do the men end their feud?

5. **(a) Speculate:** How might the story have continued if the two men had been rescued? **(b) Support:** Why do you think so?

6. **(a) Evaluate:** Considering the cause of their predicament, do you think the two men deserved their fate? Why or why not? **(b) Extend:** What lesson can be learned from the experiences of Ulrich and Georg?

7. **(a) Apply:** What is it about human nature that leads to feuds like the one in the story? **(b) Speculate:** Will it ever be possible to end such feuds? Explain.

Saki

(1870–1916)

Saki is the pen name of the British writer H. H. Munro. Born in Burma, he was sent at age two to live in England, where he was raised in a strict household by two aunts. As a young adult, he returned to Burma to serve in the police force. Two years later, however, poor health forced him to return to England, where he began working as a jounalist. After serving as a newspaper correspondent in Russia and France, Saki settled in London.

In 1904, his first collection of short stories was published. He later wrote more short stories and two novels.

Saki was killed in France during World War I. In his honor, the king of England issued a scroll that concludes, "Let those who come after see to it that his name is not forgotten."

Review and Assess

Literary Analysis

Conflict

1. What **external conflict** pits a character against another character in "The Interlopers"?
2. Identify a conflict that pits a character against a force of nature.
3. Give an example of an **internal conflict** within Ulrich or Georg.
4. Using a chart like the one shown, analyze a conflict that changes or develops as the story continues.

Developing conflict	Reason for change

Connecting Literary Elements

5. Using a character-trait diagram like this one, list the traits you detect in each man. Cite examples from the story.

Character   **Traits**   **Examples**

6. How does the use of **indirect characterization** illuminate the conflict between the two men? Give specific details.

Reading Strategy

Identifying Causes and Effects

7. (a) What **causes** the beech tree to fall over? (b) What is the **effect** of that event?
8. (a) Why do the men shout together at the end? (b) What is the effect of their shouting? (c) Is it the effect they expect?

Extend Understanding

9. **Social Studies Connection:** (a) Explain the options for resolving a bitter territorial dispute among nations in today's world. (b) Why are such problems so complicated?

Integrate Language Skills

Vocabulary Development Lesson

Word Analysis: Latin Root *-dol-*

The Latin root *-dol-* means "pain." The root appears in the word *condolence*, meaning "an expression of sympathy with a grieving person's pain." Using the meaning of *-dol-*, define *doleful* and *indolent* and use each in a sentence.

Spelling Strategy

For many verbs ending in *y*, you must change the *y* to *i* or *ie* when you add an ending such as *-s* or *-ed*. For those that end in *y* preceded by a vowel, however, the spelling remains unchanged. For example, *medley* + *-s* = *medleys*.

For each item, add the ending shown and write the new word created.

1. spy + *-s*
2. journey + *-ed*
3. stray + *-ed*
4. fly + *-s*

Fluency: Words in Context

Write sentences as described below, using one word from the vocabulary list on page 303 for each sentence.

1. Write the lead sentence of a news article describing a robbery.
2. Describe the site of a rock-climbing expedition.
3. Explain what a group of rescue workers provides for flood victims.
4. Begin a letter to a friend who has lost an elderly family member.
5. Describe your feelings after spending a week in bed with the flu.
6. Write a description of a program honoring the composer of many famous songs.

Grammar Lesson

Different Kinds of Conjunctions

A main clause is a group of words with a subject and a verb that makes sense even when it stands alone. In contrast, a subordinate clause makes sense only when it is linked to a main clause. **Conjunctions** connect words, word groups, or clauses.

A **subordinating conjunction** links a subordinate clause to the main clause of a sentence.

> **Subordinating:** *Before* they moved, the tree fell on them.

A **coordinating conjunction** joins main clauses or words of equal importance.

> **Coordinating:** They waited, *but* no one arrived.

Correlative conjunctions are pairs of conjunctions that link words of equal rank.

> **Correlative:** Ulrich watched, *not* in quest of quarry *but* to wait for thieves.

Practice Identify the conjunctions and classify each as *subordinating*, *coordinating*, or *correlative*.

1. Ulrich and Georg were enemies.
2. A tree fell, and the two men were trapped.
3. Neither Ulrich nor Georg was brave.
4. They yelled so that help would come.
5. Interlopers arrived, but they were wolves.

Writing Application Summarize the story, making use of at least one of each type of conjunction.

W̶G̶ Prentice Hall Writing and Grammar Connection: Chapter 19, Section 2

Writing Lesson

News Story

Nature's own violence spells doom for Ulrich and Georg. Imagine you are a news reporter. Write a story about the freak accident and its aftermath.

Prewriting   Focus on the questions *who? what? when? where? why?* and *how?* Include facts, quotations, and details below each heading in a chart. Then, plan your lead, or opening paragraph, which should summarize the news story.

Model: Recording Details in an Organizer

Who?	What?	When?	Where?	Why?	How?
Ulrich and Georg	Hit by a tree limb	Night	Ulrich's land	A beech tree fell on them	Tree blown down by storm

Drafting   As you write the body of your story, use elaboration—the development of ideas and details—to help readers understand the news event. Clarify as much of the event as you can.

Revising   Read your story aloud to a classmate. Change any part of the story that is unclear or requires further elaboration.

W̸G Prentice Hall Writing and Grammar Connection: Chapter 6, Section 2

Extension Activities

Listening and Speaking To present a **debate** about the disputed land, form groups to represent each man. Each group should

- offer reasons why its character is entitled to the land.
- use quotations and other citations from the story to support its point of view.
- present an introductory statement, a rebuttal, and a closing statement.

Allot each team the same amount of time, and then ask the audience to decide which group was more persuasive. **[Group Activity]**

Research and Technology The chilling ending of "The Interlopers" comes about because of the unexpected arrival of wolves. Create a **brochure** that presents information about wolves. Design and publish your document with software and graphics programs that make charts, maps, or other graphics. Show where wolves live and how they raise their young, form packs, and hunt.

 **Take It to the Net**   www.phschool.com

Go online for an additional research activity using the Internet.

Prepare to Read

The Rug Merchant

Preview

Connecting to the Literature

Sometimes you make up your mind and then find yourself changing it. You think you have someone sized up and then discover that a bit more measuring tape is needed. James Michener finds himself in this position in "The Rug Merchant."

Background

Persian rugs—like the ones sold by Zaqir, the rug merchant in the essay—are mostly made of wool, but the finest are made of silk. Different designs are linked with specific regions. Most designs are abstract or geometric patterns, although some depict people, plants, and animals.

Literary Analysis

Characterization in Essays

Writers create and in essays develop their characters by means of a process called **characterization.** In an essay, a person's speech and actions, the reactions of others, and the author's comments all contribute to the person's characterization. Look at this description of Zaqir, a rug merchant in Afghanistan:

> . . . a very thin, toothy man with longish black hair and a perpetual smile entered and started throwing onto the dirt floor twenty or thirty of the most enchantingly beautiful Persian rugs I had ever seen.

Note how the author focuses on the man's appearance and behavior. While reading "The Rug Merchant," look for more details that characterize the seller.

Connecting Literary Elements

"The Rug Merchant" is a nonfiction essay that uses **first-person narration**—the author is part of the story and thus makes use of the words *I*, *me*, and *my*. Michener relates his own experiences with a rug merchant. In so doing, Michener ends up characterizing not only Zaqir but also himself. Authors using first-person narration inevitably tell readers as much about themselves as about other characters.

Reading Strategy

Making Inferences About Characters

When you **make inferences about characters,** you draw conclusions about them by using details such as the following:

- Their appearance and actions
- What they say—including what they say about themselves—in narration and dialogue

Use a chart like the one shown to record details from "The Rug Merchant." For each detail you note, jot down the inference you draw.

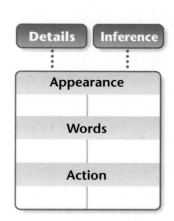

Vocabulary Development

improvised (im′ prə vīzd) *adj.* put together spontaneously (p. 317)

laden (lād′ 'n) *adj.* burdened (p. 317)

encompassed (en kum′ pəst) *v.* surrounded (p. 317)

impose (im pōz′) *v.* put to some trouble (p. 319)

ingeniously (in jēn′ yəs lē) *adv.* very cleverly (p. 320)

The Rug Merchant

from *The World Is My Home: A Memoir*

James Michener

I once made a long trip over the Dasht-i-Margo, the desert in Afghanistan, to the ancient city of Herat (he rät′), where I lodged in a former mosque with earthen floors. I had been in my improvised quarters only a few minutes when a very thin, toothy man with longish black hair and a perpetual smile entered and started throwing onto the dirt floor twenty or thirty of the most enchantingly beautiful Persian rugs I had ever seen. Their designs were miraculous—intricate interweavings of Koranic symbols framed in geometric patterns that teased the eye—but their colors were also sheer delight: reds, yellows, greens and especially dark blues that were radiant.

They made my room a museum, one rug piled atop another, all peeking out at me, and when they were in place and the smiling man was satisfied with his handiwork—I supposed that this was a service of the so-called hotel—to my amazement he handed me a scrap of paper on which was written in pencil in English: "muhammad zaqir, rug merchant, herat."

Aware at last of how I had been trapped, I protested: "No! No! No rugs!" but without relaxing his smile the least bit he said in English: "No necessity to buy. I leave here. You study, you learn to like," and before I could protest further he was gone. I ran out to make him take back his rugs, for I wanted none of them, but he was already leading his laden camel away from the old mosque.

I assumed he had learned from the hotel manager that I was to be in Herat for five days, and it was obvious that he felt confident that within that period he could wear me down and persuade me to buy a rug. He started on the evening of that first day; he came back after supper to sit with me in the shadowy light cast by a flickering lamp. He said: "Have you ever seen lovelier rugs? That one from my friend in Meshed. Those two from the dealer in Bukhara. This one from a place you know, maybe? Samarkand."

When I asked him how he was able to trade with such towns in the Soviet Union[1] he shrugged: "Borders? Out here we don't bother," and with a sweep of his hand that encompassed all the rugs he said: "Not one woven in Afghanistan," and I noted the compelling pronunciation he gave that name: Ahf-han-ee-stahn.

He sat for more than an hour with me that evening, and next day he was back before noon to start his serious bargaining: "Michener-sahib,[2] name German perhaps?" I told him it was more likely English, at which he laughed: "English, Afghans, many battles, English always win but next day you march back to India, nothing change." When I corrected him: "I'm not English," he said: "I know. Pennsylvania. Three, four, maybe five of your rugs look great your place Pennsylvania."

"But I don't need rugs there. I don't really want them."

"Would they not look fine Pennsylvania?" and as if the rugs were of

---

1. **Soviet Union** The Union of Soviet Socialist Republics consisted of fifteen republics strictly controlled by the country's central government until independence movements in 1991.
2. **Michener-sahib** (sä′ ib) Mr. Michener.

improvised (im′ prə vīzd) *adj.* put together spontaneously

Literary Analysis
Characterization in Essays How would you describe Michener, based on where he is lodging?

laden (lād′ 'n) *adj.* burdened

encompassed (en kum′ pəst) *v.* surrounded

Reading Check
What does the visitor bring to Michener's room?

The Rug Merchant ◆ 317

little value, he kicked the top ones aside to reveal the glowing wonders of those below.

When he returned that second night he got down to even more serious business: "The big white and gold one you like, six hundred dollars." On and on he went, and when it was clear that I had no interest whatever in the big ones, he subtly covered them over with the smaller six- by four-foot ones already in the room; then he ran out to his camel to fetch seven or eight of the size that I had in some unconscious way disclosed I might consider, and by the end of that session he knew that I was at least a possible purchaser of four or five of the handsome rugs.

"Ah, Michener-sahib, you have fine eye. That one from China, silk and wool, look at those tiny knots." Then he gave me a lesson in rug making; he talked about the designs, the variation in knots, the wonderful compactness of the Chinese variety, the dazzling colors of the Samarkand. It was fascinating to hear him talk, and all the while he was wearing me down.

He was a persistent rascal, always watching till he saw me return to my mosque after work, then pouncing on me. On the third day, as he sat drinking tea with me while our chairs were perched on his treasury of rugs, four and five deep at some places and covering the entire floor, he knocked down one after another of my objections: "You can't take them with you? No traveler can. I send them to you, camel here, ship Karachi, train New York, truck to your home Pennsylvania." Pasted onto the pages of his notebook were addresses of buyers from all parts of the world to whom he had shipped his rugs, and I noticed that they had gone out from Meshed in Iran, Mazar-e-Sharif in Afghanistan and Bukhara (bü kär´ ə) in Russia; apparently he really moved about with his laden camel. But he also had, pasted close to the shipping address, letters from his customers proving that the rugs had finally reached their new owners. In our dealings he seemed to me an honest man.

On that third night, when it began to look as if I might escape without making a purchase even though I had shown an interest in six rugs, he hammered at me regarding payments: "Now, Michener-sahib, I can take American dollars, you know."

"I have no American dollars." Rapidly he ran through the currencies that he would accept, British, Indian, Iranian, Pakistani, Afghani, in that descending order, until I had to stop him with a truthful statement: "Muhammad, my friend, I have no money, none of any kind," and before the last word had been uttered he cried: "I take traveler's checks, American Express, Bank America in California," and then I had to tell him the sad news: "Muhammad, friend. I have no traveler's checks. Left them all locked up in the American embassy in Kabul. Because there are robbers on the road to Meshed."

Literary Analysis
Characterization in Essays What do Zaqir's persistence and sales technique suggest about his understanding of people?

Reading Strategy
Making Inferences About Characters What causes Michener to conclude that Zaqir is an honest man?

"I know. I know. But you are an honest man, Michener-sahib. I take your personal check."

When I said truthfully that I had none, he asked simply: "You like those six rugs?"

"Yes, you have made me appreciate them. I do."

With a sweeping gesture he gathered the six beauties, rolled them deftly into a bundle and thrust them into my arms: "You take them. Send me a check when you get to Pennsylvania."

"You would trust me?"

"You look honest. Don't I look honest?" And he picked up one of his larger rugs, a real beauty, and showed me the fine knots: "Bukhara. I got it there, could not pay. I send the money when I sell. Man in Bukhara trusts me. I trust you."

I said I could not <u>impose</u> on him in that way. Something might happen to me or I might prove to be a crook, and the discussion ended, except that as he left me he asked: "Michener, if you had the money, what rugs would you take with you?" and I said "None, but if you could ship them, I'd take those four," and he said: "Those four you shall have. I'll find a way."

Next day he was back in the mosque right after breakfast with an astonishing proposal: "Michener-sahib, I can let you have those four rugs, special price, four hundred fifty dollars." Before I could repeat my inability to pay, he said: "Bargain like this you never see again. Tell you what to do. You write me a check."

When I said, distressed at losing such a bargain: "But I really have no blank checks," he said: "You told me yesterday. I believe you. But draw me one," and from his folder he produced a sheet of ordinary paper and a pencil. He showed me how to draw a copy of a blank check, bearing the name of the bank, address, amount, etc.—and for the first time in my life I actually drew a blank check, filled in the amount and signed it, whereupon Muhammad Zaqir placed it in his file, folded the four rugs I had bought, tied them with string and attached my name and address.

He piled the rugs onto his camel, and then mounted it to proceed on his way to Samarkand.

Back home in Pennsylvania I started to receive two different kinds of letters, perhaps fifteen of each. The following is a sample of the first category:

> I am a shipping agent in Istanbul and a freighter arrived here from Karachi bringing a large package, well wrapped, addressed to you in Pennsylvania. Upon receipt of your check for $19.50 American I will forward the package to you.

From Karachi, Istanbul, Trieste, Marseilles and heavens knows where else I received a steady flow of letters over a three-year period, and always the sum demanded was less than twenty dollars, so that I would say to myself: "Well, I've invested so much in it already, I may as well

risk a little more." And off the check would go, with the rugs never getting any closer. Moreover, I was not at all sure that if they ever did reach me they would be my property, for my unusual check had never been submitted for payment, even though I had forewarned my local bank: "If it ever does arrive, pay it immediately, because it's a debt of honor."

The second group of letters explained the long delay:

> I am serving in Kabul as the Italian ambassador and was lately in Herat where a rug merchant showed me that remarkable check you gave him for something like five hundred dollars. He asked me if I thought it would be paid if he forwarded it and I assured him that since you were a man of good reputation it would be. When I asked him why he had not submitted it sooner, he said: "Michener-sahib a good name. I show his check everybody like you, sell many rugs."

These letters came from French commercial travelers, English explorers, Indian merchants, almost anyone who might be expected to reach out-of-the-way Herat and take a room in that miserable old mosque.

In time the rugs arrived, just as Muhammad Zaqir had predicted they would, accompanied by so many shipping papers they were a museum in themselves. And after my improvised check had been used as an advertisement for nearly five years, it too came home to roost and was honored. Alas, shortly thereafter the rugs were stolen, but I remember them vividly and with longing. Especially do I remember the man who spent four days ingeniously persuading me to buy.

ingeniously (in jēn´ yəs lē) *adv.* cleverly

James Michener

(1907–1997)

James Michener was raised as a Quaker by his adoptive mother in Doylestown, Pennsylvania. After graduating from college, he worked as a book editor before joining the navy during World War II.

Michener's war experiences inspired him to write *Tales of the South Pacific* (1947), which won the Pulitzer Prize—a remarkable achievement for a first-time novelist.

Michener was a tireless portrayer of other lands and peoples. Among the many places he wrote about were the Holy Land, in *The Source* (1965), and South Africa, in *The Covenant* (1980).

Review and Assess

Thinking About the Selection

1. **Respond:** Would you have bought rugs from Zaqir? Explain.

2. **(a) Recall:** What does Zaqir do after Michener first protests that he does not want the rugs? **(b) Infer:** Why does Michener keep discussing the rugs with Zaqir?

3. **(a) Recall:** When Zaqir returns on the second night, how has he altered his sales pitch? **(b) Distinguish:** Zaqir's behavior prompts Michener to describe him as both "an honest man" and "a rascal." What provokes this reaction?

4. **(a) Recall:** What business proposal does Zaqir eventually make to Michener? **(b) Generalize:** What does the proposal suggest about the differences between Zaqir's culture and Michener's?

5. **Speculate:** What do you think Michener finally concludes about Zaqir as a result of their dealings?

6. **Extend:** What could this essay teach someone about trust and honesty?

Review and Assess

Literary Analysis

Characterization in Essays

1. As first **characterized,** does Zaqir seem believable to you? Write your response in the center of a cluster map like the one shown. Then, show which actions and words support your opinion.

Actions/words

Throws rugs on the floor

Zaqir

Actions/words

2. Does your overall impression of Zaqir change over the course of the story? Explain.
3. Describe Michener as a character. Base your answer on his actions, attitudes, and words.

Connecting Literary Elements

4. **First-person narration** reveals the ideas and opinions of the writer. In which specific ways is your opinion of Zaqir influenced by Michener's narration?
5. Cite specific ways in which your impression of Zaqir might be different if he had narrated the story.

Reading Strategy

Making Inferences About Characters

6. Michener pays shipping charges for three years while awaiting the rugs' arrival. What does this fact lead you to **infer** about him?
7. One detail and the responses it generates can reveal the traits of two characters. (a) What inferences can you draw about Michener based on the blank check he draws? (b) What can you infer about Zaqir based on his interaction with the check?

Extend Understanding

8. **Cultural Connection:** Which cultural differences influence the nature of the salesperson-customer relationship in this essay?

Quick Review

Characterization involves an author's use of speech, actions, reactions, and comments to create and develop characters.

In nonfiction, **first-person narration** allows the author to be part of the action and to use the words *I, me,* and *my.*

To **make inferences about characters**, draw conclusions about them from their appearance, actions, and words.

 Take It to the Net
www.phschool.com
Take the interactive self-test online to check your understanding of the selections.

Integrate Language Skills

Vocabulary Development Lesson

Word Analysis: Latin Root -vis-

The Latin root -vis- means "see." The root appears in the word *improvised*, which literally means "not seen before." It also appears in these words and phrases:

visitor	revise
supervisor	visual aid
invisible	envision

Identify the word or phrase above that matches each clue.

1. A person who oversees and directs you in your work
2. Not able to be seen
3. One who comes to see you
4. Something you see that helps explain an idea
5. To see in your mind
6. To "see again" and change

Concept Development: Synonyms

Identify the synonym, or word with nearly the same meaning, for the first word in each item.

1. laden: (a) spoon, (b) burdened, (c) hurt
2. improvised: (a) unplanned, (b) entertaining, (c) careful
3. encompassed: (a) directed, (b) watched, (c) surrounded
4. ingeniously: (a) cleverly, (b) dishonestly, (c) stupidly
5. impose: (a) arrange, (b) trouble, (c) stand

Spelling Strategy

For a word that ends in a double consonant, do not drop the final consonant before adding an ending: *encompass* + *-ed* = *encompassed*.

Identify the misspelled word or words below and correct the spelling.

1. enthraling   2. embarrasment   3. reference

Grammar Lesson

Interjections

An **interjection** is a word or phrase that expresses a feeling or an emotion and functions independently of the other words in a sentence. An interjection might express pain, joy, annoyance, or surprise.

In the following example, the interjection expresses a feeling of discovery.

Example:
Oh, Michener-sahib, you have a fine eye.

Punctuate mild interjections with commas and strong ones with exclamation marks.

Practice Identify the interjections below. Then, describe the emotion that each expresses.

1. No! I want no rugs!
2. Ah, Michener-sahib, I can take American dollars.
3. Well, you make me appreciate them.
4. My goodness, I've already invested so much.
5. Alas, the rugs were stolen.

Writing Application Select three sentences from "The Rug Merchant" and rewrite them, using interjections to add emotion.

W̶G̶ *Prentice Hall Writing and Grammar Connection: Chapter 19, Section 2*

Writing Lesson

Letter of Recommendation

If a problem had arisen with the rugs that Michener bought from Zaqir, he might have written a letter of complaint to the merchant. Instead, he seems to have been pleased with his purchase. As Michener, write a letter encouraging others to buy from Zaqir.

Prewriting   Review the story to find examples of Zaqir's behavior and sales approach. Also, note Michener's evolving responses to Zaqir.

Drafting   Write your letter, clearly stating your feelings about the rug merchant. As a testimonial, your letter should explain Michener's experiences and draw generalizations about them.

Revising   Review your draft, underlining the main impression you want to convey to other consumers. Where necessary, add more examples to support this idea.

Model: Revising to Create a Main Impression

Working with Zaqir is entertainment in itself.

Personally, I received my goods years after I purchased them, but the memory of this persistent salesman—piling rug over rug—lingers.

> The added text elaborates on the writer's positive memories.

WG *Prentice Hall Writing and Grammar Connection: Chapter 7, Section 4*

Extension Activities

Listening and Speaking With a classmate, **role-play** a conversation between Michener and Zaqir. Combine dialogue from the essay with original dialogue. Follow these points:

- Analyze the situation the men are in before constructing your dialogue.
- Use nonverbal techniques—voice, gestures, and eye contact—to convey the characters' essence.

Rehearse your conversation together, using a tape recorder to check its effectiveness. Then, present the conversation to your class. [**Group Activity**]

Research and Technology Search the Internet for additional information about Persian rugs, like those described in "The Rug Merchant." Display what you learn in an **oral presentation.** Use graphics, such as pictures of vibrant rugs, to enhance the appeal and accuracy of your report, and prepare concise notes to help you in your delivery.

 Take It to the Net   www.phschool.com

Go online for an additional research activity using the Internet.

Prepare to Read

Combing ◆ Women ◆ maggie and milly and molly and may ◆ Astonishment

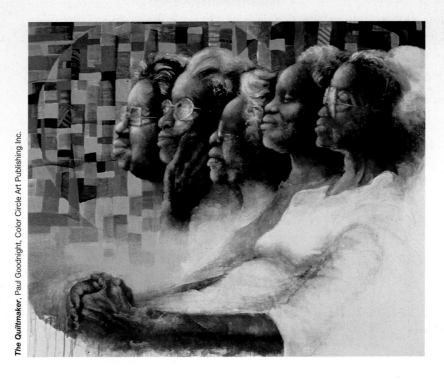

The Quiltmaker, Paul Goodnight, Color Circle Art Publishing Inc.

Preview

Connecting to the Literature

Throughout our lives, we make discoveries that show us who we are. Each of the poems that follow presents such a discovery. You may find that the discoveries of the poems' speakers lead you to discoveries of your own.

Background

In "Women," the speaker expresses admiration for African American women who fought for public school desegregation in the American South. Until the 1950s, these schools were segregated—that is, black and white students attended different schools. In 1954, the U.S. Supreme Court ruled that segregated public schooling was not permissible because it was inherently unequal. Some state governments and local school districts resisted the new ruling.

Literary Analysis

Moment of Insight

A **moment of insight** is a fresh, new thought that arises from a poet's musings or reflections. Specific details in a poem add up to a general insight into life. This excerpt from "Combing" offers one such insight:

> Bending, I bow my head
> And lay my hand upon
> Her hair, combing, and think
> How women do this for
> Each other.

The poet connects her own action with something all women have done. Look for other moments of insight as you read the four selections. Use a chart like the one shown to record the details and insights you find.

Details

She combs her daughter's hair.

Insight

She realizes that this is something all women do.

Comparing Literary Works

A moment of insight is usually closely related to a poem's **theme,** or central message about life. The poems that follow all focus on a theme, related to the issue of identity. Each poem explores a different way of thinking about identity—through family connections, nature, and an appreciation of the surrounding world. As you read, compare and contrast the messages about identity that the poems convey. With which poet's message do you most identify? Why?

Reading Strategy

Interpreting Meaning

When you **interpret the meaning** of a poem, you seek to understand the point or insight that the poet communicates. To help interpret the meaning of a poem, apply the following techniques:

- Use sensory images—things you can see, hear, taste, smell, or touch—to picture what is being described.
- Ask yourself why the poet has chosen those specific images.
- Connect what is being said to your own experience.

As you read, try to interpret the meaning of each poem.

Vocabulary Development

intent (in tent´) *adj.* firmly fixed; concentrated (p. 326)

plaiting (plāt´ iŋ) *v.* braiding (p. 326)

stout (stout) *adj.* sturdy (p. 327)

languid (laŋ´ gwid) *adj.* drooping; weak (p. 329)

Combing

Gladys Cardiff

ending, I bow my head
And lay my hand upon
　Her hair, combing, and think
How women do this for
5　Each other. My daughter's hair
Curls against the comb,
Wet and fragrant—orange
Parings. Her face, downcast,
Is quiet for one so young.

10　I take her place. Beneath
My mother's hands I feel
The braids drawn up tight
As a piano wire and singing,
Vinegar-rinsed. Sitting
15　Before the oven I hear
The orange coils tick
The early hour before school.

She combed her grandmother
Mathilda's hair using
20　A comb made out of bone.
Mathilda rocked her oak wood
Chair, her face downcast,
<u>Intent</u> on tearing rags
In strips to braid a cotton
25　Rug from bits of orange
And brown. A simple act,

Preparing hair. Something
Women do for each other,
<u>Plaiting</u> the generations.

Reading Strategy
Interpreting Meaning
Identify the sensory language in this stanza that helps you interpret the poem's meaning.

intent (in tent´) *adj.* firmly fixed; concentrated

plaiting (plāt´ iŋ) *v.* braiding

Gladys Cardiff

(b. 1942)

Born in Montana, where her Cherokee father and Irish/Welsh mother taught school on a Blackfoot reservation, Gladys Cardiff grew up in Seattle, Washington, and received both Bachelor and Master of Arts degrees in creative writing from the University of Washington.

The Quiltmakers, Paul Goodnight, Color Circle Art Publishing, Inc.

▲**Critical Viewing** Draw conclusions about the artist's attitude toward these women. Is it similar to the one expressed by Alice Walker? **[Draw Conclusions]**

Women
Alice Walker

They were women then
My mama's generation
Husky of voice—<u>Stout</u> of
Step
5 With fists as well as
Hands
How they battered down
Doors
And ironed
10 Starched white
Shirts
How they led
Armies
Headragged Generals
15 Across mined
Fields
Booby-trapped
Ditches
To discover books
20 Desks
A place for us
How they knew what we
Must know
Without knowing a page
25 Of it
Themselves.

stout (stout) *adj.* sturdy

Alice Walker

(b. 1944)
Alice Walker was born in Eatonton, Georgia. From the age of eight, she kept a journal and wrote poems. Many teachers encouraged her love of reading and writing.

Walker has written poetry, short stories, nonfiction, and novels, including the highly acclaimed *The Color Purple*.

maggie and milly and molly and may

E. E. Cummings

maggie and milly and molly and may
went down to the beach (to play one day)

and maggie discovered a shell that sang
so sweetly she couldn't remember her troubles, and

5 milly befriended a stranded star
whose rays five languid fingers were;

and molly was chased by a horrible thing
which raced sideways while blowing bubbles: and

may came home with a smooth round stone
10 as small as a world and as large as alone.

For whatever we lose (like a you or a me)
it's always ourselves we find in the sea

Reading Strategy
Interpreting Meaning
What does the poet mean
by "a shell that sang"?

languid (laŋ´ gwid) *adj.*
drooping; weak

Review and Assess

Thinking About the Selections

1. **Respond:** Which of these poems did you like best? Why?

2. **(a) Recall:** How many generations of her family does the speaker in "Combing" mention? **(b) Analyze:** What do you think "plaiting the generations" means to the poet?

3. **(a) Recall:** Whom does the speaker in "Women" describe as being "husky of voice" and "stout of step"? **(b) Support:** What do these words convey about the women?

4. **(a) Interpret:** What makes women who "knew . . . without knowing" remarkable? **(b) Speculate:** How might these women have described themselves?

5. **(a) Recall:** Who are the four characters in Cummings's poem? **(b) Infer:** Do they seem different from one another? Explain.

6. **Infer:** According to Cummings, what kinds of things can you find out about yourself at sea?

7. **(a) Speculate:** Would the speaker in "Combing" or "Women" be more likely to agree with the insight in Cummings's poem? **(b) Support:** Which specific details influenced your choice?

8. **Evaluate:** Do you think a person can gain a better understanding of him- or herself by reflecting on past generations or by reflecting on individual experiences? Explain.

E. E. Cummings

(1894–1962)
Born in Cambridge, Massachusetts, E. E. Cummings graduated from Harvard University. Serving in Europe during World War I, he was briefly imprisoned because of his connection to an American who French authorities thought was critical of the war effort.

Both as poet and playwright, Cummings became notorious for his unconventional style, which reflected his individualistic outlook. Though much of his work is playful and lyrical, he often disregarded rules of grammar, spelling, and punctuation. In addition, he frequently coined his own words and ran sentences together.

Astonishment

Wisława Szymborska

Translated by Grażyna Drabik, Austin Flint, and Sharon Olds

Why as one person, and one only?
Why this one, not another? And why here?
On Tuesday? At home, not in a nest?
Why in skin, not scales? With a face, not a leaf?
5 And why do I come, I myself, only once?
On this earth? Near a small star?
After many epochs[1] of absence?
Instead of always, and as all?
As all insects, and all horizons?
10 And why right now? Why bone and blood?
Myself as myself with myself? Why—
not nearby or a hundred miles away,
not yesterday or a hundred years ago—
do I sit and stare into a dark corner,
15 just as it looks up, suddenly raising its head,
this growling thing that is called a dog?

---

1. **epochs** (ep′ əks) *n.* periods or spans of time.

Reading Strategy
Interpreting Meaning To which "small star" does the speaker refer in line 6?

Wisława Szymborska

(b. 1923)

In her poem "Astonishment," Wisława Szymborska uses the word *why* eight times. "Question authority" might be the motto of this Polish poet. During World War II, when the Nazis closed Polish secondary schools and universities, Szymborska attended school illegally.

Today, Szymborska lives quietly in Poland. She prefers letting her poetry speak for her. In 1996, she was awarded the Nobel Prize for Literature.

Review and Assess

Thinking About the Selection

1. **Respond:** How do you react to the poet's style of presenting the entire poem as a series of questions? Explain.

2. **(a) Recall:** Which questioning word is used the most?
   (b) Infer: What do the questions indicate about the speaker?
   (c) Draw Conclusions: Do they all seem to point in the same direction, or not? Explain.

3. **(a) Interpret:** What does the speaker find astonishing?
   (b) Connect: How do the final lines reinforce this idea?

4. **(a) Speculate:** Would E. E. Cummings be likely to agree with the insight expressed in this poem? **(b) Support:** Draw on images and ideas in both poems to support your answer.

5. **Evaluate:** Do you think pondering the meaning of life, as the speaker does, can enrich a person's life? Why or why not?

Review and Assess

Literary Analysis

Moment of Insight

1. (a) Which details lead to the **moments of insight** in "Combing" and "Women"? (b) At what line in each poem is the insight revealed?
2. Which words express the moment of insight in "maggie and milly and molly and may"?
3. (a) What is the insight expressed in "Astonishment"? (b) What provokes it?

Comparing Literary Works

4. Exploring identity is the **theme** common to all four poems. How does each poet address this theme? In the center of a chart like this one, record the similarities you find. In the outer boxes, note the differences in the poems' ideas.

5. Of the four moments of insight, which came as the greatest surprise to you? Explain your answer.
6. Which moment of insight meant the most to you? Explain.

Reading Strategy

Interpreting Meaning

7. Which images and interpretations came to mind while you read "Combing" and "Women"?
8. In his poem, Cummings focuses on playing, while in hers, Szymborska focuses on the single question *why?* What is the effect of each poet's strategy?

Extend Understanding

9. **Career Connection:** What value might the insights in the four poems have for a teacher, a counselor, or anyone in the position of giving guidance to young people?

Quick Review

A **moment of insight** is a fresh, new thought that arises from a poet's musings.

The **theme** is the message or central insight at the heart of a work of literature.

To **interpret the meaning** of a poem, work to understand the point or insight that the poet is making.

 Take It to the Net

www.phschool.com
Take the interactive self-test online to check your understanding of the selections.

Integrate Language Skills

Vocabulary Development Lesson

Word Analysis: Words With Multiple Meanings

Some words have more than one meaning. For example, in "Women," the poet uses the word *stout* to mean "sturdy." *Stout* can also mean "courageous" or "heavyset." When a word has multiple meanings, its context determines the meaning that applies.

Write two definitions for each italicized word. Underline the definition that applies in the sentence based on the context.

1. The growling dog made its *intent* plain.
2. I was saddened to see her *downcast* expression.
3. Maggie found a *shell* on the beach that made her forget her troubles.
4. He understood the book without having read a *page* of it.

Concept Development: Antonyms

Write the word from the vocabulary list on page 325 that is an antonym for, or has the opposite meaning of, each of these words.

1. vigorous
2. unbraiding
3. distracted
4. weak

Spelling Strategy

For a word that ends in the pattern *vowel-vowel-consonant*, do not double the consonant before adding an ending.

Example: *plait + -ing = plaiting*

Think of an ending for each word shown, and use it to write a new word. Use each ending only once.

1. ghoul
2. scream
3. braid
4. appear

Grammar Lesson

Parenthetical Expressions

As you have seen in Cummings's poem, parentheses are sometimes used to set off a nonessential phrase within a sentence. Commas can also set off these **parenthetical expressions,** or nonessential words or phrases that interrupt the sentence's general flow. Look at how parenthetical expressions are used below:

Direct Address: Please help me, *Milly*.
Mild Interjection: *Well*, I never saw such a beautiful shell.
Common Expression: It is, *in my opinion*, tiny.
Transition: The ocean, *however*, is huge.
Contrast: This one, *unlike mine*, is blue.

Practice Copy each sentence, inserting any commas necessary to set off the parenthetical expression.

1. It is I think a powerful poem.
2. Oh I was amazed by what I saw.
3. Her hair was braided neatly and beautifully I might add.
4. Yes they certainly were determined and strong women.
5. Yours like mine is a smooth shell.

Writing Application Write a paragraph about one or two of the poems you liked best. Use at least two parenthetical expressions.

WG *Prentice Hall Writing and Grammar Connection: Chapter 29, Section 2*

Writing Lesson

Journal Entry on a Moment of Insight

Writing poetry is one way of exploring ideas and feelings. Journal writing is another. Write a journal entry about a moment of insight that you had in the recent past as a result of something that happened either locally or nationally.

Prewriting	Start by jotting down important events that have occurred over the past several years. Then, choose one of those as your topic. Gather details by noting the sensory details of the event or experience. These will add emotional depth to your entry.
Drafting	Using your notes as a starting point, recount the experience or event. Include details that will help your readers *feel* what you are describing. Reveal the moment of insight at the end of your journal entry.
Revising	Read over your journal entry. Delete details that do not add to your insight. Look for places where more sensory details would add to the emotional depth of your writing.

Model: Eliminating Unnecessary Information

moving through the frenzy with silent focus

The rescue workers—dressed in blue coveralls—treated the

accident victims with great compassion.

> Words like *frenzy* and *silent focus* add to the emotional depth of the writing.

W̶G *Prentice Hall Writing and Grammar Connection: Chapter 1, Section 1*

Extension Activities

Listening and Speaking With three classmates, prepare an **oral reading** of "maggie and milly and molly and may."

- Plan individual speaking assignments, but read the first and last stanzas together.
- Consider your audience, and practice changing your tone of voice to improve the presentation's impact on your audience.

After you have rehearsed, perform your interpretation for your classmates and invite them to offer their reactions. **[Group Activity]**

Research and Technology Using "Combing" and "Women" as inspiration, prepare a **photo essay** about mothers and daughters. Try to include women of varying ages and backgrounds. Use the Internet to help you find photos, or take pictures of subjects you know. Then, prepare captions that reflect your response to each photo. Present a display in your classroom or school library.

 **Take It to the Net**   www.phschool.com

Go online for an additional research activity using the Internet.

Writing WORKSHOP

Persuasion: Persuasive Essay

A **persuasive essay** is a work in which a writer presents a case for or against a particular position. In this workshop, you will write a persuasive essay on a topic of importance to you.

Assignment Criteria. Your persuasive essay should have the following characteristics:

- A clear thesis statement—a statement of your position on an issue
- Evidence that supports your position and anticipates your readers' counterarguments
- An effective organization
- Persuasive language that builds your argument

To preview the criteria on which your persuasive essay may be assessed, see the Rubric on page 337.

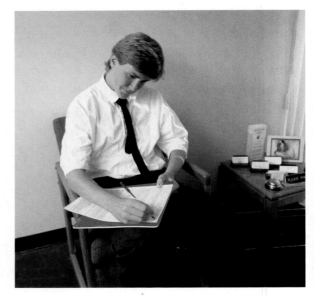

Prewriting

Choose a topic. Pair up with a classmate and brainstorm for topics that are important to each of you, noting those that cause the most disagreement. Select an issue that has compelling arguments on both sides. Then, choose a position to support.

Look at both sides. A persuasive essay is always more effective if it acknowledges and addresses counterarguments. Make a chart like the one below by jotting down facts and ideas that support or contradict your position.

Evidence for school uniforms	Evidence against school uniforms
• May reduce violence and discrimination	• Take choice away from students
• Promote school image	• Can cause resentment among students

Gather evidence. Gather evidence from a wide variety of sources. Collect quotations and facts. As you investigate, keep track of any ideas or phrases that are not your own so that you can give appropriate credit.

Write a thesis statement. Review your notes and the evidence that you have gathered from additional research. Develop a thesis statement that clearly expresses your position.

Student Model

Before you begin drafting your persuasive essay, read this student model and review the characteristics of powerful persuasion.

Braden Danbury
Cumming, GA

Dress Codes May Succeed Where School Uniforms Have Failed

School uniforms are becoming increasingly popular as a way to combat school violence and discrimination. Uniforms, while they may help somewhat, cause problems of their own. Students argue that it is their right to wear what they choose and uniforms violate that right. A less strict code is the answer to both of these problems, keeping appropriate attire in the schools while allowing individuals to choose what they wear.

> The author offers a clear thesis statement in the form of a proposal that addresses a key problem.

Uniforms require students to wear specific shirt and pant types, thus eliminating the element of choice. Dress codes, on the other hand, are less restrictive than school uniforms and cause less resentment among students. Students enjoy choosing what to wear to school each day, coordinating what they wear with how they feel. School uniforms may cause friction between students and school officials, which can have negative consequences.

While it might make sense to have students' safety as a leading justification for requiring uniforms, safety hits the bottom of the list in a press release from the National Association of Elementary School Principals. Safety ranks below such trivial things as school image. This calls into question why uniforms are touted as the answer to school safety issues. Dress codes make the difference where it counts. They keep students safe while forcing them to do nothing other than make sure their clothes meet acceptable standards. An added benefit of dress codes is that schools with uniform policies pay much more than schools with dress codes. Schools with uniforms have to design, order, sell, and distribute the uniforms they wish to have for their school. Dress codes are much less expensive to implement and follow.

> Braden finds a way to deal with counterarguments based on safety concerns.

> Braden offers evidence that supports his position.

With the rise in violence, students and their dress often come under suspicion and scrutiny. In addition, the wide variety of clothing in our high schools may lead students to make prejudicial judgments about each other. Dress codes address the problems of violence without causing resentment among students. They are less strict, giving the students more freedom in how they dress, while allowing school officials to set general guidelines. The amount of money it would take to implement a dress code is a fraction of the cost of school uniforms. Dress codes are not the only answer, but they are a step toward combating violence and discrimination in schools.

> The author restates his thesis and summarizes his evidence. He also offers an additional insight.

Drafting

Organize your arguments. It is useful to sketch out a logical structure for your essay before you write it. Decide which arguments you will present in support of your thesis statement and the order of presentation. Be sure to include a place in your outline to address counterarguments. The organization at right demonstrates one effective way to write a persuasive essay.

Provide evidence. For each point you make, provide evidence to back up your argument. Types of effective evidence include the following:

- **Statistics:** Cite numbers that show the impact of your proposal.

- **Expert opinions:** Include the advice of those who have training and experience related to your topic.

- **Personal observations:** Tell your readers about your own experiences with the topic.

- **Testimonials:** Include statements from peers that reinforce your argument.

Write with a respectful tone. Let your ideas be the strength of your essay. Avoid insulting the opposition. Instead, use a tone that shows respect.

Revising

Revise to address readers' concerns. To convince those who may not agree with your position, show them that you understand their concerns.

1. Look over your draft to highlight controversial claims that a critic of your position would oppose.

2. For each of these claims, determine strong counterarguments that you can make with explanations and evidence.

3. Look for a place where you can insert this information and incorporate it into your draft.

Organizing Your Arguments

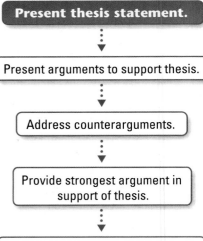

Present thesis statement.

↓

Present arguments to support thesis.

↓

Address counterarguments.

↓

Provide strongest argument in support of thesis.

↓

Conclude by restating thesis and presenting a memorable final thought or quotation.

Model: Addressing the Opposition

Dress codes make the difference where it counts. They keep students safe while forcing them to do nothing other than make sure their clothes meet acceptable standards.

Braden could provide evidence *and* address concerns by finding a statistic that shows that schools with dress codes are just as safe as, or safer than, schools with uniforms.

Revise to strengthen persuasive language. Look for words that can be replaced with more persuasive language. For example, in the following example, *refused* creates a stronger impression than *did not want*.

Example: She *did not want* to leave her home.
She *refused* to leave her home.

Compare the model and the nonmodel. Why is the model more effective than the nonmodel?

Nonmodel	Model
Students argue that it is their right to wear what they choose and that uniforms withdraw that right.	Students argue that it is their right to wear what they choose and that uniforms violate that right.

Publishing and Presenting

Present your writing to a wider audience. Sharing your persuasive essay might possibly achieve results—your ideas could inspire a positive change in behavior, open minds to a new perspective, or help change an unfair policy.

Speaking Connection

To learn more about analyzing persuasive arguments, see the **Listening and Speaking Workshop**, page 338.

Deliver an oral presentation. Read your persuasive composition aloud in front of your classmates. After you have finished reading, take an unofficial poll to determine whether or not you convinced your audience of your position.

Publish in a newspaper. Send your essay as an opinion piece to your school or community newsletter, or condense it into a letter to the editor.

 Prentice Hall Writing and Grammar Connection: Chapter 7

Rubric for Self-Assessment

Evaluate your persuasive essay using the following criteria and rating scale:

Criteria	Rating Scale				
	Not very				Very
How clear is the thesis statement?	1	2	3	4	5
How well is the thesis supported by evidence?	1	2	3	4	5
How well are readers' concerns anticipated and addressed?	1	2	3	4	5
How effectively are arguments organized?	1	2	3	4	5
How powerful is the persuasive language?	1	2	3	4	5

Listening and Speaking WORKSHOP

Analyzing Types of Arguments

We normally think of an argument as a shouting match or disagreement. However, an argument, as it is used to describe speeches, essays, and debates, is a series of statements that support a particular conclusion. Learning how to analyze an argument will improve your own ability to build persuasive arguments.

Recognize Argument Structure

Just as the human body is supported by its skeleton, the body of an argument is bolstered with supporting statements, or premises. Recognizing an argument's structure will help you figure out whether it is strong—supported by many powerful premises—or weak.

Identify the conclusion. The conclusion is the main idea of an argument. It should be easy to identify because it is broadly stated, general, and supported by individual pieces of evidence.

Identify premises. Premises are the basic building blocks of an argument. The best way to find individual premises is to work backward from a conclusion to find its supporting statements or evidence.

Identify Argument Types

Persuasive speakers use a variety of argument types to convince audiences. For example, if you had to prepare a persuasive speech on why solar energy is better than energy from coal, you might use the following argument types:

- **Analogy (Making a comparison):** You could argue that not using solar energy is like paying to drive your car to school when you could take a free school bus.

- **Authority (Citing expert opinion):** You might point to specific research that links the burning of coal to air pollution.

- **Emotion (Appealing to sense of right and wrong):** You could indicate the harmful effects that pollution might have on a child with asthma.

- **Logic (Using reasoning):** You could indicate that solar energy is cleaner than coal and exists in greater supply.

- **Causation (Using cause-and-effect analysis):** You could walk your audience through the coal energy process, from the burning of coal to its effect on living organisms.

Analyzing Types of Arguments

Argument Structure

Conclusion: _____

Premise: _____   Premise: _____

Premise: _____

Argument Types

Type	Example
Analogy	
Authority	
Emotion	
Logic	
Causation	

(Activity:)
Observation and Analysis Watch a video of a debate or an important speech, such as a presidential address. As you listen, complete a chart like the one shown. Note an example of each type of argument you hear in the speech. Use the flowchart to diagram one of the main arguments.

Assessment WORKSHOP

Stated and Implied Main Idea

In the reading sections of some tests, you are required to read passages and answer multiple-choice questions about stated and implied main ideas. Use the following strategies to answer such questions:

- Look for a topic sentence that is a statement of the main idea of a passage.
- If a main idea is not stated, it may be implied or suggested.
- To identify an implied main idea, read the passage and summarize the author's message in a single statement.
- To make sure that you have identified the topic sentence correctly, check that the other sentences support the idea of the sentence you have chosen.

Test-Taking Strategies

- Check implied main ideas by making sure all of the sentences support your one-sentence summary.
- Consider the title you might assign a passage. This may reinforce the main idea.

Sample Test Item

Directions: Read the passage, and then answer the question that follows.

Despite dropping temperatures and decreased daylight, finches, sparrows, and mockingbirds are birds commonly seen in winter. These species feed primarily on seeds and berries, which are plentiful even through the coldest months.

1. What is the main idea implied in this passage?

   A Birds feed on seeds and berries in winter.

   B Birds that are seen in winter are finches, sparrows, and mockingbirds.

   C During winter, birds look for food near trees and shrubs.

   D Finches, sparrows, and mockingbirds can survive the coldest winter months.

Answer and Explanation

The correct answer is **D,** because both sentences support the main idea. **A** and **B** are details, but they are not the central idea of the passage. **C** is not stated in the passage.

▶ Practice

Directions: Read the passage, and then answer the question that follows.

Everyone has a fever at some point. A fever is a symptom, not a disease. It is an indication that your body is fighting an infection or illness. While it causes discomfort, a fever may be a sign of recovery.

You do not need to call a doctor immediately if you develop a low-grade fever. You should drink fluids and get plenty of rest. Record your temperature every two hours, and note any change in symptoms.

1. What is the stated main idea of the first paragraph?

   A Everyone gets a fever at some point.

   B A fever is a symptom of a disease, not the disease itself.

   C A fever indicates that your body is fighting an infection or illness.

   D A fever may be a sign of your body's recovery.

Exploring the Theme

What's so funny? It might be an animal trainer teaching 5,000 flies how to "act." It might be an overstressed husband taking a mental leave of absence, or it might be an outlandish poem told in nonsense language. Check out these stories, essays, poems, and more. You are sure to find something to make you smile.

You may never have played football on a crowded street in Philadelphia, like Bill Cosby in **"Go Deep to the Sewer."** But you will probably still laugh when you recognize yourself—and the games you improvised with your friends—in Cosby's humorous reminiscence. This is only one of the many types of laughter you will find in the pieces that follow—the laughter of recognition.

▲ **Critical Viewing** Which aspects of this drawing add to its humorous impact? **[Analyze]**

Why Read Literature?

Whenever you read, you have a purpose, or reason. You might read to find a particular type of information, to be entertained, or to further your understanding of a certain kind of literature. Preview three purposes you could set for yourself before reading works in this unit.

1 Read for the Love of Literature

In Russian literature there is a tradition of poking fun at government officials that has landed some writers in trouble. The negative reaction to Nikolai Gogol's play *The Inspector-General* caused Gogol to seek exile. See how dramatist Anton Chekhov takes Gogol's play, in which townspeople mistake a local scoundrel for a government inspector, and turns it on its head in his version of **The Inspector-General,** page 358.

You know something is not quite right when you read a poem like "Jabberwocky." Maybe it is the fact that author Lewis Carroll invents his own language as he goes along. Maybe it is the feeling that, in spite of all the bizarre phrases, you still understand what he is saying. Test your wits and chortle along with the inspired nonsense of **"Jabberwocky,"** page 400.

The Jabberwock, 1872, John Tenniel

2 Read for Information

You might be surprised at some of the trickery trainers use to get animals to do what movie directors want. Find out how one trainer coaxed five thousand winged extras to fly on cue as he takes you behind the scenes in **"Fly Away,"** page 373.

If you have ever wondered what insects eat or hungered to know the name of that bug you found crawling across your bathroom floor, you can find the answers in Patricia Volk's essay **"An Entomological Study of Apartment 4A,"** page 386.

3 Read to Be Entertained

We all have moments when we take a mental break and pretend to be somewhere or someone we are not. James Thurber attempts to answer the question "What would it be like to daydream all the time?" in his humorous story entitled **"The Secret Life of Walter Mitty,"** page 346.

 Take It to the Net

Visit the Web site for online instruction and activities related to each selection in this unit.
www.phschool.com

How to Read Literature

Use Interactive Reading Strategies

To get the most out of many things in life, you have to get involved. This rule is as true in reading as it is in playing sports or visiting new places. Use these strategies to interact with what you are reading.

1. Read back or read ahead.

Even the best readers can find themselves confused when they encounter difficult passages. If you lose focus or encounter complex sentences with unfamiliar words, follow these steps:

- Pause to think about what you have just read and to look up new words. If necessary, go back to the last portion of the text you understood and reread from that point.

- Read ahead to clear up confusion—especially when reading texts in which the action is presented before explanations are given.

2. Read between the lines.

- Notice details that might provide indications of a deeper message or future plot development.

- Keep track of suspicions you might have about characters and their motives by using a chart like the one shown.

Read Between the Lines	
Character	Driver in *The Inspector-General*
What I already know about the character	Driver knows many personal details about the new Inspector-General.
What the author might be suggesting	Driver might be able to recognize the Inspector-General if he were to meet him.

3. Recognize situational humor.

When you laugh because you relate to the set of circumstances an author is describing, you are recognizing situational humor. Keep in mind the following tips:

- Look for humor that involves familiar experiences.

- Notice techniques like contrast or exaggeration that play up the humor of a given situation.

4. Question characters' actions.

As you read, ask questions and offer explanations for why characters act the way they do. Base your answers on characters' past actions and your own experiences. For example, you might want to determine the main character's motive in this passage.

> Mr. Johnson . . . came forward and, touching his hat civilly, said, "Perhaps I can keep an eye on your little boy for you."
>
> —*from* "One Ordinary Day, With Peanuts"

Start by asking why a character might offer help. He might be acting out of kindness or expecting something in return. Use your answers to evaluate the character's behavior as you continue reading.

As you read, review these reading strategies and use the notes in the selection margin to interact with the text.

Prepare to Read

The Secret Life of Walter Mitty

Portrait XIV, Donald C. Martin, Private Collection

 Take It to the Net

Visit www.phschool.com for interactive activities and instruction related to "The Secret Life of Walter Mitty," including
- background
- graphic organizers
- literary elements
- reading strategies

Preview

Connecting to the Literature

There you are, a movie star, accepting an Academy Award. . . . Suddenly, a dog barks, bringing you back to the real world . . . in a bus on your way home. Perhaps you can recall daydreams that seemed sweeter than reality. "The Secret Life of Walter Mitty" is about a man whose frequent daydreams are more real to him than his workaday existence.

Background

Psychologists say that a person's thoughts often consist of seemingly unconnected insights, memories, and reflections, and that single incidents can prompt an unpredictable mental response. In James Thurber's story, random events cause Walter Mitty's thoughts to jump back and forth between his exciting "secret" life and his humdrum everyday life.

Literary Analysis

Point of View

In stories told in the **first-person point of view,** the narrator is one of the characters. In the **third-person point of view,** the narrator does not participate in the action. The third-person point of view can be either *omniscient,* in which the narrator sees into the minds of all the characters, or *limited,* in which the narrator sees the world through one character's eyes and reveals only that character's thoughts.

This story is written from the third-person point of view. As you read, notice that the narrator lets you see Mitty's thoughts and feelings in a way you would not experience in real life.

Connecting Literary Elements

Walter Mitty, a bumbling husband but a man of action in his dreams, is an example of a **round character**—a character who exhibits many traits, including faults as well as virtues. Mrs. Mitty, a wife who does nothing but scold Walter, is an example of a **flat character**—a character who seems to have only a single surface or aspect to her personality. As you read, notice the many traits of Walter Mitty.

Reading Strategy

Reading Back and Reading Ahead

Walter Mitty's thoughts consistently shift from fantasy to reality. To understand the shifts in the story, read back and read ahead.

- **Read back** to see if you have overlooked any important facts.
- **Read ahead** to clarify an unclear situation.

Use a chart like this one to clarify insights you gain by reading back and reading ahead.

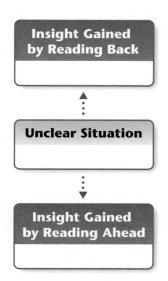

Vocabulary Development

rakishly (rāk´ ish lē) *adv.* with a trim, casual look; dashingly (p. 347)

hurtling (hʉrt´ liŋ) *adj.* moving swiftly and with great force (p. 347)

distraught (di strôt´) *adj.* extremely troubled; confused; distracted (p. 348)

haggard (hag´ ərd) *adj.* having a worn look, as from sleeplessness (p. 348)

insolent (in´ sə lənt) *adj.* boldly disrespectful (p. 349)

insinuatingly (in sin´ yoo āt´ iŋ lē) *adv.* suggesting indirectly (p. 349)

cur (kʉr) *n.* mean, contemptible person; mean, ugly dog (p. 349)

cannonading (kan´ ən ād´ iŋ) *n.* continuous firing of artillery (p. 350)

derisive (di rī´ siv) *adj.* showing contempt or ridicule (p. 352)

inscrutable (in skrŌŌt´ ə bəl) *adj.* baffling; mysterious (p. 352)

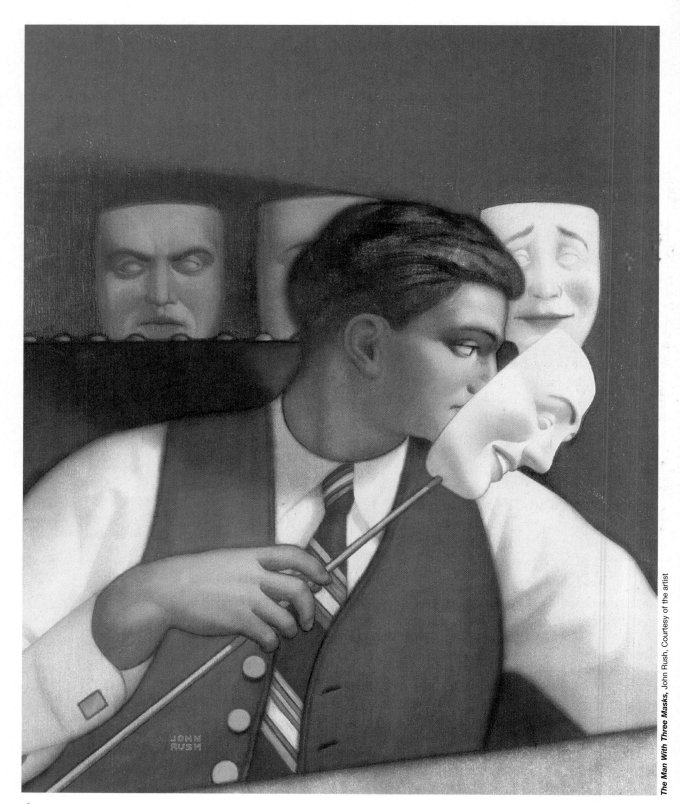

The Man With Three Masks, John Rush, Courtesy of the artist

▲ **Critical Viewing** Analyze the significance of the mask in this painting. Why might the man hold one mask up to his face and have other masks nearby? **[Analyze]**

The Secret Life of Walter Mitty

James Thurber

We're going through!" The Commander's voice was like thin ice breaking. He wore his full-dress uniform, with the heavily braided white cap pulled down rakishly over one cold gray eye. "We can't make it, sir. It's spoiling for a hurricane, if you ask me." "I'm not asking you, Lieutenant Berg," said the Commander. "Throw on the power lights! Rev her up to 8,500! We're going through!" The pounding of the cylinders increased: ta-pocketa-pocketa-pocketa-*pocketa-pocketa*. The Commander stared at the ice forming on the pilot window. He walked over and twisted a row of complicated dials. "Switch on No. 8 auxiliary!" he shouted. "Switch on No. 8 auxiliary!" repeated Lieutenant Berg. "Full strength in No. 3 turret!" shouted the Commander. "Full strength in No. 3 turret!" The crew, bending to their various tasks in the huge, hurtling eight-engined Navy hydroplane,[1] looked at each other and grinned. "The Old Man'll get us through," they said to one another. "The Old Man ain't afraid of Hell!". . .

"Not so fast! You're driving too fast!" said Mrs. Mitty. "What are you driving so fast for?"

"Hmm?" said Walter Mitty. He looked at his wife, in the seat beside him, with shocked astonishment. She seemed grossly unfamiliar, like a strange woman who had yelled at him in a crowd. "You were up to fifty-five," she said. "You know I don't like to go more than forty. You were up to fifty-five." Walter Mitty drove on toward Waterbury in silence, the roaring of the SN202 through the worst storm in twenty years of Navy flying fading in the remote, intimate airways of his mind. "You're tensed up again," said Mrs. Mitty. "It's one of your days. I wish you'd let Dr. Renshaw look you over."

Walter Mitty stopped the car in front of the building where his wife went to have her hair done. "Remember to get those overshoes while

---

rakishly (rāk´ ish lē) *adv.* with a trim, casual look; dashing

hurtling (hurt´ lin) *adj.* moving swiftly and with great force

✔ **Reading Check**
Why is Mrs. Mitty upset?

---

1. **hydroplane** (hī´ drō plān´) *n.* seaplane.

I'm having my hair done," she said. "I don't need overshoes," said Mitty. She put her mirror back into her bag. "We've been all through that," she said, getting out of the car. "You're not a young man any longer." He raced the engine a little. "Why don't you wear your gloves? Have you lost your gloves?" Walter Mitty reached in a pocket and brought out the gloves. He put them on, but after she had turned and gone into the building and he had driven on to a red light, he took them off again. "Pick it up, brother!" snapped a cop as the light changed, and Mitty hastily pulled on his gloves and lurched ahead. He drove around the streets aimlessly for a time, and then he drove past the hospital on his way to the parking lot.

. . . "It's the millionaire banker, Wellington McMillan," said the pretty nurse. "Yes?" said Walter Mitty, removing his gloves slowly. "Who has the case?" "Dr. Renshaw and Dr. Benbow, but there are two specialists here, Dr. Remington from New York and Mr. Pritchard-Mitford from London. He flew over." A door opened down a long, cool corridor and Dr. Renshaw came out. He looked <u>distraught</u> and <u>haggard</u>. "Hello, Mitty," he said. "We're having the devil's own time with McMillan, the millionaire banker and close personal friend of Roosevelt. Obstreosis of the ductal tract.[2] Tertiary. Wish you'd take a look at him." "Glad to," said Mitty.

In the operating room there were whispered introductions: "Dr. Remington, Dr. Mitty. Mr. Pritchard-Mitford, Dr. Mitty." "I've read your book on streptothricosis," said Pritchard-Mitford, shaking hands. "A brilliant performance, sir." "Thank you," said Walter Mitty. "Didn't know you were in the States, Mitty," grumbled Remington. "Coals to Newcastle,[3] bringing Mitford and me up here for tertiary." "You are very kind," said Mitty. A huge, complicated machine, connected to the operating table, with many tubes and wires, began at this moment to go pocketa-pocketa-pocketa. "The new anesthetizer is giving way!" shouted an intern. "There is no one in the East who knows how to fix it!" "Quiet, man!" said Mitty, in a low, cool voice. He sprang to the machine, which was now going pocketa-pocketa-queep-pocketa-queep. He began fingering delicately a row of glistening dials. "Give me a fountain pen!" he snapped. Someone handed him a fountain pen. He pulled a faulty piston out of the machine and inserted the pen in its place. "That will hold for ten minutes," he said. "Get on with the operation." A nurse hurried over and whispered to Renshaw, and Mitty saw the man turn pale. "Coreopsis has set in," said Renshaw nervously. "If you would take over, Mitty?" Mitty looked at him and at the craven figure of Benbow, who drank, and at the grave, uncertain faces of the two great specialists. "If you wish," he said. They slipped a white gown on him; he adjusted a mask and drew on thin gloves; nurses handed him shining . . .

"Back it up, Mac! Look out for that Buick!" Walter Mitty jammed on

distraught (di strôt') *adj.* extremely troubled; confused; distracted

haggard (hag' ərd) *adj.* having a worn look, as from sleeplessness

**Literary Analysis
Point of View and Round Characters** How does this shift in scenes show that Walter Mitty is a round character?

---

2. **obstreosis of the ductal tract** Thurber has invented this and other medical terms.
3. **coals to Newcastle** The proverb "bringing coals to Newcastle" means bringing things to a place unnecessarily—Newcastle, England, was a coal center and so did not need coal brought to it.

the brakes. "Wrong lane, Mac," said the parking-lot attendant, looking at Mitty closely. "Gee. Yeh," muttered Mitty. He began cautiously to back out of the lane marked "Exit Only." "Leave her sit there," said the attendant. "I'll put her away." Mitty got out of the car. "Hey, better leave the key." "Oh," said Mitty, handing the man the ignition key. The attendant vaulted into the car, backed it up with <u>insolent</u> skill, and put it where it belonged.

They're so cocky, thought Walter Mitty, walking along Main Street; they think they know everything. Once he had tried to take his chains off, outside New Milford, and he had got them wound around the axles. A man had had to come out in a wrecking car and unwind them, a young, grinning garageman. Since then Mrs. Mitty always made him drive to a garage to have the chains taken off. The next time, he thought, I'll wear my right arm in a sling; they won't grin at me then. I'll have my right arm in a sling and they'll see I couldn't possibly take the chains off myself. He kicked at the slush on the sidewalk. "Overshoes," he said to himself, and he began looking for a shoe store.

When he came out into the street again, with the overshoes in a box under his arm, Walter Mitty began to wonder what the other thing was his wife had told him to get. She had told him, twice, before they set out from their house for Waterbury. In a way he hated these weekly trips to town—he was always getting something wrong. Kleenex, he thought, Squibb's, razor blades? No. Toothpaste, toothbrush, bicarbonate, carborundum, initiative and referendum?[4] He gave it up. But she would remember it. "Where's the what's-its-name?" she would ask. "Don't tell me you forgot the what's-its-name." A newsboy went by shouting something about the Waterbury trial.

. . . "Perhaps this will refresh your memory." The District Attorney suddenly thrust a heavy automatic at the quiet figure on the witness stand. "Have you ever seen this before?" Walter Mitty took the gun and examined it expertly. "This is my Webley-Vickers 50.80," he said calmly. An excited buzz ran around the courtroom. The Judge rapped for order. "You are a crack shot with any sort of firearms, I believe?" said the District Attorney, <u>insinuatingly</u>. "Objection!" shouted Mitty's attorney. "We have shown that the defendant could not have fired the shot. We have shown that he wore his right arm in a sling on the night of the fourteenth of July." Walter Mitty raised his hand briefly and the bickering attorneys were stilled. "With any known make of gun," he said evenly, "I could have killed Gregory Fitzhurst at three hundred *feet with my left hand.*" Pandemonium broke loose in the courtroom. A woman's scream rose above the bedlam and suddenly a lovely, dark-haired girl was in Walter Mitty's arms. The District Attorney struck at her savagely. Without rising from his chair, Mitty let the man have it on the point of the chin. "You miserable <u>cur</u>!" . . .

---

4. **carborundum** (kär′ bə run′ dəm), **initiative** (i nish′ ē ə tiv) **and referendum** (ref ə ren′ dəm) Thurber is purposely making a nonsense list; *carborundum* is a hard substance used for scraping, *initiative* is the right of citizens to introduce ideas for laws, and *referendum* is the right of citizens to vote on laws.

insolent (in′ sə lənt) *adj.* boldly disrespectful

insinuatingly (in sin′ yōō āt′ iŋ lē) *adv.* suggesting indirectly

cur (kʉr) *n.* mean, contemptible person; mean, ugly dog

✔**Reading Check**
Why does Mitty say that next time he will wear his arm in a sling?

"Puppy biscuit," said Walter Mitty. He stopped walking and the buildings of Waterbury rose up out of the misty courtroom and surrounded him again. A woman who was passing laughed. "He said 'Puppy biscuit,'" she said to her companion. "That man said 'Puppy biscuit' to himself." Walter Mitty hurried on. He went into an A. & P., not the first one he came to but a smaller one farther up the street. "I want some biscuit for small, young dogs," he said to the clerk. "Any special brand, sir?" The greatest pistol shot in the world thought a moment. "It says 'Puppies Bark for It' on the box," said Walter Mitty.

His wife would be through at the hairdresser's in fifteen minutes, Mitty saw in looking at his watch, unless they had trouble drying it; sometimes they had trouble drying it. She didn't like to get to the hotel first; she would want him to be there waiting for her as usual. He found a big leather chair in the lobby, facing a window, and he put the overshoes and the puppy biscuit on the floor beside it. He picked up an old copy of *Liberty* and sank down into the chair. "Can Germany Conquer the World Through the Air?" Walter Mitty looked at the pictures of bombing planes and of ruined streets.

Literary Analysis
Point of View Through whose eyes do you obtain this view of Mrs. Mitty?

. . . "The cannonading has got the wind up in young Raleigh,[5] sir," said the sergeant. Captain Mitty looked up at him through tousled hair. "Get him to bed," he said wearily. "With the others. I'll fly alone." "But you can't, sir," said the sergeant anxiously. "It takes two men to handle that bomber and the Archies[6] are pounding hell out of the air. Von Richtman's circus[7] is between here and Saulier." "Somebody's got to get that ammunition dump," said Mitty. "I'm going over. Spot of brandy?" He poured a drink for the sergeant and one for himself. War thundered and whined around the dugout and battered at the door. There was a rending of wood and splinters flew through the room. "A bit of a near thing," said Captain Mitty carelessly. "The box barrage is closing in," said the sergeant. "We only live once, Sergeant," said Mitty, with his faint, fleeting smile. "Or do we?" He poured another brandy and tossed it off. "I never see a man could hold his brandy like you, sir," said the sergeant. "Begging your pardon, sir." Captain Mitty stood up and strapped on his huge Webley-Vickers automatic. "It's forty kilometers through hell, sir," said the sergeant. Mitty finished one last brandy. "After all," he said softly, "what isn't?" The pounding of the cannon increased; there was the rat-tat-tatting of machine guns, and from somewhere came the menacing pocketa-pocketa-pocketa of the new flame-throwers. Walter Mitty walked to the door of the dugout humming "Auprès de Ma Blonde."[8] He turned and waved to the sergeant. "Cheerio!" he said. . . .

Something struck his shoulder. "I've been looking all over this hotel

cannonading (kan' ən ād' iŋ) *n.* continuous firing of artillery

Reading Strategy
Reading Back and Reading Ahead To clarify Mitty's location, would you read ahead or read back at this point? Explain.

---

5. **has got the wind up in young Raleigh** has made young Raleigh nervous.
6. **Archies** slang term for antiaircraft guns.
7. **Von Richtman's circus** German airplane squadron.
8. **"Auprès de Ma Blonde"** (ō prā' də mä blôn' də) "Next to My Blonde," a popular French song.

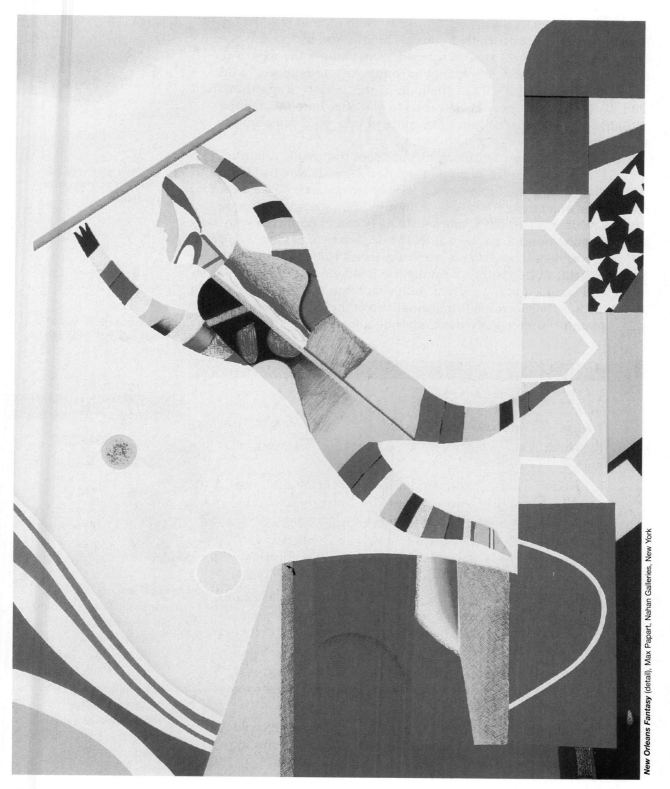

New Orleans Fantasy (detail), Max Papart, Nahan Galleries, New York

▲ **Critical Viewing** Describe a situation that might make Walter Mitty daydream about being a circus performer like the one shown. **[Hypothesize]**

for you," said Mrs. Mitty. "Why do you have to hide in this old chair? How did you expect me to find you?" "Things close in," said Walter Mitty vaguely. "What?" Mrs. Mitty said. "Did you get the what's-its-name? The puppy biscuit? What's in that box?" "Overshoes," said Mitty. "Couldn't you have put them on in the store?" "I was thinking," said Walter Mitty. "Does it ever occur to you that I am sometimes thinking?" She looked at him. "I'm going to take your temperature when I get you home," she said.

They went out through the revolving doors that made a faintly <u>derisive</u> whistling sound when you pushed them. It was two blocks to the parking lot. At the drugstore on the corner she said, "Wait here for me. I forgot something. I won't be a minute." She was more than a minute. Walter Mitty lighted a cigarette. It began to rain, rain with sleet in it. He stood up against the wall of the drugstore, smoking. . . . He put his shoulders back and his heels together. "To hell with the hand-kerchief," said Walter Mitty scornfully. He took one last drag on his cig-arette and snapped it away. Then, with that faint, fleeting smile playing about his lips, he faced the firing squad; erect and motionless, proud and disdainful, Walter Mitty the Undefeated, <u>inscrutable</u> to the last.

derisive (di rī′ siv) *adj.* showing contempt or ridicule

inscrutable (in skrōōt′ ə bəl) *adj.* baffling; mysterious

Review and Assess

Thinking About the Selection

1. **Respond:** Do you feel sorry for Walter Mitty? Why or why not?

2. **(a) Recall:** In the "real" world, what are Mitty and his wife actually doing? **(b) Deduce:** Does Mrs. Mitty understand the reasons for Walter's absentmindedness? Explain.

3. **(a) Recall:** What jars Mitty out of his first daydream? **(b) Compare and Contrast:** How does he behave in this daydream? In his real life?

4. **(a) Recall:** What event triggers Mitty's courtroom daydream? **(b) Draw Conclusions:** Explain the significant difference between the way people treat Mitty in his real life and the way they treat him in his daydreams.

5. **(a) Infer:** Which aspects of Mrs. Mitty's personality trigger Mitty's last daydream? **(b) Draw Conclusions:** In what way is this daydream a comment on his fate in real life?

6. **Hypothesize:** How might Mitty's life be altered if he could transfer the self-esteem he experiences in his daydreams into his conscious life?

7. **Take a Position:** Can daydreaming ever benefit a person? Explain.

James Thurber

(1894–1961)

Born in Columbus, Ohio, James Thurber began his writing career at the *Columbus Evening Dispatch*, where he was a reporter. He later achieved fame as a humor-ous writer and cartoonist during his many years at *The New Yorker* magazine.

Thurber's plays, stories, essays, fables, reminiscences, and verse fill more than twenty volumes. He lost his sight in the 1940s but con-tinued to write until his death. In 1960, he won the Antoinette Perry award for his revue *A Thurber Carnival*.

Review and Assess

Literary Analysis

Point of View

1. Is there a moment when you realize that you are seeing Walter Mitty's world through his eyes? Explain.
2. How are your feelings about Mitty influenced by seeing things from his **point of view**?
3. If the **limited third-person narration** had focused on Mrs. Mitty instead of Walter, how would the story have been different? Use a Venn diagram to gather details for a response.

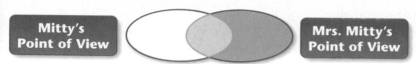

Connecting Literary Elements

4. (a) What evidence suggests that Walter Mitty is a **round character**? (b) What evidence shows Mrs. Mitty is a **flat character**?
5. Using a chart like the one shown here, analyze the characters in Walter's daydreams.

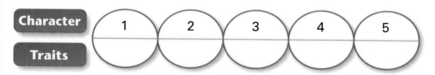

6. (a) Do the characters in Mitty's daydreams seem as flat as those in his real life? (b) How does this characterization influence the story?

Reading Strategy

Reading Back and Reading Ahead

7. Cite two places where **reading back or ahead** helped you fully understand the meaning of a scene in the story.

Extend Understanding

8. **Career Connection:** (a) In reality, could Mitty perform the work he thinks about in his daydreams? Why or why not? (b) Suggest a fulfilling career for Walter. Explain your choice.

Quick Review

Point of view is the perspective from which a story is told.

A **limited third-person narrator** reveals the thoughts of only one character, through whose eyes you see the other characters.

A **round character** exhibits many traits, including both virtues and faults.

A **flat character** exhibits only a single quality or trait.

You **read back** to see if you have overlooked any important facts.

You **read ahead** to look for an explanation of a passage you do not understand.

 Take It to the Net
www.phschool.com

Take the interactive self-test online to check your understanding of the selection.

Integrate Language Skills

Vocabulary Development Lesson

Word Analysis: Latin Root -scrut-

The Latin root -scrut- means "to search carefully or examine." The word *inscrutable* literally means "not able to be searched or examined" or "not easily understood." Define each of the following words.

1. scrutiny   **2.** scrutinize   **3.** inscrutability

Spelling Strategy

When a word ends in silent *e*, you often drop the *e* before adding an ending that begins with a vowel. For example, *cannonade + -ing = cannonading*. However, there are many exceptions to this rule. For example, *manage + -able = manageable*. Write the new word that is formed when you combine these words and suffixes.

1. rake + *-ing*   **3.** courage + *-ous*

2. cure + *-ative*   **4.** sane + *-ity*

Concept Development: Synonyms

On your paper, write the letter of the word in the second column that is closest in meaning to each word in the first column. To help you, review the vocabulary list on page 345.

1.	rakishly	**a.**	baffling
2.	hurtling	**b.**	bombarding
3.	distraught	**c.**	implying
4.	haggard	**d.**	scoundrel
5.	insolent	**e.**	speeding
6.	insinuatingly	**f.**	insulting
7.	cur	**g.**	exhausted
8.	cannonading	**h.**	disrespectful
9.	derisive	**i.**	troubled
10.	inscrutable	**j.**	stylishly

Grammar Lesson

Complete Subjects and Predicates

The **complete subject** of a sentence consists of the simple subject and all the words associated with it. The **complete predicate** consists of the simple predicate, or verb, and all the words associated with it.

COMPLETE SUBJ	COMPLETE PRED
A woman's scream	rose above the bedlam.

Practice Copy each sentence. Underline the complete subject once and the complete predicate twice.

1. The Commander spoke seriously.

2. He looked at his wife in astonishment.

3. A huge machine, connected to the operating table, was very noisy.

4. He could not remember what she asked him to buy.

5. The District Attorney spoke to the man on the witness stand.

6. War rumbled and whined at the door.

Writing Application Write two or three sentences to add more details to one of Walter Mitty's adventures in the story. Underline each complete subject once and each complete predicate twice.

W̶G Prentice Hall Writing and Grammar Connection: Chapter 20, Section 1

Writing Lesson

Character Profile

Walter Mitty sees himself as one fearless character after another. Use one of Mitty's daydreams to inspire a character profile that vividly describes a personality he becomes in his dreams.

Prewriting   Use a cluster map like the one shown to jot down details that capture the character's appearance, personality, achievements, and feelings.

Model: Creating a Character Profile

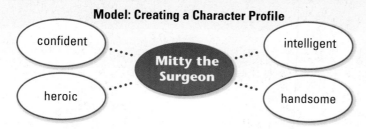

Drafting   Decide on the impression you want to convey, and present details so that they all point toward it. Build toward the most important point.

Revising   Review your work to be sure you have used details from each prewriting category. Ask a classmate to identify the main impression of your character description. If the response is not what you expected, revise to clarify your focus. Provide more details that support the main impression, and eliminate those that do not.

W̸G Prentice Hall Writing and Grammar Connection: Chapter 13, Section 2

Extension Activities

Listening and Speaking Take these steps to adapt one of Walter Mitty's daydreams as a **dramatic skit:**

- In a group, choose the daydream you find most appealing.
- Decide who will play the various roles.

Consider incorporating the phrase *ta-pocketa-pocketa* to ensure that the scene truly captures Mitty. Perform your skit for the class. **[Group Activity]**

Research and Technology Use library resources, including the Internet, to research scientific facts and theories about daydreaming. Record the information in a **learning log,** a written record of what you discover about the topic. Compare your findings to the story. Decide whether Walter Mitty is really as different from others as he seems.

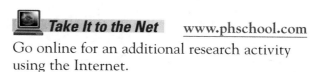 **Take It to the Net**   www.phschool.com

Go online for an additional research activity using the Internet.

Prepare to Read

The Inspector-General

Valmondois Sous la Neige, Maurice Vlaminck

Take It to the Net

Visit www.phschool.com
for interactive activities
and instruction related to
The Inspector-General,
including
- background
- graphic organizers
- literary elements
- reading strategies

Preview

Connecting to the Literature

Sometimes, people hide their identities or pretend to be someone else. They may be trying to impress someone or play a practical joke. Unexpectedly, the results can be embarrassing or even funny, as the title character of this selection discovers.

Background

The Inspector-General is set in imperial Russia, before the 1917 communist revolution, when the country was ruled by an emperor, or czar. To oversee the many minor officials in Russia's vast expanse, the czars employed people called inspectors general. They observed how local schools, courts, and hospitals were functioning. Many people resented the czar's authority, however, and inspectors general were as unpopular as other officials.

Literary Analysis

Irony

When a literary work like *The Inspector-General* takes a surprising turn, it creates **irony**—a contrast between what is expected or believed and what is actual. Following are some of the types of irony used in literature:

- **Verbal irony:** A word or phrase is used to suggest the opposite of its usual meaning.
- **Dramatic irony:** There is a contradiction between what a character thinks and what the reader knows is true.
- **Situational irony:** An event directly contradicts the expectations of readers or characters.

As you will see, irony can create humor.

Connecting Literary Elements

In this play, **dialogue**—the conversation between characters—helps to convey the irony. Through dialogue, the driver's vivid descriptions paint a picture for his traveler, and the irony of the situation is revealed. Watch for the driver's descriptions of the inspector general, as revealed through his dialogue, and decide how accurate they are.

Reading Strategy

Reading Between the Lines

When you read a drama, **read between the lines,** or draw conclusions about a person or idea by using the information provided through dialogue. These tips can help you read between the lines:

- Think critically about a character based on what he or she says or does, or based on details of appearance, as revealed through dialogue.
- Pay attention to questions that one character asks another.

Use a diagram like the one shown here to record ideas that you find between the lines.

Information Provided

Traveler wants to talk about himself.

Conclusion

He thinks he is an important man.

Vocabulary Development

incognito (in käg´ ni tō´) *n.* a disguised condition (p. 359)

anonymous (ə nän´ ə məs) *adj.* without a known or acknowledged name (p. 359)

trundle (trun´ dəl) *v.* to roll along; to rotate (p. 359)

valet (val´ it) *n.* a man's personal servant who takes care of the man's clothes (p. 360)

buffet (bə´ fā´) *n.* restaurant with a counter or table where refreshments are served (p. 362)

The Inspector-General

Anton Chekhov Adapted by Michael Frayn

Valmondois Sous la Neige, Maurice de Vlaminck

▲ **Critical Viewing** What might life be like in a setting such as this one? **[Speculate]**

The curtain goes up to reveal falling snow and a cart facing away from us. Enter the STORYTELLER, who begins to read the story. Meanwhile, the TRAVELER enters. He is a middle-aged man of urban appearance, wearing dark glasses and a long overcoat with its collar turned up. He is carrying a small traveling bag. He climbs into the cart and sits facing us.

STORYTELLER. The Inspector General. In deepest <u>incognito</u>, first by express train, then along back roads, Pyotr Pavlovich Posudin[1] was hastening toward the little town of N, to which he had been summoned by an <u>anonymous</u> letter. "I'll take them by surprise," he thought to himself. "I'll come down on them like a thunderbolt out of the blue. I can just imagine their faces when they hear who I am . . ." [*Enter the DRIVER, a peasant, who climbs onto the cart, so that he is sitting with his back to us, and the cart begins to <u>trundle</u> slowly away from us.*] And when he'd thought to himself for long enough, he fell into conversation with the driver of the cart. What did he talk about? About himself, of course. [*Exit the STORYTELLER.*]

TRAVELER. I gather you've got a new Inspector-General in these parts.

DRIVER. True enough.

TRAVELER. Know anything about him? [*The driver turns and looks at the TRAVELER, who turns his coat collar up a little higher.*]

DRIVER. Know anything about him? Of course we do! We know everything about all of them up there! Every last little clerk—we know the color of his hair and the size of his boots! [*He turns back to the front, and the TRAVELER permits himself a slight smile.*]

TRAVELER. So, what do you reckon? Any good, is he? [*The DRIVER turns around.*]

DRIVER. Oh, yes, he's a good one, this one.

TRAVELER. Really?

DRIVER. Did one good thing straight off.

TRAVELER. What was that?

DRIVER. He got rid of the last one. Holy terror he was! Hear him coming five miles off! Say he's going to this little town. Somewhere like we're going, say. He'd let all the world know about it a month before. So now he's on his way, say, and it's like thunder and lightning coming down the road. And when he gets where he's going he has a good sleep, he has a good eat and drink—and then he starts. Stamps his feet, shouts his head off. Then he has another good sleep, and off he goes.

---

1. **Pyotr Pavlovich Posudin** (pyōˊ tr pávˊ lōˊ vich pō syŌŌˊ dən)

incognito (in kägˊ ni tōˊ) *n.* a disguised condition

anonymous (ə nänˊ ə məs) *adj.* without a known or acknowledged name

trundle (trunˊ dəl) *v.* to roll along; to rotate

Literary Analysis
Irony What is ironic about the driver's words here?

 Reading Check
What does the driver say about the last inspector general?

TRAVELER. But the new one's not like that?

DRIVER. Oh, no, the new one goes everywhere on the quiet, like. Creeps around like a cat. Don't want no one to see him, don't want no one to know who he is. Say he's going to this town down the road here. Someone there sent him a letter on the sly, let's say. "Things going on here you should know about." Something of that kind. Well, now, he creeps out of his office, so none of them up there see him go. He hops on a train just like anyone else, just like you or me. Then when he gets off he don't go jumping into a cab or nothing fancy. Oh, no. He wraps himself up from head to toe so you can't see his face, and he wheezes away like an old dog so no one can recognize his voice.

TRAVELER. Wheezes? That's not wheezing! That's the way he talks! So I gather.

DRIVER. Oh, is it? But the tales they tell about him. You'd laugh till you burst your tripes![2]

TRAVELER [*sourly*]. I'm sure I would.

DRIVER. He drinks, mind!

TRAVELER [*startled*]. Drinks?

DRIVER. Oh, like a hole in the ground. Famous for it.

TRAVELER. He's never touched a drop! I mean, from what I've heard.

DRIVER. Oh, not in public, no. Goes to some great ball—"No thank you, not for me." Oh, no, he puts it away at home! Wakes up in the morning, rubs his eyes, and the first thing he does, he shouts, "Vodka!" So in runs his <u>valet</u> with a glass. Fixed himself up a tube behind his desk, he has. Leans down, takes a pull on it, no one the wiser.

TRAVELER [*offended*]. How do you know all this, may I ask?

DRIVER. Can't hide it from the servants, can you? The valet and the coachman have got tongues in their heads. Then again, he's on the road, say, going about his business, and he keeps the bottle in his little bag. [*The* TRAVELER *discreetly pushes the traveling bag out of the* DRIVER's *sight.*] And his housekeeper . . .

TRAVELER. What about her?

DRIVER. Runs circles around him, she does, like a fox round his tail. She's the one who wears the trousers.[3] The people aren't half so frightened of him as they are of her.

TRAVELER. But at least he's good at his job, you say?

DRIVER. Oh, he's a blessing from heaven, I'll grant him that.

TRAVELER. Very cunning—you were saying.

---

2. **tripes** (trīps) *n.* parts of the stomach, usually of an ox or a sheep.
3. **wears the trousers** has the greatest authority; is really in charge.

valet (val' it) *n.* a man's personal servant who takes care of the man's clothes

White Night, Edvard Munch, National Gallery, Oslo

◀ **Critical Viewing**
How well does the mood of this painting match the mood of this play? Explain. **[Connect]**

DRIVER. Oh, he creeps around all right.

TRAVELER. And then he pounces, yes? I should think some people must get the surprise of their life, mustn't they?

DRIVER. No, no—let's be fair, now. Give him his due. He don't make no trouble.

TRAVELER. No, I mean, if no one knows he's coming . . .

DRIVER. Oh, that's what *he* thinks, but *we* all know.

TRAVELER. You know?

DRIVER. Oh, some gentleman gets off the train at the station back there with his greatcoat up to his eyebrows and says, "No, I don't want a cab, thank you, just an ordinary horse and cart for me." Well, we'd put two and two together, wouldn't we! Say it was you, now, creeping along down the road here. The lads would be down there in a cab by now! By the time you got there the whole town would be as regular

Literary Analysis
Irony What makes the driver's description funny?

✔**Reading Check**

What does the driver say that the new inspector general does at night?

as clockwork! And you'd think to yourself, "Oh, look at that! As clean as a whistle! And they didn't know I was coming!" No, that's why he's such a blessing after the other one. This one believes it!

TRAVELER. Oh, I see.

DRIVER. What, you thought we wouldn't know him? Why, we've got the electric telegraph these days! Take today, now. I'm going past the station back there this morning, and the fellow who runs the <u>buffet</u> comes out like a bolt of lightning. Arms full of baskets and bottles. "Where are you off to?" I say. "Doing drinks and refreshments for the Inspector-General!" he says, and he jumps into a carriage and goes flying off down the road here. So there's the old Inspector-General, all muffled up like a roll of carpet, going secretly along in a cart somewhere—and when he gets there, nothing to be seen but vodka and cold salmon!

TRAVELER [*shouts*]. Right—turn around, then . . . !

DRIVER [*to the horse*]. Whoa, boy! Whoa! [*To the* TRAVELER.] Oh, so what's this, then? Don't want to go running into the Inspector-General, is that it? [*The* TRAVELER *gestures impatiently for the* DRIVER *to turn the cart around.* DRIVER *to the horse.*] Back we go, then, boy. Home we go. [*He turns the cart around, and the* TRAVELER *takes a swig from his traveling bag.*] Though if I know the old devil, he's like as not turned around and gone home again himself. [*Blackout.*]

> **buffet** (bə fā´) *n.* restaurant with a counter or table where refreshments are served

Review and Assess

Thinking About the Selection

1. **Respond:** Did you feel any sympathy for the inspector general? Why or why not?

2. **(a) Recall:** What have townspeople learned about the inspector general's habits? **(b) Draw Conclusions:** What do these habits reveal about the official's character?

3. **(a) Recall:** What does the traveler do when the driver mentions that the inspector general keeps a flask of vodka? **(b) Infer:** What does this action tell you about the traveler?

4. **(a) Recall:** How does the driver describe the preparations for the inspector general's arrival? **(b) Interpret:** Why does this account provoke the traveler's demand to turn around?

5. **Speculate:** What kind of report might the inspector general make to the czar about his mission? Give specific details.

6. **Assess:** Based on his actions, what kind of leader do you think the inspector general will be?

7. **Evaluate:** Who do you think is the wiser man, the driver or the traveler? Explain.

Anton Chekhov

(1860–1904)

The grandson of a former serf who had purchased his freedom, Chekhov grew up in a small Russian coastal town. He later attended medical school in Moscow, where he began writing humorous sketches and short stories. Writing soon became his major focus, but he practiced medicine part-time throughout his life.

Chekhov wrote more than one thousand short stories as well as several acclaimed plays, including *The Seagull* (1896), *Uncle Vanya* (1899), and *The Three Sisters* (1901). He is considered one of the finest playwrights and short-story writers who ever lived.

Review and Assess

Literary Analysis

Irony

1. The humor in *The Inspector-General* comes from the use of **irony.** In a chart like the one shown here, note the traveler's assumptions and the driver's ironic observations.

2. Explain why the traveler's attempt to hide his identity presents **situational irony.**

3. Explain why the driver's remark that the inspector general is "a good one" is an example of **verbal irony.**

Connecting Literary Elements

4. (a) What image of the inspector general is revealed through the **dialogue**? (b) Explain the irony in the driver's description of the new inspector general.

5. As the dialogue between the men continues, the situation becomes ever funnier. Use a flowchart like the one shown here to record the most important details leading to the comic reversal.

Reading Strategy

Reading Between the Lines

6. (a) When did you first realize that the traveler is the inspector general? (b) Which details led you to this conclusion?

7. As the driver goes on speaking, the traveler resorts to saying "so I gather" and "from what I've heard." **Read between the lines** to explain why he uses these expressions.

Extend Understanding

8. **Cultural Connection:** What makes a person of authority popular or unpopular in the public eye?

Integrate Language Skills

Vocabulary Development Lesson

Word Analysis: Greek Root -nym-

The Greek root -nym-, meaning "name," is used in many English words, including *anonymous*, which means "without a known name." Use a dictionary to define the following words.

1. patronymic   2. synonym   3. acronym

Spelling Strategy

When you add a suffix that begins with a vowel to a word that ends in a consonant, the spelling of the original word does not change. For example, *inspect* + *-or* = *inspector*.

Add *-ance*, *-ish*, or *-er* to each word below to form three properly spelled words.

1. child   2. travel   3. accept

Fluency: Sentence Completions

In your notebook, complete each sentence with a word from the vocabulary list on page 357.

1. The heavy trucks slowly ____?____ along the bumpy road.
2. An ____?____ donor gave ten thousand dollars to the hospital fund. We're still not sure who made the donation.
3. The ____?____ cleaned and ironed the pants of the hotel guest.
4. The ____?____ featured delicious main courses and desserts. Everyone moved along, placing their favorite foods on their plates.
5. Traveling ____?____, with sunglasses, a fake mustache, and a hat, the spy checked into the motel under a false name.

Grammar Lesson

Compound Subjects and Compound Predicates

A sentence may have two or more subjects with the same verb (a **compound subject**) or two or more verbs, or predicates, with the same subject (a **compound predicate**). It may even have both at once. The parts of a compound subject or predicate are joined by a conjunction, such as *and* or *or*.

Compound subject: Glasses and an overcoat were worn by the inspector general. Glasses, an overcoat, and a traveling bag were some of his belongings.

Compound predicate: They traveled and talked in the cart. The driver turns, looks, and nods at the traveler.

Practice Copy each sentence. Underline each compound subject once and each compound predicate twice.

1. Snow and ice make travel difficult.
2. The driver and the traveler took a ride.
3. As they ride, the traveler asks questions and hopes for the right response.
4. The driver's manner and his ideas reveal an interesting situation.
5. He makes a decision and chooses to leave.

Writing Application Write two sentences about *The Inspector-General*, using a compound subject in one and a compound predicate in the other.

W̶G̶ Prentice Hall Writing and Grammar Connection: Chapter 20, Section 1

Writing Lesson

Ad for a New Inspector General

Imagine that you are the czar and have just fired the old inspector general. Write a newspaper ad to find a replacement. Your ad should provide information that will appeal to potential applicants and clarify whether they are qualified for the job.

Prewriting   Jot down ideas in the following categories: (a) job title and responsibilities; (b) necessary experience and background; (c) salary and benefits; (d) contact information, such as the company's phone number or address.

Drafting   Begin with an attention-grabbing introduction. Then, devote a short paragraph to each of the four categories.

> ### Model: Grabbing Your Reader's Attention
>
> Love to travel? Ready to take on fascinating new responsibilities? Consider becoming an inspector general!

An effective ad is based on a catchy and memorable message.

Revising   Compare your ad to your prewriting notes, underlining key details in your draft. If you discover information that is unclear or incomplete, revise to present a more accurate picture of the job.

WG Prentice Hall Writing and Grammar Connection: Chapter 8, Section 3

Extension Activities

Listening and Speaking With two other students, prepare to perform a **Readers Theater presentation** of *The Inspector-General.* Do not provide props or staging; instead, focus on a well-prepared reading of the play.

- Choose roles—the traveler, the driver, and a narrator who reads the introduction and any stage directions you feel should be shared.
- Experiment to find the tone of voice and style of delivery that seem to work best.

Then, perform the play in front of a small group or the entire class. **[Group Activity]**

Research and Technology Research what life was like in Russia during the rule of the czars. Explain the responsibilities of inspectors general during this time. Use two or more Internet search engines to broaden the scope of your findings. Display your findings in a **concept map** or another graphic organizer and present it to your class. Ask your class to compare inspectors general in history to the inspector general in this story.

 **Take It to the Net**   www.phschool.com

Go online for an additional research activity using the Internet.

Prepare to Read

Go Deep to the Sewer ◆ Fly Away

Take It to the Net

Visit www.phschool.com
for interactive activities
and instruction related to
the selections, including

- background
- graphic organizers
- literary elements
- reading strategies

Preview

Connecting to the Literature

When life hands out lemons, some people make lemonade. Other people make big lemon meringue pies to toss so that others will laugh. Maybe you are one of those people who can find something funny even in difficult situations. These selections focus on the lighter side of personal experiences.

Background

For years, Ralph Helfer, an animal trainer and the author of "Fly Away," used an animal-training method based on fear. After being injured several times, Helfer developed a new system, "affection training," with which the trainer wins an animal's loyalty through understanding, patience, and love. Since using this system, neither Helfer nor any of his animals have been injured.

Literary Analysis

Humorous Remembrance

A **humorous remembrance** is a story that emphasizes what is funny in a writer's past experiences. The following excerpt from "Go Deep to the Sewer" relates a ten-year-old quarterback's instructions to his team, whose football field was an urban street in Philadelphia.

> ". . . Arnie, you go down to the corner of Locust an' fake takin' the bus. An' Cos, you do a zig out to the bakery. See if you can shake your man before you hit the rolls."

As you read the selections, notice how both writers find something to laugh about in experiences that may have had their painful moments as well.

Comparing Literary Works

Humorous remembrances are all amusing, whether or not the writers initially intended them to be. Humor is the most important ingredient in both of these stories, and laughter may be the reader's most frequent reaction. Compare the humorous and serious sides of the experiences these authors convey in each of their stories.

Reading Strategy

Recognizing Situational Humor

Situational humor, as found in these humorous remembrances, arises from conditions that mix people, actions, and settings in funny and often improbable ways:

- In "Go Deep to the Sewer," a stickball player is tagged out at third base because the car that takes the place of the base is suddenly driven away.
- In "Fly Away," the trainer amazingly gets several thousand flies to take to the air on cue.

Use a chart like this one to capture and categorize specific examples of situational humor you find as you read.

What Is Being Done?	Who Is Doing It?
Where?	**Using What?**

Vocabulary Development

lateral (lat´ ər əl) *adj.* sideways (p. 368)

yearned (yʉrnd) *v.* longed for (p. 370)

decoy (dē´ koĭ) *n.* person used to lure others into a trap (p. 370)

interpretation (in tʉr´ prə tā´ shən) *n.* explanation (p. 371)

skeptical (skep´ ti kəl) *adj.* doubting; questioning (p. 375)

Go Deep to the Sewer

Bill Cosby

The essence of childhood, of course, is play, which my friends and I did endlessly on streets that we reluctantly shared with traffic. As a daring receiver in touch football, I spent many happy years running up and down those asphalt fields, hoping that a football would hit me before a Chevrolet did.

My mother was often a nervous fan who watched me from her window.

"Bill, don't get run over!" she would cry in a moving concern for me.

"Do you see me getting run over?" I would cleverly reply.

And if I ever *had* been run over, my mother had a seat for it that a scalper[1] would have prized.

Because the narrow fields of those football games allowed almost no <u>lateral</u> movement, an end run was possible only if a car pulled out and blocked for you. And so I worked on my pass-catching, for I knew I had little chance of ever living my dream: taking a handoff and sweeping to glory along the curb, dancing over the dog dung like Red Grange.

The quarterback held this position not because he was the best passer but because he knew how to drop to one knee in the huddle and diagram plays with trash.

"Okay, Shorty," Junior Barnes would say, "this is you: the orange peel."

"I don' wanna be the orange peel," Shorty replied. "The orange peel is Albert. I'm the gum."

lateral (lat´ ər əl) *adj.* sideways

Reading Strategy
Recognizing Situational Humor Why did few players get to make "end runs"? What is funny about this situation?

---

1. scalper (skalp´ ər) *n.* person who buys tickets and sells them later at higher than regular prices.

◀ **Critical Viewing**
How does this painting
help you picture the setting
and the characters in
Cosby's essay? **[Connect]**

Young Brothers in the Hood, Tom McKinney

"But let's make 'em *think* he's the orange peel," I said, "an' let 'em think Albert's the manhole."

"Okay, Shorty," said Junior, "you go out ten steps an' then cut left behind the black Oldsmobile."

"I'll sorta go *in* it first to shake my man," said Shorty, "an' then, when he don' know where I am, you can hit me at the fender."

"Cool. An' Arnie, you go down to the corner of Locust an' fake takin' the bus. An' Cos, you do a zig out to the bakery. See if you can shake your man before you hit the rolls."

"Suppose I start a fly pattern to the bakery an' then do a zig out to the trash can," I said.

"No, they'll be expecting that."

**Reading Check**

Where do Cosby and his
friends play football?

I spent most of my boyhood trying to catch passes with the easy grace of my heroes at Temple;[2] but easy grace was too hard for me. Because I was short and thin, my hands were too small to catch a football with arms extended on the run. Instead, I had to stagger backwards and smother the ball in my chest. How I <u>yearned</u> to grab the ball in my hands while striding smoothly ahead, rather than receiving it like someone who was catching a load of wet wash. Often, after a pass had bounced off my hands, I returned to the quarterback and glumly said, "Jeeze, Junior, I don' know what happened." He, of course, knew what had happened: he had thrown the ball to someone who should have been catching it with a butterfly net.

Each of these street games began with a quick review of the rules: two-hand touch, either three or four downs, always goal-to-go, forward passing from anywhere, and no touchdowns called back because of traffic in motion. If a receiver caught a ball near an oncoming car while the defender was running for his life, the receiver had guts, and possibly a long excuse from school.

I will never forget one particular play from those days when I was trying so hard to prove my manhood between the manholes. In the huddle, as Junior, our permanent quarterback, dropped to one knee to arrange the garbage offensively, I said, "Hey, Junior, make me a <u>decoy</u> on this one."

Pretending to catch the ball was what I did best.

"What's a decoy?" he said.

"Well, it's—"

"I ain't got time to learn. Okay, Eddie, you're the Dr Pepper cap an' you go deep toward New Jersey."

"An' I'll fool around short," I said.

"No, Cos, you fake goin' deep an' then buttonhook at the DeSoto. An' Harold, you do a zig out between 'em. *Somebody* get free."

Moments later, the ball was snapped to him and I started sprinting down the field with my defender, Jody, who was matching me stride for stride. Wondering if I would be able to get free for a pass sometime within the next hour, I stopped at the corner and began sprinting back to Junior, whose arm had been cocked for about fifteen seconds, as if he'd been posing for a trophy. Since Eddie and Harold also were covered, and since running from scrimmage was impossible on that narrow field, I felt that this might be touch football's first eternal play: Junior still standing there long after Eddie, Harold, and I had dropped to the ground, his arm still cocked as he tried to find some way to pass to himself.

But unlimited time was what we had and it was almost enough for us. Often we played in the street until the light began to fade and the ball became a blur in the dusk. If there is one memory of my

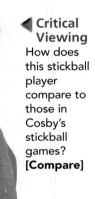

yearned (yɥrnd) *v.* longed for

decoy (dē′ koi′) *n.* person used to lure others into a trap

◀ **Critical Viewing**
How does this stickball player compare to those in Cosby's stickball games? **[Compare]**

---

2. **Temple** Temple University in Philadelphia, Pennsylvania.

childhood that will never disappear, it is a bunch of boys straining to find a flying football in the growing darkness of a summer night.

There were, of course, a couple of streetlamps on our field, but they were useful only if your pattern took you right up to one of them to make your catch. The rest of the field was lost in the night; and what an adventure it was to refuse to surrender to that night, to hear the quarterback cry "Ball!" and then stagger around in a kind of gridiron blindman's buff.

"Hey, you guys, dontcha think we should call the game?" said Harold one summer evening.

"Why do a stupid thing like that?" Junior replied.

"'Cause I can't see the ball."

"Harold, that don't make you special. Nobody can see the ball. But y' *know* it's up there."

And we continued to stagger around as night fell on Philadelphia and we kept looking for a football that could have been seen only on radar screens.

One day last year in a gym, I heard a boy say to his father, "Dad, what's a Spal*deen*?"

This shocking question left me depressed, for it is one thing not to know the location of the White House or the country that gave its name to Swiss cheese, but when a boy doesn't know what a Spal*deen* is, our educational system has failed. For those of you ignorant of basic American history, a Spal*deen* was a pink rubber ball with more bounce than can be imagined today. Baseball fans talk about the lively ball, but a lively baseball is a sinking stone compared to a Spal*deen*, which could be dropped from your eye level and bounce back there again, if you wanted to do something boring with it. And when you connected with a Spal*deen* in stickball, you put a pink rocket in orbit, perhaps even over the house at the corner and into another neighborhood, where it might gently bop somebody's mother sitting on a stoop.

I love to remember all the street games that we could play with a Spal*deen*. First, of course, was stickball, an organized version of which is also popular and known as baseball. The playing field was the same rectangle that we used for football: it was the first rectangular diamond. And for this game, we had outfield walls in which people happened to live and we had bases that lacked a certain uniformity: home and second were manhole covers, and first and third were the fenders of parked cars.

One summer morning, this offbeat infield caused a memorable <u>interpretation</u> of the official stickball rules. Junior hit a two-sewer shot and was running toward what should have been third when third suddenly drove away in first. While the bewildered Junior tried to arrive safely in what had become a twilight zone, Eddie took my throw from center field and tagged him out.

"I'm not out!" cried Junior in outrage. "I'm right here on third!"

And he did have a point, but so did Eddie, who replied, not without a certain logic of his own, "But third ain't there anymore."

Literary Analysis
Humorous Remembrance
Which details about playing at night are exaggerated?

interpretation (in tur´ prə ta´ shən) *n.* explanation

Reading Check

What is the one memory Cosby has of his childhood that he says will never disappear?

In those games, our first base was as mobile as our third; and it was a floating first that set off another lively division of opinion on the day that Fat Albert hit a drive over the spot from which first base had just driven away, leaving us without a good part of the right field foul line. The hit would have been at least a double for anyone with movable legs, but Albert's destination was first, where the play might have been close had the right fielder hit the cutoff man instead of a postman.

"Foul ball!" cried Junior, taking a guess that happened to be in his favor.

"You're out of your mind, Junior!" cried Albert, an observation that often was true, no matter what Junior was doing. "It went right over the fender!"

"What fender?"

"If that car comes back, you'll see it's got a fender," said Albert, our automotive authority.

However, no matter how many pieces of our field drove away, nothing could ever take away the sweetness of having your stick connect with a Spal*deen* in a magnificent *whoppp* and drive it so high and far that it bounced off a window with a view of New Jersey and then caromed back to the street, where Eddie would have fielded it like Carl Furillo[3] had he not backed into a coal chute.

---

3. **Carl Furillo** (kärl fər il′ ō) baseball player for the Brooklyn Dodgers in the 1950s.

Reading Strategy
Recognizing Situational Humor What do you find most humorous in this passage?

Review and Assess

Thinking About the Selection

1. **Respond:** Would you enjoy playing stickball or football by the rules Bill Cosby describes? Explain.

2. **(a) Recall:** What does Cosby regret about his physical size during his boyhood? **(b) Compare and Contrast:** How was Cosby like and unlike his heroes at Temple University?

3. **(a) Recall:** Why was Junior always the quarterback for the neighborhood football games? **(b) Analyze:** Was Junior's method of calling plays successful? Explain.

4. **(a) Recall:** How does Cosby describe the experience of connecting with a Spaldeen? **(b) Interpret:** Does Cosby really mean what he says about hitting a Spaldeen? Explain.

5. **(a) Speculate:** What does Cosby mean when he says "The essence of childhood . . . is play"? **(b) Evaluate:** Do you agree with this idea? Explain.

Bill Cosby

(b. 1937)
The son of a navy cook and a domestic worker, Bill Cosby grew up in the housing projects of Philadelphia. Although he left high school to join the navy, he earned a diploma through a correspondence course. During the 1960s, he performed stand-up comedy in Philadelphia and soon became nationally famous.

Cosby has won awards for his television shows and his books, which include *Fatherhood* (1986) and *Time Flies* (1987).

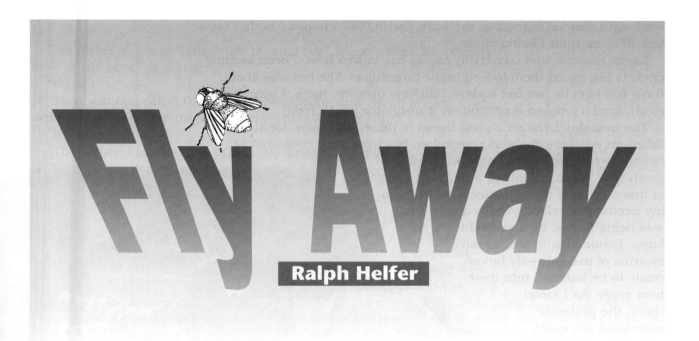

Fly Away

Ralph Helfer

"I need 5,000 trained flies. Can you do it? Yes or no!" The voice at the other end of the phone was insistent.

"Well, I . . ."

"Of course you can't, Helfer. *Nobody* can. Look, I told the director I'd make a couple of calls. So, now I have. The answer is obviously NO!"

"I *can* do it," I said, fitting my sentence neatly in between my caller's constant jabber, "but I'll need a couple of days."

The voice on the phone was silent a moment. Then: "You're kidding."

"No, really. Two days, and I'll be ready. What do they have to do?"

"There's this artificial, dead-looking 'thing' lying on the ground in the forest. The director wants thousands of flies to be crawling on it without flying away."

"Okay," I said. "Consider it done."

"No, wait. Then, he wants them *all* to fly away, on command—but not before."

"Okay, no problem," I said. "Two days."

"Wait. Did you hear what I said? They can't leave until he says okay. How are you going to keep them there, let alone have them fly away when he wants them to??"

"I'll stick each of their 20,000 legs in glue! Look, don't worry. Call me later, and I'll give you the figure. 'Bye."

Sometimes affection training was not the only answer. One could not "pet" a fly or earn its respect. I knew I would have to resort to the laws of nature for the answer to this one. I'd had the opportunity to

Reading Strategy
Recognizing Situational Humor How does the caller's attitude create humor?

**Reading Check**

What does the director's assistant ask Helfer to do?

The crew, absolutely bug-eyed (forgive the pun), was hypnotized.
"One," I counted. They looked from the flies to me.
"Two."
"Three!" I yelled, clapping my hands and stamping my foot at the same time. Five thousand twenty-one flies flew up, up, around and around. The camera hummed until the director, rousing himself from his amazed state, said, "Cut!"

The entire crew was silent for a moment, and then they burst into applause and delighted laughter.

"You did it, you really did it!" said the director, slapping me heartily on the back. "I'm not even going to ask you how. I don't even want to know. But if I ever need a trained *anything*, you're the man I'll call!"

Straight-faced, I said, "Well, actually, I've recently trained 432 flies to form a chorus line on my arm, and on cue they all kick a leg at the same time."

The director, poker-faced, looked straight at me. "Which one?" he asked.
"Which one what?"
"Which leg?"
"The left one, of course!"
We all broke up laughing and headed home.

Review and Assess

Thinking About the Selection

1. **Respond:** What did you find most interesting about Ralph Helfer's remembrance? Explain.

2. **(a) Recall:** What plan does Helfer develop to make the flies do what is needed for the movie? **(b) Draw Conclusions:** Why do you think he feels comfortable making the deal?

3. **(a) Recall:** How does Helfer know that the flies will not fly away as soon as they are released? **(b) Infer:** Why does he speak to the flies as if they understand him?

4. **(a) Recall:** What is the director's reaction to the fly stunt? **(b) Infer:** Would he want to work with Helfer again? Why?

5. **Assess:** Would it have benefited Helfer to tell the director how he did the fly trick? Explain.

6. **Speculate:** What specific skills are needed to be a good animal trainer? Explain.

7. **(a) Evaluate:** Do you think Helfer's live effects are still needed in the computer age? **(b) Support:** What would be gained or lost by using only computers for special effects?

Ralph Helfer

(b. 1937)

Ralph Helfer, one of the world's leading animal trainers, has worked in more than 5,000 movies and television programs. In his book *The Beauty of the Beasts* (1989), Helfer describes being "clawed by lions, attacked by bears, bitten by poisonous snakes, and nearly suffocated by pythons."

Since instituting affection training, however, Helfer has been bite-free. He and his trained animals have won 18 PATSY awards for the best animal performances on screen.

Review and Assess

Literary Analysis

Humorous Remembrance

1. Use a chart like the one below to record details that identify "Go Deep to the Sewer" as a **humorous remembrance.**

Cosby's Story

2. How does Cosby give readers the sense that they are part of the action as they move through the story?

3. (a) What overall impression of his work does Helfer communicate in his remembrance? (b) Which humorous details make the writing entertaining?

Comparing Literary Works

4. (a) Review each selection and compare the serious elements or ideas in each of these humorous remembrances. (b) Which selection conveyed the more serious ideas? Explain.

5. Cosby's story strings together experiences of childhood play. Helfer's memoir focuses on one memorable job. Which piece do you find more appealing? Why?

Reading Strategy

Recognizing Situational Humor

6. How does Cosby use his **situation**—being obliged to play football and stickball in the street—to humorous advantage?

7. Helfer pretends to count the sleeping flies. Why is this funny?

8. How does the audience's reaction to Helfer's achievement add to the situation's humor?

Extend Understanding

9. **Cultural Connection:** Do you think Cosby's story could only be appreciated by people who have lived in a city? Explain.

Integrate Language Skills

Vocabulary Development Lesson

Concept Development: Sports Jargon

Jargon is special language related to a particular activity, profession, sport, or art. Use a dictionary to find the meanings of the following sports terms. Then, explain how each term might be used in everyday speech.

1. slam dunk
2. punt
3. on deck
4. huddle

Spelling Strategy

When you add -*ly* to a word ending with a short vowel followed by an *l*, keep the final *l*. For example, *lateral* + *-ly= laterally*.

Identify the misspelled words in the following list and correct their spelling.

1. wonderfuly
2. civily
3. thoughtfully
4. politically

Concept Development: Analogies

Complete the following analogies by analyzing the word relationship in the first pair of words. Then, create the same relationship in the second pair by choosing the most suitable word.

1. forward : ahead :: lateral : ____?____
   (a) nearby (b) quickly (c) sideways (d) far
2. dislike : like :: yearn : ____?____
   (a) long for (b) realize (c) reject
   (d) behave
3. false : wrong :: decoy : ____?____
   (a) duck (b) bait (c) coach (d) invite
4. seasoning : spice :: interpretation : ____?____
   (a) version (b) behavior (c) satisfaction
   (d) play
5. prisoner : pardon :: skeptic : ____?____
   (a) remedy (b) lightly (c) convince
   (d) enemy

Grammar Lesson

Direct Objects

A **direct object** is the noun or pronoun that receives the action of a verb. You can determine whether a word is a direct object by asking *whom?* or *what?* after an action verb.

Examples:

Junior threw the *football* to Cosby. (threw *what?*)

He told *Albert* to pass the ball. (told *whom?*)

Junior devised elaborate *plans* for the team. (devised *what?*)

The boy asked his *father*. (asked *whom?*)

Practice In each sentence, identify the direct object and the verb whose action it completes.

1. I will never forget one particular play.
2. Suppose I start a fly pattern to the bakery.
3. "No," said Junior, "they'll be expecting that."
4. "Now, Ralph, I'll roll the camera whenever you say—okay?"
5. The professor gave me a batch of fly larvae.

Writing Application Write a short paragraph about a sports experience you have had. Try to include a direct object in every sentence. Then, underline each direct object.

W͜G Prentice Hall Writing and Grammar Connection: Chapter 20, Section 3

Writing Lesson

Humorous Personal Narrative

Choose a memorable experience and write a humorous narrative about it. Catch your readers' attention and help them anticipate the comedy in your writing. Use the essays by Cosby and Helfer as inspirations for your own brand of humor.

Prewriting   Jot down details that you know will make your readers laugh. Focus on details that can be exaggerated for comic effect.

Drafting   The best groundwork for any kind of narrative writing—especially a humorous narrative—is a strong introduction. A striking quotation is one of a number of things that will make a good start.

> ### Model: Writing a Strong Introduction
>
> The voice on the phone was insistent: "I need a dozen rabbits, and I need them now!"

An interesting quotation or a surprising observation can provide a strong introduction to a narrative.

Revising   Review your draft to evaluate whether your introduction will make your readers want to read further. Then, check that your narrative maintains its humorous tone throughout.

*W*G *Prentice Hall Writing and Grammar Connection: Chapter 4, Section 3*

Extension Activities

Listening and Speaking   Bill Cosby's memoir originated as part of his stand-up comedy routine. Working with a partner, use a real or imagined incident from your own life or one you have seen in a book, movie, or television show as the basis for a brief **monologue.** Your partner can help you judge whether the incident has comic potential.

- Emphasize the humor of the situation.
- End the story in a satisfying way.

Use your partner's feedback to revise your monologue before presenting it to a small group of friends or classmates. **[Group Activity]**

Research and Technology   Use books, magazines, reference materials, or online resources to do research about current methods of training animals. Focus on learning about the training methods used with two or three specific kinds of animals. Organize what you learn into a **visual report** using charts, graphs, or other appropriate visual aids. Share your findings with your class.

 **Take It to the Net**   www.phschool.com

Go online for an additional research activity using the Internet.

Prepare to Read

An Entomological Study of Apartment 4A

 Take It to the Net

Visit www.phschool.com
for interactive activities
and instruction related to
"An Entomological Study of
Apartment 4A," including

- background
- graphic organizers
- literary elements
- reading strategies

Preview

Connecting to the Literature

Often, we are fascinated by creatures that repel us. Even if you would rather not look at that many-legged thing that just scurried under the stove, you may still want to know what it is. This natural curiosity inspired writer Patricia Volk to collect the bugs she found in her apartment and take them to an expert for identification.

Background

In everyday speech, the words *insect* and *bug* are used for all sorts of pests, but no entomologist, like Louis Sorkin in this article, would use these terms loosely. An entomologist studies insects—their behavior, their eating habits, and the differences among the dozens of species that are often smaller than a human fingernail.

Literary Analysis

Feature Article

A **feature article** is a newspaper or magazine story written to entertain readers or to provide information on a subject of human interest. Such an article may be designed to evoke an emotional response to its subject's achievements or problems. One way a writer can evoke a strong response from readers is by sharing a personal experience. In this excerpt, note how Patricia Volk personalizes a common problem.

> A black crawly thing with more legs than the Rockettes had staked out the north bedroom wall . . . and a bug as shiny as patent leather had moved into the water gauge of our electric coffee maker.

Notice how Volk's subject matter entertains while informing you.

Connecting Literary Elements

A well-written article holds your attention because it never wanders far from its main idea. The **main idea** is the central or underlying point of an article. The fact that every sentence in "An Entomological Study of Apartment 4A" is related to the writer's investigation of insects and bugs shapes the article and gives it impact. By the end of the article, Volk reveals the main idea and the insights it generates.

Reading Strategy

Establishing a Purpose for Reading

To get the most out of what you read, **establish a purpose** for reading and then read to achieve this purpose. Your purpose may be

- to discover something new or to gather information for a report; if so, focus on obtaining useful facts.
- simply to enjoy reading; if so, look for fascinating details and descriptions.

Set a purpose for reading this selection and use a chart like this one to jot down notes that will help fulfill your purpose.

Vocabulary Development

microcosms (mī′ krō käz′əms) *n.* little worlds (p. 386)

metaphors (met′ə fôrz) *n.* ways of speaking of things as though they were something else (p. 386)

poignant (poin′ yənt) *adj.* drawing forth compassion; moving (p. 389)

malevolence (mə lev′ ə ləns) *n.* bad or evil feelings or intentions (p. 389)

immortalized (i môr′ tə līzd) *v.* given lasting fame (p. 390)

An Entomological Study of Apartment 4A

Patricia Volk

Louis Sorkin has a prominent forehead, gently rounded abdomen and powerful bandy legs. During the day, he can be found in the entomology department of the American Museum of Natural History. Sorkin, a senior scientific assistant, has agreed to identify the insects that have been calling my home home since we asked Fred, the building pest control operator, to stop spraying.

"God bless you," Fred used to say at the door, as if we might be seeing each other for the last time.

"What's in this stuff, anyway?" I said to him one day. Malathion, a controversial pesticide, was on the list.

Normally I admire bugs, which happens to be the scientific name for insects that have a modified beaklike mouth. As a child, I collected them in glass cigar tubes my father brought home from his restaurant. Bugs are <u>microcosms</u> and microcosms are <u>metaphors</u>. But something was eating grooves in my favorite brown hat. A black crawly thing with more legs than the Rockettes had staked out the north bedroom wall. There was a fauna in the freezer and a bug as shiny as patent leather had moved into the water gauge of our electric coffee maker. Darkest of

microcosms (mī´ krō kāz´əms) *n.* little worlds

metaphors (met´ə fôrz´) *n.* ways of speaking of things as though they were something else

all, there were definite signs of wildlife in the back-room closet a former tenant had jury-rigged into a shower. Whatever it was, it was big.

What I'm hoping Louis N. Sorkin will tell me is what eats what and whether biological warfare is an apartment possibility. California used Australian ladybugs to get rid of cottony-cushion scale. The Mormons lucked out when sea gulls saved them from the locusts. Could my pests have natural enemies on the food chain, something besides the Tokay gecko that barks at night and looks like a Tokay gecko?

Sorkin greets me in a hall stacked six feet high with drawers of Pyraustinae, a moth. We scuttle into a room crammed with journals, papers and boxes of stoppered vials. On the wall, a sign reads, "Feeling Lousy?" Sorkin's desk is littered with dental tools, mail, baby food jars and mugs with spoons—roach heaven.

I hand him my hat. He tweezes something off the brim and puts it under his microscope.

"This is a shed skin of one of the dermestid beetles in the larval stage," he says. "I think this one is the Anthrenus species. They've been grazing along it here . . . here . . . they like wool. In New York City, they live under the parquet floor.[1] Hair is a very good food source for them."

"What do they eat on hair?"

"The hair itself. It's protein."

I empty two shopping bags filled with takeout containers and hand over the freezer specimen.

It turns out that it's an immature German cockroach, which means, Sorkin says, it could have been found anywhere. Of my 21 specimens, 11 are German cockroaches. This comes as a big surprise because some look like black dots, some are pear-shaped with pale dorsal banding and some look like greasy pecan shells. Sorkin explains that roaches have a three-stage metamorphosis, going from egg to wingless nymph to adult. During the nymph stage, they molt up to seven times.

Reading Strategy
Establishing a Purpose for Reading What purpose have you set for reading this article?

"German cockroaches are called Belgian cockroaches in Germany," Sorkin says, scratching his arm. I scratch mine too. "They're also called steam-bugs, shiners and Yankee settlers."

He studies a bug I found in my colander under the grapes.

"Oh! Otiorhynchus ovatus! A strawberry root weevil. It's an outdoor weevil that sometimes comes into homes as it migrates."

"How would it get into a fourth-floor apartment?"

"They crawl."

"Would it eat my roaches?"

"It would starve."

I show him an arachnid that has spun a web in its container. Maybe it eats strawberry root weevils.

---

1. **parquet** (pär kā′) **floor** wooden floor in which the pieces of wood fit together to form a pattern.

Reading Check

What does Sorkin say is a very good food source for dermestid beetles?

"This is a jumping spider. Normally it would be outside."

Sorkin peers into the container with the north-wall stalker.

"A house centipede!" His mustache twitches. "This is a neat animal! Chilopoda have their front legs modified to inject venom. They're predators. They live on roaches and spiders and probably other centipedes."

Bingo! A natural roach enemy. "So if I introduce more Chilopods, they'll get rid of the roaches?"

"Not completely. You'd have to isolate your apartment. If you could keep them from gaining access through cracks and wall voids and holes around pipes and the door to the hallway, yeah, you could have a really insect-free zone."

The phone rings. It rings all day. Louis Sorkin is the 911 of insect emergencies. If you open your safe and bugs fly in your face or you need to know whether New Mexican centipedes produce cyanide, Sorkin's your man.

He studies two flies I found on the bathroom windowsill. There's no masking his disgust.

"These are a little moldy or fungus-y. They look like houseflies, Musca domestica."

He checks a dust ball from under our bed for dust mites, which spend their days with their mouths open, waiting for scales to drop from our skin.

"Can't see much here."

"Is it true that there are things that live on our eyelids?"

"There are two species of certain follicle mites around the nose and forehead."

"What's the reason for us to have them?"

"They're just there. Demidex folliculorum. They feed on the material in the hair follicles and usually don't cause any trouble whatsoever. Hold your skin tight like this"—Sorkin pulls his forehead to the side with four fingers—"and push it with a 3-by-5 card and look at what you pushed on a slide, you might even find them."

I try it, but even with magnification of 200, nothing shows up. Maybe moisturizer kills them.

Sorkin checks sweepings from the back-room closet shower.

"This is an American cockroach. You also have the shed skin of what looks like another Anthrenus species and an Odd beetle. The reason it has that name is because the male and female don't look alike. So you've got three different things in here."

On deck is my strangest bug. It suspends itself in liquid, like a peanut in pudding.

"Oh yeah." Sorkin recognizes it instantly. "This is a tortoise beetle. When they're alive they're sometimes gold-colored."

"How did it get in the apartment?"

"Flew."

Sorkin helps me load the containers back into the

Literary Analysis
Feature Article Which humorous lines add human interest to the article?

Reading Strategy
Establishing a Purpose for Reading What reading purpose do these odd and interesting facts support?

shopping bag. I head home thinking about the high drama that goes on behind the kitchen pegboard and wondering about the strawberry root weevil. What compelled it to climb four stories to a place where it would find nothing to eat? A strawberry root weevil entering an apartment is a suicidal gesture . . . .

The next morning, while I'm getting coffee, a juvenile roach heads for the food processor. Although I can do 3.8 m.p.h. on the treadmill and the fastest roach in the world can only go 2.9, I'm no match for it. In the sink, there's a mature female that looks like she's carrying a purse. She died with her egg case stuck in her. Before Sorkin, I never would have found this <u>poignant</u>. Sipping coffee, I gaze at the ceiling. That's when it hits me: I've neglected my prime bug habitat.

Back at the museum, Sorkin rotates a new container with hundreds of insects and insect fragments I've retrieved from our glass ceiling fixture.

"There's . . . a hover fly . . . a spotted cucumber beetle . . . staphylinid beetles . . . a carabid stink beetle . . . ichneumon wasps . . . leaf hoppers . . . a ladybird beetle . . . a fungus beetle . . . a silverfish . . . mirid plant bugs . . . a chironomid midge . . . drugstore beetles . . . and . . . more dermestids. All these insects are attracted to light and they fly in. Then they die and the dermestids eat them."

"How do the dermestids know they're in there?"

"They smell them."

I ask Sorkin about my most surprising insect encounter:

"One night, I was making guacamole and when I put in the chili powder it started to move. How could insects live on something so hot?"

"Oh, cigarette beetles are very common in dried pepper. They do quite well. Some insects feed on insecticide."

I follow Sorkin to another room. He points to a heap of black molts from his tarantula (they would make terrific earmuffs), then lifts the lid off a plastic tray. There it is, ready to pounce, a furry ball of <u>malevolence</u>. Sorkin shows me a jar of preserved insects saved at the 100th anniversary dinner of the New York Entomological Society. There's a cerambycid larva as big as a parsnip, giant meal worms and a black thing the size of a small hamburger.

"This is a belostomadid, or true water bug, from Thailand. The body has a Gorgonzola cheese flavor."

Sorkin's personal favorite is grubs over easy.

"Tastes like bacon," he says.

"Are bugs kosher?"[2]

"Uh, well, yes and no. There are references in the Bible that say six species of locust are kosher, but there's some discussion that people were really referring to locust *beans*."

Sorkin is encyclopedic. Sorkin can answer anything. Talking to Sorkin is like playing "Stump the Stars": No, a roach cannot live on the glue of one postage stamp for a year. Even though we find them that

---

2. **kosher** (kō´ shər) *adj.* fit to eat according to Jewish dietary laws.

poignant (poin´ yənt) *adj.* drawing forth compassion; moving

malevolence (mə lev´ ə ləns) *n.* bad or evil feelings or intentions

✔ **Reading Check**

What happens to Volk's guacamole when she adds chili powder?

way, insects don't always die on their backs. (Their legs bend in or they twitch and fall over.) There is no such thing as a *hen*-roach. It would not destroy the balance of nature if all pest species were eliminated from apartments, since that's not their natural habitat anyway. Roaches probably got into Biosphere 2 on packaging, same as we import them from the supermarket. After you've finished the bananas, fruit flies go back outside. Centipedes don't have a hundred legs. They have one pair per body segment, and 20 to 30 segments is normal. New insects are being discovered all the time. Recently Sorkin was <u>immortalized</u> by a parasitic moth mite, *Charletonia sorkini*.

"Can you look at a bite and tell what did it?"

"Sometimes," Sorkin says. "Bedbugs bite in a line. Fleas," he taps his sock, "usually bite at ground level."

I show him the back of my neck.

"None of your samples did that."

I thank Sorkin for his help. While my problem hasn't been solved, at least I know more about it. And I don't have cereal mites, black carpet beetles, termites, bedbugs, furniture carpet beetles, Trogoderma beetles, fleas and Anthrenus carpet beetles. Head lice, now that the kids are out of elementary school, are a thing of the past. If many of my insects come in with fresh air, what's the alternative? When you think about it, living close to nature, even on a tiny scale, is a privilege in a city.

When greeting, insects antennate, tapping each other with their antennae to check out who they're dealing with. Sorkin and I nod goodbye and shake hands, a *Homo sapiens*-specific ritual.

immortalized (i môr´ tə līzd) *v.* given lasting fame

Review and Assess

Thinking About the Selection

1. **Respond:** What was the most interesting thing you learned from this article?

2. **(a) Recall:** What reason does Patricia Volk give for visiting the entomologist? **(b) Analyze:** Does her stated reason strike you as a sensible response? Why?

3. **(a) Recall:** What do most of the bugs in the first batch turn out to be? **(b) Deduce:** Why does this surprise Volk?

4. **(a) Infer:** How is the author's attitude toward bugs changed by what she learns? **(b) Analyze:** How does she demonstrate her change in attitude? **(c) Speculate:** Do you think her new attitude will be temporary or long-term?

5. **Evaluate:** The author seems to imply that problems and annoyances are easier to cope with if you maintain a light, easygoing attitude. Do you agree or disagree? Explain.

Patricia Volk

(b. 1943)

In her youth, Volk focused on the visual arts. She worked as an art director at advertising agencies and at magazines such as *Seventeen* and *Harper's Bazaar*. A passion for writing soon emerged, and in 1988 she became a full-time writer.

Her short stories, articles, and novels—even the award-winning advertisements she has written—display her quirky sense of humor. Having spent almost all her life in New York City, she has a keen sense of the everyday humor of modern urban life.

Review and Assess

Literary Analysis

Feature Article

1. How well does "An Entomological Study of Apartment 4A" fit the criteria for a **feature article**?
2. What is one entertaining aspect of the article? Explain.
3. Using a chart like the one shown here, identify at least four facts you found in the article. For each, identify how it is useful or valuable.

Information ···▶ **How Is It Useful?**

4. Do you consider Patricia Volk's article to be a genuine human-interest story? Why?

Connecting Literary Elements

5. By the end of the article, the **main idea** is revealed to the reader. (a) What is this central point? (b) Use a chart like this to explain which details from the article help to convey the main idea.

Main Idea:		
Details:	Details:	Details:

6. The author finds a dead cockroach and describes the scene as "poignant." Does a moment like this reinforce or depart from the main idea? Explain.

Reading Strategy

Establishing a Purpose for Reading

7. (a) What was your own **purpose for reading**? (b) Why did you select this particular purpose?
8. Identify at least three facts or incidents from the article that helped you achieve your purpose.

Extend Understanding

9. **Science Connection:** The use of pesticides is often a subject of debate. Do you agree with Patricia Volk's approach to pest control? Explain why or why not.

Integrate Language Skills

Vocabulary Development Lesson

Word Analysis: Greek Prefix *micro-*

The Greek prefix *micro-* means "small." Thus, the word *microcosm* means "small world." Using this information, match each of the following words with its definition.

a. microorganism **b.** microfilm **c.** microcomputer

   1. an electronic device of reduced size
   2. a tiny life form
   3. a format for storing reduced-size images

Spelling Strategy

When you attach a prefix to a word, the spelling of the original word does not change. For example, *im- + mortal = immortal*.

Add *il-*, *mis-*, or *hemi-* to each word below to form three properly spelled words.

   1. fire   **2.** sphere   **3.** legal

Fluency: Sentence Completions

On your paper, write the following sentences. Then, fill in the blanks with a form of the most appropriate word from the vocabulary list on page 389.

   1. In poems and stories, a road is often a ____?____ for life.
   2. The wicked villain planned to blow up the city out of sheer ____?____.
   3. Philosophers have said that human beings are ____?____ of nature; by understanding people, you can understand nature.
   4. The hero's adventures were ____?____ in song and story.
   5. The ____?____ plot had us all sniffling by the end of the movie.

Grammar Lesson

Indirect Objects

An **indirect object** is a noun or pronoun that names the person or thing that receives the action of the verb. You can tell whether a word is the indirect object by finding the direct object and asking *to / for whom?* or *to / for what?* after the action verb. An indirect object always comes between the subject and its direct object, and it never appears in a sentence without a direct object.

	S	V	IO
Example: Patricia Volk	gave	Louis Sorkin

  DO
some insects. *(gave insects to whom?)*

Practice Identify the indirect object in each sentence.

   1. Fred gave Patricia Volk a promise that he would stop spraying.
   2. I handed the entomologist my hat with the grooves in it.
   3. Sorkin offered her some information on the bugs in her house.
   4. The bugs gave them an itchy feeling.
   5. Later, Sorkin showed her a jar of insects.

Writing Application Use each word below as an indirect object in a sentence.

   1. cockroaches   **2.** apartment

W̶G Prentice Hall Writing and Grammar Connection: Chapter 20, Section 3

Writing Lesson

A Letter to an Expert

The entomologist Louis Sorkin played an important part in Patricia Volk's article. Write a letter asking him for information on an interesting insect you have found.

Prewriting   List insects that you frequently see around your neighborhood. Choose one that interests you. Then, jot down some questions about it.

Drafting   In the body of the letter, identify yourself, explain why you are interested in the insect, and ask your questions. Your letter should be straightforward and have the right level of formality: In this case, use the recipient's title and last name, be polite, and avoid slang.

Revising   Make sure that your letter includes a heading, an inside address, a salutation, body, closing, and signature. Then, revise to eliminate any language that may be too informal.

Model: Revising for the Right Level of Formality

several

I have noticed ~~tons of~~ gray fuzzy insects on the sidewalks

near my house. ~~Gross!~~ They appeared one day last week.

> When in doubt, use formal language. It is better to be considered too proper rather than impolite.

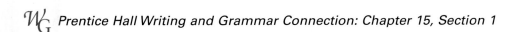

Prentice Hall Writing and Grammar Connection: Chapter 15, Section 1

Extension Activities

Listening and Speaking Patricia Volk has grown wary of pesticides. Work with a partner or a group to conduct a **print and television ad review** for pest-control products. You should

- identify the techniques used to sell these products.
- compare advertising claims for the various pesticides.

Follow up with a small-group discussion of what you have learned. **[Group Activity]**

Research and Technology Volk's feature article is meant to entertain, yet it addresses a broad subject—the world of insects. Use the article as a springboard for your own **entomological study.** Identify the categories or criteria you will use to classify the insects you study. Then, generate a database that provides information on a variety of bugs.

 **Take It to the Net**   www.phschool.com

Go online for an additional research activity using the Internet.

READING INFORMATIONAL MATERIALS

Newspaper Articles

About Newspaper Articles

A newspaper is a form of print media. Its main purpose is to inform the public by presenting news and commentary.

- A *daily newspaper* covers international, national, state, and local news with articles on topics such as politics, economics, education, and science. Newspapers also present feature articles that showcase trends, unusual people and events, and other topics of continuing interest.

- A *weekly newspaper* usually has a smaller readership than a daily. Its articles report more personal kinds of news, such as local weddings or fires.

- A *special-interest newspaper* runs articles of interest to one particular group of people, such as teachers, parents, or immigrants.

Reading Strategy

Analyzing Text Structure

Text structure is the way a piece of writing is organized and presented. Writers use different structures for a variety of needs. In a front-page news article, for example, the first paragraph contains the basic facts of the story. In a feature article, the structure may be more relaxed.

"Cows on Parade" is a feature article written for a special-interest business newspaper, *The Business Journal* of Milwaukee. The writer adopts a casual tone and does not present any financial information until the fourth paragraph. As you read the article, use a chart like the one below to note the kinds of information—factual details, quotations, summaries—included in the text. Indicate the location of each type of information you find.

	Vivid Scene	Summary of Central Event	Details: who, what, when, where, or how	Quotation	General Background Information
Paragraph 1			*Where:* Chicago *What:* the cow		
Paragraph 2	320 painted fiberglass cows				

'Cows on parade' find sweet home in Chicago

After success in big city, cow caravan not herded for dairy state

David Schuyler

The city of Chicago has adopted one of Wisconsin's dearest symbols—the cow.

Make that 320 of them, to be exact. They're made of fiberglass, painted, prettied up by local artists and displayed about the city's streets in what may be the country's goofiest and most well-received public art project ever.

Chicago's "Cows on Parade" public art spectacle, a project of the Public Art Program of the Department of Cultural Affairs, is being credited for a boom in the tourism trade that could add an extra $100 million or more to the city's economy. Not bad for a bunch of beautified bovines that only had to hang around—literally, for some—for four months.

"We really didn't anticipate the effect they would have on people," said Dorothy Coyle, director of tourism for the city of Chicago. "The publicity was tremendous and it did result in people traveling to Chicago just to see the cows."

Given the success of the cows in the big city, what about the idea of displaying the cows in their true home state as a tourist attraction?

Members of the Milwaukee Riverwalk District

Board recently visited Chicago to view the display and consider the possibility of bringing the cows to Milwaukee, said board member Marsha Sehler.

"They were terrific, but what was more terrific was the reaction. Everybody was buying film and cameras at that Walgreens on Michigan Avenue," said Sehler.

NOT A COWTOWN

The organization, however, has since decided not to pursue the project.

Fellow Riverwalk District Board member Lisa Bailey believed that Milwaukee would not receive any benefit from hosting the cows, particularly with a number of other American cities considering a similar display.

"It didn't make sense to bring the cows here to Milwaukee," she said. "We don't want to look like a secondhand city."

If any plans to bring the cows to Wisconsin are in the works, they have yet to be made public.

The life-size cow replicas were displayed in Chicago from June 15 to Oct. 31, and received with open arms by both natives and visitors of the city with big shoulders. People crowded around cows in a variety of settings: on the sidewalks along North Michigan Avenue, outside of the Museum of Science and Industry, floating in the terminal of O'Hare International Airport, and climbing up the sides of buildings.

Cows appeared along

A quotation by someone directly involved in the event provides important information for readers.

Background information about the event helps you understand the current situation better.

continued next page

city streets adorned as ladybugs, as waiters, as Picasso paintings and, of course, as the cow that jumped over the moon. One of three representations of Mrs. O'Leary's cow, long-blamed for starting the Chicago fire of 1871, still had monkeys on its back. In one bad pun, a cow, sponsored by Harry Caray's Restaurant, had holes drilled through it to represent the late WGN sportscaster's exclamation, "Holy cow!"

This paragraph would be of particular interest to a business newspaper's readers.

Chicago adapted the idea from the Swiss. Chicago businessman Peter Hanig saw a similar display while on vacation in Zurich, Switzerland, last year and promoted the concept for the city, said Coyle.

Zurich displayed 800 cows in its "Cow Parade" project, resulting in approximately $100 million in additional tourism dollars coming into the city, Coyle said.

Chicago tourism officials won't have any figures on the project's economic impact until December, but they are confident of its success.

"We believe that we will actually surpass that amount," Coyle said.

A brief subhead signals that a new main idea will follow. You can find the main idea and its supporting details in the section that follows.

OUT-MOO-NEUVERING NYC

Chicago, however, wasn't the only city that had heard of the Zurich event. When the city discovered that New York City was also considering having a cow parade, Chicago officials moved quickly.

The city negotiated a licensing agreement with the Swiss government to exclusively feature a United States cow event for 1999.

The city received a $100,000 grant from the state of Illinois to help fund the project. An additional $100,000 was raised from Michigan Avenue businesses by the Cows on Parade Committee, co-chaired by Hanig.

The city purchased 320 fiberglass cows and charged local businesses and individuals $3,500 each to have an artist produce a cow with a design approved by the city. Businesses could also choose to have an artist draw up their own design, which still had to be approved by city officials, Coyle said.

Some more renowned artists demanded more, a cost which was picked up by the company buying the cow. One cow was reportedly sold for $11,000.

ALLEN-EDMONDS HAS A COW

Footwear businessman Hanig contacted Port Washington-based Allen-Edmonds Shoe Corp. about purchasing one of the cows, said Louis Ripple, director of sales and marketing.

The company became interested in its industry colleague's pitch and decided to buy a cow and have it displayed in front of its Michigan Avenue store.

"The customers really enjoyed it," he said. "We certainly had a lot of comments."

Ripple credits the cow—Shoe Horn—for bringing people into the store and even purchasing shoes. With the Chicago project now completed, the company plans to bring the cow to Wisconsin and have it displayed in its Port Washington headquarters, Ripple said.

The cows' combination of public art with something recognizably down-home may account for their popularity, said Curtis Carter, director of the Haggerty Museum of Art in Milwaukee.

"They are easily accessible to a wide range of the population," he said. "You don't need a degree in art history to appreciate these."

Juxtaposing a rural symbol with an urban setting also fits well with the socially provocative nature of public art and adds to the irony and wit of the sculptures, Carter said.

While Milwaukee takes a pass, at least 28 other cities are exploring their own cow parades, Coyle said. Variations on the theme are also being considered, such as pigs, lizards, lions, coffee cups and basketballs, she said.

As for Chicago, "we will come up with something completely different," said Coyle.

Check Your Comprehension

1. What effect did the cows have on tourism in Chicago?
2. Why did Milwaukee officials vote against the cows?
3. Where did the idea of the cows originate?

Applying the Reading Strategy

Analyzing Text Structure

4. How does "Cows on Parade" differ in format from an article you might see on the front page of a daily newspaper?
5. How does the paragraph about cows appearing as ladybugs, waiters, and Picasso paintings help reinforce the writer's purpose?

Activity

Developing a K-W-L Chart

Having read a newspaper article about painted fiberglass cows, you now possess a certain amount of knowledge on the subject. However, you may wish to learn even more about the topic.

Create a K-W-L chart like the one shown here. In the first column, write down important details that you already **know** about the cows. In the second column, list questions indicating what you still **want** to learn about them. Consult newspapers and magazines in a library and go to Internet Web sites to find information that can answer your questions. In the third column of the chart, record what you **learned** and how you obtained the information.

What I *Know*	What I *Want* to Know	What I *Learned* and Where
Cows were a success in Chicago.	What reaction did they generate in New York City?	
One cow was sold for $11,000.	What is the most anyone paid for a cow?	

Contrasting Informational Materials

Feature Articles, Art Reviews, and Advertisements

1. "Cows on Parade" is a feature article: The author draws in readers with humor and does not present hard facts for several paragraphs. Imagine that the cow display had been the subject of an art critic's review instead of a reporter's feature story. Explain how the information and details would have been structured differently.
2. Imagine that the cow exhibit were the subject of an advertisement or brochure meant to draw tourists to Chicago. How would the writing differ in structure from the feature article?

Prepare to Read

Jabberwocky ◆ Macavity: The Mystery Cat ◆ Problems With Hurricanes

 Take It to the Net

Visit www.phschool.com for interactive activities and instruction related to the selections, including

- background
- graphic organizers
- literary elements
- reading strategies

Preview

Connecting to the Literature

You can probably remember enjoying silly nursery rhymes and songs when you were young. Not all funny poems are written for children, though. As you will see, poems like the ones you are about to read can make you laugh out loud.

Background

The farmer, or "campesino," in "Problems With Hurricanes" says, "Don't worry about the water / Don't worry about the wind—," but that is exactly what you should worry about in such a storm. As a hurricane approaches land, strong rains form huge ocean waves, called storm surges, that can cause severe flooding. Puerto Rico, the poet's homeland, is in a hurricane region where the storm season extends from August to October.

Literary Analysis

Humorous Diction

A writer's **diction**, or word choice, can help create a humorous effect. For example, writers may intentionally use the wrong word, use formal or informal English, or even invent unusual words. In the following line from "Macavity: The Mystery Cat," notice how the sophisticated words used to describe a cat contribute to the humor:

> For he's a fiend in feline shape, a monster of depravity.

As you read these three poems, think about how each writer's word choice makes you smile.

Comparing Literary Works

In each of the poems you are about to read, repetition is used to create a unique effect. **Repetition** is the use of any element of language—a sound, word, phrase, clause, or sentence—more than once. Poets use many kinds of repetition to add emphasis, drama, or musical rhythm to a poem. Compare the way lines, words, or stanzas are repeated in these poems, and consider the effect of the repetition.

Reading Strategy

Contrasting the Serious and the Ridiculous

One way in which these poems achieve humor is by combining the **serious** with the **ridiculous**. Consider, for example, these lines from "Problems With Hurricanes":

> How would your family / feel if they had to tell
> The generations that you / got killed by a flying / Banana.

Death is serious indeed, but a flying banana is just plain silly, and the combination of the two details makes most readers chuckle. To help you contrast the serious and ridiculous details, use a chart like this one.

Vocabulary Development

chortled (chôrt´ 'ld) v. made a jolly, chuckling sound (p. 401)

bafflement (baf´ əl mənt) n. puzzlement; bewilderment (p. 403)

levitation (lev i tā´ shən) n. the illusion of keeping a heavy body in the air without visible support (p. 403)

feline (fē´ līn) adj. catlike (p. 403)

depravity (dē prav´ ə tē) n. crookedness; corruption (p. 403)

larder (lärd´ ər) n. place where food is kept; pantry (p. 403)

suavity (swä´ və tē) n. quality of being socially smooth (p. 404)

projectiles (prō jek´ təlz) n. objects that are hurled through the air (p. 405)

Jabberwocky

Lewis Carroll

'Twas brillig, and the slithy toves
    Did gyre and gimble in the wabe;
All mimsy were the borogoves,
    And the mome raths outgrabe.

5   "Beware the Jabberwock, my son!
    The jaws that bite, the claws that catch!
Beware the Jubjub bird, and shun
    The frumious Bandersnatch!"

He took his vorpal sword in hand:
10   Long time the manxome foe he sought—
So rested he by the Tumtum tree,
    And stood awhile in thought.

Literature in context   Language Connection

Alice encounters a creature called a Jabberwock in the first chapter of *Through the Looking-Glass*. She cannot understand it, so the character Humpty Dumpty explains some of its words, including these:

brillig: four o'clock in the afternoon, the time when you begin broiling things for dinner

toves: creatures that are something like badgers, something like lizards, and something like corkscrews

gyre: go round and round like a gyroscope

gimble: make holes like a gimlet (a hand tool that bores holes)

wabe: grass plot around a sundial

mome: having lost the way home

raths: something like green pigs

The Jabberwock, 1872, John Tenniel

And as in uffish thought he stood,
    The Jabberwock, with eyes of flame,
15 Came whiffling through the tulgey wood,
    And burbled as it came!

One, two! One, two! And through and through
    The vorpal blade went snicker-snack!
He left it dead, and with its head
20   He went galumphing back.

"And hast thou slain the Jabberwock?
    Come to my arms, my beamish boy!
O frabjous day! Callooh! Callay!"
    He <u>chortled</u> in his joy.

25 'Twas brillig, and the slithy toves
    Did gyre and gimble in the wabe;
All mimsy were the borogoves,
    And the mome raths outgrabe.

chortled (chôrt′ 'ld) *v.*
made a jolly, chuckling
sound

Review and Assess

Thinking About the Selection

1. **Respond:** What images did this poem bring to mind?

2. **(a) Recall:** State in your own words the warning given in the second stanza of the poem. **(b) Analyze:** How would you describe the overall mood of "Jabberwocky"?

3. **(a) Recall:** What does the hero do after being warned about the Jabberwock? **(b) Evaluate:** One critic said that "Jabberwocky," despite its odd language, tells a story like many legends of knights and dragons. Do you agree? Why or why not? **(c) Assess:** Do you think the poem pokes fun at knighthood? Explain.

4. **(a) Interpret:** You can often tell the part of speech of a word even if you do not understand it. Identify the part of speech of three of the made-up words in this poem. Explain how you arrived at each answer. **(b) Apply:** How can a poem like "Jabberwocky" give readers a better understanding of language?

5. **Speculate:** Do you think it is easier or more challenging to write a poem with invented language? Explain.

Lewis Carroll

(1832–1898)

Charles Lutwidge Dodgson was a professor of mathematics, an ordained deacon in the Church of England, and a talented early photographer. Yet today, he is best remembered for two children's books he wrote under the pen name Lewis Carroll: *Alice's Adventures in Wonderland* (1865) and its sequel, *Through the Looking-Glass* (1871). Both feature a young girl named Alice whose curiosity leads her into amazing fantasy worlds. Huge bestsellers almost from the moment they appeared, the *Alice* books have been the basis of numerous stage plays, television adaptations, and live and animated movies.

Macavity:

T. S. Eliot

Illustration from *Old Possum's Book of Practical Cats*, Edward Gorey

◄ **Critical Viewing**
Judging from this
illustration, what do you
think is the spirit
of the poem? **[Infer]**

The Mystery Cat

Macavity's a Mystery Cat: he's called the Hidden Paw—
For he's the master criminal who can defy the Law.
He's the <u>bafflement</u> of Scotland Yard,[1] the Flying Squad's[2]
    despair:
5 For when they reach the scene of crime—*Macavity's not*
    there!

Macavity, Macavity, there's no one like Macavity,
He's broken every human law, he breaks the law of gravity.
His powers of <u>levitation</u> would make a fakir[3] stare,
10 And when you reach the scene of crime—*Macavity's not there!*
You may seek him in the basement, you may look up in the
    air—
But I tell you once and once again, *Macavity's not there!*

Macavity's a ginger cat, he's very tall and thin;
15 You would know him if you saw him, for his eyes are sunken in.
His brow is deeply lined with thought, his head is highly
    domed;
His coat is dusty from neglect, his whiskers are uncombed.
He sways his head from side to side, with movements like a
20   snake;
And when you think he's half asleep, he's always wide awake.

Macavity, Macavity, there's no one like Macavity,
For he's a fiend in <u>feline</u> shape, a monster of <u>depravity</u>.
You may meet him in a by-street, you may see him in the
25   square—
But when a crime's discovered, then *Macavity's not there!*

He's outwardly respectable. (They say he cheats at cards.)
And his footprints are not found in any file of Scotland Yard's.
And when the <u>larder</u>'s looted, or the jewel-case is rifled,
30 Or when the milk is missing, or another Peke's[4] been stifled,
Or the greenhouse glass is broken, and the trellis past repair—
Ay, there's the wonder of the thing! *Macavity's not there!*

---

1. **Scotland Yard** London police.
2. **Flying Squad** criminal-investigation department.
3. **fakir** (fə kir´) *n.* Muslim or Hindu beggar who claims to perform miracles.
4. **Peke** short for Pekingese, a small dog with long, silky hair and a pug nose.

bafflement (baf´ əl mənt) *n.* puzzlement; bewilderment

levitation (lev i tā´ shən) *n.* the illusion of keeping a heavy body in the air without visible support

feline (fē´ līn) *adj.* catlike

depravity (dē prav´ ə tē) *n.* crookedness; corruption

larder (lärd´ ər) *n.* place where food is kept; pantry

**Reading Check**

Which unusual detail links or separates Macavity from crime scenes?

Death by drowning has honor
15 If the wind picked you up
and slammed you
Against a mountain boulder
This would not carry shame
But
20 to suffer a mango smashing
Your skull
or a plantain hitting your
Temple at 70 miles per hour
is the ultimate disgrace.

25 The campesino takes off his hat—
As a sign of respect
toward the fury of the wind
And says:
Don't worry about the noise
30 Don't worry about the water
Don't worry about the wind—
If you are going out
beware of mangoes
And all such beautiful
35 sweet things.

Review and Assess

Thinking About the Selection

1. **Respond:** What amusing images does this poem create?

2. **(a) Recall:** According to the campesino, which causes of death would be worse than drowning or being slammed into a mountain by the wind? **(b) Distinguish:** What seems to be the difference for him between a noble and a shameful hurricane death?

3. **(a) Recall:** Which question does the campesino ask in the second stanza? **(b) Infer:** What is he suggesting about how one family member's death affects future generations? **(c) Assess:** Do you think the campesino is a reliable judge of human behavior?

4. **Modify:** How would the poem be affected if the last four lines were not included?

5. **(a) Analyze:** How would you describe the tone or mood of this poem? **(b) Support:** Which words or images create this tone?

Victor Hernández Cruz

(b. 1949)

A native of Puerto Rico, Victor Hernández Cruz moved to New York City with his family while still a boy. As a poet, Cruz pioneered a style called Nuyorican, a combination of English and Spanish dotted with slang that became popular among New York poets of Puerto Rican descent. He is also known for powerful oral readings that twice saw him crowned World Heavyweight Poetry Champion in Taos, New Mexico.

Review and Assess

Literary Analysis

Humorous Diction

1. Find at least three words or phrases in "Macavity" that seem typical of mystery or crime fiction. How do these words contribute to the poem's **humorous diction**?
2. (a) Rewrite three sentences from "Jabberwocky" using familiar words. (b) Is it still funny? Explain.

Comparing Literary Works

3. (a) Using a chart like the one below, compare the humorous diction found in each poem. (b) Does diction play an equally strong role in creating humor in each poem? Explain.

Poem	Serious Subject	Humorous Diction

4. (a) Compare the technique of **repetition** used in each of the poems. (b) In your opinion, which poem makes the best use of repetition?

Reading Strategy

Contrasting the Serious and the Ridiculous

5. Sum up what is most serious and most ridiculous in each of the three poems.
6. What point do you think each poet is making through this contrast?
7. Of the three, which poem do you think is the most serious? Explain your choice.

Extend Understanding

8. **Cultural Connection:** "Macavity: The Mystery Cat" refers to several qualities of cats. Cats have played an important role in human society for thousands of years. "Curiosity killed the cat" is a common saying in our society. Explain the meaning of this saying. Come up with two more sayings or legends about cats and explain their meanings.

Integrate Language Skills

Vocabulary Development Lesson

Word Origins: Portmanteau Words

"Jabberwocky" contains many invented words, including some formed by blending two words into one—like *chortled*, combining *chuckle* and *snort*, or *mimsy*, combining *miserable* and *flimsy*. Such words are now known as **portmanteau words**.

Use a dictionary, if necessary, to explain the origins of these portmanteau words:

    1. smog   **2.** brunch   **3.** motel

Spelling Strategy

The *shun/zhun* sound in a suffix is spelled *ssion* or *tion/sion*. The *shun* sound can be heard in *fission* and *levitation*; the *zhun* sound, in *invasion*.

Complete each word below with the correct form of the *shun/zhun* sound.

    1. deci___   **2.** transmi___   **3.** transla___

Fluency: Sentence Completion

Complete each sentence with a vocabulary word from the list on page 399.

1. The magician seemed to perform ___?___, for it looked as if a person floated in air.
2. Bullets and darts are types of ___?___.
3. Lions are part of the ___?___ family.
4. The poem was written in invented language, to the ___?___ of many readers.
5. Store the food in the ___?___.
6. The sinner had engaged in many forms of ___?___.
7. Jack ___?___ as he observed the outcome of his practical joke.
8. Cary Grant was an actor of great sophistication and ___?___.

Grammar Lesson

Predicate Adjectives

In sentences formed with linking verbs, the verb can be completed with a predicate adjective. A **predicate adjective** is an adjective that appears with a linking verb and describes the subject of the sentence. Linking verbs, including forms of the verb *be*, express a state of being.

                  S   V PA
Example: The cat was *tall*.

A **compound predicate adjective** is two or more adjectives that appear with the linking verb and describe the subject.

                  S   V PA   PA
Example: The cat was *sneaky* and *mischievous*.

Practice Copy the following sentences. Circle the linking verb. Then, underline each predicate adjective and draw an arrow to the word it modifies.

1. His brow is deep.
2. Macavity was good at escaping.
3. He appears respectable and smart.
4. The whiskers are uncombed.
5. They have looked for him everywhere because they are thorough.

Writing Application Write two sentences using the following items as predicate adjectives.

1. deceitful
2. shocked and dismayed

WG *Prentice Hall Writing and Grammar Connection: Chapter 20, Section 3*

Writing Lesson

Fantastic Poem

The poems in this section are unusual, to say the least. Write your own unusual poem about one of the fantastic creatures or events you have just read about.

Prewriting List precise details that you might use to describe this unusual creature or event. Choose details that you think will help you achieve an overall mood—humorous, eerie, or something else.

Drafting Write either a free-verse poem—one without a regular rhythm or rhyme scheme—or one with a regular rhythm and rhyme scheme. Use descriptive details that contribute to your overall mood.

Revising Read your poem aloud. Highlight weak or vague words, and replace them with more precise language.

Model: Revising to Add Precise Details

>   *leaped*   *gripping*
> Macavity ~~came~~ out, ~~holding~~ a key in one paw,
>   *gazed*   *admired*
> Curious, he ~~looked~~ around and ~~liked~~ what he saw.

> Words like *leaped* and *gazed* add precise details to the poem.

WG *Prentice Hall Writing and Grammar Connection: Chapter 6, Connected Assignment*

Extension Activities

Research and Technology The poet of "Problems With Hurricanes" is a native of Puerto Rico, a hurricane region. In a group, research and present a **television news report** on weather conditions and foods grown in Puerto Rico.

- Find maps, photographs, and other visuals.
- Look for generalizations you can draw about the climate of the region.

Rehearse and then present your broadcast to the class. **[Group Activity]**

Listening and Speaking Write a **news article** reporting the events found in "Macavity: The Mystery Cat." Give a description of Macavity's appearance. Then, explain why he is considered a master criminal. Try to stay objective, reporting only the facts without including personal opinions. Present the news article to your class.

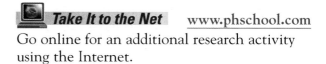 **Take It to the Net**   www.phschool.com

Go online for an additional research activity using the Internet.

Prepare to Read

Talk

 Take It to the Net

Visit www.phschool.com
for interactive activities
and instruction related to
"Talk," including
• background
• graphic organizers
• literary elements
• reading strategies

Preview

Connecting to the Literature

Your breakfast muffin somersaults out of your hands and lands jam side down on the floor. Although the muffin may be called an "inanimate object," it seems to have a mischievous mind of its own. "Talk" is an African folk tale that whimsically nudges this idea a step further.

Background

"Talk" is set on the west coast of Africa, in the country now known as the Republic of Ghana. Many of the story's details reflect the everyday reality of life there. For example, yams, mentioned often in the story, are one of the staples of the diet of rural Ghanaians. In addition, the characters include a fisherman and a weaver, common occupations in Ghana, a country known for its beautiful hand-woven fabrics.

Literary Analysis
Humorous Folk Tale

A **folk tale** is an anonymous story passed down by word of mouth from one generation to the next. With everyday language, folk tales express the beliefs and values of the cultures that create them, and they typically present simple characters and far-fetched situations. A **humorous folk tale**, meant to entertain and to instruct, uses humor or exaggeration to appeal to its audiences. Look at the following example from "Talk":

> . . . a country man went out to his garden to dig up some yams to take to market. While he was digging, one of the yams said to him, "Well at last you're here . . ."

You will see that this fantastic idea of objects that suddenly speak is repeated throughout the story for humorous effect.

Connecting Literary Elements

Personification, often used in folk tales, occurs when a nonhuman subject is given human characteristics. In "Talk," personification contributes to the humor in the folk tale by giving objects the ability to speak. As you read, notice the nonhuman things that seem to come to life.

Reading Strategy
Recognizing Illogical Situations

When reading a folk tale, you might come across situations that could not possibly happen in real life. Illogical situations can make a work of fantasy more fantastic and entertaining. However, these situations can distract you, so it is important to **recognize illogical situations** when you read. To prevent illogical situations from distracting you, follow these strategies:

- Jot down confusing or unusual situations.
- Decide why a situation is illogical.
- Consider what the situation adds to the story.

Use a chart like the one shown here to keep track of the illogical situations you come across in "Talk."

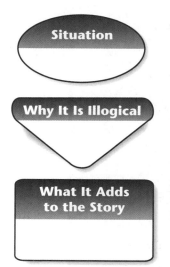

Vocabulary Development

ford (fôrd) *n.* shallow place in a river that can be crossed (p. 413)

refrain (ri frān´) *v.* hold back (p. 414)

scowling (skou´ iŋ) *v.* contracting the eyebrows and frowning to show displeasure (p. 414)

"I went out to my garden to dig yams," the farmer said, waving his arms. "Then everything began to talk! My yam said, 'Leave me alone!' My dog said, 'Pay attention to your yam!' The tree said, 'Put that branch down!' The branch said, 'Do it softly!' And the stone said, 'Take it off me!'"

"And my fish trap said, 'Well, did he take it off?'" the fisherman said.

"And my cloth said, 'You'd run too!'" the weaver said.

"And the river said the same," the bather said hoarsely, his eyes bulging.

The chief listened to them patiently, but he couldn't <u>refrain</u> from <u>scowling</u>. "Now this is really a wild story," he said at last. "You'd better all go back to your work before I punish you for disturbing the peace."

So the men went away, and the chief shook his head and mumbled to himself, "Nonsense like that upsets the community."

"Fantastic, isn't it?" his stool said. "Imagine, a talking yam!"

refrain (ri frān´) v. hold back

scowling (skoul´ iŋ) v. contracting the eyebrows and frowning to show displeasure

Review and Assess

Thinking About the Selection

1. **Respond:** Which situation in "Talk" struck you as the funniest? Why?

2. **(a) Recall:** How does the fisherman react when the country man tells his crazy story? **(b) Analyze:** Why does he get so upset when his fish trap speaks to him?

3. **(a) Recall:** What upsets each man who joins the country man? **(b) Deduce:** What reason might the objects and animals have for speaking all of a sudden?

4. **(a) Recall:** What does the chief say to the men when they come rushing in to tell their stories? **(b) Modify:** What do you think the chief should have said to the men?

5. **(a) Hypothesize:** What might the chief say when his stool talks back to him? **(b) Evaluate:** Would the story have been funnier if it had included what the chief said or did after the stool spoke? Explain.

6. **(a) Compare and Contrast:** What aspects of the story are unique to its West African setting? What elements of the story are universal? **(b) Make a Judgment:** Would most Americans find "Talk" funny? Explain.

7. **(a) Recall:** What happens to every human character after he insults each man who is afraid? **(b) Draw Conclusions:** Which aspects of human nature does the story hold up to ridicule?

Harold Courlander

(b. 1908)

Harold Courlander has had a long, distinguished career as a builder of bridges between different cultures. The settings for his novels range from eighteenth-century Africa to rural Mississippi to the Hopi Nation before the arrival of the Europeans.

George Herzog

(1901–1983)

Born in Budapest, Hungary, George Herzog was a pioneer in the field of ethnomusicology, the study of music for its cultural values and social significance. He also taught courses in linguistics and cultural anthropology and published numerous books on folk music.

Review and Assess

Literary Analysis

Humorous Folk Tale

1. Use a chart like the one below to show how "Talk" fits the criteria of a **humorous folk tale.**

Characters	Simple Language	Far-fetched Situations	Point About Human Nature

2. What image of its culture does "Talk" seem to project? Why?

Connecting Literary Elements

3. Use a chart like the one below to show how the nonhuman characters are **personified** in the folk tale. Write the words that are spoken and the feelings that are conveyed by each character.

Words		Character		Feelings
	◄···		···►	

4. How does personification create a humorous effect in the story?

Reading Strategy

Recognizing Illogical Situations

5. What is illogical about what happens to each man in "Talk"?
6. Does the use of **illogical situations** grow funnier or less funny as the story goes on? Explain.
7. (a) Is the chief's reaction to the men logical or illogical? Explain. (b) How does his response add to the humor?

Extend Understanding

8. **Cultural Connection:** (a) If objects or animals in the United States could speak for a day, which ones might have the most to say? (b) What might they say? Explain.

Quick Review

Humorous folk tales are stories from the oral tradition that both entertain and instruct.

Personification is the attribution of human characteristics to animals or inanimate objects.

To **recognize illogical situations,** test them against your own experiences and knowledge. Then, decide how the illogical situations add to a story.

 Take It to the Net
www.phschool.com
Take the interactive self-test online to check your understanding of the selection.

Integrate Language Skills

Vocabulary Development Lesson

Word Analysis: Latin Prefix *re-*

The word *refrain* uses the Latin prefix *re-*, which means "back" or "again." Thus, the word *refrain* means "to hold oneself back." Other words that use the Latin prefix *re-* include *rewrite* (to write something *again*) and *reflect* (to think *back*).

Using the meaning of *re-*, write the word from the following list that is the best match for each definition below.

   a. rethink   **c.** regenerate

   b. refresh   **d.** redo

1. Produce or grow again
2. Make cooler than before
3. Start over; try again
4. Give something another thought

Concept Development: Antonyms

Write the letter of the word whose meaning is most nearly opposite to that of the first word.

1. scowling: (a) frowning, (b) smiling, (c) resting
2. ford: (a) icy canal, (b) shallow underwater spot, (c) deep underwater spot
3. refrain: (a) continue, (b) stop, (c) begin

Spelling Strategy

In words ending in two vowels plus a consonant, do not double the final consonant before adding an ending that starts with a vowel. For example, *refrain* + *-ed* = *refrained*. In your notebook, write the correct spelling of each word. Then, use each word in a sentence.

   1. shout + *-ed* **2.** look + *-ing* **3.** weed + *-ed*

Grammar Lesson

Predicate Nominatives

A **predicate nominative** is a noun or pronoun that appears with a linking verb (commonly a form of *be*). A predicate nominative renames, identifies, or explains the subject of the sentence. The linking verb acts as an equal sign between the subject and the predicate nominative; both the subject and the predicate nominative name the same person or thing.

In the examples below, the subject is in boldface, the linking verb is in italics, and the predicate nominative is underlined.

>   S   LV   PN
> **Examples:** The **yam** *was* the <u>first</u> to talk.
>
>   S LV   PN
> Now **this** *is* really a wild <u>story</u>.

Practice Copy the following sentences. Label the subject and verb. Then, underline the predicate nominative in each.

1. The story is a folk tale.
2. The chief was a skeptic.
3. The men were sprinters.
4. The branch and stone were talkers.
5. One object in the story was the yam.

Writing Application Use each of the following in a sentence, and then underline the predicate nominative.

1. are talking objects
2. The chief will become

W͜G *Prentice Hall Writing and Grammar Connection: Chapter 20, Section 3*

Writing Lesson

Humorous Folk Tale

Think of your school as a community, with its own culture, customs, and values. Write your own humorous folk tale set in your school. Use simple characters, simple language, and a far-fetched situation. To add humor, personify some of the objects in your school, just as nonhuman things were personified in "Talk."

Prewriting   Choose an event that has happened in your school. Add unusual details to the real-life event to create a far-fetched situation. Gather details about your characters, using a chart like the one shown.

Character	Actions	Description
desk	It can walk and talk.	When it "wakes up," it has a friendly and boisterous personality.

Drafting   As you draft, show, rather than tell, what is happening in the story. Use characters' actions, details of setting, and dialogue to show readers what you want them to see.

Revising   Ask a partner to read your folk tale aloud. Listen closely to the language you have included in your story. Rewrite any dialogue that sounds unnatural to make your characters sound more realistic.

W͞G Prentice Hall Writing and Grammar Connection: Chapter 5, Section 2

Extension Activities

Listening and Speaking Imagine that a famous television interviewer or talk-show host conducts an **interview** with one of the nonhuman characters in "Talk." With another student, role-play this situation.

- Ask questions that will inform and entertain your audience.
- Use appropriate mannerisms and gestures as you talk.

Present your interview to your class. **[Group Activity]**

Research and Technology "Talk" is set in West Africa, near the Gulf of Guinea. Prepare a **cultural report** about this region. Include as many multimedia elements as you can: a map; photographs of people, land, and art; tapes of voices and music; and actual art objects and clothes, if you can find them. Consider creating a multimedia presentation to share your findings.

 Take It to the Net   www.phschool.com

Go online for an additional research activity using the Internet.

Prepare to Read

One Ordinary Day, With Peanuts

 Take It to the Net

Visit www.phschool.com for interactive activities and instruction related to "One Ordinary Day, With Peanuts," including

- background
- graphic organizers
- literary elements
- reading strategies

Preview

Connecting to the Literature

Sometimes it may seem as though there are not enough hours in the day. People often criticize the pace of modern life, complaining that they find it too hectic. As you will see, several of the characters in Shirley Jackson's story are experiencing one of life's frenzied days.

Background

Shirley Jackson's story is set in New York City. More than 8 million people live in the five boroughs that officially make up the city. On a typical workday, a few million more travel in from the suburbs—most of them to work in the island borough of Manhattan. For many people, Manhattan defines their image of New York City.

Literary Analysis

Surprise Ending

A **surprise ending** is an unexpected twist at the close of a story. The writer makes a surprise ending believable by hinting at it earlier in the story, without giving the surprise away. This example shows that the writer carefully conceals some ideas from the reader, hinting at a surprise ending:

> Finally, from half a block away, he saw what he wanted, and moved out into the center of the traffic to intercept a young man, who was hurrying . . .

Based on what you learn in the story, try to predict the ending.

Connecting Literary Elements

The **plot** is the sequence of events that drives the action. In "One Ordinary Day, With Peanuts," the story focuses on the actions of Mr. Johnson after he leaves his apartment early one morning. Events take a surprising twist when he returns home at the end of the day. Notice how the events of the plot lead you to anticipate the story's conclusion.

Reading Strategy

Questioning Characters' Actions

The title of the story suggests that Mr. Johnson's actions are ordinary, but the reader must decide if that is really the case. One way to do so is to **question a character's actions.** For each event, ask these questions:

- What reasons might the character have for this action?
- What behavior on the part of other characters may have led to this action?
- Does the action seem consistent with the character's personality or past behavior?

Use a chart like this one to record your questions and answers.

Action
Mr. Johnson offers to watch the little boy.

Question
What are his motives?

Answer

Vocabulary Development

irradiated (ir rā′ dē āt′ id) v. gave out; radiated (p. 421)

loitered (loit′ ərd) v. hung about; lingered (p. 421)

endeavoring (en dev′ ər iŋ) v. trying; attempting (p. 421)

ominously (äm′ ə nəs lē) adv. in a threatening way (p. 423)

buffeted (buf′ it ed) v. jostled; knocked about (p. 427)

insatiable (in sā′ shə bəl) adj. unable to be satisfied (p. 427)

omen (ō′ mən) n. sign foretelling a future event, either good or evil (p. 428)

impertinent (im pʉrt′ 'n ənt) adj. rude; impolite (p. 430)

"Yep," said the boy.

"Where you going?"

"Vermont."

"Nice place. Plenty of snow there. Maple sugar, too; you like maple sugar?"

"Sure."

"Plenty of maple sugar in Vermont. You going to live on a farm?"

"Going to live with Grandpa."

"Grandpa like peanuts?"

"Sure."

"Ought to take him some," said Mr. Johnson, reaching into his pocket. "Just you and Mommy going?"

"Yep."

"Tell you what," Mr. Johnson said. "You take some peanuts to eat on the train."

The boy's mother, after glancing at them frequently, had seemingly decided that Mr. Johnson was trustworthy, because she had devoted herself wholeheartedly to seeing that the movers did not—what movers rarely do, but every housewife believes they will—crack a leg from her good table, or set a kitchen chair down on a lamp. Most of the furniture was loaded by now, and she was deep in that nervous stage when she knew there was something she had forgotten to pack—hidden away in the back of a closet somewhere, or left at a neighbor's and forgotten, or on a clothesline—and was trying to remember under stress what it was.

"This all, lady?" the chief mover said, completing her dismay.

Uncertainly, she nodded.

"Want to go on the truck with the furniture, sonny?" the mover asked the boy, and laughed. The boy laughed too and said to Mr. Johnson, "I guess I'll have a good time at Vermont."

"Fine time," said Mr. Johnson, and stood up. "Have one more peanut before you go," he said to the boy.

The boy's mother said to Mr. Johnson, "Thank you so much; it was a great help to me."

"Nothing at all," said Mr. Johnson gallantly. "Where in Vermont are you going?"

The mother looked at the little boy accusingly, as though he had given away a secret of some importance, and said unwillingly, "Greenwich."

"Lovely town," said Mr. Johnson. He took out a card, and wrote a name on the back. "Very good friend of mine lives in Greenwich," he said. "Call on him for anything you need. His wife makes the best doughnuts in town," he added soberly to the little boy.

"Swell," said the little boy.

"Goodbye," said Mr. Johnson.

He went on, stepping happily with his new-shod feet, feeling the warm sun on his back and on the top of his head. Halfway down the block he met a stray dog and fed him a peanut.

Reading Strategy
Questioning Characters' Actions Why do you think Mr. Johnson watched the boy?

At the corner, where another wide avenue faced him, Mr. Johnson decided to go on uptown again. Moving with comparative laziness, he was passed on either side by people hurrying and frowning, and people brushed past him going the other way, clattering along to get somewhere quickly. Mr. Johnson stopped on every corner and waited patiently for the light to change, and he stepped out of the way of anyone who seemed to be in any particular hurry, but one young lady came too fast for him, and crashed wildly into him when he stooped to pat a kitten which had run out onto the sidewalk from an apartment house and was now unable to get back through the rushing feet.

"Excuse me," said the young lady, trying frantically to pick up Mr. Johnson and hurry on at the same time, "terribly sorry."

The kitten, regardless now of danger, raced back to its home. "Perfectly all right," said Mr. Johnson, adjusting himself carefully. "You seem to be in a hurry."

"Of course I'm in a hurry," said the young lady. "I'm late."

She was extremely cross and the frown between her eyes seemed well on its way to becoming permanent. She had obviously awakened late, because she had not spent any extra time in making herself look pretty, and her dress was plain and unadorned with collar or brooch, and her lipstick was noticeably crooked. She tried to brush past Mr. Johnson, but, risking her suspicious displeasure, he took her arm and said, "Please wait."

"Look," she said <u>ominously</u>, "I ran into you and your lawyer can see my lawyer and I will gladly pay all damages and all inconveniences suffered therefrom but please this minute let me go because *I am late.*"

"Late for what?" said Mr. Johnson; he tried his winning smile on her but it did no more than keep her, he suspected, from knocking him down again.

▲ **Critical Viewing** This scene is filled with anonymous people moving about. What might Mr. Johnson think about these people? **[Speculate]**

ominously (ăm′ ə nəs lē) *adv.* in a threatening way

**Reading Check**

What happens to Mr. Johnson when he stoops to pat a kitten?

One Ordinary Day, With Peanuts ◆ 423

"Late for work," she said between her teeth. "Late for my employ-ment. I have a job and if I am late I lose exactly so much an hour and I cannot really afford what your pleasant conversation is costing me, be it *ever* so pleasant."

"I'll pay for it," said Mr. Johnson. Now these were magic words, not necessarily because they were true, or because she seriously expected Mr. Johnson to pay for anything, but because Mr. Johnson's flat statement, obviously innocent of irony, could not be, coming from Mr. Johnson, anything but the statement of a responsible and truthful and respectable man.

"What *do* you mean?" she asked.

"I said that since I am obviously responsible for your being late I shall certainly pay for it."

"Don't be silly," she said, and for the first time the frown disap-peared. "I wouldn't expect you to pay for anything—a few minutes ago I was offering to pay *you*. Anyway," she added, almost smiling, "it *was* my fault."

"What happens if you don't go to work?"

She stared. "I don't get paid."

"Precisely," said Mr. Johnson.

"What do you mean, precisely? If I don't show up at the office exactly twenty minutes ago I lose a dollar and twenty cents an hour, or two cents a minute or . . . " She thought. ". . . Almost a dime for the time I've spent talking to you."

Mr. Johnson laughed, and finally she laughed, too. "You're late already," he pointed out. "Will you give me another four cents worth?"

"I don't understand why."

"You'll see," Mr. Johnson promised. He led her over to the side of the walk, next to the buildings, and said, "Stand here," and went out into the rush of people going both ways. Selecting and considering, as one who must make a choice involving perhaps whole years of lives, he estimated the people going by. Once he almost moved, and then at the last minute thought better of it and drew back. Finally, from half a block away, he saw what he wanted, and moved out into the center of the traffic to intercept a young man, who was hurrying, and dressed as though he had awakened late, and frowning.

"Oof," said the young man, because Mr. Johnson had thought of no better way to intercept anyone than the one the young woman had unwittingly used upon him. "Where do you think you're going?" the young man demanded from the sidewalk.

"I want to speak to you," said Mr. Johnson ominously.

The young man got up nervously, dusting himself and eyeing Mr. Johnson. "What for?" he said. "What'd *I* do?"

"That's what bothers me most about people nowadays," Mr. Johnson complained broadly to the people passing. "No matter whether they've done anything or not, they always figure someone's after them. About what you're going to do," he told the young man.

"Listen," said the young man, trying to brush past him, "I'm late,

Reading Strategy
Questioning Characters' Actions What could be Mr. Johnson's motive for offering to pay for the young woman's time?

Reading Strategy
Questioning Characters' Actions What is unusual about Mr. Johnson's actions?

▲ **Critical Viewing** Based upon this photograph, what can you infer about the setting of this story? **[Infer]**

and I don't have any time to listen. Here's a dime, now get going."

"Thank you," said Mr. Johnson, pocketing the dime. "Look," he said, "what happens if you stop running?"

"I'm late," said the young man, still trying to get past Mr. Johnson, who was unexpectedly clinging.

"How much you make an hour?" Mr. Johnson demanded.

"A communist, are you?" said the young man. "Now will you please let me—"

"No," said Mr. Johnson insistently, "*how* much?"

"Dollar fifty," said the young man. "And *now* will you—"

"You like adventure?"

The young man stared, and, staring, found himself caught and held by Mr. Johnson's genial smile; he almost smiled back and then

✔**Reading Check**

How does Mr. Johnson respond when the woman says she is late for work?

repressed it and made an effort to tear away. "I got to *hurry*," he said.

"Mystery? Like surprises? Unusual and exciting events?"

"You selling something?"

"Sure," said Mr. Johnson. "You want to take a chance?"

The young man hesitated, looking longingly up the avenue toward what might have been his destination and then, when Mr. Johnson said, "I'll pay for it," with his own peculiar convincing emphasis, turned and said, "Well, okay. But I got to see it first, what I'm buying."

Mr. Johnson, breathing hard, led the young man over to the side where the girl was standing; she had been watching with interest Mr. Johnson's capture of the young man and now, smiling timidly, she looked at Mr. Johnson as though prepared to be surprised at nothing.

Mr. Johnson reached into his pocket and took out his wallet. "Here," he said, and handed a bill to the girl. "This about equals your day's pay."

"But no," she said, surprised in spite of herself. "I mean, I *couldn't*."

"Please do not interrupt," Mr. Johnson told her. "And *here*," he said to the young man, "this will take care of *you*." The young man accepted the bill dazedly, but said, "Probably counterfeit," to the young woman out of the side of his mouth. "Now," Mr. Johnson went on, disregarding the young man, "what is your name, miss?"

"Kent," she said helplessly. "Mildred Kent."

"Fine," said Mr. Johnson. "And you, sir?"

"Arthur Adams," said the young man stiffly.

"Splendid," said Mr. Johnson. "Now, Miss Kent, I would like you to meet Mr. Adams. Mr. Adams, Miss Kent."

Miss Kent stared, wet her lips nervously, made a gesture as though she might run, and said, "How do you do?"

Mr. Adams straightened his shoulders, scowled at Mr. Johnson, made a gesture as though he might run, and said, "How do you do?"

"Now *this*," said Mr. Johnson, taking several bills from his wallet, "should be enough for the day for both of you. I would suggest, perhaps, Coney Island◆—although I personally am not fond of the place—or perhaps a nice lunch somewhere, and dancing, or a matinee,[1] or even a movie, although take care to choose a really good one;

---

1. **matinee** here, an afternoon performance of an on- or off-Broadway show.

Literature
in context Geography Connection

◆ **Coney Island**

Coney Island—the place to which Mr. Johnson suggests Miss Kent and Mr. Adams might go—is a famous beach area and amusement park in Brooklyn, one of the five boroughs of New York City. During the first half of the twentieth century, it was one of the largest amusement areas in the world. Millions of New Yorkers were drawn to its rides, games, entertainment, restaurants, and swimming each year. Although attendance was down during the early 1950s because of the polio epidemic and the resulting fear of contagion, by 1955—when this story was published—attendance was back up to 1.5 million on July 4th.

The Cyclone at Coney Island

Reading Strategy
Questioning Characters' Actions Why might Mr. Johnson have "captured" the young man?

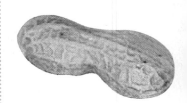

there are so many bad movies these days. "You might," he said, struck with an inspiration, "visit the Bronx Zoo, or the Planetarium.[2] Anywhere, as a matter of fact," he concluded, "that you would like to go. Have a nice time."

As he started to move away, Arthur Adams, breaking from his dumbfounded stare, said, "But see here, mister, you *can't* do this. Why—how do you know—I mean, *we* don't even know—I mean, how do you know we won't just take the money and not do what you said?"

"You've taken the money," Mr. Johnson said. "You don't have to follow any of my suggestions. You may know something you prefer to do—perhaps a museum, or something."

"But suppose I just run away with it and leave her here?"

"I know you won't," said Mr. Johnson gently, "because you remembered to ask *me* that. Goodbye," he added, and went on.

As he stepped up the street, conscious of the sun on his head and his good shoes, he heard from somewhere behind him the young man saying, "Look, you know you don't have to if you don't want to," and the girl saying, "But unless you don't want to . . ." Mr. Johnson smiled to himself and then thought that he had better hurry along; when he wanted to he could move very quickly, and before the young woman had gotten around to saying, "Well, *I* will if *you* will," Mr. Johnson was several blocks away and had already stopped twice, once to help a lady lift several large packages into a taxi and once to hand a peanut to a seagull. By this time he was in an area of large stores and many more people and he was <u>buffeted</u> constantly from either side by people hurrying and cross and late and sullen. Once he offered a peanut to a man who asked him for a dime, and once he offered a peanut to a bus driver who had stopped his bus at an intersection and had opened the window next to his seat and put out his head as though longing for fresh air and the comparative quiet of the traffic. The man wanting a dime took the peanut because Mr. Johnson had wrapped a dollar bill around it, but the bus driver took the peanut and asked ironically, "You want a transfer, Jack?"

On a busy corner Mr. Johnson encountered two young people—for one minute he thought they might be Mildred Kent and Arthur Adams—who were eagerly scanning a newspaper, their backs pressed against a storefront to avoid the people passing, their heads bent together. Mr. Johnson, whose curiosity was <u>insatiable</u>, leaned onto the storefront next to them and peeked over the man's shoulder; they were scanning the "Apartments Vacant" columns.

Mr. Johnson remembered the street where the woman and her little boy were going to Vermont and he tapped the man on the shoulder and said amiably, "Try down on West Seventeen. About the middle of the block, people moved out this morning."

---

2. **Planetarium** the Hayden Planetarium, adjoining the American Museum of Natural History in New York City.

buffeted (buf´ it ed) v. jostled; knocked about

insatiable (in sā´ she bel) *adj.* unable to be satisfied

✔Reading Check
What does Mr. Johnson offer to the man who asks him for a dime?

"Say, what do you—" said the man, and then, seeing Mr. Johnson clearly, "Well thanks. Where did you say?"

"West Seventeen," said Mr. Johnson. "About the middle of the block." He smiled again and said, "Good luck."

"Thanks," said the man.

"Thanks," said the girl, as they moved off.

"Goodbye," said Mr. Johnson.

He lunched alone in a pleasant restaurant, where the food was rich, and only Mr. Johnson's excellent digestion could encompass two of their whipped-cream-and-chocolate-and-rum-cake pastries for dessert. He had three cups of coffee, tipped the waiter largely, and went out into the street again into the wonderful sunlight, his shoes still comfortable and fresh on his feet. Outside he found a beggar staring into the windows of the restaurant he had left and, carefully looking through the money in his pocket, Mr. Johnson approached the beggar and pressed some coins and a couple of bills into his hand. "It's the price of the veal cutlet lunch plus tip," said Mr. Johnson. "Goodbye."

After his lunch he rested; he walked into the nearest park and fed peanuts to the pigeons. It was late afternoon by the time he was ready to start back downtown, and he had refereed two checker games and watched a small boy and girl whose mother had fallen asleep and awakened with surprise and fear which turned to amusement when she saw Mr. Johnson. He had given away almost all of his candy, and had fed all the rest of his peanuts to the pigeons, and it was time to go home. Although the late afternoon sun was pleasant, and his shoes were still entirely comfortable, he decided to take a taxi downtown.

He had a difficult time catching a taxi, because he gave up the first three or four empty ones to people who seemed to need them more; finally, however, he stood alone on the corner and—almost like netting a frisky fish—he hailed desperately until he succeeded in catching a cab which had been proceeding with haste uptown and seemed to draw in towards Mr. Johnson against its own will.

"Mister," the cab driver said as Mr. Johnson climbed in, "I figured you was an <u>omen</u>, like. I wasn't going to pick you up at all."

"Kind of you," said Mr. Johnson ambiguously.

"If I'd of let you go it would of cost me ten bucks," said the driver.

"Really?" said Mr. Johnson.

"Yeah," said the driver. "Guy just got out of the cab, he turned around and give me ten bucks, said take this and bet it in a hurry on a horse named Vulcan,[3] right away."

"Vulcan?" said Mr. Johnson, horrified. "A fire sign[4] on a Wednesday?"

"What?" said the driver. "Anyway, I said to myself if I got no fare between here and there I'd bet the ten, but if anyone looked like they

Literary Analysis
Surprise Ending When she awoke and saw Mr. Johnson, the mother's fear changed to amusement. What do you think the story's tone will be at the end?

omen (ō´ mən) *n.* sign foretelling a future event, either good or evil

---

3. **Vulcan** also the name of the Roman god of fire.
4. **fire sign** term borrowed from astrology, referring here to Vulcan.

needed the cab I'd take it as an omen and I'd take the ten home to the wife."

"You were very right," said Mr. Johnson heartily. "This is Wednesday, you would have lost your money. Monday, yes, or even Saturday. But never never never a fire sign on a Wednesday. Sunday would have been good, now."

"Vulcan don't run on Sunday," said the driver.

"You wait till another day," said Mr. Johnson. "Down this street, please, driver. I'll get off on the next corner."

"He *told* me Vulcan, though," said the driver.

"I'll tell you," said Mr. Johnson, hesitating with the door of the cab half open. "You take that ten dollars and I'll give you another ten dollars to go with it, and you go right ahead and bet that money on any Thursday on any horse that has a name indicating . . . let me see, Thursday . . . well, grain. Or any growing food."

"Grain?" said the driver. "You mean a horse named, like, Wheat or something?"

"Certainly," said Mr. Johnson. "Or, as a matter of fact, to make it even easier, any horse whose name includes the letters C, R, L. Perfectly simple."

"Tall corn?" said the driver, a light in his eye. "You mean a horse named, like, Tall Corn?"

"Absolutely," said Mr. Johnson. "Here's your money."

"Tall Corn," said the driver. "Thank *you*, mister."

"Goodbye," said Mr. Johnson.

He was on his own corner and went straight up to his apartment. He let himself in and called "Hello?" and Mrs. Johnson answered from the kitchen, "Hello, dear, aren't you early?"

"Took a taxi home," Mr. Johnson said. "I remembered the cheesecake, too. What's for dinner?"

Mrs. Johnson came out of the kitchen and kissed him; she was a comfortable woman, and smiling as Mr. Johnson smiled. "Hard day?" she asked.

"Not very," said Mr. Johnson, hanging his coat in the closet. "How about you?"

"So-so," she said. She stood in the kitchen doorway while he settled into his easy chair and took off his good shoes and took out the paper he had bought that morning. "Here and there," she said.

"I didn't do so badly," Mr. Johnson said. "Couple young people."

"Fine," she said. "I had a little nap this afternoon, took it easy most of the day. Went into a department store this morning and accused

Reading Strategy
Questioning Characters' Actions Is Mr. Johnson's behavior in the cab consistent with the impression you have of him up to this point? Why or why not?

✓ **Reading Check**
Why does Mr. Johnson have a hard time catching a cab?

Integrate Language Skills

Vocabulary Development Lesson

Related Words: *omen*

An *omen* is "a sign or event that foretells the future." Such signs can be positive or negative, but the word *ominously* focuses only on the negative: It means "in a way that seems to foretell doom." Write the meaning of each word below, using the meaning of the related word.

1. *irradiated*—related word: *radiant*
2. *planetarium*—related word: *planet*
3. *insatiable*—related word: *satisfy*

Spelling Strategy

When you add an ending to a word that ends with two or more consonants, never double the final consonant. Thus, *impertinent* becomes *impertinently*, but *final* becomes *finally*. Write the correct spelling for each item below.

1. pass + *-ed* 2. dumb + *-ly* 3. tick + *-ing*

Concept Development: Synonyms

Choose the letter of the word that is most nearly the same in meaning as the first word.

1. irradiated: (a) darkened, (b) glowed, (c) frozen
2. loitered: (a) dirtied, (b) delivered, (c) lingered
3. endeavoring: (a) trying, (b) asking, (c) preparing
4. ominously: (a) threateningly, (b) brightly, (c) loudly
5. buffeted: (a) cooked, (b) shined, (c) shoved
6. insatiable: (a) unquenchable, (b) indefinite, (c) odd
7. omen: (a) stamp, (b) signal, (c) cause
8. impertinent: (a) impatient, (b) unrelated, (c) impolite

Grammar Lesson

Direct Object or Object of a Preposition?

A **direct object** is a noun or pronoun that receives the action of a transitive action verb. The **object of the preposition** is the noun or pronoun at the end of a prepositional phrase. Look at the following examples.

>   S   V   DO
> **Direct Object:** Mr. Johnson ate *lunch*. (*lunch* receives the action of *ate*)
>
>   S   V
> **Object of a Preposition:** Mr. Johnson ate
>   PREP PHRASE
> at a pleasant *restaurant*. (*restaurant* is the object of the preposition *at*)

Practice Copy each sentence. Label the subjects and verbs. Circle each direct object. Underline each object of a preposition.

1. The woman ran into Mr. Johnson.
2. Mr. Johnson spoke to the people.
3. She watched Mr. Johnson with interest.
4. He gave peanuts to the people he met.
5. He paid her for the hours she missed.

Writing Application Write a paragraph about "One Ordinary Day, With Peanuts" that includes at least one direct object and one prepositional phrase.

WG Prentice Hall Writing and Grammar Connection: Chapter 20, Section 3

Writing Lesson

Summary

A summary provides only the most important details of a story or event. Write a summary of Mrs. Johnson's day.

Prewriting	Start by imagining Mrs. Johnson's unusual day. Fill out an hour-by-hour schedule showing all her activities. Underline the most important events in your list.
Drafting	Recount the events of the day in chronological order. Use transitions like *next, meanwhile,* and *later* to clarify the order of events.
Revising	Reread your summary to make sure that you have included all of the important details of the day. Place boxes between sentences to help you evaluate whether you need to add transitions. Where necessary, add transition words to make your writing clearer.

Model: Revising to Add Transitions

☑ She shut the door, ready to start her day. ☐ *First,* She bought

the paper, giving everyone an angry snarl. ☐ *Then,* She looked

for her first victim.

> Transition words smooth out the writing and make the sequence of events clear.

W̸G ***Prentice Hall Writing and Grammar Connection: Chapter 7, Section 4***

Extension Activities

Listening and Speaking Imagine meeting both Mr. Johnson and Mrs. Johnson on this not-so-ordinary day. Prepare a **monologue** describing your feelings before and after the encounter. Review the story before you write.

- Notice how people reacted to Mr. Johnson's generosity.
- Think about how Mrs. Johnson probably treated people and how her actions would compare with Mr. Johnson's.

Rehearse your monologue, and present it to your class.

Research and Technology In a small group, put together a **research report** about the setting of the story, New York City in the 1950s. Before starting your research, generate research questions about the tourist attractions in New York City and the kinds of changes that took place in the 1950s. Use library sources, including encyclopedias on CD-ROM, to help you. **[Group Activity]**

 ***Take It to the Net*** www.phschool.com

Go online for an additional research activity using the Internet.

Writing WORKSHOP

Writing for Assessment: Test Essay

To make sure that you are learning the information and skills you need to succeed, teachers frequently assess your knowledge. Tests, oral reports, and research papers are ways of evaluating your progress. Essay tests are the most common type of **writing for assessment.**

Assignment Criteria. Successful writing for assessment usually has the following characteristics:

- a direct response to the test question
- a thesis statement that is clearly worded and well supported
- specific information about the topic, drawn from your reading or from class discussion
- a clear organization

To preview the criteria on which your writing for assessment may be judged, see the Rubric on page 437.

Prewriting

Choose a topic. On some essay tests, a single topic is assigned. In cases in which you have the opportunity to choose a topic, use the following techniques:

- **Consider what you know.** Jot down specific details for each topic. You should choose a topic that you know well.
- **Pinpoint your strengths.** The question may ask you to *analyze,* to *predict,* or to *explain.* Choose a topic for which you can provide facts to support the type of response required.

Narrow your response. As you prepare to write your essay, circle key words in the question and take notes to help you interpret the directions. The chart on this page shows how specific verbs should direct the purpose of your writing.

Draft a single sentence. Identify in a single sentence the main idea you will develop in your essay. Once you choose your topic, jot down this sentence and refer to it to remind you of your position. Use your main idea to formulate your thesis statement when you draft.

> **Example**
> **Essay Question:** Discuss how someone you admire overcame an obstacle in order to succeed.
>
> **Main Idea:** I will discuss how Stevie Wonder and Jackie Joyner-Kersee overcame their disabilities.

Narrow Your Response

Key Words	Essay Objectiv
Analyze	Examine how vario elements contribut to the whole.
Describe	Give main features and examples of e
Compare and Contrast	Stress how two wo or other items are alike and different.
Discuss	Support a generali- zation with facts a examples.
Explain	Clarify by probing reasons, causes, results, and effects
Defend	Support your positi with examples fro the text.

Student Model

Before you begin drafting your writing for assessment, read this student model and review the characteristics of effective writing for assessment.

Eddie Harris
Chicago, IL

Question: *In an essay, discuss how someone you admire overcame an obstacle in order to succeed.*

The best way to overcome a disability is to face it head-on and not let it prevent you from achieving great things. This is the lesson I draw from the lives of two people whom I admire—the musician Stevie Wonder and the track-and-field star Jackie Joyner-Kersee. I respect them for their courage and strength in overcoming obstacles. Both are African Americans with disabilities who defied obstacles in order to be successful in their fields.

> The author uses a general statement to introduce his response to the essay question.

> This author presents a thesis statement that focuses his answer to the essay question.

Stevie Wonder became blind after he was born prematurely and received too much oxygen. But that did not stop him from becoming one of the best musicians ever. He started out singing rock and roll songs outside a church in Detroit. Eventually, he found his way to Motown Studios at a time when Motown was one of the top recording studios in America. There his career skyrocketed. He became one of the best Motown singers even though he was only ten years old.

He has since been nominated for more Grammy awards than any other musician. His blindness is no disability for him. On the music charts, Stevie Wonder opened the gates for a new sound . . . not just for African Americans but for everyone else as well.

Another person that I admire for the way she overcame obstacles is Jackie Joyner-Kersee, a famous track-and-field star. She was born in East St. Louis, Illinois, and her family was very poor. Her parents thought that track and field were inappropriate for a girl. When she was nine, she entered her first track-and-field competition. Even though she lost, she didn't give up. Jackie entered another race. Her parents were shocked when she won.

In the late 1980s, she was diagnosed with asthma. This has not interfered with her performance as an athlete. Jackie is a world champion in both the long jump and heptathlon and has many Olympic medals to prove it.

> In the body of the essay, the author supports his general statement with specific factual information.

Jackie Joyner-Kersee continues to be a role model for young people with disabilities like me. I think that Jackie Joyner-Kersee and Stevie Wonder are admirable for overcoming their disabilities. Stevie Wonder overcame blindness to bring music to the world. Joyner-Kersee stunned us with her athleticism, despite her asthma. They teach me to never give up, no matter how intimidating the obstacles I face in life.

> The author concludes by restating his thesis and reinforcing it with personal insight.

Drafting

Find a focus. Once you choose your topic, develop a focus for your essay. Consider the type of writing you are creating, and draft a statement that directly responds to the question. Use the information at right to help you focus your ideas.

Plan a structure. When you sketch an outline for your essay, divide it into three parts: introduction, body, and conclusion.

- The **introduction** should state your thesis.
- The **body** of the essay should present at least two main points that support your thesis.
- The **conclusion** should restate the answer to the essay question and sum up the main points in the body.

Fill in the details. In a test situation, you normally have limited time. List the evidence, facts, examples, and quotations you will need to prove your point. Jot down as many details as you can remember or generate. Refer to this list as you draft.

Find Your Focus

Exposition

Develop a thesis statement to address the question, gearing your response to the expectation of problem-and-solution, cause-and-effect, or comparison-and-contrast essays.

Persuasion

Choose a position to argue, and identify the support you'll use to defend it.

Response to Literature

In a single sentence, identify your focus. You may decide to evaluate a character or analyze a setting.

Revising

Revise for coherence. When you have finished writing, compare the first paragraph of your essay with the last:

1. The first paragraph should contain your focus or thesis in response to the essay question.

2. The final paragraph should restate the thesis statement and summarize your supporting evidence.

3. If the main points in the first and final paragraphs do not match, revise either paragraph to make the writing more coherent. If necessary, revise body paragraphs or add transitional sentences to make sure that the essay flows and holds together well.

Model: Revising a Conclusion

Stevie Wonder overcame blindness to bring music to the world. Joyner-Kersee stunned us with her athleticism, despite her asthma.

I think that Jackie Joyner-Kersee and Stevie Wonder are admirable for overcoming their disabilities. They teach me to never give up, no matter how intimidating the obstacles I face in my life.

Eddie could summarize his supporting arguments to give greater weight and clarity to his thesis.

Revise for formal language. Look for words in your writing that can be replaced with words that are more appropriate to your purpose. In the following example, *element* creates a more formal effect than *thing*.

Informal: The railroad was the *thing* that most contributed to the success of new businesses.

Formal: The railroad was the *element* that most contributed to the success of new businesses.

Compare the model and the nonmodel. Why is the model more effective than the nonmodel?

Nonmodel	Model
The first person I want to talk about is a great African American musician by the name of Stevie Wonder.	One person who serves as a powerful example of someone who has overcome a disability is the African American musician Stevie Wonder.

Publishing and Presenting

After you receive an essay back from your teacher with comments, keep a copy in your portfolio. Consider this suggestion to make further use of it:

Organize a study group. Compare your response with those of your classmates. Read the essays and discuss with other members of the study group the ways you could improve your essay writing. If it is helpful, list the strengths and weaknesses of each essay. Use the lists to improve your performance on your next essay test.

Rubric for Self-Assessment

Evaluate your writing for assessment using the following criteria and rating scale:

Criteria	Rating Scale				
	Not very				Very
How directly does the essay answer the question?	1	2	3	4	5
How well is the thesis supported by evidence?	1	2	3	4	5
How specific is the supporting information?	1	2	3	4	5
How effectively is information drawn from reading or discussion incorporated?	1	2	3	4	5
How effectively are arguments organized?	1	2	3	4	5

Listening and Speaking WORKSHOP

Delivering a Descriptive Presentation

In a **descriptive presentation**, you communicate an experience by describing it in detail. The ability to deliver a memorable descriptive presentation is as important for telling a good story as it is for telling someone how to operate machinery. The following techniques will help you organize and deliver a descriptive presentation.

Prepare the Presentation

Much of the creative work that goes into putting together a descriptive presentation involves gathering details and organizing them logically.

Picture the topic that you are describing. Project yourself into the situation you are describing. Think about what you see, hear, and feel around you. Make a list of these sensory details, selecting those that would best help your audience to picture the situation. For example, you might describe the feeling of terror when the person teaching you to ride your bike let go, and you suddenly forgot how to brake.

Define your topic. Too much descriptive detail can slow you down or get you sidetracked. To avoid this problem, start off with a single generalization that sums up your presentation and suits your purpose. Then, consider whether details are essential or inessential to capturing your generalization. Adjust the balance if you feel you have too much or too little detail.

Defining Your Topic

Purpose: To entertain
Audience: Fellow students

Essential Details	Inessential Details
I received a bike for my sixth birthday.	
I felt the wheel shake when I was first gaining my balance.	My bike was a three speed.
I didn't know how to brake when my dad let go.	

Deliver the Presentation

When it comes time to deliver your presentation, use the following techniques to provide greater impact.

Be dynamic. An audience will pay closer attention to a speaker who is animated and varies his or her voice. The more interested you are in your topic, the easier it will be to give a dynamic presentation.

Gauge audience reaction. Look at the audience frequently to check how people are reacting. If you feel your audience is losing interest, leave out some details and pick up your pace. If people are actively engaged, do not be afraid to elaborate on aspects that seem to play well with your audience.

Activity:
Analyzing a Speech
Pair up with another student. Choose a topic that you know well but your partner does not. Take turns presenting to each other, using as much description as you feel necessary. When you have finished, ask your partner to recall as many details as possible. Use this feedback to evaluate your presentation.

Assessment WORKSHOP

Cause and Effect

The reading sections of some tests often require you to read a passage and answer multiple-choice questions about cause-and-effect relationships. Use these strategies to help you answer test questions on cause and effect:

- Remember that a *cause* is an event that makes something happen, and an *effect* is a result of that event.
- To recognize cause and effect, ask yourself, "What happened in this passage? Why did this event come about?"
- Do not limit your search to a single cause and effect. One cause may have several effects, and one effect may have several causes.

Sample Test Item

Directions: Read the passage, and then answer the question that follows.

Marcus dressed quickly, gulped breakfast, and bolted out the door. As he hurried to school, he mentally reviewed his notes and realized that he felt confident. He had been unprepared for the last biology exam. This would be his last chance to improve his final grade. This time, he had made a serious effort to study for the exam.

1 Why did Marcus feel confident?

  A This was his last chance to pass biology.

  B He arrived at school on time.

  C He had not done well on the last exam.

  D He had studied hard for the exam.

Answer and Explanation

The correct answer is *D*. *A* and *C* might make Marcus more nervous, but not confident. *B* is not found in the paragraph.

▶ Practice

Directions: Read the passage, and then answer the question that follows.

Lauren looked at the car repair bill. She thought about the day that Shelly, her sister, had borrowed her car. Lauren had reluctantly given her the keys. Shelly had promised to be back in time for Lauren to go to work, so five hours later, Shelly returned and sheepishly explained how she had crushed the rear fender. Lauren had lost a day's pay. "Well, I've learned something," she thought.

1 Why did Lauren lose a day's pay?

  A She had to have her car repaired.

  B Shelly had an accident.

  C She couldn't go to work.

  D Shelly begged her for the car.

2 Why did Lauren give Shelly the keys to her car?

  A She needed money to pay a bill.

  B It was a rainy day.

  C They were sisters.

  D Shelly made a promise to be back on time.

UNIT 5 Visions of the Future

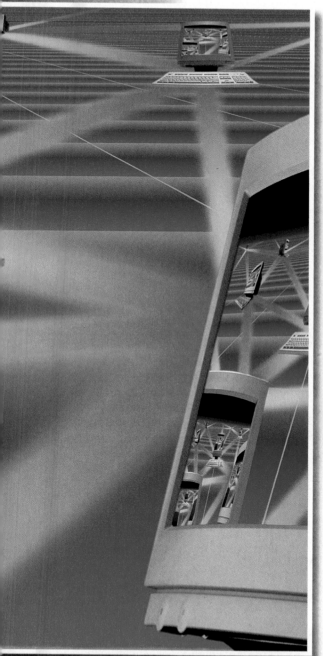

Exploring the Theme

People have always tried to imagine the future. Some have worried that today's human carelessness will produce the problems of tomorrow. Others have looked optimistically toward the future, hoping that technological progress will offer us a way to solve our current problems. Still others have predicted that each set of advancements will bring its own set of problems and solutions, in an endless cycle of human wisdom and folly.

Bryan Woolley incorporates elements of all three outlooks in his time capsule essay, "To the Residents of A.D. 2029." Addressing future citizens, Woolley acknowledges the problems of our time. Through it all, though, he manages to find perspective, humor, and a glimmer of hope.

▲ **Critical Viewing** Which elements of this picture suggest that computer technology opens infinite possibilities? **[Infer]**

Read Literature?

Whenever you read science fiction, you have a purpose, or reason. You might read to appreciate a new view of the future, or because the social issues an author raises interest you. Preview the three purposes you might set before reading works in this unit.

1

Read for the Love of Literature

Science fiction is particularly compelling when a writer interweaves technological progress with great moral dilemmas. If you have ever wondered—or worried—what it might be like when humans rely completely on technology, you may find a surprising answer in Isaac Asimov's **"The Machine That Won the War,"** page 456.

Many works of science fiction are tales of wayward computers destroying the world with murderous abandon. But why not try to imagine a world where technology and nature coexist peacefully? If this concept intrigues you, read Richard Brautigan's **"All Watched Over by Machines of Loving Grace,"** page 476.

2

Read for Information

In 1993, when the first Internet browser was introduced, few could have predicted how important the Internet would become. How difficult is it for you to imagine the state of technology five years from now? Find out Bill Gates's vision for the future in video technology and see if it matches your own in **"The Road Ahead,"** page 446.

In 1962, pesticide use was widespread and companies dumped toxins into our streams. It took a biologist named Rachel Carson to draw the vital connection between technology and destruction of the environment. Read an excerpt from *Silent Spring*—the book that helped spawn the environmental movement—on page 491.

3

Read to Be Inspired

Imprisoned for twenty-seven years for his opposition to racial segregation, Nelson Mandela served as the conscience of South Africa. After he was released and elected president, Mandela was faced with the overwhelming task of creating a just society out of poverty and inequality. See how he viewed this as an opportunity to issue a stirring call to action in **"Glory and Hope,"** page 506.

 Take It to the Net

Visit the Web site for online instruction and activities related to each selection in this unit.
www.phschool.com

How to Read Literature

Use Critical Reading Strategies

When you read a work that presents an individual's perspective, it is a good idea to read critically. Reading critically involves examining and questioning the author's ideas. Use these strategies to help you read critically:

1. Recognize bias.

No matter how impartial writers seem, they inevitably bring some of their own experiences and beliefs to their writing. The bias that results influences both their writing and your reaction. To increase your awareness of bias:

- Weigh the facts that support or contradict the author's position. Then, see if your conclusion is the same as the author's.

- Consider what the author is omitting, as well as including.

- Learn about the author's background to determine which experiences may have influenced his or her writing.

2. Identify relevant details.

To help process information as you read, it is useful to screen passages for relevant detail.

- Details that have the most relevance are those that are essential to your understanding of the story's plot, characters, and setting.

- Do not expect to know what is or is not relevant from the very beginning. As you read further, the distinction will become clearer.

3. Recognize a poet's purpose.

- Look for recurring ideas and images in the poem that may provide clues to a poet's reason for writing.

- Pay close attention to the opening and closing lines of a poem. Poets will often announce their intentions in these lines.

- Remember that a poet may have multiple purposes and that every reader may bring a slightly different interpretation to a poem.

Fact vs. Opinion

Selection
"To the Residents of A.D. 2029"

Fact (Verifiable)
▶ 20th C. U.S. has the world's highest standard of living.

Opinion (Belief)
▶ We need art to feed our souls and America does not have enough art.

4. Distinguish fact from opinion.

- Facts can be verified for accuracy by checking a reference book; opinions cannot. Note the examples of the distinction between fact and opinion at right.

- Opinions, though often stated strongly, will always be an interpretation based on a writer's beliefs or values.

As you read the selections in this unit, review the critical reading strategies and apply them to interact with the text.

Prepare to Read

from The Road Ahead

Take It to the Net

Visit www.phschool.com
for interactive activities
and instruction related to
The Road Ahead, including
- background
- graphic organizers
- literary elements
- reading strategies

Preview

Connecting to the Literature

Technology changes at an astounding pace. Computers that were marvels of technology a few years ago now lack the processing power, memory, and features to complete the new tasks people take for granted. Let this essay by computer mogul Bill Gates encourage you to speculate how future innovations will replace today's cutting-edge technology and affect your life.

Background

The Internet consists of thousands of computer networks connected via telephone lines and cable wires. The Internet provides access to vast amounts of information, including text, graphics, and sound, with links to other sites and "pages." In *The Road Ahead,* Gates envisions a new Internet service—the delivery of high-quality video programming when customers want it.

Literary Analysis

Expository Writing

Expository writing informs the reader, explaining its subject by presenting details, examples, and facts. This passage from the selection uses details to explain the concept of conventional television:

> Conventional television allows us to decide what we watch but not when we watch it. . . . Viewers have to synchronize their schedules with the time of a broadcast. . . .

Although the focus of expository writing is to present information, the writer may also express personal opinions based on experience. As you read this excerpt from *The Road Ahead*, note how the author uses facts and examples to explain his subject and support his views.

Connecting Literary Elements

In expository writing, an **author's purpose** is his or her reason for writing—to inform, to entertain, or to persuade, for example. Of course, an author may have more than one purpose: Bill Gates writes persuasively to convince you of his opinions. At the same time, he informs and entertains you. To help you organize the opinions and supporting facts in Gates's essay, use a chart like the one shown here.

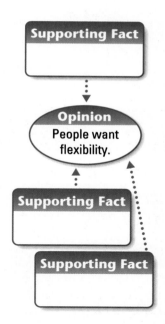

Reading Strategy

Recognizing a Writer's Bias

Even within expository writing, an author may show bias—a strong feeling for or against something. To **recognize a writer's bias**, pay attention to the following:

- loaded words—words that trigger a positive or negative response
- a single viewpoint that does not address an opposing viewpoint
- an opinion or assumption that is not backed up with facts

In this selection, Gates's involvement in his software company probably influences his positive attitude toward technology.

Vocabulary Development

simultaneously (sī´ məl tā´ nē əs lē) *adv.* at the same time (p. 447)

capacious (kə pā´ shəs) *adj.* able to hold much; roomy (p. 449)

precursors (prē kur´ sərz) *n.* things that prepare the way for what will follow (p. 450)

infrared (in´ frə red´) *adj.* of light waves that lie just beyond the red end of the visible spectrum (p. 450)

parlance (pär´ ləns) *n.* style of speaking or writing; language (p. 450)

years ago, the only form of communication was the spoken word and the listener had to be in the presence of the speaker or miss his message. Once the message could be written, it could be stored and read later by anybody, at his or her convenience. I'm writing these words at home on a summer evening, but I have no idea where or when you'll read them. One of the benefits the communications revolution will bring to all of us is more control over our schedules.

Once a form of communication is asynchronous, you also get an increase in the variety of selection possibilities. Even people who rarely record television programs routinely rent movies from the thousands of choices available at local video rental stores for just a few dollars each. The home viewer can spend any evening with Elvis, the Beatles—or Greta Garbo.

Television has been around for fewer than sixty years, but in that time it has become a major influence in the life of almost everyone in the developed nations. In some ways, though, television was just an

▼ **Critical Viewing** Computers and the Internet are now a part of everyday life. How do Gates's predictions about future technologies relate to your own experiences? **[Apply]**

enhancement of commercial radio, which had been bringing electronic entertainment into homes for twenty years. But no broadcast medium we have right now is comparable to the communications media we'll have once the Internet evolves to the point at which it has the broadband capacity[2] necessary to carry high-quality video.

Because consumers already understand the value of movies and are used to paying to watch them, video-on-demand is an obvious development. There won't be any intermediary VCR. You'll simply select what you want from countless available programs.

No one knows when residential broadband networks capable of supporting video-on-demand will be available in the United States and other developed countries, let alone in developing countries. Many corporate networks already have enough bandwidth,[3] but . . . even in the U.S. most homes will have to make do for some time—maybe more than a decade—with narrowband and midband access. Fortunately, these lower-capacity bandwidths work fine for many Internet-based services such as games, electronic mail, and banking. For the next few years, interactivity in homes will be limited to these kinds of services, which will be delivered to personal computers and other information appliances.

Even after broadband residential networks have become common, television shows will continue to be broadcast as they are today, for synchronous consumption. But after they air, these shows—as well as thousands of movies and virtually all other kinds of video—will also be available whenever you want to view them. If a new episode of *Seinfeld* is on at 9:00 P.M. on Thursday night, you'll also be able to see it at 9:13 P.M., 9:45 P.M., or 11:00 A.M. on Saturday. And there will be thousands of other choices. Your request for a specific movie or TV show episode will register, and the bits[4] will be routed to you across the network. It will feel as if there's no intermediary machinery between you and the object of your interest. You'll indicate what you want, and presto! you'll get it.

Movies, TV shows, and other kinds of digital information will be stored on "servers," which are computers with <u>capacious</u> disks. Servers will provide information for use anywhere on the network, just as they do for today's Internet. If you ask to see a particular movie, check a fact, or retrieve your electronic mail, your request will be routed by switches to the server or servers storing that information. You won't know whether the movie, TV show, query response, or e-mail that arrives at your house is stored on a server down the road or on the other side of the country, and it won't matter to you.

The digitized data will be retrieved from the server and routed by switches back to your television, personal computer, or telephone—your "information appliance." These digital devices will succeed for

---

2. **broadband capacity** *n.* ability to transmit a huge amount of electronic information quickly.
3. **bandwidth** *n.* amount of electronic information that can be transmitted in a given amount of time; capacity.
4. **bits** *n.* units of electronic information.

Literary Analysis
Expository Writing and Author's Purpose What is Gates's purpose in this part of his essay?

Reading Strategy
Recognizing a Writer's Bias How does Gates's bias toward technology affect his views and enthusiasm in this paragraph?

capacious (kə pā´ shəs) *adj.* able to hold much; roomy

Reading Check

In the future, where will digital information be stored, according to the writer?

the same reason their analog <u>precursors</u> did—they'll make some aspect of life easier. Unlike the dedicated word processors[5] that brought the first microprocessors to many offices, most of these information appliances will be general-purpose, programmable computers connected to the network.

Even if a show is being broadcast live, you'll be able to use your <u>infrared</u> remote control to start it, stop it, or go to any earlier part of the program, at any time. If somebody comes to the door, you'll be able to pause the program for as long as you like. You'll be in absolute control—except, of course, you won't be able to forward past part of a live show as it's taking place.

Most viewers can appreciate the benefits of video-on-demand and will welcome the convenience it gives them. Once the costs to build a broadband network are low enough, video-on-demand has the potential to be what in computer <u>parlance</u> is called a "killer application," or just "killer app"—a use of technology so attractive to consumers that it fuels market forces and makes the underlying invention on which it depends all but indispensable. Killer applications change technological advances from curiosities into moneymaking essentials.

---

5. **dedicated word processors** *n.* machines that can be used only for word processing. Unlike personal computers, dedicated machines perform only one function.

precursors (prē kur´ sərz) *n.* things that prepare the way for what will follow

infrared (in´ frə red´) *adj.* of light waves that lie just beyond the red end of the visible spectrum

parlance (pär´ ləns) *n.* style of speaking or writing; language

Review and Assess

Thinking About the Selection

1. **Respond:** What do you think about an Internet video service like the one Gates describes?

2. **(a) Recall:** Which television show does Gates cite at the start of his essay? **(b) Connect:** Why is its popularity important to the point he is trying to make?

3. **(a) Recall:** How did video delivery work when Gates wrote his essay? **(b) Compare and Contrast:** In what ways does Gates think future video delivery will be different? **(c) Infer:** Why will the Internet's broadband development be significant?

4. **(a) Recall:** How long does Gates estimate Americans will have to wait for video-on-demand to be available? **(b) Infer:** How do you think Gates feels about the length of time this development will take?

5. **Speculate:** How might the advances that Gates predicts directly affect your future?

6. **(a) Extend:** What negative impacts might video-on-demand have on our society? **(b) Assess:** Do you think the benefits outweigh the negative impacts? Explain.

Bill Gates

(b. 1955)

In 1997, *Newsweek* magazine called Bill Gates "the richest man in the world, and maybe the smartest." He is chief executive officer and cofounder of Microsoft Corporation, the world's largest computer software company.

In the eighth grade, Gates taught himself the computer language BASIC and began writing programs. In 1975, he and Paul Allen wrote the first version of BASIC for a microcomputer. They soon started Microsoft, which now has over 20,000 employees. In *The Road Ahead* (1996), Gates examines the future of computer technology.

Review and Assess

Literary Analysis

Expository Writing

1. Using a chart like the one shown here, identify the main idea Gates proposes. Then, identify three facts that support this idea.

2. Which details and descriptions help Gates give the essay a personal flavor?
3. Which opinions does the author introduce in his essay?

Connecting Literary Elements

4. (a) Is Gates's idea persuasive? (b) Which supporting details are most or least convincing?
5. What is the **author's** primary **purpose**? Explain.

Reading Strategy

Recognizing a Writer's Bias

6. How does Gates show a **bias** in the way he describes and explains videocassette recorders of the early 1980s?
7. (a) Use a chart like the one shown to categorize the biases in Gates's writing. Identify those details that help Gates make his case and those that do not help. (b) Do Gates's biases ultimately make his writing more or less effective for a general audience? Explain.

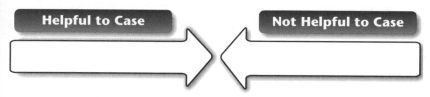

Extend Understanding

8. **Technology Connection:** In your opinion, which technological development is the most important for the present and future—the communications revolution or something else? Why?

Quick Review

Expository writing informs the reader, explaining something by presenting details, examples, and facts.

An **author's purpose** is his or her reason for writing—for example, it may be to inform, to entertain, or to persuade.

A writer's work may exhibit **bias**, a strong feeling for or against something, based on knowledge or personal experience.

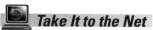 **Take It to the Net**
www.phschool.com

Take the interactive self-test online to check your understanding of the selection.

Integrate Language Skills

Vocabulary Development Lesson

Word Analysis: Latin Root *-simul-*

The Latin root *-simul-* means "same" or "at the same time." This fact explains the meaning of *simultaneously*—"happening at the same time." This root also appears in *simulate* and *simulcast*; identify the definition that matches each word.

1. broadcast at the same time on radio and television
2. look or act like; feign

Spelling Strategy

Do not change the spelling of a base word when you add a prefix to it. For example, *infra-* + *red* = *infrared*.

Add *un-*, *mis-*, or *pre-* to each word below to form three properly spelled words.

1. record   2. spell   3. necessary

Fluency: Word Choice

In each sentence, replace the italicized words with the appropriate one from the word list on page 445. Rephrase as necessary.

1. The expert hiker could pack an amazing amount of gear in the *large and roomy* backpack.
2. The two runners reached the finish line *at the same time*.
3. In computer *language*, restarting a computer is called "rebooting."
4. Ultraviolet radiation is more dangerous than *that of light waves beyond the red end of the spectrum*.
5. Vinyl records were the *things that came before and prepared the way for* compact discs.

Grammar Lesson

Main and Subordinate Clauses

A **clause** is a group of words with a subject and a verb. A **main,** or **independent, clause** can stand by itself as a complete sentence. In contrast, a **subordinate clause** cannot stand by itself.

In a sentence, a subordinate clause may either follow or precede a main clause.

> **Main Clause:**
> The Internet is expanding.
> **Main Clause, Subordinate Clause:**
> It offers more *as time passes*.
> **Subordinate Clause, Main Clause:**
> *If we let it,* it can change our lives.

Practice Copy each sentence. Underline the main clause and circle the subordinate clause.

1. If you cared about a program, you taped it.
2. This medium will offer shows that you can watch any time.
3. The demand is growing, even as I write.
4. Before much more time passes, the revolution will succeed.
5. Viewers welcome convenience, which video-on-demand will give them.

Writing Application Rephrase each of the preceding sentences by converting main clauses to subordinate ones and subordinate clauses to main ones.

WG Prentice Hall Writing and Grammar Connection: Chapter 21, Section 2

Writing Lesson

Consumer Response

Bill Gates uses his experience as a businessman and technology specialist to offer his views about the future. In an essay that responds to his, use your experiences as a television viewer or computer user to tell technology developers which advances you would like to see.

Prewriting Review the essay, noting key advances that Gates mentions. Evaluate the worth of each one to you. Then, brainstorm to add your own ideas for innovation. For each idea, list the benefits of your proposal.

Model: Brainstorming to Identify Benefits

Idea	Benefit
1. full-screen, real-time videophones	1. Allows people to see each other clearly, without choppiness of current technology.

This idea comes from the writer's disappointment with existing video applications.

Drafting Begin with an introduction that establishes your authority as a consumer. Then, devote a paragraph to each of your ideas, explaining both your innovation and its benefits.

Revising Evaluate the body paragraphs to decide whether you have effectively argued the effects of your proposal. If necessary, add more details about current technology's shortcomings to support the need for change.

 Prentice Hall Writing and Grammar Connection: Chapter 10, Section 2

Extension Activities

Listening and Speaking Working in a group, organize a **presentation** on important inventions of the past one hundred years.

- The group should agree on the inventions to be discussed.
- Each student should research a single invention.
- Use charts and other visuals in creating a display to support the discussion.

Conclude your presentation by inviting questions from your audience. [**Group Activity**]

Research and Technology The future is likely to see many more technological advances besides video-on-demand. Use the Internet to learn what Bill Gates and three (or more) other experts think will be the big technological breakthroughs in the coming decades. Prepare a handout with an **annotated list** of Web sites you found most helpful.

 Take It to the Net   www.phschool.com

Go online for an additional research activity using the Internet.

Prepare to Read

The Machine That Won the War

 Take It to the Net

Visit www.phschool.com for interactive activities and instruction related to "The Machine That Won the War," including
- background
- graphic organizers
- literary elements
- reading strategies

Preview

Connecting to the Literature

The success of everyday life has come to depend on computers. Machines track store purchases, banking transactions, and school records. Sometimes, as you will see in "The Machine That Won the War," computers run important military applications.

Background

When Isaac Asimov wrote this story, computers were big, bulky machines; small, personal computers had not yet been invented. Solving problems required the setting of thousands of cables and switches by hand. The early computers had names like UNIVAC and ENIAC. Perhaps Asimov was thinking of them when he devised the name "Multivac"—the powerful computer in this story.

Literary Analysis

Science Fiction

Science fiction is a form of literature in which the writer makes free use of his or her imagination to create settings, characters, and situations not found in reality. Whatever changes the author introduces, however, are based on real science. This passage from Asimov's story describes an unreal setting and situation:

> "What do you know of the data Multivac had to use: predigested from a hundred subsidiary computers here on Earth, on the Moon, on Mars, even on Titan. . . ."

In addition to the names of actual planets and moons that Asimov cites, notice how many of the details in "The Machine That Won the War" combine imagination with scientific fact.

Connecting Literary Elements

A story's **setting** is the time and place in which the action occurs. In science fiction, the setting may be

- an alternative past.
- an altered present.
- a possible future.

Many details of Asimov's story suggest that it is set in a possible future.

Reading Strategy

Identifying Relevant Details

Relevant details are those descriptions or events that are important in helping you understand the plot, characters, and setting of a story. Asimov's story mentions computers on the Moon, Mars, and Titan. These details are relevant because they make it clear that the setting is in the future.

Use a chart like the one shown to record specific details about characters, setting, technology, or the war found in the story, and explain why each is relevant.

Details	Relevance

Vocabulary Development

erratic (er rat′ ik) *adj.* irregular; random (p. 457)

grisly (griz′ lē) *adj.* horrifying; gruesome (p. 457)

imperturbable (im′ pər tur′ bə bəl) *adj.* unable to be excited or disturbed (p. 457)

oracle (ôr′ ə kəl) *n.* source of knowledge or wise counsel (p. 457)

surcease (sur′ sēs′) *n.* end (p. 459)

subsidiary (səb sid′ ē er′ ē) *adj.* secondary; supporting (p. 459)

circumvent (sur′ kəm vent′) *v.* avoid; go around (p. 460)

The Machine That Won the War

Isaac Asimov

The celebration had a long way to go and even in the silent depths of Multivac's underground chambers, it hung in the air.

If nothing else, there was the mere fact of isolation and silence. For the first time in a decade, technicians were not scurrying about the vitals of the giant computer, the soft lights did not wink out their <u>erratic</u> patterns, the flow of information in and out had halted.

It would not be halted long, of course, for the needs of peace would be pressing. Yet now, for a day, perhaps for a week, even Multivac might celebrate the great time, and rest.

Lamar Swift took off the military cap he was wearing and looked down the long and empty main corridor of the enormous computer. He sat down rather wearily in one of the technician's swing-stools, and his uniform, in which he had never been comfortable, took on a heavy and wrinkled appearance.

He said, "I'll miss it all after a <u>grisly</u> fashion. It's hard to remember when we weren't at war with Deneb, and it seems against nature now to be at peace and to look at the stars without anxiety."

The two men with the Executive Director of the Solar Federation were both younger than Swift. Neither was as gray. Neither looked quite as tired.

John Henderson, thin-lipped and finding it hard to control the relief he felt in the midst of triumph, said, "They're destroyed! They're destroyed! It's what I keep saying to myself over and over and I still can't believe it. We all talked so much, over so many years, about the menace hanging over Earth and all its worlds, over every human being, and all the time it was true, every word of it. And now we're alive and it's the Denebians who are shattered and destroyed. They'll be no menace now, ever again."

"Thanks to Multivac," said Swift, with a quiet glance at the <u>imperturbable</u> Jablonsky, who through all the war had been Chief Interpreter of science's <u>oracle</u>. "Right, Max?"

Jablonsky shrugged. He said, "Well, that's what *they* say." His broad thumb moved in the direction of his right shoulder, aiming upward.

"Jealous, Max?"

"Because they're shouting for Multivac? Because Multivac is the big hero of mankind in this war?" Jablonsky's craggy face took on an air of suitable contempt. "What's that to me? Let Multivac be the machine that won the war, if it pleases them."

Henderson looked at the other two out of the corners of his eyes. In this short interlude that the three had instinctively sought out

erratic (er rat´ ik) *adj.* irregular; random

grisly (griz´ lē) *adj.* horrifying; gruesome

imperturbable (im´ pər tur´ bə bəl) *adj.* unable to be excited or disturbed

oracle (ôr´ ə kəl) *n.* source of knowledge or wise counsel

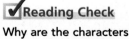
Reading Check

Why are the characters enjoying a brief rest as the story begins?

▲ **Critical Viewing** What attraction might the night sky, as shown here, have for science-fiction writers? **[Hypothesize]**

in the one peaceful corner of a metropolis gone mad; in this entr'acte[1] between the dangers of war and the difficulties of peace; when, for one moment, they might all find <u>surcease</u>; he was conscious only of his weight of guilt.

surcease (sur´ sēs´) n. end

Suddenly, it was as though that weight were too great to be borne longer. It had to be thrown off, along with the war; now!

Henderson said, "Multivac had nothing to do with victory. It's just a machine."

"A big one," said Swift.

"Then just a big machine. No better than the data fed it." For a moment, he stopped, suddenly unnerved at what he was saying.

Jablonsky looked at him. "You should know. You supplied the data. Or is it just that you're taking the credit?"

"*No,*" said Henderson angrily. "There is no credit. What do you know of the data Multivac had to use: predigested from a hundred <u>subsidiary</u> computers here on Earth, on the Moon, on Mars, even on Titan. With Titan always delayed and always feeling that its figures would introduce an unexpected bias."

subsidiary (səb sid´ ē er´ ē) adj. secondary; supporting

"It would drive anyone mad," said Swift, with gentle sympathy.

Henderson shook his head. "It wasn't just that. I admit that eight years ago when I replaced Lepont as Chief Programmer, I was nervous. But there was an exhilaration about things in those days. The war was still long range; an adventure without real danger. We hadn't reached the point where manned vessels had had to take over and where interstellar warps could swallow up a planet clean, if aimed correctly. But then, when the real difficulties began—"

Angrily—he could finally permit anger—he said, "You know nothing about it."

"Well," said Swift. "Tell us. The war is over. We've won."

"Yes." Henderson nodded his head. He had to remember that. Earth had won, so all had been for the best. "Well, the data became meaningless."

"Meaningless? You mean that literally?" said Jablonsky.

"Literally. What would you expect? The trouble with you two was that you weren't out in the thick of it. You never left Multivac, Max, and you, Mr. Director, never left the Mansion except on state visits where you saw exactly what they wanted you to see."

"I was not as unaware of that," said Swift, "as you may have thought."

"Do you know," said Henderson, "to what extent data concerning our production capacity, our resource potential, our trained manpower—everything of importance to the war effort, in fact—had become unreliable and untrustworthy during the last half of the war? Group leaders, both civilian and military, were intent on projecting their own improved image, so to speak, so they obscured the bad and magnified the good. Whatever the machines might do, the men who programmed

Reading Strategy
Identifying Relevant Details Which details in this paragraph are relevant to helping you understand the plot?

✔**Reading Check**
What does Henderson say about Multivac's role in winning the war?

---

1. entr'acte (än trakt´) *n.* interval.

them and interpreted the results had their own skins to think of and competitors to stab. There was no way of stopping that. I tried, and failed."

"Of course," said Swift, in quiet consolation. "I can see that you would."

"Yet I presume you provided Multivac with data in your programming?" Jablonsky said. "You said nothing to us about unreliability."

"How could I tell you? And if I did, how could you afford to believe me?" demanded Henderson, savagely. "Our entire war effort was geared to Multivac. It was the one great weapon on our side, for the Denebians had nothing like it. What else kept up morale in the face of doom but the assurance that Multivac would always predict and <u>circumvent</u> any Denebian move, and would always direct and prevent the circumvention of our moves? Great Space, after our Spy-warp was blasted out of hyperspace we lacked any reliable Denebian data to feed Multivac and we didn't dare make *that* public."

circumvent (sʉr´ kəm vent´) *v.* avoid; go around

"True enough," said Swift.

"Well, then," said Henderson, "if I told you the data was unreliable, what could you have done but replace me and refuse to believe me? I couldn't allow that."

"What did you do?" said Jablonsky.

"Since the war is won, I'll tell you what I did. I corrected the data."

"How?" asked Swift.

"Intuition, I presume. I juggled them till they looked right. At first, I hardly dared. I changed a bit here and there to correct what were obvious impossibilities. When the sky didn't collapse about us, I got braver. Toward the end, I scarcely cared. I just wrote out the necessary data as it was needed. I even had the Multivac Annex prepare data for me according to a private programming pattern I had devised for the purpose."

"Random figures?" said Jablonsky.

"Not at all. I introduced a number of necessary biases."

Jablonsky smiled, quite unexpectedly, his dark eyes sparkling behind the crinkling of the lower lids. "Three times a report was brought to me about unauthorized uses of the Annex, and I let it go each time. If it had mattered, I would have followed it up and spotted you, John, and found out what you were doing. But, of course, nothing about Multivac mattered in those days, so you got away with it."

"What do you mean, nothing mattered?" asked Henderson, suspiciously.

"Nothing did. I suppose if I had told you this at the time, it would have spared you your agony, but then if you had told me what you were doing, it would have spared me mine. What made you think Multivac was in working order, whatever the data you supplied it?"

"Not in working order?" said Swift.

"Not really. Not reliably. After all, where were my technicians in the last years of the war? I'll tell you, they were feeding computers on a thousand different space devices. They were gone! I had to make do

Reading Strategy
Identifying Relevant Details What are the most relevant details in this paragraph?

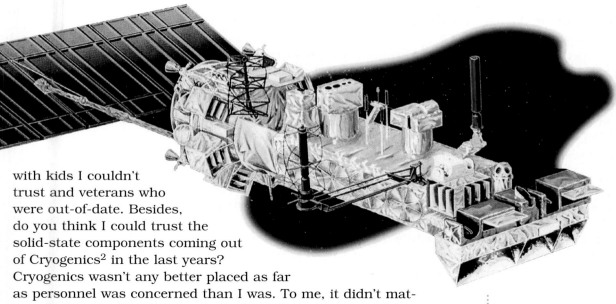

with kids I couldn't trust and veterans who were out-of-date. Besides, do you think I could trust the solid-state components coming out of Cryogenics[2] in the last years? Cryogenics wasn't any better placed as far as personnel was concerned than I was. To me, it didn't matter whether the data being supplied Multivac were reliable or not. The results weren't reliable. That much I knew."

"What did you do?" asked Henderson.

"I did what you did, John. I introduced the bugger factor. I adjusted matters in accordance with intuition—and that's how the machine won the war."

Swift leaned back in the chair and stretched his legs out before him. "Such revelations. It turns out then that the material handed me to guide me in my decision-making capacity was a man-made interpretation of man-made data. Isn't that right?"

"It looks so," said Jablonsky.

"Then I perceive I was correct in not placing too much reliance upon it," said Swift.

"You didn't?" Jablonsky, despite what he had just said, managed to look professionally insulted.

"I'm afraid I didn't. Multivac might seem to say, Strike here, not there; do this, not that; wait, don't act. But I could never be certain that what Multivac seemed to say, it really did say; or what it really said, it really meant. I could never be certain."

"But the final report was always plain enough, sir," said Jablonsky.

"To those who did not have to make the decision, perhaps. Not to me. The horror of the responsibility of such decisions was unbearable and not even Multivac was sufficient to remove the weight. But the point is I was justified in doubting and there is tremendous relief in that."

Caught up in the conspiracy of mutual confession, Jablonsky put titles aside. "What was it you did then, Lamar? After all, you did make decisions. How?"

---

2. **Cryogenics** (krī ō jen′ iks) here, a department concerned with the science of low-temperature phenomena.

✔️**Reading Check**

What kind of data and interpretation of data were given to Swift during the war?

"Well, it's time to be getting back perhaps, but—I'll tell you first. Why not? I did make use of a computer, Max, but an older one than Multivac, much older."

He groped in his own pocket and brought out a scattering of small change; old-fashioned coins dating to the first years before the metal shortage had brought into being a credit system tied to a computer-complex.

Swift smiled rather sheepishly. "I still need these to make money seem substantial to me. An old man finds it hard to abandon the habits of youth." He dropped the coins, one by one, back into his pocket.

He held the last coin between his fingers, staring absently at it. "Multivac is not the first computer, friends, nor the best-known, nor the one that can most efficiently lift the load of decision from the shoulders of the executive. A machine *did* win the war, John; at least a very simple computing device did; one that I used every time I had a particularly hard decision to make."

With a faint smile of reminiscence, he flipped the coin he held. It glinted in the air as it spun and came down in Swift's outstretched palm. His hand closed over it and brought it down on the back of his left hand. His right hand remained in place, hiding the coin.

"Heads or tails, gentlemen?" said Swift.

Review and Assess

Thinking About the Selection

1. **Respond:** How did your opinion of Multivac change as you read the story?

2. **(a) Recall:** What is behind the celebration mentioned at the opening of the story? **(b) Connect:** Do the three men join in the celebratory mood? Explain.

3. **(a) Recall:** What are the job titles of the three men in the story? **(b) Compare and Contrast:** How are the men's jobs related yet different?

4. **(a) Recall:** What was Multivac's expected role in the war? **(b) Draw Conclusions:** What was its true role in the war?

5. **(a) Recall:** What did the men do to the data fed to Multivac? **(b) Deduce:** Did their actions make Multivac less reliable than Swift's "simple computing device"? Explain.

6. **Speculate:** If all three men had done their jobs properly, would the war's outcome have been different? Explain.

7. **Take a Position:** Do you think it is better to rely on information from humans or from computers? Why?

Isaac Asimov

(1920–1992)

Asimov came to the United States from Russia at the age of three. His parents spoke no English, but he taught himself to read the language before entering first grade.

Disliking the need to return library books and wanting a permanent library of his own, Asimov decided to write his own books. Overall, he wrote more than 470 books on subjects including science, history, Shakespeare, and the Bible, as well as science fiction, for which he is best known.

Some of his most famous works include *I Robot* (1950), the *Foundation* trilogy (1951–53), and *Fantastic Voyage* (1966), which was made into a movie.

Review and Assess

Literary Analysis

Science Fiction

1. In **science fiction,** some elements must be based on scientific ideas. Use a chart like this to classify key elements of the story.

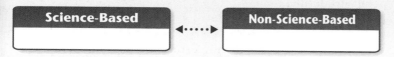

2. Which plot details indicate that the story is science fiction?
3. Could the characters in this story exist in real life? Why or why not?
4. Good science fiction carefully balances scientific and imaginative elements. Is this story good science fiction? Explain.

Connecting Literary Elements

5. Which details of time and place indicate that the story's **setting** is the future? Record your answers in a chart like the one below.

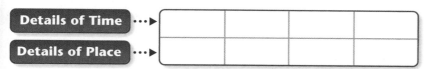

6. On the basis of what you know about the present and the past, does Asimov's future seem genuinely possible? Explain.
7. Could a story have the same setting as Asimov's and *not* be science fiction? Explain.

Reading Strategy

Identifying Relevant Details

8. In this story, the space program is both vast and advanced. (a) Find two details that support this statement. (b) Are these details **relevant** to the plot? Explain your answer.
9. (a) Which detail in the story shows how the monetary system in Asimov's future world differs from the present system? (b) Is the changed system relevant? Explain.

Extend Understanding

10. **Technology Connection:** Computers solve many—but not all—problems. Name areas where they are not useful now, and then speculate whether future computers might be useful in those areas.

Quick Review

Science fiction is a form of fiction in which the writer makes free use of imagination to create settings, characters, and situations not found in reality.

A story's **setting** is the time and place in which its action occurs.

To **identify relevant details,** find those that make the plot, characters, and setting understandable.

 Take It to the Net

www.phschool.com
Take the interactive self-test online to check your understanding of the selection.

Integrate Language Skills

Vocabulary Development Lesson

Word Analysis: Latin Prefix *circum-*

The Latin prefix *circum-* means "around." *Circumvent*, for instance, means "go around" or "avoid." Apply the meaning of *circum-* to define each word below. Then, use each word in a sentence.

1. circumference
2. circumscribe
3. circumstance
4. circumnavigate

Spelling Strategy

To add the suffix *-ly* to a word that ends in *-ic*, spell the suffix *-ally*. For example, *erratic* becomes *erratically*. (An exception to this rule is *publicly*.) Add *-ally* to the following adjectives to make them adverbs. Then, use each adverb in a sentence.

1. realistic
2. hectic
3. terrific

Concept Development: Synonyms

Choose the letter of the word or phrase that has the same meaning as the first word.

1. erratic: (a) slow, (b) random, (c) rapid
2. grisly: (a) private, (b) oily, (c) horrifying
3. imperturbable: (a) unexcitable, (b) increasing, (c) unhappy
4. oracle: (a) wise person, (b) loyal pet, (c) generous host
5. surcease: (a) a beginning, (b) an overabundance, (c) an end
6. subsidiary: (a) foremost, (b) subsiding, (c) secondary
7. circumvent: (a) avoid, (b) encourage, (c) reward

Grammar Lesson

Adverb Clauses and Noun Clauses

A **subordinate clause** is a group of words with a subject and verb that cannot stand alone as a sentence. An **adverb clause** is a subordinate clause that modifies a verb, an adjective, or an adverb. It tells *where*, *when*, *why*, *how*, or *to what extent*.

> **Adverb Clause:** Swift was surprised *when he heard the news*. (modifies the adjective *surprised* by telling *when*)

A **noun clause** is a subordinate clause that acts as a noun.

> **Noun Clause:** The decision was *whether they should trust Multivac*. (acts as predicate nominative)

Practice Identify the subordinate clause in each sentence, and tell whether it functions as an adverb clause or a noun clause.

1. The three men confessed after the war ended.
2. Each man's secret was that he had changed the rules.
3. Multivac was valuable if it was used right.
4. The computer didn't know that it was a hero.
5. Swift tossed a coin before he made a decision.

Writing Application "Since the war is won, I'll tell you what I did." Using this sentence as a model, write two original sentences that incorporate both an adverb clause and a noun clause.

W͟G Prentice Hall Writing and Grammar Connection: Chapter 21, Section 2

Writing Lesson

Newspaper Story

Write a newspaper story about the end of the war between Earth and Deneb. Use references from "The Machine That Won the War" and your own ideas to explain what the war was about and what the victory might mean for Earthlings.

Prewriting   Start by jotting down answers to the five W's—*who, what, where, when,* and *why.* Then, plan an attention-grabbing headline.

Drafting   Begin your news story with a striking lead sentence that captures the effect the war has had on both Earthlings and Denebians. As you write the body of your article, make sure that each of the questions is addressed and answered.

Model: Writing an Attention-Grabbing Lead

After a ten-year struggle, Earth is at peace.

Denebians are no longer a threat, and Earthlings

must now begin to rebuild a planet shattered by war.

> Words like *struggle, peace, threat,* and *shattered* immediately grab the reader's attention.

Revising   Ask a classmate to read your draft aloud to you. As you listen, consider which scenes are unclear, and then provide further elaboration.

W̶G̶ Prentice Hall Writing and Grammar Connection: Chapter 13, Section 3

Extension Activities

Listening and Speaking   In Asimov's story, the three main characters relied on intuition to adjust the data fed to Multivac. In a small group, conduct a **discussion** on the role of intuition in any decision. Use these questions to guide you:

- When is it proper to ignore instructions and follow your instincts?
- When may using your intuition be the wrong thing to do?

Take notes on the points group members make. Then, use your notes to share a summary of the discussion with the class. [**Group Activity**]

Research and Technology   Prepare an **illustrated report** on the history of computers, including an essay accompanied by drawings, photos, and magazine ads. Incorporate Asimov's Multivac into your writing, explaining how it compares to computers throughout history. Design and publish your illustrated report by using desktop software and graphic programs.

 **Take It to the Net**   www.phschool.com

Go online for an additional research activity using the Internet.

AHA MOMENT

Julia Alvarez

I was in the tiny bathroom in the back of the plane when I
felt the slamming jolt, then the horrible swerve that threw
me against the door. Oh, Lord, I thought, this is it! Somehow
I managed to unbolt the door and scramble out. The flight
attendants, already strapped in, waved wildly for me to sit
down. As I lunged ahead toward my seat, passengers looked
up at me with the stricken expression of creatures who know
they are about to die.

"I think we got hit by lightning," the girl in the seat next to mine said. She was from a small town in east Texas, and this was only her second time on an airplane. She had won a trip to England by competing in a high school geography bee and was supposed to make a connecting flight when we landed in Newark.

In the next seat, at the window, sat a young businessman who had been confidently working. Now he looked worried—something that really worries me: when confident-looking businessmen look worried. The laptop was put away. "Something's not right," he said.

The pilot's voice came over the speaker. I heard vaguely through my fear, "Engine number two. . .hit. . .emergency landing. . .New Orleans." When he was done, the voice of a flight attendant came on, reminding us of the emergency procedures she had reviewed before takeoff. Of course I never paid attention to this drill, always figuring that if we ever got to the point where we needed to use life jackets, I would have already died of terror.

Now we began a roller-coaster ride through the thunderclouds. I was ready to faint, but when I saw the face of the girl next to me I pulled myself together. I reached for her hand and reassured her that we were going to make it. "What a story you're going to tell when you get home!" I said. "After this, London's going to seem like small potatoes."

"Yes, ma'am," she mumbled.

I wondered where I was getting my strength. Then I saw that my other hand was tightly held by a ringed hand. Someone was comforting *me*—a glamorous young woman across the aisle, the female equivalent of the confident businessman. She must have seen how scared I was and reached over.

"I tell you," she confided, "the problems I brought up on this plane with me sure don't seem real big right now." I loved her southern <u>drawl</u>, her <u>indiscriminate</u> use of perfume, her soulful squeezes. I was sure that even if I survived a plane crash, I'd have a couple of broken fingers from all the T.L.C.[1] "Are you okay?" she kept asking me.

Among the many feelings going through my head during those excruciating 20 minutes was pride—pride in how well everybody was behaving. No one panicked. No one screamed. As we jolted and screeched our way downward, I could hear small pockets of soothing conversation everywhere.

I thought of something I had heard a friend say about the wonderful gift his dying father had given the family: He had died peacefully, as if not to alarm any of them about an experience they would all have to go through someday.

And then—yes!—we landed safely. Outside on the ground, attendants and officials were waiting to transfer us to alternate flights. But we passengers clung together. We chatted about the lives we now felt blessed to be living, as difficult or rocky as they might be. The young

---

1. T.L.C. abbreviation for "Tender Loving Care"

Thematic Connection
What do the descriptions of passengers and their varied reactions show us about dependence on technology?

drawl (drôl) *n.* a slow speech pattern, characterized by prolonged vowels

indiscriminate (in′di skrim′ i nit) *adj.* ignoring standards of good taste

businessman <u>lamented</u> that he had not had a chance to buy his two little girls a present. An older woman offered him her box of expensive Lindt chocolates, still untouched, tied with a lovely bow. "I shouldn't be eating them anyhow," she said. My glamorous aisle mate took out her cell phone and passed it around to anyone who wanted to make a call to hear the reassuring voice of a loved one.

There was someone I wanted to call. Back in Vermont, my husband, Bill, was anticipating my arrival late that night. He had been complaining that he wasn't getting to see very much of me because of my book tour. That's why I had decided to take this particular flight—oh, yes, one of those stories! I had planned to surprise him by getting in a few hours early. Now I just wanted him to know I was okay and on my way.

When my name was finally called to board my new flight, I felt almost tearful to be parting from people whose lives had so intensely, if briefly, touched mine.

Even now, back on terra firma,[2] walking down a Vermont road, I sometimes hear an airplane and look up at that small, glinting piece of metal. I remember the passengers on that fateful, lucky flight and wish I could thank them for the many acts of kindness I witnessed and received. I am indebted to my fellow passengers and wish I could pay them back.

But then, remembering my aisle mate's hand clutching mine while I clutched the hand of the high school student, I feel struck by lightning all over again: The point is not to pay back kindness but to pass it on.

<hr>

2. **terra firma** (ter′ə fur′mə) *n.* Latin phrase meaning "solid ground."

---

lamented (lə ment′ id) *v.* expressed sorrow; regretted

Julia Alvarez

(b. 1950)

Julia Alvarez immigrated to the United States from the Dominican Republic when she was ten years old. This sudden adjustment to an unfamiliar country with a strange language influenced her decision to write. ". . . I realized that language was going to be how I connected with these babbles. . . . Language was a portable homeland." Since this early realization, Alvarez has written several successful novels and volumes of poetry, in addition to teaching writing to college students, senior citizens, and bilingual students. Alvarez's work has been praised for its humor, sensitivity, and insight into the way people think and interact.

Connecting Literature Past and Present

1. How does Alvarez's story reflect the often hidden role technology plays in our lives?

2. Why do you think the passengers reacted the way they did when their plane was hit?

3. (a) How does the narrative reflect an "aha moment"? (b) In what ways might the experience change the writer's life? Explain.

4. (a) In what ways were the situations of the men in "The Machine That Won the War" and the passengers in the Alvarez story similar? (b) How did they differ?

5. What do both of these stories have to tell us about human faith in technology?

Prepare to Read

Fire and Ice ◆ "There Will Come Soft Rains" ◆ The Horses ◆ All Watched Over by Machines of Loving Grace

Wild Mustang, Red Desert, Wyoming

Take It to the Net

Visit www.phschool.com for interactive activities and instruction related to the selections, including
- background
- graphic organizers
- literary elements
- reading strategies

Preview

Connecting to the Literature

Is the world heading toward a gloomy destruction or a golden age of harmony? The poets in these four works explore their individual visions of the future. As you read the poems, consider your own ideas on the subject.

Background

Sara Teasdale's poem mentions "the war" without specifying which one. She and her husband both opposed World War I (1914–1918), even though their position was unpopular. Called at the time the Great War, it was the first one fought with machine guns, weapons that could spit out 600 to 700 bullets a minute. Soldiers on the battlefield knew that large numbers of them would be brutally cut down by machine-gun fire. The impersonality of this type of warfare horrified many.

Literary Analysis

Alliteration

Alliteration is the repetition of a consonant sound at the beginning of two or more words. Poets use this sound technique mainly to emphasize certain words but also to create musical effects and to help create a mood. In these lines from "The Horses," four words begin with *w*:

> We saw the heads
> Like a wild wave charging and were afraid.

The repetition of the sound draws attention to these words and their meaning. When read aloud, the words slow the reader's pace and suggest a sense of awe. Look for other examples of alliteration in the selections, and think about how it affects the poems' sound and meaning.

Comparing Literary Works

Each poem in this section presents a vision of the future. While one poem's vision may be more or less disturbing than another's, each poet sends a particular message or warning to people. Compare and contrast the visions presented in each poem. Decide whether a particular poem presents a hopeful, gloomy, or frightening vision of the future, and consider how effectively a message is conveyed.

Reading Strategy

Recognizing a Poet's Purpose

Each poem in this group calls attention to a troubling situation or attitude. To **recognize a poet's purpose,** or reason for writing a poem, read the work closely. Follow these suggestions:

- Look for the meaning behind the words in the poem.
- Note words that seem startling or jarring.
- Consider why the poet chose those specific words.

Use a chart like the one shown to note key details. Jot down the effects of each and determine the poet's purpose.

Key Words
perish
twice

Effects
surprising,
scary

Poet's Purpose

Vocabulary Development

perish (per´ ish) *v.* die (p. 472)

suffice (sə fīs´) *v.* be enough (p. 472)

tremulous (trem´ yoo ləs) *adj.* quivering (p. 473)

covenant (kuv´ ə nənt) *n.* agreement; pact (p. 474)

confounds (kən foundz´) *v.* bewilders; confuses (p. 474)

steeds (stēdz) *n.* horses (p. 475)

archaic (är kā´ ik) *adj.* seldom used; old-fashioned (p. 475)

Fire and Ice

Robert Frost

Some say the world will end in fire,
Some say in ice.
From what I've tasted of desire
I hold with those who favor fire.
5   But if it had to perish twice,
I think I know enough of hate
To say that for destruction ice
Is also great
And would suffice.

perish (per´ ish) v. die

suffice (sə fīs´) v. be enough

Robert Frost

(1874–1963)
Like the title of his poem "Fire and Ice," Robert Frost seemed witty and warm to some, cold and bitter to others. All agreed, however, that poetry came first in his life. Frost is known for being the poet called upon to recite two poems at the inauguration of John F. Kennedy in 1961.

Frost produced a large body of work and became the most popular American poet of his time, winning four Pulitzer Prizes.

Review and Assess

Thinking About the Selection

1. **Respond:** How does the speaker's view of the future make you feel? Explain.

2. **(a) Recall:** With which opinion of the world's end does Frost first side? **(b) Interpret:** How might desire bring an end to the world?

3. **(a) Recall:** Why does Frost think the world might end in ice? **(b) Interpret:** In what way is ice a fitting metaphor for hatred?

4. **Assess:** How do the rhyming words affect the poem's mood?

5. **Speculate:** How have desire and hatred already affected the safety of people in the world?

"There Will Come Soft Rains"

(War Time)

Sara Teasdale

There will come soft rains and the smell of the ground,
And swallows circling with their shimmering sound;

And frogs in the pools singing at night,
And wild plum-trees in <u>tremulous</u> white;

5 Robins will wear their feathery fire
Whistling their whims on a low fence-wire;

And not one will know of the war, not one
Will care at last when it is done.

Not one would mind, neither bird nor tree
10 If mankind perished utterly;

And Spring herself, when she woke at dawn,
Would scarcely know that we were gone.

tremulous (trem´ yōō ləs)
adj. quivering

Sara Teasdale

(1884–1933)

Sara Teasdale's poetry—much of it on the subject of love—was rooted in her own difficulties with personal relationships. Teasdale had a sad life and often expressed her sadness through poetry.

She once commented that "poems are written because of a state of emotional irritation" and that the poem "free[s] the poet from an emotional burden."

Review and Assess

Thinking About the Selection

1. **Respond:** Do you think that nature "has an attitude" toward humans, as this poem suggests? Explain.

2. **(a) Recall:** According to the poet, what will animals do after the war is over? **(b) Compare and Contrast:** How will the animals' fate differ from people's?

3. **Recall:** What will be Spring's reaction to human absence after the war? **(b) Generalize:** What theme about war does Spring's reaction, in combination with other details in the poem, suggest?

4. **Speculate:** Teasdale died before an even more destructive war broke out. What might her reaction have been to World War II?

The Horses

Edwin Muir

Barely a twelvemonth after
The seven days war that put the world to sleep,
Late in the evening the strange horses came.
By then we had made our <u>covenant</u> with silence,
5 But in the first few days it was so still
We listened to our breathing and were afraid.
On the second day
The radios failed; we turned the knobs; no answer.
On the third day a warship passed us, heading north,
10 Dead bodies piled on the deck. On the sixth day
A plane plunged over us into the sea. Thereafter
Nothing. The radios dumb;
And still they stand in corners of our kitchens,
And stand, perhaps, turned on, in a million rooms
15 All over the world. But now if they should speak,
If on a sudden they should speak again,
If on the stroke of noon a voice should speak,
We would not listen, we would not let it bring
That old bad world that swallowed its children quick
20 At one great gulp. We would not have it again.
Sometimes we think of the nations lying asleep,
Curled blindly in impenetrable sorrow,
And then the thought <u>confounds</u> us with its strangeness.

The tractors lie about our fields; at evening
25 They look like dank sea-monsters couched and waiting.
We leave them where they are and let them rust:

covenant (kuv´ ə nənt) *n.*
agreement; pact

Literary Analysis
Alliteration What
examples of alliteration
do you see in line 20?

confounds (kən foundz´) *v.*
bewilders; confuses

▼ **Critical Viewing** In
what ways do these
horses compare to those
the poet describes?
[Connect]

'They'll moulder away and be like other loam'.[1]
We make our oxen drag our rusty ploughs,
Long laid aside. We have gone back
30 Far past our fathers' land.
                        And then, that evening
Late in the summer the strange horses came.
We heard a distant tapping on the road,
A deepening drumming; it stopped, went on again
35 And at the corner changed to hollow thunder.
We saw the heads
Like a wild wave charging and were afraid.
We had sold our horses in our fathers' time
To buy new tractors. Now they were strange to us
40 As fabulous <u>steeds</u> set on an ancient shield
Or illustrations in a book of knights.
We did not dare go near them. Yet they waited,
Stubborn and shy, as if they had been sent
By an old command to find our whereabouts
45 And that long-lost <u>archaic</u> companionship.
In the first moment we had never a thought
That they were creatures to be owned and used.
Among them were some half-a-dozen colts
Dropped in some wilderness of the broken world,
50 Yet new as if they had come from their own Eden.[2]
Since then they have pulled our ploughs and borne our loads,
But that free servitude still can pierce our hearts.
Our life is changed; their coming our beginning.

steeds (stēdz) *n.* horses

archaic (är kā´ ik) *adj.* seldom used; old-fashioned

1. **loam** (lōm) *n.* dark, rich soil.
2. **Eden** in the Bible, the garden where life began with Adam and Eve; paradise.

Review and Assess

Thinking About the Selection

1. **Respond:** How did the arrival of the horses in the poem make you feel? Explain.

2. **(a) Recall:** What has been the result of the "seven days war"? **(b) Support:** What words led you to this opinion?

3. **(a) Recall:** What did the "old bad world" do to its children? **(b) Analyze:** Is this event a sufficient explanation for the sorrow and confusion the speaker refers to?

4. **(a) Recall:** What has happened to the tractors? **(b) Interpret:** Why are the tractors and the horses placed side by side?

5. **Speculate:** Do you see any reason to believe that the note of hope the speaker associates with the horses' arrival will survive into the future? Explain your response.

Edwin Muir

(1887–1959)

A prolific writer who produced many volumes of poetry and several novels, Muir had visions of the future that were rooted in his past. He spent his first fourteen years on a farm in the Orkney Islands north of the Scottish mainland. Much of his imagery comes from this place.

All Watched Over by Machines of Loving Grace

Richard Brautigan

I like to think (and
the sooner the better!)
of a cybernetic meadow
where mammals and computers
5 live together in mutually
programming harmony
like pure water
touching clear sky.

I like to think
   (right now, please!)
10 of a cybernetic forest
filled with pines and electronics
where deer stroll peacefully
past computers
as if they were flowers
15 with spinning blossoms.

I like to think
   (it has to be!)
of a cybernetic ecology
where we are free of our labors
and joined back to nature,
20 returned to our mammal
brothers and sisters,
and all watched over
by machines of loving grace.

Richard Brautigan

(1935–1984)
With his 1967 novel *Trout Fishing in America,* Brautigan became a spokesperson of the hippie genera-tion. Ironically, though, he was at least fifteen years older than the hippies and thus a product of the beat generation that preceded them. Nevertheless, he was certainly a free spirit in his writing.

Review and Assess

Thinking About the Selection

1. **Respond:** What emotions does this poem evoke in you?

2. **(a) Recall:** Why does Brautigan describe computers as "machines of loving grace"? **(b) Draw Conclusions:** On the basis of your answer, describe Brautigan's vision of the future.

3. **(a) Assess:** Does he describe a peaceful or a stressful environment? **(b) Speculate:** Has Brautigan's vision become a reality yet?

Review and Assess

Literary Analysis
Alliteration
1. Using a chart like the one below, record examples of **alliteration** in "There Will Come Soft Rains" and "The Horses," along with the effect they produce.

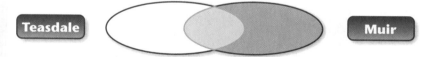

Poem	Lines	Alliteration	Effect

2. Find two examples of alliteration in "Fire and Ice," and explain their effect on the poem's meaning.

Comparing Literary Works
3. (a) Compare the visions of the future that Frost and Brautigan introduce in their poems. (b) Do you think the ideas in Brautigan's poem are more optimistic than those in Frost's? Explain.
4. Both Teasdale and Muir imagine the world after a devastating war. Use a Venn diagram to compare and contrast Teasdale's and Muir's visions of the future.

Teasdale   **Muir**

5. What similar ideas do you think Teasdale and Muir had about the war itself?

Reading Strategy
Recognizing a Poet's Purpose
6. (a) Briefly describe each poet's **purpose.** (b) What words, phrases, and ideas led you to your answer in each case?
7. In "All Watched Over by Machines of Loving Grace," how does the phrase "cybernetic meadow" help you recognize the poet's purpose?

Extend Understanding
8. **World Events Connection:** If these poets were alive today, which present-day conflicts or events might inspire their response? Explain.

Integrate Language Skills

Vocabulary Development Lesson

Word Analysis: Latin Suffix -ous

The Latin suffix -ous means "full of " or "characterized by," as in the word *tremulous*, which means "characterized by trembling." Match each word below with its definition.

1. perilous   **2.** courageous   **3.** clamorous
a. characterized by bravery
b. noisy; loud; marked by vehemence
c. risky; full of danger

Spelling Strategy

If a word ends in a vowel-vowel-consonant combination, do not double the consonant before adding a suffix. For example, *archaic* + *-ally* = *archaically*. Add *-ness*, *-ance*, or *-al* to each word below to form a properly spelled new word.

1. tremulous   **2.** avoid   **3.** stoic

Concept Development: Synonyms

Identify the word that is a synonym for, or is closest in meaning to, each word from the vocabulary list on page 471.

1. perish: (a) live, (b) die, (c) decide
2. suffice: (a) help, (b) satisfy, (c) mistake
3. steeds: (a) rewards, (b) cattle, (c) horses
4. confounds: (a) irritates, (b) surprises, (c) confuses
5. tremulous: (a) quivering, (b) huge, (c) emotional
6. archaic: (a) curved, (b) simple, (c) old-fashioned
7. covenant: (a) church, (b) argument, (c) agreement

Grammar Lesson

Adjective Clauses

A **subordinate clause** is a group of words with a subject and verb that cannot stand on its own in a sentence.

An **adjective clause** is a subordinate clause that modifies a noun or pronoun by answering the question *what kind?* or *which one?* It is usually introduced by a **relative pronoun,** such as *who, whom, whose, which,* or *that,* or by a **conjunction,** such as *where, when,* or *why.*

In this example, the adjective clause is underlined and the noun it modifies is in italics.

> **Example:** I see a *meadow* where they live together. (which *meadow?*)

Practice Write each sentence on your paper. Underline the adjective clauses and circle the word that each one modifies.

1. It was a seven days war that put the world to sleep.
2. There was a time when people used tractors.
3. I hold with those who favor fire.
4. We saw the horses, which could help us with our labor.
5. Listen to the plains where robins whistle.

Writing Application Write a short paragraph about the poem you liked best. Use at least three adjective clauses in your paragraph.

Prentice Hall Writing and Grammar Connection: Chapter 21, Section 2

Writing Lesson

Poem to a Future Generation

The poems in this section describe the future in order to make you think critically about the present. Write a short poem that describes the positive aspects of today's world for people of the future.

Prewriting	Decide on a positive message. Then, make a list of images drawn from the present-day world that will help convey your message. Try to use words that create alliteration and convey a particular mood.
Drafting	Use precise language and sensory details to present a clear picture of the present. Make sure that you present each image in as few words as possible.
Revising	As you discuss your poem with a classmate, highlight any words that do not create a clear picture or do not seem necessary. Consider rephrasing for clarity or eliminating the unnecessary words.

Model: Rephrasing to Clarify an Image

> *awash in   silvery*
> The sky was ~~streaming with a beautiful~~ light,
>
> *the somber ravens soared*
> As we sat in silence, ~~watching the birds overhead.~~

> Precise adjectives like *silvery* and *somber* help build and clarify the images while keeping them forceful and brief.

WG *Prentice Hall Writing and Grammar Connection: Chapter 6, Section 4*

Extension Activities

Listening and Speaking Prepare and present a **dramatic reading** of "Fire and Ice," "All Watched Over by Machines of Loving Grace," or "There Will Come Soft Rains."

- Concentrate on your tone of voice and use of facial expressions to express meaning.
- Practice making eye contact with your audience.

Videotape your rehearsal for later review, or practice in front of a mirror. After presenting, invite listeners to comment on the effectiveness of your reading.

Research and Technology Watch a video or TV program set in the future. As you watch, jot down some specific futuristic elements at work. As a participant in a **panel discussion,** discuss whether the program presents a positive or negative vision of the future. Then, compare this vision to the visions of the poems in this section. **[Group Activity]**

 **Take It to the Net**   www.phschool.com

Go online for an additional research activity using the Internet.

READING INFORMATIONAL MATERIALS

Product Information

About Product Information

Product information is printed material that comes packaged with a manufactured item. Two common types of product information are **technical directions** and **warranties.**

- Technical directions explain the safe, proper, and efficient uses of a product and may include diagrams to help convey information.
- Warranties explain the contractual obligations between a consumer and the manufacturer.

You might find these printed features after opening a new item such as a camera, computer, or calculator.

Reading Strategy

Analyzing the Purpose of Product Information

To get the most out of product information, you need to know where to locate the information you want.

Technical directions offer step-by-step instructions for using the item. They may explain procedures such as the following:

- How to assemble the item
- How to turn the item on and off
- How to operate specific features

A **warranty** explains what the manufacturer agrees to provide the consumer in terms of service and maintenance. It may tell, for example, how long the manufacturer will repair a part at no additional charge. Often, the consumer must mail in a signed warranty card to the manufacturer in order for the agreement to become effective.

As you read product information, check to see that it contains the features and purposes outlined in the chart below.

Product Information	Features	Purpose
Technical directions	• Assembling, operating, maintenance instructions • Informal language	Explains how to assemble, use, and protect the merchandise
Warranty	• Charts or graphs • Printed contract between manufacturer and user • Formal language	Details manufacturer's service obligation to user

Technical Directions

Following are technical directions for using a graphing calculator. The product manual, included with the purchase, outlines the procedures for a variety of calculating functions. The directions on this page specifically offer step-by-step instructions for displaying and tracing a graph. They assume the user has a basic knowledge of the calculator.

The heading conveniently indicates the function being explained.

DISPLAYING AND TRACING THE GRAPH

Now that you have defined the function to be graphed and the WINDOW in which to graph it, you can display and explore the graph. You can trace along a function with TRACE.

1. Press **GRAPH** to graph the selected function in the viewing **WINDOW**.

   The graph of $Y_1=(W-2X)(L/2-X)X$ is shown in the display.

The directions provide visual aids to accompany the instructional text.

2. Press ▶ once to display the free-moving graph cursor just to the right of the center of the screen. The bottom line of the display shows the **X** and **Y** coordinate values for the position of the graph cursor.

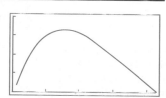

X=2.1702128 _ Y=20

3. Use the cursor-keys (◀, ▶, ▲ and ▼) to position the free-moving cursor at the apparent maximum of the function.

   As you move the cursor, **X** and **Y** coordinate values are updated continually with the cursor position.

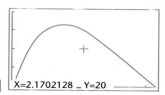

X=1.6276596 _ Y=32.903226

Directions are numbered to show the user the exact order of the steps.

4. Press **TRACE**. The **TRACE** cursor appears on the Y_1 function near the middle of the screen. 1 in the upper right corner of the display shows that the cursor is on Y_1. As you press ◀ and ▶, you **TRACE** along Y_1, one **X** dot at a time, evaluating Y_1 at each **X**.

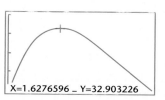

X=1.5824468 _ Y=33.074029

These directions assume a certain level of knowledge, using vocabulary that is not defined in the instructions.

   Press ◀ and ▶ until you are on the maximum **Y** value. This is the maximum of $Y_1(X)$ for the X pixels. (There may be a maximum "in between" pixels.)

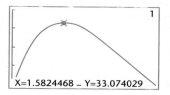

One-Year Limited Warranty

The warranty below is included in the product manual for the graphing calculator. Its language outlines the manufacturer's and the consumer's responsibilities. The warranty also explains the process a consumer should follow to get the product repaired.

The warranty specifies the person or persons covered by this agreement.

Subheads help the user locate specific conditions in the agreement.

The agreement states, in detail, what the manufacturer promises the consumer.

One-Year Limited Warranty

This electronic calculator warranty extends to the original consumer purchaser of the product.

Warranty Duration

This calculator is warranted to the original consumer purchaser for a period of one (1) year from the original purchase date.

Warranty Coverage

This calculator is warranted against defective materials or workmanship. This warranty is void if the product has been damaged by accident, unreasonable use, neglect, improper service, or other causes not arising out of defects in material or workmanship.

Warranty Disclaimers

Any implied warranties arising out of this sale, including but not limited to the implied warranties of merchantability and fitness for a particular purpose, are limited in duration to the above one-year period. This company shall not be liable for loss of use of the calculator or other incidental or consequential costs, expenses, or damages incurred by the consumer or any other user.

Some states do not allow the exclusion or limitations of implied warranties or consequential damages, so the above limitations or exclusions may not apply to you.

Legal Remedies

This warranty gives you specific legal rights, and you may also have other rights that vary from state to state.

Warranty Performance

During the above one-year warranty period, a defective calculator will either be repaired or replaced with a reconditioned comparable model when the product is returned, postage prepaid, to a service facility.

The repaired or replacement calculator will be in warranty for the remainder of the original warranty period or for six months, whichever is longer. Other than the postage requirement, no charge will be made for such repair or replacement.

It is strongly recommended that you insure the product for value prior to mailing.

Check Your Comprehension

1. What is the first thing you must do in order to graph the selected function in the viewing window?
2. How long does the warranty on this graphing calculator last?
3. Who must pay the postage when a damaged calculator is shipped to a service facility for repair?

Applying the Reading Strategy

Analyzing Purpose of Product Information

4. What purpose do the technical directions serve for the consumer?
5. Why do the technical directions include visuals?
6. Why would it be necessary for the manufacturer to have verification of the calculator's purchase date?
7. Why does the manufacturer recommend insuring the product prior to mailing?

Activity

Using Information From Consumer Documents

Find the product information that accompanies a product such as a VCR or a digital alarm clock. Read the manufacturer's technical directions and warranty. Use the chart below to record the three important pieces of information from each document. Explain their importance.

Product Information for _____		
	Key Information	Reasons
Technical Directions		
Warranty		

Contrasting Informational Materials

Product Information, Advertisements, and Consumer Articles

1. Technical directions and warranties are two types of product information. Advertisements are also a kind of product information since they, too, offer details about a product. However, an advertisement does not share the same purpose or language as technical directions or a warranty. Explain the differences in purpose and language between (a) technical directions and an advertisement, and (b) a warranty and an advertisement.
2. Find a product review in a magazine such as *Consumer Reports*. Explain how the purpose and language of the review differ from those found in technical directions and a warranty.

Prepare to Read

"If I Forget Thee, Oh Earth . . ." ◆ *from* Silent Spring ◆ To the Residents of A.D. 2029

Preview

Connecting to the Literature

Perhaps you are aware of local dangers to the environment and of individuals or groups that are seeking to correct them. In these selections, the authors encourage readers to think about environmental problems and their solutions.

Background

Many environmentalists today are concerned with the ozone layer, which shields Earth from 95 to 99 percent of the sun's harmful ultraviolet rays. Since the mid-1970s, scientists have worried about a breakdown in the ozone layer caused by the use of CFCs found in aerosol sprays and refrigerants. Environmental scientists continue to monitor the situation.

Literary Analysis

Persuasive Appeal

A **persuasive appeal** is an urgent appeal or warning that aims to convince the reader to think or act in a certain way. A persuasive appeal may exist in fiction or nonfiction, and it may be stated or implied. In this excerpt from *Silent Spring*, Rachel Carson warns how the indiscriminate use of pesticides threatens our environment:

> Then a strange blight crept over the area and everything began to change . . . mysterious maladies swept the flocks of chickens; the cattle and sheep sickened and died.

As you read, find other warnings about environmental conditions.

Comparing Literary Works

The writers of these selections use **imagery**, or descriptive language, to create pictures in the reader's mind. Imagery is intended to appeal to one or more of the senses—sight, hearing, touch, taste, or smell. Compare the imagery in each selection, and decide how it strengthens the warning.

Reading Strategy

Distinguishing Between Fact and Opinion

When you read literature that makes a persuasive appeal, it is important to distinguish between fact and opinion. A **fact** is a statement that can be proved, or tested for accuracy. An **opinion** is a statement of personal preference and cannot be proved. Look at the following examples from "To the Residents of A.D. 2029."

Fact: Parts of our land are overcrowded, parts neglected, parts abused, parts destroyed.

Opinion: Our present disrespect for the natural world is our most serious stupidity to date.

Use a chart like this one to separate facts from opinions as you read.

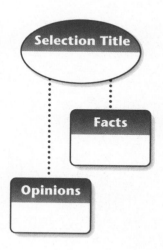

Vocabulary Development

purged (pʉrjd) *v.* cleansed (p. 487)

pyre (pīr) *n.* pile of wood on which a body is burned at a funeral (p. 489)

perennial (pər en´ ē əl) *adj.* constant (p. 489)

blight (blīt) *n.* something that destroys or prevents growth (p. 492)

moribund (môr´ i bund´) *adj.* dying (p. 493)

postulated (päs´ chə lāt´ ed) *v.* claimed (p. 497)

beleaguered (bē lē´ gərd) *adj.* worried; tormented (p. 498)

schism (siz´ əm) *n.* division (p. 498)

"If I Forget Thee, Oh Earth..."

Arthur C. Clarke

When Marvin was ten years old, his father took him through the long, echoing corridors that led up through Administration and Power, until at last they came to the uppermost levels of all and were among the swiftly growing vegetation of the Farmlands. Marvin liked it here: it was fun watching the great, slender plants creeping with almost visible eagerness toward the sunlight as it filtered down through the plastic domes to meet them. The smell of life was everywhere, awakening inexpressible longings in his heart: no longer was he breathing the dry, cool air of the residential levels, <u>purged</u> of all smells but the faint tang of ozone.1 He wished he could stay here for a little while, but Father would not let him. They went onward until they had reached the entrance to the Observatory, which he had never visited: but they did not stop, and Marvin knew with a sense of rising excitement that there could be only one goal left. For the first time in his life, he was going Outside.

There were a dozen of the surface vehicles, with their wide balloon tires and pressurized cabins, in the great servicing chamber. His father must have been expected, for they were led at once to the little scout car waiting by the huge circular door of the airlock. Tense with expectancy, Marvin settled himself down in the cramped cabin while his father started the motor and checked the controls. The inner door of the lock slid open and then closed behind them: he heard the roar of the great air pumps fade slowly away as the pressure dropped to zero. Then the "Vacuum" sign flashed on, the outer door parted, and before Marvin lay the land which he had never yet entered.

He had seen it in photographs, of course: he had watched it imaged on television screens a hundred times. But now it was lying all around him, burning beneath the fierce sun that crawled so slowly across the jet-black sky. He stared into the west, away from the blinding splendor of the sun—and there were the stars, as he had been told but had never quite believed. He gazed at them for a long time, marveling that anything could be so bright and yet so tiny. They were intense unscintillating points, and suddenly he remembered a rhyme he had once read in one of his father's books:

Twinkle, twinkle, little star,
How I wonder what you are.

Well, *he* knew what the stars were. Whoever asked that question must have been very stupid. And what did they mean by "twinkle"? You could see at a glance that all the stars shone with the same steady, unwavering light. He abandoned the puzzle and turned his attention to the landscape around him.

---

1. **ozone** (ō´ zōn) *n.* form of oxygen with a sharp odor.

purged (pʉrjd) *v.* cleansed

Reading Strategy
Distinguishing Between Fact and Opinion Is the statement "They were intense unscintillating points" a fact or an opinion? Explain.

✔**Reading Check**

Where is Marvin going for the first time in his life?

They were racing across a level plain at almost a hundred miles an hour, the great balloon tires sending up little spurts of dust behind them. There was no sign of the Colony: in the few minutes while he had been gazing at the stars, its domes and radio towers had fallen below the horizon. Yet there were other indications of man's presence, for about a mile ahead Marvin could see the curiously shaped structures clustering round the head of a mine. Now and then a puff of vapor would emerge from a squat smokestack and would instantly disperse.

They were past the mine in a moment: Father was driving with a reckless and exhilarating skill as if—it was a strange thought to come into a child's mind—he were trying to escape from something. In a few minutes they had reached the edge of the plateau on which the Colony had been built. The ground fell sharply away beneath them in a dizzying slope whose lower stretches were lost in shadow. Ahead, as far as the eye could reach, was a jumbled wasteland of craters, mountain ranges, and ravines. The crests of the mountains, catching the low sun, burned like islands of fire in a sea of darkness: and above them the stars still shone as steadfastly as ever.

There could be no way forward—yet there was. Marvin clenched his fists as the car edged over the slope and started the long descent. Then he saw the barely visible track leading down the mountainside, and relaxed a little. Other men, it seemed, had gone this way before.

Night fell with a shocking abruptness as they crossed the shadow line and the sun dropped below the crest of the plateau. The twin searchlights sprang into life, casting blue-white bands on the rocks ahead, so that there was scarcely need to check their speed. For hours they drove through valleys and past the foot of mountains whose peaks seemed to comb the stars, and sometimes they emerged for a moment into the sunlight as they climbed over higher ground.

And now on the right was a wrinkled, dusty plain, and on the left, its ramparts and terraces rising mile after mile into the sky, was a wall of mountains that marched into the distance until its peaks sank from sight below the rim of the world. There was no sign that men had ever explored this land, but once they passed the skeleton of a crashed rocket, and beside it a stone cairn[2] surmounted by a metal cross.

It seemed to Marvin that the mountains stretched on forever: but at last, many hours later, the range ended in a towering, precipitous headland[3] that rose steeply from a cluster of little hills. They drove down into a shallow valley that curved in a great arc toward the far side of the mountains: and as they did so, Marvin slowly realized that something very strange was happening in the land ahead.

The sun was now low behind the hills on the right: the valley before them should be in total darkness. Yet it was awash with a cold white

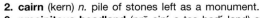

2. **cairn** (kern) *n.* pile of stones left as a monument.
3. **precipitous headland** (prē sip′ ə təs hed′ land) steep cliff.

radiance that came spilling over the crags beneath which they were driving. Then, suddenly, they were out in the open plain, and the source of the light lay before them in all its glory.

It was very quiet in the little cabin now that the motors had stopped. The only sound was the faint whisper of the oxygen feed and an occasional metallic crepitation as the outer walls of the vehicle radiated away their heat. For no warmth at all came from the great silver crescent that floated low above the far horizon and flooded all this land with pearly light. It was so brilliant that minutes passed before Marvin could accept its challenge and look steadfastly into its glare, but at last he could discern the outlines of continents, the hazy border of the atmosphere, and the white islands of cloud. And even at this distance, he could see the glitter of sunlight on the polar ice.

It was beautiful, and it called to his heart across the abyss of space. There in that shining crescent were all the wonders that he had never known—the hues of sunset skies, the moaning of the sea on pebbled shores, the patter of falling rain, the unhurried benison of snow. These and a thousand others should have been his rightful heritage, but he knew them only from the books and ancient records, and the thought filled him with the anguish of exile.

Why could they not return? It seemed so peaceful beneath those lines of marching cloud. Then Marvin, his eyes no longer blinded by the glare, saw that the portion of the disk that should have been in darkness was gleaming faintly with an evil phosphorescence:[4] and he remembered. He was looking upon the funeral <u>pyre</u> of a world—upon the radioactive aftermath of Armageddon.[5] Across a quarter of a million miles of space, the glow of dying atoms was still visible, a <u>perennial</u> reminder of the ruinous past. It would be centuries yet before that deadly glow died from the rocks and life could return again to fill that silent, empty world.

And now Father began to speak, telling Marvin the story which until this moment had meant no more to him than the fairy tales he had once been told. There were many things he could not understand: it was impossible for him to picture the glowing, multicolored pattern of life on the planet he had never seen. Nor could he comprehend the forces that had destroyed it in the end, leaving the Colony, preserved by its isolation, as the sole survivor. Yet he could share the agony of those final days, when the Colony had learned at last that never again would the supply ships come flaming down through the stars with gifts from home. One by one the radio stations had ceased to call: on the shadowed globe the lights of the cities had dimmed and died, and they were alone at last, as no men had ever been alone before, carrying in their hands the future of the race.

Then had followed the years of despair, and the long-drawn battle

---

4. **phosphorescence** (fäs´ fə res´ əns) *n.* emission of light resulting from exposure to radiation.
5. **Armageddon** (är´ mə ged´ ən) *n.* in the Bible, the place where the final battle between good and evil is to be fought.

Literary Analysis
Persuasive Appeal What warning is implied in this description of Earth?

pyre (pīr) *n.* pile of wood on which a body is burned at a funeral

perennial (pə ren´ ē əl) *adj.* constant

**Reading Check**
What does Marvin realize he is seeing?

Along the roads, laurel, viburnum and alder, great ferns and wild-flowers delighted the traveler's eye through much of the year. Even in winter the roadsides were places of beauty, where countless birds came to feed on the berries and on the seed heads of the dried weeds rising above the snow. The countryside was, in fact, famous for the abundance and variety of its bird life, and when the flood of migrants was pouring through in spring and fall people traveled from great distances to observe them. Others came to fish the streams, which flowed clear and cold out of the hills and contained shady pools where trout lay. So it had been from the days many years ago when the first settlers raised their houses, sank their wells, and built their barns.

Then a strange <u>blight</u> crept over the area and everything began to change. Some evil spell had settled on the community: mysterious maladies swept the flocks of chickens; the cattle and sheep sickened and died. Everywhere was a shadow of death. The farmers spoke of

blight (blīt) *n.* something that destroys or prevents growth

much illness among their families. In the town the doctors had become more and more puzzled by new kinds of sickness appearing among their patients. There had been several sudden and unexplained deaths, not only among adults but even among children, who would be stricken suddenly while at play and die within a few hours.

There was a strange stillness. The birds, for example—where had they gone? Many people spoke of them, puzzled and disturbed. The feeding stations in the backyards were deserted. The few birds seen anywhere were <u>moribund</u>; they trembled violently and could not fly. It was a spring without voices. On the mornings that had once throbbed with the dawn chorus of robins, catbirds, doves, jays, wrens, and scores of other bird voices there was now no sound; only silence lay over the fields and woods and marsh.

On the farms the hens brooded, but no chicks hatched. The farmers complained that they were unable to raise any pigs—the litters were small and the young survived only a few days. The apple trees

Literary Analysis
Persuasive Appeal What persuasive appeal does the author present in this paragraph?

moribund (môr´ i bund´) *adj.* dying

▼ **Critical Viewing**
What might the author think about the aerial spraying of crops to kill pests? **[Connect]**

were coming into bloom but no bees droned among the blossoms, so there was no pollination and there would be no fruit.

The roadsides, once so attractive, were now lined with browned and withered vegetation as though swept by fire. These, too, were silent, deserted by all living things. Even the streams were now lifeless. Anglers no longer visited them, for all the fish had died.

In the gutters under the eaves and between the shingles of the roofs, a white granular powder still showed a few patches; some weeks before it had fallen like snow upon the roofs and the lawns, the fields and streams.

No witchcraft, no enemy action had silenced the rebirth of new life in this stricken world. The people had done it themselves.

This town does not actually exist, but it might easily have a thousand counterparts in America or elsewhere in the world. I know of no community that has experienced all the misfortunes I describe. Yet every one of these disasters has actually happened somewhere, and many real communities have already suffered a substantial number of them. A grim specter has crept upon us almost unnoticed, and this imagined tragedy may easily become a stark reality we all shall know.

Review and Assess

Thinking About the Selection

1. **Respond:** Is Carson's technique of describing environmental problems in a fictional town effective? Explain.

2. **(a) Recall:** What is the condition of life at the beginning of Carson's story? **(b) Compare and Contrast:** How does the condition of life change as the story continues?

3. **(a) Recall:** What happens to the farm animals? **(b) Infer:** What causes this sudden change?

4. **(a) Recall:** What becomes of the vegetation in the town? **(b) Connect:** Why does the fate of the vegetation affect the fate of humans?

5. **(a) Recall:** What information about the town does Carson reveal at the end of her story? **(b) Speculate:** Would Carson's story have been more effective had the town been real? Why or why not?

6. **(a) Recall:** According to Carson, who caused the problem? **(b) Draw Conclusions:** What suggestions do you think Carson would make to humans?

7. **Apply:** Does a warning like Carson's motivate you to become more involved in environmental issues? Explain.

Rachel Carson

(1907–1964)

As a young woman, Rachel Carson studied writing at the Pennsylvania College for Women. A lifelong love of science and nature, however, caused her to change her field of study to marine biology. She was later able to pursue both fields by writing eloquently about nature.

Carson's widely praised book *The Sea Around Us* (1951) came out of her years as a biologist and editor at the United States Fish and Wildlife Service. Her most significant work was *Silent Spring* (1962), a chilling and well-documented warning about the dangers of pesticides. Before her book, few people understood the dangers of pollution or the interconnectedness of all life.

To the Residents of Residents of A.D. 2029

Bryan Woolley

Every writer's secret dream has been fulfilled for me. I know, as surely as anyone can know such things, that my works will be read fifty years from now. Well, one work, anyway.

This is because Collin County is about to dedicate a new courthouse and jail in McKinney, and somewhere in the vicinity of that structure the Collin County Historical Commission is going to bury a time capsule that will be opened in A.D. 2029, assuming that somebody's still around then, and that he can read. And I've been asked to contribute something to the capsule, probably because Mrs. Elisabeth Pink—the lady responsible for its contents—and I knew each other slightly long ago, in an era that by 2029 will be known as Prehistory.

My contribution, Mrs. Pink's letter says, "could be either on our current status or what you think the future will hold."

I wish I could report to the future that our current status is hunky-dory, that we live in the Golden Age of something or other. Until recently it was possible for Americans to believe that. There's no doubt that in the twentieth century, at least, the people of the United States have enjoyed the highest standard of living that the world has known up to this point in history. We've had so much of everything, in fact, that we've thought our supplies of the essentials of life—land, food, air, water, fuel—would last forever, and we've been wasteful. Sometimes we've even been wasteful of human life itself.

Lately, though, a sense of decline has set in. We've begun to realize that we're in trouble. We've poured so much filth into our water that much of it is undrinkable, and no life can live in it. Even the life of the ocean, the great mother of us all, is threatened. Scientists say the last wisp of pure, natural air in the continental United States was absorbed into our generally polluted atmosphere over Flagstaff, Arizona, several years ago. Parts of our land are overcrowded, parts neglected, parts abused, parts destroyed. We continue to depend on unrenewable resources—petroleum; natural gas, and coal—for most of the fuel that heats and cools our homes; runs our industry, agriculture, and business; and propels our transportation. We've suddenly discovered that those resources are disappearing forever. Without usable land, air, water, and fuel, food production would be impossible, of course. In addition, the United States and the Soviet Union are at this moment trying to make treaties that we hope will keep us from destroying all life and the possibility of life if we decide to destroy each other before the fuel runs out.

Literary Analysis
Persuasive Appeal Which words indicate that the author's persuasive appeal is beginning?

Reading Strategy
Distinguishing Between Fact and Opinion Which facts here support the writer's opinion about a sense of decline?

◀ **Critical Viewing** How can respect for wildflowers and other parts of nature improve the quality of human life? **[Speculate]**

So I would classify the current status that Mrs. Pink mentions as shaky, which makes the outlook for the future—even so near a future as A.D. 2029—uncertain.

An uncertain future is no new thing, of course. The future has always existed only in the imagination, a realm of hope and dread with which we can do little more than play games. But the games sometimes become serious. The Europeans <u>postulated</u> another land across the ocean for centuries and then came and found it. Jules Verne traveled under the sea and to the moon in his mind many years before we could make the machines to catch up with him. If, as we say, Necessity is the mother of Invention, then Desire is the father of Possibility.

Because of man's amazing record of making his dreams come true, I refuse to be pessimistic about the future, despite the frightening aspects of the present. As long as we—both as a race and as a crowd of individuals—retain our capacity for dreaming, we also keep the possibility of doing. And when doing becomes necessary, we invent a means to do so. Especially when we're in danger, as we are now.

Some of our present dangers surely will be around in 2029, for they're part of being human. We're too far from solving poverty, disease, and probably even war to be done with them in another half-century. Collin County probably will still need its courts and its jail—

▲ **Critical Viewing** How does this image relate to Woolley's vision? **[Connect]**

postulated (päs´ chə lāt´ ed) v. claimed

✔**Reading Check**

What does Woolley say the United States and the Soviet Union are doing "at this moment"?

maybe more courts and a newer, stronger jail.

But if my generation and my sons' generation do what we must to prolong the possibility of survival and the likelihood of this being read, most of the problems about which I'm worrying may seem quaint. If so, they'll be replaced by others that will seem as serious to those who gather to open the time capsule as mine do to me. Golden Ages exist only in retrospect, never for those who are trying to cope with them.

So for the <u>beleaguered</u> residents of 2029 I wish four things:

—A deeper understanding of history, to better avoid repeating the errors of the past, for if each generation keeps on inventing its own mistakes, some of the old ones will have to be thrown out.

—A healing of the <u>schism</u> between man and the rest of nature. Our present disrespect for the natural world is our most serious stupidity to date. We must realize that man can't long outlive the other living creatures.

—A wider and more profound appreciation of beauty. Music, poetry, pictures, and stories feed the soul as surely as wheat and meat and rice feed the body, and the soul of America is malnourished.

—A sense of humor. If man ever stops laughing at himself, he can no longer endure life, nor will he have reason to.

beleaguered (bi lē′ gərd) *adj.* worried; tormented

schism (siz′ əm) *n.* division

Review and Assess

Thinking About the Selection

1. **Respond:** Based on Woolley's ideas, do you take a pessimistic or an optimistic view of the future? Why?

2. **(a) Recall:** Why is the author guaranteed an audience in the future? **(b) Infer:** What prompted the author to accept the invitation to write this essay?

3. **(a) Recall:** Name two environmental problems mentioned by the author. **(b) Analyze:** Identify at least two pessimistic signs for the future that Woolley foresees.

4. **Support:** What specific evidence does Woolley offer to support his assertion that human beings have a record of making dreams come true?

5. **(a) Analyze:** What does Woolley mean when he says "Golden Ages exist only in retrospect, never for those who are trying to cope with them"? **(b) Connect:** What does this statement reveal about the author's fears for 2029?

6. **(a) Categorize:** Review the four wishes Woolley makes at the end of his essay, and rank them in order from most important to least important. **(b) Support:** Explain the priorities you have set.

Bryan Woolley

(b. 1937)
Born in Texas, Bryan Woolley has been a teacher, a journalist, and a novelist. His novel *November 22*, about the events in Dallas on the day President John F. Kennedy was assassinated, was praised by *Texas Monthly* as an outstanding book. In 1979, the author wrote "To the Residents of A.D. 2029," addressing his concerns for the present and his hopes for the future.

Review and Assess

Literary Analysis

Persuasive Appeal

1. What details does Clarke include to make his science-fiction story believable enough to be taken seriously as **persuasive appeal**?
2. Carson creates a fictional place to show many examples of the dangers of pesticides. What effect does this have on her warning?
3. (a) What argument for an optimistic outlook does Woolley use in his writing? (b) What is the effect of his positive outlook?

Comparing Literary Works

4. (a) Using a chart like the one below, compare the **imagery** used in each selection. (b) How does each author's use of imagery strengthen the persuasive appeal?

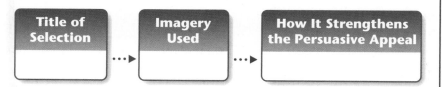

Title of Selection	Imagery Used	How It Strengthens the Persuasive Appeal

5. In your opinion, which selection is most powerful or persuasive? Explain.

Reading Strategy

Distinguishing Between Fact and Opinion

6. Identify one **fact** and one **opinion** mentioned in Clarke's story.
7. (a) What is one opinion expressed in the chapter from *Silent Spring*? (b) Which facts support this opinion?
8. Using a chart like the one below, identify at least two facts and two opinions in Woolley's essay, and explain what makes each a fact or an opinion.

Statement	Fact or Opinion?	Why?

Extend Understanding

9. **Media Link:** Which of the three selections would be the best choice for adaptation as a science-fiction movie? Why?

Quick Review

In all forms of literature, writers may use **persuasive appeals** to warn readers and urge action. The message of such appeals may be stated or implied.
Imagery is the use of descriptive language to create pictures in the reader's mind.

A **fact** is a statement that can be proved, or tested for accuracy.
An **opinion** is a statement of personal preference and cannot be proved.

 Take It to the Net
www.phschool.com
Take the interactive self-test online to check your understanding of these selections.

Integrate Language Skills

Vocabulary Development Lesson

Word Analysis: Latin Root -ann-

The Latin root -ann- means "year." The root appears, in modified form, in the word *perennial*, meaning "through the years." Perennial flowers blossom year after year, whereas annual flowers blossom for only one season, then die. Use the meaning of -ann- to write the correct definition of each of the following words.

1. annually **2.** biannual **3.** semiannual

Spelling Strategy

When a word ends in two or more consonants, do not double the final consonant before adding a suffix. For example, *blight* + *-ed* = *blighted*. Add each suffix shown below to form a new word. Then, use each new word in a sentence.

1. quick + *-ly*   **3.** expect + *-ation*
2. catch + *-ing*   **4.** warn + *-ing*

Fluency: Sentence Completion

On your paper, rewrite the following sentences, filling in each blank with a word from the vocabulary list on page 485.

1. The ___?___ politician pleaded with his colleagues to revive the ___?___ bill he had proposed.
2. Brown spots on the shrubs warned of a ___?___ in the ___?___ garden.
3. After his death, the holy man was cremated on a ___?___.
4. The police ___?___ that the burglar would return.
5. There was a ___?___ in the group because some members of the group disagreed about an issue.
6. She wished she had ___?___ all negativity from her group.

Grammar Lesson

Compound and Complex Sentences

A **compound sentence** consists of two or more independent clauses. The clauses can be joined by a comma and a coordinating conjunction or by a semicolon. A **complex sentence** consists of one independent clause, which can stand by itself, and at least one subordinate clause, which cannot stand by itself as a sentence. In the following examples, the independent clauses are underlined and the subordinate clause is italicized.

Compound sentence: The stars shone, and he remembered an old nursery rhyme.

Complex sentence: *When the stars shone,* he remembered an old nursery rhyme.

Practice Identify each sentence below as *compound* or *complex*. For compound sentences, identify the coordinating conjunction. For complex sentences, identify the subordinate clause.

1. When he was ten, Marvin went outside.
2. He saw Earth, but no one lived there.
3. Life changed after pesticide was sprayed.
4. The animals grew ill, and vegetation died.
5. We must act now if we care about the world.

Writing Application Write a paragraph about one of these selections. Use and identify two compound sentences and two complex sentences in your writing.

WG Prentice Hall Writing and Grammar Connection: Chapter 21, Section 2

Writing Lesson

Environmental Report

Rachel Carson's *Silent Spring* had an enormous impact on the way people viewed pest control, due partly to its well-documented facts. Using information from the selections and additional research, prepare a factual report on an environmental issue.

Prewriting   Choose an environmental issue of interest to you. Decide which facts from the selections and from your research are the most valuable. Jot these key findings on note cards. Put your cards in an order that makes sense and use your cards to make an outline.

Drafting   Write a strong introduction, body, and conclusion for your report. As you write, elaborate with facts and statistics to prove your point.

Model: Elaborating to Prove a Point

In 1995, our town had 35 ducks swimming on Birch Pond. Today, only 8 ducks remain. Why? The answer comes in a single word: pollution.

> The author provides an exact year and specific statistics to help prove the point that the waters are polluted.

Revising   Reread your draft and add any facts that would strengthen the main point you want to convey.

Prentice Hall Writing and Grammar Connection: Chapter 12, Section 3

Extension Activities

Listening and Speaking Prepare a **speech** about an environmental issue that concerns you. As you prepare and rehearse your speech, consider these tips:

- Offer strong arguments supported with facts and statistics to help you win over your audience.
- Tell listeners exactly which action you wish them to take.

After delivering the speech, invite your audience to evaluate the effectiveness of your arguments.

Research and Technology   Imagine that you are a descendant of Marvin in "If I Forget Thee, Oh Earth. . . ." You and the other members of the Colony are preparing to return to Earth. In a group, research information about the ozone layer. Write a **memo** that gives suggestions to your fellow travelers about ways they can protect Earth when they return. **[Group Activity]**

 Take It to the Net   www.phschool.com

Go online for an additional research activity using the Internet.

Prepare to Read

Gifts ◆ Glory and Hope

 Take It to the Net

Visit www.phschool.com
for interactive activities
and instruction related to
the selections, including
- background
- graphic organizers
- literary elements
- reading strategies

Preview

Connecting to the Literature

As you watch the newscast of a demonstration for freedom in a foreign land, you may not feel personally affected. Yet, as these selections show, freedom is a concern shared by people throughout the world.

Background

Apartheid, which means "apartness" in Afrikaans (one of the languages of South Africa), is the policy of segregation and discrimination that was once practiced against nonwhites by the South African government. When apartheid became law in 1948, it affected housing, education, and transportation. In order to help end apartheid, many nations reduced trade with South Africa. Apartheid was finally abolished in 1991.

Literary Analysis

Tone

Tone is the attitude a writer takes toward an audience or subject. The tone might be formal or informal, playful or serious. Recognizing the author's word choice is key to understanding the tone of a piece. Consider the formal and hopeful tone of this passage from "Glory and Hope."

> Today, all of us do, by our presence here, and by our celebrations in other parts of our country and the world, confer glory and hope to newborn liberty.

As you read, notice the tone conveyed through the author's word choice.

Comparing Literary Works

You will discover that these selections share a common theme: hope for a peaceful future and freedom for all people. Though the authors represent different lands and people, both writers show concern for peace and freedom for all. While reading, compare the ways that each author expresses his or her hopes, and pay special attention to the tone used to express the theme.

Reading Strategy

Evaluating the Writer's Message

Tone helps convey a writer's message—the idea that he or she wants to communicate. To **evaluate a writer's message,** first identify the message, and then determine whether the message meets these criteria:

- Is it logical, or clearly reasoned-out?
- Is it well-supported, or backed up with facts or personal experience?

You can evaluate a message without necessarily agreeing with it. Use a chart like the one shown to evaluate the writer's message.

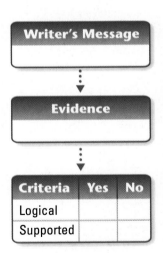

Vocabulary Development

pinions (pin´ yənz) *n.* last bony sections of a bird's wings (p. 505)

hieroglyphics (hī´ ər ō´ glif´ iks) *n.* pictures that represent words or ideas (p. 505)

confer (kən fʉr´) *v.* to give (p. 506)

pernicious (pər nish´ əs) *adj.* destructive (p. 507)

ideology (ī´ dē äl´ ə jē) *n.* ideas on which a political, economic, or social system is based (p. 507)

chasms (kaz´ əmz) *n.* deep cracks in Earth's surface (p. 507)

covenant (kuv´ ə nənt) *n.* agreement or contract (p. 507)

inalienable (in āl´ yən ə bəl) *adj.* not able to be taken away (p. 507)

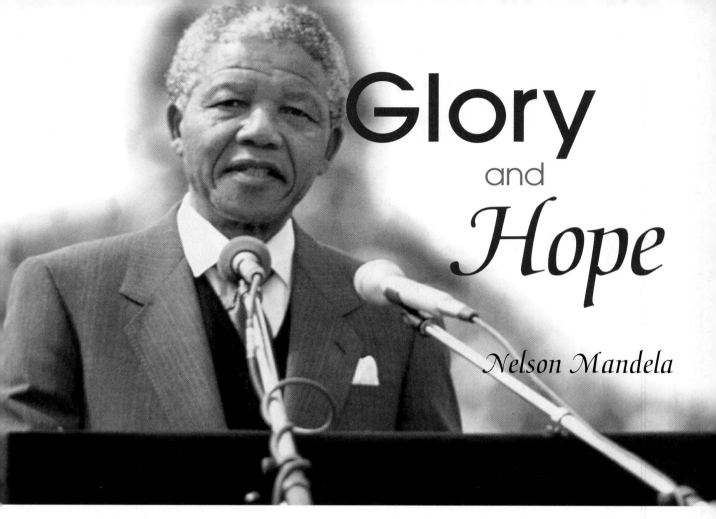

Glory and Hope

Nelson Mandela

Your majesties, your royal highnesses, distinguished guests, comrades and friends: Today, all of us do, by our presence here, and by our celebrations in other parts of our country and the world, <u>confer</u> glory and hope to newborn liberty.

Out of the experience of an extraordinary human disaster that lasted too long must be born a society of which all humanity will be proud.

Our daily deeds as ordinary South Africans must produce an actual South African reality that will reinforce humanity's belief in justice, strengthen its confidence in the nobility of the human soul and sustain all our hopes for a glorious life for all.

All this we owe both to ourselves and to the peoples of the world who are so well represented here today.

To my compatriots, I have no hesitation in saying that each one of us is as intimately attached to the soil of this beautiful country as are the famous jacaranda trees of Pretoria and the mimosa trees of the bushveld.[1]

---

1. **bushveld** (boosh′ velt) *n.* South African grassland with abundant shrubs and thorny vegetation.

▲ **Critical Viewing**
How do you think Mandela felt when this picture was taken as he presented this speech? **[Interpret]**

confer (kən fur′) *v.* to give

Literary Analysis
Tone How does the speaker establish a tone of pride in this passage?

Each time one of us touches the soil of this land, we feel a sense of personal renewal. The national mood changes as the seasons change.

We are moved by a sense of joy and exhilaration when the grass turns green and the flowers bloom.

That spiritual and physical oneness we all share with this common homeland explains the depth of the pain we all carried in our hearts as we saw our country tear itself apart in terrible conflict, and as we saw it spurned, outlawed and isolated by the peoples of the world, precisely because it has become the universal base of the pernicious ideology and practice of racism and racial oppression.

We, the people of South Africa, feel fulfilled that humanity has taken us back into its bosom, that we, who were outlaws not so long ago, have today been given the rare privilege to be host to the nations of the world on our own soil.

We thank all our distinguished international guests for having come to take possession with the people of our country of what is, after all, a common victory for justice, for peace, for human dignity.

We trust that you will continue to stand by us as we tackle the challenges of building peace, prosperity, nonsexism, nonracialism and democracy.

We deeply appreciate the role that the masses of our people and their democratic, religious, women, youth, business, traditional and other leaders have played to bring about this conclusion. Not least among them is my Second Deputy President, the Honorable F. W. de Klerk.

We would also like to pay tribute to our security forces, in all their ranks, for the distinguished role they have played in securing our first democratic elections and the transition to democracy, from bloodthirsty forces which still refuse to see the light.

The time for the healing of the wounds has come.

The moment to bridge the chasms that divide us has come.

The time to build is upon us.

We have, at last, achieved our political emancipation. We pledge ourselves to liberate all our people from the continuing bondage of poverty, deprivation, suffering, gender and other discrimination.

We succeeded to take our last steps to freedom in conditions of relative peace. We commit ourselves to the construction of a complete, just and lasting peace.

We have triumphed in the effort to implant hope in the breasts of the millions of our people. We enter into a covenant that we shall build the society in which all South Africans, both black and white, will be able to walk tall, without any fear in their hearts, assured of their inalienable right to human dignity—a rainbow nation at peace with itself and the world.

As a token of its commitment to the renewal of our country, the new Interim Government of National Unity will, as a matter of urgency, address the issue of amnesty for various categories of our people who are currently serving terms of imprisonment.

We dedicate this day to all the heroes and heroines in this country and the rest of the world who sacrificed in many ways and surrendered their lives so that we could be free.

Their dreams have become reality. Freedom is their reward.

We are both humbled and elevated by the honor and privilege that you, the people of South Africa, have bestowed on us, as the first President of a united, democratic, nonracial and nonsexist South Africa, to lead our country out of the valley of darkness.

We understand it still that there is no easy road to freedom.

We know it well that none of us acting alone can achieve success.

We must therefore act together as a united people, for national reconciliation, for nation building, for the birth of a new world.

Let there be justice for all.

Let there be peace for all.

Let there be work, bread, water and salt for all.

Let each know that for each the body, the mind and the soul have been freed to fulfill themselves.

Never, never and never again shall it be that this beautiful land will again experience the oppression of one by another and suffer the indignity of being the skunk of the world.

The sun shall never set on so glorious a human achievement!

Let freedom reign. God bless Africa!

Nelson Mandela

(b. 1918)
Nelson Mandela was born in South Africa, a nation whose white government maintained a strict policy of apartheid, or legal discrimination against blacks. In 1944, Mandela began protesting apartheid. Twenty years later, after several arrests, he was sentenced to life in prison for acts of sabotage.

After twenty-seven years of imprisonment, Mandela was released in 1990. He continued to fight for equal rights for all South Africans. In 1991, apartheid was finally abolished and, in 1993, Mandela and South African president F. W. de Klerk shared the Nobel Peace Prize. The next year, Mandela became the first black man to be elected president of South Africa.

Review and Assess

Thinking About the Selection

1. **Respond:** What do you admire most about the message in Mandela's speech? Why?

2. **(a) Recall:** According to Mandela, what is "newborn" in South Africa? **(b) Interpret:** Which emotion does the word "newborn" add to his remarks?

3. **(a) Recall:** Citing examples, describe what life was like in the old South Africa. **(b) Draw Conclusions:** Describe the new South Africa that Mandela envisions.

4. **(a) Recall:** What "covenant" does Mandela say the South African people are now entering? **(b) Generalize:** Which ideas in the speech are especially important for safeguarding the human rights of all people throughout today's world?

5. **(a) Connect:** How does the title of the speech connect with the ideas that Mandela conveys? **(b) Compare and Contrast:** What are the similarities and differences between "glory" and "hope"?

6. **Extend:** How do you think the people of South Africa reacted to Mandela's inaugural speech?

7. **Take a Position:** Basing your answer on Mandela's speech, what do you think was the new leader's greatest challenge? Why?

Review and Assess

Literary Analysis

Tone

1. Using a chart like the one below, analyze the **tone** of "Glory and Hope" and "Gifts."

Title	Memorable Words or Phrases	Tone	Effect of the Tone

2. Given the format of each selection, would you say the tone is appropriate in each case? Explain.

Comparing Literary Works

3. Using a chart like the one below, compare the ways that Shu Ting and Nelson Mandela express hope for a peaceful future.

4. Which selection do you feel does a better job of justifying its optimism for the future? Explain.

Reading Strategy

Evaluating the Writer's Message

5. (a) What is Nelson Mandela's **message**? (b) How does he support his message?
6. Which evidence from your own knowledge or experience would support—or challenge—the validity of Mandela's message?
7. Evaluate Shu Ting's message in "Gifts."

Extend Understanding

8. **Social Studies Connection:** What is currently being done to help oppressed people in other parts of the world attain their human rights and freedom?

Quick Review

Tone is the attitude a writer takes toward an audience or subject.

To **evaluate a writer's message,** decide whether the ideas of the writer are logical and well-supported.

 Take It to the Net
www.phschool.com
Take the interactive self-test online to check your understanding of these selections.

Integrate Language Skills

Vocabulary Development Lesson

Word Analysis: Greek Suffix -logy

The Greek suffix -logy means "the study, science, or theory of." The suffix appears in the word ideology, which means "the study of ideas" or "a set of ideas." Define each of the following words.

1. zoology   2. sociology   3. biology

Spelling Strategy

If a word ends in a single consonant preceded by a single vowel and the last syllable is accented, double the final consonant before adding most endings. For example, confer becomes conferred. However, do not double the final consonant before adding -ence, as in conference. (Occurrence is an exception to this rule.) For each item, add the suffix shown and write the new word. Then, use each new word in a sentence.

1. refer + -ed   2. infer + -ence   3. defer + -ing

Fluency: Sentence Completion

Identify the word from the vocabulary list on page 503 that correctly completes each sentence below.

1. The general will ____?____ a medal upon the heroic soldier.
2. In a free society, liberty and freedom are ____?____ rights for everyone.
3. A term to describe a destructive system of ideas is a ____?____ ____?____.
4. Once you enter into a ____?____, you are not supposed to back out.
5. The ____?____ on the birds' wings were red with spots of white.
6. The scientist studied the ____?____ that had been scratched into the cave wall.
7. If you should go out walking after an earthquake, do not fall into any ____?____.

Grammar Lesson

Parallelism: Clauses

Parallelism is the repetition of grammatically similar words or groups of words. The parallelism may appear in the form of related **clauses**—groups of words with subjects and verbs—if a clause is presented for the first time, and then its pattern is repeated in subsequent clauses or sentences. Parallelism gives the writing a sense of rhythm, evenness, and structure. Look at this example from "Gifts."

> **Example:** My dream is the dream of a pond.
> My joy is the joy of sunlight.
> My grief is the grief of birds.

Practice Copy each pair of sentences below. Underline the words that are repeated in order to create parallelism.

1. Let there be justice. Let there be peace.
2. To be free is a gift. To be free is a treasure.
3. The time to heal has come. The time to build has come.
4. I shall sing to life. I shall dance to love.
5. Freedom is a privilege. Life is a privilege.

Writing Application Using the parallelism you have identified, add another sentence to each practice item.

𝒲𝒢 *Prentice Hall Writing and Grammar Connection: Chapter 21, Section 2*

Writing Lesson

Letter to Nelson Mandela

In his speech "Glory and Hope," Nelson Mandela presents a memorable message about the future of South Africa. Write a letter to Nelson Mandela in which you share the parts of his speech that you found most inspiring.

Prewriting   Make a list of words that describe how Mandela's speech makes you feel. Next to each word, write the section of the speech that evoked that particular emotion.

Model: Listing Words to Describe Feelings

Feeling	Example From Speech
hope	The sun shall never set on so glorious a human achievement!

> The example from the speech explains the hopeful feeling.

Drafting   As you draft, use a friendly yet respectful tone. Your opening paragraph should address your reason for writing. The body of your letter should address your feelings about his speech. In your closing paragraph, sum up the way in which the speech inspired you.

Revising   Read your letter to a classmate to make sure that you have maintained a respectful tone throughout your letter.

W *Prentice Hall Writing and Grammar Connection: Chapter 15, Section 1*

Extension Activities

Listening and Speaking In a group, hold a **panel discussion** on the kind of world you would like to leave to future generations. Keep in mind the human rights issues that Nelson Mandela addresses in "Glory and Hope." Consider these tips:

- Make note cards to use for extemporaneous, or unrehearsed, delivery of your ideas.
- During your discussion, show respect for everyone's opinions and speak in turn.

Afterward, analyze the process to decide how you might improve future discussions. [**Group Activity**]

Research and Technology Write a **research report** about the changes in South Africa since the end of apartheid. Use library resources, including the Internet, to gather information from at least three sources, synthesizing the details and facts you find into your writing. Then, share your report with classmates..

 Take It to the Net   www.phschool.com

Go online for an additional research activity using the Internet.

Writing WORKSHOP

Exposition: How-to Essays

A how-to essay or manual provides detailed step-by-step instructions that tell you how to perform a certain task. In this workshop, you will write a how-to essay on a process you know well.

Assignment Criteria. Your how-to essay should have the following characteristics:

- Specific factual information presented logically and accurately
- Rules of behavior for each particular situation
- Examples and definitions that demonstrate key concepts
- Instructions that anticipate readers' potential mistakes

To preview the criteria on which your how-to essay may be assessed, see the Rubric on page 515.

Prewriting

Choose a topic. Make a calendar of your schedule. For each day of the week, write down your activities. Then, identify an activity from your calendar to describe in a how-to manual. Or, if you prefer, describe another activity with which you are familiar.

Use a target diagram. Once you have chosen an activity to describe in a how-to manual, use the diagram on this page to narrow your topic. In the outer circle, write your general topic. Then, consider the aspect of your topic on which you will focus in your manual; write this in the inner circle. To complete the diagram, write an even narrower topic in the center of the target.

Gather information. As you prepare to draft your how-to manual, remember to provide your reader with all the tools needed to perform the activity you are describing:

- Make a list of materials needed
- Note all the steps involved, in the order in which they occur
- Collect any additional information or hints of use to the reader

Narrowing Your Topic With a Target Diagram

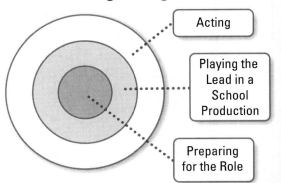

Acting

Playing the Lead in a School Production

Preparing for the Role

Student Model

Before you begin drafting, read this student model and review the characteristics of effective how-to essays.

Carmen Rose Viviano-Crafts
Syracuse, NY

Preparing for a Dramatic Role

One of the first challenges of a new dramatic role is the task of memorizing lines. Use the following guidelines to memorize lines more efficiently:

1. Read the entire play at least twice to familiarize yourself with the setting and situations. When performing, it is essential to know what is going on around you in order to provide the appropriate reactions.

2. Highlight or underline all your lines to identify when your character speaks.

3. Begin to concentrate solely on your parts. Look at the script scene by scene, memorizing one or two scenes a day, depending on how much time you have. Reading the lines out loud speeds up the process by making the lines more memorable.

4. Once you feel confident enough, begin to "run" your lines (read them aloud), with another person reading the other characters' lines. This prepares you for being onstage with other actors.

5. When you begin rehearsing with fellow cast members, you will be able to try out different ways of saying things, and you'll start to develop your character. Here are the steps to use when developing a character:
   - If your role is based on a real person, research that person or observe someone in a similar situation. Try to find out as much information as you can so that you can play the part realistically.
   - If you are playing a fictional character, study the script closely. The character's words can tell you about his or her feelings, likes, and dislikes.
   - Once you have learned some aspects of your character, begin to delve into the mind and soul of the person. Make up an entire life story for your character. The more you know about the person, the easier it is to put yourself in his or her place. Think of a past experience to relate to something your character is going through. Bring the emotions you felt in that situation to your character's situation.
   - Finally, conduct general conversations with other cast members, with each of you speaking from your own character's point of view. Ask things like "How do you feel about me?" and "How do you think I feel about you?" This lets you know how you are perceived by the other actors/characters in the play, and allows you to react more realistically.

6. After each rehearsal, consider what worked well and what felt wrong to you. Use your after-rehearsal notes as feedback to improve your performance.

Margin notes (partially visible):

...mbering sys-
...ows Carmen
...ent informa-
...gically.

...ring time
...tions, the
...anticipates
...s' questions
...ncerns.

...ation about
...ching demon-
...the writer's
...stions.

...ideas offer
...f conduct,
...ing the value
...strategy.

Drafting

Organize information. Now that you have gathered all the information you want to include in your draft, choose an organization that will make sense to your reader. Chronological, or step-by-step, order is usually best suited to this kind of writing. Use the chart at right to help you organize your information effectively.

Elaborate each stage in a process. Provide information to fully explain each step in the process:

- Explain why each step is important.
- Define terms.
- Include graphics where necessary.

Give thorough descriptions and explanations so your readers can complete the task you describe.

Organize Information

1. State the purpose of your technical document.
2. List the materials and conditions necessary to complete the activity.
3. Provide examples to demonstrate the activity.
4. List steps to complete in consecutive order.
5. Suggest solutions to common problems when performing the activity.

Use graphic devices. Photographs, diagrams, and drawings are a great way to help readers follow an explanation. Create or locate graphics to reinforce your instructions, and place them at the appropriate points in your essay. To work effectively, each graphic must be clear and complete. Each should illustrate a step in the process you are explaining. Finally, a graphic should include labels to make strong connections back to your essay.

Consider formatting techniques. In your how-to essay, lengthy paragraphs may not be the best way to present information. Brief paragraphs, bullets, or numbered lists will help keep your how-to essay clear and easy for readers to manage.

Revising

Revise for clarity. Look over your draft to identify instructions, steps, or information that may be unclear to your reader. Mark these sections and go back to them, rewriting any confusing passages with language that informs in a logical manner.

Model: Revising for Clarity

—*read aloud*—

4. Once you feel confident enough, begin to "run" your lines with another person. ∧ *This prepares you for being onstage with other actors.*

Carmen defined a term that may be unfamiliar to readers and added information to explain the value of a strategy.

Revise for transitions. Look for sections in your draft that need transitional language to connect the steps in your activity. In the following example, adding the words *first* and *then* makes the instruction easier to understand.

> **Example:** Wash the bowl and add the eggs.
> *First,* wash the bowl, and *then* add the eggs.

Compare the model and the nonmodel. Why is the model more effective than the nonmodel?

Nonmodel	Model
Look at the script scene by scene, memorizing one or two scenes a day. Begin to "run" your lines. This prepares you for being onstage with other actors.	Begin to concentrate solely on your parts. Look at the script scene by scene, memorizing one or two scenes a day, depending on how much time you have. Once you feel confident, begin to "run" your lines. This prepares you for being onstage with other actors.

Publishing and Presenting

How-to essays or manuals are meant to be shared. Consider this option for sharing your writing with a wider audience.

Deliver an oral presentation. Prepare and distribute a handout of your draft for your classmates. Give an instructional presentation, providing elaboration if you feel something is unclear. Ask for feedback on the clarity of your how-to manual and presentation. If possible, have a classmate attempt the activity you described in order to gauge the effectiveness of your manual and presentation.

Rubric for Self-Assessment

Evaluate your how-to essay using the following criteria and rating scale:

Criteria	Rating Scale				
	Not very				Very
Is factual information expressed logically and correctly?	1	2	3	4	5
Are the rules of behavior or action for a specific situation clearly conveyed?	1	2	3	4	5
How well incorporated are examples and definitions that demonstrate concepts?	1	2	3	4	5
How well are readers' mistakes anticipated?	1	2	3	4	5

Listening and Speaking WORKSHOP

Effective Listening and Note Taking

Even when they are presenting information to an audience, some people speak very rapidly, leaving you struggling to keep up. The good news is that you can keep up with even the fastest speakers through careful listening. Once you have perfected your listening and note-taking skills, you can use them any time you need to remember something you have heard.

Listen Carefully

Listen to how something is said. Speakers often give you clues to what they consider important. If someone adds emphasis, changes his or her tone of voice, or repeats certain aspects often, then these are points you should capture in your notes.

Recognize barriers to listening. A major barrier to effective listening is the distractions all around you. Make sure to sit in a place that is as close to the speaker as possible, away from side conversations or visual distractions. Try not to let your mind wander—stay focused on what the speaker is saying.

Take Notes

Understand what the speaker is saying. Sometimes, we are too busy with the act of taking notes to think about what the speaker is saying. Focus on the speaker's ideas to decide which points are important and what form your notes should take.

Write main points and key details. You should not try to take down in your notes every word a speaker says. Instead, determine the speaker's main points and capture a few supporting details that illustrate each main point.

Rephrase and rewrite. To save time, try to rephrase the speaker's words using minimal punctuation, partial phrases, and abbreviations wherever possible. Also, the more you can rewrite the information simply, in your own words, the better you will understand it later.

Review your notes. To reinforce what you heard, review your notes as soon as possible after writing them. While your memory is still fresh, add significant details, rewrite confusing notes, and highlight important information.

Activity:
Observation and Discussion
With other students, watch a video of a television interview. Take notes without stopping the video. Afterward, use your notes to present a summary of the speaker's main points. Use the chart to evaluate and compare notes to see how they differ in length and emphasis.

Note-Taking Evaluation

Rating System
+ = Excellent   ✔ = Average   – = Weak

Notes:
Organization:
____ Inappropriate   ____ Sensible
Coherence:
____ Confusing   ____ Clear
Length:
____ Too Long   ____ Adequate   ____ Too Short

Summaries:
How did your note taking affect your summary?

Did you feel you missed any main points that the other students found?

Did you have any main points that you now feel should be considered supporting details (or vice versa)?

Assessment WORKSHOP

Generalizations

The reading sections of some tests require you to read a passage and answer multiple-choice questions about generalizations. Use the following strategies to help you answer these kinds of test questions:

- Remember that a generalization is a broad statement that can be applied to a variety of situations.
- Generalizations often illustrate a key theme, or lesson, of a passage.
- To make a generalization, list the main points or events in the passage. Then, devise a general principle that applies to all of the items in your list.

Test-Taking Strategies

- Generalizations can be easily recognized when they use signal words such as "in general," "most," "often," and "usually."
- Test a generalization by checking to see whether it can be applied to multiple elements of the passage.

Sample Test Item

Directions: Read the passage, and then answer the question that follows.

When you vote for class president, remember this: If you don't care about class trips or adequate funding, vote for Jessie Smith again. If you want to have more outings and more money, vote for Helen Aquino. Her plans include three fund-raising events and a class outing after each one! Make this year one to remember—vote for Helen Aquino!

1 Which of these statements is a generalization about the passage?

- **A** Class elections are often pointless.
- **B** Political ads try to make opponents look bad.
- **C** A new candidate is always better.
- **D** Most students don't vote.

Answer and Explanation

The correct answer is *B.* The advertisement characterizes her opponent as uncaring about issues that Aquino considers important. Answers *A, C,* and *D* may be applicable in other situations, but they do not reflect ideas contained in this specific passage.

▶ Practice

Directions: Read the passage, and then answer the question that follows.

When we moved to this city a month ago, I never expected to have to make so many adjustments. I have had to consult so many transit schedules and I have gotten lost so many times that I am no longer interested in exploring my new surroundings. I also thought I would have some new friends by now.

1 Which generalization applies to the passage?

- **A** Getting lost is part of adjusting to a new city.
- **B** Transit schedules are often complicated.
- **C** It takes a long time to meet people.
- **D** Adjusting to new situations and surroundings can be difficult.

Reading, 1973, by Billy Morrow Jackson

Exploring the Genre

A short story is a brief visit to an imaginary world. This world could be nineteenth-century Paris, the American Southwest, or the swamp country of South Carolina. Wherever you travel, you will meet characters who deal with problems that are surprisingly real—for example, how to win someone's love or how to treat a younger brother. As you live through these problems with the characters, you may gain a deeper understanding of the world around you.

Despite their varied content, almost all short stories have the following elements in common:

- **Plot**— the sequence of events that catches your interest and takes you through the story.

- **Characters**— the people, animals, or other beings that take part in the story's action.

- **Setting**— the time and location in which the story takes place.

- **Theme**— the message about life that the story conveys.

This unit highlights the elements of the short story while showing the power and variety of the form.

▲ **Critical Viewing** How does the mood of this painting match your notion of reading? **[Compare]**

Why Read Literature?

Whenever you read fiction, you have a purpose, or reason. You might find the topic interesting or love the characters a certain author creates. Preview three purposes you might set before reading works in this unit.

1 Read for the Love of Literature

We may no longer use pocket watches or sell our hair like the main characters in "The Gift of the Magi." Nevertheless, this story of a couple in love is still widely read and admired today. Find out why generations of people have treasured this simple O. Henry tale when you read **"The Gift of the Magi,"** page 524.

A powerful story may teach a lesson yet still entertain. When a woman sacrifices the financial stability of her household to appear wealthier than she is, you might appreciate the irony of her downfall in Guy de Maupassant's story, **"The Necklace,"** page 608.

2 Read to Appreciate an Author's Style

Some may associate lying in bed with laziness, but Mark Twain found it to be the best position to inspire good writing. Propped up with pillows, Twain would write stories with an informal, humorous style that reflected the good-natured ease of his surroundings. Fall under the spell of a master storyteller as you read Twain's **"The Invalid's Story,"** page 596.

Realism blends with fantasy in Isabel Allende's stories. Enjoy her unique style in the tale of an eccentric uncle who turns his family's town upside down in **"Uncle Marcos,"** page 577.

3 Read for Information

Advertisements can convey a great deal of information about a society and culture at a specific point in time. Place yourself in the shoes of a customer looking for a good automotive deal in 1913 as you scan the **"Advertisement for Automobile,"** page 536.

Stories that examine the intersection of two cultures usually end up revealing something hidden about each one. Native American ritual combines with Catholicism in unexpected ways in Leslie Marmon Silko's **"The Man to Send Rain Clouds,"** page 590.

 Take It to the Net

Visit the Web site for online instruction and activities related to each selection in this unit.
www.phschool.com

How to Read Literature

Use Strategies for Reading Fiction

Fiction is literature of the imagination. Authors of fiction invent the characters and events that populate their short stories and novels. Fiction can be closely associated with real people and events or it can be entirely fabricated. The following strategies will help you get more out of the fiction you read.

1. Ask questions.

Pause occasionally when reading to jot down two types of questions:

- Basic questions about what is happening in the story.
- Deeper-level questions about characters' motivations or the author's overall message.

2. Draw conclusions.

As soon as you find answers to your questions, you are ready to draw conclusions. Put details together to arrive at an understanding of the story, as the chart at right demonstrates.

- Carefully examine the evidence before drawing a conclusion. For example, look at characters' past actions before you attribute a general habit pattern to them.
- Make sure that your conclusions fit the general theme or tone of the story.

Drawing Conclusions

Character: Madame Loisel in Guy de Maupassant's "The Necklace"	
Details	**Conclusions**
Character's Action	**Reason for the Action**
She cries when she receives invitation to an evening party.	She is afraid she will be ridiculed if she goes to the party.

3. Identify with a character.

If you have ever sympathized with a character you might never have known in real life, you have identified with a character. Here are some tips to help you relate to the characters you encounter as you read:

- Imagine yourself in the character's situation.
- Think about how you might feel or react in that situation.

4. Use your senses.

Many stories are rich with descriptions of sensory details such as sights, sounds, and smells. As you read, make these descriptions come alive.

- Match the descriptions of sights, sounds, smells, and feelings with similar situations that you have personally experienced.
- Use your imagination and the details that the author provides to picture the action in your mind.

As you read the selections in this unit, review the reading strategies and apply them to interact with the text.

Prepare to Read

The Gift of the Magi

Wishful Thinking, Peter Szumowski, Private Collection

 Take It to the Net

Visit www.phschool.com for interactive activities and instruction related to "The Gift of the Magi," including

- background
- graphic organizers
- literary elements
- reading strategies

Preview

Connecting to the Literature

With excitement, you tear the wrapping paper off a birthday gift, only to be disappointed by the present you uncover. You hide your feelings, remembering it is the thought that counts. Gifts may be either less appropriate or more meaningful than they first appear. In "The Gift of the Magi," a husband and wife discover the problems and joys of giving gifts.

Background

In a story that was written years ago, any prices quoted may seem very low. Inflation, the steady increase in the prices of most things, is the reason: It reduces money's purchasing power. In this story, written around 1905, $32 is roughly a month's rent for Della and Jim. Today, for many people, that amount would not cover one week's rent.

Literary Analysis

Plot

Plot is the sequence of events that make up a story. Plot is divided into five stages:

- **Exposition**—the scene is set and background information is provided
- **Rising action**—the central conflict, or struggle, is introduced
- **Climax**—the high point of the conflict
- **Falling action**—the conflict lessens
- **Resolution**—the conflict concludes and loose ends get tied up

As you read "The Gift of the Magi," notice how its events apply to the stages of plot development.

Connecting Literary Elements

During the resolution, you learn how a story will end. In "The Gift of the Magi," the resolution reveals a **surprise ending,** a conclusion that differs from the reader's expectations, but in a way that is both logical and believable. As you read, look for clues to the surprise ending.

Reading Strategy

Asking Questions

To fully understand the plot of a story, **ask questions** about characters and events. Ask yourself these kinds of questions while you read:

- Why does a character act in a certain way?
- What does an event really mean?
- Why does the narrator reveal or conceal information?

Use a chart like the one shown to help you as you look for the answers to your questions in the story.

Vocabulary Development

instigates (in´ stə gāts´) *v.* urges on; stirs up (p. 525)

depreciate (dē prē´ shē āt´) *v.* reduce in value (p. 526)

cascade (kas kād´) *n.* waterfall (p. 526)

chaste (chāst) *adj.* pure or clean in style; not ornate (p. 526)

meretricious (mer´ ə trish´ əs) *adj.* attractive in a cheap, flashy way (p. 526)

ravages (rav´ ij iz) *n.* ruins (p. 527)

discreet (di skrēt´) *adj.* tactful; respectful (p. 529)

The Gift of the Magi

O. Henry

One dollar and eighty-seven cents. That was all. And sixty cents of it was in pennies. Pennies saved one and two at a time by bulldozing the grocer and the vegetable man and the butcher until one's cheeks burned with the silent imputation of parsimony[1] that such close dealing implied. Three times Della counted it. One dollar and eighty-seven cents. And the next day would be Christmas.

There was clearly nothing to do but flop down on the shabby little couch and howl. So Della did it. Which instigates the moral reflection that life is made up of sobs, sniffles, and smiles, with sniffles predominating.

Reading Strategy
Asking Questions What question might you ask, based on this paragraph?

instigates (in´ stə gāts´) v. urges on; stirs up

While the mistress of the home is gradually subsiding from the first stage to the second, take a look at the home. A furnished flat[2] at $8 per week. It did not exactly beggar description,[3] but it certainly had that word on the lookout for the mendicancy squad.[4]

In the vestibule below was a letter-box into which no letter would go, and an electric button from which no mortal finger could coax a ring. Also appertaining thereunto was a card bearing the name "Mr. James Dillingham Young."

The "Dillingham" had been flung to the breeze during a former period of prosperity when its possessor was being paid $30 per week. Now, when the income was shrunk to $20, the letters of "Dillingham" looked blurred, as though they were thinking seriously of contracting to a modest and unassuming D. But whenever Mr. James Dillingham Young came home and reached his flat above he was called "Jim" and greatly hugged by Mrs. James Dillingham Young, already introduced to you as Della. Which is all very good.

Della finished her cry and attended to her cheeks with the powder rag. She stood by the window and looked out dully at a gray cat walking a gray fence in a gray backyard. Tomorrow would be Christmas Day, and she had only $1.87 with which to buy Jim a present. She had been saving every penny she could for months, with this result. Twenty dollars a week doesn't go far. Expenses had been greater than she had calculated. They always are. Only $1.87 to buy a present for Jim. Her Jim. Many a happy hour she had spent planning for something nice for him.

Something fine and rare and sterling—something just a little bit near to being worthy of the honor of being owned by Jim.

There was a pier glass[5] between the windows of the room. Perhaps you have seen a pier glass in an $8 flat.

Literary Analysis
Plot What conflict is introduced at this point?

---

1. **imputation** (im pyōō tā´ shən) **of parsimony** (pär´ sə mō´ nē) accusation of stinginess.
2. **flat** *n.* apartment.
3. **beggar description** resist description.
4. **it certainly . . . mendicancy** (men´ di kən´ sē) **squad** it would have been noticed by the police who arrested beggars.
5. **pier** (pir) **glass** tall mirror.

☑**Reading Check**

How much money does Della have to buy a present for Jim?

A very thin and very agile person may, by observing his reflection in a rapid sequence of longitudinal strips, obtain a fairly accurate conception of his looks. Della, being slender, had mastered the art.

Suddenly she whirled from the window and stood before the glass. Her eyes were shining brilliantly, but her face had lost its color within twenty seconds. Rapidly she pulled down her hair and let it fall to its full length.

Now, there were two possessions of the James Dillingham Youngs in which they both took a mighty pride. One was Jim's gold watch that had been his father's and his grandfather's. The other was Della's hair. Had the Queen of Sheba[6] lived in the flat across the airshaft, Della would have let her hair hang out the window some day to dry just to depreciate Her Majesty's jewels and gifts. Had King Solomon been the janitor, with all his treasures piled up in the basement, Jim would have pulled out his watch every time he passed, just to see him pluck at his beard from envy.

So now Della's beautiful hair fell about her rippling and shining like a cascade of brown waters. It reached below her knee and made itself almost a garment for her. And then she did it up again nervously and quickly. Once she faltered for a minute and stood still while a tear or two splashed on the worn red carpet.

On went her old brown jacket; on went her old brown hat. With a whirl of skirts and with the brilliant sparkle still in her eyes, she fluttered out the door and down the stairs to the street.

Where she stopped the sign read: "Mme. Sofronie. Hair Goods of All Kinds." One flight up Della ran, and collected herself, panting. Madame, large, too white, chilly, hardly looked the "Sofronie."

"Will you buy my hair?" asked Della.

"I buy hair," said Madame. "Take yer hat off and let's have a sight at the looks of it."

Down rippled the brown cascade.

"Twenty dollars," said Madame, lifting the mass with a practiced hand.

"Give it to me quick," said Della.

Oh, and the next two hours tripped by on rosy wings. Forget the hashed metaphor. She was ransacking the stores for Jim's present.

She found it at last. It surely had been made for Jim and no one else. There was no other like it in any of the stores, and she had turned all of them inside out. It was a platinum fob chain* simple and chaste in design, properly proclaiming its value by substance alone and not by meretricious ornamentation—as all good things should do. It was even worthy of The Watch. As soon as she saw it she knew that

Literature
in context Cultural Connection

♦ **Watch Fob Chain**

A fob chain is central to the plot of "The Gift of the Magi." The word *fob* probably entered the English language from the German dialect word *Fuppe*, meaning "pocket." During the nineteenth century, before the wristwatch became common, a man would carry a pocket watch that fit in a special vest pocket. To keep the watch from falling or becoming lost, it was fastened to the vest by means of a strap or chain (sometimes with an ornament, or fob, at the end) that was attached to a pin with a locking clasp, making it quite secure. Sometimes, as pictured at right, a chain had finely detailed metalwork, making it a work of art.

A fob chain was often handed down from father to son, as was Jim Young's in O. Henry's story. This fact alone made it very precious to its owner, despite its modest intrinsic value.

depreciate (dē prē′ shē āt′) *v.* reduce in value

cascade (kas kād′) *n.* waterfall

chaste (chāst) *adj.* pure or clean in style; not ornate

meretricious (mer′ ə trish′ əs) *adj.* attractive in a cheap, flashy way

---

6. **Queen of Sheba** in the Bible, the beautiful queen who visited King Solomon to test his wisdom.

it must be Jim's. It was like him. Quietness and value—the description applied to both. Twenty-one dollars they took from her for it, and she hurried home with the 87 cents. With that chain on his watch Jim might be properly anxious about the time in any company. Grand as the watch was he sometimes looked at it on the sly on account of the old leather strap that he used in place of a chain.

When Della reached home her intoxication gave way a little to prudence and reason. She got out her curling irons and lighted the gas and went to work repairing the <u>ravages</u> made by generosity added to love. Which is always a tremendous task, dear friends—a mammoth task.

Within forty minutes her head was covered with tiny, close-lying curls that made her look wonderfully like a truant schoolboy. She looked at her reflection in the mirror long, carefully, and critically.

"If Jim doesn't kill me," she said to herself, "before he takes a second look at me, he'll say I look like a Coney Island[7] chorus girl. But what could I do—oh! what could I do with a dollar and eighty-seven cents?"

At 7 o'clock the coffee was made and the frying-pan was on the back of the stove hot and ready to cook the chops.

Jim was never late. Della doubled the fob chain in her hand and sat on the corner of the table near the door that he always entered. Then she heard his step on the stair away down on the first flight, and she turned white for just a moment. She had a habit of saying little silent prayers about the simplest every-day things, and now she whispered: "Please God, make him think I am still pretty."

The door opened and Jim stepped in and closed it. He looked thin and very serious. Poor fellow, he was only twenty-two—and to be burdened with a family! He needed a new overcoat and he was without gloves.

Jim stopped inside the door, as immovable as a setter at the scent of quail. His eyes were fixed upon Della, and there was an expression in them that she could not read, and it terrified her. It was not anger, nor surprise, nor disapproval, nor horror, nor any of the sentiments that she had been prepared for. He simply stared at her fixedly with that peculiar expression on his face.

Della wriggled off the table and went for him.

"Jim, darling," she cried, "don't look at me that way. I had my hair cut off and sold it because I couldn't have lived through Christmas without giving you a present. It'll grow out again—you won't mind, will you? I just had to do it. My hair grows awfully fast. Say 'Merry Christmas!' Jim, and let's be happy. You don't know what a nice—what a beautiful, nice gift I've got for you."

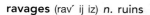

ravages (rav´ ij iz) *n.* ruins

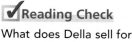

✔**Reading Check**

What does Della sell for twenty dollars?

---

7. **Coney Island** beach and amusement park in Brooklyn, New York.

The Gift of the Magi ◆ 527

Hairdresser's Window, 1907, John Sloan, Wadsworth Atheneum, Hartford, Connecticut

▲ **Critical Viewing** How do you think Della felt as she approached Madame Sofronie's shop? **[Analyze]**

"You've cut off your hair?" asked Jim, laboriously, as if he had not arrived at that patent fact yet even after the hardest mental labor.

"Cut it off and sold it," said Della. "Don't you like me just as well, anyhow? I'm me without my hair, ain't I?"

Jim looked about the room curiously.

"You say your hair is gone?" he said, with an air almost of idiocy.

"You needn't look for it," said Della. "It's sold, I tell you—sold and gone, too. It's Christmas Eve, boy. Be good to me, for it went for you. Maybe the hairs of my head were numbered," she went on with a sudden serious sweetness, "but nobody could ever count my love for you. Shall I put the chops on, Jim?"

Out of his trance Jim seemed quickly to wake. He enfolded his Della. For ten seconds let us regard with <u>discreet</u> scrutiny some inconsequential object in the other direction. Eight dollars a week or a million a year—what is the difference? A mathematician or a wit would give you the wrong answer. The Magi brought valuable gifts, but that was not among them. This dark assertion will be illuminated later on.

Jim drew a package from his overcoat pocket and threw it upon the table.

"Don't make any mistake, Dell," he said, "about me. I don't think there's anything in the way of a haircut or a shave or a shampoo that could make me like my girl any less. But if you'll unwrap that package you may see why you had me going a while at first."

White fingers and nimble tore at the string and paper. And then an ecstatic scream of joy; and then, alas! a quick feminine change to hysterical tears and wails, necessitating the immediate employment of all the comforting powers of the lord of the flat.

For there lay The Combs—the set of combs, side and back, that Della had worshipped for long in a Broadway window. Beautiful combs, pure tortoise shell, with jeweled rims—just the shade to wear in the beautiful vanished hair. They were expensive combs, she knew, and her heart had simply craved and yearned over them without the least hope of possession. And now, they were hers, but the tresses that should have adorned the coveted adornments were gone.

But she hugged them to her bosom, and at length she was able to look up with dim eyes and a smile and say: "My hair grows so fast, Jim!"

And then Della leaped up like a little singed cat and cried, "Oh, oh!" Jim had not yet seen his beautiful present. She held it out to him

discreet (di skrēt´) *adj.* tactful; respectful

▼ **Critical Viewing**
How might Della have felt about an elaborate, expensive comb like this one? **[Connect]**

✓ **Reading Check**

What gift does Jim give to Della?

eagerly upon her open palm. The dull precious metal seemed to flash with a reflection of her bright and ardent spirit.

"Isn't it a dandy, Jim? I hunted all over town to find it. You'll have to look at the time a hundred times a day now. Give me your watch. I want to see how it looks on it."

Instead of obeying, Jim tumbled down on the couch and put his hands under the back of his head and smiled.

"Dell," said he, "let's put our Christmas presents away and keep 'em a while. They're too nice to use just at present. I sold the watch to get the money to buy your combs. And now suppose you put the chops on."

The Magi, as you know, were wise men—wonderfully wise men—who brought gifts to the Babe in the manger. They invented the art of giving Christmas presents. Being wise, their gifts were no doubt wise ones, possibly bearing the privilege of exchange in case of duplication. And here I have lamely related to you the uneventful chronicle of two foolish children in a flat who most unwisely sacrificed for each other the greatest treasures of their house. But in a last word to the wise of these days let it be said that of all who give gifts these two were the wisest. Of all who give and receive gifts, such as they are wisest. Everywhere they are wisest. They are the magi.

O. Henry

(1862–1910)
William Sydney Porter, alias O. Henry, was born in Greensboro, North Carolina, and left school at sixteen to work at his uncle's drugstore. In 1882, he moved to Texas. In Austin he worked at a ranch, a general land office, and then the First National Bank. In Houston, he became a reporter, columnist, and cartoonist for the *Houston Post*.

In 1896, Porter was indicted for embezzling bank funds. He fled to Honduras but returned to Texas when he learned his wife was dying. After her death, Porter was arrested, convicted, and sent to prison in Ohio, where he began writing short stories that made him immensely popular.

Released from prison, he changed his name to O. Henry and moved to New York City. Many of his stories, including "The Gift of the Magi," draw upon his observations of the lives of everyday New Yorkers.

Review and Assess

Thinking About the Selection

1. **Respond:** If you were Jim or Della, how would you feel about the gift you received?

2. **(a) Recall:** How do Jim and Della feel toward each other?
   (b) Support: What evidence from the story leads you to your opinion?

3. **(a) Recall:** What does Della do to get money for Jim's present?
   (b) Infer: What does her action suggest about her character?

4. **(a) Recall:** How does Jim react when he sees that Della has cut her hair? **(b) Analyze:** Why does Della misunderstand Jim's reaction?

5. **(a) Recall:** How did Jim get the money for Della's gift?
   (b) Connect: How does he react to the watch chain?
   (c) Infer: Why does he react in such a way?

6. **Draw Conclusions:** O. Henry says of these "two foolish children" that they were "the wisest." How do you think he would define wisdom?

7. **Take a Position:** Do you believe it is wise to give up your most treasured possessions to buy something meaningful for a loved one? Why or why not?

Review and Assess

Literary Analysis

Plot

1. What is the central conflict, or struggle, in the **plot** of "The Gift of the Magi"?
2. What occurs at the climax, or high point, of the story?
3. Which events form the resolution?
4. The exposition extends to the introduction of the central conflict. Use this graphic organizer to help you describe the remaining stages in the plot of "The Gift of the Magi."

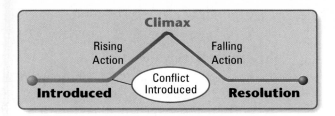

Connecting Literary Elements

5. In what ways was the ending different from what you expected?
6. Look back at the story. Which hints point to the **surprise ending**?
7. Although it was a surprise, did you find the ending logical and believable? Explain.

Reading Strategy

Asking Questions

8. Which **questions** about Della and Jim came to your mind as you read?
9. (a) List three details that the narrator reveals and three that he does not reveal. (b) What is the effect of the narrator's choice of details?

Extend Understanding

10. **History Connection:** This story takes place about a hundred years ago. How might the story—and especially Della and Jim—be different if the story took place today?

Quick Review

Plot is the sequence of events that make up a story. Plot is divided into five stages: **exposition** (the scene is set and background information is provided), **rising action** (the central conflict, or struggle, is introduced), **climax** (the high point of the conflict), **falling action** (the conflict lessens), and **resolution** (the conflict concludes and loose ends get tied up).

A **surprise ending** is a conclusion that differs from what a reader expects.

To fully understand the plot, **ask questions** about characters, events, and information the narrator reveals or conceals.

 Take It to the Net
www.phschool.com
Take the interactive self-test online to check your understanding of the selection.

Integrate Language Skills

Vocabulary Development Lesson

Word Analysis: Latin Prefix *de-*

In "The Gift of the Magi," you will encounter the word *depreciate,* meaning "to reduce in value." This word is derived from a Latin word meaning "price" and contains the Latin prefix *de-,* which in this case means "down." When something *depreciates,* its price goes down. The prefix *de-* can also mean "away from," as in *deviate,* or "undo," as in *defrost.*

Using what you know about the meaning of *de-,* match each phrase shown here with one of the words below.

a. demerit   **b.** derail   **c.** deform

1. run off the tracks
2. undo something's shape
3. grade for poor work

Concept Development: Synonyms

Write the word that is a synonym for, or means the same as, the vocabulary word on the left.

1.	instigates	**a.**	waterfall
2.	depreciate	**b.**	gaudy
3.	cascade	**c.**	cheapen
4.	meretricious	**d.**	pure
5.	chaste	**e.**	tactful
6.	discreet	**f.**	ruins
7.	ravages	**g.**	provokes

Spelling Strategy

If a word ends in a single consonant that is preceded by two vowels, do not double the final consonant when you add an ending. Thus, *discreet* + *-ly* = *discreetly.* Add *-ly, -ing,* or *-ed* to each word below to form a properly spelled new word.

1. chain   **2.** hour   **3.** kneel

Grammar Lesson

Adverb Phrases

An **adverb phrase** is a prepositional phrase that modifies a verb, an adjective, or an adverb. An adverb phrase answers the question *how? in what way? where? when?* or *to what extent?*

In this example, the adverb phrase is italicized.

> **Example:** She let her hair fall *to its full length.* (to what extent did it fall?)

Practice Copy each of these sentences from the story. Underline the adverb phrases, and write the word or words each adverb phrase modifies.

1. Had the Queen of Sheba lived in the next flat across the airshaft, Della would have let her hair hang out the window.
2. The next two hours tripped by on rosy wings.
3. Within forty minutes her head was covered with tiny, close-lying curls.
4. He simply stared at her fixedly with that peculiar expression on his face.
5. She held it out to him eagerly upon her open palm.

Writing Application Write four sentences that contain adverb phrases. Each sentence should include a response to at least one of these questions: *How? Where? When?* Underline the phrases you have included.

W̶G̶ Prentice Hall Writing and Grammar Connection: Chapter 21, Section 1

Writing Lesson

Story From Jim's Point of View

As you read "The Gift of the Magi," you learn about the experiences of Della and Jim through a narrator who stands outside the story. Rewrite the story, telling it from Jim's point of view.

Prewriting   Review the story and use a chart like the one shown to jot down information that is revealed about Jim. Next to each piece of information, write a sentence from Jim's perspective.

Model: Writing From a First-Person Perspective

Information From the Story	In Jim's Words
They took great pride in Jim's gold watch, which had been passed down to him.	I always cherished this watch, not for the gold, but for the memory of my father.

Drafting   Using Jim's words, draft your story. Remember that the entire narrative must be from Jim's perspective. Any information about Della that you include must be from Jim's point of view.

Revising   Reread your draft, checking for any inconsistencies in viewpoint. Decide whether Jim would truly know the information you provide. Rewrite any passage that is not written from Jim's perspective.

WG Prentice Hall Writing and Grammar Connection: Chapter 5, Section 2

Extension Activities

Listening and Speaking In a small group, prepare a **performance** of "The Gift of the Magi."

- Consider the best approach to take to show the characters and the setting.
- Work out the best way to include the information the narrator provides.
- Decide who will play each part.

If possible, tape your rehearsals for review. Perform the play for your classmates. Invite them to write a brief response. [**Group Activity**]

Research and Technology Prepare an **illustrated report** about life in New York or any other large American city around 1905, when "The Gift of the Magi" was written. Use reference books as well as an Internet search engine to find information and period illustrations. Look especially for pictures of clothing that appears very different from what people wear today.

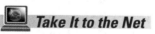 **Take It to the Net**   www.phschool.com

Go online for an additional research activity using the Internet.

Gift-Giving in the Technological World

In "The Gift of the Magi," Della spends the day before Christmas frantically searching stores for Jim's present. Had she lived in modern times, she could have saved time and trouble by shopping online via the Internet.

Search Engines

Della had no idea which store carried the platinum watch chain she sought. Today, she could use the Internet to locate the store and item. After logging on to the search engine of her choice, she would simply enter the object of her search: "watch-chain store." If her search yielded 500 watch stores in 12 different countries, she might wish to narrow her search further by doing an "AND" search. In this case, she would use the search engine's advanced search screen to add "New York City" to her search terms. The results would list only New York City watch-chain stores, saving Della the cost of travel.

Store Web Sites

If Della already knew of stores that sold watch chains online, she could log on directly to each store's Web site. Sites sometimes include a "Search" box for typing in the name of a particular item. If the watch chain were in stock, Della might even be able to order it online and have it rush-delivered in time for Christmas. However, because online merchants are not likely to accept hair as payment, Della might have to apply for a credit card—another advance in the modern world.

Online Auctions

Della might have saved some money by bidding for her watch chain at an online auction. After logging on to an auction Web site, she would have identified the item she was seeking and found a list of available items. Della could then have bid against other buyers, with the item going to the highest bidder.

Connecting Literature and Society

1. Which method of online shopping do you think would have suited Della's needs best? Why?
2. What are the advantages of shopping online as opposed to shopping the way Della and Jim did? What are the disadvantages?

Advertisements

About Advertisements

An **advertisement** is a message intended to promote a product, a service, or an idea. People use advertisements for many purposes:

- Manufacturers advertise to persuade consumers to buy their goods.
- Companies advertise to create a positive public image of themselves.
- Politicians advertise to win votes.
- Special-interest groups advertise to promote causes they favor.
- Individuals advertise to sell homes, cars, and other property.

You can find advertisements in many places—in newspapers and magazines, on television and radio, on billboards and posters, and in your mail and e-mail.

Reading Strategy

Analyzing Persuasive Techniques: Appeal Through Expertise

Advertisers use many techniques to persuade consumers to buy products. One technique is the **appeal through expertise,** which takes advantage of the average customer's ignorance about the product.

The automobile advertisement on the next page states that the R-C-H automobile has a "semi-floating type" of rear axle. However, there is no explanation of what a semi-floating axle is or why it should be considered a unique and valuable feature. For all you know, every car is made with such an axle. Yet, the phrase sounds impressive. The ad reads as if it were written by experts, and readers might trust it, based solely on the technical language the copywriter uses.

As you read the entire ad, list each feature that it describes. Ask yourself: Is this feature likely to be familiar to customers? If the answer is no, list it in your notebook as an appeal through expertise.

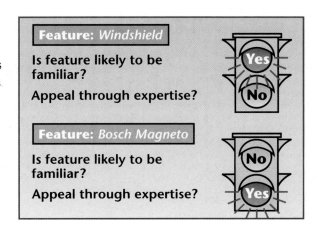

Advertisement for Automobile

Before 1908, owning an automobile was a luxury. Henry Ford and other manufacturers changed that, producing affordable cars such as the R-C-H "Twenty-Five." The following is an advertisement for the car.

Including a handsome profile of the car appeals to consumers' desire for status and pride of ownership.

The ad uses the superlative *best* to convince readers that no other car is as good as this one.

Extra suggests that buyers are getting even more than they are paying for.

The words *Jiffy* and *instantaneously* are appealing because they imply the greatest possible speed.

R-C-H Announcement 191

RC

R-C-H "Twenty-Five"

We are determined to build the best all 'round five-passenger touring car in the world and sell it, completely equipped, for

$900

The Car

Motor— Long-stroke; 4 cylinders cast en bloc; $3\frac{1}{4}$ inch bore, 5 inch stroke. Two-bearing crank shaft.

Drive— **Left Side**. Irreversible worm gear, 16 inch steering wheel. Spark and throttle control on steering column.

Axles— Front, I-beam, drop-forged; rear, semi-floating type.

The Equipment

Non-skid tires—$32x3\frac{1}{2}$.

12-inch Bullet electric head lights with double parabolic lens.

Bosch Magneto.

Demountable rims.

Extra rim and holders.

Tally-ho horn.

Jiffy curtains—up or down instantaneously.

R-C-H CORPORATION, 133 Lycaste Street, Detroit, Mich

Check Your Comprehension

1. How many passengers was the car designed to carry?
2. Which appealing details describe the car's headlights?

Applying the Reading Strategy

Analyzing Persuasive Techniques: Appeal Through Expertise

3. On a separate piece of paper, list each feature described in the ad. Which of those features suggest an appeal through expertise?

Activity

Researching a Product

An appeal through expertise can be effective only if consumers are unfamiliar with the product's advertised features. The best way for consumers to protect themselves is by finding out as much about the product as possible. Then, they can better evaluate the advertisement.

Find a current advertisement for a product. In a chart like the one shown, list the advertised features that may be unfamiliar to many consumers. Then, conduct research using an encyclopedia, owner's manual, Internet Web site, or other resource to learn the function and importance of each feature.

Feature	Function	Importance
crank shaft	controls timing and motion of pistons, which fire to power the engine	significant
convertible top	allows the car's top to be raised and lowered	minor

Comparing Informational Texts

Persuasive Techniques Then and Now

1. Review current advertisements to determine persuasive techniques being used today. Identify examples of (a) slogans or catchy phrases, (b) testimonials, (c) celebrity endorsements, (d) sales or financial incentives, and (e) statistics.

2. Locate newspapers and magazines to find current car advertisements. Compare the ads you find with the one for the R-C-H "Twenty-Five." Use these points of comparison:

   • Analyze the way the ads persuade readers, noting the appealing words and phrases employed in each advertisement.

   • Notice the use of images and fonts to create an impression.

Share your findings with the class.

Prepare to Read

Sonata for Harp and Bicycle

Preview

Connecting to the Literature

Mysteries are everywhere. Some people find safety in ignoring them or simply wondering about them without trying to figure them out. Certain people, however, feel compelled to solve these mysteries—even if danger is involved. In this story, a young man stumbles into a strange situation and tries to get to the bottom of it, come what may.

Background

A sonata [sə nät′ ə] is a musical composition in several movements, or parts, for one or more instruments. Sonatas are frequently written for solo piano or for piano and another instrument (such as a harp). In titling her story "Sonata for Harp and Bicycle," Joan Aiken playfully suggests a musical structure that will, like a sequence of chords, be resolved at the end.

Literary Analysis

Rising Action

The most suspenseful part of a story is the **rising action**—the part that introduces and develops the main conflict of the plot. The rising action of "Sonata for Harp and Bicycle" includes a complicated, puzzling mystery that fuels suspense as this passage from the story suggests:

> "—fire escape," he heard, as they came into the momentary hush of the carpeted entrance hall. And "—it's to do with a bicycle. A bicycle and a harp."

As you read, watch for the way in which a harp and a bicycle surprisingly converge.

Connecting Literary Elements

The rising action builds until it reaches the **climax,** or high point of interest. The climax is the emotional peak of the story—the moment toward which the plot builds. It is also the point from which the action winds down toward the resolution. As you read, use a chart like this one to record details leading to the climax and to explain the mystery.

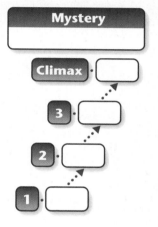

Reading Strategy

Predicting

When you **predict,** you guess what will happen on the basis of what you already know. While reading the story,

- make predictions by looking for clues about future events.
- record each clue you find, along with a prediction of where it will lead.

Revise your predictions as you read, and compare them with what actually happens at the end.

Vocabulary Development

encroaching (en krōch´ iŋ) *adj.* intruding in a sneaking way (p. 541)

tantalizingly (tan´ tə līz´ iŋ lē) *adv.* in a teasing way (p. 542)

furtive (fur´ tiv) *adj.* sneaky (p. 543)

menacing (men´ əs iŋ) *v.* threatening (p. 544)

reciprocate (ri sip´ rə kāt) *v.* return (p. 546)

ardent (ärd´ 'nt) *adj.* passionate (p. 546)

gossamer (gäs´ ə mər) *adj.* light, thin, and filmy (p. 546)

preposterous (prē päs´ tər əs) *adj.* absurd (p. 546)

engendered (en jen´ dərd) *adj.* produced (p. 547)

improbably (im präb´ ə blē) *adv.* unlikely to happen (p. 548)

Sonata for Harp and Bicycle

Joan Aiken

"No

one is allowed to remain in the building after five o'clock," Mr. Manaby told his new assistant, showing him into the little room that was like the inside of a parcel.

"Why not?"

"Directorial policy," said Mr. Manaby. But that was not the real reason.

Gaunt and sooty, Grimes Buildings lurched up the side of a hill toward Clerkenwell.[1] Every little office within its dim and crumbling exterior owned one tiny crumb of light—such was the proud boast of the architect—but toward evening the crumbs were collected as by an immense vacuum cleaner, absorbed and demolished, yielding to an uncontrollable mass of dark that came tumbling in through windows and doors to take their place. Darkness infested the building like a flight of bats returning willingly to roost.

"Wash hands, please. Wash hands, please," the intercom began to bawl in the passages at a quarter to five. Without much need of prompting, the staff hustled like lemmings along the corridors to green- and blue-tiled washrooms that mocked with an illusion of cheerfulness the encroaching dusk.

"All papers into cases, please," the voice warned, five minutes later. "Look at your desks, ladies and gentlemen. Any documents left lying about? Kindly put them away. Desks must be left clear and tidy. Drawers must be shut."

A multitudinous shuffling, a rustling as of innumerable bluebottle flies might have been heard by the attentive ear after this injunction, as the employees of Moreton Wold and Company thrust their papers into cases, hurried letters and invoices into drawers, clipped statistical abstracts together and slammed them into filing cabinets, dropped discarded copy into wastepaper baskets. Two minutes later, and not a desk throughout Grimes Buildings bore more than its customary coating of dust.

---

1. **Clerkenwell** district of London.

☑ **Reading Check**

What is the new assistant told about being in the building after five o'clock?

"Hats and coats on, please. Hats and coats on, please. Did you bring an umbrella? Have you left any shopping on the floor?" At three minutes to five the homegoing throng was in the lifts[2] and on the stairs; a clattering, staccato-voiced flood darkened momentarily the great double doors of the building, and then as the first faint notes of St. Paul's[3] came echoing faintly on the frosty air, to be picked up near at hand by the louder chimes of St. Biddulph's-on-the-Wall, the entire premises of Moreton Wold stood empty.

"But why is it?" Jason Ashgrove, the new copywriter, asked his secretary one day. "Why are the staff herded out so fast? Not that I'm against it, mind you; I think it's an admirable idea in many ways, but there is the liberty of the individual to be considered, don't you think?"

"Hush!" Miss Golden, the secretary, gazed at him with large and terrified eyes. "You mustn't ask that sort of question. When you are taken onto the Established Staff you'll be told. Not before."

"But I want to know now," Jason said in discontent. "Do you know?"

"Yes, I do," Miss Golden answered <u>tantalizingly</u>. "Come on, or we shan't have finished the Oat Crisp layout by a quarter to." And she stared firmly down at the copy in front of her, lips folded, candyfloss hair falling over her face, lashes hiding eyes like peridots,[4] a girl with a secret.

Jason was annoyed. He rapped out a couple of rude and witty rhymes which Miss Golden let pass in a withering silence.

"What do you want for your birthday, Miss Golden? Sherry? Fudge? Bubble bath?"

"I want to go away with a clear conscience about Oat Crisps," Miss Golden retorted. It was not true; what she chiefly wanted was Mr. Jason Ashgrove, but he had not realized this yet.

"Come on, don't tease! I'm sure you haven't been on the Established Staff all that long," he coaxed her. "What happens when one is taken on, anyway? Does the Managing Director have us up for a confidential chat? Or are we given a little book called *The Awful Secret of Grimes Buildings*?"

Miss Golden wasn't telling. She opened her drawer and took out a white towel and a cake of rosy soap.

"Wash hands, please! Wash hands, please!"

Jason was frustrated. "You'll be sorry," he said. "I shall do something desperate."

"Oh no, you mustn't!" Her eyes were large with fright. She ran from the room and was back within a couple of moments, still drying her hands.

"If I took you out for a coffee, couldn't you give me just a tiny hint?"

Side by side Miss Golden and Mr. Ashgrove ran along the green-floored passages, battled down the white marble stairs among the hundred other employees from the tenth floor, the nine hundred from the floors below.

Literary Analysis
Rising Action What conflict is introduced here to begin the rising action?

tantalizingly (tan´ tə līz´ iŋ lē) *adv.* in a teasing way

Reading Strategy
Predicting Do you think the relationship between Miss Golden and Jason will develop into a romance? Which details help you decide?

---

2. lifts *n.* British term for elevators.
3. St. Paul's famous church in London.
4. peridots (per´ i däts´) *n.* yellowish-green gems.

He saw her lips move as she said something, but in the clatter of two thousand feet the words were lost.

"—fire escape," he heard, as they came into the momentary hush of the carpeted entrance hall. And "—it's to do with a bicycle. A bicycle and a harp."

"I don't understand."

Now they were in the street, chilly with the winter dusk smells of celery on carts, of swept-up leaves heaped in faraway parks, and cold layers of dew sinking among the withered evening primroses in the bombed areas. London lay about them wreathed in twilit mystery and fading against the barred and smoky sky. Like a ninth wave the sound of traffic overtook and swallowed them.

"Please tell me!"

But, shaking her head, she stepped onto a scarlet homebound bus and was borne away from him.

Literary Analysis
Rising Action What effect does Miss Golden's silence have on the rising action?

Jason stood undecided on the pavement, with the crowds dividing around him as around the pier of a bridge. He scratched his head, looked about him for guidance.

An ambulance clanged, a taxi hooted, a drill stuttered, a siren wailed on the river, a door slammed, a brake squealed, and close beside his ear a bicycle bell tinkled its tiny warning.

A bicycle, she had said. A bicycle and a harp.

Jason turned and stared at Grimes Buildings.

Somewhere, he knew, there was a back way in, a service entrance. He walked slowly past the main doors, with their tubs of snowy chrysanthemums, and up Glass Street. A tiny <u>furtive</u> wedge of dark-ness beckoned him, a snicket, a hacket, an alley carved into the thickness of the building. It was so narrow that at any moment, it seemed, the overtopping walls would come together and squeeze it out of existence.

furtive (fur´ tiv) *adj.* sneaky

Walking as softly as an Indian, Jason passed through it, slid by a file of dustbins,[5] and found the foot of the fire escape. Iron treads rose into the mist, like an illustration to a Gothic[6] fairy tale.

He began to climb.

When he had mounted to the ninth story he paused for breath. It was a lonely place. The lighting consisted of a dim bulb at the foot of every flight. A well of gloom sank beneath him. The cold fingers of the wind nagged and fluttered at the tails of his jacket, and he pulled the string of the fire door and edged inside.

Grimes Buildings were triangular, with the street forming the base of the triangle, and the fire escape the point. Jason could see two long pas-sages coming toward him, meeting at an acute angle where he stood. He started down the left-hand one, tiptoeing in the cavelike silence. Nowhere was there any sound, except for the faraway drip of a tap.

☑**Reading Check**
Which question does Jason Ashgrove want answered by Miss Golden?

---

5. dustbins British term for garbage cans.
6. Gothic *adj.* mysterious.

No night watchman would stay in the building; none was needed. Burglars gave the place a wide berth.

Jason opened a door at random; then another. Offices lay everywhere about him, empty and forbidding. Some held lipstick-stained tissues, spilled powder, and orange peels; others were still foggy with cigarette smoke. Here was a Director's suite of rooms—a desk like half an acre of frozen lake, inch-thick carpet, roses, and the smell of cigars. Here was a conference room with scattered squares of doodled blotting paper. All equally empty.

He was not sure when he first began to notice the bell. Telephone, he thought at first, and then he remembered that all the outside lines were disconnected at five. And this bell, anyway, had not the regularity of a telephone's double ring: there was a tinkle, and then silence; a long ring, and then silence; a whole volley of rings together, and then silence.

Jason stood listening, and fear knocked against his ribs and shortened his breath. He knew that he must move or be paralyzed by it. He ran up a flight of stairs and found himself with two more endless green corridors beckoning him like a pair of dividers.

Another sound now: a waft of ice-thin notes, riffling up an arpeggio[7] like a flurry of snowflakes. Far away down the passage it echoed. Jason ran in pursuit, but as he ran the music receded. He circled the building, but it always outdistanced him, and when he came back to the stairs he heard it fading away to the story below.

He hesitated, and as he did so heard again the bell; the bicycle bell. It was approaching him fast, bearing down on him, urgent, <u>menacing</u>. He could hear the pedals, almost see the shimmer of an invisible wheel. Absurdly, he was reminded of the insistent clamor of an ice-cream vendor, summoning children on a sultry Sunday afternoon.

There was a little fireman's alcove beside him, with buckets and pumps. He hurled himself into it. The bell stopped beside him, and then there was a moment while his heart tried to shake itself loose in his chest. He was looking into two eyes carved out of expressionless air; he was held by two hands knotted together out of the width of dark.

"Daisy, Daisy?" came the whisper. "Is that you, Daisy? Have you come to give me your answer?"

Jason tried to speak, but no words came.

---

7. arpeggio (är pej´ ō) *n.* notes of a chord played one after the other instead of together.

Literary Analysis
Rising Action What effect does the sound of the bell have on the plot?

menacing (men´ əs iŋ) *v.* threatening

▼ **Critical Viewing**
How does the mood of these buildings compare to the mood of the setting of the story? **[Compare]**

"It's not Daisy! Who are you?" The sibilants[8] were full of threat. "You can't stay here. This is private property."

He was thrust along the corridor. It was like being pushed by a whirlwind—the fire door opened ahead of him without a touch, and he was on the openwork platform, clutching the slender railing. Still the hands would not let him go.

"How about it?" the whisper mocked him. "How about jumping? It's an easy death compared with some."

Jason looked down into the smoky void. The darkness nodded to him like a familiar.[9]

"You wouldn't be much loss, would you? What have you got to live for?"

Miss Golden, Jason thought. She would miss me. And the syllables Berenice Golden lingered in the air like a chime. Drawing on some unknown deposit of courage he shook himself loose from the holding hands and ran down the fire escape without looking back.

Next morning when Miss Golden, crisp, fragrant, and punctual, shut the door of Room 492 behind her, she stopped short of the hatpegs with a horrified gasp.

"Mr. Ashgrove, your hair!"

"It makes me look more distinguished, don't you think?" he said.

It had indeed this effect, for his impeccable dark cut had turned to a stippled silver which might have been envied by many a diplomat.

"How did it happen? You've not—" her voice sank to a whisper—*"you've not been in Grimes Buildings after dark?"*

"Miss Golden—Berenice," he said earnestly. "Who was Daisy? Plainly you know. Tell me the story."

"Did you see him?" she asked faintly.

"Him?"

"William Heron—The Wailing Watchman. Oh," she exclaimed in terror, "I can see you did. Then you are doomed—doomed!"

"If I'm doomed," said Jason, "let's have coffee, and you tell me the story quickly."

"It all happened over fifty years ago," said Berenice, as she spooned out coffee powder with distracted extravagance. "Heron was the night watchman in this building, patrolling the corridors from dusk to dawn every night on his bicycle. He fell in love with a Miss Bell who taught the harp. She rented a room—this room—

---

8. **sibilants** (sib´ əl əntz) *n.* hissing sounds.
9. **a familiar** a spirit.

☑ **Reading Check**

What happens to Jason inside the Grimes Buildings?

and gave lessons in it. She began to <u>reciprocate</u> his love, and they used to share a picnic supper every night at eleven, and she'd stay on a while to keep him company. It was an idyll,[10] among the fire buckets and the furnace pipes.

"On Halloween he had summoned up the courage to propose to her. The day before he had told her he was going to ask her a very important question, and he came to the Buildings with a huge bunch of roses and a bottle of wine. But Miss Bell never turned up.

"The explanation was simple. Miss Bell, of course, had been losing a lot of sleep through her nocturnal romance, and so she used to take a nap in her music room between seven and ten, to save going home. In order to make sure that she would wake up, she persuaded her father, a distant relative of Graham Bell,[11] to attach an alarm-waking fixture to her telephone which called her every night at ten. She was too modest and shy to let Heron know that she spent those hours in the building, and to give him the pleasure of waking her himself.

"Alas! On this important evening the line failed, and she never woke up. The telephone was in its infancy at that time, you must remember.

"Heron waited and waited. At last, mad with grief and jealousy, having called her home and discovered that she was not there, he concluded that she had betrayed him; he ran to the fire escape, and cast himself off it, holding the roses and the bottle of wine.

"Daisy did not long survive him but pined away soon after. Since that day their ghosts have haunted Grimes Buildings, he vainly patrolling the corridors on his bicycle, she playing her harp in the room she rented. *But they never meet.* And anyone who meets the ghost of William Heron will himself, within five days, leap down from the same fatal fire escape."

She gazed at him with tragic eyes.

"In that case we must lose no time," said Jason, and he enveloped her in an embrace as prompt as it was <u>ardent</u>. Looking down at the <u>gossamer</u> hair sprayed across his pin-stripe, he added, "Just the same it is a <u>preposterous</u> situation. Firstly, I have no intention of jumping off the fire escape—" here, however, he repressed a shudder as he remembered the cold, clutching hands of the evening before— "and secondly, I find it quite nonsensical that those two inefficient ghosts have spent fifty years in this building without coming across each other. We must remedy the matter, Berenice. We must not begrudge our new-found happiness to others."

He gave her another kiss so impassioned that the electric typewriter against which they were leaning began chattering to itself in a frenzy of enthusiasm.

"This very evening," he went on, looking at his watch, "we will put matters right for that unhappy couple and then, if I really have only five more days to live, which I don't for one moment believe, we will

---

10. **idyll** (ī´ dəl) *n.* romantic scene, usually in the country.
11. **Graham Bell** Alexander Graham Bell (1847–1922), the inventor of the telephone.

reciprocate (ri sip´ rə kāt) *v.* return

Literary Analysis
Rising Action How does this information change the nature of the story's conflict?

ardent (ärd´ 'nt) *adj.* passionate

gossamer (gäs´ ə mər) *adj.* light, thin, and filmy

preposterous (prē päs´ tər əs) *adj.* absurd

Reading Strategy
Predicting How do you think Jason plans to "remedy the matter"?

proceed to spend them together, my bewitching Berenice, in the most advantageous manner possible."

She nodded, spellbound.

"Can you work a switchboard?" he added. She nodded again. "My love, you are perfection itself. Meet me in the switchboard room then, at ten this evening. I would say, have dinner with me, but I shall need to make one or two purchases and see an old R.A.F.[12] friend. You will be safe from Heron's curse in the switchboard room if he always keeps to the corridors."

"I would rather meet him and die with you," she murmured.

"My angel, I hope that won't be necessary. Now," he said, sighing, "I suppose we should get down to our day's work."

Strangely enough the copy they wrote that day, although <u>engendered</u> from such agitated minds, sold more packets of Oat Crisps than any other advertising matter before or since.

That evening when Jason entered Grimes Buildings he was carrying two bottles of wine, two bunches of red roses, and a large canvas-covered bundle. Miss Golden, who had concealed herself in the switchboard room before the offices closed for the night, eyed these things with surprise.

"Now," said Jason, after he had greeted her, "I want you first to ring our own extension."

"No one will reply, surely?"

"I think she will reply."

Sure enough, when Berenice rang Extension 170 a faint, sleepy voice, distant and yet clear, whispered, "Hullo?"

"Is that Miss Bell?"

"Yes."

Berenice went a little pale. Her eyes sought Jason's and, prompted by him, she said formally, "Switchboard here, Miss Bell. Your ten o'clock call."

"Thank you," the faint voice said. There was a click and the line went blank.

"Excellent," Jason remarked. He unfastened his package and slipped its straps over his shoulders. "Now plug into the intercom."

Berenice did so, and then said, loudly and clearly, "Attention. Night watchman on duty, please. Night watchman on duty. You have an urgent summons to Room 492. You have an urgent summons to Room 492." The intercom echoed and reverberated through the empty corridors, then coughed itself to silence.

"Now we must run. You take the roses, sweetheart, and I'll carry the bottles."

Together they raced up eight flights of stairs and along the passages to Room 492. As they neared the door a burst of music met them—harp music swelling out, sweet and triumphant. Jason took a bunch of roses from Berenice, opened the door a little way, and gently deposited them,

12. R.A.F. Royal Air Force.

engendered (en jen′ dərd) *adj.* produced

Literary Analysis
Rising Action and Climax
Which details in this paragraph suggest that the story is nearing its climax?

**Reading Check**

According to Berenice, what happens to anyone who meets the ghost of William Heron?

with a bottle, inside the door. As he closed it again Berenice said breathlessly, "Did you see anyone?"

"No," he said. "The room was too full of music." She saw that his eyes were shining.

They stood hand in hand, reluctant to move away, waiting for they hardly knew what. Suddenly the door opened again. Neither Berenice nor Jason, afterward, would speak of what they saw but each was left with a memory, bright as the picture on a Salvador Dali[13] calendar, of a bicycle bearing on its saddle a harp, a bottle of wine, and a bouquet of red roses, sweeping <u>improbably</u> down the corridor and far, far away.

"We can go now," Jason said.

He led Berenice to the fire door, tucking the bottle of Médoc in his jacket pocket. A black wind from the north whistled beneath them as they stood on the openwork platform, looking down.

"We don't want our evening to be spoiled by the thought of a curse hanging over us," he said, "so this is the practical thing to do. Hang onto the roses." And holding his love firmly, Jason pulled the rip cord of his R.A.F. friend's parachute and leaped off the fire escape.

A bridal shower of rose petals adorned the descent of Miss Golden, who was possibly the only girl to be kissed in midair in the district of Clerkenwell at ten minutes to midnight on Halloween.

---

13. **Salvador Dali** (sal´ və dôr´ dä´ lē) modern artist (1904–1989) famous for his unusual pictures.

Review and Assess

Thinking About the Selection

1. **Respond:** If you were Jason, would you try to solve the mystery of the Grimes Buildings? Explain.

2. **(a) Recall:** What three things does Miss Golden mention to Jason as they leave the Grimes Buildings at five P.M.?
   (b) Connect: How does he use this information?

3. **(a) Recall:** How has Jason changed when he sees Miss Golden the next day? **(b) Analyze Cause and Effect:** What evidence is there that his encounter in the closed building causes the change?

4. **(a) Recall:** How does Jason avoid the curse that awaits anyone who sees Heron's ghost? **(b) Speculate:** Who was more concerned about the curse—Jason or Berenice? Explain.
   (c) Infer: Why do you think Berenice agrees to assist Jason?

5. **Generalize:** What lesson do the circumstances of William Heron's death teach about the danger of making rash decisions?

Joan Aiken

(b. 1924)

Joan Aiken, the daughter of the poet Conrad Aiken, was born in England and lived with her family in an eerie old house, an experience that helped foster her fascination with mystery and the unexplained.

Aiken began writing at five and published her first story at sixteen. After working in London for a magazine, an advertising agency, and the United Nations, she decided to pursue what she has called "the family trade." Her immense output includes novels, poems, plays, and stories.

Known for her wit, Aiken called her first short-story collection *All You Ever Wanted* and her second *More Than You Bargained For.*

Like other writers, she sometimes uses personal experiences in her work. Jason Ashgrove, the main character of "Sonata for Harp and Bicycle," writes advertising copy, as Aiken once did.

Review and Assess

Literary Analysis

Rising Action

1. At what point in the story does the **rising action** begin? Explain.
2. Why do the sounds that Jason hears in the empty building increase the tension and suspense of the rising action?
3. What information keeps the action of the plot rising on the morning after Jason's escape from Heron?

Connecting Literary Elements

4. Using a chart like the one shown, identify two events in the rising action and determine which event marks the **climax** of the story.

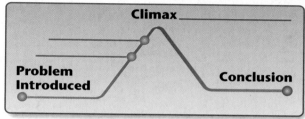

5. What makes the climax the true emotional peak?
6. Which specific events preceding the climax lead you to believe that the climax is imminent? Explain.

Reading Strategy

Predicting

7. Jason enters the Grimes Buildings after closing and hears a bicycle bell tinkling. What **predictions** did you make based on this event?
8. Using a chart like the one shown, explain which clues in the story helped you make the most accurate predictions.

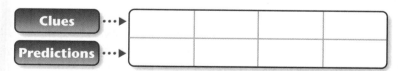

Extend Understanding

9. **Cultural Connection:** This story is set in London and refers to local landmarks. Does the effect of the story depend on its setting, or could it just as well be set in any large city? Explain.

Quick Review

The **rising action** introduces the conflict and builds to the climax of the story.

The **climax** concludes the rising action and is the point of highest interest in the story.

When you **predict**, you guess what will happen next on the basis of what you already know.

 Take It to the Net

www.phschool.com
Take the interactive self-test online to check your understanding of the selection.

Integrate Language Skills

Vocabulary Development Lesson

Word Analysis: Words From Myths

Many English words derive their meaning from names in Greek mythology. *Echo* is a nymph who pined away until only her voice remained. *Hercules* is a son of Zeus known for his strength. *Narcissus* is a handsome youth in love with his reflection.

Use the clues above to write a definition for each word below.

1. echo   2. herculean   3. narcissism

Spelling Strategy

If a word ends in two consonants, do not change the consonants when you add a word ending. Thus, *encroach* + *-ing* = *encroaching*. Add *-ful*, *-ive*, or *-en* to the words below to create three properly spelled new words.

1. gold   2. help   3. collect

Concept Development: Synonyms

Correctly match each word on the left with its synonym on the right. To help you, review the vocabulary list on p. 539.

1. encroaching	a.	passionate
2. tantalizingly	b.	threatening
3. furtive	c.	created
4. menacing	d.	delicate
5. reciprocate	e.	teasingly
6. ardent	f.	unlikely
7. gossamer	g.	secretive
8. preposterous	h.	intruding
9. engendered	i.	nonsensical
10. improbably	j.	return

Grammar Lesson

Participial Phrases

A **participle** is a verb form that acts as an adjective. A **participial phrase** is a participle with an accompanying adverb, adverb phrase, or complement. To avoid misplaced modifiers—participles or participial phrases that seem to modify the wrong words—place a participle or participial phrase as close to the word it modifies as possible.

> **Participle:** He heard a *clattering* noise. (modifies *noise*)
> **Participial Phrase:** He heard them *clattering down the stairs.* (modifies *them*)
> **Misplaced Modifier:** *Converging,* Jason saw down the corridors. (modifies *Jason*)
> **Correct:** Jason saw down the *converging* corridors. (modifies *corridors*)

Practice Identify each participle or participial phrase. Indicate the word each one modifies and correct any misplaced modifiers.

1. Frightened by what she saw, she told him the story.
2. Heron was the watchman, patrolling from dusk to dawn.
3. We will spend our time together, my bewitching Berenice.
4. He carried red roses and a covered bundle.
5. Hanging in the air, Jason felt danger.

Writing Application Rewrite three sentences from the story, using a participle or participial phrase correctly in each.

WG *Prentice Hall Writing and Grammar Connection: Chapter 21, Section 1*

Writing Lesson

Critical Review

Joan Aiken has said, "A flat or unsatisfactory ending is the worst sin a writer can commit." Write a critical review evaluating the ending of "Sonata for Harp and Bicycle," and indicate whether Aiken has provided a satisfactory or unsatisfactory ending.

Prewriting   Make a list of the qualities that you think create satisfactory and unsatisfactory endings to stories. Then, check off the qualities that relate to Aiken's story.

Model: Evaluating a Story's Ending

Satisfactory	Unsatisfactory
☑ when problems are resolved for characters	☐ when events are predictable

Drafting   The first sentence of your review should state your opinion about the ending. Follow up by referring to examples from the story to provide support for your views.

Revising   Reread your draft. Circle any descriptive words you use to convey positive or negative criticism. If you have used vague or overused words, consider replacing them with more precise words.

*W*G *Prentice Hall Writing and Grammar Connection: Chapter 13, Section 2*

Extension Activities

Listening and Speaking   Develop and perform a **talk-show interview** featuring Berenice, Jason, the two ghosts, and the host of the program.

- Review the story and jot down the experiences of Berenice and Jason and the two ghosts.
- Plan the interview so that the two pairs of guests tell what happened at the Grimes Buildings from their own perspectives.
- Practice your interview, providing enough time for each character to speak.

Present your interview to your class. [**Group Activity**]

Research and Technology   Research a famous real-life mystery, and create a **timeline** outlining the facts and summarizing the details. Search the Internet or the library for help in locating information about your subject. Compare the elements of the real-life mystery to those of the mystery in "Sonata for Harp and Bicycle." Present the timeline and your comparison to the class.

 **Take It to the Net**   www.phschool.com

Go online for an additional research activity using the Internet.

Prepare to Read

The Scarlet Ibis

Preview

Connecting to the Literature

Sometimes your best pal is also the biggest pain in your neck. The narrator of "The Scarlet Ibis" has these conflicting feelings toward his younger brother. Although his brother is his closest companion, the narrator is embarrassed by him and makes tremendous demands on him.

Background

Found mostly in the South American tropics, the strikingly beautiful scarlet ibis is a wading bird with long legs, a long, slender neck, black-tipped wings, and a wingspan of more than three feet. Since it seldom appears in the United States north of Florida, the discovery of such a bird in coastal North Carolina, the setting of this story, is unexpected and dramatic.

Literary Analysis

Point of View

Point of view is the perspective from which a story is told. In **third-person point of view,** the narrator does not participate in the story. In **first-person point of view,** the narrator is a character who refers to himself or herself as "I." Look at this passage from "The Scarlet Ibis":

> . . . one afternoon as I watched him, my head poked between the iron posts of the foot of the bed, he looked straight at me and grinned. I skipped through the room, . . . shouting, "Mama, he smiled. He's all there! He's all there!" and he was.

In using this point of view, the writer enables you to experience the narrator's feelings firsthand.

Connecting Literary Elements

A first-person point of view lets you see firsthand how a character changes. A **dynamic character** is one who develops and grows during the course of a story. In contrast, a **static character** does not change. In "The Scarlet Ibis," Doodle's brother is a dynamic character whose emotions range among love, frustration, anger, and sadness over the course of the story.

Reading Strategy

Identifying With a Character

Authors who write from a first-person point of view invite you to walk through the story in the shoes of one of the characters. **Identify with the character** using these steps:

- Put yourself in his or her place.
- Consider how you would respond if you were in the same situation.

Use a chart like this one to record events from the story, the narrator's reaction to each event, and how *you* might have reacted.

Vocabulary Development

imminent (im´ ə nənt) *adj.* likely to happen soon (p. 558)

iridescent (ir´ ə des´ ənt) *adj.* having shifting, rainbowlike colors (p. 559)

vortex (vôr´ teks´) *n.* rushing whirl, drawing in all that surrounds it (p. 559)

infallibility (in fal´ ə bil´ ə tē) *n.* condition of being unable to fail (p. 559)

entrails (en´ trālz) *n.* internal organs, specifically intestines (p. 560)

precariously (prē ker´ ē əs lē) *adv.* insecurely (p. 561)

evanesced (ev´ ə nest´) *v.* faded away (p. 563)

The Scarlet Ibis

James Hurst

It was in the clove of seasons, summer was dead but autumn had not yet been born, that the ibis lit in the bleeding tree. The flower garden was stained with rotting brown magnolia petals and ironweeds grew rank amid the purple phlox. The five o'clocks by the chimney still marked time, but the oriole nest in the elm was untenanted and rocked back and forth like an empty cradle. The last graveyard flowers were blooming, and their smell drifted across the cotton field and through every room of our house, speaking softly the names of our dead.

It's strange that all this is still so clear to me, now that the summer has long since fled and time has had its way. A grindstone stands where the bleeding tree stood, just outside the kitchen door, and now if an oriole sings in the elm, its song seems to die up in the leaves, a silvery dust. The flower garden is prim, the house a gleaming white, and the pale fence across the yard stands straight and spruce. But sometimes (like right now), as I sit in the cool, green-draped parlor, the grindstone begins to turn, and time with all its changes is ground away—and I remember Doodle.

▲ **Critical Viewing**
The narrator uses a description of nature to introduce a story from the past. Why might a natural setting, like the one shown here, spark a memory? **[Hypothesize]**

Reading Strategy
Identifying With a Character What provokes the narrator to refer to time as being "ground away"?

Doodle was just about the craziest brother a boy ever had. Of course, he wasn't a crazy crazy like old Miss Leedie, who was in love with President Wilson and wrote him a letter every day, but was a nice crazy, like someone you meet in your dreams. He was born when I was six and was, from the outset, a disappointment. He seemed all head, with a tiny body which was red and shriveled like an old man's. Everybody thought he was going to die—everybody except Aunt Nicey, who had delivered him. She said he would live because he was born in a caul[1] and cauls were made from Jesus' nightgown. Daddy had Mr. Heath, the carpenter, build a little mahogany coffin for him. But he didn't die, and when he was three months old Mama and Daddy decided they might as well name him. They named him William Armstrong, which was like tying a big tail on a small kite. Such a name sounds good only on a tombstone.

I thought myself pretty smart at many things, like holding my breath, running, jumping, or climbing the vines in Old Woman Swamp, and I wanted more than anything else someone to race to Horsehead Landing, someone to box with, and someone to perch with in the top fork of the great pine behind the barn, where across the fields and swamps you could see the sea. I wanted a brother. But Mama, crying, told me that even if William Armstrong lived, he would never do these things with me. He might not, she sobbed, even be "all there." He might, as long as he lived, lie on the rubber sheet in the center of the bed in the front bedroom where the white marquisette curtains billowed out in the afternoon sea breeze, rustling like palmetto fronds.[2]

It was bad enough having an invalid brother, but having one who possibly was not all there was unbearable, so I began to make plans to kill him by smothering him with a pillow. However, one afternoon as I watched him, my head poked between the iron posts of the foot of the bed, he looked straight at me and grinned. I skipped through the rooms, down the echoing halls, shouting, "Mama, he smiled. He's all there! He's all there!" and he was.

When he was two, if you laid him on his stomach, he began to try to move himself, straining terribly. The doctor said that with his weak heart this strain would probably kill him, but it didn't. Trembling, he'd push himself up, turning first red, then a soft purple, and finally collapse back onto the bed like an old worn-out doll. I can still see Mama watching him, her hand pressed tight across her mouth, her eyes wide and unblinking. But he learned to crawl (it was his third winter), and we brought him out of the front bedroom, putting him on the rug before the fireplace. For the first time he became one of us.

As long as he lay all the time in bed, we called him William Armstrong, even though it was formal and sounded as if we were referring to one of our ancestors, but with his creeping around on the deerskin rug and beginning to talk, something had to be done about

---

1. **caul** (kôl) *n.* membrane enclosing a baby at birth.
2. **palmetto fronds** palm leaves.

Literary Analysis
Point of View Which details indicate the point of view from which this story is written?

✔**Reading Check**

How does William Armstrong respond when the narrator pokes his head through the posts of the bed to look at him?

his name. It was I who renamed him. When he crawled, he crawled backwards, as if he were in reverse and couldn't change gears. If you called him, he'd turn around as if he were going in the other direction, then he'd back right up to you to be picked up. Crawling backward made him look like a doodle-bug, so I began to call him Doodle, and in time even Mama and Daddy thought it was a better name than William Armstrong. Only Aunt Nicey disagreed. She said caul babies should be treated with special respect since they might turn out to be saints. Renaming my brother was perhaps the kindest thing I ever did for him, because nobody expects much from someone called Doodle.

Although Doodle learned to crawl, he showed no signs of walking, but he wasn't idle. He talked so much that we all quit listening to what he said. It was about this time that Daddy built him a go-cart and I had to pull him around. At first I just paraded him up and down the piazza, but then he started crying to be taken out into the yard and it ended up by my having to lug him wherever I went. If I so much as picked up my cap, he'd start crying to go with me and Mama would call from wherever she was, "Take Doodle with you."

He was a burden in many ways. The doctor had said that he mustn't get too excited, too hot, too cold, or too tired and that he must always be treated gently. A long list of don'ts went with him, all of which I ignored once we got out of the house. To discourage his coming with me, I'd run with him across the ends of the cotton rows and career him around corners on two wheels. Sometimes I accidentally turned him over, but he never told Mama. His skin was very sensitive, and he had to wear a big straw hat whenever he went out. When the going got rough and he had to cling to the sides of the go-cart, the hat slipped all the way down over his ears. He was a sight. Finally, I could see I was licked. Doodle was my brother and he was going to cling to me forever, no matter what I did, so I dragged him across the burning cotton field to share with him the only beauty I knew, Old Woman Swamp. I pulled the go-cart through the saw-tooth fern, down into the green dimness where the palmetto fronds whispered by the stream. I lifted him out and set him down in the soft rubber grass beside a tall pine. His eyes were round with wonder as he gazed about him, and his little hands began to stroke the rubber grass. Then he began to cry.

"For heaven's sake, what's the matter?" I asked, annoyed.

Two Boys in a Punt, N. C. Wyeth, Courtesy of Dr. and Mrs. William A. Morton, Jr.

▲ **Critical Viewing**
What can you tell about the brothers' relationship from this illustration and the details in the story? **[Infer]**

"It's so pretty," he said. "So pretty, pretty, pretty."

After that day Doodle and I often went down into Old Woman Swamp. I would gather wildflowers, wild violets, honeysuckle, yellow jasmine, snakeflowers, and water lilies, and with wire grass we'd weave them into necklaces and crowns. We'd bedeck ourselves with our handiwork and loll about thus beautified, beyond the touch of the everyday world. Then when the slanted rays of the sun burned orange in the tops of the pines, we'd drop our jewels into the stream and watch them float away toward the sea.

There is within me (and with sadness I have watched it in others) a knot of cruelty borne by the stream of love, much as our blood sometimes bears the seed of our destruction, and at times I was mean to Doodle. One day I took him up to the barn loft and showed him his casket, telling him how we all had believed he would die. It was covered with a film of Paris green[3] sprinkled to kill the rats, and screech owls had built a nest inside it.

Doodle studied the mahogany box for a long time, then said, "It's not mine."

"It is," I said. "And before I'll help you down from the loft, you're going to have to touch it."

"I won't touch it," he said sullenly.

"Then I'll leave you here by yourself," I threatened, and made as if I were going down.

Doodle was frightened of being left. "Don't go leave me, Brother," he cried, and he leaned toward the coffin. His hand, trembling, reached out, and when he touched the casket he screamed. A screech owl flapped out of the box into our faces, scaring us and covering us with Paris green. Doodle was paralyzed, so I put him on my shoulder and carried him down the ladder, and even when we were outside in the bright sunshine, he clung to me, crying, "Don't leave me. Don't leave me."

When Doodle was five years old, I was embarrassed at having a brother of that age who couldn't walk, so I set out to teach him. We were down in Old Woman Swamp and it was spring and the sick-sweet smell of bay flowers hung everywhere like a mournful song. "I'm going to teach you to walk, Doodle," I said.

He was sitting comfortably on the soft grass, leaning back against the pine. "Why?" he asked.

I hadn't expected such an answer. "So I won't have to haul you around all the time."

"I can't walk, Brother," he said.

---

3. **Paris green** poisonous green powder.

Literary Analysis
Point of View How would this part of the story be different if a third-person narrator told it?

Reading Check
What does the narrator force Doodle to touch?

"Who says so?" I demanded.

"Mama, the doctor—everybody."

"Oh, you can walk," I said, and I took him by the arms and stood him up. He collapsed onto the grass like a half-empty flour sack. It was as if he had no bones in his little legs.

"Don't hurt me, Brother," he warned.

"Shut up. I'm not going to hurt you. I'm going to teach you to walk." I heaved him up again, and again he collapsed.

This time he did not lift his face up out of the rubber grass. "I just can't do it. Let's make honeysuckle wreaths."

"Oh yes you can, Doodle," I said. "All you got to do is try. Now come on," and I hauled him up once more.

It seemed so hopeless from the beginning that it's a miracle I didn't give up. But all of us must have something or someone to be proud of, and Doodle had become mine. I did not know then that pride is a wonderful, terrible thing, a seed that bears two vines, life and death. Every day that summer we went to the pine beside the stream of Old Woman Swamp, and I put him on his feet at least a hundred times each afternoon. Occasionally I too became discouraged because it didn't seem as if he was trying, and I would say, "Doodle, don't you *want* to learn to walk?"

He'd nod his head, and I'd say, "Well, if you don't keep trying, you'll never learn." Then I'd paint for him a picture of us as old men, white-haired, him with a long white beard and me still pulling him around in the go-cart. This never failed to make him try again.

Finally one day, after many weeks of practicing, he stood alone for a few seconds. When he fell, I grabbed him in my arms and hugged him, our laughter pealing through the swamp like a ringing bell. Now we knew it could be done. Hope no longer hid in the dark palmetto thicket but perched like a cardinal in the lacy toothbrush tree, brilliantly visible. "Yes, yes," I cried, and he cried it too, and the grass beneath us was soft and the smell of the swamp was sweet.

With success so <u>imminent</u>, we decided not to tell anyone until he could actually walk. Each day, barring rain, we sneaked into Old Woman Swamp, and by cotton-picking time Doodle was ready to show what he could do. He still wasn't able to walk far, but we could wait no longer. Keeping a nice secret is very hard to do, like holding your breath. We chose to reveal all on October eighth, Doodle's sixth birthday, and for weeks ahead we mooned around the house, promising everybody a most spectacular surprise. Aunt Nicey said that, after so much talk, if we produced anything less tremendous than the Resurrection,[4] she was going to be disappointed.

At breakfast on our chosen day, when Mama, Daddy, and Aunt Nicey were in the dining room, I brought Doodle to the door in the go-cart just as usual and had them turn their backs, making them cross

Reading Strategy
Identifying With a Character How would you feel if you were in Doodle's situation? Why?

imminent (im′ ə nənt) *adj.* likely to happen soon

---

4. the Resurrection (rez′ ə rek′ shən) the rising of Jesus Christ from the dead after his death and burial.

their hearts and hope to die if they peeked. I helped Doodle up, and when he was standing alone I let them look. There wasn't a sound as Doodle walked slowly across the room and sat down at his place at the table. Then Mama began to cry and ran over to him, hugging him and kissing him. Daddy hugged him too, so I went to Aunt Nicey, who was thanks praying in the doorway, and began to waltz her around. We danced together quite well until she came down on my big toe with her brogans, hurting me so badly I thought I was crippled for life.

Doodle told them it was I who had taught him to walk, so everyone wanted to hug me, and I began to cry.

"What are you crying for?" asked Daddy, but I couldn't answer. They did not know that I did it for myself; that pride, whose slave I was, spoke to me louder than all their voices, and that Doodle walked only because I was ashamed of having a crippled brother.

Within a few months Doodle had learned to walk well and his go-cart was put up in the barn loft (it's still there) beside his little mahogany coffin. Now, when we roamed off together, resting often, we never turned back until our destination had been reached, and to help pass the time, we took up lying. From the beginning Doodle was a terrible liar and he got me in the habit. Had anyone stopped to listen to us, we would have been sent off to Dix Hill.

My lies were scary, involved, and usually pointless, but Doodle's were twice as crazy. People in his stories all had wings and flew wherever they wanted to go. His favorite lie was about a boy named Peter who had a pet peacock with a ten-foot tail. Peter wore a golden robe that glittered so brightly that when he walked through the sunflowers they turned away from the sun to face him. When Peter was ready to go to sleep, the peacock spread his magnificent tail, enfolding the boy gently like a closing go-to-sleep flower, burying him in the gloriously <u>iridescent</u>, rustling <u>vortex</u>. Yes, I must admit it. Doodle could beat me lying.

Doodle and I spent lots of time thinking about our future. We decided that when we were grown we'd live in Old Woman Swamp and pick dog-tongue for a living. Beside the stream, he planned, we'd build us a house of whispering leaves and the swamp birds would be our chickens. All day long (when we weren't gathering dog-tongue) we'd swing through the cypresses on the rope vines, and if it rained we'd huddle beneath an umbrella tree and play stickfrog. Mama and Daddy could come and live with us if they wanted to. He even came up with the idea that he could marry Mama and I could marry Daddy. Of course, I was old enough to know this wouldn't work out, but the picture he painted was so beautiful and serene that all I could do was whisper Yes, yes.

Once I had succeeded in teaching Doodle to walk, I began to believe in my own <u>infallibility</u> and I prepared a terrific development program for him, unknown to Mama and Daddy, of course. I would teach him to run, to swim, to climb trees, and to fight. He, too, now

Literary Analysis
Point of View What effect does the narrator's admission of his motive have on your perception of his development?

iridescent (ir´ ə des´ ənt) *adj.* having shifting, rainbowlike colors

vortex (vôr´ teks´) *n.* rushing whirl, drawing in all that surrounds it

infallibility (in fal´ ə bil´ ə tē) *n.* condition of being unable to fail

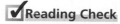**Reading Check**

What surprise do the narrator and Doodle present to their parents?

believed in my infallibility, so we set the deadline for these accomplishments less than a year away, when, it had been decided, Doodle could start to school.

That winter we didn't make much progress, for I was in school and Doodle suffered from one bad cold after another. But when spring came, rich and warm, we raised our sights again. Success lay at the end of summer like a pot of gold, and our campaign got off to a good start. On hot days, Doodle and I went down to Horsehead Landing and I gave him swimming lessons or showed him how to row a boat. Sometimes we descended into the cool greenness of Old Woman Swamp and climbed the rope vines or boxed scientifically beneath the pine where he had learned to walk. Promise hung about us like the leaves, and wherever we looked, ferns unfurled and birds broke into song.

That summer, the summer of 1918, was blighted. In May and June there was no rain and the crops withered, curled up, then died under the thirsty sun. One morning in July a hurricane came out of the east, tipping over the oaks in the yard and splitting the limbs of the elm trees. That afternoon it roared back out of the west, blew the fallen oaks around, snapping their roots and tearing them out of the earth like a hawk at the <u>entrails</u> of a chicken. Cotton bolls were wrenched from the stalks and lay like green walnuts in the valleys between the rows, while the cornfield leaned over uniformly so that the tassels touched the ground. Doodle and I followed Daddy out into the cotton field, where he stood, shoulders sagging, surveying the ruin. When his chin sank down onto his chest, we were frightened, and Doodle slipped his hand into mine. Suddenly Daddy straightened his shoulders, raised a giant knuckly fist, and with a voice that seemed to rumble out of the earth itself began cursing heaven, hell, the weather, and the Republican Party. Doodle and I, prodding each other and giggling, went back to the house, knowing that everything would be all right.

And during that summer, strange names were heard through the house: Chateau Thierry, Amiens, Soissons, and in her blessing at the supper table, Mama once said, "And bless the Pearsons, whose boy Joe was lost at Belleau Wood."[5]

So we came to that clove of seasons. School was only a few weeks away, and Doodle was far behind schedule. He could barely clear the ground when climbing up the rope vines and his swimming was certainly not passable. We decided to double our efforts, to make that last drive and reach our pot of gold. I made him swim until he turned blue and row until he couldn't lift an oar. Wherever we went, I purposely walked fast, and although he kept up, his face turned red and his eyes became glazed. Once, he could go no further, so he collapsed on the ground and began to cry.

entrails (en´ trālz) *n.* internal organs, specifically intestines

Literary Analysis
Point of View Based on this passage, what do you learn about the narrator and his wishes for his brother?

---

5. **Château Thierry** (shä´ tō´ tē er´ ē), **Amiens** (à myan´), **Soissons** (swä sôn´), . . . **Belleau** (be lō´) **Wood** places in France where battles were fought during World War I.

"Aw, come on, Doodle," I urged. "You can do it. Do you want to be different from everybody else when you start school?"

"Does it make any difference?"

"It certainly does," I said. "Now, come on," and I helped him up.

As we slipped through dog days, Doodle began to look feverish, and Mama felt his forehead, asking him if he felt ill. At night he didn't sleep well, and sometimes he had nightmares, crying out until I touched him and said, "Wake up, Doodle. Wake up."

It was Saturday noon, just a few days before school was to start. I should have already admitted defeat, but my pride wouldn't let me. The excitement of our program had now been gone for weeks, but still we kept on with a tired doggedness. It was too late to turn back, for we had both wandered too far into a net of expectations and had left no crumbs behind.

Daddy, Mama, Doodle, and I were seated at the dining-room table having lunch. It was a hot day, with all the windows and doors open in case a breeze should come. In the kitchen Aunt Nicey was humming softly. After a long silence, Daddy spoke. "It's so calm, I wouldn't be surprised if we had a storm this afternoon."

"I haven't heard a rain frog," said Mama, who believed in signs, as she served the bread around the table.

"I did," declared Doodle. "Down in the swamp."

"He didn't," I said contrarily.

"You did, eh?" said Daddy, ignoring my denial.

"I certainly did," Doodle reiterated, scowling at me over the top of his iced-tea glass, and we were quiet again.

Suddenly, from out in the yard, came a strange croaking noise. Doodle stopped eating, with a piece of bread poised ready for his mouth, his eyes popped round like two blue buttons. "What's that?" he whispered.

I jumped up, knocking over my chair, and had reached the door when Mama called, "Pick up the chair, sit down again, and say excuse me."

By the time I had done this, Doodle had excused himself and had slipped out into the yard. He was looking up into the bleeding tree. "It's a great big red bird!" he called.

The bird croaked loudly again, and Mama and Daddy came out into the yard. We shaded our eyes with our hands against the hazy glare of the sun and peered up through the still leaves. On the topmost branch a bird the size of a chicken, with scarlet feathers and long legs, was perched <u>precariously</u>. Its wings hung down loosely, and as we watched, a feather dropped away and floated slowly down through the green leaves.

"It's not even frightened of us," Mama said.

"It looks tired," Daddy added. "Or maybe sick."

Doodle's hands were clasped at his throat, and I had never seen him stand still so long. "What is it?" he asked.

Daddy shook his head. "I don't know, maybe it's—"

Reading Strategy
Identifying With a Character How do you think Doodle feels when his brother asks him if he wants to be different from everybody else?

precariously (prē ker´ ē əs lē) adv. insecurely

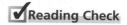Reading Check

What does Doodle find in the yard?

At that moment the bird began to flutter, but the wings were uncoordinated, and amid much flapping and a spray of flying feathers, it tumbled down, bumping through the limbs of the bleeding tree and landing at our feet with a thud. Its long, graceful neck jerked twice into an S, then straightened out, and the bird was still. A white veil came over the eyes and the long white beak unhinged. Its legs were crossed and its clawlike feet were delicately curved at rest. Even death did not mar its grace, for it lay on the earth like a broken vase of red flowers, and we stood around it, awed by its exotic beauty.

"It's dead," Mama said.

"What is it?" Doodle repeated.

"Go bring me the bird book," said Daddy.

I ran into the house and brought back the bird book. As we watched, Daddy thumbed through its pages. "It's a scarlet ibis," he said, pointing to a picture. "It lives in the tropics—South America to Florida. A storm must have brought it here."

Sadly, we all looked back at the bird. A scarlet ibis! How many miles it had traveled to die like this, in our yard, beneath the bleeding tree.

"Let's finish lunch," Mama said, nudging us back toward the dining room.

"I'm not hungry," said Doodle, and he knelt down beside the ibis.

"We've got peach cobbler for dessert," Mama tempted from the doorway.

Doodle remained kneeling. "I'm going to bury him."

"Don't you dare touch him," Mama warned. "There's no telling what disease he might have had."

"All right," said Doodle. "I won't."

Daddy, Mama, and I went back to the dining-room table, but we watched Doodle through the open door. He took out a piece of string from his pocket and, without touching the ibis, looped one end around its neck. Slowly, while singing softly "Shall We Gather at the River," he carried the bird around to the front yard and dug a hole in the flower garden, next to the petunia bed. Now we were watching him through the front window, but he didn't know it. His awkwardness at digging the hole with a shovel whose handle was twice as long as he was made us laugh, and we covered our mouths with our hands so he wouldn't hear.

When Doodle came into the dining room, he found us seriously eating our cobbler. He was pale and lingered just inside the screen door. "Did you get the scarlet ibis buried?" asked Daddy.

Doodle didn't speak but nodded his head.

"Go wash your hands, and then you can have some peach cobbler," said Mama.

"I'm not hungry," he said.

"Dead birds is bad luck," said Aunt Nicey, poking her head from the kitchen door. "Specially *red* dead birds!"

As soon as I had finished eating, Doodle and I hurried off to

▶ **Critical Viewing** How would you react if this exotic bird showed up in your back yard? **[Relate]**

Reading Strategy
Identifying With a Character With whose response toward the ibis do you identify most strongly? Why?

Scarlet Ibis, John James Audubon, New-York Historical Society

Horsehead Landing. Time was short, and Doodle still had a long way to go if he was going to keep up with the other boys when he started school. The sun, gilded with the yellow cast of autumn, still burned fiercely, but the dark green woods through which we passed were shady and cool. When we reached the landing, Doodle said he was too tired to swim, so we got into a skiff and floated down the creek with the tide. Far off in the marsh a rail was scolding, and over on the beach locusts were singing in the myrtle trees. Doodle did not speak and kept his head turned away, letting one hand trail limply in the water.

After we had drifted a long way, I put the oars in place and made Doodle row back against the tide. Black clouds began to gather in the southwest, and he kept watching them, trying to pull the oars a little faster. When we reached Horsehead Landing, lightning was playing across half the sky and thunder roared out, hiding even the sound of the sea. The sun disappeared and darkness descended, almost like night. Flocks of marsh crows flew by, heading inland to their roosting trees, and two egrets, squawking, arose from the oyster-rock shallows and careened away.

Doodle was both tired and frightened, and when he stepped from the skiff he collapsed onto the mud, sending an armada of fiddler crabs rustling off into the marsh grass. I helped him up, and as he wiped the mud off his trousers, he smiled at me ashamedly. He had failed and we both knew it, so we started back home, racing the storm. We never spoke (What are the words that can solder cracked pride?), but I knew he was watching me, watching for a sign of mercy. The lightning was near now, and from fear he walked so close behind me he kept stepping on my heels. The faster I walked, the faster he walked, so I began to run. The rain was coming, roaring through the pines, and then, like a bursting Roman candle, a gum tree ahead of us was shattered by a bolt of lightning. When the deafening peal of thunder had died, and in the moment before the rain arrived, I heard Doodle, who had fallen behind, cry out, "Brother, Brother, don't leave me! Don't leave me!"

The knowledge that Doodle's and my plans had come to naught was bitter, and that streak of cruelty within me awakened. I ran as fast as I could, leaving him far behind with a wall of rain dividing us. The drops stung my face like nettles, and the wind flared the wet glistening leaves of the bordering trees. Soon I could hear his voice no more.

I hadn't run too far before I became tired, and the flood of childish spite <u>evanesced</u> as well. I stopped and waited for Doodle. The sound of rain was everywhere, but the wind had died and it fell straight down in parallel paths like ropes

Literary Analysis
Point of View What might you learn about Doodle's silence here if the story were told from his point of view?

Reading Strategy
Identifying With a Character How do you think the narrator feels about his brother's failure?

evanesced (ev´ ə nest´) v. faded away

✔**Reading Check**
What does Doodle do with the dead ibis?

hanging from the sky. As I waited, I peered through the downpour, but no one came. Finally I went back and found him huddled beneath a red nightshade bush beside the road. He was sitting on the ground, his face buried in his arms, which were resting on his drawn-up knees. "Let's go, Doodle," I said.

He didn't answer, so I placed my hand on his forehead and lifted his head. Limply, he fell backwards onto the earth. He had been bleeding from the mouth, and his neck and the front of his shirt were stained a brilliant red.

"Doodle! Doodle!" I cried, shaking him, but there was no answer but the ropy rain. He lay very awkwardly, with his head thrown far back, making his vermilion neck appear unusually long and slim. His little legs, bent sharply at the knees, had never before seemed so fragile, so thin.

I began to weep, and the tear-blurred vision in red before me looked very familiar. "Doodle!" I screamed above the pounding storm and threw my body to the earth above his. For a long long time, it seemed forever, I lay there crying, sheltering my fallen scarlet ibis from the heresy[6] of rain.

---

6. **heresy** (her´ i sē) idea opposed to the beliefs of a religion or philosophy.

Review and Assess

Thinking About the Selection

1. **Respond:** Do you blame the narrator for Doodle's death? Why or why not?

2. **(a) Recall:** How does Doodle react to Old Woman Swamp? **(b) Analyze:** What does Doodle's reaction suggest about his character?

3. **(a) Recall:** What do the brothers reveal on Doodle's sixth birthday? **(b) Deduce:** Do you think the family guessed the reason for the narrator's tears? Explain.

4. **(a) Recall:** What does the narrator want to teach Doodle to do next? **(b) Interpret:** Why do you think he sets such demanding goals for Doodle?

5. **(a) Recall:** What happens after the appearance of the scarlet ibis? **(b) Infer:** What do you think motivates Doodle to treat the ibis as he does?

6. **Compare:** How is Doodle like the scarlet ibis?

7. **Extend:** Do you think it is normal to have mixed feelings about a brother or sister? Why or why not?

James Hurst

(b. 1922)

James Hurst grew up in coastal North Carolina, a place of quiet landscapes and violent storms. Before becoming a writer, he studied both chemical engineering and opera, served in the army during World War II, and eventually took a job in a New York bank. Hurst's career at the bank lasted for thirty-four years.

While at the bank, Hurst spent his evenings writing short stories. "The Scarlet Ibis," his most popular story, was published in 1960. One of the qualities that makes it such a powerful story is Hurst's use of symbols—objects, people, or ideas that have an underlying meaning. Hurst wrote, "I wanted [the ibis] to represent [the character of Doodle]—not Doodle's physical self, but his spirit."

Review and Assess

Literary Analysis

Point of View

1. Does Hurst's use of the **first-person point of view** make you feel more involved in the story? Why or why not?
2. What is the effect of having the narrator look back at the events years after they occurred?
3. If it were told from another point of view, the story would be very different. In a chart like the one shown, record how various events might be seen from Daddy's and Mama's perspective.

Connecting Literary Elements

4. Is Doodle a **dynamic** or a **static character**? Using a chart like this one, cite story details that will help you answer the question.

5. Are the mother and father in the story **dynamic characters?** Explain.
6. (a) Do you think a first-person narrator must always be a dynamic character? (b) Would "The Scarlet Ibis" be an effective story if the narrator never changed? Why or why not?

Reading Strategy

Identifying With a Character

7. **Identify** with the narrator by describing how you might have treated Doodle if he had been your little brother.
8. What can you learn from the narrator's experiences that you can apply to your relationships?

Extend Understanding

9. **Cultural Connection:** The story refers briefly to World War I, then raging in Europe. What connections can be made between the horrors of war and the pain of ordinary life? Explain.

Prepare to Read

Blues Ain't No Mockin Bird ◆ Uncle Marcos

Take It to the Net

Visit www.phschool.com
for interactive activities
and instruction related to
the selections, including
- background
- graphic organizers
- literary elements
- reading strategies

Preview

Connecting to the Literature

Certain people you meet in childhood may become etched in memory forever because of their unique personality traits or the lessons they teach you. In these stories, you will meet two memorable characters who leave an indelible impression on the stories' narrators.

Background

Imagine a world in which people can float in the air and it can rain continuously for years. These fantastic details capture the way a group of writers, including Isabel Allende, use words. The authors practice a style of writing known as "magical realism," in which fantastic details blend with realistic ones to stretch the boundaries of readers' imaginations.

Literary Analysis

Characterization

Characterization refers to the way a writer reveals a character's personality traits. With **direct characterization,** writers directly state a character's personality traits. In **indirect characterization,** a writer uses a character's actions, thoughts, and feelings to suggest a character's traits. In this passage from "Uncle Marcos," the writer characterizes Marcos indirectly:

> He spent the whole night making incomprehensible movements in the drawing room; later they turned out to be exercises . . .

Notice how the authors of these selections let their characters' words and actions, along with the reactions of others, reveal what they are like.

Comparing Literary Works

A character's personality traits are often revealed through the **narrator**—the person from whose perspective a story is told.

- A **third-person narrator** is not a character in the story.
- A **first-person narrator** is a character within the story.

The narrator in "Blues Ain't No Mockin Bird" is part of the story, while the narrator of "Uncle Marcos" stands outside the story. Compare the author's choice of narrator in each selection.

Reading Strategy

Making Inferences About Characters

When you **make an inference about a character,** you draw a conclusion using details the author provides. For example, in "Uncle Marcos," you will learn that Marcos once serenaded a woman. From this, you can infer that he is romantic and unpredictable.

To make inferences, look beyond the words on the page, and ask yourself what the author implies about the characters. On a chart like this one, list details from the selections and the inferences you make from them.

Vocabulary Development

lassoed (las′ ōd′) *adj.* wrapped around (p. 570)

formality (fôr mal′ ə tē) *n.* established rules or customs (p. 574)

pallid (pal′ id) *adj.* pale (p. 577)

vanquished (vaŋ′ kwisht) *adj.* defeated (p. 577)

fetid (fet′ id) *adj.* smelly (p. 577)

impassive (im pas′ iv) *adj.* showing no emotion (p. 578)

disconsolately (dis kän′ sə lit lē) *adv.* unhappily (p. 581)

unrequited (un ri kwīt′ id) *adj.* not reciprocated (p. 583)

BLUES AIN'T NO MOCKIN BIRD

Toni Cade Bambara

The puddle had frozen over, and me and Cathy went stompin in it. The twins from next door, Tyrone and Terry, were swingin so high out of sight we forgot we were waitin our turn on the tire. Cathy jumped up and came down hard on her heels and started tap-dancin. And the frozen patch splinterin every which way underneath kinda spooky. "Looks like a plastic spider web," she said. "A sort of weird spider, I guess, with many mental problems." But really it looked like the crystal paperweight Granny kept in the parlor. She was on the back porch, Granny was, making the cakes drunk. The old ladle drip-ping rum into the Christmas tins, like it used to drip maple syrup into the pails when we lived in the Judson's woods, like it poured cider into the vats when we were on the Cooper place, like it used to scoop butter-milk and soft cheese when we lived at the dairy.

"Go tell that man we ain't a bunch of trees."

"Ma'am?"

"I said to tell that man to get away from here with that camera." Me and Cathy look over toward the meadow where the men with the station wagon'd been roamin around all mornin. The tall man with a huge cam-era <u>lassoed</u> to his shoulder was buzzin our way.

"They're makin movie pictures," yelled Tyrone, stiffenin his legs and twistin so the tire'd come down slow so they could see.

"They're makin movie pictures," sang out Terry.

"That boy don't never have anything original to say," say Cathy grown-up.

lassoed (las´ ōd´) *adj.* wrapped around

Sharecropper, Elizabeth Catlett, Courtesy Evan Tibbs Collection

▲ **Critical Viewing** As you read, compare Granny with the woman in the illustration. **[Compare and Contrast]**

By the time the man with the camera had cut across our neighbor's yard, the twins were out of the trees swingin low and Granny was onto the steps, the screen door bammin soft and scratchy against her palms. "We thought we'd get a shot or two of the house and everything and then—"

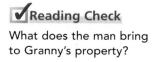

Reading Check

What does the man bring to Granny's property?

Blues Ain't No Mockin Bird ◆ 571

"Good mornin," Granny cut him off. And smiled that smile.

"Good mornin," he said, head all down the way Bingo does when you yell at him about the bones on the kitchen floor. "Nice place you got here, aunty. We thought we'd take a—"

"Did you?" said Granny with her eyebrows. Cathy pulled up her socks and giggled.

"Nice things here," said the man, buzzin his camera over the yard. The pecan barrels, the sled, me and Cathy, the flowers, the printed stones along the driveway, the trees, the twins, the toolshed.

"I don't know about the thing, the it, and the stuff," said Granny, still talkin with her eyebrows. "Just people here is what I tend to consider."

Camera man stopped buzzin. Cathy giggled into her collar.

"Mornin, ladies," a new man said. He had come up behind us when we weren't lookin. "And gents," discoverin the twins givin him a nasty look. "We're filmin for the county," he said with a smile. "Mind if we shoot a bit around here?"

"I do indeed," said Granny with no smile. Smilin man was smiling up a storm. So was Cathy. But he didn't seem to have another word to say, so he and the camera man backed on out the yard, but you could hear the camera buzzin still. "Suppose you just shut that machine off," said Granny real low through her teeth, and took a step down off the porch and then another.

"Now, aunty," Camera said, pointin the thing straight at her.

"Your mama and I are not related."

Smilin man got his notebook out and a chewed-up pencil. "Listen," he said movin back into our yard, "we'd like to have a statement from you . . . for the film. We're filmin for the county, see. Part of the food stamp campaign. You know about the food stamps?"

Granny said nuthin.

"Maybe there's somethin you want to say for the film. I see you grow your own vegetables," he smiled real nice. "If more folks did that, see, there'd be no need—"

Granny wasn't sayin nuthin. So they backed on out, buzzin at our clothesline and the twins' bicycles, then back on down to the meadow. The twins were danglin in the tire, lookin at Granny. Me and Cathy were waitin, too, cause Granny always got somethin to say. She teaches steady with no let-up. "I was on this bridge one time," she started off. "Was a crowd cause this man was goin to jump, you understand. And a minister was there and the police and some other folks. His woman was there, too."

"What was they doin?" asked Tyrone.

"Tryin to talk him out of it was what they was doin. The minister talkin about how it was a mortal sin, suicide. His woman takin bites out of her own hand and not even knowin it, so nervous and cryin and talkin fast."

Literature in context Cultural Connection

Dialect

"Blues Ain't No Mockin Bird" is written in dialect—a way of speaking that is common to people in a particular region or group. Dialect affects pronunciation, word choice, and sentence structure. You will notice, for example, that the characters in Bambara's story do not pronounce the g on the ends of -ing words—a common speech pattern in the American South. Bambara's use of dialect makes her story sound informal and intimate, as if it were being related orally.

Literary Analysis
Characterization and Narrator Who is the narrator? How do you know?

"So what happened?" asked Tyrone.

"So here comes . . . this person . . . with a camera, takin pictures of the man and the minister and the woman. Takin pictures of the man in his misery about to jump, cause life so bad and people been messin with him so bad. This person takin up the whole roll of film practically. But savin a few, of course."

"Of course," said Cathy, hatin the person. Me standin there wonderin how Cathy knew it was "of course" when I didn't and it was *my* grandmother.

After a while Tyrone say, "Did he jump?"

"Yeh, did he jump?" say Terry all eager. And Granny just stared at the twins till their faces swallow up the eager and they don't even care any more about the man jumpin. Then she goes back onto the porch and lets the screen door go for itself. I'm lookin to Cathy to finish the story cause she knows Granny's whole story before me even. Like she knew how come we move so much and Cathy ain't but a third cousin we picked up on the way last Thanksgivin visitin. But she knew it was on account of people drivin Granny crazy till she'd get up in the night and start packin. Mumblin and packin and wakin everybody up sayin, "Let's get on away from here before I kill me somebody." Like people wouldn't pay her for things like they said they would. Or Mr. Judson bringin us boxes of old clothes and raggedy magazines. Or Mrs. Cooper comin in our kitchen and touchin everything and sayin how clean it all was. Granny goin crazy, and Granddaddy Cain pullin her off the people, sayin, "Now, now, Cora." But next day loadin up the truck, with rocks all in his jaw, madder than Granny in the first place.

"I read a story once," said Cathy soundin like Granny teacher. "About this lady Goldilocks who barged into a house that wasn't even hers. And not invited, you understand. Messed over the people's groceries and broke up the people's furniture. Had the nerve to sleep in the folks' bed."

"Then what happened?" asked Tyrone. "What they do, the folks, when they come in to all this mess?"

"Did they make her pay for it?" asked Terry, makin a fist. "I'd've made her pay me."

I didn't even ask. I could see Cathy actress was very likely to just walk away and leave us in mystery about this story which I heard was about some bears.

"Did they throw her out?" asked Tyrone, like his father sounds when he's bein extra nasty-plus to the washin-machine man.

"Woulda," said Terry. "I woulda gone upside her head with my fist and—"

"You woulda done whatcha always do—go cry to Mama, you big baby," said Tyrone. So naturally Terry starts hittin on Tyrone, and next thing you know they tumblin out the tire and rollin on the ground. But Granny didn't say a thing or send the twins home or step out on the steps to tell us about how we can't afford to be fightin amongst ourselves. She didn't say nuthin. So I get into the tire to take my turn. And I could see her leanin up against the pantry table, staring at the cakes

Reading Strategy
Making Inferences About Characters What can you infer about the attitudes of the children toward Granny?

Reading Check

How does Granny respond when the camera crew ask her to make a statement?

she was puttin up for the Christmas sale, mumblin real low and grumpy and holdin her forehead like it wanted to fall off and mess up the rum cakes.

Behind me I hear before I can see Granddaddy Cain comin through the woods in his field boots. Then I twist around to see the shiny black oilskin cuttin through what little left there was of yellows, reds, and oranges. His great white head not quite round cause of this bloody thing high on his shoulder, like he was wearin a cap on sideways. He takes the shortcut through the pecan grove, and the sound of twigs snapping overhead and under-foot travels clear and cold all the way up to us. And here comes Smilin and Camera up behind him like they was goin to do somethin. Folks like to go for him sometimes. Cathy say it's because he's so tall and quiet and like a king. And people just can't stand it. But Smilin and Camera don't hit him in the head or nuthin. They just buzz on him as he stalks by with the chicken hawk slung over his shoulder, squawkin, drippin red down the back of the oil-skin. He passes the porch and stops a second for Granny to see he's caught the hawk at last, but she's just starin and mumblin, and not at the hawk. So he nails the bird to the toolshed door, the hammerin crackin through the eardrums. And the bird flappin himself to death and droolin down the door to paint the gravel in the driveway red, then brown, then black. And the two men movin up on tiptoe like they was invisible or we were blind, one.

"Get them persons out of my flower bed, Mister Cain," say Granny moanin real low like at a funeral.

"How come your grandmother calls her husband 'Mister Cain' all the time?" Tyrone whispers all loud and noisy and from the city and don't know no better. Like his mama, Miss Myrtle, tell us never mind the <u>formality</u> as if we had no better breeding than to call her Myrtle, plain. And then this awful thing—a giant hawk—come wailin up over the meadow, flyin low and tilted and screamin, zigzaggin through the pecan grove, breakin branches and hollerin, snappin past the clothes-line, flyin every which way, flyin into things reckless with crazy.

"He's come to claim his mate," say Cathy fast, and ducks down. We all fall quick and flat into the gravel driveway, stones scrapin my face. I squinch my eyes open again at the hawk on the door, tryin to fly up out of her death like it was just a sack flown into by mistake. Her body holdin her there on that nail, though. The mate beatin the air overhead and clutchin for hair, for heads, for landin space.

The camera man duckin and bendin and runnin and fallin, jigglin the

Reading Strategy
Making Inferences About Characters What inferences can you make about the camera crew from their reaction to Granddaddy Cain?

formality (fôr maľ ə tē) n. established rules or customs

camera and scared. And Smilin jumpin up and down swipin at the huge bird, tryin to bring the hawk down with just his raggedy ole cap. Granddaddy Cain straight up and silent, watchin the circles of the hawk, then aimin the hammer off his wrist. The giant bird fallin, silent and slow. Then here comes Camera and Smilin all big and bad now that the awful screechin thing is on its back and broken, here they come. And Granddaddy Cain looks up at them like it was the first time noticin, but not payin them too much mind cause he's listenin, we all listenin, to that low groanin music comin from the porch. And we figure any minute, somethin in my back tells me any minute now, Granny gonna bust through that screen with somethin in her hand and murder on her mind. So Granddaddy say above the buzzin, but quiet, "Good day, gentlemen." Just like that. Like he'd invited them in to play cards and they'd stayed too long and all the sandwiches were gone and Reverend Webb was droppin by and it was time to go.

They didn't know what to do. But like Cathy say, folks can't stand Granddaddy tall and silent and like a king. They can't neither. The smile the men smilin is pullin the mouth back and showin the teeth. Lookin like the wolf man, both of them. Then Granddaddy holds his hand out— this huge hand I used to sit in when I was a baby and he'd carry me through the house to my mother like I was a gift on a tray. Like he used to on the trains. They called the other men just waiters. But they spoke of Granddaddy separate and said, The Waiter. And said he had engines in his feet and motors in his hands and couldn't no train throw him off and couldn't nobody turn him round. They were big enough for motors, his hands were. He held that one hand out all still and it gettin to be not at all a hand but a person in itself.

"He wants you to hand him the camera," Smilin whispers to Camera, tiltin his head to talk secret like they was in the jungle or somethin and come upon a native that don't speak the language. The men start untyin the straps, and they put the camera into that great hand speckled with the hawk's blood all black and crackly now. And the hand don't even drop with the weight, just the fingers move, curl up around the machine. But Granddaddy lookin straight at the men. They lookin at each other and everywhere but at Granddaddy's face.

"We filmin for the county, see," say Smilin. "We puttin together a movie for the food stamp program . . . filmin all around these parts. Uhh, filmin for the county."

"Can I have my camera back?" say the tall man with no machine on his shoulder, but still keepin it high like the camera was still there or needed to be. "Please, sir."

Then Granddaddy's other hand flies up like a sudden and gentle bird, slaps down fast on top of the camera and lifts off half like it was a calabash[1] cut for sharing.

"Hey," Camera jumps forward. He gathers up the parts into his chest and everything unrollin and fallin all over. "Whatcha tryin to do? You'll

---

1. calabash (kal´ ə bash) *n.* large gourdlike fruit.

Literary Analysis
Characterization and Narrator How do the narrator's memories of Granddaddy influence your reaction to him?

Reading Check
What does Granddaddy do to let the camera crew know he wants their camera?

ruin the film." He looks down into his chest of metal reels and things like he's protectin a kitten from the cold.

"You standin in the misses' flower bed," say Granddaddy. "This is our own place."

The two men look at him, then at each other, then back at the mess in the camera man's chest, and they just back off. One sayin over and over all the way down to the meadow, "Watch it, Bruno. Keep ya fingers off the film." Then Granddaddy picks up the hammer and jams it into the oilskin pocket, scrapes his boots, and goes into the house. And you can hear the squish of his boots headin through the house. And you can see the funny shadow he throws from the parlor window onto the ground by the string-bean patch. The hammer draggin the pocket of the oilskin out so Granddaddy looked even wider. Granny was hummin now—high not low and grumbly. And she was doin the cakes again, you could smell the molasses from the rum.

"There's this story I'm goin to write one day," say Cathy dreamer. "About the proper use of the hammer."

"Can I be in it?" Tyrone say with his hand up like it was a matter of first come, first served.

"Perhaps," say Cathy, climbin onto the tire to pump us up. "If you there and ready."

Review and Assess

Thinking About the Selection

1. **Respond:** Which character from the story would you most like to meet? Why?

2. **(a) Recall:** How does Granny react when she notices the man with the camera? **(b) Analyze:** What does she mean when she says "we ain't a bunch of trees"?

3. **(a) Recall:** Why are the photographers filming in the area? **(b) Generalize:** What kind of message is Granny giving the men through her speech and actions?

4. **(a) Generalize:** What is the main point of Granny's story about the man who attempted suicide? **(b) Draw Conclusions:** How does the story help explain Granny's behavior?

5. **(a) Recall:** How is Granddaddy described when he first appears on the scene? **(b) Connect:** What does Granny ask Granddaddy to do when he appears? **(c) Infer:** What does the description of his actions suggest about his character?

6. **Evaluate:** Is Granddaddy's treatment of the photographers justified? Support your view with details from the story.

Toni Cade Bambara

(1939–1995)

Toni Cade Bambara's interest in her African American heritage comes through clearly in her writing. Her cultural identity is evident even in her name, Bambara—the name of an African tribe known for its textiles—which she made her own after finding it on a sketchbook belonging to her great-grandmother.

Bambara wrote two collections of short stories—*Gorilla, My Love,* where "Blues Ain't No Mockin Bird" appeared, and *The Sea Birds Are Still Alive*—as well as a novel, *The Salt Eaters.*

Uncle Marcos

from *The House of the Spirits*

Isabel Allende

. . . It had been two years since Clara had last seen her Uncle Marcos, but she remembered him very well. His was the only perfectly clear image she retained from her whole childhood, and in order to describe him she did not need to consult the daguerreotype[1] in the drawing room that showed him dressed as an explorer leaning on an old-fashioned double-barreled rifle with his right foot on the neck of a Malaysian tiger, the same triumphant position in which she had seen the Virgin standing between plaster clouds and <u>pallid</u> angels at the main altar, one foot on the <u>vanquished</u> devil. All Clara had to do to see her uncle was close her eyes and there he was, weather-beaten and thin, with a pirate's mustache through which his strange, sharklike smile peered out at her. It seemed impossible that he could be inside that long black box that was lying in the middle of the courtyard.

Each time Uncle Marcos had visited his sister Nivea's home, he had stayed for several months, to the immense joy of his nieces and nephews, particularly Clara, causing a storm in which the sharp lines of domestic order blurred. The house became a clutter of trunks, of animals in jars of formaldehyde,[2] of Indian lances and sailor's bundles. In every part of the house people kept tripping over his equipment, and all sorts of unfamiliar animals appeared that had traveled from remote lands only to meet their death beneath Nana's irate broom in the farthest corners of the house. Uncle Marcos's manners were those of a cannibal, as Severo put it. He spent the whole night making incomprehensible movements in the drawing room; later they turned out to be exercises designed to perfect the mind's control over the body and to improve digestion. He performed alchemy[3] experiments in the kitchen, filling the house with <u>fetid</u> smoke and ruining pots and pans with solid substances that stuck to their bottoms and were impossible to remove. While the rest of the household tried to sleep, he dragged his suitcases up and down the halls, practiced making strange, high-pitched sounds

pallid (pal´ id) *adj.* pale

vanquished (vaŋ´ kwisht) *adj.* defeated

fetid (fet´ id) *adj.* smelly

---

1. **daguerreotype** (də ger´ ō tīp´) *n.* early type of photograph.
2. **formaldehyde** (for mal´ də hīd´) *n.* solution used as a preservative.
3. **alchemy** (al´ kə mē) *adj.* early form of chemistry, with philosophic and magical associations.

**Reading Check**

How long does Uncle Marcos stay when he visits Nivea's home?

on savage instruments, and taught Spanish to a parrot whose native language was an Amazonic dialect. During the day, he slept in a hammock that he had strung between two columns in the hall, wearing only a loincloth that put Severo in a terrible mood but that Nivea forgave because Marcos had convinced her that it was the same costume in which Jesus of Nazareth had preached. Clara remembered perfectly, even though she had been only a tiny child, the first time her Uncle Marcos came to the house after one of his voyages. He settled in as if he planned to stay forever. After a short time, bored with having to appear at ladies' gatherings where the mistress of the house played the piano, with playing cards, and with dodging all his relatives' pressures to pull himself together and take a job as a clerk in Severo del Valle's law practice, he bought a barrel organ and took to the streets with the hope of seducing his Cousin Antonieta and entertaining the public in the bargain. The machine was just a rusty box with wheels, but he painted it with seafaring designs and gave it a fake ship's smokestack. It ended up looking like a coal stove. The organ played either a military march or a waltz, and in between turns of the handle the parrot, who had managed to learn Spanish although he had not lost his foreign accent, would draw a crowd with his piercing shrieks. He also plucked slips of paper from a box with his beak, by way of selling fortunes to the curious. The little pink, green, and blue papers were so clever that they always divulged the exact secret wishes of the customers. Besides fortunes there were little balls of sawdust to amuse the children. The idea of the organ was a last desperate attempt to win the hand of Cousin Antonieta after more conventional means of courting her had failed. Marcos thought no woman in her right mind could remain <u>impassive</u> before a barrel-organ serenade. He stood beneath her window one evening and played his military march and his waltz just as she was taking tea with a group of female friends. Antonieta did not realize the music was meant for her until the parrot called her by her full name, at which point she appeared in the window. Her reaction was not what her suitor had hoped for. Her friends offered to spread the news to every salon[4] in the city, and the next day people thronged the downtown streets hoping to see Severo del Valle's brother-in-law playing the organ and selling little sawdust balls with a motheaten parrot, for the sheer pleasure of proving that even in the best of families there could be good reason for embarrassment. In the face of this stain to the family reputation, Marcos was

▲ **Critical Viewing** In this story, a man tries to build a flying machine. Which character traits might you find in someone who would try to do this? **[Speculate]**

impassive (im pas´ iv) *adj.* showing no emotion

---

4. **salon** (sə län´) *n.* regular gathering of distinguished guests that meets in a private home.

forced to give up organ grinding and resort to less conspicuous ways of winning over his Cousin Antonieta, but he did not renounce his goal. In any case, he did not succeed, because from one day to the next the young lady married a diplomat who was twenty years her senior; he took her to live in a tropical country whose name no one could recall, except that it suggested negritude,[5] bananas, and palm trees, where she managed to recover from the memory of that suitor who had ruined her seventeenth year with his military march and his waltz. Marcos sank into a deep depression that lasted two or three days, at the end of which he announced that he would never marry and that he was embarking on a trip around the world. He sold his organ to a blind man and left the parrot to Clara, but Nana secretly poisoned it with an overdose of cod-liver oil, because no one could stand its lusty glance, its fleas, and its harsh, tuneless hawking of paper fortunes and sawdust balls.

That was Marcos's longest trip. He returned with a shipment of enormous boxes that were piled in the far courtyard, between the chicken coop and the woodshed, until the winter was over. At the first signs of spring he had them transferred to the parade grounds, a huge park where people would gather to watch the soldiers file by on Independence Day, with the goosestep they had learned from the Prussians. When the crates were opened, they were found to contain loose bits of wood, metal, and painted cloth. Marcos spent two weeks assembling the contents according to an instruction manual written in English, which he was able to decipher thanks to his invincible imagination and a small dictionary. When the job was finished, it turned out to be a bird of prehistoric dimensions, with the face of a furious eagle, wings that moved, and a propeller on its back. It caused an uproar. The families of the oligarchy[6] forgot all about the barrel organ, and Marcos became the star attraction of the season. People took Sunday outings to see the bird; souvenir vendors and strolling photographers made a fortune. Nonetheless, the public's interest quickly waned. But then Marcos announced that as soon as the weather cleared he planned to take off in his bird and cross the mountain range. The news spread, making this the most talked-about event of the year. The contraption lay with its stomach on terra firma,[7] heavy and sluggish and looking more like a wounded duck than like one of those newfangled airplanes they were starting to produce in the United States. There was nothing in its appearance to suggest that it could move, much less take flight across the snowy peaks. Journalists and the curious flocked to see it. Marcos smiled his immutable[8] smile before the avalanche of questions and posed for photographers without offering

---

5. **negritude** (neg′ rə tood′) *n.* blacks and their cultural heritage.
6. **oligarchy** (äl′ i gär′ kē) *n.* government ruled by a few.
7. **terra firma** (ter′ a fur′ ma) *n.* Latin term meaning "firm earth; solid ground."
8. **immutable** (im myoot′ ə bəl) *adj.* never changing.

Literary Analysis
Direct and Indirect Characterization What does the fact that Uncle Marcos's deep depression lasted only a few days tell you about his character?

✓**Reading Check**
What does Uncle Marcos do with the barrel organ?

the least technical or scientific explanation of how he hoped to carry out his plan. People came from the provinces to see the sight. Forty years later his great-nephew Nicolás, whom Marcos did not live to see, unearthed the desire to fly that had always existed in the men of his lineage. Nicolás was interested in doing it for commercial reasons, in a gigantic hot-air sausage on which would be printed an advertisement for carbonated drinks. But when Marcos announced his plane trip, no one believed that his contraption could be put to any practical use. The appointed day dawned full of clouds, but so many people had turned out that Marcos did not want to disappoint them. He showed up punctually at the appointed spot and did not once look up at the sky, which was growing darker and darker with thick gray clouds. The astonished crowd filled all the nearby streets, perching on rooftops and the balconies of the nearest houses and squeezing into the park. No political gathering managed to attract so many people until half a century later, when the first Marxist candidate attempted, through strictly democratic channels, to become President. Clara would remember this holiday as long as she lived. People dressed in their spring best, thereby getting a step ahead of the official opening of the season, the men in white linen suits and the ladies in the Italian straw hats that were all the rage that year. Groups of elementary-school children paraded with their teachers, clutching flowers for the hero. Marcos accepted their bouquets and joked that they might as well hold on to them and wait for him to crash, so they could take them directly to his funeral. The bishop himself, accompanied by two incense bearers, appeared to bless the bird without having been asked, and the police band played happy, unpretentious music that pleased everyone. The police, on horseback and carrying lances, had trouble keeping the crowds far enough away from the center of the park, where Marcos waited dressed in mechanic's overalls, with huge racer's goggles and an explorer's helmet. He was also equipped with a compass, a telescope, and several strange maps that he had traced himself based on various theories of Leonardo da Vinci and on the polar knowledge of the Incas.[9] Against all logic, on the second try the bird lifted off without mishap and with a certain elegance, accompanied by the creaking of its skeleton and the roar of its motor. It rose flapping its wings and disappeared into the clouds, to a send-off of applause, whistlings, handkerchiefs, drumrolls, and the sprinkling of holy water. All that remained on earth were the comments of the amazed crowd below and a multitude of experts, who attempted to provide a reasonable explanation of the miracle. Clara continued to stare at the sky long after her uncle had become invisible. She thought she saw him ten minutes later, but it was only a migrating sparrow. After three days the initial euphoria that had accompanied the first airplane flight in the country died down and no one gave the episode another thought, except for Clara, who continued to peer at the horizon.

9. **Leonardo da Vinci** (lē´ ə när´ dō də vin´ chē) . . . **Incas** Leonardo da Vinci (1452–1519) was an Italian painter, sculptor, architect, and scientist. The Incas were Native Americans who dominated ancient Peru until the Spanish conquest.

Literary Analysis

Characterization What does the people's reaction to Marcos's plan for a plane trip tell you about him?

Reading Strategy

Making Inferences About Characters What can you infer about Uncle Marcos's motives for attempting to fly in his "bird"?

After a week with no word from the flying uncle, people began to speculate that he had gone so high that he had disappeared into outer space, and the ignorant suggested he would reach the moon. With a mixture of sadness and relief, Severo decided that his brother-in-law and his machine must have fallen into some hidden crevice of the cordillera,[10] where they would never be found. Nivea wept <u>disconsolately</u> and lit candles to San Antonio, patron of lost objects. Severo opposed the idea of having masses said, because he did not believe in them as a way of getting into heaven, much less of returning to earth, and he maintained that masses and religious vows, like the selling of indulgences, images, and scapulars,[11] were a dishonest business. Because of his attitude, Nivea and Nana had the children say the rosary,[12] behind their father's back for nine days. Meanwhile, groups of volunteer explorers and mountain climbers tirelessly searched peaks and passes, combing every accessible stretch of land until they finally returned in triumph to hand the family the mortal remains of the deceased in a sealed black coffin. The intrepid traveler was laid to rest in a grandiose funeral. His death made him a hero and his name was on the front page of all the papers for several days. The same multitude that had gathered to see him off the day he flew away in his bird paraded past his coffin. The entire family wept as befit the occasion, except for Clara, who continued to watch the sky with the patience of an astronomer. One week after he had been buried, Uncle Marcos, a bright smile playing behind his pirate's mustache, appeared in person in the doorway of Nivea and Severo del Valle's house. Thanks to the surreptitious[13] prayers of the women and children, as he himself admitted, he was alive and well and in full possession of his faculties, including his sense of humor. Despite the noble lineage of his aerial maps, the flight had been a failure. He had lost his airplane and had to return on foot, but he had not broken any bones and his adventurous spirit was intact. This confirmed the family's eternal devotion to San Antonio, but was not taken as a warning by future generations, who also tried to fly, although by different means. Legally, however, Marcos was a corpse. Severo del Valle was obliged to use all his legal ingenuity to bring his brother-in-law back to life and the full rights of citizenship. When the coffin was pried open in the presence of the appropriate authorities, it was found to contain a bag of sand. This discovery ruined the reputation, up till then untarnished, of the volunteer explorers and mountain climbers, who from that day on were considered little better than a pack of bandits.

Marcos's heroic resurrection made everyone forget about his barrel-organ phase. Once again he was a sought-after guest in all the city's salons and, at least for a while, his name was cleared. Marcos stayed in

disconsolately (dis kän´ sə lit lē) *adv.* unhappily

Reading Strategy
Making Inferences About Characters What inference can you make about Clara from her belief concerning her uncle and his fate?

---

10. cordillera (kôr´ dil yer´ə) *n.* system or chain of mountains.
11. indulgences, images, and scapulars (skap´ yə lərz) Indulgences are pardons for sins, images are pictures or sculptures of religious figures, and scapulars are garments worn by Roman Catholics as tokens of religious devotion.
12. say the rosary use a set of beads to say prayers.
13. surreptitious (sur´ əp tish´ əs) *adj.* secretive.

Reading Check
What happens to Uncle Marcos after he loses his airplane?

his sister's house for several months. One night he left without saying goodbye, leaving behind his trunks, his books, his weapons, his boots, and all his belongings. Severo, and even Nivea herself, breathed a sigh of relief. His visit had gone on too long. But Clara was so upset that she spent a week walking in her sleep and sucking her thumb. The little girl, who was only seven at the time, had learned to read from her uncle's storybooks and been closer to him than any other member of the family because of her prophesying powers. Marcos maintained that his niece's gift could be a source of income and a good opportunity for him to culti-vate his own clairvoyance.[14] He believed that all human beings pos-sessed this ability, particularly his own family, and that if it did not function well it was simply due to a lack of training. He bought a crystal ball in the Persian bazaar, insisting that it had magic powers and was from the East (although it was later found to be part of a buoy from a fishing boat), set it down on a background of black velvet, and announced that he could tell people's fortunes, cure the evil eye, and improve the quality of dreams, all for the modest sum of five centavos.[15] His first customers were the maids from around the neighborhood. One of them had been accused of stealing, because her employer had mis-placed a valuable ring. The crystal ball revealed the exact location of the object in question: it had rolled beneath a wardrobe. The next day there was a line outside the front door of the house. There were coachmen, storekeepers, and milkmen; later a few municipal employees and distinguished ladies made a discreet appearance, slinking along the side walls of the house to keep from being recognized. The customers were received by Nana, who ushered them into the waiting room and collected their fees. This task kept her busy throughout the day and demanded so much of her time that the family began to complain that all there ever was for din-ner was old string beans and jellied quince.[16] Marcos decorated the carriage house with some frayed curtains that had once belonged in the drawing room but that neglect and age had turned to dusty rags. There he and Clara received the cus-tomers. The two divines wore tunics "color of the men of light," as Marcos called the color yellow. Nana had dyed them with saffron powder, boiling them in pots usually reserved for rice and pasta. In addition to his tunic, Marcos wore a turban around his head and an Egyptian amulet around his neck. He had grown a beard and let his hair grow long and he was thinner than ever before. Marcos and Clara were utterly convincing, especially because the child had no need to look into the crystal ball to guess what her clients wanted to hear. She would whisper in her Uncle Marcos's ear, and he in turn would transmit the

Literary Analysis
Characterization and Narrator Which words does the narrator use here to characterize Clara directly?

▼ **Critical Viewing** This sketch of a helicopter by Italian artist and inventor Leonardo da Vinci predates the first working helicopters by about 450 years. What do you think Uncle Marcos would have thought of Leonardo da Vinci? **[Speculate]**

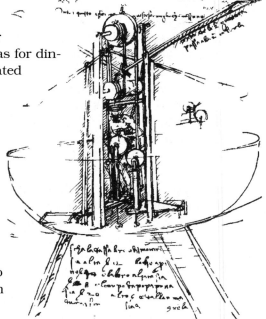

---

14. **clairvoyance** (kler voi´ əns) *n.* supposed ability to perceive unseen things.
15. **centavos** (sen tä´ vōs) *n.* coins equal to 1/100 of a cruzeiro, the basic monetary unit of Brazil.
16. **quince** (kwins) golden or greenish-yellow, hard, apple-shaped fruit.

message to the client, along with any improvisations of his own that he thought pertinent. Thus their fame spread, because all those who arrived sad and bedraggled at the consulting room left filled with hope.

<u>Unrequited</u> lovers were told how to win over indifferent hearts, and the poor left with foolproof tips on how to place their money at the dog tracks. Business grew so prosperous that the waiting room was always packed with people, and Nana began to suffer dizzy spells from being on her feet so many hours a day. This time Severo had no need to intervene to put a stop to his brother-in-law's venture, for both Marcos and Clara, realizing that their unerring guesses could alter the fate of their clients, who always followed their advice to the letter, became frightened and decided that this was a job for swindlers. They abandoned their carriage-house oracle and split the profits, even though the only one who had cared about the material side of things had been Nana.

Of all the del Valle children, Clara was the one with the greatest interest in and stamina for her uncle's stories. She could repeat each and every one of them. She knew by heart words from several dialects of the Indians, was acquainted with their customs, and could describe the exact way in which they pierced their lips and earlobes with wooden shafts, their initiation rites, the names of the most poisonous snakes, and the appropriate antidotes for each. Her uncle was so eloquent that the child could feel in her own skin the burning sting of snakebites, see reptiles slide across the carpet between the legs of the jacaranda[17] room divider, and hear the shrieks of macaws behind the drawing-room drapes. She did not hesitate as she recalled Lope de Aguirre's search for El Dorado,[18] or the unpronounceable names of the flora and fauna her extraordinary uncle had seen; she knew about the lamas who take salt tea with yak lard and she could give detailed descriptions of the opulent women of Tahiti, the rice fields of China, or the white prairies of the North, where the eternal ice kills animals and men who lose their way, turning them to stone in seconds. Marcos had various travel journals in which he recorded his excursions and impressions, as well as a collection of maps and books of stories and fairy tales that he kept in the trunks he stored in the junk room at the far end of the third courtyard. From there they were hauled out to inhabit the dreams of his descendants, until they were mistakenly burned half a century later on an infamous pyre.

Now Marcos had returned from his last journey in a coffin. He had died of a mysterious African plague that had turned him as yellow and wrinkled as a piece of parchment. When he realized he was ill, he set out for home with the hope that his sister's ministrations and Dr. Cuevas's knowledge would restore his health and youth, but he was unable to withstand the sixty days on ship and died at the latitude of

---

unrequited (un ri kwit′ id) *adj.* not reciprocated

17. **jacaranda** (jak′ ə ran′ də) type of tropical American tree.
18. **Lope de Aguirre's** (lō′ pā dā ä gēr′ rās) **. . . El Dorado** Lope de Aguirre was a Spanish adventurer (1510–1561) in colonial South America who searched for a legendary country called El Dorado, which was supposedly rich in gold.

Reading Check

What power does Marcos believe Clara holds?

Guayaquil,[19] ravaged by fever and hallucinating about musky women and hidden treasure. The captain of the ship, an Englishman by the name of Longfellow, was about to throw him overboard wrapped in a flag, but Marcos, despite his savage appearance and his delirium, had made so many friends on board and seduced so many women that the passengers prevented him from doing so, and Longfellow was obliged to store the body side by side with the vegetables of the Chinese cook, to preserve it from the heat and mosquitoes of the tropics until the ship's carpenter had time to improvise a coffin. At El Callao[20] they obtained a more appropriate container, and several days later the captain, furious at all the troubles this passenger had caused the shipping company and himself personally, unloaded him without a backward glance, surprised that not a soul was there to receive the body or cover the expenses he had incurred. Later he learned that the post office in these latitudes was not as reliable as that of far-off England, and that all his telegrams had vaporized en route. Fortunately for Longfellow, a customs lawyer who was a friend of the del Valle family appeared and offered to take charge, placing Marcos and all his paraphernalia in a freight car, which he shipped to the capital to the only known address of the deceased: his sister's house. . . .

19. **Guayaquil** (gwĭ ä kēl´) seaport in western Ecuador.
20. **El Callao** (kə yä´ ō) seaport in western Peru.

Review and Assess

Thinking About the Selection

1. **Respond:** Which of Uncle Marcos's adventures would you most like to share with him? Why?

2. **(a) Recall:** What does Uncle Marcos do to try to win the hand of Cousin Antonieta? **(b) Connect:** Is her reaction what Uncle Marcos expects? **(c) Compare and Contrast:** What subsequent actions does each take in the wake of his courtship?

3. **(a) Recall:** What does Uncle Marcos make from the materials in the "enormous boxes"? **(b) Infer:** What do you think motivates Uncle Marcos to undertake this project?

4. **(a) Recall:** How do various people in the family and community react to Uncle Marcos's disappearance? **(b) Deduce:** Do you think Marcos wanted to fool everyone about his fate? Explain.

5. **Speculate:** In the story, you see the reactions of people who knew Uncle Marcos. How do you think people who did not know him might have reacted to him? Explain.

Isabel Allende

(b. 1942)

Isabel Allende has said, "I had a very lonely life when I was a child but very interesting—only adults around me . . . a very extravagant family." She grew up in Chile, where she lived with her grandparents. Her uncle was the former Chilean president Salvador Allende.

Allende's first novel, *The House of the Spirits* (1985), from which "Uncle Marcos" is excerpted, was inspired by her family. Her other books include *Of Love and Shadows* (1987), *Eva Luna* (1988), *The Stories of Eva Luna* (1991), *The Infinite Plan* (1993), and *Paula* (1995).

Review and Assess

Literary Analysis

Characterization

1. Using a chart like this one, find examples of **indirect characterization** for two people in each story. Rewrite each example to **directly characterize** the person.

Indirect Characterization → Character ← Direct Characterization

2. Which character does Isabel Allende indirectly characterize in the most detail? Support your answer.
3. Which form of characterization does each writer seem to prefer? Explain and support your answer.

Comparing Literary Works

4. Using the Venn diagram below, compare the information revealed about the characters through the **narration** in each story. Consider each character's appearance, traits, actions, and thoughts.

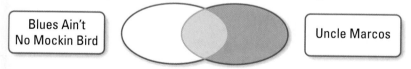

Blues Ain't No Mockin Bird   Uncle Marcos

5. How would these stories be different if their narration styles were switched? Provide specific examples.

Reading Strategy

Making Inferences About Characters

6. **Make an inference** to explain how the photographer in "Blues Ain't No Mockin Bird" feels about the people he is filming.
7. In "Uncle Marcos," which details might lead you to infer that Clara is an unusual child?

Extend Understanding

8. **Media Connection:** (a) What insights might journalists gain from reading Bambara's story? (b) Are there any times when the public's right to know outweighs individual privacy? Explain.

Quick Review

Characterization is the set of techniques writers use to reveal the personalities of characters in fiction.

With **direct characterization,** a writer simply states a fact about a character.

With **indirect characterization,** a writer implies facts about a character through the character's words and actions and the reactions of others.

A **first-person narrator** relates events from the perspective of a character in the story.

A **third-person narrator** relates a story's events, but he or she is not a character in the story.

To make inferences about characters, draw conclusions using details the author provides.

 Take It to the Net

www.phschool.com

Take the interactive self-test online to check your understanding of the selections.

Integrate Language Skills

Vocabulary Development Lesson

Word Analysis: Latin Prefix *dis-*

The Latin prefix *dis-* means "opposite." Thus, *disconsolate* means "the opposite of consolable," or "dejected; cheerless."

Match each word on the left with its definition on the right.

1. dishonest
2. disassemble
3. distrust

a. take apart
b. doubt
c. not truthful

Spelling Strategy

When you add a prefix to a word, do not change the spelling of the original word. For example, *un-* + *requited* = *unrequited*. Add *in-*, *im-*, *non-*, or *un-* to each word below to form four properly spelled new words.

1. formality
2. cover
3. passive
4. sense

Concept Development: Analogies

For each item, complete the analogy.

1. disconsolately : joyously :: rain : ___?___
   a. sunshine b. leaf c. spring d. grass
2. fetid : smelly :: pond : ___?___
   a. rain b. duck c. pool d. egg
3. formality : tuxedo :: relaxation : ___?___
   a. chair b. snow c. red d. swimsuit
4. impassive : calm :: search : ___?___
   a. find b. explore c. begin d. reason
5. lassoed : released :: day : ___?___
   a. sad b. week c. pocket d. night
6. pallid : ruddy :: bend : ___?___
   a. straighten b. swirl c. trade d. fry
7. unrequited : shared :: calm : ___?___
   a. dry b. windy c. excited d. cold
8. vanquished : beaten :: survived : ___?___
   a. persevered b. horse c. hunter d. peril

Grammar Lesson

Infinitive Phrases

An **infinitive** is a verb form preceded by the word *to* that acts as a noun, adjective, or adverb. An **infinitive phrase** is an infinitive with its modifiers or complements. Like infinitives, infinitive phrases can function as nouns, adjectives, or adverbs. Unlike a **prepositional phrase** that begins with *to* and ends with a noun, an infinitive phrase always ends with a verb.

> **Infinitive:** Granny decided *to stare*. (noun)
>
> **Infinitive Phrase:** Clara was afraid *to speak her mind*. (acts as an adverb by modifying *afraid*)
>
> **Prepositional Phrase:** Antonieta did not speak *to Marcos*.

Practice Copy the sentences below. Circle the infinitives and underline the infinitive phrases. Identify the part of speech of each phrase.

1. The men wanted to get a statement from Granny.
2. Soon there were no more hawks to chase.
3. He wanted to throw him overboard.
4. The machine was made to soar over the mountains to a new life.
5. The organ was a last attempt to win the hand of Cousin Antonieta.

Writing Application Write two sentences about each selection, using infinitives and infinitive phrases in each.

WG Prentice Hall Writing and Grammar Connection: Chapter 21, Section 1

Writing Lesson

Magazine Feature

These selections feature amazing characters, brought to life with vivid details. Use one of the characters in this section as the basis for a magazine feature—an article that is meant to entertain or provide information on a subject of interest.

Prewriting As you prepare, decide what makes the character truly remarkable. To help you gather relevant ideas, list specific details concerning the person's appearance, personality, and achievements.

Model: Organizing Details

Talents	Goals
adventurous	to fly
eccentric	to travel the world

> These specific details, under the general ideas *Talents* and *Goals,* will support the main impression and make a feature article believable.

Drafting Use your notes to focus your writing on the main impression: the amazing qualities of your character. As you write, provide examples illustrating each characteristic you mention.

Revising Review your work to ensure that you communicate your main impression. Add more details if necessary, and discard any details that are not relevant or that detract from your focus.

WG *Prentice Hall Writing and Grammar Connection: Chapter 13, Section 2*

Extension Activities

Research and Technology Sometimes, a person like Uncle Marcos is seen as irresponsible. However, imaginative and adventurous people like him are responsible for making some of the most important discoveries in history.

- In a group, research people in history who, through their adventures, made great discoveries.
- Show how these people compare to Marcos.

Compile your notes to create a **comparison-and-contrast brochure.**

Listening and Speaking Assume that you are the cameraman in "Blues Ain't No Mockin Bird," and prepare a **monologue** explaining to your boss what happened to your camera. Do not omit anything important, and do not exaggerate. Be polite, and use language appropriate to your situation. Read or perform the monologue for a friend or a small group.

 **Take It to the Net**   www.phschool.com

Go online for an additional research activity using the Internet.

Prepare to Read

The Man to Send Rain Clouds ◆ The Invalid's Story

Feast Day, San Juan Pueblo, 1921, William Penhallow Henderson,
National Museum of American Art, Smithsonian Institution

 Take It to the Net

Visit www.phschool.com
for interactive activities
and instruction related to
the selections, including
- background
- graphic organizers
- literary elements
- reading strategies

Preview

Connecting to the Literature

People cope with the loss of a loved one in different ways. Some try to preserve their memories of the deceased; others try to fulfill the loved one's last wishes. These stories offer two sets of circumstances surrounding death and others' responses to it.

Background

"The Man to Send Rain Clouds" explores the traditions of the Pueblo people of the southwestern United States. Over time, the Pueblo people have tried to maintain their ancient belief that if they live in harmony with the natural world, nature will give them what they need. The Pueblos' balancing of traditional and modern ways provides the central conflict in Leslie Marmon Silko's story.

Literary Analysis

Setting

In each of these stories, **setting**—the time and place in which the story unfolds—strongly influences the action. Time may include not only the historical period but also a specific year, season, or time of day. Place may involve not only the geographical place but also the social, economic, and cultural environment. The following excerpt reveals the cultural environment of "The Man to Send Rain Clouds":

> Leon stared at the new moccasins that Teofilo had made for the ceremonial dances in the summer. They were nearly hidden by the red blanket.

In some stories, the setting simply provides a backdrop for the action; in other stories, including these, setting shapes the character's actions.

Comparing Literary Works

Although both stories deal with death, the settings of the stories are very different. One is the high desert of New Mexico; the other is a train on its way to Wisconsin. While reading, compare and contrast the brief journey of the aged Pueblo with the somewhat longer one of John B. Hackett. Note the way story events seem to emerge from each distinctive setting.

Reading Strategy

Using Your Senses

The setting of each story, like a stifling boxcar with a smelly package, gives your **senses** a virtual workout. Draw from your own experiences to see, hear, smell, taste, or feel what each author describes. Then, try to re-create senses in your mind. Use a chart like the one shown to record key details appealing to each sense.

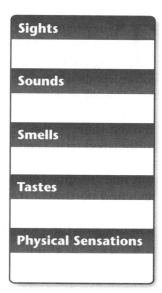

| Sights |
| Sounds |
| Smells |
| Tastes |
| Physical Sensations |

Vocabulary Development

cloister (klois´ tər) n. place devoted to religious seclusion (p. 594)

pagans (pā´ gənz) n. people who are not Christians, Muslims, or Jews (p. 594)

perverse (pər vʉrs´) adj. continuing in a stubborn way to do what is wrong or harmful (p. 594)

prodigious (pro dij es) adj. enormous (p. 597)

deleterious (del´ ə tir´ ē əs) adj. harmful to health or well-being (p. 598)

ominous (äm´ ə nəs) adj. threatening (p. 599)

judicious (jōō dish´ əs) adj. showing good judgment (p. 599)

placidly (plas´ id lē) adv. calmly; quietly (p. 599)

desultory (des´ əl tôr´ ē) adj. random (p. 600)

"Thank God for that. Teofilo is a very old man. You really shouldn't allow him to stay at the sheep camp alone."

"No, he won't do that any more now."

"Well, I'm glad you understand. I hope I'll be seeing you at Mass[1] this week—we missed you last Sunday. See if you can get old Teofilo to come with you." The priest smiled and waved at them as they drove away.

Louise and Teresa were waiting. The table was set for lunch, and the coffee was boiling on the black iron stove. Leon looked at Louise and then at Teresa.

"We found him under a cottonwood tree in the big arroyo near sheep camp. I guess he sat down to rest in the shade and never got up again." Leon walked toward the old man's bed. The red plaid shawl had been shaken and spread carefully over the bed, and a new brown flannel shirt and pair of stiff new Levi's were arranged neatly beside the pillow. Louise held the screen door open while Leon and Ken carried in the red blanket. He looked small and shriveled, and after they dressed him in the new shirt and pants he seemed more shrunken.

It was noontime now because the church bells rang the Angelus.[2] They ate the beans with hot bread, and nobody said anything until after Teresa poured the coffee.

Ken stood up and put on his jacket. "I'll see about the gravediggers. Only the top layer of soil is frozen. I think it can be ready before dark."

Leon nodded his head and finished his coffee. After Ken had been gone for a while, the neighbors and clanspeople came quietly to embrace Teofilo's family and to leave food on the table because the gravediggers would come to eat when they were finished.

The sky in the west was full of pale yellow light. Louise stood outside with her hands in the pockets of Leon's green army jacket that was too big for her. The funeral was over, and the old men had taken their candles and medicine bags[3] and were gone. She waited until the body was laid into the pickup before she said anything to Leon. She touched his arm, and he noticed that her hands were still dusty from the corn meal that she had sprinkled around the old man. When she spoke, Leon could not hear her.

"What did you say? I didn't hear you."

"I said that I had been thinking about something."

"About what?"

"About the priest sprinkling holy water for Grandpa. So he won't be thirsty."

Leon stared at the new moccasins that Teofilo had made for the ceremonial dances in the summer. They were nearly hidden by the red blanket. It was getting colder, and the wind pushed gray dust down the

Literary Analysis
Setting Which cultural elements are represented in Louise's request to the priest?

---

1. **Mass** (mas) church service celebrated by Roman Catholics.
2. **Angelus** (an´ jə ləs) bell rung at morning, noon, and evening to announce a prayer.
3. **medicine bags** bags containing objects that were thought to have special powers.

Feast Day, San Juan Pueblo, 1921, William Penhallow Henderson, National Museum of American Art, Smithsonian Institution

narrow pueblo road. The sun was approaching the long mesa where it disappeared during the winter. Louise stood there shivering and watching his face. Then he zipped up his jacket and opened the truck door. "I'll see if he's there."

Ken stopped the pickup at the church, and Leon got out: and then Ken drove down the hill to the graveyard where people were waiting. Leon knocked at the old carved door with its symbols of the Lamb.[4] While he waited he looked up at the twin bells from the king of Spain with the last sunlight pouring around them in their tower.

The priest opened the door and smiled when he saw who it was.

---

4. **the Lamb** Jesus Christ, as the sacrificial Lamb of God.

▲ Critical Viewing
How do the images in this painting compare to images created by the story? **[Compare]**

☑ Reading Check
What do the old men take with them when the funeral is over?

"Come in! What brings you here this evening?"

The priest walked toward the kitchen, and Leon stood with his cap in his hand, playing with the earflaps and examining the living room—the brown sofa, the green armchair, and the brass lamp that hung down from the ceiling by links of chain. The priest dragged a chair out of the kitchen and offered it to Leon.

"No thank you, Father. I only came to ask you if you would bring your holy water to the graveyard."

The priest turned away from Leon and looked out the window at the patio full of shadows and the dining-room windows of the nuns' cloister across the patio. The curtains were heavy, and the light from within faintly penetrated; it was impossible to see the nuns inside eating supper. "Why didn't you tell me he was dead? I could have brought the Last Rites[5] anyway."

Leon smiled. "It wasn't necessary, Father."

The priest stared down at his scuffed brown loafers and the worn hem of his cassock. "For a Christian burial it was necessary."

His voice was distant, and Leon thought that his blue eyes looked tired.

"It's O.K. Father, we just want him to have plenty of water."

The priest sank down into the green chair and picked up a glossy missionary magazine. He turned the colored pages full of lepers and pagans without looking at them.

"You know I can't do that, Leon. There should have been the Last Rites and a funeral Mass at the very least."

Leon put on his green cap and pulled the flaps down over his ears. "It's getting late, Father. I've got to go."

When Leon opened the door Father Paul stood up and said, "Wait." He left the room and came back wearing a long brown overcoat. He followed Leon out the door and across the dim churchyard to the adobe steps in front of the church. They both stooped to fit through the low adobe entrance. And when they started down the hill to the graveyard only half of the sun was visible above the mesa.

The priest approached the grave slowly, wondering how they had managed to dig into the frozen ground; and then he remembered that this was New Mexico, and saw the pile of cold loose sand beside the hole. The people stood close to each other with little clouds of steam puffing from their faces. The priest looked at them and saw a pile of jackets, gloves, and scarves in the yellow, dry tumbleweeds that grew in the graveyard. He looked at the red blanket, not sure that Teofilo was so small, wondering if it wasn't some perverse Indian trick—something they did in March to ensure a good harvest—wondering if maybe old Teofilo was actually at sheep camp corraling the sheep for the night. But there he was, facing into a cold dry wind and squinting at the last sunlight, ready to bury a red wool blanket while the faces of his parishioners were in shadow with the last warmth of the sun on their backs.

---

5. the Last Rites religious ceremony for a dying person or for someone who has just died.

cloister (klois´ tər) *n.* place devoted to religious seclusion

pagans (pā´ gənz) *n.* people who are not Christians, Muslims, or Jews

perverse (pər vurs´) *adj.* continuing in a stubborn way to do what is wrong or harmful

His fingers were stiff, and it took him a long time to twist the lid off the holy water. Drops of water fell on the red blanket and soaked into dark icy spots. He sprinkled the grave and the water disappeared almost before it touched the dim, cold sand; it reminded him of something—he tried to remember what it was, because he thought if he could remember he might understand this. He sprinkled more water; he shook the container until it was empty, and the water fell through the light from sundown like August rain that fell while the sun was still shining, almost evaporating before it touched the wilted squash flowers.

The wind pulled at the priest's brown Franciscan robe[6] and swirled away the corn meal and pollen that had been sprinkled on the blanket. They lowered the bundle into the ground, and they didn't bother to untie the stiff pieces of new rope that were tied around the ends of the blanket. The sun was gone, and over on the highway the eastbound lane was full of headlights. The priest walked away slowly. Leon watched him climb the hill, and when he had disappeared within the tall, thick walls, Leon turned to look up at the high blue mountains in the deep snow that reflected a faint red light from the west. He felt good because it was finished, and he was happy about the sprinkling of the holy water; now the old man could send them big thunderclouds for sure.

Literary Analysis
Setting In what ways does the setting described in the last paragraph contribute to the action in the story?

---

6. **Franciscan** (fran sis´ kən) **robe** robe worn by a member of the Franciscan religious order, founded in 1209 by Saint Francis of Assisi.

Review and Assess

Thinking About the Selection

1. **Respond:** What did you think about the way in which the tribespeople buried Teofilo's body? Why?

2. **(a) Recall:** What do Leon and Ken find at the opening of the story? **(b) Analyze:** Why doesn't Leon tell Father Paul about Teofilo's death at first?

3. **(a) Recall:** Why does Louise ask Leon to bring the priest to Teofilo's grave? **(b) Compare and Contrast:** What does this story reveal about the contrasts between Pueblo and Christian beliefs?

4. **(a) Analyze:** Why is Father Paul upset about the burial ceremony? **(b) Infer:** What insight into the Pueblo people do you think Father Paul gained during the ceremony?

5. **(a) Recall:** How are Leon's feelings described at the end of the story? **(b) Draw Conclusions:** What do Leon's thoughts after Teofilo's burial suggest about his views of death?

6. **Extend:** What lesson can be taken from this story about working out differences in cultural beliefs?

Leslie Marmon Silko

(b. 1948)

Storytelling has always been an important part of Leslie Marmon Silko's life. Raised on the Laguna Pueblo reservation in New Mexico, she grew up listening to tribal stories told by her great-grandmother and great-aunts.

In her stories, novels, and poems, Silko explores what life is like for Native Americans in today's world. Many of her works capture the contrast between traditional values and beliefs and the elements of modern-day life.

The Man to Send Rain Clouds ◆ 595

The
Invalid's
Story
Mark Twain

I seem sixty and married, but these effects are due to my condition and sufferings, for I am a bachelor, and only forty-one. It will be hard for you to believe that I, who am now but a shadow, was a hale, hearty man two short years ago—a man of iron, a very athlete!—yet such is the simple truth. But stranger still than this fact is the way in which I lost my health. I lost it through helping to take care of a box of guns on a two-hundred-mile railway journey one winter's night. It is the actual truth, and I will tell you about it.

I belong in Cleveland, Ohio. One winter's night, two years ago, I reached home just after dark, in a driving snowstorm, and the first thing I heard when I entered the house was that my dearest boyhood friend and schoolmate, John B. Hackett, had died the day before, and that his last utterance had been a desire that I would take his remains home to his poor old father and mother in Wisconsin. I was greatly shocked and grieved, but there was no time to waste in emotions; I must start at once. I took the card, marked "Deacon Levi Hackett, Bethlehem, Wisconsin," and hurried off through the whistling storm to the railway station. Arrived there I found the long white-pine box which had been described to me; I fastened the card to it with some tacks, saw it put safely aboard the express car, and then ran into the eating room to provide myself with a sandwich and some cigars. When I returned, presently, there was my coffin-box *back again*, apparently, and a young fellow examining around it, with a card in his hands, and some tacks and a hammer! I was astonished and puzzled. He began to nail on his card, and I rushed out to the express car, in a good deal of a state of mind, to ask for an explanation. But no—there was my box, all right, in the express car; it hadn't been disturbed. [The fact is that without my suspecting it a <u>prodigious</u> mistake had been made. I was carrying off a box of *guns* which that young fellow had come to the station to ship to a rifle company in Peoria, Illinois, and *he* had got my corpse.] Just then the conductor sang out "All aboard," and I jumped into the express car and got a comfortable seat on a bale of buckets. The expressman was there, hard at work—a plain man of fifty, with a simple, honest, good-natured face, and a breezy, practical heartiness in his general style. As the train moved off a stranger skipped into the car and set a package of peculiarly mature and capable Limburger cheese[1] on one end of my coffin-box—I mean my box of guns. That is to say, I know now that it was Limburger cheese, but at that time I never had heard of the article in my life, and of course was wholly ignorant of its character. Well, we sped through the wild night, the bitter storm raged on, a cheerless misery stole over me, my heart went down, down, down! The old expressman made a brisk remark or two about the tempest and the arctic weather, slammed his sliding doors to, and bolted them, closed his window down tight, and then went bustling around, here and there and yonder, setting things to rights, and all the time contentedly humming "Sweet By and By" in a low tone, and flatting a good deal. Presently I

---

1. Limburger cheese cheese with a strong odor.

◀ **Critical Viewing** How do the sensory details in this image compare to the sensory details in the story? **[Compare]**

Literary Analysis
Setting Describe the setting at the beginning of this paragraph.

prodigious (prō dij′ əs) *adj.* enormous

✔ **Reading Check**
What is the first thing the narrator hears when he enters his house during a snowstorm?

The Invalid's Story ◆ 597

began to detect a most evil and searching odor stealing about on the frozen air. This depressed my spirits still more, because of course I attributed it to my poor departed friend. There was something infinitely saddening about his calling himself to my remembrance in this dumb, pathetic way, so it was hard to keep the tears back. Moreover, it distressed me on account of the old expressman, who, I was afraid, might notice it. However, he went humming tranquilly on, and gave no sign; and for this I was grateful. Grateful, yes, but still uneasy; and soon I began to feel more and more uneasy every minute, for every minute that went by that odor thickened up the more, and got to be more and more gamy and hard to stand. Presently, having got things arranged to his satisfaction, the expressman got some wood and made up a tremendous fire in his stove. This distressed me more than I can tell, for I could not but feel that it was a mistake. I was sure that the effect would be <u>deleterious</u> upon my poor departed friend. Thompson— the expressman's name was Thompson, as I found out in the course of the night—now went poking around his car, stopping up whatever stray cracks he could find, remarking that it didn't make any difference what kind of a night it was outside, he calculated to make us comfortable, anyway. I said nothing, but I believed he was not choosing the right way. Meantime he was humming to himself just as before; and meantime, too, the stove was getting hotter and hotter, and the place closer and closer. I felt myself growing pale and qualmish,[2] but grieved

---

2. **qualmish** (kwäm´ ish) *adj.* slightly ill.

Reading Strategy
Using Your Senses Which senses can you use to experience this description? How can an "odor" be "searching"?

deleterious (del´ ə tir´ ē əs) *adj.* injurious; harmful to health or well-being

▼ **Critical Viewing**
Examine this painting of a railway station in 1874. How difficult do you think it was to get from one place to another at this time in history? Which details in the painting support your ideas?
[Support]

Sacramento Railroad Station, 1874, William Hahn, The Fine Arts Museum of San Francisco

in silence and said nothing. Soon I noticed that the "Sweet By and By" was gradually fading out; next it ceased altogether, and there was an <u>ominous</u> stillness. After a few moments Thompson said—

"Pfew! I reckon it ain't no cinnamon't I've loaded up thish-year stove with!"

He gasped once or twice, then moved toward the cof—gun-box, stood over that Limburger cheese part of a moment, then came back and sat down near me, looking a good deal impressed. After a contemplative pause, he said, indicating the box with a gesture—

"Friend of yourn?"

"Yes," I said with a sigh.

"He's pretty ripe, ain't he!"

Nothing further was said for perhaps a couple of minutes, each being busy with his own thoughts; then Thompson said, in a low awed voice—

"Sometimes it's uncertain whether they're really gone or not—*seem* gone, you know—body warm, joints limber—and so, although you *think* they're gone, you don't really know. I've had cases in my car. It's perfectly awful, becuz *you* don't know what minute they'll rise up and look at you!" Then, after a pause, and slightly lifting his elbow toward the box,—"But *he* ain't in no trance! No, sir, I go bail for *him*!"

We sat some time, in meditative silence, listening to the wind and the roar of the train; then Thompson said, with a good deal of feeling:

"Well-a-well, we've all got to go, they ain't no getting around it. Man that is born of woman is of few days and far between, as Scriptur'[3] says. Yes, you look at it any way you want to, it's awful solemn and cur'us: they ain't *nobody* can get around it; *all's* got to go—just *everybody*, as you may say. One day you're hearty and strong"—here he scrambled to his feet and broke a pane and stretched his nose out at it a moment or two, then sat down again while I struggled up and thrust my nose out at the same place, and this we kept on doing every now and then—"and next day he's cut down like the grass, and the places which knowed him then knows him no more forever, as Scriptur' says. Yes'ndeedy, it's awful solemn and cur'us; but we've all got to go, one time or another; they ain't no getting around it."

There was another long pause; then—

"What did he die of?"

I said I didn't know.

"How long has he ben dead?"

It seemed <u>judicious</u> to enlarge the facts to fit the probabilities; so I said:

"Two or three days."

But it did no good: for Thompson received it with an injured look which plainly said. "Two or three *years*, you mean." Then he went right along, <u>placidly</u> ignoring my statement, and gave his views at considerable length upon the unwisdom of putting off burials too long. Then he lounged off toward the box, stood a moment, then came back on a

---

3. Scriptur' scripture; the Bible.

ominous (äm´ ə nəs) *adj.* threatening

Reading Strategy
Using Your Senses How does Twain rely on sound to set the mood for the following scene?

judicious (jōō dish´ əs) *adj.* showing good judgment

placidly (plas´ id lē) *adv.* calmly; quietly

**Reading Check**

What does the narrator say depressed his spirits?

sharp trot and visited the broken pane, observing:

"'Twould 'a' ben a durn sight better, all around, if they'd started him along last summer."

Thompson sat down and buried his face in his red silk handkerchief, and began to slowly sway and rock his body like one who is doing his best to endure the almost unendurable. By this time the fragrance—if you may call it fragrance—was just about suffocating, as near as you can come at it. Thompson's face was turning gray: I knew mine hadn't any color left in it. By and by Thompson rested his forehead in his left hand, with his elbow on his knee, and sort of waved his red handkerchief toward the box with his other hand, and said:

"I've carried a many a one of 'em—some of 'em considerable overdue, too—but, lordy, he just lays over 'em all!—and does it *easy*. Cap, they was heliotrope[4] to *him*!"

This recognition of my poor friend gratified me, in spite of the sad circumstances, because it had so much the sound of a compliment.

Pretty soon it was plain that something had got to be done. I suggested cigars. Thompson thought it was a good idea. He said:

"Likely it'll modify him some."

We puffed gingerly along for a while, and tried hard to imagine that things were improved. But it wasn't any use. Before very long, and without any consultation, both cigars were quietly dropped from our nerveless fingers at the same moment. Thompson said, with a sigh:

"No, Cap, it don't modify him worth a cent. Fact is, it makes him worse, becuz it appears to stir up his ambition. What do you reckon we better do, now?"

I was not able to suggest anything: indeed, I had to be swallowing and swallowing all the time, and did not like to trust myself to speak. Thompson fell to maundering,[5] in a <u>desultory</u> and low-spirited way, about the miserable experiences of this night: and he got to referring to my poor friend by various titles—sometimes military ones, sometimes civil ones; and I noticed that as fast as my poor friend's effectiveness grew, Thompson promoted him accordingly—gave him a bigger title. Finally he said:

"I've got an idea. Suppos'n' we buckle down to it and give the Colonel a bit of a shove toward t'other end of the car?—about ten foot, say. He wouldn't have so much influence, then, don't you reckon?"

I said it was a good scheme. So we took in a good fresh breath at the broken pane, calculating to hold it till we got through: then we went there and bent over that deadly cheese and took a grip on the box. Thompson nodded "All ready," and then we threw ourselves forward with all our might: but Thompson slipped, and slumped down with his nose on the cheese, and his breath got loose. He gagged and gasped, and floundered up and made a break for the door, pawing the air and saying hoarsely, "Don't hender me!—gimme the road! I'm a-dying;

---

4. **heliotrope** (hē´ lē ə trōp´) *n.* sweet-smelling plant.
5. **maundering** (môn´ dər iŋ) *v.* talking in an unconnected way.

gimme the road!" Out on the cold platform I sat down and held his head awhile, and he revived. Presently he said:

"Do you reckon we started the Gen'rul any?"

I said no: we hadn't budged him.

"Well, then, *that* idea's up the flume. We got to think up something else. He's suited wher' he is, I reckon; and if that's the way he feels about it, and has made up his mind that he don't wish to be disturbed, you bet he's a-going to have his own way in the business. Yes, better leave him right wher' he is, long as he wants it so; becuz he holds all the trumps, don't you know, and so it stands to reason that the man that lays out to alter his plans for him is going to get left."

But we couldn't stay out there in that mad storm; we should have frozen to death. So we went in again and shut the door, and began to suffer once more and take turns at the break in the window. By and by, as we were starting away from a station where we had stopped a moment Thompson pranced in cheerily, and exclaimed:

"We're all right, now! I reckon we've got the Commodore this time. I judge I've got the stuff here that'll take the tuck out of him."

It was carbolic acid. He had a carboy[6] of it. He sprinkled it all around everywhere; in fact he drenched everything with it, rifle-box, cheese and all. Then we sat down, feeling pretty hopeful. But it wasn't for long. You see the two perfumes began to mix, and then—well, pretty soon we made a break for the door; and out there Thompson swabbed his face with his bandanna and said in a kind of disheartened way:

"It ain't no use. We can't buck agin *him*. He just utilizes everything we put up to modify him with, and gives it his own flavor and plays it back on us. Why, Cap, don't you know, it's as much as a hundred times worse in there now than it was when he first got a-going. I never *did* see one of 'em warm up to his work so, and take such a dumnation interest in it. No, sir, I never did, as long as I've ben on the road: and I've carried a many a one of 'em, as I was telling you."

We went in again after we were frozen pretty stiff; but my, we couldn't stay in, now. So we just waltzed back and forth, freezing, and thawing, and stifling, by turns. In about an hour we stopped at another station; and as we left it Thompson came in with a bag, and said—

"Cap, I'm a-going to chance him once more—just this once; and if we don't fetch him this time, the thing for us to do, is to just throw up the sponge and withdraw from the canvass.[7] That's the way *I* put it up."

He had brought a lot of chicken feathers, and dried apples, and leaf tobacco, and rags, and old shoes, and sulphur, and asafetida,[8]

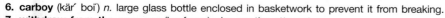

6. **carboy** (kär′ boi′) *n.* large glass bottle enclosed in basketwork to prevent it from breaking.
7. **withdraw from the canvass** (kan′ vəs) give up the attempt.
8. **asafetida** (as′ ə fet′ ə də) *n.* bad-smelling substance from certain plants, used as medicine.

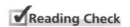

The Invalid's Story ◆ 601

and one thing or another: and he piled them on a breadth of sheet iron in the middle of the floor, and set fire to them.

When they got well started. I couldn't see, myself, how even the corpse could stand it. All that went before was just simply poetry to that smell—but mind you, the original smell stood up out of it just as sublime as ever—fact is, these other smells just seemed to give it a better hold: and my, how rich it was! I didn't make these reflections there—there wasn't time—made them on the platform. And breaking for the platform, Thompson got suffocated and fell: and before I got him dragged out, which I did by the collar, I was mighty near gone myself. When we revived, Thompson said dejectedly:

"We got to stay out here, Cap. We got to do it. They ain't no other way. The Governor wants to travel alone, and he's fixed so he can outvote us."

And presently he added:

"And don't you know, we're *pisoned*. It's our last trip, you can make up your mind to it. Typhoid fever is what's going to come of this. I feel it a-coming right now. Yes, sir, we're elected, just as sure as you're born."

We were taken from the platform an hour later, frozen and insensible, at the next station, and I went straight off into a virulent fever, and never knew anything again for three weeks. I found out, then, that I had spent that awful night with a harmless box of rifles and a lot of innocent cheese; but the news was too late to save me; imagination had done its work, and my health was permanently shattered; neither Bermuda nor any other land can ever bring it back to me. This is my last trip; I am on my way home to die.

Review and Assess

Thinking About the Selection

1. **Respond:** Did you find this story entertaining? Why or why not?

2. **(a) Recall:** What is the purpose of the narrator's journey?
   (b) Speculate: Would the story be as effective if it were not set on a train? Why or why not?

3. **(a) Recall:** What do the men believe is creating the awful smell?
   (b) Recall: What is actually creating the smell? **(c) Compare and Contrast:** How does the contrast between what they think is true and what is really true contribute to the humor?

4. **(a) Recall:** Find at least three places in the story where the narrator exaggerates details. **(b) Analyze:** How does the use of exaggeration contribute to the story's humor?

5. **Analyze:** How does Thompson's description of the corpse as deliberately trying to smell bad add to the story's humor?

6. **Extend:** Would this story make a good movie? Why or why not?

Mark Twain

(1835–1910)

Born Samuel Langhorne Clemens, this great American humorist grew up in the river town of Hannibal, Missouri. Even though Twain traveled and lived all over the United States, it is the great Mississippi River that courses through the heart of his life and work.

As a young man, Twain learned the trade of the riverboat pilot and took his name from a sounding cry used on steamboats on the Mississippi: 'By the mark—twain,' which means the water is two fathoms deep. Although Twain worked as a printer, prospector, reporter, editor, and lecturer, writing was his true calling. Some of his most popular works include *Tom Sawyer, The Adventures of Huckleberry Finn,* and *Life on the Mississippi.*

Review and Assess

Literary Analysis

Setting

1. (a) In "The Man to Send Rain Clouds," which aspects of the Native American culture affect the action, and how? (b) Why is the desert important to the action? Use a chart like the one below to analyze the story's **setting.**

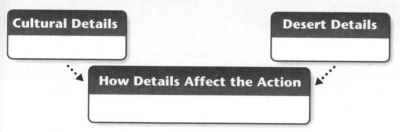

2. (a) In "The Invalid's Story," describe the physical environment in which the narrator and Thompson sit. (b) Which factors in this setting drive the action of the story?

Comparing Literary Works

3. (a) Compare both stories to evaluate how the setting influences the action in each. (b) In which story is the setting more critical to the action? Explain.

4. (a) Compare the details of the winter settings found in each story. (b) How would each story be affected if it were set during a different season? Explain.

Reading Strategy

Using Your Senses

5. In "The Man to Send Rain Clouds," to which two **senses** would you say Silko appeals the most? Support your answer.

6. "The Invalid's Story" is one of the few stories to play almost exclusively to the sense of smell. Find two images in the story that most vividly capture the smell of the cheese. Explain your choice.

Extend Understanding

7. **Cultural Connection:** Silko's story illustrates conflict between cultures. (a) Describe another situation in which two cultures have clashed. (b) What can be done to resolve such conflicts?

Integrate Language Skills

Vocabulary Development Lesson

Word Analysis: Latin Suffix -ous

Several words in "The Invalid's Story" end in -ous. The Latin suffix -ous generally means "full of" or "characterized by," as in *courageous*, meaning "full of courage." Add -ous to each word to form a new word. Then, define each new word.

1. melody   2. prestige   3. riot

Spelling Strategy

When adding a suffix to words ending in y preceded by a consonant, change the y to i unless the suffix itself starts with i. For example, *desultory + -ly = desultorily*. However, *try + -ing = trying*.

Write the new word formed by adding each suffix.

1. lonely + -est
2. unnecessary + -ly
3. fly + -ing

Concept Development: Synonyms

Choose the word that is closest in meaning to the first word.

1. deleterious: (a) delaying, (b) tasty, (c) harmful
2. cloister: (a) retreat, (b) group, (c) injury
3. judicious: (a) legal, (b) prudent, (c) rash
4. desultory: (a) kind, (b) evil, (c) random
5. placidly: (a) quietly, (b) coldly, (c) politely
6. pagans: (a) aliens, (b) villains, (c) non-believers
7. ominous: (a) threatening, (b) dishonest, (c) dark
8. prodigious: (a) inventive, (b) enormous, (c) joyous
9. perverse: (a) untidy, (b) improper, (c) clean

Grammar Lesson

Prepositional Phrase or Infinitive?

An **infinitive** is a verbal consisting of the word *to* and a verb. A **prepositional phrase**, however, consists of a preposition and a noun or pronoun, as well as any modifiers.

It is important not to confuse a prepositional phrase beginning with *to* with an infinitive. A prepositional phrase always ends with a noun or pronoun, while an infinitive always ends with a verb.

> **Examples: Infinitive:** He needed *to bring* the coffin on a train.
>
> **Prepositional Phrase:** Leon carried Teofilo *to the truck*.

Practice Copy each sentence in your notebook, circling each phrase beginning with *to*. Then, label each a *prepositional phrase* or an *infinitive*.

1. Neighbors came to embrace Teofilo's family.
2. They asked the priest to help them by sprinkling holy water.
3. He walked to the railway station.
4. Thompson reacted strongly to the smell.
5. The cheese was causing them to suffer.

Writing Application Write a short paragraph about your reaction to either story, including at least two infinitives and two prepositional phrases in your writing.

W̶G̶ Prentice Hall Writing and Grammar Connection: Chapter 21, Section 1

Writing Lesson

Letter From Father Paul

Imagine that you are Father Paul in "The Man to Send Rain Clouds." Write a letter to a friend addressing the cultural differences you have encountered and how you would like to deal with them.

Prewriting   Review the story. Jot down the ways Father Paul deals with the differences in the cultures. Then, note additional ways you think the two cultures can work together.

Drafting   In your opening paragraph, express the feelings of Father Paul. Next, explain the differences in the cultures from his point of view. Finally, explain the way he intends to work with the Native American culture in the future.

Model: Drafting a Strong Opening Sentence

I am very fortunate to be working in this community, but I feel a conflict within myself and I struggle to know the best way to handle our differences.

> Words like *fortunate* and *struggle* convey the varied feelings of Father Paul.

Revising   Reread your letter. Make sure that you have addressed and explained each of the ways you think the two cultures can work together.

Prentice Hall Writing and Grammar Connection: Chapter 11, Section 3

Extension Activities

Listening and Speaking Prepare a **monologue** in which Thompson from "The Invalid's Story" explains the experience on the train from his perspective.

- Review the story to gain a better understanding of Thompson.
- Use the tone of voice and gestures you think Thompson would use.
- Maintain a humorous tone.

Present your monologue to the class, and ask classmates if they agree with your interpretation of Thompson.

Research and Technology In a small group, prepare a **research report** about the Pueblo people. Use library resources, including the Internet and books about Native Americans, to gather information about their traditions and beliefs. In your report, explain which elements of Silko's story reflect the Pueblo culture best. **[Group Activity]**

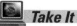 **Take It to the Net**   www.phschool.com

Go online for an additional research activity using the Internet.

Prepare to Read

The Necklace ◆ The Harvest

Campesino, 1976, Daniel DeSiga. Wright Art Gallery, University of California, Los Angeles

 Take It to the Net

Visit www.phschool.com
for interactive activities
and instruction related to
the selections, including
• background
• graphic organizers
• literary elements
• reading strategies

Preview

Connecting to the Literature

You may remember a time when a simple or surprising discovery made a strong impression on your life. Both of these stories capture the lasting impact of a character's discovery. Watch for the moment of discovery, and think about how it changes each character's world.

Background

Moving from place to place, harvesting and processing crops for low pay, migrant workers face many obstacles in the United States, such as difficulty in obtaining unemployment compensation, disability insurance, and sufficient education for their children. A former migrant worker himself, Tomás Rivera's concern is reflected in both "The Harvest" and his work as an educator.

Literary Analysis

Theme

The **theme** of a literary work is the insight about life that it communicates. Sometimes, the theme of a work is stated directly. More often, however, the theme is expressed indirectly through the experiences of the characters, through the events and the setting of the work, or through the use of devices such as irony or symbols. The following excerpt from "The Necklace" raises questions about the importance of money and attention:

> She had no dowry, no hopes, not the slightest chance of being appreciated, understood, loved, and married by a rich and distinguished man; so she slipped into marriage with a minor civil servant at the Ministry of Education.

As you read these stories, pay attention to insights into life that are indirectly expressed.

Comparing Literary Works

Although the cultures and settings presented in the following stories are very different, both stories include a moment of discovery that greatly affects a character's life and indirectly expresses each story's theme. Compare the moments of insight the characters experience in the following stories.

Reading Strategy

Drawing Conclusions

In determining a theme, you usually need to **draw conclusions** about characters and events. Follow these steps:

- Gather details about characters and events in the story.
- Make decisions about the underlying meaning of the details.

Using a chart like the one shown here, note details and draw conclusions about each character's actions. Then, decide how these actions might relate to each theme.

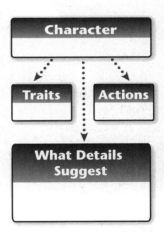

Vocabulary Development

déclassée (dā´ klä sā´) *French fem. adj.* lowered in social status (p. 609)

rueful (roo͞´ fəl) *adj.* feeling sorrow or regret (p. 609)

resplendent (ri splen´ dənt) *adj.* shining brightly (p. 611)

disheveled (di shev´ əld) *adj.* disarranged and untidy (p. 614)

profoundly (prō found´ lē) *adv.* deeply and intensely (p. 615)

harrowed (har´ ōd) *v.* broken up by a harrow, a frame with spikes drawn by a horse or tractor (p. 619)

astutely (ə stoot´ lē) *adv.* cleverly or cunningly (p. 619)

"What do you expect me to do with that?"

"Why, I thought you'd be pleased, dear. You never go out and this would be an occasion for you, a great one! I had a lot of trouble getting it. Everyone wants an invitation; they're in great demand and there are only a few reserved for the employees. All the officials will be there."

She looked at him, irritated, and said impatiently:

"I haven't a thing to wear. How could I go?"

It had never even occurred to him. He stammered:

"But what about the dress you wear to the theater? I think it's lovely. . . ."

He fell silent, amazed and bewildered to see that his wife was crying. Two big tears escaped from the corners of her eyes and rolled slowly toward the corners of her mouth. He mumbled:

"What is it? What is it?"

But, with great effort, she had overcome her misery; and now she answered him calmly, wiping her tear-damp cheeks:

"It's nothing. It's just that I have no evening dress and so I can't go to the party. Give the invitation to one of your colleagues whose wife will be better dressed than I would be."

He was overcome. He said:

"Listen, Mathilde [ma tēld´], how much would an evening dress cost—a suitable one that you could wear again on other occasions, something very simple?"

She thought for several seconds, making her calculations and at the same time estimating how much she could ask for without eliciting an immediate refusal and an exclamation of horror from this economical government clerk.

At last, not too sure of herself, she said:

"It's hard to say exactly but I think I could manage with four hundred francs."

He went a little pale, for that was exactly the amount he had put aside to buy a rifle so that he could go hunting the following summer near Nanterre, with a few friends who went shooting larks around there on Sundays.

However, he said:

"Well, all right, then. I'll give you four hundred francs. But try to get something really nice."

As the day of the ball drew closer, Madame Loisel seemed depressed, disturbed, worried—despite the fact that her dress was ready. One evening her husband said:

"What's the matter? You've really been very strange these last few days."

And she answered:

"I hate not having a single jewel, not one stone, to wear. I shall look so dowdy.[3] I'd almost rather not go to the party."

Reading Strategy
Drawing Conclusions
What conclusions can you draw about the feelings of Madame Loisel on the basis of her reaction to this invitation?

Literary Analysis
Theme Which details do you learn in these paragraphs that might suggest the story's ending and theme?

---

3. **dowdy** (dou´dē) *adj.* shabby.

He suggested:

"You can wear some fresh flowers. It's considered very chic[4] at this time of year. For ten francs you can get two or three beautiful roses."

That didn't satisfy her at all.

"No . . . there's nothing more humiliating than to look poverty-stricken among a lot of rich women."

Then her husband exclaimed:

"Wait—you silly thing! Why don't you go and see Madame Forestier [fôr əs tyā´] and ask her to lend you some jewelry. You certainly know her well enough for that, don't you think?"

She let out a joyful cry.

"You're right. It never occurred to me."

The next day she went to see her friend and related her tale of woe.

Madame Forestier went to her mirrored wardrobe, took out a big jewel case, brought it to Madame Loisel, opened it, and said:

"Take your pick, my dear."

Her eyes wandered from some bracelets to a pearl necklace, then to a gold Venetian cross set with stones, of very fine workmanship. She tried on the jewelry before the mirror, hesitating, unable to bring herself to take them off, to give them back. And she kept asking:

"Do you have anything else, by chance?"

"Why yes. Here, look for yourself. I don't know which ones you'll like."

All at once, in a box lined with black satin, she came upon a superb diamond necklace, and her heart started beating with overwhelming desire. Her hands trembled as she picked it up. She fastened it around her neck over her high-necked dress and stood there gazing at herself ecstatically.

Hesitantly, filled with terrible anguish, she asked:

"Could you lend me this one—just this and nothing else?"

"Yes, of course."

She threw her arms around her friend's neck, kissed her ardently, and fled with her treasure.

The day of the party arrived. Madame Loisel was a great success. She was the prettiest woman there—<u>resplendent</u>, graceful, beaming, and deliriously happy. All the men looked at her, asked who she was, tried to get themselves introduced to her. All the minister's aides wanted to waltz with her. The minister himself noticed her.

She danced enraptured—carried away, intoxicated with pleasure, forgetting everything in this triumph of her beauty and the glory of her success, floating in a cloud of happiness formed by all this homage, all this admiration, all the desires she had stirred up—by this victory so complete and so sweet to the heart of a woman.

When she left the party, it was almost four in the morning. Her husband had been sleeping since midnight in a small, deserted sitting room, with three other gentlemen whose wives were having a wonderful time.

---

4. **chic** (shēk) *adj.* fashionable.

Reading Strategy
Drawing Conclusions
What conclusions can you draw about Madame Loisel's feelings toward her husband?

resplendent (ri splen´ dənt) *adj.* shining brightly

Reading Check

Why does Madame Loisel visit Madame Forestier?

Madame Loisel came to know the awful life of the poverty-stricken. However, she resigned herself to it with unexpected fortitude. The crushing debt had to be paid. She would pay it. They dismissed the maid; they moved into an attic under the roof.

She came to know all the heavy household chores, the loathsome work of the kitchen. She washed the dishes, wearing down her pink nails on greasy casseroles and the bottoms of saucepans. She did the laundry, washing shirts and dishcloths which she hung on a line to dry; she took the garbage down to the street every morning, and carried water upstairs, stopping at every floor to get her breath. Dressed like a working-class woman, she went to the fruit store, the grocer, and the butcher with her basket on her arm, bargaining, outraged, contesting each sou[8] of her pitiful funds.

Every month some notes had to be honored and more time requested on others.

Her husband worked in the evenings, putting a shopkeeper's ledgers in order, and often at night as well, doing copying at twenty-five centimes a page.

And it went on like that for ten years.

After ten years, they had made good on everything, including the usurious rates and the compound interest.

Madame Loisel looked old now. She had become the sort of strong woman, hard and coarse, that one finds in poor families. <u>Disheveled</u>, her skirts askew, with reddened hands, she spoke in a loud voice, slopping water over the floors as she washed them. But sometimes, when her husband was at the office, she would sit down by the window and muse over that party long ago when she had been so beautiful, the belle of the ball.

How would things have turned out if she hadn't lost that necklace? Who could tell? How strange and fickle life is! How little it takes to make or break you!

Then one Sunday when she was strolling along the Champs Elysées[9] to forget the week's chores for a while, she suddenly caught sight of a woman taking a child for a walk. It was Madame Forestier, still young, still beautiful, still charming.

Madame Loisel started to tremble. Should she speak to her? Yes, certainly she should. And now that she had paid everything back, why shouldn't she tell her the whole story?

She went up to her.

"Hello, Jeanne."

The other didn't recognize her and was surprised that this plainly dressed woman should speak to her so familiarly. She murmured:

"But . . . madame! . . . I'm sure . . . You must be mistaken."

"No, I'm not. I am Mathilde Loisel."

Literary Analysis
Theme What insight into hardship does this description of Madame Loisel suggest?

disheveled (di shev´ əld) *adj.* disarranged and untidy

Her friend gave a little cry.

"Oh! Oh, my poor Mathilde, how you've changed!"

"Yes, I've been through some pretty hard times since I last saw you and I've had plenty of trouble—and all because of you!"

"Because of me? What do you mean?"

"You remember the diamond necklace you lent me to wear to the party at the Ministry?"

"Yes. What about it?"

"Well, I lost it."

"What are you talking about? You returned it to me."

"What I gave back to you was another one just like it. And it took us ten years to pay for it. You can imagine it wasn't easy for us, since we were quite poor. . . . Anyway, I'm glad it's over and done with."

Madame Forestier stopped short.

"You say you bought a diamond necklace to replace that other one?"

"Yes. You didn't even notice then? They really were exactly alike."

And she smiled, full of a proud, simple joy.

Madame Forestier, profoundly moved, took Mathilde's hands in her own.

"Oh, my poor, poor Mathilde! Mine was false. It was worth five hundred francs at the most!"

profoundly (prō found′ lē) *adv.* deeply and intensely

Review and Assess

Thinking About the Selection

1. **Respond:** Do you feel sorry for Mathilde? Why or why not?

2. **(a) Recall:** As the story begins, why is Madame Loisel so unhappy with her life? **(b) Infer:** Do you think the author wants readers to sympathize with her unhappiness at this time? Why or why not?

3. **(a) Recall:** How does Madame Loisel's husband respond to her disappointment over the invitation? **(b) Compare and Contrast:** How is Madame Loisel different from her husband?

4. **(a) Recall:** Why is Madame Loisel so happy when her husband suggests that she go to see her wealthy friend, Madame Forestier? **(b) Interpret:** What symbolic meaning does the necklace have for Madame Loisel when she wears it?

5. **(a) Recall:** How does Madame Loisel change over the ten years she works to pay off the cost of the necklace? **(b) Analyze:** What actually causes her to change?

6. **Interpret:** How is the ending of the story ironic or surprising?

7. **Speculate:** Do you think people who value material possessions too much are likely to face hardship in life? Why or why not?

Guy de Maupassant

(1850–1893)

Perhaps the best-known short-story writer in the world, Guy de Maupassant is known for his realistic stories that capture the surprising twists and turns of life. Maupassant was raised in northern France. As a young man, he served in the Franco-Prussian War, gathering experiences that would later appear in some of his stories. Later, he became a government clerk and devoted his spare time to writing. Eventually, Maupassant became the literary apprentice of well-known writer Gustave Flaubert, who introduced him to other illustrious writers of the day.

Despite the wealth he accumulated, Maupassant's later years were shadowed by ill health and depression.

Campesino, 1976, Daniel DeSiga, Wright Art Gallery, University of California, Los Angeles

The Harvest

Tomás Rivera

The end of September and the beginning of October. That was the best time of the year. First, because it was a sign that the work was coming to an end and that the return to Texas would start. Also, because there was something in the air that the folks created, an aura of peace and death. The earth also shared that feeling. The cold came more frequently, the frosts that killed by night, in the morning covered the earth in whiteness. It seemed that all was coming to an end. The folks felt that all was coming to rest. Everyone took to thinking more. And they talked more about the trip back to Texas, about the harvests, if it had gone well or bad for them, if they would return or not to the same place next year. Some began to take long walks around the grove. It seemed like in these last days of work there was a wake over the earth. It made you think.

Literary Analysis
Theme What insights about life might be provided in this paragraph?

That's why it wasn't very surprising to see Don Trine take a walk by himself through the grove and to walk along the fields every afternoon. This was at the beginning, but when some youngsters asked him if they could tag along, he even got angry. He told them he didn't want anybody sticking behind him.

"Why would he want to be all by hisself, anyway?"

"To heck with him: it's his business."

"But, you notice, it never fails. Every time, why, sometimes I don't even think he eats supper, he takes his walk. Don't you think that's a bit strange?"

"Well, I reckon. But you saw how he got real mad when we told him we'd go along with him. It wasn't anything to make a fuss over. This ain't his land. We can go wherever we take a liking to. He can't tell us what to do."

"That's why I wonder, why'd he want to walk by hisself?"

And that's how all the rumors about Don Trine's walks got started. The folks couldn't figure out why or what he got out of taking off by himself every afternoon. When he would leave, and somebody would spy on him, somehow or other he would catch on, then take a little walk, turn around and head right back to his chicken coop. The fact of the matter is that everybody began to say he was hiding the money he had earned that year or that he had found some buried treasure and every day, little by little, he was bringing it back to his coop. Then they began to say that when he was young he had run around with a gang in Mexico and that he always carried around a lot of money with him. They said, too, that even if it was real hot, he carried a belt full of money beneath his undershirt. Practically all the speculation centered on the idea that he had money.

◀ **Critical Viewing** What does this painting suggest about the lives of the migrant workers in this story? **[Infer]**

Reading Check

What does everyone see Don Trine do every afternoon?

"Let's see, who's he got to take care of? He's an old bachelor. He ain't never married or had a family. So, with him working so many years . . . Don't you think he's bound to have money? And then, what's that man spend his money on? The only thing he buys is his bit of food every Saturday. Once in a while, a beer, but that's all."

"Yeah, he's gotta have a pile of money, for sure. But, you think he's going to bury it around here?"

"Who said he's burying anything? Look, he always goes for his food on Saturday. Let's check close where he goes this week, and on Saturday, when he's on his errand, we'll see what he's hiding. Whadda you say?"

"Good'nuff. Let's hope he doesn't catch on to us."

▼ **Critical Viewing**
Does this image capture the setting of the story as you imagine it? Why or why not? **[Evaluate]**

Farmworker de Califas, Tony Ortega, Courtesy of the artist

That week the youngsters closely watched Don Trine's walks. They noticed that he would disappear into the grove, then come out on the north side, cross the road then cross the field until he got to the irrigation ditch. There he dropped from sight for a while, then he reappeared in the west field. It was there where he would disappear and linger the most. They noticed also that, so as to throw people off his track, he would take a different route, but he always spent more time around the ditch that crossed the west field. They decided to investigate the ditch and that field the following Saturday.

When that day arrived, the boys were filled with anticipation. The truck had scarcely left and they were on their way to the west field. The truck had not yet disappeared and they had already crossed the grove. What they found they almost expected. There was nothing in the ditch, but in the field that had been <u>harrowed</u> after pulling the potatoes they found a number of holes.

"You notice all the holes here? The harrow didn't make these. Look, here's some foot prints, and notice that the holes are at least a foot deep. You can stick your arm in them up to your elbow. No animal makes these kind of holes. Whadda you think?"
"Well, it's bound to be Don Trine. But, what's he hiding? Why's he making so many holes? You think the landowner knows what he's up to?"
"Naw, man. Why, look, you can't see them from the road. You gotta come in a ways to notice they're here. What's he making them for? What's he using them for? And, look, they're all about the same width. Whadda you think?"
"Well, you got me. Maybe we'll know if we hide in the ditch and see what he does when he comes here."
"Look, here's a coffee can. I bet you this is what he digs with."
"I think you're right."

The boys had to wait until late the following Monday to discover the reason for the holes. But the word had spread around so that everybody already knew that Don Trine had a bunch of holes in that field. They tried not to let on but the allusions they made to the holes while they were out in the fields during the day were very obvious. Everybody thought there had to be a big explanation. So, the youngsters spied more carefully and <u>astutely</u>.

That afternoon they managed to fool Don Trine and saw what he was doing. They saw, and as they had suspected, Don Trine used the coffee can to dig a hole. Every so often, he would measure with his arm the depth of the hole. When it went up to his elbow, he stuck in his left arm, then filled dirt in around it with his right hand, all the way up to the elbow. Then he stayed like that for some time. He seemed very satisfied and even tried to light a cigarette with one hand. Not being able to, he just let it hang from his lips. Then he dug another hole and repeated the process. The boys could not understand why

Reading Strategy
Drawing Conclusions
What conclusion would you draw about Don Trine from his mysterious behavior?

harrowed (har´ ōd) v. broken up by a harrow, a frame with spikes drawn by a horse or tractor

Reading Strategy
Drawing Conclusions
What conclusion can you draw, so far, about Don Trine based on his actions?

astutely (ə stoōt´ lē) adv. cleverly or cunningly

✔**Reading Check**

What do the youngsters witness Don Trine doing with the dirt?

he did this. That was what puzzled them the most. They had believed that, with finding out what it was he did, they would understand everything. But it didn't turn out that way at all. The boys brought the news to the rest of the folks in the grove and nobody there understood either. In reality, when they found out that the holes didn't have anything to do with money, they thought Don Trine was crazy and even lost interest in the whole matter. But not everybody.

The next day one of the boys who discovered what Don Trine had been up to went by himself to a field. There he went through the same procedure that he had witnessed the day before. What he experienced and what he never forgot was feeling the earth move, feeling the earth grasp his fingers and even caressing them. He also felt the warmth of the earth. He sensed he was inside someone. Then he understood what Don Trine was doing. He was not crazy, he simply liked to feel the earth when it was sleeping.

That's why the boy kept going to the field every afternoon, until one night a hard freeze came on so that he could no longer dig any holes in the ground. The earth was fast asleep. Then he thought of next year, in October at harvest time, when once again he could repeat what Don Trine did. It was like when someone died. You always blamed yourself for not loving him more before he died.

Tomás Rivera

(1935–1984)

Born in Crystal City, Texas, Tomás Rivera soon joined what he called the "migrant labor stream" that traveled throughout the farmlands of the United States. Faced with the challenge of alternating schooling with work in the fields, Rivera pursued his education tirelessly. His persistence paid off, as he eventually earned a Ph.D. in Spanish Literature.

Rivera's concern for the education of minorities led him to a career as an educator, limiting the time he could devote to his writing. Nevertheless, he has become one of the most renowned Mexican American authors in the United States. His work most often focuses on the experiences of migrant farm workers.

Review and Assess

Thinking About the Selection

1. **Respond:** What do you think of Don Trine at the end of the story? Why?

2. **(a) Recall:** At what time of year does this story take place? **(b) Apply:** How does the opening paragraph foreshadow, or hint at, the ending of the story?

3. **(a) Recall:** What do the boys think Don Trine is doing every afternoon? **(b) Infer:** What do the boys' speculations about Don Trine reveal about them?

4. **(a) Recall:** When the one boy goes into the field later, what does he learn about Don Trine? **(b) Recall:** What does he realize when he imitates Don Trine's actions? **(c) Infer:** What does this ability to understand Don Trine suggest about the boy?

5. **(a) Extend:** Don Trine finds a way to make a connection with nature. In what other ways do people connect with nature? **(b) Speculate:** Do you think most people would benefit from taking time to appreciate nature? Why or why not?

Review and Assess

Literary Analysis

Theme

1. Toward the end of "The Necklace," Madame Loisel thinks, "How strange and fickle life is! How little it takes to make or break you!" What does this statement suggest about the complexity of life?

2. Considering the course of events for Madame Loisel, what would you say is the **theme** of "The Necklace"? Explain.

3. Using a chart like the one below, analyze the last two paragraphs of "The Harvest" and explain the theme of the story.

Words From the Text	Insights
Theme:	

Comparing Literary Works

4. (a) Summarize the moment of insight for Madame Loisel in "The Necklace" and for the boy at the end of the "The Harvest."
   (b) Using a Venn diagram like the one below, explain how their discoveries are similar and different.

5. Who do you think will be affected more by their insight? Explain.

Reading Strategy

Drawing Conclusions

6. Madame Loisel places a high value on material goods. On the basis of the story, what **conclusion** can you draw about such values?

7. Based on the ending of "The Harvest," what conclusion can you draw about the importance of nature to the human spirit?

Extend Understanding

8. **Cultural Connection:** (a) What does "The Necklace" show you about life in middle-class French society in the late nineteenth century? (b) Do you think there are parallels in modern American society? Explain.

Quick Review

The **theme** of a literary work is the insight about life that it communicates.

To **draw conclusions**, gather details and make decisions about the underlying meaning of these details.

 Take It to the Net
www.phschool.com
Take the interactive self-test online to check your understanding of the selections.

Writing WORKSHOP

Narration: Short Story

A **short story** is a work of fiction that combines plot, setting, and characters to present a brief narrative. In this workshop, you will write and revise a short story.

Assignment Criteria. Your short story should have the following characteristics:

- A main character who takes part in the action
- Details that describe a particular time and place
- A conflict, or problem, to be introduced, developed, and resolved
- A succession of events that make up the plot, incorporating changes in time and mood
- A central theme or generalization about life

To preview the criteria on which your short story may be assessed, see the Rubric on page 627.

Prewriting

Choose a topic. Use **sentence starters** to spark your creativity when brainstorming for a topic. Use one sentence starter to write freely for five minutes without worrying about grammar or sentence structure. Draw from your memories or imagination to develop interesting situations. Then, circle intriguing conflicts or themes and choose one to build into a story. Consider these sentence starters or make up your own:

- *What would happen if . . .*
- *One person I will never forget is . . .*

Based on your work, choose an idea as the basis for a story.

Summarize the plot. Briefly describe the incidents that make up the plot of your story. If you need more than a few sentences to do this, you may be trying to do too much in your writing.

Develop characters. Bring the characters and conflict of your story to life by providing enough detail for readers to imagine the world you create. Establish details about each of your characters to incorporate into your draft later.

Character	Details
Grandfather Clock	• Lonely, because everyone grows up and moves away • Wants to be loved and cared for • Is winding down from lack of human care

Student Model

Before you begin drafting your short story, read this abridged student model and its side notes. The full text of the story can be found at www.phschool.com

Katie Hartwell
Newberry, Florida

The main character in this first-person story is the grandfather clock.

Grandfather Clock

Tick, tock, tick, tock. I'm sitting here, watching the moments of my existence pass slowly away. My house has been empty for such a long time, and I'm lonely and forgotten. As I sit here, by myself, all that I can do is look back and reminisce. I could tell you stories that only walls would know. But walls can't speak.

In the opening paragraph, the author describes setting and mood.

I came to this place many years ago, tugged along behind an old man. . . . Sadly, he was with me for only three short years before he passed on. . . .

For a time, I was left alone, while people came and looked at the house. . . . Then, one day a nice couple moved in with a young son. From the beginning, their son Danny was fascinated by me, and I was completely taken with him. He always looked as if he loved the stories I told, most of which began with, "Back in my day . . ." and "When I was younger. . . ." I sometimes thought that he didn't really understand what I was saying, but it felt good to be loved. . . . When Danny went off to college, I was crushed. Soon afterward, his parents sold the house. . . .

The mood changes as time passes and new events occur.

New owners came and went. Then, one day I heard a new family was moving into the house. You can't even imagine my surprise when, out of the blue, Danny walked through the front door. He had a wife and kids now. I was so overjoyed when I saw him that I put all my energy into my daily activities. . . . I spent the next twenty years watching Danny's kids grow up, with a mixture of pride and anxiety about what would happen next.

The kids finally grew up and Danny sold the house. That was about five years ago. . . . Some of the local kids have started the rumor that the house is haunted—and, in a fashion, it is. It is haunted by the memories of all the people who have lived in it. Every second has left its mark on me. I have been counting them down and they are almost up for me. . . . I hope that someday somebody will remember me, and come to wind me again. Maybe then I'll get a new home and a chance for a whole new set of memories.

The author restates the problem and central theme in the closing lines of the story.

Drafting

Organize details. As you draft your short story, check that you have included the following story components:

- **Characters**—actors in the story with unique characteristics, attitudes, and relationships to one another
- **Setting**—the specific time and place of the action of your story
- **Conflict**—a struggle between opposing forces or characters
- **Action**—specific events in the plot that show how the conflict intensifies and how it is resolved

Elaborate. If you find yourself writing sentences that tell readers what you want them to think, challenge yourself to be a better storyteller. Provide details that will make the writing speak for itself. Follow up "telling" sentences with "showing" ones. Use the chart at right as a guide for drafting more revealing sentences.

Elaborate: Show, Don't Tell

Telling	Showing
Danny seemed to like me.	He would spend hours in front of me, staring up at my face, and raptly listening to everything I said. When I spoke, the little boy would stare up at me, smiling.

Revising

Revise to emphasize changes in mood. The power of a story depends on its ability to appeal to a reader's emotions. One dramatic technique that writers use is an abrupt shift in mood to keep the reader emotionally involved. Review your story and note instances where events occur that would fit naturally with a change in mood. Then, add descriptions to show how the characters might react emotionally to the new event.

Model: Stressing a Change in Mood

For a time I was left alone, while people came and looked at

I lost hope that the house would ever be occupied again.

the house. ⋀Then, one day a nice couple moved in with a

Naturally, I was ecstatic.

young son. ⋀From the beginning, their son Danny was

fascinated by me, and I was completely taken with him.

> Katie adds description and insight to show the clock's shifting emotions.

Revise to use the active voice. In sentences whose verbs take the active voice, the subject performs the action of a sentence. To create dynamic sentences in which characters are acting instead of being acted upon, choose the active voice instead of the passive voice. In the following example, the active voice makes the writing stronger.

Passive Voice: The bus was caught by Daniel.

Active Voice: Daniel caught the bus.

Compare the model and the nonmodel. Why is the model more effective than the nonmodel?

Nonmodel	Model
I hope that someday I will be remembered by somebody and that I will be wound again.	I hope that someday someone will remember me, and come to wind me again.

Publishing and Presenting

When you are satisfied with your short story, share your writing with a wider audience.

Deliver an oral presentation. Read your short story aloud to your classmates. As you read passages with dialogue, alter your voice to convey the different personalities of your characters. Ask for feedback from your classmates and consider revisions based on their comments. Then, compile your work with that of your classmates to publish an anthology or collection of your short stories in book form.

 Speaking Connection

To learn more about analyzing presentations, see the **Listening and Speaking Workshop,** p. 628.

 Prentice Hall Writing and Grammar Connection: Chapter 5

Rubric for Self-Assessment

Evaluate your short story using the following criteria and rating scale:

| Criteria | Rating Scale |
	Not very				Very
How well do you establish your setting?	1	2	3	4	5
Is the main character well developed?	1	2	3	4	5
How well do you develop, introduce, and resolve your central conflict?	1	2	3	4	5
How well developed is your plot?	1	2	3	4	5
How effectively does the story convey a theme or generalization about life?	1	2	3	4	5

Listening and Speaking WORKSHOP

Analyzing a Media Presentation

People enjoy watching a movie review and then agreeing—or vehemently disagreeing—with the critic's opinions. In order to explain your own reaction to a movie or television show, it is useful to know how to **analyze a media presentation.** As with any type of analysis, interpreting involves breaking different elements of a program apart and examining them.

Analyze the Media Presentation

Establish categories. Since they cannot address every aspect of a production, critics use established categories to analyze and evaluate media presentations.

- For *fiction,* including movies and television programs, critics use categories such as plot, setting, dialogue, and believability.
- For *nonfiction,* including news programs, documentaries, and infomercials, critics use categories such as clarity of presentation, credibility of sources, and appropriateness of special effects.

Note your responses. As you watch the presentation, use a chart like the one shown to record your impressions. For each category, make brief notes about aspects that struck you favorably or unfavorably. Compare the presentation to movies or shows you have seen in the past.

Evaluate the Media Presentation

When you have finished viewing, review your notes to find a central idea.

Indicate strengths and weaknesses. Describe your overall impression of the media presentation, and then assess the movie's individual aspects. You can do this by assigning numerical ratings or by choosing adjectives to convey your impressions of various aspects of the program—for example, identify a *weak* plot, *shallow* characters, *clever* dialogue, *brilliant* special effects, or *inventive* camera work.

Cite examples to support your view. Since others may not share your opinion, use your analysis as an opportunity for persuasion. Cite examples from the movie or show to justify your opinions. For example, if you criticized the dialogue as unrealistic, you might cite a ridiculous conversation between two characters to support this view.

Rating a Media Presentation

	Category	Opinion	Evidence
FICTION	Plot		
	Setting		
	Dialogue		
	Realistic Portrayal		
NONFICTION	Clarity of Presentation		
	Credibility of Sources		
	Organization		
	Added Effects		

(Activity: Analysis and Discussion) In a small group, watch a movie, a news report, or another type of media presentation. Using the chart shown, analyze the program. Share your reviews with the other members of the group to discuss differences in opinion.

Assessment WORKSHOP

Author's Point of View

The reading sections of some tests require you to read a passage and answer multiple-choice questions about the author's point of view. Use these strategies to help you answer test questions about the author's point of view:

- Look for language to help you understand the author's perspective or thoughts on a subject.
- Use the author's tone and choice of details as clues to his or her point of view.
- Remember that the author's point of view is often implied, not directly stated.

Test-Taking Strategies

- Look for strong language that seems calculated to sway readers' emotions. Then, infer the author's approval or disapproval.
- Examine the opening and closing statements carefully as an indication of an author's attitude.

Sample Test Item

Directions: Read the passage, and then answer the question that follows.

Jane Addams founded a settlement house in Chicago, Illinois, in 1889. Hull House offered hot lunches, child care, and tutoring in English and other subjects. Most important, Hull House developed a neighborhood spirit among recent immigrants. Addams said that she was just "a simple person," but her ideas and actions had far-reaching consequences.

1. The author views Jane Addams with _____?_____.
   A suspicion
   B affection
   C admiration
   D fear

Answer and Explanation

The correct answer is *C*. The author selects facts that highlight Addams's positive qualities. The passage mentions no negative characteristics, which might justify *A* or *D*. The author does not discuss Addams in an openly personal way, so *B* is not the best answer.

▷ Practice

Directions: Read the passage, and then answer the question that follows.

Jonah Hart, a student, was in-line skating when he fell and hit his head. He was unconscious for several days. Jonah probably would have walked away with only scrapes and bruises if he had been wearing a helmet. The National Safe Kids Campaign says that wearing helmets lowers the risk of head injury by 85 percent. Kids should always wear helmets when they skate. A helmet could save your life!

1. The author's point of view is that _____?_____.
   A helmets are not expensive
   B everyone should join the National Safe Kids Campaign
   C Jonah Hart could have avoided injury if he had been a better skater
   D kids risk injury if they skate without helmets

Mural on PAL center depicts the diverse community in Santa Monica, CA

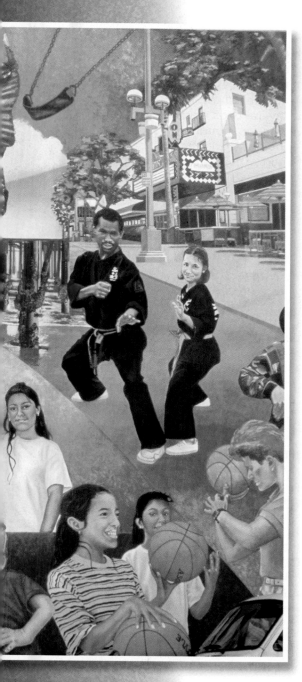

Exploring the Genre

If fiction takes you on imaginative flights of fancy, nonfiction grounds you in reality. This does not make nonfiction any less fascinating or diverse. When you want to encounter real people with interesting experiences, learn a new skill, or read viewpoints on a controversial issue, you can turn to nonfiction.

The nonfiction in this unit falls into several categories:

- An **autobiography** is the writer's own story, describing notable events of his or her life.

- A **biography** is the story of a life from another person's perspective.

- An **essay** is a short nonfiction work that addresses a specific subject. A **reflective essay** shares the writer's inner thoughts and feelings. A **narrative essay** tells a story about an actual event or person. An **expository essay** explains certain aspects of a subject. A **persuasive essay** attempts to convince the reader to think or act in a certain way.

- A **speech** is a talk or an address presented to an audience.

▲ **Critical Viewing** Which nonfiction subjects could this image effectively illustrate? **[Hypothesize]**

Why Read Literature?

Whenever you read nonfiction, you have a purpose, or reason. You might be curious about a topic or fascinated by an author's memory of an important event. Preview three purposes you might set before reading works in this unit.

1 Read for the Love of Literature

Even your longest-held opinions can change, if you keep an open mind. As a child, Lorraine Hansberry strongly disliked summer. Learn how her initial feelings turned into an enthusiastic embrace of the season in her eloquent essay **"On Summer,"** page 656.

Powerful literature can make unlikely heroes out of ordinary people. Some people might not think twice about an old woman walking in the snow, bent under the weight of several bags of laundry. For Isaac Bachevis Singer, though, this woman presents an opportunity to memorialize a personal hero in **"The Washwoman,"** page 650.

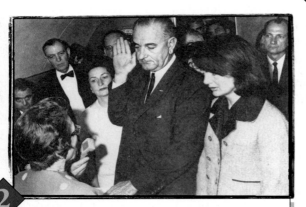

2 Read for Information

Lady Bird Johnson became First Lady as a result of one of the most traumatic episodes in American history: the assassination of President John F. Kennedy in 1963. Observe Johnson's impressions as momentous events swirled around her when you read **from *A White House Diary*,** page 674.

Not many people have viewed Earth from a vantage point two hundred miles away. Discover the complex answer to the question "What was it like?" when you read astronaut Sally Ride's essay **"Single Room, Earth View,"** page 636.

3 Read to Be Inspired

After you read Steve Gietschier's enthusiastic book review **"In These Girls, Hope Is a Muscle,"** page 715, you just might be tempted to pick up the book, which traces the emotional highs and lows of a women's high school basketball team.

In a sport known for emotional behavior, tennis champion Arthur Ashe never lost his cool. Yet, when others expected such a cool player to play cautiously, he attacked the ball with a fierce intensity. Learn more about this remarkable athlete in John McPhee's essay **"Arthur Ashe Remembered,"** page 682.

 Take It to the Net

Visit the Web site for online instruction and activities related to each selection in this unit.
www.phschool.com

How to Read Literature

Use Strategies for Reading Nonfiction

Although works of nonfiction vary in topic, type, and purpose, they all share one common characteristic: They all claim to be true. This does not mean that you should accept everything an author writes without question. Use these strategies to help you judge the facts and form your own opinions.

1. Identify the author's attitude.

To identify an author's attitude, examine the selection of language and evidence presented in the text.

- If the text includes language with strong positive or negative connotations, this can provide you with valuable clues to the author's attitude.
- When an author uses neutral language, he or she may wish to be perceived as even-handed and objective.
- If the author highlights certain facts or details and omits others, note it as possible evidence of personal bias.

2. Find the writer's main points and support.

Taking apart a writer's argument for analysis is the first step to forming your own opinion on the subject. Use the model at right to guide you.

- To determine the main points of a selection, ask yourself what the author wants you to learn or think as a result of reading the text.
- Summarize the ideas of individual paragraphs or chapters to determine how an author is supporting the main points.

Finding Main Points and Support:

"Arthur Ashe Remembered"

Ashe was a great tennis player.
- Maintained control, even in tight spots
- Played with energy, grace, and power
- Willing to take risks to win games

Ashe was difficult to read.
- Didn't react emotionally, kept cool
- Would attempt unpredictable shots

3. Vary your reading rate.

- To find specific information, skim the text quickly, looking for key words and phrases.
- To absorb a complex argument or appreciate descriptive passages, slow your reading pace.

4. Use visuals as a key to meaning.

Nonfiction authors frequently use drawings, charts, and graphs to supplement their written text. To get the most out of visuals, first summarize the main point that the visual attempts to convey. Then, determine how the illustration, chart, or graph complements the main points that the author is trying to make.

As you read the selections in this unit, review the reading strategies and apply them to interact with the text.

Prepare to Read

Single Room, Earth View

Take It to the Net

Visit www.phschool.com for interactive activities and instruction related to "Single Room, Earth View," including
- background
- graphic organizers
- literary elements
- reading strategies

Preview

Connecting to the Literature

At street level, a city can be a confusing place. When you look at that city from a high floor of a tall building, however, its layout becomes apparent. In this essay, you will see what it is like to look down on Earth, as the astronaut Sally Ride describes her view from space.

Background

On June 18, 1983, when she soared aloft as flight engineer and mission specialist aboard the shuttle *Challenger*—the same shuttle that would explode shortly after liftoff three years later—Sally Ride became the first American woman in space. Her historic mission allowed her to experience what she recounts in "Single Room, Earth View."

Literary Analysis

Observation

An **observation** describes an event that a writer witnessed firsthand. It includes many details and uses vivid, precise words to re-create the event for readers. In this example, the vivid details are set in italics:

> We could see the Ganges River dumping *its murky, sediment-laden water* into the Indian Ocean and watch *ominous hurricane clouds expanding and rising like biscuits in the oven* . . .

As you read, notice Ride's clear, expressive observations of Earth.

Connecting Literary Elements

To enhance a written observation, writers use **description**—a portrait in words of a person, place, or object. Descriptive writing uses sensory details that appeal to sight, hearing, taste, smell, and touch. A writer may also use figurative language to draw unique and surprising comparisons that bring a subject's key qualities into focus. Notice how Sally Ride uses a variety of techniques to vividly describe her view of Earth.

Reading Strategy

Varying Your Reading Rate

When you **vary your reading rate,** you adjust your reading speed to suit your purpose.

- Read quickly if you are scanning for a particular piece of information or just want the overall idea of a nonfiction work.
- Read slowly and carefully when seeking to understand more details or more complex information.

Use a chart like this one to record changes in your reading rate.

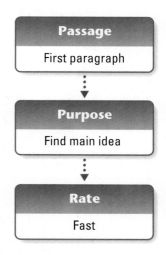

Vocabulary Development

articulate (är tik′ yoo lit) *adj.* expressing oneself clearly and easily (p. 637)

surreal (sər rē′ əl) *adj.* strange (p. 637)

ominous (äm′ ə nəs) *adj.* threatening (p. 637)

novice (näv′ is) *adj.* beginner (p. 637)

muted (myoot′ əd) *adj.* weaker; less intense (p. 638)

eddies (ed′ ēz) *n.* circular currents (p. 639)

subtle (sut′ 'l) *adj.* not obvious (p. 639)

eerie (ir′ ē) *adj.* mysterious (p. 639)

diffused (di fyoozd′) *v.* spread out (p. 640)

extrapolating (ek strap′ ə lāt′ iŋ) *v.* arriving at a conclusion by making inferences based on known facts (p. 640)

rifts and seas. I also became an instant believer in plate tectonics;[*] India really *is* crashing into Asia, and Saudi Arabia
and Egypt really *are* pulling apart, making the Red Sea
wider. Even though their respective motion is really no
more than mere inches a year, the view from overhead
makes theory come alive.

Spectacular as the view is from 200 miles up, the Earth
is not the awe-inspiring "blue marble" made famous by the
photos from the moon. From space shuttle height, we can't
see the entire globe at a glance, but we can look down the
entire boot of Italy, or up the East Coast of the United
States from Cape Hatteras to Cape Cod. The panoramic
view inspires an appreciation for the scale of some of
nature's phenomena. One day, as I scanned the sandy
expanse of Northern Africa, I couldn't find any of the familiar landmarks—colorful outcroppings of rock in Chad, irrigated patches of the Sahara. Then I realized they were
obscured by a huge dust storm, a cloud of sand that
enveloped the continent from Morocco to the Sudan.

Since the space shuttle flies fairly low (at least by orbital
standards; it's more than 22,000 miles lower than a typical TV
satellite), we can make out both natural and manmade features in
surprising detail. Familiar geographical features like San Francisco
Bay, Long Island, and Lake Michigan are easy to recognize, as are
many cities, bridges, and airports. The Great Wall of China is *not* the
only man-made object visible from space.

The signatures of civilization are usually seen in straight lines
(bridges or runways) or sharp delineations (abrupt transitions from
desert to irrigated land, as in California's Imperial Valley). A modern
city like New York doesn't leap from the canvas of its surroundings,
but its straight piers and concrete runways catch the eye—and
around them, the city materializes. I found Salina, Kansas (and
pleased my in-laws, who live there) by spotting its long runway amid
the wheat fields near the city. Over Florida, I could see the launch
pad where we had begun our trip, and the landing strip, where we
would eventually land.

Some of civilization's more unfortunate effects on the environment
are also evident from orbit. Oil slicks glisten on the surface of the
Persian Gulf, patches of pollution-damaged trees dot the forests of
central Europe. Some cities look out of focus, and their colors <u>muted</u>,
when viewed through a pollutant haze. Not surprisingly, the effects
are more noticeable now than they were a decade ago. An astronaut
who has flown in both Skylab and the space shuttle reported that the
horizon didn't seem quite as sharp, or the colors quite as bright, in
1983 as they had in 1973.

Of course, informal observations by individual astronauts are one
thing, but more precise measurements are continually being made
from space: The space shuttle has carried infrared film to document

*L*iterature
in context Science Connection

♦ Plate Tectonics

In the 1960s, scientists proposed a
theory that Earth's outer shell consists
of a number of rigid segments, or
"plates." The shell, called the litho-
sphere, is about 45 to 95 miles thick
and seems to be in constant motion.
The plates slowly slide on a soft, flexible layer of rock and move from 0.5 to
4 inches a year.

If one plate pushes against another,
the collision can form mountains. Major
earthquakes occur when two plates
slide past each other. Not all scientists,
however, are as convinced as Sally Ride
was, circling the planet 22 miles up,
that the plate tectonic theory is valid.

Reading Strategy
**Varying Your Reading
Rate** How quickly would
you read this paragraph if
you wanted to learn about
effects on the environ-
ment viewed from space?

muted (myōot′ əd) *adj.*
weaker; less intense

damage to citrus trees in Florida and in rain forests along the Amazon. It has carried even more sophisticated sensors in the payload bay. Here is one example: sensors used to measure atmospheric carbon monoxide levels, allowing scientists to study the environmental effects of city emissions and land-clearing fires.

Most of the Earth's surface is covered with water, and at first glance it all looks the same: blue. But with the right lighting conditions and a couple of orbits of practice, it's possible to make out the intricate patterns in the oceans—<u>eddies</u> and spirals become visible because of the <u>subtle</u> differences in water color or reflectivity.

eddies (ed´ ēz) *n.* circular currents

subtle (sut´ 'l) *adj.* not obvious

Observations and photographs by astronauts have contributed significantly to the understanding of ocean dynamics, and some of the more intriguing discoveries prompted the National Aeronautics and Space Administration to fly an oceanographic observer for the express purpose of studying the ocean from orbit. Scientists' understanding of the energy balance in the oceans has increased significantly as a result of the discoveries of circular and spiral eddies tens of kilometers in diameter, of standing waves hundreds of kilometers long, and of spiral eddies that sometimes trail into one another for thousands of kilometers. If a scientist wants to study features on this scale, it's much easier from an orbiting vehicle than from the vantage point of a boat.

Believe it or not, an astronaut can also see the wakes of large ships and the contrails[2] of airplanes. The sun angle has to be just right, but when the lighting conditions are perfect, you can follow otherwise invisible oil tankers on the Persian Gulf and trace major shipping lanes through the Mediterranean Sea. Similarly, when atmospheric conditions allow contrail formation, the thousand-mile-long condensation trails let astronauts trace the major air routes across the northern Pacific Ocean.

Part of every orbit takes us to the dark side of the planet. In space, night is very, very black—but that doesn't mean there's nothing to look at. The lights of cities sparkle; on nights when there was no moon, it was difficult for me to tell the Earth from the sky—the twinkling lights could be stars or they could be small cities. On one nighttime pass from Cuba to Nova Scotia, the entire East Coast of the United States appeared in twinkling outline.

When the moon is full, it casts an <u>eerie</u> light on the Earth. In its light, we see ghostly clouds and bright reflections on the water. One night, the Mississippi River flashed into view, and because of our viewing angle and orbital path, the reflected moonlight seemed to flow downstream—as if Huck Finn[3] had tied a candle to his raft.

eerie (ir´ ē) *adj.* mysterious

Of all the sights from orbit, the most spectacular may be the

---

2. **contrails** (kän´ trāls´) *n.* white trails of condensed water vapor that sometimes form in the wake of aircraft.
3. **Huck Finn** hero of Mark Twain's novel *The Adventures of Huckleberry Finn.*

Reading Check

What is the infrared film carried in a space shuttle used to document?

magnificent displays of lightning that ignite the clouds at night. On Earth, we see lightning from below the clouds; in orbit, we see it from above. Bolts of lightning are <u>diffused</u> by the clouds into bursting balls of light. Sometimes, when a storm extends hundreds of miles, it looks like a transcontinental brigade is tossing fireworks from cloud to cloud.

As the shuttle races the sun around the Earth, we pass from day to night and back again during a single orbit—hurtling into darkness, then bursting into daylight. The sun's appearance unleashes spectacular blue and orange bands along the horizon, a clockwork miracle that astronauts witness every 90 minutes. But I really can't describe a sunrise in orbit. The drama set against the black backdrop of space and the magic of the materializing colors can't be captured in an astronomer's equations or an astronaut's photographs.

I once heard someone (not an astronaut) suggest that it's possible to imagine what spaceflight is like by simply <u>extrapolating</u> from the sensations you experience on an airplane. All you have to do, he said, is mentally raise the airplane 200 miles, mentally eliminate the air noise and the turbulence, and you get an accurate mental picture of a trip in the space shuttle.

Not true. And while it's natural to try to liken spaceflight to familiar experiences, it can't be brought "down to Earth"—not in the final sense. The environment is different, the perspective is different. Part of the fascination with space travel is the element of the unknown—the conviction that it's different from earthbound experiences. And it is.

diffused (di fyo͞ozd′) v. spread out

extrapolating (ek strap′ ə lāt′ iŋ) v. arriving at a conclusion by making inferences based on known facts

Sally Ride

(b. 1951)

Although best known as an astronaut, Sally Ride was also a talented athlete in her youth. She received both undergraduate and graduate degrees from Stanford University.

In 1978, she read about NASA's search for astronauts and ultimately was chosen as one of the six women and twenty-five men accepted from among 8,000 applicants. In 1983, Sally Ride became the first American woman in space. She played a key role in the investigation of the *Challenger* tragedy in 1986.

Ride retired from NASA in 1987. She currently teaches physics at the University of California and is the author of several books on space.

Review and Assess

Thinking About the Selection

1. **Respond:** Would you like to be an astronaut? Why or why not?

2. **(a) Recall:** On which space shuttle did Ride travel?
   (b) Compare and Contrast: According to Ride, how is travel on the space shuttle different from travel on an airplane?

3. **(a) Recall:** Which geological features did Ride observe from orbit? **(b) Interpret:** Why did Ride find it easier to imagine geological forces from space?

4. **(a) Recall:** Which "unfortunate effects" did Ride see from orbit? **(b) Infer:** Why would these effects make colors seen in 1983 seem not as bright as those seen in 1973?

5. **(a) Draw Conclusions:** Does space travel aid in understanding conditions on Earth? **(b) Support:** Cite evidence from Ride's essay to explain your point of view.

6. **Connect:** How have Ride's descriptions of Earth changed the way you think about our planet?

Review and Assess

Literary Analysis

Observation

1. Which details in the essay show Ride's talent for **observation** in finding civilization's "signatures"?
2. How does Ride prove herself to be a careful observer of Earth's oceans?
3. Choose a particularly powerful observation of Ride's, and explain what makes it memorable. Use a chart like the following to record facts, events, and vivid details.

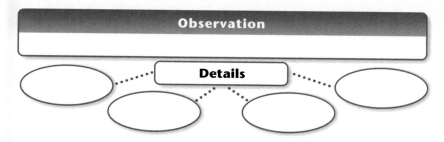

Connecting Literary Elements

4. Find an example from Ride's selection of **descriptive** language that appeals to the sense of touch.
5. How does Ride use comparisons to everyday phenomena to help readers follow her observations?
6. Does Ride's attention to descriptive details compromise her ability to be objective or strengthen her ability to convey her ideas?

Reading Strategy

Varying Your Reading Rate

7. (a) If you were reading to learn about Ride's description of cities in the United States, which paragraphs could you skim through quickly? (b) Which paragraphs would you read more carefully?
8. Why might you recommend that someone else read the entire essay slowly? Refer to the selection as you answer.

Extend Understanding

9. **Science Connection:** How has Sally Ride's essay affected what you think about the space program? Explain.

Quick Review

An **observation** describes an event that a writer saw firsthand, and it includes many details and vivid, precise words.

A **description** is a portrait in words of a person, place, or object.

To **vary your reading rate**, adjust your reading speed according to your purpose for reading.

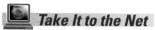 **Take It to the Net**

www.phschool.com
Take the interactive self-test online to check your understanding of the selection.

Integrate Language Skills

Vocabulary Development Lesson

Word Analysis: Latin Root -nov-

The Latin root -nov- means "new." The root appears in the word *novice*, which means "someone new to an activity; a beginner."

Use your knowledge of the root -nov- to define each of the following words, incorporating *new* into each definition.

1. novel (*adj.*)   **2.** renovate   **3.** innovate

Spelling Strategy

If a word ends in silent *e*, drop the *e* before adding a suffix that starts with a vowel. Thus, *extrapolate* + -*ing* = *extrapolating* and *diffuse* + -*ion* = *diffusion*.

Add -*able*, -*ing*, or -*est* to each word below to form three properly spelled new words.

1. rare   **2.** use   **3.** articulate

Fluency: Context

Fill in each blank with a word (or a form of the word) from the vocabulary list on page 635.

1. Normally ____?____, the veteran scientist felt like a tongue-tied ____?____ speaker.

2. The low, ____?____ murmuring of her audience was frightening and ____?____, giving her a bad feeling.

3. She turned on the projector, and the smell of burning dust, ____?____ but unmistakable, ____?____ through the air.

4. "This will seem weird, even ____?____," she said, putting on the strange first slide.

5. "However, what we can ____?____ from the facts and evidence is clear."

6. "The odd, ____?____ patterns of ____?____ and whirlpools on Planet X are mysterious signs of intelligent life."

Grammar Lesson

Subject-Verb Agreement

The **subject** is the word or group of words in a sentence that tells whom or what the sentence is about. The **verb,** or *predicate,* is the word or group of words in a sentence that expresses an action, condition, or state of being.

Subjects and verbs must agree in number. A singular subject requires a singular verb. A plural subject requires a plural verb.

	S V
Singular:	The <u>astronaut</u> *orbits* Earth.

	S V
Plural:	The <u>astronauts</u> *orbit* Earth.

Practice In each sentence, choose the form of the verb that agrees with the subject.

1. The shuttle (circle, circles) the planet.

2. Cameras (capture, captures) the experience.

3. A mountain and a river (come, comes) into view.

4. Bolts of lightning (flash, flashes) quickly.

5. Sally Ride (describe, describes) her trip.

Writing Application Find three sentences in "Single Room, Earth View" that have a plural subject and verb, and rewrite each with a singular subject and verb.

W͟G Prentice Hall Writing and Grammar Connection: Chapter 25, Section 1

Writing Lesson

Observation From Space

Imagine that you are an astronaut in space, like Sally Ride. Perhaps you are orbiting this planet in a space shuttle or planting a flag on the surface of Mars. Write an observation that describes the event for readers back home on Earth.

Prewriting   Consult actual photographs taken from space to gain a sense of what you might see as an astronaut. Make a list of the features on Earth that you want to include in your observation.

Drafting   To ensure that you get all your ideas on paper, write a first draft without stopping to change what you have written. Concentrate on getting across what you perceive through your senses.

Revising   Look for places where you can add vivid adjectives to enliven your description. Replace vague words with more exact ones.

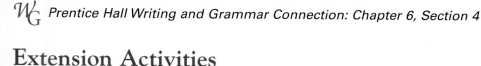

Model: Revising to Incorporate Vivid Adjectives

gray, rocky, and desolate

I stepped onto the ∧ surface of the moon. Seeing the great

awesome

bulk of Earth overhead was an ∧ ~~interesting~~ experience.

> Vivid adjectives such as *gray, rocky, desolate,* and *awesome* make the description come to life.

Prentice Hall Writing and Grammar Connection: Chapter 6, Section 4

Extension Activities

Listening and Speaking   In a group, study detailed photographs of Earth taken from space. Design a **presentation** to share one of the images you choose.

- Conduct research to learn about the features you want to highlight.
- Let your viewers know exactly what they see in the photograph.
- Describe each important feature.

Encourage your classmates to ask questions about the information in your presentation. [**Group Activity**]

Research and Technology   Prepare a **report** on one aspect of space exploration, such as women astronauts or the space shuttle. Access NASA's Web site and related sites to obtain information and illustrations for your report. Where needed, identify and explain any discrepancies you find among the various Web sites.

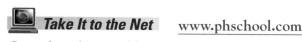 **Take It to the Net**   www.phschool.com

Go online for an additional research activity using the Internet.

Persuasive Speeches

About Persuasive Speeches

A **persuasive speech** is an oral presentation whose purpose is to convince listeners to accept a particular opinion or to take a specific action. For example, a speaker might deliver a speech that explains why democracy is the best form of government, or that urges audience members to vote for a particular political candidate.

Persuasive speeches are only as good as the arguments they set forth. Speakers, therefore, must support their opinions with strong arguments in order to be convincing. Speakers may appeal to logic or emotion and may use facts, statistics, examples, or anecdotes to reinforce their arguments.

Reading Strategy

Evaluating the Author's Purpose

Evaluating the speaker's purpose helps you put the overall argument into a framework that is easier to understand. Once you have identified the purpose, you can then determine which details the speaker uses to achieve that purpose.

Evaluate John F. Kennedy's purpose for giving the following speech by locating the main ideas he uses to support his argument. Then, determine if the purpose is reasonable and whether Kennedy achieves his purpose through the speech.

Evaluating Purpose				
Purpose: To convince Americans of the need to continue the peaceful exploration of space in the name of progress and national pride.				
➤ Detail:				
➤ Detail:				
➤ Detail:				

Evaluation:	**Not Very**				**Very**
Is Kennedy's purpose reasonable?	1	2	3	4	5
How effectively does Kennedy achieve his purpose?	1	2	3	4	5

The New Frontier

John F. Kennedy

Speech at Rice University, Houston, Texas, 1962

. . . No man can fully grasp how far and how fast [humanity has] come, but condense, if you will, the 50,000 years of man's recorded history in a time span of but a half-century. Stated in these terms, we know very little about the first forty years, except at the end of them advanced man had learned to use the skins of animals to cover him. Then about ten years ago, under this standard, man emerged from his caves to construct other kinds of shelter. Only five years ago man learned to write and use a cart with wheels. Christianity began less than two years ago. The printing press came this year, and then less than two months ago, during this whole fifty-year span of human history, the steam engine provided a new source of power.

Newton[1] explored the meaning of gravity. Last month electric lights and telephones and automobiles and airplanes became available. Only last week did we develop penicillin and television and nuclear power, and now if America's new space craft succeeds in reaching Venus, we will have literally reached the stars before midnight tonight.

This is a breathtaking pace, and such a pace cannot help but create new ills as it dispels old, new ignorance, new problems, new dangers. Surely the opening vistas of space promise high costs and hardships, as well as high reward.

So it is not surprising that some would have us stay where we are a little longer to rest, to wait. But this city of Houston, this State of Texas, this country of the United States was not built by those who waited and rested and wished to look behind them. This country was conquered by those who moved forward—and so will space.

William Bradford, speaking in 1630 of the founding of the Plymouth Bay Colony,[2] said that all great and honorable actions are accompanied with great difficulties,

---

1. **Newton** Sir Isaac Newton (1642–1727), English scientist and mathematician who formulated the idea of gravity.
2. **William Bradford . . . Plymouth Bay Colony** Bradford (1590–1657), a Pilgrim leader, was the second governor of Plymouth Colony, an early English colony in America, established by the Pilgrims in 1620.

> The listing of past milestones is intended to persuade readers that the space program is equally as important.

Prepare to Read

The Washwoman ◆ On Summer ◆ A Celebration of Grandfathers

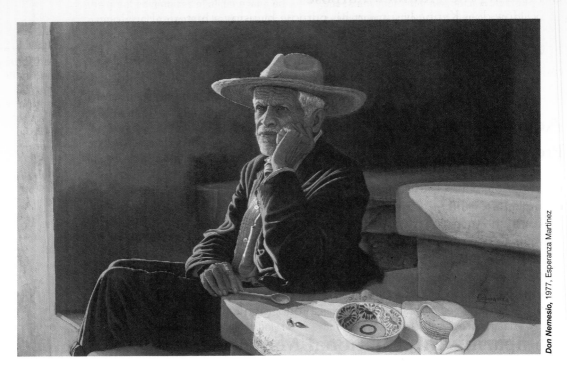

Don Nemesio, 1977, Esperanza Martinez

Preview

Connecting to the Literature

The authors of these selections journey deep into their past to find people who gave them gifts that were not boxed or tied with bows. Think about similar special gifts in your life, about the people who gave them to you, and about what these gifts have meant to you.

Background

In the early 1900s, Russia, Austria-Hungary, and Germany ruled the territories that make up modern Poland, the scene of "The Washwoman." In this area, few people were well off—most worked long hours merely to earn enough to survive. The area had a sizable Jewish population, most of whom spoke Yiddish and maintained their own cultural traditions. These conditions form the backdrop for Isaac Bashevis Singer's narrative essay.

Literary Analysis

Essay

An **essay** is a short piece of nonfiction in which a writer expresses a personal view on a topic. In this example, Rudolfo Anaya tells why he thinks his dying grandfather acted with uncharacteristic impatience:

> It was because he could not care for himself, because he was returning to that state of childhood, and all those wishes and desires were now wrapped in a crumbling body.

As you read, look for details that express each writer's point of view.

Comparing Literary Works

Within the broad range of essays, there are specific types, each with a different purpose.

- **Narrative essays** tell a story.
- **Persuasive essays** present an opinion in order to convince readers to accept a position or take a course of action.
- **Reflective essays** reveal a writer's feelings about a topic of personal importance.

Compare these essays by considering which category each one represents. Then, compare the specific effects each essay has on the reader.

Reading Strategy

Identifying the Author's Attitude

In an essay, the **author's attitude** toward the subject colors the presentation of information. For example, a writer describing someone he or she respects will use descriptive words and details that convey that respect.

Use a diagram like the one shown to help you identify the author's attitude. Note words or details that hint at the author's feelings. Then, indicate what these hints suggest about the author's attitude.

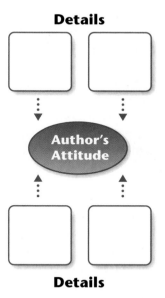

Vocabulary Development

forebears (fôr´ bərs´) *n.* ancestors (p. 650)

rancor (raŋ´ kər) *n.* deep spite or bitter hate (p. 651)

obstinacy (äb´ stə nə sē) *n.* stubbornness (p. 653)

pious (pī´ əs) *adj.* showing religious devotion (p. 654)

aloofness (ə lo͞of´ nəs) *n.* state of being distant or removed (p. 656)

perplexes (pər pleks´ iz) *v.* confuses or makes hard to understand (p. 662)

permeate (pur´ mē āt´) *v.* spread or flow throughout (p. 663)

epiphany (ē pif´ ə nē) *n.* moment of sudden understanding (p. 664)

The Washwoman

Isaac Bashevis Singer

Our home had little contact with Gentiles.[1] The only Gentile in the building was the janitor. Fridays he would come for a tip, his "Friday money." He remained standing at the door, took off his hat, and my mother gave him six groschen.[2]

Besides the janitor there were also the Gentile washwomen who came to the house to fetch our laundry. My story is about one of these.

She was a small woman, old and wrinkled. When she started washing for us, she was already past seventy. Most Jewish women of her age were sickly, weak, broken in body. All the old women in our street had bent backs and leaned on sticks when they walked. But this washwoman, small and thin as she was, possessed a strength that came from generations of peasant <u>forebears</u>. Mother would count out to her a bundle of laundry that had accumulated over several weeks. She would lift the unwieldy pack, load it on her narrow shoulders, and carry it the long way home. She lived on Krochmalna Street too, but at the other end, near the

forebears (fôr′ bərs′) *n.* ancestors

---

1. **Gentiles** any persons not Jewish; here, specifically Christians.
2. **groschen** (grō′ shən) Austrian cent or penny.

Wola section. It must have been a walk of an hour and a half.

She would bring the laundry back about two weeks later. My mother had never been so pleased with any washwoman. Every piece of linen sparkled like polished silver. Every piece was neatly ironed. Yet she charged no more than the others. She was a real find. Mother always had her money ready, because it was too far for the old woman to come a second time.

Laundering was not easy in those days. The old woman had no faucet where she lived but had to bring in the water from a pump. For the linens to come out so clean, they had to be scrubbed thoroughly in a washtub, rinsed with washing soda, soaked, boiled in an enormous pot, starched, then ironed. Every piece was handled ten times or more. And the drying! It could not be done outside because thieves would steal the laundry. The wrung-out wash had to be carried up to the attic and hung on clotheslines. In the winter it would become as brittle as glass and almost break when touched. And there was always a to-do with other housewives and washwomen who wanted the attic clothesline for their own use. Only God knows all the old woman had to endure each time she did a wash!

She could have begged at the church door or entered a home for the penniless and aged. But there was in her a certain pride and love of labor with which many Gentiles have been blessed. The old woman did not want to become a burden, and so she bore her burden.

My mother spoke a little Polish, and the old woman would talk with her about many things. She was especially fond of me and used to say I looked like Jesus. She repeated this every time she came, and Mother would frown and whisper to herself, her lips barely moving, "May her words be scattered in the wilderness."

The woman had a son who was rich. I no longer remember what sort of business he had. He was ashamed of his mother, the washwoman, and never came to see her. Nor did he ever give her a groschen. The old woman told this without <u>rancor</u>. One day the son was married. It seemed that he had made a good match. The wedding took place in a church. The son had not invited the old mother to his wedding, but she went to the church and waited at the steps to see her son lead the "young lady" to the altar.

The story of the faithless son left a deep impression on my mother. She talked about it for weeks and months. It was an affront not only to the old woman but to the entire institution of motherhood. Mother would argue, "Nu, does it pay to make sacrifices for children? The mother uses up her last strength, and he does not even know the meaning of loyalty."

And she would drop dark hints to the effect that she was not certain of her own children: Who knows what they would do some day? This, however, did not prevent her from dedicating her life to us. If there was any delicacy in the house, she would put it aside for the children and invent all sorts of excuses and reasons why she herself did not want to taste it. She knew charms that went back to ancient times, and she

Literary Analysis
Essay Which type of essay do you think Singer is writing? Why?

Reading Strategy
Identifying the Author's Attitude Which words and phrases indicate the author's admiration for the washwoman?

rancor (raŋ´ kər) n. deep spite or bitter hate

✔**Reading Check**

Why does the washwoman's son never come to see her?

◀ **Critical Viewing**
Based on her clothing and her expression, what do you imagine this woman is like? Why? **[Infer]**

used expressions she had inherited from generations of devoted mothers and grandmothers. If one of the children complained of a pain, she would say, "May I be your ransom and may you outlive my bones!" Or she would say, "May I be the atonement for the least of your fingernails." When we ate she used to say, "Health and marrow in your bones!" The day before the new moon she gave us a kind of candy that was said to prevent parasitic worms. If one of us had something in his eye, Mother would lick the eye clean with her tongue. She also fed us rock candy against coughs, and from time to time she would take us to be blessed against the evil eye. This did not prevent her from studying *The Duties of the Heart, The Book of the Covenant,* and other serious philosophic works.

But to return to the washwoman. That winter was a harsh one. The streets were in the grip of a bitter cold. No matter how much we heated our stove, the windows were covered with frostwork and decorated with icicles. The newspapers reported that people were dying of the cold. Coal became dear. The winter had become so severe that parents stopped sending children to cheder,[3] and even the Polish schools were closed.

On one such day the washwoman, now nearly eighty years old, came to our house. A good deal of laundry had accumulated during the past weeks. Mother gave her a pot of tea to warm herself, as well as some bread. The old woman sat on a kitchen chair trembling and shaking, and warmed her hands against the teapot. Her fingers were gnarled from work, and perhaps from arthritis too. Her fingernails were strangely white. These hands spoke of the stubbornness of mankind, of the will to work not only as one's strength permits but beyond the limits of one's power. Mother counted and wrote down the list: men's undershirts, women's vests, long-legged drawers, bloomers, petticoats, shifts, featherbed covers, pillowcases, sheets, and the men's fringed garments. Yes, the Gentile woman washed these holy garments as well.

The bundle was big, bigger than usual. When the woman placed it on her shoulders, it covered her completely. At first she swayed, as though she were about to fall under the load. But an inner <u>obstinacy</u> seemed to call out: No, you may not fall. A donkey may permit himself to fall under his burden, but not a human being, the crown of creation.

It was fearful to watch the old woman staggering out with the enormous pack, out into the frost, where the snow was dry as salt and the air was filled with dusty white whirlwinds, like goblins dancing in the cold. Would the old woman ever reach Wola?

She disappeared, and Mother sighed and prayed for her.

Usually the woman brought back the wash after two or, at the most, three weeks. But three weeks passed, then four and five, and nothing was heard of the old woman. We remained without linens. The cold had become even more intense. The telephone wires were now as thick as ropes. The branches of the trees looked like glass. So much snow had fallen that the streets had become uneven, and sleds were able to glide

---

3. **cheder** (khā´ dər) *n.* religious school.

The Washwoman ◆ 653

Reading Strategy
Identifying the Author's Attitude Based on this paragraph, what do you think the author's attitude is toward his mother?

Literary Analysis
Essay Which personal view does the author express here?

obstinacy (äb´ stə nə sē) *n.* stubbornness

Reading Check

How does the washwoman handle the unusually large bundle of laundry?

down many streets as on the slopes of a hill. Kindhearted people lit fires in the streets for vagrants[4] to warm themselves and roast potatoes in, if they had any to roast.

For us the washwoman's absence was a catastrophe. We needed the laundry. We did not even know the woman's address. It seemed certain that she had collapsed, died. Mother declared she had had a premonition, as the old woman left our house that last time, that we would never see our things again. She found some old torn shirts and washed and mended them. We mourned, both for the laundry and for the old, toil-worn woman who had grown close to us through the years she had served us so faithfully.

More than two months passed. The frost had subsided, and then a new frost had come, a new wave of cold. One evening, while Mother was sitting near the kerosene lamp mending a shirt, the door opened and a small puff of steam, followed by a gigantic bundle, entered. Under the bundle tottered the old woman, her face as white as a linen sheet. A few wisps of white hair straggled out from beneath her shawl. Mother uttered a half-choked cry. It was as though a corpse had entered the room. I ran toward the old woman and helped her unload her pack. She was even thinner now, more bent. Her face had become more gaunt, and her head shook from side to side as though she were saying no. She could not utter a clear word, but mumbled something with her sunken mouth and pale lips.

After the old woman had recovered somewhat, she told us that she had been ill, very ill. Just what her illness was, I cannot remember. She had been so sick that someone had called a doctor, and the doctor had sent for a priest. Someone had informed the son, and he had contributed money for a coffin and for the funeral. But the Almighty had not yet wanted to take this pain-racked soul to Himself. She began to feel better, she became well, and as soon as she was able to stand on her feet once more, she resumed her washing. Not just ours, but the wash of several other families too.

"I could not rest easy in my bed because of the wash," the old woman explained. "The wash would not let me die."

"With the help of God you will live to be a hundred and twenty," said my mother, as a benediction.

"God forbid! What good would such a long life be? The work becomes harder and harder . . . my strength is leaving me . . . I do not want to be a burden on anyone!" The old woman muttered and crossed herself, and raised her eyes toward heaven.

Fortunately there was some money in the house and Mother counted out what she owed. I had a strange feeling: the coins in the old woman's washed-out hands seemed to become as worn and clean and <u>pious</u> as she herself was. She blew on the coins and tied them in a kerchief. Then she left, promising to return in a few weeks for a new load of wash.

Literary Analysis
Essay Which words convey strong personal feelings about the washwoman's absence?

Reading Strategy
Identifying the Author's Attitude How would you describe the author's attitude toward the washwoman, based on this information about her illness?

pious (pī′ əs) *adj.* showing religious devotion

---

4. vagrants (vā′ grənts) *n.* people who wander from place to place, especially those without regular jobs.

But she never came back. The wash she had returned was her last effort on this earth. She had been driven by an indomitable will to return the property to its rightful owners, to fulfill the task she had undertaken.

And now at last her body, which had long been no more than a shard[5] supported only by the force of honesty and duty, had fallen. Her soul passed into those spheres where all holy souls meet, regardless of the roles they played on this earth, in whatever tongue, of whatever creed. I cannot imagine paradise without this Gentile washwoman. I cannot even conceive of a world where there is no recompense for such effort.

Reading Strategy
Identifying the Author's Attitude Which attitude toward the washwoman does Singer express here?

---

5. **shard** (shärd) *n.* fragment or broken piece.

Review and Assess

Thinking About the Selection

1. **Respond:** Why do you think the washwoman gives so much and asks so little in return?

2. **(a) Recall:** Which job does the washwoman perform for Singer's family? **(b) Connect:** Which laborious obstacles to doing the job well does Singer describe?

3. **(a) Recall:** How does Singer's mother feel about the washwoman? **(b) Compare and Contrast:** In what ways is the washwoman like and unlike the author's mother?

4. **(a) Recall:** What prevents the washwoman from returning to the family for several months? **(b) Draw Conclusions:** What does the washwoman's eventual return tell you about her character?

5. **(a) Interpret:** What significance, beyond her work alone, does the washwoman have for Singer? **(b) Speculate:** In light of his own words, how might Singer's life have been different if he had never known her?

6. **(a) Interpret:** What difficulties does Singer imply about the washwoman? **(b) Assess:** Which details of her life are omitted from the essay? **(c) Evaluate:** What effect do these omissions have on the effectiveness of the selection?

7. **(a) Assess:** Do you think the washwoman had a fulfilling life? Explain. **(b) Apply:** What lessons can we learn from the washwoman?

8. **(a) Evaluate:** What are the benefits of a life of service? **(b) Extend:** What are the costs?

Isaac Bashevis Singer

(1904–1991)

I. B. Singer once said that he believed that "life itself is a story." This belief is reflected in his many short stories, novels, and essays that capture the lessons of everyday life.

Born in Poland, Singer moved to New York City in 1935 and later took American citizenship. Writing in Yiddish, the language of some Eastern European Jews and their descendants, Singer became a widely popular and respected writer. He won the Nobel Prize for Literature in 1978.

On Summer

Lorraine Hansberry

It has taken me a good number of years to come to any measure of respect for summer. I was, being May-born, literally an "infant of the spring" and, during the later childhood years, tended, for some reason or other, to rather worship the cold <u>aloofness</u> of winter. The adolescence, admittedly lingering still, brought the traditional passionate commitment to melancholy autumn—and all that. For the longest kind of time I simply thought that *summer* was a mistake.

In fact, my earliest memory of anything at all is of waking up in a darkened room where I had been put to bed for a nap on a summer's afternoon, and feeling very, very hot. I acutely disliked the feeling then and retained the bias for years. It had originally been a matter of the heat but, over the years, I came actively to associate displeasure with most of the usually celebrated natural features and social by-products of the season: the too-grainy texture of sand; the too-cold coldness of the various waters we constantly try to escape into, and the icky-perspiry feeling of bathing caps.

It also seemed to me, esthetically[1] speaking, that nature had got inexcusably carried away on the summer question and let the whole thing get to be rather much. By duration alone, for instance, a summer's day seemed maddeningly excessive; an utter overstatement. Except for those few hours at either end of it, objects always appeared in too sharp a relief against backgrounds; shadows too pronounced and light too blinding. It always gave me the feeling of walking around in a motion picture which had been too artsily-craftsily exposed. Sound also had a way of coming to the ear without that muting influence, marvelously common to winter, across patios or beaches or through the woods. I suppose I found it too stark and yet too intimate a season.

---

1. **esthetically** (es thet′ ik lē) *adv.* artistically.

Literary Analysis
Essay What personal view does Hansberry express?

My childhood Southside[2] summers were the ordinary city kind, full of the street games which other rememberers have turned into fine ballets these days and rhymes that anticipated what some people insist on calling modern poetry:

Oh, Mary Mack, Mack, Mack
With the silver buttons, buttons, buttons
All down her back, back, back
She asked her mother, mother, mother
For fifteen cents, cents, cents
To see the elephant, elephant, elephant
Jump the fence, fence, fence
Well, he jumped so high, high, high
'Til he touched the sky, sky, sky
And he didn't come back, back, back
'Til the Fourth of Ju-ly, ly, ly!

2. **Southside** section of Chicago, Illinois.

▲ **Critical Viewing**
How well does this photograph fit the essay? Explain. **[Evaluate]**

✔**Reading Check**
What is Hansberry's earliest memory?

Evenings were spent mainly on the back porches where screen doors slammed in the darkness with those really very special summertime sounds. And, sometimes, when Chicago nights got too steamy, the whole family got into the car and went to the park and slept out in the open on blankets. Those were, of course, the best times of all because the grownups were invariably reminded of having been children in rural parts of the country and told the best stories then. And it was also cool and sweet to be on the grass and there was usually the scent of freshly cut lemons or melons in the air. And Daddy would lie on his back, as fathers must, and explain about how men thought the stars above us came to be and how far away they were. I never did learn to believe that anything could be as far away as *that*. Especially the stars.

▼ Critical Viewing
How does this photograph of the Maine coast add to the descriptions in the essay? [Connect]

My mother first took us south to visit her Tennessee birthplace one summer when I was seven or eight, I think. I woke up on the back seat of the car while we were still driving through some place called Kentucky and my mother was pointing out to the beautiful hills on both sides of the highway and telling my brothers and my sister about how her father had run away and hidden from his master in those very hills when he was a little boy. She said that his mother had wandered among the wooded slopes in the moonlight and left food for him in secret places. They were very beautiful hills and I looked out at them for miles and miles after that wondering who and what a *master* might be.

I remember being startled when I first saw my grandmother rocking away on her porch. All my life I had heard that she was a great

Literary Analysis
Essay Which details suggest that Hansberry is trying to convince you to accept her opinion about summer?

✔**Reading Check**
Whom does Hansberry visit in Tennessee?

beauty and no one had ever remarked that they meant a half century before. The woman that I met was as wrinkled as a prune and could hardly hear and barely see and always seemed to be thinking of other times. But she could still rock and talk and even make wonderful cupcakes which were like cornbread, only sweet. She was captivated by automobiles and, even though it was well into the Thirties,[3] I don't think she had ever been in one before we came down and took her driving. She was a little afraid of them and could not seem to negotiate the windows, but she loved driving. She died the next summer and that is all that I remember about her, except that she was born in slavery and had memories of it and they didn't sound anything like *Gone With the Wind*.[4]

Like everyone else, I have spent whole or bits of summers in many different kinds of places since then: camps and resorts in the Middle West and New York State; on an island; in a tiny Mexican village; Cape Cod, perched atop the Truro bluffs at Longnook Beach that Millay[5] wrote about; or simply strolling the streets of Provincetown[6] before the hours when the parties begin.

And, lastly, I do not think that I will forget days spent, a few summers ago, at a beautiful lodge built right into the rocky cliffs of a bay on the Maine coast. We met a woman there who had lived a purposeful and courageous life and who was then dying of cancer. She had, characteristically, just written a book and taken up painting. She had also been of radical viewpoint all her life; one of those people who energetically believe that the world *can* be changed for the better and spend their lives trying to do just that. And that was the way she thought of cancer; she absolutely refused to award it the stature of tragedy, a devastating instance of the brooding doom and inexplicability[7] of the absurdity of human destiny, etc., etc. The kind of characterization given, lately, as we all know, to far less formidable foes in life than cancer.

But for this remarkable woman it was a matter of nature in imperfection, implying, as always, work for man to do. It was an *enemy*, but a palpable one with shape and effect and source; and if it existed, it could be destroyed. She saluted it accordingly, without despondency, but with a lively, beautiful and delightfully ribald anger. There was one thing, she felt, which would prove equal to its relentless ravages and that was the genius of man. Not his mysticism, but man with tubes and slides and the stubborn human notion that the stars are very much within our reach.

The last time I saw her she was sitting surrounded by her paintings with her manuscript laid out for me to read, because, she said,

Reading Strategy
Identifying the Author's Attitude How would you describe the author's attitude toward her grandmother?

Literary Analysis
Essay Which words convey the reflective nature of Hansberry's essay?

---

3. **Thirties** the 1930s.
4. ***Gone With the Wind*** novel set in the South during the Civil War period.
5. **Millay** Edna St. Vincent Millay (1892–1950), American poet.
6. **Provincetown** resort town at the northern tip of Cape Cod, Massachusetts.
7. **inexplicability** (in eks′ pli kə bil′ ə tē) *n.* condition that cannot be explained.

she wanted to know what a *young person* would think of her thinking; one must always keep up with what *young people* thought about things because, after all, they were *change*.

Every now and then her jaw set in anger as we spoke of things people should be angry about. And then, for relief, she would look out at the lovely bay at a mellow sunset settling on the water. Her face softened with love of all that beauty and, watching her, I wished with all my power what I knew that she was wishing: that she might live to see at least one more *summer*. Through her eyes I finally gained the sense of what it might mean; more than the coming autumn with its pretentious melancholy; more than an austere and silent winter which must shut dying people in for precious months; more even than the frivolous spring, too full of too many false promises, would be the gift of another summer with its stark and intimate assertion of neither birth nor death but life at the apex; with the gentlest nights and, above all, the longest days.

I heard later that she did live to see another summer. And I have retained my respect for the noblest of the seasons.

Review and Assess

Thinking About the Selection

1. **Respond:** How do Hansberry's ideas about summer compare with your own?

2. **(a) Recall:** What are some of Hansberry's memories of childhood summers? **(b) Compare and Contrast:** Do her memories seem to support or contradict the opinion of summer she stated earlier? Explain.

3. **(a) Recall:** When does Hansberry first visit her grandmother? **(b) Infer:** Why do you think she includes the section about her grandmother in her essay?

4. **(a) Recall:** When does Hansberry's attitude toward summer change? **(b) Connect:** At the end, she calls summer "the noblest of the seasons." What do you think she means by this phrase?

5. **(a) Analyze:** What point of view does Hansberry try to persuade you to accept in her essay? **(b) Support:** What emotional appeals does she use to reach this goal?

6. **(a) Extend:** What experience have you had to cause your attitude about a season to change? **(b) Synthesize:** Is such a transformation of childhood opinions an important part of growing up? Why?

7. **Take a Position:** Which do you think affects a person's opinions more—personal experience or some other kind of learning? Explain.

Lorraine Hansberry

(1930–1965)

Lorraine Hansberry was born and raised in Chicago, Illinois. After high school, she studied art for two years before moving to New York City, where she worked for an African American newspaper called *Freedom*. While in New York, she wrote *A Raisin in the Sun*, which takes its name from a Langston Hughes poem, and in 1959 it became the first play by an African American woman to be produced on Broadway.

The essay "On Summer" comes from *To Be Young, Gifted, and Black*, a collection of Hansberry's writings that was published after her death.

A Celebration of
Grandfathers

Rudolfo A. Anaya

"Buenos días le de Dios, abuelo."[1] God give you a good day, grandfather. This is how I was taught as a child to greet my grandfather, or any grown person. It was a greeting of respect, a cultural value to be passed on from generation to generation, this respect for the old ones.

The old people I remember from my childhood were strong in their beliefs, and as we lived daily with them we learned a wise path of life to follow. They had something important to share with the young, and when they spoke the young listened. These old abuelos and abuelitas[2] had worked the earth all their lives, and so they knew the value of nurturing, they knew the sensitivity of the earth. The daily struggle called for cooperation, and so every person contributed to the social fabric, and each person was respected for his contribution.

The old ones had looked deep into the web that connects all animate and inanimate forms of life, and they recognized the great design of the creation.

These *ancianos*[3] from the cultures of the Río Grande, living side by side, sharing, growing together, they knew the rhythms and cycles of time, from the preparation of the earth in the spring to the digging of the acequias[4] that brought the water to the dance of harvest in the fall. They shared good times and hard times. They helped each other through the epidemics and the personal tragedies, and they shared what little they had when the hot winds burned the land and no rain came. They learned that to survive one had to share in the process of life.

Hard workers all, they tilled the earth and farmed, ran the herds and spun wool, and carved their saints and their kachinas[5] from cottonwood late in the winter nights. All worked with a deep faith which <u>perplexes</u> the modern mind.

Their faith shone in their eyes; it was in the strength of their grip, in the creases time wove into their faces. When they spoke, they spoke plainly and with few words, and they meant what they said.

---

1. **Buenos días le de Dios, abuelo** (bwā´ nəs dē´ äs lā dā dē´ ōs ä bwā´ lō)
2. **abuelitas** (a bwā lē´ täs) grandmothers.
3. *ancianos* (än cē ä´ nōs) old people; ancestors.
4. **acequias** (ä sā kē´ əs) irrigation ditches.
5. **kachinas** (kə chē´ nəz) small wooden dolls, representing the spirit of an ancestor or a god.

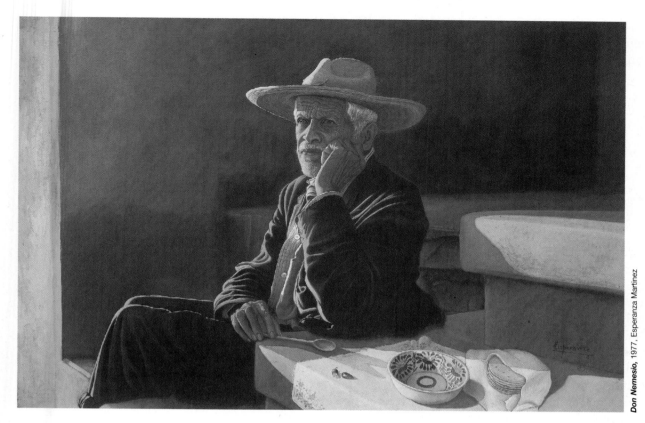

When they prayed, they went straight to the source of life. When there were good times, they knew how to dance in celebration and how to prepare the foods of the fiestas.[6] All this they passed on to the young, so that a new generation would know what they had known, so the string of life would not be broken.

Today we would say that the old abuelitos lived authentic lives.

Newcomers to New Mexico often say that time seems to move slowly here. I think they mean they have come in contact with the inner strength of the people, a strength so solid it causes time itself to pause. Think of it. Think of the high, northern New Mexico villages, or the lonely ranches on the open llano.[7] Think of the Indian pueblo[8] which lies as solid as rock in the face of time. Remember the old people whose eyes seem like windows that peer into a distant past that makes absurdity of our contemporary world. That is what one feels when one encounters the old ones and their land, a pausing of time.

We have all felt time stand still. We have all been in the presence of power, the knowledge of the old ones, the majestic peace of a mountain stream or an aspen grove or red buttes rising into blue sky. We have all felt the light of dusk <u>permeate</u> the earth and cause time to pause in its flow.

---

6. **fiestas** (fē es´ təz) celebrations; feasts.
7. **llano** (yä´ nō) plain.
8. **pueblo** (pweb´ lō) village or town.

▲ Critical Viewing
Which aspects of the man in this painting are similar to the description of the elders in the essay? **[Compare and Contrast]**

permeate (pʉr´ mē āt´) v. spread or flow throughout

✔ Reading Check
Why was Anaya taught as a child to give his grandfather a proper greeting?

A Celebration of Grandfathers ◆ 663

I felt this when first touched by the spirit of Ultima, the old *curandera*[9] who appears in my first novel, *Bless Me, Ultima.* This is how the young Antonio describes what he feels:

> When she came the beauty of the llano unfolded before my eyes, and the gurgling waters of the river sang to the hum of the turning earth. The magical time of childhood stood still, and the pulse of the living earth pressed its mystery into my living blood. She took my hand, and the silent, magic powers she possessed made beauty from the raw, sun-baked llano, the green river valley, and the blue bowl which was the white sun's home. My bare feet felt the throbbing earth, and my body trembled with excitement. Time stood still . . .

Literary Analysis
Essay Which of Anaya's personal experiences help him reflect on his feelings about the strength and power of the old ones?

At other times, in other places, when I have been privileged to be with the old ones, to learn, I have felt this inner reserve of strength upon which they draw. I have been held motionless and speechless by the power of curanderas. I have felt the same power when I hunted with Cruz, high on the Taos [tä′ ōs] mountain, where it was more than the incredible beauty of the mountain bathed in morning light, more than the shining of the quivering aspen, but a connection with life, as if a shining strand of light connected the particular and the cosmic. That feeling is an <u>epiphany</u> of time, a standing still of time.

epiphany (ē pif′ ə nē) *n.* moment of sudden understanding

But not all of our old ones are curanderos or hunters on the mountain. My grandfather was a plain man, a farmer from Puerto de Luna[10] on the Pecos River. He was probably a descendent of those people who spilled over the mountain from Taos, following the Pecos River in search of farmland. There in that river valley he settled and raised a large family.

Bearded and walrus-mustached, he stood five feet tall, but to me as a child he was a giant. I remember him most for his silence. In the summers my parents sent me to live with him on his farm, for I was to learn the ways of a farmer. My uncles also lived in that valley, the valley called Puerto de Luna, there where only the flow of the river and the whispering of the wind marked time. For me it was a magical place.

I remember once, while out hoeing the fields, I came upon an anthill, and before I knew it I was badly bitten. After he had covered my welts with the cool mud from the irrigation ditch, my grandfather calmly said: "Know where you stand." That is the way he spoke, in short phrases, to the point.

One very dry summer, the river dried to a trickle, there was no water for the fields. The young plants withered and died. In my sadness and with the impulses of youth I said, "I wish it would rain!" My grandfather touched me, looked up into the sky and whispered, "Pray for rain." In his language there was a difference. He felt connected to the cycles that brought the rain or kept it from us. His prayer was a

Reading Strategy
Identifying the Author's Attitude What attitude toward his grandfather is the author communicating?

---

9. curandera (kōō rän dä′ rä) medicine woman.
10. Puerto de Luna (pwer′ tō dä lōō′ nə) Port of the Moon, the name of a town.

El Lenador, 1934, Tom Lea, Museum of Fine Arts, Museum of New Mexico

◀ **Critical Viewing**
How does the elderly farmer in this painting compare with the image you have of the author's grandfather? [**Compare and Contrast**]

meaningful action, because he was a participant with the forces that filled our world, he was not a bystander.

A young man died at the village one summer. A very tragic death. He was dragged by his horse. When he was found I cried, for the boy was my friend. I did not understand why death had come to one so young. My grandfather took me aside and said: "Think of the death of the trees and the fields in the fall. The leaves fall, and everything rests, as if dead. But they bloom again in the spring. Death is only this small transformation in life."

These are the things I remember, these fleeting images, few words.

I remember him driving his horse-drawn wagon into Santa Rosa in the fall when he brought his harvest produce to sell in the town. What a tower of strength seemed to come in that small man huddled on the seat of the giant wagon. One click of his tongue and the horses obeyed, stopped or turned as he wished. He never raised his

✓**Reading Check**

What does Anaya's grandfather tell him to do when there is no water for the fields?

A Celebration of Grandfathers ◆ 665

whip. How unlike today when so much teaching is done with loud words and threatening hands.

I would run to greet the wagon, and the wagon would stop. "Buenos días le de Dios, abuelo," I would say. This was the pre-scribed greeting of esteem and respect. Only after the greeting was given could we approach these venerable old people. "Buenos días te de Dios, mi hijo,"[11] he would answer and smile, and then I could jump up on the wagon and sit at his side. Then I, too, became a king as I rode next to the old man who smelled of earth and sweat and the other deep aromas from the orchards and fields of Puerto de Luna.

We were all sons and daughters to him. But today the sons and daughters are breaking with the past, putting aside los abuelitos. The old values are threatened, and threatened most where it comes to these relationships with the old people. If we don't take the time to watch and feel the years of their final transformation, a part of our humanity will be lessened.

Reading Strategy
Identifying the Author's Attitude How would you describe the author's attitude toward the potential loss of old values?

I grew up speaking Spanish, and oh! how difficult it was to learn English. Sometimes I would give up and cry out that I couldn't learn. Then he would say, "Ten paciencia."[12] Have patience. *Paciencia*, a word with the strength of centuries, a word that said that someday we would overcome. *Paciencia*, how soothing a word coming from this old man who could still sling hundred-pound bags over his shoulder, chop wood for hours on end, and hitch up his own horses and ride to town and back in one day.

"You have to learn the language of the Americanos,"[13] he said. "Me, I will live my last days in my valley. You will live in a new time, the time of the gringos."[14]

A new time did come, a new time is here. How will we form it so it is fruitful? We need to know where we stand. We need to speak softly and respect others, and to share what we have. We need to pray not for material gain, but for rain for the fields, for the sun to nurture growth, for nights in which we can sleep in peace, and for a harvest in which everyone can share. Simple lessons from a simple man. These lessons he learned from his past which was as deep and strong as the currents of the river of life, a life which could be stronger than death.

Literary Analysis
Essay Which words in this paragraph signify that the purpose of Anaya's essay has shifted from reflection to persuasion?

He was a man; he died. Not in his valley, but nevertheless cared for by his sons and daughters and flocks of grandchildren. At the end, I would enter his room which carried the smell of medications and Vicks, the faint pungent odor of urine, and cigarette smoke. Gone were the aroma of the fields, the strength of his young manhood. Gone also was his patience in the face of crippling old age. Small things bothered him; he shouted or turned sour when his expecta-tions were not met. It was because he could not care for himself, because he was returning to that state of childhood, and all those

---

11. mi hijo (mē ē′ hō) my son.
12. Ten paciencia (ten pä sē en′ sē ä)
13. Americanos (ä mer′ ē kä′ nōs) Americans.
14. gringos (grin′ gōs) foreigners; North Americans.

wishes and desires were now wrapped in a crumbling old body.

"Ten paciencia," I once said to him, and he smiled. "I didn't know I would grow this old," he said. "Now, I can't even roll my own cigarettes." I rolled a cigarette for him, placed it in his mouth and lit it. I asked him why he smoked, the doctor had said it was bad for him. "I like to see the smoke rise," he said. He would smoke and doze, and his quilt was spotted with little burns where the cigarettes dropped. One of us had to sit and watch to make sure a fire didn't start.

I would sit and look at him and remember what was said of him when he was a young man. He could mount a wild horse and break it, and he could ride as far as any man. He could dance all night at a dance, then work the acequia the following day. He helped neighbors, they helped him. He married, raised children. Small legends, the kind that make up everyman's life.

He was 94 when he died. Family, neighbors, and friends gathered; they all agreed he had led a rich life. I remembered the last years, the years he spent in bed. And as I remember now, I am reminded that it is too easy to romanticize old age. Sometimes we forget the pain of the transformation into old age, we forget the natural breaking down of the body. Not all go gentle into the last years, some go crying and cursing, forgetting the names of those they loved the most, withdrawing into an internal anguish few of us can know. May we be granted the patience and care to deal with our ancianos.

Literary Analysis
Essay What reflections does Anaya convey in this part of his essay?

For some time we haven't looked at these changes and needs of the old ones. The American image created by the mass media is an image of youth, not of old age. It is the beautiful and the young who are praised in this society. If analyzed carefully, we see that same damaging thought has crept into the way society views the old. In response to the old, the mass media have just created old people who act like the young. It is only the healthy, pink-cheeked, outgoing, older persons we are shown in the media. And they are always selling something, as if an entire generation of old people were salesmen in their lives. Commercials show very lively old men, who must always be in excellent health according to the new myth, selling insurance policies or real estate as they are out golfing; older women selling coffee or toilet paper to those just married. That image does not illustrate the real life of the old ones.

Real life takes into account the natural cycle of growth and change. My grandfather pointed to the leaves falling from the tree. So time brings with its transformation the often painful, wearing-down process. Vision blurs, health wanes; even the act of walking carries with it the painful reminder of the autumn of life. But this process is something to be faced, not something to be hidden away by false images. Yes, the old can be young at heart, but in their own way, with their own dignity. They do not have to copy the always-young image of the Hollywood star.

My grandfather wanted to return to his valley to die. But by then the families of the valley had left in search of a better future. It is only now that there seems to be a return to the valley, a revival. The

**Reading Check**
What does Anaya's grandfather say to him as the writer struggles to learn English?

new generation seeks its roots, that value of love for the land moves us to return to the place where our ancianos formed the culture.

I returned to Puerto de Luna last summer, to join the community in a celebration of the founding of the church. I drove by my grandfather's home, my uncles' ranches, the neglected adobe[15] washing down into the earth from whence it came. And I wondered, how might the values of my grandfather's generation live in our own? What can we retain to see us through these hard times? I was to become a farmer, and I became a writer. As I plow and plant my words, do I nurture as my grandfather did in his fields and orchards? The answers are not simple.

"They don't make men like that anymore," is a phrase we hear when one does honor to a man. I am glad I knew my grandfather. I am glad there are still times when I can see him in my dreams, hear him in my reverie. Sometimes I think I catch a whiff of that earthy aroma that was his smell, just as in lonely times sometimes I catch the fragrance of Ultima's herbs. Then I smile. How strong these people were to leave such a lasting impression.

So, as I would greet my abuelo long ago, it would help us all to greet the old ones we know with this kind and respectful greeting: "Buenos días le de Dios."

---

15. adobe (ə dō´ bē) *n.* sun-dried clay brick.

Rudolfo Anaya

(b. 1937)

Rudolfo Anaya was born in Pastura, New Mexico, and his writing reflects his Mexican American heritage.

Many of his novels, stories, and articles concern the past. His first novel, *Bless Me, Ultima* (1972), was acclaimed for its depiction of the culture and history of New Mexico. Anaya has also published *Heart of Aztlan* (1976) and *Tortuga* (1979).

His essay "A Celebration of Grandfathers" reflects on the "old ones" he remembers from his childhood.

Review and Assess

Thinking About the Selection

1. **Respond:** How would you describe the author's attitude toward the "old ones"?

2. **(a) Recall:** What qualities of old people does Anaya remember from his childhood? **(b) Distinguish:** How are these qualities different from the images created by American mass media?

3. **(a) Recall:** What kind of work did Anaya's grandfather do? **(b) Compare and Contrast:** How do the author's work and values differ from those of his grandfather?

4. **(a) Recall:** What is the "new time" that Anaya's grandfather mentions? **(b) Infer:** What does the author imply about this "new time"?

5. **(a) Analyze:** Why do you think the essay ends with the very same words with which it begins? **(b) Support:** Use evidence from the essay to support your view.

6. **(a) Generalize:** What perspective does Anaya offer on the way old people should be treated as they age and die? **(b) Take a Position:** Do you agree with him? Explain.

Review and Assess

Literary Analysis

Essay

1. Using a chart like the one shown, analyze the ideas presented in each of these **essays.**

2. What personal views about life does Singer express in his essay?
3. What are some of the facts and reasons Hansberry presents to persuade you to accept her opinion about summer?
4. Rudolfo Anaya celebrates his grandfather and other "old ones." Which people or things seem, in his view, less worthy of praise?

Comparing Literary Works

5. Which essay is the most **persuasive**?
6. Which essay includes the most **reflections** by the author?
7. Which essay has the strongest emotional effect on the reader? Why?
8. How are the three authors' attitudes toward elderly people similar and different? Cite specific details.

Reading Strategy

Identifying the Author's Attitude

9. Which three adjectives might Singer use to describe his attitude toward the washwoman? Explain your answer.
10. Do you think Anaya could convince others who do not share his background to adopt his attitude? Explain.

Extend Understanding

11. **Cultural Connection:** Are today's elderly treated with what the three authors would consider appropriate respect? Explain.

Integrate Language Skills

Vocabulary Development Lesson

Word Analysis: Anglo-Saxon Prefix *fore-*

The Anglo-Saxon prefix *fore-* means "before." The prefix appears in the word *forebears*, which means "ancestors" or "those who came before us."

Use the meaning of *fore-* to define each word below.

1. foreground   **2.** foresee   **3.** forethought

Spelling Strategy

To form the plural (or some verb forms) of words ending in *z*, *x*, *sh*, *ch*, or *s*, add *-es* instead of *-s*. Thus, *perplex* + *-es* = *perplexes*.

Add *-es* to each word below. Then, find four other words in the selections that would follow this rule.

1. box   **2.** fizz   **3.** clash

Fluency: Word Choice

For each item below, write the word from the vocabulary list on page 649 that best matches each clue.

1. creates confusion
2. the condition of showing disinterest, distance, or uninvolvement
3. one's relatives who lived long ago
4. the opposite of peaceful agreement and harmony
5. a sudden feeling of discovery
6. a quality of donkeys
7. deeply religious
8. what a heavy rain does when it falls on dry soil

Grammar Lesson

Consistency of Verb Tense

A **verb** is a word that expresses an action or a state of being. A verb has various **tenses,** such as past, present, and future. These forms of the verb are used to show the time of the action or condition.

To maintain a **consistency of verb tense,** analyze the verbs in your writing. If you begin a passage in the past tense, for instance, do not suddenly switch to present tense to talk about the past.

> **Unnecessary Tense Shift:** We *paid* the wash-woman. She *thanks* us.
>
> **Correct:** We *paid* the washwoman. She *thanked* us.

Practice Rewrite each of the following items to maintain consistency of verb tense.

1. Yesterday I worked. Then, I will rest.
2. The woman comes early. She left late.
3. When Grandmother sings to me, I recorded her.
4. Tomorrow, we will travel and visited friends.
5. I ran to greet the wagon, and the wagon stops.

Writing Application Change the tense of the first verb in each of the practice sentences above, and then adjust the tense of the second verb to match the first.

WG **Prentice Hall Writing and Grammar Connection: Chapter 23, Section 1**

Writing Lesson

Essay on Summer

Write an essay that summarizes the ideas Hansberry presents in her essay "On Summer." Provide your own personal connections to agree or disagree with her views.

Prewriting   List Hansberry's reflections on summer, and then list personal experiences that connect to the reflection. If you find that you do not connect with her experience, explain why.

Model: Connecting to the Author's Experience

Hansberry's Reflection	My Connection
Sleeping outside on hot summer nights	It reminds me of my camping trips to Vermont.

Drafting   As you draft, make sure to support each opinion with a specific example. In the closing paragraph of your essay, state your final views on summer.

Revising   Read your draft to a classmate. Ask your classmate if your views on summer are clear. Add any necessary details to strengthen your description of your experiences and to improve your analysis.

WG *Prentice Hall Writing and Grammar Connection: Chapter 13, Section 2*

Extension Activities

Listening and Speaking To learn more about the authors, watch the movie version of either Lorraine Hansberry's *A Raisin in the Sun* or Isaac B. Singer's *Yentl*. Then, prepare a **movie review** for your classmates.

- Determine what you liked and disliked about the film's acting, directing, and costuming.
- Find any connection between the movie and the author's essay in this book.
- Prepare concise notes to use in an oral presentation of your review.

Later, invite your audience to evaluate the effectiveness of your review. **[Group Activity]**

Research and Technology Conduct an **interview** with an older person whom you know and admire. Find out key details about the person's life and important lessons that he or she has learned. Videotape the interview and share it with your class. After you present the video, compare the elderly person in your interview with the grandfather in "A Celebration of Grandfathers."

 Take It to the Net   www.phschool.com

Go online for an additional research activity using the Internet.

Prepare to Read

from A White House Diary ◆ Arthur Ashe Remembered ◆ Georgia O'Keeffe

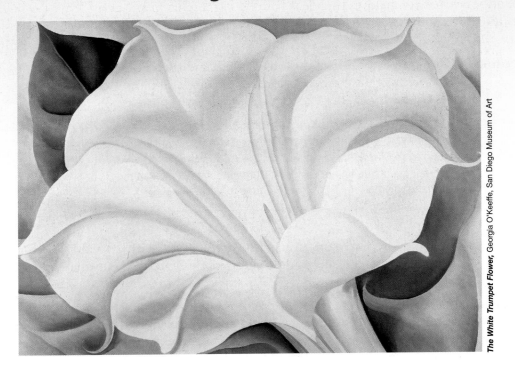

The White Trumpet Flower, Georgia O'Keeffe, San Diego Museum of Art

Take It to the Net

Visit www.phschool.com for interactive activities and instruction related to the selections, including
- background
- graphic organizers
- literary elements
- reading strategies

Preview

Connecting to the Literature

In the following selections, you will have a rare chance to see the private sides of three famous Americans. As you read, think about how the triumphs and tragedies in your own life have led you to discover what really matters.

Background

The assassination of President John F. Kennedy on November 22, 1963, was a stunning and unforgettable event. As the news media reported the tragedy, the United States came to a halt. People wept openly in their homes and in the streets. Kennedy had been a young, vibrant, and popular leader. A mournful nation agreed with his successor, Lyndon Johnson, who said of the assassination, "We have suffered a loss that cannot be weighed."

Literary Analysis

Biographical and Autobiographical Writing

Biographical writing is nonfiction in which a writer tells the story of another person's life. **Autobiographical writing** is nonfiction in which a writer tells the story of his or her own life. This excerpt from *A White House Diary* lets you share Lady Bird Johnson's thoughts and feelings:

> One last happy moment I had was looking up and seeing Mary Griffith leaning out of a window waving at me.

As you read, notice the emotions conveyed through each piece.

Comparing Literary Works

Biographical and autobiographical writing offer readers two distinctly different experiences. The differences in the presentation of views and experiences in each type of writing can influence the way readers interpret the events. Compare the selections and consider how each type of writing influences your attitude toward the person at the center of the work.

Reading Strategy

Finding the Writer's Main Points and Support

A key to understanding biographies and autobiographies is the ability to **find the writer's main points** and the details that **support** those points.

- Read each paragraph to determine the main idea it conveys.
- Locate the facts, events, details, or quotations that elaborate, develop, or support the main idea.
- Once you have finished reading a selection, try to determine the main points of the work as a whole.

Use a chart like the one shown here to help you as you read.

Vocabulary Development

tumultuous (tōō mul′ chōō əs) *adj.* greatly disturbed (p. 676)

implications (im′ pli kā′ shənz) *n.* indirect indications (p. 677)

poignant (poin′ yənt) *adj.* drawing forth pity or compassion (p. 678)

legacy (leg′ ə sē) *n.* anything handed down from an ancestor (p. 683)

enigma (i nig′ mə) *n.* puzzling or baffling matter; riddle (p. 683)

condescending (kän′ di sen′ diŋ) *adj.* characterized by looking down on someone (p. 685)

sentimental (sen′ tə ment′ 'l) *adj.* excessively emotional (p. 686)

genesis (jen′ ə sis) *n.* origin (p. 686)

rancor (raŋ′ kər) *n.* hatred (p. 689)

immutable (im myōōt′ ə bəl) *adj.* never changing (p. 689)

from

A White House Diary

Lady Bird Johnson

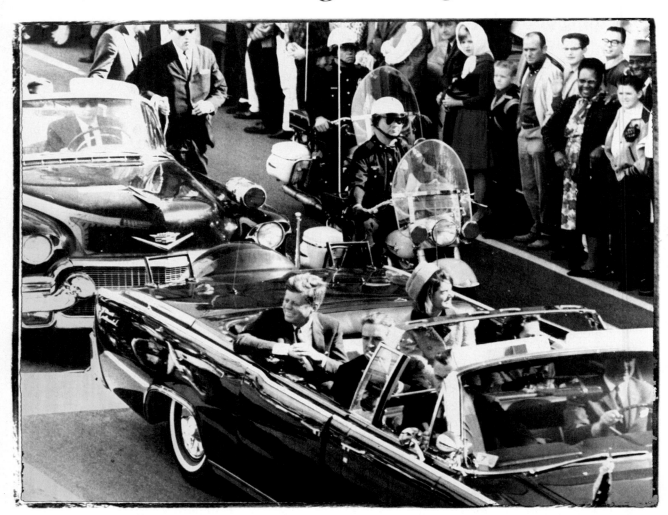

▲ **Critical Viewing** What does this photograph reveal about the mood in the moments leading up to the assassination? **[Infer]**

DALLAS, FRIDAY, NOVEMBER 22, 1963

It all began so beautifully. After a drizzle in the morning, the sun came out bright and clear. We were driving into Dallas. In the lead car were President and Mrs. Kennedy, John and Nellie Connally,[1] a Secret Service[2] car full of men, and then our car with Lyndon and me and Senator Ralph Yarborough.

The streets were lined with people—lots and lots of people—the children all smiling, placards, confetti, people waving from windows. One last happy moment I had was looking up and seeing Mary Griffith leaning out of a window waving at me. (Mary for many years had been in charge of altering the clothes which I purchased at Neiman-Marcus.)

Then, almost at the edge of town, on our way to the Trade Mart for the Presidential luncheon, we were rounding a curve, going down a hill, and suddenly there was a sharp, loud report. It sounded like a shot. The sound seemed to me to come from a building on the right above my shoulder. A moment passed, and then two more shots rang out in rapid succession. There had been such a gala air about the day that I thought the noise must come from firecrackers—part of the celebration. Then the Secret Service men were suddenly down in the lead car. Over the car radio system, I heard "Let's get out of here!" and our Secret Service man, Rufus Youngblood, vaulted over the front seat on top of Lyndon, threw him to the floor, and said, "Get down."

Senator Yarborough and I ducked our heads. The car accelerated terrifically—faster and faster. Then, suddenly, the brakes were put on so hard that I wondered if we were going to make it as we wheeled left and went around the corner. We pulled up to a building. I looked up and saw a sign, "HOSPITAL." Only then did I believe that this might be what it was. Senator Yarborough kept saying in an excited voice, "Have they shot the President? Have they shot the President?" I said something like, "No, it can't be."

As we ground to a halt—we were still the third car—Secret Service men began to pull, lead, guide, and hustle us out. I cast one last look over my shoulder and saw in the President's car a bundle of pink, just like a drift of blossoms, lying on the back seat. It was Mrs. Kennedy lying over the President's body.

The Secret Service men rushed us to the right, then to the left, and then onward into a quiet room in the hospital—a very small room. It was lined with white sheets, I believe.

People came and went—Kenny O'Donnell, the President's top aide, Congressman Homer Thornberry, Congressman Jack Brooks. Always there was Rufe right there and other Secret Service agents—Emory Roberts, Jerry Kivett, Lem Johns, and Woody Taylor. People spoke of how widespread this might be. There was talk about where we would go—to the plane, to our house, back to Washington.

---

1. **John and Nellie Connally** John Connally, then Governor of Texas, and his wife, Nellie.
2. **Secret Service** division of the U.S. Treasury Department, responsible for protecting the president.

Literary Analysis
Biographical and Autobiographical Writing
Which words in this passage tell you that Johnson's writing is autobiographical?

Reading Strategy
Finding the Writer's Main Points and Support
Which details does the writer use to support her main point that she was in disbelief about the shooting?

 **Reading Check**
Where are the Johnsons taken after a shot is heard?

Mrs. Kennedy had arrived by this time, as had the coffin. There, in the very narrow confines of the plane—with Jackie standing by Lyndon, her hair falling in her face but very composed, with me beside him, Judge Hughes in front of him, and a cluster of Secret Service people, staff, and Congressmen we had known for a long time around him—Lyndon took the oath of office.

It's odd the little things that come to your mind at times of utmost stress, the flashes of deep compassion you feel for people who are really not at the center of the tragedy. I heard a Secret Service man say in the most desolate voice—and I hurt for him: "We never lost a President in the Service." Then, Police Chief Curry of Dallas came on the plane and said, "Mrs. Kennedy, believe me, we did everything we possibly could." That must have been an agonizing moment for him.

We all sat around the plane. The casket was in the corridor. I went in the small private room to see Mrs. Kennedy, and though it was a very hard thing to do, she made it as easy as possible. She said things like, "Oh, Lady Bird, we've liked you two so much. . . . Oh, what if I had not been there. I'm so glad I was there."

I looked at her. Mrs. Kennedy's dress was stained with blood. One leg was almost entirely covered with it and her right glove was caked, it was caked with blood—her husband's blood. Somehow that was one of the most <u>poignant</u> sights—that immaculate woman exquisitely dressed, and caked in blood.

I asked her if I couldn't get someone in to help her change and she said, "Oh, no. Perhaps later I'll ask Mary Gallagher but not right now." And then with almost an element of fierceness—if a person that

▲ **Critical Viewing** This photograph shows Lyndon Johnson beginning to assume his duties as president. Based on the details in the photo, how do you think he felt at that time? Why? **[Analyze]**

poignant (poin´ yənt) *adj.* drawing forth pity or compassion

gentle, that dignified, can be said to have such a quality—she said, "I want them to see what they have done to Jack."

I tried to express how we felt. I said, "Oh, Mrs. Kennedy, you know we never even wanted to be Vice President and now, dear God, it's come to this." I would have done anything to help her, but there was nothing I could do, so rather quickly I left and went back to the main part of the airplane where everyone was seated.

The flight to Washington was silent, each sitting with his own thoughts. One of mine was a recollection of what I had said about Lyndon a long time ago—he's a good man in a tight spot. I remembered one little thing he had said in that hospital room—"Tell the children to get a Secret Service man with them."

Finally we got to Washington, with a cluster of people waiting and many bright lights. The casket went off first, then Mrs. Kennedy, and then we followed. The family had come to join her. Lyndon made a very simple, very brief, and, I think, strong statement to the people there. Only about four sentences. We got in helicopters, dropped him off at the White House, and I came home in a car with Liz Carpenter.[5]

---

5. Liz Carpenter Mrs. Johnson's press secretary.

Review and Assess

Thinking About the Selection

1. **Respond:** What do you admire most about Lady Bird Johnson? Why?

2. **(a) Recall:** What are the writer's thoughts about Mrs. Kennedy at the hospital? **(b) Deduce:** In what ways is Mrs. Kennedy alone?

3. **(a) Recall:** What is the most noticeable aspect of Mrs. Kennedy's appearance when Mrs. Johnson speaks with her on *Air Force One*? **(b) Interpret:** In what way is wearing the clothing a tribute to her husband?

4. **(a) Recall:** Where does Lyndon Johnson take the oath of office? **(b) Support:** Which details from the text indicate that the Johnsons are up to the tasks before them?

5. **(a) Recall:** How does Mrs. Kennedy behave after the death of her husband? **(b) Compare and Contrast:** What similarities do you find between Mrs. Kennedy and Mrs. Johnson? Explain your answer.

6. **Assess:** Why might a diary entry be an effective way for a person to grieve and cope with a tragic event?

Lady Bird Johnson

(b. 1912)

Texas-born Claudia Alta Taylor received her nickname at age two, when a nurse said she was as pretty as a lady bird. In 1934, she married Lyndon Johnson, then a congressional secretary. Throughout her husband's political career, Lady Bird was a most valued advisor and campaigner.

On November 22, 1963, after President John F. Kennedy was killed by an assassin in Dallas, Texas, Lady Bird Johnson became First Lady of the United States. Aboard *Air Force One*, the president's airplane, Vice President Johnson took the oath of office to become the thirty-sixth president of the United States. On his left stood Kennedy's widow, Jackie, her clothing still spattered with her husband's blood. On his right stood his wife, Lady Bird.

The Role of the First Lady

The excerpt from *A White House Diary* by Lady Bird Johnson offers a keen insight into the kinds of pressures and responsibilities that a president's spouse can face. Despite these pressures, first ladies often carve out their own niches by advancing special causes. Johnson went on to become a respected advocate for natural resource conservation. Throughout our nation's history, first ladies have applied their own style and personalities to the ways in which they defined and carried out their duties as the wife of the president.

Eleanor Roosevelt: Social Activist

Eleanor Roosevelt was married to Franklin D. Roosevelt, president of the United States from 1933 to 1945. During her years in the White House, Mrs. Roosevelt became the most socially active first lady in American history. Because of her husband's physical restrictions due to polio, Mrs. Roosevelt often went on fact-finding tours on his behalf. During the Depression, she spoke in cities across America to bring hope to the poor and desperate. She also traveled to Europe, Latin America, and many other parts of the world, working for young people and minority groups. Privately, Mrs. Roosevelt urged her husband to take stronger actions on social problems like racial inequality. She raised money for humanitarian causes by writing magazine articles and a daily newspaper column. During World War II, she visited American troops overseas.

©White House Collection, Courtesy White House Historical Association

Roosevelt's Legacy

Roosevelt's activism inspired a more recent first lady, Hillary Clinton. When Mrs. Clinton worked on issues ranging from health care to children's welfare, she explicitly mentioned her debt to Mrs. Roosevelt in redefining the role of first lady. Like Mrs. Roosevelt, who went on to become a United Nations delegate, Mrs. Clinton also took on a high visibility, post-White House career—as a United States senator representing New York.

Mamie Eisenhower: Hostess and Housewife

Mamie Eisenhower was married to Dwight D. Eisenhower, president of the United States from 1953 to 1961. Mrs. Eisenhower defined her role in the White House primarily as a popular hostess. As a result of increased air travel in the 1950s, the Eisenhowers entertained more state and foreign leaders than any previous presidential couple. Beloved for her unpretentious yet dignified style, Mrs. Eisenhower personally greeted thousands of tourists at the White House. The American public regarded her as the ideal American woman of the 1950s. She described herself as "perfectly satisfied as a housewife," and served as an inspiration to homemakers across the country who felt she reflected their own values.

©White House Collection, Courtesy White House Historical Association

Eisenhower's Legacy

When emotional issues, such as school desegregation, were on people's minds, Mrs. Eisenhower largely refrained from taking public positions. On the rare occasions when she did speak out, she did so with gracious impartiality. In the 1952 election, for instance, she urged Americans to vote, even if they chose to vote for her husband's opponent, Adlai Stevenson. Her legacy can be seen in the highly visible roles that subsequent first ladies have assumed in serving as coordinators of White House social and diplomatic events.

Connecting Literature and Social Studies

1. Based on these descriptions, how did Eleanor Roosevelt and Mamie Eisenhower view their role as first lady?

2. Which first lady defined her role similarly to Lady Bird Johnson? Why?

3. What type of first lady would appeal to most Americans today? Explain your opinion.

And of course he never did—not in the height of his athletic power, not in the statesmanship of the years that followed, and not in the endgame of his existence. If you wished to choose a single image, you would see him standing there in his twenties, his lithe body a braid of cables, his energy without apparent limit, in a court situation indescribably bad, and all he does is put his index finger on the bridge of his glasses and push them back up the bridge of his nose. In the shadow of disaster, he hits out. Faced with a choice between a conservative, percentage return or a one-in-ten flat-out blast, he chooses the blast. In a signature manner, he extends his left arm to point upward at lobs as they fall toward him. His overheads, in fire bursts, put them away. His backhand is, if anything, stronger than his forehand, and his shots from either side for the most part are explosions. In motions graceful and decisive, though, and with reactions as fast as the imagination, he is a master of drop shots, of cat-and-mouse, of miscellaneous dinks and chips and (riskiest of all) the crosscourt half-volley. Other tennis players might be wondering who in his right mind would attempt something like that, but that is how Ashe plays the game: at the tensest moment, he goes for the all but impossible. He is predictably unpredictable. He is unreadable. His ballistic serves move in odd patterns and come off the court in unexpected ways. Behind his impassive face—behind the enigmatic glasses, the lifted chin, the first-mate-on-the-bridge look—there seems to be, even from this distance, a smile.

Reading Strategy
Finding the Writer's Main Points and Support What is the writer's main point in this paragraph?

Review and Assess

Thinking About the Selection

1. **Respond:** After reading this selection, what are your feelings about Arthur Ashe? Why?

2. **(a) Recall:** How did Ashe once describe his life?
   (b) Connect: What later proved to be tragically ironic about this statement?

3. **(a) Recall:** Which "weapon" did Ashe use against opponents on the court? **(b) Interpret:** Why did Ashe's opponents often think he was toying with them?

4. **(a) Recall:** According to his father, how was Ashe like his mother? **(b) Recall:** What does Ashe say he likes best about himself on the court? **(c) Draw Conclusions:** Based on this article, how would you describe Ashe's character?

5. **(a) Connect:** Use examples to show how the writer uses the way Arthur Ashe played tennis to illustrate how Ashe lived life. **(b) Apply:** How can one aspect of Ashe's approach to tennis—going for the difficult shot when in trouble—be applied as an approach to life?

John McPhee

(b. 1931)

After graduating from Princeton University, John McPhee worked at *Time* magazine and then at *The New Yorker*. McPhee has written many nonfiction books and essays.

McPhee has found success in writing about topics that fascinate him. One such subject is sports. In his book *Levels of the Game* (1969), an account of the 1968 U.S. Open Tennis Championship, McPhee reveals his admiration for Arthur Ashe.

The White Trumpet Flower, Georgia O'Keeffe, San Diego Museum of Art

Georgia O'Keeffe
Joan Didion

"**W**here I was born and where and how I have lived is unimportant," Georgia O'Keeffe told us in the book of paintings and words published in her ninetieth year on earth. She seemed to be advising us to forget the beautiful face in the Stieglitz[1] photographs. She appeared to be dismissing the rather <u>condescending</u> romance that had attached to her by then, the romance of extreme good looks and advanced age and deliberate isolation. "It is what I have done with where I have been that should be

---

1. Stieglitz (stēg´ lits) Alfred Stieglitz (1864–1946); U.S. photographer and husband of Georgia O'Keeffe.

▲ **Critical Viewing**
What can you guess about the personality of the artist from her work? **[Deduce]**

condescending (kän´ di sen´ diŋ) *adj.* characterized by looking down on someone

of interest." I recall an August afternoon in Chicago in 1973 when I took my daughter, then seven, to see what Georgia O'Keeffe had done with where she had been. One of the vast O'Keeffe "Sky Above Clouds" canvases floated over the back stairs in the Chicago Art Institute that day, dominating what seemed to be several stories of empty light, and my daughter looked at it once, ran to the landing, and kept on looking. "Who drew it," she whispered after a while. I told her. "I need to talk to her," she said finally.

My daughter was making, that day in Chicago, an entirely unconscious but quite basic assumption about people and the work they do. She was assuming that the glory she saw in the work reflected a glory in its maker, that the painting was the painter as the poem is the poet, that every choice one made alone—every word chosen or rejected, every brush stroke laid or not laid down—betrayed one's character. *Style is character.* It seemed to me that afternoon that I had rarely seen so instinctive an application of this familiar principle, and I recall being pleased not only that my daughter responded to style as character but that it was Georgia O'Keeffe's particular style to which she responded: this was a hard woman who had imposed her 192 square feet of clouds on Chicago.

"Hardness" has not been in our century a quality much admired in women, nor in the past twenty years has it even been in official favor for men. When hardness surfaces in the very old we tend to transform it into "crustiness" or eccentricity, some tonic pepperiness to be indulged at a distance. On the evidence of her work and what she has said about it, Georgia O'Keeffe is neither "crusty" nor eccentric. She is simply hard, a straight shooter, a woman clean of received wisdom and open to what she sees. This is a woman who could early on dismiss most of her contemporaries as "dreamy," and would later single out one she liked as "a very poor painter." (And then add, apparently by way of softening the judgment: "I guess he wasn't a painter at all. He had no courage and I believe that to create one's own world in any of the arts takes courage.") This is a woman who in 1939 could advise her admirers that they were missing her point, that their appreciation of her famous flowers was merely <u>sentimental</u>. "When I paint a red hill," she observed coolly in the catalogue for an exhibition that year, "you say it is too bad that I don't always paint flowers. A flower touches almost everyone's heart. A red hill doesn't touch everyone's heart." This is a woman who could describe the <u>genesis</u> of one of her most well-known paintings—the "Cow's Skull: Red, White and Blue" owned by the Metropolitan[2]—as an act of quite deliberate and derisive orneriness. "I thought of the city men I had been seeing in the East," she wrote. "They talked so often of writing the Great American Novel—the Great American Play—the Great American Poetry. . . . So as I was painting my cow's head on blue I thought to

---

2. **Metropolitan** Metropolitan Museum of Art in New York City.

Literary Analysis
Biographical and Autobiographical Writing
How does the author personalize her biographical writing about O'Keeffe?

Reading Strategy
Finding the Writer's Main Points and Support What is the writer's main point in this paragraph?

sentimental (sen′ tə ment′ 'l) *adj.* excessively emotional

genesis (jen′ ə sis) *n.* origin

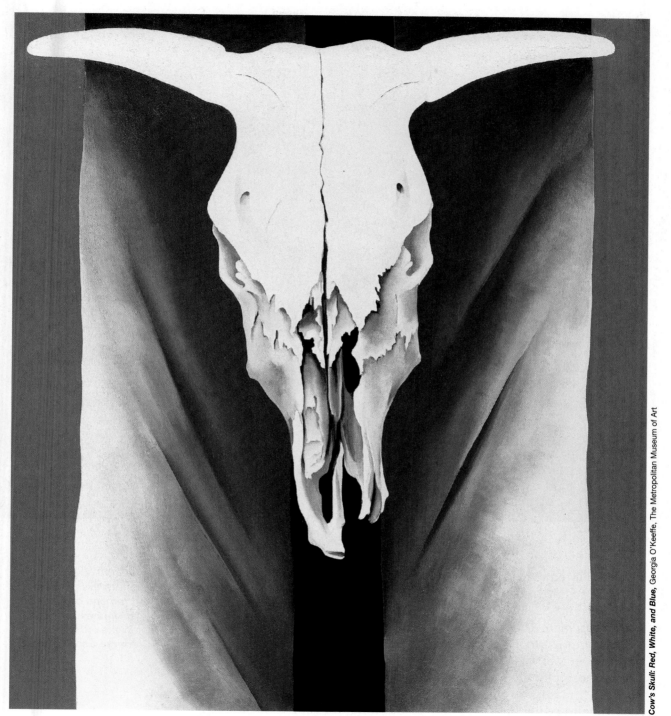

*Cow's Skull: **Red, White, and Blue**, Georgia O'Keeffe, The Metropolitan Museum of Art*

▲ **Critical Viewing** What information in the text helps you understand this painting better? **[Connect]**

myself, 'I'll make it an American painting. They will not think it great with the red stripes down the sides—Red, White and Blue—but they will notice it.'"

The city men. The men. They. The words crop up again and again as this astonishingly aggressive woman tells us what was on her mind when she was making her astonishingly aggressive paintings. It was those city men who stood accused of sentimentalizing her flowers: "I made you take time to look at what I saw and when you took time to really notice my flower you hung all your associations with flowers on my flower and you write about my flower as if I

▲ **Critical Viewing**
Compare this painting with the one on page 685. What do they suggest about the artist? **[Compare and Contrast]**

think and see what you think and see—and I don't." *And I don't.* Imagine those words spoken, and the sound you hear is *don't tread on me.*[3] "The men" believed it impossible to paint New York, so Georgia O'Keeffe painted New York. "The men" didn't think much of her bright color, so she made it brighter. The men yearned toward Europe so she went to Texas, and then New Mexico. The men talked about Cézanne,[4] "long involved remarks about the 'plastic quality' of his form and color," and took one another's long involved remarks, in the view of this angelic rattlesnake in their midst, altogether too seriously. "I can paint one of those dismal-colored paintings like the men," the woman who regarded herself always as an outsider remembers thinking one day in 1922, and she did: a painting of a shed "all low-toned and dreary with the tree beside the door." She called this act of <u>rancor</u> "The Shanty" and hung it in her next show. "The men seemed to approve of it," she reported fifty-four years later, her contempt undimmed. "They seemed to think that maybe I was beginning to paint. That was my only low-toned dismal-colored painting."

Some women fight and others do not. Like so many successful guerrillas in the war between the sexes, Georgia O'Keeffe seems to have been equipped early with an <u>immutable</u> sense of who she was and a fairly clear understanding that she would be required to prove it. On the surface her upbringing was conventional. She was a child on the Wisconsin prairie who played with china dolls and painted watercolors with cloudy skies because sunlight was too hard to paint and, with her brother and sisters, listened every night to her mother read stories of the Wild West, of Texas, of Kit Carson and Billy the Kid. She told adults that she wanted to be an artist and was embarrassed when they asked what kind of artist she wanted to be: she had no idea "what kind." She had no idea what artists did. She had never seen a picture that interested her, other than a pen-and-ink Maid of Athens in one of her mother's books, some Mother Goose illustrations printed on cloth, a tablet cover that showed a little girl with pink roses, and the painting of Arabs on horseback that hung in her grandmother's parlor. At thirteen, in a Dominican convent, she was mortified when the sister corrected her drawing. At Chatham Episcopal Institute in Virginia she painted lilacs and sneaked time alone to walk out to where she could see the line of the Blue Ridge Mountains on the horizon. At the Art Institute in Chicago she was shocked by the presence of live models and wanted to abandon anatomy lessons. At the Art Students League in New York one of her fellow students advised her that, since he would be a great painter and she would end up teaching painting in a girls' school, any work of hers was less important than modeling for him. Another painted over her work to show her how the Impressionists did trees. She had

---

3. **Don't tread on me** motto of the first official American flag to be flown by a naval vessel, on December 3, 1775.
4. **Cézanne** (sā zän) Paul Cézanne (1839–1906), French Impressionist and Post-Impressionist painter.

Literary Analysis
Biographical and Autobiographical Writing
What does this paragraph reveal about O'Keeffe?

rancor (raŋ′ kər) *n.* hatred

immutable (im myo͞ot′ ə bəl) *adj.* never changing

Reading Check
What made O'Keeffe's childhood "conventional"?

not before heard how the Impressionists did trees and she did not much care.

At twenty-four she left all these opinions behind and went for the first time to live in Texas, where there were no trees to paint and no one to tell her how not to paint them. In Texas there was only the horizon she craved. In Texas she had her sister Claudia with her for a while, and in the late afternoons they would walk away from town and toward the horizon and watch the evening star come out. "That evening star fascinated me," she wrote. "It was in some way very exciting to me. My sister had a gun, and as we walked she would throw bottles into the air and shoot as many as she could before they hit the ground. I had nothing but to walk into nowhere and the wide sunset space with the star. Ten watercolors were made from that star." In a way one's interest is compelled as much by the sister Claudia with the gun as by the painter Georgia with the star, but only the painter left us this shining record. Ten watercolors were made from that star.

Review and Assess

Thinking About the Selection

1. **Respond:** Which of O'Keeffe's qualities do you admire most? Why?

2. **(a) Recall:** Which primary character trait does the writer attribute to O'Keeffe? **(b) Interpret:** What does the writer mean by "hardness"? Give examples.

3. **(a) Recall:** How does O'Keeffe respond when " 'the men' didn't think much of her bright color"? **(b) Draw Conclusions:** What does her response tell you about her character?

4. **(a) Recall:** Where does O'Keeffe move and find what she craves? **(b) Infer:** What do you think she found attractive about this place?

5. **Interpret:** What does Didion mean when she says O'Keeffe had "an immutable sense of who she was"?

6. **(a) Analyze:** What do the words "style is character" mean? **(b) Draw Conclusions:** Explain how the statement is appropriate for Georgia O'Keeffe. Cite evidence from the text to support your answer.

7. **(a) Speculate:** To what extent do you think O'Keeffe's disregard for the opinions of others contributed to her success? **(b) Assess:** Do you think an artist needs to be bold and individualistic to be successful?

Joan Didion

(b. 1934)

Joan Didion is descended from a long line of pioneers. Her great-great-grandmother went west in a covered wagon in 1846.

As a young woman, Didion won a writing contest sponsored by *Vogue* magazine. Eventually, she became an editor there. Her reputation in the literary world, however, is based on her novels and essays. Didion has said, "I write entirely to find out what I'm thinking, what I'm looking at, what I see and what it means."

The essay "Georgia O'Keeffe" pays tribute to an artist who herself displayed a strong pioneer spirit.

Review and Assess

Literary Analysis

Biographical and Autobiographical Writing

1. Using a chart like this one, provide evidence to show whether each selection is a **biography** or an **autobiography.**

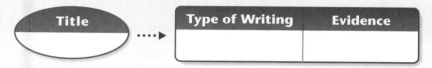

2. What are two details from *A White House Diary* that reveal the compassion of Lady Bird Johnson?
3. What does McPhee reveal about Ashe's personal nature?
4. In what ways was Georgia O'Keeffe portrayed as a "loner"?

Comparing Literary Works

5. (a) Which of the three selections reveals the most to you about the qualities of the person portrayed? (b) Which of the three selections evokes the most emotion in you? Why?
6. (a) How would *A White House Diary* be different if it were written as a biography? (b) Use a Venn diagram like this one to compare the ways each type of writing would present Lady Bird Johnson.

Reading Strategy

Finding the Writer's Main Points and Support

7. For each main point below, explain which details the writer provides to support the main point:
   (a) Mrs. Kennedy made Lady Bird's visit with her as easy as possible.
   (b) Remaining cool on the court was a potent weapon for Ashe.
   (c) Georgia O'Keeffe was a hard, straight shooter.

Extend Understanding

8. **Social Studies Connection:** Why are biographical and autobiographical writings valuable sources for historians and teachers?

Quick Review

Biographical writing is nonfiction in which a writer tells the story of another person's life.

Autobiographical writing is nonfiction in which a writer tells the story of his or her own life.

A writer's **main points** are the main ideas expressed in a selection. **Support** for these points can include facts, events, quotations, and other details that prove or elaborate each main idea.

 Take It to the Net

www.phschool.com
Take the interactive self-test online to check your understanding of these selections.

Integrate Language Skills

Vocabulary Development Lesson

Word Analysis: Latin Root -sent-/-sens-

The Latin root -sent-/-sens- means "feeling." The root appears in the word *sentimental*, which means "having excessive feelings." Using the meaning of -sent-/-sens-, define each word below.

1. sensitize **2.** sensitively **3.** sentimentality

Spelling Strategy

Do not change the spelling of a base word when adding a prefix to it. For example, *im-* + *mutable* = *immutable*.

Add the prefix shown to form the new word. Then, use each word in a sentence.

1. *pre-* + eminent   **3.** *un-* + natural

2. *dis-* + service   **4.** *im-* + proper

Fluency: Definitions

Review the vocabulary list on page 673. Then, match each of the following phrases on the left with its correct definition on the right.

1. poignant genesis   **a.** emotional riddle
2. tumultuous implications **b.** unchangeable inheritance
3. immutable legacy   **c.** patronizing hatred
4. sentimental enigma   **d.** turbulent indications
5. condescending rancor   **e.** moving beginning

Grammar Lesson

Subject-Verb Agreement: Confusing Subjects

The **subject** and **verb** in a sentence must agree in number. A singular subject takes the singular form of the verb. A plural subject takes the plural form of the verb. If a subject follows a verb in a sentence, the subject and verb must still agree.

In the following examples, the verbs are italicized and the subjects are underlined.

Singular:	There *was* a sharp, loud report.
Plural:	There *were* sharp, loud reports.

If the subject is *any* or *all*, the verb agrees with the noun to which the pronoun refers.

Singular:	All the danger *was* over.
Plural:	All the shades *were* lowered.

Practice Identify the subject in each sentence. Then, choose the correct verb to complete each sentence.

1. There (was, were) Secret Service men all over.
2. His entire life (was, were) a series of victories.
3. Some of his opponents (was, were) baffled.
4. There on the wall (was, were) her paintings.
5. Each painting in the group (was, were) a masterpiece.

Writing Application Use each item as the subject in a sentence. Make sure you use a verb that agrees in number with the subject.

1. tennis players   **2.** painter

Prentice Hall Writing and Grammar Connection: Chapter 25, Section 1

Writing Lesson

Awards Speech

Imagine that you are an official at an awards ceremony for Lady Bird Johnson, Arthur Ashe, or Georgia O'Keeffe. Using the selections you have just read, write a speech that introduces the award winner.

Prewriting   Select the person from these selections whom you admire most. Jot down the points you would like to make about that person.

Drafting   Begin your speech with an attention-grabbing opening. In the body of your speech, present your main points in a logical order.

Revising   Read your speech and ask a classmate to suggest places where you can add details to make your ideas more coherent. Add transition words, such as *then* and *as a result*, to clarify your speech.

Model: Adding Smooth Transitions

Tonight we are honoring an admirable woman.

But even more importantly,

⋀We are honoring a great American. She has worked tirelessly

As a result,

for our country.⋀ She has brought all of us closer together.

> The inserted words create smoother transitions between sentences.

𝒲𝒢 Prentice Hall Writing and Grammar Connection: Chapter 7, Section 4

Extension Activities

Listening and Speaking In a small group, develop and present a **radio news report** on the assassination of President Kennedy.

- Use library resources to find relevant information on the subject.
- Use details such as quotations and anecdotes in your report.
- Organize the information in the best possible order, using transition words where helpful.

Present your radio news report to the class. **[Group Activity]**

Research and Technology Prepare a **visual presentation** on the paintings of Georgia O'Keeffe. Find reproductions of her paintings and use them as your primary source of information. Then, use the Internet to find more information about her and her paintings. Write informational captions for each painting. Present your findings to your class.

 **Take It to the Net**   www.phschool.com

Go online for an additional research activity using the Internet.

Prepare to Read

excerpt from Understanding Comics

Take It to the Net

Visit www.phschool.com
for interactive activities
and instruction related to
Understanding Comics,
including
- background
- graphic organizers
- literary elements
- reading strategies

Preview

Connecting to the Literature

Most people associate comics with superheroes, humorous animals, and amusing people with exaggerated facial features. As you read this excerpt from *Understanding Comics,* consider how much the writer/illustrator changes your impressions and ideas about a typical comic strip.

Background

Comics first appeared in American newspapers in the late 1800s. One early strip featuring a character called the Yellow Kid was so popular that it boosted sales for its newspaper. Soon, other newspapers were running their own comics, too. Comic books first appeared in the 1930s. The *Superman* comic began in 1938 and is still popular today. In recent years, the popularity of comic books has increased dramatically among adults.

Literary Analysis

Visual Essay

A **visual essay** is an exploration of a topic that conveys its ideas through visual elements as well as language. Like a standard essay, a visual essay presents an author's views of a topic. Unlike other essays, however, much of the meaning in a visual essay is conveyed through illustrations or photographs. For example, the following excerpt from *Understanding Comics* will take on new meaning when you read it along with a visual element in the comic:

> The artform—the *medium*—known as comics is a *vessel* which can hold any *number* of *ideas* and *images*.

Note how the visual elements of *Understanding Comics* heighten your understanding and appreciation of the text.

Connecting Literary Elements

The **tone** of a visual essay is the writer's attitude toward his or her audience and subject, and it can be conveyed through both words and images. Often, the tone can be described in a single adjective, such as *formal* or *informal*, *serious* or *playful*, *bitter* or *ironic*. As you read a comic, consider how the pictures and the letters—for example, the size of the letters and the repetition of words—contribute to the author's overall tone.

Reading Strategy

Using Visuals as a Key to Meaning

You can **use visuals as a key to meaning** by looking carefully at each illustration or photograph and deciding how it adds to the ideas presented in the written text. Pictures can reinforce and extend words in the following ways:

- They add humor to apparently straightforward statements.
- They add details, without having to use additional words.
- They signal flashbacks in time or the element of fantasy.

Use a chart like the one shown to record details about the text and the illustrations. Then, explain how the visual extends meaning.

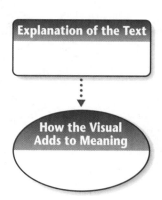

Vocabulary Development

obsessed (əb sest´) *adj.* greatly occupied with

aesthetic (es thet´ ik) *adj.* relating to the appreciation of beauty

arbitrary (är´ bə trer´ē) *adj.* not fixed by rules, but left to one's judgment

IN LESS THAN A *YEAR*, I BECAME *TOTALLY OBSESSED* WITH COMICS! I DECIDED TO BECOME A *COMICS ARTIST* IN *10TH GRADE* AND BEGAN TO *PRACTICE*, *PRACTICE*, *PRACTICE*!

I FELT THAT THERE WAS SOMETHING *LURKING* IN COMICS... SOMETHING THAT HAD *NEVER BEEN DONE.*

SOME KIND OF *HIDDEN POWER!*

BUT WHENEVER I TRIED TO *EXPLAIN* MY FEELING, I FAILED *MISERABLY.*

COMIC BOOKS?! HA! HA! HA!

BUT IT-- BUT IT'S-- BUH...

SURE, I REALIZED THAT COMIC BOOKS WERE USUALLY *CRUDE, POORLY-DRAWN, SEMILITERATE, CHEAP, DISPOSABLE KIDDIE FARE*--

--BUT--

THEY DON'T *HAVE* TO BE!

THE *PROBLEM* WAS THAT FOR *MOST PEOPLE,* THAT WAS WHAT *"COMIC BOOK"* MEANT!

DON'T GIMME THAT *COMIC BOOK* TALK, BARNEY!

IF PEOPLE FAILED TO *UNDERSTAND* COMICS, IT WAS BECAUSE THEY DEFINED WHAT COMICS COULD BE *TOO NARROWLY!*

A *PROPER DEFINITION,* IF WE COULD *FIND* ONE, MIGHT GIVE *LIE* TO THE STEREOTYPES--

--AND SHOW THAT THE *POTENTIAL* OF COMICS IS *LIMITLESS* AND *EXCITING!*

THIS IS WHERE OUR JOURNEY *BEGINS.*

© and ™ 1994 Scott McCloud

--WHILE NOT BEING *SO* BROAD AS TO INCLUDE ANYTHING WHICH IS CLEARLY *NOT* COMICS.

"COMICS" IS THE WORD WORTH DEFINING, AS IT REFERS TO THE MEDIUM *ITSELF,* NOT A SPECIFIC *OBJECT* AS "COMIC BOOK" OR "COMIC STRIP" DO.

WE CAN ALL VISUALIZE *A* COMIC.

BUT WHAT--

--IS--

--COMICS?

THE WORLD OF COMICS IS A *HUGE* AND *VARIED* ONE. OUR DEFINITION MUST ENCOMPASS ALL THESE TYPES--

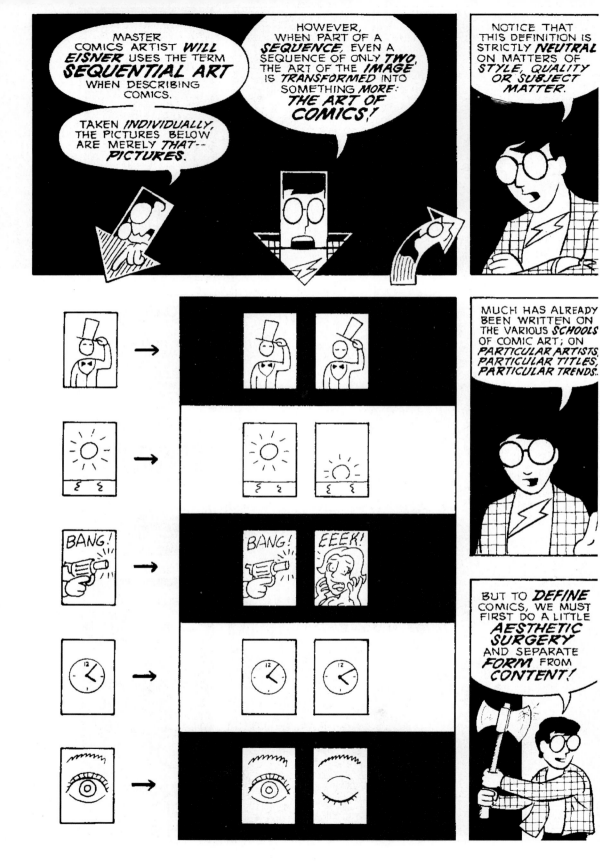

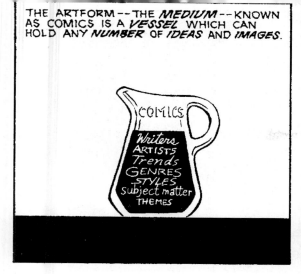

THE ARTFORM -- THE *MEDIUM* -- KNOWN AS COMICS IS A *VESSEL* WHICH CAN HOLD ANY *NUMBER* OF *IDEAS* AND *IMAGES*.

COMICS
Writers
ARTISTS
Trends
GENRES
STYLES
Subject matter
THEMES

THE *"CONTENT"* OF THOSE IMAGES AND IDEAS IS, OF COURSE, UP TO *CREATORS*, AND WE ALL HAVE DIFFERENT *TASTES*.

=GLUG=
=GLUG=

PTU!!!

=GAAK=
=WHEEEEZ=
=KAF! KAF!=
GLUGH·GGH...

-ahem-

THE *TRICK* IS TO NEVER MISTAKE THE *MESSAGE* --

--FOR THE *MESSENGER*.

COMICS

AT ONE TIME OR ANOTHER VIRTUALLY *ALL* THE GREAT MEDIA HAVE RECEIVED *CRITICAL EXAMINATION*, IN AND OF *THEMSELVES*.

WRITTEN WORD   MUSIC   VIDEO

THEATRE   VISUAL ART   FILM

BUT FOR *COMICS*, THIS ATTENTION HAS BEEN *RARE*. *

LET'S SEE IF WE CAN HELP *RECTIFY* THE SITUATION.

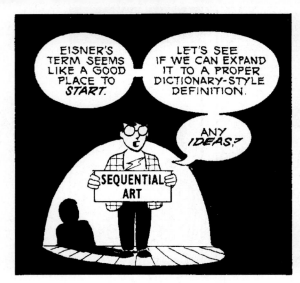

EISNER'S TERM SEEMS LIKE A GOOD PLACE TO *START.*

LET'S SEE IF WE CAN EXPAND IT TO A PROPER DICTIONARY-STYLE DEFINITION.

ANY *IDEAS?*

SEQUENTIAL ART

THERE ARE A LOT OF DIFFERENT *KINDS* OF ART. HOW ABOUT SOMETHING A LITTLE MORE *SPECIFIC?*

OKAY.

HOW'S *THIS?*

SEQUENTIAL *VISUAL* ART

HEY, WHAT ABOUT *ANIMATION?!*

BEG PARDON?

SEQUENTIAL VISUAL ART

ISN'T ANIMATED FILM JUST *VISUAL ART IN SEQUENCE?*

HMM... GOOD POINT.

I GUESS THE BASIC DIFFERENCE IS THAT ANIMATION IS SEQUENTIAL IN *TIME* BUT NOT SPATIALLY *JUXTAPOSED** AS COMICS ARE.

EACH SUCCESSIVE FRAME OF A *MOVIE* IS PROJECTED ON EXACTLY THE *SAME* SPACE -- THE *SCREEN* -- WHILE EACH FRAME OF *COMICS* MUST OCCUPY A *DIFFERENT* SPACE.

WHRRRRRRRR

SPACE DOES FOR *COMICS* WHAT *TIME* DOES FOR *FILM!*

The complete *Understanding Comics* is 215 pages in 9 chapters and examines all aspects of comics. The above excerpt is from Chapter One.

Review and Assess

Thinking About the Selection

1. **Respond:** Did you enjoy this selection? Why or why not?

2. **(a) Recall:** How does McCloud's view of comics change from his early childhood view to his present view? **(b) Make a Judgment:** Do you accept McCloud's final definition of comics, which says nothing about their entertainment value? Explain.

3. **Evaluate:** Do you think McCloud is justified in comparing comics to art forms such as film, music, and theater? Explain.

Scott McCloud

(b. 1960)

Scott McCloud started drawing comics at the age of twelve. After graduating from Syracuse University in 1982, he began his career as a cartoonist. He has since published an award-winning comic book series called *Zot!* as well as *Destroy!*, a parody of superhero comics.

Review and Assess

Literary Analysis

Visual Essay

1. Using a chart like this one, identify the main idea of this selection. Show how both the visuals and the text convey this idea.

2. Would the selection lose its impact if either the words or the visuals were eliminated? Explain.

3. How does McCloud's selection fit Will Eisner's description of comics as "sequential art"?

Connecting Literary Elements

4. Using a chart like this, analyze the varying **tone** of the selection.

Text	Visuals	Tone

5. Which word best describes the overall tone of the essay? Explain.

Reading Strategy

Using Visuals as a Key to Meaning

6. Find three places in which visuals add humor to text that is straightforward and serious. Explain each example.

7. Identify two illustrations that add meaning to McCloud's definition of a comic. Explain.

8. Find two illustrations that help explain the meaning of the term "sequential art." Explain how the visuals illustrate the meaning.

Extend Understanding

9. **Media Connection:** McCloud briefly addresses the difference between comics and animation. (a) What are some additional differences between comics and animation? (b) Which medium do you think is more effective in conveying a message? Why?

Quick Review

A **visual essay** is a piece of nonfiction that conveys its ideas through visual elements as well as language.

The **tone** in a literary work is the writer's attitude toward his or her audience and subject.

To **use visuals as a key to meaning,** rely on illustrations or photographs to help you understand and appreciate the meaning of accompanying text.

 Take It to the Net
www.phschool.com
Take the interactive self-test online to check your understanding of the selection.

Prepare to Read

Earhart Redux ◆ In These Girls, Hope Is a Muscle

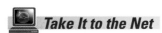

Take It to the Net

Visit www.phschool.com
for interactive activities
and instruction related to
the selections, including

- background
- graphic organizers
- literary elements
- reading strategies

Preview

Connecting to the Literature

Sometimes a failure can be the most powerful incentive for a new victory. If you have ever wanted something, lost it, and then wanted it even more, you will know the truth at the heart of these true stories.

Background

In 1932, at age thirty-five, Amelia Earhart became the first woman to fly solo across the Atlantic Ocean. Five years later, she attempted to fly around the world, accompanied only by a navigator. After circling three quarters of the globe, the pair disappeared on July 1, 1937, near New Guinea. Earhart's final message reported empty fuel tanks. Her plane was never found. In 1997, Linda Finch successfully re-created and completed Earhart's flight around the world in a similar aircraft.

Literary Analysis

Career Writing

Writing is an important part of a wide range of occupations—for example, television reporting, advertising, even police work. **Career writing** is any writing that is done as part of a person's job responsibilities. In this example, writer Tracy Kidder presents his review of a fellow reporter's work:

> This book is the product of a perfect marriage. The subject is timely and fascinating, and Madeleine Blais is a first-rate reporter and writer.

As you read the selections, note the type of career writing that each represents. Then, consider the qualities that the pieces share.

Comparing Literary Works

Each of the following selections tells about real women who are defined by the challenges they take on. As you read, compare the different experiences and challenges of the women in each piece, as well as the ways these writers address their subjects' struggles.

Reading Strategy

Determining the Author's Purpose

Career writing is shaped most of all by its purpose—the goal the writer sets out to achieve. When you **determine the author's purpose,** you seek to understand the writer's goal, which may be to inform, to entertain, or to persuade. You can determine the writer's purpose by paying close attention to details in the writing. Use a chart like the one shown to record details and identify each writer's purpose.

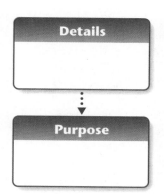

Vocabulary Development

aerodynamics (er´ ō dī nam´ iks) *n.* branch of mechanics dealing with the forces exerted by air or other gases in motion (p. 711)

hydraulic (hī drô´ lik) *adj.* operated by the movement and pressure of liquid (p. 713)

pursue (pər soo´) *v.* seek (p. 715)

improbable (im präb´ ə bəl) *adj.* unlikely to happen (p. 715)

derides (di rīdz´) *v.* ridicules (p. 715)

legacy (leg´ ə sē) *n.* anything handed down from an ancestor (p. 715)

riveting (riv´ it iŋ) *adj.* firmly holding attention (p. 717)

ruminative (roo´ mə nə təv) *adj.* meditative (p. 717)

adept (ə dept´) *adj.* highly skilled; expert (p. 717)

compelling (kəm pel´ iŋ) *adj.* forceful (p. 718)

Earhart Redux

Alex Chadwick

On March 17, 1997, national interest was piqued as Linda Finch set off to complete the flight that Amelia Earhart had attempted sixty years earlier. Alex Chadwick, a radio reporter for National Public Radio, conducted a radio interview with Linda Finch before her flight. The following is the script of Chadwick's interview.

BOB EDWARDS, HOST: This is *Morning Edition.* I'm Bob Edwards.

In Oakland, California, this morning, pilot Linda Finch takes off on an adventure that actually started 60 years ago. On this day in 1937, Amelia Earhart began her attempt to become the first person to fly around the world at the equator. She failed.

Her plane disappeared over the Pacific Ocean, but in that, she achieved a measure of immortality.

In the latest National Geographic Radio Expedition, NPR's[1] Alex Chadwick reports Linda Finch hopes to finish what Amelia Earhart began.

SOUNDS OF MACHINERY

ALEX CHADWICK, NPR REPORTER: The door to the hangar is bigger than any big theater movie screen. And it's opening slowly and improbably, folding outward on a horizontal midline and upward from the bottom. And there is Linda Finch's amazing airplane: 1930s aerodynamics, like an artifact from an old movie, or a dream.

LINDA FINCH, PILOT: The aircraft is very rare. There were only fifteen manufactured initially in the twenties and thirties, and there are only two left in the world.

CHADWICK: Ms. Finch is pretty rare herself. A 46-year-old grandmother who owns several nursing homes in Texas, and a pilot who restores and flies vintage fighters. Even so, replicating Amelia Earhart's flight is difficult. And though she doesn't like to say so, a little risky.

SOUNDS OF DOORS OPENING AND CLOSING

FINCH: We'll be flying in an aircraft that is the exact same model Amelia flew. And we'll be following the same route that she flew around the world.

CHADWICK: Well, I'm sure some people hearing about this flight would say, what is the point of setting off in an aircraft that's already failed in this once? I mean, it's dangerous. Maybe recklessly dangerous.

FINCH: Well, I have a lot of advantages that Amelia didn't have. We will have modern navigation, communication, and flight instruments that she just didn't have available at the time. The flight, I believe, needs to be done in the right airplane, to be historically correct, to generate the excitement in order to communicate our message.

I started learning about Amelia and really feel like I came to know her. And although I think that flying was definitely a part of her being,

---

1. NPR's National Public Radio's.

aerodynamics (er´ ō dī nam´ iks) *n.* branch of mechanics dealing with the forces exerted by air or other gases in motion

Reading Strategy
Determining the Author's Purpose
What is the author's goal in this passage?

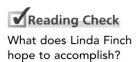**Reading Check**
What does Linda Finch hope to accomplish?

that she really flew to get the recognition to convince people that they could do what they wanted. Especially women in the 1930s. That people weren't limited to small lives. That they could have their dreams.

CHADWICK: Amelia Earhart was an aviation pioneer, daring and determined. The second flyer after Lindbergh[2] to solo across the Atlantic. Fourteen others had died trying to repeat his flight, and Amelia nearly did when a crucial instrument failed in bad weather.

Here's that earlier flyer after her Atlantic flight, when President Hoover presented her with a gold medal from the National Geographic Society.

AMELIA EARHART, PILOT: I came down until I could see the flight path blinking in the darkness. If it had been a smooth sea, I might have come too far. Whether I was 50 feet off the water or 150, I do not know, without my altimeter. I was too close, however.

CHADWICK: The plane that Amelia used on her round-the-world attempt, the Lockheed Electra 10-E, is 38.5 feet long, with a 55-foot wingspan. The tail angles back on a small, solid rubber rear wheel. The nose tilts upwards toward the sky. She glows like a polished aluminum athlete, broad-shouldered. Beautiful as a swan dive.

SOUND OF AIRPLANE ENGINE

She carries two nine-cylinder radial Pratt and Whitney Wasp engines. These are the first air-cooled engines developed. At 650 pounds, they produced more than 400 horsepower when they were introduced in 1926, and that was an extraordinary weight-power ratio for the time.

Linda Finch's plane has later, more powerful versions of that engine, as did Amelia Earhart's. Except for new navigation and communication gear, their planes are identical.

FINCH: The aircraft was in boxes and pieces and parts. And one of the things that I discovered was that prior to World War II, there were no parts manuals. You get just a big box of pieces, and it's like a jigsaw puzzle, you have to figure out how to put it together.

CHADWICK: She describes the Electra as graceful and slow in flight. Almost peaceful. Amelia did all her flying, but carried a navigator co-pilot. And so will Linda. The cockpit is a narrow, confined space, barely enough room for twin controls. And the enormous, banquet-sized steering wheels.

SOUND OF WHEELS TURNING

What do these wheels feel like? They look like they came out of

Literary Analysis
Career Writing
What information did Chadwick need to research in order to prepare this writing assignment?

---

2. **Lindbergh** Charles Lindbergh (1902–1974) made the first solo nonstop flight across the Atlantic Ocean on May 20–21, 1927.

1940s British sports cars or something.

FINCH: Exactly, and the wood is so worn. We actually had some new ones we could have put in. But I like these because they're worn and they've been in the airplane, obviously, since it was new.

CHADWICK: So, this is all human-powered controls for turning things and making the airplane fly?

FINCH: Absolutely. People are very surprised that there is just a thin cable and actually you move the cable. Everyone always says, does it have <u>hydraulic</u> controls? Absolutely not.

CHADWICK: These things here, these switches and hand controls. Those are original on the plane. This is what Amelia Earhart flew.

FINCH: Exactly. There are many things, the controls, throttle, and the propeller and mixture controls, the fuel selector gauges, the magneto switches, the gear indicator. All of the things that have to do with the airplane mechanically are in fact the same as Amelia's.

CHADWICK: The plane was in the airport in Memphis, en route for tests elsewhere. Linda, and navigator Bob Fodge, had refilled the main battery the evening before, and something had gone wrong. Overnight it leaked acid, eating away at a small panel of the undercarriage. They had to remove it.

The technology is 60 and 70 years old. Linda Finch knows how it works. Why it works. Why it's reliable. But she is attempting to fly around the world in an airplane where the rivets all show. And the cockpit windows slide open, and little accidents cause the flawless aluminum skin to weaken and decay.

The navigation electronics are as good as you could get. She has an on-board satellite link to the Internet. Schools can check her progress hourly. But the actual airplane is decades older than Linda Finch herself. And on many portions of this flight, she's going to have to overload that plane with fuel in order to cross open water.

What does your daughter think? What does your family think, when you are setting off to re-create a flight that Amelia Earhart did not survive?

FINCH: Well, my daughter is very supportive and excited and pleased. And is real involved in the project. On the other hand, she's a worrier. So, she always worries.

And she's most happy that we'll actually be sending the airplane's position back on the Internet every hour. So, I think she'll be watching that quite closely to see where we are.

CHADWICK: Oakland; across the country to Miami; then San Juan, Puerto Rico; Cumana, Venezuela; Paramari, Vos Serena; down to Natale in Brazil, and across to Africa. Dakkar, Injamana, Khartoum. It'll be hot over the desert. Karachi, Calcutta, Rangoon. In a couple of

hydraulic (hī drô′ lik) *adj.* operated by the movement and pressure of liquid

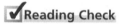

✓ Reading Check

How does Finch say her family has responded to her adventure?

months, she'll get to Lahe, New Guinea, the last place that Amelia Earhart was ever seen.

Here's Amelia, after flying the Atlantic.

EARHART: I hope that the flight has meant something to women in aviation. If it has, I shall feel it justified. But I can't claim anything else.

CHADWICK: And here is Linda Finch. In a tan wool gabardine flight suit, strains showing in her face a little from the work and the stress, but mostly looking eager to go finish that great adventure.

FINCH: Well, I don't know what happened to Amelia Earhart, and neither does anyone else, certainly. When I'm reading a book about Amelia and I get to the last communications that they heard from her, that's really where I stop reading. Because I just think it doesn't matter. What does matter is what Amelia did with her life, and that's really the focus of our project.

SOUND OF AN AIRPLANE PROPELLER

CHADWICK: Pilot Linda Finch, who sets out today to fly around the world in a Lockheed Electra 10-E, the plane Amelia Earhart flew.

For Radio Expeditions, this is Alex Chadwick reporting.

Alex Chadwick

(b. 1947)

As you read "Earhart Redux," you may have noticed the references to sound effects. Alex Chadwick's work as a correspondent for National Public Radio for more than twenty years has been marked by his use of such sounds to anchor his stories in reality.

Before becoming a radio correspondent, Chadwick earned a degree in communications from American University in Washington, D.C., and worked in Maine as both a radio reporter and a commercial fisherman.

Chadwick's accomplishments in radio include his essays and features on the critically acclaimed radio programs *Morning Edition* and *All Things Considered*. He also co-hosted the Public Broadcasting Service television series *Childhood* in 1991.

Review and Assess

Thinking About the Selection

1. **Respond:** Do you admire Linda Finch for undertaking her adventure? Explain.

2. **(a) Recall:** As the interview begins, what words does Alex Chadwick use to describe Finch? **(b) Analyze:** How does Chadwick seem to feel about Finch and her mission?

3. **(a) Recall:** What happened to Amelia Earhart when she attempted to fly around the world at the equator?
   (b) Evaluate: What details of the report add to the suspense about the outcome of Finch's endeavor?

4. **(a) Recall:** How often is Amelia Earhart's voice heard in the interview? **(b) Speculate:** What effect does Chadwick create by including the voice of Earhart?

5. **(a) Recall:** What sound effects does Chadwick use in his interview? **(b) Draw a Conclusion:** Why does Chadwick use the sound effects in his work?

6. **Evaluate:** In the interview, Earhart says, "I hope that the flight has meant something to women in aviation." What do you think Finch's flight might mean to these women?

7. **Assess:** How might Finch inspire the general public?

In These Girls, Hope Is a Muscle

Book Review by *Steve Gietschier*

If you have not yet had the opportunity to give your heart to a women's high school basketball team or to feel the passion of women's athletics in general, reading this book may be the start of something big. Although its poetic title alone could win an award, the text is even better: beautifully written, heartfelt, gently humorous but most important, forthright in its insistence that women as well as men should be able to <u>pursue</u> genuine excellence through sports.

Blais explains how <u>improbable</u> it is to find a championship basketball team of either gender, John Calipari's Massachusetts' squad[1] excluded, in Amherst, Mass., a town she <u>derides</u> as "probably the only place in the United States where men can wear berets and not get beaten up." Amherst, she says, "is, for the most part, smoke free, nuclear free and eager to free Tibet."[2] It is the proud home of Bread & Circus, the self-proclaimed world's largest health food store. More significantly, Amherst is, in Blais' view, "an achingly democratic sort of place in which tryouts for Little League, with their inevitable rejections, have caused people to suggest that more teams should be created so that no one is left out."

Far from an athlete herself, Blais nevertheless was still able to find unfolding within Amherst's "self-absorbed loftiness" the glistening struggle of superb competitors, the Lady Hurricanes of Amherst Regional High School. Picking up their story with the final game of the 1991–92 season, Blais followed their efforts throughout 1992–93, an epic campaign dedicated to overcoming a long <u>legacy</u> of being good, but just not good enough.

On the surface, then, this book is a simple tale of a singular basketball season. . . . Readers looking for no more than a good story

pursue (pər soo′) *v.* seek

improbable (im präb′ ə bəl) *adj.* unlikely to happen

derides (di rīdz′) *v.* ridicules

Reading Strategy
Determining the Author's Purpose Why does Gietschier include Blais's quote about the qualities of Amherst?

legacy (leg′ ə sē) *n.* anything handed down from an ancestor

---

1. **John Calipari's Massachusetts' squad** coach of an excellent basketball team at University of Massachusetts.
2. **to free Tibet** Once a semi-independent state, Tibet has been part of China since the 1950s.

can chart the season game by game and turn one page after another in anticipation of the next victory.

But there is so much more here to savor and absorb. The young women who give themselves so completely to their team's quest are extraordinary each in her own way. Burdened with the pains of adolescence, the duties that high school imposes and, in some cases, the tough circumstances of families rent asunder,[3] they learn from one another how to dig deep to find the resources they need to reach their goal.

In the process, they journey in so many ways to places Amherst women have never gone before, proving to themselves, their families, their town and all who will look with open eyes that women's sports can be an astoundingly fulfilling and moving experience.

---

3. **rent asunder** (ə sun′ dər) torn apart.

▶ **Critical Viewing**
How might this player's facial expression reflect the experiences of the Lady Hurricanes? **[Infer]**

As part of the marketing of a book, many publishers include brief reviews by well-known writers or public figures. Following are some of the comments that appeared on the book jacket of Madeleine Blais's book.

Book Jacket Copy for

In These Girls, Hope Is a Muscle Madeleine Blais

Advance praise for *In These Girls, Hope Is a Muscle*:

This book is the product of a perfect marriage. The subject is timely and fascinating, and Madeleine Blais is a first-rate reporter and writer.
—Tracy Kidder

Blais's narrative gift has produced a touching, exciting book about a subject largely ignored until now, namely women athletes. Her story of a year in the life of a high school basketball team and its hometown goes far beyond the obvious to illuminate how people really feel, how things really work.
—Anne Bernays

Begun as an article that appeared in the *New York Times Magazine*, *In These Girls, Hope Is a Muscle* offers a riveting close-up of the girls on a high school basketball team whose passion for the sport is rivaled only by their loyalty to one another. Reminiscent of John McPhee's *A Sense of Where You Are* and H. G. Bissinger's *Friday Night Lights*, Pulitzer Prize–winning journalist Madeleine Blais's book takes the reader through a singular season in the history of the Lady Hurricanes of Amherst, Massachusetts.

For years they had been known as a finesse team, talented and hard-working players who in the end lacked that final hardscrabble ingredient that would take them over the top to the state championship. They seemed doomed to mirror the college town they represented: kindly, ruminative, at times ineffectual; more adept at quoting Emily Dickinson[1] and singing nature songs than going to the basket.

One season, all that changed. Madeleine Blais takes us from try-outs to practices during the regular season, up through the final championship game against the mighty Hillies from Haverhill. The result is an astoundingly moving narrative that captures the complexities of girls' experiences in high school, in sports, and in our society.

---

1. **Emily Dickinson** (1830–1886), poet who was born and lived most of her life in Amherst, Massachusetts.

riveting (riv´ it iŋ) *adj.* firmly holding attention

ruminative (rōō´ mə nə təv) *adj.* meditative

adept (ə dept´) *adj.* highly skilled; expert

Reading Strategy
Determining the Author's Purpose What are two goals the writer exhibits in this passage?

In These Girls, Hope Is a Muscle ◆ 717

As their coach says, unlike training boys—whose arrogance and confidence often have to be eroded before a team can pull together—working with girls is all constructive. The way to build a girls' team is to build each player's self-confidence. During the course of this season we see the Amherst Lady Hurricanes in their fierce, funny, sisterhood-is-powerful quest for excellence.

As Blais reports, "This is just one team in one season. It alone cannot change the discrimination against girls and their bodies throughout history." But it is a <u>compelling</u>, funny, and touching literary exploration of one group of girls' fight for success and, perhaps most of all, respect. *In These Girls, Hope Is a Muscle* is both a dramatization of the success of the women's movement and a testimony to all the changes that have yet to come.

compelling (kəm pel′ iŋ)
adj. forceful

Madeleine Blais worked at the *Miami Herald* for eight years. A collection of her work, *The Heart Is an Instrument: Portraits in Journalism*, was published by the University of Massachusetts Press in 1992. Now a resident of Amherst, she has been on the faculty at the University of Massachusetts for six years.

Review and Assess

Thinking About the Selection

1. **Respond:** Does reading the review and the book-jacket blurb of *In These Girls, Hope Is a Muscle* make you want to read the book itself? Explain.

2. **(a) Recall:** In the opening of his review, which words does Gietschier use to describe Blais's book? **(b) Analyze:** Why do you think Gietschier likes Blais's book?

3. **(a) Recall:** What is the subject of the book *In These Girls, Hope Is a Muscle*? **(b) Infer:** Based on Gietschier's review, why do you think Blais chose to write the book?

4. **(a) Recall:** According to the book review, what do the girls prove about women's sports? **(b) Speculate:** Who do you think would be most persuaded to buy this book after reading the review?

5. **(a) Recall:** What two people are quoted in the book-jacket copy? **(b) Compare:** What do their comments have in common? **(c) Summarize:** Since the information following the quotes closely echoes the author's writing in the book, what would you say is Blais's main idea and attitude toward the subject?

6. **Compare and Contrast:** How is the format of the book-jacket blurb different from that of Gietschier's review?

Steve Gietschier

(b. 1948)
Steve Gietschier holds the game of basketball dear to his heart: His experiences coaching his daughter's team led him to seek out the assignment of reviewing *In These Girls, Hope Is a Muscle*, Madeleine Blais's gripping account of a high-school girls' basketball team's championship season.

Born in New York City, Gietschier earned his bachelor's degree from Georgetown University in Washington, D.C., and his doctorate from Ohio State University.

Since 1986, Gietschier has been the Director of Historical Records at *The Sporting News* in St. Louis, Missouri, the newspaper that originally published his review of Blais's book.

Review and Assess

Literary Analysis

Career Writing

1. Why is it important for a radio journalist to be a good writer?
2. Using a chart like the one below, list the characteristics of good radio journalism, as well as the characteristics of a well-written book review and book-jacket blurb.

Radio Journalism	Book Review	Book-Jacket Blurb

3. Based on your chart, how effective is each selection that you read?

Comparing Literary Works

4. Using a chart like the one below, compare the challenges faced by Linda Finch and the Lady Hurricanes.

Person/Group		Challenges	Strengths
	····▶		

5. How is a challenge to a team different from a challenge to an individual?
6. In your opinion, which selection is more successful at conveying the challenge its subject faces?

Reading Strategy

Determining the Author's Purpose

7. What do you think is Chadwick's **purpose** in conducting his interview with Linda Finch?
8. (a) Explain the different purposes of the book-jacket copy and the review. (b) Do you think the book review or the book-jacket copy is more effective in persuading people to read the book? Why?

Extend Understanding

9. **Career Link:** What other occupations can you think of in which writing is particularly important?

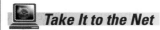

Writing WORKSHOP

Exposition: Problem-and-Solution Essay

A **problem-and-solution essay** identifies and explains a problem and then proposes a practical solution. In this workshop, you will write a problem-and-solution essay.

Assignment Criteria. Your problem-and-solution essay should have the following characteristics:

- A statement of the problem and a suggested solution
- Facts, statistics, and details that show the problem's scope and indicate how it can be solved
- Language appropriate to the level of knowledge of your audience
- A logical organization

To preview the criteria on which your problem-and-solution essay may be assessed, see the Rubric on page 725.

Prewriting

Choose a topic. Write your problem-and-solution essay about an issue of interest to you. One strategy is to conduct a **media scan,** reviewing local newspapers and television news programs for items about community issues and problems. List problems for which you can imagine practical solutions. Choose one as your essay topic.

Create a problem profile. Once you have chosen a topic, create a profile to help you determine which aspect of the problem you will address in your essay. Answer the following questions about the problem:

- Who or what is affected by the problem?
- What causes the problem to occur?
- What are some possible solutions to the problem?

Gather information. Collect the information you will need to start your draft. Assess all the possible solutions and weed out the less practical ones to narrow your list.

Identify your audience. Keep a specific audience in mind while you write: readers who have the ability to implement your suggestions. As you narrow your list of solutions, identify the aspects of each idea that will most likely appeal to your target audience.

Problem Profile

Problem: Litter is creating an unsafe environment.

Who is affected? *Everyone on Earth.*

What causes the problem?

Lack of:

- *responsibility*
- *environmental education*
- *sense of ownership*

What are possible solutions? *Stiffer fines, more policing, more environmental education, volunteer trash pickup*

Student Model

Before you begin drafting your problem-and-solution essay, read this student model and review the characteristics of effective problem-and-solution essays.

Naomi Barrowclough
Maplewood, NJ

Environmental Un-Consciousness

During a recent Earth Day cleanup, I became disgusted by the amount of trash I picked up within a two-hour period. People had thrown little papers, bits of plastic, and candy wrappers until the mess formed a multicolored carpet over the green grass. What people who litter may not realize is that litter creates serious environmental problems, in addition to prompting concerns over appearance.

> In the opening paragraph, the author provides a general statement of the problem.

We've all been told not to litter, but it does not seem to sink in. One person may think his or her contribution is only a microscopic addition when viewed against the whole. But if every person shared this sense of irresponsibility, Earth would soon be overwhelmed by pollution.

Litter is harmful for many reasons. For one, roadside litter is eventually washed into our waterways and oceans—water we use for drinking and recreation. Also, animals might entangle themselves or mistake trash for food and swallow it. In our public spaces, children spend a great deal of time in areas where they could be physically harmed by the pollution caused by litter.

> Here, the author provides greater detail to explain the problem more fully.

There is no simple solution to the problem of litter, only an array of possible solutions with one strategy in common: Create a feeling of ownership over public spaces. Some of the most popular sites for litter are beaches and parks because people feel no sense of ownership over these places. These same people might think twice about littering in their own homes.

> The author introduces a general solution here.

To create a feeling of ownership, it is necessary to educate children early about the environmental consequences of littering. Schools could lead field trips to local beaches or parks where students pick up trash and test water quality. If kids have to fish two shopping carts from the side of a stream, as I did, they might think twice about throwing something else on the ground. If they see that contaminated water is harmful to humans and wildlife, they might stop someone they see littering.

> In this paragraph, specific strategies for achieving the solution are introduced.

There is no easy way to stop littering. Fines and policing alone will not do the trick because people will just look before they litter. Until people understand that littering is irresponsible and has devastating environmental consequences, there will continue to be litterbugs. The solution lies in education and creating a sense of ownership about our public spaces.

> In the final paragraph, the author addresses a potential concern and then restates her solution.

Drafting

Organize your ideas. An effective organization for your essay breaks your ideas into clear categories. After an introduction that raises your audience's interest, develop the problem with detailed examples. Next, offer a solution. Use your conclusion to drive home the soundness of your ideas.

Elaborate. In order to persuade your readers, consider these types of evidence:

- **Statistics:** Provide numbers to show how many people would be affected by your solution.
- **Expert opinions:** Include the advice of those who have training and experience related to your topic.
- **Personal anecdotes:** Tell your readers about your own experiences with the problem or solution.
- **Testimonials:** Include comments from others on the effectiveness of your proposed solution.

Address readers' concerns. To convince those who may not approve of your solution, show them that you understand their concerns. Address their objections with explanations and evidence that suggest your solution is the best course of action.

Elaborate to Provide Evidence

Subject: Problem-and-solution essay on litter

Statistics to include:

    Number of tons of litter deposited in local park/year

    Water quality studies related to pollution from litter

Experts to cite:

    Environmental organizations

    Park and beach sanitation officials

    Local police

Anecdote to include:

    Earth Day trash pickup experience

Testimonials to provide:

    Educators involved with environmental issues

    Park officials

Revising

Revise to support generalizations. Look at each paragraph to be sure that the details support or explain the main idea of its topic sentence. Use the following strategies:

1. Highlight your topic sentence, the general statement from which the rest of the paragraph flows.

2. Underline the supporting sentences that develop this main idea.

3. Eliminate any sentences that do not support the main idea and cut those that simply restate it.

Model: Supporting Generalizations

Litter is harmful for many reasons. For one, roadside litter is eventually washed into our waterways and oceans— water we use for drinking and recreation. ~~It is also unpleasant to see trash floating in the water.~~ Also, animals might entangle themselves or mistake trash for food and swallow it.

> Naomi chose to eliminate the third sentence since it did not relate directly to her topic sentence.

Revise to evaluate and refine word choice. Review your draft as if you were a member of your target audience. Find terms that need to be defined, or vocabulary that seems too difficult or easy for your readers. Then, make changes accordingly.

General Audience: Another way to fight fatigue is to exercise regularly.

Target Audience of Experts: Another way to raise low levels of blood sugar is to get more exercise.

Compare the two sentences below. Why would the model be more appropriate than the nonmodel if you were presenting an essay to third graders?

Nonmodel	Model
But if every person shared this sense of irresponsibility, Earth would soon be overwhelmed by pollution.	If no one cared about how much pollution he or she caused, Earth would be completely polluted.

Publishing and Presenting

To make the best use of your problem-and-solution essay, share it with the people who can help you make a difference.

Send a letter. Send your essay to the appropriate government official, agency, or group. Share any responses you receive with classmates.

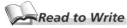
Read to Write

To see another example of problem-and-solution writing, see "To the Residents of A.D. 2029" on page 495.

 Prentice Hall Writing and Grammar Connection: Chapter 11

Rubric for Self-Assessment

Evaluate your problem-and-solution essay using the following criteria and rating scale:

Criteria	Rating Scale				
	Not very				Very
Is the problem explored adequately in the essay?	1	2	3	4	5
How effective is the suggested solution?	1	2	3	4	5
Do facts, statistics, and details effectively illustrate the problem and solution?	1	2	3	4	5
How appropriate is the language for the audience's knowledge level?	1	2	3	4	5
Was the information logically organized and presented?	1	2	3	4	5

Listening and Speaking WORKSHOP

Evaluating a Speech

Public speaking can be daunting for someone who is not used to presenting ideas in front of an audience. It may be easier to be evaluating the speech as an audience member. The two skills are closely related. In this workshop, you will learn how to **evaluate a speech**, which will give you a solid basis for preparing your own oral presentation.

Evaluate Content

Assess arguments for quality. A convincing speech should present arguments that are easily understood. While evaluating speeches, you may catch flaws or "holes" in poorly presented arguments. To find errors in arguments, use the following tips:

● Determine the type of argument the speaker uses.

● Decide whether you can identify a potential flaw, or consider whether you know of specific information that contradicts the argument.

Use the chart at right to anticipate common weaknesses in these types of arguments.

Type of Argument	Potential Flaw
Analogy: Compares one situation to another	Are the two situations really alike?
Authority: Cites the opinion of an expert	Is the expert knowledgeable and unbiased?
Emotion: Appeals to audience's feelings	Is the full argument balanced between logic and emotion?
Logic: Appeals to sense of rationalism	
Causation: Shows cause-and-effect relationship	Does the argument oversimplify?

Evaluate development of arguments. A good speech has a logical development and organization. Main points are introduced and developed with supporting evidence in the form of facts, statistics, anecdotes, charts, or graphs. In a conclusion, the speaker summarizes the main argument. The speaker might vary this organization slightly, but the structure should always be apparent to the audience.

Evaluate Delivery

Observe the speaker's choice of language. Speakers often include powerful language to make their speech more memorable and persuasive. As you listen, note instances where the speaker uses words or phrases with strong positive or negative *connotations,* or associations. Think about how the use of this language influences your own attitude toward the topic. Be alert to the fact that some speakers may rely on powerful or emotional language instead of reasoned arguments to advance their ideas.

Listen to the speaker's voice. Determine whether the speaker's voice is varied enough to hold an audience's attention and whether key points are emphasized. Also, think about whether the speaker's delivery creates a mood and tone that are appropriate to the subject.

Activity:
Analyzing a Speech Evaluate a famous speech, such as Martin Luther King's "I Have a Dream" speech, with your classmates. As a group, assess the argument for quality and generate a list of positive and negative qualities of that speech.

Assessment WORKSHOP

Connotation and Denotation

The reading sections of some tests require you to read a passage and answer multiple-choice questions about the meaning of a word or phrase. Use these strategies to help you distinguish between two different types of meaning:

- *Denotation* refers to the literal, or exact, meaning of a word. Denotations are characterized by a neutral, objective tone. For example, *thin* and *skinny* have similar denotations. They each describe a quality of depth or size.

- *Connotation* is the implied, or suggested, meaning of a word or phrase. A connotation can be positive or negative, depending on its context and each reader's past experience. For example, many people would say *thin* has a positive connotation but *skinny* has a negative one.

Test-Taking Strategies

- To determine a word's connotation, notice the reaction a word or phrase elicits from you.
- When searching for a denotation, look for a synonym that defines the word exactly, without placing it in a positive or negative light.

Sample Test Item

Directions: Read the passage, and then answer the question that follows.

Arlene Johnson's 1956 Cadillac convertible was a <u>battleship</u>. With its long silver body and huge chrome tail fins, this well-cared-for antique cruised through the streets of Coberton every morning with Arlene sitting proudly at the wheel. She was a petite woman, and even with the top down, the car swallowed her up.

1. What is the connotation of <u>battleship</u> in this passage?
   A large warship with guns and armor
   B large, powerful vehicle
   C compact, new vehicle
   D dilapidated, unsafe vehicle

Answer and Explanation

The correct answer is *B,* the implied meaning of *battleship*. *A* is a literal definition of battleship and is therefore a denotation that does not make sense in the context of the passage. *C* and *D* are incorrect because the passage indicates an older, larger vehicle that is well maintained.

▶ Practice

Directions: Read the passage, and then answer the questions that follow.

The Elmont High School Blazers struggled through their <u>worst</u> football season ever. Each week, they walked onto Elmont Field with the hope of victory and walked off with another loss. After four losses, with the stands nearly empty, the team still <u>strode</u> onto the field with pride.

1. What is the denotation of <u>worst</u> in this passage?
   A most embarrassing
   B most stunning
   C most difficult
   D most bad

2. What is the connotation of <u>strode</u> in this passage?
   A walked slowly and dejectedly
   B walked purposefully
   C raced at a quick pace
   D moved hesitantly

Why Read Literature?

A dramatic work can have multiple dimensions. You might explore one dimension while reading and then find something completely new after learning more about its history. Preview these examples that show how you can explore many sides of a single work of literature.

1

Read for the Love of Literature

No other author has been as widely read and admired as William Shakespeare. Discover Shakespeare for yourself as you read *Romeo and Juliet,* page 770.

2

Read for Information

It is one thing to imagine the action as you read *Romeo and Juliet,* but quite another to picture a performance in Shakespeare's time. Find out why the role of Juliet was always played by a young boy—along with other interesting facts—when you travel back to the stage of seventeenth-century England in **"The Shakespearean Theater,"** page 764.

One reason Shakespeare's plays have gained worldwide popularity is that they touch on so many aspects of the human experience. You may be amazed at just how adaptable his plays are when you read this unit's *Connections* feature, **"Shakespeare in Today's World,"** page 878.

3

Read to Be Inspired

Shakespeare's story of two young lovers kept apart by a senseless feud still retains its power today. In 1993, when a young Serb man and his Muslim lover died in each other's arms during bitter ethnic warfare in Bosnia, they were instantly dubbed "Romeo and Juliet." As you read *Romeo and Juliet,* you will understand why this story continues to inspire comparison today.

 Take It to the Net

Visit the Web site for online instruction and activities related to each selection in this unit.
www.phschool.com

How to Read Literature

Use Strategies for Reading Drama

While drama shares many elements with prose, fiction, and poetry, the greatest difference is that dramas are designed to be performed on a stage before an audience. Since you will not have the benefit of a performance to help you interpret the text, use the following strategies when reading drama.

1. Picture the action.

- Use stage directions to form a mental image of the way characters move around on stage and interact with one another.

- Pay close attention to stage directions related to setting. For example, if the action takes place in a 1950s drugstore, it will have a much different feel than if it is set in a character's living room.

2. Use text aids.

Text aids are notes outside the main text that clarify the meaning of a word or phrase or add detailed information.

- Try not to let text aids interrupt the flow of your reading. If you come to an unfamiliar phrase, first try to figure it out from context.

- If you need to use a text aid, substitute the footnoted language directly into the original sentence, and then reread the new sentence with the surrounding text.

3. Read blank verse.

Blank verse is a poetic form that uses a regular meter to create a certain mood and rhythm. The author often uses blank verse to create a more formal atmosphere. To get used to the feel of blank verse, read passages aloud, stressing every second syllable. Read at a steady pace, and pause only when you see punctuation, as the model at right suggests.

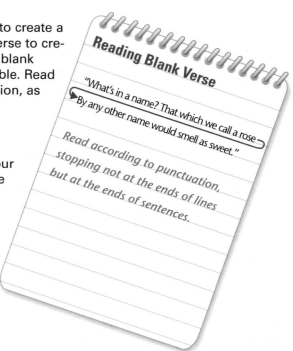

Reading Blank Verse

"What's in a name? That which we call a rose
By any other name would smell as sweet."

Read according to punctuation, stopping not at the ends of lines but at the ends of sentences.

4. Paraphrase.

Paraphrase, or summarize, a key idea or passage in your own words to ensure that you understand what you have read.

- Replace formal language with words that are more commonly used.

- When summarizing, eliminate ideas that are not essential to the meaning of the passage.

As you read the selections in this unit, review the reading strategies and apply them to strengthen your understanding of the text.

Prepare to Read

The Dancers

Take It to the Net

Visit www.phschool.com
for interactive activities
and instruction related to
"The Dancers," including
- background
- graphic organizers
- literary elements
- reading strategies

Preview

Connecting to the Literature

Like most people, you probably experience times when your social life does not go smoothly. You might go to a party and find that you do not know anyone, or mistakenly make plans with two different people for the same evening. As you read this play, notice how the characters respond to such awkward situations.

Background

In the 1950s, the setting for "The Dancers," people danced differently from the way they do now. Partners held each other, and their movements were synchronized and determined by the type of dance they were doing. It was not uncommon for children to take dance lessons in which they learned ballroom dances such as the waltz, the fox trot, and the cha-cha.

Literary Analysis

Staging

Staging is one of the ways in which a script is brought to life. It includes the sets, lighting, sound effects, costumes, and the way the actors move and deliver their lines. Staging is based on the stage directions, which are often bracketed and italicized. The staging excerpt below provides a brief description of the appearance and actions of one character, Emily, as she arrives on stage. In addition, it gives the time of day in which the scene takes place:

> [ELIZABETH CREWS *and her daughter* EMILY *come into the drugstore.* EMILY *is about seventeen and very pretty. This afternoon, however, it is evident that she is unhappy.*]

As you read the play, use the dialogue, stage directions, and your imagination to stage the play in your mind's eye.

Connecting Literary Elements

A drama relies completely on staging and dialogue to tell a story. **Dialogue** is a conversation between characters. It is used to reveal the qualities and situations of the characters and to advance the action of the play. As you read, notice how the staging and dialogue work together to reveal the events of the play.

Reading Strategy

Picturing the Action

Plays are meant to be performed, so it is important to **picture the action** as you read. To picture the action, you should use these strategies:

- Read stage directions carefully and draw from your own experience to connect to the scene being set.
- Notice subtleties about characters' emotions, insecurities, or hopes.

Using a chart like the one on the right, note descriptions of characters and details of setting to help you picture the action.

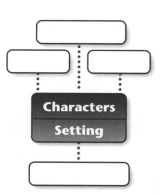

Vocabulary Development

genteel (jen tēl´) *adj.* polite (p. 741)

mortified (môrt´ ə fīd´) *v.* humiliated (p. 742)

defiance (dē fī´ əns) *n.* open resistance (p. 743)

console (kən sōl´) *v.* comfort (p. 751)

The

CHARACTERS

A **WAITRESS** in the local drugstore

INEZ STANLEY, Horace's older sister

ELIZABETH CREWS, Emily's mother

EMILY CREWS, a popular seventeen
year old

HERMAN STANLEY, Inez's husband

HORACE, a sensitive eighteen year old

MARY CATHERINE DAVIS, a
plainer girl of Emily's
age

VELMA MORRISON, another
young girl

TOM DAVIS, Mary Catherine's
father

MRS. DAVIS, Mary Catherine's mother

SETTING

Harrison, Texas

Dancers

Horton Foote

[*Scene: The stage is divided into four acting areas: downstage left is the living room of* INEZ *and* HERMAN STANLEY. *Downstage right is part of a small-town drugstore. Upstage right is the living room of* ELIZABETH CREWS. *Upstage left, the yard and living room of* MARY CATHERINE DAVIS. *Since the action should flow continuously from one area to the other, only the barest amount of furnishings should be used to suggest what each area represents. The lights are brought up on the drugstore, downstage right.* WAITRESS *is there.* INEZ STANLEY *comes into the drugstore. She stands for a moment thinking. The* WAITRESS *goes over to her.*]

WAITRESS. Can I help you?

INEZ. Yes, you can if I can think of what I came in here for. Just gone completely out of my mind. I've been running around all day. You see, I'm expecting some company tonight. My brother Horace. He's coming on a visit.

[ELIZABETH CREWS *and her daughter* EMILY *come into the drugstore.* EMILY *is about seventeen and very pretty. This afternoon, however, it is evident that she is unhappy.*]

Hey . . .

ELIZABETH. We've just been by your house.

Literary Analysis
Staging What images do these stage directions create for you?

✔**Reading Check**

How does Emily look when she comes into the drugstore?

INEZ. You have? Hello, Emily.

EMILY. Hello.

ELIZABETH. We made some divinity[1] and took it over for Horace.

INEZ. Well, that's so sweet of you.

ELIZABETH. What time is he coming in?

INEZ. Six-thirty.

ELIZABETH. Are you meeting him?

INEZ. No—Herman. I've got to cook supper. Can I buy you all a drink?

ELIZABETH. No, we have to get Emily over to the beauty parlor.

INEZ. What are you wearing tonight, Emily?

ELIZABETH. She's wearing that sweet little net[2] I got her the end of last summer. She's never worn it to a dance here.

INEZ. I don't think I've ever seen it. I'll bet it looks beautiful on her. I'm gonna make Horace bring you by the house so I can see you before the dance.

WAITRESS. Excuse me. . . .

INEZ. Yes?

WAITRESS. Have you thought of what you wanted yet? I thought I could be getting it for you.

INEZ. That's sweet, honey . . . but I haven't thought of what I wanted yet. [*To* ELIZABETH *and* EMILY.] I feel so foolish, I came in here for something, and I can't remember what.

WAITRESS. Cosmetics?

INEZ. No . . . you go on. I'll think and call you.

WAITRESS. All right. [*She goes.*]

INEZ. Emily, I think it's so sweet of you to go to the dance with Horace. I know he's going to be thrilled when I tell him.

ELIZABETH. Well, you're thrilled too, aren't you, Emily?

EMILY. Yes, ma'm.

ELIZABETH. I told Emily she'd thank me some day for not permitting her to sit home and miss all the fun.

EMILY. Mama, it's five to four. My appointment is at four o'clock.

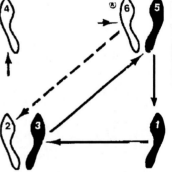

Reading Strategy
Picturing the Action
What kind of expression do you think Emily has on her face when she responds to her mother? Why?

---

1. **divinity** soft, creamy candy made of sugar, egg whites, corn syrup, flavoring, and nuts.
2. **sweet little net** dress made of delicate, lacy fabric.

ELIZABETH. Well, you go on in the car.

EMILY. How are you gonna get home?

ELIZABETH. I'll get home. Don't worry about me.

EMILY. OK. [*She starts out.*]

INEZ. 'Bye, Emily.

EMILY. 'Bye. [*She goes on out.*]

ELIZABETH. Does Horace have a car for tonight?

INEZ. Oh, yes. He's taking Herman's.

ELIZABETH. I just wondered. I wanted to offer ours if he didn't have one.

INEZ. That's very sweet—but we're giving him our car every night for the two weeks of his visit. Oh—I know what I'm after. Flowers. I have to order Emily's corsage for Horace. I came in here to use the telephone to call you to find out what color Emily's dress was going to be.

ELIZABETH. Blue.

INEZ. My favorite color. Walk me over to the florist.

ELIZABETH. All right.

[*They go out as the lights fade. The lights are brought up downstage left on the living room of* INEZ STANLEY. HERMAN STANLEY *and his brother-in-law,* HORACE, *come in.* HERMAN *is carrying* HORACE'*s suitcase.* HERMAN *is in his middle thirties.* HORACE *is eighteen, thin, sensitive, but a likable boy.*]

HERMAN. Inez. Inez. We're here.

[*He puts the bag down in the living room.* INEZ *comes running in from stage right.*]

INEZ. You're early.

HERMAN. The bus was five minutes ahead of time.

INEZ. Is that so? Why, I never heard of that. [*She kisses her brother.*] Hello, honey.

HORACE. Hello, sis.

INEZ. You look fine.

HORACE. Thank you.

INEZ. You haven't put on a bit of weight though.

HORACE. Haven't I?

INEZ. Not a bit. I'm just going to stuff food down you and put some weight on you while you're here. How's your appetite?

HORACE. Oh, it's real good. I eat all the time.

Reading Strategy
Picturing the Action
Picture in your mind how Emily looks as she starts to leave the drugstore. Is she in a hurry?

Literary Analysis
Staging What kind of staging do you think could be added to this dialogue between Horace and Inez?

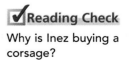Reading Check

Why is Inez buying a corsage?

INEZ. Fine. Why, I think he dances real well. Don't you, Herman?

HERMAN. Yes, I do. Just fine, Inez.

INEZ. Just a lovely dancer, all he needs is confidence. He is very light on his feet. And he has a fine sense of rhythm—why, brother, you're a born dancer—

[HORACE *is smiling over the compliments, half wanting to believe what they say, but then not so sure. He is dancing with her around the room as the lights fade. They are brought up on the area upstage right.* EMILY CREWS *is in her living room. She has on her dressing gown.*[3] *She is crying.* ELIZABETH, *her mother, comes in from upstage right.*]

ELIZABETH. Emily.

EMILY. Yes, ma'm.

ELIZABETH. Do you know what time it is?

EMILY. Yes, ma'm.

ELIZABETH. Then why in the world aren't you dressed?

EMILY. Because I don't feel good.

ELIZABETH. Emily . . .

EMILY. I don't feel good . . . [*She begins to cry.*] Oh, Mother. I don't want to go to the dance tonight. Please, ma'm, don't make me. I'll do anything in this world for you if you promise me . . .

ELIZABETH. Emily. This is all settled. You are going to that dance. Do you understand me. You are going to that dance. That sweet, nice brother of Inez Stanley's will be here any minute. . . .

EMILY. Sweet, nice brother. He's a goon. That's what he is. A regular goon. A bore and a goon. . . .

ELIZABETH. Emily . . .

EMILY. That's all he is. Just sits and doesn't talk. Can't dance. I'm not going to any dance or any place else with him and that's final.

[*She runs out stage right.*]

ELIZABETH. Emily . . . Emily . . . You get ready this minute . . . [*The doorbell rings. Yelling.*] Emily . . . Emily . . . Horace is here. I want you down those stairs in five minutes . . . dressed.

[*She goes out stage left and comes back in followed by* HORACE, *all dressed up. He has a corsage box in his hand.*]

Hello, Horace.

---

3. **dressing gown** loose robe.

HORACE. Good evening.

ELIZABETH. Sit down, won't you, Horace? Emily is a little late getting dressed. You know how girls are.

HORACE. Yes, ma'm.

[*He sits down. He seems a little awkward and shy.*]

ELIZABETH. Can I get you something to drink, Horace?

HORACE. No, ma'm.

[*A pause.* ELIZABETH *is obviously very nervous about whether* EMILY *will behave or not.*]

ELIZABETH. Are you sure I can't get you a coca-cola or something?

HORACE. No. Thank you.

ELIZABETH. How's your family?

HORACE. Just fine, thank you.

ELIZABETH. I bet your sister was glad to see you.

HORACE. Yes, she was.

ELIZABETH. How's your family? Oh, I guess I asked you that, didn't I?

HORACE. Yes, you did.

[ELIZABETH *keeps glancing off stage right, praying that* EMILY *will put in an appearance.*]

ELIZABETH. I understand you've become quite an accomplished dancer. . . .

HORACE. Oh . . . well . . . I . . .

ELIZABETH. Inez tells me you do all the new steps.

HORACE. Well—I . . .

ELIZABETH. Excuse me. Let me see what is keeping that girl.

[*She goes running off stage right.* HORACE *gets up. He seems very nervous. He begins to practice his dancing. He seems more unsure of himself and awkward. . . . We can hear* ELIZABETH *offstage knocking on* EMILY's *door. At first* HORACE *isn't conscious of the knocking or the ensuing conversation and goes on practicing his dancing. When he first becomes conscious of what's to follow he tries to pay no attention. Then gradually he moves over to the far left side of the stage. The first thing we hear is* ELIZABETH's <u>genteel</u> *tapping at* EMILY's *door. Then she begins to call, softly at first, then louder and louder.*]

Emily. Emily. Emily Crews. Emily Carter Crews. . . . [*The pounding offstage is getting louder and louder.*] Emily. I can hear you in there. Now open that door.

Literary Analysis
Staging and Dialogue
Does the dialogue effectively convey Elizabeth's nervousness mentioned in the stage directions? Explain.

Reading Strategy
Picturing the Action
Describe how you picture Horace's body language as he overhears the conversation going on offstage.

genteel (jen tēl′) *adj.* polite

**Reading Check**

Why is Emily still in her dressing gown and crying when Horace arrives?

EMILY. [*Screaming back.*] I won't. I told you I won't.

ELIZABETH. Emily Carter Crews. You open that door immediately.

EMILY. I won't.

ELIZABETH. I'm calling your father from downtown if you don't open that door right this very minute.

EMILY. I don't care. I won't come out.

ELIZABETH. Then I'll call him. [*She comes running in from stage right.* HORACE *quickly gets back to his chair and sits.*] Excuse me, Horace.

[*She crosses through the room and goes out upstage right.* HORACE *seems very ill at ease. He looks at the box of flowers. He is very warm. He begins to fan himself.* ELIZABETH *comes back in the room from upstage right. She is very nervous. But she tries to hide her nervousness in an overly social manner.* ELIZABETH *has decided to tell a fib.*]

Horace, I am so sorry to have to ruin your evening, but my little girl isn't feeling well. She has a headache and a slight temperature and I've just called the doctor and he says he thinks it's very advisable that she stay in this evening. She's upstairs insisting she go, but I do feel under the circumstances I had just better keep her in. I hope you understand.

HORACE. Oh, yes ma'm. I do understand.

ELIZABETH. How long do you plan to visit us, Horace?

HORACE. Two weeks.

ELIZABETH. That's nice. [*They start walking offstage left.*] Please call Emily tomorrow and ask her out again. She'll just be heartbroken if you don't.

HORACE. Yes, ma'm. Good night.

ELIZABETH. Good night, Horace. [HORACE *goes out.* ELIZABETH *calls out after him.*] Can you see, Horace? [*In the distance we hear* HORACE *answer.*]

HORACE. Yes, ma'm.

ELIZABETH. Now you be sure and call us tomorrow. You hear? [*She stands waiting for a moment. Then she walks back across stage to upstage right, screaming at the top of her voice.*] Emily Carter Crews. You have mortified me. You have mortified me to death. I have, for your information, called your father and he is interrupting his work and is coming home this very minute and he says to tell you that you are not to be allowed to leave this house again for two solid weeks. Is that perfectly clear?

[*She is screaming as she goes out upstage right. The lights are brought down. They are brought up immediately downstage right on*

Reading Strategy
Picturing the Action
How do you picture the facial expressions of Horace and Elizabeth as she apologizes to him?

mortified (môrt′ ə fīd) *v.* humiliated

the drugstore. It is half an hour later. HORACE *comes in. He seats himself at the counter. He still has the box of flowers. The drugstore is deserted. A* WAITRESS *is up near the front with her arms on the counter. She keeps glancing at a clock.* HORACE *is examining a menu . . .*]

HORACE. Can I have a chicken salad sandwich?

WAITRESS. We're all out of that.

HORACE. Oh.

[*He goes back to reading the menu.*]

WAITRESS. If it's all the same to you, I'd rather not make a sandwich. I'm closing my doors in ten minutes.

HORACE. Oh. Well, what would you like to make?

WAITRESS. Any kind of ice cream or soft drinks. [*She looks up at the ice cream menu.*] Coffee is all gone.

HORACE. How about a chocolate ice cream soda?

WAITRESS. O.K. Coming up. [*She starts to mix the soda. She talks as she works.*] Going to the dance?

HORACE. No.

WAITRESS. The way you're all dressed up I thought for sure you were going.

HORACE. No. I was, but I changed my mind.

[MARY CATHERINE DAVIS *comes in the drugstore from downstage right. Somehow in her young head she has gotten the idea that she is a plain girl and in <u>defiance</u> for the pain of that fact she does everything she can to make herself look plainer.*]

WAITRESS. Hello, Mary Catherine. Been to the movies?

MARY CATHERINE. Yes, I have.

[*The* WAITRESS *puts the drink down in front of* HORACE. *He begins to drink.*]

WAITRESS. What'll you have, Mary Catherine?

MARY CATHERINE. Vanilla ice cream.

▲ **Critical Viewing**
What does this photograph reveal about life in the 1950s, the setting for "The Dancers"? **[Infer]**

defiance (dē fī′ əns) *n.* open resistance

✔**Reading Check**
What excuse does Elizabeth give for Emily's refusal to go to the dance?

The Dancers ◆ 743

WAITRESS. O.K. [*She gets the ice cream. She talks as she does so.*] There weren't many at the picture show tonight, I bet. I can always tell by whether we have a crowd in here or not after the first show. I guess everybody is at the dance.

MARY CATHERINE. I could have gone, but I didn't want to. I didn't want to miss the picture show. Emily Crews didn't go. Leo couldn't get home from summer school and she said she was refusing to go. Her mother made a date for her with some bore from out of town without consulting her and she was furious about it. I talked to her this afternoon. She said she didn't know yet how she would get out of it, but she would. She said she had some rights. Her mother doesn't approve of Leo and that's a shame because they are practically engaged.

WAITRESS. I think Emily is a very cute girl, don't you?

MARY CATHERINE. Oh, yes. I think she's darling.

[HORACE *has finished his drink and is embarrassed by their talk. He is trying to get the* WAITRESS'*s attention but doesn't quite know how. He finally calls to the* WAITRESS.]

HORACE. Miss . . .

WAITRESS. Yes?

HORACE. How much do I owe you?

WAITRESS. Twenty cents.

HORACE. Thank you.

[*He reaches in his pocket for the money.*]

WAITRESS. Emily has beautiful clothes, doesn't she?

MARY CATHERINE. Oh, yes. She does.

WAITRESS. Her folks are rich?

MARY CATHERINE. She has the prettiest things. But she's not a bit stuck up. . . .

[*He holds the money out to the* WAITRESS.]

HORACE. Here you are.

WAITRESS. Thank you. [*She takes the money and rings it up in the cash register.* HORACE *goes on out.* WAITRESS *shakes her head as he goes.*] There's a goofy nut if I ever saw one. He's got flowers under his arm. He's wearing a tux and yet he's not going to the dance. Who is he?

MARY CATHERINE. I don't know. I never saw him before.

[*The* WAITRESS *walks to the edge of the area and looks out. She comes back shaking her head. She sits on the stool beside* MARY CATHERINE.]

Literary Analysis
Staging What do you think Horace is doing in this scene to get the waitress's attention?

Reading Strategy
Picturing the Action How do you picture Horace, based on the waitress's description?

WAITRESS. [*While laughing and shaking her head.*] I ought to call the Sheriff and have him locked up. Do you know what he's doing?

MARY CATHERINE. No. What?

WAITRESS. Standing on the corner. Dancing back and forth. He's holding his arm up like he's got a girl and everything. Wouldn't it kill you? [*Goes to the front and looks out.*] See him?

MARY CATHERINE. No. He's stopped.

WAITRESS. What's he doing?

MARY CATHERINE. Just standing there. Looking kind of lost.

[MARY CATHERINE *comes back to the counter. She starts eating her ice cream again.*]

WAITRESS. Well—it takes all kinds.

MARY CATHERINE. I guess so.

[*She goes back to eating her ice cream. The lights are brought down. The lights are brought up on the area downstage left. The living room of the* STANLEYS. INEZ *is there reading a book.* HERMAN *comes in.*]

HERMAN. Hi, hon.

INEZ. Hello. . . .

HERMAN. What's the matter with you? You look down in the dumps.

INEZ. No, I'm just disgusted.

HERMAN. What are you disgusted about?

INEZ. Horace. I had everything planned so beautifully for him and then that silly Emily has to go and hurt his feelings.

HERMAN. Well, honey, that was pretty raw, the trick she pulled.

INEZ. I know. But he's a fool to let that get him down. He should have just gone to the dance by himself and proved her wrong. . . . Why like I told him. Show her up. Rush a different girl every night. Be charming. Make yourself popular. But it's like trying to talk to a stone wall. He refused to go out any more. He says he's going home tomorrow.

HERMAN. Where is he now?

INEZ. Gone to the movies.

HERMAN. Well, honey. I hate to say it, but in a way it serves you right. I've told you a thousand times if I've told you once. Leave the boy alone. He'll be all right. Only don't push him. You and your mother have pushed the boy and pushed him and pushed him.

INEZ. And I'm going to keep on pushing him. I let him off tonight

Literary Analysis
Staging Would additional stage directions convey a clearer image of Horace, or is the dialogue sufficient? Explain.

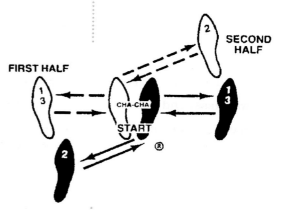

✓**Reading Check**
Why is Inez disgusted?

EMILY. Hello, Horace. . . . Do you know Mary Catherine Davis?

HORACE. No. How do you do.

MARY CATHERINE. How do you do.

EMILY. I feel awfully bad about last night, Horace. My mother says that you know I wasn't really sick. I just wanted to tell you that it had nothing to do with you, Horace. It was a battle between me and my mother. Mary Catherine can tell you. I promised the boy I go with not to go with any other boys . . .

HORACE. Oh, that's all right, I understand.

EMILY. You see, we've gone steady for two years. All the other boys in town understand it and their feelings are not a bit hurt if I turn them down. Are they, Mary Catherine?

MARY CATHERINE. No.

EMILY. Mary Catherine is my best friend and she can tell you I'm not stuck up. And I would have gone, anyway, except I was so mad at my mother . . .

MARY CATHERINE. Emily is not stuck up a bit. Emily used to date all the boys before she began going with Leo steadily. . . . Didn't you, Emily?

EMILY. Uh-huh. How long are you going to be here, Horace?

HORACE. Well, I haven't decided, Emily.

EMILY. Well, I hope you're not still hurt with me.

HORACE. No, I'm not, Emily.

EMILY. Well, I'm glad for that. Mary Catherine, can you come with us?

MARY CATHERINE. No, I can't, Emily. Velma came in after the first show started and I promised to wait here for her and we'd walk home together.

EMILY. Come on. We can ride around and watch for her.

MARY CATHERINE. No. I don't dare. You know how sensitive Velma is. If she looked in here and saw I wasn't sitting at this counter she'd go right home and not speak to me again for two or three months.

EMILY. Velma's too sensitive. You shouldn't indulge her in it.

MARY CATHERINE. I'm willing to grant you that. But you all are going off to college next year and Velma and I are the only ones that are going to be left here and I can't afford to get her mad at me.

EMILY. O.K. I'll watch out for you and if we're still riding around when Velma gets out, we'll pick you up.

MARY CATHERINE. Fine. . . .

EMILY. 'Bye. . . .

Literary Analysis
Staging and Dialogue
Would staging enhance the dialogue in this scene? Explain.

Reading Strategy
Picturing the Action How do you picture Horace as Emily apologizes to him?

MARY CATHERINE. 'Bye. . . .

EMILY. 'Bye, Horace.

HORACE. Good-bye, Emily.

[*She goes out downstage right.*]

MARY CATHERINE. She's a lovely girl. She was my closest friend until this year. Now we're still good friends, but we're not as close as we were. We had a long talk about it last week. I told her I understood. She and Eloise Dayton just naturally have a little more in common now. They're both going steady and they're going to the same college. [*A pause.*] They're going to Sophie Newcomb.[4] Are you going to college?

HORACE. Uh-huh.

MARY CATHERINE. You are? What college?

HORACE. The University. . . .

MARY CATHERINE. Oh. I know lots of people there. [*A pause.*] I had a long talk with Emily about my not getting to go. She said she thought it was wonderful that I wasn't showing any bitterness about it. [*A pause.*] I'm getting a job next week so I can save up enough money to go into Houston to Business School. I'll probably work in Houston some day. If I don't get too lonely. Velma Morrison's oldest sister went into Houston and got herself a job but she almost died from loneliness. She's back here now working at the Court House. Oh, well . . . I don't think I'll get lonely. I think a change of scenery would be good for me.

[VELMA MORRISON *comes in downstage right. She is about the same age as* MARY CATHERINE. *She is filled with excitement.*]

VELMA. Mary Catherine, you're going to be furious with me. But Stanley Sewell came in right after you left and he said he'd never forgive me if I didn't go riding with him. . . . I said I had to ask you first. As I had asked you to wait particularly for me and that I knew you were very sensitive.

MARY CATHERINE. I'm very sensitive. You're very sensitive. . . . I have never in my life stopped speaking to you over anything.

---

4. **Sophie Newcomb** H. Sophie Newcomb College for Women in New Orleans, Louisiana.

Literature in context   Cultural Connection

The 1950s Drugstore

Many of the scenes in "The Dancers" are set in a drugstore. In addition to selling medicine, soap, and other necessities, the drugstore of the 1950s offered people a place to hear local gossip and get something to eat at the soda fountain. Few drugstores today have soda fountains that sell ice cream cones and sundaes.

Back in the 1950s, you could sit at the counter and have a small sandwich and a soda while you listened to the jukebox. Many owners expanded their stores by adding booths and tables and by extending the menu to include hot dogs, hamburgers, and French fries. Many booths had their own "private" jukeboxes, on which couples could play their favorite songs. Horton Foote's play captures just this type of shop.

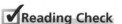

Reading Check

Why does Mary Catherine want to wait for Velma?

MARY CATHERINE. I love to dance.

HORACE. Well . . . I don't dance too well.

MARY CATHERINE. There's nothing to it but confidence.

HORACE. That's what my sister says . . .

MARY CATHERINE. I didn't learn for the longest kind of time for lack of confidence and then Emily gave me a long lecture about it and I got confidence and went ahead and learned. Would you like to come in for a while?

HORACE. Well . . . if it's all right with you. . . .

MARY CATHERINE. I'd be glad to have you.

HORACE. Thank you.

[*They go into the area.* MARY CATHERINE'S *father,* TOM DAVIS, *is seated there in his undershirt. He works in a garage.*]

MARY CATHERINE. Hello, Daddy.

TOM. Hello, baby.

MARY CATHERINE. Daddy, this is Horace.

TOM. Hello, son.

HORACE. Howdy do, sir.

[*They shake hands.*]

MARY CATHERINE. Horace is Mrs. Inez Stanley's brother. He's here on a visit.

TOM. That's nice. Where's your home, son?

HORACE. Flatonia.

TOM. Oh, I see. Well, are you young people going to visit for a while?

MARY CATHERINE. Yes, sir.

TOM. Well, I'll leave you then. Good night.

MARY CATHERINE. Good night, Daddy.

HORACE. Good night, sir. [*He goes out upstage left.*] What does your father do?

MARY CATHERINE. He works in a garage. He's a mechanic. What does your father do?

HORACE. He's a judge.

MARY CATHERINE. My father worries so because he can't afford to send me to college. My mother told him that was all foolishness. That I'd rather go to business school anyway.

HORACE. Had you rather go to business school?

Reading Strategy
Picturing the Action Do the staging directions or the dialogue provide a clearer image of Mary Catherine's dad? Explain.

Literary Analysis
Staging If you could add a description of the set at this point, what would it be?

MARY CATHERINE. I don't know. [*A pause.*] Not really. But I'd never tell him that. When I was in the seventh grade I thought I would die if I couldn't get there, but then when I was in the ninth, Mother talked to me one day and told me Daddy wasn't sleeping at nights for fear I'd be disappointed if he couldn't send me, so I told him the next night I decided I'd rather go to business school. He seemed relieved. [*A pause.*]

HORACE. Mary Catherine. I . . . uh . . . heard you say a while ago that you didn't dance because you lacked confidence and uh . . . then I heard you say you talked it over with Emily and she told you what was wrong and you got the confidence and you went ahead . . .

MARY CATHERINE. That's right. . . .

HORACE. Well . . . It may sound silly and all to you . . . seeing I'm about to start my first year at college . . . but I'd like to ask you a question. . . .

MARY CATHERINE. What is it, Horace?

HORACE. How do you get confidence?

MARY CATHERINE. Well, you just get it. Someone points it out to you that you lack it and then you get it. . . .

HORACE. Oh, is that how it's done?

MARY CATHERINE. That's how I did it.

HORACE. You see I lack confidence. And I . . . sure would like to get it. . . .

MARY CATHERINE. In what way do you lack confidence, Horace? . . .

HORACE. Oh, in all kinds of ways. [*A pause.*] I'm not much of a mixer[6]. . .

MARY CATHERINE. I think you're just mixing fine tonight.

HORACE. I know. That's what's giving me a little encouragement. You're the first girl I've ever really been able to talk to. I mean this way. . . .

MARY CATHERINE. Am I, Horace . . . ?

HORACE. Yes.

MARY CATHERINE. Well, I feel in some ways that's quite a compliment.

HORACE. Well, you should feel that way. [*A pause.*] Mary Catherine . . .

MARY CATHERINE. Yes, Horace?

HORACE. I had about decided to go back home tomorrow or the next day, but I understand there's another dance at the end of the week . . .

MARY CATHERINE. Uh-huh. Day after tomorrow.

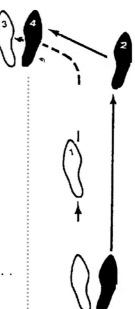

START

---

6. **a mixer** someone who socializes easily.

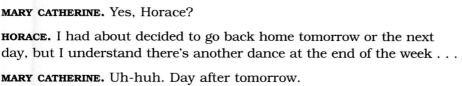

✔ Reading Check

What does Horace say he lacks?

HORACE. What do you mean?

INEZ. She has crawled on her knees.

HORACE. She's crawled on her knees? I don't get it. . . .

INEZ. She has eaten dirt.

HORACE. Sister, what's this all about?

INEZ. Last night around ten o'clock she called in the meekest kind of voice possible and said, Inez, I've called up to apologize to you. I have apologized to Horace in the drugstore. Did she?

HORACE. Uh. Huh.

INEZ. And now I want to apologize to you and to tell you how sorry I am I behaved so badly. . . .

HORACE. Well. Isn't that nice of her, Inez?

INEZ. Wait a minute. You haven't heard the whole thing. And then her highness added, tell Horace if he would like to invite me to the dance to call me and I'd be glad to accept. And furthermore, Elizabeth called this morning and said they were leaving for Houston to buy her the most expensive evening dress in sight. Just to impress you with.

HORACE. Oh . . . [*He sits down on a chair.*]

INEZ. Brother. What is the matter with you? Now are you gonna start worrying about this dancin' business all over again? You are the biggest fool sometimes. We've got today and tomorrow to practice.

HORACE. Inez . . .

INEZ. Yes?

HORACE. I already have a date with someone tomorrow. . . .

INEZ. You do?

HORACE. Yes. I met a girl last night at the drugstore and I asked her.

INEZ. What girl did you ask?

HORACE. Mary Catherine Davis. . . .

INEZ. Well, you've got to get right out of it. You've got to call her up and explain just what happened.

HORACE. But, Inez . . .

INEZ. You've got to do it, Horace. They told me they are spending all kinds of money for that dress. I practically had to threaten Elizabeth with never speaking to her again to bring this all about. Why, she will never forgive me now if I turn around and tell her you can't go. . . . Horace. Don't look that way. I can't help it. For my sake, for your sister's sake you've got to get out of this date with Mary Catherine Davis . . . tell her . . . tell her . . . anything . . .

Literary Analysis
Staging and Dialogue
What image of Emily is conveyed through Inez's words?

Reading Strategy
Picturing the Action
What expression do you imagine Horace wears now?

HORACE. O.K. [*A pause. He starts out.*] What can I say?

INEZ. I don't know, Horace. [*A pause.*] Say . . . well just tell her the truth. That's the best thing. Tell her that Emily's mother is your sister's best friend and that Emily's mother has taken her into Houston to buy her a very expensive dress . . .

HORACE. What if Mary Catherine has bought a dress . . .

INEZ. Well, she can't have bought an expensive dress. . . .

HORACE. Why not?

INEZ. Because her people can't afford it. Honey, you'll be the envy of every young man in Harrison, bringing Emily Crews to the dance. . . . Why, everybody will wonder just what it is you have . . .

HORACE. I'm not going to do it.

INEZ. Horace . . .

HORACE. I don't want to take Emily, I want to take Mary Catherine and that's just what I'm going to do.

INEZ. Horace . . .

HORACE. My mind is made up. Once and for all. . . .

INEZ. Then what am I gonna do? [*She starts to cry.*] Who's gonna speak to Elizabeth? She'll bless me out putting her to all this trouble. Making her spend all this money and time . . . [*She is crying loudly now.*] Horace. You just can't do this to me. You just simply can't. . . .

HORACE. I can't help it. I'm not taking Emily Crews—

INEZ. Horace . . .

HORACE. I am not taking Emily Crews.

[*He is firm. She is crying as the lights fade. The lights are brought up on the upstage left area.* MARY CATHERINE's *father is seated there. He is in his undershirt. In the distance dance music can be heard.* MRS. DAVIS *comes in from stage left.*]

MRS. DAVIS. Don't you think you'd better put your shirt on, Tom? Mary Catherine's date will be here any minute.

TOM. What time is it?

MRS. DAVIS. Nine o'clock.

TOM. The dance has already started. I can hear the music from here.

MRS. DAVIS. I know. But you know young people, they'd die before they'd be the first to a dance. Put your shirt on, Tom.

TOM. O.K.

Literary Analysis
Staging What does "a pause" convey about Horace's feelings?

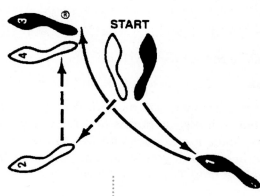

✔ **Reading Check**

What does Inez tell Horace about Emily?

MRS. DAVIS. As soon as her date arrives we'll go.

TOM. O.K.

[MARY CATHERINE *comes in from stage left. She has on an evening dress and she looks very pretty.*]

MRS. DAVIS. Why, Mary Catherine. You look lovely. Doesn't she look lovely, Tom?

TOM. Yes, she does.

MRS. DAVIS. Turn around, honey, and let me see you from the back. [*She does so.*] Just as pretty as you can be, Mary Catherine.

MARY CATHERINE. Thank you.

[HORACE *comes in downstage left in his tux with a corsage box. He walks up the center of the stage to the upstage left area.*]

That's Horace. [*She goes to the corner of the area.*] Hello, Horace.

HORACE. Hello, Mary Catherine.

MARY CATHERINE. You've met my mother and father.

HORACE. Yes. I have. I met your father the other night and your mother yesterday afternoon.

MRS. DAVIS. Hello, Horace.

TOM. Hello, son.

MRS. DAVIS. Well, we were just going. You all have a good time tonight.

HORACE. Thank you.

MRS. DAVIS. Come on, Tom.

TOM. All right. Good night and have a nice time.

MARY CATHERINE. Thank you, Daddy. [*They go out stage left.* HORACE *hands her the corsage box. She takes it and opens it.*] Oh, thank you, Horace. Thank you so much. [*She takes the flowers out.*] They're just lovely. Will you pin them on for me?

HORACE. I'll try. [*He takes the corsage and the pin. He begins to pin it on.*] Will about here be all right?

MARY CATHERINE. Just fine. [*He pins the corsage on.*] Emily told me about the mix-up between your sister and her mother. I appreciate your going ahead and taking me anyway. If you had wanted to get out of it I would have understood. Emily and I are very good friends . . . and . . .

Reading Strategy
Picturing the Action
How do you picture the expressions on both characters' faces at this point? Why?

HORACE. I didn't want to get out of it, Mary Catherine. I wanted to take you.

MARY CATHERINE. I'm glad you didn't want to get out of it. Emily offered to let me wear her new dress. But I had already bought one of my own.

HORACE. It's very pretty, Mary Catherine.

MARY CATHERINE. Thank you. [*A pause.*] Well, the dance has started. I can hear the music. Can't you?

HORACE. Yes.

MARY CATHERINE. Well, we'd better get going. . . .

HORACE. All right. [*They start out.*] Mary Catherine. I hope you don't think this is silly, but could we practice just once more . . .

MARY CATHERINE. Certainly we could. . . .

[*They start to dance.* HORACE *has improved although he is no Fred Astaire. They are dancing around and suddenly* HORACE *breaks away.*]

HORACE. Mary Catherine. I'm not good enough yet. I can't go. I'm sorry. Please let's just stay here.

MARY CATHERINE. No, Horace. We have to go.

HORACE. Please, Mary Catherine . . .

MARY CATHERINE. I know just how you feel, Horace, but we have to go. [*A pause.*] I haven't told you the whole truth, Horace. This is my first dance, too. . . .

HORACE. It is?

MARY CATHERINE. Yes. I've been afraid to go. Afraid I wouldn't be popular. The last two dances I was asked to go and I said no.

HORACE. Then why did you accept when I asked you?

MARY CATHERINE. I don't know. I asked myself that afterwards. I guess

Reading Check

What does Horace want to do once more before the dance?

because you gave me a kind of confidence. [*A pause. They dance again.*] You gave me confidence and I gave you confidence. What's the sense of getting confidence, Horace, if you're not going to use it?

[*A pause. They continue dancing.*]

HORACE. That's a pretty piece.

MARY CATHERINE. Yes, it is.

[*A pause. They dance again.* HORACE *stops.*]

HORACE. I'm ready to go if you are, Mary Catherine.

MARY CATHERINE. I'm ready. [*They start out.*] Scared?

HORACE. A little.

MARY CATHERINE. So am I. But let's go.

HORACE. O.K.

[*They continue out the area down the center of the stage and off downstage right as the music from the dance is heard.*]

Review and Assess

Thinking About the Selection

1. **Respond:** Do you admire Horace? Why or why not?

2. **(a) Recall:** Why is Inez determined to set up Horace with Emily? **(b) Recall:** Why is Elizabeth determined to set up Emily with Horace? **(c) Compare and Contrast:** Which qualities do Elizabeth and Inez seem to have in common?

3. **(a) Recall:** Why does Emily refuse to go to the dance with Horace? **(b) Make a Judgment:** Do you think Emily's behavior is justified? Explain.

4. **(a) Recall:** What does Emily tell Horace the next day about why she did not go to the dance? **(b) Analyze:** What does this action tell you about Emily's character?

5. **(a) Recall:** How does Horace meet Mary Catherine? **(b) Infer:** In what ways are Horace and Mary Catherine well suited to be friends? **(c) Analyze:** After asking Mary Catherine to the dance, how does Horace demonstrate that he is a sensitive and considerate person?

6. **Speculate:** Do you think the adults or the teenagers acted more maturely in this play?

7. **(a) Extend:** Identify one insight about human relationships that you gained from this play. **(b) Apply:** How can this insight be applied to your own life?

Horton Foote

(b. 1916)

Born in Wharton, Texas, Horton Foote left his hometown after high school to attend acting school. While studying in New York, he formed friendships with several fellow actors; together, they formed an off-Broadway theater company. He began writing plays, and since then, writing has been the focus of his career.

During the 1950s and early 1960s, television's "golden age," Foote wrote scripts for live television. One of his first teleplays, *The Trip to Bountiful*, was later made into an award-winning film. Many of Foote's plays are set in the fictional town of Harrison, Texas, based on his hometown and the people he has known.

He says that his plays are often concerned "with defining what home is and where home is and how we get to home." Recurring themes include human shortcomings, family issues, and relationships between generations.

Review and Assess

Literary Analysis

Staging

1. (a) Using a chart like the one below, select two examples of stage directions in "The Dancers" that leave most of the specifics up to the imagination. (b) How might you add to the **staging** you have listed to better explain the place, action, or event described in your examples? (c) Why might the author have left staging vague?

Existing Stage Directions ··▶ **Expanded Stage Directions**

2. (a) What kind of lighting would be most effective in the drugstore scenes? (b) What kind of lighting would be most effective when Horace is dancing with Mary Catherine? Why?

Connecting Literary Elements

3. Using a chart like the one below, explain which **dialogue** in the play reveals the most about each character.

Character | **Dialogue** ··▶ **Reveals**

4. Give two examples of staging directions that enhance the dialogue and provide a clearer image of a character or situation. Explain your answer.

Reading Strategy

Picturing the Action

5. In the opening scene, you learn that Emily is unhappy. How might Emily's face, posture, and actions show this?

6. **Picture** the scene in which Mary Catherine tells the waitress about the date Emily Crews wanted to break. (a) How do you think Horace might act as he sits at the counter? (b) What do you think the waitress might do as she listens?

Extend Understanding

7. **Drama Connection:** The characters spend most of their time in a drugstore. If you were to update this play, where might you set it to reflect today's trends? Why?

Quick Review

Staging is one of the ways a script is brought to life. It includes descriptions of the sets, lighting, sound effects, costumes, and directions about the way the actors should move and deliver their lines.

Dialogue is a conversation between characters that reveals the qualities and situations of the characters and advances the action of the play.

To **picture the action** in a play, read descriptions carefully, and draw from your own experience to see characters and actions in your mind's eye.

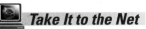 **Take It to the Net**

www.phschool.com

Take the interactive self-test online to check your understanding of the selection.

The Shakespearean Theater

ROMEO AND JULIET

Of all the love stories ever written, that of Romeo and Juliet is the most famous. To many people, Shakespeare's tragic lovers represent the essence of romantic love. When Shakespeare wrote *The Tragedy of Romeo and Juliet*, he was a young man, and the play is a young man's play about young love.

The Theater in Shakespeare's Day

Romeo and Juliet, like most of Shakespeare's plays, was produced in a public theater. Public theaters were built around roofless courtyards without artificial light. Performances, therefore, were given only during daylight hours. Surrounding the courtyard were three levels of galleries with benches on which wealthier playgoers sat. Less wealthy spectators, called groundlings, stood and watched a play from the courtyard, which was called the pit.

Most of Shakespeare's plays were performed in the Globe theater. No one is certain exactly what the Globe looked like, though Shakespeare tells us it was round or octagonal. We know that it was open to the sky and held between 2,500 and 3,000 people. Scholars disagree about its actual dimensions and size. The discovery of its foundation in 1990 was exciting because the eventual excavation will reveal clues about the plays, the actors, and the audience. The tiny

▼ **Critical Viewing**
Which attribute of the Globe theater is emphasized in this painting? **[Analyze]**

GLOBE. SOUTHWARKE.

The Globe Theatre, London

part of the foundation initially uncovered yielded a great number of hazelnut shells. Hazelnuts were Elizabethan popcorn; people munched on them all during the performance.

The stage was a platform that extended into the pit. Actors entered and left the stage from doors located behind the platform. The portion of the galleries behind and above the stage was used primarily as dressing and storage rooms. The second-level gallery right above the stage, however, was used as an upper stage. It would have been here that the famous balcony scene in *Romeo and Juliet* was enacted.

▲ **Critical Viewing**
Which part of the replica of the Globe theater do you think is being built in this picture? **[Speculate]**

There was no scenery in the theaters of Shakespeare's day. Settings were indicated by references in the dialogue. As a result, one scene could follow another in rapid succession. The actors wore elaborate clothing. It was, in fact, typical Elizabethan clothing, not costuming. Thus, the plays produced in Shakespeare's day were fast-paced, colorful productions. Usually, a play lasted two hours.

One other difference between Shakespeare's theater and today's is that acting companies in the sixteenth century were made up only of men and boys. Women did not perform on the stage. This was not considered proper for a woman. As a general rule, boys of eleven, twelve, or thirteen—before their voices changed—performed the female roles.

The Globe Today

Building a replica of Shakespeare's Globe was the dream of American actor Sam Wanamaker. After long years of fund-raising and construction, the theater opened in London to its first full season on June 8, 1997, with a production of *Henry V*. Like the earlier Globe, this one is made of wood, with a thatched roof and lime plaster covering the walls. The stage and the galleries are covered, but the "bear pit," where the modern-day groundlings stand, is open to the skies, exposing the spectators to the weather.

Prepare to Read

The Tragedy of Romeo and Juliet, Act I

 Take It to the Net

Visit www.phschool.com for interactive activities and instruction related to *The Tragedy of Romeo and Juliet,* including

- background
- graphic organizers
- literary elements
- reading strategies

Preview

Connecting to the Literature

The world is filled with rivalries—among countries, families, schools, even groups of friends. Occasionally, rivalries become so fierce that the members of one group refuse to associate with their rivals. In extreme cases, as you will see in this play, rivalries can even erupt into violence.

Background

Shakespeare based his play about star-crossed lovers from feuding Italian families on a poem published in 1562 by Arthur Brooke. Brooke's 3,000-line poem has a highly moral tone: Disobedience, as well as fate, leads to the deaths of the two lovers. Brooke's poem, in turn, was based on a French version of the story, written in 1559.

Literary Analysis

Character

Characters are the people or animals who take part in a literary work. Some characters are fully developed, while others are not as complex.

- A **round character** has many personality traits, like a real person.
- A **flat character** is one-dimensional, embodying only a single trait. Shakespeare's plays often include flat characters who provide comic relief.

As you read the play, use a chart like the one shown to note round and flat characters and their personality traits.

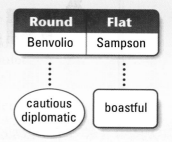

Connecting Literary Elements

A **dramatic foil** is a character who highlights the traits of another character through contrast. For example, in Act I, Benvolio, who tries to quiet a group of brawling servants, is a foil to Tybalt, who has a fiery hot temper. As you read, look for foils by identifying characters who possess contrasting personality traits. This will help you determine key differences among characters.

Reading Strategy

Using Text Aids

The way the characters speak in Shakespeare's play, which was written over 400 years ago, will probably be unfamiliar to you. To make sure that you understand the dialogue, it is crucial that you use the **text aids**—the numbered explanations of Shakespeare's language that appear alongside the text.

- If you are confused by a passage, check to see if there is a footnote and read the corresponding explanation.
- Reread the passage, using your new knowledge from the footnote, to be sure that you grasp the meaning of the passage.

The footnotes should add to your enjoyment of the play by clarifying confusing language.

Vocabulary Development

pernicious (pər nish´ əs) *adj.* causing great injury or ruin (p. 774)

augmenting (ôg ment´ iŋ) *v.* increasing; enlarging (p. 775)

grievance (grēv´ əns) *n.* injustice; complaint (p. 776)

transgression (trans gresh´ ən) *n.* wrongdoing; sin (p. 777)

heretics (her´ ə tiks) *n.* those who hold to a belief opposed to the established teachings of a church (p. 780)

GREGORY. But thou art not quickly moved to strike.

SAMPSON. A dog of the house of Montague moves me.

GREGORY. To move is to stir, and to be valiant is to stand. Therefore, if thou art moved, thou run'st away.

10 **SAMPSON.** A dog of that house shall move me to stand. I will take the wall[6] of any man or maid of Montague's.

GREGORY. That shows thee a weak slave; for the weakest goes to the wall.

SAMPSON. 'Tis true; and therefore women, being the weaker
15 vessels, are ever thrust to the wall. Therefore I will push Montague's men from the wall and thrust his maids to the wall.

GREGORY. The quarrel is between our masters and us their men.

SAMPSON. Tis all one. I will show myself a tyrant. When I have fought with the men, I will be civil with the maids—I will cut
20 off their heads.

GREGORY. The heads of the maids?

SAMPSON. Ay, the heads of the maids or their maidenheads. Take it in what sense thou wilt.

GREGORY. They must take it in sense that feel it.

25 **SAMPSON.** Me they shall feel while I am able to stand; and 'tis known I am a pretty piece of flesh.

GREGORY. Tis well thou art not fish; if thou hadst, thou hadst been Poor John. Draw thy tool![7] Here comes two of the house of Montagues.

[*Enter two other Servingmen,* ABRAM *and* BALTHASAR.]

30 **SAMPSON.** My naked weapon is out. Quarrel! I will back thee.

GREGORY. How? Turn thy back and run?

SAMPSON. Fear me not.

GREGORY. No, marry. I fear thee!

SAMPSON. Let us take the law of our sides;[8] let them begin.

35 **GREGORY.** I will frown as I pass by, and let them take it as they list.[9]

SAMPSON. Nay, as they dare. I will bite my thumb[10] at them, which is disgrace to them if they bear it.

ABRAM. Do you bite your thumb at us, sir?

SAMPSON. I do bite my thumb, sir.

40 **ABRAM.** Do you bite your thumb at us, sir?

SAMPSON. [*Aside to* GREGORY] Is the law of our side if I say ay?

---

6. **take the wall** assert superiority by walking nearer the houses and therefore farther from the gutter

Literary Analysis
Character What does this conversation reveal about the Capulets and the Montagues?

7. **tool** weapon.

8. **take . . . sides** make sure the law is on our side.
9. **list** please.
10. **bite . . . thumb** make an insulting gesture.

Reading Strategy
Using Text Aids How does footnote 8 help you understand Sampson's logic in line 34?

GREGORY. [*Aside to* SAMPSON] No.

SAMPSON. No, sir, I do not bite my thumb at you, sir; but I bite my thumb, sir.

45 **GREGORY.** Do you quarrel, sir?

ABRAM. Quarrel, sir? No, sir.

SAMPSON. But if you do, sir, I am for you. I serve as good a man as you.

ABRAM. No better.

SAMPSON. Well, sir.

[*Enter* BENVOLIO.]

50 **GREGORY.** Say "better." Here comes one of my master's kinsmen.

SAMPSON. Yes, better, sir.

ABRAM. You lie.

SAMPSON. Draw, if you be men. Gregory, remember thy
swashing[11] blow.   [*They fight.*]

55 **BENVOLIO.** Part, fools!
Put up your swords. You know not what you do.

[*Enter* TYBALT.]

TYBALT. What art thou drawn among these heartless hinds?[12]
Turn thee, Benvolio; look upon thy death.

BENVOLIO. I do but keep the peace. Put up thy sword,
60   Or manage it to part these men with me.

TYBALT. What, drawn, and talk of peace? I hate the word
As I hate hell, all Montagues, and thee.
Have at thee, coward!   [*They fight.*]

[*Enter an* OFFICER, *and three or four* CITIZENS *with clubs or partisans.*[13]]

OFFICER. Clubs, bills,[14] and partisans! Strike! Beat them down!
65   Down with the Capulets! Down with the Montagues!

[*Enter old* CAPULET *in his gown, and his* WIFE.]

CAPULET. What noise is this? Give me my long sword, ho!

LADY CAPULET. A crutch, a crutch! Why call you for a sword?

CAPULET. My sword, I say! Old Montague is come
And flourishes his blade in spite[15] of me.

[*Enter old* MONTAGUE *and his* WIFE.]

70 **MONTAGUE.** Thou villain Capulet!—Hold me not; let me go.

LADY MONTAGUE. Thou shalt not stir one foot to seek a foe.

Literary Analysis
Character How would you describe Gregory and Sampson in this scene?

11. **swashing** hard downward swordstroke.

12. **heartless hinds** cowardly servants. *Hind* also meant "a female deer."

Literary Analysis
Character and Dramatic Foil Which contrasting personality traits do Benvolio and Tybalt reveal in their brief conversation?

13. **partisans** spearlike weapons with broad blades.

14. **bills** weapons consisting of hook-shaped blades with long handles.

15. **spite** defiance.

✔ Reading Check
Whom does Tybalt fight?

[*Enter* PRINCE ESCALUS, *with his Train.*[16]]

PRINCE. Rebellious subjects, enemies to peace,
Profaners[17] of this neighbor-stainèd steel—
Will they not hear? What, ho! You men, you beasts,
75   That quench the fire of your <u>pernicious</u> rage
With purple fountains issuing from your veins!
On pain of torture, from those bloody hands
Throw your mistempered[18] weapons to the ground
And hear the sentence of your moved prince.
80   Three civil brawls, bred of an airy word
By thee, old Capulet, and Montague,
Have thrice disturbed the quiet of our streets
And made Verona's ancient citizens
Cast by their grave beseeming ornaments[19]
85   To wield old partisans, in hands as old,
Cank'red with peace, to part your cank'red hate.[20]
If ever you disturb our streets again,
Your lives shall pay the forfeit of the peace.
For this time all the rest depart away.
90   You, Capulet, shall go along with me;
And, Montague, come you this afternoon,
To know our farther pleasure in this case,
To old Freetown, our common judgment place.
Once more, on pain of death, all men depart.

                [*Exit all but* MONTAGUE, *his* WIFE, *and* BENVOLIO.]

95 **MONTAGUE.** Who set this ancient quarrel new abroach?[21]
Speak, nephew, were you by when it began?

BENVOLIO. Here were the servants of your adversary
And yours, close fighting ere I did approach.
I drew to part them. In the instant came
100   The fiery Tybalt, with his sword prepared;
Which, as he breathed defiance to my ears,
He swung about his head and cut the winds,
Who, nothing hurt withal, hissed him in scorn.
While we were interchanging thrusts and blows,
105   Came more and more, and fought on part and part,[22]
Till the Prince came, who parted either part.

LADY MONTAGUE. O, where is Romeo? Saw you him today?
Right glad I am he was not at this fray.

BENVOLIO. Madam, an hour before the worshiped sun
110   Peered forth the golden window of the East,
A troubled mind drave me to walk abroad:
Where, underneath the grove of sycamore
That westward rooteth from this city side,
So early walking did I see your son.

16. Train attendants.

17. Profaners those who show disrespect or contempt.

pernicious (pər nish´ əs) *adj.* causing great injury or ruin

18. mistempered hardened for a wrong purpose; bad-tempered.

19. Cast . . . ornaments put aside their dignified and appropriate clothing.

20. Cank'red . . . hate rusted from lack of use, to put an end to your malignant feuding.

21. Who . . . abroach? Who reopened this old fight?

22. on . . . part on one side and the other.

Literary Analysis
Character What can you infer about Benvolio based on his interaction with Romeo's parents?

115	Towards him I made, but he was ware[23] of me
	And stole into the covert[24] of the wood.
	I, measuring his affections[25] by my own,
	Which then most sought where most might not be found,[26]
	Being one too many by my weary self,
120	Pursued my humor not pursuing his,[27]
	And gladly shunned who gladly fled from me.

MONTAGUE. Many a morning hath he there been seen,
With tears <u>augmenting</u> the fresh morning's dew,
Adding to clouds more clouds with his deep sighs;
125 But all so soon as the all-cheering sun
Should in the farthest East begin to draw
The shady curtains from Aurora's* bed,
Away from light steals home my heavy[28] son
And private in his chamber pens himself,
130 Shuts up his windows, locks fair daylight out,
And makes himself an artificial night.
Black and portentous[29] must this humor prove
Unless good counsel may the cause remove.

BENVOLIO. My noble uncle, do you know the cause?

135 MONTAGUE. I neither know it nor can learn of him.

BENVOLIO. Have you importuned[30] him by any means?

MONTAGUE. Both by myself and many other friends;
But he, his own affections' counselor,
Is to himself—I will not say how true—
140 But to himself so secret and so close,
So far from sounding[31] and discovery,
As is the bud bit with an envious worm
Ere he can spread his sweet leaves to the air
Or dedicate his beauty to the sun.
145 Could we but learn from whence his sorrows grow,
We would as willingly give cure as know.

23. ware aware; wary.

24. covert hidden place.

25. measuring . . . affections judging his feelings.

26. Which . . . found which wanted to be where there was no one else.

27. Pursued . . . his followed my own mind by not following after Romeo.

augmenting (ôg ment′ iŋ) v. increasing; enlarging

28. heavy sad, moody.

29. portentous promising bad fortune.

30. importuned questioned deeply.

31. sounding understanding.

✓**Reading Check**

How does the Prince respond to the fight between Benvolio and Tybalt?

Literature
in context Humanities Connection

♦ *Aurora*

Aurora was the Latin goddess of the dawn who began each day riding a chariot from the River Oceanus to heaven to announce the coming of the sun. She was said to dip her rosy fingers into a cup filled with dew and sprinkle drops on flowers and trees. Aurora had special feelings for young people like Romeo, whose lives were just dawning. Unlike Aurora, the moody Romeo roams at night and shuts himself in his room at dawn (I, i, 127).

[*Enter* ROMEO.]

BENVOLIO. See, where he comes. So please you step aside;
    I'll know his <u>grievance</u>, or be much denied.

MONTAGUE. I would thou wert so happy by thy stay
150 To hear true shrift.[32] Come, madam, let's away.

[Exit MONTAGUE and WIFE.]

BENVOLIO. Good morrow, cousin.

ROMEO.   Is the day so young?

BENVOLIO. But new struck nine.

ROMEO.   Ay me! Sad hours seem long.
    Was that my father that went hence so fast?

BENVOLIO. It was. What sadness lengthens Romeo's hours?

155 **ROMEO.** Not having that which having makes them short.

BENVOLIO. In love?

ROMEO. Out—

BENVOLIO. Of love?

ROMEO. Out of her favor where I am in love.

160 **BENVOLIO.** Alas that love, so gentle in his view,[33]
    Should be so tyrannous and rough in proof![34]

ROMEO. Alas that love, whose view is muffled still,[35]
    Should without eyes see pathways to his will!
    Where shall we dine? O me! What fray was here?
165   Yet tell me not, for I have heard it all.
    Here's much to do with hate, but more with love.[36]
    Why then, O brawling love, O loving hate,
    O anything, of nothing first created!
    O heavy lightness, serious vanity,
170   Misshapen chaos of well-seeming forms,

grievance (grēv′ əns) *n.*
injustice; complaint

32. I . . . shrift I hope you
are lucky enough to hear
him confess the truth.

Literary Analysis
Character Which
personality traits are
revealed by Benvolio's
concern for Romeo?

33. view appearance.
34. in proof when experienced.

35. whose . . . still Cupid is
traditionally represented as
blindfolded.

36. but . . . love loyalty to
family and love of fighting. In
the following lines, Romeo
speaks of love as a series of
contradictions—a union of
opposites.

▶ **Critical Viewing**
How would you describe
the feelings of each
character, based on this
photograph? **[Analyze]**

Feather of lead, bright smoke, cold fire, sick health,
Still-waking sleep, that is not what it is!
This love feel I, that feel no love in this.
Dost thou not laugh?

BENVOLIO.   No, coz,[37] I rather weep.

ROMEO.   Good heart, at what?

175   **BENVOLIO.**   At thy good heart's oppression.

ROMEO.   Why, such is love's <u>transgression</u>.
Griefs of mine own lie heavy in my breast,
Which thou wilt propagate, to have it prest
With more of thine.[38] This love that thou hast shown
180   Doth add more grief to too much of mine own.
Love is a smoke made with the fume of sighs;
Being purged, a fire sparkling in lovers' eyes;
Being vexed, a sea nourished with loving tears.
What is it else? A madness most discreet,[39]
185   A choking gall,[40] and a preserving sweet.
Farewell, my coz.

BENVOLIO.   Soft![41] I will go along.
And if you leave me so, you do me wrong.

ROMEO.   Tut! I have lost myself; I am not here;
This is not Romeo, he's some other where.

190   **BENVOLIO.**   Tell me in sadness,[42] who is that you love?

ROMEO.   What, shall I groan and tell thee?

BENVOLIO.   Groan? Why, no;
But sadly tell me who.

ROMEO.   Bid a sick man in sadness make his will.
Ah, word ill urged to one that is so ill!
195   In sadness, cousin, I do love a woman.

BENVOLIO.   I aimed so near when I supposed you loved.

ROMEO.   A right good markman. And she's fair I love.

BENVOLIO.   A right fair mark, fair coz, is soonest hit.

ROMEO.   Well, in that hit you miss. She'll not be hit
200   With Cupid's arrow. She hath Dian's wit,[43]
And, in strong proof[44] of chastity well armed,
From Love's weak childish bow she lives uncharmed.
She will not stay[45] the siege of loving terms,
Nor bide th' encounter of assailing eyes,
205   Nor ope her lap to saint-seducing gold.
O, she is rich in beauty; only poor
That, when she dies, with beauty dies her store.[46]

BENVOLIO.   Then she hath sworn that she will still live chaste?

Romeo and Juliet, Act I, Scene i ◆ 777

Literary Analysis
Character What do Romeo's words in lines 171–174 reveal about his personality?

37. **coz** cousin.

transgression (trans gresh´ ən) *n.* wrongdoing; sin

38. **Which . . . thine** Which griefs you will increase by adding your own sorrow to them.

39. **discreet** intelligently sensitive.

40. **gall** a bitter liquid.
41. **Soft!** Hold on a minute.

Reading Strategy
Using Text Aids Why is footnote 41 helpful here?

42. **in sadness** seriously.

Literary Analysis
Character Which details in line 195 indicate that Romeo is a round character?

43. **Dian's wit** the mind of Diana, goddess of chastity.
44. **proof** armor.
45. **stay** endure; put up with.
46. **That . . . store** In that her beauty will die with her if she does not marry and have children.

✔ **Reading Check**
What reason for his sadness does Romeo give to Benvolio?

ROMEO. She hath, and in that sparing make huge waste;
210 For beauty, starved with her severity,
Cuts beauty off from all posterity.[47]
She is too fair, too wise, wisely too fair
To merit bliss by making me despair.[48]
She hath forsworn to[49] love, and in that vow
215 Do I live dead that live to tell it now.

BENVOLIO. Be ruled by me; forget to think of her.

ROMEO. O, teach me how I should forget to think!

BENVOLIO. By giving liberty unto thine eyes.
Examine other beauties.

ROMEO.   'Tis the way
220 To call hers, exquisite, in question more.[50]
These happy masks that kiss fair ladies' brows,
Being black puts us in mind they hide the fair.
He that is strucken blind cannot forget
The precious treasure of his eyesight lost.
225 Show me a mistress that is passing fair:
What doth her beauty serve but as a note
Where I may read who passed that passing fair?[51]
Farewell. Thou canst not teach me to forget.

BENVOLIO. I'll pay that doctrine, or else die in debt.[52]   [*Exit all.*]

Scene ii. *A street.*

[*Enter* CAPULET, COUNTY PARIS, *and the* CLOWN, *his servant.*]

CAPULET. But Montague is bound as well as I,
In penalty alike; and 'tis not hard, I think,
For men so old as we to keep the peace.

PARIS. Of honorable reckoning[1] are you both,
5 And pity 'tis you lived at odds so long.
But now, my lord, what say you to my suit?

CAPULET. But saying o'er what I have said before:
My child is yet a stranger in the world,
She hath not seen the change of fourteen years;
10 Let two more summers wither in their pride
Ere we may think her ripe to be a bride.

PARIS. Younger than she are happy mothers made.

CAPULET. And too soon marred are those so early made.
Earth hath swallowed all my hopes[2] but she;
15 She is the hopeful lady of my earth.[3]
But woo her, gentle Paris, get her heart;
My will to her consent is but a part.

47. in . . . posterity By denying herself love and marriage, she wastes her beauty, which will not live on in future generations.

48. She . . . despair She is being too good—she'll earn happiness in heaven by dooming me to live without her love.

49. forsworn to sworn not to.

50. 'Tis . . . more That way will only make her beauty more strongly present in my mind.

Literary Analysis
Character and Dramatic Foil What contrasting attitudes are revealed in this exchange between Romeo and Benvolio?

51. who . . . fair who surpassed in beauty that very beautiful woman.

52. I'll. . . debt I'll teach you to forget, or else die trying.

1. reckoning reputation.

Literary Analysis
Character What can you tell about Lord Capulet's character traits based on his talk with Paris?

2. hopes children.

3. She . . . earth My hopes for the future rest in her; she will inherit all that is mine.

An she agree, within her scope of choice
Lies my consent and fair according voice,[4]
20 This night I hold an old accustomed feast,
Whereto I have invited many a guest,
Such as I love; and you among the store,
One more, most welcome, makes my number more.
At my poor house look to behold this night
25 Earth-treading stars[5] that make dark heaven light.
Such comfort as do lusty young men feel
When well-appareled April on the heel
Of limping Winter treads, even such delight
Among fresh fennel buds shall you this night
30 Inherit at my house. Hear all, all see,
And like her most whose merit most shall be;
Which, on more view of many, mine, being one,
May stand in number, though in reck'ning none.[6]
Come, go with me. [*To* SERVANT, *giving him a paper*]
   Go, sirrah, trudge about
35 Through fair Verona; find those persons out
Whose names are written there, and to them say
My house and welcome on their pleasure stay.[7] [*Exit with* PARIS.]

SERVANT. Find them out whose names are written here? It is written
that the shoemaker should meddle with his yard and the tailor
40 with his last, the fisher with his pencil and the painter with his
nets;[8] but I am sent to find those persons whose names are
here writ, and can never find what names the writing person
hath here writ. I must to the learned. In good time![9]

[*Enter* BENVOLIO *and* ROMEO.]

BENVOLIO. Tut, man, one fire burns out another's burning;
45   One pain is less'ned by another's anguish;
Turn giddy, and be holp by backward turning;[10]
   One desperate grief cures with another's languish.
Take thou some new infection to thy eye,
And the rank poison of the old will die.

50 **ROMEO.** Your plantain leaf[11] is excellent for that.

BENVOLIO. For what, I pray thee?

ROMEO.   For your broken shin.

BENVOLIO. Why, Romeo, art thou mad?

ROMEO. Not mad, but bound more than a madman is;
Shut up in prison, kept without my food,
55 Whipped and tormented and—God-den,[12] good fellow.

SERVANT. God gi' go-den. I pray, sir, can you read?

ROMEO. Ay, mine own fortune in my misery.

SERVANT. Perhaps you have learned it without book.
But, I pray, can you read anything you see?

60 **ROMEO.** Ay, if I know the letters and the language.

SERVANT. Ye say honestly. Rest you merry.[13]

ROMEO. Stay, fellow; I can read. [*He reads the letter.*]
"Signior Martino and his wife and daughters;
County Anselm and his beauteous sisters;
65 The lady widow of Vitruvio;
Signior Placentio and his lovely nieces;
Mercutio and his brother Valentine;
Mine uncle Capulet, his wife and daughters;
My fair niece Rosaline; Livia;
70 Signior Valentio and his cousin Tybalt;
Lucio and the lively Helena."
A fair assembly. Whither should they come?

SERVANT. Up.

ROMEO. Whither? To supper?

75 **SERVANT.** To our house.

ROMEO. Whose house?

SERVANT. My master's.

ROMEO. Indeed I should have asked you that before.

SERVANT. Now I'll tell you without asking. My master is the great
80 rich Capulet; and if you be not of the house of Montagues, I pray
come and crush a cup of wine. Rest you merry.   [*Exit.*]

BENVOLIO. At this same ancient[14] feast of Capulet's
Sups the fair Rosaline whom thou so loves;
With all the admirèd beauties of Verona.
85 Go thither, and with unattainted[15] eye
Compare her face with some that I shall show,
And I will make thee think thy swan a crow.

ROMEO. When the devout religion of mine eye
Maintains such falsehood, then turn tears to fires:
90 And these, who, often drowned, could never die,
Transparent <u>heretics</u>, be burnt for liars![16]
One fairer than my love? The all-seeing sun
Ne'er saw her match since first the world begun.

BENVOLIO. Tut! you saw her fair, none else being by,
95 Herself poised with herself in either eye;[17]
But in that crystal scales[18] let there be weighed
Your lady's love against some other maid
That I will show you shining at this feast,
And she shall scant show well that now seems best.

13. Rest you merry May God keep you happy—a way of saying farewell.

Literary Analysis
Character Is the servant a round or flat character? Why?

14. ancient long-established; traditional.

15. unattainted unprejudiced.

heretics (her′ ə tiks) *n.* those who hold to a belief opposed to the established teachings of a church

16. When . . . liars! When I see Rosaline as just a plain-looking girl, may my tears turn to fire and burn my eyes out!

Reading Strategy
Using Text Aids How does footnote 16 convey Romeo's feelings for Rosaline?

17. Herself . . . eye Rosaline compared with no one else.

18. crystal scales your eyes.

100 **ROMEO.** I'll go along, no such sight to be shown,
But to rejoice in splendor of mine own.[19] [*Exit all.*]

19. **mine own** my own love, Rosaline.

S**cene iii.** *A room in* CAPULET'*s house.*

[*Enter* CAPULET'S WIFE, *and* NURSE.]

LADY CAPULET. Nurse, where's my daughter? Call her forth to me.

NURSE. Now, by my maidenhead at twelve year old,
I bade her come. What, lamb! What, ladybird!
God forbid, where's this girl? What, Juliet!

[*Enter* JULIET.]

5 **JULIET.** How now? Who calls?

NURSE. Your mother.

JULIET. Madam, I am here
What is your will?

LADY CAPULET. This is the matter—Nurse, give leave[1] awhile;
We must talk in secret. Nurse, come back again.
I have rememb'red me; thou's hear our counsel.[2]
10 Thou knowest my daughter's of a pretty age.

NURSE. Faith, I can tell her age unto an hour.

LADY CAPULET. She's not fourteen.

NURSE. I'll lay fourteen of my teeth—
And yet, to my teen[3] be it spoken, I have but four—
She's not fourteen. How long is it now
To Lammastide?[4]

15 **LADY CAPULET.** A fortnight and odd days.[5]

NURSE. Even or odd, of all days in the year,
Come Lammas Eve at night shall she be fourteen.
Susan and she (God rest all Christian souls!)

1. **give leave** Leave us alone.

2. **thou's . . . counsel** You shall hear our conference.

Reading Strategy
Using Text Aids Based on footnotes 1 and 2, what facial expression might the Nurse have during Lady Capulet's speech?

3. **teen** sorrow.

4. **Lammastide** August 1, a holiday celebrating the summer harvest.

5. **A fortnight and odd days** two weeks plus a few days.

◀ **Critical Viewing**
What do this picture and the conversation among Juliet, Lady Capulet, and the Nurse tell you about their relationship? **[Infer]**

✔**Reading Check**
What does Romeo agree to do with Benvolio?

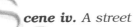

Scene iv. *A street*

[*Enter* ROMEO, MERCUTIO, BENVOLIO, *with five or six other* MASKERS; TORCHBEARERS.]

<blockquote>

ROMEO. What, shall this speech[1] be spoke for our excuse?
    Or shall we on without apology?

BENVOLIO. The date is out of such prolixity.[2]
    We'll have no Cupid hoodwinked with a scarf,
5   Bearing a Tartar's painted bow of lath,
    Scaring the ladies like a crowkeeper,
    Nor no without-book prologue, faintly spoke
    After the prompter, for our entrance;
    But, let them measure us by what they will,
10   We'll measure them a measure and be gone.

ROMEO. Give me a torch. I am not for this ambling.
    Being but heavy,[3] I will bear the light.

MERCUTIO. Nay, gentle Romeo, we must have you dance.

ROMEO. Not I, believe me. You have dancing shoes
15   With nimble soles; I have a soul of lead
    So stakes me to the ground I cannot move.

MERCUTIO. You are a lover. Borrow Cupid's wings
    And soar with them above a common bound

ROMEO. I am too sore enpiercèd with his shaft
20   To soar with his light feathers; and so bound

</blockquote>

Reading Strategy

Using Text Aids How would you restate Romeo's questions in lines 1–2 in contemporary English?

1. this speech Romeo asks whether he and his companions, being uninvited guests, should follow custom by announcing their arrival in a speech.

2. The . . . prolixity Such wordiness is outdated. In the following lines, Benvolio says, in sum: "Let's forget about announcing our entrance with a show. The other guests can look over as they see fit. We'll dance a while, then leave."

3. heavy weighed down with sadness.

▼ Critical Viewing
Which details in this photograph show how Romeo and his friends prepare to attend the feast? **[Infer]**

I cannot bound a pitch above dull woe.
Under love's heavy burden do I sink.

MERCUTIO. And, to sink in it, should you burden love—
Too great oppression for a tender thing.

25 **ROMEO.** Is love a tender thing? It is too rough,
Too rude, too boist'rous, and it pricks like thorn.

MERCUTIO. If love be rough with you, be rough with love.
Prick love for pricking, and you beat love down.
Give me a case to put my visage[4] in.
30 A visor for a visor![5] What care I
What curious eye doth quote deformities?[6]
Here are the beetle brows shall blush for me.

BENVOLIO. Come, knock and enter; and no sooner in
But every man betake him to his legs.[7]

35 **ROMEO.** A torch for me! Let wantons light of heart
Tickle the senseless rushes[8] with their heels;
For I am proverbed with a grandsire phrase,[9]
I'll be a candleholder and look on;
The game was ne'er so fair, and I am done.[10]

40 **MERCUTIO.** Tut! Dun's the mouse, the constable's own word![11]
If thou art Dun,[12] we'll draw thee from the mire
Of this sir-reverence love, wherein thou stickest
Up to the ears. Come, we burn daylight, ho!

ROMEO. Nay, that's not so.

MERCUTIO.   I mean, sir, in delay
45 We waste our lights in vain, like lights by day.
Take our good meaning, for our judgment sits
Five times in that ere once in our five wits.[13]

ROMEO. And we mean well in going to this masque,
But 'tis no wit to go.

MERCUTIO.   Why, may one ask?

ROMEO. I dreamt a dream tonight.

50 **MERCUTIO.**   And so did I.

ROMEO. Well, what was yours?

MERCUTIO.   That dreamers often lie.

ROMEO. In bed asleep, while they do dream things true.

MERCUTIO. O, then I see Queen Mab[14] hath been with you.
She is the fairies' midwife, and she comes
55 In shape no bigger than an agate stone
On the forefinger of an alderman,
Drawn with a team of little atomies[15]

4. **visage** mask.

5. **A visor . . . visor!** A mask for a mask—which is what my real face is like!

6. **quote deformities** notice my ugly features.

7. **betake . . . legs** start dancing.

8. **Let . . . rushes** Let fun-loving people dance on the floor coverings.

9. **proverbed . . . phrase** directed by an old saying.

10. **The game . . . done** No matter how much enjoyment may be had, I won't have any.

11. **Dun's . . . word!:** Lie low like a mouse—that's what a constable waiting to make an arrest might say.

12. **Dun** proverbial name for a horse.

13. **Take . . . wits** Understand my intended meaning. That shows more intelligence than merely following what your senses perceive.

14. **Queen Mab** the queen of fairyland.

Literary Analysis
Character and Dramatic Foil In what way is Mercutio a foil for the sulky Romeo?

15. **atomies** creatures.

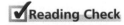**Reading Check**

What advice about love does Mercutio give Romeo?

Over men's noses as they lie asleep;
Her wagon spokes made of long spinners'[16] legs,
60 The cover, of the wings of grasshoppers;
Her traces, of the smallest spider web;
Her collars, of the moonshine's wat'ry beams;
Her whip, of cricket's bone; the lash, of film;[17]
Her wagoner, a small gray-coated gnat,
65 Not half so big as a round little worm
Pricked from the lazy finger of a maid;
Her chariot is an empty hazelnut,
Made by the joiner squirrel or old grub,[18]
Time out o' mind the fairies' coachmakers.
70 And in this state she gallops night by night
Through lovers' brains, and then they dream of love;
On courtiers' knees, that dream on curtsies straight;
O'er lawyers' fingers, who straight dream on fees;
O'er ladies' lips, who straight on kisses dream,
75 Which oft the angry Mab with blisters plagues,
Because their breath with sweetmeats[19] tainted are.
Sometimes she gallops o'er a courtier's nose,
And then dreams he of smelling out a suit;[20]
And sometime comes she with a tithe pig's[21] tail
80 Tickling a parson's nose as 'a lies asleep,
Then he dreams of another benefice.[22]
Sometime she driveth o'er a soldier's neck,
And then dream he of cutting foreign throats,
Of breaches, ambuscadoes,[23] Spanish blades,
85 Of healths[24] five fathom deep; and then anon
Drums in his ear, at which he starts and wakes,
And being thus frighted, swears a prayer or two
And sleeps again. This is that very Mab
That plats[25] the manes of horses in the night
90 And bakes the elflocks[26] in foul sluttish hairs,
Which once untangled much misfortune bodes.
This is the hag, when maids lie on their backs,
That presses them and learns them first to bear,
Making them women of good carriage.[27]
This is she—

95 **ROMEO.**   Peace, peace, Mercutio, peace!
Thou talk'st of nothing.

MERCUTIO.   True, I talk of dreams;
Which are the children of an idle brain,
Begot of nothing but vain fantasy;
Which is as thin of substance as the air,
100 And more inconstant than the wind, who woos
Even now the frozen bosom of the North
And, being angered, puffs away from thence,
Turning his side to the dew-dropping South.

16. **spinners** spiders.

17. **film** spider's thread.

18. **old grub** an insect that bores holes in nuts.

Literary Analysis
Character Which character traits does Mercutio reveal in his Queen Mab speech?

19. **sweetmeats** candy.

20. **smelling . . . suit** finding someone who has a petition (suit) for the king and who will pay the courtier to gain the king's favor for the petition.

21. **tithe pig** a pig donated to a parson.

22. **benefice** a church appointment that included a guaranteed income.

23. **ambuscadoes** ambushes.

24. **healths** toasts ("To your health!").

25. **plats** tangles.

26. **elflocks** tangled hair.

27. **carriage** posture.

Literary Analysis
Character and Dramatic Foil How do lines 95–96 emphasize the contrast between Romeo and Mercutio?

BENVOLIO. This wind you talk of blows us from ourselves.
105 Supper is done, and we shall come too late.

ROMEO. I fear, too early; for my mind misgives
Some consequence yet hanging in the stars
Shall bitterly begin his fearful date
With this night's revels and expire the term
110 Of a despisèd life, closed in my breast,
By some vile forfeit of untimely death.[28]
But he that hath the steerage of my course
Direct my sail! On, lusty gentlemen!

BENVOLIO. Strike, drum.

[They march about the stage, and retire to one side.]

Scene v. *A hall in* CAPULET'S *house.*

*[*SERVINGMEN *come forth with napkins.]*

FIRST SERVINGMAN. Where's Potpan, that he helps not to
take away? He shift a trencher![1] He scrape a trencher!

SECOND SERVINGMAN. When good manners shall lie all in one or two
men's hands, and they unwashed too, 'tis a foul thing.

5 **FIRST SERVINGMAN.** Away with the join-stools, remove the
court cupboard, look to the plate. Good thou, save me a
piece of marchpane,[2] and, as thou loves me, let the porter
let in Susan Grindstone and Nell. Anthony, and Potpan!

SECOND SERVINGMAN. Ay, boy, ready.

10 **FIRST SERVINGMAN.** You are looked for and called for,
asked for and sought for, in the great chamber.

THIRD SERVINGMAN. We cannot be here and there too.
Cheerly, boys! Be brisk awhile, and the longer liver
take all. *[Exit.]*

[Enter CAPULET, *his* WIFE, JULIET, TYBALT, NURSE, *and all the* GUESTS *and*
GENTLEWOMEN *to the* MASKERS.]

15 **CAPULET.** Welcome, gentlemen! Ladies that have their toes
Unplagued with corns will walk a bout[3] with you.
Ah, my mistresses, which of you all
Will now deny to dance? She that makes dainty,[4]
She I'll swear hath corns. Am I come near ye now?
20 Welcome, gentlemen! I have seen the day
That I have worn a visor and could tell
A whispering tale in a fair lady's ear,
Such as would please. 'Tis gone, 'tis gone, 'tis gone.
You are welcome, gentlemen! Come, musicians, play.

[Music plays, and they dance.]

25 A hall,[5] a hall! Give room! And foot it, girls.

28. **my mind . . . death** My mind is fearful that some future event, fated by the stars, shall start to run its course tonight and cut my life short.

Reading Strategy
Using Text Aids Using note 28 as a text aid, restate Romeo's words in lines 109–111 in modern English.

1. **trencher** wooden platter.

2. **marchpane** marzipan, a confection made of sugar and almonds.

Literary Analysis
Character How do flat characters like the servingmen add to the play?

3. **walk a bout** dance a turn.

4. **makes dainty** hesitates, acts shy.

5. **A hall** clear the floor, make room for dancing.

✔ **Reading Check**

What does Romeo fear might happen in the near future?

More light, you knaves, and turn the tables up,
And quench the fire; the room is grown too hot.
Ah, sirrah, this unlooked-for sport comes well.
Nay, sit; nay, sit, good cousin Capulet;
30 For you and I are past our dancing days.
How long is't now since last yourself and I
Were in a mask?

SECOND CAPULET.   By'r Lady, thirty years.

CAPULET. What, man? 'Tis not so much, 'tis not so much;
35 'Tis since the nuptial of Lucentio,
Come Pentecost as quickly as it will,
Some five-and-twenty years, and then we masked.

SECOND CAPULET. 'Tis more, 'tis more. His son is elder, sir;
His son is thirty.

CAPULET.   Will you tell me that?
40 His son was but a ward[6] two years ago.

ROMEO. [*To a* SERVINGMAN] What lady's that which doth
enrich the hand
Of yonder knight?

SERVINGMAN. I know not, sir.

ROMEO. O, she doth teach the torches to burn bright!
It seems she hangs upon the cheek of night
45 As a rich jewel in an Ethiop's ear—
Beauty too rich for use, for earth too dear!
So shows a snowy dove trooping with crows
As yonder lady o'er her fellows shows.
The measure done, I'll watch her place of stand
50 And, touching hers, make blessèd my rude hand.
Did my heart love till now? Forswear[7] it, sight!
For I ne'er saw true beauty till this night.

TYBALT. This, by his voice, should be a Montague.
Fetch me my rapier, boy. What! Dares the slave
55 Come hither, covered with an antic face,[8]
To fleer[9] and scorn at our solemnity?
Now, by the stock and honor of my kin,
To strike him dead I hold it not a sin.

CAPULET. Why, how now, kinsman? Wherefore storm you so?

60 **TYBALT.** Uncle, this is a Montague, our foe,
A villain, that is hither come in spite
To scorn at our solemnity this night.

CAPULET. Young Romeo is it?

TYBALT.   'Tis he, that villain Romeo.

▲ **Critical Viewing**
What can you tell about Romeo's personality from the fact that he has taken off his mask? **[Draw Conclusions]**

6. **ward** minor.

7. **Forswear** deny.

8. **antic face** strange, fantastic mask.

9. **fleer** mock.

Reading Strategy
Using Text Aids What does Tybalt mean by saying that Romeo has come to the party with an "antic face, / To fleer and scorn at our solemnity"?

CAPULET. Content thee, gentle coz,[10] let him alone.
65 'A bears him like a portly gentleman,[11]
    And, to say truth, Verona brags of him
    To be a virtuous and well-governed youth.
    I would not for the wealth of all this town
    Here in my house do him disparagement.[12]
70 Therefore be patient; take no note of him.
    It is my will, the which if thou respect,
    Show a fair presence and put off these frowns,
    An ill-beseeming semblance[13] for a feast.

TYBALT. It fits when such a villain is a guest.
    I'll not endure him.

75 **CAPULET.**   He shall be endured.
    What, goodman[14] boy! I say he shall. Go to![15]
    Am I the master here, or you? Go to!
    You'll not endure him, God shall mend my soul![16]
    You'll make a mutiny among my guests!
80 You will set cock-a-hoop.[17] You'll be the man!

TYBALT. Why, uncle, 'tis a shame.

CAPULET.   Go to, go to!
    You are a saucy boy. Is't so, indeed?
    This trick may chance to scathe you.[18] I know what.
    You must contrary me! Marry, 'tis time–
85 Well said, my hearts!—You are a princox[19]—go!
    Be quiet, or—more light, more light!—For shame!
    I'll make you quiet. What!—Cheerly, my hearts!

TYBALT. Patience perforce with willful choler meeting[20]
    Makes my flesh tremble in their different greeting.
90 I will withdraw; but this intrusion shall,
    Now seeming sweet, convert to bitt'rest gall.   [*Exit.*]

ROMEO. If I profane with my unworthiest hand
        This holy shrine,[21] the gentle sin is this:
    My lips, two blushing pilgrims, ready stand
95   To smooth that rough touch with a tender kiss.

JULIET. Good pilgrim, you do wrong your hand too much,
        Which mannerly devotion shows in this;
    For saints have hands that pilgrims' hands do touch
        And palm to palm is holy palmers'[22] kiss.

100 **ROMEO.** Have not saints lips, and holy palmers too?

JULIET. Ay, pilgrim, lips that they must use in prayer.

ROMEO. O, then, dear saint, let lips do what hands do!
    They pray; grant thou, lest faith turn to despair.

JULIET. Saints do not move,[23] though grant for prayers' sake.

10. coz Here coz is used as a term of address for a relative.

11. 'A . . . gentleman He behaves like a dignified gentleman.

12. disparagement insult.

13. ill-beseeming semblance inappropriate appearance.

14. goodman term of address for someone below the rank of gentleman.

15. Go to! expression of angry impatience.

16. God . . . soul! expression of impatience, equivalent to, "God save me!"

17. You will set cock-a-hoop You want to swagger like a barnyard rooster.

18. This . . . you This trait of yours may turn to hurt you.

19. princox rude youngster; wise guy.

20. Patience . . . meeting enforced self-control mixing with strong anger.

Literary Analysis
Character Which character traits do Romeo and Juliet reveal in their words to each other?

21. shrine Juliet's hand.

22. palmers pilgrims who at one time carried palm branches from the Holy Land.

23. move initiate involvement in earthly affairs.

✓**Reading Check**

How does Capulet respond when Tybalt says he will not tolerate Romeo's presence at the party?

105 **ROMEO.** Then move not while my prayer's effect I take.
       Thus from my lips, by thine my sin is purged.   [*Kisses her.*]

JULIET. Then have my lips the sin that they have took.

ROMEO. Sin from my lips? O trespass sweetly urged!²⁴
       Give me my sin again.   [*Kisses her.*]

JULIET.   You kiss by th' book.²⁵

110 **NURSE.** Madam, your mother craves a word with you.

ROMEO. What is her mother?

NURSE.   Marry, bachelor,
       Her mother is the lady of the house,
       And a good lady, and a wise and virtuous.
       I nursed her daughter that you talked withal.
115   I tell you, he that can lay hold of her
       Shall have the chinks.²⁶

ROMEO.   Is she a Capulet?
       O dear account! My life is my foe's debt.²⁷

BENVOLIO. Away, be gone; the sport is at the best.

ROMEO. Ay, so I fear; the more is my unrest.

120 **CAPULET.** Nay, gentlemen, prepare not to be gone;
       We have a trifling foolish banquet towards.²⁸
       Is it e'en so?²⁹ Why then, I thank you all.
       I thank you, honest gentlemen. Good night.
       More torches here! Come on then; let's to bed.
125   Ah, sirrah, by my fay,³⁰ it waxes late;
       I'll to my rest.   [*Exit all but* JULIET *and* NURSE.]

▲ Critical Viewing

What does this picture suggest about Romeo and Juliet's feelings for each other? [**Infer**]

24. O . . . urged! Romeo is saying, in substance, that he is happy. Juliet calls his kiss a sin, for now he can take it back—by another kiss.

25. by th' book as if you were following a manual of courtly love.

26. chinks cash.

27. My life . . . debt Since Juliet is a Capulet, Romeo's life is at the mercy of the enemies of his family.

Reading Strategy

Using Text Aids What do you learn from the text aid that helps you understand Romeo's conflict?

28. towards being prepared.

29. Is . . . so? Is it the case that you really must leave?

30. fay faith.

JULIET. Come hither, nurse. What is yond gentleman?

NURSE. The son and heir of old Tiberio.

JULIET. What's he that now is going out of door?

130 **NURSE.** Marry, that, I think, be young Petruchio.

JULIET. What's he that follows here, that would not dance?

NURSE. I know not.

JULIET. Go ask his name—If he is married,
My grave is like to be my wedding bed.

135 **NURSE.** His name is Romeo, and a Montague,
The only son of your great enemy.

JULIET. My only love, sprung from my only hate!
Too early seen unknown, and known too late!
Prodigious³¹ birth of love it is to me

140 That I must love a loathèd enemy.

NURSE. What's this? What's this?

JULIET.   A rhyme I learnt even now.
Of one I danced withal.   [*One calls within,* "Juliet."]

NURSE.   Anon, anon!
Come, let's away; the strangers all are gone.   [*Exit all.*]

31. Prodigious monstrous; foretelling misfortune.

Review and Assess

Thinking About Act I

1. **Respond:** If you were Romeo or Juliet, would you pursue a relationship? Explain.

2. **(a) Recall:** Based on Act I, what facts do you know about Romeo's and Juliet's lives? **(b) Compare and Contrast:** How are these characters' personalities alike and different?

3. **(a) Recall:** What information about the two households is presented in the Prologue? **(b) Connect:** How does Juliet's comment in Act I, Scene v, lines 137–138, echo the Prologue?

4. **Analyze:** How do the comments of Montague and Benvolio in Act I help you understand the character of Romeo?

5. **(a) Analyze:** What threats to Romeo and Juliet's love already exist in Act I? **(b) Support:** How does Shakespeare use these threats to generate suspense in the first act?

6. **Evaluate:** Based on Romeo's behavior in Act I, do you think Shakespeare accurately portrays a teenager in love? Explain.

Prepare to Read

The Tragedy of Romeo and Juliet, Act II

Literary Analysis

Blank Verse

Blank verse is unrhymed poetry written in iambic pentameter, or lines of five stressed beats in which every second syllable is stressed. For example, when Romeo sees Juliet appear at her window, he exclaims,

> But soft! What light through yonder window breaks?
> It is the east, and Juliet is the sun!

Much of *Romeo and Juliet* is written in blank verse. This formal meter is well suited to serious subjects. As you read, say some of the lines aloud and note the effect of the stressed syllables and words spoken in blank verse.

Connecting Literary Elements

In a play, you generally learn about characters from the things they say and do and the way they speak. In Shakespeare's plays, blank verse helps reinforce **character rank:** Important or aristocratic characters typically speak in blank verse. Minor or comic characters often do not speak in verse. Use a chart like the one shown to identify a character's rank in this play.

Reading Strategy

Reading Blank Verse

When **reading blank verse,** remember that thoughts or phrases often run past the end of a line. To determine its full meaning, read blank verse in sentences, pausing according to the punctuation and not necessarily at the end of each line.

Vocabulary Development

cunning (kun´ iŋ) *n.* cleverness; slyness (p. 799)

procure (prō kyoor´) *v.* get (p. 801)

vile (vīl) *adj.* worthless (p. 803)

predominant (prē däm´ ə nənt) *adj.* having dominating influence over others (p. 803)

intercession (in´ tər sesh´ ən) *n.* the act of pleading on behalf of another (p. 804)

sallow (sal´ ō) *adj.* of a sickly, pale-yellowish complexion (p. 804)

waverer (wā´ vər ər) *n.* one who changes or is unsteady (p. 805)

lamentable (lə men´ tə bəl) *adj.* distressing; sad (p. 806)

unwieldy (un wēl´ dē) *adj.* awkward; clumsy (p. 811)

Review and Anticipate

Act I reveals a bitter, long-standing feud between the Montagues and the Capulets. It also introduces the play's title characters, who meet at a feast and immediately fall in love, only to discover that they come from opposing sides of the feud.

Based on what you have learned about the personalities of Romeo and Juliet, how do you expect them to respond to their love for each other and to the problems it poses? How do you think their families will react?

[*Enter* CHORUS.]

CHORUS. Now old desire[1] doth in his deathbed lie,
　　　And young affection gapes to be his heir;[2]
　　That fair[3] for which love groaned for and would die,
　　　With tender Juliet matched, is now not fair.
5　Now Romeo is beloved and loves again,
　　　Alike bewitchèd[4] by the charm of looks;
　　But to his foe supposed he must complain,[5]
　　　And she steal love's sweet bait from fearful hooks.
　　Being held a foe, he may not have access
10　　To breathe such vows as lovers use to swear,

1. **old desire** Romeo's love for Rosaline.

2. **young . . . heir** Romeo's new love for Juliet is eager to replace his love for Rosaline.

3. **fair** beautiful woman (Rosaline).

4. **Alike bewitched** Both Romeo and Juliet are enchanted.

5. **complain** address his words of love.

And she as much in love, her means much less
    To meet her new belovèd anywhere;
But passion lends them power, time means to meet,
Temp'ring extremities with extreme sweet.[6]   [*Exit.*]

Scene i. *Near* CAPULET's *orchard.*

[*Enter* ROMEO *alone.*]

    ROMEO. Can I go forward when my heart is here?
      Turn back, dull earth,[1] and find thy center[2] out.

[*Enter* BENVOLIO *with* MERCUTIO. ROMEO *retires.*]

    BENVOLIO. Romeo! My cousin Romeo! Romeo!

    MERCUTIO.   He is wise.
      And, on my life, hath stol'n him home to bed.

5   **BENVOLIO.** He ran this way and leapt this orchard wall.
      Call, good Mercutio.

    MERCUTIO.   Nay, I'll conjure[3] too.
      Romeo! Humors! Madman! Passion! Lover!
      Appear thou in the likeness of a sigh;
      Speak but one rhyme, and I am satisfied!
10   Cry but "Ay me!" pronounce but "love" and "dove";
      Speak to my gossip[4] Venus one fair word,
      One nickname for her purblind son and heir,
      Young Abraham Cupid, he that shot so true
      When King Cophetua loved the beggar maid!
15   He heareth not, he stirreth not, he moveth not;
      The ape is dead,[5] and I must conjure him.
      I conjure thee by Rosaline's bright eyes,
      By her high forehead and her scarlet lip,
      By her fine foot, straight leg, and quivering thigh,
20   And the demesnes that there adjacent lie,
      That in thy likeness thou appear to us!

    BENVOLIO. And if he hear thee, thou wilt anger him.

    MERCUTIO. This cannot anger him. 'Twould anger him
      To raise a spirit in his mistress' circle
25   Of some strange nature, letting it there stand
      Till she had laid it and conjured it down.
      That were some spite; my invocation
      Is fair and honest; in his mistress' name,
      I conjure only but to raise up him.

30   **BENVOLIO.** Come, he hath hid himself among these trees
      To be consorted[6] with the humorous[7] night.
      Blind is his love and best befits the dark.

    MERCUTIO. If love be blind, love cannot hit the mark.

---

6. Temp'ring . . . sweet easing their difficulties with great delights.

1. dull earth lifeless body.
2. center heart, or possibly soul (Juliet).

Literary Analysis
Blank Verse Line 3 breaks the pattern of blank verse. Why is this break suited to the emotion of the line?

3. conjure recite a spell to make Romeo appear.

4. gossip merry old lady.

Reading Strategy
Reading Blank Verse When reading Mercutio's speech (lines 6–21), where should you pause and where should you come to a complete stop?

5. The ape is dead Romeo, like a trained monkey, seems to be playing.

6. consorted associated.
7. humorous humid; moody, like a lover.

Now will he sit under a medlar tree
35   And wish his mistress were that kind of fruit
As maids call medlars[8] when they laugh alone.
O, Romeo, that she were, O that she were
An open *et cetera*, thou a pop'rin pear!
Romeo, good night. I'll to my truckle bed;[9]
40   This field bed is too cold for me to sleep.
Come, shall we go?

BENVOLIO.   Go then, for 'tis in vain
To seek him here that means not to be found.

                         [*Exit with others.*]

Scene ii. CAPULET's orchard.

ROMEO. [*Coming forward*] He jests at scars that never felt a wound.

[*Enters* JULIET *at a window.*]

But soft! What light through yonder window breaks?
It is the East, and Juliet is the sun!
Arise, fair sun, and kill the envious moon,
5   Who is already sick and pale with grief
That thou her maid art far more fair than she.
Be not her maid, since she is envious.
Her vestal livery[1] is but sick and green,
And none but fools do wear it. Cast it off.
10   It is my lady! O, it is my love!
O, that she knew she were!
She speaks, yet she says nothing. What of that?
Her eye discourses; I will answer it.
I am too bold; 'tis not to me she speaks.
15   Two of the fairest stars in all the heaven,
Having some business, do entreat her eyes
To twinkle in their spheres[2] till they return.
What if her eyes were there, they in her head?
The brightness of her cheek would shame those stars
20   As daylight doth a lamp; her eyes in heaven
Would through the airy region stream so bright
That birds would sing and think it were not night.
See how she leans her cheek upon that hand,
O, that I were a glove upon that hand,
That I might touch that cheek!

JULIET.   Ay me!

25   **ROMEO.**   She speaks.
O, speak again, bright angel, for thou art
As glorious to this night, being o'er my head,
As is a wingèd messenger of heaven
Unto the white-upturnèd wond'ring eyes

---

8. medlars applelike fruits.

9. truckle bed trundlebed, placed under a larger bed when not in use.

Literary Analysis
Blank Verse What effect does Shakespeare achieve by breaking up a rhymed couplet—a pair of rhyming lines—into two separate scenes?

1. livery clothing or costume worn by a servant.

2. spheres orbits.

Reading Strategy
Reading Blank Verse Why does reading Romeo's speech in complete sentences instead of line by line help you grasp its meaning?

**Reading Check**

Whom does Romeo see at the window?

Which is the god of my idolatry,
And I'll believe thee.

115 **ROMEO.**   If my heart's dear love—

JULIET. Well, do not swear. Although I joy in thee,
I have no joy of this contract[20] tonight.
It is too rash, too unadvised, too sudden;
Too like the lightning, which doth cease to be
120 Ere one can say it lightens. Sweet, good night!
This bud of love, by summer's ripening breath,
May prove a beauteous flow'r when next we meet.
Good night, good night! As sweet repose and rest
Come to thy heart as that within my breast!

125 **ROMEO.** O, wilt thou leave me so unsatisfied?

JULIET. What satisfaction canst thou have tonight?

ROMEO. Th' exchange of thy love's faithful vow for mine.

JULIET. I gave thee mine before thou didst request it;
And yet I would it were to give again.

130 **ROMEO.** Wouldst thou withdraw it? For what purpose, love?

JULIET. But to be frank[21] and give it thee again.
And yet I wish but for the thing I have.
My bounty[22] is as boundless as the sea,
My love as deep; the more I give to thee,

20. **contract** betrothal.

Reading Strategy
Reading Blank Verse
How would you rephrase
in Standard English what
Romeo and Juliet are say-
ing to each other?

21. **frank** generous.

22. **bounty** what I have
to give.

◀ **Critical Viewing**
How does Juliet's
expression in this picture
match the feelings she has
conveyed in the play so
far? [**Connect**]

135 The more I have, for both are infinite,
I hear some noise within. Dear love, adieu!

[NURSE *calls within.*]

Anon, good nurse! Sweet Montague, be true.
Stay but a little, I will come again.   [*Exit.*]

ROMEO. O blessèd, blessèd night! I am afeard,
140 Being in night, all this is but a dream,
Too flattering-sweet to be substantial.[23]

[*Enter* JULIET *again.*]

JULIET. Three words, dear Romeo, and good night indeed.
If that thy bent[24] of love be honorable,
Thy purpose marriage, send me word tomorrow,
145 By one that I'll <u>procure</u> to come to thee,
Where and what time thou wilt perform the rite;
And all my fortunes at thy foot I'll lay
And follow thee my lord throughout the world.

NURSE. [*Within*] Madam!

150 **JULIET.** I come anon.—But if thou meanest not well,
I do beseech thee—

NURSE.   [*Within*] Madam!

JULIET.   By and by[25] I come.—
To cease thy strife[26] and leave me to my grief.
Tomorrow will I send.

ROMEO.   So thrive my soul—

JULIET. A thousand times good night!   [*Exit.*]

155 **ROMEO.** A thousand times the worse, to want thy light!
Love goes toward love as schoolboys from their books;
But love from love, toward school with heavy looks.

[*Enter* JULIET *again.*]

JULIET. Hist! Romeo, hist! O for a falc'ner's voice
To lure this tassel gentle[27] back again!
160 Bondage is hoarse[28] and may not speak aloud,
Else would I tear the cave where Echo[29] lies
And make her airy tongue more hoarse than mine
With repetition of "My Romeo!"

ROMEO. It is my soul that calls upon my name.
165 How silver-sweet sound lovers' tongues by night,
Like softest music to attending ears!

JULIET. Romeo!

ROMEO.   My sweet?

JULIET. What o'clock tomorrow
Shall I send to thee?

ROMEO. By the hour of nine.

JULIET. I will not fail. 'Tis twenty year till then.
170 I have forgot why I did call thee back.

ROMEO. Let me stand here till thou remember it.

JULIET. I shall forget, to have thee still stand there,
Rememb'ring how I love thy company.

ROMEO. And I'll stay, to have thee still forget,
175 Forgetting any other home but this.

JULIET. 'Tis almost morning. I would have thee gone—
And yet no farther than a wanton's[30] bird,
That lets it hop a little from his hand,
Like a poor prisoner in his twisted gyves,[31]
180 And with a silken thread plucks it back again,
So loving-jealous of his liberty.

ROMEO. I would I were thy bird.

JULIET. Sweet, so would I.
Yet I should kill thee with much cherishing.
Good night, good night! Parting is such sweet sorrow
185 That I shall say good night till it be morrow. *[Exit.]*

ROMEO. Sleep dwell upon thine eyes, peace in thy breast!
Would I were sleep and peace, so sweet to rest!
Hence will I to my ghostly friar's[32] close cell,[33]
His help to crave and my dear hap[34] to tell. *[Exit.]*

Scene iii. FRIAR LAWRENCE's cell.

[Enter FRIAR LAWRENCE alone, with a basket.]

FRIAR. The gray-eyed morn smiles on the frowning night,

Literature
in context Literature Connection

Hyperbole
   Hyperbole is deliberate exaggeration in writing or speech. For example, in lines 71–72, when Romeo says the look in Juliet's eyes is more dangerous than twenty of her kinsmen's swords, he uses hyperbole to express the power in the beauty of her eyes. Several times in this scene, as in line 169, both young lovers use hyperbole to emphasize their love.

Check'ring the eastern clouds with streaks of light;
And fleckèd[1] darkness like a drunkard reels
From forth day's path and Titan's burning wheels.[2]
5   Now, ere the sun advance his burning eye
The day to cheer and night's dank dew to dry,
I must upfill this osier cage[3] of ours
With baleful[4] weeds and precious-juicèd flowers.
The earth that's nature's mother is her tomb.
10   What is her burying grave, that is her womb;
And from her womb children of divers kind[5]
We sucking on her natural bosom find,
Many for many virtues excellent,
None but for some, and yet all different.
15   O, mickle[6] is the powerful grace[7] that lies
In plants, herbs, stones, and their true qualities;
For naught so <u>vile</u> that on the earth doth live
But to the earth some special good doth give;
Nor aught so good but, strained[8] from that fair use,
20   Revolts from true birth,[9] stumbling on abuse.
Virtue itself turns vice, being misapplied,
And vice sometime by action dignified.

[*Enter* ROMEO.]

Within the infant rind[10] of this weak flower
Poison hath residence and medicine power;[11]
25   For this, being smelt, with that part cheers each part;[12]
Being tasted, stays all senses with the heart.[13]
Two such opposèd kings encamp them still[14]
In man as well as herbs—grace and rude will;
And where the worser is <u>predominant</u>,
30   Full soon the canker[15] death eats up that plant.

ROMEO. Good morrow, father.

FRIAR.   *Benedicite!*[16]
What early tongue so sweet saluteth me?
Young son, it argues a distemperèd head[17]
So soon to bid good morrow to thy bed.
35   Care keeps his watch in every old man's eye,
And where care lodges, sleep will never lie;
But where unbruisèd youth with unstuffed[18] brain
Doth couch his limbs, there golden sleep doth reign,
Therefore thy earliness doth me assure
40   Thou art uproused with some distemp'rature;[19]
Or if not so, then here I hit it right—
Our Romeo hath not been in bed tonight.

ROMEO. That last is true. The sweeter rest was mine.

FRIAR. God pardon sin! Wast thou with Rosaline?

1. **fleckèd** spotted.
2. **Titan's burning wheels** wheels of the sun god's chariot.
3. **osier cage** willow basket.
4. **baleful** poisonous.
5. **divers kind** different kinds.
6. **mickle** great.
7. **grace** divine power.
8. **strained** turned away.

vile (vīl) *adj.* worthless

9. **Revolts . . . birth** conflicts with its real purpose.
10. **infant rind** tender skin.
11. **and medicine power** and medicinal quality has power.
12. **with . . . part** with that quality—odor—revives each part of the body.
13. **stays . . . heart** kills (stops the working of the five senses along with the heart).

predominant (prē däm' ə nənt) *adj.* having dominating influence over others

14. **still** always.
15. **canker** a destructive caterpillar.
16. *Benedicite!* God bless you!
17. **distemperèd head** troubled mind.
18. **unstuffed** not filled with cares.
19. **distemp'rature** illness.

**Reading Check**

When Romeo leaves Juliet, what reason does he give for visiting the Friar?

ROMEO. With Rosaline, my ghostly father? No.
45   I have forgot that name and that name's woe.

FRIAR. That's my good son! But where hast thou been then?

ROMEO. I'll tell thee ere thou ask it me again.
    I have been feasting with mine enemy,
50   Where on a sudden one hath wounded me
    That's by me wounded. Both our remedies
    Within thy help and holy physic[20] lies.
    I bear no hatred, blessèd man, for, lo,
    My <u>intercession</u> likewise steads my foe.[21]

55 **FRIAR.** Be plain, good son, and homely in thy drift.[22]
    Riddling confession finds but riddling shrift.[23]

ROMEO. Then plainly know my heart's dear love is set
    On the fair daughter of rich Capulet;
    As mine on hers, so hers is set on mine,
60   And all combined, save[24] what thou must combine
    By holy marriage. When and where and how
    We met, we wooed, and made exchange of vow,
    I'll tell thee as we pass; but this I pray,
    That thou consent to marry us today.

65 **FRIAR.** Holy Saint Francis! What a change is here!
    Is Rosaline, that thou didst love so dear,
    So soon forsaken? Young men's love then lies
    Not truly in their hearts, but in their eyes.
    Jesu Maria! What a deal of brine[25]
70   Hath washed thy <u>sallow</u> cheeks for Rosaline!
    How much salt water thrown away in waste
    To season love, that of it doth not taste!
    The sun not yet thy sighs from heaven clears,
    Thy old groans ring yet in mine ancient ears.
75   Lo, here upon thy cheek the stain doth sit
    Of an old tear that is not washed off yet.
    If e'er thou wast thyself, and these woes thine,
    Thou and these woes were all for Rosaline.
    And art thou changed? Pronounce this sentence then:
80   Women may fall[26] when there's no strength[27] in men.

ROMEO. Thou chidst me oft for loving Rosaline.

FRIAR. For doting,[28] not for loving, pupil mine.

ROMEO. And badst[29] me bury love.

FRIAR.   Not in a grave
    To lay one in, another out to have.

85 **ROMEO.** I pray thee chide me not. Her I love now
    Doth grace[30] for grace and love for love allow.[31]
    The other did not so.

20. physic (fiz´ ik) medicine.

21. My . . . foe my plea also helps my enemy (Juliet, a Capulet).

intercession (in´ tər sesh´ ən) *n.* the act of pleading on behalf of another

22. and . . . drift and simple in your speech.

23. Riddling . . . shrift A confusing confession will get you uncertain forgiveness. The Friar means that unless Romeo speaks clearly, he will not get clear and direct advice.

24. And . . . save and we are united in every way, except for (save).

25. brine salt water (tears).

sallow (sal´ ō) *adj.* of a sickly, pale-yellowish complexion

26. fall be weak or inconstant.

Literary Analysis
Blank Verse Which important words are stressed in the last six lines of the Friar's speech?

27. strength constancy; stability.

28. doting being infatuated.

29. badst urged.

30. grace favor.
31. allow give.

FRIAR.   O, she knew well
Thy love did read by rote, that could not spell.[32]
But come, young <u>waverer</u>, come go with me.

90   In one respect I'll thy assistant be;
For this alliance may so happy prove
To turn your households' rancor[33] to pure love.

ROMEO. O, let us hence! I stand on[34] sudden haste.

FRIAR. Wisely and slow. They stumble that run fast.   *[Exit all.]*

Scene iv. *A street.*

[Enter BENVOLIO *and* MERCUTIO.]

MERCUTIO. Where the devil should this Romeo be?
Came he not home tonight?

BENVOLIO. Not to his father's. I spoke with his man.

MERCUTIO. Why, that same pale hardhearted wench, that Rosaline,
5   Torments him so that he will sure run mad.

BENVOLIO. Tybalt, the kinsman to old Capulet,
Hath sent a letter to his father's house.

MERCUTIO. A challenge, on my life.

BENVOLIO. Romeo will answer it.

10   **MERCUTIO.** Any man that can write may answer a letter.

BENVOLIO. Nay, he will answer the letter's master, how he dares,
being dared.

MERCUTIO. Alas, poor Romeo, he is already dead: stabbed
with a white wench's black eye; run through the ear
15   with a love song; the very pin of his heart cleft with the
blind bow-boy's butt-shaft;[1] and is he a man to encounter Tybalt?

BENVOLIO. Why, what is Tybalt?

MERCUTIO. More than Prince of Cats.[2] O, he's the courageous captain of compliments.[3] He fights as you sing
20   pricksong[4]—keeps time, distance, and proportion; he
rests his minim rests,[5] one, two, and the third in your
bosom! The very butcher of a silk button,[6] a duelist, a
duelist! A gentleman of the very first house,[7] of the first
and second cause.[8] Ah, the immortal *passado!* The
25   *punto reverso!* The hay![9]

BENVOLIO. The what?

MERCUTIO. The pox of such antic, lisping, affecting fantas-
ticoes—these new tuners of accent![10] "By Jesu, a very
good blade! A very tall man! A very good whore!" Why,

---

32. Thy . . . spell your love recited words from memory with no under-standing of them.

waverer (wā′ vər ər) *n.* one who changes or is unsteady

33. rancor hatred.

34. stand on insist on.

1. blind bow-boy's butt-shaft Cupid's blunt arrow.

2. Prince of Cats Tybalt, or a variation of it, is the name of the cat in medieval stories of Reynard the Fox.

3. captain of compliments master of formal behavior.

4. as you sing prick-song with attention to precision.

5. rests . . . rests observes all formalities.

6. button an exact spot on his opponent's shirt.

7. first house finest school of fencing.

8. the first and second cause reasons that would cause a gentle-man to challenge another to a duel.

9. *passado!* . . . *punto reverso!* . . . hay! lunge . . . backhanded stroke . . . home thrust.

10. The pox . . . accent May the plague strike these absurd characters with their phony man-ners—these men who speak in weird, newfan-gled ways!

✓ **Reading Check**

What does the Friar think Romeo and Juliet's love will do for the Capulets and Montagues?

30   is not this a <u>lamentable</u> thing, grandsir, that we
    should be thus afflicted with these strange flies, these
    fashionmongers, these pardon-me's,[11] who stand so
    much on the new form that they cannot sit at ease on
    the old bench? O, their bones, their bones!

[*Enter* ROMEO.]

35 **BENVOLIO.** Here comes Romeo! Here comes Romeo!

   MERCUTIO. Without his roe, like a dried herring.[12] O flesh,
    flesh, how art thou fishified! Now is he for the num-
    bers[13] that Petrarch flowed in. Laura,[14] to his lady, was
    a kitchen wench (marry, she had a better love to be-
40   rhyme her), Dido a dowdy, Cleopatra a gypsy, Helen
    and Hero hildings and harlots, Thisbe a gray eye or so,
    but not to the purpose. Signior Romeo, *bon jour!*
    There's a French salutation to your French slop. You
    gave us the counterfeit fairly last night.

45 **ROMEO.** Good morrow to you both. What counterfeit did I
    give you?

   MERCUTIO. The slip,[15] sir, the slip. Can you not conceive?

   ROMEO. Pardon, good Mercutio. My business was great,
    and in such a case as mine a man may strain courtesy.

---

lamentable (lə men′ tə bəl)
adj. distressing; sad

11. these pardon-me's
these men who are
always saying "Pardon
me" (adopting ridiculous
manners).

**12. Without . . . her-
ring** worn out.

13. numbers verses of
love poems.

14. Laura Laura and the
other ladies mentioned
are all notable figures of
European love literature.
Mercutio is saying that
Romeo thinks that none
of them compare with
Rosaline.

15. slip escape. *Slip* is
also a term for counter-
feit coin.

Literary Analysis
Blank Verse Why do you
think the conversation
between Romeo and his
friends is not in blank
verse?

◀ **Critical Viewing**
How is the rowdy
behavior of the young
Montagues, as shown in
this picture, typical of a
group of teenage friends?
[Generalize]

◀ **Critical Viewing**
How do the men in this picture compare with your image of the three men in this scene? **[Generalize]**

50   **MERCUTIO.** That's as much as to say, such a case as yours constrains a man to bow in the hams.[16]

ROMEO. Meaning, to curtsy.

MERCUTIO. Thou hast most kindly hit it.

ROMEO. A most courteous exposition.

55   **MERCUTIO.** Nay, I am the very pink of courtesy.

ROMEO. Pink for flower.

MERCUTIO. Right.

ROMEO. Why, then is my pump[17] well-flowered.

MERCUTIO. Sure wit, follow me this jest now till thou hast
60   worn out thy pump, that, when the single sole of it is worn, the jest may remain, after the wearing, solely singular.[18]

ROMEO. O single-soled jest, solely singular for the single-ness![19]

65   **MERCUTIO.** Come between us, good Benvolio! My wits faints.

ROMEO. Swits and spurs, swits and spurs; or I'll cry a match.[20]

MERCUTIO. Nay, if our wits run the wild-goose chase, I am done; for thou hast more of the wild goose in one of

16. hams hips.

17. pump shoe.

18. when . . . singular the jest will outwear the shoe and will then be all alone.

19. O . . . singleness! O thin joke, unique for only one thing—weakness!

20. Swits . . . match Drive your wit harder to beat me or else I'll claim victory in this match of word play.

✔**Reading Check**

How does Romeo respond when Mercutio says Romeo gave them "the slip" the night before?

Romeo and Juliet, Act II, Scene iv ◆ 807

70 thy wits than, I am sure, I have in my whole five. Was I with you there for the goose?

ROMEO. Thou wast never with me for anything when thou wast not there for the goose.

MERCUTIO. I will bite thee by the ear for that jest.

75 **ROMEO.** Nay, good goose, bite not!

MERCUTIO. Thy wit is a very bitter sweeting;²¹ it is a most sharp sauce.

ROMEO. And is it not, then, well served in to a sweet goose?

MERCUTIO. O, here's a wit of cheveril,²² that stretches from an inch
80 narrow to an ell broad!

ROMEO. I stretch it out for that word "broad," which added to the goose, proves thee far and wide a broad goose.

MERCUTIO. Why, is not this better now than groaning for love? Now art thou sociable, now art thou Romeo; now
85 art thou what thou art, by art as well as by nature. For this driveling love is like a great natural²³ that runs lolling²⁴ up and down to hide his bauble²⁵ in a hole.

BENVOLIO. Stop there, stop there!

MERCUTIO. Thou desirest me to stop in my tale against the hair.²⁶

90 **BENVOLIO.** Thou wouldst else have made thy tale large.

MERCUTIO. O, thou art deceived! I would have made it short; for I was come to the whole depth of my tale, and meant indeed to occupy the argument²⁷ no longer.

ROMEO. Here's goodly gear!²⁸

[*Enter* NURSE *and her Man*, PETER.]

95 A sail, a sail!

MERCUTIO. Two, two! A shirt and a smock.²⁹

NURSE. Peter!

PETER. Anon.

NURSE. My fan, Peter.

100 **MERCUTIO.** Good Peter, to hide her face; for her fan's the fairer face.

NURSE. God ye good morrow, gentlemen.

MERCUTIO. God ye good-den, fair gentlewoman.

NURSE. Is it good-den?

105 **MERCUTIO.** 'Tis no less, I tell ye; for the bawdy hand of the

---

21. sweeting a kind of apple.

22. cheveril easily stretched kid leather.

23. natural idiot.

24. lolling with tongue hanging out.

25. bauble toy.

Literary Analysis
Blank Verse and Character Rank How does Shakespeare reveal Mercutio's intelligence despite the fact that the character does not speak in blank verse?

26. the hair natural inclination.

27. occupy the argument talk about the matter.

28. goodly gear good stuff for joking (Romeo sees Nurse approaching).

29. A shirt and a smock a man and a woman.

dial is now upon the prick of noon.

NURSE. Out upon you! What a man are you!

ROMEO. One, gentlewoman, that God hath made, himself to mar.

NURSE. By my troth, it is well said. "For himself to mar,"
110   quoth 'a? Gentlemen, can any of you tell me where I
    may find the young Romeo?

ROMEO. I can tell you; but young Romeo will be older
    when you have found him than he was when you sought
    him. I am the youngest of that name, for fault[30] of a
115   worse.

NURSE. You say well.

MERCUTIO. Yea, is the worst well? Very well took,[31] i' faith! Wisely,
    wisely.

NURSE. If you be he, sir, I desire some confidence[32] with you.

120 **BENVOLIO.** She will endite him to some supper.

MERCUTIO. A bawd, a bawd, a bawd! So ho!

ROMEO. What hast thou found?

MERCUTIO. No hare, sir; unless a hare, sir, in a lenten pie,
    that is something stale and hoar ere it be spent.

              [*He walks by them and sings.*]

125   An old hare hoar,
              And an old hare hoar,
            Is very good meat in Lent;
              But a hare that is hoar
              Is too much for a score
130   When it hoars ere it be spent.

Romeo, will you come to your father's? We'll to dinner thither.

ROMEO. I will follow you.

MERCUTIO. Farewell, ancient lady. Farewell, [*singing*] "Lady, lady,
    lady."[33]
                           [*Exit* MERCUTIO, BENVOLIO.]

135 **NURSE.** I pray you, sir, what saucy merchant was this that
    was so full of his ropery?[34]

ROMEO. A gentleman, nurse, that loves to hear himself talk
    and will speak more in a minute than he will stand to
    in a month.

140 **NURSE.** And 'a[35] speak anything against me, I'll take him
    down, and 'a were lustier than he is, and twenty such
    Jacks; and if I cannot, I'll find those that shall. Scurvy
    knave! I am none of his flirt-gills;[36] I am none of his

30. fault lack.

31. took understood.

32. confidence Nurse means *conference.*

33. "Lady . . . lady" line from an old ballad, "Chaste Susanna."

34. ropery Nurse means *roguery,* the talk and conduct of a rascal.

35. 'a he.

36. flirt-gills common girls.

☑ **Reading Check**

Who interrupts Romeo and his friends to ask about Romeo?

145   skainsmates.[37] And thou must stand by too, and suffer every knave to use me at his pleasure!

PETER. I saw no man use you at his pleasure. If I had, my weapon should quickly have been out, I warrant you. I dare draw as soon as another man, if I see occasion in a good quarrel, and the law on my side.

150 **NURSE.** Now, afore God, I am so vexed that every part about me quivers. Scurvy knave! Pray you, sir, a word; and, as I told you, my young lady bid me inquire you out. What she bid me say, I will keep to myself; but first let me tell ye, if ye should lead her in a fool's paradise, as

155   they say, it were a very gross kind of behavior, as they say; for the gentlewoman is young; and therefore, if you should deal double with her, truly it were an ill thing to be off'red to any gentlewoman, and very weak[38] dealing.

160 **ROMEO.** Nurse, commend[39] me to thy lady and mistress. I protest unto thee—

NURSE. Good heart, and i' faith I will tell her as much. Lord, Lord, she will be a joyful woman.

ROMEO. What wilt thou tell her, nurse? Thou dost not

165   mark me.

NURSE. I will tell her, sir, that you do protest, which, as I take it, is a gentlemanlike offer.

ROMEO. Bid her devise
Some means to come to shrift[40] this afternoon;

170   And there she shall at Friar Lawrence' cell
Be shrived and married. Here is for thy pains.

NURSE. No, truly, sir; not a penny.

ROMEO. Go to! I say you shall.

NURSE. This afternoon, sir? Well, she shall be there.

175 **ROMEO.** And stay, good nurse, behind the abbey wall.
Within this hour my man shall be with thee
And bring thee cords made like a tackled stair.[41]
Which to the high topgallant[42] of my joy
Must be my convoy[43] in the secret night.

180   Farewell. Be trusty, and I'll quit[44] thy pains.
Farewell. Commend me to thy mistress.

NURSE. Now God in heaven bless thee! Hark you, sir.

ROMEO. What say'st thou, my dear nurse?

NURSE. Is your man secret? Did you ne'er hear say,

185   Two may keep counsel, putting one away?[45]

---

37. skainsmates criminals; cutthroats.

Literary Analysis
Blank Verse and Character Rank Why do you think Shakespeare chose to write the Nurse's lines without attention to blank verse?

38. weak unmanly.

39. commend convey my respect and best wishes.

40. shrift confession.

Reading Strategy
Reading Blank Verse How would you rephrase Romeo's words in lines 170–171?

41. tackled stair rope ladder.

42. topgallant summit.

43. convoy conveyance.

44. quit reward; pay you back for.

45. Two . . . away Two can keep a secret if one is ignorant, or out of the way.

ROMEO. Warrant thee my man's as true as steel.

NURSE. Well, sir, my mistress is the sweetest lady. Lord,
Lord! When 'twas a little prating[46] thing— O, there is a
nobleman in town, one Paris, that would fain lay knife
190   aboard;[47] but she, good soul, had as lieve[48] see a toad,
a very toad, as see him. I anger her sometimes, and tell
her that Paris is the properer man; but I'll warrant
you, when I say so, she looks as pale as any clout[49]
in the versal world.[50] Doth not rosemary and Romeo
195   begin both with a letter?

ROMEO. Ay, nurse; what of that? Both with an *R.*

NURSE. Ah, mocker! That's the dog's name.[51] *R* is for the—
No; I know it begins with some other letter; and she
hath the prettiest sententious[52] of it, of you and rosemary,
200   that it would do you good to hear it.

ROMEO. Commend me to thy lady.

NURSE. Ay, a thousand times. [*Exit* ROMEO.] Peter!

PETER. Anon.

NURSE. Before, and apace.[53]   [*Exit, after* PETER.]

Scene v. CAPULET's *orchard.*

[*Enter* JULIET.]

JULIET. The clock struck nine when I did send the nurse;
In half an hour she promised to return.
Perchance she cannot meet him. That's not so.
O, she is lame! Love's heralds should be thoughts,
5   Which ten times faster glides than the sun's beams
Driving back shadows over low'ring[1] hills.
Therefore do nimble-pinioned doves draw Love,[2]
And therefore hath the wind-swift Cupid wings.
Now is the sun upon the highmost hill
10   Of this day's journey, and from nine till twelve
Is three long hours; yet she is not come.
Had she affections and warm youthful blood,
She would be as swift in motion as a ball;
My words would bandy her[3] to my sweet love,
15   And his to me.
But old folks, many feign[4] as they were dead—
Unwieldy, slow, heavy and pale as lead.

[*Enter* NURSE *and* PETER.]

O God, she comes! O honey nurse, what news?
Hast thou met with him? Send thy man away.

---

46. prating babbling.

47. fain . . . aboard eagerly seize Juliet for himself.

48. had as lieve would as willingly.

49. clout cloth.

50. versal world universe.

51. dog's name *R* sounds like a growl.

52. sententious Nurse means *sentences*—clever, wise sayings.

53. Before, and apace Go ahead of me, and quickly.

1. low'ring darkening.

2. Therefore . . . Love therefore, doves with quick wings pull the chariot of Venus, goddess of love.

Literary Analysis
Blank Verse What is the effect of hearing Juliet's blank verse right after the Nurse's prose speeches?

3. bandy her send her rapidly.

4. feign act.

unwieldy (un wēl′ dē) *adj.* awkward; clumsy

✓**Reading Check**

What does Romeo ask the Nurse to tell Juliet?

NURSE.   O God's Lady dear!
Are you so hot?[11] Marry come up, I trow.[12]
Is this the poultice[13] for my aching bones?
Henceforward do your messages yourself.

65 **JULIET.** Here's such a coil![14] Come, what says Romeo?

NURSE. Have you got leave to go to shrift today?

JULIET. I have.

NURSE. Then hie you hence to Friar Lawrence' cell;
There stays a husband to make you a wife.
70 Now comes the wanton[15] blood up in your cheeks:
They'll be in scarlet straight at any news.
Hie you to church: I must another way,
To fetch a ladder, by the which your love
Must climb a bird's nest soon when it is dark.
75 I am the drudge, and toil in your delight:
But you shall bear the burden soon at night.
Go; I'll to dinner; hie you to the cell.

JULIET. Hie to high fortune! Honest nurse, farewell.   [*Exit all.*]

*S*cene vi. FRIAR LAWRENCE's *cell.*

[*Enter* FRIAR LAWRENCE *and* ROMEO.]

FRIAR. So smile the heavens upon this holy act
That afterhours with sorrow chide us not![1]

ROMEO. Amen, amen! But come what sorrow can,
It cannot countervail[2] the exchange of joy
5 That one short minute gives me in her sight.
Do thou but close our hands with holy words,
Then love-devouring death do what he dare—
It is enough I may but call her mine.

FRIAR. These violent delights have violent ends
10 And in their triumph die, like fire and powder,[3]
Which, as they kiss, consume. The sweetest honey
Is loathsome in his own deliciousness
And in the taste confounds[4] the appetite.
Therefore love moderately: long love doth so;
15 Too swift arrives as tardy as too slow.

[*Enter* JULIET.]

Here comes the lady. O, so light a foot
Will ne'er wear out the everlasting flint.[5]
A lover may bestride the gossamers[6]
That idles in the wanton summer air,
20 And yet not fall; so light is vanity.[7]

11. **hot** impatient; hot-tempered.

12. **Marry . . . trow** Indeed, cool down, I say.
13. **poultice** remedy.
14. **coil** disturbance.

Literary Analysis
Blank Verse Why do you think Shakespeare broke the pattern of blank verse in line 67?

15. **wanton** excited.

Literary Analysis
Blank Verse What effect is created by making Juliet's last line rhyme with the Nurse's last line?

1. **That . . . not!** that the future does not punish us with sorrow.
2. **countervail** equal.

3. **powder** gunpowder.

4. **confounds** destroys.

5. **flint** stone.

6. **gossamers** spider webs.

7. **vanity** foolish things that cannot last.

JULIET. Good even to my ghostly confessor.

FRIAR. Romeo shall thank thee, daughter, for us both.

JULIET. As much to him,[8] else is his thanks too much.

ROMEO. Ah, Juliet, if the measure of thy joy
25   Be heaped like mine, and that thy skill be more
To blazon it,[9] then sweeten with thy breath
This neighbor air, and let rich music's tongue
Unfold the imagined happiness that both
Receive in either by this dear encounter.

30 **JULIET.** Conceit, more rich in matter than in words,
Brags of his substance, not of ornament.[10]
They are but beggars that can count their worth;
But my true love is grown to such excess
I cannot sum up sum of half my wealth.

35 **FRIAR.** Come, come with me, and we will make short work;
For, by your leaves, you shall not stay alone
Till Holy Church incorporate two in one.   [*Exit all.*]

8. As . . . him the same greeting to him.

Reading Strategy
Reading Blank Verse
How can you read Romeo's lines most effectively to grasp their meaning as well as their poetry?

9. and . . . it and if you are better able to proclaim it.

10. Conceit . . . ornament Understanding does not need to be dressed up in words.

Review and Assess

Thinking About Act II

1. **Respond:** Do you think Friar Lawrence is wise to agree to marry Romeo and Juliet? Explain.

2. **(a) Recall:** Where do Romeo and Juliet first mutually declare their love for each other? **(b) Interpret:** What role does darkness play in the scene?

3. **(a) Recall:** What doubts and fears does Juliet express even as she realizes that Romeo loves her? **(b) Make a Judgment:** Do you think the couple will be able to overcome these problems? Explain.

4. **(a) Recall:** What weakness in Romeo does the Friar point out before agreeing to help? **(b) Compare and Contrast:** How do the Friar's motives differ from the couple's own motives?

5. **(a) Recall:** For whom does Juliet wait in Act II, Scene v? **(b) Interpret:** What are Juliet's feelings as she waits to hear the message Romeo has sent?

6. **Analyze:** What tragic events to come are foreshadowed in Act II?

7. **Evaluate:** Why do you think the love scene in Capulet's garden is one of the most famous in all of literature?

Review and Assess

Literary Analysis

Blank Verse

1. Copy the following passages of **blank verse.** Then, indicate the pattern of accented (´) and unaccented (˘) syllables in each line.
   (a) Act II, Scene ii, lines 43–51
   (b) Act II, Scene vi, lines 3–8
2. Using a chart like the one shown, rewrite the lines below, marking stressed and unstressed syllables. Then, indicate which key words are stressed in each line and explain why those words are important to the drama.
   (a) ROMEO. Can I go forward when my heart is here?
   (b) JULIET. But my true love is grown to such excess.

Blank Verse Pattern	Key Words	Significance

Connecting Literary Elements

3. Identify the aristocratic and common people in Acts I and II, based on whether or not they speak in blank verse.
4. (a) Why do you think Shakespeare chose to have aristocratic characters speak in blank verse instead of ordinary prose? (b) What is the effect of such a choice?

Reading Strategy

Reading Blank Verse

5. How many sentences are in lines 1–8 in Act II, Scene v?
6. Copy Act II, Scene v, lines 1–8 as a paragraph. Read your paragraph aloud, and mark it to indicate where it is natural to take a breath or pause.
7. Rewrite the paragraph in your own words.

Extend Understanding

8. **Cultural Connection:** How does the attitude that Romeo and Juliet appear to have toward marriage compare with the attitudes of teenagers in our time?

Integrate Language Skills

Vocabulary Development Lesson

Word Analysis: Latin Prefix *inter-*

The Latin prefix *inter-*, which means "between" or "among," appears in *intercession,* meaning "the act of going between." Use the meaning of *inter-* to define each word below.

1. international   **2.** interpersonal   **3.** interstate

Spelling Strategy

If a word ends in one consonant preceded by one vowel and the final syllable is not accented, do not double the final consonant when adding a suffix. For example, *waver* + *-er* = *waverer.* Add the suffix shown and write the new word.

1. peril (*-ous*)   **2.** gather (*-ed*)   **3.** travel (*-ing*)

Fluency: Clarify Word Meaning

Review the vocabulary words on page 794. In your notebook, match each expression on the left with its meaning on the right.

1. lamentable intercession	**a.** low slyness
2. procure quickly	**b.** dominating hue
3. vile cunning	**c.** sickly skin tone
4. predominant color	**d.** awkward tool
5. sallow complexion	**e.** sad pleading
6. unwieldy implement	**f.** cowardly fluctuator
7. spineless waverer	**g.** obtain fast

Grammar Lesson

Possessive Case of Personal Pronouns

The **possessive case of personal pronouns** shows possession before nouns and gerunds. Possessive pronouns can also be used alone.

> **Before Noun:** By *her* high forehead and *her* scarlet lip . . .
>
> **Before Gerund:** Romeo did not mind *their* joking.
>
> **Alone:** In such a case as *mine* a man may strain courtesy.

Practice Copy the following sentences, and underline the personal pronouns in the possessive case. Identify the function each serves.

1. Is the money yours?
2. He seems to have lost his reason.
3. Her ramblings frustrated them.
4. Our families will never understand.
5. The choice to act is ours.

Writing Application In three sentences, demonstrate all three ways to use possessive pronouns.

*W*G *Prentice Hall Writing and Grammar Connection: Chapter 24, Section 1*

Extension Activities

Writing In an **adaptation,** place Shakespeare's famous balcony scene in another time and place, such as medieval Japan, the United States during the Civil War, or your hometown today. Change the language and setting, but retain the underlying meaning of the original dialogue.

Listening and Speaking Romeo persuades the Friar to perform his marriage. Practice your powers of persuasion by conducting a **role play** of the situation of your choice with a partner. After your experience, ask for feedback from your partner. **[Group Activity]**

MERCUTIO. Come, come, thou art as hot a Jack in thy mood as any in Italy; and as soon moved to be moody, and as soon moody to be moved.[2]

BENVOLIO. And what to?

15 **MERCUTIO.** Nay, and there were two such, we should have none shortly, for one would kill the other. Thou! Why, thou wilt quarrel with a man that hath a hair more or a hair less in his beard than thou hast. Thou wilt quarrel with a man for cracking nuts, having no other reason but because thou hast hazel eyes. What eye but

20 such an eye would spy out such a quarrel? Thy head is as full of quarrels as an egg is full of meat; and yet thy head hath been beaten as addle[3] as an egg for quarreling. Thou hast quarreled with a man for coughing in the street, because he hath wakened thy dog that hath lain asleep in the sun. Didst thou not fall out

25 with a tailor for wearing his new doublet[4] before Easter? With another for tying his new shoes with old riband?[5] And yet thou wilt tutor me from quarreling![6]

BENVOLIO. And I were so apt to quarrel as thou art, any man should buy the fee simple[7] of my life for an hour and a quarter.[8]

30 **MERCUTIO.** The fee simple? O simple![9]

[*Enter* TYBALT, PETRUCHIO, *and* OTHERS.]

BENVOLIO. By my head, here comes the Capulets.

MERCUTIO. By my heel, I care not.

TYBALT. Follow me close, for I will speak to them.
35 Gentlemen, good-den. A word with one of you.

MERCUTIO. And but one word with one of us? Couple it with something; make it a word and a blow.

TYBALT. You shall find me apt enough to that, sir, and you will give me occasion.[10]

40 **MERCUTIO.** Could you not take some occasion without giving?

TYBALT. Mercutio, thou consortest[11] with Romeo.

MERCUTIO. Consort?[12] What, dost thou make us minstrels? And thou make minstrels of us, look to hear nothing but discords.[13] Here's my fiddlestick; here's that shall make you dance.
45 Zounds,[14] consort!

BENVOLIO. We talk here in the public haunt of men.
Either withdraw unto some private place,
Or reason coldly of your grievances,
Or else depart. Here all eyes gaze on us.

50 **MERCUTIO.** Men's eyes were made to look, and let them gaze.
I will not budge for no man's pleasure, I.

Literary Analysis
Soliloquy, Aside, and Monologue Which details of Mercutio's speech indicate that it is a monologue and not a soliloquy?

Reading Strategy
Paraphrasing How would you paraphrase the exchange between Tybalt and Mercutio to make its tone and meaning understandable to a reader today?

[*Enter* ROMEO.]

TYBALT. Well, peace be with you, sir. Here comes my man.[15]

MERCUTIO. But I'll be hanged, sir, if he wear your livery.[16]
Marry, go before to field,[17] he'll be your follower!
55   Your worship in that sense may call him man.

TYBALT. Romeo, the love I bear thee can afford
No better term than this: thou art a villain.[18]

ROMEO. Tybalt, the reason that I have to love thee
Doth much excuse the appertaining[19] rage
60   To such a greeting. Villain am I none.
Therefore farewell. I see thou knowest me not.

TYBALT. Boy, this shall not excuse the injuries
That thou hast done me; therefore turn and draw.

ROMEO. I do protest I never injured thee,
65   But love thee better than thou canst devise[20]
Till thou shalt know the reason of my love;
And so, good Capulet, which name I tender[21]
As dearly as mine own, be satisfied.

MERCUTIO. O calm, dishonorable, vile submission!
70   *Alla stoccata*[22] carries it away.   [*Draws.*]
Tybalt, you ratcatcher, will you walk?

TYBALT. What wouldst thou have with me?

MERCUTIO. Good King of Cats, nothing but one of your nine lives.
That I mean to make bold withal,[23] and, as you shall use me
75   here-after, dry-beat[24] the rest of the eight. Will you pluck your
sword out of his pilcher[25] by the ears? Make haste, lest mine be
about your ears ere it be out.

TYBALT. I am for you.   [*Draws.*]

ROMEO. Gentle Mercutio, put thy rapier up.

80 **MERCUTIO.** Come, sir, your *passado!*   [*They fight.*]

ROMEO. Draw, Benvolio; beat down their weapons.
Gentlemen, for shame! Forbear this outrage!
Tybalt, Mercutio, the Prince expressly hath
Forbid this bandying in Verona streets.
85   Hold, Tybalt! Good Mercutio!

[TYBALT *under* ROMEO'S *arm thrusts* MERCUTIO *in, and flies.*]

MERCUTIO.   I am hurt.
A plague a[26] both houses! I am sped.[27]
Is he gone and hath nothing?

BENVOLIO.   What, art thou hurt?

---

15. man the man I'm looking
for; "man" also meant
"manservant."

16. livery servant's
uniform.

17. field dueling place.

18. villain low, vulgar
person.

19. appertaining
appropriate.

20. devise understand;
imagine.

21. tender value.

22. *Alla stoccata* at
the thrust—an Italian
fencing term that Mer-
cutio uses as a nick-
name for Tybalt.

23. make bold withal
make bold with; take.

24. dry-beat thrash.

25. pilcher scabbard.

26. a on.

27. sped wounded;
done for.

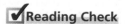Reading Check

What is the outcome of
the duel between Tybalt
and Mercutio?

MERCUTIO. Ay, ay, a scratch, a scratch. Marry, 'tis enough.
Where is my page? Go, villain, fetch a surgeon.   [*Exit* PAGE.]

90 **ROMEO.** Courage, man. The hurt cannot be much.

MERCUTIO. No, 'tis not so deep as a well, nor so wide as a church
door; but 'tis enough, 'twill serve. Ask for me tomorrow, and you
shall find me a grave man. I am peppered,[28] I warrant, for this
world. A plague a both your houses! Zounds, a dog, a rat, a
95 mouse, a cat, to scratch a man to death! A braggart, a rogue, a
villain, that fights by the book of arithmetic![29] Why the devil came
you between us? I was hurt under your arm.

ROMEO. I thought all for the best.

MERCUTIO. Help me into some house, Benvolio,
100 Or I shall faint. A plague a both your houses!
They have made worms' meat of me. I have it,[30]
And soundly too. Your houses!   [*Exit* MERCUTIO *and* BENVOLIO.]

ROMEO. This gentleman, the Prince's near ally,[31]
My very friend, hath got his mortal hurt
105 In my behalf—my reputation stained
With Tybalt's slander—Tybalt, that an hour
Hath been my cousin. O sweet Juliet,
Thy beauty hath made me effeminate
And in my temper soft'ned valor's steel!

[*Enter* BENVOLIO.]

110 **BENVOLIO.** O Romeo, Romeo, brave Mercutio is dead!
That <u>gallant</u> spirit hath aspired[32] the clouds,
Which too untimely here did scorn the earth.

ROMEO. This day's black fate on moe[33] days doth depend;[34]
This but begins the woe others must end.

[*Enter* TYBALT.]

115 **BENVOLIO.** Here comes the furious Tybalt back again.

ROMEO. Alive in triumph, and Mercutio slain?
Away to heaven respective lenity,[35]
And fire-eyed fury be my conduct[36] now!
Now, Tybalt, take the "villain" back again
120 That late thou gavest me; for Mercutio's soul
Is but a little way above our heads,
Staying for thine to keep him company.
Either thou or I, or both, must go with him.

TYBALT. Thou, wretched boy, that didst consort him here,
125 Shalt with him hence.

ROMEO.   This shall determine that.
                         [*They fight.* TYBALT *falls.*]

---

28. **peppered** finished off.

29. **by . . . arithmetic** by formal rules.

30. **I have it** I've got my deathblow.

31. **ally** relative.

Reading Strategy
Paraphrasing How does Romeo say Juliet has changed him? What does he mean?

gallant (gal′ ənt) *adj.* brave and noble

32. **aspired** climbed to.
33. **moe** more.
34. **depend** hang over.

Reading Strategy
Paraphrasing How would you paraphrase Romeo's words to Tybalt?

35. **respective lenity** thoughtful mercy.

36. **conduct** guide.

BENVOLIO. Romeo, away, be gone!
    The citizens are up, and Tybalt slain.
    Stand not amazed. The Prince will doom thee death
    If thou art taken. Hence, be gone, away!

130 **ROMEO.** O, I am fortune's fool!^{37}

BENVOLIO.   Why dost thou stay?   [*Exit* ROMEO.]

[*Enter* CITIZENS.]

CITIZEN. Which way ran he that killed Mercutio?
    Tybalt, that murderer, which way ran he?

BENVOLIO. There lies that Tybalt.

CITIZEN.   Up, sir, go with me.
    I charge thee in the Prince's name obey.

[*Enter* PRINCE, OLD MONTAGUE, CAPULET, *their* WIVES, *and all.*]

135 **PRINCE.** Where are the vile beginners of this <u>fray</u>?

BENVOLIO. O noble Prince, I can discover^{38} all
    The unlucky manage^{39} of this fatal brawl.
    There lies the man, slain by young Romeo,
    That slew thy kinsman, brave Mercutio.

140 **LADY CAPULET.** Tybalt, my cousin! O my brother's child!
    O Prince! O cousin! Husband! O, the blood is spilled
    Of my dear kinsman! Prince, as thou art true,

Reading Strategy
Paraphrasing What urgent warning is Benvolio giving Romeo?

37. fool plaything.

fray (frā) *n.* noisy fight

38. discover reveal.

Reading Strategy
Paraphrasing Has Benvolio reported the facts accurately?

39. manage course.

◀ **Critical Viewing**
Using this picture, explain the emotions on the street after Romeo kills Tybalt. **[Make a Judgment]**

☑ **Reading Check**
What does Romeo do to Tybalt?

Romeo and Juliet, Act III, Scene i ◆ 823

For blood of ours shed blood of Montague.
O cousin, cousin!

145 **PRINCE.** Benvolio, who began this bloody fray?

BENVOLIO. Tybalt, here slain, whom Romeo's hand did slay.
Romeo, that spoke him fair, bid him bethink
How nice[40] the quarrel was, and urged withal
Your high displeasure. All this—utterèd
150 With gentle breath, calm look, knees humbly bowed—
Could not take truce with the unruly spleen[41]
Of Tybalt deaf to peace, but that he tilts[42]
With piercing steel at bold Mercutio's breast;
Who, all as hot, turns deadly point to point,
155 And, with a martial scorn, with one hand beats
Cold death aside and with the other sends
It back to Tybalt, whose dexterity
Retorts it. Romeo he cries aloud,
"Hold, friends! Friends, part!" and swifter than his tongue,
160 His agile arm beats down their fatal points,
And 'twixt them rushes; underneath whose arm
An envious[43] thrust from Tybalt hit the life
Of stout Mercutio, and then Tybalt fled;
But by and by comes back to Romeo,
165 Who had but newly entertained[44] revenge,
And to't they go like lightning; for, ere I
Could draw to part them, was stout Tybalt slain;
And, as he fell, did Romeo turn and fly.
This is the truth, or let Benvolio die.

170 **LADY CAPULET.** He is a kinsman to the Montague;
Affection makes him false, he speaks not true.
Some twenty of them fought in this black strife,
And all those twenty could but kill one life.
I beg for justice, which thou, Prince, must give.
175 Romeo slew Tybalt; Romeo must not live.

PRINCE. Romeo slew him; he slew Mercutio.
Who now the price of his dear blood doth owe?

MONTAGUE. Not Romeo, Prince; he was Mercutio's friend;
His fault concludes but what the law should end,
The life of Tybalt.[45]

180 **PRINCE.** And for that offense
Immediately we do exile him hence.
I have an interest in your hate's proceeding.
My blood[46] for your rude brawls doth lie a-bleeding;
But I'll amerce[47] you with so strong a fine
185 That you shall all repent the loss of mine.
I will be deaf to pleading and excuses;

Reading Strategy
Paraphrasing What does Lady Capulet ask the Prince to do?

40. **nice** trivial.

41. **spleen** angry nature.
42. **tilts** thrusts.

martial (mär′ shəl) *adj.* military

Literary Analysis
Soliloquy, Aside, and Monologue Is Benvolio's monologue describing the fight factual or biased? How do you know?

43. **envious** full of hatred.
44. **entertained** considered.

45. **His fault . . . Tybalt** by killing Tybalt, he did what the law would have done.

Reading Strategy
Paraphrasing Restate Montague's remarks in your own words.

exile (eks′ īl′) *v.* banish

46. **My blood** Mercutio was related to the Prince.

47. **amerce** punish.

Nor tears nor prayers shall purchase out abuses.
Therefore use none. Let Romeo hence in haste,
Else, when he is found, that hour is his last.
190 Bear hence this body and attend our will.[48]
Mercy but murders, pardoning those that kill.

[*Exit with others.*]

 cene ii. CAPULET'S *orchard.*

[*Enter* JULIET *alone.*]

    JULIET. Gallop apace, you fiery-footed steeds,[1]
    Towards Phoebus' lodging![2] Such a wagoner
    As Phaëton[3] would whip you to the west
    And bring in cloudy night immediately.
5   Spread thy close curtain, love-performing night,
    That runaways' eyes may wink,[4] and Romeo
    Leap to these arms untalked of and unseen.
    Lovers can see to do their amorous rites,
    And by their own beauties; or, if love be blind,
10   It best agrees with night. Come, civil night,
    Thou sober-suited matron all in black,
    And learn me how to lose a winning match,
    Played for a pair of stainless maidenhoods.
    Hood my unmanned blood, bating in my cheeks,[5]
15   With thy black mantle till strange[6] love grow bold,
    Think true love acted simple modesty,
    Come, night; come, Romeo; come, thou day in night;
    For thou wilt lie upon the wings of night
    Whiter than new snow upon a raven's back.
20   Come, gentle night; come, loving, black-browed night;
    Give me my Romeo; and when I shall die,
    Take him and cut him out in little stars,
    And he will make the face of heaven so fine
    That all the world will be in love with night
25   And pay no worship to the garish sun
    O, I have bought the mansion of a love,
    But not possessed it; and though I am sold,
    Not yet enjoyed. So tedious is this day
    As is the night before some festival
30   To an impatient child that hath new robes
    And may not wear them. O, here comes my nurse,

[*Enter* NURSE, *with cords.*]

    And she brings news; and every tongue that speaks
    But Romeo's name speaks heavenly <u>eloquence</u>.
    Now, nurse, what news? What hast thou there, the cords
    That Romeo bid thee fetch?
35   **NURSE.**   Ay, ay, the cords.

48. attend our will await my decision.

1. fiery-footed steeds horses of the sun god, Phoebus.

2. Phoebus' lodging below the horizon.

3. Phaëton Phoebus' son, who tried to drive his father's horses but was unable to control them.

4. That runaways' eyes may wink so that the eyes of busybodies may not see.

5. Hood . . . cheeks hide the untamed blood that makes me blush.

6. strange unfamiliar.

Literary Analysis
Soliloquy, Aside, and Monologue Should Juliet's speech be classified as a monologue, a soliloquy, or an aside? Why?

eloquence (el´ ə kwəns) *n.* speech that is vivid, forceful, graceful, and persuasive

✔**Reading Check**

What punishment does the Prince order for Romeo?

JULIET. Ay me! What news? Why dost thou wring thy hands?

NURSE. Ah, weraday![7] He's dead, he's dead, he's dead!
We are undone, lady, we are undone!
Alack the day! He's gone, he's killed, he's dead!

JULIET. Can heaven be so envious?

40 **NURSE.**   Romeo can,
Though heaven cannot. O Romeo, Romeo!
Who ever would have thought it? Romeo!

JULIET. What devil art thou that dost torment me thus?
This torture should be roared in dismal hell.
45 Hath Romeo slain himself? Say thou but "Ay,"
And that bare vowel "I" shall poison more
Than the death-darting eye of cockatrice.◆
I am not I, if there be such an "Ay,"[8]
Or those eyes' shot[9] that makes thee answer "Ay."
50 If he be slain, say "Ay"; or if not, "No."
Brief sounds determine of my weal or woe.

NURSE. I saw the wound, I saw it with mine eyes,
(God save the mark![10]) here on his manly breast.
A piteous corse,[11] a bloody piteous corse;
55 Pale, pale as ashes, all bedaubed in blood,
All in gore-blood. I sounded[12] at the sight.

JULIET. O, break, my heart! Poor bankrout,[13] break at once!
To prison, eyes; ne'er look on liberty!
Vile earth, to earth resign;[14] end motion here,
60 And thou and Romeo press one heavy bier![15]

NURSE. O Tybalt, Tybalt, the best friend I had!
O courteous Tybalt! Honest gentleman!
That ever I should live to see thee dead!

---

7. **Ah, weraday!** alas!

Literary Analysis
Allusions What is the effect of Juliet's allusions to hell in lines 43–44? Explain.

8. **"Ay"** yes.
9. **eyes' shot** the Nurse's glance.

10. **God save the mark!** may God save us from evil!

11. **corse** corpse.

12. **sounded** swooned; fainted.

13. **bankrout** bankrupt.
14. **Vile . . . resign** let my body return to the earth.

15. **bier** platform on which a corpse is displayed before burial.

Literature
in context Humanities Connection

◆ *Cockatrice*

In a play on words, Juliet links "Ay" with the dangerous "eye" of a cockatrice (III, ii, 47). The cockatrice is a serpent that, according to myth, could kill with a look or transform people into stone. The creature resembled a snake with the head and yellow feathers of a rooster. It feared the song of the rooster as well as its own reflection in the mirror. Juliet alludes to a cockatrice to reinforce the tormenting nature of her conversation with the Nurse.

JULIET. What storm is this that blows so contrary?[16]
65 Is Romeo slaught'red, and is Tybalt dead?
My dearest cousin, and my dearer lord?
Then, dreadful trumpet, sound the general doom![17]
For who is living, if those two are gone?

NURSE. Tybalt is gone, and Romeo banishèd;
70 Romeo that killed him, he is banishèd.

JULIET. O God! Did Romeo's hand shed Tybalt's blood?

NURSE. It did, it did! Alas the day, it did!

JULIET. O serpent heart, hid with a flow'ring face!
Did ever dragon keep so fair a cave?
75 Beautiful tyrant! Fiend angelical!
Dove-feathered raven! Wolvish-ravening lamb!
Despisèd substance of divinest show!
Just opposite to what thou justly seem'st—
A damnèd saint, an honorable villain!
80 O nature, what hadst thou to do in hell
When thou didst bower the spirit of a fiend
In mortal paradise of such sweet flesh?
Was ever book containing such vile matter
So fairly bound? O, that deceit should dwell
In such a gorgeous palace!

85 **NURSE.**   There's no trust,
No faith, no honesty in men; all perjured,
All forsworn,[18] all naught, all dissemblers.[19]
Ah, where's my man? Give me some *aqua vitae*.[20]
These griefs, these woes, these sorrows make me old.
Shame come to Romeo!

90 **JULIET.**   Blistered be thy tongue
For such a wish! He was not born to shame.
Upon his brow shame is ashamed to sit;
For 'tis a throne where honor may be crowned
Sole monarch of the universal earth.
95 O, what a beast was I to chide at him!

NURSE. Will you speak well of him that killed your cousin?

JULIET. Shall I speak ill of him that is my husband?
Ah, poor my lord, what tongue shall smooth thy name
When I, thy three-hours wife, have mangled it?
100 But wherefore, villain, didst thou kill my cousin?
That villain cousin would have killed my husband.
Back, foolish tears, back to your native spring!
Your tributary[21] drops belong to woe,
Which you, mistaking, offer up to joy.
105 My husband lives, that Tybalt would have slain;

16. **contrary** in opposite directions.

17. **dreadful . . . doom** let the trumpet that announces doomsday be sounded.

Reading Strategy
Paraphrasing Restate lines 78–79 in your own words.

18. **forsworn** are liars.
19. **dissemblers** hypocrites.
20. *aqua vitae* brandy.

21. **tributary** in tribute.

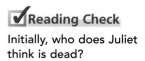
Reading Check

Initially, who does Juliet think is dead?

And Tybalt's dead, that would have slain my husband.
All this is comfort; wherefore weep I then?
Some word there was, worser than Tybalt's death,
That murd'red me. I would forget it fain;
110 But O, it presses to my memory
Like damnèd guilty deeds to sinners' minds!
"Tybalt is dead, and Romeo—banishèd."
That "banishèd," that one word "banishèd,"
Hath slain ten thousand Tybalts. Tybalt's death
115 Was woe enough, if it had ended there;
Or, if sour woe delights in fellowship
And needly will be ranked with[22] other griefs,
Why followed not, when she said "Tybalt's dead,"
Thy father, or thy mother, nay, or both,
120 Which modern[23] lamentation might have moved?
But with a rearward[24] following Tybalt's death,
"Romeo is banishèd"—to speak that word
Is father, mother, Tybalt, Romeo, Juliet,
All slain, all dead. "Romeo is banishèd"—
125 There is no end, no limit, measure, bound,
In that word's death; no words can that woe sound.
Where is my father and my mother, nurse?

NURSE. Weeping and wailing over Tybalt's corse.
Will you go to them? I will bring you thither.

130 **JULIET.** Wash they his wounds with tears? Mine shall be spent,
When theirs are dry, for Romeo's banishment.
Take up those cords. Poor ropes, you are beguiled,
Both you and I, for Romeo is exiled.
He made you for a highway to my bed;
135 But I, a maid, die maiden-widowèd.
Come, cords; come, nurse. I'll to my wedding bed;
And death, not Romeo, take my maidenhead!

NURSE. Hie to your chamber. I'll find Romeo
To comfort you. I wot[25] well where he is.
140 Hark ye, your Romeo will be here at night.
I'll to him; he is hid at Lawrence' cell.

JULIET. O, find him! Give this ring to my true knight
And bid him come to take his last farewell.   [*Exit* with NURSE]

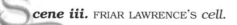 **cene iii.** FRIAR LAWRENCE'S *cell.*

[*Enter* FRIAR LAWRENCE.]

FRIAR. Romeo, come forth; come forth, thou fearful man.
Affliction is enamored of thy parts,[1]
And thou art wedded to calamity.

[Enter ROMEO.]

ROMEO. Father, what news? What is the Prince's doom?[2]
5   What sorrow craves acquaintance at my hand
That I yet know not?

FRIAR.   Too familiar
Is my dear son with such sour company.
I bring thee tidings of the Prince's doom.

ROMEO. What less than doomsday[3] is the Prince's doom?

10 **FRIAR.** A gentler judgment vanished[4] from his lips—
Not body's death, but body's banishment.

ROMEO. Ha, banishment? Be merciful, say "death";
For exile hath more terror in his look,
Much more than death. Do not say "banishment."

15 **FRIAR.** Here from Verona art thou banishèd.
Be patient, for the world is broad and wide.

ROMEO. There is no world without[5] Verona walls,
But purgatory, torture, hell itself.
Hence banishèd is banished from the world,
20   And world's exile is death. Then "banishèd"
Is death mistermed. Calling death "banishèd,"
Thou cut'st my head off with a golden ax
And smilest upon the stroke that murders me.

FRIAR. O deadly sin! O rude unthankfulness!
25   Thy fault our law calls death;[6] but the kind Prince,
Taking thy part, hath rushed[7] aside the law,
And turned that black word "death" to "banishment."
This is dear mercy, and thou seest it not.

ROMEO. 'Tis torture, and not mercy. Heaven is here,
30   Where Juliet lives; and every cat and dog
And little mouse, every unworthy thing,
Live here in heaven and may look on her;
But Romeo may not. More validity,[8]
More honorable state, more courtship lives
35   In carrion flies than Romeo. They may seize
On the white wonder of dear Juliet's hand
And steal immortal blessing from her lips,
Who, even in pure and vestal modesty,
Still blush, as thinking their own kisses sin;
40   But Romeo may not, he is banishèd.
Flies may do this but I from this must fly;
They are freemen, but I am banishèd.
And sayest thou yet that exile is not death?
Hadst thou no poison mixed, no sharp-ground knife,

2. doom final decision.

3. doomsday my death.

4. vanished escaped; came forth.

5. without outside.

6. Thy fault . . . death for what you did our law demands the death penalty.

7. rushed pushed.

Reading Strategy
Paraphrasing Restate Romeo's complaint in lines 29–33.

8. validity value.

**Reading Check**

What punishment does the Friar say Romeo could have received for his crime?

What simpleness[14] is this.—I come, I come! [*Knock.*]
Who knocks so hard? Whence come you? What's your will?

[*Enter* NURSE.]

NURSE. Let me come in, and you shall know my errand.
I come from Lady Juliet.

80 **FRIAR.** Welcome then.

NURSE. O holy friar, O, tell me, holy friar,
Where is my lady's lord, where's Romeo?

FRIAR. There on the ground, with his own tears made drunk.

NURSE. O, he is even in my mistress' case,
85 Just in her case! O woeful sympathy!
Piteous predicament! Even so lies she,
Blubb'ring and weeping, weeping and blubb'ring.
Stand up, stand up! Stand, and you be a man.
For Juliet's sake, for her sake, rise and stand!
90 Why should you fall into so deep an O?[15]

ROMEO. [*Rises.*] Nurse—

NURSE. Ah sir, ah sir! Death's the end of all.

ROMEO. Spakest thou of Juliet? How is it with her?
Doth not she think me an old murderer,
95 Now I have stained the childhood of our joy
With blood removed but little from her own?
Where is she? And how doth she? And what says
My concealed lady[16] to our canceled love?

NURSE. O, she says nothing, sir, but weeps and weeps;
100 And now falls on her bed, and then starts up,
And Tybalt calls; and then on Romeo cries,
And then down falls again.

ROMEO. As if that name,
Shot from the deadly level[17] of a gun,
Did murder her; as that name's cursèd hand
105 Murdered her kinsman. O, tell me, friar, tell me,
In what vile part of this anatomy
Doth my name lodge? Tell me, that I may sack[18]
The hateful mansion.

[*He offers to stab himself, and* NURSE *snatches the dagger away.*]

FRIAR. Hold thy desperate hand.
Art thou a man? Thy form cries out thou art;
110 Thy tears are womanish, thy wild acts denote
The unreasonable fury of a beast.
Unseemly[19] woman in a seeming man!
And ill-beseeming beast in seeming both![20]

---

14. **simpleness** silly behavior (Romeo does not move).

15. **O** cry of grief.

16. **concealed lady** secret bride.

17. **level** aim.

18. **sack** plunder.

19. **Unseemly** inappropriate (because unnatural).

20. **And . . . both!** Romeo has inappropriately lost his human nature because he seems like a man and woman combined.

Thou hast amazed me. By my holy order,
115 I thought thy disposition better tempered.
Hast thou slain Tybalt? Wilt thou slay thyself?
And slay thy lady that in thy life lives,
By doing damnèd hate upon thyself?
Why railest thou on thy birth, the heaven, and earth?
120 Since birth and heaven and earth, all three do meet
In thee at once; which thou at once wouldst lose.
Fie, fie, thou shamest thy shape, thy love, thy wit,[21]
Which, like a usurer,[22] abound'st in all,
And usest none in that true use indeed
125 Which should bedeck[23] thy shape, thy love, thy wit.
Thy noble shape is but a form of wax,
Digressing from the valor of a man;
Thy dear love sworn but hollow prejury,
Killing that love which thou hast vowed to cherish;
130 Thy wit, that ornament to shape and love,
Misshapen in the conduct[24] of them both,
Like powder in a skilless soldier's flask,[25]
Is set afire by thine own ignorance,
And thou dismemb'red with thine own defense.[26]
135 What, rouse thee, man! Thy Juliet is alive,
For whose dear sake thou wast but lately dead.[27]
There art thou happy.[28] Tybalt would kill thee,
But thou slewest Tybalt. There art thou happy.
The law, that threat'ned death, becomes thy friend
140 And turns it to exile. There art thou happy.
A pack of blessings light upon thy back;
Happiness courts thee in her best array;
But, like a misbehaved and sullen wench,[29]
Thou puts up[30] thy fortune and thy love.
145 Take heed, take heed, for such die miserable.
Go get thee to thy love, as was decreed,
Ascend her chamber, hence and comfort her.
But look thou stay not till the watch be set,[31]
For then thou canst not pass to Mantua,
150 Where thou shalt live till we can find a time
To blaze[32] your marriage, reconcile your friends,
Beg pardon of the Prince, and call thee back
With twenty hundred thousand times more joy
Than thou went'st forth in lamentation.
155 Go before, nurse. Commend me to thy lady,
And bid her hasten all the house to bed,
Which heavy sorrow makes them apt unto.[33]
Romeo is coming.

NURSE. O Lord, I could have stayed here all the night
160 To hear good counsel. O, what learning is!
My lord, I'll tell my lady you will come.

21. **wit** mind; intellect.
22. **Which, like a usurer** who, like a rich money-lender.

23. **bedeck** do honor to.

Literary Analysis
Soliloquy, Aside, and Monologue Is the Friar's long speech addressed to another character? Is it a monologue or a soliloquy?

24. **conduct** management.
25. **flask** powder flask.
26. **And thou . . . defense** the friar is saying that Romeo's mind, which is now irrational, is destroying rather than aiding him.

27. **but lately dead** only recently declaring yourself dead.

28. **happy** fortunate.
29. **wench** low, common girl.

30. **puts up** pouts over.

31. **watch be set** watchmen go on duty.

32. **blaze** announce publicly.

33. **apt unto** likely to do.

**Reading Check**

What three reasons does the Friar give to persuade Romeo to change his attitude?

ROMEO. Do so, and bid my sweet prepare to chide.[34]

[NURSE *offers to go in and turns again.*]

NURSE. Here, sir, a ring she bid me give you, sir.
Hie you, make haste, for it grows very late.   [*Exit.*]

165 **ROMEO.** How well my comfort is revived by this!

FRIAR. Go hence; good night; and here stands all your state:[35]
Either be gone before the watch be set,
Or by the break of day disguised from hence.
Sojourn[36] in Mantua. I'll find out your man,
170 And he shall signify[37] from time to time
Every good hap to you that chances here.
Give me thy hand. 'Tis late. Farewell; good night.

ROMEO. But that a joy past joy calls out on me,
It were a grief so brief to part with thee.
175 Farewell.   [*Exit all.*]

Scene iv. *A room in* CAPULET'S *house.*

[*Enter old* CAPULET, *his* WIFE, *and* PARIS.]

CAPULET. Things have fall'n out, sir, so unluckily
That we have had no time to move[1] our daughter.
Look you, she loved her kinsman Tybalt dearly,
And so did I. Well, we were born to die.
5 'Tis very late; she'll not come down tonight.
I promise you, but for your company,
I would have been abed an hour ago.

PARIS. These times of woe afford no times to woo.
Madam, good night. Commend me to your daughter.

10 **LADY.** I will, and know her mind early tomorrow;
Tonight she's mewed up to her heaviness.[2]

CAPULET. Sir, Paris, I will make a desperate tender[3]
Of my child's love. I think she will be ruled
In all respects by me; nay more, I doubt it not.
15 Wife, go you to her ere you go to bed;
Acquaint her here of my son[4] Paris' love
And bid her (mark you me?) on Wednesday next—
But soft! What day is this?
PARIS.   Monday, my lord.

CAPULET. Monday! Ha, ha! Well, Wednesday is too soon.
20 A[5] Thursday let it be—a Thursday, tell her,
She shall be married to this noble earl.
Will you be ready? Do you like this haste?
We'll keep no great ado[6]—a friend or two;
For hark you, Tybalt being slain so late,

---

34. chide rebuke me (for slaying Tybalt).

Reading Strategy
Paraphrasing What does Romeo mean when he says, "Bid my sweet prepare to chide"?

35. here . . . state this is your situation.

36. Sojourn remain.

37. signify let you know.

Reading Strategy
Paraphrasing Is Romeo's parting with the Friar angry, sad, or something else? Explain.

1. move discuss your proposal with.

Literary Analysis
Soliloquy, Aside, and Monologue Is Lady Capulet's brief remark in lines 10–11 an aside? Why or why not?

2. mewed . . . heaviness locked up with her sorrow.

3. desperate tender risky offer.

4. son son-in-law.

5. A on.

6. We'll . . . ado We won't make a great fuss.

25 It may be thought we held him carelessly,[7]
Being our kinsman, if we revel much.
Therefore we'll have some half a dozen friends,
And there an end. But what say you to Thursday?

PARIS. My lord, I would that Thursday were tomorrow.

30 **CAPULET.** Well, get you gone. A Thursday be it then.
Go you to Juliet ere you go to bed;
Prepare her, wife, against[8] this wedding day.
Farewell, my lord.—Light to my chamber, ho!
Afore me,[9] it is so very late
35 That we may call it early by and by.
Good night.   [*Exit all.*]

Scene v. CAPULET'S *orchard.*

[*Enter* ROMEO *and* JULIET *aloft.*]

JULIET. Wilt thou be gone? It is not yet near day.
It was the nightingale, and not the lark,[1]
That pierced the fearful hollow of thine ear.
Nightly she sings on yond pomegranate tree.
5 Believe me, love, it was the nightingale.

ROMEO. It was the lark, the herald of the morn;
No nightingale. Look, love, what envious streaks
Do lace the severing[2] clouds in yonder East.
Night's candles[3] are burnt out, and jocund day
10 Stands tiptoe on the misty mountaintops.
I must be gone and live, or stay and die.

JULIET. Yond light is not daylight; I know it, I.
It is some meteor that the sun exhales[4]
To be to thee this night a torchbearer
15 And light thee on thy way to Mantua.
Therefore stay yet; thou need'st not to be gone.

ROMEO. Let me be ta'en, let me be put to death.
I am content, so thou wilt have it so.
I'll say yon gray is not the morning's eye,
20 'Tis but the pale reflex of Cynthia's brow;[5]
Nor that is not the lark whose notes do beat
The vaulty heaven so high above our heads.
I have more care to stay than will to go.
Come, death, and welcome! Juliet wills it so.
25 How is't, my soul? Let's talk; it is not day.

JULIET. It is, it is! Hie hence, be gone, away!
It is the lark that sings so out of tune,
Straining harsh discords and unpleasing sharps.[6]
Some say the lark makes sweet division;[7]

---

7. held him carelessly did not respect him enough.

Reading Strategy
Paraphrasing Paraphrase lines 25–26 to explain why Capulet wants to hold a small wedding.

8. against for.

9. Afore me indeed (a mild oath).

1. nightingale . . . lark The nightingale was associated with the night; the lark, with dawn.

2. severing parting.
3. Night's candles stars.

4. exhales sends out.

5. reflex . . . brow reflection of the moon (Cynthia was a name for the moon goddess).

6. sharps shrill high notes.

7. division melody.

**Reading Check**

What do the Capulets plan for Juliet on Thursday?

30 This doth not so, for she divideth us.
  Some say the lark and loathèd toad change eyes;[8]
  O, now I would they had changed voices too,
  Since arm from arm that voice doth us affray,[9]
  Hunting thee hence with hunt's-up[10] to the day.
35 O, now be gone! More light and light it grows.

  ROMEO. More light and light—more dark and dark our woes.

[*Enter* NURSE.]

  NURSE. Madam!

  JULIET. Nurse?

  NURSE. Your lady mother is coming to your chamber.
40 The day is broke; be wary, look about.   [*Exit.*]

  JULIET. Then, window, let day in, and let life out.

  ROMEO. Farewell, farewell! One kiss, and I'll descend.
              [*He goeth down.*]

  JULIET. Art thou gone so, love-lord, ay husband-friend?
  I must hear from thee every day in the hour,
45 For in a minute there are many days.
  O, by this count I shall be much in years[11]
  Ere I again behold my Romeo!

  ROMEO. Farewell!
  I will omit no opportunity
50 That may convey my greetings, love, to thee.

  JULIET. O, think'st thou we shall ever meet again?

  ROMEO. I doubt it not; and all these woes shall serve
  For sweet discourses[12] in our times to come.

  JULIET. O God, I have an ill-divining[13] soul!
55 Methinks I see thee, now thou art so low,
  As one dead in the bottom of a tomb.
  Either my eyesight fails, or thou lookest pale.

  ROMEO. And trust me, love, in my eye so do you.
  Dry sorrow drinks our blood.[14] Adieu, adieu! [*Exit.*]

60 **JULIET.** O Fortune, Fortune! All men call thee <u>fickle</u>.
  If thou art fickle, what dost thou[15] with him
  That is renowned for faith? Be fickle, Fortune,
  For then I hope thou wilt not keep him long
  But send him back.

[*Enter* MOTHER.]

65 **LADY CAPULET.** Ho, daughter! Are you up?

  JULIET. Who is't that calls? It is my lady mother.

---

8. change eyes exchange eyes (because the lark has a beautiful body with ugly eyes and the toad has an ugly body with beautiful eyes).

9. affray frighten.

10. hunt's-up morning song for hunters.

Reading Strategy
Paraphrasing Restate Romeo's complaint in line 36 to explain the contrast he makes between light and dark.

11. much in years much older.

Reading Strategy
Paraphrasing Translate Romeo and Juliet's conversation in lines 48–53 into modern English.

12. discourses conversations.

13. ill-divining predicting evil.

14. Dry sorrow . . . blood it was once believed that sorrow drained away the blood.

fickle (fik´əl) *adj.* changeable

15. dost thou do you have to do.

Literary Analysis
Allusion To which quality of Fortune, the Greek goddess of chance, does Juliet allude?

Is she not down so late,[16] or up so early?
What unaccustomed cause procures her hither?[17]

LADY CAPULET. Why, how now, Juliet?

JULIET.   Madam, I am not well.

70 **LADY CAPULET.** Evermore weeping for your cousin's death?
What, wilt thou wash him from his grave with tears?
And if thou couldst, thou couldst not make him live.
Therefore have done. Some grief shows much of love;
But much of grief shows still some want of wit.

75 **JULIET.** Yet let me weep for such a feeling[18] loss.

LADY CAPULET. So shall you feel the loss, but not the friend
Which you weep for.

JULIET.   Feeling so the loss,
I cannot choose but ever weep the friend.

LADY CAPULET. Well, girl, thou weep'st not so much for his death
80   As that the villain lives which slaughtered him.

JULIET. What villain, madam?

LADY CAPULET.   That same villain Romeo.

JULIET. [*Aside*] Villain and he be many miles asunder.[19]—
God pardon him! I do, with all my heart;
And yet no man like he doth grieve my heart.

85 **LADY CAPULET.** That is because the traitor murderer lives.

JULIET. Ay, madam, from the reach of these my hands.
Would none but I might venge my cousin's death!

LADY CAPULET. We will have vengeance for it, fear thou not.
Then weep no more. I'll send to one in Mantua,
90   Where that same banished runagate[20] doth live,
Shall give him such an unaccustomed dram[21]
That he shall soon keep Tybalt company;
And then I hope thou wilt be satisfied.

JULIET. Indeed I never shall be satisfied
95   With Romeo till I behold him—dead[22]—
Is my poor heart so for a kinsman vexed.
Madam, if you could find out but a man
To bear a poison, I would temper[23] it;
That Romeo should, upon receipt thereof,
100   Soon sleep in quiet. O, how my heart abhors
To hear him named and cannot come to him,
To wreak[24] the love I bore my cousin
Upon his body that hath slaughtered him!

LADY CAPULET. Find thou the means, and I'll find such a man.

16. Is she . . . late Has she stayed up so late?

17. What . . . hither? What unusual reason brings her here?

18. feeling deeply felt.

Literary Analysis
Soliloquy, Aside, and Monologue Which characteristics of an aside do you find in Juliet's words in lines 82–84?

19. asunder apart.

20. runagate renegade; runaway.

21. unaccustomed dram unexpected dose of poison.

22. dead Juliet is deliberately ambiguous here. Her mother thinks *dead* refers to Romeo. But Juliet is using the word with the following line, in reference to her heart.

23. temper mix; weaken.

24. wreak (reek) avenge; express.

✔ **Reading Check**

Who leaves Juliet's chambers just before Lady Capulet arrives?

105　　　But now I'll tell thee joyful tidings, girl.

JULIET. And joy comes well in such a needy time.
　　　What are they, beseech your ladyship?

LADY CAPULET. Well, well, thou hast a careful[25] father, child;
　　　One who, to put thee from thy heaviness,
110　　　Hath sorted out[26] a sudden day of joy
　　　That thou expects not nor I looked not for.

JULIET. Madam, in happy time![27] What day is that?

LADY CAPULET. Marry, my child, early next Thursday morn
　　　The gallant, young, and noble gentleman,
115　　　The County Paris, at Saint Peter's Church,
　　　Shall happily make thee there a joyful bride.

JULIET. Now by Saint Peter's Church, and Peter too,
　　　He shall not make me there a joyful bride!
　　　I wonder at this haste, that I must wed
120　　　Ere he that should be husband comes to woo.
　　　I pray you tell my lord and father, madam,
　　　I will not marry yet; and when I do, I swear
　　　It shall be Romeo, whom you know I hate,
　　　Rather than Paris. These are news indeed!

125 **LADY CAPULET.** Here comes your father. Tell him so yourself,
　　　And see how he will take it at your hands.

[*Enter* CAPULET *and* NURSE.]

CAPULET. When the sun sets the earth doth drizzle dew,
　　　But for the sunset of my brother's son
　　　It rains downright.
130　　　How now? A conduit,[28] girl? What, still in tears?
　　　Evermore show'ring? In one little body
　　　Thou counterfeits a bark,[29] a sea, a wind:
　　　For still thy eyes, which I may call the sea,
　　　Do ebb and flow with tears; the bark thy body is,
135　　　Sailing in this salt flood; the winds, thy sighs,
　　　Who, raging with thy tears and they with them,
　　　Without a sudden calm will overset
　　　Thy tempest-tossèd body. How now, wife?
　　　Have you delivered to her our decree?

140 **LADY CAPULET.** Ay, sir; but she will none, she gives you
　　　　　thanks.[30]
　　　I would the fool were married to her grave!

CAPULET. Soft! Take me with you,[31] take me with you, wife.
　　　How? Will she none? Doth she not give us thanks?
　　　Is she not proud?[32] Doth she not count her blest,
145　　　Unworthy as she is, that we have wrought[33]

---

25. careful considerate.

26. sorted out selected.

Reading Strategy
Paraphrasing Restate Lady Capulet's remarks in lines 108–111 in your own words.

27. in happy time just in time.

28. conduit water pipe.

29. bark boat.

30. she will none . . . thanks she'll have nothing to do with it, thank you.

31. Soft! Take . . . you Wait a minute. Let me understand you.

32. proud pleased.

33. wrought arranged.

▼ **Critical Viewing** Do you think this picture accurately conveys Juliet's response to her parents' plan for her marriage? **[Analyze]**

So worthy a gentleman to be her bride?

JULIET.   Not proud you have, but thankful that you have.
Proud can I never be of what I hate,
But thankful even for hate that is meant love.

150 **CAPULET.**   How, how, how, how, chopped-logic?³⁴ What is this?
"Proud"—and "I thank you"—and "I thank you not"—
And yet "not proud"? Mistress minion³⁵ you,
Thank me no thankings, nor proud me no prouds,
But fettle³⁶ your fine joints 'gainst Thursday next
155 To go with Paris to Saint Peter's Church,
Or I will drag thee on a hurdle³⁷ thither.
Out, you greensickness carrion!³⁸ Out, you baggage!³⁹
You tallow-face!⁴⁰

LADY CAPULET.   Fie, fie! What, are you mad?

JULIET.   Good father, I beseech you on my knees,
160 Hear me with patience but to speak a word.

CAPULET.   Hang thee, young baggage! Disobedient wretch!
I tell thee what—get thee to church a Thursday
Or never after look me in the face.
Speak not, reply not, do not answer me!
165 My fingers itch. Wife, we scarce thought us blest
That God had lent us but this only child;
But now I see this one is one too much,
And that we have a curse in having her.
Out on her, hilding!⁴¹

NURSE.   God in heaven bless her!
170 You are to blame, my lord, to rate⁴² her so.

CAPULET.   And why, my Lady Wisdom? Hold your tongue,
Good Prudence. Smatter with your gossips, go!⁴³

NURSE.   I speak no treason.

CAPULET.   O, God-i-god-en!

NURSE.   May not one speak?

CAPULET.   Peace, you mumbling fool!
175 Utter your gravity⁴⁴ o'er a gossip's bowl,
For here we need it not.

LADY CAPULET.   You are too hot.

CAPULET.   God's bread!⁴⁵ It makes me mad.
Day, night; hour, tide, time; work, play;
Alone, in company; still my care hath been
180 To have her matched; and having now provided
A gentleman of noble parentage,
Of fair demesnes,⁴⁶ youthful, and nobly trained,

34. chopped-logic
contradictory, unsound
thought and speech.

35. Mistress minion Miss
Uppity.

36. fettle prepare.

37. hurdle sled on
which prisoners were
taken to their execution.

38. greensickness carrion
anemic lump of flesh.

39. baggage naughty girl.

40. tallow-face wax-
pale face.

41. hilding worthless
person.

42. rate scold; berate.

43. Smatter . . . go! Go
chatter with the other old
women.

44. gravity wisdom.

45. God's bread! By
the holy Eucharist!

46. demesnes property.

✓ **Reading Check**

What does Capulet say
will happen if Juliet does
not get married at the
church on Thursday?

Stuffed, as they say, with honorable parts,[47]
Proportioned as one's thought would wish a man—
185 And then to have a wretched puling[48] fool,
A whining mammet,[49] in her fortune's tender,[50]
To answer "I'll not wed, I cannot love;
I am too young, I pray you pardon me"!
But, and you will not wed, I'll pardon you!
190 Graze where you will, you shall not house with me.
Look to't, think on't; I do not use to jest.
Thursday is near; lay hand on heart, advise:[51]
And you be mine, I'll give you to my friend;
And you be not, hang, beg, starve, die in the streets,
195 For, by my soul, I'll ne'er acknowledge thee,
Nor what is mine shall never do thee good.
Trust to't. Bethink you. I'll not be forsworn.[52]   [*Exit.*]

JULIET. Is there no pity sitting in the clouds
That sees into the bottom of my grief?
200 O sweet my mother, cast me not away!
Delay this marriage for a month, a week;
Or if you do not, make the bridal bed
In that dim monument where Tybalt lies.

LADY CAPULET. Talk not to me, for I'll not speak a word.
205 Do as thou wilt, for I have done with thee.   [*Exit.*]

JULIET. O God!—O nurse, how shall this be prevented?
My husband is on earth, my faith in heaven.[53]
How shall that faith return again to earth
Unless that husband send it me from heaven
210 By leaving earth?[54] Comfort me, counsel me.
Alack, alack, that heaven should practice stratagems[55]
Upon so soft a subject as myself!
What say'st thou? Hast thou not a word of joy?
Some comfort, nurse.

NURSE.   Faith, here it is.
Romeo is banished; and all the world to nothing[56]
That he dares ne'er come back to challenge[57] you;
Or if he do, it needs must be by stealth.
Then, since the case so stands as now it doth,
I think it best you married with the County.
220 O, he's a lovely gentleman!
Romeo's a dishclout to him.[58] An eagle, madam,
Hath not so green, so quick, so fair an eye
As Paris hath. Beshrew my very heart,
I think you are happy in this second match,
225 For it excels your first; or if it did not,
Your first is dead—or 'twere as good he were
As living here and you no use of him.

47. **parts** qualities.

48. **puling** whining.
49. **mammet** doll.
50. **in . . . tender** when good fortune is offered her.

51. **advise** consider.

52. **forsworn** made to violate my promise.

Reading Strategy
Paraphrasing In lines 200–204, what options does Juliet offer her mother?

53. **my faith in heaven** my marriage vow is recorded in heaven.

54. **leaving earth** dying.
55. **stratagems** tricks; plots.

56. **all . . . nothing** the odds are overwhelming.

57. **challenge** claim.

58. **a dishclout to him** a dishcloth compared with him.

JULIET. Speak'st thou from thy heart?

NURSE. And from my soul too; else beshrew them both.

230 **JULIET.** Amen!

NURSE. What?

JULIET. Well, thou hast comforted me marvelous much.
    Go in; and tell my lady I am gone,
    Having displeased my father, to Lawrence' cell,
235   To make confession and to be absolved.[59]

NURSE. Marry, I will; and this is wisely done.   *[Exit.]*

JULIET. Ancient damnation![60] O most wicked fiend!
    Is it more sin to wish me thus forsworn,
    Or to dispraise my lord with that same tongue
240   Which she hath praised him with above compare
    So many thousand times? Go, counselor!
    Thou and my bosom henceforth shall be twain.[61]
    I'll to the friar to know his remedy.
    If all else fail, myself have power to die.   *[Exit.]*

59. absolved receive forgiveness for my sins.

60. Ancient damnation! Old devil!

61. Thou . . . twain You will from now on be separated from my trust.

Review and Assess

Thinking About Act III

1. **Respond:** What would you do if you were in Romeo or Juliet's situation?

2. **(a) Recall:** Why do Mercutio and Tybalt fight in Act III, Scene i? **(b) Interpret:** What does Mercutio mean by his dying exclamation, "A plague on both your houses!"? **(c) Connect:** How do these lines echo the ideas set forth in the play's prologue?

3. **(a) Recall:** How and why does Romeo kill Tybalt? **(b) Interpret:** What does Romeo mean when he says, after killing Tybalt, "I am fortune's fool!"?

4. **(a) Recall:** What punishment does the prince order for Romeo? **(b) Draw Conclusions:** Why does the Prince decide not to sentence Romeo to death, despite his threat in Act I?

5. **(a) Recall:** Describe the clashing emotions Juliet feels when Nurse reports Tybalt's death and Romeo's punishment. **(b) Compare and Contrast:** What reactions—both similar and different—do Juliet and Romeo have to Romeo's punishment?

6. **Speculate:** Do you think Romeo's punishment is fair? Support your answer.

Prepare to Read

The Tragedy of Romeo and Juliet, Act IV

Literary Analysis

Dramatic Irony

Dramatic irony is a contradiction between what a character thinks or says and what the audience or reader knows to be true. For example, in Act III, Lord Capulet decides that the way to ensure Juliet's future happiness is to have her wed Paris. He does not know what you know—that Juliet is already married. Dramatic irony involves you emotionally in the story. You may even feel the urge to step into the play to help the characters see a situation correctly.

Connecting Literary Elements

Suspense is a feeling of curiosity or uncertainty about the outcome of events in a literary work. Suspense often results from the use of dramatic irony, as the audience anxiously wonders whether characters will discover the truth before it is too late. As you read the events of Act IV, notice how Shakespeare builds suspense through Juliet's words and actions.

Reading Strategy

Predicting

When you **predict,** you make educated guesses about what may happen next in a literary work. To predict, consider each character's personality and what information he or she knows. Also, look for places where the author hints at future events. In this passage, Juliet's remark hints at deadly consequences:

> If in thy wisdom thou canst give no help,
> Do thou but call my resolution wise
> And with this knife I'll help it presently.

Use a chart like this one to make and assess predictions as you read.

What I Predict

Juliet will not marry Paris.

Why?

She says she will kill herself instead.

Actual Outcome

Vocabulary Development

pensive (pen´ siv) *adj.* thinking deeply or seriously (p. 846)

vial (vī´ əl) *n.* small bottle containing medicine or other liquids (p. 848)

enjoined (en joind´) *v.* ordered (p. 849)

wayward (wā´ wərd) *adj.* headstrong; willful (p. 850)

dismal (diz´ məl) *adj.* causing gloom or misery (p. 850)

loathsome (lōth´ səm) *adj.* disgusting (p. 851)

pilgrimage (pil´ grim ij) *n.* long journey, often for religious purposes (p. 855)

 placed.

Review and Anticipate

Romeo and Juliet are married for only a few hours when disaster strikes. In Act III, Juliet's cousin Tybalt kills Mercutio, and then Romeo kills Tybalt. This leads to Romeo's banishment from Verona. To make matters worse, Juliet's parents are determined to marry her to Paris. Will Romeo and Juliet ever be able to live together as husband and wife? What, if anything, can the lovers now do to preserve their relationship?

Scene i. FRIAR LAWRENCE'S *cell.*

[*Enter* FRIAR LAWRENCE *and* COUNTY PARIS.]

FRIAR. On Thursday, sir? The time is very short.

PARIS. My father[1] Capulet will have it so,
And I am nothing slow to slack his haste.[2]

FRIAR. You say you do not know the lady's mind.
Uneven is the course;[3] I like it not.

5

PARIS. Immoderately she weeps for Tybalt's death,
And therefore have I little talked of love;
For Venus smiles not in a house of tears.
Now, sir, her father counts it dangerous

1. father future father-in-law.

2. I . . . haste I won't slow him down by being slow myself.

3. Uneven . . . course irregular is the plan.

✔**Reading Check**

What is the Friar's complaint to Paris about the impending wedding?

10   That she do give her sorrow so much sway,
And in his wisdom hastes our marriage
To stop the inundation[4] of her tears,
Which, too much minded[5] by herself alone,
May be put from her by society.

15   Now do you know the reason of this haste.

FRIAR. [*Aside*] I would I knew not why it should be slowed.—
Look, sir, here comes the lady toward my cell.

[*Enter* JULIET.]

PARIS. Happily met, my lady and my wife!

JULIET. That may be, sir, when I may be a wife.

20 **PARIS.** That "may be" must be, love, on Thursday next.

JULIET. What must be shall be.

FRIAR.   That's a certain text.[6]

PARIS. Come you to make confession to this father?

JULIET. To answer that, I should confess to you.

PARIS. Do not deny to him that you love me.

25 **JULIET.** I will confess to you that I love him.

PARIS. So will ye, I am sure, that you love me.

JULIET. If I do so, it will be of more price,[7]
Being spoke behind your back, than to your face.

PARIS. Poor soul, thy face is much abused with tears.

30 **JULIET.** The tears have got small victory by that,
For it was bad enough before their spite.[8]

PARIS. Thou wrong'st it more than tears with that report.

JULIET. That is no slander, sir, which is a truth;
And what I spake, I spake it to my face.

35 **PARIS.** Thy face is mine, and thou hast sland'red it.

JULIET. It may be so, for it is not mine own.
Are you at leisure, holy father, now,
Or shall I come to you at evening mass?

FRIAR. My leisure serves me, <u>pensive</u> daughter, now.
40   My lord, we must entreat the time alone.[9]

PARIS. God shield[10] I should disturb devotion!
Juliet, on Thursday early will I rouse ye.
Till then, adieu, and keep this holy kiss.   [*Exit.*]

JULIET. O, shut the door, and when thou hast done so,
45   Come weep with me—past hope, past care, past help!

FRIAR. O Juliet, I already know thy grief;
      It strains me past the compass of my wits.[11]
      I hear thou must, and nothing may prorogue[12] it,
      On Thursday next be married to this County.

50 **JULIET.** Tell me not, friar, that thou hearest of this,
      Unless thou tell me how I may prevent it.
      If in thy wisdom thou canst give no help,
      Do thou but call my resolution wise
      And with this knife I'll help it presently.[13]
55   God joined my heart and Romeo's, thou our hands;
      And ere this hand, by thee to Romeo's sealed,
      Shall be the label to another deed,[14]
      Or my true heart with treacherous revolt
      Turn to another, this shall slay them both.
60   Therefore, out of thy long-experienced time,
      Give me some present counsel; or, behold,
      'Twixt my extremes and me[15] this bloody knife
      Shall play the umpire, arbitrating[16] that
      Which the commission of thy years and art
65   Could to no issue of true honor bring.[17]
      Be not so long to speak. I long to die
      If what thou speak'st speak not of remedy.

    FRIAR. Hold, daughter. I do spy a kind of hope,
      Which craves[18] as desperate an execution
70   As that is desperate which we would prevent.
      If, rather than to marry County Paris,
      Thou hast the strength of will to slay thyself,
      Then is it likely thou wilt undertake
      A thing like death to chide away this shame,
75   That cop'st with death himself to scape from it;[19]
      And, if thou darest, I'll give thee remedy.

    JULIET. O, bid me leap, rather than marry Paris,
      From off the battlements of any tower,
      Or walk in thievish ways,[20] or bid me lurk
80   Where serpents are; chain me with roaring bears,
      Or hide me nightly in a charnel house,[21]
      O'ercovered quite with dead men's rattling bones,
      With reeky[22] shanks and yellow chapless[23] skulls;
      Or bid me go into a new-made grave
85   And hide me with a dead man in his shroud—
      Things that, to hear them told, have made me tremble—
      And I will do it without fear or doubt,
      To live an unstained wife to my sweet love.

    FRIAR. Hold, then. Go home, be merry, give consent
90   To marry Paris. Wednesday is tomorrow.
      Tomorrow night look that thou lie alone;

11. **past . . . wits** beyond the ability of my mind to find a remedy.

12. **prorogue** delay.

Reading Strategy

Predicting What do you predict Juliet will do if there is no way to prevent her marriage to Paris?

13. **presently** at once.

14. **Shall . . . deed** shall give the seal of approval to another marriage contract.

15. **'Twixt . . . me** between my misfortunes and me.

16. **arbitrating** deciding.

17. **Which . . . bring** which the authority that derives from your age and ability could not solve honorably.

18. **craves** requires.

19. **That cop'st . . . it** that bargains with death itself to escape from it.

20. **thievish ways** roads where criminals lurk.

21. **charnel house** vault for bones removed from graves to be reused.

22. **reeky** foul-smelling.

23. **chapless** jawless.

✓**Reading Check**

What does the Friar tell Juliet she should do when she goes home?

Let not the nurse lie with thee in thy chamber.
Take thou this <u>vial</u>, being then in bed,
And this distilling liquor drink thou off;
95 When presently through all thy veins shall run
A cold and drowsy humor;[24] for no pulse
Shall keep his native[25] progress, but surcease;[26]
No warmth, no breath, shall testify thou livest;
The roses in thy lips and cheeks shall fade
100 To wanny ashes,[27] thy eyes' windows[28] fall
Like death when he shuts up the day of life;
Each part, deprived of supple government,[29]
Shall, stiff and stark and cold, appear like death;
And in this borrowed likeness of shrunk death
105 Thou shalt continue two-and-forty hours,
And then awake as from a pleasant sleep.
Now, when the bridegroom in the morning comes
To rouse thee from thy bed, there art thou dead.
Then, as the manner of our country is,
110 In thy best robes uncovered on the bier[30]
Thou shalt be borne to that same ancient vault
Where all the kindred of the Capulets lie.
In the meantime, against[31] thou shalt awake,
Shall Romeo by my letters know our drift;[32]
115 And hither shall he come; and he and I
Will watch thy waking, and that very night
Shall Romeo bear thee hence to Mantua.
And this shall free thee from this present shame,
If no inconstant toy[33] nor womanish fear
120 Abate thy valor[34] in the acting it.

JULIET. Give me, give me! O, tell not me of fear!

vial (vī´ əl) *n.* small bottle containing medicine or other liquids

24. **humor** fluid; liquid.
25. **native** natural.
26. **surcease** stop.

27. **wanny ashes** to the color of pale ashes.

28. **eyes' windows** eyelids.

29. **supple government** ability for maintaining motion.

30. **uncovered on the bier** displayed on the funeral platform.

31. **against** before.
32. **drift** purpose; plan.

33. **inconstant toy** passing whim.
34. **Abate thy valor** lessen your courage.

◀ **Critical Viewing**
According to the play, what power does the vial hold? **[Connect]**

FRIAR. Hold! Get you gone, be strong and prosperous
In this resolve. I'll send a friar with speed
To Mantua, with my letters to thy lord.

125 **JULIET.** Love give me strength, and strength shall help afford.
Farewell, dear father. [*Exit with* FRIAR.]

Scene ii. *Hall in* CAPULET'*s house.*

[*Enter* FATHER CAPULET, MOTHER, NURSE, *and* SERVINGMEN, *two or three.*]

CAPULET. So many guests invite as here are writ. [*Exit a* SERVINGMAN.]
Sirrah, go hire me twenty cunning¹ cooks.

SERVINGMAN. You shall have none ill, sir; for I'll try² if they can lick
their fingers.

5 **CAPULET.** How canst thou try them so?

SERVINGMAN. Marry, sir, 'tis an ill cook that cannot lick his own fin-
gers.³ Therefore he that cannot lick his fingers goes not with me.

CAPULET. Go, begone. [*Exit* SERVINGMAN.]
We shall be much unfurnished⁴ for this time.
10 What, is my daughter gone to Friar Lawrence?

NURSE. Ay, forsooth.⁵

CAPULET. Well, he may chance to do some good on her.
A peevish self-willed harlotry it is.⁶

[*Enter* JULIET.]

NURSE. See where she comes from shrift with merry look.

15 **CAPULET.** How now, my headstrong? Where have you been gadding?

JULIET. Where I have learnt me to repent the sin
Of disobedient opposition
To you and your behests,⁷ and am <u>enjoined</u>
By holy Lawrence to fall prostrate⁸ here
20 To beg your pardon. Pardon, I beseech you!
Henceforward I am ever ruled by you.

CAPULET. Send for the County. Go tell him of this.
I'll have this knot knit up tomorrow morning.

JULIET. I met the youthful lord at Lawrence' cell
25 And gave him what becomèd⁹ love I might,
Not stepping o'er the bounds of modesty.

CAPULET. Why, I am glad on't. This is well. Stand up.
This is as't should be. Let me see the County.
Ay, marry, go, I say, and fetch him hither.
30 Now, afore God, this reverend holy friar,
All our whole city is much bound¹⁰ to him.

Literary Analysis
Dramatic Irony What information does Juliet now know that Romeo does not?

1. **cunning** skillful.

2. **try** test.

3. **'tis . . . fingers** It's a bad cook that won't taste his own cooking.
4. **unfurnished** unprepared.

5. **forsooth** in truth.

6. **A peevish . . . it is** It is the ill-tempered, self-ish behavior of a woman without good breeding.

7. **behests** requests.
enjoined (en joind´) *v.* ordered

8. **fall prostrate** lie face down in humble submission.

9. **becomèd** suitable; proper.

10. **bound** indebted.

Reading Check

What does the Friar say will happen when Juliet drinks the contents of the vial?

JULIET. Nurse, will you go with me into my closet[11]
    To help me sort such needful ornaments[12]
    As you think fit to furnish me tomorrow?

35 **LADY CAPULET.** No, not till Thursday. There is time enough.

CAPULET. Go, nurse, go with her. We'll to church tomorrow.
                                [*Exit* JULIET *and* NURSE.]

LADY CAPULET. We shall be short in our provision.[13]
    'Tis now near night.

CAPULET.   Tush, I will stir about,
    And all things shall be well, I warrant thee, wife.
40   Go thou to Juliet, help to deck up her.[14]
    I'll not to bed tonight; let me alone.
    I'll play the housewife for this once. What, ho![15]
    They are all forth; well, I will walk myself
    To County Paris, to prepare up him
45   Against tomorrow. My heart is wondrous light,
    Since this same <u>wayward</u> girl is so reclaimed.   [*Exit with* MOTHER.]

Scene iii. JULIET'*s chamber.*

[*Enter* JULIET *and* NURSE.]

JULIET. Ay, those attires are best; but, gentle nurse,
    I pray thee leave me to myself tonight;
    For I have need of many orisons[1]
    To move the heavens to smile upon my state,[2]
5   Which, well thou knowest, is cross[3] and full of sin.

[*Enter* MOTHER.]

LADY CAPULET. What, are you busy, ho? Need you my help?

JULIET. No, madam; we have culled[4] such necessaries
    As are behoveful[5] for our state tomorrow.
    So please you, let me now be left alone,
10   And let the nurse this night sit up with you:
    For I am sure you have your hands full all
    In this so sudden business.

LADY CAPULET.   Good night.
    Get thee to bed, and rest: for thou hast need.
                               [*Exit* MOTHER *and* NURSE.]

JULIET. Farewell! God knows when we shall meet again.
15   I have a faint cold fear thrills through my veins
    That almost freezes up the heat of life.
    I'll call them back again to comfort me.
    Nurse!—What should she do here?
    My <u>dismal</u> scene I needs must act alone.

---

11. closet private room.
12. ornaments clothes.

13. short . . . provision lacking time for preparation.

14. deck up her dress her; get her ready.

15. What, ho! Capulet is calling for his servants.

wayward (wā′ wərd) *adj.* headstrong; willful

Literary Analysis
Dramatic Irony What is ironic about Lord Capulet's relief and joy?

1. orisons prayers.
2. state condition.
3. cross selfish; disobedient.

4. culled chosen.
5. behoveful desirable; appropriate.

Literary Analysis
Dramatic Irony and Suspense In what ways does Juliet's statement— "I have a faint cold fear thrills through my veins"—add suspense to the drama?

dismal (diz′ məl) *adj.* causing gloom or misery

20 Come, vial.
What if this mixture do not work at all?
Shall I be married then tomorrow morning?
No, no! This shall forbid it. Lie thou there.   [*Lays down a dagger.*]
What if it be a poison which the friar
25 Subtly hath minist'red[6] to have me dead,
Lest in this marriage he should be dishonored
Because he married me before to Romeo?
I fear it is; and yet methinks it should not,
For he hath still been tried[7] a holy man.
30 How if, when I am laid into the tomb,
I wake before the time that Romeo
Come to redeem me? There's a fearful point!
Shall I not then be stifled in the vault,
To whose foul mouth no healthsome air breathes in,
35 And there die strangled ere my Romeo comes?
Or, if I live, is it not very like
The horrible conceit[8] of death and night,
Together with the terror of the place—
As in a vault, an ancient receptacle
40 Where for this many hundred years the bones
Of all my buried ancestors are packed;
Where bloody Tybalt, yet but green in earth,[9]
Lies fest'ring in his shroud; where, as they say,
At some hours in the night spirits resort—
45 Alack, alack, is it not like[10] that I,
So early waking—what with <u>loathsome</u> smells,
And shrieks like mandrakes[11] torn out of the earth,
That living mortals, hearing them, run mad—
O, if I wake, shall I not be distraught,[12]
50 Environèd[13] with all these hideous fears,
And madly play with my forefathers' joints,
And pluck the mangled Tybalt from his shroud,
And, in this rage, with some great kinsman's bone
As with a club dash out my desp'rate brains?
55 O, look! Methinks I see my cousin's ghost
Seeking out Romeo, that did spit his body
Upon a rapier's point. Stay, Tybalt, stay!
Romeo, Romeo, Romeo, I drink to thee.
                    [*She falls upon her bed within the curtains.*]

Scene iv. *Hall in* CAPULET'*s house.*

[*Enter* LADY OF THE HOUSE *and* NURSE.]

LADY CAPULET. Hold, take these keys and fetch more spices, nurse.

NURSE. They call for dates and quinces[1] in the pastry.[2]

---

6. minist'red given me.

7. tried proved.

Literary Analysis
Dramatic Irony and Suspense How do Juliet's anxieties add to the suspense for readers or audiences?

8. conceit idea; thought.

9. green in earth newly entombed.

10. like likely.

loathsome (lōth´ səm) *adj.* disgusting

11. mandrakes plants with forked roots that resemble human legs. The mandrake was believed to shriek when uprooted and cause the hearer to go mad.

12. distraught insane.
13. Environèd surrounded.

Reading Strategy
Predicting What do you think will happen when Juliet's "lifeless" body is found on her bed?

1. quinces golden apple-shaped fruit.
2. pastry baking room.

✓ Reading Check
What does Juliet do after her mother and the Nurse leave her chambers?

The County Paris hath set up his rest
That you shall rest but little. God forgive me!
Marry, and amen. How sound is she asleep!
I needs must wake her. Madam, madam, madam!
10 Ay, let the County take you in your bed;
He'll fright you up, i' faith. Will it not be?

[*Draws aside the curtains.*]

What, dressed, and in your clothes, and down again?[3]
I must needs wake you. Lady! Lady! Lady!
Alas, alas! Help, help! My lady's dead!
15 O weraday that ever I was born!
Some *aqua vitae*, ho! My lord! My lady!

[*Enter* MOTHER.]

LADY CAPULET. What noise is here?

NURSE.   O lamentable day!

LADY CAPULET. What is the matter?

NURSE.   Look, look! O heavy day!

LADY CAPULET. O me, O me! My child, my only life!
20 Revive, look up, or I will die with thee!
Help, help! Call help.

[*Enter* FATHER.]

CAPULET. For shame, bring Juliet forth; her lord is come.

NURSE. She's dead, deceased; she's dead, alack the day!

LADY CAPULET. Alack the day, she's dead, she's dead, she's dead!

25 **CAPULET.** Ha! Let me see her. Out alas! She's cold,
Her blood is settled, and her joints are stiff;
Life and these lips have long been separated.
Death lies on her like an untimely frost
Upon the sweetest flower of all the field.

NURSE. O lamentable day!

30 **LADY CAPULET.**   O woeful time!

CAPULET. Death, that hath ta'en her hence to make me wail,
Ties up my tongue and will not let me speak.

[*Enter* FRIAR LAWRENCE *and the* COUNTY PARIS, *with* MUSICIANS.]

FRIAR. Come, is the bride ready to go to church?

CAPULET. Ready to go, but never to return.
35 O son, the night before thy wedding day
Hath Death lain with thy wife. There she lies,
Flower as she was, deflowerèd by him.
Death is my son-in-law, Death is my heir;

Literary Analysis
Dramatic Irony How does the Nurse's carefree chatter add to the irony of the scene?

3. **down again** back in bed.

Reading Strategy
Predicting Predict what Lord and Lady Capulet will say when they see their daughter's body.

Literary Analysis
Dramatic Irony What is ironic about the Capulets' behavior in lines 24–30?

My daughter he hath wedded. I will die
40 And leave him all. Life, living, all is Death's.

PARIS. Have I thought, love, to see this morning's face,
And doth it give me such a sight as this?

LADY CAPULET. Accursed, unhappy, wretched, hateful day!
Most miserable hour that e'er time saw
45 In lasting labor of his <u>pilgrimage</u>!
But one, poor one, one poor and loving child,
But one thing to rejoice and solace[4] in,
And cruel Death hath catched it from my sight.

NURSE. O woe! O woeful, woeful, woeful day!
50 Most lamentable day, most woeful day
That ever ever I did yet behold!
O day, O day, O day! O hateful day!
Never was seen so black a day as this.
O woeful day! O woeful day!

55 **PARIS.** Beguiled,[5] divorcèd, wrongèd, spited, slain!
Most detestable Death, by thee beguiled,
By cruel, cruel thee quite overthrown.
O love! O life!—not life, but love in death!

CAPULET. Despised, distressèd, hated, martyred, killed!
60 Uncomfortable[6] time, why cam'st thou now
To murder, murder our solemnity?[7]
O child, O child! My soul, and not my child!
Dead art thou—alack, my child is dead,
And with my child my joys are burièd!

65 **FRIAR.** Peace, ho, for shame! Confusion's cure lives not
In these confusions.[8] Heaven and yourself
Had part in this fair maid—now heaven hath all,
And all the better is it for the maid.
Your part in her you could not keep from death,
70 But heaven keeps his part in eternal life.
The most you sought was her promotion,
For 'twas your heaven she should be advanced;
And weep ye now, seeing she is advanced
Above the clouds, as high as heaven itself?
75 O, in this love, you love your child so ill
That you run mad, seeing that she is well.[9]
She's not well married that lives married long,
But she's best married that dies married young.
Dry up your tears and stick your rosemary[10]
80 On this fair corse, and, as the custom is,
And in her best array bear her to church:
For though fond nature[11] bids us all lament,
Yet nature's tears are reason's merriment.[12]

Literary Analysis
Dramatic Irony How do Paris' words contribute to the dramatic irony?

pilgrimage (pil′ grim ij) *n.* long journey, often for religious purposes

4. **solace** find comfort.

5. **Beguiled** cheated.

6. **Uncomfortable** painful, upsetting.

7. **solemnity** solemn rites.

Reading Strategy
Predicting What might Capulet's remarks in lines 63–64 foreshadow about the future?

8. **Confusion's . . . confusions** The remedy for this calamity is not to be found in these outcries.

9. **well** blessed in heaven.

10. **rosemary** an ever-green herb signifying love and remembrance.

11. **fond nature** mistake-prone human nature.

12. **Yet . . . merriment** while human nature causes us to weep for Juliet, reason should cause us to be happy (since she is in heaven).

✔Reading Check

What does the Nurse find when she draws aside the curtains in Juliet's chamber?

CAPULET. All things that we ordainèd festival[13]
85 Turn from their office to black funeral—
Our instruments to melancholy bells,
Our wedding cheer to a sad burial feast;
Our solemn hymns to sullen dirges[14] change;
Our bridal flowers serve for a buried corse;
90 And all things change them to the contrary.

FRIAR. Sir, go you in; and, madam, go with him;
And go, Sir Paris. Everyone prepare
To follow this fair corse unto her grave.
The heavens do low'r[15] upon you for some ill;
95 Move them no more by crossing their high will.

[*Exit, casting rosemary on her and shutting the curtains.
The* NURSE *and* MUSICIANS *remain.*]

FIRST MUSICIAN. Faith, we may put up our pipes and be gone.

NURSE. Honest good fellows, ah, put up, put up!
For well you know this is a pitiful case.[16]   [*Exit.*]

FIRST MUSICIAN. Ay, by my troth, the case may be amended.

[*Enter* PETER.]

100 **PETER.** Musicians, O, musicians, "Heart's ease," "Heart's ease"! O,
and you will have me live, play "Heart's ease."

FIRST MUSICIAN. Why "Heart's ease"?

PETER. O, musicians, because my heart itself plays "My heart is
full."
O, play me some merry dump[17] to comfort me.

105 **FIRST MUSICIAN.** Not a dump we! 'Tis no time to play now.

PETER. You will not then?

FIRST MUSICIAN. No.

PETER. I will then give it you soundly.

FIRST MUSICIAN. What will you give us?

110 **PETER.** No money, on my faith, but the gleek.[18] I will give you[19] the
minstrel.[20]

FIRST MUSICIAN. Then will I give you the serving-creature.

PETER. Then will I lay the serving-creature's dagger on your pate.
I will carry no crotchets.[21] I'll *re* you, I'll *fa* you. Do you note me?

115 **FIRST MUSICIAN.** And you *re* us and *fa* us, you note us.

SECOND MUSICIAN. Pray you put up your dagger, and put out your wit.
Then have at you with my wit!

PETER. I will dry-beat you with an iron wit, and put up my iron

---

13. ordainèd festival
planned to be part of a
celebration.

14. dirges funeral hymns.

15. low'r frown.

16. case situation;
instrument case.

17. dump sad tune.

18. gleek scornful speech.

19. give you call you.

20. minstrel a contemptuous term (as opposed
to *musician*).

21. crotchets whim;
quarter notes.

dagger. Answer me like men.

120 "When griping grief the heart doth wound,
 And doleful dumps the mind oppress,
Then music with her silver sound"—

Why "silver sound"? Why "music with her silver sound"? What say you, Simon Catling?

125 **FIRST MUSICIAN.** Marry, sir, because silver hath a sweet sound.

PETER. Pretty! What say you, Hugh Rebeck?

SECOND MUSICIAN. I say "silver sound" because musicians sound for silver.

PETER. Pretty too! What say you, James Soundpost?

130 **THIRD MUSICIAN.** Faith, I know not what to say.

PETER. O, I cry you mercy,[22] you are the singer. I will say for you. It is "music with her silver sound" because musicians have no gold for sounding.
 "Then music with her silver sound
135 With speedy help doth lend redress." [*Exit.*]

FIRST MUSICIAN. What a pestilent knave is this same!

SECOND MUSICIAN. Hang him, Jack! Come, we'll in here, tarry for the mourners, and stay dinner. [*Exit with others.*]

22. **cry you mercy** beg your pardon.

Reading Strategy
Predicting Do you predict that the Friar's plan will succeed? Why or why not?

Review and Assess

Thinking About Act IV

1. **Respond:** Should Romeo and Juliet have followed Friar Lawrence's advice? Why or why not?

2. **(a) Recall:** What event are Paris and Juliet discussing at the beginning of Act IV? **(b) Compare and Contrast:** How do their feelings about the event differ?

3. **(a) Recall:** What is Friar Lawrence's plan for Juliet? **(b) Analyze:** Why do you think Juliet trusts the Friar?

4. **(a) Recall:** What three fears does Juliet reveal in her soliloquy in Scene iii? **(b) Interpret:** What does the soliloquy reveal about her personality?

5. **(a) Evaluate:** Do you think drinking the potion is a courageous or a foolish act? Explain. **(b) Draw Conclusions:** How has Juliet changed during the play? Explain.

6. **Evaluate:** Do you think it is appropriate for a religious person like the Friar to deceive people with the hope of positive outcomes?

Prepare to Read

The Tragedy of Romeo and Juliet, Act V

Literary Analysis

Tragedy

A **tragedy** is a drama in which the central character, who is usually of noble stature, meets with disaster or great misfortune. The tragic hero's downfall is usually the result of fate, a serious character flaw, or a combination of both. A great tragedy is not necessarily depressing, however. It uplifts the audience by showing the greatness of spirit of which people are capable. This spirit is reflected in these lines near the end of the play:

> For I will raise her statue in pure gold,
> That whiles Verona by that name is known,
> There shall no figure at such rate be set
> As that of true and faithful Juliet.

As you read Act V of *Romeo and Juliet*, consider the reasons for the tragic events and analyze how the events make you feel about the human spirit.

Connecting Literary Elements

A **character's motive** is the reason behind an individual's thoughts or actions. In Shakespeare's tragedies, the hero's motives are basically good, although sometimes misguided. The character's fate, therefore, often seems worse than what he or she deserves.

Reading Strategy

Identifying Causes and Effects

Tragedies often involve a chain of causes and effects that advances the plot and leads to the final tragic outcome.

- A **cause** is an action, an event, or a situation that produces a result.
- An **effect** is the result produced by a cause.

Use a chart like this one to record the causes and effects in Act V.

Vocabulary Development

remnants (rem′ nənts) *n.* remaining persons or things (p. 862)

penury (pen′ yōō rē) *n.* extreme poverty (p. 862)

haughty (hôt′ ē) *adj.* arrogant (p. 866)

sepulcher (sep′ əl kər) *n.* tomb (p. 869)

ambiguities (am′ bə gyōō′ ə tēz) *n.* statements or events whose meanings are unclear (p. 872)

scourge (skʉrj) *n.* whip or other instrument for inflicting punishment (p. 873)

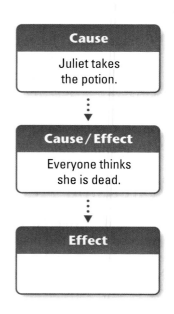

Cause

Juliet takes the potion.

Cause / Effect

Everyone thinks she is dead.

Effect

Review and Anticipate

To prevent her marriage to Paris, Juliet has taken the Friar's potion and, as Act V begins, is in a temporary deathlike sleep. Her unsuspecting family plans her funeral. Meanwhile, the Friar has sent a messenger to Mantua to tell Romeo of the ruse, so that he may return and rescue Juliet from her family tomb. What do you think might go wrong with the Friar's plan?

Scene i. *Mantua. A street.*

[*Enter* ROMEO.]

    ROMEO. If I may trust the flattering truth of sleep,[1]
      My dreams presage[2] some joyful news at hand.
      My bosom's lord[3] sits lightly in his throne,
      And all this day an unaccustomed spirit
5   Lifts me above the ground with cheerful thoughts.
      I dreamt my lady came and found me dead
      (Strange dream that gives a dead man leave to think!)
      And breathed such life with kisses in my lips
      That I revived and was an emperor.
10   Ah me! How sweet is love itself possessed,
      When but love's shadows[4] are so rich in joy!

1. flattering . . . sleep pleasing illusions of dreams.

2. presage foretell.

3. bosom's lord heart.

4. shadows dreams; unreal images.

✔ **Reading Check**

Why is Romeo in a good mood?

Romeo and Juliet, Act V, Scene i ◆ 861

[*Enter* ROMEO'S MAN, BALTHASAR, *booted.*]

News from Verona! How now, Balthasar?
Dost thou not bring me letters from the friar?
How doth my lady? Is my father well?
How fares my Juliet? That I ask again,
For nothing can be ill if she be well.

MAN. Then she is well, and nothing can be ill.
Her body sleeps in Capels' monument,[5]
And her immortal part with angels lives.
I saw her laid low in her kindred's vault
And presently took post[6] to tell it you.
O, pardon me for bringing these ill news,
Since you did leave it for my office,[7] sir.

ROMEO. Is it e'en so? Then I defy you, stars!
Thou knowest my lodging. Get me ink and paper
And hire post horses. I will hence tonight.

MAN. I do beseech you, sir, have patience.
Your looks are pale and wild and do import
Some misadventure.[8]

ROMEO.   Tush, thou art deceived.
Leave me and do the thing I bid thee do.
Hast thou no letters to me from the friar?

MAN. No, my good lord.

ROMEO.   No matter. Get thee gone.
And hire those horses. I'll be with thee straight. [*Exit* BALTHASAR.]
Well, Juliet, I will lie with thee tonight.
Let's see for means. O mischief, thou art swift
To enter in the thoughts of desperate men!
I do remember an apothecary,[9]
And hereabouts 'a dwells, which late I noted
In tatt'red weeds, with overwhelming brows,
Culling of simples.[10] Meager were his looks,
Sharp misery had worn him to the bones;
And in his needy shop a tortoise hung,
An alligator stuffed, and other skins
Of ill-shaped fishes; and about his shelves
A beggarly account[11] of empty boxes,
Green earthen pots, bladders, and musty seeds,
Remnants of packthread, and old cakes of roses[12]
Were thinly scatterèd, to make up a show.
Noting this penury, to myself I said,
"And if a man did need a poison now
Whose sale is present death in Mantua,
Here lives a caitiff[13] wretch would sell it him."
O, this same thought did but forerun my need,

15

20

25

30

35

40

45

50

Literary Analysis
Tragedy and Character's Motive What motivates Romeo's questions?

5. **Capels' monument** the Capulets' burial vault.

6. **presently took post** immediately set out on horseback.

7. **office** duty.

Literary Analysis
Tragedy Which words in the exchange between Romeo and the man suggest that fate plays a role in the tragedy?

8. **import / Some misadventure** suggest some misfortune.

9. **apothecary** one who prepares and sells drugs and medicines.

10. **In tatt'red . . . simples** in torn clothing, with overhanging eyebrows, sorting out herbs.

11. **beggarly account** small number.

12. **cakes of roses** pressed rose petals (used for perfume).

remnants (rem´ nənts) *n.* remaining persons or things

penury (pen´ yo͞o rē) *n.* extreme poverty

13. **caitiff** miserable.

And this same needy man must sell it me.
55 As I remember, this should be the house.
Being holiday, the beggar's shop is shut.
What, ho! Apothecary!

[*Enter* APOTHECARY.]

APOTHECARY.   Who calls so loud?

ROMEO. Come hither, man. I see that thou art poor.
Hold, there is forty ducats.[14] Let me have
60 A dram of poison, such soon-speeding gear[15]
As will disperse itself through all the veins
That the life-weary taker may fall dead,
And that the trunk[16] may be discharged of breath
As violently as hasty powder fired
65 Doth hurry from the fatal cannon's womb.

APOTHECARY. Such mortal drugs I have; but Mantua's law
Is death to any he that utters[17] them.

ROMEO. Art thou so bare and full of wretchedness
And fearest to die? Famine is in thy cheeks,
70 Need and oppression starveth in thy eyes,
Contempt and beggary hangs upon thy back:
The world is not thy friend, nor the world's law;
The world affords no law to make thee rich;
Then be not poor, but break it and take this.

75 APOTHECARY. My poverty but not my will consents.

ROMEO. I pay thy poverty and not thy will.

APOTHECARY. Put this in any liquid thing you will
And drink it off, and if you had the strength
Of twenty men, it would dispatch you straight.

80 ROMEO. There is thy gold—worse poison to men's souls,
Doing more murder in this loathsome world,
Than these poor compounds[18] that thou mayst not sell.
I sell thee poison; thou hast sold me none.
Farewell. Buy food and get thyself in flesh.
85 Come, cordial[19] and not poison, go with me
To Juliet's grave; for there must I use thee.   [*Exit all.*]

Scene ii. FRIAR LAWRENCE'S *cell.*

[*Enter* FRIAR JOHN *to* FRIAR LAWRENCE.]

JOHN. Holy Franciscan friar, brother, ho!

[*Enter* FRIAR LAWRENCE.]

LAWRENCE. This same should be the voice of Friar John.

Reading Strategy
Identifying Causes and Effects What causes Romeo to buy poison from the apothecary?

14. **ducats** (duk′ əts) gold coins.

15. **soon-speeding gear** fast-working stuff.

16. **trunk** body.

17. **utters** sells.

Literary Analysis
Tragedy and Character's Motive What motivates the apothecary to sell Romeo poison?

18. **compounds** mixtures.

19. **cordial** health-giving drink.

✓**Reading Check**

What does Romeo learn from Balthasar?

35 By heaven, I will tear thee joint by joint
And strew this hungry churchyard with thy limbs.
The time and my intents are savage-wild,
More fierce and more inexorable⁹ far
Than empty¹⁰ tigers or the roaring sea.

40 **BALTHASAR.** I will be gone, sir, and not trouble ye.

ROMEO. So shalt thou show me friendship. Take thou that.
Live, and be prosperous; and farewell, good fellow.

BALTHASAR. [*Aside*] For all this same, I'll hide me hereabout.
His looks I fear, and his intents I doubt. [*Retires.*]

45 **ROMEO.** Thou detestable maw,¹¹ thou womb of death,
Gorged with the dearest morsel of the earth,
Thus I enforce thy rotten jaws to open,
And in despite¹² I'll cram thee with more food.
[ROMEO *opens the tomb.*]

PARIS. This is that banished <u>haughty</u> Montague
50 That murd'red my love's cousin—with which grief
It is supposed the fair creature died—
And here is come to do some villainous shame
To the dead bodies. I will apprehend¹³ him.
Stop thy unhallowèd toil, vile Montague!

9. inexorable uncontrollable.
10. empty hungry.

11. maw stomach.

12. despite scorn.

Literary Analysis
Tragedy and Character's Motive Why is Romeo's intention to feed himself to the tomb especially tragic?

haughty (hôt´ ē) *adj.* arrogant

13. apprehend seize; arrest.

▼ **Critical Viewing** In the tomb, Romeo pulls back the shroud to reveal what he thinks is Juliet's dead body. What clues about her appearance, as it is shown here, should have led him to realize she was still alive? **[Support]**

55   Can vengeance be pursued further than death?
       Condemnèd villain, I do apprehend thee.
       Obey, and go with me; for thou must die.

ROMEO. I must indeed; and therefore came I hither.
       Good gentle youth, tempt not a desp'rate man.
60   Fly hence and leave me. Think upon these gone;
       Let them affright thee. I beseech thee, youth,
       Put not another sin upon my head
       By urging me to fury. O, be gone!
       By heaven, I love thee better than myself,
65   For I come hither armed against myself.
       Stay not, be gone. Live, and hereafter say
       A madman's mercy bid thee run away.

PARIS. I do defy thy conjurations.[14]
       And apprehend thee for a felon[15] here.

70 **ROMEO.** Wilt thou provoke me? Then have at thee, boy! [*They fight.*]

    PAGE. O Lord, they fight! I will go call the watch. [*Exit.* PARIS *falls.*]

    PARIS. O, I am slain! If thou be merciful,
       Open the tomb, lay me with Juliet.   [*Dies.*]

    ROMEO. In faith, I will. Let me peruse[16] this face.
75   Mercutio's kinsman, noble County Paris!
       What said my man when my betossèd[17] soul
       Did not attend[18] him as we rode? I think
       He told me Paris should have married Juliet.
       Said he not so, or did I dream it so?
80   Or am I mad, hearing him talk of Juliet,
       To think it was so? O, give me thy hand,
       One writ with me in sour misfortune's book!
       I'll bury thee in a triumphant grave.
       A grave? O, no, a lanthorn,[19] slaught'red youth,
85   For here lies Juliet, and her beauty makes
       This vault a feasting presence[20] full of light.
       Death, lie thou there, by a dead man interred.
                  [*Lays him in the tomb.*]
       How oft when men are at the point of death
       Have they been merry! Which their keepers[21] call
90   A lightning before death. O, how may I
       Call this a lightning? O my love, my wife!
       Death, that hath sucked the honey of thy breath,
       Hath had no power yet upon thy beauty.
       Thou art not conquered. Beauty's ensign[22] yet
95   Is crimson in thy lips and in thy cheeks,
       And death's pale flag is not advancèd there.
       Tybalt, liest thou there in thy bloody sheet?
       O, what more favor can I do to thee

Reading Strategy
Identifying Causes and Effects What do you think will be the effect of Paris' condemnation of Romeo? Why?

14. **conjurations** solemn appeals.

15. **felon** criminal.

16. **peruse** look over.

17. **betossèd** upset.
18. **attend** give attention to.

19. **lanthorn** windowed structure on top of a room to admit light; also, a lantern.

20. **feasting presence** chamber fit for a celebration.

21. **keepers** jailers.
22. **ensign** banner.

Reading Strategy
Identifying Causes and Effects What is the real cause for Romeo's observation that "death's pale flag is not yet advanced" in Juliet's face?

✔**Reading Check**

What happens to Paris at the tomb?

Than with that hand that cut thy youth in twain
100 To sunder[23] his that was thine enemy?
Forgive me, cousin! Ah, dear Juliet,
Why art thou yet so fair? Shall I believe
That unsubstantial Death is amorous,[24]
And that the lean abhorrèd monster keeps
105 Thee here in dark to be his paramour?
For fear of that I still will stay with thee
And never from this pallet[25] of dim night
Depart again. Here, here will I remain
With worms that are thy chambermaids. O, here
110 Will I set up my everlasting rest
And shake the yoke of inauspicious[26] stars
From this world-wearied flesh. Eyes, look your last!
Arms, take your last embrace! And, lips, O you
The doors of breath, seal with a righteous kiss
115 A dateless[27] bargain to engrossing[28] death!
Come, bitter conduct;[29] come, unsavory guide!
Thou desperate pilot,[30] now at once run on
The dashing rocks thy seasick weary bark!
Here's to my love! [*Drinks.*] O true apothecary!
120 Thy drugs are quick. Thus with a kiss I die.   [*Falls.*]

[*Enter* FRIAR LAWRENCE, *with lanthorn, crow, and spade.*]

FRIAR. Saint Francis be my speed![31] How oft tonight
    Have my old feet stumbled[32] at graves! Who's there?

BALTHASAR. Here's one, a friend, and one that knows you well.

FRIAR. Bliss be upon you! Tell me, good my friend,
125   What torch is yond that vainly lends his light
    To grubs[33] and eyeless skulls? As I discern,
    It burneth in the Capels' monument.

BALTHASAR. It doth so, holy sir; and there's my master,
    One that you love.

FRIAR.   Who is it?

BALTHASAR.   Romeo.

FRIAR. How long hath he been there?

130 **BALTHASAR.**   Full half an hour.

FRIAR. Go with me to the vault.

BALTHASAR.   I dare not, sir.
    My master knows not but I am gone hence,
    And fearfully did menace me with death
    If I did stay to look on his intents.

135 **FRIAR.** Stay then; I'll go alone. Fear comes upon me.
    O, much I fear some ill unthrifty[34] thing.

---

23. **sunder** cut off.

24. **amorous** full of love.

25. **pallet** bed.

26. **inauspicious** promising misfortune.
27. **dateless** eternal.
28. **engrossing** all-encompassing.
29. **conduct** guide (poison).
30. **pilot** captain (Romeo himself).
31. **speed** help.
32. **stumbled** stumbling was thought to be a bad omen.

Reading Strategy
Identifying Causes and Effects How is Friar Lawrence's late arrival another example of chance contributing to this tragedy?
33. **grubs** worms.

Literary Analysis
Tragedy Do you think Balthasar could have prevented this tragedy?

34. **unthrifty** unlucky.

BALTHASAR. As I did sleep under this yew tree here,
I dreamt my master and another fought,
And that my master slew him.

FRIAR. Romeo!
140 Alack, alack, what blood is this which stains
The stony entrance of this sepulcher?
What mean these masterless[35] and gory swords
To lie discolored by this place of peace? *[Enters the tomb.]*
Romeo! O, pale! Who else? What, Paris too?
145 And steeped in blood? Ah, what an unkind[36] hour
Is guilty of this lamentable chance!
The lady stirs. *[JULIET rises.]*

JULIET. O comfortable[37] friar! Where is my lord?
I do remember well where I should be,
150 And there I am. Where is my Romeo?

FRIAR. I hear some noise. Lady, come from that nest
Of death, contagion, and unnatural sleep.
A greater power than we can contradict
Hath thwarted our intents. Come, come away.
155 Thy husband in thy bosom there lies dead;
And Paris too. Come, I'll dispose of thee
Among a sisterhood of holy nuns.
Stay not to question, for the watch is coming.
Come, go, good Juliet. I dare no longer stay.

160 **JULIET.** Go, get thee hence, for I will not away. *[Exit FRIAR.]*
What's here? A cup, closed in my truelove's hand?
Poison, I see, hath been his timeless[38] end.
O churl![39] Drunk all, and left no friendly drop
To help me after? I will kiss thy lips.
165 Haply some poison yet doth hang on them
To make me die with a restorative.[40] *[Kisses him.]*
Thy lips are warm!

CHIEF WATCHMAN. *[Within]* Lead, boy. Which way?

JULIET. Yea, noise? Then I'll be brief. O happy[41] dagger!
[Snatches ROMEO'S dagger.]
170 This is thy sheath; there rust, and let me die.
[She stabs herself and falls.]

[Enter PARIS' BOY and WATCH.]

BOY. This is the place. There, where the torch doth burn.

CHIEF WATCHMAN. The ground is bloody. Search about the churchyard.
Go, some of you; whoe'er you find attach.[42]
[Exit some of the WATCH.]
Pitiful sight! Here lies the County slain;
175 And Juliet bleeding, warm, and newly dead,

sepulcher (sep´ əl kər) *n.* tomb

35. masterless discarded (without masters).

36. unkind unnatural.

37. comfortable comforting.

Reading Strategy
Identifying Causes and Effects What do you think will be the effect once Juliet discovers that Romeo is dead?

Literary Analysis
Tragedy and Character's Motive Why do you think Friar Lawrence wants to "dispose of Juliet" in a sisterhood of nuns?

38. timeless untimely; too soon.

39. churl rude fellow.

40. restorative medicine.

41. happy convenient; opportune.

42. attach arrest.

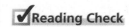
Reading Check
What does the Friar find when he enters the vault?

Integrate Language Skills

Vocabulary Development Lesson

Word Analysis: Latin Prefix *ambi-*

The Latin prefix *ambi-* means "both." It appears in *ambiguities*, which means "statements or events having two or more possible meanings." In your notebook, complete each sentence below with one of the following words.

   a. ambidextrous   **b.** ambilateral

1. The __?__ man used both hands with equal skill.
2. The __?__ pain hurt both sides of my body.

Spelling Strategy

If a noun ends in *y* preceded by a consonant, change the *y* to *i* and add *-es* to form the plural. For example, *ambiguities* is the plural of *ambiguity*. Write the plural of each of these nouns.

   1. tragedy   **2.** fury   **3.** enmity

Concept Development: Synonyms

In your notebook, write the word that is the best synonym for the first word. To help you, review the vocabulary list on page 860.

1. remnants: (a) cloths, (b) remains, (c) factors
2. penury: (a) poverty, (b) currency, (c) disease
3. haughty: (a) timid, (b) friendly, (c) arrogant
4. sepulcher: (a) monument, (b) tomb, (c) cemetery
5. ambiguities: (a) vows, (b) details, (c) uncertainties
6. scourge: (a) sorrow, (b) punishment, (c) hatred

Grammar Lesson

Agreement With Indefinite Pronouns

Indefinite pronouns refer to people, places, or things, often without specifying which ones. Indefinite pronouns may be singular (such as *each*, *neither*, or *one*) or plural (such as *both* or *many*).

When you write a sentence with a personal pronoun that has an indefinite pronoun as its antecedent, you must make sure the pronouns agree in number. In the examples below, the indefinite pronoun is underlined and the personal pronoun is in italics.

Singular:	<u>One</u> of the friars stayed in *his* quarters.
Plural:	<u>Both</u> of the friars were quarantined in *their* house.

Practice Write each sentence, circling the indefinite pronoun and choosing the personal pronoun that completes the sentence correctly.

1. Both of the lovers lost (his, their) lives.
2. Each of the fathers mourned (his, their) child.
3. Many were shocked by (its, their) discovery.
4. One of the lovers poisoned (his, their) lips.
5. Neither of the families was happy with (its, their) loss.

Writing Application Write two sentences about Act V, using a singular indefinite pronoun and personal pronoun in one and a plural indefinite pronoun and personal pronoun in the other.

W͚G *Prentice Hall Writing and Grammar Connection: Chapter 25, Section 2*

Writing Lesson

Persuasive Letter

A letter from Friar Lawrence to both families, urging them to end their feud, might have saved Romeo and Juliet's lives. As the Friar, develop a persuasive letter to send to both families right after you have married their children.

Prewriting   Your letter should appeal both to reason and to emotion. Make a list of factual evidence and emotional pleas that might convince the families to end their feud.

Drafting   Begin your draft by announcing the marriage ceremony you have just performed. Then, arrange your persuasive appeals in a logical order.

Revising   Read your draft as if you were Montague or Capulet. Determine whether the letter appeals equally to both your mind and heart. If not, revise it so that the appeals are both strong and balanced.

Model: Revising to Balance Persuasive Appeals

They each live behind gated walls and have to sneak into each other's homes to be together.

The hatred between your families is forcing your children to be apart and is threatening their happiness. They are even afraid that something bad might happen if they attempt to tell their families of their marriage. Do you want your children to be miserable?

Adding factual information makes the letter more persuasive by balancing appeals to reason and emotion.

WG *Prentice Hall Writing and Grammar Connection: Chapter 7, Section 4*

Extension Activities

Listening and Speaking Hold a **mock trial** to investigate the causes of the tragedy. Follow these steps:

- Assign roles—the main characters, the lawyer, the judge, and the jury.
- Take depositions in which each character tells the story from his or her perspective.

When the court is in session, lawyers should question and cross-examine witnesses before the jury reaches a verdict. **[Group Activity]**

Research and Technology Imagine that you and a group of classmates have been hired to create a **set design** for a modern-day version of *Romeo and Juliet*. Decide on an appropriate setting for the adaptation, such as in a large modern city. Then, use computer software or posterboard to create diagrams for your set design.

 Take It to the Net   www.phschool.com

Go online for an additional research activity using the Internet.

READING INFORMATIONAL MATERIALS

Atlas Entries

About Atlas Entries

An atlas is a book of maps showing physical features of the world, such as cities, mountains, rivers, and roads. Some atlases include facts and statistics about the places depicted. Many modern atlases, like the Dorling Kindersley atlas (whose pages are shown here), provide brief articles on topics such as these:

- Population
- Climate
- Government
- Transportation
- Tourism

The maps in an atlas usually are accompanied by a *legend,* a key that explains the symbols and colors used in the map. For example, symbols might represent features such as national or state capitals. Color codes might be used to indicate land height or density of population. The legend also indicates to what mileage the map is scaled.

Reading Strategy

Skimming and Scanning

Atlases and other reference materials provide a broad range of information. To find what you need, adjust your reading rate by skimming or scanning.

- By **skimming,** you can get an idea of the organization and scope of a work before reading it. To skim, read quickly, taking in words in groups. Stop for headings and other text that is set off, such as bold text.

- By **scanning,** you can locate specific information fast. Move your eyes quickly over the page. Look for words related to the information you are seeking. Stop and read the paragraphs that contain the words you are seeking.

Skim the atlas entry on the following pages. Use a graphic organizer like the one at right to record each kind of information you can find on the page.

Subjects Covered	How I Know
Climate of Italy	Listed as a heading on the page
Transportation in Italy	Listed as a heading on the page, shown with icons of a ship and a plane

ITALY

Adapted from *Dorling Kindersley World Reference Atlas*

ITALY

Total Land Area : 294 060 sq. km
(301 270 sq. miles)

POPULATION

over 1 000 000
over 500 000
over 100 000
over 50 000
over 10 000

The legend explains the meaning of the symbols found on the map.

LAND HEIGHT

3000m/9843ft
2000m/6562ft
1000m/3281ft
500m/1640ft
200m/656ft
Sea Level

The map shows the cities and towns of Italy.

Writing WORKSHOP

Response to Literature

When you write a **response to literature,** you explore *how, what,* and *why* a piece of writing communicates to you. In this workshop, you will write a response to a piece of literature that engages you as a reader.

Assignment Criteria. Your response to literature should have the following characteristics:

- An analysis of the work's content, its related ideas, or its effect on the reader
- A thesis statement that characterizes your response
- A focus on a single aspect or an overall view of the work
- Evidence from the literary work or other texts to support the opinions you present

To preview the criteria on which your response to literature may be assessed, see the Rubric on page 887.

Prewriting

Choose a topic. Think of novels, poems, and other works of literature that you consider memorable. Create a top-ten list by writing down the titles and authors of these works. Next to each, note any ideas you would like to share about the literature. Review your list and choose a topic.

Gather details. Return to the piece of literature you have selected to find examples, excerpts, and direct quotations that relate directly to your topic. You will use this evidence to help frame your main idea and supporting ideas.

Gathering Details

What I want to prove:
General Zaroff's civilized exterior conceals a ruthless, cunning, heartless murderer.

How I can prove it:
- Describe the wealth of his castle
- Include quote: "The weak were created to please the strong."

Clarify your purpose. Whether you are sharing your enthusiasm for a new writer, interpreting a well-known poem, or responding to a short story, include details that support your writing goal. Consider these tips:

- **To praise,** include concrete details about what you liked.
- **To analyze,** back up your ideas with evidence from the text.
- **To explain a personal response,** show how the work connects to your own experience or ideas.

Student Model

Before you begin drafting your response to literature, read this student model and review the characteristics of effective responses to literature.

Jeff Rutherford
Broken Arrow, OK

Characterization of General Zaroff

What lies at the heart of a refined man? In Richard Connell's short story "The Most Dangerous Game," the deranged, yet cunning and elegant, General Zaroff shares his taste for hunting with an unsuspecting visitor. Although he is civilized in his choice of lifestyle, Zaroff's beliefs reveal the murderous mind behind the illusion of a charming, charismatic man.

When we first encounter General Zaroff, our initial reaction is one of delight and admiration for his wealth and charm. Zaroff lives in a massive castle, feasts on the finest delicacies, and wears expensive clothes. His luxurious surroundings and lifestyle reflect a highly civilized, eloquent, and proper gentleman. As readers soon learn, however, there is more to Zaroff than food and elegance.

Beneath Zaroff's fine qualities, though, lies an overwhelming attitude of arrogance. This attitude comes from his firm belief that his way of thinking is superior to that of the average person. Zaroff also fancies himself a phenomenal hunter: "My hand was made for the trigger," he claims. It is this deadly mixture of arrogance, superior hunting skills, and belief that it is natural for the strong to prevail over the weak that makes him disregard the value of human life.

Zaroff's extreme beliefs lead him to conclude that only the intelligent mind of a human being can provide him with the dangerous game he desires. Rationalizing that "the weak were created to please the strong," he chooses to hunt humans instead of animals. Unfortunately, Rainsford steps into this situation. The major conflicts in "The Most Dangerous Game" demonstrate what happens during such an inhumane hunt.

However, the general's arrogance and disregard for human life blind him to the fear and desperation of his prey. His attitude leads to his own demise at the hands of Rainsford, his prey. The characterization of Zaroff as a murderer hiding behind a mask of civility shows that beneath even the most beautiful rose can lie a sharp and deadly thorn.

> The title indicates that the essay is limited to a single character.

> Jeff uses strong language to clearly state his thesis.

> Direct quotations provide evidence for this characterization of Zaroff.

> Jeff concludes his response with an analogy that neatly summarizes his analysis.

Listening and Speaking WORKSHOP

Presenting an Oral Response to Literature

Certain works of literature provoke a strong emotional response. Capturing those feelings in words can be a challenging task. When you present an **oral response to literature,** you articulate your response and support it with evidence from the text.

Define Your Response

Before you present a response to others, you must first determine how you feel about a selection. Review the Writing Workshop on pages 884–887. Use these steps to help you focus and define your feelings:

Summarize the main ideas. Finding the main idea gives you a basic skeleton around which to organize your response. In nonfiction, the main idea is generally found in the introduction or conclusion. For a fictional work, limit yourself to the most important ideas. Then, gather details from the work that are especially important or memorable to you.

Characterize your response. Decide whether you agree or disagree with the main ideas you have selected and determine why. Turn these reactions into a single thesis statement that captures the way you feel, and jot down at least three reasons for your reaction. These reasons will be your supporting arguments.

Find evidence to support your response. Use examples from the literature as evidence to support your arguments. Direct quotations or paraphrases give greater depth and power to the arguments you develop in your oral response.

Offer Your Response

Organize your thoughts. If possible, keep your organization clear and simple, and include these elements:

- A brief introduction outlining your thesis
- A body presenting supporting arguments along with key evidence
- A summary of your main argument

Use evocative language. To make your presentation more memorable, choose words and phrases that will have powerful associations for your audience and generate a reaction.

(Activity: **Book Club)** Forming a book club can enhance your enjoyment of reading by exchanging views with others. Discuss a work of literature in a small group. Take turns presenting and evaluating all of the group's presentations, using the chart shown. Discuss interesting variations in interpretation or response.

> ### Feedback Form for Oral Response to Literature
>
> **Rating System**
> + = Excellent   ✔ = Average   – = Weak
>
> **Content**
> _____ Clarity of thesis
> _____ Support of ideas with evidence
> _____ Validity of interpretation
>
> **Delivery**
> _____ Presentation clearly organized and presented
> _____ Use of appropriate language to describe response
>
> *Answer the following questions:*
>
> Do you agree with the interpretation of the work?
>
> What would have made the presentation more effective?

Assessment WORKSHOP

Responses and Interpretations

The reading sections of some tests require you to read a passage and write short, essay-type answers that respond to and interpret the written text. Use the following strategies to help you defend your responses and interpretations:

- To determine your reaction, think about how the text makes you feel and how it might influence your opinions.
- When you interpret a text, give your own ideas about what the text means.
- Base your response and interpretation on information contained in the text, supporting your opinions with references.

Test-Taking Strategies

- To defend your ideas about a fictional work, use the language, plot details, and character descriptions as support.
- Search for facts, quotations, and statistics to support your interpretation of nonfiction.

Sample Test Item

Directions: Read the passage, and then answer the question that follows.

Geographers use globes and maps to represent Earth. A globe is more accurate than a map. Shaped like Earth, a globe gives a true picture of the size and shape of landmasses and of distance across oceans. Globes are awkward to carry around, however, so most people use maps instead. Even so, maps have a major drawback. Because Earth's surface is curved and maps are flat, all maps distort Earth's image in some way.

1. For what reason would you use a map? For what reason would you use a globe? Support your answers.

Answers and Explanations

Possible Answers:

You might use a map to find out how to drive to a new place. You might use a globe to see how far the United States is from China.

A successful answer should incorporate the different attributes of globes and maps.

Practice

Directions: Read the passage, and then answer the questions that follow.

Hoover Dam was built in the 1930s during the Great Depression to control the Colorado River and irrigate the farmlands of the southwestern United States. It has also provided electric power and formed a giant reservoir, Lake Mead, for drinking water, swimming, boating, and fishing. However, Hoover Dam has also changed the river's ecology, hurting some native fish and other species and flooding some parts of the Grand Canyon.

1. In what ways have technology and human intervention served the needs of the United States?

2. Do you think the advantages outweighed the disadvantages in the construction of Hoover Dam? Support your answer with evidence from the text.

Poetry

Garden of Delights, watercolor, 11" x17", Sandy Novak, Omni-Photo Communications, Inc.

Exploring the Genre

The poet T. S. Eliot said that poetry can be enjoyed before it is understood. A powerful poem uses language to draw you in, invite you to reread, and inspire you to find a new layer of meaning each time. A poet carefully chooses words to capture a unique and personal vision. Poetry combines meaning with sound to add music and rhythm to ideas. Each reader brings a different set of associations to a poem based on the people, places, and experiences that he or she has known.

These terms will help you discuss the variety of poems in this unit:

- **Lyric poetry** expresses vivid thoughts and feelings.

- **Narrative poetry** tells a story.

- **Dramatic poetry** uses techniques of drama, such as speaker and conflict, to tell a story.

- **Musical devices** such as alliteration, ono-matopoeia, assonance, consonance, meter, repetition, and rhyme give poems a melo-dious quality.

- **Figurative language** uses simile, lyrical metaphor, and personification in creative, unexpected comparisons and descriptions.

▲ **Critical Viewing** Which details of this picture suggest poetry to you? **[Connect]**

Why Read Literature?

There are many different reasons to read a poem. You might read poetry because you like the way certain poets put words together or because you find their perspectives unique and intriguing. Preview three purposes you might set before reading the poems in this unit.

Read for the Love of Literature

A poem can provide a window into the writing process. Find out how choosing the right words for a poem is a little like eating overripe blackberries in Galway Kinnell's **"Blackberry Eating,"** page 914.

Good literature makes connections and illustrates universal themes. If you ever have been forced to stay inside and clean while others played, you can appreciate the way Julia Alvarez transforms household drudgery into personal discovery in **"Woman's Work,"** page 920.

Read for Information

With the rapid advances in science and technology in the last century, you might wonder how doctors, scientists, and librarians keep up with recent developments in their fields. Explore the world of professional journals in this unit's **Reading Informational Materials,** page 964.

Read to Appreciate an Author's Style

The eagle, subject of Alfred, Lord Tennyson's poem, has long been one of the most recognizable symbols of grace, power, and authority. See how Tennyson adds majesty to the list when you read **"The Eagle,"** page 906.

When the playwright Lorraine Hansberry read one of Langston Hughes's poems, she was so moved by his insights that she used a line from one of his works to name her play *A Raisin in the Sun*. Read Hughes's powerful poem **"Dream Deferred,"** page 904.

 Take It to the Net

Visit the Web site for online instruction and activities related to each selection in this unit.
www.phschool.com

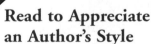

How to Read Literature

Use Strategies for Reading Poetry

If you are used to reading prose, getting accustomed to poetry may take a slight adjustment. The payoff comes when you suddenly gain insight into a poet's ideas. Here are some strategies to help make the shift from prose to poetry:

1. Use your senses.

One way to appreciate a poem more fully is to use all of your senses to place yourself in the situation the poet describes.

- Determine the poem's setting before you try to imagine individual sensations.

- Look for descriptive words that convey a specific physical sensation.

- Be aware of words that appeal to sight, sound, taste, touch, and smell.

2. Paraphrase.

Since the language of a poem can be abstract, it is helpful to rephrase lines to make sure that you understand their meaning.

- Choose words you commonly use when rephrasing what the author is saying.

- Use simple sentences and change the word order if it helps you understand the meaning better.

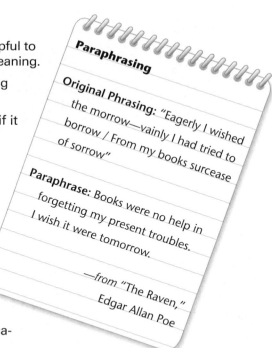

Paraphrasing

Original Phrasing: "Eagerly I wished the morrow—vainly I had tried to borrow / From my books surcease of sorrow"

Paraphrase: Books were no help in forgetting my present troubles. I wish it were tomorrow.

—from "The Raven," Edgar Allan Poe

3. Draw inferences about the speaker.

When you read a poem, you hear the voice of the poem's speaker, or the imaginary voice assumed by the poet. As you read, think about how you might describe the person voicing those particular lines of poetry. Use this knowledge to achieve a deeper understanding of the poem's meaning.

4. Read in sentences.

- Use punctuation, not the ends of lines, as the indication of where to pause when reading a poem.

- Periods, commas, colons, semicolons, and dashes signal where to pause or to stop reading.

As you read the selections in this unit, review the reading strategies and look at the notes in the side columns. Use the suggestions to apply the strategies and interact with the text.

Prepare to Read

I Wandered Lonely as a Cloud

 Take It to the Net

Visit www.phschool.com for interactive activities and instruction related to "I Wandered Lonely as a Cloud," including

- background
- graphic organizers
- literary elements
- reading strategies

Preview

Connecting to the Literature

You probably have moments in your life that you replay in your memory—images to which photographs or videos cannot do justice because they cannot capture your feelings. In this poem, William Wordsworth captures both the images and the feelings connected to a special moment in his life.

Background

Dorothy Wordsworth was William's friend as well as his sister. She kept a journal of their activities, including what they saw as they took walks through England's Lake District. On April 15, 1802, she recorded her impressions after they suddenly saw a field crowded with daffodils. Wordsworth used his sister's comments as inspiration for this poem.

Literary Analysis

Rhyme Scheme

A **rhyme scheme** is a regular pattern of rhyming words that appear at the ends of lines in a poem. You indicate the pattern of a poem's rhymes by using letters of the alphabet, assigning a new letter to each rhyme. The first stanza of "I Wandered Lonely as a Cloud" follows a rhyme scheme of *ababcc*. Look at the first three lines of the stanza:

> I wandered lonely as a cloud (a)
> That floats on high o'er vales and hills, (b)
> When all at once I saw a crowd, (a)

Since *cloud* and *crowd* are rhyming words, lines 1 and 3 are assigned the letter *a*. *Hills* does not rhyme with *cloud*, so line 2 is assigned the letter *b*. As you read the other stanzas, determine whether Wordsworth keeps to his rhyme scheme or if he breaks the pattern he has established.

Connecting Literary Elements

A **simile** is a figure of speech in which *like* or *as* is used to make a comparison between ideas that are basically dissimilar. The title of Wordsworth's poem contains a simile in which the speaker compares himself to a cloud. As with the rhyme scheme in a poem, similes require writers to carefully consider their use of language—assessing both the words that they choose and the impressions that those words make.

Reading Strategy

Using Your Senses

Once you have a basic idea of what is happening in a poem, **using your senses** can give you a greater appreciation of the ideas the poem conveys.

- Pay attention to images that appeal to your senses of sight, smell, sound, taste, and touch.
- Consider the impression each image conveys.

As you read, use a chart like the one shown to note the images that appeal to your senses, and then record how they make you feel.

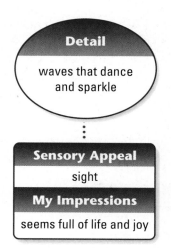

Vocabulary Development

host (hōst) *n.* great number (p. 897)

glee (glē) *n.* joy (p. 898)

pensive (pen′ siv) *adj.* thinking deeply (p. 898)

bliss (blis) *n.* great joy or happiness (p. 898)

I Wandered Lonely

as a Cloud

William Wordsworth

I wandered lonely as a cloud
That floats on high o'er vales[1] and hills,
When all at once I saw a crowd,
A <u>host</u>, of golden daffodils;
5   Beside the lake, beneath the trees,
Fluttering and dancing in the breeze.

Continuous as the stars that shine
And twinkle on the milky way,
They stretched in never-ending line
10   Along the margin of a bay:
Ten thousand saw I at a glance,
Tossing their heads in sprightly dance.

---

1. o'er vales over valleys.

host (hōst) *n.* great number

Reading Check

What was most remarkable about the flowers that the speaker saw?

Integrate Language Skills

Vocabulary Development Lesson

Specialized Vocabulary: Poetic Contractions

Poets sometimes use **poetic contractions**—words in which one or more letters are left out—to sustain a rhythm or rhyme scheme. For example, Wordsworth uses the contraction *o'er*—short for *over*—to maintain the rhythm of line 2.

Identify the meanings of these contractions.

1. 'twill   **2.** 'twasn't   **3.** fore'er

Spelling Strategy

When adding a suffix that begins with a consonant to a word that ends in silent *e*, do not drop the *e*. For example, *pensive* + *-ly* = *pensively*. Add the suffix to each word below.

1. grace + *-ful*   **2.** love + *-ly*   **3.** place + *-ment*

Concept Development: Antonyms

Review the vocabulary list on page 895 and notice Wordsworth's use of the words in the poem. Then, in your notebook, write the word that is the antonym, or the opposite in meaning, of the first word.

1. glee: (a) intelligence, (b) happiness, (c) sorrow
2. pensive: (a) careless, (b) cheerful, (c) thoughtful
3. host: (a) army, (b) small number, (c) innkeeper
4. bliss: (a) intelligence, (b) happiness, (c) misery

Grammar Lesson

Semicolons and Colons

A **semicolon** is used to join independent clauses that are closely related. It is also used to separate independent clauses or items in a series that already contain a number of commas.

A **colon** is used mainly to list items following an independent clause. Look at how the semicolon and the colon are used in the following sentences:

Semicolon:	The field of daffodils appeared unexpectedly; the sight greatly impressed Wordsworth.
Colon:	The flowers moved in ways that seemed almost human: fluttering, nodding, and dancing.

Practice Write these sentences on your paper, adding semicolons or colons wherever necessary.

1. Dorothy Wordsworth was many things a sister, a friend, and an inspiration.
2. She wrote often in her journal her comments are fascinating.
3. She described the field of daffodils vividly many of her details appear in this poem.
4. According to her journal, the daffodils did the following things tossed, reeled, danced, and laughed.
5. He used her journal entries to create his poem it was written just as beautifully.

Writing Application Write two sentences about Wordsworth's poem. Use a semicolon in one sentence and a colon in the other.

W/*G* *Prentice Hall Writing and Grammar Connection: Chapter 29, Section 3*

Writing Lesson

Description of a Natural Scene

Wordsworth uses words to create a vivid portrait of a natural scene. Create your own descriptive word picture in the form of either a few paragraphs or a brief poem. Describe a beautiful natural scene that you have witnessed or seen in photographs.

Prewriting Jot down details that are related to the scene you have chosen. Next, decide on the purpose for your description. Eliminate details that do not fit your purpose and replace them with more precise details.

Drafting Decide whether your description will be a poem or a set of paragraphs. Use your notes to write your first draft.

Revising As you evaluate your writing, circle vague words and replace them with words that are more appealing to the senses. Also, eliminate details that confuse the purpose.

Model: Avoiding Unnecessary Details

Breathless,
I stood on the side of the crater. ~~I wondered what time it was.~~
                                        massive
The sun threw shadows across the crater's ~~large~~ bowl.

> Taking out unnecessary details and adding more precise words adds to the appeal of the word picture.

Prentice Hall Writing and Grammar Connection: Chapter 6, Section 4

Extension Activities

Listening and Speaking Prepare a **visual presentation** about England's Lake District, where Wordsworth grew up. Follow this plan:

- Look for pictures of the region.
- Find connections between the landscape and the imagery that Wordsworth used.
- Practice giving the presentation so that you will feel comfortable speaking and displaying the visuals.

In your presentation, read Wordsworth's poem aloud to the class, and then explain your findings.

Research and Technology Wordsworth is one of the most famous British Romantic poets. With a few classmates, find out about the other Romantic poets, such as John Keats or Samuel Taylor Coleridge. Collect examples of their poetry. Using word-processing software, create an **anthology** of the poems and include an explanation of each choice. [**Group Activity**]

 **Take It to the Net**   www.phschool.com

Go online for an additional research activity using the Internet.

Bernard's Daddy, Raymond Lark, Edward Smith and Company

▲ **Critical Viewing** Explain why you do or do not think this piece of art is an effective illustration for the two poems. **[Evaluate]**

Dream Deferred

Langston Hughes

Harlem

What happens to a dream <u>deferred</u>?

    Does it dry up
    like a raisin in the sun?
5   Or <u>fester</u> like a sore——
    And then run?
    Does it stink like rotten meat?
    Or crust and sugar over——
    like a syrupy sweet?

10   Maybe it just sags
    like a heavy load.

    Or does it explode?

deferred (di furd´) *adj.* put off until a future time

fester (fes´ tər) *v.* form pus

Dreams

Langston Hughes

Hold fast to dreams
For if dreams die
Life is a broken-winged bird
That cannot fly.

5   Hold fast to dreams
For when dreams go
Life is a <u>barren</u> field
Frozen with snow.

barren (bar´ən) *adj.* empty

Langston Hughes

(1902–1967)
Langston Hughes, born in Joplin, Missouri, was the first African American to have a strictly literary career. As a young man, he held a variety of jobs—teacher, ranch hand, farmer, seaman, and night-club cook, among others. He drew on all of these experiences, but even more so on his experience as an African American man, to create his great body of work. "Dream Deferred" and "Dreams" illustrate his ability to express the spirit of black America.

Review and Assess

Thinking About the Selections

1. **Respond:** Which poem affected you more? Why?

2. **(a) Recall:** What is the first question asked in "Dream Deferred"? **(b) Infer:** How is the question answered? **(c) Speculate:** Why does Hughes use six questions and only one statement in the poem?

3. **(a) Compare and Contrast:** How does the last line of "Dream Deferred" contrast with the rest of the poem? **(b) Draw Conclusions:** What is the effect of this contrast?

4. **(a) Recall:** To what two things does the speaker in "Dreams" compare life? **(b) Interpret:** Restate in your own words the advice that "Dreams" offers.

5. **Apply:** How might you apply the advice Hughes gives in "Dreams" to your own life?

6. **(a) Assess:** What might your life be like if you were prevented from pursuing your dreams or goals? **(b) Extend:** Which personal qualities are needed to hold on to dreams in adversity?

The Eagle

Alfred, Lord Tennyson

He clasps the crag[1] with crooked hands;
Close to the sun in lonely lands,
Ring'd with the <u>azure</u> world, he stands.

azure (azh´ ər) *adj.* blue

The wrinkled sea beneath him crawls;
5   He watches from his mountain walls,
And like a thunderbolt he falls.

---

1. crag (krag) *n.* steep, rugged rock that juts out from a rock mass.

Review and Assess

Thinking About the Selection

1. **Respond:** How did you feel as you read "The Eagle"? Why?

2. **(a) Recall:** When the poem opens, where is the eagle?
   (b) Interpret: Why does Tennyson place the eagle in that setting?

3. **(a) Interpret:** What is meant by the words "close to the sun"?
   (b) Assess: What effect does this phrase have on your response to the eagle?

4. **(a) Recall:** What is the eagle doing? **(b) Make a Judgment:** Is "falls" the right word for the action of the eagle in line 6? Explain.

5. **(a) Compare and Contrast:** How is the first stanza different from the second? **(b) Evaluate:** Why do you think Tennyson breaks such a short poem into two stanzas?

6. **(a) Assess:** Which words would you use to describe an eagle? **(b) Extend:** Why do you think an eagle is the national emblem of the United States?

Alfred, Lord Tennyson

(1809–1892)

The most popular of British poets during his lifetime, Alfred, Lord Tennyson rose from the quiet of humble beginnings to the glory of the position of poet laureate of England. Although he was enthralled by the technological advances of the Victorian era, Tennyson remained a poet of nature, bringing both imagination and feeling to the landscape and its inhabitants.

"Hope"
is the thing with
feathers—

Emily Dickinson

"Hope" is the thing with feathers—
That perches in the soul—
And sings the tune without the words—
And never stops—at all—

5   And sweetest—in the Gale[1]—is heard—
And <u>sore</u> must be the storm—
That could <u>abash</u> the little Bird
That kept so many warm—

I've heard it in the chillest land—
10 And on the strangest Sea—
Yet, never, in Extremity,
It asked a crumb—of Me.

---

1. **gale** (gāl) *n.* strong wind.

sore (sôr) *adj.* fierce; cruel

abash (ə bash´) *v.* embarrass

Emily Dickinson

(1830–1886)
Shy, solitary, and brilliant, Emily Dickinson led a life filled with loneliness in Amherst, Massachusetts. Yet, despite her quiet exterior, an inner life continually raged, enabling her to produce at least 1,775 poems.

Dickinson is known for her deceptively simple subjects from nature—flies buzzing at the moment of human death, birds coming down a walk. She wrote most frequently about death, love, and some of her religious beliefs. Whatever her subject, however, Dickinson's treatment was imaginative, complex, and thought-provoking.

Review and Assess

Thinking About the Selection

1. **Respond:** How do your views about hope compare with those expressed in Dickinson's poem?
2. **(a) Recall:** What is hope compared to in the poem?
   (b) Analyze: What do the two items have in common?
3. **(a) Recall:** According to the speaker, what does hope do?
   (b) Interpret: Why is it significant that hope sings a tune without words?
4. **(a) Infer:** When does hope sing the "sweetest" tune?
   (b) Interpret: Why would it sing so well at this time?
5. **Extend:** In what kinds of situations might hope keep people "warm"?

Review and Assess

Literary Analysis

Figurative Language

1. List the similes found in "Dream Deferred." Which similes are the most effective? Why?
2. (a) Change the two metaphors in "Dreams" into similes by adding *like*. (b) Does this alter the effect or meaning of the poem? Explain.
3. Using a chart like the one shown, list the **figurative language** in "'Hope' is the thing with feathers—" and "The Eagle." Then, write the comparison being made for each.

Poem		

→

Simile	Metaphor	Personification

Comparing Literary Works

4. Using a chart like the one shown, compare the **connotations** of the figurative language found in each of the poems.

Poem	Figurative Language

→

Connotation

5. (a) Which poem connotes, or suggests, a feeling of despair? How?
   (b) Which poem connotes optimism and perseverance? How?

Reading Strategy

Paraphrasing

6. (a) **Paraphrase** the last stanza of "Dreams." (b) According to the poem, how would your life feel if it were empty of dreams?
7. Paraphrase the last stanza of "'Hope' is the thing with feathers—". Be sure to supply a noun to take the place of the pronoun *it*.

Extend Understanding

8. **Social Studies Connection:** How might civil rights leaders have used any of these poems in support of their cause?

Prepare to Read

Blackberry Eating ◆ Memory ◆ Eulogy for a Hermit Crab ◆ Meciendo ◆ Woman's Work

 Take It to the Net

Visit www.phschool.com
for interactive activities
and instruction related to
the selections, including

- background
- graphic organizers
- literary elements
- reading strategies

Preview

Connecting to the Literature

With a little thought, you can often find deeper meaning in routine events and observations. For example, gazing upon the ocean might make you think of the immensity and timelessness of nature. As these poems illustrate, one of the great qualities of poetry is that it can lead you toward such insights.

Background

One of the poems in this group is about a hermit crab, an animal that carries around an abandoned shell to cover its soft, unprotected abdomen. As a hermit crab grows, it must continually find larger shells—a dilemma that causes much competition among hermit crabs.

Literary Analysis

Imagery

Imagery is the descriptive language that paints pictures in readers' minds. An image may appeal to any of the five senses: sight, sound, taste, smell, or touch. The following example from Margaret Walker's "Memory" uses imagery that appeals to the senses of touch and sight:

> I can remember wind-swept streets of cities
> on cold and blustery nights, on rainy days;

As you read, use a chart like this one to note memorable images and to analyze the senses to which each image appeals.

Image: fat, overripe, icy, black blackberries	
Sight	✓
Sound	
Taste	✓
Smell	
Touch	✓

Comparing Literary Works

Two poets can use the same word to create different images, or they can describe similar images in different ways. For example, one poet uses *icy* to describe juicy blackberries, but another uses *icy* to describe the painful, sharp wind. Similarly, one poet describes the movement of the sea as *spinning*, whereas another describes it as *rocking*. Compare the imagery in each of the following poems and determine the effect each has on you as a reader.

Reading Strategy

Picturing the Imagery

To appreciate the ideas that are being presented in a poem, form a mental **picture** of **each image.**

- Pay attention to descriptive words in the poem, and consider each word's descriptive meaning.
- Using your imagination, try to place yourself in the poem and experience what the speaker experiences at that moment.
- If possible, relate the image in the poem to something that you yourself have experienced.

As you relate to each image, remember to not only *see* but also *hear*, *feel*, *taste*, and *smell* what the poet describes.

Vocabulary Development

unbidden (un bid´ 'n) *adj.* without being asked; uninvited (p. 914)

sinister (sin´ is tər) *adj.* threatening harm; ominous (p. 915)

meticulously (mə tik´ yōō ləs lē) *adv.* very carefully; scrupulously (p. 916)

divine (də vīn´) *adj.* holy; sacred (p. 919)

primed (prīmd) *v.* prepared (p. 920)

BLACKBERRY EATING

Galway Kinnell

I love to go out in late September
among the fat, overripe, icy, black blackberries
to eat blackberries for breakfast,
the stalks very prickly, a penalty
5 they earn for knowing the black art
of blackberry-making; and as I stand among them
lifting the stalks to my mouth, the ripest berries
fall almost <u>unbidden</u> to my tongue,
as words sometimes do, certain peculiar words
10 like *strengths* or *squinched*,
many-lettered, one-syllabled lumps,
which I squeeze, squinch open, and splurge well
in the silent, startled, icy, black language
of blackberry-eating in late September.

unbidden (un bid´ 'n) *adj.*
without being asked;
uninvited

Review and Assess

Thinking About the Selection

1. **Respond:** Which description in this poem is most appealing?
2. **(a) Recall:** Identify two words that the speaker compares to blackberries. **(b) Compare and Contrast:** What do these words have in common with blackberries?
   c) **Analyze:** What special meaning does eating blackberries have for the speaker?
3. **Make a Judgment:** Which aspect of writing does "Blackberry Eating" capture in lines 9–13? Explain.
4. **Speculate:** Do you think the speaker of this poem enjoys writing poetry? Why or why not?

Galway Kinnell

(b. 1927)

Galway Kinnell is an American poet whose writing addresses the themes of the inevitability of death, selfhood, and the power of nature. He has taught at various universities and has been active in the civil rights movement.

Memory

Margaret Walker

I can remember wind-swept streets of cities
on cold and blustery nights, on rainy days;
heads under shabby felts[1] and parasols
and shoulders hunched against a sharp concern;
5   seeing hurt bewilderment on poor faces,
smelling a deep and <u>sinister</u> unrest
these brooding people cautiously caress;
hearing ghostly marching on pavement stones
and closing fast around their squares of hate.
10 I can remember seeing them alone,
at work, and in their tenements at home.
I can remember hearing all they said:
their muttering protests, their whispered oaths,
and all that spells their living in distress.

sinister (sin´ is tər) *adj.*
threatening harm; ominous

---

1. **felts** felt hats.

Review and Assess

Thinking About the Selection

1. **Respond:** What thoughts and feelings did "Memory" evoke in you? Explain.

2. **(a) Recall:** Describe the setting and weather in Walker's poem. **(b) Interpret:** What effect does the weather have on your understanding of the lives of the people in "Memory"?

3. **Interpret:** Explain how "Memory" can be seen as a criticism of an injustice in society.

4. **Speculate:** What do you think is a possible result of a life lived in distress? Explain.

Margaret Walker

(1915–1998)
A poet and novelist, Margaret Walker is considered one of the legends of African American literature. She is best known for *Jubilee* (1966), her narrative on the life of the daughter of a slave and a slave owner. As a writer, Walker focused on the experiences and hardships of African Americans.

Woman's Work

Julia Alvarez

Who says a woman's work isn't high art?
She'd challenge as she scrubbed the bathroom tiles.
Keep house as if the address were your heart.

We'd clean the whole upstairs before we'd start
5   downstairs. I'd sigh, hearing my friends outside.
Doing her woman's work was a hard art

to practice when the summer sun would bar
the floor I swept till she was satisfied.
She kept me prisoner in her housebound heart.

10 She'd shine the tines of forks, the wheels of carts,
cut lacy lattices[1] for all her pies.
Her woman's work was nothing less than art.

And, I, her masterpiece since I was smart,
was <u>primed</u>, praised, polished, scolded and advised
15 to keep a house much better than my heart.

I did not want to be her counterpart!
I struck out . . . but became my mother's child:
a woman working at home on her art,
housekeeping paper as if it were her heart.

---

1. **lattices** (lat´ is əz) narrow strips of pastry laid on the pie in a crisscross pattern.

Literary Analysis
Imagery Compare the image of the way the mother treats her daughter to the image of the way she treats her house.

primed (prīmd) v. prepared

Review and Assess

Thinking About the Selection

1. **Respond:** How do you feel about the mother in this poem? Why?
2. **(a) Recall:** What ambition does the mother have for her daughter? **(b) Analyze:** Why does the speaker reject that ambition? **(c) Infer:** How can you tell that the daughter both admires and resents her mother?
3. **Compare and Contrast:** How does the final stanza suggest that the daughter is similar to her mother, after all?
4. **Assess:** Do you think housekeeping can be considered an art? Explain.

Julia Alvarez

(b. 1950)

Julia Alvarez moved from the Dominican Republic to New York City with her family when she was ten years old. She says that the complexity of the many cultures in the United States is "part of what makes us rich and makes us strong."

Review and Assess

Literary Analysis

Imagery

1. Which **images** in "Memory" appeal to your sense of hearing?
2. Which images in "Eulogy for a Hermit Crab" reveal the most about the crab's world?
3. An image that appeals to the sense of touch or movement runs throughout "Meciendo." Name that image and explain its appeal.

Comparing Literary Works

4. (a) Use a chart like the one shown to identify words in "Blackberry Eating" and "Memory" that convey emotion.
   (b) Which poem conveys a feeling of contentment?

5. How do the images of the ocean in "Meciendo" and "Eulogy for a Hermit Crab" differ?

Reading Strategy

Picturing the Imagery

6. "Blackberry Eating" contains the adjectives *icy* and *prickly*, which seem unpleasant. Why, then, is picturing the images in this poem a pleasant experience?
7. Using a chart like the one below, name three images from the poems in this section that appeal to your senses, and explain how you picture the imagery.

Image	Sense Used	How I Picture It

Extend Understanding

8. **Science Connection:** (a) What can you learn about marine biology by reading "Eulogy for a Hermit Crab"? (b) What does the poem achieve that a biology book could not?

Quick Review

Imagery is the descriptive language used to create mental pictures by appealing to sight, sound, taste, touch, or smell.

To **picture the imagery,** imagine experiencing what the speaker experiences at that moment, or relate the image in the poem to something that you yourself have experienced.

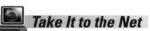 **Take It to the Net**

www.phschool.com
Take the interactive self-test online to check your understanding of the selections.

Integrate Language Skills

Vocabulary Development Lesson

Word Analysis: Latin Root -prim-

The word *prime* comes from the Latin root *-prim-*, which means "first in time or in importance." In "Woman's Work," *primed* means "coached beforehand." Using your knowledge of *-prim-*, define each of these words or phrases:

1. prime witness
2. primitive
3. primary election
4. primary color

Spelling Strategy

Before adding an ending that begins with a vowel to a word that ends in silent *e*, drop the *e*: *prime* + *-ed* = *primed*. Write the new word formed by adding the suffix to each word below. Then, use each new word in a sentence.

1. dive + *-ing*   2. revise + *-ing*   3. confide + *-ence*

Concept Development: Synonyms

In your notebook, write the letter of the word that means about the same as the first word. To help you, review the vocabulary list on page 913.

1. unbidden: (a) uninvited, (b) unusual, (c) ordered
2. sinister: (a) innocent, (b) evil, (c) sisterly
3. primed: (a) allowed, (b) coached, (c) followed
4. meticulously: (a) carefully, (b) quickly, (c) sloppily
5. divine: (a) godlike, (b) congested, (c) divided

Grammar Lesson

Ellipsis Points

Ellipsis points (. . .) are punctuation marks that are used to show that something has not been expressed. Usually, ellipsis points indicate one of the following situations:

- Words have been left out of a quotation
- A series continues beyond the items mentioned
- Time passes or action occurs in a narrative

This example, from the final stanza of "Woman's Work," indicates the passage of time or action:

> **Example:**   I struck out . . . but became my mother's child.

Practice Choose the blank that marks the most reasonable place to insert ellipsis points.

1. Her memories of the city ____ are clear, vivid ____ and poignant.
2. Walker refers to ____ "wind-swept streets of cities ____ on rainy days."
3. The people ____ who live in "Memory" face ____ conditions that are windy, cold, ____ and generally unpleasant.
4. The speaker remembers ____ seeing them "alone, at work, and ____ at home."
5. They keep their discontent to ____ themselves ____ but will they ____ do so forever?

Writing Application Write about one of the poems in this group, and illustrate at least two of the ellipsis rules in your sentences.

W̶G Prentice Hall Writing and Grammar Connection: Chapter 29

Writing Lesson

Letter About a Memorable Moment

These five poems use imagery to describe memorable moments. Choose a moment that was memorable for you, whether it occurred in real life or in a picture or a movie. Write a letter about that remarkable time and place, using imagery to capture your experience.

Prewriting   Once you have chosen an important moment, list sensory details that convey the main impression, such as joy, fear, pride, or awe. Gather details to show how the place or event appealed to your senses of sight, sound, taste, touch, and smell.

Drafting   Use your prewriting notes to draft your letter, focusing on the main impression you want to convey. Organize your details in order of time, space, or importance.

Revising   As you reread your letter, ask yourself whether each sensory detail contributes to the main impression. Add or change details to strengthen the main impression.

Model: Revising to Strengthen the Main Impression

teemed with life

Every inch of the rain forest ~~was alive.~~ Trees, brushes, and

jostled for position

vines ~~were everywhere.~~

> These revisions build the image of a vibrant and living landscape.

 Prentice Hall Writing and Grammar Connection: Chapter 6, Section 4

Extension Activities

Listening and Speaking   In her poem, Rogers offers a description of the hermit crab that is both beautiful and highly accurate. Plan a visual **presentation of artwork** that combines the same qualities.

- Look for art that you consider to be both beautiful and true to life.
- Make brief notes about each picture.
- Practice making your presentation while displaying your pictures.

Present your findings to your class and ask them for feedback on your art choices.

Research and Technology   In a small group, prepare a **research report** about how women's roles have changed over the past several decades. You might use "Woman's Work" to help you generate questions for research. Use library resources, including the Internet, and personal interviews to help you gather facts and information. **[Group Activity]**

 Take It to the Net   www.phschool.com
Go online for an additional research activity using the Internet.

Prepare to Read

Uphill ◆ Summer ◆ Ecclesiastes 3:1–8 ◆ The Bells

Preview

Connecting to the Literature

Sweating through an August afternoon, you realize that the summer heat will soon change to the chill of autumn. You see parents and children enjoying the outdoors and realize that toddlers grow to adulthood. Nature and life have predictable cycles and stages. The following poems explore these cycles.

Background

Throughout the ages, poets have explored the stages and patterns of life. Scientists, too, describe life as comprising cycles and seasons, stages and patterns. Advances in medicine may extend life expectancy, but medicine has not been able to alter the basic cycle of life in which we are born, grow, and inevitably die.

Literary Analysis

Lyric Poetry and Sound Devices

These poems are examples of **lyric poetry**—verse that expresses the observations and feelings of a single speaker through a highly musical style. That style comes from various **sound devices,** including the following:

- **Rhythm:** the pattern of beats or stresses in language
- **Alliteration:** the repetition of initial consonant sounds
- **Rhyme:** the repetition of sounds at the ends of words
- **Onomatopoeia:** the use of words, like *buzz* and *whirr,* that imitate the sounds that they name

As you read, notice the musical sounds in each poem.

Comparing Literary Works

As these poems suggest, life is filled with cycles and stages. Whether addressing life milestones, the journey from birth to death, or the natural progression of seasons, each poem reveals patterns that apply to life. As you move from one poem to the next, compare and contrast the patterns and cycles presented in each to determine whether each presents a hopeful or a despairing message.

Reading Strategy

Listening to Poetic Sounds

To appreciate the musical quality of lyric poems, read them aloud and **listen to the sound** of the lines. Follow these points to help you:

- Read the poem aloud to yourself or to a partner. If you wish, record your reading.
- Listen for the musical sounds created by the words.
- Consider the mood or feeling created by the sounds.

Use a chart like the one shown to help you analyze how the sound reinforces the poem's meaning.

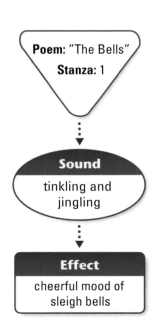

Vocabulary Development

wayfarers (wā′ fer′ ərz) *n.* travelers (p. 926)

voluminously (və lōōm′ ə nəs lē) *adv.* fully; in great volume (p. 932)

palpitating (pal′ pə tāt′ iŋ) *adj.* beating rapidly; throbbing (p. 933)

monotone (män′ ə tōn′) *n.* uninterrupted repetition of the same tone (p. 933)

pæan (pē′ ən) *n.* song of joy or triumph (p. 933)

II

15　Hear the mellow wedding bells,
Golden bells!
What a world of happiness their harmony foretells!
Through the balmy air of night
How they ring out their delight!
20　From the molten golden-notes,
And all in tune,
What a liquid ditty[4] floats
To the turtle-dove[5] that listens, while she gloats
On the moon!
25　Oh, from out the sounding cells,
What a gush of euphony[6] <u>voluminously</u> wells!
How it swells!
How it dwells
On the future! how it tells
30　Of the rapture that impels
To the swinging and the ringing
Of the bells, bells, bells,
Of the bells, bells, bells, bells
Bells, bells, bells—
35　To the rhyming and the chiming of the bells!

III

Hear the loud alarum[7] bells!
Brazen[8] bells!
What a tale of terror now their turbulency tells!
In the startled ear of night
40　How they scream out their affright!
Too much horrified to speak,
They can only shriek, shriek,
Out of tune,
In a clamorous appealing to the mercy of the fire,
45　In a mad expostulation[9] with the deaf and frantic fire
Leaping higher, higher, higher,
With a desperate desire,
And a resolute endeavor
Now—now to sit or never,
50　By the side of the pale-faced moon.
Oh, the bells, bells, bells!
What a tale their terror tells

voluminously (və lōōm′ ə nəs lē) *adv.* fully; in great volume

Reading Strategy
Listening to Poetic Sounds What do the sounds in these lines suggest? Explain.

---

4. **ditty** (dit′ ē) *n.* song.
5. **turtle-dove** The turtle-dove is traditionally associated with love.
6. **euphony** (yōō′ fə nē) *n.* pleasing sound.
7. **alarum** (ə ler′ əm) *adj.* sudden call to arms; alarm.
8. **brazen** (brā′ zən) *adj.* made of brass; having the sound of brass.
9. **expostulation** (eks päs′ chə lā′ shən) *n.* objection; complaint.

Of Despair!
How they clang, and clash, and roar!
55   What a horror they outpour
On the bosom of the <u>palpitating</u> air!
Yet the ear it fully knows,
By the twanging
And the clanging,
60   How the danger ebbs and flows;
Yet the ear distinctly tells,
In the jangling,
And the wrangling,
How the danger sinks and swells,
65 By the sinking or the swelling in the anger of the bells—
Of the bells—
Of the bells, bells, bells, bells,
Bells, bells, bells—
In the clamor and the clangor of the bells!

IV
70   Hear the tolling of the bells—
Iron bells!
What a world of solemn thought their monody[10] compels!
In the silence of the night,
How we shiver with affright
75   At the melancholy menace of their tone!
For every sound that floats
From the rust within their throats
Is a groan.
And the people—ah, the people—
80   They that dwell up in the steeple,
All alone,
And who tolling, tolling, tolling,
In that muffled <u>monotone</u>,
Feel a glory in so rolling
85   On the human heart a stone—
They are neither man nor woman—
They are neither brute nor human—
They are Ghouls:[11]
And their king it is who tolls;
90   And he rolls, rolls, rolls,
Rolls
A <u>pæan</u> from the bells!
And his merry bosom swells
With the pæan of the bells!

---

10. monody (män´ ə dē) *n.* poem of mourning; a steady sound; music in which one
instrument or voice is dominant.
11. Ghouls (goolz) *n.* evil spirits that rob graves.

palpitating (pal´ pə tāt´ iŋ)
adj. beating rapidly;
throbbing

Literary Analysis
**Lyric Poetry and Sound
Devices** What effect is
created by the sound
devices in lines 73–78?

monotone (män´ ə tōn´) *n.*
uninterrupted repetition
of the same tone

pæan (pē´ ən) *n.* song of
joy or triumph

☑ **Reading Check**

What kind of story do the
wedding bells tell?

Integrate Language Skills

Vocabulary Development Lesson

Word Analysis: Greek Prefix *mono-*

The word *monotone* contains the Greek prefix *mono-*, which means "one." You might guess, therefore, that *monotone* means "one tone," which is close to the actual meaning, "uninterrupted repetition of the same tone."

Match each word containing the prefix *mono-* with its definition on the right.

1. monorail
2. monopoly
3. monochromatic
4. monolith

  a. exclusive control of the selling of something
  b. single large block of stone
  c. railway with a single rail as a track
  d. having or being of one color

Fluency: Clarify Word Meaning

Copy the paragraph below, completing it with words from the vocabulary list on page 925.

Commuters, ___?___ heading home from work, ___?___ packed the railroad platform. With their hearts ___?___, they listened to an announcement delivered in a ___?___. When the voice proclaimed that their train was about to arrive, they sang a ___?___ as one!

Spelling Strategy

A prefix attached to a word does not affect the spelling of the original word. For example, *mono-* + *tone* = *monotone*. Rewrite each word below by adding the given prefix. Then, use each new word in a sentence.

1. *un-* + necessary
2. *dis-* + satisfied
3. *re-* + construct
4. *pre* + determine

Grammar Lesson

End Punctuation

End punctuation is the period, question mark, or exclamation mark at the end of a sentence. A **period** indicates the end of a sentence or an abbreviation. A **question mark** follows a word, phrase, or sentence that asks a question. An **exclamation mark** indicates strong feeling or emotion, including surprise. In the following examples, notice how the end punctuation affects the meaning of these sentences:

Statement:	The road winds uphill.
Question:	The road winds uphill?
Exclamation:	The road winds uphill!

Practice Write each item below, using the appropriate end punctuation for the emotion indicated in parentheses.

1. I will meet other wayfarers at night (anxiety)
2. You like hot days (disbelief)
3. Please, listen to the bells (anger)
4. The time has come to dig up what we have planted (informative)
5. I hear the sound of the bells (excitement)

Writing Application Write five sentences that reflect on one of the poems you have just read. Use each type of end punctuation at least once.

W̶G Prentice Hall Writing and Grammar Connection: Chapter 29, Section 1

Writing Lesson

Rap Song

Like lyric poems, rap songs are musical expressions of a speaker's thoughts and feelings. Write a rap song that conveys your feelings about a season, a stage of life, or another topic that interests you.

Prewriting   Choose your topic and make preliminary notes about it. Decide on your message and your key ideas. Then, think about which words or lines you could repeat to help drive home your points.

Drafting   As you draft your rap song, focus on establishing a strong rhythm. Use rhymes at the ends of lines to create a musical effect. Also, consider including a refrain, a line or group of lines that is repeated throughout the song.

Revising   Read your rap song aloud to check its rhythm. Make sure that your use of repetition highlights your main ideas. Make any revisions needed to improve the sound of the song.

Model: Analyzing Word Choice for Use of Repetition

abound

Fall—everywhere I look I find leaves ~~all over~~!

falling

Yellow, red, orange, brown are ~~going~~ to the ground.

> The rhyming words *abound* and *ground* and the repeated use of *fall* improve the sound of the song.

WG Prentice Hall Writing and Grammar Connection: Chapter 6, Connected Assignment

Extension Activities

Listening and Speaking Prepare and present a **dramatic reading** of "The Bells" to capture the poem's musical quality.

- Read the poem aloud to yourself.
- Make notes about which words to emphasize and when to change your reading pace.
- Practice your reading, recording yourself, if possible, so that you can hear and fix problem spots.

After you present your dramatic reading, ask your listeners what they liked best about it.

Research and Technology In a group, create an **illustrated version** of the poem "Summer." Look on the Internet for images, or use photographs and original artwork that you prepare. As you conduct your visual research, try to capture the mood of the poem. Combine the poem with the art and share it with classmates. **[Group Activity]**

 **Take It to the Net**   www.phschool.com

Go online for an additional research activity using the Internet.

The Raven

Edgar Allan Poe

Once upon a midnight dreary, while I pondered, weak and weary,
Over many a <u>quaint</u> and curious volume of forgotten lore,[1]
While I nodded, nearly napping, suddenly there came a tapping,
As of someone gently rapping, rapping at my chamber door.
5   "'Tis some visitor," I muttered, "tapping at my chamber door—
        Only this, and nothing more."

Ah, distinctly I remember it was in the bleak December,
And each separate dying ember wrought its ghost upon the floor.
Eagerly I wished the morrow—vainly I had tried to borrow
10   From my books surcease[2] of sorrow—sorrow for the lost Lenore—
For the rare and radiant maiden whom the angels name Lenore—
        Nameless here for evermore.

And the silken, sad, uncertain rustling of each purple curtain
Thrilled me—filled me with fantastic terrors never felt before;
15   So that now, to still the beating of my heart, I stood repeating
"'Tis some visitor entreating entrance at my chamber door—
Some late visitor entreating entrance at my chamber door—
        This it is and nothing more."

Presently my soul grew stronger; hesitating then no longer,
20   "Sir," said I, "or Madam, truly your forgiveness I implore;
But the fact is I was napping, and so gently you came rapping,
And so faintly you came tapping, tapping at my chamber door,
That I scarce was sure I heard you"—here I opened wide the door—
        Darkness there, and nothing more.

25   Deep into that darkness peering, long I stood there wondering,
        fearing,
Doubting, dreaming dreams no mortal ever dared to dream before;
But the silence was unbroken, and the darkness gave no token,[3]
And the only word there spoken was the whispered word, "Lenore!"
This *I* whispered, and an echo murmured back the word, "Lenore!"
30   Merely this, and nothing more.

---

1. **quaint . . . lore** strange book of ancient learning.
2. **surcease** (sʉr sēs´) *n.* end.
3. **token** (tō´ kən) *n.* sign.

quaint (kwānt) *adj.*
strange; unusual

Literary Analysis
Narrative and Dramatic Poetry Which background details does the speaker provide in the first two stanzas to set the scene for the story?

Reading Strategy
Drawing Inferences About the Speaker Which words or actions by the speaker show that he is getting more and more nervous?

Then into the chamber turning, all my soul within me burning,
Soon I heard again a tapping somewhat louder than before.
"Surely," said I, "surely that is something at my window lattice;[4]
Let me see, then, what thereat[5] is, and this mystery explore—
35 Let my heart be still a moment and this mystery explore—
    'Tis the wind, and nothing more!"

Open here I flung the shutter, when, with many a flirt[6] and flutter,
In there stepped a stately raven of the saintly days of yore;
Not the least obeisance[7] made he; not an instant stopped or
    stayed he;
40 But, with mien[8] of lord or lady, perched above my chamber door—
Perched upon a bust of Pallas[9] just above my chamber door—
    Perched, and sat, and nothing more.

Then this ebony bird beguiling my sad fancy[10] into smiling,
By the grave and stern decorum of the countenance[11] it wore,
45 "Though thy crest be shorn and shaven, thou," I said, "art sure
    no craven,[12]
Ghastly grim and ancient raven wandering from the Nightly shore—
Tell me what thy lordly name is on the Night's Plutonian[13] shore!"
    Quoth[14] the raven, "Nevermore."

Much I marveled this ungainly fowl to hear discourse so plainly,
50 Though its answer little meaning—little relevancy bore;
For we cannot help agreeing that no sublunary[15] being
Ever yet was blessed with seeing bird above his chamber door—
Bird or beast upon the sculptured bust above his chamber door,
    With such name as "Nevermore."

55 But the raven, sitting lonely on the placid bust, spoke only
That one word, as if his soul in that one word he did outpour.
Nothing farther then he uttered—not a feather then he fluttered—
Till I scarcely more than muttered, "Other friends have flown before—
On the morrow *he* will leave me, as my hopes have flown before."
60   Quoth the raven, "Nevermore."

Literary Analysis
Narrative and Dramatic Poetry Which elements of a story plot are evident in the first eight stanzas of the poem?

---

4. lattice (lat´ is) *n.* framework of wood or metal.
5. thereat (*th*er at´) *adv.* there.
6. flirt (flurt) *n.* quick, uneven movement.
7. obeisance (ō bā´ səns) *n.* bow or another sign of respect.
8. mien (mēn) *n.* manner.
9. bust of Pallas (pal´ əs) sculpture of the head and shoulders of Pallas Athena (ə thē´ nə), the ancient Greek goddess of wisdom.
10. fancy (fan´ sē) *n.* imagination.
11. countenance (koun´ tə nəns) *n.* facial appearance.
12. craven (krā´ vən) *n.* coward (usually an adjective).
13. Plutonian (plⁿ tō´ nē ən) *adj.* like the underworld, ruled over by the ancient Roman god Pluto.
14. quoth (kwōth) *v.* said.
15. sublunary (sub lōōn´ ər ē) *adj.* earthly.

**Reading Check**

What is tapping at the speaker's chamber door?

Wondering at the stillness broken by reply so aptly spoken,
"Doubtless," said I, "what it utters is its only stock and store,
Caught from some unhappy master whom unmerciful Disaster
Followed fast and followed faster—so, when Hope he would adjure,[16]
65 Stern Despair returned, instead of the sweet Hope he dared adjure—
    That sad answer, 'Nevermore.'"

But the raven still beguiling all my sad soul into smiling,
Straight I wheeled a cushioned seat in front of bird, and bust, and
    door;
Then upon the velvet sinking, I betook myself to linking
70 Fancy unto fancy, thinking what this ominous bird of yore—
What this grim, ungainly, ghastly, gaunt, and ominous bird of yore
    Meant in croaking "Nevermore."

This I sat engaged in guessing, but no syllable expressing
To the fowl whose fiery eyes now burned into my bosom's core;
75 This and more I sat divining,[17] with my head at ease reclining
On the cushion's velvet lining that the lamplight gloated o'er,
But whose velvet violet lining with the lamplight gloating o'er,
    She shall press, ah, nevermore!

Then, methought, the air grew denser, perfumed from an unseen
    censer[18]
80 Swung by angels whose faint footfalls tinkled on the tufted floor.
"Wretch," I cried, "thy God hath lent thee—by these angels he hath
    sent thee
Respite—respite and Nepenthe[19] from thy memories of Lenore!
Let me quaff[20] this kind Nepenthe and forget this lost Lenore!"
    Quoth the raven, "Nevermore."

85 "Prophet!" said I, "thing of evil!—prophet still, if bird or devil!—
Whether Tempter[21] sent, or whether tempest tossed thee here
    ashore,
Desolate, yet all undaunted, on this desert land enchanted—
On this home by Horror haunted—tell me truly, I implore—
Is there—is there balm in Gilead?[22]—tell me—tell me, I implore!"
90   Quoth the raven, "Nevermore."

"Prophet!" said I, "thing of evil!—prophet still, if bird or devil!
By that Heaven that bends above us—by that God we both adore—

Reading Strategy
Drawing Inferences About the Speaker What does the speaker's action in line 68 suggest about his state of mind?

beguiling (bi gīl´ iŋ) *adj.* tricking; charming

respite (res´ pit) *n.* rest; relief

desolate (des´ ə lit) *adj.* deserted

---

16. **adjure** (ə joor´) *v.* appeal to.
17. **divining** (də vīn´ iŋ) *v.* guessing.
18. **censer** (sen´ sər) *n.* container for burning incense.
19. **Nepenthe** (ni pen´ thē) *n.* drug used in ancient times to cause forgetfulness of sorrow.
20. **quaff** (kwäf) *v.* drink.
21. **Tempter** devil.
22. **balm** (bäm) **in Gilead** (gil´ ē əd) cure for suffering; the Bible refers to a medicinal ointment, or balm, made in a region called Gilead.

Tell this soul with sorrow laden if, within the distant Aidenn,[23]
It shall clasp a sainted maiden whom the angels name Lenore—
95 Clasp a rare and radiant maiden whom the angels name Lenore."
    Quoth the raven, "Nevermore."

"Be that word our sign of parting, bird or fiend!" I shrieked, upstarting—
"Get thee back into the tempest and the Night's Plutonian shore!
Leave no black plume as a token of that lie thy soul hath spoken!
100 Leave my loneliness unbroken!—quit the bust above my door!
Take thy beak from out my heart, and take thy form from off my door!"
    Quoth the raven, "Nevermore."

And the raven, never flitting, still is sitting, still is sitting
On the <u>pallid</u> bust of Pallas just above my chamber door;
105 And his eyes have all the seeming of a demon that is dreaming,
And the lamplight o'er him streaming throws his shadow on the floor;
And my soul from out that shadow that lies floating on the floor
    Shall be lifted—nevermore!

pallid (pal´ id) *adj.* pale

---

23. **Aidenn** name meant to suggest Eden or paradise.

Review and Assess

Thinking About the Selection

1. **Respond:** How do you feel about the poem's speaker? Why?
2. **(a) Recall:** Who is Lenore and what has happened to her?
   (b) Infer: What can you infer about the speaker's relationship with Lenore? Explain.
3. **(a) Recall:** Which two adjectives does the speaker use to describe his mood at the beginning of the poem? **(b) Draw Conclusions:** Which adjectives would you use to describe the speaker's mood at the end of the poem? Explain. **(c) Analyze Cause and Effect:** What has caused the speaker's mood to change?
4. **(a) Recall:** What one word does the Raven speak? **(b) Draw Conclusions:** Do you think the raven is merely repeating a sound, or is it responding to each of the narrator's questions?
5. **(a) Connect:** Describe how your impression of the raven changes as the poem progresses. **(b) Analyzing Cause and Effect:** What causes your impression to change?
6. **Evaluate:** Poe considered having a parrot repeat the word "Nevermore." Would the poem have been as effective if Poe had used a parrot instead of a raven? Explain.

Edgar Allan Poe

(1809–1849)

Although he is re-membered mostly for his eerie short stories, Edgar Allan Poe was also a gifted poet. The haunting mood of "The Raven," his best-known poem, reflects the impact of the many misfortunes that Poe experienced during his brief, tragic life. As a young boy, Poe lost both of his parents and was taken in by a wealthy Virginia merchant, John Allan, but their relationship was often stormy.

During his literary career, Poe published numerous short stories and poems but never achieved financial success as a writer. Despite his financial struggles, Poe experienced a period of happiness following his marriage to Virginia Clemm in 1835. This happiness was shattered, however, by his wife's death in 1847. (For more on Edgar Allan Poe, see pp. 12 and 934.)

Integrate Language Skills

Vocabulary Development Lesson

Word Analysis: Latin Root -sol-

The Latin root -sol- means "alone." This root contributes to the definition of *desolate*, meaning "deserted" or "abandoned." Use the meaning of -sol- to write a definition of each italicized word.

1. A *solitary* tree remains where a forest once stood.
2. Maria enjoyed the *solitude* of the morning.
3. The *isolated* cottage is surrounded by fields.

Spelling Strategy

When a word ends in silent *e*, drop the *e* when adding a suffix that begins with a vowel. For example, *beguile* + *-ing* = *beguiling*.

Add the suffix in italics to each item below, and write the new word in your notebook.

1. rustle (*-ing*) **2.** forgive (*-able*) **3.** donate (*-tion*)

Concept Development: Analogies

For each sentence below, write the word from the vocabulary list on page 939 that best completes each comparison. Then, explain your reasoning.

1. *Tired* is to *energetic* as ___?___ is to *crowded*.
2. *Baritone* is to *man* as ___?___ is to *child*.
3. *Amusing* is to *entertaining* as ___?___ is to *strange*.
4. *Faded* is to *fabric* as ___?___ is to *skin*.
5. *Tiny* is to *enormous* as ___?___ is to *joyful*.
6. *Teasing* is to *tormenting* as ___?___ is to *tricking*.
7. *Work* is to *exert* as ___?___ is to *relax*.

Grammar Lesson

Punctuation With Quotation Marks

In direct quotations, quotation marks enclose the exact words a person speaks. Interrupting expressions, such as *he said* or *she asked*, are set off with commas. A comma or period is placed inside the final quotation mark, but a question mark or exclamation mark is set inside the final quotation mark only if the end mark is part of the quotation.

> **Example:**
>
> "There is a visitor," he remarked, "knocking on my door." (interrupter set off with commas)
>
> I yelled, "There's someone at my door!" (exclamation mark is part of quote)

Practice Copy the following sentences, adding the proper punctuation.

1. The only word spoken was the word *Lenore!*
2. Surely said I, something's at my window
3. That's the last word I'll hear from you! I shrieked.
4. The lover declares She is lovely!
5. The soldier, he said, is quick to exclaim Let's fight!

Writing Application Expand each sentence to include a direct quotation. Punctuate correctly.

1. The school boy whined.
2. I remember said the old man.

W͟G Prentice Hall Writing and Grammar Connection: Chapter 29, Section 4

Writing Lesson

Scene for a Movie

Imagine that you have been hired by a film studio to create a movie based on "The Raven." Write a detailed description of the scene that a scriptwriter could use to develop a script. In your description, provide detailed instructions about the mood, setting, characters, and events of the scene.

Prewriting   Start by thinking about how the poem could be expanded into a movie. Review the poem to jot down details about people, events, and setting that might appear in the opening scene.

Drafting   Using the ideas you have gathered, draft your description. Start with a paragraph describing the mood you want to establish. Then, follow with paragraphs about the plot, characters, and setting.

Revising   Look for places where you can add precise details to set a gloomy mood. Have one of your classmates assume the role of a scriptwriter to read your description and tell you if you have conveyed the feeling of the poem. Add further details if they are needed.

Model: Revising to Add Descriptive Details

lit by a single lamp that casts soft, eerie shadows on the wall,

In a darkened room ∧ a man sits reading a heavy book.

> Words such as *single lamp* and *eerie* help develop the scene.

 Prentice Hall Writing and Grammar Connection: Chapter 6, Section 4

Extension Activities

Listening and Speaking   Stage a **debate** based on "The Seven Ages of Man."

- Form two teams of two to four speakers.
- One team should support the views expressed in "The Seven Ages of Man," while the second team should support a more optimistic view.
- Speakers for each group should present their side to the class, backing up points with examples from real life.

Afterward, have the class decide which side presented the stronger argument. **[Group Activity]**

Research and Technology   Gather information for a **fact sheet** on ravens. Include details on what the birds look like, where they are found, what they eat, and other key facts. If possible, include information from Internet or encyclopedia sources that provide photos or film footage of ravens. Compare the details in your fact sheet to details about the raven found in Poe's poem.

 **Take It to the Net**   www.phschool.com

Go online for an additional research activity using the Internet.

to stay on top of it. I worked out constantly. Watched what I ate. Checked my hairline in the mirror. I had gone from being proud to say my age—because of all I had done so young—to not bringing it up, for fear I was getting too close to forty and, therefore, professional oblivion.

Morrie had aging in better perspective.

"All this emphasis on youth—I don't buy it," he said. "Listen, I know what a misery being young can be, so don't tell me it's so great. All these kids who came to me with their struggles, their strife, their feelings of inadequacy, their sense that life was miserable. . . .

"And, in addition to all the miseries, the young are not wise. They have very little understanding about life. Who wants to live every day when you don't know what's going on? When people are manipulating you, telling you to buy this perfume and you'll be beautiful, or this pair of jeans and you'll be sexy—and you believe them! It's such nonsense."

Weren't you *ever* afraid to grow old, I asked?

"Mitch, I *embrace* aging."

Embrace it?

"It's very simple. As you grow, you learn more. If you stayed at twenty-two, you'd always be as ignorant as you were at twenty-two. Aging is not just decay, you know. It's growth. It's more than the negative that you're going to die, it's also the positive that you *understand* you're going to die, and that you live a better life because of it."

Yes, I said, but if aging were so valuable, why do people always say, "Oh, if I were young again." You never hear people say, "I wish I were sixty-five."

He smiled. "You know what that reflects? Unsatisfied lives. Unfulfilled lives. Lives that haven't found meaning. Because if you've found meaning in your life, you don't want to go back. You want to go forward. You want to see more, do more. You can't wait until sixty-five.

"Listen. You should know something. All younger people should know something. If you're always battling against getting older, you're always going to be unhappy, because it will happen anyhow.

"And Mitch?"

He lowered his voice.

"The fact is, *you* are going to die eventually."

I nodded.

"It won't matter what you tell yourself."

I know.

"But hopefully," he said, "not for a long, long time."

He closed his eyes with a peaceful look, then asked me to adjust the pillows behind his head. His body needed constant adjustment to stay comfortable. It was propped up in the chair with white pillows, yellow foam, and blue towels. At a quick glance, it seemed as if Morrie were being packed for shipping.

"Thank you," he whispered as I moved the pillows.

oblivion (ə bliv′ ē ən) *n.* condition of being forgotten

Thematic Connection
How does Morrie's view of aging contrast with that of Jacques, the speaker of "The Seven Ages of Man"?

No problem, I said.

"Mitch. What are you thinking?"

I paused before answering. Okay, I said, I'm wondering how you don't envy younger, healthy people.

"Oh, I guess I do." He closed his eyes. "I envy them being able to go to the health club, or go for a swim. Or dance. Mostly for dancing. But envy comes to me, I feel it, and then I let it go. Remember what I said about detachment? Let it go. Tell yourself, 'That's envy, I'm going to separate from it now.' And walk away."

He coughed—a long, scratchy cough—and he pushed a tissue to his mouth and spit weakly into it. Sitting there, I felt so much stronger than he, ridiculously so, as if I could lift him and toss him over my shoulder like a sack of flour. I was embarrassed by this superiority, because I did not feel superior to him in any other way.

How do you keep from envying . . .

"What?"

Me?

He smiled.

"Mitch, it is impossible for the old not to envy the young. But the issue is to accept who you are and <u>revel</u> in that. This is your time to be in your thirties. I had my time to be in my thirties, and now is my time to be seventy-eight.

"You have to find what's good and true and beautiful in your life as it is now. Looking back makes you competitive. And, age is not a competitive issue."

He exhaled and lowered his eyes, as if to watch his breath scatter into the air.

"The truth is, part of me is every age. I'm a three-year-old, I'm a five-year-old, I'm a thirty-seven-year-old, I'm a fifty-year-old. I've been through all of them, and I know what it's like. I delight in being a child when it's appropriate to be a child. I delight in being a wise old man when it's appropriate to be a wise old man. Think of all I can be! I am every age, up to my own. Do you understand?"

I nodded.

"How can I be envious of where you are—when I've been there myself?"

revel (rev´əl) v. take delight or pleasure

Mitch Albom

(b. 1958)

Building a career in newspaper journalism, nonfiction writing, and television commentary, Mitch Albom accomplished a great deal at an early age. He has been voted America's best sportswriter thirteen times by the Associated Press Sports Editors for his columns in the *Detroit Free Press*. He appears regularly on television and has his own radio show. Still, the impending death of his former professor made him take a step back to reevaluate his own life. *Tuesdays with Morrie* (1997) was the result of this soul-searching. More than 5 million copies of the book have been sold, securing its place on bestseller lists since its publication.

Connecting Literature Past and Present

1. How might you apply Morrie's advice on growing older to your own life?

2. How might the author's perspective have changed after hearing Morrie's views on aging and death?

3. Assess the different views on aging presented by "The Seven Ages of Man" and by Morrie. With which do you agree more?

Three Haiku

Temple bells die out.
The fragrant blossoms remain.
A perfect evening!

—BASHŌ

Dragonfly catcher,
How far have you gone today
In your wandering?

—CHIYOJO

Bearing no flowers,
I am free to toss madly
Like the willow tree.

—CHIYOJO

Haiku Poets

Bashō (1644–1694)

Bashō [bash′ō] is regarded as one of the greatest Japanese poets. In his youth, he lived in luxury as the companion to the son of a lord. Later, however, he lived apart and devoted himself to writing haiku.

Chiyojo (1887–1959)

Chiyojo [chē yō jō] was the wife of a samurai's servant. When her husband died, she became a nun and began studying poetry with a well-known teacher of haiku. Scholars celebrate the lightness of spirit in her poems.

Hokku Poems

Richard Wright

Make up your mind snail!
You are half inside your house
And halfway out!

In the falling snow
A laughing boy holds out his palms
Until they are white

Keep straight down this block
Then turn right where you will find
A peach tree blooming

Whose town did you leave
O wild and drowning spring rain
And where do you go?

Review and Assess

Thinking About the Selections

1. **Respond:** Which of the seven haiku do you like best? Why?

2. **(a) Recall:** To which senses does Bashō's haiku appeal?
   (b) Analyze Cause and Effect: In what ways do the two things that are sensed help to make the evening perfect?

3. **(a) Recall:** In what two ways does Chiyojo say she is like a willow tree? **(b) Interpret:** What impression is she trying to convey by the comparison?

4. **(a) Recall:** Which two weather events does Richard Wright describe in his haiku? **(b) Interpret:** What different feelings does he convey about these two weather events? **(c) Analyze:** Which words in each poem help to convey the feelings?

5. **(a) Distinguish:** Which of the haiku convey humor, and which seem serious? **(b) Make a Judgment:** Do you think that the haiku form works better with a more solemn or a more humorous content? Explain.

Richard Wright

(1908–1960)

Richard Wright is best known for his acclaimed novel *Native Son* (1940), which chronicles the life of an African American boy raised in poverty in Chicago. However, Wright also produced a wide range of other types of works, including essays and poems. As a poet, Wright experimented with different forms, including the traditional Japanese haiku.

On the Grasshopper and the Cricket

John Keats

The poetry of earth is never dead:
When all the birds are faint with the hot sun,
And hide in cooling trees, a voice will run
From hedge to hedge about the new-mown mead;[1]
5 That is the Grasshopper's—he takes the lead
In summer luxury,—he has never done
With his delights; for when tired out with fun
He rests at ease beneath some pleasant weed.
The poetry of earth is <u>ceasing</u> never:
10 On a lone winter evening, when the frost
Has <u>wrought</u> a silence, from the stove there shrills
The Cricket's song, in warmth increasing ever,
And seems to one in <u>drowsiness</u> half lost,
The Grasshopper's among some grassy hills.

ceasing (sēs´ iŋ) v.
stopping

wrought (rôt) v. formed;
fashioned

drowsiness (drou´ zē nes)
n. sleepiness

---

1. mead (mēd) n. meadow.

Review and Assess

Thinking About the Selection

1. **Respond:** Which scene painted by the poet appeals more to you? Why?

2. **(a) Compare and Contrast:** In what ways are the two insects alike and different? **(b) Associate:** How are the two insects connected in the speaker's mind?

3. **(a) Interpret:** What does the speaker mean by saying "The poetry of earth is never dead"? **(b) Analyze:** In which other line of the poem do you find this line closely echoed?
   (c) Interpret: Do you think there is a difference in meaning between these related lines? Explain.

4. **Generalize:** What one word would you use to describe this poem? Explain your choices.

5. **Make a Judgment:** Does the sonnet form help or hinder Keats in getting across his meaning? Explain.

6. **Apply:** In your environment, what "poetry of nature" do you experience at different times of the year? Explain, citing examples from at least two seasons.

John Keats

(1795–1821)

The poems of John Keats are among the most admired in the English language. Remarkably, Keats accomplished this distinction in spite of his premature death at the age of twenty-five.

Keats is considered one of the main poets of the Romantic Movement, a group of writers who stressed the importance of individual experience and the spiritual connection between people and nature.

SONNET 30

William Shakespeare

When to the sessions of sweet silent thought
I summon up remembrance of things past,
I sigh the lack of many a thing I sought,
And with old <u>woes</u>' new wail my dear times waste:[1]
5 Then can I drown an eye, unused to flow,
For precious friends hid in death's dateless[2] night,
And weep afresh love's long since cancelled woe,
And moan the expense[3] of many a vanished sight:
Then can I grieve at grievances foregone,[4]
10 And heavily from woe to woe tell o'er[5]
The sad account of fore-bemoanèd moan,[6]
Which I new pay as if not paid before.
But if the while I think on thee, dear friend,
All losses are restored and sorrows end.

woes (wōz) *n.* great sorrows

---

1. **And . . . waste** and by grieving anew for past sorrows, ruin the precious present.
2. **dateless** endless.
3. **expense** loss.
4. **foregone** past and done with.
5. **tell o'er** count up.
6. **fore-bemoanèd moan** sorrows suffered in the past.

Review and Assess

Thinking About the Selection

1. **Respond:** Would you want the speaker of the poem as a friend? Explain?

2. **(a) Recall:** In the opening lines of Sonnet 30, how does the speaker refer to his memories? **(b) Infer:** In general, how does the speaker feel when he remembers the past? Explain.

3. **(a) Infer:** In line 5, what does "drown an eye" mean? **(b) Analyze Cause and Effect:** Which thoughts cause the speaker to "drown an eye"? Why?

4. **Clarify:** What is the speaker describing in lines 10–12?

5. **Hypothesize:** How would the effect of this poem be different without the final two lines?

6. **Evaluate:** Do you agree with the assessment of the value of friendship? Why or why not?

William Shakespeare

(1564–1616)

William Shakespeare was as much a poet as a playwright. He not only wrote his 37 plays in verse, but also composed 154 sonnets. Taken together, the sonnets seem to tell a story. The "plot" is not always clear, but it seems obvious that the main characters are a young nobleman, a lady, a poet (probably Shakespeare himself), and a rival poet. Some of the best sonnets, like Sonnet 30, are addressed to the nobleman. (For more on William Shakespeare, see p. 766.)

Review and Assess

Literary Analysis

Haiku and Sonnets

1. (a) What are the two main images in Wright's second **haiku**? (b) What is the connection between these images?

2. A Shakespearean **sonnet** usually presents an idea or question in the first quatrain (four lines), explores the idea in the next two quatrains, and reaches a conclusion in the couplet (two lines) at the end. Use a chart like this to analyze the content of Sonnet 30.

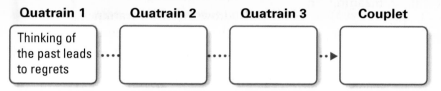

Quatrain 1	Quatrain 2	Quatrain 3	Couplet
Thinking of the past leads to regrets			

3. Keats's **sonnet** is Petrarchan, a form consisting of an octave (eight lines) and a sestet (six lines). In his poem, how is the content of the octave and the sestet related?

Comparing Literary Works

4. (a) Which of these poets use images from the natural world to explain something about human nature? (b) Which of these poets seem to focus primarily on the natural world rather than on people?

5. Do you think the haiku writers would agree with Keats that "the poetry of earth is never dead"? Explain your answer.

Reading Strategy

Reading in Sentences

6. In Sonnet 30, why do lines 1 and 10 lack punctuation marks?

7. In "On the Grasshopper and the Cricket," why do lines 1 and 9 end in colons rather than in periods?

8. How do the haiku writers use or omit punctuation to convey a dominant impression in their poems?

Extend Understanding

9. **Science Connection:** In what ways can scientists develop a different understanding of nature by reading poems that focus on natural images?

Quick Review

A **haiku** is a poem in three unrhymed lines (of five, seven, and five syllables each) that conveys a single, dominant impression by means of images from nature.

A **sonnet** is a lyric poem of fourteen lines, usually written in rhymed iambic pentameter.

To understand the literal meaning of a poem, **read in sentences** rather than lines, using punctuation to determine when to pause or stop.

 Take It to the Net

www.phschool.com
Take the interactive self-test online to check your understanding of these selections.

Journalism

CD-ROMs

Chronicle of the 20th Century. 1996. $39.95.

Ages 9–up. A charmingly anachronistic newspaper editor's office, complete with a manual typewriter and a ticker tape machine, is the starting point for this exploration of twentieth-century history up to the early days of 1996. There are multiple access points for young people searching for specific events, dates, or names, as well as some intriguing opportunities for browsing and for more in-depth research on eight major focus areas, such as the Russian Revolution, the two world wars, space exploration, and the fall of Communism. All entries contain visual materials as well as text, and many also include sound or video clips, such as Orson Welles' famous "War of the Worlds" broadcast and Yasir Arafat addressing the United Nations in Arabic. With newspapers and headlines making up the framework for this CD-ROM, it also makes a good springboard to books about journalism.

Books

Fleischman, Paul. *Dateline: Troy.* 1996. 79p. $15.99 (1-56402-469-5).

Ages 11–up. The author juxtaposes the history of the Trojan War with newspaper clippings of contemporary events, making the parallels between Homer's world and our own unmistakably clear.

Granfield, Linda. *Extra! Extra! The Who, What, Where, When, and Why of Newspapers.* Illus. by Bill Slavin. 1994. 72p. $16.99 (0-531-98683-6); paper, $7.95 (0-531-07049-2).

Ages 9–12. This book contains everything kids ever wanted to know about how a newspaper is published—including information on how to publish their own.

The Gold Rush

CD-ROMs

Klondike Gold. 1996. $39.95.

Ages 11–up. American children more familiar with the California gold rush will find some interesting differences and similarities in the Klondike gold rush that took place in the far north of Canada in 1896. A pan of gold nuggets serves as the main menu on this CD-ROM, leading to information about this rip-roaring episode in Yukon history, an interactive exploration of the placer mining process, and a rich segment on "The Cremation of Sam McGee" by Robert Service, the bard of the Yukon. Historical photographs form the foundation for multiple hypertext links to related topics, and honky-tonk music sets the tone.

Books

Fleischman, Sid. *Bandit's Moon.* Illus. by Jos. A. Smith. 1998. 136p. $15 (0-688-15830-7).

Ages 9–12. Twelve-year-old orphan Annyrose tells what happened when she was taken in by Joaquin Murieta and his band of outlaws during the California gold rush.

Service, Robert W. *The Cremation of Sam McGee.* Illus. by Ted Harrison. 1987. 32p. $18 (0-688-06903-7).

Ages 9–up. An illustrated edition of the poetic tall tale about a frozen gold miner that is featured in the *Klondike Gold* CD-ROM.

Yee, Paul. *Tales from Gold Mountain.* Illus. by Simon Ng. 1999. 64p. $18.95 (0-88899-098-7).

Ages 9–12. Yee blends folklore, fact, and fiction in these eight haunting stories about Chinese immigrants in North America.

> Information is presented in three categories: *Castles*, *Journalism,* and *The Gold Rush.*

> Teachers and librarians may find the inclusion of books and CD-ROMS especially useful.

> Formatting, such as the use of titles and subheads, helps readers locate the content they wish to find.

Check Your Comprehension

1. What is the advantage to children in learning from a CD-ROM, according to Virginia A. Walter?
2. What is the subject of Paul Fleischman's book *Dateline: Troy*?
3. How does Walter organize the materials that she recommends?

Applying the Reading Strategy

Identifying a Target Audience's Purpose

4. Use a chart like the one shown to identify three purposes that either a librarian or a teacher might have for reading the article in *Book Links*. For each, indicate which details in the article meet that purpose.

Purposes of Specific Audiences

A. Librarian Purpose
  1.
  2.   Details
  3.
B. Teacher Purpose
  1.
  2.   Details
  3.

Activity

Writing an Annotated Discography

The article presented here offers reviews of books and CD-ROMs devoted to certain subjects. When the subject of a review is music, it often takes the form of an annotated discography. An annotated discography lists songs or CDs by a particular artist or in a specific genre and offers opinions about their quality. Using the chart below as a guide, write an annotated discography reviewing a category of music. Include your evaluation of each item and provide details to support our opinions.

Music Title	Your Reaction	Supporting Detail

Contrasting Informational Materials

Professional Journals and General Newspapers

1. Imagine that the books presented by Walter were reviewed in a daily newspaper with a general adult readership. (a) What book information does the professional journal article contain that a newspaper might omit? (b) What details might be expanded in a newspaper review? (c) What other information might a newspaper include that was omitted in this article?
2. Suppose that the same books in this article were reviewed in a magazine or newspaper written for young people. (a) How would the content of such a review differ from the content in the article presented here? (b) How would the style of the two kinds of reviews be different?

Writing WORKSHOP

Exposition: Comparison-and-Contrast Essay

A **comparison-and-contrast essay** addresses two or more subjects to show their similarities and differences. It may describe or explain, reveal strengths and weaknesses, or persuade readers to value one subject over another. In this workshop, you will write a comparison-and-contrast essay on subjects that are suitable to this type of exposition.

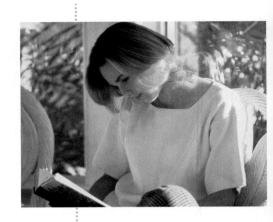

Assignment Criteria. Your comparison-and-contrast essay should have the following characteristics:

- Analysis and discussion of similarities and differences between two or more things, people, places, or ideas
- Factual details about each subject
- A purpose for comparison and contrast
- Equal presentation of each subject using one of two organizations: subject-by-subject or point-by-point

To preview the criteria on which your comparison-and-contrast essay may be assessed, see the Rubric on page 971.

Prewriting

Choose a topic. Explore topics in terms of clear opposites (winter/summer), clear similarities (baseball/cricket), or close relationships (book/movie). **Brainstorm** for topics by starting with names of people, places, objects, or ideas. Then, note related subjects that come to mind. Notice relationships that interest you, and then choose one to develop.

Identify your audience. Your intended audience will direct the type of information you include—from the level of vocabulary you use to the level of analysis you pursue. Consider your audience as you gather information.

Specify your purpose. To identify a purpose for your essay, consider the following possibilities:

- *To persuade*—You want readers to accept your opinion that one subject is preferable to another.
- *To explain*—You want readers to understand something special about the subjects.
- *To describe*—You want readers to understand the basic similarities and differences between your subjects.

Gather details. As you generate the details to use in your comparison-and-contrast essay, look at the ideas you have collected and consider the main elements you will discuss.

Brainstorming for Topic Pairs

hockey vs. soccer
middle school vs. high school
love for my town vs. boredom with it
music vs. literature
video vs. DVD

Student Model

Before you begin drafting your comparison-and-contrast essay, read this student model and review the characteristics of an effective comparison-and-contrast essay.

Lauren DeLoach
Bernice, Louisiana

Ambivalence

When I consider my conflicting feelings about my hometown, I see that there are things that I love and hate about living in Bernice, Louisiana, a nineties version of Mayberry. I love the security of a small town, and I hate it. I love the way that my town is not clouded by the smog of a city, and I hate it too. I love it and I hate that I love it.

I love and hate the security in my town for a number of reasons. I love it because I know that it is my dogs scratching at my door at 5:30 in the morning and not some dangerous stranger. In my town, a fifteen-car traffic jam is front-page news. On the other hand, I hate that it gets a little boring sometimes. I don't want criminals at my door, but a little excitement would be nice.

I am fond of the size of Bernice and I detest it, too. I'm glad that only fifteen cars is a major traffic jam. But I hate that I have to drive sixteen miles to the nearest major store. I love and hate that my town is so small that I know everybody's first, middle, and last names. I like it because I have a "tab" at the grocery story and the drug store, so that eliminates the necessity of money. I hate that everybody knows me because that means that everybody finds out about whom I'm dating, whom I once dated, my height, weight, and age. I also hate that we all know each other so well that the most entertaining news we can come up with to put in the Bernice Banner is that Peggy Jane and her brother JC visited their Aunt Goosey Lou in the nursing home. But by knowing everyone so well, I've made friends who are trustworthy because we know all of each other's deepest secrets.

Even though I say that I detest some things, home wouldn't be home without these silly quirks. I love that my parents and their friends are known as the "elite group" because they have traveled beyond Texas, Arkansas, and Mississippi. I love saying that I have read the *Iliad* to people who think I would not read such a book. I know that it sounds like I love the provincialism that small towns can impose, but the smells of fresh-cut grass and the gardenia bush outside my door are what make my home my home.

This is what I love and what I say I hate, but I don't really. The overall feeling I get from living in Bernice is ambivalence. I love it and I hate that I love such goofy things. But the parts of home that seem so trivial are the ones that make you who you are. That makes a place your home.

Lauren's essay will compare two feelings: what she loves and what she hates about her hometown.

Using a point-by-point organization, Lauren addresses the first contrast in her attitudes about her town: She feels ambivalence about its security.

These facts support the writer's ideas and opinions.

Lauren's comparison allows her to be funny, but also helps her reflect on her ideas.

Listening and Speaking WORKSHOP

Comparing Media Coverage

Whether information comes from the Internet or a 24-hour cable network, it is useful to know how to analyze and compare media coverage.

Prepare to View

Every news format and news source has strengths and weaknesses. As you follow news stories, consider the way they are filtered and presented to you.

Consider your sources. Certain types of news media are designed to cover specific types of news events. Consider these sources and the variety and quality of reporting they represent:

- nightly network news or local television news
- Internet Web pages of news organizations
- public radio
- national magazines or daily newspapers
- cable news channels

Recognize differences. Before you compare media coverage, think about the differences you are likely to find among sources. A good general news source might present news coverage of a variety of topics—science, politics, and entertainment. However, if you are looking for coverage of one issue, you might be concerned with the depth of coverage rather than variety.

Identify bias. Bias occurs when an organization has a special interest in reporting the news in a particular way. If you anticipate bias, you will have a heightened awareness when you view the news source. Find out which organization sponsors the coverage, and think about how that might influence reporting of a particular issue or group of issues.

Using Criteria to Compare Coverage

Accuracy
- Are there any mistakes in the facts presented?
- Are the news reports misleading viewers by leaving out essential information?

Comprehensiveness
- Do the news reports support their assertions with evidence?
- Do the reports present an adequate level of detail and complexity?

Credibility
- How close were the reporters to the events they are reporting?
- Do the reports cite well-known authorities or published studies?

Objectivity
- Do news sources present more than one side of an issue?
- Does any source have a vested interest in presenting facts in a particular way?

View and Compare

Use consistent criteria. When you watch or listen to coverage of a news story reported by several sources, you are likely to notice differences. Consider the questions in the chart shown on this page.

Make comparisons. Once you have evaluated each news source, a side-by-side comparison, using the same criteria, should be straightforward. Notice the similarities and differences among the reports you find to determine the news sources you can trust.

Activity:
Research and Discussion
Choose a current issue to research as a group. Find three sources from television, radio, or the Internet. Compare coverage of that issue and discuss your findings.

Analogies

The reading sections of some tests often require you to answer multiple-choice questions to complete analogies. Use the following strategies to help you:

- An *analogy* establishes a relationship between one pair of words so that a similar relationship can be established between a second pair.

- To complete an analogy, identify the relationship between the initial pair of words, and then look for a second pair with a similar relationship.

- Common relationships to look for are synonyms, antonyms, cause and effect, part and whole, example and group, and product and function.

Test-Taking Strategies

- Say the relationship of the first word pair aloud to yourself in a test sentence. For example, "joy/smile" would be "When you feel joy, you smile."
- Use the same relationship when putting the second pair of words into a sentence. Discard pairs that do not make sense in your test sentence.

Sample Test Item

Directions: Read the word pair, and then choose the letter of the word pair that is most similar to the example.

1. MINT : HERB ::

   A garage : car

   B score : game

   C snow : precipitation

   D sow : harvest

Answer and Explanation

C is the correct answer. To arrive at the correct answer, identify the relationship first: "Mint is a type of herb." Then, look for a word pair that has a similar relationship. Since garage is *not* a type of car, score is *not* a type of game, and sow is *not* a type of harvest, the answer cannot be *A, B,* or *D.* Snow is a type of precipitation, therefore *C* is the correct choice.

Practice

Directions: Read each word pair, and then choose the letter of the word pair that is most similar to the example.

1. SUNSCREEN : PROTECT ::

   A shampoo : rinse

   B sand : bucket

   C curtains : drapes

   D label : inform

2. STATEMENT : CONFIDENCE ::

   A excitement : happiness

   B proposal : intuition

   C question : confusion

   D interruption : disappointment

3. CONDUCTOR : SYMPHONY ::

   A orchestra : violin

   B driver : bus

   C tour guide : argument

   D official : relaxation

The Epic

Ulysses Deriding Polyphemus, 1819, J.M.W. Turner, The National Gallery, London

Exploring the Genre

Turn the page to enter a world of heroes, gods, and sweeping adventures. Tradition tells us that the blind poet Homer wrote the *Odyssey* after it had been passed down by generations of Greek singers. If it had not been for this ancient scribe, many generations of readers would never have learned about the heroic exploits of Odysseus and his companions.

An **epic** is a long narrative poem about the deeds of gods or heroes. Early in the *Odyssey*, Homer presents an epic question. Odysseus asks:

> "Where shall a man find sweetness to surpass his own home and his parents? In far lands he shall not, though he find a house of gold. What of my sailing, then, from Troy?"

The *Odyssey* itself is the answer.

▲ **Critical Viewing** In this painting, inspired by the *Odyssey*, which dangers seem to present themselves? **[Interpret]**

Read Literature?

As you read an ancient work of literature, it is interesting to think about its influence on subsequent generations of authors and readers. The *Odyssey* is a powerful tale that has been read for many different reasons since it was first written down. Here is a sampling of reasons to read this epic and the works that follow:

1 Read for the Love of Literature

The singers who spread the tale of the *Odyssey* before it was written down were highly skilled poets. Each would change the tale slightly, embellishing certain parts to create his own dramatic effects and style. Enjoy the final product of many skillful poets as you read an excerpt from the ***Odyssey***, page 980.

A powerful story can take on new life when it is read by authors who are inspired to create works of their own. See which lesson Constantine Cavafy took from Odysseus' long absence from home when you read his poem **"Ithaca,"** page 1058.

2 Read to Be Entertained

Great adventures are not limited to the pages of ancient epics. Find the connection between ancient Greek adventure and a heart-pounding modern-day odyssey through space as you read the excerpt from ***Lost Moon***, page 1064.

3 Read for Information

In 1962, John Glenn was the first American to orbit Earth. Thirty-six years later, at the age of 77, he joined the crew of the space shuttle to go into orbit again, eliciting both admiration and controversy. Read both sides of the debate over Glenn's 1998 space flight in **Reading Informational Materials: Newspaper Editorials,** page 1066.

 Take It to the Net

Visit the Web site for online instruction and activities related to each selection in this unit.

www.phschool.com

How to Read Literature

Use Strategies for Reading an Epic

In ancient societies, wandering storytellers told stories of gods and heroes that would sometimes take days to complete. To help the storytellers remember such lengthy pieces, epic tales were composed in poetry and recited to musical accompaniment. Their language and sentence structure may present some difficulty for you as you read. Apply the following strategies to help you.

1. Summarize.

You can be certain that you have understood a passage when you are able to offer a clear, concise summary of the action. Stop to summarize what has happened at each pause in the action. Eliminate any aspects or events that are not directly related to the basic plot.

2. Read in sentences.

You may become confused if you stop at the end of every line of verse in an epic because sentences frequently flow to the next line.

- Be guided by the punctuation, not simply the ends of lines, in determining where to pause.
- Use periods and the ends of paragraphs to maintain the natural flow of words.

3. Compare and contrast.

Finding similarities and recognizing differences can help you understand your reactions to different texts.

- Choose basic categories such as style, subject, and viewpoint to compare and contrast.
- Compare specific passages that are similar enough to enable you to draw effective comparisons and contrasts.

> The lovely voices in ardor appealing over the water made me crave to listen, . . .
>
> —from the *Odyssey*

> I don't enjoy singing
> this trio, fatal and valuable.
>
> —from "Siren Song"

Summarizing

Passage: But the man skilled in all ways of contending, / satisfied by the great bow's look and heft, . . .
—from the *Odyssey*

Summary: The man was a great warrior, and the large bow looked and felt good to him.

The subject of these two passages is the same, but the lines express different viewpoints. The *Odyssey* uses formal, elevated language, whereas "Siren Song" uses informal language. The *Odyssey* passage simply tells the story, but "Siren Song" hints at a deeper meaning.

As you read the selections in this unit, review the reading strategies and look at the notes in the side column. Use the suggestions to apply the strategies and interact with the text.

Prepare to Read

from the Odyssey, Part 1

"*Circe Meanwhile had gone her Ways . . .*," 1924, William Russell Flint, New York Public Library

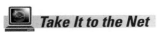 **Take It to the Net**

Visit www.phschool.com for interactive activities and instruction related to the *Odyssey*, including
- background
- graphic organizers
- literary elements
- reading strategies

Preview

Connecting to the Literature

Whether you are journeying across town or to another country, it sometimes seems to take forever to reach your destination. Just getting there can be quite an adventure! In the *Odyssey*, you will follow a journey that took far longer than expected and experience the amazing adventures that took place along the way.

Background

The *Odyssey* describes what happened to the Greek hero Odysseus on his way home after the Trojan War. According to legend, the Trojan War was sparked when Paris, son of the king of Troy, ran off with Helen, the most beautiful woman in the world and the wife of Menelaus of Sparta. A Greek force attacked Troy (in modern-day Turkey) to recapture her and was finally victorious after ten years of fighting.

Literary Analysis

The Epic Hero

An epic is a long poem about the adventures of gods or heroes. The epic's central character, its **epic hero,** is a larger-than-life figure from history or legend. The hero undertakes a dangerous voyage, demonstrating traits—such as courage, loyalty, and honor—that are valued by the society in which the epic originates. In this passage, Odysseus shows his bravery and leadership:

> Now, by the gods, I drove my big hand spike
> deep in the embers, charring it again,
> and cheered my men along with battle talk
> to keep their courage up; no quitting now.

As you read, use a chart like the one shown to record traits or actions that prove Odysseus to be an epic hero.

Connecting Literary Elements

At the center of every epic is a **conflict**—a struggle between opposing forces. Conflicts may occur between characters, between a character and nature, or within a character's mind. In an epic, conflicts often put the traits of the epic hero on display. In the *Odyssey*, notice that conflicts arise as the hero confronts his enemies and as he wrestles with his own thoughts.

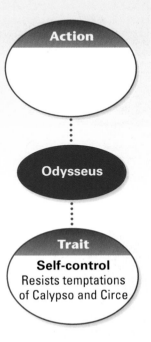

Reading Strategy

Reading in Sentences

To get the most out of a story told in verse, ignore the line breaks and **read in sentences.** Although the line breaks reveal the structure of the verse, they may make it harder for you to follow the meaning. Read the *Odyssey* the same way you might read a magazine article or a novel: Let the words flow to you in complete sentences. In some cases, you may need to rephrase the sentences in your own words to make the meaning clearer.

Vocabulary Development

plundered (plun´ dərd) *v.* took goods by force; looted (p. 981)

squall (skwôl) *n.* brief, violent storm (p. 984)

dispatched (di spacht´) *v.* finished quickly (p. 990)

mammoth (mam´ əth) *adj.* enormous (p. 993)

titanic (tī tan´ ik) *adj.* of great size or strength (p. 997)

assuage (ə swāj´) *v.* calm; pacify (p. 1000)

bereft (bi reft´) *adj.* deprived (p. 1003)

ardor (är´ dər) *n.* passion; enthusiasm (p. 1007)

insidious (in sid´ ē əs) *adj.* characterized by craftiness and betrayal (p. 1011)

CHARACTERS

Alcinous (al sin´ ō əs)—king of the Phaeacians, to whom Odysseus tells his story

Odysseus (ō dis´ ē əs)—king of Ithaca

Calypso (kə lip´ sō)—sea goddess who loved Odysseus

Circe (sʉr´ sē)—enchantress who helped Odysseus

Zeus (zoōs)—king of the gods

Apollo (ə päl´ ō)—god of music, poetry, prophecy, and medicine

Agamemnon (ag´ ə mem´ nän´)—king and leader of Greek forces

Poseidon (pō sī´ dən)—god of sea, earthquakes, horses, and storms at sea

Athena (ə thē´ nə)—goddess of wisdom, skills, and warfare

Polyphemus (päl´ i fē´ məs)—the Cyclops who imprisoned Odysseus

Laertes (lā ʉr´ tēz´)—Odysseus' father

Cronus (krō´ nəs)—Titan ruler of the universe; father of Zeus

Perimedes (per´ ə mē´ dēz)—member of Odysseus' crew

Eurylochus (yoō ril´ ə kəs)—another member of the crew

Tiresias (tī rē´ sē əs)—blind prophet who advised Odysseus

Persephone (pər sef´ ə nē)—wife of Hades

Telemachus (tə lem´ ə kəs)—Odysseus and Penelope's son

Sirens (sī´ rənz)—creatures whose songs lure sailors to their deaths

Scylla (sil´ ə)—sea monster of gray rock

Charybdis (kə rib´ dis)—enormous and dangerous whirlpool

Lampetia (lam pē´ shə)—nymph

Hermes (hʉr´ mēz´)—herald and messenger of the gods

Eumaeus (yoō mē´ əs)—old swineherd and friend of Odysseus

Antinous (an tin´ ō əs)—leader among the suitors

Eurynome (yoō rin´ ə mē)—housekeeper for Penelope

Penelope (pə nel´ ə pē)—Odysseus' wife

Eurymachus (yoō ri´ mə kəs)—suitor

Amphinomus (am fin´ ə məs)—suitor

Sailing from Troy

Ten years after the Trojan War, Odysseus departs from the goddess Calypso's island. He arrives in Phaeacia, ruled by Alcinous. Alcinous offers a ship to Odysseus and asks him to tell of his adventures.

"I am Laertes'[5] son, Odysseus.

               Men hold me
formidable for guile[6] in peace and war:
20 this fame has gone abroad to the sky's rim.

My home is on the peaked sea-mark of Ithaca[7]
under Mount Neion's wind-blown robe of leaves,
in sight of other islands—Dulichium,
Same, wooded Zacynthus—Ithaca
25 being most lofty in that coastal sea,
and northwest, while the rest lie east and south.
A rocky isle, but good for a boy's training;
I shall not see on earth a place more dear,
though I have been detained long by Calypso,[8]
30 loveliest among goddesses, who held me
in her smooth caves, to be her heart's delight,
as Circe of Aeaea,[9] the enchantress,
desired me, and detained me in her hall.
But in my heart I never gave consent.
35 Where shall a man find sweetness to surpass
his own home and his parents? In far lands
he shall not, though he find a house of gold.

What of my sailing, then, from Troy?

               What of those years
of rough adventure, weathered under Zeus?
40 The wind that carried west from Ilium[10]
brought me to Ismarus, on the far shore,
a strongpoint on the coast of Cicones.[11]
I stormed that place and killed the men who fought.
Plunder we took, and we enslaved the women,
45 to make division, equal shares to all—
but on the spot I told them: 'Back, and quickly!
Out to sea again!' My men were mutinous,[12]
fools, on stores of wine. Sheep after sheep
they butchered by the surf, and shambling cattle,

---

5. Laertes (lā ʉr´ tēz´)

6. guile (gīl) *n.* craftiness; cunning.

7. Ithaca (ith´ ə kə) island off the west coast of Greece.

Reading Strategy
Reading in Sentences
Why do these opening lines sound more natural when you ignore the line breaks?

8. Calypso (kə lip´ sō)

9. Circe (sʉr´ sē) **of Aeaea** (ē´ ē ə)

10. Ilium (il ē əm) Troy.

11. Cicones (si kō´ nēz)

12. mutinous (myo͞ot´ ən əs) *adj.* rebellious.

✔**Reading Check**
Who has asked Odysseus to tell his tale?

50 feasting,—while fugitives went inland, running
    to call to arms the main force of Cicones.
    This was an army, trained to fight on horseback
    or, where the ground required, on foot. They came
    with dawn over that terrain like the leaves
55 and blades of spring. So doom appeared to us,
    dark word of Zeus for us, our evil days.
    My men stood up and made a fight of it—
    backed on the ships, with lances kept in play,
    from bright morning through the blaze of noon
60 holding our beach, although so far outnumbered;
    but when the sun passed toward unyoking time,
    then the Achaeans,[13] one by one, gave way.
    Six benches were left empty in every ship
    that evening when we pulled away from death.
65 And this new grief we bore with us to sea:
    our precious lives we had, but not our friends.
    No ship made sail next day until some shipmate
    had raised a cry, three times, for each poor ghost
    unfleshed by the Cicones on that field.

The Lotus-Eaters

70 Now Zeus the lord of cloud roused in the north
    a storm against the ships, and driving veils
    of <u>squall</u> moved down like night on land and sea.
    The bows went plunging at the gust; sails
    cracked and lashed out strips in the big wind.
75 We saw death in that fury, dropped the yards,
    unshipped the oars, and pulled for the nearest lee:[14]
    then two long days and nights we lay offshore
    worn out and sick at heart, tasting our grief,
    until a third Dawn came with ringlets shining.
80 Then we put up our masts, hauled sail, and rested,
    letting the steersmen and the breeze take over.

    I might have made it safely home, that time,
    but as I came round Malea the current
    took me out to sea, and from the north
85 a fresh gale drove me on, past Cythera.
    Nine days I drifted on the teeming sea
    before dangerous high winds. Upon the tenth
    we came to the coastline of the Lotus-Eaters,
    who live upon that flower. We landed there

13. Achaeans (ə kē´ ənz)
Greeks; here, Odysseus' men.

squall (skwôl) *n.* brief,
violent storm

14. lee (lē) *n.* area sheltered
from the wind.

90 to take on water. All ships' companies
mustered alongside for the mid-day meal.
Then I sent out two picked men and a runner
to learn what race of men that land sustained.
They fell in, soon enough, with Lotus-Eaters,
95 who showed no will to do us harm, only
offering the sweet Lotus to our friends—
but those who ate this honeyed plant, the Lotus,
never cared to report, nor to return:
they longed to stay forever, browsing on
100 that native bloom, forgetful of their homeland.
I drove them, all three wailing, to the ships,
tied them down under their rowing benches,
and called the rest: 'All hands aboard;
come, clear the beach and no one taste
105 the Lotus, or you lose your hope of home.'
Filing in to their places by the rowlocks
my oarsmen dipped their long oars in the surf,
and we moved out again on our sea faring.

Reading Strategy
Reading in Sentences
Read lines 94–98 as a complete sentence. How does doing so help your understanding of the passage?

Literary Analysis
The Epic Hero Which characteristics of a hero and leader does Odysseus show in the episode with the Lotus-Eaters?

Review and Assess

Thinking About the Selection

1. **Respond:** What is your first impression of Odysseus? Which of his qualities do you admire?

2. **(a) Recall:** Describe the events on Ismarus.
   (b) Interpret: What lessons can be learned from the defeat of Odysseus and his men at Ismarus?

3. **(a) Recall:** Where is Odysseus' home? **(b) Interpret:** What significant role does his home play in Odysseus' epic journey?

4. **(a) Recall:** How do Calypso and Circe keep Odysseus from reaching home? **(b) Interpret:** What were Odysseus' feelings when he was with Calypso and Circe?

5. **(a) Recall:** What happens to the men who eat the Lotus?
   (b) Infer: What does this episode suggest about the main problem that Odysseus has with his men? **(c) Speculate:** What do you think about the way Odysseus responds to the three men who long to stay with the Lotus-Eaters?

6. **Compare and Contrast:** In what ways is the world of the *Odyssey* similar to today's world? In what ways is it different?

7. **Take a Position:** Do you admire Odysseus? Why or why not?

The Cyclops

In the next land we found were Cyclopes,[15]
110 giants, louts, without a law to bless them.
In ignorance leaving the fruitage of the earth in mystery
to the immortal gods, they neither plow
nor sow by hand, nor till the ground, though grain—
wild wheat and barley—grows untended, and
115 wine-grapes, in clusters, ripen in heaven's rains.
Cyclopes have no muster and no meeting,
no consultation or old tribal ways,
but each one dwells in his own mountain cave
dealing out rough justice to wife and child,
120 indifferent to what the others do. . . .

As we rowed on, and nearer to the mainland,
at one end of the bay, we saw a cavern
yawning above the water, screened with laurel,
and many rams and goats about the place
125 inside a sheepfold—made from slabs of stone
earthfast between tall trunks of pine and rugged
towering oak trees.

A prodigious[16] man
slept in this cave alone, and took his flocks
to graze afield—remote from all companions,
130 knowing none but savage ways, a brute
so huge, he seemed no man at all of those
who eat good wheaten bread; but he seemed rather
a shaggy mountain reared in solitude.
We beached there, and I told the crew
135 to stand by and keep watch over the ship:
as for myself I took my twelve best fighters
and went ahead. I had a goatskin full
of that sweet liquor that Euanthes' son,
Maron, had given me. He kept Apollo's[17]
140 holy grove at Ismarus; for kindness
we showed him there, and showed his wife and child,
he gave me seven shining golden talents[18]
perfectly formed, a solid silver winebowl,
and then this liquor—twelve two-handled jars
145 of brandy, pure and fiery. Not a slave
in Maron's household knew this drink; only
he, his wife and the storeroom mistress knew;
and they would put one cupful—ruby-colored,
honey-smooth—in twenty more of water,

15. **Cyclopes** (sī klō′ pēz′) *n.* plural form of **Cyclops** (sī′ kläps′), a race of giants with one eye in the middle of the forehead.

Literary Analysis
The Epic Hero and Conflict Based on Odysseus' description of Cyclopes, what conflicts might arise for Odysseus and his men?

16. **prodigious** (prō dij′ əs) *adj.* enormous.

Reading Strategy
Reading in Sentences Rephrase the description of the Cyclops in lines 130–133, using your own words.

17. **Apollo** (ə päl′ ō) god of music, poetry, prophecy, and medicine.

18. **talents** units of money in ancient Greece.

150 but still the sweet scent hovered like a fume
over the winebowl. No man turned away
when cups of this came round.

                                    A wineskin full
I brought along, and victuals[19] in a bag,
for in my bones I knew some towering brute
155 would be upon us soon—all outward power,
a wild man, ignorant of civility.

We climbed, then, briskly to the cave. But Cyclops
had gone afield, to pasture his fat sheep,
so we looked round at everything inside:
160 a drying rack that sagged with cheeses, pens
crowded with lambs and kids,[20] each in its class:
firstlings apart from middlings, and the 'dewdrops,'

19. victuals (vit´ əls) *n.*
food or other provisions.

20. kids *n.* young goats.

✔ **Reading Check**
What does Odysseus bring along when he goes to inspect the Cyclops' cave?

◀ **Critical Viewing** How does this image of Apollo compare with your impressions of the other gods Odysseus has encountered? **[Compare and Contrast]**

or newborn lambkins, penned apart from both.
And vessels full of whey[21] were brimming there—
165 bowls of earthenware and pails for milking.
My men came pressing round me, pleading:

'Why not

take these cheeses, get them stowed, come back,
throw open all the pens, and make a run for it?
We'll drive the kids and lambs aboard. We say
170 put out again on good salt water!'

Ah,

how sound that was! Yet I refused. I wished
to see the cave man, what he had to offer—
no pretty sight, it turned out, for my friends.
We lit a fire, burnt an offering,
175 and took some cheese to eat; then sat in silence
around the embers, waiting. When he came
he had a load of dry boughs[22] on his shoulder
to stoke his fire at suppertime. He dumped it
with a great crash into that hollow cave,
180 and we all scattered fast to the far wall.
Then over the broad cavern floor he ushered
the ewes he meant to milk. He left his rams
and he-goats in the yard outside, and swung
high overhead a slab of solid rock
185 to close the cave. Two dozen four-wheeled wagons,
with heaving wagon teams, could not have stirred
the tonnage of that rock from where he wedged it
over the doorsill. Next he took his seat
and milked his bleating ewes. A practiced job
190 he made of it, giving each ewe her suckling;
thickened his milk, then, into curds and whey,
sieved out the curds to drip in withy[23] baskets,
and poured the whey to stand in bowls
cooling until he drank it for his supper.
195 When all these chores were done, he poked the fire,
heaping on brushwood. In the glare he saw us.

'Strangers,' he said, 'who are you? And where from?
What brings you here by seaways—a fair traffic?
Or are you wandering rogues, who cast your lives
200 like dice, and ravage other folk by sea?'

21. whey (hwā) *n.* thin, watery part of milk separated from the thicker curds.

22. boughs (bȯuz) *n.* tree branches.

23. withy (with´ ē) *adj.* made from tough, flexible twigs.

We felt a pressure on our hearts, in dread
of that deep rumble and that mighty man.
But all the same I spoke up in reply:

'We are from Troy, Achaeans, blown off course
205 by shifting gales on the Great South Sea;
homeward bound, but taking routes and ways
uncommon; so the will of Zeus would have it.
We served under Agamemnon,[24] son of Atreus—
the whole world knows what city
210 he laid waste, what armies he destroyed.
It was our luck to come here; here we stand,
beholden for your help, or any gifts
you give—as custom is to honor strangers.
We would entreat you, great Sir, have a care
215 for the gods' courtesy; Zeus will avenge
the unoffending guest.'

                                        He answered this
from his brute chest, unmoved:

                                        'You are a ninny,
or else you come from the other end of nowhere,
telling me, mind the gods! We Cyclops
220 care not a whistle for your thundering Zeus
or all the gods in bliss; we have more force by far.
I would not let you go for fear of Zeus—
you or your friends—unless I had a whim[25] to.
Tell me, where was it, now, you left your ship—
225 around the point, or down the shore, I wonder?'

He thought he'd find out, but I saw through this,
and answered with a ready lie:

                                        'My ship?
Poseidon[26] Lord, who sets the earth a-tremble,
broke it up on the rocks at your land's end.
230 A wind from seaward served him, drove us there.
We are survivors, these good men and I.'

Neither reply nor pity came from him,
but in one stride he clutched at my companions
and caught two in his hands like squirming puppies
235 to beat their brains out, spattering the floor.
Then he dismembered them and made his meal,
gaping and crunching like a mountain lion—
everything: innards, flesh, and marrow bones.

Literary Analysis
The Epic Hero Which quality of an epic hero does Odysseus demonstrate by addressing the mighty man?

24. Agamemnon (ag´ ə mem´ nän´) king who led the Greek army during the Trojan War.

Literary Analysis
The Epic Hero and Conflict What conflict is revealed in lines 217–223?

25. whim (hwim) *n.* sudden thought or wish to do something.

26. Poseidon (pō sī´ dən) god of the sea, earthquakes, horses, and storms at sea.

Reading Check

What does Odysseus tell Cyclops happened to their ship?

'Nohbdy's my meat, then, after I eat his friends.
Others come first. There's a noble gift, now.'

Even as he spoke, he reeled and tumbled backward,
320 his great head lolling to one side; and sleep
took him like any creature. Drunk, hiccuping,
he dribbled streams of liquor and bits of men.

Now, by the gods, I drove my big hand spike
deep in the embers, charring it again,
325 and cheered my men along with battle talk
to keep their courage up: no quitting now.
The pike of olive, green though it had been,
reddened and glowed as if about to catch.
I drew it from the coals and my four fellows
330 gave me a hand, lugging it near the Cyclops
as more than natural force nerved them; straight
forward they sprinted, lifted it, and rammed it
deep in his crater eye, and leaned on it
turning it as a shipwright turns a drill
335 in planking, having men below to swing
the two-handled strap that spins it in the groove.
So with our brand we bored[34] that great eye socket
while blood ran out around the red-hot bar.
Eyelid and lash were seared; the pierced ball
340 hissed broiling, and the roots popped.

                                        In a smithy
one sees a white-hot axehead or an adze
plunged and wrung in a cold tub, screeching steam—
the way they make soft iron hale and hard—:
just so that eyeball hissed around the spike.
345 The Cyclops bellowed and the rock roared round him,
and we fell back in fear. Clawing his face
he tugged the bloody spike out of his eye,
threw it away, and his wild hands went groping;
then he set up a howl for Cyclopes
350 who lived in caves on windy peaks nearby.
Some heard him; and they came by divers[35] ways
to clump around outside and call:
                                    'What ails you,
Polyphemus?[36] Why do you cry so sore
in the starry night? You will not let us sleep.
355 Sure no man's driving off your flock? No man
has tricked you, ruined you?'

34. bored (bôrd) v.
made a hole in.

35. divers (dī´ vərz) adj.
several; various.

36. Polyphemus (päl´ i
fē´ məs)

Out of the cave
the <u>mammoth</u> Polyphemus roared in answer:

'Nohbdy, Nohbdy's tricked me, Nohbdy's ruined me!'

To this rough shout they made a sage[37] reply:

360 'Ah well, if nobody has played you foul
there in your lonely bed, we are no use in pain
given by great Zeus. Let it be your father,
Poseidon Lord, to whom you pray.'

So saying
they trailed away. And I was filled with laughter
365 to see how like a charm the name deceived them.
Now Cyclops, wheezing as the pain came on him,
fumbled to wrench away the great doorstone
and squatted in the breach with arms thrown wide
for any silly beast or man who bolted—
370 hoping somehow I might be such a fool.
But I kept thinking how to win the game:
death sat there huge; how could we slip away?
I drew on all my wits, and ran through tactics,
reasoning as a man will for dear life,
375 until a trick came—and it pleased me well.
The Cyclops' rams were handsome, fat, with heavy
fleeces, a dark violet.

Three abreast
I tied them silently together, twining
cords of willow from the ogre's bed;
380 then slung a man under each middle one
to ride there safely, shielded left and right.
So three sheep could convey each man. I took
the woolliest ram, the choicest of the flock,
and hung myself under his kinky belly,
385 pulled up tight, with fingers twisted deep
in sheepskin ringlets for an iron grip.
So, breathing hard, we waited until morning.

When Dawn spread out her fingertips of rose
the rams began to stir, moving for pasture,
390 and peals of bleating echoed round the pens
where dams with udders full called for a milking.
Blinded, and sick with pain from his head wound,
the master stroked each ram, then let it pass,

mammoth (mam′ əth) *adj.*
enormous

37. sage (sāj) *adj.* wise.

Reading Strategy
Reading in Sentences
How many questions do
the other Cyclopes ask
Polyphemus? What two
basic things do they want
to know?

Literary Analysis
The Epic Hero Which
heroic quality does
Odysseus demonstrate in
lines 371–375?

**Reading Check**

What do the other
Cyclopes think
Polyphemus is saying
when he says, "Nohbdy's
tricked me"?

you damned cannibal? Eater of guests
435 under your roof! Zeus and the gods have paid you!'

The blind thing in his doubled fury broke
a hilltop in his hands and heaved it after us.
Ahead of our black prow it struck and sank
whelmed in a spuming geyser, a giant wave
440 that washed the ship stern foremost back to shore.
I got the longest boathook out and stood
fending us off, with furious nods to all
to put their backs into a racing stroke—
row, row, or perish. So the long oars bent
445 kicking the foam sternward, making head
until we drew away, and twice as far.
Now when I cupped my hands I heard the crew
in low voices protesting:

                              'Godsake, Captain!
Why bait the beast again? Let him alone!'

450 'That tidal wave he made on the first throw
all but beached us.'

                              'All but stove us in!'
'Give him our bearing with your trumpeting,
he'll get the range and lob a boulder.'

                                          'Aye
He'll smash our timbers and our heads together!'
455 I would not heed them in my glorying spirit,
but let my anger flare and yelled:

                              'Cyclops,
if ever mortal man inquire
how you were put to shame and blinded, tell him
Odysseus, raider of cities, took your eye:
460 Laertes' son, whose home's on Ithaca!'

At this he gave a mighty sob and rumbled:
'Now comes the weird[40] upon me, spoken of old.
A wizard, grand and wondrous, lived here—Telemus,[41]
a son of Eurymus;[42] great length of days
465 he had in wizardry among the Cyclopes,
and these things he foretold for time to come:
my great eye lost, and at Odysseus' hands.

Literary Analysis
The Epic Hero Despite his heroism, which human weaknesses does Odysseus reveal as he sails away?

Reading Strategy
Reading in Sentences Rephrase the sentence in lines 450–451.

40. **weird** *n.* fate or destiny.
41. **Telemus** (tel e′ məs)
42. **Eurymus** (yōō rim′ əs)

Always I had in mind some giant, armed
in giant force, would come against me here.
470 But this, but you—small, pitiful and twiggy—
you put me down with wine, you blinded me.
Come back, Odysseus, and I'll treat you well,
praying the god of earthquake[43] to befriend you—
his son I am, for he by his avowal
475 fathered me, and, if he will, he may
heal me of this black wound—he and no other
of all the happy gods or mortal men.'

Few words I shouted in reply to him:

'If I could take your life I would and take
480 your time away, and hurl you down to hell!
The god of earthquake could not heal you there!'

At this he stretched his hands out in his darkness
toward the sky of stars, and prayed Poseidon:

'O hear me, lord, blue girdler of the islands,
485 if I am thine indeed, and thou art father:
grant that Odysseus, raider of cities, never
see his home: Laertes' son, I mean,
who kept his hall on Ithaca. Should destiny
intend that he shall see his roof again
490 among his family in his father land,
far be that day, and dark the years between.
Let him lose all companions, and return
under strange sail to bitter days at home.'

In these words he prayed, and the god heard him.
495 Now he laid hands upon a bigger stone
and wheeled around, <u>titanic</u> for the cast,
to let it fly in the black-prowed vessel's track.
But it fell short, just aft the steering oar,
and whelming seas rose giant above the stone
500 to bear us onward toward the island.
⠀⠀⠀⠀⠀⠀⠀⠀⠀⠀⠀⠀⠀⠀There
as we ran in we saw the squadron waiting,
the trim ships drawn up side by side, and all
our troubled friends who waited, looking seaward.
We beached her, grinding keel in the soft sand,
505 and waded in, ourselves, on the sandy beach.
Then we unloaded all the Cyclops' flock

43. god of earthquake
Poseidon.

Reading Strategy
Reading in Sentences
Rephrase the second
sentence of Cyclops'
prayer to Poseidon.

titanic (tī tan´ ik) *adj.* of
great size or strength

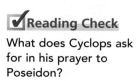**Reading Check**

What does Cyclops ask
for in his prayer to
Poseidon?

Odysseus in the Land of the Dead, N. C. Wyeth, Delaware Art Museum

▲ **Critical Viewing** What can you infer about ancient Greek beliefs concerning death and the afterlife from the text and this illustration? **[Infer]**

to make division, share and share alike,
only my fighters voted that my ram,
the prize of all, should go to me. I slew him
510 by the seaside and burnt his long thighbones
to Zeus beyond the stormcloud, Cronus'[44] son,
who rules the world. But Zeus disdained my offering:
destruction for my ships he had in store
and death for those who sailed them, my companions.
515 Now all day long until the sun went down
we made our feast on mutton and sweet wine,
till after sunset in the gathering dark
we went to sleep above the wash of ripples.

When the young Dawn with fingertips of rose
520 touched the world, I roused the men, gave orders
to man the ships, cast off the mooring lines;
and filing in to sit beside the rowlocks
oarsmen in line dipped oars in the gray sea.
So we moved out, sad in the vast offing,[45]
525 having our precious lives, but not our friends.

The Land of the Dead

*Odysseus and his men sail to Aeolia,[46] where Aeolus, king of the
winds, sends Odysseus on his way with a gift: a sack containing
all the winds except the favorable west wind. When they are near
home, Odysseus' men open the sack, letting loose a storm that
drives them back to Aeolia. Aeolus casts them out, having decided
that they are detested by the gods. They sail for seven days and
arrive in the land of the Laestrygonians,[47] a race of cannibals.
These creatures destroy all of Odysseus' ships except the one he is
sailing in. Odysseus and his reduced crew escape and reach
Aeaea, the island ruled by the sorceress-goddess Circe. She transforms half of the men into swine. Protected by a magic herb,
Odysseus demands that Circe change his men back into human
form. Before Odysseus departs from the island a year later, Circe
informs him that in order to reach home he must journey to the
land of the dead, Hades, and consult the blind prophet Tiresias.*

Literary Analysis
The Epic Hero Which admirable quality does Odysseus show in his actions with the stolen sheep?

44. Cronus (krō´ nəs) Titan who was ruler of the universe until he was overthrown by his son Zeus.

45. offing *n.* distant part of the sea visible from the shore.

46. Aeolia (ē ō´ lē ə)

47. Laestrygonians (les tri gō´ ni anz)

✔**Reading Check**

What does Circe say Odysseus must do in order to reach home?

We bore down on the ship at the sea's edge
and launched her on the salt immortal sea,
stepping our mast and spar in the black ship;
embarked the ram and ewe and went aboard
530   in tears, with bitter and sore dread upon us.
But now a breeze came up for us astern—
a canvas-bellying landbreeze, hale shipmate
sent by the singing nymph with sunbright hair;[48]
so we made fast the braces, took our thwarts,
535   and let the wind and steersman work the ship
with full sail spread all day above our coursing,
till the sun dipped, and all the ways grew dark
upon the fathomless unresting sea.

                                                    By night
our ship ran onward toward the Ocean's bourne,
540   the realm and region of the Men of Winter,
hidden in mist and cloud. Never the flaming
eye of Helios lights on those men
at morning, when he climbs the sky of stars,
nor in descending earthward out of heaven;
545   ruinous night being rove over those wretches.
We made the land, put ram and ewe ashore,
and took our way along the Ocean stream
to find the place foretold for us by Circe.
There Perimedes and Eulylochus[49]
550   pinioned[50] the sacred beasts. With my drawn blade
I spaded up the votive[51] pit, and poured
libations[52] round it to the unnumbered dead:
sweet milk and honey, then sweet wine, and last
clear water; and I scattered barley down.
555   Then I addressed the blurred and breathless dead,
vowing to slaughter my best heifer for them
before she calved, at home in Ithaca,
and burn the choice bits on the altar fire;
as for Tiresias, I swore to sacrifice
560   a black lamb, handsomest of all our flock.
Thus to <u>assuage</u> the nations of the dead
I pledged these rites, then slashed the lamb and ewe,
letting their black blood stream into the wellpit.
Now the souls gathered, stirring out of Erebus,[53]
565   brides and young men, and men grown old in pain,
and tender girls whose hearts were new to grief;
many were there, too, torn by brazen lanceheads,
battle-slain, bearing still their bloody gear.

**48. singing nymph . . .
hair** Circe.

Reading Strategy
Reading in Sentences
Reread the sentences in
lines 539–541 to explain
what happens to their
ship by night.

49. Perimedes (per´ ə mē´
dēz) **and Eurylochus** (yōō
ril´ ə kəs)

50. pinioned (pin´ yənd)
v. confined or shackled.

51. votive (vōt´ iv) *adj.*
done in fulfillment of a
vow or pledge.

52. libations (lī bā´ shənz)
n. wine or other liquids
poured upon the ground
as a sacrifice to a god.

assuage (ə swāj´) *v.* calm;
pacify

53. Erebus (er´ ə bəs) dark
region under the earth
through which the dead
pass before entering the
realm of Hades.

From every side they came and sought the pit
570 with rustling cries; and I grew sick with fear.
But presently I gave command to my officers
to flay those sheep the bronze cut down, and make
burnt offerings of flesh to the gods below—
to sovereign Death, to pale Persephone.[54]
575 Meanwhile I crouched with my drawn sword to keep
the surging phantoms from the bloody pit
till I should know the presence of Tiresias.[55]

One shade came first—Elpenor, of our company,
who lay unburied still on the wide earth
580 as we had left him—dead in Circe's hall,
untouched, unmourned, when other cares compelled us.
Now when I saw him there I wept for pity
and called out to him:

     'How is this, Elpenor,
how could you journey to the western gloom
585 swifter afoot than I in the black lugger?'
He sighed, and answered:

     'Son of great Laertes,
Odysseus, master mariner and soldier,
bad luck shadowed me, and no kindly power;
ignoble death I drank with so much wine.
590 I slept on Circe's roof, then could not see
the long steep backward ladder, coming down,
and fell that height. My neckbone, buckled under,
snapped, and my spirit found this well of dark.
Now hear the grace I pray for, in the name
595 of those back in the world, not here—your wife
and father, he who gave you bread in childhood,
and your own child, your only son, Telemachus,[56]
long ago left at home.

     When you make sail
and put these lodgings of dim Death behind,
600 you will moor ship, I know, upon Aeaea Island;
there, O my lord, remember me, I pray,
do not abandon me unwept, unburied,
to tempt the gods' wrath, while you sail for home;
but fire my corpse, and all the gear I had,
605 and build a cairn[57] for me above the breakers—
an unknown sailor's mark for men to come.

Literary Analysis
The Epic Hero and Conflict Which outside forces and inner feelings does Odysseus confront as he faces the spirits of the dead?

54. Persephone (pər səf´ ə nē) wife of Hades.

55. Tiresias (tī rē´ sē əs)

Reading Strategy
Reading in Sentences As you read Elpenor's words, where do you pause if you read in sentences?

56. Telemachus (tə lem´ ə kəs)

57. cairn (kern) *n.* conical heap of stones built as a monument.

✔**Reading Check**
What does Elpenor say happened to him on Circe's roof?

Heap up the mound there, and implant upon it
the oar I pulled in life with my companions.'

He ceased, and I replied:

'Unhappy spirit,
610   I promise you the barrow and the burial.'

So we conversed, and grimly, at a distance,
with my long sword between, guarding the blood,
while the faint image of the lad spoke on.
Now came the soul of Anticlea, dead,
615   my mother, daughter of Autolycus,[58]
dead now, though living still when I took ship
for holy Troy. Seeing this ghost I grieved,
but held her off, through pang on pang of tears,
till I should know the presence of Tiresias.
620   Soon from the dark that prince of Thebes[59] came forward
bearing a golden staff; and he addressed me:

'Son of Laertes and the gods of old,
Odysseus, master of landways and seaways,
why leave the blazing sun, O man of woe,
625   to see the cold dead and the joyless region?
Stand clear, put up your sword;
let me but taste of blood, I shall speak true.'

At this I stepped aside, and in the scabbard
let my long sword ring home to the pommel silver,
630   as he bent down to the somber blood. Then spoke
the prince of those with gift of speech:

'Great captain,
a fair wind and the honey lights of home
are all you seek. But anguish lies ahead;
the god who thunders on the land prepares it,
635   not to be shaken from your track, implacable,
in rancor for the son whose eye you blinded.
One narrow strait may take you through his blows:
denial of yourself, restraint of shipmates.
When you make landfall on Thrinacia first
640   and quit the violet sea, dark on the land
you'll find the grazing herds of Helios
by whom all things are seen, all speech is known.

58. Autolycus (ô tăl´ i kəs)

59. Thebes (thēbz)

Reading Strategy
Reading in Sentences
In ordinary language,
rephrase the lines in which
Odysseus puts away his
sword.

Avoid those kine,[60] hold fast to your intent,
and hard seafaring brings you all to Ithaca.
645 But if you raid the beeves, I see destruction
for ship and crew. Though you survive alone,
<u>bereft</u> of all companions, lost for years,
under strange sail shall you come home, to find
your own house filled with trouble: insolent men
650 eating your livestock as they court your lady.
Aye, you shall make those men atone in blood!
But after you have dealt out death—in open
combat or by stealth—to all the suitors,
go overland on foot, and take an oar,
655 until one day you come where men have lived
with meat unsalted, never known the sea,
nor seen seagoing ships, with crimson bows

60. kine (kīn) *n.* cattle.

bereft (bi reft´) *adj.*
deprived

✔Reading Check

What does Odysseus
learn has happened to his
mother?

▲ **Critical Viewing** How does the description of the characters in this art compare
to your image of the characters in the *Odyssey*? **[Compare and Contrast]**

and oars that fledge light hulls for dipping flight.
The spot will soon be plain to you, and I
660 can tell you how: some passerby will say,
"What winnowing fan is that upon your shoulder?"
Halt, and implant your smooth oar in the turf
and make fair sacrifice to Lord Poseidon:
a ram, a bull, a great buck boar; turn back,
665 and carry out pure hecatombs[61] at home
to all wide heaven's lords, the undying gods,
to each in order. Then a seaborne death
soft as this hand of mist will come upon you
when you are wearied out with rich old age,
670 your country folk in blessed peace around you.
And all this shall be just as I foretell.'

61. hecatombs (hek´ ə tōmz´) *n.* large-scale sacrifices in ancient Greece; often, the slaughter of 100 cattle at one time.

Review and Assess

Thinking About the Selection

1. **Respond:** What do you think of Odysseus' plan for escaping from Polyphemus?

2. **(a) Recall:** Before the meeting with the Cyclops, what had Odysseus received from Maron at Ismarus?
   (b) Generalize: What does the encounter with Maron reveal about ancient Greek attitudes regarding hospitality?

3. **(a) Recall:** How do Odysseus and his companions expect to be treated by the Cyclops? **(b) Infer:** What "laws" of behavior and attitude does Polyphemus violate in his treatment of the Greeks?

4. **(a) Recall:** How do Odysseus and his crew ultimately escape from the Cyclops? **(b) Evaluate:** Which positive and negative character traits does Odysseus demonstrate in his adventure with the Cyclops?

5. **(a) Recall:** Whom does Odysseus encounter in the Land of the Dead? **(b) Interpret:** Which character trait does Odysseus display in the Land of the Dead that he did not reveal earlier?

6. **(a) Recall:** What difficulties does Tiresias predict for the journey to come? **(b) Speculate:** Why would Odysseus continue, despite the grim prophecies?

7. **(a) Assess:** Based on Tiresias' prediction, which heroic qualities will Odysseus need to rely upon as he continues his journey? Explain.

The Sirens

Odysseus returns to Circe's island. The goddess reveals his course to him and gives advice on how to avoid the dangers he will face: the Sirens, who lure sailors to their destruction; the Wandering Rocks, sea rocks that destroy even birds in flight; the perils of the sea monster Scylla and, nearby, the whirlpool Charybdis;[62] and the cattle of the sun god, which Tiresias has warned Odysseus not to harm.

62. Charybdis (kə rib′ dis)

As Circe spoke, Dawn mounted her golden throne,
and on the first rays Circe left me, taking
her way like a great goddess up the island.
675 I made straight for the ship, roused up the men
to get aboard and cast off at the stern.
They scrambled to their places by the rowlocks
and all in line dipped oars in the gray sea.
But soon an offshore breeze blew to our liking—
680 a canvas-bellying breeze, a lusty shipmate
sent by the singing nymph with sunbright hair.
So we made fast the braces, and we rested,
letting the wind and steersman work the ship.
The crew being now silent before me, I
685 addressed them, sore at heart:

                              'Dear friends,
more than one man, or two, should know those things
Circe foresaw for us and shared with me,
so let me tell her forecast: then we die
with our eyes open, if we are going to die,
690 or know what death we baffle if we can. Sirens
weaving a haunting song over the sea
we are to shun, she said, and their green shore
all sweet with clover; yet she urged that I
alone should listen to their song. Therefore
695 you are to tie me up, tight as a splint,
erect along the mast, lashed to the mast,
and if I shout and beg to be untied,
take more turns of the rope to muffle me.'

I rather dwelt on this part of the forecast,
700 while our good ship made time, bound outward down
the wind for the strange island of Sirens.

Literary Analysis
The Epic Hero What does Odysseus reveal about his character by sharing information with his men?

✓**Reading Check**

What has Odysseus asked his shipmates to do in order to deal with the Sirens?

were fixed upon that yawning mouth in fear
of being devoured.

                              Then Scylla made her strike,

810 whisking six of my best men from the ship.
I happened to glance aft at ship and oarsmen
and caught sight of their arms and legs, dangling
high overhead. Voices came down to me
in anguish, calling my name for the last time.

815 A man surfcasting on a point of rock
for bass or mackerel, whipping his long rod
to drop the sinker and the bait far out,
will hook a fish and rip it from the surface
to dangle wriggling through the air:

                                      so these

820 were borne aloft in spasms toward the cliff.

She ate them as they shrieked there, in her den,
in the dire grapple, reaching still for me—
and deathly pity ran me through
at that sight—far the worst I ever suffered,
825 questing the passes of the strange sea.

                                We rowed on.

The Rocks were now behind; Charybdis, too,
and Scylla dropped astern.

The Cattle of the Sun God

In the small hours of the third watch, when stars
that shone out in the first dusk of evening
830 had gone down to their setting, a giant wind
blew from heaven, and clouds driven by Zeus
shrouded land and sea in a night of storm;
so, just as Dawn with fingertips of rose
touched the windy world, we dragged our ship
835 to cover in a grotto, a sea cave
where nymphs had chairs of rock and sanded floors.
I mustered all the crew and said:

Reading Strategy
Reading in Sentences By reading in sentences rather than line breaks, explain what happens in lines 810–814.

Literary Analyis
The Epic Hero How does Odysseus show the heroic quality of loyalty in lines 823–825?

         'Old shipmates,
our stores are in the ship's hold, food and drink;
the cattle here are not for our provision,
840 or we pay dearly for it.
        Fierce the god is
who cherishes these heifers and these sheep:
Helios; and no man avoids his eye.'

To this my fighters nodded. Yes. But now
we had a month of onshore gales, blowing
845 day in, day out—south winds, or south by east.
As long as bread and good red wine remained
to keep the men up, and appease their craving,
they would not touch the cattle. But in the end,
when all the barley in the ship was gone,
850 hunger drove them to scour the wild shore
with angling hooks, for fishes and seafowl,
whatever fell into their hands; and lean days
wore their bellies thin.
        The storms continued.
So one day I withdrew to the interior
855 to pray the gods in solitude, for hope
that one might show me some way of salvation.
Slipping away, I struck across the island
to a sheltered spot, out of the driving gale.
I washed my hands there, and made supplication
860 to the gods who own Olympus,[71] all the gods—
but they, for answer, only closed my eyes
under slow drops of sleep.
      Now on the shore Eurylochus
made his insidious plea:
        'Comrades,' he said,
'You've gone through everything; listen to what I say.
865 All deaths are hateful to us, mortal wretches,
but famine is the most pitiful, the worst
end that a man can come to.
       Will you fight it?
Come, we'll cut out the noblest of these cattle
for sacrifice to the gods who own the sky;
870 and once at home, in the old country of Ithaca,

Reading Strategy
Reading in Sentences
Explain the instructions that Odysseus gives his crew in lines 838–840.

Literary Analysis
The Epic Hero and Conflict What conflict is likely to arise from the crew's hunger?

71. Olympus (ō lim´ pəs) Mount Olympus, home of the gods.

insidious (in sid´ ē əs) *adj.* characterized by craftiness and betrayal

☑**Reading Check**
What does Scylla do to the six men she takes from the ship?

920 —Calypso later told me of this exchange,
as she declared that Hermes[75] had told her.
Well, when I reached the sea cave and the ship,
I faced each man, and had it out; but where
could any remedy be found? There was none.
925 The silken beeves[76] of Helios were dead.
The gods, moreover, made queer signs appear:
cowhides began to crawl, and beef, both raw
and roasted, lowed like kine upon the spits.

Now six full days my gallant crew could feast
930 upon the prime beef they had marked for slaughter
from Helios' herd; and Zeus, the son of Cronus,
added one fine morning.

                                      All the gales
had ceased, blown out, and with an offshore breeze
we launched again, stepping the mast and sail,
935 to make for the open sea. Astern of us
the island coastline faded, and no land
showed anywhere, but only sea and heaven,
when Zeus Cronion piled a thunderhead
above the ship, while gloom spread on the ocean.
940 We held our course, but briefly. Then the squall
struck whining from the west, with gale force, breaking
both forestays, and the mast came toppling aft
along the ship's length, so the running rigging
showered into the bilge.

                                  On the afterdeck
945 the mast had hit the steersman a slant blow
bashing the skull in, knocking him overside,
as the brave soul fled the body, like a diver.
With crack on crack of thunder, Zeus let fly
a bolt against the ship, a direct hit,
950 so that she bucked, in reeking fumes of sulphur,
and all the men were flung into the sea.
They came up 'round the wreck, bobbing awhile
like petrels[77] on the waves.

                          No more seafaring
homeward for these, no sweet day of return;
955 the god had turned his face from them.

                            I clambered

75. Hermes (hur´ mēz) herald and messenger of the gods.

76. beeves (bēvz) *n.* plural of *beef.*

Reading Strategy
Reading in Sentences By reading in sentences, explain what happens to the ship.

77. petrels (pe´ trəlz) small, dark sea birds.

fore and aft my hulk until a comber
split her, keel from ribs, and the big timber
floated free; the mast, too, broke away.
A backstay floated dangling from it, stout
960 rawhide rope, and I used this for lashing
mast and keel together. These I straddled,
riding the frightful storm.

                                        Nor had I yet
seen the worst of it: for now the west wind
dropped, and a southeast gale came on—one more
965 twist of the knife—taking me north again,
straight for Charybdis. All that night I drifted,
and in the sunrise, sure enough, I lay
off Scylla mountain and Charybdis deep.
There, as the whirlpool drank the tide, a billow
970 tossed me, and I sprang for the great fig tree,
catching on like a bat under a bough.
Nowhere had I to stand, no way of climbing,
the root and bole[78] being far below, and far
above my head the branches and their leaves,
975 massed, overshadowing Charybdis pool.
But I clung grimly, thinking my mast and keel
would come back to the surface when she spouted.
And ah! how long, with what desire, I waited!
till, at the twilight hour, when one who hears
980 and judges pleas in the marketplace all day
between contentious men, goes home to supper,
the long poles at last reared from the sea.

Now I let go with hands and feet, plunging
straight into the foam beside the timbers,
985 pulled astride, and rowed hard with my hands
to pass by Scylla. Never could I have passed her
had not the Father of gods and men,[79] this time,
kept me from her eyes. Once through the strait,
nine days I drifted in the open sea
990 before I made shore, buoyed up by the gods,
upon Ogygia[80] Isle. The dangerous nymph
Calypso lives and sings there, in her beauty,
and she received me, loved me.

Literary Analysis
The Epic Hero Which of Odysseus' heroic qualities are revealed in lines 959–962?

78. **bole** (bōl) *n.* tree trunk.

79. **Father . . . men** Zeus.

80. **Ogygia** (o jij´ ī a).

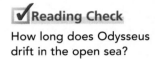

Reading Check

How long does Odysseus drift in the open sea?

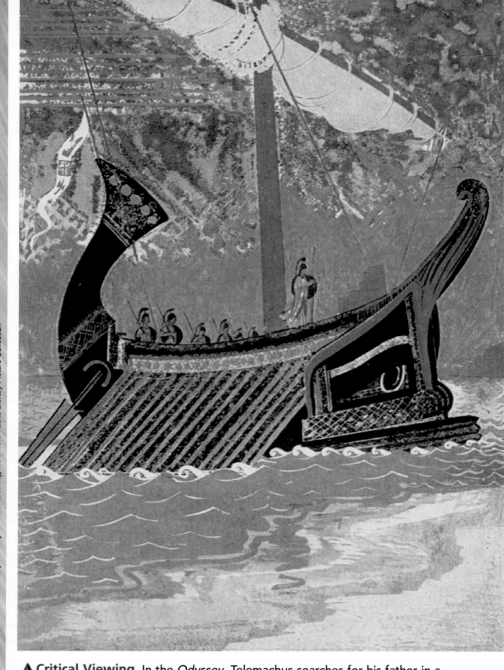

▲ **Critical Viewing** In the *Odyssey*, Telemachus searches for his father in a ship like this one. From what you observe in the painting, how does this ship compare with modern ships? **[Compare and Contrast]**

But why tell
the same tale that I told last night in hall
995 to you and to your lady? Those adventures
made a long evening, and I do not hold
with tiresome repetition of a story."

Review and Assess

Thinking About the Selection

1. **Respond:** In which adventure in this section does Odysseus act most heroically? Explain.

2. **(a) Recall:** How do the Sirens lure travelers to their destruction? **(b) Compare and Contrast:** How does the danger posed by the Sirens compare to that posed by the Lotus-Eaters?

3. **(a) Recall:** What are Scylla and Charybdis, and why do they pose dangers for travelers? **(b) Analyze:** Why does Odysseus choose to sail toward Scylla rather than Charybdis?

4. **(a) Make a Judgment:** Was Odysseus right not to tell his men about his decision to sail toward Scylla? **(b) Hypothesize:** What would have happened if Odysseus had told them everything?

5. **(a) Recall:** What does Eurylochus say to persuade Odysseus' men to slaughter and eat the cattle of Helios, the sun god? **(b) Analyze:** Why is Odysseus unable to keep his men from killing the cattle? **(c) Apply:** If you had been in their situation, do you think you would have eaten the cattle? Why or why not?

6. **Make a Judgment:** Do the members of the crew deserve the punishment they receive for killing the cattle?

Review and Assess

Literary Analysis

The Epic Hero

1. As an **epic hero,** Odysseus has both heroic and mortal qualities. Identify some of his qualities in both categories.
2. When Odysseus introduces himself in lines 18–37, which heroic traits does he reveal?
3. Based on Odysseus' actions in these episodes, which values did the ancient Greeks admire?

Connecting Literary Elements

4. Some of Odysseus' **conflicts** involve battles with enemies, and some involve clashes with thoughts and feelings within himself. On a chart like the one shown, list Odysseus' external and internal conflicts.

External Conflicts

Internal Conflicts

External Conflicts

5. In which of the adventures does Odysseus come into conflict with forces of nature?
6. Which character traits help Odysseus to be victorious in most of his conflicts?

Reading Strategy

Reading in Sentences

7. (a) How many complete stops should you make in reading lines 398–408? (b) Where are they?
8. Rewrite lines 704–715 as a paragraph, using your own words.

Extend Understanding

9. **History Connection:** Which political or military leader whom you have read or heard about seems similar to Odysseus? Explain.

Integrate Language Skills

Vocabulary Development Lesson

Word Origins: Words From Myths

Titanic, meaning "huge or powerful," comes from *Titans*, giant Greek gods who once ruled the world. Define each word and explain its link to mythology.

1. helium   2. odyssey   3. museum   4. siren

Spelling Strategy

If a word of more than one syllable has a vowel-consonant ending and the accent is not on the last syllable, do not double the final consonant before adding a suffix beginning with a vowel: *plunder + -ed = plundered*. Correct any misspellings below.

1. mentorring   2. flowerred   3. travelers

Concept Development: Antonyms

After reviewing the vocabulary on page 979, match each word below with its opposite.

1. dispatched   a. restored to its owner
2. bereft   b. begun
3. plundered   c. joyfully acquired
4. squall   d. tiny
5. mammoth   e. small and weak
6. assuage   f. calm, sunny weather
7. insidious   g. honest
8. titanic   h. aggravate
9. ardor   i. indifference

Grammar Lesson

Usage: *like, as,* and *as if*

The words *like, as,* and *as if* all suggest comparisons, but they are often used incorrectly. **Like** is a preposition and should not be used instead of the conjunctions **as** or **as if** to introduce a clause.

Incorrect: *Like* he had boasted, he was mighty.
Correct: *As* he had boasted, he was mighty.

Incorrect: He held the men *like* they were squirming puppies.
Correct: He held the men *as if* they were squirming puppies.
Correct: He held the men *like* squirming puppies.

Practice Write these sentences on your paper, using the correct word(s) in parentheses.

1. He ate (as if, like) he had been starving.
2. The men wept (as if, like) children.
3. (Like, As) a dead man, he slept unmoving.
4. The men felt (like, as if) they were doomed.
5. Odysseus' bragging sounded (like, as) a donkey's bray to the Cyclops.

Writing Application Write three sentences about Odysseus, using *like, as,* or *as if* in one sentence each.

*W*_G *Prentice Hall Writing and Grammar Connection: Chapter 27, Section 2*

Extension Activities

Listening and Speaking Pick one episode from Part 1 of the *Odyssey*, and describe the action as a **play-by-play broadcast**. Reread the episode and jot down the key actions. Draft a script. Practice your broadcast and record it to play for the class.

Writing In a **comparison-and-contrast essay,** explore the concept of the hero. In your essay, show similarities and differences between Odysseus and other heroes, real or imaginary. Include several different points of comparison.

Prepare to Read

from the Odyssey, Part 2

Literary Analysis

Epic Simile

An **epic simile**, sometimes called a Homeric simile, is an elaborate comparison that may extend for several lines. Epic similes may use the words *like, as, just as,* or *so* to make the comparison. In Part 1, lines 268–271, Odysseus uses an epic simile to describe the fallen tree from which he creates the weapon used to blind the Cyclops.

> And it was like a mast / a lugger of twenty oars, broad in the beam— / a deep-sea-going craft—might carry: / so long, so big around, it seemed.

As you read, notice Homer's use of epic similes to bring descriptions to life.

Connecting Literary Elements

Similes are one example of **imagery**—descriptive language that creates word pictures. These pictures, or images, are created with details of sight, sound, taste, touch, smell, or movement. An epic simile contains imagery that shows how something looks or acts by comparing it to something else. For example, comparing a fallen tree to a broad mast stresses the size of the tree.

Reading Strategy

Summarizing

You can better understand the events in an epic like the *Odyssey*—or in any other work of literature with a complicated plot—by **summarizing** the events as you read. Retell the plot briefly in your own words, jotting down details about what events occurred and why.

Use a chart like the one shown to summarize episodes in the *Odyssey*.

What Happens

As a beggar, Odysseus meets Telemachus. He is changed by Athena. He reveals his identity.

Why?

His disguise helps him find out what has changed in Ithaca. He needs his son's help.

Summary

Vocabulary Development

dissemble (di sem´ bəl) *v.* conceal under a false appearance; disguise (p. 1022)

lithe (līth) *adj.* supple; limber (p. 1024)

incredulity (in´ krə dōō´ lə tē) *n.* inability to believe (p. 1024)

bemusing (bi myōōz´ iŋ) *adj.* stupefying or muddling (p. 1027)

glowering (glou´ ər iŋ) *adj.* staring with sullen anger; scowling (p. 1029)

equity (ek´ wit ē) *n.* fairness; impartiality; justice (p. 1032)

maudlin (môd´ lin) *adj.* tearfully or foolishly sentimental (p. 1032)

contempt (kən tempt´) *n.* disdain or scorn; scornful feelings or actions (p. 1040)

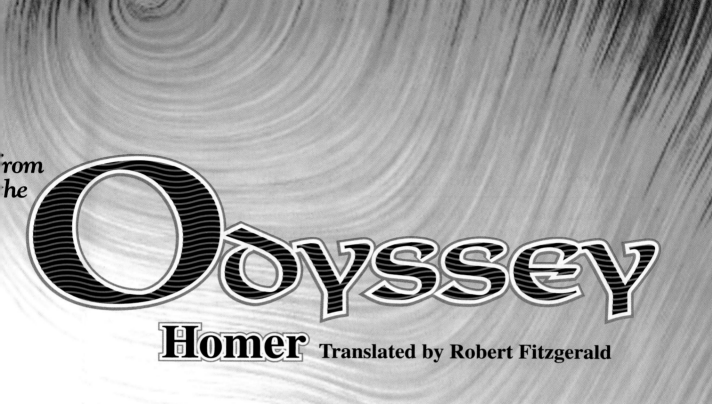

from the

Odyssey

Homer   Translated by Robert Fitzgerald

PART 2
The Return of Odysseus

Review and Anticipate

In Part 1 of the *Odyssey*, Odysseus and his companions face many perils on their voyage from Troy to Ithaca. At some moments, they are tempted by others to forsake their voyage; at others, their lives are endangered by powerful enemies. Ultimately, Odysseus' men bring about their own destruction at the hand of Zeus when they kill the cattle belonging to Helios.

As Part 2 begins, Odysseus is alone when he reaches Ithaca after a twenty-year absence. What do you predict will happen when Odysseus arrives home?

                              Saying no more,
she tipped her golden wand upon the man,
making his cloak pure white, and the knit tunic
fresh around him. <u>Lithe</u> and young she made him,
ruddy with sun, his jawline clean, the beard
1020 no longer gray upon his chin. And she
withdrew when she had done.
                              Then Lord Odysseus
reappeared—and his son was thunderstruck.
Fear in his eyes, he looked down and away
as though it were a god, and whispered:
                                        "Stranger,
1025 you are no longer what you were just now!
Your cloak is new; even your skin! You are
one of the gods who rule the sweep of heaven!
Be kind to us, we'll make you fair oblation[2]
and gifts of hammered gold. Have mercy on us!"

1030 The noble and enduring man replied:

"No god. Why take me for a god? No, no.
I am that father whom your boyhood lacked
and suffered pain for lack of. I am he."

Held back too long, the tears ran down his cheeks
1035 as he embraced his son.
                              Only Telemachus,
uncomprehending, wild
with <u>incredulity</u>, cried out:
                                  "You cannot
be my father Odysseus! Meddling spirits
conceived this trick to twist the knife in me!
1040 No man of woman born could work these wonders
by his own craft, unless a god came into it
with ease to turn him young or old at will.
I swear you were in rags and old,
and here you stand like one of the immortals!"

1045 Odysseus brought his ranging mind to bear
and said:
                    "This is not princely, to be swept
away by wonder at your father's presence.
No other Odysseus will ever come,
for he and I are one, the same; his bitter
1050 fortune and his wanderings are mine.

---

lithe (līth) *adj.* supple; limber

2. oblation (äb lā´ shən) *n.* offering to a god.

incredulity (in´ krə doo´ lə tē) *n.* inability to believe

Twenty years gone, and I am back again
on my own island.
                            As for my change of skin,
that is a charm Athena, Hope of Soldiers,
uses as she will; she has the knack
1055 to make me seem a beggar man sometimes
and sometimes young, with finer clothes about me.
It is no hard thing for the gods of heaven
to glorify a man or bring him low."

When he had spoken, down he sat.
                            Then, throwing
1060 his arms around this marvel of a father
Telemachus began to weep. Salt tears
rose from the wells of longing in both men,
and cries burst from both as keen and fluttering
as those of the great taloned hawk,
1065 whose nestlings farmers take before they fly.
So helplessly they cried, pouring out tears,
and might have gone on weeping so till sundown,
had not Telemachus said:
                            "Dear father! Tell me
what kind of vessel put you here ashore
1070 on Ithaca? Your sailors, who were they?
I doubt you made it, walking on the sea!"

Then said Odysseus, who had borne the barren sea:

"Only plain truth shall I tell you, child.
Great seafarers, the Phaeacians, gave me passage
1075 as they give other wanderers. By night
over the open ocean, while I slept,
they brought me in their cutter,[3] set me down
on Ithaca, with gifts of bronze and gold
and stores of woven things. By the gods' will
1080 these lie all hidden in a cave. I came
to this wild place, directed by Athena,
so that we might lay plans to kill our enemies.
Count up the suitors for me, let me know
what men at arms are there, how many men.
1085 I must put all my mind to it, to see
if we two by ourselves can take them on
or if we should look round for help."
                                        Telemachus
replied:

Reading Strategy
Summarizing How does Odysseus explain the change in his appearance?

Literary Analysis
Epic Simile In this epic simile, what is being compared?

3. cutter (kut´ər) *n.* small, swift ship or boat carried aboard a large ship to transport personnel or supplies.

Reading Check
Why is Telemachus initially doubtful of Odysseus' words?

Reading Strategy
Summarizing Summarize Telemachus' response to his father in lines 1089–1092. What is his concern?

4. in their prime in the best or most vigorous stage of their lives.

▼ **Critical Viewing**
Why do you think scenes such as this were depicted on Greek pottery? **[Speculate]**

                    "O Father, all my life your fame
as a fighting man has echoed in my ears—
1090   your skill with weapons and the tricks of war—
but what you speak of is a staggering thing,
beyond imagining, for me. How can two men
do battle with a houseful in their prime?[4]
For I must tell you this is no affair
1095   of ten or even twice ten men, but scores,
throngs of them. You shall see, here and now.
The number from Dulichium alone
is fifty-two picked men, with armorers,
a half dozen; twenty-four came from Same,
1100   twenty from Zacynthus; our own island
accounts for twelve, high-ranked, and their retainers,
Medon the crier, and the Master Harper,
besides a pair of handymen at feasts.
If we go in against all these
1105   I fear we pay in salt blood for your vengeance.
You must think hard if you would conjure up
the fighting strength to take us through."

                                        Odysseus

who had endured the long war and the sea
answered:

                                "I'll tell you now.
1110   Suppose Athena's arm is over us, and Zeus
her father's, must I rack my brains for more?"

Clearheaded Telemachus looked hard and said:

"Those two are great defenders, no one doubts it,
but throned in the serene clouds overhead;
1115   other affairs of men and gods they have
to rule over."

                        And the hero answered:

"Before long they will stand to right and left of us
in combat, in the shouting, when the test comes—
our nerve against the suitors' in my hall.
1120   Here is your part: at break of day tomorrow
home with you, go mingle with our princes.
The swineherd later on will take me down
the port-side trail—a beggar, by my looks,
hangdog and old. If they make fun of me
1125   in my own courtyard, let your ribs cage up

1026 ◆ *The Epic*

your springing heart, no matter what I suffer,
no matter if they pull me by the heels
or practice shots at me, to drive me out.
Look on, hold down your anger. You may even
1130 plead with them, by heaven! in gentle terms
to quit their horseplay—not that they will heed you,
rash as they are, facing their day of wrath.
Now fix the next step in your mind.

                                                    Athena,
counseling me, will give me word, and I
1135 shall signal to you, nodding: at that point
round up all armor, lances, gear of war
left in our hall, and stow the lot away
back in the vaulted storeroom. When the suitors
miss those arms and question you, be soft
1140 in what you say: answer:

                                    'I thought I'd move them
out of the smoke. They seemed no longer those
bright arms Odysseus left us years ago
when he went off to Troy. Here where the fire's
hot breath came, they had grown black and drear.
1145 One better reason, too, I had from Zeus:
suppose a brawl starts up when you are drunk,
you might be crazed and bloody one another,
and that would stain your feast, your courtship. Tempered
iron can magnetize a man.'

                                                    Say that.

1150 But put aside two broadswords and two spears
for our own use, two oxhide shields nearby
when we go into action. Pallas Athena
and Zeus All-Provident will see you through,
bemusing our young friends.

                                    Now one thing more.
1155 If son of mine you are and blood of mine,
let no one hear Odysseus is about.
Neither Laertes, nor the swineherd here,
nor any slave, nor even Penelope.
But you and I alone must learn how far
1160 the women are corrupted; we should know
how to locate good men among our hands,
the loyal and respectful, and the shirkers⁵
who take you lightly, as alone and young."

Reading Strategy
Summarizing Summarize Athena's role in Odysseus' plan.

Reading Strategy
Summarizing Summarize the events of Odysseus' reunion with Telemachus.

bemusing (bi myo͞oz´ iŋ) *adj.* stupefying or muddling

5. shirkers (shʉrk´ ərz) *n.* people who get out of doing (or leave undone) something that needs to be done.

✔**Reading Check**

How does Odysseus tell his son to respond if the suitors "practice shots" on Odysseus?

Argus

Odysseus heads for town with Eumaeus. Outside the palace, Odysseus' old dog, Argus, is lying at rest as his long-absent master approaches.

While he spoke

an old hound, lying near, pricked up his ears
1165 and lifted up his muzzle. This was Argus,
trained as a puppy by Odysseus,
but never taken on a hunt before
his master sailed for Troy. The young men, afterward,
hunted wild goats with him, and hare, and deer,
1170 but he had grown old in his master's absence.
Treated as rubbish now, he lay at last
upon a mass of dung before the gates—
manure of mules and cows, piled there until
fieldhands could spread it on the king's estate.
1175 Abandoned there, and half destroyed with flies,
old Argus lay.

But when he knew he heard

Odysseus' voice nearby, he did his best
to wag his tail, nose down, with flattened ears,
having no strength to move nearer his master.
1180 And the man looked away,
wiping a salt tear from his cheek; but he
hid this from Eumaeus. Then he said:

"I marvel that they leave this hound to lie
here on the dung pile;
1185 he would have been a fine dog, from the look of him,
though I can't say as to his power and speed
when he was young. You find the same good build
in house dogs, table dogs landowners keep
all for style."

And you replied, Eumaeus:

1190 "A hunter owned him—but the man is dead
in some far place. If this old hound could show
the form he had when Lord Odysseus left him,
going to Troy, you'd see him swift and strong.
He never shrank from any savage thing
1195 he'd brought to bay in the deep woods; on the scent
no other dog kept up with him. Now misery

Reading Strategy
Summarizing Summarize Argus' situation since Odysseus' departure.

has him in leash. His owner died abroad,
and here the women slaves will take no care of him.
You know how servants are: without a master
1200 they have no will to labor, or excel.
For Zeus who views the wide world takes away
half the manhood of a man, that day
he goes into captivity and slavery."

Eumaeus crossed the court and went straight forward
1205 into the megaron[6] among the suitors:
but death and darkness in that instant closed
the eyes of Argus, who had seen his master,
Odysseus, after twenty years.

The Suitors

Still disguised as a beggar, Odysseus enters his home.
He is confronted by the haughty[7] suitor Antinous.[8]

But here Antinous broke in, shouting:

                                                "God!
1210 What evil wind blew in this pest?

                                        Get over,
stand in the passage! Nudge my table, will you?
Egyptian whips are sweet
to what you'll come to here, you nosing rat,
making your pitch to everyone!
1215 These men have bread to throw away on you
because it is not theirs. Who cares? Who spares
another's food, when he has more than plenty?"

With guile Odysseus drew away, then said:

"A pity that you have more looks than heart.
1220 You'd grudge a pinch of salt from your own larder
to your own handyman. You sit here, fat
on others' meat, and cannot bring yourself
to rummage out a crust of bread for me!"

Then anger made Antinous' heart beat hard,
1225 and, <u>glowering</u> under his brows, he answered:

Reading Strategy
Summarizing Summarize the account of Argus in your own words.

6. **megaron** (meg´ ə rön)
n. great, central hall of the house, usually containing a center hearth.

7. **haughty** (hôt´ ē) *adj.*
arrogant.
8. **Antinous** (an tin´ ō əs)

glowering (glou´ ər iŋ) *adj.*
staring with sullen anger; scowling

Reading Check

What is Argus' relationship to Odysseus?

And he replied:

"My lady, never a man in the wide world
should have a fault to find with you. Your name
has gone out under heaven like the sweet
honor of some god-fearing king, who rules
in <u>equity</u> over the strong: his black lands bear
both wheat and barley, fruit trees laden bright,
new lambs at lambing time—and the deep sea
gives great hauls of fish by his good strategy,
so that his folk fare well.

O my dear lady,
this being so, let it suffice to ask me
of other matters—not my blood, my homeland.
Do not enforce me to recall my pain.
My heart is sore; but I must not be found
sitting in tears here, in another's house:
it is not well forever to be grieving.
One of the maids might say—or you might think—
I had got <u>maudlin</u> over cups of wine."

And Penelope replied:

"Stranger, my looks,
my face, my carriage,[12] were soon lost or faded
when the Achaeans crossed the sea to Troy,
Odysseus my lord among the rest.
If he returned, if he were here to care for me,
I might be happily renowned!
But grief instead heaven sent me—years of pain.
Sons of the noblest families on the islands,
Dulichium, Same, wooded Zacynthus,[13]
with native Ithacans, are here to court me,
against my wish; and they consume this house.
Can I give proper heed to guest or suppliant
or herald on the realm's affairs?

How could I?
wasted with longing for Odysseus, while here
they press for marriage.

Ruses[14] served my turn
to draw the time out—first a close-grained web
I had the happy thought to set up weaving
on my big loom in hall. I said, that day:
'Young men—my suitors, now my lord is dead,
let me finish my weaving before I marry,

1290
1295
1300
1305
1310
1315
1320
1325

equity (ek´ wit ē) *n.* fairness; impartiality; justice

Literary Analysis
Epic Simile To what does Odysseus compare his wife in the epic simile in lines 1290–1297?

maudlin (môd´ lin) *adj.* tearfully or foolishly sentimental

12. carriage (kar´ ij) *n.* posture.

13. Zacynthus (za sin´ thus)

14. ruses (rōōz´ əz) *n.* tricks.

or else my thread will have been spun in vain.
It is a shroud I weave for Lord Laertes
when cold Death comes to lay him on his bier.
The country wives would hold me in dishonor
1330 if he, with all his fortune, lay unshrouded.'
I reached their hearts that way, and they agreed.
So every day I wove on the great loom,
but every night by torchlight I unwove it;
and so for three years I deceived the Achaeans.
1335 But when the seasons brought a fourth year on,
as long months waned, and the long days were spent,
through impudent folly in the slinking maids
they caught me—clamored up to me at night;
I had no choice then but to finish it.
1340 And now, as matters stand at last,
I have no strength left to evade a marriage,
cannot find any further way; my parents
urge it upon me, and my son
will not stand by while they eat up his property.
1345 He comprehends it, being a man full-grown,
able to oversee the kind of house
Zeus would endow with honor.

                        But you too
confide in me, tell me your ancestry.
You were not born of mythic oak or stone."

---

*Penelope again asks the beggar to tell about himself. He makes
up a tale in which Odysseus is mentioned and declares that
Penelope's husband will soon be home.*

1350 "You see, then, he is alive and well, and headed
homeward now, no more to be abroad
far from his island, his dear wife and son.
Here is my sworn word for it. Witness this,
god of the zenith, noblest of the gods,[15]
1355 and Lord Odysseus' hearthfire, now before me:
I swear these things shall turn out as I say.
Between this present dark and one day's ebb,
after the wane, before the crescent moon,
Odysseus will come."

Reading Strategy
Summarizing Summarize what Penelope tells the disguised Odysseus. How has she demonstrated her loyalty to her husband?

15. god of the zenith, noblest of the gods Zeus.

 **Reading Check**

How does Odysseus initially respond to Penelope's questions about his past?

The Trial of the Bow, N. C. Wyeth, Delaware Art Museum

▲ **Critical Viewing** The winner of the archery contest will win Penelope's hand in marriage. How does the artist capture the tension in this scene? **[Interpret]**

The Challenge

Pressed by the suitors to choose a husband from among them, Penelope says she will marry the man who can string Odysseus' bow and shoot an arrow through twelve axhandle sockets. The suitors try and fail. Still in disguise, Odysseus asks for a turn and gets it.

And Odysseus took his time,

1360 turning the bow, tapping it, every inch,
for borings that termites might have made
while the master of the weapon was abroad.
The suitors were now watching him, and some
jested among themselves:

"A bow lover!"

1365 "Dealer in old bows!"

"Maybe he has one like it

at home!"

"Or has an itch to make one for himself."

"See how he handles it, the sly old buzzard!"

And one disdainful suitor added this:

"May his fortune grow an inch for every inch he bends it!"

1370 But the man skilled in all ways of contending,
satisfied by the great bow's look and heft,
like a musician, like a harper, when
with quiet hand upon his instrument
he draws between his thumb and forefinger
1375 a sweet new string upon a peg: so effortlessly
Odysseus in one motion strung the bow.
Then slid his right hand down the cord and plucked it,
so the taut gut vibrating hummed and sang
a swallow's note.

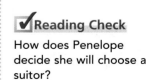

Reading Check

How does Penelope decide she will choose a suitor?

In the hushed hall it smote the suitors
1380 and all their faces changed. Then Zeus thundered
overhead, one loud crack for a sign.
And Odysseus laughed within him that the son
of crooked-minded Cronus had flung that omen down.
He picked one ready arrow from his table
1385 where it lay bare: the rest were waiting still
in the quiver for the young men's turn to come.
He nocked[16] it, let it rest across the handgrip,
and drew the string and grooved butt of the arrow,
aiming from where he sat upon the stool.

Now flashed

1390 arrow from twanging bow clean as a whistle
through every socket ring, and grazed not one,
to thud with heavy brazen head beyond.

Then quietly

Odysseus said:

"Telemachus, the stranger
you welcomed in your hall has not disgraced you.

▲ **Critical Viewing**
Compare Odysseus'
grace, described in line
1375, with the grace of
the hunter pictured here.
[Compare and Contrast]

16. nocked set an
arrow against the bow-
string.

1395   I did not miss, neither did I take all day
    stringing the bow. My hand and eye are sound,
    not so contemptible as the young men say.
    The hour has come to cook their lordships' mutton—
    supper by daylight. Other amusements later,
1400   with song and harping that adorn a feast."

    He dropped his eyes and nodded, and the prince
    Telemachus, true son of King Odysseus,
    belted his sword on, clapped hand to his spear,
    and with a clink and glitter of keen bronze
1405   stood by his chair, in the forefront near his father.

Review and Assess

Thinking About the Selection

1. **Respond:** If you were Telemachus or Penelope, how would you react to the stranger's arrival?

2. **(a) Recall:** Who does Telemachus think Odysseus is when they first reunite? **(b) Compare and Contrast:** Compare Odysseus' emotions with those of Telemachus at their reunion.

3. **(a) Recall:** Who is Argus? **(b) Recall:** How does Argus react to Odysseus' return? **(c) Analyze:** Is it a coincidence that Argus dies just when Odysseus returns? Explain.

4. **(a) Recall:** Describe Antinous' treatment of Odysseus. **(b) Analyze Causes and Effects:** Why do you think Antinous treats Odysseus so badly?

5. **(a) Analyze:** How does Penelope feel about the suitors in her house? **(b) Compare and Contrast:** How might Odysseus' feelings about the suitors differ from Penelope's?

6. **(a) Recall:** What does Odysseus tell Penelope about himself? **(b) Infer:** Why do you think Odysseus chooses not to reveal his identity to his wife?

7. **Take a Position:** Is it wrong for Odysseus to deceive his wife? Explain.

Contempt was all you had for the gods who rule wide heaven,
contempt for what men say of you hereafter.
Your last hour has come. You die in blood."

1445 As they all took this in, sickly green fear
pulled at their entrails, and their eyes flickered
looking for some hatch or hideaway from death.
Eurymachus[19] alone could speak. He said:

"If you are Odysseus of Ithaca come back,
1450 all that you say these men have done is true.
Rash actions, many here, more in the countryside.
But here he lies, the man who caused them all.
Antinous was the ringleader, he whipped us on
to do these things. He cared less for a marriage
1455 than for the power Cronion has denied him
as king of Ithaca. For that
he tried to trap your son and would have killed him.
He is dead now and has his portion. Spare
your own people. As for ourselves, we'll make
1460 restitution of wine and meat consumed,
and add, each one, a tithe of twenty oxen
with gifts of bronze and gold to warm your heart.
Meanwhile we cannot blame you for your anger."

Odysseus glowered under his black brows
1465 and said:
                    "Not for the whole treasure of your fathers,
all you enjoy, lands, flocks, or any gold
put up by others, would I hold my hand.
There will be killing till the score is paid.
You forced yourselves upon this house. Fight your way out,
1470 or run for it, if you think you'll escape death.
I doubt one man of you skins by."

They felt their knees fail, and their hearts—but heard
Eurymachus for the last time rallying them.

"Friends," he said, "the man is implacable.
1475 Now that he's got his hands on bow and quiver
he'll shoot from the big doorstone there
until he kills us to the last man.
                                        Fight, I say,
let's remember the joy of it. Swords out!
Hold up your tables to deflect his arrows.
1480 After me, everyone: rush him where he stands.

contempt (kən tempt´) n.
disdain or scorn; scornful
feelings or actions

19. Eurymachus (yo͞o
ri´ mə kəs)

Reading Strategy
Summarizing Summarize
the plea made by
Eurymachus to Odysseus.

If we can budge him from the door, if we can pass
into the town, we'll call out men to chase him.
This fellow with his bow will shoot no more."

He drew his own sword as he spoke, a broadsword of fine
    bronze,
1485 honed like a razor on either edge. Then crying hoarse and loud
he hurled himself at Odysseus. But the kingly man let fly
an arrow at that instant, and the quivering feathered butt
sprang to the nipple of his breast as the barb stuck in his liver.
The bright broadsword clanged down. He lurched and fell aside,
1490 pitching across his table. His cup, his bread and meat,
were spilt and scattered far and wide, and his head slammed
    on the ground.
Revulsion, anguish in his heart, with both feet kicking out,
he downed his chair, while the shrouding wave of mist closed on
    his eyes.

Amphinomus now came running at Odysseus,
1495 broadsword naked in his hand. He thought to make
the great soldier give way at the door.
But with a spear throw from behind Telemachus hit him
between the shoulders, and the lancehead drove
clear through his chest. He left his feet and fell
1500 forward, thudding, forehead against the ground.
Telemachus swerved around him, leaving the long dark spear
planted in Amphinomus. If he paused to yank it out
someone might jump him from behind or cut him down with a
    sword
at the moment he bent over. So he ran—ran from the tables
1505 to his father's side and halted, panting, saying:

"Father let me bring you a shield and spear,
a pair of spears, a helmet.
I can arm on the run myself; I'll give
outfits to Eumaeus and this cowherd.
1510 Better to have equipment."

                                    Said Odysseus:

"Run then, while I hold them off with arrows
as long as the arrows last. When all are gone
if I'm alone they can dislodge me."

                                    Quick

upon his father's word Telemachus

Literary Analysis
Epic Simile Why is the
comparison of
Eurymachus' sharp sword
to a razor a simile but not
an epic simile?

Reading Strategy
Summarizing In your own
words, briefly describe
the events of the battle of
Odysseus and Telemachus
with the suitors thus far.

☑**Reading Check**

What does Telemachus
want to bring to his father
to help him fight the
suitors?

1515 ran to the room where spears and armor lay.
He caught up four light shields, four pairs of spears,
four helms of war high-plumed with flowing manes,
and ran back, loaded down, to his father's side.
He was the first to pull a helmet on
1520 and slide his bare arm in a buckler strap.
The servants armed themselves, and all three took their stand
beside the master of battle.
                                    While he had arrows
he aimed and shot, and every shot brought down
one of his huddling enemies.
1525 But when all barbs had flown from the bowman's fist,
he leaned his bow in the bright entryway
beside the door, and armed: a four-ply shield
hard on his shoulder, and a crested helm,
horsetailed, nodding stormy upon his head,
1530 then took his tough and bronze-shod spears. . . .

Aided by Athena, Odysseus, Telemachus, Eumaeus, and other
 faithful herdsmen kill all the suitors.

And Odysseus looked around him, narrow-eyed,
for any others who had lain hidden
while death's black fury passed.
                                    In blood and dust
he saw that crowd all fallen, many and many slain.

1535 Think of a catch that fishermen haul in to a half-moon bay
in a fine-meshed net from the whitecaps of the sea:
how all are poured out on the sand, in throes for the salt sea,
twitching their cold lives away in Helios' fiery air:
so lay the suitors heaped on one another.

Penelope's Test

Penelope tests Odysseus to prove he really is her husband.

1540 Greathearted Odysseus, home at last,
was being bathed now by Eurynome
and rubbed with golden oil, and clothed again
in a fresh tunic and a cloak. Athena
lent him beauty, head to foot. She made him
1545 taller, and massive, too, with crisping hair

Literary Analysis
Imagery and Epic Simile
In reading the epic simile
in lines 1535–1539, what
do you picture?

Literary Analysis
Epic Simile To what is
Odysseus' hair compared?
Is this comparison an epic
simile?

in curls like petals of wild hyacinth
but all red-golden. Think of gold infused
on silver by a craftsman, whose fine art
Hephaestus♦ taught him, or Athena: one
1550 whose work moves to delight: just so she lavished
beauty over Odysseus' head and shoulders.
He sat then in the same chair by the pillar,
facing his silent wife, and said:

                      "Strange woman,
the immortals of Olympus made you hard,
1555 harder than any. Who else in the world
would keep aloof as you do from her husband
if he returned to her from years of trouble,
cast on his own land in the twentieth year?

Nurse, make up a bed for me to sleep on.
1560 Her heart is iron in her breast."

                          Penelope
spoke to Odysseus now. She said:

                      "Strange man,
if man you are . . . This is no pride on my part
nor scorn for you—not even wonder, merely.
I know so well how you—how he—appeared
1565 boarding the ship for Troy. But all the same . . .

Make up his bed for him, Eurycleia.
Place it outside the bedchamber my lord
built with his own hands. Pile the big bed
with fleeces, rugs, and sheets of purest linen."

1570 With this she tried him to the breaking point,
and he turned on her in a flash raging:

"Woman, by heaven you've stung me now!
Who dared to move my bed?
No builder had the skill for that—unless
1575 a god came down to turn the trick. No mortal
in his best days could budge it with a crowbar.
There is our pact and pledge, our secret sign,
built into that bed—my handiwork
and no one else's!

                   An old trunk of olive
1580 grew like a pillar on the building plot,

*L*iterature
in context   **Mythology Connection**

♦ *Hephaestus*

Any craftsman taught by Hephaestus, the Greek god of fire and metalworking, would be worth his weight in gold. His counterpart in Roman mythology was the mighty fire god Vulcan. Hephaestus was renowned for his work at the forge, crafting such items as Athena's spear, Achilles' shield, and Zeus' thunderbolts. Hephaestus was the only god with a physical deformity, caused when his father Zeus hurled him from Olympus. During his recovery, he learned how to craft beautiful objects from underwater coral and metals.

Statue of Vulcan, Hephaestus'
Roman counterpart

✔ Reading Check

How does Odysseus describe Penelope's attitude toward him?

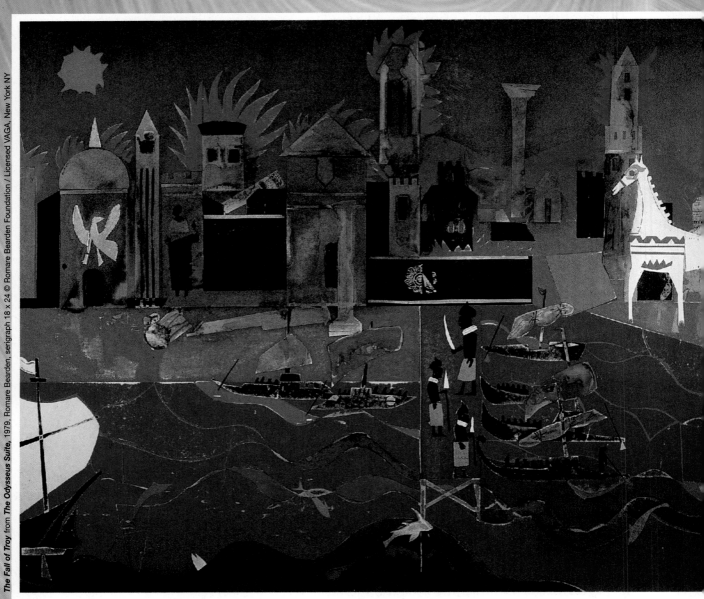

▲ **Critical Viewing** How does your image of the events in the *Odyssey* compare to this artist's interpretation of the events? **[Compare]**

and I laid out our bedroom round that tree,
lined up the stone walls, built the walls and roof,
gave it a doorway and smooth-fitting doors.
Then I lopped off the silvery leaves and branches,
1585 hewed and shaped that stump from the roots up
into a bedpost, drilled it, let it serve
as model for the rest. I planed them all,
inlaid them all with silver, gold and ivory,
and stretched a bed between—a pliant web
1590 of oxhide thongs dyed crimson.
                                        There's our sign!
I know no more. Could someone else's hand
have sawn that trunk and dragged the frame away?"

Their secret! as she heard it told, her knees
grew tremulous and weak, her heart failed her.
1595 With eyes brimming tears she ran to him,
throwing her arms around his neck, and kissed him,
murmuring:
                              "Do not rage at me, Odysseus!
No one ever matched your caution! Think
what difficulty the gods gave: they denied us
1600 life together in our prime and flowering years,
kept us from crossing into age together.
Forgive me, don't be angry. I could not
welcome you with love on sight! I armed myself
long ago against the frauds of men,
1605 impostors who might come—and all those many
whose underhanded ways bring evil on! . . .
But here and now, what sign could be so clear
as this of our own bed?
No other man has ever laid eyes on it—
1610 only my own slave, Actoris, that my father
sent with me as a gift—she kept our door.
You make my stiff heart know that I am yours."

Now from his breast into his eyes the ache
of longing mounted, and he wept at last,
1615 his dear wife, clear and faithful, in his arms,

Reading Strategy
Summarizing How would you describe Penelope's feelings in lines 1593–1596?

✔ **Reading Check**
What difficulty does Penelope say the gods gave to her and Odysseus?

longed for as the sunwarmed earth is longed for by a swimmer
spent in rough water where his ship went down
under Poseidon's blows, gale winds and tons of sea.
Few men can keep alive through a big surf

1620 to crawl, clotted with brine, on kindly beaches
in joy, in joy, knowing the abyss[20] behind:
and so she too rejoiced, her gaze upon her husband,
her white arms round him pressed as though forever.

20. **abyss** (ə bis´) *n.* ocean depths.

The Ending

Odysseus is reunited with his father. Athena commands that peace prevail between Odysseus and the relatives of the slain suitors. Odysseus has regained his family and his kingdom.

Homer

(circa 800 B.C.)

A legendary poet and historian, Homer is credited with two of the most famous and enduring epics of all time: the *Iliad* and the *Odyssey*. Their impressive length and scope have resulted in the coining of an adjective from the author's name: *homeric,* meaning "large-scale, massive, or enormous."

Facts about Homer's life have been lost over time. Scholars even disagree about whether the *Iliad* and the *Odyssey* were written by the same person—and whether Homer existed at all! According to tradition, however, Homer was born in western Asia Minor, and he was blind.

In later centuries, the *Iliad* and the *Odyssey* were the basis of Greek and Roman education.

Review and Assess

Thinking About the Selection

1. **Respond:** Do you think that Odysseus' revenge is justified? Why or why not?

2. **(a) Recall:** Which act begins Odysseus' revenge on the suitors? **(b) Analyze:** Why does this act catch the suitors by surprise?

3. **(a) Recall:** What planning does Odysseus do before battling the suitors? **(b) Analyze:** How does his planning help him defeat his opponents?

4. **(a) Recall:** How does the fight turn out? **(b) Analyze:** Even though some suitors have been crueler than others, why does Odysseus take equal revenge on all of them?

5. **(a) Recall:** What is Penelope's test, and how does Odysseus pass it? **(b) Infer:** Why does Penelope feel the need to test Odysseus, even though he has abandoned his disguise? **(c) Interpret:** Is the mood after the test altogether happy? Explain.

6. **(a) Connect:** Are Odysseus' actions in dealing with the suitors consistent with his actions in earlier episodes of the epic? Explain. **(b) Assess:** Do you consider him heroic?

7. **Evaluate:** How do you think the problem of the suitors should have been handled? Why?

Review and Assess

Literary Analysis

Epic Simile

1. Identify at least three **epic similes** in Part 2 of the *Odyssey*.
2. Using a chart like the one shown, note what is being compared in each of the epic similes you identified and the purpose of the comparison.

Lines	Comparison	Purpose

Connecting Literary Elements

3. What **imagery** involving sight, sound, and movement does Homer include in the epic simile in lines 1061–1065?
4. In lines 1412–1425, to which senses do the images used in describing Antinous' death appeal?
5. (a) What is the epic simile in lines 1613–1624? (b) Why is this simile a powerful image for the conclusion of the epic?

Reading Strategy

Summarizing

6. To **summarize** Part 2, use a timeline like this to list, in order, the main events.

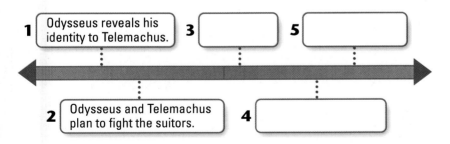

1 Odysseus reveals his identity to Telemachus.   3   5

2 Odysseus and Telemachus plan to fight the suitors.   4

7. Explain the cause and effect of each event that you listed.

Extend Understanding

8. **Cultural Connection:** Why do you think contemporary readers still relate to the characters and the events in the *Odyssey*?

Integrate Language Skills

Vocabulary Development Lesson

Word Analysis: Latin Root -equi-

The Latin root -equi-, meaning "same" or "equal," appears in the word *equity*, which means "fairness" or "justice." Complete each sentence below with one of the following -equi- words.

a. equinox   **b.** equivalent   **c.** equidistant

1. Two nickels are _____?_____ to a dime.
2. Since the two restaurants are _____?_____, we could reach either one in the same time.
3. At the vernal _____?_____, day and night are of the same duration.

Spelling Strategy

When adding a suffix beginning with a vowel to a word that ends in silent *e*, drop the *e* and add the suffix: *bemuse* + *-ing* = *bemusing*.

Add the suffix in italics to each word below, and write the new word in your notebook.

1. believe + *-able*   **2.** sense + *-ible*   **3.** secure + *-ity*

Concept Development: Synonyms

Review the words in the vocabulary list on page 1020. Then, choose the word or phrase whose meaning is closest to that of the first word.

1. dissemble: (a) resemble, (b) take apart, (c) disguise
2. lithe: (a) alert, (b) young, (c) limber
3. incredulity: (a) disbelief, (b) anger, (c) naiveté
4. bemusing: (a) allowing, (b) muddling, (c) entertaining
5. glowering: (a) shining, (b) scowling, (c) laughing
6. equity: (a) fairness, (b) horses, (c) calmness
7. maudlin: (a) boring, (b) tired, (c) sentimental
8. contempt: (a) scorn, (b) pity, (c) doubt

Grammar Lesson

Usage: *among* and *between*

The prepositions *among* and *between* are sometimes used incorrectly. **Among** always implies a relationship involving three or more items, while **between** generally is used with only two.

> **Among:** Eumaeus went into the megaron *among* the suitors. (many suitors)
>
> **Between:** Odysseus will come *between* this present dark and one day's ebb. (two times)

Practice Copy these sentences, using *among* or *between* to complete each one.

1. Suddenly a beggar stood _____?_____ all of the suitors.
2. A clash _____?_____ him and Antinous quickly developed.
3. Sounds of protest spread _____?_____ the onlookers, but Antinous paid them no heed.
4. Odysseus' deadly arrow struck _____?_____ Antinous' neck and shoulder.
5. Odysseus' skill as an archer is well known _____?_____ the Greeks.

Writing Application Write four sentences about events in the *Odyssey*. Use *among* correctly in two of the sentences and *between* correctly in the other two.

W̶G Prentice Hall Writing and Grammar Connection: Chapter 27, Section 2

Writing Lesson

Character Study

Odysseus is an epic hero, but he may not be a good role model. In a character study, evaluate Odysseus' status as a hero by analyzing his actions and motives. Support your analysis with examples and quotations from the epic.

Prewriting   Decide what you want to prove about Odysseus. To get started, write several different completions to this statement: *What I want to prove is* . . . Then, for each statement, list lines from the poem that can help you prove your point.

Drafting   Develop a thesis statement that expresses your main idea. Then, organize your points in a logical order. As you draft, be sure to include quotations from the text to illustrate your ideas.

Model: Using Quotations to Illustrate Points

When the men are escaping from the Cyclops, Odysseus taunts Polyphemus against his crew's wishes. He notes, "I would not heed them in my glorying spirit, but let my anger flare and yelled" (lines 455–456).

> Quotations from the text and line citations help readers see a strong connection between an argument and the text.

Revising   Review your draft to determine whether your ideas come across clearly and are well supported with quotations.

W͏G Prentice Hall Writing and Grammar Connection: Chapter 13, Section 3

Extension Activities

Listening and Speaking With several classmates, prepare a **debate** to determine whether Odysseus should be prosecuted for murder in the slaying of Penelope's suitors.

- Divide into two opposing teams.
- Prepare an argument expressing your team's position, and support it with details from the *Odyssey* or from actual legal cases found in library or Internet sources.
- Present arguments before the class.

Ask class members to decide which side presented its argument most successfully. **[Group Activity]**

Research and Technology Create an ***Odyssey* map** that traces Odysseus' voyage. Conduct library and Internet research to help you determine locations and distances between them. You might also refer to the map on page 1013. When you have completed your map, calculate the actual straight-line distance from Troy to Ithaca. Then, based on your map, approximate how far Odysseus traveled.

 Take It to the Net   www.phschool.com

Go online for an additional research activity using the Internet.

Prepare to Read

An Ancient Gesture ◆ Siren Song ◆ Prologue and Epilogue *from the* Odyssey ◆ Ithaca

Penelope and the Suitors, 1912, J.M. Waterhouse, Aberdeen Art Gallery and Museum, Scotland

Take It to the Net

Visit www.phschool.com
for interactive activities
and instruction related to
the selections, including

- background
- graphic organizers
- literary elements
- reading strategies

Preview

Connecting to the Literature

Two or more people looking at the same event are likely to describe it in distinctly different ways. In these selections, four writers bring their own perspectives to the events in the *Odyssey*.

Background

The authors of these four poems are twentieth-century men and women. Thus, their views of society and of men's and women's roles in society are very different from Homer's. For much of history in most cultures, women have had fewer legal rights and fewer opportunities than men. In fact, women in the United States did not even have the right to vote until 1920. Further progress for women was slow; they did not gain career and educational opportunities until the last few decades of the twentieth century.

Literary Analysis

Contemporary Interpretations

The characters and events of the *Odyssey* are timeless and universal in their interest and significance. They are so rich in meaning that every generation sees in them ideas and values that ring true. **Contemporary interpretations** of the epic—present-day conceptions or understandings— have produced poems, plays, novels, and essays by countless writers. For instance, in "Ithaca," Constantine Cavafy transforms Ithaca from a physical place to a spiritual ideal:

> Ithaca has given you the beautiful voyage.
> Without her you would never have taken the road.

Notice how the poets use ideas from Homer's work to convey contemporary thoughts, values, beliefs, and feelings.

Comparing Literary Works

Contemporary interpretations of an epic like the *Odyssey* can differ widely in purpose, theme, and artistic method. Consider the impact the backgrounds, ideas, and feelings of these writers may have had on their interpretations of the *Odyssey*. Then, compare the ways each poet reflects and adapts ideas from Homer's epic.

Reading Strategy

Comparing and Contrasting

In reading a piece of literature based on an earlier work, look for the similarities and differences between the original and the updated work.

- **Compare** an updated work with its original to discover how elements in the works are alike.
- **Contrast** an updated work with its original to decide how elements in the works are different.

As you read, use a Venn diagram like the one shown to identify similarities and differences between each poem and Homer's *Odyssey*.

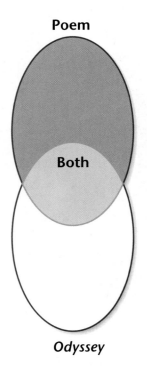

Poem

Both

Odyssey

Vocabulary Development

beached (bēcht) *adj.* washed up and lying on a beach (p. 1054)

picturesque (pik´ chər esk´) *adj.* like or suggesting a picture (p. 1055)

tempests (tem´ pists) *n.* violent storms with strong winds (p. 1056)

amber (am´ bər) *n.* yellowish resin used in jewelry (p. 1059)

ebony (eb´ ə nē) *n.* hard, dark wood used for furniture (p. 1059)

defrauded (dē frôd´ id) *v.* cheated (p. 1060)

▲ **Critical Viewing** The poet uses classical images from the *Odyssey*, like those pictured here, to make a connection to modern life. Which experiences in your life could correspond to some of the classical images mentioned in the poem? **[Connect]**

ITHACA

Constantine Cavafy

When you start on your journey to Ithaca,
then pray that the road is long,
full of adventure, full of knowledge.
Do not fear the Lestrygonians[1]
5   and the Cyclopes and the angry Poseidon.
You will never meet such as these on your path,
if your thoughts remain lofty, if a fine
emotion touches your body and your spirit.
You will never meet the Lestrygonians,
10   the Cyclopes and the fierce Poseidon,
if you do not carry them within your soul,
if your soul does not raise them up before you.

Then pray that the road is long.
That the summer mornings are many,
15   that you will enter ports seen for the first time
with such pleasure, with such joy!
Stop at Phoenician markets,
and purchase fine merchandise,
mother-of-pearl and corals, <u>amber</u> and <u>ebony</u>,

---

1. **Lestrygonians** (les tri gō′ nē ənz) cannibals who destroy all of Odysseus' ships except his own and kill the crews.

amber (am′ bər) *n.* yellowish resin used in jewelry

ebony (eb′ ə nē) *n.* hard, dark wood used for furniture

✔Reading Check

What advice does the speaker give listeners or readers about meeting the Lestrygonians?

20 and pleasurable perfumes of all kinds,
    buy as many pleasurable perfumes as you can;
    visit hosts of Egyptian cities,
    to learn and learn from those who have knowledge.

    Always keep Ithaca fixed in your mind.
25 To arrive there is your ultimate goal.
    But do not hurry the voyage at all.
    It is better to let it last for long years;
    and even to anchor at the isle when you are old,
    rich with all that you have gained on the way,
30 not expecting that Ithaca will offer you riches.

    Ithaca has given you the beautiful voyage.
    Without her you would never have taken the road.
    But she has nothing more to give you.

    And if you find her poor, Ithaca has not <u>defrauded</u> you.
35 With the great wisdom you have gained, with so much experience,
    You must surely have understood by then what Ithaca means.

defrauded (dē frôd´ id) v.
cheated

Review and Assess

Thinking About the Selection

1. **Respond:** Does the journey to Ithaca as described in this poem appeal to you? Explain.

2. **(a) Recall:** According to the speaker, how can you avoid meeting the Lestrygonians, the Cyclopes, and Poseidon on the road to Ithaca? **(b) Infer:** Why might a person carry such terrors as these in his or her own soul?

3. **(a) Recall:** What three things does the speaker say you should pray for on the journey to Ithaca?
   (b) Connect: What activities and pleasures are linked to these prayers?

4. **(a) Recall:** Why is Ithaca important? **(b) Interpret:** What might Ithaca symbolize to the poet?

5. **(a) Infer:** What message is conveyed in the last three lines of the poem? **(b) Apply:** Do you agree with this message?

6. **(a) Speculate:** What do you think the speaker might have said to Odysseus if he could have advised him during his journey? **(b) Take a Position:** Do you agree with this advice? Explain.

Constantine Cavafy

(1863–1933)
Considered the most important Greek poet of the first half of the twentieth century, Cavafy was born to Greek parents in Alexandria, Egypt.
    "Ithaca" showcases his basic creative method: using the world of Greek mythology to write poems that speak to today's reader.

Review and Assess

Literary Analysis

Contemporary Interpretations

1. What timeless theme does Edna St. Vincent Millay express in her **contemporary interpretation** of the *Odyssey*?
2. Use a chart like the one shown to explain how Atwood uses similarities and differences between her Siren and Homer's to make a point about modern women.

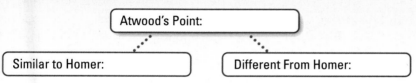

3. How does Walcott make the *Odyssey* seem contemporary?
4. Why is Odysseus' journey home good material for a poem that, like Constantine Cavafy's, concerns the course of human life?

Comparing Literary Works

5. Use a Venn diagram to identify the ways in which the attitudes toward men and women expressed in Atwood's and Millay's poems are similar or different.

6. How is Cavafy's poem different in tone from one or more of the other poems? Explain your answer.
7. Which of the other three poets might enjoy Walcott's treatment of the *Odyssey*? Cite details from their poems that support your answer.

Reading Strategy

Comparing and Contrasting

8. How is the journey that Cavafy describes essentially different from the one that Homer describes?

Extend Understanding

9. **Fine Arts Connection:** What other classical literary works can you think of that are especially well suited for modern interpretations? Explain your answer.

Quick Review

Contemporary interpretations are present-day conceptions or understandings of a classical work whose ideas and values are relevant to the present.

To **compare** an updated work with its original, determine how the two works are alike.

To **contrast** an updated work with its original, decide how the two works are different.

 Take It to the Net
www.phschool.com
Take the interactive self-test online to check your understanding of these selections.

Integrate Language Skills

Vocabulary Development Lesson

Word Analysis: French Suffix -esque

The French suffix -esque means "like" or "having the quality of." In "Siren Song," one of the Sirens complains of having to look too *picturesque*, which means "like or suggesting a picture." The suffix also appears in *statuesque* and *arabesque*.

Complete each sentence with one of the -esque words below:

a. picturesque **b.** statuesque **c.** arabesque

1. The ____?____ mountain view lingered in my mind for several days.
2. The carpet was covered with ____?____ designs resembling Moorish calligraphy.
3. The ____?____ actress commanded the attention of the audience with her regal bearing and stunning diamonds.

Concept Development: Analogies

Complete each analogy below with a word from the vocabulary list on page 1051.

1. *Melodious* is to *voice* as __?__ is to *appearance*.
2. *Marble* is to *statue* as __?__ is to *necklace*.
3. *Fallen* is to *leaves* as __?__ is to *shells*.
4. *Floods* are to *water* as __?__ are to *wind*.
5. *Aluminum* is to *can* as __?__ is to *table*.
6. *Spoke* is to *conversed* as __?__ is to *cheated*.

Spelling Strategy

If a word ends in a vowel-vowel-consonant combination, do not double the final consonant before adding a suffix. Thus, *defraud* + *-ed* = *defrauded*. Add the suffix to each word below and then use the new word in a sentence.

1. sweet + *-est* 2. break + *-age* 3. veil + *-ed*

Grammar Lesson

Varying Sentence Length

When you **vary sentence length,** you alternate between long and short sentences in order to make your sentences more interesting and readable. The varied rhythm of the passage below helps emphasize its meaning.

> **Example:** Cavafy uses the journey to Ithaca as a metaphor for one's own life journey. Enjoy life, says the poet. (*Long sentence followed by short sentence*)

If you write many long sentences, it will help the flow of your writing if you break some into shorter sentences.

Practice Rewrite each sentence as two shorter sentences. Simplify where possible.

1. Penelope cries for Odysseus, who is her husband, who has been away for years.
2. Sailors cannot resist the call of the Sirens' song, which lures men to their deaths.
3. Walcott introduces Billy Blue, who substitutes for Homer, narrator of the *Odyssey*.
4. Ithaca, which may symbolize the end of life, is the goal to focus on.
5. Each poet offers an interpretation of the *Odyssey*, the epic by Homer, who lived long ago.

Writing Application Write a paragraph describing your reaction to one of the poems. Work to vary your sentence lengths.

Writing Lesson

Comparison-and-Contrast Essay

All four of the poems in this section draw their inspiration from Homer's *Odyssey*. Write an essay in which you compare and contrast one of the selections with the appropriate portion of Homer's original work.

Prewriting After choosing the selection you wish to compare and contrast, list the ways that the poem and the *Odyssey* are similar and different. Prepare a comparison chart to organize the information.

Model: Finding Points of Comparison

Cavafy's "Ithaca"	Homer's *Odyssey*
1. Hopes the journey is long.	1. Hopes the journey will end.
2.	2.
3.	3.

> A comparison chart is a useful tool for organizing the information to be used in an essay.

Drafting Use the notes in your chart as the starting point from which to write your draft. Use words such as *like, unlike, similarly,* and *in contrast* to show points of difference and resemblance.

Revising When you revise your essay, make sure that it is clearly organized by points of comparison and contrast. In addition to checking for accuracy, be sure you have clarified the meaning of the passages to which you draw your readers' attention.

𝒲G *Prentice Hall Writing and Grammar Connection: Chapter 9, Section 2*

Extension Activities

Listening and Speaking Watch a film version of the *Odyssey*. Then, prepare a **movie review** for your classmates. In writing your review, consider these key elements of the task:

- Focus on the movie's themes and imagery.
- Formulate your own judgments about the film.
- Support those judgments with evidence.

Read your review aloud to your classmates and invite them to ask questions. **[Group Activity]**

Research and Technology Organize a **collection of literary works** inspired by the *Odyssey*. Use the Internet to help you search. Find enough information so that you can include a summary of each work you choose. If possible, use software to design your collection.

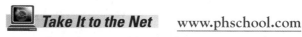 **Take It to the Net**   www.phschool.com

Go online for an additional research activity using the Internet.

CONNECTIONS
Literature Past and Present
Modern-day Odyssey

The *Odyssey* recounts the trials and adventures of Odysseus. Two decades is a long time to be away from home, dependent on the whims of the gods and facing dangers in battle with men and monsters. Still, risk has its rewards, and ultimately the story has a happy ending.

In April 1970, the three-man crew of the *Apollo 13* spacecraft embarked on a modern-day odyssey to the moon. Like Odysseus, they set out with a spirit of anticipation and adventure. But the exploration of space has its own perils. On the third day of their mission, just as they were getting ready to sleep in the command module nicknamed Odyssey, an onboard oxygen tank ruptured. After several nerve-wracking days, the crew finally managed to return safely to Earth. In this case, survival was the ultimate reward. The following excerpt from one astronaut's narrative describes the moment when the gas leak was first discovered.

Lost Moon
The Perilous Voyage of
Apollo 13
Jim Lovell
and
Jeffrey Kluger

"It looks to me," Lovell told the ground uninflectedly, "that we are venting something." Then, for impact, and perhaps to persuade himself, he repeated: "We are venting something into space."

"Roger," Lousma responded in the mandatory matter-of-factness of the Capcom, "we copy your venting."

"It's a gas of some sort," Lovell said.

"Can you tell us anything about it? Where is it coming from?"

"It's coming out of window one right now, Jack," Lovell answered, offering only as much detail as his limited vantage point provided.

The understated report from the spacecraft tore through the control room like a bullet.

"Crew thinks they're venting something," Lousma said to the loop at large.

"I heard that," Kranz said.

"Copy that, Flight?" Lousma asked, just to be sure.

"Rog," Kranz assured him. "O.K. everybody, let's think of the kinds of things we'd be venting. GNC, you got anything that looks abnormal on your system?"

"Negative, Flight."

"How about you, EECOM? You see anything with the instrumentation you've got that could be venting?"

"That's affirmed, Flight," Liebergot said, thinking, of course, of oxygen tank two. If a tank of gas is suddenly reading empty and a cloud of gas is surrounding the spacecraft, it's a good bet the two are connected, especially if the whole mess had been preceded by a suspicious, ship-shaking bang. "Let me look at the system as far as venting is concerned," Liebergot said to Flight.

"O.K., let's start scanning," Kranz agreed. "I assume you've called in your backup EECOM to see if we can get some more brain power on this thing."

"We got one here."

"Rog."

The change on the loop and in the room was palpable. No one said anything out loud, no one declared anything officially, but the controllers began to recognize that Apollo 13, which had been launched in triumph just over two days earlier, might have just metamorphosed from a brilliant mission of exploration to one of simple survival.

Jim Lovell

(b. 1928)

Jim Lovell was a test pilot for U.S. Navy fighter aircraft before joining the space program as an astronaut. Lovell was the first man to rendezvous two spacecraft and to journey twice to the moon. He coauthored this account of the harrowing journey of *Apollo 13*'s three-man crew.

Jeffrey Kluger

(b. 1954)

Jeffrey Kluger, a senior writer for *Time* magazine, frequently writes on science and space issues. With *Apollo 13* astronaut Jim Lovell, he coauthored the book *Lost Moon*, which served as the basis for the Ron Howard film about the mission.

Connecting Literature Past and Present

1. How would you have reacted to the discovery of the oxygen leak?
2. Did the astronauts deal with adversity in a manner similar to Odysseus'? If not, how did they differ?
3. Do the roles played by the gods have any type of counterpart in the account of the flight of *Apollo 13*? Explain

The Wrong Orbit

Senator Has No Legitimate Business Blasting Into Space

Editorial in *The Kansas City Star*, January 20, 1998

Most Americans think of political lobbying as something done by special interest groups trying to curry favor with lawmakers to affect some legislation. Not so in the case of Sen. John Glenn and his former employer, the National Aeronautics and Space Administration.

Glenn, a Democratic senator from Ohio, has lobbied NASA for some time in hope of returning to space. Glenn, who will turn 77 in July, was the first American to orbit the Earth.

He plans to retire from the Senate, but for his next engagement he wants to strap on a space suit under the pretense of scientific merit. Glenn says his space jaunt would help the space program understand the effects of weightlessness on the aging human form. (C'mon, Senator, it's doubtful even you believe that, so don't expect anyone else to.)

There are much better uses for the taxpayers' money than Glenn's planned junket in space via the Discovery mission in October. Besides, as the senator ought to know, workers in the space program are being laid off around the country due to downsizing at NASA. And there's something questionable, if not downright indecent, about a U.S. senator who has been a NASA ally in Congress, calling on the space agency for a favor. Whether on this planet or another, a quid pro quo is the same.

. . .

John Glenn became a hero after his pioneering space flight, and he parlayed that status into what was said to be a successful political career. His political career was jeopardized by his involvement in the Keating Five scandal, and he became excessively shrill this year during committee hearings as the Senate defender of the Democratic presidential fund-raising debacle.

Certainly, there are times when good science and good politics mix, as happened with the launch of the U.S. space program as part of the space race with former Soviet Union.

But Glenn's proposed junket in space is neither good science nor good politics.

> The writer uses the loaded word "pretense" in this paragraph.

> Here, the writer acknowledges an opposing point of view. Later, the writer will argue that the position is wrong.

> The editorial concludes with a restatement of the writer's opinion.

Check Your Comprehension

1. What were John Glenn's two careers?
2. What is unusual about Glenn's proposed ride in space?
3. Which editorial opposes Glenn's planned space ride?

Applying the Reading Strategy

Analyzing Bias

4. Cite two uses of loaded words in each editorial.
5. Identify two issues raised by the Kansas City editorial that are ignored by the Minneapolis editorial.

Activity

Writing an Editorial Analysis

These two editorials offer opposing points of view about John Glenn's proposed space trip. Create an outline like the one shown, listing the arguments in each editorial. Then, explain which editorial you find more convincing and why.

Contrasting Informational Texts

Editorials and News Reports

Editorials serve a different purpose from news reports. You read an editorial to discover a different perspective, or opinion, of an event. You watch a news report to collect information that is largely free of opinion.

1. Consider the differences between the two types of writing and answer the following questions:
   (a) How would a news article presenting John Glenn's proposed space voyage differ in tone and content from an editorial on the subject?
   (b) What is the benefit of each kind of writing?

2. In a current newspaper, find two letters to the editor that present opposing views on the same topic. Summarize the arguments that each writer presents.

I. Minneapolis Star and Tribune
   A. Main idea_____
   _____
   B. Supporting arguments
      1._____
      2._____
      3._____
   C. My conclusion_____
   _____

II. The Kansas City Star
   A. Main idea_____
   _____
   B. Supporting arguments
      1._____
      2._____
      3._____
   C. My conclusion_____
   _____

Writing WORKSHOP

Research Writing: Research Report

A **research report** interprets and presents information gathered through the extensive study of a subject. In this workshop, you will write a research report that presents your findings on a subject.

Assignment Criteria. Your research report should have the following characteristics of research writing:

- A thesis statement that is clearly expressed
- Factual support from a variety of credited sources
- A clear organization that includes an introduction, body, and conclusion
- A bibliography or works-cited list that provides a complete listing of research sources

To preview the criteria on which your research report may be assessed, see the Rubric on page 1075.

Prewriting

Choose a topic. Identify an area of general interest, and **brainstorm** for a list of more specific categories. For example, from the general area of art, you might choose the following categories: sculpture, Impressionism, and Pop Art. Using these categories, find a topic you would like to research.

Identify your purpose. Before you begin your report, consider a question that you would like to answer through your research. Review your notes and jot down a question that expresses this idea clearly. You may want to incorporate this information in a slightly different form into your draft when you start writing.

Question: How did the school of painting called Impressionism begin?

Gather and organize information. As you locate information, take notes to aid you in drafting your paper and creating a reference list.

- **Source cards:** Create a separate card to note the author, title, publisher, city, date of publication, and page number of each source you consult.
- **Note cards:** For each item of information, create a separate note card to record facts accurately, as in the chart shown.

If you choose to keep an electronic log of information, be sure to include all source details. Electronic logs offer you the advantage of using key word searches to locate source details.

Organize Information with Note Cards

> Marsh, Peter, M.D. *Eye to Eye: How People Interact.* Topsfield, MA: Salem House Publishers, 1988. (p. 54)
>
> Gestures vary from culture to culture. The American "OK" symbol (thumb and forefinger) is considered insulting in Greece and Turkey.

Student Model

Before you begin your research report, read this student model and review the characteristics of an effective research report.

Lyndsey Regan
Canyon Country, CA

Body Language

When we speak to other people, they are not only listening to our actual words, but sensing our facial expression, tone of voice, gestures, level of eye contact, posture, and movements as well. Nonverbal communication, or body language, makes up approximately 65 percent of human communication (Aylesworth 3). Body language has a major impact on how others perceive what we say. It can also be a tool for miscommunication when the speaker and listener are from different cultures or are communicating through technology that deprives them of visual cues. In fact, we often realize the importance of body language only when we cannot interpret someone else's body language correctly.

In *Eye to Eye: How People Interact*, Dr. Peter Marsh explains that before we speak, our gestures, posture and facial expressions are already broadcasting messages to those around us. While we are speaking, these gestures continue to communicate messages—usually clarifying what we are saying, but sometimes contradicting us in telltale ways (Marsh 116–119).

Often, body language is an unconscious act that triggers the most developed senses in other people—hearing and sight (Aylesworth 18). That is why body language is such a great way to emphasize words and ideas. Many people take advantage of this. Advertisers, for example, hire actors in their commercials who use body language that appeals to viewers.

Studies have shown that people's body language changes when they are not telling the truth (Vrij, Edward, Roberts, and Bull 239–263). If someone's body language is inconsistent with what he or she is saying, people tend to believe what the body is telling them. A good way for people to convey a positive message is to avoid certain movements, like fidgeting or letting your eyes wander. Instead, good communicators maintain steady eye contact, nod in agreement, and smile. You may notice that people on television, like hosts of infomercials and talk-show hosts, generally display this positive body language when speaking.

> The opening line is meant to capture the reader's attention by presenting a surprising perspective.

> The author expresses her thesis statement clearly and concisely.

Body language is usually learned, but it can also be inherited. It is affected by age, gender, background, and situation. The meaning of body language can change depending on cultural context. According to Dr. Marsh, each culture has developed its own repertoire of symbolic gestures, many with original associations that have now been long forgotten (Marsh 53–54). This causes people to be alarmed by foreign visitors or nervous around people when they visit new countries.

In the United States, people have a wide variety of regional influences because the country is a melting pot of diverse cultures. A gesture that means the same thing throughout the United States is the "OK" sign made with the thumb and the forefinger. This gesture is interpreted similarly in some European countries, but if you were to perform this sign in Greece or Turkey, it would be considered very insulting (Marsh 54).

There are other cultural differences in body language within Europe. In Germany, body language often reflects social status, and Germans often use body language for emphasis. Italian gestures are usually passionate, emotional expressions communicated with the face, arms, and shoulders. Italians often use body language to clarify themselves or to express urgency. In France, people tend to use more formal gestures. They are generally not as expressive or insistent as Italians. The body language of the French is not nearly as casual as we are used to in America (Ruesch and Kees 23–25). As you can see by exploring a few examples from different cultures, there are many differences in body language. Therefore, when you communicate with people from other countries, take special care in your use of body language.

Technological advancements in our society affect the way we communicate. For example, when we speak on the telephone, we are unable to see the person on the other end of the line. The message that a person may be trying to convey may be misinterpreted without the additional visual information provided by his or her body language. With electronic mail, there is no visual or verbal communication whatsoever. As a result, people cannot completely understand the meaning of what is being communicated. Therefore, people using e-mail should be careful about what they write. To avoid miscommunication, communicating the old-fashioned way—in person—may be the best approach.

> Whenever Lyndsey presents a specific piece of evidence that is not her own idea or common knowledge, she cites it using the appropriate format.

> The author's organizational structure is logical and clear. First, she discusses how body language is used in a variety of cultures. Next, she gives examples of what happens when we do not have body language to guide us.

In conclusion, body language is a significant component of communication, even though we are often not aware of it. Body language, like facial expressions and gestures, frequently enables people to clearly understand one another, but we must remember that people cannot always be read like a book. With cultural differences, body language can take on different meanings, and this allows for potential miscommunication. Changes in technology present a different kind of problem but with a similar result. When body language cannot be seen, people may misinterpret the meaning of the communicator, making them angry or confused. As you can see, the additional information we provide with our body language plays a major role in how we communicate our thoughts and ideas.

Works-Cited List

After her conclusion, Lyndsey presents the complete information for the works cited in her report using MLA, a common style for citation.

Aylesworth, Thomas G. *Understanding Body Talk.* New York :
F. Watts, 1979.

Marsh, Peter, M.D. *Eye to Eye: How People Interact.* Topsfield, MA:
Salem House Publishers, 1988.

Ruesch, Jurgen, and Weldon Kees. *Nonverbal Communication:
Notes on the Visual Perception of Human Relations.* Berkeley, CA:
University of California Press, 1969.

Vrij, Aldert, Katherine Edward, Kim P. Roberts, and Ray Bull.
"Detecting Deceit via Analysis of Verbal and Nonverbal Behavior."
Journal of Nonverbal Behavior, Winter 2000: 239–263.

Drafting

Propose a thesis statement. An effective thesis statement expresses an idea that can be supported by research. Review your notes and take a focused position that can be supported by most of the data you have gathered. Incorporate this position into your draft in the form of a statement.

> **Sample Thesis Statement**
> Claude Monet's handling of light in his water lily paintings is typical of Impressionist techniques.

Create an outline. To expand your ideas before writing the draft, use an outline. Organize your outline by using headings, as modeled in the chart shown. To construct a sentence outline, identify a topic sentence in each section. You can use these sentences to develop your draft.

Prepare to credit sources. When you include a direct quotation, present an original idea that is not your own, or report a fact that is available in only one source, you must include documentation. As you draft, circle ideas or words that are not your own. Use parentheses to note the author's last name and the page numbers of the material used. Later, you can use this record to create formal citation.

Outline Using Headings

Thesis Statement: Body language has a major impact on how others perceive what we say.
I. Introduction—Body language definition and thesis
II. Importance of body language
A. To emphasize key points
B. To recognize falsehoods
III. Poorly understood body language
A. Cultural differences
B. Text or voice technology
IV. Summary and conclusion

Revising

Revise to consider your sources. When presenting material as *fact*—information that is true and can be proven—you must confirm that the source of your information is reliable.

Underline any fact in your draft that may not have a trustworthy source. For example, you may have found an idea on another student's Web site or in a newspaper known for exaggerating ideas or events. Check to see if the fact you have marked is repeated in another, more reliable source, such as an established encyclopedia, a scholarly Web site, or a more trustworthy newspaper or magazine. If the fact is essential to your argument, you *must* find the fact in another source. If this fact is not essential to your argument, consider removing it from your draft.

Model: Evaluating Sources

A good way to convey a positive message is to avoid certain movements. ~~When people cross their arms it is always a sign of defensiveness.~~

> Lyndsey found that this was a controversial claim that was supported by only one source. Since it was inessential to her basic argument, she chose to eliminate it.

Revise to examine word choice. Except for the specific terminology associated with your topic, avoid using the same word over and over. Identify words that are key to your topic, and review your writing to find words that you have repeated. Circle them as you read. Using a thesaurus, generate a list of possible synonyms, and substitute them as appropriate. Look at these examples:

Example Synonym Banks

technology: innovation, invention, product, brainchild

theory: belief, policy, system, position, idea

Ronald Reagan: president, government official, leader

Finalize your research report. Before you publish your research report, you should document your sources of information. A works-cited page provides readers with complete information on each source you cite in your paper. A bibliography lists every work you used when researching, even if you did not cite it in the body of the report.

Standards for documentation are set by several organizations. Identify the format your teacher prefers. Following that format, check that each entry is complete and properly punctuated. (For more information, see Writing Criticism and Citing Sources, pages R30 and R31.)

Publishing and Presenting

Share your writing with a wider audience.

Deliver an oral presentation. Read your research report aloud in front of your classmates. You may want to provide classmates with a copy of your bibliography or works-cited page if they care to learn more about your topic.

 Prentice Hall Writing and Grammar Connection: Chapter 12

Rubric for Self-Assessment

Evaluate your research report using the following criteria and rating scale:

Criteria	Rating Scale Not very				Very
How clearly is the thesis statement expressed?	1	2	3	4	5
How sufficient is factual support from a variety of sources?	1	2	3	4	5
Is the research report well organized?	1	2	3	4	5
How comprehensive is the bibliography or works-cited list?	1	2	3	4	5

Listening and Speaking WORKSHOP

Delivering an Expository Presentation

In an **expository presentation,** a speaker explains a topic for an audience. Expository presentations are common in the business, scientific, and academic worlds. As with any public speech, the success of an expository presentation depends on thoughtful preparation and enthusiastic delivery.

Prepare the Presentation

Chose a topic. Decide what information you will present. You may decide to introduce your audience to your favorite hobby, to explain an interesting development in current events, or to discuss a musician whose work you admire. Narrow your topic so that you can address it in a brief presentation.

Consider your audience. The content of your presentation depends on the level of knowledge your audience already possesses. If they know little to nothing about your topic, do not present high-level material with complex detail. Conversely, do not expect an audience that is already familiar with a topic to be interested in basic-level description.

Prepare visuals. Plan to incorporate visuals to add interest to your presentation. These enhancements may include charts, graphs, bulleted outlines, illustrations, and fine art. Visuals should meet these criteria:

- They should be concise but clear.
- They should support your main thesis.
- They should present material in a new and interesting way.

Deliver the Presentation

Choose an appropriate tone. Develop a tone appropriate to the subject. If you are delivering a presentation on a serious subject, such as a bloody battle of the Civil War, adopt a serious tone. Use dramatic language and graphic visuals. Consider adding humor only when you want to put your audience at ease and inject some appropriate variety into your presentation.

Make use of source material. Direct references and quotations from source material can bring a presentation to life. Whenever appropriate, cite your sources or quote experts.

Offer varying interpretations. If a topic is controversial, address the varying interpretations of the subject. Stay on the subject when doing this, and offer your own conclusions to clarify ideas for your audience. Visual aids can help to eliminate confusion when you discuss complex topics.

(Activity: Presentation and Feedback) Choose a historical topic to present. Research your topic, and then deliver an expository presentation that incorporates visual aids as well as material culled from a variety of sources. Critique your presentation with the feedback form at right, and ask other students to offer their feedback.

Feedback Form for Expository Presentation

Rating System
+ = excellent   ✔ = average   – = weak

Preparation
Scope of Topic _____
Level of Detail _____
Use of Visuals _____

Delivery
Tone _____
Reference to Source Materials _____
Introduction of Varying Interpretations _____

Answer the following questions:
What did you learn that you did not know before?

What questions do you have about the content?

What improvements to the presentation would you recommend? Why?

Assessment WORKSHOP

Grammar, Usage, and Mechanics

The reading portions of some standardized tests require you to read a sentence or passage and answer multiple-choice questions about grammar, usage, and mechanics. Use the following information to help you:

- Grammar and usage questions test your knowledge of the parts of speech and the rules of sentence structure.
- To answer grammar and usage questions, check to see if all the parts of the sentence agree in number (singular or plural) and gender (masculine or feminine). Then, look to see whether every sentence expresses a complete thought.
- *Mechanics* refers to correct punctuation and capitalization. As you read each passage, determine whether the text makes correct use of these elements of writing.

Test-Taking Strategies

- Try to "hear" each sentence. If it sounds incorrect, check to see if all the parts of the sentence agree. If it is so long that you run out of breath, check for missing punctuation.
- If a word looks wrong, examine its spelling and capitalization.

Sample Test Item

Directions: Read the sentence and choose the best correction for the underlined word or words. If no correction is required, choose "Correct as is."

1. The use of sundials for telling time <u>span</u> many centuries.

   A are spanning

   B is spanning

   C spans

   D Correct as is

Answer and Explanation

The correct answer is *C*. *Use* is the subject and is singular. Therefore, the verb with which it agrees should be in its singular form, *spans*. *A* is plural and is therefore incorrect. *B* is incorrect because it describes an action in the present progressive tense, which does not make sense in the context of this sentence. *D* is incorrect because the verb does not agree in number with the subject.

▶ Practice

Directions: Read each sentence and choose the best correction for the underlined word or words. If no correction is required, choose "Correct as is."

1. Harold went to the barber <u>shop he</u> also went to the store.

   A shop. He

   B shop, he

   C shop—he

   D Correct as is

2. Although we want more <u>information. We</u> don't know where to look.

   A information: we

   B information, we

   C information—we

   D Correct as is

3. The pile of books on the table <u>are</u> heavy.

   A is

   B were

   C are not

   D Correct as is

RESOURCES

Following are some suggestions for longer works that will give you the opportunity to experience the fun of sustained reading. Each of the suggestions further explores one of the themes in this book. Many of the titles are included in the **Prentice Hall Literature Library**.

Unit One

A Tale of Two Cities
Charles Dickens

This historical novel, set in London and Paris during the French Revolution, is filled with suspenseful plot twists such as false accusations, look-alike characters, and bitter people thirsting for revenge. At the center of it all is beautiful Lucy Manette—whose father wavers between sanity and madness after spending eighteen years in a French prison, and whose husband is later unjustly imprisoned and sentenced to die by the guillotine.

To Kill a Mockingbird
Harper Lee

This novel, set in the South in the early 1930s, is narrated by a strong-willed girl named Scout. Through Scout's narration, readers meet her older brother, Jem, and her beloved father, Atticus, a respected lawyer who defends an African American accused of attacking a white woman. Scout also recounts the chilling legend of Boo Radley, a neighborhood recluse, feared by all the children, who seems to be following Scout and her brother.

The Strange Case of Dr. Jekyll and Mr. Hyde
Robert Louis Stevenson

This is the story of a mild-mannered doctor who explores his dark side—with terrifying results. Fascinated with the idea of evil, the story's main character, Dr. Jekyll, develops a potion that changes him into the violent Mr. Hyde. Before long, however, Jekyll finds himself transforming into Hyde without the aid of the potion, leaving him, along with terrified readers, to wonder which personality will finally win out.

Unit Two

The Old Man and the Sea
Ernest Hemingway

This novel tells of a man's heroic struggle with nature. The battle begins when the old fisherman Santiago hooks a giant marlin after months without a catch. The old man puts up a fierce effort to conquer the huge and powerful fish, fighting exhaustion, hunger, injury, and even a pack of sharks. This story, told in Hemingway's lean, straightforward style, is a timeless tale of courage and adventure.

The Miracle Worker
William Gibson

This moving play is based on the true story of Helen Keller, who was left blind, deaf, and unable to speak following an illness when she was an infant. The title refers to Helen's teacher, Annie Sullivan, a young woman determined to meet the challenge of helping Helen to communicate. This play, Gibson's most famous, inspired an Academy Award-winning movie.

Rosa Parks: My Story
Rosa Parks with Jim Haskins

One of the pivotal moments of the American civil rights movement occurred on December 1, 1955, when Rosa Parks, an African American, chose not to give up her seat to a white rider on a bus in Montgomery, Alabama. Through this memoir, readers get a firsthand account of that dramatic event and its aftermath, as well as biographical information about one of the leaders of the civil rights movement.

Unit Three

Great Expectations
Charles Dickens

Set in nineteenth-century England, this classic novel traces the passage of a boy called Pip into adulthood. Along the way, he encounters many memorable characters, including a pair of escaped convicts, a wealthy old woman who hasn't left her house since being jilted on her wedding day, and a beautiful young girl who captures his heart. Through a series of adventures, Pip makes many discoveries about himself, the people close to him, and the society in which he lives.

When the Legends Die
Hal Borland

This is the story of a young man who discovers his identity and cultural heritage as he struggles with the challenges of nature. After his father kills another brave, Thomas Black Bull and his parents flee the Ute reservation in southwestern Colorado to live in the wilderness. There, they follow the old ways of Native Americans—hunting, fishing, and fighting for survival. Life is good until Thomas's parents die and he is left on his own.

The House on Mango Street
Sandra Cisneros

This book, a mixture of poetry and prose, tells the story of Esperanza Cordero, a young girl living in Chicago. Through her neighbors on Mango Street, Esperanza makes many discoveries about life as she explores questions such as these: Should a girl get married or pursue her education? How does writing help people express their ideas and solve their problems? Why is growing up so confusing?

Unit Four

The Prince and the Pauper
Mark Twain

In this social satire, set in sixteenth-century England, a young prince and a London street beggar exchange identities. Twain uses both understatement and exaggeration to describe the confusing events that follow. The amusing twists and turns of the plot ultimately reveal a deeper message—that it is wrong to judge people by their outward appearances and that anyone can be a king.

Alice's Adventures in Wonderland
Lewis Carroll

In this fanciful story, a young girl falls down a rabbit hole and finds herself in a strange country where nothing seems to make sense. At times, she grows huge as a giant; at other times, she shrinks to the size of a mouse. Along the way, Alice meets an assortment of extraordinary characters, including a talking rabbit, a sleepy dormouse, and a grinning Cheshire cat. More than just a children's story, this book uses satire and symbolism to poke fun at society.

Childhood
Bill Cosby

In this entertaining book, funnyman Bill Cosby shares humorous reminiscences of his childhood. He recalls getting scolded for his bad manners, acting up in school, suffering through crushes on girls, and playing sports on the streets of Philadelphia. Each tale is told in the sidesplitting style that has secured for Cosby his place as one of the country's best-loved comedians.

Unit Five

Fahrenheit 451
Ray Bradbury

This book is set in a time when firemen start fires—fires that burn books. Guy Montag is a fireman who enjoys his job and never thinks of questioning the system. Then, he meets a teenage girl who tells him of a time when people were not afraid to think for themselves. Suddenly Montag realizes that he can no longer blindly accept the laws of his society.

The Time Machine
H. G. Wells

In this classic science-fiction tale, written more than one hundred years ago, H. G. Wells provides a grim view of the future. The story focuses on an inventor who travels into the future in a time machine he has built. During his travels, he views the progressive destruction of society and even life itself, eventually witnessing a time when giant crabs are the only surviving life form and the sun and Earth are dying.

Dragonsong
Anne McCaffrey

Set in the imaginary world of Pern, *Dragonsong* tells the story of Menolly, a young musician. When the laws of her society prevent Menolly from developing her musical talents, she wanders away from her home and discovers a group of rare and enchanting fire lizards. Menolly's relationship with the fire lizards and her unshakeable love for her music are the basis of this fantasy story.

abash (ə bash´) *v.*: Embarrass

acclaimed (ə klāmd´) *v.*: Greeted with loud applause or approval; hailed

acutely (ə kyōōt´ lē) *adv.*: Sharply

adept (ə dept´) *adj.*: Highly skilled; expert

aerodynamics (er´ ō dī nam´ iks) *n.*: Branch of mechanics dealing with the forces exerted by air or other gases in motion

aloofness (ə lōōf´ nes) *n.*: State of being distant, removed, or uninvolved

amber (am´ bər) *n.*: Yellowish resin used in jewelry

ambiguities (am´ bə gyōō´ ə tēz) *n.*: Statements or events whose meanings are unclear

amicably (am´ i kə blē) *adv.*: Agreeably

anonymous (ə nän´ ə məs) *adj.*: Without a known or acknowledged name

archaeologist (är´ kē äl´ ə jist) *n.*: Person who practices the scientific study of the remains of ancient ways of life

archaic (är kā´ ik) *adj.*: Seldom used; old-fashioned

ardent (ärd´ ´nt) *adj.*: Passionate

ardor (är´ dər) *n.*: Passion; enthusiasm

articulate (är tik´ yōō lāt) *v.*: Express in words

articulate (är tik´ yōō lit) *adj.*: Expressing oneself clearly and easily

assuage (ə swāj´) *v.*: Calm; pacify

astutely (ə stōōt´ lē) *adv.*: Cleverly or cunningly

astuteness (ə stōōt´ nis) *n.*: Shrewdness

augmenting (ôg ment´ iŋ) *v.*: Increasing; enlarging

avail (ə vāl´) *v.*: Be of help

awry (ə rī´) *adj.*: Not straight

azure (azh´ ər) *adj.*: Blue

bafflement (baf´ əl mənt) *n.*: Puzzlement; bewilderment

barren (bar´ ən) *adj.*: Empty

beached (bēcht´) *adj.*: Washed up and lying on a beach

beguiling (bi gīl´ iŋ) *adj.*: Tricking; charming

beleaguered (bi lē´ gərd) *adj.*: Worried; tormented

bemusing (bi myōōz´ iŋ) *adj.*: Stupefying or muddling

benevolently (bə nev´ ə lənt lē) *adv.*: In a kind and well-meaning way

bereft (bi reft´) *adj.*: Deprived

bizarre (bi zär´) *adj.*: Odd in appearance

blandly (bland´ lē) *adv.*: In a mild and soothing way

blight (blīt) *n.*: Something that destroys or prevents growth

bliss (blis) *n.*: Great joy or happiness

brazen (brā´ zən) *adj.*: Shamelessly bold

buffet (bə fā´) *n.*: Counter or table where refreshments are served

buffeted (buf´ it ed) *v.*: Jostled; knocked about

cannonading (kan´ ən ād´ iŋ) *n.*: Continuous firing of artillery

capacious (kə pā´ shəs) *adj.*: Able to hold much; roomy

ceasing (sēs´ iŋ) *v.*: Stopping

censure (sen´ shər) *n.*: Strong disapproval

charged (chärjd) *adj.*: Tensely expectant; intense

chasms (kaz´ əmz) *n.*: Deep cracks in Earth's surface; narrow gorges

chaste (chāst) *adj.*: Pure or clean in style; not ornate

chattel (chat´ əl) *n.*: Movable item of personal property

chortled (chôrt´ əld) *v.*: Made a jolly, chuckling sound

cipher (sī´ fər) *adj.*: Code

circumvent (sʉr´ kəm vent´) *v.*: Avoid; go around

cloister (klois´ tər) *n.*: Place devoted to religious seclusion

compelling (kəm pel´ iŋ) *adj.*: Forceful

complied (kəm plīd´) *v.*: Carried out or fulfilled a request

concessions (kən sesh´ ənz) *n.*: Things given or granted as privileges

condescending (kän´ di sen´ diŋ) *adj.*: Characterized by looking down on someone

condolence (kən dō´ ləns) *n.*: Expression of sympathy for a grieving person

confer (kən fʉr´) *v.*: To give

confounds (kən foundz´) *v.*: Bewilders; confuses

console (kən sōl´) *v.*: Comfort

contempt (kən tempt´) *n.*: Actions or attitude of a person toward someone or something he or she considers low or worthless

conundrums (kə nun´ drəmz) *n.*: Puzzling questions or problems

covenant (kuv´ ə nənt) *n.*: Agreement; pact

creed (krēd) *n.*: Statement of belief

cunning (kun´ iŋ) *n.*: Clever; sly

cur (kʉr) *n.*: Mean, contemptible person; mean, ugly dog

dallying (dal´ ē iŋ) *v.*: Wasting time; loitering

déclassée (dā´ klä sā´) *French fem. adj.*: Lowered in social status

decoy (dē´ koi) *n.*: Person or thing used to lure others into a trap

deferred (di fʉrd´) *adj.*: Put off until a future time

defiance (di fī´ əns) *n.*: Open resistance

defrauded (di frôd´ əd) *v.*: Cheated

deity (dē´ ə tē) *n.*: A god

deleterious (del´ ə tir´ ē əs) *adj.*: Injurious; harmful to health or well-being

demure (di myōōr´) *adj.*: Shy or modest

depravity (dē prav´ ə tē) *n.*: Wickedness; corruption

derides (di rīdz´) *v.*: Ridicules

derisive (di rī´ siv) *adj.*: Showing contempt or ridicule

desolate (des´ ə lit) *adj.*: Deserted; abandoned

despair (di sper´) *n.*: Hopelessness

despotic (des pät´ ik) *adj.*: Like or in the manner of an absolute ruler or tyrant

desultory (des´ əl tôr´ ē) *adj.*: Random

determination (dē tʉr´ mi nā´ shən) *n.*: Firm intention

detritus (di trīt´ əs) *n.*: Debris

diffused (di fyōōzd´) *v.*: Spread out

discreet (dis krēt´) *adj.*: Tactful; respectful

disheveled (di shev´ əld) *adj.*: Disarranged and untidy

dishevelment (di shev´ əl mənt) *n.*: A state of being untidy

dismal (diz´ məl) *adj.*: Causing gloom or misery

dispatched (dis pacht´) *v.*: Finished quickly

disperse (di spʉrs´) *v.*: Drive off or scatter in different directions

dissemble (di sem´ bəl) *v.*: Conceal with false appearances; disguise

distraught (di strôt´) *adj.*: Extremely troubled; confused; distracted

diverged (dī vʉrjd´) *v.*: Branched out in different directions

divine (də vīn´) *adj.*: Holy; sacred

dogmas (dôg´ məz) *n.*: Firmly held beliefs or doctrines

droll (drōl) *adj.*: Comic and amusing in an odd way

drowsiness (drou´ zē nes) *n.*: Sleepiness

ebony (eb´ ə nē) *n.*: Hard, dark wood used for furniture

eddies (ed´ ēz) *n.*: Circular currents

eerie (ir´ ē) *adj.*: Mysterious

effervesce (ef´ ər ves´) *v.*: To be lively

effigies (ef´ i jēz) *n.*: Crude figures or dummies representing hated people or a group

eloquence (el´ ə kwəns) *n.*: Speech that is vivid, forceful, graceful, and persuasive

elucidate (i lōō´ sə dāt´) *v.*: Explain

encompassed (en kum´ pəst) *v.*: Surrounded

encroaching (en krōch´ iŋ) *adj.*: Intruding in a gradual or sneaking way

endeavoring (en dev´ ər iŋ) *n.*: Trying; attempting

endurance (en dʉr´ əns) *n.*: Ability to withstand hardship and stress and to carry on

engendered (en jen´ dərd) *v.*: Produced

enigma (i nig´ mə) *n.*: Puzzling or baffling matter; riddle

enjoined (en joind´) *v.*: Ordered

entrails (en´ trālz) *n.*: Internal organs, specifically intestines

epiphany (ē pif´ ə nē) *n.*: Moment of sudden understanding

epithets (ep´ ə thetz) *n.*: Abusive words or phrases; slurs

equity (ek´ wit ē) *n.*: Fairness; impartiality; justice

erratic (er rat´ ik) *adj.*: Irregular; random

evanesced (ev ə nest´) *v.*: Faded away

exalted (eg zôlt´ əd) *v.*: Lifted up

exile (eks´ īl´) *v.*: Banish

extrapolating (ek strap´ ə lāt´ iŋ) *v.*: Arriving at a conclusion by making inferences based on known facts

extrapolation (ek strap′ ə lā′ shən) n.: Conclusions drawn by speculation on the basis of facts

feint (fānt) v.: Pretended move to catch an opponent off guard

feline (fē′ līn) adj.: Catlike

fester (fes′ tər) v.: Form pus

fickle (fik′ əl) adj.: Changeable

ford (fôrd) n.: Shallow place in a river that can be crossed

forebears (fôr′ bərs′) n.: Ancestors

formality (fôr mal′ ə tē) n.: Established rules or customs

formidable (fôr′ mə də bəl) adj.: Awe-inspiring

fray (frā) n.: Noisy fight

fretful (fret′ fəl) adj.: Irritable and discontented

furtive (fur′ tiv) adj.: Preventing observation; sneaky

furtively (fur′ tiv lē) adv.: Stealthily, so as to avoid being heard

futile (fyo͞ot′ əl) adj.: Useless; hopeless

gallant (gal′ ənt) adj.: Brave and noble

garish (gar′ ish) adj.: Too bright or gaudy

gaunt (gônt) adj.: Thin and bony

genesis (jen′ ə sis) n.: Birth; origin; beginning

genteel (jen tēl′) adj.: Refined; polite

glee (glē) n.: Joy

glowering (glou′ ər iŋ) adj.: Staring with sullen anger; scowling

gossamer (gäs′ ə mər) adj.: Light, thin, and filmy

grievance (grēv′ əns) n.: Injustice; complaint

grisly (griz′ lē) adj.: Horrifying; gruesome

grotesque (grō tesk′) adj.: Having a strange, bizarre design

haggard (hag′ ərd) adj.: Having a wild, worn look, as from sleeplessness

hamlet (ham′ lit) n.: Very small village

harness (här′ nis) v.: Attach, as with straps for pulling or controlling

harried (har′ ēd) adj.: Worried

harrowed (har′ ōd) v.: Broken up and leveled by a harrow, a frame with spikes or disks, drawn by a horse or tractor

haughty (hôt′ ē) adj.: Arrogant

heretics (her′ ə tiks) n.: Those who hold to a belief opposed to the established teachings of a church

hieroglyphics (hī′ ər ō′ glif′ iks) n.: Pictures or symbols that represent words or ideas

hoax (hōks) n.: Deceitful trick

host (hōst) n.: A great number

hurtling (hurt′ liŋ) adj.: Moving swiftly and with great force

hydraulic (hī drô′ lik) adj.: Operated by the movement and pressure of liquid

ideology (ī′ dē äl′ ə jē) n.: Ideas on which a political, economic, or social system is based

imbued (im byo͞od′) v.: Inspired

imminent (im′ ə nənt) adj.: Likely to happen soon

immortalized (im môrt′ ′l īzd) v.: Given lasting fame

immutable (im′ myo͞ot′ ə bəl) adj.: Never changing

imperative (im per′ ə tiv) adj.: Absolutely necessary; urgent

imperialist (im pir′ ē əl ist) adj.: Here, describing a person from a country that seeks to dominate weaker countries

impertinent (im purt′ ən ənt) adj.: Rude; impolite

imperturbable (im′ pər tur′ bə bəl) adj.: Unable to be excited or disturbed

implications (im′ pli kā′ shənz) n.: Suggestions or indirect indications

impose (im pōz′) v.: Put to some trouble

improbable (im präb′ ə bəl) adj.: Unlikely to happen

improvised (im′ prə vīzd) adj.: Put together on the spur of the moment

inalienable (in āl′ yən ə bəl) adj.: Not able to be taken away or transferred

incognito (in käg′ ni tō′) n.: A disguised condition

incredulity (in′ krə do͞o′ lə tē) n.: Inability to believe

indolently (in′ də lənt lē) adv.: Lazily; idly

ineffable (in ef′ ə bəl) adj.: Too overwhelming to be expressed in words

infallibility (in fal′ ə bil′ ə tē) n.: Condition of being unable to fail

infrared (in′ frə red′) adj.: Of light waves that lie just beyond the red end of the visible spectrum

ingeniously (in jēn′ yəs lē) adv.: Cleverly

insatiable (in sā′ shə bəl) adj.: Unable to be satisfied

inscrutable (in skro͞ot′ ə bəl) adj.: That which cannot be easily understood; baffling; mysterious

insidious (in sid′ ē əs) adj.: Treacherous in a sly, tricky way

insinuatingly (in sin′ yo͞o āt′ iŋ lē) adv.: Hinting or suggesting indirectly; implying

insolent (in′ sə lənt) adj.: Boldly disrespectful in speech or behavior

instigates (in′ stə gāts′) v.: Urges on; stirs up

intent (in tent′) adj.: Firmly fixed; concentrated

intercession (in′ tər sesh′ ən) n.: The act of pleading on behalf of another

interpretation (in tur′ prə tā′ shən) n.: Explanation

introspective (in′ trō spek′ tiv) adj.: Causing one to look into one's own thoughts and feelings

intuition (in′ to͞o ish′ ən) n.: Knowledge of something without reasoning

iridescent (ir′ i des′ ənt) adj.: Having shifting, rainbowlike colors

irradiated (ir rā′ dē āt′ id) v.: Gave out; radiated

jibed (jībd) v.: Stopped short and turned from side to side

judicious (jo͞o dish′ əs) adj.: Showing good judgment

keener (kēn′ ər) adj.: More clear; sharper

kindred (kin′ drid) n.: Relatives

laden (lād′ ən) adj.: Burdened

lamentable (lam′ ən tə bəl) adj.: Distressing; sad

languid (laŋ′ gwid) adj.: Drooping; weak

languor (laŋ′ gər) n.: Lack of vigor; weakness

larder (lärd′ ər) n.: Place where food is kept; pantry

lassoed (las′ ōd) adj.: Wrapped around

lateral (lat′ ər əl) adj.: Sideways

legacy (leg′ ə sē) n.: Anything handed down from an ancestor

legendary (lej′ ən der′ ē) adj.: Based on legends, or stories handed down for generations

levitation (lev ə tā′ shən) n.: The illusion of keeping a heavy body in the air without visible support

lingered (liŋ′ gərd) v.: Stayed on, as if unwilling to leave

literally (lit′ ər əl ē) adv.: Actually; in fact

lithe (līth) adj.: Supple; limber

loathsome (lōth′ səm) adj.: Disgusting

loitered (loit′ ərd) v.: Hung about; lingered

longevity (län jev′ə tē) n.: The length or duration of a life

malevolence (mə lev′ ə ləns) n.: Bad or evil feelings or intentions

malodorous (mal ō′ dər əs) adj.: Having a bad smell

mammoth (mam′ əth) adj.: Enormous

manhandled (man′ han′ dəld) v.: Treated roughly

marauders (mə rôd′ ərz) n.: Raiders; people who take goods by force

martial (mär′ shəl) adj.: Military

maudlin (môd′ lin) adj.: Tearfully or foolishly sentimental

medley (med′ lē) n.: Mixture of things not usually found together

menacing (men′ əs iŋ) v.: Threatening

meretricious (mer′ ə trish′ əs) adj.: Attractive in a cheap, flashy way

metaphors (met′ə fôrz′) n.: Figures of speech in which things are spoken of as if they were something else

metaphysical (met′ ə fiz′ i kəl) adj.: Spiritual; beyond the physical

meticulously (mə tik′ yo͞o ləs lē) adv.: Very carefully; scrupulously

microcosms (mī′ krō kä′ zəmz) n.: Little worlds

monotone (män′ ə tōn′) n.: Uninterrupted repetition of the same tone

moribund (môr′ i bund′) adj.: Dying

mortified (môrt′ ə fīd′) v.: Embarrassed

muted (myo͞ot′ əd) adj.: Weaker; less intense

myriad (mir′ ē əd) adj.: Countless; innumerable

naive (nä ēv′) adj.: Unsophisticated

novice (näv′ is) adj.: Beginner

oasis (ō ā′ sis) n.: Fertile place in the desert

obstinacy (äb′ stə nə sē) n.: Stubbornness

omen (ō′ mən) n.: Sign foretelling a future event, either good or evil

ominous (äm′ ə nəs) adj.: Threatening; menacing

ominously (äm′ ə nəs lē) adv.: In a threatening way

oppression (ə presh′ ən) n.: Keeping others down by the unjust use of power

oracle (ō′ rə kəl) n.: Source of knowledge or wise counsel

paean (pē′ ən) n.: Song of joy or triumph

pagans (pā′ gənz) n.: People who are not Christians, Muslims, or Jews

pallid (pal′ id) adj.: Pale

pallor (pal´ ər) n.: Paleness

palpable (pal´ pə bəl) adj.: Able to be touched or felt

palpitating (pal´ pə tāt iŋ) adj.: Beating rapidly; throbbing

pandemonium (pan´ də mō´ nē əm) n.: Wild disorder, noise, or confusion

parched (pärcht) adj.: Dried up by heat

parlance (pär´ ləns) n.: Style of speaking or writing; language

pensive (pen´ siv) adj. Thinking deeply or seriously

penury (pen´ yōō rē) n.: Extreme poverty

perennial (pə ren´ ē əl) adj.: Lasting through the year or for a long time

perish (per´ ish) v.: Die

permeate (pur´ mē āt) v.: Spread or flow throughout

pernicious (pər nish´ əs) adj.: Causing great injury or ruin; destructive

perpetuated (pər pech´ ōō āt id) v.: Caused to continue indefinitely; prolonged

perplexed (pər plekst´) adj.: Puzzled; full of doubt

perplexes (pər´ pleks´ iz) v.: Confuses or makes hard to understand

perverse (pər vurs´) adj.: Continuing in a stubborn way to do what is wrong or harmful; improper; willful

picturesque (pik´ chər esk´) adj.: Like or suggesting a picture

pilgrimage (pil´ grim ij) n.: Long journey

pinions (pin´ yənz) n.: The last bony sections of a bird's wings

pious (pī´ əs) adj.: Showing religious devotion

placid (plas´ id) adj.: Tranquil; calm

placidly (plas´ id lē) adv.: Calmly; quietly

plaiting (plāt´ iŋ) v.: Braiding

plundered (plun´ dərd) v.: Took goods by force; looted

poignant (poin´ yənt) adj.: Drawing forth pity or compassion; moving

portents (pôr´ tentz) n.: Things that are thought to be signs of events to come; omens

postulated (päs´ chə lāt ed) v.: Claimed

precariously (prē ker´ ē əs lē) adv.: Insecurely

precipitous (prē sip´ ə təs) adj.: Steep; sheer

precluded (prē klōōd´ id) v.: Prevented; made impossible in advance

precursors (prē kur´ sərz) n.: Things that prepare the way for what will follow

predominant (prē däm´ ə nənt) adj.: Having dominating influence over others

preposterous (pri päs´ tər əs) adj.: Absurd

primed (prīmd) v.: Made ready; prepared

procure (prō kyōōr´) v.: Get; obtain

prodigious (prō dij´ əs) adj.: Wonderful; of great size

prodigy (präd´ ə jē) n.: Person who is amazingly talented or intelligent

profoundly (prō found´ lē) adv.: Deeply and intensely

projectiles (prō jek´ təlz) n.: Objects that are hurled through the air

pungent (pun´ jənt) adj.: Producing a sharp sensation of smell

purged (purjd) v.: Cleansed; emptied

pursue (pər sōō´) v.: Seek

pyre (pīr) n.: Pile of wood on which a body is burned at a funeral

quaint (kwānt) adj.: Strange; unusual

rakishly (rāk´ ish lē) adv.: With a careless, casual look; dashing

rancor (raŋ´ kər) n.: Deep spite or bitter hate

ravages (rav´ ij iz) n.: Ruins; devastating damages

ravenous (rav´ ə nəs) adj.: Greedily hungry

reciprocate (ri sip´ rə kāt) v.: Return

reconcile (rek´ ən sīl´) v.: Bring into agreement

reconciled (rek´ ən sīld) adj.: Became friends again

reconnaissance (ri kän´ ə səns) adj.: Exploratory in nature, as when examining or observing to seek information

recounted (ri kount´ ed) v.: Told in detail; narrated

refrain (ri frān´) v.: To hold back

remnants (rem´ nənts) n.: Remaining persons or things

respite (res´ pit) n.: Rest; relief

resplendent (ri splen´ dənt) adj.: Shining brightly

retort (ri tôrt´) n.: Sharp or clever reply

retribution (re trə byōō´ shən) n.: Payback; punishment for a misdeed or reward for a good deed

revelry (rev´ əl rē) n.: Party

reverie (rev´ ər ē) n.: Dreamy thought of pleasant things

riveting (riv´ it iŋ) adj.: Firmly holding attention

rueful (rōō´ fəl) adj.: Feeling sorrow or regret

ruminative (rōō´ mə nə təv) adj.: Meditative

sallow (sal´ ō) adj.: Of a sickly, pale-yellowish complexion

schism (siz´ əm) n.: Split or division

scourge (skurj) n.: Whip or other instrument for inflicting punishment

scowling (skoul´ iŋ) v.: Contracting the eyebrows and frowning to show displeasure

scruples (skrōō´ pəlz) n.: Misgivings about something one feels is wrong

sentimental (sen´ tə ment´ əl) adj.: Excessively or foolishly emotional

sepulcher (sep´ əl kər) n.: Tomb

shards (shärdz) n.: Broken pieces

simultaneously (sī´ məl tā´ nē əs lē) adv.: At the same time

singular (siŋ´ gyə lər) adj.: Extraordinary; rare

sinister (sin´ is tər) adj.: Threatening harm; ominous

skeptical (skep´ ti kəl) adj.: Doubting; questioning

slouching (slouch´ iŋ) adj.: Drooping

sobriety (sə brī´ ə tē) n.: Moderation, especially in the use of alcoholic beverages

sore (sôr) adj.: Fierce; cruel

specters (spek´ tərz) n.: Ghostly images; phantoms

spurn (spurn) v.: Reject in a scornful way

squall (skwôl) n.: Brief, violent storm

steeds (stēdz) n.: Horses

stout (stout) adj.: Sturdy; forceful

strafing (strāf´ iŋ) adj.: Attacking with machine-gun fire

suavity (swäv´ ə tē) n.: Quality of being socially smooth

subjugation (sub´ jə gā´ shən) n.: Enslavement

submerged (səb murjd´) adj.: Covered with something; underwater

subsidiary (səb sid´ ē er´ ē) adj.: Secondary; supporting

subtle (sut´ 'l) adj.: Not obvious

succor (suk´ ər) n.: Aid; help; relief

suffice (sə fīs´) v.: To be enough

sullen (sul´ ən) adj.: Gloomy; dismal

surcease (sur sēs´) n.: An end

surge (surj) v.: Increase suddenly; speed up

surreal (sə rē´ əl) adj.: Strange

tantalizingly (tan´ tə līz´ iŋ glē) adv.: In a teasing or tormenting way

tempests (tem´ pists) n.: Violent storms with strong winds

thronging (throŋ´ iŋ) adj.: Crowding into

titanic (tī tan´ ik) adj.: Of great size or strength

transgression (trans gresh´ ən) n.: Wrongdoing; sin

treble (treb´ əl) n.: High-pitched voice

tremulous (trem´ yōō ləs) adj.: Quivering

trundle (trun´ dəl) v.: To roll along; to rotate

tumult (tōō´ məlt) n.: Noisy commotion

tumultuous (tōō mul´ chōō əs) adj.: Greatly disturbed

unbidden (un bid´ ən) adj.: Without being asked; uninvited

unpalatable (un pal´ ət ə bəl) adj.: Distasteful; unpleasant

unwieldy (un wēl´ dē) adj.: Awkward; clumsy

valet (val´ it) n.: A man's personal servant who takes care of the man's clothes

vanquished (vaŋ´ kwisht) adj.: Defeated

venture (ven´ chər) n.: Chance

vex (veks) v.: Annoy

vial (vī´ əl) n.: Small bottle containing medicine or other liquids

vile (vīl) adj.: Evil; wicked; worthless; cheap; low

voluminously (və lōōm´ ə nəs lē) adv.: Fully; in great volume

vortex (vôr´ teks) n.: Center of a situation, which draws in all that surrounds it

warp (wôrp) v.: Bend or twist out of shape; distort

waverer (wā´ vər ər) n.: One who changes or is unsteady

wavering (wā´ vər iŋ) adj.: Flickering

wayfarers (wā´ fer ərz) n.: Travelers

wayward (wā´ wərd) adj.: Insistent upon having one's own way; headstrong

woeful (wō´ fəl) adj.: Full of sorrow

woes (wōz) n.: Great sorrows

wreathed (rēthd) v.: Curled around

writhing (rīth´ iŋ) v.: Twisting; turning

wrought (rôt) v.: Formed; fashioned

yearned (yurnd) v.: Longed for; desired

ACT *See* Drama.

ALLEGORY An *allegory* is a story or tale with two or more levels of meaning—a literal level and one or more symbolic levels. The events, setting, and characters in an allegory are symbols for ideas and qualities.

ALLITERATION *Alliteration* is the repetition of initial consonant sounds. Writers use alliteration to give emphasis to words, to imitate sounds, and to create musical effects. In the following lines from Walter de la Mare's "The Listeners," notice how the *s* sound imitates a whisper:

Ay, they heard his foot upon the stirrup,
    And the sound of iron on stone,
    And how the silence surged softly backward. . .

ALLUSION An *allusion* is a reference to a well-known person, place, event, literary work, or work of art. In "The Gift of the Magi" (p. 524), O. Henry writes about a young couple and the Christmas gifts they give to each other. At the end of the story, the narrator explains the biblical allusion in the title: "The Magi, as you know, were wise men—wonderfully wise men—who brought gifts to the Babe in the manger. They invented the art of giving Christmas presents. Being wise, their gifts were no doubt wise ones. . . ."

ANALOGY An *analogy* makes a comparison between two or more things that are similar in some ways but otherwise unalike.

ANECDOTE An *anecdote* is a brief story about an interesting, amusing, or strange event told to entertain or to make a point. In "A Lincoln Preface" (p. 152), Carl Sandburg tells anecdotes about Abraham Lincoln.
See also Narrative.

ANTAGONIST An *antagonist* is a character or force in conflict with a main character, or protagonist.

ANTICLIMAX Like a climax, an *anticlimax* is the turning point in a story. However, an anticlimax is always a letdown. It's the point at which you learn that the story will not turn out the way you had expected. In Thayer's "Casey at the Bat," the anticlimax occurs when Casey strikes out instead of hitting a game-winning run as everyone had expected.

ASIDE An *aside* is a short speech delivered by an actor in a play. Traditionally, the aside is directed to the audience and is presumed to be inaudible to the other actors.

ASSONANCE *Assonance* is the repetition of vowel sounds followed by different consonants in two or more stressed syllables. Assonance is found in the phrase "weak and weary" in Edgar Allan Poe's "The Raven" (p. 940).

ATMOSPHERE *See* Mood.

AUTOBIOGRAPHY An *autobiography* is a form of nonfiction in which a writer tells his or her own life story. An autobiography may tell about the person's whole life or only a part of it.
See also Biography *and* Nonfiction.

BALLAD A *ballad* is a songlike poem that tells a story, often one dealing with adventure and romance. Most ballads are written in four- to six-line stanzas and have regular rhythms and rhyme schemes. A ballad often features a refrain—a regularly repeated line or group of lines.
See also Oral Tradition.

BIOGRAPHY A *biography* is a form of nonfiction in which a writer tells the life story of another person. Biographies have been written about many famous people, historical and contemporary, but they can also be written about "ordinary" people.
See also Autobiography *and* Nonfiction.

BLANK VERSE *Blank verse* is poetry written in unrhymed iambic pentameter lines. This verse form was widely used by William Shakespeare.
See also Meter.

CHARACTER A *character* is a person or an animal who takes part in the action of a literary work. The main character, or protagonist, is the most important character in a story. This character often changes in some important way as a result of the story's events. In Richard Connell's "The Most Dangerous Game" (p. 18), Rainsford is the main character and General Zaroff is the antagonist, or character who opposes the main character.

Characters are sometimes classified as round or flat, dynamic or static. A *round character* shows many different traits—faults as well as virtues. A *flat character* shows only one trait. A *dynamic character* develops and grows during the course of the story; a *static character* does not change.
See also Characterization and Motivation.

CHARACTERIZATION *Characterization* is the act of creating and developing a character. In *direct characterization*, the author directly states a character's traits. In

"Uncle Marcos," for example, a character states that "Uncle Marcos's manners were those of a cannibal."

In *indirect characterization*, an author tells what a character looks like, does, and says, as well as how other characters react to him or her. It is up to the reader to draw conclusions about the character based on this indirect information.

The most effective indirect characterizations usually result from showing characters acting or speaking.
See also Character.

CLIMAX The *climax* of a story, novel, or play is the high point of interest or suspense. The events that make up the rising action lead up to the climax. The events that make up the falling action follow the climax.
See also Conflict, Plot, *and* Anticlimax.

COMEDY A *comedy* is a literary work, especially a play, that has a happy ending. Comedies often show ordinary characters in conflict with society. These conflicts are resolved through misunderstandings, deceptions, and concealed identities, which result in the correction of moral faults or social wrongs. Types of comedy include *romantic comedy*, which involves problems among lovers, and the *comedy of manners*, which satirically challenges the social customs of a sophisticated society. Comedy is often contrasted with tragedy, in which the protagonist meets an unfortunate end.

COMIC RELIEF *Comic relief* is a technique that is used to interrupt a serious part of a literary work by introducing a humorous character or situation.

CONFLICT A *conflict* is a struggle between opposing forces. Characters in conflict form the basis of stories, novels, and plays.

There are two kinds of conflict: external and internal. In an external conflict, the main character struggles against an outside force. This force may be another character, as in Richard Connell's "The Most Dangerous Game" (p. 18), in which Rainsford struggles with General Zaroff. The outside force could also be the standards or expectations of a group, such as the family prejudices that Romeo and Juliet struggle against. Their story (p. 770) shows them in conflict with society. The outside force may be nature itself, a person-against-nature conflict. The two men who are trapped by a fallen tree in Saki's "The Interlopers" (p. 304) face such a conflict.

An *internal conflict* involves a character in conflict with himself or herself. In "Checkouts" (p. 282), two young people who meet by chance in a supermarket agonize over whether they should speak to each other.
See also Plot.

CONNOTATION The *connotation* of a word is the set of ideas associated with it in addition to its explicit meaning. In his poem "Sympathy" (p. 292), Paul Laurence Dunbar speaks of a "caged bird," which connotes a sad, trapped creature.
See also Denotation.

COUPLET A *couplet* is a pair of rhyming lines, usually of the same length and meter. In the following couplet from a poem by William Shakespeare, the speaker comforts himself with the thought of his love:

For thy sweet love remember'd such wealth brings
That then I scorn to change my state with kings.

See also Stanza.

DENOTATION The *denotation* of a word is its dictionary meaning, independent of other associations that the word may have. The denotation of the word *lake*, for example, is an inland body of water. "Vacation spot" and "place where the fishing is good" are connotations of the word *lake*.
See also Connotation.

DENOUEMENT *See* Plot.

DESCRIPTION A *description* is a portrait in words of a person, place, or object. Descriptive writing uses sensory details, those that appeal to the senses: sight, hearing, taste, smell, and touch. Description can be found in all types of writing. Rudolfo Anaya's essay "A Celebration of Grandfathers" (p. 662) contains descriptive passages.

DEVELOPMENT *See* Plot.

DIALECT *Dialect* is the form of language spoken by people in a particular region or group. Pronunciation, vocabulary, and sentence structure are affected by dialect. In "The Invalid's Story" (p. 596), Mark Twain uses dialect:

"Friends of *yourn*?"
"Yes," I said with a sigh.
"He's pretty ripe, *ain't* he!"

DIALOGUE A *dialogue* is a conversation between characters. It is used to reveal character and to advance action. In a story or novel, quotation marks are generally used to indicate a speaker's exact words. A new paragraph usually indicates a change of speaker. Look at an example from "The Scarlet Ibis" (p. 554). The narrator is a boy who is urging his frail younger brother, Doodle, to stand up and walk fast:

> "Aw, come on Doodle," I urged. "You can do it. Do you want to be different from everybody else when you start school?"
>
> "Does it make any difference?"
>
> "It certainly does," I said. "Now come on," and I helped him up.

A drama depends entirely on dialogue and actions. Quotation marks are not used in the *script*, which is the printed version of a play. Instead, the dialogue follows the name of the speaker. Here is an example from *The Dancers* (p. 734):

> HORACE. Miss . . .
>
> WAITRESS. Yes?
>
> HORACE. How much do I owe you?

DICTION *Diction* is word choice, including the vocabulary used, the appropriateness of the words, and the vividness of the language. Diction can be formal, as in this excerpt from O. Henry's "The Gift of the Magi" (p. 524):

> In the vestibule below was a letter-box into which no letter would go, and an electric button from which no mortal finger could coax a ring.

Diction can also be informal and conversational, as in these lines from Ernest Lawrence Thayer's "Casey at the Bat" (p. 42):

> It looked extremely rocky for the Mudville nine
>   that day;
> The score stood two to four; with but an inning
>   left to play.
> So, when Cooney died at second, and Burrows
>   did the same,
> A pallor wreathed the features of the patrons of
>   the game.

See also Connotation *and* Denotation.

DIRECT CHARACTERIZATION *See* Characterization.

DRAMA A *drama* is a story written to be performed by actors. The script of a drama is made up of *dialogue*—the words the actors say—and *stage directions*, which are comments on how and where action happens.

The drama's *setting* is the time and place in which the action occurs. It is indicated by one or more sets that suggest interior or exterior scenes. *Props* are objects, such as a sword or a cup of tea, that are used onstage.

At the beginning of most plays, a brief exposition gives the audience some background information about the characters and the situation. Just as in a story or novel, the plot of a drama is built around characters in conflict.

Dramas are divided into large units called *acts,* which are divided into smaller units called *scenes*. A long play may include many sets that change with the scenes, or it may indicate a change of scene with lighting.

See also Dialogue, Genre, Stage Directions, *and* Tragedy.

DRAMATIC IRONY *See* Irony.

DRAMATIC MONOLOGUE A *dramatic monologue* is a poem or speech in which a fictional character addresses the listener.

DRAMATIC POETRY *Dramatic poetry* is poetry that utilizes the techniques of drama. The dialogue used in Edgar Allan Poe's "The Raven" (p. 940) makes it dramatic dialogue. A *dramatic monologue* is a poem spoken by one person, addressing a silent listener.

END RHYME *See* Rhyme.

EPIC An *epic* is a long narrative poem about the deeds of gods or heroes. Homer's *Odyssey* (p. 980) is an example of epic poetry. It tells the story of the Greek hero Odysseus, the king of Ithaca.

An epic is elevated in style and usually follows certain patterns. The poet begins by announcing the subject and asking a Muse—one of the nine goddesses of the arts, literature, and sciences—to help.

See also Epic Simile *and* Narrative Poem.

EPIC SIMILE An *epic simile*, also called *Homeric simile*, is an elaborate comparison of unlike subjects. In this example from the *Odyssey* (p. 980), Homer compares the bodies of men killed by Odysseus to a fisherman's catch heaped up on the shore:

> Think of a catch that fishermen haul in to a
>   half-moon bay
> in a fine-meshed net from the whitecaps of the sea:
> how all are poured out on the sand, in throes
>   for the salt sea,
> twitching their cold lives away in Helios' fiery air:
>   so lay the suitors heaped on one another.

See also Figurative Language *and* Simile.

ESSAY An *essay* is a short nonfiction work about a particular subject. While classification is difficult, five types of essays are sometimes identified.

A *descriptive essay* seeks to convey an impression about a person, place, or object. In "A Celebration of Grandfathers" (p. 662), Rudolfo Anaya describes the cultural values that his grandfather and other "old ones" from his childhood passed down.

A *narrative essay* tells a true story. In "The Washwoman," Isaac Bashevis Singer tells of his childhood in Poland.

An *expository essay* gives information, discusses ideas, or explains a process. In "Single Room, Earth View" (p. 636), Sally Ride describes what it is like to be in outer space.

A *persuasive essay* tries to convince readers to do something or to accept the writer's point of view. In the essay, "To the Residents of A.D. 2029" (p. 495), Bryan Woolley advises future generations how to avoid calamities.

A *visual essay* is an exploration of a topic that conveys its ideas through visual elements as well as language. Like a standard essay, a visual essay presents an author's views of a single topic. Unlike other essays, however, much of the meaning in a visual essay is conveyed through illustrations or photographs.
See also Description, Exposition, Genre, Narration, Nonfiction, *and* Persuasion.

EXPOSITION *Exposition* is writing or speech that explains a process or presents information. In the plot of a story or drama, the exposition is the part of the work that introduces the characters, the setting, and the basic situation.

EXTENDED METAPHOR In an *extended metaphor*, as in regular metaphor, a writer speaks or writes of a subject as though it were something else. An extended metaphor sustains the comparison for several lines or for an entire poem. The "caged bird" of Paul Laurence Dunbar's "Sympathy" (p. 292) is an extended metaphor for a person who is not free.
See also Figurative Language *and* Metaphor.

FALLING ACTION *See* Plot.

FANTASY A *fantasy* is highly imaginative writing that contains elements not found in real life. Examples of fantasy include stories that involve supernatural elements, stories that resemble fairy tales, and stories that deal with imaginary places and creatures.
See also Science Fiction.

FICTION *Fiction* is prose writing that tells about imaginary characters and events. The term is usually used for novels and short stories, but it also applies to dramas and narrative poetry. Some writers rely on their imaginations alone to create their works of fiction. Others base their fiction on actual events and people, to which they add invented characters, dialogue, and plot situations.
See also Genre, Narrative, *and* Nonfiction.

FIGURATIVE LANGUAGE *Figurative language* is writing or speech not meant to be interpreted literally. It is often used to create vivid impressions by setting up comparisons between dissimilar things.

Some frequently used figures of speech are *metaphors, similes*, and *personifications*.
See also Literal Language.

FOIL A *foil* is a character who provides a contrast to another character. In *Romeo and Juliet* (p. 770), the fiery temper of Tybalt serves as a foil to the good nature of Benvolio.

FOOT *See* Meter.

FORESHADOWING *Foreshadowing* is the use in a literary work of clues that suggest events that have yet to occur. This technique helps to create suspense, keeping readers wondering about what will happen next.
See also Suspense.

FREE VERSE *Free verse* is poetry not written in a regular rhythmical pattern, or meter. Free verse seeks to capture the rhythms of speech.
See also Meter.

GENRE A *genre* is a category or type of literature. Literature is commonly divided into three major genres: poetry, prose, and drama. Each major genre is in turn divided into smaller genres, as follows:
1. Poetry: Lyric Poetry, Concrete Poetry, Dramatic Poetry, Narrative Poetry, and Epic Poetry
2. Prose: Fiction (Novels and Short Stories) and Nonfiction (Biography, Autobiography, Letters, Essays, and Reports)
3. Drama: Serious Drama and Tragedy, Comic Drama, Melodrama, and Farce

See also Drama, Poetry, *and* Prose.

HAIKU The *haiku* is a three-line verse form. The first and third lines of a haiku each have five syllables. The second line has seven syllables. A haiku seeks to convey a single vivid emotion by means of images from nature.

HOMERIC SIMILE *See* Epic Simile.

HYPERBOLE A *hyperbole* is a deliberate exaggeration or overstatement. In Mark Twain's "The Notorious Jumping Frog of Calaveras County," the claim that Jim Smiley would follow a bug as far as Mexico to win a bet is a hyperbole. As this example shows, hyperboles are often used for comic effect.

IAMB *See* Meter.

IMAGE An *image* is a word or phrase that appeals to one or more of the five senses—sight, hearing, touch, taste, or smell. Writers use images to re-create sensory experiences in words.
See also Description.

IMAGERY *Imagery* is the descriptive or figurative language used in literature to create word pictures for the reader. These pictures, or images, are created by details of sight, sound, taste, touch, smell, or movement.

INDIRECT CHARACTERIZATION *See* Characterization.

INTERNAL RHYME *See* Rhyme.

IRONY *Irony* is the general term for literary techniques that portray differences between appearance and reality, or expectation and result. In *verbal irony*, words are used to suggest the opposite of what is meant. In *dramatic irony*, there is a contradiction between what a character thinks and what the reader or audience knows to be true. In *irony of situation*, an event occurs that directly contradicts the expectations of the characters, the reader, or the audience.

LITERAL LANGUAGE *Literal language* uses words in their ordinary senses. It is the opposite of *figurative language*. If you tell someone standing on a diving board to jump in, you speak literally. If you tell someone on the street to jump in a lake, you are speaking figuratively.
See also Figurative Language.

LYRIC POEM A *lyric poem* is a highly musical verse that expresses the observations and feelings of a single speaker. In ancient times, lyric poems were sung to the accompaniment of the lyre, a type of stringed instrument. Modern lyric poems are not usually sung. However, they still have a musical quality that is achieved through rhythm and other devices such as alliteration and rhyme.

MAIN CHARACTER *See* Character.

METAPHOR A *metaphor* is a figure of speech in which one thing is spoken of as though it were something else. Unlike a simile, which compares two things using *like* or *as*, a metaphor implies a comparison between them. In "Dreams" (p. 905), Langston Hughes uses a metaphor to show what happens to a life without dreams:

. . . if dreams die
Life is a broken-winged bird
That cannot fly.

See also Extended Metaphor *and* Figurative Language.

METER The *meter* of a poem is its rhythmical pattern. This pattern is determined by the number and types of stresses, or beats, in each line. To describe the meter of a poem, you must scan its lines. Scanning involves marking the stressed and unstressed syllables, as shown with the following two lines from "I Wandered Lonely as a Cloud" by William Wordsworth (p. 896):

I wan|dered lone|ly as| a cloud

That floats |on high| o'er vales| and hills.

As you can see, each strong stress is marked with a slanted line (´) and each unstressed syllable with a horseshoe symbol (˘). The stressed and unstressed syllables are then divided by vertical lines (|) into groups called *feet*. The following types of feet are common in English poetry:

1. *Iamb:* a foot with one unstressed syllable followed by a stressed syllable, as in the word "again"

2. *Trochee:* a foot with one stressed syllable followed by an unstressed syllable, as in the word "wonder"

3. *Anapest:* a foot with two unstressed syllables followed by one strong stress, as in the phrase "on the beach"

4. *Dactyl:* a foot with one strong stress followed by two unstressed syllables, as in the word "wonderful"

5. *Spondee:* a foot with two strong stresses, as in the word "spacewalk"

Depending on the type of foot that is most common in them, lines of poetry are described as *iambic*, *trochaic*, *anapestic*, and so forth.

Lines are also described in terms of the number of feet that occur in them, as follows:

1. *Monometer:* verse written in one-foot lines
All things
Must pass
Away.

2. *Dimeter:* verse written in two-foot lines
Thomas | Jefferson
What do | you say
Under the | gravestone
Hidden | away?
—Rosemary and Stephen Vincent Benét,
"Thomas Jefferson, 1743–1826"

3. *Trimeter:* verse written in three-foot lines
   I know | not whom | I meet
   I know | not where | I go.

4. *Tetrameter:* verse written in four-foot lines

5. *Pentameter:* verse written in five-foot lines

6. *Hexameter:* verse written in six-foot lines

7. *Heptameter:* verse written in seven-foot lines

   Blank verse is poetry written in unrhymed iambic pentameter. Poetry that does not have a regular meter is called *free verse*.

MONOLOGUE A *monologue* is a speech by one character in a play, story, or poem. An example from Shakespeare's *Romeo and Juliet* (p. 770) is the speech in which the Prince of Verona commands the Capulets and Montagues to cease feuding (Act 1, Scene i, lines 62–84).
See also Dramatic Poetry *and* Soliloquy.

MONOMETER *See* Meter.

MOOD *Mood*, or *atmosphere*, is the feeling created in the reader by a literary work or passage. The mood is often suggested by descriptive details. Often the mood can be described in a single word, such as lighthearted, frightening, or despairing. Notice how this passage from Edgar Allan Poe's "The Cask of Amontillado" (p. 6) contributes to an eerie, fearful mood:

> "The niter!" I said; "see, it increases. It hangs like moss upon the vaults. We are below the river's bed. The drops of moisture trickle among the bones. Come, we will go back ere it is too late."

See also Tone.

MORAL A *moral* is a lesson taught by a literary work. A fable usually ends with a moral that is directly stated.

MOTIVATION *Motivation* is a reason that explains or partially explains why a character thinks, feels, acts, or behaves in a certain way. Motivation results from a combination of the character's personality and the situation he or she must deal with. Nat Hocken in "The Birds" (p. 50) is motivated by his fear of being killed by birds to board up windows and stay inside.
See also Character *and* Characterization.

MYTH A *myth* is a fictional tale that explains the actions of gods or the causes of natural phenomena. Unlike legends, myths have little historical truth and involve supernatural elements. Every culture has its collections of myths. Among the most familiar are the myths of the ancient Greeks and Romans. The *Odyssey* (p. 980) is a mythical story attributed to the ancient poet Homer.
See also Oral Tradition.

NARRATION *Narration* is writing that tells a story. The act of telling a story in speech is also called narration. Novels and short stories are fictional narratives. Nonfiction works—such as news stories, biographies, and autobiographies—are also narratives. A narrative poem tells a story in verse.
See also Anecdote, Essay, Narrative Poem, Nonfiction, Novel, *and* Short Story.

NARRATIVE A *narrative* is a story told in fiction, non-fiction, poetry, or drama.
See also Narration.

NARRATIVE POEM A *narrative poem* is one that tells a story. "Casey at the Bat" (p. 42) is a humorous narrative poem about the last inning of a baseball game. Edgar Allan Poe's "The Raven" (p. 940) is a serious narrative poem about a man's grief over the loss of a loved one.
See also Dramatic Poetry, Epic, *and* Narration.

NARRATOR A *narrator* is a speaker or character who tells a story. The writer's choice of narrator determines the story's *point of view*, which directs the type and amount of information the writer reveals.

When a character in the story tells the story, that character is a *first-person narrator*. This narrator may be a major character, a minor character, or just a witness. Readers see only what this character sees, hear only what he or she hears, and so on. The first-person narrator may or may not be reliable. We have reason, for example, to be suspicious of the first-person narrator of Edgar Allan Poe's "The Cask of Amontillado" (p. 6).

When a voice outside the story narrates, the story has a *third-person narrator*. An omniscient, or all-knowing, third-person narrator can tell readers what any character thinks and feels. For example, in Guy de Maupassant's "The Necklace" (p. 608), we know the feelings of both Monsieur and Madame Loisel. A limited third-person narrator sees the world through one character's eyes and reveals only that character's thoughts. In James Thurber's "The Secret Life of Walter Mitty" (p. 346), the narrator reveals only Mitty's experiences and feelings.
See also Speaker.

NONFICTION *Nonfiction* is prose writing that presents and explains ideas or that tells about real people, places, ideas, or events. To be classified as nonfiction, a work must be true. "Single Room, Earth View" (p. 636) is a nonfictional account of the view of Earth from space.

See also Autobiography, Biography, *and* Essay.

NOVEL A *novel* is a long work of fiction. It has a plot that explores characters in conflict. A novel may also have one or more subplots, or minor stories, and several themes.

OCTAVE *See* Stanza.

ONOMATOPOEIA *Onomatopoeia* is the use of words that imitate sounds. *Whirr, thud, sizzle*, and *hiss* are typical examples. Writers can deliberately choose words that contribute to a desired sound effect.

ORAL TRADITION The *oral tradition* is the passing of songs, stories, and poems from generation to generation by word of mouth. Many folk songs, ballads, fairy tales, legends, and myths originated in the oral tradition.

See also Myth.

PARADOX A *paradox* is a statement that seems contradictory but that actually may be true. Because a paradox is surprising, it catches the reader's attention.

PENTAMETER *See* Meter.

PERSONIFICATION *Personification* is a type of figurative language in which a nonhuman subject is given human characteristics. William Wordsworth personifies daffodils when he describes them as "Tossing their heads in sprightly dance" (p. 896).

See also Figurative Language.

PERSUASION *Persuasion* is writing or speech that attempts to convince the reader to adopt a particular opinion or course of action.

PLOT *Plot* is the sequence of events in a literary work. In most novels, dramas, short stories, and narrative poems, the plot involves both characters and a central conflict. The plot usually begins with an *exposition* that introduces the setting, the characters, and the basic situation. This is followed by the *inciting incident*, which introduces the central conflict. The conflict then increases during the *development* until it reaches a high point of interest or suspense, the *climax*. All the events leading up to the climax make up the *rising action*. The climax is followed by the *falling action*, which leads to the *denouement*, or *resolution*, in which a general insight or change is conveyed.

POETRY *Poetry* is one of the three major types of literature, the others being prose and drama. Most poems make use of highly concise, musical, and emotionally charged language. Many also make use of imagery, figurative language, and special devices of sound such as rhyme. Poems are often divided into lines and stanzas and often employ regular rhythmical patterns, or meters. However, some poems are written out just like prose, while others are written in free verse.

See also Genre.

POINT OF VIEW *See* Narrator.

PROSE *Prose* is the ordinary form of written language. Most writing that is not poetry, drama, or song is considered prose. Prose is one of the major genres of literature and occurs in two forms: fiction and nonfiction.

See also Fiction, Genre, *and* Nonfiction.

PROTAGONIST The *protagonist* is the main character in a literary work.

See also Antagonist *and* Character.

QUATRAIN A *quatrain* is a stanza or poem made up of four lines, usually with a definite rhythm and rhyme scheme.

REPETITION *Repetition* is the use of any element of language—a sound, a word, a phrase, a clause, or a sentence—more than once.

Poets use many kinds of repetition. Alliteration, assonance, rhyme, and rhythm are repetitions of certain sounds and sound patterns. A refrain is a repeated line or group of lines. In both prose and poetry, repetition is used for musical effects and for emphasis.

See also Alliteration, Assonance, Rhyme, *and* Rhythm.

RESOLUTION *See* Plot.

RHYME *Rhyme* is the repetition of sounds at the ends of words. *End rhyme* occurs when the rhyming words come at the ends of lines, as in "The Desired Swan Song" by Samuel Taylor Coleridge:

Swans sing before they die—'twere no bad *thing*
Should certain persons die before they *sing*.

Internal rhyme occurs when the rhyming words appear in the same line, as in the first line of Edgar Allan Poe's "The Raven" (p. 940):

Once upon a midnight *dreary*, while I pondered, weak and *weary*,

See also Repetition *and* Rhyme Scheme.

RHYME SCHEME A *rhyme scheme* is a regular pattern of rhyming words in a poem. The rhyme scheme of a poem is indicated by using different letters of the alphabet for each new rhyme. In an *aabb* stanza, for example, line 1 rhymes with line 2 and line 3 rhymes with line 4. William Wordsworth's poem "I Wandered Lonely as a Cloud" (p. 896) uses an *ababcc* rhyme pattern:

I wandered lonely as a cloud	a
That floats on high o'er vales and hills,	b
When all at once I saw a crowd,	a
A host, of golden daffodils;	b
Beside the lake, beneath the trees,	c
Fluttering and dancing in the breeze.	c

Many poems use the same pattern of rhymes, though not the same rhymes, in each stanza.

See also Rhyme.

RHYTHM *Rhythm* is the pattern of *beats*, or *stresses*, in spoken or written language. Some poems have a very specific pattern, or meter, whereas prose and free verse use the natural rhythms of everyday speech.

See also Meter.

RISING ACTION *See* Plot.

ROUND CHARACTER *See* Character.

SCENE *See* Drama.

SCIENCE FICTION *Science fiction* is writing that tells about imaginary events involving science or technology. Many science-fiction stories are set in the future. Arthur C. Clarke's "If I Forget Thee, Oh Earth . . ." (p. 486) is set on the moon after a nuclear disaster on Earth.

See also Fantasy.

SENSORY LANGUAGE *Sensory language* is writing or speech that appeals to one or more of the senses.

See also Image.

SESTET *See* Stanza.

SETTING The *setting* of a literary work is the time and place of the action. Time can include not only the historical period—past, present, or future—but also a specific year, season, or time of day. Place may involve not only the geographical place—a region, country, state, or town—but also the social, economic, or cultural environment.

In some stories, setting serves merely as a backdrop for action, a context in which the characters move and speak. In others, however, setting is a crucial element.

See also Mood.

SHORT STORY A *short story* is a brief work of fiction. In most short stories, one main character faces a conflict that is resolved in the plot of the story. Great craftsmanship must go into the writing of a good story, for it has to accomplish its purpose in relatively few words.

See also Fiction *and* Genre.

SIMILE A *simile* is a figure of speech in which *like* or *as* is used to make a comparison between two basically unlike ideas. "Claire is as flighty as Roger" is a comparison, not a simile. "Claire is as flighty as a sparrow" is a simile.

See also Figurative Language.

SOLILOQUY A *soliloquy* is a long speech expressing the thoughts of a character alone on stage. In William Shakespeare's *Romeo and Juliet* (p. 861), Romeo gives a soliloquy after the servant has fled and Paris has died (Act V, Scene iii, lines 74–120).

See also Monologue.

SONNET A *sonnet* is a fourteen-line lyric poem, usually written in rhymed iambic pentameter. The *English*, or *Shakespearean*, sonnet consists of three quatrains (four-line stanzas) and a couplet (two lines), usually rhyming *abab cdcd efef gg*. The couplet usually comments on the ideas contained in the preceding twelve lines. The sonnet is usually not printed with the stanzas divided, but a reader can see distinct ideas in each. See the English sonnet by William Shakespeare on page 960.

The *Italian*, or *Petrarchan*, sonnet consists of an octave (eight-line stanza) and a sestet (six-line stanza). Often, the octave rhymes *abbaabba* and the sestet rhymes *cdecde*. The octave states a theme or asks a question. The sestet comments on or answers the question.

See also Lyric Poem, Meter, *and* Stanza.

SPEAKER The *speaker* is the imaginary voice assumed by the writer of a poem. In many poems, the speaker is not identified by name. When reading a poem, remember that the speaker within the poem may be a person, an animal, a thing, or an abstraction. The speaker in the following stanza by Emily Dickinson is a person who has died:

Because I could not stop for Death—
He kindly stopped for me—
The Carriage held but just Ourselves—
And Immortality.

STAGE DIRECTIONS *Stage directions* are notes included in a drama to describe how the work is to be performed or staged. These instructions are printed in italics and are not spoken aloud. They are used to describe sets, lighting, sound effects, and the appearance, personalities, and movements of characters. *See also* Drama.

STANZA A *stanza* is a formal division of lines in a poem, considered as a unit. Often, the stanzas in a poem are separated by spaces.

Stanzas are sometimes named according to the number of lines found in them. A *couplet*, for example, is a two-line stanza. A *tercet* is a stanza with three lines. Other types of stanzas include the following:

1. *Quatrain:* a four-line stanza
2. *Cinquain:* a five-line stanza
3. *Sestet:* a six-line stanza
4. *Heptastich:* a seven-line stanza
5. *Octave:* an eight-line stanza

See also Haiku *and* Sonnet.

STATIC CHARACTER *See* Character.

SURPRISE ENDING A *surprise ending* is a conclusion that violates the expectations of the reader but in a way that is both logical and believable.

O. Henry's "The Gift of the Magi" (p. 524) and Guy de Maupassant's "The Necklace" (p. 608) have surprise endings. Both authors were masters of this form.

SUSPENSE *Suspense* is a feeling of uncertainty about the outcome of events in a literary work. Writers create suspense by raising questions in the minds of their readers.

SYMBOL A *symbol* is anything that stands for or represents something else. An object that serves as a symbol has its own meaning, but it also represents abstract ideas. Marks on paper can symbolize spoken words. A flag symbolizes a country. A flashy car may symbolize wealth. Writers sometimes use such conventional symbols in their work, but they may also create symbols of their own through emphasis or repetition.

In James Hurst's "The Scarlet Ibis" (p. 554), the ibis symbolizes the character named Doodle. Doodle and the ibis have many traits in common. Both are beautiful and otherworldly. Both struggle against great odds. Both meet an unfortunate fate. Since a story says something about life or people in general, the ibis, in a larger sense, becomes a symbol for those who struggle.

TETRAMETER *See* Meter.

THEME A *theme* is a central message or insight into life revealed through a literary work.

The theme of a literary work may be stated directly or implied. When the theme of a work is implied, readers think about what the work suggests about people or life.

TONE The *tone* of a literary work is the writer's attitude toward his or her audience and subject. The tone can often be described by a single adjective, such as *formal* or *informal*, *serious* or *playful*, *bitter* or *ironic*. When O. Henry discusses the young couple in "The Gift of the Magi" (p. 524), he uses a sympathetic tone. By contrast, Margaret Walker uses a grieving tone in her poem "Memory" (p. 915). *See also* Mood.

TRAGEDY A *tragedy* is a work of literature, especially a play, that results in a catastrophe for the main character. In ancient Greek drama, the main character was always a significant person—a king or a hero—and the cause of the tragedy was a tragic flaw, or weakness, in his or her character. In modern drama, the main character can be an ordinary person, and the cause of the tragedy can be some evil in society itself. Tragedy not only arouses fear and pity in the audience, but also, in some cases, conveys a sense of the grandeur and nobility of the human spirit.

Shakespeare's *Romeo and Juliet* (p. 770) is a tragedy. Romeo and Juliet both suffer from the tragic flaw of impulsiveness. This flaw ultimately leads to their deaths. *See also* Drama.

TRIMETER *See* Meter.

UNIVERSAL THEME A *universal theme* is a message about life that can be understood by most cultures. Many folk tales and examples of classic literature address universal themes such as the importance of courage, the effects of honesty, or the danger of greed.

VERBAL IRONY *See* Irony.

VILLANELLE A *villanelle* is a lyric poem written in three-line stanzas, ending with a four-line stanza. It has two refrain lines that appear initially in the first and third lines of the first stanza; they then appear alternately as the third line of subsequent stanzas and finally as the last two lines of the poem.

VISUAL ESSAY A *visual essay* is an exploration of a topic that conveys its ideas through visual elements as well as language. Like a standard essay, a visual essay presents an author's views of a single topic. Unlike other essays, however, much of the meaning in a visual essay is conveyed through illustrations or photographs.

THE WRITING PROCESS

A polished piece of writing can seem to have been effortlessly created, but most good writing is the result of a process of writing, rethinking, and rewriting. The process can roughly be divided into stages: prewriting, drafting, revising, editing, proofreading, and publishing.

It is important to remember that the writing process is one that moves backward as well as forward. Even while you are moving forward in the creation of your composition, you may still return to a previous stage—to rethink or rewrite.

Following are stages of the writing process, with key points to address during each stage.

Prewriting

In this stage, you plan out the work to be done. You prepare to write by exploring ideas, gathering information, and working out an organization plan. Following are the key steps to take at this stage.

Step 1: Analyze the writing situation. Start by clarifying your assignment, so that you know exactly what you are supposed to do.

- *Focus your topic.* If necessary, narrow the topic—the subject you are writing about—so that you can write about it fully in the space you have.
- *Know your purpose.* What is your goal for this paper? What do you want to accomplish? Your purpose will determine what you include in the paper.
- *Know your audience.* Who will read your paper influences what you say and how you say it.

Step 2: Gather ideas and information. You can do this in a number of ways:

- *Brainstorm.* When you brainstorm, either alone or with others, you come up with possible ideas to use in your paper. Not all of your ideas will be useful or suitable. You will need to evaluate them later.
- *Consult other people about your subject.* Speaking informally with others may suggest an idea or an approach you did not see at first.
- *Make a list of questions about your topic.* When your list is complete, find the answers to your questions.
- *Do research.* Your topic may require information that you do not have, so you will need to go to other sources to find information. There are numerous ways to find information on a topic.

The ideas and information you gather will become the content of your paper. Not all of the information you gather will be needed. As you develop and revise your paper, you will make further decisions about what to include and what to leave out.

Drafting

When you draft, you put down your ideas on paper in rough form. Working from your prewriting notes and your outline or plan, you develop and present your ideas in sentences and paragraphs.

Organize. First, make a rough plan for the way you want to present your information. Sort your ideas and notes. Decide what goes with what and which points are the most important. You can make an outline to show the order of ideas, or you can use some other organizing plan that works for you.

There are many ways in which you can organize and develop your material. Use a method that works for your topic. Following are common methods of organizing information in the development of a paper:

- *Chronological Order* In this method, events are presented in the order in which they occurred. This organization works best for presenting narrative material or explaining in a "how-to" format.
- *Spatial Order* In spatial order, details are presented as seen in space; for example, from left to right, top to bottom, or from foreground to background. This order is good for descriptive writing.
- *Order of Importance* This order helps readers see the relative importance of ideas. You present ideas from the most to least important or from the least to most important.
- *Main Idea and Details* This logical organization works well to support an idea or opinion. Present each main idea, and back it up with appropriate support.

Once you have chosen an organization, begin writing your draft. Do not worry about getting everything perfect at the drafting stage. Concentrate on getting your ideas down.

Write your draft in a way that works for you. Some writers work best by writing a quick draft—putting down all their ideas without stopping to evaluate them. Other writers prefer to develop each paragraph carefully and thoughtfully, making sure that each main idea is supported by details.

As you are developing your draft, keep in mind your purpose and your audience. These determine what you say and how you say it.

Do not be afraid to change your original plans during drafting. Some of the best ideas are those that were not planned at the beginning. Write as many drafts as you like, until you are happy with the results.

Develop an Essay Most papers, regardless of the topic, are developed with an introduction, a body, and a conclusion. Here are tips for developing these parts:

Introduction In the introduction to a paper, you want to engage your readers' attention and let them know the purpose of your paper. You may use the following strategies in your introduction:

- Startle your readers.
- Take a stand.
- Use an anecdote.
- Quote someone.

Body of the Paper In the body of your paper, you present your information and make your points. Your organization is an important factor in leading readers through your ideas. Elaborating on your main ideas is also important. Elaboration is the development of ideas to make your written work precise and complete. You can use the following kinds of details to elaborate your main ideas:

- Facts and statistics
- Anecdotes
- Sensory details
- Examples
- Explanations and definitions
- Quotations

Conclusion The ending of your paper is the final impression you leave with your readers. Your conclusion should give readers the sense that you have pulled everything together. Following are some effective ways to end your paper:

- Summarize and restate.
- Ask a question.
- State an opinion.
- Tell an anecdote.
- Call for action.
- Provide an insight.

Revising

Once you have a draft, you can look at it critically or have others review it. This is the time to make changes—on many levels. Revising is the process of reworking what you have written to make it as good as it can be.

Revising Your Overall Structure Start by examining the soundness of your structure, or overall organization. Your ideas should flow logically from beginning to end. You may strengthen the structure by reordering paragraphs or by adding information to fill in gaps.

Revising Your Paragraphs Next, examine each paragraph in your writing. Consider the way each sentence contributes to the point of the paragraph. As you evaluate

your draft, rewrite or eliminate any sentences that are not effective.

Revising Your Sentences When you study the sentences in your draft, check to see that they flow smoothly from one to the next. Look to see that you have avoided the pattern of beginning most of your sentences in the same way, and vary your sentence length.

Revising Your Word Choice The final step in the process of revising your work is to analyze your choice of words. Consider the connotations, or associations each word suggests, and make sure that each word conveys the exact meaning you intended. Also, look for the repetition of words, and make revisions to polish your writing.

Peer Review After you have finished revising your draft, work with one or more classmates to get a fresh perspective on your writing. First, have your reviewer look at one element of your writing, and ask your reviewer a specific question to get the most focused feedback possible. Weigh the responses you receive, and determine which suggestions you want to incorporate in your draft.

Editing

When you edit, you look more closely at the language you have used to ensure that the way you expressed your ideas is the most effective.

- Replace dull language with vivid, precise words.
- Cut or change unnecessary repetition.
- Cut empty words and phrases—those that do not add anything to the writing.
- Check passive voice. Usually, active voice is more effective.
- Replace wordy expressions with shorter, more precise ones.

Proofreading

After you finish your final draft, proofread it, either on your own or with the help of a partner.

It is useful to have both a dictionary and a usage handbook available to help you check that your work is correct. Here are the tasks in proofreading:

- Correct errors in grammar and usage.
- Correct errors in punctuation and capitalization.
- Correct errors in spelling.

Publishing

Now your paper is ready to be shared with others. Consider sharing your writing with classmates, family, or a wider audience.

THE MODES OF WRITING

Writing is a process that begins with the exploration of ideas and ends with the presentation of a final draft. Often, the types of writing are grouped into modes according to form and purpose.

The modes addressed in this handbook are

- Narration
- Description
- Persuasion
- Exposition
- Research Writing
- Response to Literature
- Writing for Assessment
- Workplace Writing

NARRATION

Whenever writers tell any type of story, they are using **narration.** Although there are many kinds of narration, most narratives share certain elements, such as characters, a setting, a sequence of events, and, often, a theme. Following are some types of narration:

Autobiographical Writing Autobiographical writing tells a true story about an important period, experience, or relationship in the writer's life. An autobiographical narrative can be as simple as a description of a recent car trip or as complex as the entire story of a person's life. Effective autobiographical writing includes

- A series of events that involve the writer as the main character
- Details, thoughts, feelings, and insights from the writer's perspective
- A conflict or an event that affects the writer
- A logical organization that tells the story clearly
- Insights that the writer gained from the experience

A few types of autobiographical writing are autobiographical incidents, personal narratives, autobiographical narratives or sketches, reflective essays, eyewitness accounts, anecdotes, and memoirs.

Short Story A short story is a brief, creative narrative—a retelling of events arranged to hold a reader's attention. Most short stories include

- Details that establish the setting in time and place
- A main character who undergoes a change or learns something during the course of the story
- A conflict or a problem to be introduced, developed, and resolved
- A plot, the series of events that make up the action of the story
- A theme or generalization about life

A few types of short stories are realistic stories, fantasies, historical narratives, mysteries, thrillers, science-fiction stories, and adventure stories.

DESCRIPTION

Descriptive writing is writing that creates a vivid picture of a person, place, thing, or event. Descriptive writing can stand on its own or be part of a longer work, such as a short story. Most descriptive writing includes

- Sensory details—sights, sounds, smells, tastes, and physical sensations
- Vivid, precise language
- Figurative language or comparisons
- Adjectives and adverbs that paint a word picture
- An organization suited to the subject

Some examples of descriptive writing include description of ideas, observations, travel brochures, physical descriptions, functional descriptions, remembrances, and character sketches.

PERSUASION

Persuasion is writing or speaking that attempts to convince people to accept a position or take a desired action. When used effectively, persuasive writing has the power to change people's lives. As a reader and a writer, you will find yourself engaged in many forms of persuasion. Here are a few of them:

Persuasive Essay A persuasive essay presents your position on an issue, urges your readers to accept that position, and may encourage them to take an action. An effective persuasive essay

- Explores an issue of importance to the writer
- Addresses an issue that is arguable
- Uses facts, examples, statistics, or personal experiences to support a position
- Tries to influence the audience through appeals to the readers' knowledge, experiences, or emotions
- Uses clear organization to present a logical argument

Persuasion can take many forms. A few forms of persuasion include editorials, position papers, persuasive speeches, grant proposals, advertisements, and debates.

Advertisements An advertisement is a planned communication meant to be seen, heard, or read. It attempts to persuade an audience to buy a product or service, accept an idea, or support a cause. Advertisements may appear in printed form—in newspapers and magazines, on billboards, or as posters or flyers. They may appear on radio or television, as commercials or public-service announcements. An effective advertisement includes

- A memorable slogan to grab the audience's attention
- A call to action, which tries to rally the audience to do something
- Persuasive and/or informative text
- Striking visual or aural images
- Details that provide such information as price, location, date, and time

Several common types of advertisements are public-service announcements, billboards, merchandise ads, service ads, online ads, product packaging, and political campaign literature.

EXPOSITION

Exposition is writing that informs or explains. The information you include in expository writing is factual or based on fact. Effective expository writing reflects a well-thought-out organization—one that includes a clear introduction, body, and conclusion. The organization should be appropriate for the type of exposition you are writing. Here are some types of exposition:

Comparison-and-Contrast Essay A comparison-and-contrast essay analyzes the similarities and differences between two or more things. You may organize your essay either point by point or subject by subject. An effective comparison-and-contrast essay

- Identifies a purpose for comparison and contrast
- Identifies similarities and differences between two or more things, people, places, or ideas
- Gives factual details about the subjects being compared
- Uses an organizational plan suited to its topic and purpose

Types of comparison-and-contrast essays are product comparisons, essays on economic or historical developments, comparison and contrast of literary works, and plan evaluations.

Cause-and-Effect Essay A cause-and-effect essay examines the relationship between events, explaining how one event or situation causes another. A successful cause-and-effect essay includes

- A discussion of a cause, event, or condition that produces a specific result
- An explanation of an effect, outcome, or result

- Evidence and examples to support the relationship between cause and effect
- A logical organization that makes the explanation clear

Some appropriate subjects for cause-and-effect essays are science reports, current-events articles, health studies, historical accounts, and cause-and-effect investigations.

Problem-and-Solution Essay A problem-and-solution essay describes a problem and offers one or more solutions to it. It describes a clear set of steps to achieve a result. An effective problem-and-solution essay includes

- A clear statement of the problem, with its causes and effects summarized for the reader
- The most important aspects of the problem
- A proposal of at least one realistic solution
- Facts, statistics, data, or expert testimony to support the solution
- Language appropriate to the audience's knowledge and ability levels
- A clear organization that makes the relationship between problem and solution obvious

Some types of issues that might be addressed in a problem-and-solution essay include consumer issues, business issues, time-management issues, and local issues.

RESEARCH WRITING

Research writing is based on information gathered from outside sources, and it gives a writer the power to become an expert on any subject. A research paper—a focused study of a topic—helps writers explore and connect ideas, make discoveries, and share their findings with an audience. Effective research writing

- Focuses on a specific, narrow topic, which is usually summarized in a thesis statement
- Presents relevant information from a wide variety of sources
- Structures the information logically and effectively
- Identifies the sources from which the information was drawn

Besides the formal research report, there are many other specialized types of writing that depend on accurate and insightful research, including multimedia presentations, statistical reports, annotated bibliographies, and experiment journals.

Documented Essay A documented essay uses research gathered from outside sources to support an idea. What distinguishes this essay from other categories of research is the level and intensity of the research. In a documented essay, the writer consults a limited number of sources to elaborate an idea. In contrast, a formal research paper may include many more research sources. An effective documented essay includes

- A well-defined thesis that can be fully discussed in a brief essay
- Facts and details to support each main point
- Expert or informed ideas gathered from interviews and other sources
- A clear, coherent method of organization
- Full internal documentation to show sources of information

Subjects especially suited to the documented essay format include health issues, current events, and cultural trends.

Research Paper A research paper presents and interprets information gathered through an extensive study of a subject. An effective research paper has

- A clearly stated thesis statement
- Convincing factual support from a variety of outside sources, including direct quotations whose sources are credited
- A clear organization that includes an introduction, body, and conclusion
- A bibliography, or works-cited list, that provides a complete listing of research sources

Some research formats you may encounter include lab reports, annotated bibliographies, and multigenre research papers.

RESPONSE TO LITERATURE

When you write a **response-to-literature essay,** you give yourself the opportunity to discover *what, how,* and *why* a piece of writing communicated to you. An effective response

- Contains a reaction to a poem, story, essay, or other work of literature
- Analyzes the content of a literary work, its related ideas, or the work's effect on the reader
- Presents a thesis statement to identify the nature of the response
- Focuses on a single aspect of the work or gives a general overview

- Supports opinion with evidence from the work addressed

The following are just a few of the ways you might respond in writing to a literary work: reader's response journals, character analyses, literary letters, and literary analyses.

WRITING FOR ASSESSMENT

One of the most common types of school **assessment** is the written test. Most often, a written test is announced in advance, allowing you time to study and prepare. When a test includes an essay, you are expected to write a response that includes

- A clearly stated and well-supported thesis or main idea
- Specific information about the topic derived from your reading or from class discussion
- A clear organization

In your school career, you will probably encounter questions that ask you to address each of the following types of writing: explain a process; defend a position; compare, contrast, or categorize; and show cause and effect.

WORKPLACE WRITING

Workplace writing is probably the format you will use most after you finish school. It is used in offices, factories, and by workers on the road. Workplace writing includes a variety of formats that share common features. In general, workplace writing is fact-based writing that communicates specific information to readers in a structured format. Effective workplace writing

- Communicates information concisely to make the best use of both the writer's and the reader's time
- Includes a level of detail that provides necessary information and anticipates potential questions
- Reflects the writer's care if it is error-free and neatly presented

Some common types of workplace writing include business letters, memorandums, résumés, forms, and applications.

SUMMARY OF GRAMMAR

Nouns A **noun** names a person, place, or thing. **Common nouns** name any one of a class of people, places, or things. **Proper nouns** name specific people, places, or things.

Common Noun	Proper Noun
city	Washington, D.C.

Pronouns A **pronoun** is a word that stands for a noun or for a word that takes the place of a noun.

A **personal pronoun** refers to (1) the person speaking, (2) the person spoken to, or (3) the person, place, or thing spoken about.

	Singular	Plural
First Person	I, me, my, mine	we, us, our, ours
Second Person	you, your, yours	you, your, yours
Third Person	he, him, his,	they, them,
	she, her, hers,	their, theirs
	it, its	

A **reflexive pronoun** ends in -*self* or -*selves* and adds information to a sentence by pointing back to a noun or pronoun earlier in the sentence.

As I said these words I busied *myself* among the pile of bones of which I have before spoken.
—"The Cask of Amontillado," p. 6

An **intensive pronoun** ends in -*self* or -*selves* and simply adds emphasis to a noun or a pronoun in the same sentence.

And Spring *herself*, when she woke at dawn, Would scarcely know that we were gone.
—"There Will Come Soft Rains," p. 473

Demonstrative pronouns (*this*, *these*, *that*, and *those*) direct attention to a specific person, place, or thing.

These are the juiciest pears I have ever tasted.

A **relative pronoun** begins a subordinate (relative) clause and connects it to another idea in the sentence.

The poet *who* wrote "Fire and Ice" is Robert Frost.

The poet *whom* I admire is Frost.

An **indefinite pronoun** refers to a person, place, or thing, often without specifying which one.

Some of the flowers were in bloom.

Everybody chose something.

Verbs A **verb** is a word that expresses time while showing an action, a condition, or the fact that something exists.

An **action verb** indicates the action of someone or something.

An action verb is **transitive** if it directs action toward someone or something named in the same sentence.

Henderson *shook* his head.
—"The Machine That Won the War," p. 456

An action verb is **intransitive** if it does not direct action toward something or someone named in the same sentence.

Earth *had won* so all *had been* for the best.
—"The Machine That Won the War," p. 456

A **linking verb** is a verb that connects the subject of a sentence with a noun or pronoun that renames or describes the subject. All linking verbs are intransitive.

Life *is* a broken-winged bird . . .
—"Dreams," p. 905

A **helping verb** is a verb that can be added to another verb to make a verb phrase.

Nor *did* I suspect that these experiences could be part of a novel's meaning.

Adjectives An **adjective** describes a noun or a pronoun or gives a noun or a pronoun a more specific meaning. Adjectives answer these questions:

What kind?	*blue* lamp, *large* tree
Which one?	*this* table, *those* books
How many?	*five* stars, *several* buses
How much?	*less* money, *enough* votes

The articles *the, a,* and *an* are adjectives. *An* is used before a word beginning with a vowel sound.

A noun may sometimes be used as an adjective.

diamond necklace	*summer* vacation

Adverbs An **adverb** modifies a verb, an adjective, or another adverb. Adverbs answer the questions *where, when, in what way,* or *to what extent.*

He could stand *there.* (modifies verb *stand*)

He was *blissfully* happy. (modifies adjective *happy*)

It ended *too* soon. (modifies adverb *soon*)

Prepositions A **preposition** relates a noun or a pronoun that appears with it to another word in the sentence.

the scene *before* the end   stood *near* me

Conjunctions A **conjunction** connects other words or groups of words.

A **coordinating conjunction** connects similar kinds or groups of words.

mother *and* father   simple *yet* stylish

Correlative conjunctions are used in pairs to connect similar words or groups of words.

both Sue *and* Meg   *neither* he *nor* I

A **subordinating conjunction** connects two complete ideas by placing one idea below the other in rank or importance.

You would know him *if* you saw him.

Interjections An **interjection** expresses feeling or emotion and functions independently of a sentence.

"*Oh*, my poor, poor, Mathilde!"

—"The Necklace," p. 608

Sentences A **sentence** is a group of words with a subject and a predicate. Together, these parts express a complete thought.

I closed my eyes and pondered my next move.

—"Rules of the Game," p. 262

A **fragment** is a group of words that does not express a complete thought.

The Swan Theater in London

Subject and Verb Agreement A singular verb must be used with a singular subject; a plural verb must be used with a plural subject.

Raegan is going home now.

Many *storms are* the cause of beach erosion.

In a sentence with combined singular and plural subjects, the verb should agree with the subject closest to it.

Either the *cats* or the *dog is* hungry.

Neither *Angie* nor her *sisters were* present.

Phrase A **phrase** is a group of words, without a subject and a verb, that functions in a sentence as one part of speech.

A **prepositional phrase** is a group of words that includes a preposition and a noun or a pronoun that is the object of the preposition.

outside my window   below the counter

An **adjective phrase** is a prepositional phrase that modifies a noun or a pronoun by telling *what kind* or *which one.*

The wooden gates *of that lane* stood open.

An **adverb phrase** is a prepositional phrase that modifies a verb, an adjective, or an adverb by pointing out *where, when, in what way,* or *to what extent.*

"They rose and fell *in the trough of the seas,* heads to the wind, like a mighty fleet at anchor. . . ."

—"The Birds," p. 50

An **appositive phrase** is a noun or pronoun with modifiers, placed next to a noun or a pronoun to add information and details.

"It is a very great pleasure and honor to welcome Mr. Sanger Rainsford, *the celebrated hunter,* to my home."

—"The Most Dangerous Game," p. 18

A **participial phrase** is a participle with its modifiers or complements. The entire phrase acts as an adjective.

"Try the settee," said Holmes, *relapsing into his armchair . . .*

—"The Red-headed League," p. 96

A **gerund phrase** is a gerund with modifiers or a complement, all acting together as a noun.

The baying of the hounds drew nearer, . . .

—"The Most Dangerous Game," p. 18

An **infinitive phrase** is an infinitive (*to* and a verb) with modifiers, complements, or a subject, all acting together as a single part of speech.

I continued, as was my wont, *to smile in his face,* . . .

—"The Cask of Amontillado," p. 6

Clauses A **clause** is a group of words with a subject and a verb.

An **independent clause** has a subject and a verb and can stand by itself as a complete sentence.

A **subordinate clause** has a subject and a verb but cannot stand by itself as a complete sentence; it can only be part of a sentence.

An **adjective clause** is a subordinate clause that modifies a noun or a pronoun by telling *what kind* or *which one*.

> Walter Mitty stopped the car in front of the building *where his wife went to have her hair done.*
>
> —"The Secret Life of Walter Mitty," p. 346

An **adverb clause** modifies a verb, an adjective, an adverb, or a verbal by telling *where, when, in what way, to what extent, under what condition,* or *why.*

> The hunter shook his head several times, *as if he was puzzled.*
>
> —"The Most Dangerous Game," p. 18

A **noun clause** is a subordinate clause that acts as a noun.

> . . . I discovered *that the intoxication had worn off . . .*
>
> —"The Cask of Amontillado," p. 6

SUMMARY OF CAPITALIZATION AND PUNCTUATION

Capitalization

Capitalize the first word of a sentence and also the first word in a quotation if the quotation is a complete sentence.

> I said to him, "My dear Fortunato, you are luckily met."　　—"The Cask of Amontillado," p. 6

Capitalize all proper nouns and adjectives.

> O. Henry　　Ganges River　　Great Wall of China

Capitalize a person's title when it is followed by the person's name or when it is used in direct address.

> Madame　　　Dr. Mitty　　　General Zaroff

Capitalize titles showing family relationships when they refer to a specific person, unless they are preceded by a possessive noun or pronoun.

> Uncle Marcos　　　Granddaddy Cain

Capitalize the first word and all other key words in the titles of books, periodicals, poems, stories, plays, paintings, and other works of art.

> *Odyssey*　　　　"I Wandered Lonely as a Cloud"

Punctuation

End Marks Use a **period** to end a declarative sentence, an imperative sentence, an indirect question, and most abbreviations.

> Mr. Jabez Wilson laughed heavily.
>
> —"The Red-headed League," p. 96

Use a **question mark** to end a direct question, an incomplete question, or a statement that is intended as a question.

> Shall I meet other wayfarers at night?
>
> —"Uphill," p. 926

Use an **exclamation mark** after a statement showing strong emotion, an urgent imperative sentence, or an interjection expressing strong emotion.

> Free at last! Free at last!
> Thank God almighty, we are Free at last!
>
> —"I Have a Dream," p. 164

Commas Use a **comma** before the coordinating conjunction to separate two independent clauses in a compound sentence.

> All at once . . . she came upon a superb diamond necklace, and her heart started beating with overwhelming desire.　　—"The Necklace," p. 608

Use commas to separate three or more words, phrases, or clauses in a series.

> My brothers and I would peer into the medicinal herb shop, watching old Li dole out onto a stiff sheet of white paper the right amount of insect shells, saffron-colored seeds, and pungent leaves for his ailing customers.
>
> —"Rules of the Game," p. 262

Use commas to separate adjectives of equal rank. Do not use commas to separate adjectives that must stay in a specific order.

> The big cottonwood tree stood apart from a small group of winterbare cottonwoods which grew in the wide, sandy arroyo.
>
> —"The Man to Send Rain Clouds," p. 590

> In autumn those that had not migrated overseas . . . were caught up in the same driving urge . . .
>
> —"The Birds," p. 50

Use a comma after an introductory word, phrase, or clause.

> When Marvin was ten years old, his father took him through the long, echoing corridors . . .
>> —"If I Forget Thee, Oh Earth . . . ," p. 486

Use commas to set off parenthetical and nonessential expressions.

> An evil place can, so to speak, broadcast vibrations of evil.
>> —"The Most Dangerous Game," p. 18

Use commas with places, dates, and titles.

> Poe was raised in Richmond, Virginia.

> On September 1, 1939, World War II began.

> Dr. Martin Luther King, Jr., was born in 1929.

Use a comma to set off a direct quotation, to prevent a sentence from being misunderstood, and to indicate the omission of a common verb in a sentence with two or more clauses.

> Michele said, "I'm going to the game tonight."

> *Faulty:* She stifled the sob that rose to her lips and lay motionless.

> *Revised:* She stifled the sob that rose to her lips, and lay motionless.

> In the *Odyssey,* the Cyclops may symbolize brutishness; the Sirens, knowledge.

Semicolons
Use a **semicolon** to join independent clauses that are not already joined by a conjunction.

> The lights of cities sparkle; on nights when there was no moon, it was difficult for me to tell the Earth from the sky. . . .
>> —"Single Room, Earth View," p. 636

Use a semicolon to join independent clauses separated by either a conjunctive adverb or a transitional expression.

> Edward Way Teale wrote nearly thirty books; moreover, he was also an artist and a naturalist.

Use semicolons to avoid confusion when independent clauses or items in a series already contain commas.

> Unable to afford jewelry, she dressed simply; but she was as wretched as a *déclassée,* for women have neither caste nor breeding—in them beauty, grace, and charm replace pride of birth.
>> —"The Necklace," p. 608

Colons
Use a **colon** in order to introduce a list of items following an independent clause.

> The authors we are reading include a number of poets: Robert Frost, Lewis Carroll, and Emily Dickinson.

Use a colon to introduce a formal quotation.

> I have a dream that one day this nation will rise up and live out the true meaning of its creed: "We hold these truths to be self-evident; . . ."
>> —"I Have a Dream," p. 164

Quotation Marks
A **direct quotation** represents a person's exact speech or thoughts and is enclosed in quotation marks.

> "Where I was born and where and how I have lived is unimportant," Georgia O'Keeffe told us in the book of paintings and words published in her ninetieth year on earth.
>> —"Georgia O'Keeffe," p. 685

An **indirect quotation** reports only the general meaning of what a person said or thought and does not require quotation marks.

> The driver of the bus saw me still sitting there, and he asked was I going to stand up . . .
>> —from *Rosa Parks: My Story,* p. 168

Always place a comma or a period inside the final quotation mark.

> "I don't know," he said slowly. "It says here the birds are hungry."   —"The Birds," p. 50

Place a question mark or an exclamation mark inside the final quotation mark if the end mark is part of the quotation; if it is not part of the quotation, place it outside the final quotation mark.

> "That pig will devour us, greedily!"
>> —"The Golden Kite, the Silver Wind," p. 178

> Have you ever read the poem "Dreams"?

Use single quotation marks for a quotation within a quotation.

> "'But,' said I, 'there would be millions of red-headed men who would apply.'"
>> —"The Red-headed League," p. 96

Use quotation marks around the titles of short written works, episodes in a series, songs, and titles of works mentioned as parts of a collection.

> "I Hear America Singing"   "Both Sides Now"

Dashes Use **dashes** to indicate an abrupt change of thought, a dramatic interrupting idea, or a summary statement.

> The streets were lined with people—lots and lots of people—the children all smiling, placards, confetti, people waving from windows.
>
> —from *A White House Diary,* p. 674

Parentheses Use **parentheses** to set off asides and explanations only when the material is not essential or when it consists of one or more sentences.

> One last happy moment I had was looking up and seeing Mary Griffith . . . (Mary for many years had been in charge of altering the clothes which I purchased) . . .
>
> —from *A White House Diary,* p. 674

Hyphens Use a **hyphen** with certain numbers, after certain prefixes, with two or more words used as one word, and with a compound modifier coming before a noun.

> seventy-six   Post-Modernist

Apostrophes Add an **apostrophe** and *-s* to show the possessive case of most singular nouns.

> Thurmond's wife   the playwright's craft

Add an apostrophe to show the possessive case of plural nouns ending in *-s* and *-es.*

> the sailors' ships   the Wattses' daughter

Add an apostrophe and *-s* to show the possessive case of plural nouns that do not end in *-s* or *-es.*

> the children's games   the people's friend

Use an apostrophe in a contraction to indicate the position of the missing letter or letters.

> You'll be lonely at first, they admitted, but you're so nice you'll make friends fast.
>
> —"Checkouts," p. 282

GLOSSARY OF COMMON USAGE

among, between
Among is usually used with three or more items. *Between* is generally used with only two items.

> *Among* the poems we read this year, Margaret Walker's "Memory" was my favorite.

> Mark Twain's "The Invalid's Story" includes a humorous encounter *between* the narrator and a character named Thompson.

amount, number
Amount refers to a mass or a unit, whereas *number* refers to individual items that can be counted. Therefore, *amount* generally appears with a singular noun, and *number* appears with a plural noun.

> Annie Sullivan's work with Helen Keller must have required a huge *amount* of patience.

> In her poem, "Uphill," Christina Rossetti uses a *number* of intriguing symbols.

any, all
Any should not be used in place of *any other* or *all.*

> Rajika liked Amy Tan's "Rules of the Game" better than *any other* short story.

> Of *all* O. Henry's short stories, "The Gift of the Magi" is one of the most famous.

around
In formal writing, *around* should not be used to mean *approximately* or *about.* These usages are allowable, however, in informal writing or in colloquial dialogue.

> Shakespeare's *Romeo and Juliet* had its first performance in *approximately* 1595.

> Shakespeare was *about* thirty when he wrote this play.

as, because, like, as to
The word *as* has several meanings and can function as several parts of speech. To avoid confusion, use *because* rather than *as* when you want to indicate cause and effect.

> *Because* Cyril was interested in the history of African American poetry, he decided to write his report on Paul Laurence Dunbar.

Do not use the preposition *like* to introduce a clause that requires the conjunction *as.*

> Dorothy Parker conversed *as* she wrote—wittily.

The use of *as to* for *about* is awkward and should be avoided.

> Rosa has an interesting theory *about* E. E. Cummings's unusual typography in his poems.

bad, badly
Use the predicate adjective *bad* after linking verbs such as *feel*, *look*, and *seem*. Use *badly* whenever an adverb is required.

> Sara Teasdale's poem "There Will Come Soft Rains" shows clearly that the author felt *bad* about the destruction of war.

> In O. Henry's "The Gift of the Magi," Della *badly* wants to buy a wonderful Christmas present for her husband, Jim.

because of, due to
Use *due to* if it can logically replace the phrase *caused by*. In introductory phrases, however, *because of* is better usage than *due to*.

> The popularity of Frank Stockton's "The Lady or the Tiger?" is largely *due to* the story's open ending.

> *Because of* her feeling that Bennie's mother had enough to worry about already, Bennie's grandmother keeps the doctor's conclusions to herself.

being as, being that
Avoid these expressions. Use *because* or *since* instead.

> *Because* the protagonist of James Hurst's "The Scarlet Ibis" is a dynamic character, he changes significantly in the course of the story.

> *Since* Romeo and Juliet were from feuding families, their relationship involved secrecy and risk.

beside, besides
Beside is a preposition meaning "at the side of" or "close to." Do not confuse *beside* with *besides,* which means "in addition to." *Besides* can be a preposition or an adverb.

> When our group discussed William Least Heat Moon's "Nameless, Tennessee," Luis sat *beside* Eileen.

> *Besides* "The Bells," can you think of any other poems by Edgar Allan Poe?

can, may
The verb *can* generally refers to the ability to act. The verb *may* generally refers to permission to act.

> The mysterious listeners in Walter de la Mare's poem *can* hear the words of the lonely traveler.

> *May* I tell you why I admire Edgar Lee Masters's "George Gray"?

compare, contrast
The verb *compare* can involve both similarities and differences. The verb *contrast* always involves differences. Use *to* or *with* after *compare.* Use *with* after *contrast.*

> Theo's paper *compared* James Weldon Johnson's style in "The Creation" *with* the style of African American sermons of the same period.

> In the opening lines of the famous speech in Shakespeare's *As You Like It*, the world is *compared to* a stage and men and women to actors or players.

> The speaker's tone of hysteria in the closing stanzas of Poe's "The Raven" *contrasts with* the quiet opening of the poem.

different from, different than
The preferred usage is *different from*.

> The structure of "The Meadow Mouse" is quite *different from* that of "I Wandered Lonely as a Cloud."

farther, further
Use *farther* when you refer to distance. Use *further* when you mean "to a greater degree" or "additional."

> The *farther* Rainsford traveled in the jungle in "The Most Dangerous Game," the nearer the baying of the hounds sounded.

> Despite his men's advice, Odysseus *further* insults the Cyclops and provokes the monster's curse.

fewer, less
Use *fewer* for things that can be counted. Use *less* for amounts or quantities that cannot be counted.

> Poetry often uses *fewer* words than prose to convey ideas and images.

> T. S. Eliot's humorous poems have received *less* critical attention than his serious verse has.

good, well
Use the adjective *good* after linking verbs such as *feel, look, smell, taste,* and *seem.* Use *well* whenever you need an adverb.

> In Walt Whitman's "I Hear America Singing," the "varied carols" sound *good* to the speaker.

> Dickens wrote especially *well* when he described eccentric characters.

hopefully

You should not loosely attach this adverb to a sentence, as in "*Hopefully*, the rain will stop by noon." Rewrite the sentence so that *hopefully* modifies a specific verb. Other possible ways of revising such sentences include using the adjective *hopeful* or a phrase such as "everyone *hopes* that."

> Dr. Martin Luther King, Jr., wrote and spoke *hopefully* about his dream of racial harmony.

> Akko was *hopeful* that he could find some of the unusual words from Lewis Carroll's "Jabberwocky" in an unabridged dictionary.

> Everyone *hopes* that the class production of *Romeo and Juliet* will be a big success.

its, it's

Do not confuse the possessive pronoun *its* with the contraction *it's*, used in place of "it is" or "it has."

> Ancient Greek society must have recognized many of *its* ideal values in the *Odyssey*.

> In Walter de la Mare's "The Listeners," the traveler thinks *it's* strange that no one replies to his call.

just, only

When you use *just* as an adverb meaning "no more than," be sure you place it directly before the word it logically modifies. Likewise, be sure you place *only* before the word it logically modifies.

> Shakespeare's Sonnet 30 offers *just* one remedy for the speaker's grief and depression: the thought of a dear friend.

> A stereotyped character exhibits *only* those traits or behavior patterns that are assumed to be typical.

kind of, sort of

In formal writing, you should not use these colloquial expressions. Instead, use a word such as *rather* or *somewhat*.

> Alfred is *rather* irresponsible in Morley Callaghan's story "All the Years of Her Life."

> In "The Secret Life of Walter Mitty," James Thurber characterizes Mitty as *somewhat* absent-minded.

lay, lie

Do not confuse these verbs. *Lay* is a transitive verb meaning "to set or put something down." Its principal parts are *lay, laying, laid, laid*. *Lie* is an intransitive verb meaning "to recline." Its principal parts are *lie, lying, lay, lain*.

> In Heyerdahl's *Kon-Tiki*, the narrator says that after the ship hit the reef, Herman *lay* pressed flat across the ridge of the cabin roof.

> Homer describes the slaughtered suitors *lying* dead in a heap on the floor of Odysseus' hall.

leave, let

Be careful not to confuse these verbs. *Leave* means "to go away" or "to allow to remain." *Let* means "to permit."

> In Tennyson's "The Eagle," the bird *leaves* the crag and plunges like a thunderbolt toward the sea.

> The lovesick Romeo asks his friends to *leave* him alone while they go to Capulet's party.

> "*Let* wantons light of heart / Tickle the senseless rushes with their heels," he says.

literally, figuratively

Literally means "word for word" or "in fact." The opposite of *literally* is *figuratively*, meaning "metaphorically." Be careful not to use *literally* as a synonym for *nearly*, as in informal expressions like this: "He was *literally* beside himself with rage."

> Certain specific details in "I Hear an Army" show that James Joyce does not intend us to interpret the army *literally*. Instead, the army and the speaker's nightmare are meant *figuratively* to suggest his despair at his abandonment by his love.

of, have

Do not use *of* in place of *have* after auxiliary verbs like *would, could, should, may,* or *might*.

> Sir Arthur Conan Doyle might *have* continued to practice medicine, but soon after the publication *of* his first Sherlock Holmes stories, he decided to write full time.

raise, rise

Raise is a transitive verb that usually takes a direct object. *Rise* is an intransitive verb and never takes a direct object.

> In "Casey at the Bat," Ernest Lawrence Thayer suspensefully *raises* the reader's expectations throughout the poem, only to end the narrative with a mighty anticlimax.

> Jorge *rose* to the challenge of interpreting Gabriel García Márquez's story "A Very Old Man With Enormous Wings."

set, sit

Do not confuse these verbs. *Set* is a transitive verb meaning "to put (something) in a certain place." Its principal parts are *set, setting, set, set. Sit* is an intransitive verb meaning "to be seated." Its principal parts are *sit, sitting, sat, sat.*

> The opening sentence of Saki's "The Interlopers" *sets* a tone of tension and conflict for the story.

> While Walter Mitty *sat* in a big leather chair in the hotel lobby, he picked up a copy of a magazine.

so, so that

Be careful not to use the coordinating conjunction *so* when your context requires *so that. So* means "accordingly" or "therefore" and expresses a cause-and-effect relationship. *So that* expresses purpose.

> He wanted to check the clues, *so* he read "The Red-headed League" again.

> The priest wanted to locate Teofilo's body *so that* he could give him the Last Rites.

than, then

The conjunction *than* is used to connect the two parts of a comparison. Do not confuse *than* with the adverb *then,* which usually refers to time.

> I enjoyed reading "Jacob Lawrence: American Painter" more *than* "Autumn Gardening."

> Sally Ride earned a doctorate in physics and *then* became the first American woman in space.

that, which, who

Use the relative pronoun *that* to refer to things or people. Use *which* only for things and *who* only for people.

> The phrase *that* James Thurber dislikes is "you know."

> Donald Justice wrote "Incident in a Rose Garden," *which* is a dramatic poem.

> The sea goddess *who* loved Odysseus was Calypso.

unique

Because *unique* means "one of a kind," you should not use it carelessly to mean "interesting" or "unusual." Avoid such illogical expressions as "most unique," "very unique," and "extremely unique."

> Homer occupies a *unique* position in the history of Western literature.

when, where

Do not directly follow a linking verb with *when* or *where.* Also, be careful not to use *where* when your context requires *that.*

> *Faulty:*   Foreshadowing is *when* an author uses clues to suggest future events.

> *Revised:*   In foreshadowing, an author uses clues to suggest future events.

> *Faulty:*   Ithaca was *where* Penelope awaited Odysseus.

> *Revised:*   Penelope awaited Odysseus on Ithaca.

who, whom

In formal writing, remember to use *who* only as a subject in clauses and sentences and *whom* only as an object.

> Richard Wright, *who* is widely admired for his novel *Native Son,* also wrote haiku verse.

> Leslie Marmon Silko, *whom* Mark quoted in his oral report, was raised on the Laguna Pueblo reservation in New Mexico.

Introduction to the Internet

The Internet is a series of networks that are interconnected all over the world. The Internet allows users to have almost unlimited access to information stored on the networks. Dr. Berners-Lee, a physicist, created the Internet in the 1980s by writing a small computer program that allowed pages to be linked together using key words. The Internet was mostly text-based until 1992, when a computer program called the NCSA Mosaic (National Center for Supercomputing Applications) was created at the University of Illinois. This program was the first Web browser. The development of Web browsers greatly eased the ability of the user to navigate through all the pages stored on the Web. Very soon, the appearance of the Web was altered as well. More appealing visuals were added, and sound, too, was implemented. This change made the Web more user-friendly and more appealing to the general public.

Using the Internet for Research

Key Word Search

Before you begin a search, you should identify your specific topic. To make searching easier, narrow your subject to a key word or a group of key words. These are your search terms, and they should be as specific as possible. For example, if you are looking for the latest concert dates for your favorite musical group, you might use the band's name as a key word. However, if you were to enter the name of the group in the query box of the search engine, you might be presented with thousands of links to information about the group that is unrelated to what you want to know. You might locate such information as band member biographies, the group's history, fan reviews of concerts, and hundreds of sites with related names containing information that is irrelevant to your search. Because you used such a broad key word, you might need to navigate through all that information before you could find a link or subheading for concert dates. In contrast, if you were to type in "Duplex Arena and [band name]," you would have a better chance of locating pages that contain this information.

How to Narrow Your Search

If you have a large group of key words and still do not know which ones to use, write out a list of all the words you are considering. Once you have completed the list, scrutinize it. Then, delete the words that are least important to your search, and highlight those that are most important.

These **key search connectors** can help you fine-tune your search:

AND: Narrows a search by retrieving documents that include both terms. For example: *baseball* AND *playoffs*

OR: Broadens a search by retrieving documents including any of the terms. For example: *playoffs* OR *championships*

NOT: Narrows a search by excluding documents containing certain words. For example: *baseball* NOT *history of*

Tips for an Effective Search

1. Remember that search engines can be case-sensitive. If your first attempt at searching fails, check your search terms for misspellings and try again.

2. If you are entering a group of key words, present them in order from the most important to the least important key word.

3. Avoid opening the link to every single page in your results list. Search engines present pages in descending order of relevancy. The most useful pages will be located at the top of the list. However, read the description of each link before you open the page.

4. Some search engines provide helpful tips for specializing your search. Take the opportunity to learn more about effective searching.

Other Ways to Search

Using Online Reference Sites   How you search should be tailored to what you are hoping to find. If you are looking for data and facts, use reference sites before you jump onto a simple search engine. For example, you can find reference sites to provide definitions of words, statistics about almost any subject, biographies, maps, and concise information on many topics. Here are some useful online reference sites:

Online libraries

Online periodicals

Almanacs

Encyclopedias

You can find these sources using subject searches.

Conducting Subject Searches As you prepare to go online, consider your subject and the best way to find information to suit your needs. If you are looking for general information on a topic and you want your search results to be extensive, consider the subject search indexes on most search engines. These indexes, in the form of category and subject lists, often appear on the first page of a search engine. When you click on a specific highlighted word, you will be presented with a new screen containing subcategories of the topic you chose.

Evaluating the Reliability of Internet Resources

Just as you would evaluate the quality, bias, and validity of any other research material you locate, check the source of information you find online. Compare these two sites containing information about the poet and writer Langston Hughes:

Site A is a personal Web site constructed by a college student. It contains no bibliographic information or links to sites that he used. Included on the site are several poems by Langston Hughes and a student essay about the poet's use of symbolism. It has not been updated in more than six months.

Site B is a Web site constructed and maintained by the English Department of a major university. Information on Hughes is presented in a scholarly format, with a bibliography and credits for the writer. The site includes links to other sites and indicates new features that are added weekly.

For your own research, consider the information you find on Site B to be more reliable and accurate than that on Site A. Because it is maintained by experts in their field who are held accountable for their work, the university site will be a better research tool than the student-generated one.

Tips for Evaluating Internet Sources

1. Consider who constructed and who now maintains the Web page. Determine whether this author is a reputable source. Often, the URL endings indicate a source.
   - Sites ending in *.edu* are maintained by educational institutions.
   - Sites ending in *.gov* are maintained by government agencies (federal, state, or local).
   - Sites ending in *.org* are normally maintained by non-profit organizations and agencies.
   - Sites ending in *.com* are commercially or personally maintained.

2. Skim the official and trademarked Web pages first. It is safe to assume that the information you draw from Web pages of reputable institutions, online encyclopedias, online versions of major daily newspapers, or government-owned sites produce information as reliable as the material you would find in print. In contrast, unbranded sites or those generated by individuals tend to borrow information from other sources without providing documentation. As information travels from one source to another, it could have been muddled, misinterpreted, edited, or revised.

3. You can still find valuable information in the less "official" sites. Check for the writer's credentials, and then consider these factors:
   - Do not be misled by official-looking graphics or presentations.
   - Make sure that the information is updated enough to suit your needs. Many Web pages will indicate how recently they have been updated.
   - If the information is borrowed, notice whether you can trace it back to its original source.

Respecting Copyrighted Material

Because the Internet is a relatively new and quickly growing medium, issues of copyright and ownership arise almost daily. As laws begin to govern the use and reuse of material posted online, they may change the way that people can access or reprint material.

Text, photographs, music, and fine art printed online may not be reproduced without acknowledged permission of the copyright owner.

Writing Criticism

Literary criticism involves studying, analyzing, interpreting, and evaluating works of literature. It can be as brief as an answer to a question or as lengthy as an essay or a book. Following are examples of three types of criticism.

Analysis

You are frequently asked to analyze, or break down into parts and examine, a passage or a work. Often you must support your analysis with specific references to the text. In this brief analysis, the writer uses words from the question to write a topic sentence and embeds quotations from the text as support.

Question In "Heat" by H.D., how does the speaker create the impression that heat is almost a solid substance?

Answer The speaker in "Heat" uses repetition and imagery to convey the impression that heat is almost a solid substance. By repeating the word *heat* in each of the three stanzas, the speaker emphasizes its physical presence. Further, the speaker uses images that appeal to the sense of touch in describing heat as if it were a substance. In the first stanza, the speaker asks the wind to "cut apart the heat," and in the third stanza, to "plow through it."

Biographical Criticism Critics who take a biographical approach use information about a writer's life to explain his or her work. In this passage of biographical criticism, Kenneth Silverman explains Edgar Allan Poe's preoccupation with death as Poe's response to the early death of his mother, Eliza.

"Much of his later writing, despite its variety of forms and styles, places and characters, is driven by the question of whether the dead remain dead. . . . The most persuasive and coherent explanation, . . . comes from the modern understanding of childhood bereavement. . . . [C]hildren who lose a parent at an early age, as Edgar lost Eliza Poe, . . . invest more feeling in and magnify the parent's image. . . . The young child . . . cannot comprehend the finality of death. . . . "

Historical Criticism Using this approach, a critic explains how an author's work responds to the events, circumstances, or ideas of the author's historical era. In the following passage of historical criticism, Jean H. Hagstrum shows how William Blake's character Urizen symbolizes the Enlightenment ideas of Newton, Locke, and Bacon that Blake detested.

"Urizen is also an active force. Dividing, partitioning, dropping the plummet line, applying Newton's compasses to the world, he creates abstract mathematical forms. Like Locke, he shrinks the senses, narrows the perceptions, binds man to natural fact. Like Bacon, he creates the laws of prudence and crucifies passion."

Using Ideas From Research

Below are three common methods of incorporating the ideas of other writers into your work. Choose the most appropriate style by analyzing your needs in each case. In all cases, you must credit your source.

- **Direct Quotation:** Use quotation marks to indicate the exact words.
- **Paraphrase:** To share ideas without a direct quotation, state the ideas in your own words.
- **Summary:** To provide information about a large body of work, identify the writer's main idea.

Avoiding Plagiarism

Whether you are presenting a formal research paper or an opinion paper on a current event, be careful to give credit for any ideas or opinions that are not your own. Presenting someone else's ideas, research, or opinion as your own—even if you have rephrased it in different words—is plagiarism, the equivalent of academic stealing, or fraud.

You can avoid plagiarism by synthesizing what you learn: Read from several sources, and let the ideas of experts help you draw your own conclusions and form your own opinions. When you choose to use someone else's ideas or work to support your view, credit the source of the material.

Preparing a Manuscript

The presentation of your written work is important. Your work should be neat, clean, and easy to read. Follow your teacher's directions for placing your name and class, along with the title and date of your work, on the paper.

Research Papers

Most formal research papers have these features:
- Title Page
- Table of Contents or Outline
- Works-Cited List or Bibliography

Citing Sources

In research writing, cite your sources. In the body of your paper, provide a footnote, an endnote, or an internal citation, identifying the sources of facts, opinions, or quotations. At the end of your paper, provide a bibliography or a works-cited list, a list of all the sources you cite. Follow an established format, such as Modern Library Association (MLA) Style.

Works-Cited List (MLA Style)

A works-cited list must contain accurate information sufficient to enable a reader to locate each source you cite. The basic components of an entry are as follows:

- Name of the author, editor, translator, or group responsible for the work
- Title
- Place and date of publication
- Publisher

For print materials, the information required for a citation generally appears on the copyright and title pages of a work. For the format of works-cited list entries, consult the examples at right and in the chart on page R32.

Internal Citations (MLA Style)

An internal citation briefly identifies the source from which you have taken a specific quotation, factual claim, or opinion. It refers the reader to one of the entries on your works-cited list. An internal citation has the following features:

- It appears in parentheses.
- It identifies the source by the last name of the author, editor, or translator.
- It gives a page reference, identifying the page of the source on which the information cited can be found.

Punctuation An internal citation generally falls outside a closing quotation mark but within the final punctuation of a clause or sentence. For a long quotation set off from the rest of your text, place the citation at the end of the excerpt without any punctuation following.

Special Cases

- If the author is an organization, use the organization's name, in a shortened version if necessary.
- If you cite more than one work by the same author, add the title or a shortened version of the title.

Sample Works-Cited Lists

Carwardine, Mark, Erich Hoyt, R. Ewan Fordyce, and Peter Gill. *The Nature Company Guides: Whales, Dolphins, and Porpoises.* New York: Time-Life Books, 1998.

Whales in Danger. "Discovering Whales." 18 Oct. 1999. <http://whales.magna.com.au/DISCOVER>

Neruda, Pablo. "Ode to Spring." *Odes to Opposites.* Trans. Ken Krabbenhoft. Ed. and illus. Ferris Cook. Boston: Little, Brown and Company, 1995.

The Saga of the Volsungs. Trans. Jesse L. Byock. London: Penguin Books, 1990.

An anonymous work is listed by title.

Both the title of the work and of the collection in which it is found are listed.

Sample Internal Citations

It makes sense that baleen whales such as the blue whale, the bowhead whale, the humpback whale, and the sei whale (to name just a few) grow to immense sizes (Carwardine, Hoyt, and Fordyce 19–21). The blue whale has grooves running from under its chin to partway along the length of its underbelly. As in some other whales, these grooves expand and allow even more food and water to be taken in (Ellis 18–21).

Author's last name

Page numbers where information can be found

MLA Style for Listing Sources

Book with one author	Pyles, Thomas. *The Origins and Development of the English Language.* 2nd ed. New York: Harcourt Brace Jovanovich, Inc., 1971.
Book with two or three authors	McCrum, Robert, William Cran, and Robert MacNeil. *The Story of English.* New York: Penguin Books, 1987.
Book with an editor	Truth, Sojourner. *Narrative of Sojourner Truth.* Ed. Margaret Washington. New York: Vintage Books, 1993.
Book with more than three authors or editors	Donald, Robert B., et al. *Writing Clear Essays.* Upper Saddle River, NJ: Prentice-Hall, Inc., 1996.
Single work from an anthology	Hawthorne, Nathaniel. "Young Goodman Brown." *Literature: An Introduction to Reading and Writing.* Ed. Edgar V. Roberts and Henry E. Jacobs. Upper Saddle River, NJ: Prentice-Hall, Inc., 1998. 376–385. [Indicate pages for the entire selection.]
Introduction in a published edition	Washington, Margaret. Introduction. *Narrative of Sojourner Truth.* By Sojourner Truth. New York: Vintage Books, 1993, pp. v–xi.
Signed article in a weekly magazine	Wallace, Charles. "A Vodacious Deal." *Time,* 14 Feb. 2000: 63.
Signed article in a monthly magazine	Gustaitis, Joseph. "The Sticky History of Chewing Gum." *American History,* Oct. 1998: 30–38.
Unsigned editorial or story	"Selective Silence." Editorial. *Wall Street Journal,* 11 Feb. 2000: A14. [If the editorial or story is signed, begin with the author's name.]
Signed pamphlet	[Treat the pamphlet as though it were a book.]
Pamphlet with no author, publisher, or date	*Are You at Risk of Heart Attack?* n.p. n.d. [n.p. n.d. indicates that there is no known publisher or date]
Filmstrips, slide programs, and videotape	*The Diary of Anne Frank.* Dir. George Stevens. Perf. Millie Perkins, Shelley Winters, Joseph Schildkraut, Lou Jacobi, and Richard Beymer. Twentieth Century Fox, 1959.
Radio or television program transcript	"The First Immortal Generation." *Ockham's Razor.* Host Robyn Williams. Guest Damien Broderick. National Public Radio. 23 May 1999. Transcript.
Internet	*National Association of Chewing Gum Manufacturers.* 19 Dec. 1999 <http://www.nacgm.org/consumer/funfacts.html> [Indicate the date you accessed the information. Content and addresses at Web sites change frequently.]
Newspaper	Thurow, Roger. "South Africans Who Fought for Sanctions Now Scrap for Investors." *Wall Street Journal,* 11 Feb. 2000: A1+ [For a multipage article, write only the first page number on which it appears, followed by a plus sign.]
Personal interview	Smith, Jane. Personal interview. 10 Feb. 2000.
CD (with multiple publishers)	Simms, James, ed. *Romeo and Juliet.* By William Shakespeare. CD-ROM. Oxford: Attica Cybernetics Ltd.; London: BBC Education; London: HarperCollins Publishers, 1995.
Signed article from an encyclopedia	Askeland, Donald R. (1991). "Welding." *World Book Encyclopedia.* 1991 ed.

Index of Authors and Titles

Page numbers in *italics* refer to biographical information.

Index of Skills

LITERARY ANALYSIS

Act, R6
Allegory, R6
Alliteration, 471, 474, 477, 925, 935, R6
Allusion, 818, 826, 842, R6
Analogy, R6
Anecdote, 151, 153, 157, 159, R6
Antagonist, 213, 223, R6
Anticlimax, 41, 43, 45, R6
Aside, 818, 842, R6
Assonance, R6
Atmosphere, R6
Author's purpose, 163, 168, 172, 173, 445, 449, 451
Autobiographical writing, 673, 691
Autobiography, 631, R6
Ballad, R6
Biographical and autobiographical writing, 675, 686, 689
Biographical writing, 673, 691
Biography, 631, R6
Blank verse, 794, 796, 797, 798, 799, 801, 802, 804, 806, 808, 810, 811, 812, 814, R6
Career writing, 709, 712, 719
Character, 519, 729, 769, 772, 773, 774, 776, 777, 778, 780, 782, 785, 786, 787, 789, 792, R6
    dynamic, 553, 565
    flat, 345, 353, 769, 792
    round, 345, 348, 353, 769, 792
    static, 553, 565
Characterization, 95, 106, 112, 117, 572, 575, 580, R6–R7
    direct, 569, 579, 582, 585
    indirect, 303, 307, 311, 569, 579, 582, 585
    in essays, 315, 317, 318, 321
Character rank, 794, 802, 808, 810, 812, 816
Character's motive, 860, 862, 863, 864, 865, 866, 869, 871, 875
Climax, 41, 43, 45, 523, 531, 539, 547, 549, R7
Comedy, R7
Comic relief, R7
Conflict, 17, 22, 30, 32, 37, 303, 305, 307, 308, 311, 979, 986, 989, 1001, 1006, 1011, 1012, 1018, R7
    external, 303, 311
    internal, 303, 311
Connotation, 903, 909, R7
Contemporary interpretations, 1051, 1056, 1061
Couplet, R7
Denotation, R7
Denouement, R7
Description, 5, 13, 635, 641, R7
Development, R7
Dialect, R7

Dialogue, 177, 182, 357, 363, 729, 733, 741, 746, 748, 756, 761, R7–R8
Diction, 121, 126, 127, R8
    humorous, 399, 407
Direct characterization, 569, 579, 582, 585, R8
Drama, R8
Dramatic foil, 769, 773, 778, 782, 785, 786, 792
Dramatic irony, 357, 363, 844, 846, 849, 850, 851, 853, 854, 855, 858, R8
Dramatic literature, IN1
    conflict, IN7
    dialogue, IN6
    monologue, IN6
    play
        comedy, IN6
        drama, IN6
        tragedy, IN6
    plot, IN7
    stage directions, IN7
Dramatic monologue, R8
Dramatic poetry, 891, 939, 940, 941, 945, 947, IN8, R8
Dynamic character, 553, 565
End rhyme, R8
Epic, R8
Epic hero, 979, 985, 986, 989, 990, 991, 993, 996, 999, 1001, 1005, 1006, 1010, 1011, 1012, 1015, 1018
Epic simile, 1020, 1022, 1025, 1031, 1032, 1039, 1041, 1042, 1047, R8
Essay, 631, 649, 651, 653, 654, 656, 659, 660, 664, 666, 667, 669, R8–R9
    expository, 631
    narrative, 631, 649, 669
    persuasive, 631, 649, 669
    reflective, 247, 253, 649, 669
Exposition, 523, 531, R9
Expository essay, 631
Expository writing, 445, 447, 449, 451
Extended metaphor, R9
External conflict, 303, 311
Fable, 177, 179, 181, 182
Falling action, 523, 531, R9
Fantasy, 201, 204, 209, R9
Feature article, 385, 391
Fiction, R9
Figurative language, 187, 189, 193, 891, 903, 909, IN9, R9
    metaphor, 903, 909
    personification, 903, 909
    simile, 903, 909
First-person narration, 315, 321
First-person narrator, 569, 585
First-person point of view, 345, 553, 565
Flat character, 345, 353, 769, 792
Foil, R9
Folk literature, IN1
    epic, IN11
    folk tale, IN10

    myth, IN10
    tall tale, IN11
Folk tale, humorous, 411, 415
Foot, R9
Foreshadowing, 49, 52, 54, 55, 58, 60, 62, 66, 67, 70, 71, 74, 78, 79, 80, 83, R9
Free verse, R9
Generational conflict, 261, 263, 265, 266, 269, 271, 273
Genre, R9
Haiku, 955, 961, R9
Heroic qualities, 223
Hero in a myth, 213, 216, 219, 220, 223
Homeric simile, R9
Humorous diction, 399, 407
Humorous folk tale, 411, 415
Humorous remembrance, 367, 371, 375, 377
Hyperbole, R9
Iamb, R9
Image, R9–R10
Imagery, 49, 52, 54, 60, 71, 78, 83, 121, 122, 123, 124, 126, 127, 485, 499, 913, 920, 921, 1020, 1022, 1039, 1042, 1047, R10
Indirect characterization, 303, 307, 311, 569, 579, 585, R10
Internal conflict, 303, 311
Internal rhyme, R10
Irony, 281, 283, 284, 287, 357, 359, 360, 361, 363, R10
    dramatic, 357, 363, 844, 846, 849, 850, 851, 853, 854, 855, 858, R8
    situational, 357, 363
    verbal, 357, 363, R14
Limited third-person narrator, 353
Literal language, R10
Lyric poem, R10
Lyric poetry, 891, 925, 933, 935
Main character, R10
Main idea, 385, 391
Metaphor, 903, 909, R10
Meter, R10–R11
Moment of insight, 325, 331
Monologue, 818, 842, R11
Monometer, R11
Mood, 5, 8, 13, R11
Moral, R11
Motivation, 261, 265, 266, 269, 273, R11
Musical devices, 891
Mystery, 95, 97, 98, 101, 102, 103, 105, 106, 108, 111, 112, 113, 117
Myth, R11
Narration, 151, R11
Narrative, 159, R11
Narrative essay, 631, 649, 669
Narrative poem, 41, 45, R11
Narrative poetry, 891, 939, 940, 941, 945, 947, IN8

READING STRATEGIES

GRAMMAR, USAGE, MECHANICS

WRITING

Writing Applications

Writing Strategies

Index of Features

ACKNOWLEDGMENTS (continued)

The Business Journal Serving Greater Milwaukee "'Cows on parade' find sweet home in Chicago" by David Schuyler. "This article appeared in Volume 17, No. 7 of *The Business Journal Serving Greater Milwaukee* on November 12, 1999. It has been reprinted by *The Business Journal* serving Greater Milwaukee and further reproduction by any other party is prohibited. Copyright © 1999 by *The Business Journal* serving greater Milwaukee, 600 W Virginia Street, Suite 500, Milwaukee, WI 53204, 414-278-7788." Used by permission.

Richard Curtis Associates, Inc. "Fly Away" from *The Beauty of the Beasts: Tales of Hollywood's Wild Animal Stars* by Ralph Helfer. Copyright © 1990 by Ralph Helfer. Reprinted by permission of Richard Curtis Associates, Inc.

Abigail de Oliveira Carvalho "Echo" by Henriqueta Lisboa, from *Poems Escolbidos: Chosen Poems,* translated by Helcio Veiga Costa, copyright © 1987 by Ed. Editora e Distribuidora, Ltda. Reprinted by permission of Abigail de Oliveira Carvalho, Henriqueta Lisboa's niece.

Curtis Brown, Ltd., London "The Birds" from *Kiss Me Again Stranger* by Daphne du Maurier. Reproduced by permission of Curtis Brown, Ltd., London, on behalf of the Chichester Partnership, copyright 1952 by Daphne du Maurier.

Jonathan Clowes Ltd., on behalf of Andrea Plunket "The Redheaded League" from *The Adventures of Sherlock Holmes* by Sir Arthur Conan Doyle. Copyright © 1996 Sir Arthur Conan Doyle Copyright Holders. Reprinted by kind permission of Jonathan Clowes Ltd., London, on behalf of Andrea Plunket, the Administrator of the Sir Arthur Conan Doyle Copyrights.

Coffee House Press "Problems With Hurricanes" by Victor Hernandez Cruz, from *Red Beans.* Copyright © 1991 by Victor Hernandez Cruz. Reprinted by permission of Coffee House Press.

Don Congdon Associates, Inc. "The Golden Kite, the Silver Wind" by Ray Bradbury. Copyright © 1953 by Epoch Associates; renewed 1981 by Ray Bradbury. Reprinted by permission of Don Congdon Associates, Inc.

Joan Daves Agency for the Estate of Gabriela Mistral "Meciendo" by Gabriela Mistral ("Rocking"), translated by Doris Dana from *Selected Poems of Gabriela Mistral,* translated and edited by Doris Dana. Copyright © 1961, 1964, 1970, 1971 by Doris Dana. Reprinted by permission of the Joan Daves Agency on behalf of the estate of the author.

Dial Books for Young Readers, a division of Penguin Putnam, Inc. From *Rosa Parks: My Story* by Rosa Parks with Jim Haskins. Copyright © 1992 by Rosa Parks. Used by permission of Dial Books for Young Readers, an imprint of Penguin Putnam Books for Young Readers, a division of Penguin Putnam, Inc.

Sandra Dijkstra Literary Agency for Amy Tan From "Joy, Luck, and Hollywood" by Amy Tan. Copyright © 1993 by Amy Tan. First appeared in the *Los Angeles Times,* Sunday, September 5, 1993. Reprinted with permission of the author and the Sandra Dijkstra Literary Agency.

Doubleday, a division of Random House, Inc. "The Machine That Won the War," copyright © 1961 by Mercury Press, Inc., from *Isaac Asimov: The Complete Stories, Vol. I* by Isaac Asimov. "The Birds," copyright 1952 by Daphne du Maurier, from *Kiss Me Again Stranger* by Daphne du Maurier. From *Tuesdays with Morrie* by Mitch Albom, copyright © 1997 by Mitch Albom. Used by permission of Doubleday, a division of Random House, Inc. "The Gift of the Magi" from *The Complete Works of O. Henry* by O. Henry. Published by Press Publications Company.

Martha Escutia "Business Letter and Agenda for the 8th Annual Southeast College Conference" by Martha Escutia. Used by permission of the author.

Faber and Faber Limited and Oxford University Press, Inc. "The Horses" from *Collected Poems* by Edwin Muir, copyright © 1960 by Willa Muir. Used by permission of Faber and Faber Limited and Oxford University Press, Inc.

Farrar, Straus & Giroux, Inc. "Georgia O'Keeffe" from *The White Album* by Joan Didion. Copyright © 1979 by Joan Didion. "The Washwoman" from *A Day of Pleasure* by Isaac Bashevis Singer. Copyright © 1969 by Isaac Bashevis Singer. Excerpts from *The Odyssey: A Stage Version* by Derek Walcott. Copyright © 1993 by Derek Walcott. From *In My Place* by Charlayne Hunter-Gault. Copyright © 1992 by Charlayne Hunter-Gault. Excerpts from the *Odyssey* by Homer, translated by R. Fitzgerald. Copyright © 1961, 1963 by Robert Fitzgerald and renewed 1989 by Benedict R. C. Fitzgerald.

Gale Group Excerpts from "The Birds" by DeWitt Bodeen from pp. 249–252 of *Magill's Survey of Cinema* edited by Frank N. Magill. Copyright © 1981 by Frank N. Magill. Reprinted by permission.

Graywolf Press and The Estate of William Stafford "Fifteen," copyright 1966, 1998 by the Estate of William Stafford. Reprinted from *The Way It Is: New & Selected Poems* with the permission of Graywolf Press, Saint Paul, Minnesota, and Kim Stafford for the Estate of William Stafford.

Alice R. Abbott "Perseus" by Edith Hamilton from *Mythology.* Copyright © 1940, 1942, by Edith Hamilton, renewed 1969. Used by permission.

Harcourt, Inc. "Women" from *Revolutionary Petunias & Other Poems,* copyright © 1972, 2000 by Alice Walker. "Macavity: The Mystery Cat" from *Old Possum's Book of Practical Cats,* copyright 1939 by T. S. Eliot and renewed 1967 by Esme Valerie Eliot. "A Lincoln Preface," copyright 1953 by Carl Sandburg and renewed 1981 by Margaret Sandburg, Janet Sandburg, and Helga Sandburg Crile. "Ithaca" from *The Complete Poems of Cavafy,* copyright © 1961 and renewed 1989 by Rae Dalven. Reprinted by permission of Harcourt, Inc.

HarperCollins Publishers "Summer" from *Brown Angels: An Album of Pictures and Verse* by Walter Dean Myers. Copyright © 1993 by Walter Dean Myers. Used by permission of HarperCollins Publishers.

Helmut Hirnschall "There is a Longing..." from *My Heart Soars* by Chief Dan George and Helmut Hirnschall. Copyright © 1974 by Clarke Irwin. Used by permission of the author.

Henry Holt and Company, Inc. "Talk" from *The Cow-Tail Switch and Other West African Stories* by Harold Courlander and George Herzog, © 1947, 1974 by Harold Courlander. "Fire and Ice" from *The Poetry of Robert Frost,* edited by Edward Connery Lathem. Copyright © 1951 by Robert Frost, Copyright © 1923, 1969 by Henry Holt and Company, Inc. Reprinted by permission of Henry Holt and Company, LLC. "The Road Not Taken" from *The Poetry of Robert Frost,* edited by Edward Connery Lathem. Published by Henry Holt and Company, Inc.

Horton Foote and The Barbara Hogenson Agency, Inc. *The Dancers* by Horton Foote. Copyright © 1955, 1983 by Horton Foote. Reprinted by arrangement with Horton Foote and the Barbara Hogenson Agency, Inc.

Rosemary Thurber and The Barbara Hogenson Agency, Inc. "The Secret Life of Walter Mitty" from *My World—And Welcome To It* copyright © 1942 by James Thurber; copyright renewed © 1971 by James Thurber. Reprinted by arrangement with Rosemary Thurber and the Barbara Hogenson Agency. All rights reserved.

Houghton Mifflin Company "Blackberry Eating" from *Mortal Acts, Mortal Words* by Galway Kinnell. Copyright © 1980 by Galway Kinnell. Excerpt from *Lost Moon: The Perilous Voyage of Apollo 13.* Copyright © 1994 by Jim Lovell and Jeffrey Kluger. "All Watched Over by Machines of Loving Grace" by Richard Brautigan, from *Trout Fishing in America, The Pill versus the Springhill Mine Disaster,* and *In Watermelon Sugar.* Copyright © 1968, by Richard Brautigan. Reprinted by permission of Houghton Mifflin Co. All rights reserved. "Siren Song" from *You Are Happy* by Margaret Atwood. Copyright © 1974 by Margaret Atwood. Reprinted by permission of Houghton Mifflin Company.

Houghton Mifflin Company and Frances Collin, Literary Agent Excerpt from *Silent Spring* (pp. 1–3) by Rachel Carson. Copyright © 1962 by Rachel L. Carson, renewed 1990 by Roger Christie. Reprinted by permission of Houghton Mifflin Co. and Frances Collin, Literary Agent. All rights reserved.

James R. Hurst "The Scarlet Ibis" by James Hurst, published in *The Atlantic Monthly*, July 1960. Copyright © 1988 by James Hurst. Reprinted by permission of the author.

International Creative Management, Inc. "Single Room, Earth View" by Sally Ride, published in the April/May 1986 issue of *Air & Space/Smithsonian Magazine*, published by The Smithsonian Institution. Reprinted by permission of International Creative Management, Inc.

Japan Publications "Three Haiku" (originally titled "Temple bells die out" by Bashō; and "Dragonfly catcher" and "Bearing no flowers" by Chiyojo) from *One Hundred Famous Haiku* by Daniel C. Buchanan, Copyright © 1973 by Japan Publications. Used by permission.

The Kansas City Star "The wrong orbit. Senator has no legitimate business blasting into space," an editorial from *The Kansas City Star, 1/20/98.* Reprinted by permission of The Kansas City Star.

Lyndon B. Johnson Library From *A White House Diary* by Lady Bird Johnson. Reprinted by permission of the L.B.J. Library c/o Betty Tilson, assistant to Mrs. Lyndon B. Johnson.

Junior League of Seattle "Combing" by Gladys Cardiff from *Puget Soundings*, March 1971. Reprinted by permission of the Junior League of Seattle.

The Estate of Martin Luther King, Jr., c/o Writer's House "I Have a Dream" from *The Words of Martin Luther King, Jr.* Copyright 1963 by Martin Luther King, Jr., copyright renewed 1991 by Coretta Scott King. Reprinted by arrangement with the Estate of Martin Luther King, Jr., c/o Writer's House as agent for the proprietor.

Alfred A. Knopf, a division of Random House, Inc. "Uncle Marcos" from *The House of the Spirits* by Isabel Allende, translated by Magda Bogin, copyright © 1985 by Alfred A. Knopf, A Division of Random House, Inc. "Dream Deferred" and "Dreams" from *The Collected Poems of Langston Hughes* by Langston Hughes. Copyright © 1994 by The Estate of Langston Hughes. "To be of use" from *Circles on the Water* by Marge Piercy, copyright © 1982 by Marge Piercy. Used by permission of Alfred A. Knopf, a division of Random House, Inc.

Little, Brown and Company, Inc. "Perseus" from *Mythology* by Edith Hamilton. Copyright © 1942 by Edith Hamilton; Copyright © renewed 1969 by Dorian Fielding Reid and Doris Fielding Reid. #254, "'Hope' is the thing with feathers—" and #1176, "We never know how high we are" from *The Complete Poems of Emily Dickinson*, edited by Thomas H. Johnson. Copyright 1929, 1935 by Martha Dickson Bianchi; Copyright © renewed 1957, 1963 by Mary L. Hampson. By permission of Little, Brown and Company, Inc.

Liveright Publishing Corporation, an imprint of W. W. Norton & Company "maggie and milly and molly and may," copyright © 1956, 1984, 1991 by The Trustees for the E. E. Cummings Trust, from *Complete Poems: 1904–1962* by E. E. Cummings. Edited by George J. Firmage. Used by permission of Liveright Publishing Corporation.

Marie-Christine MacAndrew "The Necklace" from *Boule de Suif and Selected Stories* by Guy de Maupassant, translated by Andrew MacAndrew. Translation copyright © 1964 by Andrew MacAndrew. Reprinted by permission of Marie-Christine MacAndrew.

Macmillan, a division of Simon & Schuster, Inc. "Jabberwocky" from *The Collected Verse of Lewis Carroll* (New York: Macmillan, 1933). "There Will Come Soft Rains" by Sara Teasdale. Reprinted from *The Collected Poems of Sara Teasdale.* Published by Macmillan, a division of Simon & Schuster, Inc.

John McPhee "Arthur Ashe Remembered" by John McPhee, first published in *The New Yorker,* March 1, 1993. Reprinted by permission of the author.

Methuen Publishing, Limited "The Inspector-General" from *The Sneeze: Plays and Stories* by Anton Chekhov, translated and adapted by Michael Frayn, published by Methuen Drama. Originally from *An Awl in a Sack* by Anton Chekhov, 1885. Random House, UK, Ltd. Used by permission of Methuen Publishing, Limited.

Milkweed Editions "Eulogy for a Hermit Crab" by Pattiann Rogers from *Song of the World Becoming: New and Collected Poems 1981–2001* (Minneapolis: Milkweed Editions, 2001). Copyright © 1994, 2001 by Pattiann Rogers. Reprinted with permission from Milkweed Editions.

Edna St. Vincent Millay Society "An Ancient Gesture" by Edna St. Vincent Millay. From *Collected Poems*, HarperCollins. Copyright © 1954, 1982 by Norma Millay Ellis. All rights reserved. Reprinted by permission of Elizabeth Barnett, literary executor.

National Audubon Society "Audubon Web Site" from www.audubon.org. Used by permission of the National Audubon Society.

National Public Radio "Earhart Redux" by Alex Chadwick. Copyright © National Public Radio 1997. The news report by NPR's Alex Chadwick was originally broadcast on National Public Radio's and National Geographic Society's "Radio Expeditions" on March 17, 1997, and is used with the permission of National Public Radio, Inc. and the National Geographic Society. Any unauthorized duplication is strictly prohibited.

Charles Neider "The Invalid's Story" from *The Comic Mark Twain Reader*, edited by Charles Neider. Copyright © 1977 by Charles Neider. Reprinted by permission of the author.

New American Library, a division of Penguin Putnam, Inc. From *The Tragedy of Romeo and Juliet* by William Shakespeare, edited by J. A. Bryant, Jr. Published by New American Library, a division of Penguin Putnam, Inc.

Art Credits

Cover and Title Page *The Fog Warning*, 1885, oil on canvas, 30 1/4 x 48 1/2", Winslow Homer, Courtesy, Museum of Fine Arts, Boston. Reproduced with permission. ©2000 Museum of Fine Arts, Boston. All Rights Reserved. Otis Norcross Fund, 94.72; **xxv** ©The Stock Market/John Henley; **vii** Corel Professional Photos CD-ROM™; **viii** *Peculiarsome Abe*, N.C. Wyeth, Children's Special Collections, The Free Library of Philadelphia; **ix** Corel Professional Photos CD-ROM™; **x** Murray Wilson/Omni-Photo Communications, Inc.; **xi** Corel Professional Photos CD-ROM™; **xii** ©Alon Reininger/Contact Press/The Stock Market; **xiii** *The Oldest Inhabitant*, 1876, Julian Alden Weir, oil on canvas, 65 1/2 x 32" Signed, upper left. Butler Institute of American Art, Youngstown, Ohio; **xiv** Culver Pictures, Inc.; **xv** White/Pite/International Stock Photography, Ltd.; **xvi** ©Wolfgang Kaehler/CORBIS; **xvii** ©Araldo de Luca/CORBIS; **xviii** *Keying Up—The Court Jester* (detail), 1875, William Merritt Chase, Courtesy of the Pennsylvania Academy of the Fine Arts, Philadelphia, Gift of the Chapellier Galleries; **xx** ©The Stock Market/Pete Saloutos; **xxi** *The Quiltmakers*, Paul Goodnight, 22 11/16" x 24", Color Circle Art Publishing Inc.; **xi** Corel Professional Photos CD-ROM™; **xvi–xvii** Hulton Getty/Liaison Agency; **1** *The Storm*, 1893, Edvard Munch, Oil on canvas, 36 1/8 x 51 1/2" (91.8 x 130.8cm). The Museum of Modern Art, New York, Gift of Mr. and Mrs. H. Irgens Larsen and acquired through the Lillie P. Bliss and Abby Aldrich Rockefeller Funds. ©1997 The Museum of Modern Art, New York; **2** (t) *Baseball Players Practicing*, 1875, Thomas Eakins, Museum of Art, Rhode Island School of Design, Jesse Metcalf Fund and Walter H. Kimball Fund, (b) CORBIS; **4** ©Photo Researchers, Inc.; **6** *Keying Up—The Court Jester* (detail), 1875, William Merritt Chase, Courtesy of the Pennsylvania Academy of the Fine Arts, Philadelphia, Gift of the Chapellier Galleries; **9** ©Photo Researchers, Inc.; **11** SuperStock; **12** CORBIS-Bettmann; **16** Dr. E.R. Degginger; **18–19** *Peering Through the Jungle*, Larry Noble, Sal Barracca & Associates; **21** *Hat, Knife, and Gun in Woods*, David Mann, Sal Barracca & Associates; **22** Corel Professional Photos CD-ROM™; **26** Sovfoto/Eastfoto; **28** Grace Davies/Omni-Photo Communications, Inc.; **30** CORBIS; **31** Ann Shamel/Graphicstock; **33** CORBIS; **34** ©The Stock Market/John Dominis; **36** NYT Pictures; **40** *Baseball Players Practicing*, 1875, Thomas Eakins, Museum of Art, Rhode Island School of Design, Jesse Metcalf Fund and Walter H. Kimball Fund; **42** *Baseball Players Practicing*,1875, Thomas Eakins, Museum of Art, Rhode Island School of Design, Jesse Metcalf Fund and Walter H. Kimball Fund; **48** ©The Stock Market/Zefa Germany; **50** *Attack of the Birds*, 1994, Lev Tabenkin, Oil on canvas, 59" x 78", Maya Polsky Gallery; **52–53** Corel Professional Photos CD-ROM™; **56–57** *Landscape from a Dream*, 1936–38, Paul Nash, Tate Gallery, London/Art Resource, NY; **58** Art Hudson/American Red Cross; **60–61** Corel Professional Photos CD-ROM™; **65** ©The Stock Market/Zefa Germany; **68–69** *Wheatfield with Crows,* 1890, Vincent van Gogh, Van Gogh Museum, Amsterdam, The Netherlands, Art Resource, NY; **72–73** Corel Professional Photos CD-ROM™; **76** *Over and Above #13*, 1964, Clarence Holbrook Carter, oil on canvas, Courtesy of the Artist; **80–81** Corel Professional Photos CD-ROM™; **82** AP/Wide World Photos; **86** © Stone; **88** © John Darling/Stone; **89** Sonia Moskowitz/Globe Photos, Inc.; **91** Photofest; **94** Tony Cordoza/Liaison Agency; **96** The Granger Collection, New York; **99** © Simon Jauncey/Stone; **100–106** The Granger Collection, New York; **109** Historical Picture Archive/CORBIS; **110, 114** The Granger Collection, New York; **116** *Sir Arthur Conan Doyle* (detail), H. L. Gates, The National Portrait Gallery, London; **120** *Drawing Hands*, 1948, 1995 M.C. Escher/Cordon Art - Baarn - Holland. All rights reserved.; **122** *Het Blinde Huis*, William Degouve

de Nunques, State Museum, Kröller-Müller, Otterlo, The Netherlands; **123** ©Faber & Faber Ltd; **132** Jeffery Newbury/Discover Magazine; **136** Courtesy of the author; **140** ©Tony Freeman/PhotoEdit; **146–147** *Human Achievement*, Tsing-Fang Chen, Lucia Gallery, New York City/SuperStock; **148** (b.l.) CORBIS; **148** (t) *Night Games*, Ernie Barnes, Oil on canvas, 48 x 24, Courtesy of The Company of Art, Los Angeles; **148** (b.r.) *Perseus and Andromeda* (detail), ca.1580, Paolo Veronese, Musee des Beaux-Arts, Rennes, France, Erich Lessing/Art Resource, NY; **150, 152–153** *Lincoln Proclaiming Thanksgiving*, Dean Cornwell, The Lincoln Museum, Fort Wayne, Indiana, (#1153); **154** *Peculiarsome Abe*, N.C. Wyeth, Children's Special Collections, The Free Library of Philadelphia; **156** Courtesy of the Library of Congress; **158** *Carl Sandburg*, Miriam Svet, The National Portrait Gallery, Smithsonian Institution, Washington, D.C./Art Resource, New York; **162** AP/Wide World Photos; **164** CORBIS; **166** AP/Wide World Photos; **167** Neal Preston/CORBIS; **168** *The Beginning*, Artis Lane, Courtesy of the artist; **169** AP/Wide World Photos; **170–171** *We the People*, Kathy Morrow, Original scratchboard painting with hand-loomed beadwork, Courtesy of the artist; **171** Alan Markfield/Globe Photos; **172** The Granger Collection, New York; **176** Rectangular box, detail, Woven bamboo and painted lacquer, Late Ming Dynasty, early 17th century, H. 12.1 cm x W. 34.3 cm x L. 48.3 cm, H. 4 3/4" x W. 13 1/2" x L. 19", China, Avery Brundage Collection, #B60 M427, Asian Art Museum of San Francisco; **178** *The Nymph of the Lo River*, section of a handscroll. (H.9 1/2") Attributed to Ku K'ai-chih, Courtesy of the Freer Gallery of Art, Smithsonian Institution, Washington, D.C. #14.53; **182** Thomas Victor; **186** ©The Stock Market/Alan Goldsmith; **188** ©The Stock Market/Alan Goldsmith; **189** Dimitri Kessel/Life Magazine; **190** AP/Wide World Photos; **192** Henry McGee/Globe Photos; **200** Charles Weckler/The Image Bank; **202–203** Charles Weckler/The Image Bank; **205** Historical Picture Archive/CORBIS; **207** Indian, Mughal, Leaf from a royal manuscript of the Shah-Jehan Nameh: A procession in a palace courtyard, gouache on paper, mid 17th century, 28.9 x19.7 cm. Kate S. Buckingham Endowment Fund, 1975.555. Photograph © 1996, The Art Institute of Chicago. All Rights Reserved.; **208** AP/Wide World Photos; **212** *Danae with young Perseus arriving on the island of Seripo*, Museo Archeologico, Ferrara, Italy. Scala/Art Resource, NY; **214** *Andromeda Liberated*, Pierre Mignard, Louvre, Paris, France, Erich Lessing/Art Resource, NY; **217** *Danae with young Perseus arriving on the island of Seripo*, Museo Archeologico, Ferrara, Italy. Scala/Art Resource, NY; **218** Terre del Greco Ascione Collections/Superstock; **221** *Perseus and Andromeda* (detail), ca.1580, Paolo Veronese, Musée des Beaux-Arts, Rennes, France, Erich Lessing/Art Resource, NY; **222** UPI/CORBIS–Bettmann; **226** © David Madison/Stone; **228** *Night Games*, Ernie Barnes, Oil on canvas, 48 x 24, Courtesy of The Company of Art, Los Angeles; **229** Photo by Mandy Sayer; **230** ©Allsport/Tony Duffy; **231** Photo by Isidro Rodriquez; **232** Photo by Michael Nye; **236** Corel Professional Photos CD-ROM™; **242–243** *Waiting Girl*, 1978, Yan Hsia, Asian American Arts Center; **244** (b) Corel Professional Photos CD-ROM™; **246** ©Jack Hollingsworth/Index Stock Imagery/PictureQuest; **248** ©The Stock Market/Mark Gamba; **249** Corel Professional Photos CD-ROM™; **251** ©The Stock Market/Mark Gamba; **252** Thomas Victor; **260** CORBIS; **262–267** Digital Imagery ©Copyright 2001 PhotoDisc, Inc.; **268** *Chess Mates*, 1992, Pamela Chin Lee, Courtesy of the artist, Photo by John Lei/Omni-Photo Communications, Inc.; **269, 271** Digital Imagery ©Copyright 2001 Photo-Disc, Inc.; **272** Robert Foothorap; **276** Photofest; **278** ©Robert Foothorap/Black Star Publishing/PictureQuest; **280, 282**

Food City, 1967, Richard Estes, Oil acrylic and graphite on fiberboard, 48" x 68", Collection of the Akron Art Museum, Akron, Ohio, Museum Acquisition Fund, Photo by Richman Haire, ©Richard Estes/Licensed by VAGA, New York, NY/Courtesy Marlborough Gallery, NY; **286** Kit Stafford; **290** Horrillo Iriola/A.G.E. FotoStock; **292** The Granger Collection, New York; **293** Horrillo Iriola/A.G.E. FotoStock; **294** Henry McGee/Globe Photos; **295** (t) *Bubbles,* watercolor, 39" x 29", Courtesy of Scott Burdick, (b) The Granger Collection, New York; **296** UPI/CORBIS-Bettmann; **298** AP/Wide World Photos; **302** David De Lossy/The Image Bank; **304** R. Ashenbrenner/Stock Boston; **306** David De Lossy/The Image Bank; **308–309** Kenneth Redding/The Image Bank; **310** The Granger Collection, New York; **314** Tina Buckman/Index Stock Photography, Inc.; **316** Patrick Ward/Stock Boston; **318** Tina Buckman/Index Stock Photography, Inc.; **319** Digital Imagery ©Copyright 2001 PhotoDisc, Inc.; **320** Adam Scull/Globe Photos; **324** *The Quiltmakers,* Paul Goodnight, 22 11/16" x 24", Color Circle Art Publishing Inc.; **326** Digital Imagery ©Copyright 2001 PhotoDisc, Inc.; **327** (t) *The Quiltmakers,* Paul Goodnight, 22 11/16" x 24" Color Circle Art Publishing Inc., (b) Thomas Victor; **328** (t), (m), (b) Corel Professional Photos CD-ROM™; **329** *E. E. Cummings* (detail), 1958, Self-Portrait, The National Portrait Gallery, Smithsonian Institution, Washington, D.C./Art Resource, New York; **330** AP/Wide World Photos; **334** Laima Druskis/Pearson Education; **340–341** *Scientist's Hobby: Failure #18 of the Anti-Gravity Pack,* 1992, Bruce Widdows, acrylic on canvas, 84 x 132 inches, Courtesy of George Adams Gallery, New York; **342** (t) *The Jabberwock,* 1873, John Tenniel, The Granger Collection, New York, (b), ©Danny Brass/Photo Researchers, Inc.; **344** *Portrait XIV,* Private Collection/Donald C. Martin/SuperStock; **346** *The Man With Three Masks,* John Rush, Courtesy of the artist; **351** *New Orleans Fantasy* (detail), 1985, Max Papart, Lithograph, Courtesy of Nahan Galleries, New York; **352** CORBIS-Bettmann; **356, 358** *Valmondois Sous La Neige,* Maurice de Vlaminck, Superstock; **361** *White Night,* 1901, Edvard Munch, oil on canvas, 45 1/2 x 43 1/2 in. (115.5 x 111 cm) Photo: J. Lathion ©Nasjonalgalleriet 1997; **362** CORBIS-Bettmann; **366** Chromosohm/Sohm/Stock Boston; **369** *Young Brothers in the Hood,* 17x22, Tom McKinney, Courtesy of the artist; **370** Henry Horenstein/StockBoston; **372** Globe Photos; **374** Chromosohm/Sohm/Stock Boston; **376** Courtesy of the author; **380** Michael Newman/PhotoEdit; **382** ©David Muench/CORBIS; **383** Dianne Trejo; **384** © Anthony Banniste; Gallo Images/CORBIS; **386** (t) ©Stephen Dalton/Photo Researchers, Inc., (b) ©Sturgis McKeever/Photo Researchers, Inc.; **387** ©Pat Lynch/Photo Researchers, Inc.; **388** ©R.J. Erwin/Photo Researchers, Inc.; **389** ©Louis Quitt/Photo Researchers, Inc.; **390** (t) ©John M. Burnley/Photo Researchers, Inc., (b) Photo by Larry Sillen; **395** "Hey Diddle, Diddle" by William McBride and Michael Stack, Courtesy of McBride & Kelley Architects; **398** © Churchill Kheler/Stone; **400** *The Jabberwock,* 1873, John Tenniel, The Granger Collection, New York; **401** Gernsheim Collection, Harry Ransom Humanities Research Center, The University of Texas at Austin; **402** From *Old Possum's Book of Practical Cats,* Copyright 1939 by T. S. Eliot: renewed 1967 by Esme Valerie Eliot, Reproduced by permission of Harcourt Brace Jovanovich, Inc., Illustration by Edward Gorey; **404** *T. S. Eliot* (detail), 1888–1965, Sir Gerald Kelly, National Portrait Gallery, Smithsonian Institution, Art Resource, New York; **405** (l) Corel Professional Photos CD-ROM™, (r) Corel Professional Photos CD-ROM™; **406** (t.l.), (t.r) Corel Professional Photos CD-ROM™, (b) Photo by William Lewis; **414** © 1966 by Michael Courlander; **418** ©R. Gates/Archive Photos; **420** Murray Wilson/Omni-Photo Communications, Inc.; **423** UPI/CORBIS-Bettmann; **425** ©R. Gates/Archive Photos; **426** Eugene Gordon/Pearson Education/PH College; **429** Murray Wilson/Omni-Photo Communications, Inc.; **430** AP/Wide World Photos; **434** Tony Freeman/PhotoEdit; **440** Michael Agliolo/International Stock Photography, Ltd.; **442** (r) Index Stock Photography, Inc., (l) Gideon Mendel/Magnum Photos, Inc.; **444** Digital Imagery ©Copyright 2001 PhotoDisc, Inc.; **446** Sanford/Agliolo/International Stock Photography, Ltd.; **448** Index Stock Photography, Inc.; **450** Andrea Renault/Globe Photos; **454** NASA; **456–457** Corel Professional Photos CD-ROM™; **458** Corel Professional Photos CD-ROM™; **461** NASA; **462** Thomas Victor; **466** Digital Imagery ©Copyright 2001 PhotoDisc, Inc.; **466** (inset) Corel Professional Photos CD-ROM™; **469** Prentice Hall; **470** © Eastcott/Momatiuk/Stone; **472** Dimitri Kessel/Life Magazine, (l) (r) Corel Professional Photos CD-ROM™; **473** (t) Corel Professional Photos CD-ROM™, (b) CORBIS-Bettmann; **474** Corel Professional Photos CD-ROM™; **475** Mark Gerson Photography; **476** © Vernon Merritt/Time Inc.; **484** ©Alan L. Detrick/Photo Researchers, Inc.; **486–487** NASA; **490** UPI/CORBIS-Bettmann; **491** Corel Professional Photos CD-ROM™; **492–493** Frank Whitney/The Image Bank; **494** UPI/CORBIS-Bettmann; **495** ML Sinibaldi/©The Stock Market; **496** Digital Imagery ©Copyright 2001 PhotoDisc, Inc.; **497** Ryan Williams/International Stock Photography, Ltd.; **498** Photo by Judy Walgreen; **502** Gideon Mendel/Magnum Photos, Inc.; **504** Corel Professional Photos CD-ROM™; **505** Dorothy Alexander; **506** Gideon Mendel/Magnum Photos, Inc.; **508** AP/Wide World Photos; **512** © Myrleen Cate/Stone; **518–519** *Reading,* 1973, oil on masonite, Billy Morrow Jackson, Wichita Art Museum, purchased with funds donated by Mr. and Mrs. Donald C. Slawson; **520** ©Hulton Getty/Archive Photos; **522** *Wishful Thinking,* Peter Szumowski, Private Collection/Bridgeman Art Library, London/New York; **524** Jeff Spielman/The Image Bank; **527** Corel Professional Photos CD-ROM™; **528** *Hairdresser's Window,* 1907, John Sloan, oil on canvas, 1947.240, Wadsworth Atheneum, Hartford. The Ella Gallup Sumner and Mary Catlin Sumner Collection Fund; **529** Carved Tortoiseshell Comb, mid 19th century, England or France, Cooper-Hewitt National Design Museum, Smithsonian Institution/Art Resource, NY, Bequest of Mrs. John Innes Kane, 1926-22-545, photo by Richard Goodbody; **530** CORBIS-Bettmann; **534** Amazon.Com Books, Inc.; **536** CORBIS; **538** Carl Purcell/Photo Researchers, Inc.; **540–541** ©The Stock Market/ZEFA; **544–545** ©Alon Reininger/Contact Press/The Stock Market; **552** John Kaprielian/Photo Researchers, Inc.; **556** *Two Boys in a Punt,* N. C. Wyeth, Courtesy of Dr. and Mrs. William A. Morton, Jr., Photograph from Brandywine River Museum; **562–563** *Scarlet Ibis,* John James Audubon, ©Collection of The New-York Historical Society; **568** CORBIS-Bettmann; **571** *Sharecropper,* Elizabeth Catlett, Courtesy The Estate of Thurlow E. Tibbs, Jr., ©Elizabeth Catlett/Licensed by VAGA, New York, NY; **574** Digital Imagery ©Copyright 2001 PhotoDisc, Inc.; **576** Nikky Finney; **578, 582** CORBIS-Bettmann; **584** Inge Morath/Magnum Photos; **588** *Feast Day,* San Juan Pueblo, 1921, William Penhallow Henderson, National Museum of American Art, Smithsonian Institution; Given in Memory of Joshua C. Taylor/Art Resource, New York; **590–591** Corel Professional Photos CD-ROM™; **593** *Feast Day,* San Juan Pueblo, 1921, William Penhallow Henderson, National Museum of American Art, Smithsonian Institution; Given in Memory of Joshua C. Taylor/Art Resource, New York; **595** Thomas Victor; **596** ©Hulton Getty/Archive Photos; **598** *Sacramento Railroad Station,* 1874, William Hahn, Fine Arts Museum of San Francisco; **601** The Granger Collection, New York; **602** *Samuel Langhorne Clemens (Mark Twain)* (detail), 1935, Frank Edwin Larson, National Portrait Gallery, Smithsonian Institution, Washington, D.C./Art Resource, New York; **606** *Campesino,* 1976, Oil on canvas, 50 1/2 x 59 1/2 inches, Daniel DeSiga, Wight Art Gallery, University of California, Los Angeles, Collection of Alfredo Aragon, Photo by Grey Crawford; **608** Christie's Images; **612** *The New Necklace,* 1910, William McGregor Paxton, Courtesy, Museum of Fine Arts, Boston. Reproduced with permission. Zoe Oliver Sherman Collection, 22.644 ©2000 Museum of Fine Arts, Boston. All Rights Reserved.; **615** CORBIS-Bettmann; **616** *Campesino*, 1976, Oil on canvas, 50 1/2 x 59 1/2 inches, Daniel DeSiga, Wight Art Gallery, University of California, Los Angeles, Collection of Alfredo Aragon, Photo by Grey Crawford; **618** *Farmworker de Califas*, Tony Ortega, Monotype, Courtesy of the artist; **620** Arte Público Press; **624** Tony Freeman/PhotoEdit; **630–631** David Young-Wolfe/PhotoEdit; **632** (r) Monica Almeida/NYT Permissions, (l) UPI/CORBIS-Bettmann; **634, 636, 639, 640** NASA; **645** AP/Wide World Photos; **648** *Don Nemesio*, 1977, Esperanza Martinez, Courtesy of the artist; **650** Lee Snider/CORBIS; **652** *The Oldest Inhabitant*, 1876, Julian Alden Weir, oil on canvas, 65 1/2 x 32" Signed, upper left. Butler Institute of American Art, Youngstown, Ohio; **655** Thomas Victor; **657** Enrico Ferorelli; **658–659** Robert Frerck/Woodfin Camp & Associates; **661** CORBIS-Bettmann; **663** *Don Nemesio*, 1977, Esperanza Martinez, Courtesy of the artist; **665** *El Leñador*, 1934, Tom Lea, oil on canvas, 36 x 30, Collection of the Museum of New Mexico, Museum of Fine Arts, Gift of P.E.R.A.; **668** Prentice Hall; **672** *The White Trumpet Flower*, 1932, Georgia O'Keeffe, San Diego Museum of Art, Gift of Inez Grant Parker in memory of Earle W. Grant, ©1998 The Georgia O'Keeffe Foundation/Artists Rights Society (ARS), New York; **674** CORBIS-Bettmann; **676, 677, 678** UPI/CORBIS-Bettmann; **679** ©Archive Photos; **680–681** ©White House Collection, Courtesy White House Historical Association; **682** ©Allsport/Hulton Deutsch; **684** Thomas Victor; **685** *The White Trumpet Flower*, 1932, Georgia O'Keeffe, San Diego Museum of Art, Gift of Inez Grant Parker in memory of Earle W. Grant, ©1998 The Georgia O'Keeffe Foundation/Artists Rights Society (ARS), New York; **687** *Cow's Skull: Red, White and Blue*, 1931, Georgia O'Keeffe, The Metropolitan Museum of Art, The Alfred Stieglitz Collection, 1949, Copyright © 1984 by The Metropolitan Museum of Art, Photograph by Malcolm Varon, ©1998 The Georgia O'Keeffe Foundation/Artists Rights Society (ARS), New York; **688** *The Lawrence Tree*, 1929, Georgia O'Keeffe, Wadsworth Atheneum, Hartford, The Ella Gallup Sumner and Mary Catlin Sumner Collection, ©1998 The Georgia O'Keeffe Foundation/Artists Rights Society (ARS), New York; **690** Thomas Victor; **694** *Understanding Comics* by Scott McCloud, a 215-page analysis of comics in comics form © and ™ 1994 Scott McCloud; **697–704** (t) Pages 2–9 from *Understanding Comics* by Scott McCloud, a 215-page analysis of comics in comics form. © and ™ 1994 Scott McCloud; **704** (b) Scott McCloud; **708** Monica Almeida/NYT Permissions; **710** P. DaSilva/Sygma; **712** CORBIS; **713** San Diego Aerospace Museum; **714** Photo by Max Hirshfeld; **716** Monica Almeida/NYT Permissions; **718** The Sporting News; **722** David Young-Wolff/Tony Stone Images; **728–729** *The Sheridan Theatre*, 1937, Edward Hopper, Collection of the Newark Museum, 1940, Felix Fuld Bequest Fund/Art Resource, NY; **730** (l) Culver Pictures, Inc., (r) Digital Imagery ©Copyright 2001 PhotoDisc, Inc.; **732** ©1996 Robert Brooks/FPG International Corp.; **734–735** Digital Imagery ©Copyright 2001 PhotoDisc, Inc.; **736** Footprints provided by The Arthur Murray Dance Studios; **738** FPG International Corp.; **740** Footprints provided by The Arthur Murray Dance Studios; **743** FPG International Corp.; **745** Footprints provided by The Arthur Murray Dance Studios; **747** FPG International Corp.; **749** Bettmann Archive/CORBIS; **750** FPG International Corp.; **753** Footprints provided by The Arthur Murray Dance Studio; **755** ©1996 Robert Brooks/FPG International Corp.; **757** Footprints provided by The Arthur Murray Dance Studios; **758** Digital Imagery ©Copyright 2001 PhotoDisc, Inc.; **759** ©1996 Robert Brooks/FPG International Corp.; **760** Photo by Eric H. Antoniou; **764** The Globe Theatre, London, The Granger Collection, New York; **765** Robert Harding Picture Library; **766** *William Shakespeare*

(detail), Artist Unknown, by courtesy of the National Portrait Gallery, London; **768, 770** Photofest; **775** ©Araldo de Luca/CORBIS; **776** Photofest; **781** Culver Pictures, Inc.; **784** Photofest; **788** Movie Still Archives; **790, 795** Photofest; **800** Culver Pictures, Inc.; **802** Digital Imagery ©Copyright 2001 PhotoDisc, Inc.; **806, 807, 813** Photofest; **819, 823** Memory Shop; **826** Private Collection/Bridgeman Art Library, London/New York; **830–831** Culver Pictures, Inc.; **838, 845** Memory Shop; **848** Culver Pictures, Inc.; **852** Memory Shop; **861, 865, 866, 870, 878** Photofest; **881** © Dorling Kindersley; **884** © Axel Hoedt/Stone; **890–891** *Garden of Delights*, Sandy Novak/Omni-Photo Communications, Inc.; **892** (b) *Bernard's Daddy*, Raymond Lark, Master Drawing, graphite, 20 x 30 inches, Collection of Mary Moran, New Jersey. Photo courtesy of Edward Smith and Company, (t) ©The Stock Market/Pete Saloutos; **894** Corel Professional Photos CD-ROM™; **896–897** ©Wolfgang Kaehler/CORBIS; **898** The Granger Collection, New York; **902, 904** *Bernard's Daddy*, Raymond Lark, Master Drawing, graphite, 20 x 30 inches, Collection of Mary Moran, New Jersey. Photo courtesy of Edward Smith and Company; **905** *Langston Hughes* (detail), c.1925, Winold Reiss, The National Portrait Gallery, Smithsonian Institution, Washington, D.C./Art Resource, New York; **906–907** Corel Professional Photos CD-ROM™; **907** (b) *Alfred Lord Tennyson*, c.1840, S. Laurence, by courtesy of the National Portrait Gallery, London; (t) ©The Stock Market/Pete Saloutos; **908** (b) The Granger Collection, New York, (t) Digital Imagery ©Copyright 2001 Photo-Disc, Inc.; **912** ©The Stock Market/Roy Morsch; **914** Andrea Renault/Globe Photos; **915** (t) Barry Pribula/International Stock Photography, Inc.; **917** (t) Carolina Biological/Phototake, (b) Photo by Yvonne Mozee; **918–919** (t) White/Pite/International Stock Photography, Ltd., (b) UPI/CORBIS-Bettmann; **920** Prentice Hall; **924** David De Lossy/The Image Bank; **926** (t) Index Stock Photography, Inc., (b) CORBIS-Bettmann; **927** (b) John Craig Photo, (t) Digital Imagery ©Copyright 2001 PhotoDisc, Inc.; **928** ©The Stock Market/Zefa Germany; **930** *The Bells*, Edmund Dulac, New York Public Library; Astor, Lenox and Tilden Foundations; **934** CORBIS-Bettmann; **938** Esbin/Anderson/Omni-Photo Communications, Inc.; **943** CORBIS-Bettmann; **944** By permission of the Folger Shakespeare Library, Washington,D.C.; **946** *William Shakespeare* (detail), Artist unknown, by courtesy of the National Portrait Gallery, London; **950** ©Terry Vine/CORBIS; **953** Courtesy of Detroit Free Press; **954** Digital Imagery ©Copyright 2001 PhotoDisc, Inc.; **956** The Granger Collection, New York; **957** *Richard Wright* (detail), 1949, Miriam Troop, The National Portrait Gallery, Smithsonian Institution, Washington, D.C./Art Resource, New York; **958** (b) Stephen Frisch/Stock, Boston, (b) Luis Castaneda/The Image Bank; **959** The Granger Collection, New York; **960** *William Shakespeare* (detail), Artist unknown, by courtesy of the National Portrait Gallery, London; **965** Digital Imagery ©Copyright 2001 PhotoDisc, Inc.; **966** Seaver Center for Western History Research, Natural History Museum of Los Angeles County; **968** Esbin/Anderson/Omni-Photo Communications, Inc.; **974–975** *Ulysses Deriding Polyphemus*, 1819, J.M.W. Turner, The National Gallery, London; **976** (tr) *Ulysses receives the wine with which he will make Polyphemus drunk*, Italiotic crater. Museo Eoliano, Lipari, Italy/Scala/Art Resource, NY, (tl) CORBIS-Bettmann, (b) ©Bettmann/CORBIS; **978** *Circe Meanwhile Had Gone Her Ways...*, 1924, William Russell Flint, Collection of the New York Public Library; Astor, Lenox and Tilden Foundations; **980** *Ulysses Deriding Polyphemus*, 1819, J.M.W. Turner, The National Gallery, London; **987, 990** ©Araldo de Luca/CORBIS; **995** *Polyphemus, the Cyclops from Homer's Odyssey*, N.C. Wyeth, Delaware Art Museum, Photo by Jon MacDowell; **998** *Odysseus in the Land of the Dead* from Homer's *Odyssey*, N.C. Wyeth, Delaware Art Museum, Photo by Jon MacDowell; **1003** ©Araldo de Luca/CORBIS;**1008** *Circe*

Meanwhile Had Gone Her Ways..., 1924, William Russell Flint, Collection of the New York Public Library; Astor, Lenox and Tilden Foundations; **1016** *La Nef De Telemachus (The Ship of Telemachus),* New York Public Library Picture Collection; **1023** *Eumaeus, the Swineherd* from Homer's *Odyssey,* N.C. Wyeth, Delaware Art Museum, Photo by Jon MacDowell; **1026, 1030** ©Araldo de Luca/CORBIS; **1034** *The Trial of the Bow* from Homer's *Odyssey,* N.C. Wyeth, Delaware Art Museum, Photo by Jon MacDowell; **1036** Bridgeman Art Library, London/New York; **1038** *The Slaughter of the Suitors* from Homer's *Odyssey,* N.C. Wyeth, Delaware Art Museum, photo by Jon MacDowell; **1043** ©Andrew Cowin;Travel Ink/CORBIS; **1044** *The Fall of Troy* from *The Odysseus Suite,* 1979, Romare Bearden, serigraph 18x24, © Romare Bearden Foundation/Licensed by VAGA, New York, NY; **1046** CORBIS-Bettmann; **1050** *Penelope and the Suitors,* 1912, J.M. Waterhouse, 51 1/2 x 75 in. (131 x 191 cm) City of Aberdeen Art Gallery and Museums Collections, Scotland; **1053** *Edna St. Vincent Millay* (detail), Charles Ellis, The National Portrait Gallery, Smithsonian Institution, Washington, D.C./Art Resource, New York; **1054** Werner Forman/Art Resource, NY; **1055** Thomas Victor; **1056** *Ulysses receives the wine with which he will make Polyphemus drunk,* Italiotic crater. Museo Eoliano, Lipari, Italy/Scala/Art Resource, NY; **1057** Eugene Richards/Magnum/Photos, Inc.; **1058** Amphora with Grapes, oil, 15" by 19", Loran Speck, Loran Speck Art Gallery, Carmel, CA; **1060** The Granger Collection, New York; **1064** Tsado/NASA/Tom Stack & Associates; **1065** ©Bettmann/CORBIS; **1067** AP/Wide World Photos

Staff Credits

The people who made up the **Prentice Hall Literature: Timeless Voices, Timeless Themes** team—representing design services, editorial, editorial services, market research, marketing services, media resources, online services & multimedia development, production services, project office, and publishing processes—are listed below. Bold type denotes the core team members.

Susan Andariese, Rosalyn Arcilla, Laura Jane Bird, Betsy Bostwick, **Anne M. Bray,** Evonne Burgess, **Louise B. Capuano, Pam Cardiff,** Megan Chill, Ed Cordero, Laura Dershewitz, Philip Fried, **Elaine Goldman,** Barbara Goodchild, Barbara Grant, **Rebecca Z. Graziano, Doreen Graizzaro,** Dennis Higbee, **Leanne Korszoloski,** Ellen Lees, David Liston, **Mary Luthi, George Lychock,** Gregory Lynch, Sue Lyons, **William McAllister,** Frances Medico, Gail Meyer, Jessica S. Paladini, Wendy Perri, Carolyn Carty Sapontzis, **Melissa Shustyk, Annette Simmons, Alicia Solis,** Robin Sullivan, Cynthia Sosland Summers, Lois Teesdale, **Elizabeth Torjussen, Doug Utigard,** Bernadette Walsh, Helen Young

The following persons provided invaluable assistance and support during the production of this program.

Gregory Abrom, Robert Aleman, Diane Alimena, Michele Angelucci, Gabriella Apolito, Penny Baker, Sharyn Banks, Anthony Barone, Barbara Blecher, Helen Byers, Rui Camarinha, Lorelee J. Campbell, John Carle, Cynthia Clampitt, Jaime L. Cohen, Martha Conway, Dina Curro, Nancy Dredge, Johanna Ehrmann, Josie K. Fixler, Steve Frankel, Kathy Gavilanes, Allen Gold, Michael E. Goodman, Diana Hahn, Kerry L. Harrigan, Jacki Hasko, Evan Holstrom, Beth Hyslip, Helen Issackedes, Cathy Johnson, Susan Karpin, Raegan Keida, Stephanie Kota, Mary Sue Langan, Elizabeth Letizia, Christine Mann, Vickie Menanteaux, Kathleen Mercandetti, Art Mkrtchyan, Karyl Murray, Kenneth Myett, Stefano Nese, Kim Ortell, Lissette Quinones, Erin Rehill-Seker, Patricia Rodriguez, Mildred Schulte, Adam Sherman, Mary Siener, Jan K. Singh, Diane Smith, Barbara Stufflebeem, Louis Suffredini, Lois Tatarian, Tom Thompkins, Lisa Valente, Ryan Vaarsi, Linda Westerhoff, Jeff Zoda

Prentice Hall gratefully acknowledges the following teachers who provided student models for consideration in the program.

Kate Anders, Suzanne Arkfeld, Elizabeth Bailey, Bill Brown, Diane Cappillo, Mary Chapman, Deedee Chumley, Terry Day, Cheryl Devoe, Dan Diercks, Ellen Eberly, Nancy Fahner, Terri Fields, Patty Foster, Joanne Giardino, Julie Gold, Christopher Guarraia, Dianne Hammond, Jo Higgins, Pauline Hodges, Gaye Ingram, Charlotte Jefferies, Bill Jones, Ken Kaiser, Linda Kramer, Karen Lopez, Catherine Lynn, Ashley MacDonald, Kathleen Marshall, LouAnn McCarty, Peggy Moore, Ann Okamura, Will Parker, Maureen Rippee, Tucky Roger, Terrie Saunders, Marilyn Shaw, Ken Spurlock, Mary Stevens, Sandra Sullivan, Wanda Thomas, Jennifer Watson, Amanda Wolf